Kely
3, 14, 74

ADVANCED ACCOUNTING

Sixth Edition

TO THE STUDENT A Study Guide for the textbook is available through your college bookstore under the title *Study Guide to accompany Advanced Accounting, Sixth Edition* by Andrew A. Haried, Leroy F. Imdieke, Ralph E. Smith. The Study Guide can help you with course material by acting as a tutorial, review, and study aid. If the Study Guide is not in stock, ask the bookstore manager to order a copy for you.

ACCOUNTING TEXTBOOKS FROM WILEY

ADVANCED ACCOUNTING

Sixth Edition

Andrew A. Haried, PhD, CPA
Professor of Accounting
Arizona State University

Leroy F. Imdieke, PhD, CPA
Professor of Accounting
Arizona State University

Ralph E. Smith, PhD, CPA
Professor of Accounting
Arizona State University

John Wiley & Sons, Inc.
New York / Chichester / Brisbane / Toronto / Singapore

COVER Designed by Laura Ierardi
          Photograph: FPG International/Art Montes de Oca
ACQUISITIONS EDITOR Karen Hawkins
MARKETING MANAGER Karen Allman
PRODUCTION Ingrao Associates and Deborah Herbert
DESIGNER Ann Marie Renzi
MANUFACTURING MANAGER Andrea Price
ILLUSTRATION Eugene Aiello

This book was set in ITC New Baskerville by CRWaldman Graphic Communications and printed and bound by Malloy Lithographing. The cover was printed by Lehigh Press.

Library of Congress Cataloging in Publication Data:
Haried, Andrew A.
    Advanced accounting / Andrew A. Haried, Leroy F. Imdieke, Ralph F. Smith.—6th ed.
      p. cm.
      Includes index.
      ISBN 0-471-58888-1 (alk. paper)
      1. Accounting, I, Imdieke, Leroy F. II. Smith, Ralph Eugene, 1941-   . III. Title.
HF5635.H256 1994
657′.046—dc20

                                                        93-46004
                                                           CIP

Printed in the United States of America

10 9 8 7 6 5

Printed and bound by Malloy Lithographing, Inc.

For Joyce, Lorraine, and Mary

ABOUT THE AUTHORS

Andrew A. Haried, PhD, CPA, received his doctorate degree in accounting from the University of Illinois. He is currently Professor of Accounting at Arizona State University. He has had public accounting experience with Arthur Andersen & Co. and has acted as a continuing professional education consultant to both local and regional firms of public accountants. He has instructed graduate and undergraduate courses in financial accounting, reporting, and auditing. Articles by Professor Haried have appeared in the *Journal of Accounting Research, The Accounting Review, the Journal of Accountancy,* and other professional journals. He is a member of the American Accounting Association, The American Institute of Certified Public Accountants, and The Arizona Society of Certified Public Accountants.

Leroy F. Imdieke, PhD, CPA, is Professor of Accounting at Arizona State University. He received his PhD in accounting from the University of Illinois. He has instructed graduate and undergraduate courses in financial accounting and reporting and has conducted many professional development seminars during his career. Professor Imdieke's articles on financial accounting and reporting topics have appeared in *The Accounting Review, the Journal of Accountancy,* and other professional journals. He is a member of the American Accounting Association and the Arizona State Society of Certified Public Accountants. He has served on several committees of the American Accounting Association and most recently served on the Board of Directors of the Arizona Society of Certified Public Accountants. He has served as a consultant to a number of business firms and state agencies.

Ralph E. Smith, PhD, CPA, is Professor of Accounting at Arizona State University. He has instructed graduate and undergraduate courses and seminars in financial accounting theory and problems. He has also been active in developing and conducting a number of professional development seminars. Professor Smith received his PhD in accounting from the University of Kansas. He is a CPA in the State of Kansas and is a member of the American Accounting Association and the American Institute of Certified Public Accountants. He has served on several committees of the American Accounting Association and also holds membership in Beta Gamma Sigma and Beta Alpha Psi. He has written a number of articles that have appeared in *The Accounting Review*, the *Journal of Accountancy*, the *Journal of Financial and Quantitative Analysis*, and other professional and academic journals.

PREFACE

This book is suitable for advanced courses dealing with financial accounting and reporting in the following topical areas: business combinations, consolidated financial statements, equity method of reporting investments, branches, foreign currency transactions, translation of financial statements of foreign affiliates, segment reporting and interim reporting, corporate reorganization and liquidation, partnerships, fund accounting and accounting for governmental units, accounting for non-government–nonbusiness organizations, estates and trusts, installment sales, and consignment transactions. The objective of this book is to provide a comprehensive treatment of selected topics in a clear and readable manner.

A major purpose of this revision is to continue to provide maximum flexibility to the instructor in the selection and breadth of coverage for topics dealing with consolidated financial statements. Efforts to accomplish this objective include (1) the use of a subsidiary rather than a branch to illustrate foreign currency translation, to facilitate the coverage of this topic by those instructors who prefer to omit accounting for branches; and (2) the separation of the following topics into separate chapters or self-contained units that may be omitted or included as desired.

- Pooling of interests method of accounting for investments in subsidiaries
- Deferred income tax consequences relating to differences between the assigned values and tax bases of assets and liabilities of an acquired company.

- Deferred income tax consequences of undistributed subsidiary income and unrealized intercompany profit.
- Accounting for indirect ownership and reciprocal stockholdings
- Comparing of the effects of the using of the parent company and the entity concepts in preparing consolidated financial statements

All chapters have been updated where appropriate to reflect the most recent pronouncements of the Financial Accounting Standards Board and the Governmental Accounting Standards Board. Throughout this edition, we have replaced the terms "minority interest" and "majority interest" with the terms "noncontrolling interest" and "controlling interest". This change in terminology anticipates the broadening by the FASB of the concept of control from that of simple majority ownership. In addition, all chapters have been edited thoroughly to assure accuracy, clarity, and consistency throughout the text.

In teaching consolidation concepts, a decision must be made about the recording method that should be emphasized in presenting consolidated workpaper **procedure**. Major alternatives for recording investments in subsidiaries are the (1) cost method, (2) partial equity method, and (3) complete equity method. A brief description of each method follows.

1. **Cost Method.** The investment in subsidiary is carried at its cost, with no adjustments made to the investment account for subsidiary income or dividends. Dividends received by the parent company are recorded as an increase in cash and as dividend income.

2. **Partial Equity method.** The investment account is adjusted for the parent company's share of the subsidiary's reported earnings or losses, and dividends received from the subsidiary are deducted from the investment account. Generally, no other adjustments are made to the investment in subsidiary account.

3. **Complete Equity Method.** This method is the same as the partial equity method except that additional adjustments are made to the investment in subsidiary account to reflect the effects of (a) the elimination of unrealized intercompany profits, (b) the amortization (depreciation) of the difference between cost and book value, the (c) additional stockholders' equity transactions undertaken by the subsidiary that change the parent company's share of the subsidiary's stockholders' equity.

We have elected to emphasize cost method workpaper procedures for the following reasons:

1. We believe consolidation concepts and standards are presented and understood most easily within the framework of cost method workpaper procedures.

2. The cost method is the method most widely used to **record** investments in consolidated subsidiaries. This is supported by the results of a survey of corporate controllers of Fortune 500 companies who were asked to indicate the method used to **record on their books** investments in subsidiaries that are consolidated. More than 71 percent indicate that they use the cost method. The remainder use either the partial or complete equity methods.

Since approximately 29 percent of surveyed corporate controllers said that they used some form of the equity method to record their investments in subsidiaries, **for internal management use,** in this edition we also present the partial equity method (both book entries and workpaper procedures) in a way that enables instructors to:

1. Include discussion of this method, or even emphasize it if they wish.

2. Demonstrate that the method used to record investments has no effect on consolidated balances, but only on workpaper procedures.

3. Ignore this method if they wish.

Each chapter dealing with consolidated statements topics includes ample exercises and problems for instructors to emphasize the partial equity method if they so desire. As with the fifth edition, the complete equity method of reporting investments in common stock is treated for what it is, a method of **reporting** investments. The complete equity method, along with workpaper procedures for investments recorded by using the complete equity method, is covered in Chapter 12.

Other new features in the sixth edition include:

1. A section added to Chapter 4 treating the assignment of the difference between cost and book value to assets when they have a fair value less than book value and to liabilities when they have a fair value greater than book value.

2. A revised section treating intercompany sales of nondepreciable assets placed at the beginning of Chapter 6, and a section treating intercompany interest, rents, and service fees added to Chapter 6.

3. Discussion of the pooling of interests method of recording and consolidating stock acquisitions presented in a separate section in Chapter 11.

4. A complete revision of Chapter 7 to comply with the provisions of SFAS 109, *Accounting for Income Taxes*, including the addition of a section treating deferred income taxes that arise in business combinations recorded using the purchase method because of differences between the assigned values and tax bases of assets and liabilities of the acquired company.

5. In Chapter 8, a revised treatment of changes in ownership resulting from transactions by subsidiaries in its own shares of stock to conform with recommendations of the FASB.

6. The enhancement of Chapters 21 and 22 with discussions of:
   a. The hierarchy of generally accepted accounting principles for governmental entities, and the hierarchy of generally accepted accounting principles for nongovennment, nonbusiness organizations.
   b. Reporting on service efforts and accomplishments by governmental units.
   c. The financial reporting project of the GASB.
   d. Changes in financial statement display and in accounting for contributions required by SFAS No. 117 and SFAS No. 116.

In addition, exercise and problem material are revised for all chapters, with several new exercises and problems added.

The following features that were accepted so well in the first five editions are retained.

1. All illustrations are printed upright on the page and labeled clearly for convenient study and reference.

2. Entries made on consolidated statements workpapers are also presented in general journal form, and are shaded to distinguish them from book entries, to facilitate exposition and study.

Although we continue to emphasize the three-divisional, horizontal consolidated statements workpaper format, the trial balance format is introduced and illustrated in Chapter 5. Ample problem materials are provided in Chapters 5, 6, and 7 so that instructors may require solutions to consolidated statements workpapers in the trial balance format if they so desire.

Clearly there are more topics in this text than can be covered adequately in a one-semester or one-quarter course. It is our belief that it is preferable and more satisfying to both students and instructors to cover a selected number of topics in depth rather than to undertake a superficial coverage of a larger number of topics. Modules of material that an instructor may consider for exclusion in any one semester or quarter include the following:

Chapters 7 to 11.   An expanded analysis of problems in the preparation of consolidated financial statements.

Chapter 12.   The equity method of reporting investments in common stock.

Chapters 13 to 16.   Branches, foreign currency transactions and translation, and segment and interim reporting.

Chapters 18 and 19.   Partnership accounting.

Chapters 20 to 22.   Fund accounting, accounting for governmental units, and accounting for nongovernment–nonbusiness organizations.

Chapter 17, 23, and 24.   Corporate reorganization, estates and trusts, and installment and consignment transactions.

The text is also accompanied by a full range of teaching and learning supplements, which include:

1. An instructor's manual that contains solutions (including computations) to all questions, exercises, and problems in a format suitable for the preparation of transparencies.

2. A comprehensive study guide that contains chapter synopses as well as exercises and problems, including solutions.

3. Two supplements designed to eliminate repetitive procedures in the preparation of solutions to problems requiring consolidated workpapers.

- *For Use with Micro Computers*: Floppy disks with .wk1 templates for each consolidated statements workpaper problem in the end of chapter material. This supplement makes it possible for the student to transfer a partially completed workpaper for any problem selected from the disk to a spreadsheet program that accepts .wk1 spreadsheet files. After the student enters on the computer the appropriate adjusting and eliminating entries and the amount of noncontrolling interest in combined income, the consolidated statements workpaper is completed automatically and may be printed out. These disks are available free to adopters with permission to make as many copies as necessary for their students.
- *For General use*: A set of partially completed workpapers with preprinted column and side headings and parent and subsidiary account balances.

4. A list of check figures.

5. A test manual containing an expanded number and variety of examination questions and problems for each chapter.

6. A computerized test bank.

In closing, we thank the following individuals for their assistance and suggestions in the preparation of this book: C. David Baron, New Mexico State University; Donald Berberich, Thomas More College; Michelle Blazek, University of New Mexico; John W. Buckley, University of California, Los Angeles; Barney Cargile, University of Alabama; Ronald M. Copeland, Northeastern University; David Goldman, Deloitte and Touche; William Del Principe, St. Joseph College; Abo-El-Yazeed T. Habib, University of Central Arkansas; Judith A. Harris, University of Lowell; Leon E. Hay, University of Arkansas; Douglas Heerma, Indiana University; Steven Kachelmeier, University of Texas-Austin; Orville R. Keister, The University of Akron; Sharon Kimmell, University of Akron; Hans Klein, Bentley College; Barry Kuchinsky, Mercy College; Michael Luehlfing, Louisiana State University; Ronald M. Mano, Weber State College; Paul B. Miller, University of Utah; Ali Peyvandi, California State University—Fresno; Jeanine Radtke, Our Lady of Lake University; Nezik Roufaiel, Ithaca College; Victoria Rymer, University of Maryland; D. Gerald Searfoss, Deloitte and Touche; Martha Sargent, Western Oregon State College; Lloyd Vann Seawell, Indiana University; John R. Simon, Northern Illinois University; Ray Slager, Calvin College; David Vicknair, Gonzaga University; and E. Vorwerk, Concordia Lutheran College.

Suggestions and comments from readers are appreciated.

Tempe, Arizona
November 1993

Andrew A. Haried
Leroy F. Imdieke
Ralph F. Smith

CONTENTS

Chapter 2 CONSOLIDATED FINANCIAL STATEMENTS— DATE OF ACQUISITION 47

Chapter 3 CONSOLIDATED FINANCIAL STATEMENTS AFTER ACQUISITION 75

Chapter 6   ELIMINATION OF UNREALIZED PROFIT ON INTERCOMPANY SALES OF PROPERTY AND EQUIPMENT   219

Chapter 7   DEFERRED INCOME TAX CONSEQUENCES IN BUSINESS COMBINATIONS AND CONSOLIDATED FINANCIAL STATEMENTS   257

Chapter 11 POOLING OF INTERESTS AND ALTERNATIVE CONCEPTS OF CONSOLIDATED FINANCIAL STATEMENTS 415

Chapter 12 THE EQUITY METHOD OF REPORTING INVESTMENTS IN COMMON STOCK 445

Chapter 13   ACCOUNTING FOR HOME OFFICE AND BRANCH ACTIVITIES   487

Chapter 14   ACCOUNTING FOR FOREIGN CURRENCY TRANSACTIONS   519

Chapter 15   THE TRANSLATION OF FINANCIAL STATEMENTS OF FOREIGN AFFILIATES   553

Chapter 16   REPORTING FOR SEGMENTS AND INTERIM FINANCIAL PERIODS   601

Chapter 17   INSOLVENCY—LIQUIDATION AND REORGANIZATION   635

Chapter 18 PARTNERSHIPS: FORMATION, OPERATION, AND OWNERSHIP CHANGES 673

Chapter 19 PARTNERSHIP LIQUIDATION 723

Chapter 20   INTRODUCTION TO FUND ACCOUNTING   755

Chapter 21   INTRODUCTION TO ACCOUNTING FOR STATE AND LOCAL GOVERNMENTAL UNITS   799

Chapter 22 INTRODUCTION TO ACCOUNTING FOR NONGOVERNMENT NONBUSINESS ORGANIZATIONS 867

Chapter 23 ACCOUNTING FOR ESTATES AND TRUSTS 929

Chapter 24 ACCOUNTING FOR INSTALLMENT SALES AND CONSIGNMENT TRANSACTIONS 953

APPENDIX 993

INDEX 1003

ADVANCED ACCOUNTING

Sixth Edition

1

BUSINESS COMBINATIONS

Expansion is a major objective of many business organizations. Top management often lists growth as one of its primary goals. A company may grow slowly, gradually expanding its product lines, facilities, or services, or it may skyrocket almost overnight, as many electronics firms did in the 1970s and 1980s. Some businessmen consider growth so important that they say their companies must "grow or die."

A company may expand in several ways. Some firms concentrate on *internal* expansion. A firm may expand internally by engaging in product research and development. Hewlett-Packard is an example of a company that has relied on new product development to maintain and expand its market share. A firm may choose instead to emphasize marketing and promotional activities to obtain a greater share of a given market. Although such efforts usually do not expand the total market, they may redistribute that market by increasing the company's share of it.

For other firms *external* expansion is the goal; that is, they try to expand by acquiring one or more other firms. This form of expansion produces relatively rapid growth without increasing competition. A company may achieve significant cost savings as a result of external expansion, particularly when it acquires one of its major suppliers.

BUSINESS COMBINATIONS—AN HISTORICAL PERSPECTIVE

In the past hundred years, many United States businesses have achieved their goal of expansion through business combinations. A business combination occurs when the operations of two or more companies are brought under common control.

In the United States there have been three fairly distinct periods characterized by business mergers, consolidations, and other forms of combinations. During the first period, which ran from about 1880 through 1904, huge holding companies or trusts were created by investment bankers seeking to establish monopoly control over certain industries. This type of combination is generally called *horizontal integration* because it involves the combination of companies within the same industry. Examples of the trusts formed during this period are J. P. Morgan's U.S. Steel Corporation and other giant firms such as Standard Oil, American Sugar Refining Company, and the American Tobacco Company. By 1904 more than 300 such trusts had been formed, and they controlled more than 40% of the nation's industrial capital.

The second period of business combination activity, fostered by the federal government during World War I, continued through the 1920s. In an effort to bolster the war effort, the government encouraged business combinations to obtain greater standardization of materials and parts and to discourage price competition. After the war, it was difficult to reverse this trend, and business combinations continued. These combinations were efforts to obtain better integration of operations, reduce costs, and improve competitive positions rather than attempts to establish monopoly control over an industry. This type of combination is called *vertical integration* because it involves the combination of a company with its suppliers or customers. For example, Ford Motor Company expanded by acquiring a glass company, rubber plantations, a cement plant, steel mill, and other businesses that supplied its automobile manufacturing business. Between 1925 and 1930 more than 1,200 combinations took place, and about 7,000 companies disappeared in the process.

The third period started after World War II and continues unabated today. Business combinations have been particularly strong since the late 1960s. During some years more than 4,000 individual firms disappeared through combinations. Some observers have called this activity "merger mania." Rather than attempts to control an industry or to integrate operations, the primary motivation for combination recently has been to diversify business risk by combining companies in different industries having little, if any, production or market similarities. This type of business combination is called a *conglomerate.* One conglomerate may acquire another, as Esmark did when it acquired Norton-Simon, and conglomerates may "spin off" or divest themselves of individual businesses. Management of the conglomerate hopes to increase earnings over time by counterbalancing the effects of economic forces that affect different industries at different times.

A case can be made for adding a fourth relatively distinct period involving the combination of many savings and loan associations as well as banks beginning in the late 1980s and continuing today. These combinations are characterized by the absorption of failed (or failing) savings and loan companies and banks by healthy ones with the encouragement and financial support of the federal government through action by the Federal Savings and Loan Administration, Federal Deposit Insurance Corporation, and Resolution Trust Corporation.

WHY BUSINESS COMBINATIONS?

In addition to rapid expansion, the business combination method, or external expansion, has several other important advantages over internal expansion:

1. Combination with an existing company provides management of the acquiring company with an established operating unit with its own experienced personnel, regular suppliers, productive facilities, and distribution channels. Management of the acquiring company can draw upon the operating history and the related historical data base of the acquired company for planning purposes. A history of profitable operations by the acquired company may, of course, greatly reduce the risk involved in the new undertaking.

2. Expanding by combination does not create new competition as does the construction of new facilities, the output of which competes with that of existing facilities.

3. Combination may enable a company to diversify its operations rather rapidly by entering new markets that it may need to assure its sources of supply or market outlets. Entry into new markets may also be undertaken to obtain cost savings realized by smoothing cyclical operations.

4. Business combinations are sometimes entered into to take advantage of income tax laws, for example, to obtain the advantage of significant operating loss carryforwards that can be utilized by the acquiring company.

Notwithstanding its apparent advantages, business combination may not always be the best means of expansion. An overriding emphasis on rapid growth may result in the pyramiding of one company on another without sufficient management control over the resulting conglomerate. Too often in such cases, management fails to maintain a sound enough financial equity base to sustain the company during periods of recession. In order to avoid large dilutions of equity, some companies have relied on the use of various debt and preferred stock instruments to finance expansion, only to find themselves unable to provide the required debt service during a period of decreasing economic activity. The rapid build-up of many large conglomerates during the 1960s and the near-collapse of several of them during the early 1970s are evidence of the hazards of uncontrolled or unmanaged growth stemming from business combinations.

LEGAL CONSTRAINTS ON BUSINESS COMBINATIONS

One problem encountered by business units attempting to expand by acquisition is the possibility of antitrust suits. The federal government historically has demonstrated concern for and opposition to the concentration of economic power that may result from business combinations. Two important federal statutes, the Sherman Act and the Clayton Act, were enacted in an effort to deal with antitrust problems.

The Sherman Act (1890) prohibits any contract, conspiracy, or combination of business interests that results in restraint of trade or tends to create monopolistic powers. This act, however, was not broad enough to cover many types of business contracts, acquisitions, or mergers, even though it essentially tended to restrain or lessen competition. As a result, Congress passed the Clayton Act (1914).

Sections 3 and 7 of the Clayton Act prohibit price discrimination, tying contracts (e.g., requiring the purchase of one or more slow selling models of a product to obtain one or more popular models) and exclusive selling and leasing contracts, and the acquisition by one corporation of the stock of another corporation where the effect may be to lessen competition or tend to create a monopoly. Some companies, instead of acquiring the stock of another company, acquired its assets directly, and thereby bypassed the stock acquisition provision of the Act. In 1950 Congress amended the Clayton Act to prohibit one corporation from acquiring another through the acquisition of its assets if it would have been prohibited under the 1914 act from acquiring the company's stock. These two acts have been used often by the Department of Justice and the Federal Trade Commission, with varying degrees of success, in attempts to prevent the formation of business combinations (or to break up existing ones) that restrain trade. During the 1980s and 1990s the Federal Trade Commission has been swamped with cases involving billion-dollar mergers, such as the formation of Texas Air and the AT&T-NCR merger.

TYPES OF BUSINESS COMBINATIONS

Business combinations may be classified under four schemes: one based on the nature of the combination, one based on the structure of the combination, one based on the method used to accomplish the combination, and one based on the accounting method used. The first three schemes are discussed here. Accounting methods for business combinations are discussed later.

Nature of the Combination

A business combination may consist of a friendly combination or an unfriendly one. In a *friendly combination,* the boards of directors of the potential combining companies negotiate mutually agreeable terms of a proposed combination. The proposal is then submitted to the stockholders of the involved companies for approval. Normally, a two-thirds or three-fourths positive vote is required by corporate bylaws to bind all stockholders to the combination. An *unfriendly combination* results when the board of directors of a company targeted for acquisition resists the combination. Resistance often involves various tactics by the target company, generally with colorful terms, such as the following:

1. *Greenmail.* The purchase of any shares held by the would-be acquiring company at a price substantially in excess of their fair value. The purchased shares are then held as treasury stock or retired.

2. *White knight* Encouraging a third firm more acceptable to the target company management to acquire or merge with the target company.

3. *Shark repellent* Acquiring large amounts of outstanding common stock, often by incurring substantial amounts of long-term debt in payment.

4. *Pac-man defense* Attempting an unfriendly takeover of the would-be acquiring company.

5. *Scorched earth* The sale, or spin-off to stockholders, of profitable business segments.

Structure of the Combination

As discussed earlier, combinations are classified by structure into three types—horizontal, vertical, and conglomerate. A *horizontal* combination is one that involves companies within the same industry that have previously been competitors; a *vertical* combination involves a company and its suppliers or customers; a *conglomerate* combination is one involving companies in unrelated industries having little, if any, production or market similarities.

Method of Combination

Business combinations are also classified by method of combination into three types—statutory mergers, statutory consolidations, and stock acquisitions.

A *statutory merger* results when one company acquires all the net assets of one or more other companies through an exchange of stock, payment of cash or other property, or the issue of debt instruments (or a combination of these methods). The acquiring company survives, whereas the acquired company (or companies) ceases to exist as a separate legal entity, although it may be continued as a separate division of the acquiring company. Thus, if A Company acquires B Company in a statutory merger, the combination is often expressed as

$$A \text{ Company} + B \text{ Company} = A \text{ Company}$$

The boards of directors of the companies involved normally negotiate the terms of a plan of merger, which must then be approved by the stockholders of each company involved. State laws or corporation bylaws dictate the percentage of positive votes required for approval of the plan.

A *statutory consolidation* results when a new corporation is formed to acquire two or more other corporations through an exchange of voting stock; the acquired corporations then cease to exist as separate legal entities. For example, if C Company is formed to consolidate A Company and B Company, the combination is generally expressed as

$$A \text{ Company} + B \text{ Company} = C \text{ Company}$$

Stockholders of the acquired companies (A and B) become stockholders in the new entity (C). The acquired companies may be operated as separate divisions of the new corporation, just as they may under a statutory merger. Statutory consolidations require the same type of stockholder approval as do statutory mergers.

A *stock acquisition* occurs when one corporation pays cash or issues stock or debt for all or part of the voting stock of another company, and the acquired company remains intact as a separate legal entity. When the acquiring company acquires more than 50% of the voting stock of the acquired company, for example, if A Company acquires 75% of the voting stock of B Company, a parent–subsidiary relationship results. Consolidated financial statements (explained in later chapters) are prepared and the business combination is often expressed as

Financial Statements of A Company + Financial Statements of B Company = Consolidated Financial Statements of A Company and B Company

The stock may be acquired through market purchases or through direct purchase from, or exchange with, individual stockholders of the subsidiary company. Sometimes stock is acquired through a *tender offer*, which is an open offer to purchase up to a stated number of shares of a given corporation at a stipulated price per share. The offering price is generally set somewhat above the current market price of the shares in order to provide an additional incentive to prospective sellers. The investee or subsidiary company continues its legal existence, and the investor or parent company records its acquisition in its records as a long-term investment.

Although **business combination** is a broad term encompassing all forms of combination, and the terms **merger** and **consolidation** have technical, legal definitions, the three terms are often used interchangeably in practice. Thus, one cannot always rely on the accuracy of the term used to identify the type of combination, but must look to the facts of the situation to determine its accounting treatment.

The accounting treatment of mergers and consolidations, where only the acquiring or new company survives, is discussed and illustrated in this chapter. Acquisitions in which the acquired company remains intact will be discussed in subsequent chapters.

Business combinations may create rather complex accounting problems. Two pre-operating problems, (1) determining price and method of payment and (2) determining the proper accounting method for the acquisition, are discussed next. Problems arising subsequent to acquisition are treated later.

DETERMINING PRICE AND METHOD OF PAYMENT IN BUSINESS COMBINATIONS

When a business combination is effected through an open-market acquisition of stock, no particular problems arise in connection with determining price or method of payment. Price is determined by the normal functioning of the stock market, and payment is generally in cash, although some or all of the cash may have to be raised by the acquiring company through debt or equity issues. Effecting a combination may present some difficulty if there are not enough willing sellers at the open-market price to permit the acquiring company to buy a majority of the outstanding shares of the company being acquired. In that event, the acquiring company must either negotiate a price directly with individuals holding large blocks of shares or revert to an open tender offer. Regardless of the method used, the acquisition is recorded at its total purchase cost including expenses incurred in acquisition.

When a business combination constitutes a true merger and is effected by an exchange of securities, both price and method of payment problems do arise. In this case, the price is expressed in terms of a ***stock exchange ratio***, which is generally expressed as the number of shares of the acquiring company to be exchanged for each share of the acquired company, and constitutes a ***negotiated price***. It is important to understand that each constituent of the combination makes two kinds of contributions to the new entity—net assets and future earnings. The accountant often becomes deeply involved in the determination of the values of these contributions. The problems that arise are discussed in the following section. Although the discussion is in terms of a ***consolidation***, the basic principles involved apply to other types of acquisitions as well.

Net Asset and Future Earnings Contributions

Determination of an equitable price for each constituent company, and of the resulting exchange ratio, requires the valuation of each company's net assets, as well as their expected contribution to the future earnings of the new entity. The accountant is often called upon to aid in determining net asset value by assessing, for example, the expected collectibility of accounts receivable, current replacement costs for inventories and some fixed assets, and the current value of long-term liabilities based on current interest rates. To estimate current replacement costs of real estate and other items of plant and equipment, the services of appraisal firms may be needed.

Where the constituent companies have used different accounting methods, the accountant may also need to reconstruct their financial statements on the basis of agreed-on accounting methods in order to obtain reasonably comparable data. Once comparable data have been obtained for a number of prior periods, they must be analyzed further in the process of projecting future contributions to earnings. The expected contributions to future earnings may vary widely among constituents, and the exchange ratio should reflect this fact. The whole process of valuation, of course, requires the careful exercise of professional judgment. Ultimately, however, the exchange ratio is determined by the bargaining ability of the individual parties to the combination.

Once the overall values of relative net asset and earnings contributions have been agreed on, the types of securities to be issued by the new entity in exchange for those of the combining companies must be determined. In some cases a single class of stock may be issued; in other cases equity may require the use of more than one class of security.

METHODS OF ACCOUNTING FOR BUSINESS COMBINATIONS

Companies that are considering a business combination should decide early in their negotiations on the accounting method they will use to record the combination. The accounting method may significantly affect the reported financial position and results of operations of the combined entity in the current and future periods, as well as the form of payment (cash, other assets, stock, etc.).

Two methods of accounting—*purchase* and *pooling of interests*—are accepted in practice. Any business combination, be it a merger, consolidation, or stock acquisition, must be accounted for by one of these two methods. The two accounting methods are discussed, illustrated, and contrasted in the following sections.

Purchase Accounting

As the term implies, the purchase method treats the combination as the purchase of one or more companies by another. The acquiring company records the purchase at its cost. If cash is given, the amount paid constitutes cost. If debt securities are given, the present value of future payments represents cost. Cost also includes the *direct expenses* incurred in the combination, such as accounting and consulting fees. *Indirect*, ongoing costs, such as those incurred to maintain a mergers and acquisitions department, however, are charged to expense as incurred.

Assets acquired by issuing shares of stock of the acquiring corporation are recorded at the fair values of the stock given or the assets received, whichever is more clearly evident. If the stock is actively traded, its quoted market price, after making allowance for market fluctuations, additional quantities issued, issue costs, and so on, is normally better evidence of fair value than are appraisal values of the net assets of an acquired company. Thus, an adjusted market price of the shares issued normally is used. Where the issued stock is of a new or closely held company, however, the fair value of the assets received generally must be used.

Once the total cost is determined, it must be allocated to the identifiable assets acquired (including intangibles) and liabilities assumed, both of which should be recorded at their fair values at the date of acquisition. Any excess of total cost over the sum of amounts assigned to identifiable assets and liabilities is recorded as goodwill and should be amortized over its economic life but not in excess of 40 years. Sometimes the net amount of the fair values of identifiable assets and liabilities may exceed the total cost of the acquired company. If so, the excess of fair value over cost should be allocated to reduce noncurrent assets (except investments in long-term marketable securities) in proportion to their fair values in determining their assigned values. If the allocation reduces the noncurrent assets to zero value, the remainder of the excess of fair value over cost should be classified as a deferred credit and should be amortized systematically to income over the period estimated to be benefited, but not in excess of 40 years.[1]

[1] *Opinions of the Accounting Principles Board No. 16,* ''Business Combinations'' (New York: AICPA, 1970), par. 91.

Thus, assume P Company pays $17,000 cash for all the net assets of S Company when S Company's balance sheet shows the following book values and fair values:

FV of asset exceeds cost

	BOOK VALUE	FAIR VALUE
Current assets	$ 5,000	$ 5,000
Buildings (net)	10,000	15,000
Land	3,000	5,000
Total assets	$18,000	$25,000
Liabilities	$ 2,000	$ 2,000
Common stock	9,000	
Retained earnings	7,000	
Total equities	$18,000	

20000

N/A   *23000*

Cost of the acquisition ($17,000) minus the fair value of net assets acquired ($23,000) produces an excess of fair value of net assets acquired over cost of $6,000. This $6,000 is allocated to reduce the values assigned to buildings and land in the ratio of their fair values as follows:

Buildings	$15,000/$20,000 × $6,000 =	$4,500
Land	$ 5,000/$20,000 × $6,000 =	1,500
Total		$6,000

The entry by P Company to record the acquisition is then:

Current Assets	5,000	
Buildings ($15,000 − $4,500)	10,500	
Land ($5,000 − $1,500)	3,500	
Liabilities		2,000
Cash		17,000

As a more complete example, assume that on January 1, 1995, P Company, in a merger, acquired the assets and assumed the liabilities of S Company by giving one of its $15 par value common shares to the former stockholders of S Company for every two shares of the $5 par value common stock they held. Assume also that the business combination must be accounted for by the purchase method. P Company common stock, which was selling at a range of $50 to $52 per share during an extended period prior to the combination, is considered to have a fair value per share of $48 after an appropriate reduction is made in its market value for additional shares issued and for issue costs. Balance sheets for P and S Companies (along with relevant fair value data) on January 1, 1995, are presented in Illustration 1-1. Because the book value of the bonds is $400,000, bond discount in the amount of $68,821 ($400,000 − $331,179) must be recorded to reduce the bonds payable to their present value.

ILLUSTRATION 1-1
Balance Sheets of P and S Companies
January 1, 1995

	P COMPANY	S COMPANY	
	BOOK VALUE	BOOK VALUE	FAIR VALUE
Cash and receivables	$ 250,000	$ 180,000	$ 170,000
Inventories	260,000	116,000	146,000
Land	600,000	120,000	400,000
Buildings	800,000	1,000,000	1,600,000
Accumulated depreciation—buildings	(300,000)	(400,000)	(600,000)
Equipment	180,000	120,000	140,000
Accumulated depreciation—equipment	(90,000)	(40,000)	(80,000)
Total assets	$1,700,000	$1,096,000	
Current liabilities	$ 200,000	$ 150,000	$ 150,000
Bonds payable, 9%, due 1/1/2005, interest payable semiannually on 6/30 and 12/31	–0–	400,000	331,179*
Common stock, $15 par value, 50,000 shares	750,000		
Common stock, $5 par value, 60,000 shares		300,000	
Other contributed capital	400,000	100,000	
Retained earnings	350,000	146,000	
Total equities	$1,700,000	$1,096,000	

*Assuming that the yield rate on bonds with similar risk was 12% on the date of acquisition. Thus, bonds payable are valued at their present value by discounting the future payments at 12% as follows:

Present Value of Bonds Payable:
  Present Value of Maturity Value:
    P. V. of 1, 20 periods @ 6% = .3118 × $400,000 = $124,720
  Present Value of Interest Annuity:
    P. V. of annuity of 1, 20 periods @ 6% =
      11.46992 × $18,000 semiannual interest =   206,459
Total Present Value of Bonds Payable $331,179

To record the exchange of stock for the net assets of S Company, P Company will make the following entry:

Cash and Receivables	170,000	
Inventories	146,000	
Land	400,000	
Buildings	1,000,000	
Equipment	60,000	
Discount on Bonds Payable	68,821	
Goodwill	145,179	
Current Liabilities		150,000
Bonds Payable		400,000
Common Stock (30,000 × $15)		450,000
Other Contributed Capital (30,000 × $33)		990,000

Since the business combination is a merger, S Company ceases to exist as a separate legal entity. Note that under the purchase method the cost of the net assets is measured by the fair value (30,000 shares × $48 = $1,440,000) of the shares given in exchange. Common stock is credited for the par value of the shares issued, with the remainder credited to other contributed capital. Individual assets acquired and liabilities assumed are recorded at their fair values. Plant assets are recorded net of their accumulated depreciation balances, the customary procedure for recording the purchase of assets. Bonds payable are recorded at their fair value by recording a discount on the bonds. After all assets and liabilities have been recorded at their fair values, an excess of cost over fair value of $145,179 remains and is recorded as goodwill.

A balance sheet prepared after the acquisition of S Company is presented in Illustration 1-2.

ILLUSTRATION 1-2
P Company
Balance Sheet
January 1, 1995

Cash and receivables		$ 420,000
Inventories		406,000
Land		1,000,000
Buildings		1,800,000
Accumulated depreciation—buildings		(300,000)
Equipment		240,000
Accumulated depreciation—equipment		(90,000)
Goodwill		145,179
Total assets		$3,621,179
Current liabilities		$ 350,000
Bonds payable	$400,000	
Less: Bond discount	68,821	331,179
Common stock, $15 par value, 80,000 shares outstanding		1,200,000
Other contributed capital		1,390,000
Retained earnings		350,000
Total equities		$3,621,179

If an acquisition takes place within a fiscal period, purchase accounting requires the inclusion of the acquired company's revenues and expenses in the acquiring company's income statement only from the date of acquisition forward. Income earned by the acquired company prior to the date of acquisition is considered to be included in the net assets acquired.

Income Tax Consequences in Business Combinations Accounted for by the Purchase Method

The fair values of specific assets acquired and liabilities assumed in a business combination may differ from the income tax bases of those items. *SFAS No. 109* requires that a deferred tax asset or liability be recognized for differences between the assigned values and tax bases of the assets and liabilities (except goodwill, unallocated "negative goodwill," and leveraged leases) recognized in a purchase business combination.[2] In order to concentrate on basic issues, we have deferred the treatment of income tax consequences until Chapter 7, where we discuss and illustrate tax consequences related to purchase method business combinations as well as reporting tax consequences in consolidated financial statements.

Contingent Consideration in a Purchase   Purchase agreements sometimes provide that the purchasing company will give additional consideration to the seller if certain specified future events or transactions occur. The contingency may require the payment of cash (or other assets) or the issuance of additional securities. During the contingency period, the purchaser has a contingent liability that should be properly disclosed in a footnote to the financial statements. If the specified future events or transactions occur, the purchaser must record the additional consideration given as an adjustment to the original purchase transaction. Accounting for the additional consideration depends on the nature of the contingency. The two general types of contingencies are (1) contingencies based on earnings and (2) contingencies based on security prices.

Contingency based on earnings   As discussed earlier, the expected contribution by the acquired company to the future earnings of the acquiring company is an important element in determining the price to be paid for the acquired company. Because future earnings are unknown, the purchase agreement may contain a provision that the purchaser will give additional consideration to the former stockholders of the acquired company if the combined company's earnings equal or exceed a specified amount over some specified period. In essence, the parties to the business combination agree that the total price to be paid for the acquired company will not be known until the end of the contingency period. Consequently, any additional consideration given must be considered as additional cost of the acquired company.

If goodwill was recorded as part of the original purchase transaction, the fair value of any additional consideration given should be recorded as an addition to goodwill. In the event that an excess of the fair value of net assets acquired over cost was allocated to reduce the fair value of net assets recorded, the original purchase transaction must be reevaluated. The additional consideration given is assigned to noncurrent assets to raise them to their fair values, with any remaining additional consideration assigned to goodwill. The payment of the additional consideration is treated as a change in accounting estimate. The amount of additional consideration assigned to depreciable or amortizable assets is depreciated or amortized over the assets' remaining useful lives.

As an example, assume that P Company acquired all the net assets of S Company in exchange for P Company's common stock. P Company also agreed to issue

---

[2] *Statement of Financial Accounting Standards No. 109,* "Accounting for Income Taxes," FASB (Stamford, 1992), par. 30.

contingency

additional shares of common stock with a fair value of $150,000 to the former stockholders of S Company if the average postcombination earnings over the next two years equal or exceed $800,000. Assume the contingency is met. P Company's stock has a par value of $5 per share and a market value of $25 per share at the end of the contingency period, and goodwill was recorded in the original purchase transaction. P Company will issue 6,000 additional shares ($150,000/$25) and make the following entry:[3]

Goodwill	150,000	
Common Stock (6,000 × $5)		30,000
Other Contributed Capital		120,000

The goodwill recorded must be amortized by adding it to any goodwill recorded on the original purchase date and amortizing the total over its remaining useful life. The amortization period must end within 40 years from the original business combination date.

If an excess of fair value over cost, in the amount of $50,000, was allocated to reduce the fair values assigned to equipment ($35,000) and land ($15,000) in the original purchase transaction, the issuance of the new shares to settle the contingency would be recorded as follows:

Equipment *Noncurrent assets*	35,000	
Land	15,000	
Goodwill	100,000	
Common Stock		30,000
Other Contributed Capital		120,000

The additional $35,000 cost assigned to equipment must be depreciated over the equipment's remaining useful life. The goodwill recorded must be amortized to expense as described earlier.

Contingency based on security prices In contrast to additional consideration given to satisfy a contingency based on earnings, which results in an adjustment to the total purchase price, a contingency based on security prices has no effect on the determination of cost to the acquiring company. That is, total cost is agreed on as part of the initial combination transaction. The unknown element is the future market value of the acquiring company's stock given in exchange and, consequently, the number of shares or amount of other consideration to be given. The stockholders of the acquired company may be concerned that the issuance of a significant number of additional shares by the acquiring company may decrease the market value of the shares. To allay this concern, the acquiring company may guarantee the market value of the shares given as of a specified future date. If the market value of the shares at the future date is less than the guaranteed value, the acquiring company will pay cash or issue additional shares in an amount equal to the difference between the then current market value and the guaranteed value.

---

[3] If the contingency is settled in cash, the entry is a debit to goodwill and a credit to cash.

To illustrate, assume that P Company issues 50,000 shares of common stock with a par value of $5 per share and a market price of $30 per share for the net assets of S Company. P Company guarantees that the stock will have a market price of at least $30 per share one year later. At the original transaction date, P Company made the following entry:[4]

Net Assets (50,000 × $30)	1,500,000	
Common Stock (50,000 × $5)		250,000
Other Contributed Capital		1,250,000

Assuming the market price of P Company's stock at the end of the contingency period is $25 per share, P Company must give additional consideration of $250,000 (50,000 × $5). Because the value assigned to the securities at the original transaction date was only an estimate, any additional consideration given should be recorded as an adjustment to other contributed capital. If the contingency is paid in cash, P Company will make the following entry:

Other Contributed Capital	250,000	
Cash		250,000

This adjustment will result in other contributed capital of $1,000,000, verified as follows:

Total purchase price agreed on	$1,500,000
Less: Cash paid	250,000
Payment in common stock	1,250,000
Less: Par value of stock issued	250,000
Other contributed capital	$1,000,000

If the contingency is satisfied by the issuance of additional shares of stock, P Company must issue 10,000 additional shares ($250,000/$25) to the former stockholders of S Company and will make the following entry:

Other Contributed Capital	50,000	
Common Stock (10,000 × $5)		50,000

This adjustment will result in other contributed capital of $1,200,000, verified as follows:

Total purchase price paid in stock	$1,500,000
Par value of stock issued (60,000 × $5)	300,000
Other contributed capital	$1,200,000

---

[4]The term "net assets" is used here as an expediency. The individual assets acquired and liabilities assumed would be debited and credited in the entry.

In some cases, consideration contingently issuable may depend on both future earnings and future security prices. In such cases, an additional cost of the acquired company should be recorded for the additional consideration contingent on earnings, and previously recorded consideration should be reduced to current value of the consideration contingent on security prices.

LEVERAGED BUYOUTS

A leveraged buyout (LBO) occurs when a group of employees (generally a management group) creates a new company to acquire all the outstanding common shares of their employer company. The management group contributes whatever stock they hold to the new corporation and borrows sufficient funds to acquire the remainder of the common stock. The old corporation is then merged into the new corporation. The LBO term results because most of the capital of the new corporation comes from borrowed funds. The basic accounting question relates to the net asset values (fair or book) to be used by the new corporation. Accounting procedures generally follow the rules advocated by the *Emerging Issues Task Force in Consensus Position No. 88-16.* Essentially, the consensus position is that only the portion of the net assets acquired with the borrowed funds have actually been purchased and should, therefore, be recorded at their cost. The portion of the net assets of the new corporation provided by the management group is recorded at book values since there has been no change in ownership.

To illustrate, assume Old Company has 5,000 outstanding common shares, 500 of which are held by Old Company management. New Company, which is formed to merge Old Company into New Company, then borrows $31,500 to purchase the 4,500 shares held by nonmanagers. Management then contributes its 500 shares of Old Company to New Company, after which management owns 100% of New Company. Clearly, control of Old Company has changed hands. Based on the consensus position, the net assets (90%) purchased from Old Company shareholders for cash should be recorded at their cost. The net assets acquired from the 10% interest held by managers have not been confirmed through a purchase transaction and are, therefore, recorded at their book values. A summary of Old Company's net asset position just prior to the formation of New Company follows:

	BOOK VALUE	FAIR VALUE
Plant assets	$ 9,000	$24,000
Other net assets	1,000	1,000
Total	$10,000	$25,000

Book entries to record the transactions on New Company's books are:

Investment in Old Company .1($10,000)	1,000	
No Par Common Stock—New Company		1,000
To record the contribution of 500 shares of Old		
Company stock at book value.		

Cash	31,500	
Notes Payable		31,500
To record borrowings.		
Investment in Old Company	31,500	
Cash		31,500
To record the purchase of 4,500 shares of Old Company.		
Plant Assets*	22,500	
Other Net Assets	1,000	
Goodwill	9,000	
Investment in Old Company		32,500
To record the merger of Old Company into New Company.		

*[$9,000 + .9($24,000 − $9,000)]

Plant assets are recorded at book value plus 90% of the excess of fair value over book value. Other net assets are recorded at book value, which equals fair value. The $9,000 recorded as goodwill on the purchase from outside shareholders can be confirmed as follows:

Cost of shares	$31,500
Book value of net assets acquired .9($10,000)	9,000
Excess of cost over book value	22,500
Assigned to plant assets .9($24,000 − $9,000)	(13,500)
Assigned to goodwill	$ 9,000

After the merger, New Company's balance sheet will appear as follows:

NEW COMPANY
Balance Sheet
January 1, 1995

Plant assets	$22,500
Other assets	1,000
Goodwill	9,000
Total assets	$32,500
Notes payable	$31,500
Common stock	1,000
Total equities	$32,500

Note that the total equities of New Company consist primarily of debt; thus the term *leveraged buyout*. As we will see in Chapter 11, the consensus position for recording LBOs is essentially consistent with the parent company concept of consolidated financial statements.

Pooling of Interests Accounting

The pooling of interests method interprets a business combination as a process in which two or more groups of stockholders unite their ownership interests by an exchange of common stock. No acquisition of one company or companies by another is recognized, because the combination is accomplished without disbursing resources of the constituents (a corporation's unissued stock is not considered an asset). No owners of former firms are bought out. Instead, the owners, because they continue to be stockholders, retain proprietary rights, however small, in the larger surviving firm. Accordingly, the net assets of the combining companies remain intact, although combined, and the stockholder groups also remain intact, but combined.

Proponents of pooling contend that the combination is essentially a transaction between the combining stockholder groups and, therefore, that it does not involve the corporate entities; consequently, the transaction neither requires nor justifies establishing a new basis of accountability for the assets and equities of the combined operations. Thus, fair values of assets and liabilities are ignored, except in the determination of an equitable exchange ratio of common stock, and the assets acquired and liabilities assumed are carried forward to the new or surviving entity at their recorded (book) values. The stockholders' equity of the acquired company is combined with the stockholders' equity of the acquiring company. The allocation of the acquired company's stockholders' equity among common stock, other contributed capital, and retained earnings may have to be restructured, however, because of differences in the par value of the common stock issued and the par value of the common stock acquired (retired).

To illustrate, the pooling of interests method is applied to the data given in Illustration 1-1. Thirty thousand shares of P Company common stock were exchanged for all the outstanding common stock of S Company. Under pooling, the initial exchange of stock is recorded as follows:

Cash and Receivables	180,000	
Inventories	116,000	
Land	120,000	
Buildings	1,000,000	
Equipment	120,000	
Other Contributed Capital	50,000	
Accumulated Depreciation—Buildings		400,000
Accumulated Depreciation—Equipment		40,000
Current Liabilities		150,000
Bonds Payable		400,000
Common Stock (30,000 × $15)		450,000
Retained Earnings		146,000

Notice that the entry records the assets and liabilities of S Company on P Company's books at their preacquisition book values. Common stock is recorded at its par value to comply with incorporation laws regarding legal capital. An adjustment in stockholders' equity is required because of the difference between the par value of the P Company stock issued, $450,000, and the par value of S Company stock acquired, $300,000. Where the amount of the par or stated value of the stock issued ($450,000) exceeds the total par or stated value of the acquired company's stock ($300,000), the excess should be deducted first from the *combined* other contributed capital and then from *combined* retained earnings.[5] Since the par value of the stock issued exceeds the par value of the stock acquired by $150,000, the excess serves to reduce S Company's other contributed capital ($100,000) to zero, and the remaining $50,000 reduces P Company's other contributed capital, as indicated in the foregoing entry. As a result, all of S Company's retained earnings of $146,000 will be combined with the retained earnings of P Company to constitute the surviving entity's retained earnings. A postacquisition balance sheet for P Company is given in Illustration 1-3.

Pooling
Accounting

ILLUSTRATION 1-3
P Company
Balance Sheet
January 1, 1995

Cash and receivables	$ 430,000
Inventories	376,000
Land	720,000
Buildings	1,800,000
Accumulated depreciation—buildings	(700,000)
Equipment	300,000
Accumulated depreciation—equipment	(130,000)
Total assets	$2,796,000
Current liabilities	$ 350,000
Bonds payable	400,000
Common stock, $15 par value, 80,000 shares outstanding	1,200,000
Other contributed capital	350,000
Retained earnings	496,000
Total equities	$2,796,000

Note that it is the combined other contributed capital of both companies that is reduced before any reduction in combined retained earnings. For example, if the par value of the stock issued by P Company was $900,000, the entire other contributed capital of P Company would be eliminated and the following entry made for the exchange of stock. (The assets and liabilities would be recorded at book values as in the previous entry. In the entries that follow, the net effect will be recorded as "net assets," so that attention can be directed toward the items that would be different, that is, the stockholders' equity structure.)

---

[5]*Opinions of the Accounting Principles Board No. 16,* par. 53.

Net Assets	546,000	
Other Contributed Capital	400,000	
Common Stock		900,000
Retained Earnings		46,000

Par value of P Company stock issued	$900,000
Par value of S Company stock retired	300,000
Increase in par value	600,000
Reduce S Company other contributed capital	(100,000)
Balance	500,000
Reduce P Company other contributed capital	(400,000)
Balance	100,000
Reduce S Company retained earnings recorded	$(100,000)

The par value of the stock issued ($900,000) exceeds the par value of the stock acquired ($300,000) by $600,000, which serves to reduce S Company's other contributed capital by $100,000, P Company's other contributed capital by $400,000, and S Company's retained earnings by $100,000. The remainder of S Company's retained earnings ($46,000) is then combined with P Company's retained earnings to constitute the total retained earnings of the surviving company.

In some cases, part of the acquired company's other contributed capital will be combined with that of the acquiring company. Assume, for example, that the par value of the stock issued was $375,000. The following entry would be made for the exchange of stock:

Net Assets	546,000	
Common Stock		375,000
Other Contributed Capital		25,000
Retained Earnings		146,000

Par value of P Company stock issued	$375,000
Par value of S Company stock retired	300,000
Increase in par value	75,000
Reduce S Company other contributed capital recorded	$(75,000)

The par value of stock issued exceeds the par value of the stock acquired by $75,000, which serves to reduce the amount of S Company's other contributed capital by $75,000; the remaining $25,000 represents a portion of combined other contributed capital, which is recorded in the acquisition entry.

Where the amount of the par or stated value of the combined entity is *less* than the total of the par or stated value of the combining entities, the difference is an addition to the combined other contributed capital. No portion of the difference is ever added to combined retained earnings. For example, if the par value of the stock issued was $225,000, the following stock exchange entry on the books of P Company would be appropriate:

Net Assets	546,000	
Common Stock		225,000
Other Contributed Capital		175,000
Retained Earnings		146,000

In summary, combined retained earnings may be equal to or less than the total of the precombination retained earnings of the constituents, but it can never be greater than that amount.

If the combination had taken place within one fiscal period, the individual revenue and expense balances of S Company would also have been carried forward to be combined with those of P Company. Any corporation that applies the pooling method of accounting to a combination should report results of operations for the period in which the combination occurs as though the companies had been combined as of the beginning of the period. Results of operations for that period, therefore, are the sum of results of (1) operations of the *separate* companies as if they had been combined from the beginning of the fiscal period to the date the combination is consummated and (2) the *combined* operations from that date to the end of the period.[6] Under pooling accounting, all direct and indirect costs incurred to effect a business combination are deducted in determining the net income of the resulting combined company for the period in which the expenses are incurred. Thus, the costs of registering and issuing securities, and accounting and consulting fees, for example, are deducted as expenses in the period incurred.

FINANCIAL STATEMENT DIFFERENCES BETWEEN ACCOUNTING METHODS

The purchase and pooling of interests methods cannot be considered alternatives in accounting for a specific business combination. Two business combinations may be very similar, yet one may have to be accounted for as a purchase and the other may have to be accounted for as a pooling. By careful planning of the combination, the constituents can determine which method will be used. Therefore, it is important to understand the differences in financial statements that result from the use of the two methods.

A comparison of Illustrations 1-2 and 1-3 shows that total assets under the purchase method in the situation described exceed those under the pooling method by $825,179 of which $145,179 represents the intangible, goodwill. The remaining $680,000 reflects the excess of the fair values of the assets of S Company over their precombination book values. To the extent that this $680,000 relates to inventory or depreciable assets, under the purchase method, future income charges will be greater, and reported net income less. Inventory effects are normally reflected in income during the first period subsequent to combination if the first-in,

---

[6]Ibid., par. 56.

first-out (FIFO) inventory method is used by the surviving entity; under the last-in, first-out (LIFO) method, the effect is not reflected unless inventory quantities are reduced sufficiently in future periods. Depreciation charges will be greater under the purchase method over the remaining useful lives of the depreciable assets, and goodwill must be amortized to future periods. In addition, long-term liabilities (bonds payable) under the purchase method are $68,821 less than under the pooling method. This $68,821 bond discount must also be amortized to future periods. Thus, pooling generally reports greater future earnings and related earnings per share.

Illustration 1-4 shows the amount by which income under the purchase method would be less than it would be under pooling of interests for the first period after the combination. Assume that the FIFO inventory method is used; the remaining economic lives of buildings and equipment are 20 and 8 years, respectively; goodwill is amortized over the maximum period allowed, 40 years; and bond discount is amortized on a straight-line basis.

ILLUSTRATION 1-4
Income Effects of Purchase vs. Pooling

	PURCHASE	POOLING	DIFFERENCE
Building depreciation (20 years)	$ 75,000	$ 55,000	$20,000
Equipment depreciation (8 years)	18,750	21,250	(2,500)
Amortization of goodwill (40 years)	3,629	–0–	3,629
Bond discount amortization (10 years)	6,882	–0–	6,882
Inventory added to cost of sales	406,000	376,000	30,000
Total	$510,261	$452,250	$58,011

In addition, the future sale of any S Company assets combined will normally produce a greater gain (or lower loss) under pooling of interests since the assets are carried at lower precombination book values. The stockholders' equity sections of the balance sheets are considerably different under the two methods. The purchase method reports total stockholders' equity of $2,940,000 (Illustration 1-2), whereas the pooling method reports $2,046,000 (Illustration 1-3). This combination of lower stockholders' equity and higher reported earnings under pooling tends to produce a doubling effect on return on stockholders' equity. For example, assume a reported net income of $315,000 (ignoring income taxes) under the purchase method for the first full year after combination. Computation of the return on stockholders' equity would be:

Purchase method = $315,000 ÷ $2,940,000 = 10.7%
Pooling method = $373,011 ($315,000 + $58,011) ÷ $2,046,000 = 18.2%

Thus, pooling reports a significantly greater return on stockholders' equity.

A comparison of the primary differences between the purchase and pooling of interests methods is given in Illustration 1-5.

ILLUSTRATION 1-5
Comparison of Purchase and Pooling of Interests

PURCHASE	POOLING OF INTERESTS
1. Assets and liabilities acquired are recorded at their fair values. Any excess of cost over the fair value of net assets acquired is recorded as goodwill.	Assets and liabilities acquired are recorded at their precombination book values. No excess of cost over book value exists.
2. The acquired company's retained earnings do not become a part of the acquiring company's retained earnings.	The acquired company's retained earnings become a part of the acquiring company's retained earnings. Some adjustment may be required to maintain legal capital.
3. The excess of cost over book value assigned to depreciable or amortizable assets is depreciated or amortized to reduce the reported income of the acquiring company.	No excess of cost over book value exists; thus, there is no additional depreciation or amortization expense.
4. The acquired company's earnings are included with the acquiring company's earnings only from the date of combination forward.	The acquired company's earnings are included with the acquiring company's earnings for the full fiscal year in which the combination occurs.
5. Direct costs incurred in the combination are included as part of the cost of the acquired company.	Direct costs incurred in the combination are expensed in the year in which incurred.
6. Indirect costs related to acquisitions are expensed in the year in which incurred.	Same as purchase.

PURCHASE VERSUS POOLING—AN HISTORICAL SUMMARY[7]

Prior to the 1940s the vast majority of business combinations were accounted for as purchases, that is, as the acquisition by one company of one or more other companies. Although some recognition of the possibility of combining assets and equities at their book values existed as early as the 1920s, most combinations using this approach entailed a change in form of organization without any real change in substance. For example, two subsidiaries of a given parent company might be combined into one company, or a parent company might dissolve an existing subsidiary and make it a part of the legal structure of the parent. In such situations the overall operating entity remained the same, and there seemed little reason to change the basis of accountability, particularly in the absence of arm's-length bargaining as a basis for the establishment of new values.

The term "pooling of interests" was used in the 1940s in public utility rate-base cases before the Federal Power Commission to describe a combination situa-

[7]This section draws heavily on *Accounting Research Study No. 5*, "A Critical Study of Accounting for Business Combinations," by Arthur Wyatt (New York: AICPA, 1963).

tion where the constituents were so closely related that any arm's-length bargaining was questionable. The resulting combined public utility wished, for obvious reasons, to use higher current values of assets at the time of combination as the basis for establishing appropriate rates. The Commission ruled, essentially, that no new values were appropriate, since the companies had mutually agreed to pool their interests and no sale had taken place in which one party disposed of an interest and another party acquired that interest. Thus, the term "pooling of interests" was used to describe a situation or transaction rather than a method of accounting.

During the late 1940s an increasing number of business combinations were effected through an exchange of equity securities. Combinations with similar characteristics were described as poolings of interests in some situations and as purchases in others. No definitive criteria for distinguishing purchases from poolings had been developed. The Committee on Accounting Procedure of the American Institute of Accountants (the predecessor organization to the American Institute of Certified Public Accountants) studied the situation and in 1950 issued *Accounting Research Bulletin No. 40*.[8] A pooling of interests was described as a combination in which all or substantially all of the equity interests in the predecessor companies continued in the surviving entity, essentially in proportion to their interests in the predecessor companies. In addition, *ARB No. 40* stated that a pooling would normally involve companies of relatively the same size, with continuity of management or the power to control management. Furthermore, a pooling would normally involve companies whose business activities were similar or complementary. Where these conditions did not exist, a purchase was deemed the appropriate method by which to effect a combination.

Because many combinations did not clearly meet all the criteria for pooling, and because *ARB No. 40* provided no guide as to the relative importance of the criteria, similar combinations continued to be accounted for in different ways, sometimes as poolings and sometimes as purchases. In practice, the relative-size test gradually deteriorated as a guide to determining the proper classification of the transaction. In 1957, in an effort to clarify the pooling criteria, the Committee on Accounting Procedure issued *Accounting Research Bulletin No. 48*. In *ARB No. 48* the criteria in *ARB No. 40* were reiterated, except that the relative-size test was modified to permit pooling for combinations with as great a size disparity as 90%–10% or 95%–5%. *ARB No. 48* also concluded that "no one of the factors . . . would necessarily be determinative and any one factor might have varying degrees of significance in different cases; however, their presence or absence would be cumulative in effect . . . determination as to whether a particular combination is a purchase or pooling should be made in light of all attendant circumstances."[9]

Because of its failure to specify the necessary degree of conformity with the pooling criteria, *ARB No. 48* had little impact on practice. In essence, a given combination could be accounted for either as a pooling of interests or as a purchase. Just as the relative-size test had deteriorated earlier, the "continuity of ownership interests" criterion also deteriorated. The notion that relative equity interests

---

[8]*Accounting Research Bulletin No. 40*, "Business Combinations" (New York: AIA, 1950), par. 2.
[9]*Accounting Research Bulletin No. 48*, "Business Combinations" (New York: AIA, 1957), par. 7.

should continue in the new or surviving entity implies, for example, that common stock should be issued for common stock. If preferred stock or other types of securities are issued for common stock, continuity of ownership interests does not exist, and pooling is not appropriate. During the 1960s the continuity-of-ownership-interests criterion deteriorated to such a degree that many combinations were treated as poolings even though a variety of securities such as convertible preferred stock and convertible bonds were exchanged for common stock and, as a result, the nature of the ownership interests changed substantially. In addition, a procedure of "partial pooling" developed. Under this procedure a combination was consummated by an exchange of cash and stock of the surviving company for the common stock of the other constituents, and the cash portion was accounted for as a purchase and the common stock portion as a pooling. By the latter part of the 1960s, combinors had considerable freedom in practice to account for a combination by either the purchase or pooling methods, regardless of the form of the combination. Thus, the development of better criteria to distinguish between combinations that constitute purchases and combinations that constitute poolings of interests was needed. The Accounting Principles Board made the solution of this problem one of their major tasks and issued *APB Opinion No. 16*, "Business Combinations," in August 1970.

In *Opinion No. 16* the Board concluded:

> . . . that the purchase method and the pooling of interests method are both acceptable in accounting for business combinations, although not as alternatives in accounting for the same business combination. A business combination which meets specified conditions requires accounting by the pooling of interests method. A new basis of accounting is not permitted for a combination that meets the specified conditions, and the assets and liabilities of the combining companies are combined at their recorded amounts. All other business combinations should be accounted for as an acquisition of one or more companies by a corporation.[10]

Thus, *Opinion No. 16* removes the purchase–pooling option. Only the interpretation of the facts of an actual or contemplated combination can determine which method is required.

Paragraphs 45–48 of *Opinion No. 16* spell out the specific conditions under which pooling is required. All these conditions must prevail. The main points are summarized as follows: (a) independent ownership interests are combined to continue previously separate operations; (b) all or nearly all the common shares of one company are acquired in exchange for another firm's common shares, and all stockholders retain the same relative and unrestricted rights, in a single transaction that involves no planned or contingent realignment of rights in the near future; and (c) an intention must exist to continue substantially all the operations and normal stockholder relationships of the combining companies. *Opinion No. 16* drops the relative-size and management continuity tests, attempts to define criteria

---

[10]*Opinions of the Accounting Principles Board No. 16*, par. 8.

clearly, removes any choice of method (other than that provided by judicious planning of a combination's terms), and prohibits partial pooling.

In *Opinion No. 16* the Board established 12 specific conditions; if **all** are met, use of the pooling method is required. These 12 conditions are presented in the Appendix. In simplified terms, the Board held that combinations effected by pure exchanges of common stock for common stock (with no contingency clauses, unusual extra agreements, convertible or otherwise complex securities) must be accounted for as poolings; all other combinations must be treated as purchases.

Advantages and disadvantages, both theoretical and practical, may be noted for both methods. Pooling is criticized on the ground that values given and received are ignored in a negotiated transaction. "Instant earnings" are alleged to result (a) from the early sale of newly pooled assets that are carried at their precombination (and often quite low) book values, and (b) from a reporting practice that requires that the surviving firm report earnings for the year of combination as if it had been combined during that entire year, even though the combination may have occurred well along in that year, or even after the fiscal year-end but before publication of the financial statements.

Pooling is defended, on the other hand, on the grounds that it is more objective than the purchase method (no appraisals of assets or stock values are necessary), that it properly continues generally accepted accounting principles rather than introducing extensive appraisal-based data, and that it avoids accounting for one part of the combined company on a fair value basis and the other part on an historical cost basis.

Those who endorse the purchase method believe that one company clearly acquires another in almost every business combination, and that control passes to the dominant corporation in a transaction bargained on the basis of current fair values given and received, regardless of the nature of the consideration. However, with the purchase method problems are alleged to exist with regard to objective determination of current values and the apparent inconsistency of accounting for only part of the combined company on an updated basis. Goodwill and the related amortization charges may materially affect financial reports, although, being derived from current valuations (appraisals, etc.) of stock issued and assets received, they are less than objective measures.

Opinion No. 16 reduced significantly the number of business combinations accounted for as pooling of interests (as shown in Illustration 1-6) and generally improved business combination accounting and reporting. However, the basic controversy remains.

Some officials see a possible resurgence of the use of pooling of interests accounting, particularly among financial institutions. The takeover of failing banks and savings and loans by healthy ones referred to earlier is fueling an increase in poolings since banks and savings and loans traditionally have been some of the biggest users of pooling. In addition, in recessionary periods such as the early 1990s, companies have a particular interest in protecting the bottom line. Some companies even take extraordinary steps to qualify for pooling accounting in order to avoid the large charges to income for goodwill amortization and additional depreciation.

ILLUSTRATION 1-6
Business Combinations

YEAR	TOTAL	PURCHASE		POOLING OF INTERESTS		
		NO.	PERCENT	NO.	PERCENT	
1967	260	116	44.6	144	55.4	
1968	374	190	50.8	184	49.2	
1969	380	195	51.3	185	48.7	
1970	294	155	52.7	139	47.3	*Opinion No. 16* issued
1971	233	133	57.1	100	42.9	
1972	262	160	61.1	102	38.9	
1973	253	163	64.4	90	35.6	
1974	193	143	74.1	50	25.9	
1975	106	75	70.8	31	29.2	
1976	146	103	70.5	43	29.5	
1977	166	118	71.1	48	28.9	
1978	205	149	72.7	56	27.3	
1979	224	185	82.6	39	17.4	
1980	193	159	82.4	34	17.6	
1981	186	156	83.9	30	16.1	
1982	169	145	85.8	24	14.2	
1983	180	154	85.6	26	14.4	
1984	217	194	89.4	23	10.6	
1985	224	200	89.3	24	10.7	
1986	261	239	91.6	22	8.4	
1987	215	194	90.2	21	9.8	
1988	230	216	93.9	14	6.1	
1989	237	219	92.4	18	7.6	
1990	200	190	95.0	10	5.0	

SOURCE: *Accounting Trends and Techniques*, 1966 through 1991 issues (New York: AICPA).

For example, as reported in the July 5, 1991, issue of *The Wall Street Journal*, in AT&T's $7.5 billion acquisition of NCR Corporation, AT&T sold 6.3 million of NCR shares it held in order to undo the prior two years of treasury stock purchases by NCR, which would have blocked use of pooling. Without pooling, AT&T would have had to record $5.7 billion goodwill and record amortization expense of more than $142 million yearly. Because of these and other similar manipulations, many in the accounting profession are again proposing severe restrictions in the use of pooling accounting. Some even propose the complete elmination of its use.

PRO FORMA STATEMENTS

Pro forma statements, sometimes called "as if" statements, are prepared to show the effect of planned or contemplated transactions by showing how they might have affected the historical financial statements if they had been consumated during the period covered by those statements. Pro forma statements are often used for proposed business combinations. After the boards of directors of the constituents have reached tentative agreement on a combination proposal, for example, pro forma statements showing the final effect of the proposal may be prepared for distribution to the stockholders of the constituents for their consideration prior to voting on the proposal. If the proposed combination involves the issue of new securities under Securities and Exchange Commission rules, pro forma statements may be required as part of the registration statement.

When a pro forma statement is prepared, the tentative or hypothetical nature of the statement should be clearly indicated, generally by describing it as "pro forma" in the heading and including a description of the character of the transactions given effect to. Further description of any other adjustments should be clearly stated on the statement or in related notes. A pro forma balance sheet for the preceding example of P Company's acquisition of S Company that might be prepared for use by the companies' stockholders is presented in Illustration 1-7. The normal procedure is to show the audited balance sheet as of a given date, individual adjustments for the proposed transaction, and resulting account balances.

ILLUSTRATION 1-7
P Company
Pro Forma Balance Sheet
Giving Effect to Proposed Issue of Common Stock for All the
Common Stock of S Company Under Purchase Accounting
January 1, 1995

	AUDITED BALANCE SHEET	ADJUSTMENT	PRO FORMA BALANCE SHEET
ASSETS			
Cash and receivables	$ 250,000	$ 170,000	$ 420,000
Inventories	260,000	146,000	406,000
Land	600,000	400,000	1,000,000
Buildings	800,000	1,000,000	1,800,000
Accumulated depreciation—buildings	(300,000)		(300,000)
Equipment	180,000	60,000	240,000
Accumulated depreciation—equipment	(90,000)		(90,000)
Goodwill	–0–	145,179	145,179
Total assets	$1,700,000		$3,621,179
EQUITIES			
Current liabilities	$ 200,000	150,000	350,000
Bonds payable	–0–	331,179	331,179
Common stock	750,000	450,000	1,200,000
Other contributed capital	400,000	990,000	1,390,000
Retained earnings	350,000		350,000
Total equities	$1,700,000		$3,621,179

Other types of "pro forma" presentation are required by *APB Opinion No. 16.* For example, if a business combination occurred during the year and is accounted for by the purchase method, notes to financial statements should include on a pro forma basis:

1. Results of operations for the current year as though the companies had combined at the beginning of the year, unless the acquisition was at or near the beginning of the year.

2. Results of operations for the immediately preceding period as though the companies had combined at the beginning of that period if comparative financial statements are presented.

Such pro forma presentation for prior years is limited to the immediately preceding year. Similarly, where a business combination has taken place during the period and is accounted for by the pooling method, financial statements and financial information of the separate companies presented for prior years should be restated on a combined basis beginning with the earliest year presented to furnish comparative information.

APPENDIX: SPECIFIC CONDITIONS FOR POOLING OF INTERESTS

The 12 conditions that must be met for a pooling of interests are classified into three broad categories: attributes of the combining companies; conditions relating to the exchange; and absence of planned transactions.

I. Attributes of the Combining Companies:

(a) Each of the combining companies is autonomous and has not been a subsidiary or division of another corporation within two years before the plan of combination is initiated.

A pooling of interests is essentially a transaction between *independent* stockholder groups under which they unite substantially all their ownership interests by an exchange of common stock for common stock. The disposal of a subsidiary or division is a disposal of only a segment of a business and is therefore incompatible with the concept of pooling. An exception to this condition is made when a company must divest itself of a segment to comply with an order of a governmental authority or judicial body.

(b) Each of the combining companies is independent of the other combining companies. This condition means that at the dates the plan of combination is initiated and consummated, the combining companies hold as intercorporate investments no more than 10% in total of the outstanding voting common stock of any combining company.

This condition is included to prevent a company from circumventing the requirement that combining stockholders must unite substantially all their equity interests by buying out a large group of dissenting stockholders and then entering into a pooling of interests with the remaining stockholders. Such a procedure would materially alter the equity interests of the combining stockholders.

II. Conditions Relating to the Exchange to Effect the Combination:

(a) The combination is effected in a single transaction or is completed in accordance with a specific plan within one year after the plan is initiated.

The essence of pooling is the exchange of equity securities without altering the equity interests of combining stockholders. Because the combining companies continue operations during the negotiation period, equity interests could change substantially over time. An arbitrary period of one year was selected as sufficient to negotiate the terms of the pooling.

(b) A corporation offers and issues only common stock with rights identical to those of the majority of its outstanding voting common stock in exchange for substantially all the voting common stock interest of another company at the date the plan of combination is consummated. Substantially all the voting common stock means 90% or more for this condition.

This condition contains the essence of the pooling concept. The 90% figure is an arbitrary one that was selected to prevent a relatively small group of dissenting stockholders from blocking the pooling. Thus, no more than 10% of the stock can be acquired with cash or other consideration.

(c) None of the combining companies changes the equity interest of the voting common stock in contemplation of effecting the combination either within two years before the plan of combination is initiated or between the dates the combination is initiated and consummated; changes in contemplation of effecting the combination may include distributions to stockholders and additional issuances, exchanges, and retirements of securities.

This condition was included to prevent the alteration of equity interests of the common stockholders. Extra dividend distributions, additional stock issues, and stock retirements all have the potential of changing equity interests.

(d) Each of the combining companies reacquires shares of voting common stock only for purposes other than business combinations, and no company reacquires more than a normal number of shares between the dates the plan of combination is initiated and consummated.

A pooling is an exchange of common stock for common stock without changing the equity interests of the combining stockholders. No corporate assets are distributed. If a company purchases its own shares, which are then used to consummate a business combination, the net effect is obviously a purchase rather than a pooling because corporate assets have been distributed and equity interests altered.

Thus, treasury stock can be acquired only for normal purposes like providing stock for stock options and employee stock purchase plans.

(e) The ratio of the interest of an individual common stockholder to those of other common stockholders in a combining company remains the same as a result of the exchange of stock to effect the combination.

This condition was included specifically to prevent an altering of stockholder interests.

(f) The voting rights to which the common stock ownership interests in the resulting combined corporation are entitled are exercisable by the stockholders; the stockholders are neither deprived of nor restricted in exercising those rights for a period.

Limitations on or changes in voting rights would obviously alter stockholder interests.

(g) The combination is resolved at the date the plan is consummated, and no provisions of the plan relating to the issue of securities or other consideration are pending.

This condition was included to prevent the issuance of additional shares based on future earnings or stock market prices because such additional issuances would result in a change in stockholder interests.

III. Absence of Planned Transactions:

(a) The combined corporation does not agree directly or indirectly to retire or reacquire all or part of the common stock issued to effect the combination.

An agreement to retire or reacquire all or a part of the stock issued in a pooling is obviously inconsistent with the notion of combining the entire equity interests of common stockholders.

(b) The combined corporation does not enter into other financial arrangements for the benefit of the former stockholders of a combining company, such as a guaranty of loans secured by stock issued in the combination, which in effect negates the exchange of equity securities.

Arrangements of this type are also obviously inconsistent with the notion of combining entire equity interests.

(c) The combined corporation does not intend or plan to dispose of a significant part of the assets of the combining companies within two years after the combination other than disposals in the ordinary course of business of the formerly separate companies and to eliminate duplicate facilities or excess capacity.

This condition is an attempt to prevent the recognition of "immediate" profits by pooling undervalued assets with the intention of selling them at their higher fair values shortly after the combination.

Questions

(An "A" after a question, exercise, or problem number means that the question, exercise, or problem relates to a chapter appendix.)

1. Distinguish between internal and external expansion of a firm.

2. List four advantages of a business combination as compared with expanding internally.

3. What is the primary legal constraint on business combinations? Why does such a constraint exist?

4. Business combinations are classified as to structure into three types. Identify and define these types.

5. Distinguish among a statutory merger, a statutory consolidation, and a stock acquisition.

6. Define a tender offer and describe its use.

7. When stock is exchanged for stock in a business combination, how is the stock exchange ratio generally expressed?

8. Discuss the basic differences between the purchase method and the pooling of interests method.

9. When a contingency is based on security prices and additional stock is issued, how should the additional stock issued be accounted for? Why?

10. Describe the treatment that must be applied to other contributed capital and retained earnings of constituents of a business combination under a pooling of interests (a) when the par value of the new company is more than the total of the par values of the constituents, and (b) when the par value of the new company is less than the total par values of the constituents.

11. What are pro forma financial statements? What is their purpose?

12A. In January 1995, Conglomerate Company acquired 90% of the outstanding common stock of Beatle Company in exchange for Conglomerate Company common stock as part of a business combination plan initiated in April 1994. Beatle Company was incorporated in February 1993 as a new venture. At the date the combination plan was initiated, Conglomerate company owned 5% of Beatle Company stock, which it had acquired for cash during the preceding year. One of Beatle Company's major facilities is a chemical synthesis plant similar to one operated by Conglomerate Company. Conglomerate's directors see no need to maintain two such operations and plan to dispose of Beatle's plant soon after the combination. Considering only the facts given, is this combination eligible for the pooling of interests accounting treatment? Support your answer.

Exercises

Exercise 1-1

Preston Company acquired the assets (except for cash) and assumed the liabilities of Saville Company. Immediately prior to the acquisition, Saville Company's balance sheet was as follows:

	BOOK VALUE	FAIR VALUE
Cash	$ 100,000	$ 100,000
Receivables (net)	160,000	190,000
Inventory	300,000	330,000
Plant and equipment (net)	400,000	450,000
Land	350,000	550,000
Total assets	$1,310,000	$1,620,000
Liabilities	$ 450,000	$ 495,000
Common stock ($5 par value)	400,000	
Other contributed capital	110,000	
Retained earnings	350,000	
Total equities	$1,310,000	

Required:

A. Prepare the journal entries on the books of Preston Company to record the purchase of the assets and assumption of the liabilities of Saville Company if the amount paid was $1,300,000 in cash.

B. Repeat the requirement in (A) assuming the amount paid was $825,000.

Exercise 1-2

The balance sheets of Petrello Company and Sanchez Company as of January 1, 1995, are presented below. On that date, after an extended period of negotiation, the two companies agreed to merge. To effect the merger, Petrello Company is to exchange its unissued common stock for all the outstanding shares of Sanchez Company in the ratio of $\frac{1}{2}$ share of Petrello for each share of Sanchez. Market values of the shares were agreed on as Petrello, $60; Sanchez, $30. The fair values of Sanchez Company's assets and liabilities are equal to their book values with the exception of plant and equipment, which has an estimated fair value of $900,000.

	PETRELLO	SANCHEZ
Cash	$ 600,000	$ 250,000
Receivables	600,000	300,000
Inventories	2,500,000	300,000
Plant and equipment (net)	4,800,000	1,000,000
Total assets	$8,500,000	$1,850,000
Liabilities	$1,500,000	$ 400,000
Common stock, $20 par value	4,300,000	1,000,000
Other contributed capital	500,000	–0–
Retained earnings	2,200,000	450,000
Total equities	$8,500,000	$1,850,000

Required:

Prepare a balance sheet for Petrello Company immediately after the merger under the assumption that:

A. The merger is treated as a purchase.

B. The merger is treated as a pooling of interests.

Exercise 1-3

Pretzel Company acquired the assets (except for cash) and assumed the liabilities of Salt Company on January 2, 1995. As compensation, Pretzel Company gave 30,000 shares of its common stock, 15,000 shares of its 10% preferred stock, and cash of $50,000 to the stockholders of Salt Company. On the acquisition date, Pretzel Company stock had the following characteristics:

STOCK	PAR VALUE	FAIR VALUE
Common	$ 10	$ 25
Preferred	100	100

Immediately prior to the acquisition, Salt Company's balance sheet was as follows:

SALT COMPANY
Balance Sheet
January 2, 1995

Cash	$ 150,000
Accounts receivable (net of $10,000 allowance)	200,000
Inventory—LIFO cost	250,000
Land	360,000
Buildings and equipment (net)	1,040,000
Total assets	$2,000,000
Current liabilities	$ 250,000
Bonds Payable, 10%	450,000
Common stock, $5 par value	700,000
Other contributed capital	360,000
Retained earnings	240,000
Total liabilities and stockholders' equity	$2,000,000

An appraisal of Salt Company showed that the fair values of its assets and liabilities were equal to their book values except for the following, which had fair values as indicated:

Accounts receivable	$180,000
Inventory	300,000
Land	500,000
Bonds payable	470,000

Required:

Prepare the journal entry on the books of Pretzel Company to record the acquisition of the assets and assumption of the liabilities of Salt Company.

Exercise 1-4

P Company acquired the assets and assumed the liabilities of S Company on January 1, 1995, for $425,000 when S Company's balance sheet was as follows:

S COMPANY
Balance Sheet
January 1, 1995

Cash	$ 80,000
Receivables	46,000
Inventory	92,000
Land	141,000
Plant and equipment (net)	389,000
Total	$748,000
Accounts payable	$ 37,000
Bonds payable, 10%, due 12/31/2000	400,000
Common stock, $2 par value	100,000
Retained earnings	211,000
Total	$748,000

Fair values of S Company's assets and liabilities were equal to their book values except for the following:

1. Inventory has a fair value of $105,000.
2. Land has a fair value of $165,000.
3. The bonds pay interest semiannually on June 30 and December 31. The current yield rate on bonds of similar risk is 8%.

Required:

Prepare the journal entry on P Company's books to record the acquisition of the assets and assumption of the liabilities of S Company.

Exercise 1-5

Pritano Company acquired all the net assets of Succo Company on December 31, 1993, for $1,800,000 cash. The balance sheet of Succo Company immediately prior to the acquisition showed:

	BOOK VALUE	FAIR VALUE
Current assets	$ 800,000	$ 800,000
Plant and equipment	900,000	1,200,000
Total	$1,700,000	$2,000,000
Liabilities	$ 150,000	$ 180,000
Common stock	400,000	
Other contributed capital	500,000	
Retained earnings	650,000	
Total	$1,700,000	

As part of the negotiations, Pritano agreed to pay the stockholders of Succo $300,000 cash if the postcombination earnings of Pritano averaged $1,800,000 or more per year over the next two years.

Required:

A. Prepare the journal entries on the books of Pritano to record the acquisition on December 31, 1993.

B. Assuming the earnings contingency is met, prepare the journal entry on Pritano's books needed to settle the contingency on December 31, 1995.

Exercise 1-6

On January 1, 1994, Platz Company acquired all the net assets of Satz Company by issuing 75,000 shares of its $10 par value common stock to the stockholders of Satz Company. During negotiations Platz Company agreed that their common stock would have at least its current value of $40 per share on January 1, 1995. The market price of Platz Company's common stock on January 1, 1995, was $30 per share.

Required:

Prepare the journal entry on Platz Company's books on January 1, 1995, assuming:

A. The contingency is settled in cash. *75000 × 10 = 750,000*

B. The contingency is settled by issuing additional shares of stock.
75000/30 ×10 = 25,000

Exercise 1-7

Managers of Bayco own 600 of its 10,000 outstanding common shares. Draco is formed by the managers of Bayco to take over Bayco in a leveraged buyout. The managers contribute *đóng góp* their shares in Bayco, and Draco then borrows $40,000 to purchase the remaining 9,400 outstanding shares of Bayco. Bayco is then merged into Draco. Data relevant to Bayco immediately prior to the leveraged buyout follow:

9400/10000 = .94

	BOOK VALUE	FAIR VALUE
Current assets	$ 2,000	$ 2,000
Plant assets	10,000	25,000
Stockholders' equity	$12,000	$27,000

—Net asset

Required:

Complete the following schedule showing the values to be reported in Draco's balance sheet immediately after the leveraged buyout.

Current assets	$ 2000
Plant assets	24100
Goodwill	14620
Debt	4000
Stockholders' equity	720

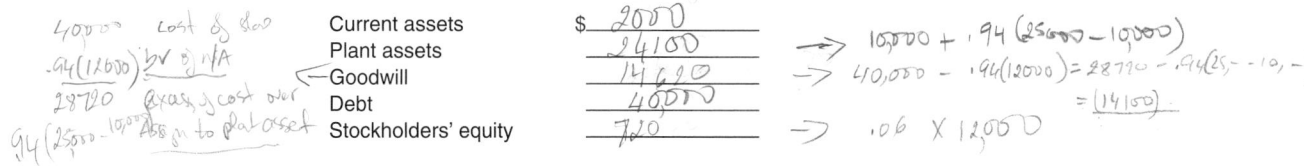

Exercise 1-8

The stockholders of Porsche Company and Saab Company agree to combine their operations through a pooling of interests. On the date of the combination, the stockholders' equity of each company is as follows:

	PORSCHE	SAAB
Current assets	$ 385,000	$126,000
Plant assets (net)	895,000	379,000
Total	$1,280,000	$505,000
Common stock, $20 par value	$ 700,000	$300,000
Other contributed capital	250,000	75,000
Retained earnings	330,000	130,000
Total	$1,280,000	$505,000

Required:

Prepare the journal entry on Porsche Company's books to record the acquisition of the net assets of Saab Company under each of the four assumptions as to the number of Porsche Company shares issued.

A. Porsche Company issues 12,000 shares.

B. Porsche Company issues 16,000 shares.

C. Porsche Company issues 19,500 shares.

D. Porsche Company issues 35,000 shares.

Exercise 1-9

Price Company issued 8,000 shares of its $20 par value common stock for all the outstanding common stock of Simmons Company in a business combination under which Simmons Company will be merged into Price Company. On the date of the combination, Price Company common stock had a fair value of $30 per share. Balance sheets for Price Company and Simmons Company immediately prior to the combination were:

	PRICE	SIMMONS
Current assets	$ 438,000	$ 64,000
Plant and equipment (net)	575,000	136,000
Total	$1,013,000	$200,000
Liabilities	$ 300,000	$ 50,000
Common stock, $20 par value	550,000	80,000
Other contributed capital	72,500	20,000
Retained earnings	90,500	50,000
Total	$1,013,000	$200,000

Required:

Select the letter of the best answer.

1. If the business combination is treated as a pooling of interests, the total other contributed capital immediately after the combination will be

(a) $12,500.
(b) $80,000.
(c) $50,000.
(d) $172,500.

2. If the business combination is treated as a pooling of interests, the total retained earnings of the pooled company immediately after the combination will be
   (a) $130,000.
   (b) $124,000.
   (c) $80,000.
   (d) $140,500.

3. If the business combination is treated as a purchase and Simmons Company's net assets have a fair value of $228,800, Price Company's balance sheet immediately after the combination will include goodwill of
   (a) $10,200.
   (b) $12,800.
   (c) $11,200.
   (d) $18,800.

4. If the business combination is treated as a purchase and the fair value of Simmons Company's current assets is $90,000, its plant and equipment is $242,000, and its liabilities are $56,000, Price Company's balance sheet immediately after the combination will include
   (a) Negative goodwill of $36,000.
   (b) Plant and equipment of $817,000.
   (c) Plant and equipment of $781,000.
   (d) Goodwill of $36,000.

Exercise 1-10

Effective December 31, 1995, Zintel Corporation proposes to issue additional shares of its common stock in exchange for all the assets and liabilities of Smith Corporation and Platz Corporation, after which Smith and Platz will distribute the Zintel stock to their stockholders in complete liquidation and dissolution. The plan of combination has been carefully developed so as to comply with the criteria for a pooling of interests. Balance sheets of each of the corporations immediately prior to merger on December 31, 1995, follow. The common stock exchange ratio was negotiated to be 1:1 for both Smith and Platz.

	ZINTEL	SMITH	PLATZ
Current assets	$1,500,000	$ 360,000	$ 15,000
Long-term assets (net)	5,800,000	1,880,000	95,000
Total	$7,300,000	$2,240,000	$110,000
Current liabilities	$ 800,000	$ 100,000	$ 8,000
Long-term debt	1,000,000	440,000	62,000
Common stock, $5 par value	2,500,000	700,000	20,000
Retained earnings	3,000,000	1,000,000	20,000
Total	$7,300,000	$2,240,000	$110,000

Required:

A. Prepare journal entries on Zintel's books to record the combination.

B. Assume that the combination fails to meet the criteria for a pooling of interests because Platz had not been an autonomous entity for two years prior to the combination. The identifiable assets and liabilities of Smith and Platz are all reflected in the balance sheets (above), and their recorded amounts are equal to their current fair values. Zintel's common stock is traded actively and has a current market price of $15 per share. Prepare journal entries on Zintel's books to record the combination.

(AICPA adapted)

Exercise 1-11A

Required:

Select the letter of the best answer.

1. The conditions required for a business combination to be accounted for as a pooling of interests have been divided into three groups. Which of the following is not one of those groups?
   (a) Conditions related to effecting the combination.
   (b) Attributes of combining companies.
   (c) Conditions related to originating the combination.
   (d) Absence of planned transactions.

2. In deciding whether a business combination meets the criteria for a pooling of interests, it is necessary to perform
   (a) A test of cash to total consideration given to acquire the shares of the combined company.
   (b) A relative-size test of the assets of the combining companies.
   (c) A test of the relative earnings of the combining companies.
   (d) A test of the number of shares exchanged in the combination.

3. Which one of the following would prevent a business combination plan from qualifying as a pooling of interests?
   (a) The combination plan cannot be consummated within one year after initiation.
   (b) One of the combining companies acquires its treasury stock for delivery under its employee stock option plan after initiation of the plan.
   (c) The other combining company was a subsidiary of a competitor company until 30 months before initiation of the combination plan.
   (d) The issuing company pays cash for the shares (a 1% interest) of a stockholder who objects to the combination plan.

4. In order to qualify for a pooling of interests, the issuing company must offer and issue only common stock for substantially all the outstanding voting stock of other combining companies. *Substantially* all means
   (a) 90% of the outstanding voting stock when the combination plan is consummated.
   (b) 90% of the outstanding voting stock less common shares and common share equivalents held by other combining companies.
   (c) 90% of the outstanding voting stock not held by other combining companies.
   (d) 90% of the outstanding voting stock when the combination plan is initiated.

5. Which of the following transactions related to a business combination would require that the combination be accounted for as a purchase?
   (a) The combined company will dispose of numerous fixed assets representing duplicate facilities subsequent to the combination.
   (b) The combined company is to retire a portion of the common stock exchanged to effect the combination within 12 months of the combination.
   (c) The combination is to be completed within 12 months from the date the plan is initiated.
   (d) 92% of one company's common stock is exchanged for only common stock in the other company.

Problems

Problem 1-1

Condensed balance sheets for Phillips Company and Solina Company on January 1, 1995, are as follows:

	PHILLIPS	SOLINA
Current assets	$182,000	$ 88,000
Plant and equipment (net)	456,000	130,000
Total assets	$638,000	$218,000
Total liabilities	$ 98,000	$ 30,000
Common stock, $10 par value	350,000	160,000
Other contributed capital	120,000	48,000
Retained earnings (deficit)	70,000	(20,000)
Total equities	$638,000	$218,000

(handwritten annotations: "Book FMV" and "520 FV" near Current assets / Plant and equipment for Phillips; "147 FV" near Solina Plant and equipment; "FMV + Book" near Total liabilities)

On January 1, 1995, the stockholders of Phillips and Solina agreed to a consolidation whereby a new corporation, McGregor Company, would be formed to consolidate Phillips and Solina. McGregor Company issued 30,000 shares of its $20 par value common stock for all the outstanding stock of Phillips and Solina.

On the date of consolidation, the fair values of Phillip's and Solina's current assets and liabilities were equal to their book values. The fair value of plant and equipment for each company was: Phillips, $520,000; Solina, $147,000.

The investment banking house of Bradly and Bradly estimated that the fair value of McGregor Company's common stock was $33 per share.

(handwritten: 30,000 × 20 / 30,000 × 33; MC 30,000 sh × $20 par; P+S $350,000 + 160,000)

Required:

Prepare the journal entries to record the consolidation on the books of McGregor Company assuming that:

A. The consolidation is accounted for as a pooling of interests.

B. The consolidation is accounted for as a purchase.

Problem 1-2

Stockholders of Acme Company, Baltic Company, and Colt Company are considering alternative arrangements for a business combination. Balance sheets and the fair values of each company's assets on October 1, 1995, were as follows:

	ACME	BALTIC	COLT
Assets	$3,700,000	$7,800,000	$ 980,000
Liabilities	$1,830,000	$2,500,000	$ 290,000
Common stock, $20 par value	2,000,000	1,800,000	540,000
Other contributed capital	–0–	600,000	190,000
Retained earnings (deficit)	(130,000)	2,900,000	(40,000)
Total equities	$3,700,000	$7,800,000	$ 980,000
Fair values of assets	$4,120,000	$8,970,000	$1,200,000

Acme Company shares have a fair value of $45. A fair (market) price is not available for shares of the other companies because they are closely held. Fair values of liabilities equal book values.

Required:

Prepare a balance sheet for the business combination for each of the following assumptions:

A. Acme Company acquires all the assets and assumes all the liabilities of Baltic and Colt Companies by issuing in exchange 130,000 shares of its common stock to Baltic Company and 40,000 shares of its common stock to Colt Company. The combination is treated as a purchase.

B. Acme Company issues shares as in (A) above, but the combination is treated as a pooling of interests.

C. A new corporation, Santele Company, is formed to take over the assets and assume the liabilities of Acme, Baltic, and Colt. The new company issues no-par stock with a stated value of $20 per share as follows: to Acme Company, 130,000 shares; to Baltic Company, 160,000 shares; to Colt Company, 20,000 shares. The combination is treated as a pooling of interests.

Problem 1-3

On January 1, 1995, Perez Company acquired all the assets and assumed all the liabilities of Stalton Company and merged Stalton into Perez. In exchange for the net assets of Stalton, Perez gave its bonds payable with a maturity value of $600,000, a stated interest rate of 10%, interest payable semiannually on June 30 and December 31, a maturity date of January 1, 2005, and a yield rate of 12%.

Balance sheets for Perez and Stalton (in addition to fair value data) on January 1, 1995, were as follows:

	PEREZ	STALTON	
	BOOK VALUE	BOOK VALUE	FAIR VALUE
Cash	$ 300,000	$112,000	$112,000
Receivables	352,700	145,000	130,000
Inventories	848,300	232,000	310,000
Land	700,000	75,000	315,000
Buildings	950,000	410,000	476,300
Accumulated depreciation—buildings	(325,000)	(170,500)	(421,400)
Equipment	262,750	136,450	123,700
Accumulated depreciation—equipment	(70,050)	(90,450)	(84,250)
Total assets	$3,018,700	$849,500	$961,350
Current liabilities	$ 342,700	$104,300	$104,300
Bonds payable, 8% due 1/1/2007, Interest payable 6/30 and 12/31		300,000	260,000
Common stock, $15 par value	1,200,000		
Common stock, $5 par value		236,500	
Other contributed capital	950,000	170,000	
Retained earnings	526,000	38,700	
Total equities	$3,018,700	$849,500	

Required:

Prepare the journal entry on the books of Perez Company to record the acquisition of Stalton Company's assets and liabilities in exchange for the bonds.

Problem 1-4

Using the data in Problem 1-3, assume that Perez Company exchanged 42,000 shares of its unissued common stock for all the outstanding common stock of Stalton Company (instead of issuing bonds) and that all conditions for pooling of interests accounting are met.

Required:

Record the exchange of stock on the books of Perez Company.

Problem 1-5

Pham Company acquired the assets (except for cash) and assumed the liabilities of Senn Company on January 1, 1996, paying $800,000 cash. Senn Company's December 31, 1995, balance sheet, reflecting both book values and fair values, showed:

	BOOK VALUE	FAIR VALUE
Accounts receivable (net)	$ 80,000	$ 72,000
Inventory	96,000	110,000
Land	122,000	180,000
Buildings (net)	410,000	500,000
Equipment (net)	263,000	320,000
Total	$971,000	$1,182,000
Accounts payable	$ 92,000	$ 92,000
Note payable	200,000	200,000
Common stock, $2 par value	170,000	
Other contributed capital	255,000	
Retained earnings	254,000	
Total	$971,000	

As part of the negotiations, Pham Company agreed to pay the former stockholders of Senn Company $120,000 cash if the postcombination earnings of the combined company (Pham) reached certain levels during 1996 and 1997.

Required:

A. Record the journal entry on the books of Pham Company to record the acquisition on January 1, 1996.

B. Assuming the earnings contingency is met, prepare the journal entry on Pham Company's books to settle the contingency on January 2, 1998.

C. Repeat requirement (B) assuming the amount of the contingent payment was $70,000 rather than $120,000.

Problem 1-6

The managers of Park Company own 2,000 of its 20,000 outstanding common shares. Step Company is formed by the managers of Park Company to take over Park Company in a leveraged buyout. The managers contribute their shares in Park Company and Step Company then borrows $80,000 to purchase the remaining 18,000 shares of Park Company for $75,000; the remaining $5,000 is used for working capital. Park Company is then merged into Step Company effective January 1, 1995. Data relevant to Park Company immediately prior to the leveraged buyout follow:

	BOOK VALUE	FAIR VALUE
Current assets	$10,000	$10,000
Plant assets	30,000	65,000
Liabilities	(5,000)	(5,000)
Stockholders' equity	$35,000	$70,000

Required:

A. Prepare journal entries on Lake Company's books to reflect the effects of the leveraged buyout.

B. Prepare a balance sheet for Lake Company immediately after the merger.

Problem 1-7

Balance sheets for Salt Company and Pepper Company on December 31, 1995, follow:

	SALT	PEPPER
ASSETS		
Cash	$ 93,400	$ 170,000
Receivables	116,600	240,000
Inventories	133,200	231,400
Plant assets	687,800	1,236,500
Total assets	$1,031,000	$1,877,900
EQUITIES		
Accounts payable	$ 190,000	$ 260,900
Mortgage payable	142,500	172,500
Common stock, $20 par value	340,000	900,000
Other contributed capital	178,500	268,500
Retained earnings	180,000	276,000
Total equities	$1,031,000	$1,877,900

Pepper Company tentatively plans to issue 29,000 shares of its $20 par value stock, which has a current market value of $40 per share net of commissions and other issue costs. Pepper Company then plans to acquire the assets and assume the liabilities of Salt Company for a cash payment of $800,000 and $300,000 in long-term 8% notes payable. Pepper Company's receivables include $57,000 owed by Salt Company. Pepper Company is willing to pay more than the book value of Salt Company assets because plant assets are undervalued by $235,000 and Salt Company has historically earned above-normal profits.

Required:

Prepare a pro forma balance sheet showing the effects of these planned transactions.

Problem 1-8

Spalding Company has offered to sell to Ping Company its assets at their book values plus $1,800,000 representing payment for goodwill. Operating data for 1994 for the two companies are as follows:

	PING COMPANY		SPALDING COMPANY	
Sales		$3,510,100		$2,365,800
Cost of goods sold		1,752,360		1,423,800
Gross profit		1,757,740		942,000
Selling expenses	$632,500		$292,100	
Other expenses	172,600		150,000	
Total expenses		805,100		442,100
Net income		$ 952,640		$ 499,900

Ping Company's management estimates the following operating changes if Spalding Company is merged with Ping Company through a purchase:

A. After the merger, the sales volume of Ping Company will be 20% in excess of the present combined sales volume, and the sale price per unit will be decreased by 10%.

B. Fixed manufacturing expenses have been 35% of cost of goods sold for each company. After the merger the fixed manufacturing expenses of Ping Company will be increased by 70% of the current fixed manufacturing expenses of Spalding Company. The current variable manufacturing expenses of Ping Company, which is 70% of cost of goods sold, is expected to increase in proportion to the increase in sales volume.

C. Selling expenses of Ping Company are expected to be 85% of the present combined selling expenses of the two companies.

D. Other expenses of Ping Company are expected to increase by 85% as a result of the merger.

Any excess of the estimated net income of the merged company over the combined present net income of the two companies is to be capitalized at 20%. If this amount exceeds the price set by Spalding Company for goodwill, Ping Company will accept the offer.

Required:

Prepare a pro forma (or projected) income statement for Ping Company for 1995 assuming the merger takes place, and indicate whether Ping Company should accept the offer.

Problem 1-9A

The boards of directors of Accent Corporation, Bent Company, Cent, Inc., and Decent Corporation are meeting jointly to discuss plans for a business combination. Each of the corporations has one class of common stock outstanding; Bent also has one class of preferred stock outstanding. Although terms have not been settled as yet, Accent will be the acquiring or issuing corporation. Because the directors want to conform to generally accepted accounting principles, they have asked you to attend the meeting as an adviser.

Required:

Consider each of the following questions independently and answer each in accordance with generally accepted accounting principles.

A. Assume that the combination will be consummated August 31, 1995. What is the philosophy underlying the accounting and how will the balance sheet accounts of each of the four corporations appear on Accent's consolidated balance sheet on September 1, 1995, if the combination is accounted for as a
   (1) Pooling of interests?
   (2) Purchase?

B. Assume that the combination will be consummated August 31, 1995. How will the income statement accounts of each of the four corporations be accounted for in preparing Accent's consolidated income statement for the year ending December 31, 1995, if the combination is accounted for as a
   (1) Pooling of interests?
   (2) Purchase?

C. Some of the directors believe that the terms of the combination should be agreed on immediately and that the method of accounting to be used (whether pooling, purchase, or a mixture) may be chosen at some later date. Others believe that the terms of the combination and the method to be used are very closely related. Which position is correct?

D. Accent and Decent are comparable in size; Cent and Bent are much smaller. How do these facts affect the choice of accounting method?

E. Bent was formerly a subsidiary of Tycoon Corporation, which has no other relationship to any of the four companies discussing combination. Eighteen months ago Tycoon voluntarily spun off Bent. What effect, if any, do these facts have on the choice of accounting method?

E. Accent holds 1,000 of Bent's 5,000 outstanding shares of preferred stock and 7,500 of Caper's 50,000 outstanding shares of common stock. All of Accent's holdings were acquired during the first three months of 1995. What effect, if any, do these facts have on the choice of accounting method?

G. It is almost certain that Mrs. Marshal Minor, Jr., who holds 5% of Decent's common stock, will object to the combination. Assume that Accent is able to acquire only 95% (rather than 100%) of Decent's stock, issuing Accent common stock in exchange. What accounting method is applicable?

H. Since the directors feel that one of Decent's major divisions will not be compatible with the operations of the combined company, they anticipate that it will be sold as soon as possible after the combination is consummated. They expect to have no trouble in finding a buyer. What effect, if any, do these facts have on the choice of accounting method?

(*AICPA adapted*)

Problem 1-10A Discussion Problem

Your client is Mega, Inc., a New York Stock Exchange company that has acquired several profitable businesses in recent years. It has subsidiaries in lines such as home computers, seismographic operations, agricultural chemicals, and solar energy. Its earnings have shown steady growth, and the stock market has valued the company with a high price-earnings ratio.

One month ago, you and Mega's treasurer discussed the proposed acquisition of Sellum, Inc., a southwestern real estate brokerage operation with subsidiaries that own and operate apartment houses. Because of the region's depressed real estate market and flat earnings, the stock of Sellum was trading at less than book value. The acquisition was to be made by a straightforward exchange of common stock for common stock using market prices. After reviewing the criteria for business combinations, the treasurer and you agreed that the accounting would follow the pooling of interests method.

But now the treasurer has suggested a complication. He tells you, "It looks like the deal for Sellum will go through. As I see it, if we intend to sell off some of the apartment house subsidiaries, or any of our other assets, we have to use the purchase method of accounting. Then we'll have a minimum of $20,000,000 negative goodwill to take into income over the next three years. We can discuss whether three is the right number of years later, but I just wanted to check and be sure that purchase accounting is OK before we close the deal." You say, "Yes, that's what the accounting standards say, provided it's a significant part of the assets and not a disposal in the ordinary course of business." The treasurer responds, "That's great; you can tell us later what is significant and that's the amount we intend to sell."

Your hesitations center around the thought that Mega may be able to "manipulate" $20,000,000 or more into its future earnings stream by expressing an intention to sell off some properties. Six months earlier you were confronted with a similar situation. Another client had acquired a ladies' apparel manufacturing complex in a pooling of interests transaction with no intention (represented in writing) of selling off any assets. But 16 months after the acquisition, it had sold off a significant, unprofitable manufacturing subsidiary.

Required:

A. Discuss how the auditor can determine a client's "intent."

B. Discuss the form versus substance of a pooling of interests versus purchase transaction.

C. Was the right answer given to Mega? Discuss.

D. Discuss the question of what constitutes a "significant part of the assets."

E. If the purchase method is followed, what should be done if Mega does not sell off a significant amount of assets?

> (*Adapted from the Touche Ross Foundation Accounting and Auditing Case Studies.*)

2

CONSOLIDATED FINANCIAL STATEMENTS—DATE OF ACQUISITION

In Chapter 1 we discussed accounting for business combinations arising from statutory mergers and consolidations. As you recall, in those situations the acquiring company survived and the acquired company or companies ceased to exist as separate legal entities. Our concern in this chapter is with accounting practices followed when one company controls the activities of another company through the direct or indirect ownership of a *majority* of its voting stock.

When this occurs, the acquiring company is generally referred to as the *parent* and the acquired company as a *subsidiary*. Those holding any remaining stock in a subsidiary are referred to as the *noncontrolling (minority) interest*. Any joint relationship is termed an *affiliation*, and the related companies are called *affiliated companies*. Each of the affiliated companies continues its separate legal existence, and the investing company carries its interest as an investment.

A corporate affiliation may, of course, consist of more than two companies. A parent may obtain a majority of the voting stock of several subsidiaries. If one or more of the subsidiaries owns a controlling interest in one or more other companies, a chain of ownership is forged by which the parent company controls, either directly or indirectly, the activities of the other companies. Many large American conglomerates have been formed by a variety of indirect ownerships.

SUBSIDIARY DEFINED

Although the term *subsidiary* is used with several meanings in practice, in this text it is used to refer to a situation in which a parent company (and/or the parent's other subsidiaries) owns more than 50% of the voting shares of another company. The critical criterion in this definition is the percentage of ownership, more than 50%, of the voting shares. The Securities and Exchange Commission defines a subsidiary as an affiliate controlled by another entity, directly or indirectly, through one or more intermediaries. Control means the possession, direct or indirect, of the power to direct or cause the direction of the management and policies of another entity, whether through the ownership of voting shares, by contract, or otherwise.

The Accounting Principles Board in *APB Opinion No. 18* explains that the term subsidiary "refers to a corporation which is controlled, directly or indirectly, by another corporation. The usual condition for control is ownership of a majority (over 50%) of the outstanding voting stock. The power to control may also exist with a lesser percentage of ownership, for example, by contract, agreement with other stockholders or by court decree."[1]

REASONS FOR SUBSIDIARY COMPANIES

There are several advantages to acquiring the *majority* of the voting stock of another company rather than all its voting stock or resources. For example:

1. Stock acquisition is relatively simple. Stock can be acquired by open market purchases or by cash tender offers to the subsidiary's stockholders. Such acquisitions avoid the often lengthy and difficult negotiations that are required in an exchange of stock for stock in a complete takeover.

2. Control of the subsidiary's operations can be accomplished with a much smaller investment, since only a majority (more than 50%) of the stock need be obtained.

3. The separate legal existence of the individual affiliates provides an element of protection of the parent's assets from attachment by creditors of the subsidiary. A parent may sometimes establish a subsidiary by forming a new corporation rather than simply adding a division to the existing company. The limited liability characteristic of the corporate form of business organization is often the primary reason for doing so.

---

[1]The SEC distinguishes majority-owned, totally held, and wholly owned subsidiaries. The term *majority-owned* means a subsidiary more than 50% of whose outstanding voting shares are owned by its parent and/or the parent's other majority-owned subsidiaries. (The definition of subsidiary used in this book is the same as the SEC's definition of a majority-owned subsidiary.) The term *totally held* means a subsidiary (1) substantially all of whose outstanding equity securities are owned by its parent and/or the parent's other totally held subsidiaries, and (2) which is not indebted to any person other than its parent and/or the parent's other totally held subsidiaries, in an amount that is material in relation to the particular subsidiary. The term *wholly owned* means a subsidiary all of whose outstanding voting shares are owned by its parent and/or the parent's other wholly owned subsidiaries.

CONSOLIDATED FINANCIAL STATEMENTS

The statements prepared for a parent company and its subsidiaries are called ***consolidated financial statements***. They include the full complement of statements normally prepared for a separate entity and represent essentially the sum of the assets, liabilities, revenues, and expenses of the affiliates after eliminating the effect of any transactions among the affiliated companies. Accountants recognize that the unconsolidated financial statements of the parent company, the ***legal entity***, are insufficient to present the financial position and results of operations of the ***economic unit*** controlled by the parent company.

As expressed by the AICPA in *Accounting Research Bulletin No. 51* (and reconfirmed by *Statement of Financial Accounting Standards No. 94*), the purpose of consolidated statements is to present, primarily for the benefit of the stockholders and creditors of the parent company, the results of operations and the financial position of a parent company and its subsidiaries essentially as if the group were a single company with one or more branches or divisions. Consolidated statements are usually presumed to be necessary for a fair presentation when one of the companies in the group directly or indirectly has a controlling financial interest in the other companies. Thus, legal aspects of the separate entities are ignored, and emphasis is placed on the economic unit under control of one management, that is, on economic substance rather than on legal form.

Although consolidated statements for the economic entity are considered to be more appropriate for use by the stockholders and creditors of the parent company, they cannot substitute for the statements prepared by the separate subsidiaries. Creditors of the subsidiaries must look to the statements of the individual legal entities in assessing the degree of protection related to their claims. Likewise, noncontrolling stockholders need the statements of the individual companies to determine the degree of investment risk involved and the amounts available for dividends. Regulatory agencies are often concerned with the net resources and results of operations of the individual subsidiaries.

REQUIREMENTS FOR THE INCLUSION OF SUBSIDIARIES IN THE CONSOLIDATED FINANCIAL STATEMENTS

Prior to the issuance of *SFAS No. 94*, "Consolidation of All Majority-Owned Subsidiaries," in 1987, many companies excluded some majority-owned subsidiaries from the consolidated statements. *Accounting Research Bulletin No. 51* provided that a subsidiary might be excluded from consolidation if the subsidiary's operations were nonhomogeneous (unrelated) to those of other subsidiaries and the parent company. This provision was often used to exclude high debt to equity companies such as finance companies, banks, and insurance companies from the consolidated statements in order to maintain lower debt to equity ratios. Consider, for example, the following simple example of P Company's fully owned finance subsidiary, S Company, with the following assets and liabilities:

	P COMPANY	S COMPANY	ELIMINATIONS DR.	ELIMINATIONS CR.	CONSOLIDATED
Investment in S Co.	$ 100	$–0–		(1) 100	$–0–
Other assets	900	500			1,400
Total	$1,000	$500			$1,400
Liabilities	$ 600	$400			$1,000
Stockholders' equity	400	100	(1) 100		400
Total	$1,000	$500			$1,300
Debt/equity ratio	1.5	4.0			2.50

(1) To eliminate the investment in S Co.

By excluding its finance subsidiary from the consolidated statements, P Company can report a substantially lower debt to equity ratio.

The purpose of consolidated statements is to present for a single accounting entity the net resources and operating results of a group of companies under common control. Given this purpose and problems related to off-balance-sheet financing, the FASB has taken the position that essentially all controlled corporations should be consolidated. Although there are several definitions of control, the FASB opted for the legal concept of majority ownership of voting stock. In addition, the FASB has reemphasized the basic position that parent-company-only financial statements are unacceptable for general purpose distribution, that is, the consolidated financial statements are the primary statements of the economic entity.[2]

Under some circumstances, majority-owned subsidiaries should be excluded from the consolidated statements. Those circumstances include:

1. Ownership is temporary. Management of the parent company should intend a long-term relationship. A parent company should not consolidate a subsidiary it expects to dispose of.

2. Control does not rest with the majority owner. For example, a subsidiary in legal reorganization or bankruptcy should not be consolidated.

3. A foreign subsidiary is domiciled in a country with foreign exchange restrictions, controls, or other governmentally imposed uncertainties so severe that they cast significant doubt on the parent's ability to control the subsidiary.

Investments in majority-owned subsidiaries that are not consolidated for one or more of the foregoing reasons are normally reported as investments using the cost method because the subsidiaries are neither controlled nor significantly influenced by the parent company.[3]

In general, the object of consolidation is to provide the most meaningful financial presentation possible in the circumstances. Considerable judgment must be exercised in accomplishing this objective. For example, summarized information about the assets, liabilities, and results of operations (or separate or combined[4]

[2]Statement of *Financial Accounting Standards No. 94* "Consolidation of All Majority-Owned Subsidiaries" (Norwalk, CT: FASB, 1987).

[3]Ibid, par. 21.

[4]Combined statements are discussed later in this chapter.

statements) of consolidated subsidiaries may be presented either individually or in groups in financial statement notes. The consolidation policy followed should be disclosed as part of the statement of significant accounting policies required by *APB Opinion No. 22*.

The FASB has an ongoing project on consolidations and related matters concerned with such things as the nature of the reporting entity, consolidation policy and procedures, reporting for unconsolidated entities, and types of disaggregated disclosures. Another part of the project deals with the issue of when, if ever, it may be appropriate to recognize a new measurement basis in the separate financial statements of an entity. The project, begun in 1982, has resulted in the issuance of *SFAS No. 94*, "Consolidation of All Majority Owned Subsidiaries," and two discussion memorandums, one dealing with "New Basis Accounting" and the other with "Consolidation Policy and Procedures." The policy and procedures memorandum considers such issues as accounting for subsidiary stock transactions, elimination of intercompany profits, and consolidation of less-than-majority-owned subsidiaries. This latter issue relates to an acceptable concept of control.

There are situations where one company effectively controls another even though owning less than a controlling interest in its voting stock. For example, A Company may own a large minority of B Company's voting stock, and the remaining voting stock is so widely held that there is little likelihood that anyone else can succeed in uniting enough other stockholders to override the votes of A Company. Some accountants hold that B Company should be included in the consolidated financial statements of A Company. These accountants believe that control should be determined on the basis of whether one company can effectively control the operating and financing policies of another company. In fact, there are many unsettled issues related to the preparation of consolidated financial statements. Significant changes may be forthcoming.

LIMITATIONS OF CONSOLIDATED STATEMENTS

As noted earlier, consolidated statements may have limited usefulness for noncontrolling stockholders, subsidiary creditors, and regulatory agencies. Noncontrolling stockholders and regulatory agencies can find little information of value to them in the consolidated statements because they contain insufficient detail about the individual subsidiaries. Then, too, creditors of a specific company have claims only against the resources of that company unless the claims are guaranteed by the parent.

In addition, consolidated statements have been criticized by financial analysts. The strong merger movement that began in the 1960s produced many highly diversified companies operating across several industries. Consolidated operating results for such companies cannot be compared with industry standards; one conglomerate cannot be compared with another. This criticism is at least partially responsible for the SEC and FASB requirements regarding segment reporting, which will be discussed in Chapter 16.

Regardless of these limitations, however, consolidated statements continue to grow in importance. The vast majority of publicly held companies own one or more subsidiaries and report on a consolidated basis. Thus, consolidated statements have assumed the position of primary statements, and the separate statements of individual subsidiaries are considered supplementary.

INVESTMENTS AT THE DATE OF ACQUISITION

The general principles used to record the merger or consolidation of one company and another were discussed in Chapter 1. The principles to be followed varied depending on whether a purchase or pooling of interests approach was appropriate. The principles followed in accounting for stock acquisitions and in preparing consolidated financial statements also depend on whether the subsidiary stock acquisition is a purchase or a pooling of interests. **In this chapter and throughout Chapters 3 through 6, we will concentrate on accounting for the acquisition of another company's voting stock under the purchase method. The pooling of interests method will be discussed in Chapter 7.**

Recording Investments at Cost

The basic guidelines for valuation discussed in Chapter 1 pertaining to business combinations apply equally to the acquisition of voting stock in another company. Under the purchase method, the stock investment is recorded at its cost as measured by the fair value of the consideration given or the consideration received, whichever is more clearly evident. Recall that the consideration given may consist of cash, other assets, debt securities, stock of the acquiring company, or a combination of these items. Only the direct costs of acquiring the stock should be included in the investment cost. Indirect costs relating to acquisitions (such as the costs of maintaining an acquisitions department) should be expensed as incurred.

If cash is used for the acquisition, the investment is recorded at its cash cost, including broker's fees and other direct costs of the investment. For example, assume that P Company acquires all 10,000 shares of the common stock of S Company for $25 per share and pays acquisition fees of $10,000. The entry to record the investment on P Company's books is:

Investment in S Company	260,000	
Cash		260,000

If P Company issues stock in the acquisition, the investment is recorded at the fair value of the stock issued, giving effect to any costs of registering the stock issue. Assume, for example, that P Company issues 20,000 of its $10 par value common shares with a fair value of $13 per share for the 10,000 shares of S Company, and that registration costs amount to $5,000, paid in cash. The entries to record the investment on P Company's books are:

Investment in S Company	260,000	
Common Stock		200,000
Other Contributed Capital		60,000
Other Contributed Capital	5,000	
Cash		5,000

In essence, the registration costs serve to reduce the other contributed capital recorded in the transaction, which is consistent with the recording of stock issuances at an amount equal to the ***net proceeds*** received.

CONSOLIDATED BALANCE SHEETS

Business units prepare two general types of financial statements—stock statements (the balance sheet or statement of financial position) and flow statements (retained earnings statement, income statement, and the statement of cash flows). Affiliated companies normally prepare this full set of financial statements. As of the date of acquisition of one company by another, however, the only relevant statement is the consolidated balance sheet. Preparation of the other consolidated financial statements is discussed in later chapters. The consolidated balance sheet reports the sum of the assets and equities of a parent and its subsidiaries as if they constituted a single company. Since the parent and its subsidiaries are being treated as a single entity, eliminations must be made to cancel the effects of transactions among them. Intercompany receivables and payables, for example, are reciprocal in nature, so they must be eliminated to avoid double counting and to avoid giving the impression that the consolidated entity owes money to itself. Likewise, any intercompany profits in assets arising from subsequent transactions must be eliminated, since an entity cannot profit on transactions with itself. The process of eliminating these types of items will be discussed in detail in this and later chapters.

Investment Elimination

An important basic elimination in the preparation of consolidated statements is the elimination of the investment account and the related subsidiary's stockholders' equity. The investment account represents the investment by the parent company in the net assets of the subsidiary and is, therefore, reciprocal to the subsidiary company's stockholders' equity. Since the subsidiary company's assets and liabilities are combined with the parent company's in the consolidated balance sheet, it is necessary to eliminate the investment account of the parent company against the related stockholders' equity of the subsidiary to avoid double counting of these net assets. In effect, when the parent company's share of the subsidiary company's equity is eliminated against the investment account, the subsidiary company's net assets are substituted for the investment account in the consolidated balance sheet.

The process of combining the individual assets and liabilities of a parent company and its subsidiary at the date of acquisition is discussed and illustrated in the following order:

1. The parent company's cost of its investment is equal to the book value of the subsidiary company's stock acquired, and
   (a) The parent company acquires 100% of the subsidiary company's stock; or
   (b) The parent company acquires less than 100% of the subsidiary company's stock.

2. The parent company's cost of its investment *exceeds* the book value of the subsidiary company's stock acquired, and less than 100% of the stock is acquired.

3. The parent company's cost of its investment is *less* than the book value of the subsidiary company's stock acquired, and less than 100% of the stock is acquired.

Examples are based on the balance sheets as of January 1, 1995, for P Company and S Company as shown in Illustration 2-1:

ILLUSTRATION 2-1
Balance Sheets for P Company and S Company
January 1, 1995

	P COMPANY	S COMPANY
Cash	$100,000	$ 20,000
Other current assets	140,000	50,000
Plant and equipment (net)	120,000	40,000
Land	40,000	20,000
Total assets	$400,000	$130,000
Liabilities	$ 60,000	$ 50,000
Common stock, $10 par value	200,000	50,000
Other contributed capital	40,000	10,000
Retained earnings	100,000	20,000
Total equities	$400,000	$130,000

Parent Company's Cost of Investment Is Equal to Book Value of Subsidiary Stock Acquired—100% of Subsidiary Stock Acquired Assume that on January 1, 1995, P Company acquired all the outstanding stock (5,000 shares) of S Company for a cash payment of $80,000, after which P Company has $20,000 in cash and $80,000 in an Investment in S Company account. Note that the $80,000 represents the recorded value of S Company's stockholders' equity. Data for the preparation of formal consolidated statements are normally accumulated on a workpaper on which any required adjusting and eliminating entries are made prior to combining remaining balances. *Adjusting entries* are those needed to correct any accounts of the affiliates that may be incorrect or to recognize the unrecorded effect of transactions that have been recorded by one party, but not by the other. Adjusting entries must be made ultimately on the books of one or more of the affiliates. *Eliminating entries* are made to cancel the effects of intercompany transactions and are made on the workpaper only. In all illustrations throughout this book, letter notation is used to identify related parts of adjusting entries, and number notation to identify related parts of eliminating entries.

A workpaper for the preparation of a consolidated balance sheet for P and S Companies on January 1, 1995, the date of acquisition, is presented in Illustration 2-2.

Purchase Accounting
Cost Equals Book Value
Wholly Owned Subsidiary
Date of Acquisition

ILLUSTRATION 2-2
Consolidated Balance Sheet Workpaper
P Company and Subsidiary
January 1, 1995

	P COMPANY	S COMPANY	ELIMINATIONS DR.	ELIMINATIONS CR.	CONSOLIDATED BALANCES
Cash	20,000	20,000			40,000
Other Current Assets	140,000	50,000			190,000
Plant and Equipment	120,000	40,000			160,000
Land	40,000	20,000			60,000
Investment in S Company	80,000			(1) 80,000	
Total Assets	400,000	130,000			450,000
Liabilities	60,000	50,000			110,000
Common Stock					
P Company	200,000				200,000
S Company		50,000	(1) 50,000		
Other Contributed Capital					
P Company	40,000				40,000
S Company		10,000	(1) 10,000		
Retained Earnings					
P Company	100,000				100,000
S Company		20,000	(1) 20,000		
Total Equities	400,000	130,000	80,000	80,000	450,000

(1) To eliminate investment in S Company.

The workpaper entry to eliminate S Company's stockholders' equity against the investment account, in general journal form, is:

(1) Common Stock—S Company	50,000	
Other Contributed Capital—S Company	10,000	
Retained Earnings—S Company	20,000	
Investment in S Company		80,000

Remember, although it is expressed in general journal form, this is a *workpaper only entry*. No entry is made on the books of either company. Note that this entry is shaded. Throughout this book, *all workpaper entries are shaded* to distinguish them clearly from book entries.

Note that the investment account and related subsidiary's stockholders' equity have been eliminated and the subsidiary company's net assets substituted for the investment account. Consolidated assets and liabilities consist of the sum of the parent and subsidiary assets and liabilities in each classification. Note also that consolidated stockholders' equity is the same as the parent company's equity. This is as it should be, since the subsidiary company's stockholders' equity has been eliminated against the parent company's investment account. The consolidated balance sheet is that of the *economic* entity, and the only ownership interest is that represented by P Company's stockholders, that is, P Company owns all of S Company's stock.

Parent Company's Cost of Investment Is Equal to Book Value of Subsidiary Company's Stock Acquired—Less than 100% of Subsidiary Stock Acquired Assume now that on January 1, 1995, P Company acquired only 90% (4,500 shares) of the stock of S Company for $72,000. Since P Company owns less than 100% of S Company's stock, consideration must be given to the existence of a noncontrolling interest (minority interest) in the net assets of S Company.[5] A workpaper for the preparation of a consolidated balance sheet at the date of acquisition in this situation is presented in Illustration 2-3.

Purchase Accounting
Cost Equals Book Value
90% Owned Subsidiary
Date of Acquisition

ILLUSTRATION 2-3
Consolidated Balance Sheet Workpaper
P Company and Subsidiary
January 1, 1995

	P COMPANY	S COMPANY	ELIMINATIONS DR.	ELIMINATIONS CR.	NONCONTROLLING INTEREST	CONSOLIDATED BALANCES
Cash	28,000	20,000				48,000
Other Current Assets	140,000	50,000				190,000
Plant and Equipment	120,000	40,000				160,000
Land	40,000	20,000				60,000
Investment in S Company	72,000			(1) 72,000		
Total Assets	400,000	130,000				458,000
Liabilities	60,000	50,000				110,000
Common stock						
P Company	200,000					200,000
S Company		50,000	(1) 45,000		5,000	
Other Contributed Capital						
P Company	40,000					40,000
S Company		10,000	(1) 9,000		1,000	
Retained Earnings						
P Company	100,000					100,000
S Company		20,000	(1) 18,000		2,000	
Noncontrolling Interest					8,000	8,000
Total Equities	400,000	130,000	72,000	72,000		458,000

(1) To eliminate investment in S Company.

In comparing Illustrations 2-2 and 2-3, it should be noted that: (1) consolidated assets are $8,000 greater in Illustration 2-3 since it took $8,000 less cash to acquire

[5]The term "minority interest" may not reflect clearly the actual nature of some items. For example, a parent company may own 25% of its subsidiary's outstanding preferred stock. In this case, the use of the term "minority interest" to represent the 75% interest held by noncontrolling shareholders is not representative of the circumstances. We have elected to use the term "noncontrolling interest" throughout this text.

the investment, and (2) and $8,000 noncontrolling interest exists. Noncontrolling interest is accumulated on the consolidated workpaper in a separate column.

The workpaper investment elimination entry is:

(1) Common Stock—S Company (.9 × $50,000)	45,000	
Other Contributed Capital—S Company (.9 × $10,000)	9,000	
Retained Earnings—S Company (.9 × $20,000)	18,000	
Investment in S Company		72,000

Only that percentage of S Company's equity acquired by P Company is eliminated against the investment account; the remainder of S Company's equity constitutes the noncontrolling interest. The purpose of the consolidated balance sheet is to report the net resources under the control of a single management, and the management of P Company effectively controls all S Company's resources. Thus, all S Company's assets and liabilities are combined with those of P Company on the consolidated balance sheet, and the noncontrolling interest represents the noncontrolling shareholders' interest in the net assets.

Determination of the proper classification of the noncontrolling interest presents some conceptual difficulty. The noncontrolling interest does not represent a liability under the normal concept of liabilities, because it does not require a future payment by the parent company or the consolidated entity. Nor does it represent a part of stockholders' equity since the only stockholders in the consolidated entity are parent company stockholders. Noncontrolling interest exists by virtue of the fact that the subsidiary's total net assets are combined with those of the parent company. Thus, the noncontrolling interest may be thought of as an equity interest in the subsidiary's net assets, although actually it represents neither creditors' nor stockholders' equity. The classification of noncontrolling interest varies in practice. Sometimes it is classified as a liability, sometimes as stockholders' equity, and, most commonly, in a separate section between liabilities and stockholders' equity.[6]

Parent Company's Cost of Investment Exceeds Book Value of Subsidiary Company's Stock Acquired—Less than 100% of the Subsidiary Company's Stock Acquired Assume that on January 1, 1995, P Company acquired 4,000 shares (80%) of the outstanding common stock of S Company for $74,000 cash, after which P Company has $26,000 in cash and $74,000 in an Investment in S Company. Since the book value of the equity interest acquired by P Company is only $64,000 (80% × $80,000), cost exceeds the book value of equity acquired by $10,000.

A workpaper for a consolidated balance sheet at date of acquisition in this situation is presented in Illustration 2-4.

The workpaper investment elimination entry is:

(1) Common Stock—S Company (.8 × $50,000)	40,000	
Other Contributed Capital—S Company (.8 × $10,000)	8,000	
Retained Earnings—S Company (.8 × $20,000)	16,000	
Land	10,000	
Investment in S Company		74,000

[6]Accountants International Study Group, *Consolidated Financial Statements*, par. 40.

Purchase Accounting
Cost Exceeds Book Value
80% Owned Subsidiary
Date of Acquisition

ILLUSTRATION 2-4
Consolidated Balance Sheet Workpaper
P Company and Subsidiary
January 1, 1995

	P COMPANY	S COMPANY	ELIMINATIONS DR.	ELIMINATIONS CR.	NONCONTROLLING INTEREST	CONSOLIDATED BALANCES
Cash	26,000	20,000				46,000
Other Current Assets	140,000	50,000				190,000
Plant and Equipment	120,000	40,000				160,000
Land	40,000	20,000	(1) 10,000			70,000
Investment in S Company	74,000			(1) 74,000		
Total Assets	400,000	130,000				466,000
Liabilities	60,000	50,000				110,000
Common stock						
P Company	200,000					200,000
S Company		50,000	(1) 40,000		10,000	
Other Contributed Capital						
P Company	40,000					40,000
S Company		10,000	(1) 8,000		2,000	
Retained Earnings						
P Company	100,000					100,000
S Company		20,000	(1) 16,000		4,000	
Noncontrolling Interest					16,000	16,000
Total Equities	400,000	130,000	74,000	74,000		466,000

(1) To eliminate investment in S Company.

When the subsidiary equity acquired is eliminated against the Investment in S Company, a $10,000 balance remains. A detailed discussion of the appropriate accounting treatment of this balance is presented in Chapter 4. At this stage of our discussion, we have assumed that the $10,000 excess cost relates to the undervaluation of the subsidiary company's land and have assigned it to land on the workpaper.

The parent company often pays an amount in excess of the book value of the subsidiary company's stock acquired. Although we have assumed here that it relates to the undervaluation of the subsidiary company's land, any one, or a combination, of the following conditions might exist:

1. The fair, or current, value of one or more specific tangible or intangible assets of the subsidiary company may exceed its recorded value because of appreciation. Or the application of conservative accounting procedures under generally accepted accounting principles often results in book values that are lower than fair values for assets. Examples are (a) the current expensing of some costs that may contain future benefits, for example, research and development expenditures, (b) the use of accelerated depreciation methods, (c) the use of the LIFO inventory method, and (d) the general prohibition against recognizing unrealized asset increments.

2. The excess payment may indicate the existence of unrecorded goodwill of the subsidiary company as reflected by its above-normal earning capacity.

3. Liabilities, generally long-term ones, may be overvalued. For example, the subsidiary company may have 8% bonds payable outstanding when acquired by the parent company even though the market rate of interest is 12% at that time.

4. A variety of market factors may affect the price paid for the stock. The mere entry of one more large buyer of stock into the market would generally have the effect of increasing the stock's market price. In essence, the parent company is willing to pay a premium for the right to acquire control and the related economic advantages it expects to obtain from integrated operations.

Parent Company's Cost of Investment Is Less than Book Value of Subsidiary Stock Acquired—Less than 100% of Subsidiary Stock Acquired Assume that on January 1, 1995, P Company acquired 4,000 shares (80%) of the outstanding common stock of S Company for $60,000, after which P Company has $40,000 in cash and $60,000 in an Investment in S Company. Since the book value of S Company equity acquired is $64,000 ($80,000 × 80%), equity acquired exceeds cost by $4,000.

A workpaper for a consolidated balance sheet at date of acquisition in this situation is presented in Illustration 2-5.

Purchase Accounting
Book Value Exceeds Cost
80% Owned Subsidiary
Date of Acquisition

ILLUSTRATION 2-5
Consolidated Balance Sheet Workpaper
P Company and Subsidiary
January 1, 1995

	P COMPANY	S COMPANY	ELIMINATIONS DR.	ELIMINATIONS CR.	NONCONTROLLING INTEREST	CONSOLIDATED BALANCES
Cash	40,000	20,000				60,000
Other Current Assets	140,000	50,000				190,000
Plant and Equipment	120,000	40,000				160,000
Land	40,000	20,000		(1) 4,000		56,000
Investment in S Company	60,000			(1) 60,000		
Total Assets	400,000	130,000				466,000
Liabilities	60,000	50,000				110,000
Common stock						
P Company	200,000					200,000
S Company		50,000	(1) 40,000		10,000	
Other Contributed Capital						
P Company	40,000					40,000
S Company		10,000	(1) 8,000		2,000	
Retained Earnings						
P Company	100,000					100,000
S Company		20,000	(1) 16,000		4,000	
Noncontrolling Interest					16,000	16,000
Total Equities	400,000	130,000	64,000	64,000		466,000

(1) To eliminate investment in S Company.

When the subsidiary equity acquired is eliminated against the Investment in S Company, a $4,000 credit balance remains. Although there may be several reasons for this difference, it generally reflects one or a combination of the following: (1) one or more of the subsidiary company's assets is overvalued, (2) one or more of the subsidiary company's liabilities is undervalued or unrecognized, (3) the parent company simply made a bargain purchase. A detailed discussion of the difference and its accounting treatment is presented in Chapter 4. Here we have assumed that it relates to the overvaluation of S Company land.

The workpaper investment elimination entry is:

Common Stock—S Company (.8 × $50,000)	40,000	
Other Contributed Capital—S Company (.8 × $10,000)	8,000	
Retained Earnings—S Company (.8 × $20,000)	16,000	
Investment in S Company		60,000
Land		4,000

Subsidiary Treasury Stock Holdings

A subsidiary may hold some of its own shares as treasury stock at the time the parent company acquires its interest. The determination of the percentage interest acquired, as well as the total equity acquired, is based on shares outstanding and should, therefore, exclude treasury shares.

For example, assume that P Company acquired 18,000 shares of S Company common stock on January 1, 1995, for a payment of $320,000 when S Company's stockholders' equity section appeared as follows:

Common stock, $10 par, 25,000 shares issued	$250,000
Other contributed capital	50,000
Retained earnings	125,000
	425,000
Less: Treasury stock at cost, 1,000 shares	20,000
Total Stockholders' Equity	$405,000

P Company's interest in S Company is 75% (18,000/24,000 shares), and total equity acquired is 75% × $405,000, or $303,750, which results in a difference between cost and book value of $16,250 ($320,000 − $303,750).

Because the treasury stock account represents a contra stockholders' equity account, the parent company's share must be eliminated by a **credit** when the investment account and subsidiary company's equity accounts are eliminated on the workpaper. Thus, the workpaper eliminating entry is:

Common Stock—S Company (.75 × $250,000)	187,500	
Other Contributed Capital—S Company (.75 × $50,000)	37,500	
Retained Earnings—S Company (.75 × $125,000)	93,750	
Land	16,250	
Investment in S Company		320,000
Treasury Stock—S Company (.75 × $20,000)		15,000

The remainder of the treasury stock ($5,000) represents a deduction in the noncontrolling interest in net assets and is, therefore, carried over as a subtraction from the noncontrolling interest.

Other Intercompany Balance Sheet Eliminations

Up to this point we have discussed the elimination of the parent company's share of the subsidiary equity acquired against the related investment account. Balance sheet eliminations of a variety of intercompany receivables and payables are also often required. Intercompany accounts receivable, notes receivable, and interest receivable, for example, must be eliminated against the reciprocal accounts payable, notes payable, and interest payable. Cash advances among affiliated companies constitute receivables and payables and must be eliminated. Eliminations also must be made for all types of intercompany accruals for such items as rent and other services. The full amount of all intercompany receivables and payables is eliminated without regard to the percentage of control held by the parent company.

Adjustments to Statement Data

At times, workpaper adjustments to accounting data may be needed before appropriate eliminating entries can be accomplished. The need for adjustments generally arises because of in-transit items where only one of the affiliates has recorded the effect of an intercompany transaction. For example, the parent company may have recorded a cash advance to one of its subsidiaries near year-end but the subsidiary may have not yet recorded the receipt of the advance. Thus, the Advances to Subsidiary account on the parent company's books has no reciprocal account on the subsidiary company's books. An adjusting workpaper entry debiting Cash and crediting Advances from Parent is required so that the asset (cash) can be appropriately included in consolidated assets and a reciprocal account established that permits the elimination of intercompany advances. The workpaper eliminations columns are used to enter these adjusting entries. Of course, it is also possible simply to adjust the subsidiary company's statements prior to their entry on the workpaper.

A COMPREHENSIVE ILLUSTRATION—MORE THAN ONE SUBSIDIARY COMPANY

No particular problem exists where the parent company owns a direct controlling interest in more than one subsidiary company. The balance sheet of each affiliate is entered on the workpaper, any adjustments needed are prepared, and all related intercompany accounts, including those between subsidiary companies, are eliminated. The remaining balances are combined, and they constitute the consolidated balance sheet.

It is useful at this point to look at an illustrative workpaper and consolidated balance sheet for a parent company, P Company, and its two subsidiaries, S Company and T Company. Assume that on January 1, 1995, P Company acquired 90% and 80% of the outstanding common stock of S Company and T Company, respectively. Immediately after the stock acquisition, balance sheets of the affiliates were:

	JANUARY 1, 1995		
	P COMPANY	S COMPANY	T COMPANY
Cash	$ 82,000	$ 36,000	$ 4,000
Accounts receivable (net)	68,000	59,000	10,000
Inventories	76,000	64,000	15,000
Advances to T Company	20,000		
Investment in S Company	250,000		
Investment in T Company	115,000		
Plant and equipment (net)	200,000	241,000	130,000
Land	24,000	10,000	6,000
Total assets	$835,000	$410,000	$165,000
Accounts payable	$ 85,000	$ 40,000	$ 25,000
Notes payable	–0–	100,000	–0–
Common stock, $10 par value	500,000	200,000	100,000
Retained earnings	250,000	70,000	40,000
Total equities	$835,000	$410,000	$165,000

(Handwritten annotations: "90%" above JANUARY 1, 1995; "80%" above T COMPANY)

Other information:

1. On the date of acquisition, P Company mailed a cash advance of $20,000 to T Company to improve T Company's working capital position. T Company had not yet received and, therefore, had not yet recorded the advance.

(Handwritten margin notes: "P owed S $6,000" / "S owed T 5,000")

2. On the date of acquisition, P Company owed S Company $6,000 for purchases on open account, and S Company owed T Company $5,000 for such purchases. All these items had been sold by the purchasing companies prior to the date of acquisition.

3. The difference between cost and the book value of equity acquired relates to the undervaluation of subsidiary land holdings. A workpaper for the preparation of a consolidated balance sheet on January 1, 1995, for P, S, and T companies is presented in Illustration 2-6.

Several items on the workpaper should be noted. The cash in transit from P Company to T Company was picked up through an adjusting entry; if it had not been, $20,000 cash would have been excluded from the consolidated balance sheet. The adjustment also provided a reciprocal account, Advance from P Company, that permitted the elimination of the intercompany transaction for advances. (The perceptive reader will have already noticed that the same net effect could have been accomplished by a combined adjusting and eliminating entry with a debit to Cash and a credit to Advance to T.)

The elimination of all intercompany accounts receivable and accounts payable, including those between subsidiary companies, was accomplished through one entry. There is no need to eliminate them individually. Notice also that the equity acquired in each subsidiary company was eliminated against each individual investment account.

Purchase Accounting
Two Partially Owned
  Subsidiaries
Date of Acquisition

ILLUSTRATION 2-6
Consolidated Balance Sheet Workpaper
P Company and Subsidiaries
January 1, 1995

	P COMPANY	S COMPANY	T COMPANY	ELIMINATIONS DR.	ELIMINATIONS CR.	NONCONTROLLING INTEREST	CONSOLIDATED BALANCES
Cash	82,000	36,000	4,000	(a) 20,000			142,000
Accounts Receivable (net)	68,000	59,000	10,000		(2) 11,000		126,000
Inventories	76,000	64,000	15,000				155,000
Advance to T Company	20,000				(1) 20,000		
Investment in S Company	250,000				(3) 250,000		
Investment in T Company	115,000				(4) 115,000		
Plant and Equipment (net)	200,000	241,000	130,000	(3) 7,000			571,000
Land	24,000	10,000	6,000	(4) 3,000			50,000
Total Assets	835,000	410,000	165,000				1,044,000
Accounts Payable	85,000	40,000	25,000	(2) 11,000			139,000
Notes Payable		100,000					100,000
Common Stock							
P Company	500,000						500,000
S Company		200,000		(3) 180,000		20,000	
T Company			100,000	(4) 80,000		20,000	
Retained Earnings							
P Company	250,000						250,000
S Company		70,000		(3) 63,000		7,000	
T Company			40,000	(4) 32,000		8,000	
Total Equities	835,000	410,000	165,000				
Advance from P Company				(1) 20,000	(a) 20,000		
Noncontrolling Interest						55,000	55,000
				416,000	416,000		1,044,000

(a) To adjust for cash advance in transit from P Company to T Company.
(1) To eliminate intercompany advances.
(2) To eliminate intercompany accounts payable and receivable.
(3) To eliminate investment in S Company.
(4) To eliminate investment in T Company.

    The formal consolidated balance sheet is prepared from the detail in the consolidated balance sheet columns of the workpaper and is presented in Illustration 2-7.

    The balance sheet data are classified according to normal balance sheet arrangements. As discussed earlier, noncontrolling interest in consolidated net assets is classified in some cases as a liability, in others as a part of stockholders' equity, and in still others in a separate section. In the treatment illustrated here, which is the most widely followed, the noncontrolling interest in consolidated net assets is reported in a single amount between liabilities and stockholders' equity.

ILLUSTRATION 2-7
Consolidated Balance Sheet
P Company and Subsidiaries
January 1, 1995

ASSETS

Current assets:		
Cash		$ 142,000
Accounts receivable (net)		126,000
Inventories		155,000
Total current assets		423,000
Plant and equipment (net)		571,000
Land		50,000
Total Assets		$1,044,000

LIABILITIES AND STOCKHOLDERS' EQUITY'

Current liabilities:		
Accounts payable		$ 139,000
Notes payable		100,000
Total liabilities		239,000
Noncontrolling interest in consolidated net assets		55,000
Stockholders' equity:		
Common stock, $10 par value	$500,000	
Retained earnings	250,000	750,000
Total Liabilities and Stockholders' Equity		$1,044,000

COMBINED FINANCIAL STATEMENTS

Some affiliations do not involve a parent–subsidiary relationship, that is, there is no equity investment in one company by another. For example, the relationship among subsidiaries of the same parent company may not involve an investment by one subsidiary in another, although the subsidiaries are affiliates. The same condition exists among several companies owned by one individual. Consolidated statements are not appropriate if there is no investment by one affiliate in another to eliminate. In these situations the most meaningful presentation may be that of combined statements in which the individual balance sheet and income statement classifications are simply summed or combined into one set of financial statements. Where such combined statements are prepared for a group of related companies, intercompany transactions, balances, and gain or loss should be eliminated in the same manner as in consolidated statements.

Assume, for example, that P Company, a manufacturing company, controls several manufacturing and retailing subsidiaries, as well as four banking subsidiaries. All the subsidiaries are consolidated. However, in order to provide details concerning the banking operations, without including four individual sets of statements, the banking subsidiaries may be combined into one set of combined statements and included in P Company's annual report, along with the consolidated statements.

Questions

1. What are the advantages of acquiring the *majority* of the voting stock of another company rather than acquiring *all* its voting stock?

2. What is the justification for preparing consolidated financial statements when, in fact, it is apparent that the consolidated group is not a legal entity?

3. Why is it often necessary to prepare separate financial statements for each legal entity in a consolidated group even though consolidated statements provide a better economic picture of the combined activities?

4. What aspects of control must exist before a subsidiary is consolidated?

5. Why are consolidated workpapers used in preparing consolidated financial statements?

6. Define noncontrolling (minority) interest. List three methods of reporting the noncontrolling interest in a consolidated balance sheet.

7. Give several reasons why a parent company would be willing to pay more than book value for subsidiary stock acquired.

8. What effect do subsidiary treasury stock holdings have at the time the subsidiary is acquired? How should the treasury stock be treated on consolidated workpapers?

9. What effect does a noncontrolling interest have on the amount of intercompany receivables and payables eliminated on a consolidated balance sheet?

Exercises

Exercise 2-1

Prepare in general journal form the workpaper entries to eliminate Prancer Company's investment in Saltez Company in the preparation of a consolidated balance sheet at the date of acquisition for each of the following independent cases:

| | | | SALTEZ COMPANY EQUITY BALANCES | | |
CASE	PERCENT OF STOCK OWNED	INVESTMENT COST	COMMON STOCK	OTHER CONTRIBUTED CAPITAL	RETAINED EARNINGS
a.	100%	$351,000	$160,000	$92,000	$43,000
b.	90	232,000	190,000	75,000	(29,000)
c.	80	159,000	180,000	40,000	(4,000)

Any difference between cost and book value of net assets acquired relates to subsidiary land.

Exercise 2-2

On January 1, 1995, Polo Company purchased 100% of the common stock of Save Company by issuing 40,000 shares of its (Polo's) $10 par value common stock with a market price of $17.50 per share. Polo incurred expenses of $20,000 for registering and issuing the common stock. The stockholders' equity section of the two companys' balance sheets on December 31, 1994, were:

	POLO	SAVE
Common stock, $10 par value	$350,000	$320,000
Other contributed capital	590,000	175,000
Retained earnings	380,000	205,000

Required:

A. Prepare the journal entry on the books of Polo Company to record the purchase of the common stock of Save Company.

B. Prepare the elimination entry required for the preparation of a consolidated balance sheet workpaper on the date of acquisition.

Exercise 2-3

On January 2, 1995, Prunce Company acquired 90% of the outstanding common stock of Sun Company for $192,000 cash. Just before the acquisition, the balance sheets of the two companies were as follows:

	PRUNCE	SUN
Cash	$260,000	$ 64,000
Accounts receivable (net)	142,000	23,000
Inventory	117,000	54,000
Plant and equipment (net)	386,000	98,000
Land	63,000	32,000
Total assets	$968,000	$271,000
Accounts payable	$104,000	$ 47,000
Mortgage payable	72,000	39,000
Common stock, $2 par value	400,000	70,000
Other contributed capital	208,000	20,000
Retained earnings	184,000	95,000
Total equities	$968,000	$271,000

The fair values of Sun Company's assets and liabilities are equal to their book values with the exception of land.

Required:

A. Prepare a journal entry to record the purchase of Sun Company's common stock.

B. Prepare a consolidated balance sheet at the date of acquisition.

Exercise 2-4

On January 1, 1995, Peach Company issued 3,000 of its $10 par value common shares with a fair value of $26 per share in exchange for the 3,500 outstanding common shares of Swartz Company in a purchase transaction. Registration costs amounted to $1,500, paid in cash. Just prior to the acquisition, the balance sheets of the two companies were as follows:

P pd,
3,9000 in d.
+1,500 in cash
31,500

for 35,000

	PEACH COMPANY	SWARTZ COMPANY
Cash	$ 63,000	$ 11,000
Accounts receivable (net)	85,000	15,000
Inventory	48,000	21,000
Plant and equipment (net)	90,000	38,000
Land	21,000	19,000
Total assets	$307,000	$104,000
Accounts payable	$ 56,000	$ 15,000
Notes payable	72,000	17,000
Common stock, $10 par value	100,000	35,000
Other contributed capital	50,000	16,000 72,000
Retained earnings	29,000	21,000
Total equities	$307,000	$104,000

The fair values of Swartz Company's assets and liabilities are equal to their book values with the exception of land holdings.

Required:

A. Prepare the journal entry on Peach Company's books to record the exchange of stock.

B. Prepare a consolidated balance sheet at the date of acquisition.

Exercise 2-5

Pool Company purchased 90% of the outstanding common stock of Spruce Company on December 31, 1995, for cash. At that time the balance sheet of Spruce Company was as follows:

Current assets	$1,050,000
Plant and equipment	990,000
Land	170,000
Total assets	$2,210,000
Liabilities	$ 820,000
Common stock, $20 par value	900,000
Other contributed capital	440,000
Retained earnings	150,000
Total	2,310,000
Less treasury stock at cost, 5,000 shares	100,000
Total equities	$2,210,000

Required:

A. Prepare the elimination entry required for the preparation of a consolidated balance sheet workpaper on December 31, 1995, assuming:
   (1) The purchase price of the stock was $1,400,000.
   (2) The purchase price of the stock was $1,160,000.
   Assume further that any difference between the cost of the investment and the book value of net assets acquired relates to subsidiary land.

B.   Compute the amount of the noncontrolling interest that would appear on the December 31, 1995 consolidated balance sheet.

$10\% (C/S + OCC + RE - I/S) = \square$

Exercise 2-6

On December 31, 1994, Price Company purchased a controlling interest in Shipley Company. The balance sheet of Price Company and the consolidated balance sheet on December 31, 1994 were as follows:

	PRICE COMPANY	CONSOLIDATED
Cash	$ 22,000	$ 37,900
Accounts receivable	35,000	57,000
Inventory	127,000	161,600
Investment in Shipley Company	212,000	–0–
Plant and equipment (net)	190,000	337,000
Land	120,000	218,400
Total	$706,000	$811,900
Accounts payable	$ 42,000	$112,500
Note payable	100,000	100,000
Noncontrolling interest in Shipley Company	–0–	35,400
Common stock	300,000	300,000
Other contributed capital	164,000	164,000
Retained earnings	100,000	100,000
Total	$706,000	$811,900

On the date of acquisition, the stockholders' equity section of Shipley Company's balance sheet was as follows:

Common stock	$ 90,000
Other contributed capital	90,000
Retained earnings	56,000
Total	$236,000

Required:

A.   Prepare the investment elimination entry made to prepare a consolidated balance sheet workpaper. Any difference between cost and book value relates to subsidiary land.

B.   Prepare Shipley Company's balance sheet as it appeared on December 31, 1994.

Problems

Problem 2-1

The two following separate cases show the financial position of a parent company and its subsidiary company on November 30, 1995, just after the parent had purchased 90% of the subsidiary's stock:

	CASE I		CASE II	
	P COMPANY	S COMPANY	P COMPANY	S COMPANY
Current assets	$ 880,000	$260,000	$ 780,000	$280,000
Investment in S Company	190,000		190,000	
Long-term assets	1,400,000	400,000	1,200,000	400,000
Other assets	90,000	40,000	70,000	70,000
Total	$2,560,000	$700,000	$2,240,000	$750,000
Current liabilities	$ 640,000	$270,000	$ 700,000	$260,000
Long-term liabilities	850,000	290,000	920,000	270,000
Common stock	600,000	180,000	600,000	180,000
Retained earnings	470,000	(40,000)	20,000	40,000
Total	$2,560,000	$700,000	$2,240,000	$750,000

Required:

Prepare a November 30, 1995, consolidated balance sheet workpaper for each of the foregoing cases. Any difference between the cost of the investment and the boo᠁ value of equity acquired relates to subsidiary land (included in long-term assets).

Problem 2-2

On January 1, 1995, Perry Company purchased 7,200 shares of Soho Company's common stock for $110,000. Immediately after the stock acquisition, the statements of financial position of Perry and Soho appeared as follows:

ASSETS	PERRY	SOHO
Cash	$ 41,000	$ 24,000
Accounts receivable	48,000	19,000
Inventory	39,000	17,000
Investment in Soho Company	110,000	
Plant assets	152,000	98,500
Accumulated depreciation—plant assets	(42,000)	(14,500)
Total	$348,000	$144,000

LIABILITIES AND OWNERS' EQUITY		
Current liabilities	$ 15,500	$ 23,000
Mortgage notes payable	30,000	
Common stock, $10 par value	180,000	90,000
Premium on common stock	80,000	11,000
Retained earnings	42,500	20,000
Total	$348,000	$144,000

Required:

Prepare a consolidated balance sheet workpaper as of January 1, 1995. Any difference between the cost of the investment and the book value of equity acquired relates to subsidiary land.

Problem 2-3

Balance sheets for P Company and S Company on August 1, 1995, are as follows:

	P COMPANY	S COMPANY
Cash	$ 165,500	$106,000
Receivables	366,000	126,000
Inventory	261,000	108,000
Investment in bonds	306,000	–0–
Investment in S Company stock	586,500	–0–
Plant and equipment (net)	573,000	320,000
Land	200,000	300,000
Total	$2,458,000	$960,000
Accounts payable	$ 174,000	$ 58,000
Accrued expenses	32,400	26,000
Bonds payable, 8%	–0–	200,000
Common stock	1,500,000	460,000
Other contributed capital	260,000	60,000
Retained earnings	491,600	156,000
Total	$2,458,000	$960,000

Required:

Prepare a workpaper for a consolidated balance sheet for P Company and its subsidiary on August 1, 1995, taking into consideration the following:

1. P Company acquired 90% of the outstanding common stock of S Company on August 1, 1995, for a cash payment of $586,500.
2. Included in the Investment in Bonds account are $40,000 par value of S Company bonds payable that were purchased at par by P Company in 1992. The bonds pay interest on April 30 and October 31. S Company has appropriately accrued interest expense on August 1, 1995; P Company, however, inadvertently failed to accrue interest income on the S Company bonds.
3. Included in P Company receivables is a $35,000 cash advance to S Company that was mailed on August 1, 1995. S Company had not yet received the advance at the time of the preparation of its August 1, 1995, balance sheet.
4. Any difference between the cost of the investment and the book value of equity acquired relates to subsidiary land.

Problem 2-4

On January 2, 1995, Phillips Company purchased 80% of Sanchez Company and 90% of Thomas Company for $225,000 and $168,000, respectively. Immediately before the acquisitions, the balance sheets of the three companies were as follows:

	PHILLIPS	SANCHEZ	THOMAS
Cash	$400,000	$ 43,700	$ 20,000
Accounts receivable	28,000	24,000	20,000
Note receivable	–0–	10,000	–0–
Interest receivable	–0–	300	–0–
Inventory	120,000	96,000	43,000
Equipment	60,000	40,000	30,000
Land	180,000	80,000	70,000
Total	$788,000	$294,000	$183,000
Accounts payable	$ 28,000	$ 20,000	$ 18,000
Note payable	–0–	–0–	10,000
Common stock	300,000	120,000	75,000
Other contributed capital	300,000	90,000	40,000
Retained earnings	160,000	64,000	40,000
Total	$788,000	$294,000	$183,000

The note receivable and interest receivable of Sanchez relate to a loan made to Thomas Company on October 1, 1994. Thomas failed to record the accrued interest expense on the note.

Required:

Prepare a consolidated balance sheet workpaper as of January 2, 1995. (Any difference between cost and book value relates to subsidiary land.)

Problem 2-5

On January 1, 1995, Pat Company purchased 90% of the outstanding common stock of Solo Company for $236,000 cash. The balance sheet for Pat Company just before the acquisition of Solo Company stock, along with the consolidated balance sheet prepared at the date of acquisition, follows.

	PAT COMPANY DECEMBER 31, 1994	CONSOLIDATED JANUARY 1, 1995
Cash	$ 540,000	$ 352,000
Accounts receivable	272,000	346,000
Advances to Solo Company	10,000	
Inventory	376,000	451,000
Plant and equipment	622,000	820,000
Land	350,000	421,000
Total	$2,170,000	$2,390,000
Accounts payable	$ 280,000	$ 386,000
Long-term liabilities	520,000	605,500
Noncontrolling interest in subsidiary		28,500
Common stock	890,000	890,000
Other contributed capital	300,000	300,000
Retained earnings	180,000	180,000
Total	$2,170,000	$2,390,000

One week before the acquisition, Pat Company had advanced $10,000 to Solo Company. Solo Company had not yet recorded the transaction on the date of acquisition. In addition, on the date of acquisition, Solo Company owed Pat Company $4,000 for purchases of merchandise on account. The merchandise had been sold to outside parties prior to the date of acquisition.

Required:

A. Determine the amount of cash that appeared on Solo Company's balance sheet immediately prior to the acquisition of its stock by Pat Company.

B. Determine the amount of total stockholders' equity on Solo Company's separate balance sheet at the date of acquisition.

C. Determine the amount of total assets appearing on Solo Company's separate balance sheet on the date of acquisition.

Problem 2-6

On July 31, 1995, Ping Company purchased 90% of Santos Company's common stock for $2,010,000 cash. Immediately after the acquisition, the two companies' balance sheets were as follows:

	PING	SANTOS
Cash	$ 320,000	$ 150,000
Accounts receivable	600,000	300,000
Note receivable	100,000	–0–
Inventory	1,840,000	400,000
Advance to Santos Company	60,000	–0–
Investment in Santos Company	2,010,000	–0–
Plant and equipment (net)	3,000,000	1,500,000
Land	90,000	90,000
Total	$8,020,000	$2,440,000
Accounts payable	$ 800,000	$ 140,000
Notes payable	900,000	100,000
Common stock	2,400,000	900,000
Other contributed capital	2,200,000	680,000
Retained earnings	1,720,000	620,000
Total	$8,020,000	$2,440,000

Santos Company has not yet recorded the $60,000 cash advance from Ping Company. Ping Company's accounts receivable include $20,000 due from Santos Company. Santos Company's $100,000 note payable is payable to Ping Company. Neither company has recorded $7,000 of interest accrued on the note from January 1 to July 31. Any difference between cost and book value relates to land.

Required:

Prepare a consolidated balance sheet workpaper on July 31, 1995.

Problem 2-7

Balance sheets for Prego Company and Sprague Company as of December 31, 1994, follow:

	PREGO COMPANY	SPRAGUE COMPANY
Cash	$ 700,000	$111,000
Accounts receivable (net)	892,000	230,000
Inventory	544,000	60,000

	PREGO COMPANY	SPRAGUE COMPANY
Property and equipment (net)	$1,927,000	$468,000
Land	120,000	94,000
Total assets	$4,183,000	$963,000
Accounts payable	$ 302,000	$152,000
Notes payable	588,000	61,000
Long-term debt	350,000	90,000
Common stock	1,800,000	500,000
Other contributed capital	543,000	80,000
Retained earnings	600,000	80,000
Total equities	$4,183,000	$963,000

The fair values of Sprague Company's assets and liabilities are equal to their book values.

Required:

Prepare a consolidated balance sheet as of January 1, 1995, under each of the following assumptions:

A. On January 1, 1995, Prego Company purchased 90% of the outstanding common stock of Sprague Company for $594,000.

B. On January 1, 1995, Prego Company exchanged 11,880 of its $20 par value common shares with a fair value of $50 per share for 90% of the outstanding common shares of Sprague Company. The transaction is a purchase.

Problem 2-8

On February 1, 1995, Punto Company purchased 95% of the outstanding common stock of Sara Company and 85% of the outstanding common stock of Rob Company. Immediately before the two acquisitions, balance sheets of the three companies were

	PUNTO	SARA 95%	ROB 85%
Cash	$165,000	$ 45,000	$17,000
Accounts receivable	35,000	35,000	26,000
Notes receivable	18,000	–0–	–0–
Merchandise inventory	106,000	35,500	14,000
Prepaid insurance	13,500	2,500	500
Advances to Sara Company	10,000		
Advances to Rob Company	5,000		
Land	248,000	43,000	15,000
Buildings (net)	100,000	27,000	16,000
Equipment (net)	35,000	10,000	2,500
Total	$735,500	$198,000	$91,000
Accounts payable	$ 25,500	$ 20,000	$10,500
Income taxes payable	30,000	10,000	–0–
Notes payable	–0–	6,000	10,500
Bonds payable	100,000	–0–	–0–
Common stock, $10 par value	300,000	144,000 _136,800_	42,000 _35,700_
Other contributed capital	150,000	12,000 _11,400_	38,000 _32,300_
Retained earnings (deficit)	130,000	6,000 _5,700_	(10,000) _(8,500)_
Total	$735,500	$198,000 _153,900_	$91,000 _59,500_

The following additional information is relevant.

1. One week before the acquisitions, Punto Company had advanced $10,000 to Sara Company and $5,000 to Rob Company. Sara Company recorded an increase to Accounts Payable for its advance, but Rob Company had not recorded the transaction.
2. On the date of acquisition, Punto Company owed Sara Company $12,000 for purchases on account, and Rob Company owed Punto Company $3,000 and Sara Company $6,000 for such purchases. The goods purchased had all been sold to outside parties prior to acquisition.
3. Punto Company exchanged 13,400 shares of its common stock with a fair value of $12 per share for 95% of the outstanding common stock of Sara Company. In addition, stock issue fees of $4,000 were paid in cash. The acquisition was accounted for as a purchase.
4. Punto Company paid $50,000 cash for the 85% interest in Rob Company.
5. Three thousand dollars of Sara Company's notes payable and $9,500 of Rob Company's notes payable were payable to Punto Company.
6. Any difference between cost and book value relates to subsidiary land.

Required:

A. Give the book entries to record the two acquisitions in the accounts of Punto Company.

B. Prepare a consolidated balance sheet workpaper immediately after acquisition.

C. Prepare a consolidated balance sheet at the date of acquisition for Punto Company and its subsidiaries.

Problem 2-9

On January 1, 1995, Pope Company purchased 90% of Sun Company's common stock for $5,300,000 cash. Immediately after the acquisition, the two companies' balance sheets were as follows:

	POPE	SUN
Cash	$ 330,000	$ 150,000
Accounts receivable	480,000	425,000
Notes receivable	100,000	–0–
Inventory	2,200,000	1,315,000
Investment in Sun Company	5,300,000	—
Plant and equipment (net)	6,365,000	3,400,000
Land	1,750,000	825,000
Total	$16,525,000	$6,115,000
Accounts payable	$ 775,000	$ 225,000
Notes payable	2,500,000	100,000
Common stock ($10 par)	5,790,000	4,880,000
Other contributed capital	3,840,000	360,000
Treasury stock held	–0–	(1,200,000)
Retained earnings	3,620,000	1,750,000
Total	$16,525,000	$6,115,000

Sun Compay's note payable is payable to Pope Company. Any difference between cost and book value relates to subsidiary land.

Required:

Prepare a consolidated balance sheet workpaper on January 1, 1995.

3

CONSOLIDATED FINANCIAL STATEMENTS AFTER ACQUISITION

Investments in voting stock of other companies may be consolidated, or they may be separately reported in the financial statements at cost, at market value, or at equity. The method of reporting adopted depends on a number of factors including the size of the investment, the extent to which the investor exercises control over the activities of the investee, and the marketability of the securities. *Investor* refers to a business entity that holds an investment in voting stock of another company. *Investee* refers to a corporation that issued voting stock held by an investor.

Prior to 1989 accounting standards generally required the use of the equity method to report investments in nonconsolidated subsidiaries. However, as mentioned in Chapter 2, the FASB changed that treatment. Under the new standard, with few exceptions, all subsidiaries must be consolidated and cannot be reported as separate investments in the consolidated financial statements. Exceptions are made for those cases in which there are serious questions regarding the ability of the parent company to actually control the activities of the subsidiary. In those cases, the subsidiary is not consolidated, but is reported in the consolidated financial statements as an investment at cost. Consequently, to satisfy reporting requirements, there is little reason to use methods other than the cost method to record investments in subsidiaries on the books of the parent company.

As discussed in the preface to this text, some companies have elected to *record* their investments using some form of the equity method in order to approximate the operating effects of the investments for internal decision-making purposes. Although there are several variations of the equity method, the two main forms are the partial equity method and the complete equity method. Under the partial equity method, the investor adjusts the investment account for its share of the investee's earnings and dividends only. Under the complete equity method, additional adjustments are made to the investment account for the effects of unrealized intercompany profits, the amortization of a difference between cost and book value, and stockholders' equity transactions undertaken by the subsidiary. *Remember, the cost method and various forms of the equity method are methods to record investments after acquisition, in contrast with the purchase and pooling of interests methods, which are methods used to record the initial acquisition of an investment.*

Because essentially all subsidiaries are either consolidated or reported as investments using the cost method, discussion and illustrations in this and subsequent chapters related to the recording of investments in subsidiaries and the preparation of consolidated financial statements are based primarily on the cost method. Book entries and workpaper eliminating entries assuming the use of the partial equity method are discussed and illustrated in separate sections.

Although the complete equity method is rarely used to report investments in nonconsolidated subsidiaries, the complete equity method must still be used to report common stock investments in the 20% to 50% range, which assume the investor's ability to exercise significant influence over the operating activities of the investee. In addition, although it may be unusual, a parent company may use the complete equity method to *record* investments in subsidiaries that will be consolidated. The complete equity method of reporting investments in common stock and workpaper eliminating entries required when investments in consolidated subsidiaries are recorded using the complete equity method are discussed and illustrated in Chapter 12.

RECORDING INVESTMENTS IN SUBSIDIARIES—COST METHOD

At the date an investment in a subsidiary is acquired, the investment account is debited for the cost of the investment. Under the cost method, income on the investment is recognized only as dividends are declared by the subsidiary. (When dividends are both declared and paid during the investor's fiscal period, dividend income is generally recognized when the dividends are received.) The investment account remains at cost unless (1) there is a permanent, material decline in the value of the investment, or (2) the subsidiary declares a liquidating dividend as described later.

To illustrate the accounting for an investment in a subsidiary, assume that P Company acquired 90% of the outstanding voting stock of S Company at the beginning of Year 1 for $800,000. Income (loss) of S Company and dividends declared by S Company during the next three years were:

YEAR	INCOME (LOSS)	DIVIDENDS DECLARED	CUMULATIVE INCOME OVER (UNDER) DIVIDENDS
1	$90,000	$30,000	$60,000
2	(20,000)	30,000	10,000
3	10,000	30,000	(10,000)

Journal entries on the books of P Company to account for the investment in S Company during the three years follow:

YEAR 1

Investment in S Company	800,000	
Cash		800,000
To record the initial investment.		
Cash	27,000	
Dividend Income		27,000
To record dividends received .9($30,000).		

YEAR 2

Cash	27,000	
Dividend Income		27,000
To record dividends received .9($30,000).		

YEAR 3

Cash	27,000	
Dividend Income		18,000
Investment in S Company		9,000
To record dividends received, $9,000 of which represent a return of investment.		

After these entries are posted, the investment account will appear as follows:

INVESTMENT IN S COMPANY			
Year 1 Cost	800,000	Year 3 Liquidating dividend	9,000
Year 3 Balance	791,000		

Year 1 entries record the initial investment and the receipt of dividends from S Company. In Year 2, although S Company incurred a $20,000 loss, there was a $60,000 excess of earnings over dividends in Year 1. Consequently, the dividends received are recognized as income by P Company. In Year 3, however, a *liquidating dividend* occurs. From the point of view of a parent company, a purchased subsidiary is deemed to have distributed a liquidating dividend when the cumulative amount of its dividends declared after its acquisition by the parent company exceeds the cumulative amount of its reported earnings after its acquisition. The treatment of such excess dividends as a return of capital is consistent with the purchase concept that subsidiary earnings prior to acquisition are purchased by the parent company at the time it acquires its interest in the subsidiary. Consequently, liquidating dividends are recorded as a reduction of the investment account rather than as dividend income.

CONSOLIDATED STATEMENTS AFTER ACQUISITION—COST METHOD

The preparation of consolidated financial statements after acquisition is not materially different in concept from preparing them at the acquisition date in the sense that reciprocal accounts are eliminated and remaining balances are combined. The process is more complex, however, because time has elapsed and business activity has taken place between the date of acquisition and the date of consolidated statement preparation. On the date of acquisition, the only relevant financial statement is the consolidated balance sheet; after acquisition, a complete set of consolidated financial statements—income statement, retained earnings statement, balance sheet, and statement of cash flows—must be prepared for the affiliated group of companies.

Workpaper Format

Accounting workpapers are used to accumulate, classify, and arrange data for a variety of accounting purposes, including the preparation of financial reports and statements. Although workpaper style and technique vary among firms and individuals, we have adopted a three-section workpaper for illustrative purposes in this book. The format includes a separate section for each of three basic financial statements—income statement, retained earnings statements, and balance sheet. In some cases the input to the workpaper comes from the individual financial statements of the affiliates to be consolidated, in which case the three-section workpaper is particularly appropriate. At other times, however, input may be from affiliate trial balances, and the data must be arranged in financial statement form before the workpaper can be completed. (An alternative trial balance workpaper format is illustrated in Chapter 5.)

The discussion and illustrations that follow are based on trial balances at December 31, 1995, for P Company and S Company given in Illustration 3-1.[1] (Throughout this chapter, any difference between cost of the investment and the book value of the equity interest acquired is assumed to relate to the under- or overvaluation of subsidiary land and is, therefore, assigned to land in the eliminating entry.)

Year of Acquisition

Assume that P Company purchased 80% of the outstanding shares of S Company common stock on January 1, 1995, for $165,000, and made the following entry:

Investment in S Company	165,000	
Cash		165,000

On June 6, 1995, S Company paid a $10,000 dividend, and made the following entry:

Dividends Declared	10,000	
Cash		10,000

---

[1]Throughout Chapters 3 through 11, unless stated otherwise, we assume the parent company purchased the subsidiary's shares on the open market.

ILLUSTRATION 3-1
P Company and S Company Trial Balances
December 31, 1995

	P COMPANY		S COMPANY	
	DR.	CR.	DR.	CR.
Cash	$ 79,000		$ 18,000	
Accounts Receivable (net)	64,000		28,000	
Inventory, 1/1	56,000		32,000	
Investment in S Company	165,000			
Property and Equipment (net)	180,000		165,000	
Land	35,000		17,000	
Accounts Payable		$ 35,000		$ 24,000
Other Liabilities		62,000		37,000
Common Stock, $10 par value		200,000		100,000
Other Contributed Capital		40,000		50,000
Retained Earnings, 1/1		210,000		40,000
Dividends Declared	20,000		10,000	
Sales		300,000		160,000
Dividend Income		8,000		
Purchases	186,000		95,000	
Expenses	70,000		46,000	
	$855,000	$855,000	$411,000	$411,000
Inventory, 12/31	$ 67,000		$ 43,000	

(Recall that the Dividends Declared account is a temporary account that is closed to retained earnings at year-end.) Since P Company owns 80% of S Company's common stock, the receipt of the dividend was recorded by P Company as follows:

Cash	8,000	
Dividend Income (80% × $10,000)		8,000

Note that the trial balance data in Illustration 3-1 reflect the effects of both the investment and dividend transactions.

A workpaper for the preparation of consolidated financial statements at December 31, 1995, the end of the year of acquisition, is presented in Illustration 3-2.

Data from the trial balances are arranged in statement form and entered on the workpaper. Consolidated financial statements should include only balances resulting from transactions with outsiders. Eliminating techniques are designed to accomplish this end. The consolidated income statement is essentially a combination of the revenue, expense, gain, and loss of all consolidated affiliates after elimination of amounts representing the effect of transactions among the affiliates. The combined income of the affiliates is reduced by the noncontrolling interest's share (if any) of the net income of the subsidiaries. The remainder, which is identified as *consolidated net income,* consists of parent company net income plus (minus) its share of the affiliate's income (loss) resulting from transactions with outside parties. The consolidated retained earnings statement consists of the normal ordering of

Cost Method
80% Owned Subsidiary
Year of Acquisition

ILLUSTRATION 3-2
Consolidated Statements Workpaper
P Company and Subsidiary
For the Year Ended December 31, 1995

	P COMPANY	S COMPANY	ELIMINATIONS DR.	ELIMINATIONS CR.	NONCONTROLLING INTEREST	CONSOLIDATED BALANCES
INCOME STATEMENT						
Sales	300,000	160,000				460,000
Dividend Income	8,000		(1) 8,000			
Total Revenue	308,000	160,000				460,000
Cost of Goods Sold:						
Inventory, 1/1	56,000	32,000				88,000
Purchases	186,000	95,000				281,000
	242,000	127,000				369,000
Inventory, 12/31	67,000	43,000				110,000
Cost of Goods Sold	175,000	84,000				259,000
Expenses	70,000	46,000				116,000
Total Cost and Expense	245,000	130,000				375,000
Net/Combined Income	63,000	30,000				85,000
Noncontrolling Interest in Income .2($30,000)					6,000	(6,000)
Net Income to Retained Earnings	63,000	30,000	8,000	–0–	6,000	79,000 P x S owned
RETAINED EARNINGS STATEMENT						
1/1 Retained Earnings						
P Company	210,000					210,000
S Company		40,000	(2) 32,000 Env		8,000	
Net Income from above	63,000	30,000	8,000	–0–	6,000	79,000
Dividends Declared						
P Company	(20,000)					(20,000)
S Company		(10,000)		(1) 8,000	(2,000)	
12/31 Retained Earnings to Balance Sheet	253,000	60,000	40,000	8,000	12,000	269,000 P x S owned
BALANCE SHEET						
Cash	79,000	18,000				97,000
Accounts Receivable (net)	64,000	28,000				92,000
Inventory, 12/31	67,000	43,000				110,000
Investment in S Company	165,000			(2) 165,000		
Property and Equipment (net)	180,000	165,000				345,000
Land	35,000	17,000	(2) 13,000			65,000
Total	590,000	271,000				709,000 P x S
Accounts Payable	35,000	24,000				59,000
Other Liabilities	62,000	37,000				99,000
Common Stock						
P Company	200,000					200,000
S Company		100,000	(2) 80,000		20,000	
Other Contributed Capital						
P Company	40,000					40,000
S Company		50,000	(2) 40,000		10,000	
Retained Earnings from above	253,000	60,000	40,000	8,000	12,000	269,000
Noncontrolling Interest in Net Assets					42,000	42,000
Total	590,000	271,000	173,000	173,000		709,000 P x S

(1) To eliminate intercompany dividends.
(2) To eliminate investment in S Company.

the statement, that is, beginning consolidated retained earnings plus consolidated net income or minus consolidated net loss, minus parent company dividends declared. The net balance represents consolidated retained earnings at the end of the period.

Several observations should be noted concerning the workpaper, Illustration 3-2.

1. Each section of the workpaper represents one of three consolidated financial statements.

2. The elimination of intercompany dividends is made by a debit to Dividend Income and a credit to Dividends Declared as follows:

(1) Dividend Income	8,000	
Dividends Declared—S Company		8,000

This eliminating entry is needed to prevent the double counting of income, since the subsidiary's individual income and expense items are combined with the parent's in the determination of combined income.

3. The elimination of the investment account is the same one that would be made at the date of acquisition for the preparation of a consolidated balance sheet, except that P Company's share of S Company's beginning retained earnings is eliminated in the *retained earnings section* of the workpaper, rather than in the balance sheet section.

(2) Common Stock—S Company	80,000	
Other Contributed Capital—S Company	40,000	
1/1 Retained Earnings—S Company	32,000	
Land	13,000	
Investment in S Company		165,000

4. Consolidated net income of $79,000 consists of:

P Company's reported net income	$63,000
Less dividends received from S Company	8,000
P Company's income from its independent operations	55,000
Plus P Company's share of the reported net income of	
S Company .8($30,000)	24,000
Consolidated Net Income	$79,000

Or consolidated net income may also be determined as follows:

P Company's reported net income	$63,000
Plus P Company's share of S Company's **undistributed income**	
for the year .8($30,000 − $10,000)	16,000
Consolidated Net Income	$79,000

5. Consolidated retained earnings on December 31, 1995, of $269,000 can be determined in a similar way as follows:

P Company's reported retained earnings, 1/1	$210,000
Plus consolidated net income for 1995	79,000
Less P Company's dividends declared during 1995	(20,000)
Consolidated Retained Earnings, 12/31	$269,000

Or consolidated retained earnings may be determined as:

P Company's reported retained earnings, 12/31	$253,000
Plus P Company's share of the increase in S Company's retained earnings from the date of acquisition to the end of 1995, .8($60,000 − $40,000)	16,000
Consolidated Retained Earnings, 12/31	$269,000

6. The total net income line from the income statement section of the work-paper is carried down to the retained earnings section; likewise, the ending retained earnings line in the retained earnings section is carried to the balance sheet section. Of course, the eliminations columns in each section do not balance, since individual eliminations made involve more than one section. The total eliminations for all three sections, however, are in balance.

7. The total noncontrolling interest of $42,000 is made up of the following:
   (a) A $6,000 (20% × $30,000) interest in the amount of S Company income that is included in combined income. The $6,000 is added to the non-controlling interest and deducted from combined income in determining consolidated income.
   (b) An $8,000 share in the beginning balance of S Company's retained earnings. The other $32,000 was purchased by P Company and is, therefore, eliminated.
   (c) A $2,000 (20% × $10,000) decrease for dividends distributed to the noncontrolling stockholders during the year. The other $8,000 in dividends represents parent company dividend income and is, therefore, eliminated.
   (d) A $20,000 and $10,000 interest, respectively, in the common stock and other contributed capital of S Company. The remaining common stock and other contributed capital were purchased by P Company and are, therefore, eliminated.

The sum of the noncontrolling interest column is transferred to the consolidated balance sheet as one amount since it reflects the noncontrolling stockholders' interest in the net assets of the consolidated group. Noncontrolling interest in consolidated net assets can also be determined directly by multiplying the noncontrolling interest percentage times the book value of the subsidiary's net assets. Thus,

noncontrolling interest in consolidated net assets can be verified as .2($271,000 −
$61,000) = $42,000.

(24,000+ 37,000)

After Year of Acquisition

For illustration purposes, assume continuation of the previous example with data
updated to December 31, 1996. Trial balances for P Company and S Company at
December 31, 1996 are given in Illustration 3-3. Note that the Investment in S
Company account still reflects the cost of the investment, $165,000. Also, the be-
ginning retained earnings balances for P and S companies on January 1, 1996, are
consistent with the ending balances on December 31, 1995 in Illustration 3-2.

A workpaper for the preparation of consolidated financial statements for P and
S Companies for the year ended December 31, 1996, is presented in Illustration
3-4. (Note that the detail making up cost of goods sold is provided in Illustration
3-2. In Illustration 3-4 and subsequent illustrations in this chapter, the detail will
be collapsed into one item, "Cost of Goods Sold.")

The workpaper entries in years after the year of acquisition are essentially the
same as those made for the year of acquisition (Illustration 3-2) with one major
exception. Before the elimination of the investment account, a workpaper entry,
(1) in Illustration 3-4, is made to the investment account and P Company's beginning retained earnings to recognize P Company's share of the cumulative undis-

ILLUSTRATION 3-3
P Company and S Company Trial Balances
December 31, 1996

| | P COMPANY | | S COMPANY | |
	DR.	CR.	DR.	CR.
Cash	$ 74,000		$ 41,000	
Accounts Receivable (net)	71,000		33,000	
Inventory, 1/1	67,000		43,000	
Investment in S Company	165,000			
Property and Equipment (net)	245,000		185,000	
Land	35,000		17,000	
Accounts Payable		$ 61,000		$ 30,000
Other Liabilities		70,000		45,000
Common Stock		200,000		100,000
Other Contributed Capital		40,000		50,000
Retained Earnings, 1/1		253,000		60,000
Dividends Declared, 8/10	30,000		10,000	
Sales		350,000		190,000
Dividend Income		8,000		
Purchases	215,000		90,000	
Expenses	80,000		56,000	
	$982,000	$982,000	$475,000	$475,000
Inventory, 12/31	$ 82,000		$ 39,000	

Cost Method
80% Owned Subsidiary
Subsequent to Year
of Acquisition

ILLUSTRATION 3-4
Consolidated Statements Workpaper
P Company and Subsidiary
For the Year Ended December 31, 1996

INCOME STATEMENT	P COMPANY	S COMPANY	ELIMINATIONS DR.	ELIMINATIONS CR.	NONCONTROLLING INTEREST	CONSOLIDATED BALANCES
Sales	350,000	190,000				540,000
Dividend Income	8,000		(2) 8,000			
Total Revenue	358,000	190,000				540,000
Cost of Goods Sold	200,000	94,000				294,000
Expenses	80,000	56,000				136,000
Total Cost and Expense	280,000	150,000				430,000
Net/Combined Income	78,000	40,000				110,000
Noncontrolling Interest in Income .2($40,000)					8,000	(8,000)
Net Income to Retained Earnings	78,000	40,000	8,000	–0–	8,000	102,000
RETAINED EARNINGS STATEMENT						
1/1 Retained Earnings						
P Company	253,000			(1) 16,000		269,000
S Company		60,000	(3) 48,000		12,000	
Net Income from above	78,000	40,000	8,000	–0–	8,000	102,000
Dividends Declared						
P Company	(30,000)					(30,000)
S Company		(10,000)		(2) 8,000	(2,000)	
12/31 Retained Earnings to Balance Sheet	301,000	90,000	56,000	24,000	18,000	341,000
BALANCE SHEET						
Cash	74,000	41,000				115,000
Accounts Receivable (net)	71,000	33,000				104,000
Inventory, 12/31	82,000	39,000				121,000
Investment in S Company	165,000		(1) 16,000	(3) 181,000		
Property and Equipment (net)	245,000	185,000				430,000
Land	35,000	7,000	(3) 13,000			65,000
Total	672,000	315,000				835,000
Accounts Payable	61,000	30,000				91,000
Other Liabilities	70,000	45,000				115,000
Common Stock						
P Company	200,000					200,000
S Company		100,000	(3) 80,000		20,000	
Other Contributed Capital						
P Company	40,000					40,000
S Company		50,000	(3) 40,000		10,000	
Retained Earnings from above	301,000	90,000	56,000	24,000	18,000	341,000
Noncontrolling Interest in Net Assets					48,000	48,000
Total	672,000	315,000	205,000	205,000		835,000

(1) To recognize P Company's share (80%) of S Company's *undistributed* income from date of acquisition to beginning of the current year. (Hereafter, we will use "To establish reciprocity.")
(2) To eliminate intercompany dividends.
(3) To eliminate investment in S Company.

tributed income or loss of S Company from the *date of acquisition to the beginning of the current year* as follows:

(1) Investment in S Company	16,000	
1/1 Retained Earnings—P Company		
(Consolidated Retained Earnings)		16,000
[80% × ($60,000 − $40,000)]		

Hereafter, this entry will be called the *entry to establish reciprocity.* The entry serves two main purposes:

1. As indicated earlier, consolidated retained earnings on January 1, 1996, consists of P Company's reported retained earnings plus P Company's share of the undistributed earnings of S Company from the date of stock acquisition to the beginning of 1996. S Company earned $30,000 during 1995, $10,000 of which was distributed as dividends in 1995. P Company recognized its share ($8,000) of these as dividend income which is, therefore, included in P Company's beginning retained earnings for 1996. The remaining $20,000 of S Company's 1995 earnings represents undistributed earnings, 80% ($16,000) of which accrues to P Company. The reciprocity entry adjusts P Company's beginning retained earnings balance on the workpaper to the appropriate beginning consolidated retained earnings amount. Note that, after the reciprocity entry is made, the beginning (1/1/96) consolidated retained earnings of $269,000 (Illustration 3-4) equal the ending (12/31/95) consolidated retained earnings amount (Illustration 3-2).

2. The entry also facilitates the elimination of the investment account by adjusting the balance in the investment account to include the parent company's share of the reported subsidiary's stockholders' equity as of the beginning of the year. Thus, when the parent company's share of each of the components of the subsidiary's stockholders' equity as of the beginning of the year is eliminated against the investment account, any remaining balance in the investment account represents the difference between cost and book value. (In this example, the difference of $13,000 is attributed to land.) This can be verified by reference to the investment elimination entry (3) given on page 86.

The amount needed for the workpaper entry to establish reciprocity can be most accurately computed by multiplying the parent company's percentage of ownership times the increase or decrease in the subsidiary's retained earnings from the date of stock acquisition to the beginning of the current year. This approach adjusts for complications that might arise where the subsidiary may have made direct entries to its retained earnings for prior period adjustments.[2]

---

[2]The parent company's share of any prior period adjustments to retained earnings made by the subsidiary after acquisition that relate to periods before acquisition should be adjusted to the excess of cost over book value. For example, if an excess cost was related to goodwill in the initial acquisition, the parent's share of a subsidiary's prior period adjustment reducing retained earnings serves to reduce that addition to goodwill on subsequent workpapers.

After the investment account is adjusted by this workpaper entry, intercompany dividend income is eliminated and P Company's share of S Company's equity is eliminated against the ***adjusted investment account*** as follows:

(2) Dividend Income	8,000	
Dividends Declared—S Company		8,000
(3) Common Stock—S Company	80,000	
Other Contributed Capital—S Company	40,000	
1/1 Retained Earnings—S Company	48,000	
Land	13,000	
Investment in S Company ($165,000 + $16,000)		181,000

Consolidated balances are then determined in the same manner as in previous illustrations. Remember that the entry to establish reciprocity is a cumulative one that recognizes the parent's share of the change in the subsidiary's retained earnings from the date of acquisition to the beginning of the current year. Thus, for example, the reciprocity entry for a December 31, 1997, workpaper is as follows:

Investment in S Company	40,000	
1/1 Retained Earnings—P Company		40,000
.8($90,000 − $40,000)		

An example of a consolidated statement of income and retained earnings and a consolidated balance sheet (based on Illustration 3-4) is presented in Illustration 3-5. Notice that all (100%) of S Company's revenues and expenses are included in the consolidated income statement. The noncontrolling interest's share of the subsidiary's income is then deducted as a separate item in determining consolidated

ILLUSTRATION 3-5
P Company and Subsidiary
Consolidated Statement of Income and Retained Earnings
For the Year Ended December 31, 1996

Sales	$540,000
Cost of goods sold	294,000
Gross margin	246,000
Expenses	136,000
Operating income	110,000
Noncontrolling interest in income	8,000
Net income	102,000
Retained earnings, 1/1/96	269,000
Total	371,000
Dividends declared	30,000
Retained earnings, 12/31/96	$341,000

P Company and Subsidiary
Consolidated Balance Sheet
December 31, 1996

ASSETS

Current assets:	
Cash	$115,000
Accounts receivable (net)	104,000
Inventories	121,000
Total currents assets	340,000
Property and equipment (net)	430,000
Land	65,000
Total assets	$835,000

LIABILITIES AND STOCKHOLDERS' EQUITY

Accounts payable		$ 91,000
Other liabilities		115,000
Total liabilities		206,000
Noncontrolling interest in net assets		48,000
Stockholders' equity:		
Common stock, $10 par value	$200,000	
Other contributed capital	40,000	
Retained earnings	341,000	581,000
Total liabilities and stockholders' equity		$835,000

net income. Likewise, all of S Company's assets and liabilities are included with those of P Company in the consolidated balance sheet. The noncontrolling interest's share of the net assets is then included as a separate item between liabilities and stockholders' equity in the consolidated balance sheet.

RECORDING INVESTMENTS IN SUBSIDIARIES—PARTIAL EQUITY METHOD

As indicated earlier, some companies may elect to use the partial equity method to record their investments in subsidiaries in order to estimate the operating effects of their investments for internal decision-making purposes. As with the cost method, the investment is recorded initially at its cost under the partial equity method. Subsequent to acquisition, the major differences between the cost and partial equity methods pertain to the period in which subsidiary income is formally recorded on the books of the parent company and the amount of income recognized.

As illustrated in previous sections of this chapter, no income from the subsidiary is recorded by the parent company under the cost method until it is distributed as dividends. When distributed, the parent records its share of the dividends as dividend income. Under the partial equity method, income is recorded in the books of the parent company in the same accounting period that it is reported by the subsidiary company, whether or not such income is distributed to the parent company. The amount of income recorded is the parent company's share of the subsidiary's reported income, which is debited to the Investment account and credited to Equity in Subsidiary Income. Dividends received from the subsidiary are then credited to the Investment account. Consequently, the parent company's share of the *cumulative undistributed income* of the subsidiary is accumulated over time as an addition to the investment account.

Investment Carried at Partial Equity—Year of Acquisition

Continue the situation in the preceding cost method illustration (Illustration 3-1), but assume that P Company has elected to use the partial equity method to record its investment. The investment is recorded initially at its cost; however, under the partial equity method the parent company's share of subsidiary dividends and income is recorded in the Investment account. Thus, P Company would make the following entries during 1995 relative to its investment in S Company.

Investment in S Company	165,000	
Cash		165,000
To record investment.		
Cash	8,000	
Investment in S Company		8,000
To record dividends received.		
Investment in S Company	24,000	
Equity in Subsidiary Income		24,000
To record equity in subsidiary income.		

After these entries are posted, the Investment account will appear as follows:

	INVESTMENT IN S COMPANY			
1/1/95	Cost	165,000	Dividends	8,000
	Subsidiary income	24,000		
12/31/95	Balance	181,000		

A consolidated statements workpaper under the partial equity method is presented in Illustration 3-6. Observe that the only differences in the affiliates' account data as compared with Illustration 3-2 (cost method workpaper) appear in P Company's statements. The investment account shows a balance of $181,000 (rather than $165,000), and equity in subsidiary income of $24,000 (rather than dividend income of $8,000) is listed in P Company's income statement. In addition, P Company's ending retained earnings is $16,000 larger, which reflects the effect of recognizing $24,000 of subsidiary income rather than only $8,000 of dividend income.

When the investment account is carried on the partial equity basis, it is necessary first to make a workpaper entry reversing the net effect of the parent company's entries on the investment account for subsidiary income and dividends during the current year. The entry, in general journal form, is:

(1) Equity in Subsidiary Income	24,000	
Dividends Declared—S Company		8,000
Investment in S Company		16,000

ILLUSTRATION 3-6
Consolidated Statements Workpaper
P Company and Subsidiary
For the Year Ended December 31, 1995

	P COMPANY	S COMPANY	ELIMINATIONS DR.	ELIMINATIONS CR.	NONCONTROLLING INTEREST	CONSOLIDATED BALANCES
INCOME STATEMENT						
Sales	300,000	160,000				460,000
Equity in Subsidiary Income	24,000		(1) 24,000			
Total Revenue	324,000	160,000				460,000
Cost of Goods Sold	175,000	84,000				259,000
Expenses	70,000	46,000				116,000
Total Cost and Expense	245,000	130,000				375,000
Net/Combined Income	79,000	30,000				85,000
Noncontrolling Interest in Income					6,000	(6,000)*
Net Income to Retained Earnings	79,000	30,000	24,000	–0–	6,000	79,000
RETAINED EARNINGS STATEMENT						
1/1 Retained Earnings						
P Company	210,000					210,000
S Company		40,000	(2) 32,000		8,000	
Net Income from above	79,000	30,000	24,000	–0–	6,000	79,000
Dividends Declared						
P Company	(20,000)					(20,000)
S Company		(10,000)		(1) 8,000	(2,000)	
12/31 Retained Earnings to Balance Sheet	269,000	60,000	56,000	8,000	12,000	269,000
BALANCE SHEET						
Cash	79,000	18,000				97,000
Accounts Receivable (net)	64,000	28,000				92,000
Inventory, 12/31	67,000	43,000				110,000
Investment in S Company	181,000			(1) 16,000		
				(2) 165,000		
Property and Equipment (net)	180,000	165,000				345,000
Land	35,000	17,000	(2) 13,000			65,000
Total	606,000	271,000				709,000
Accounts Payable	35,000	24,000				59,000
Other Liabilities	62,000	37,000				99,000
Common Stock						
P Company	200,000					200,000
S Company		100,000	(2) 80,000		20,000	
Other Contributed Capital						
P Company	40,000					40,000
S Company		50,000	(2) 40,000		10,000	
Retained Earnings from above	269,000	60,000	56,000	8,000	12,000	269,000
Noncontrolling Interest in Net Assets					42,000	42,000
Total	606,000	271,000	189,000	189,000		709,000

*20% × $30,000 = $6,000

(1) To reverse the effect of parent company entries during the year for subsidiary dividends and income.
(2) To eliminate investment in S Company.

This reversal has two effects. First, it eliminates the equity in subsidiary income and dividends recorded by P Company. Second, it returns the investment account to its balance as of the beginning of the year. This is necessary because it is the parent company's share of the subsidiary's retained earnings at the *beginning of the year* that is eliminated in the investment elimination entry. A second eliminating entry must then be made to eliminate the Investment account against subsidiary equity, as follows:

(2) Common Stock—S Company	80,000	
Other Contributed Capital—S Company	40,000	
1/1 Retained Earnings—S Company	32,000	
Land	13,000	
Investment in S Company		165,000
($181,000 − $16,000)		

Completion of the workpaper follows the same process as that used under the cost method.

Comparison of Illustrations 3-2 and 3-6 brings out one important observation. *The consolidated column of the workpaper is the same under both the cost and partial equity methods. Thus, the decision to use the cost or partial equity method to record investments in subsidiaries that will be consolidated will have no impact on the consolidated financial statements. Only the elimination process is affected.*

Note that P Company's reported net income of $79,000 (Illustration 3-6) and consolidated net income are identical. Likewise, P Company's December 31, 1995, retained earnings equal consolidated retained earnings at that date. This results because P Company has recorded its share of S Company's earnings.

Investment Carried at Partial Equity—After Year of Acquisition

To illustrate the preparation of a consolidated workpaper for years after the year of acquisition under the partial equity method, assume the same data as those given in Illustration 3-3, but use of the partial equity method rather than the cost method. After P Company has recorded its share of S Company's income ($32,000) and dividends declared ($8,000), the Investment in S Company account appears as follows:

INVESTMENT IN S COMPANY			
12/31/95 Balance	181,000	Dividends	8,000
Subsidiary income	32,000		
12/31/96 Balance	205,000		

A consolidated statements workpaper in this case is presented in Illustration 3-7.

Observe again that the only differences in the affiliates' account data as compared with Illustration 3-4 (cost method workpaper) appear in P Company's statements. The Investment account in P Company's balance sheet shows a balance of $205,000 rather than $165,000, and equity in subsidiary income of $32,000, rather

Partial Equity Method
80% Owned Subsidiary
Subsequent to Year
of Acquisition

ILLUSTRATION 3-7
Consolidated Statements Workpaper
P Company and Subsidiary
For the Year Ended December 31, 1996

INCOME STATEMENT	P COMPANY	S COMPANY	ELIMINATIONS DR.	ELIMINATIONS CR.	NONCONTROLLING INTEREST	CONSOLIDATED BALANCES
Sales	350,000	190,000				540,000
Equity in Subsidiary Income	32,000		(1) 32,000			
Total Revenue	382,000	190,000				540,000
Cost of Goods Sold	200,000	94,000				294,000
Expenses	80,000	56,000				136,000
Total Cost and Expense	280,000	150,000				430,000
Net/Combined Income	102,000	40,000				110,000
Noncontrolling Interest in Income					8,000	(8,000)*
Net Income to Retained Earnings	102,000	40,000	32,000	–0–	8,000	102,000

RETAINED EARNINGS STATEMENT						
1/1 Retained Earnings						
P Company	269,000					269,000
S Company		60,000	(2) 48,000		12,000	
Net Income from above	102,000	40,000	32,000	–0–	8,000	102,000
Dividends Declared						
P Company	(30,000)					(30,000)
S Company		(10,000)		(1) 8,000	(2,000)	
12/31 Retained Earnings to Balance Sheet	341,000	90,000	80,000	8,000	18,000	341,000

BALANCE SHEET						
Cash	74,000	41,000				115,000
Accounts Receivable (net)	71,000	33,000				104,000
Inventory, 12/31	82,000	39,000				121,000
Investment in S Company	205,000			(1) 24,000		
Property and Equipment (net)	245,000	185,000		(2) 181,000		430,000
Land	35,000	17,000	(2) 13,000			65,000
Total	712,000	315,000				835,000
Accounts Payable	61,000	30,000				91,000
Other Liabilities	70,000	45,000				115,000
Common Stock						
P Company	200,000					200,000
S Company		100,000	(2) 80,000		20,000	
Other Contributed Capital						
P Company	40,000					40,000
S Company		50,000	(2) 40,000		10,000	
Retained Earnings from above	341,000	90,000	80,000	8,000	18,000	341,000
Noncontrolling Interest in Net Assets					48,000	48,000
Total	712,000	315,000	213,000	213,000		835,000

*20% × $40,000 = $8,000

(1) To reverse the effect of parent company entries during the year for subsidiary dividends and income.
(2) To eliminate investment in S Company.

than dividend income of $8,000, is listed in P Company's income statement. In addition, P Company's beginning and ending retained earnings are $16,000 and $40,000 larger, respectively, which reflects the effect of recording its share (80%) of S Company's income in 1995 and 1996 rather than recording only its share of dividends distributed by S Company.

The elimination process follows the same procedures as those in Illustration 3-6. A workpaper entry (entry 1) is made to reverse the effect of parent company entries on the investment account for the current year. The effect is to eliminate P Company's share of subsidiary income recognized and subsidiary dividends declared during the year and to restate the investment account to its balance as of the beginning of the year. Completion of the workpaper follows the same process as that used in previous illustrations. Again, observe that the consolidated columns in Illustrations 3-4 and 3-7 are the same; regardless of the method used (cost or partial equity), the consolidated results are unaffected.

Summary of Workpaper Eliminating Entries

Basic consolidated financial statements workpaper eliminating entries depend on whether (1) the cost method or partial equity method is used to record the investment on the books of the parent company, and (2) the workpaper is being prepared at the end of the year of acquisition or at the end of periods after the year of acquisition. Workpaper eliminating entries for the alternatives are summarized in Illustration 3-8.

ILLUSTRATION 3-8
Summary of Basic Workpaper Eliminating Entries

COST METHOD	PARTIAL EQUITY METHOD
END OF YEAR OF ACQUISITION	
Dividend Income	**Equity in Subsidiary Income**
Dividends Declared—S	**Dividends Declared—S**
	Investment in S Company
To eliminate intercompany dividend income.	To eliminate intercompany income and dividends and return the investment account to its cost at date of acquisition.

- -

Capital Stock—S	
Other Contributed Capital—S	
Retained Earnings—S	**Same as Cost Method**
Difference Between Cost and	
** Book Value**	
** Investment in S Company**	
To eliminate P Company's share of S Company's stockholders' equity against the investment account.	

END OF PERIODS SUBSEQUENT TO YEAR OF ACQUISITION

Investment in S Company	
Retained Earnings—P	**No Entry Needed**
To recognize P Company's share of S Company's *undistributed* income from the date of acquisition to beginning of the current year.	

Dividend Income	Equity in Subsidiary Income
Dividends Declared—S	Dividends Declared—S
	Investment in S Company
To eliminate intercompany dividend income.	To eliminate intercompany income and dividends and return the investment account to its balance as of beginning of the current year.

Capital Stock—S	
Other Contributed Capital—S	
Retained Earnings—S	**Same as Cost Method**
Difference Between Cost and	
Book Value	
Investment in S Company	

To eliminate P Company's share of S Company's stockholders' equity against the investment account.

ELIMINATION OF INTERCOMPANY REVENUE AND EXPENSE ITEMS

Discussion and illustrations to this point have emphasized the procedures used to eliminate the parent company's interest in subsidiary equity against the investment account at the end of the year of stock acquisition and for subsequent periods. Before proceeding with a discussion of some special topics relating to consolidated statements in succeeding chapters, it should be noted that several types of intercompany revenue and expense items must be eliminated in the preparation of a consolidated income statement.

Affiliates often engage in numerous sale/purchase transactions with other affiliates. Procedures used to eliminate these intercompany sales (purchases) as well as any unrealized profit remaining in inventories are discussed and illustrated in Chapter 5. Eliminating workpaper entries are also needed for such intercompany revenue and expense items as interest, rent, and professional services. For example, the workpaper entry to eliminate intercompany interest revenue and expense takes the following form:

Interest Revenue	8,000	
Interest Expense		8,000

INTERIM ACQUISITIONS OF SUBSIDIARY STOCK

Discussion and illustrations to this point have been limited to situations in which the parent company acquired its interest in a subsidiary at the beginning of the subsidiary's fiscal period. That condition is unrealistic because some stock acquisitions are likely to be made during the subsidiary's fiscal period. Thus, the proper treatment in consolidated financial statements of the subsidiary's revenue and expense items before acquisition must be considered.

Two acceptable alternatives for treating the preacquisition revenue and expense items of the subsidiary in the consolidated income statement are prescribed by *Accounting Research Bulletin No. 51*:

When a subsidiary is purchased during the year, there are alternative ways of dealing with the results of operations in the consolidated income statement. One method, which usually is preferable, especially where there are several dates of acquisition of blocks of shares, is to include the subsidiary in the consolidation as though it had been acquired at the beginning of the year, and to deduct at the bottom of the consolidated income statement the preacquisition earnings applicable to each block of stock. This method presents results which are more indicative of the current status of the group, and facilitates future comparison with subsequent years. Another method of prorating income is to include in the consolidated statement only the subsidiary's revenue and expenses subsequent to the date of acquisition.[3]

As you recall from the discussion in Chapter 1, under purchase accounting, revenues and expenses of the acquired company are included with those of the acquiring company only from the date of acquisition forward. Both alternatives identified above accomplish this net effect, although through different forms. The difference is in the detail included in the consolidated income statement.

Alternative one, which includes the subsidiary in consolidation as though it had been acquired at the beginning of the year and makes a deduction at the bottom of the consolidated income statement for the applicable preacquisition earnings, is preferable, and it will be illustrated first. Alternative two, which includes only the subsidiary's revenue and expenses subsequent to acquisition, is illustrated later using the same data given here.

Interim Acquisition Under the Cost Method—Alternative One

Assume that P Company acquired 90% of the outstanding common stock of S Company on April 1, 1995, for a cash payment of $290,000. The difference between cost and book value relates to the undervaluation of S Company land. Trial balances at December 31, 1995, for P and S companies are as follows:

	P COMPANY DR.	P COMPANY CR.	S COMPANY DR.	S COMPANY CR.
Current Assets	$ 146,000		$ 71,000	
Investment in S Company	290,000			
Plant and Equipment (net)	326,000		200,000	
Land	120,000		90,000	
Liabilities		$ 100,000		$ 65,000
Common Stock		500,000		200,000
Retained Earnings, 1/1		214,000		80,000
Dividends Declared, 11/1	50,000		20,000	
Sales		600,000		160,000
Dividend Income		18,000		
Cost of Goods Sold	380,000		80,000	
Other Expense	120,000		44,000	
	$1,432,000	$1,432,000	$505,000	$505,000

[3] *Accounting Research Bulletin No. 51*, "Consolidated Financial Statements" (New York: AICPA, 1959), par. 11.

A workpaper for the preparation of consolidated statements on December 31, 1995 is presented in Illustration 3-9.

S Company's entire income statement account balances are included on the workpaper and P Company's share of S Company's net income earned before acquisition is deducted as "subsidiary income purchased." Thus, the workpaper eliminating entry for the investment account, in general journal form, is:

(2) Common Stock—S Company	180,000	
1/1 Retained Earnings—S Company	72,000	
Land	29,900	
Subsidiary Income Purchased	8,100	
Investment in S Company		290,000

In the computation of subsidiary income purchased, it is assumed that S Company's income of $36,000 was earned evenly throughout the year. Because one-fourth of the year had expired by April 1, the date of acquisition, net income purchased is computed as $36,000 \times \frac{1}{4} \times .9 = \$8,100$. If S Company earns its income unevenly throughout the year, because of the seasonal nature of its business, for example, this should be taken into consideration in estimating the amount of net income earned before April 1. In the event the subsidiary incurs a net loss for the year, a "subsidiary loss purchased" is credited in the elimination entry and added to combined income in determining consolidated net income, just as the noncontrolling interest in a net loss of a subsidiary is shown as a deduction in the noncontrolling interest column and an addition to combined income.

Noncontrolling interest in combined income is represented by the December 31, 1995, noncontrolling interest percentage times the reported subsidiary income (10% × $36,000), or $3,600, plus the $8,100 net income that was purchased from the former stockholders by the parent company on April 1, 1995. Thus, the noncontrolling interest in combined income reported in the consolidated income statement is $11,700 ($8,100 + $3,600). Note, however, that only $3,600 should be reflected as a part of noncontrolling interest in consolidated net assets on the balance sheet (the $11,700 noncontrolling interest share of combined income less the $8,100 sold by the noncontrolling shareholders to the parent company during 1995), since the $8,100 portion earned to April 1 was sold by the former shareholders to the parent company. The $3,600 is included in the noncontrolling interest column of the income statement section of the workpaper from which it is appropriately carried forward to the retained earnings section and eventually to the balance sheet section.

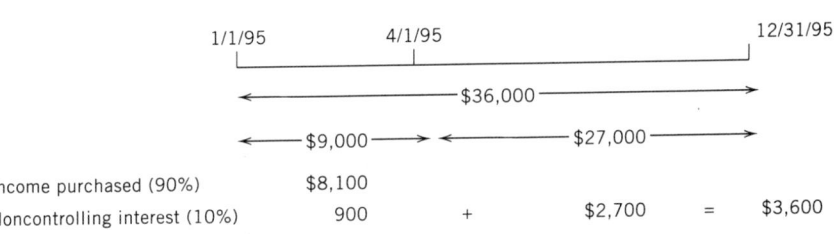

Cost Method
Interim Purchase of Stock
90% Owned Subsidiary
Alternative One

ILLUSTRATION 3-9
Consolidated Statements Workpaper
P Company and Subsidiary
For the Year Ended December 31, 1995

INCOME STATEMENT	P COMPANY	S COMPANY	ELIMINATIONS DR.	ELIMINATIONS CR.	NONCONTROLLING INTEREST	CONSOLIDATED BALANCES
Sales	600,000	160,000				760,000
Dividend Income	18,000		(1) 18,000			
Total Revenue	618,000	160,000				760,000
Cost of Goods Sold	380,000	80,000				460,000
Other Expenses	120,000	44,000				164,000
Total Cost and Expense	500,000	124,000				624,000
Net/Combined Income	118,000	36,000				136,000
Subsidiary Income Purchased			(2) 8,100			(8,100)
Noncontrolling Interest in Income .1($36,000)					3,600	(3,600)
Net Income to Retained Earnings	118,000	36,000	26,100	–0–	3,600	124,300
1/1 Retained Earnings						
P Company	214,000					214,000
S Company		80,000	(2) 72,000		8,000	
Net Income from above	118,000	36,000	26,100	–0–	3,600	124,300
Dividends Declared						
P Company	(50,000)					(50,000)
S Company		(20,000)		(1) 18,000	(2,000)	
12/31 Retained Earnings to Balance Sheet	282,000	96,000	98,100	18,000	9,600	288,300
BALANCE SHEET						
Current Assets	146,000	71,000				217,000
Investment in S Company	290,000			(2) 290,000		
Property and Equipment (net)	326,000	200,000				526,000
Land	120,000	90,000	(2) 29,900			239,900
Total	882,000	361,000				982,900
Liabilities	100,000	65,000				165,000
Common Stock						
P Company	500,000					500,000
S Company		200,000	(2) 180,000		20,000	
Retained Earnings from above	282,000	96,000	98,100	18,000	9,600	288,300
Noncontrolling Interest in Net Assets					29,600	29,600
Total	882,000	361,000	308,000	308,000		982,900

(1) To eliminate intercompany dividends.
(2) To eliminate investment in S Company.

In subsequent years, the establishment of reciprocity is based on the parent company's share of the change in subsidiary retained earnings from the date of acquisition, April 1, 1995, to the beginning of the appropriate year. S Company's retained earnings on April 1, 1995, were $89,000, consisting of the 1/1/95 balance of $80,000 plus the $9,000 income earned from January 1 to April 1, 1995. The December 31, 1996, workpaper entry to establish reciprocity, for example, would be:

Investment in S Company	6,300	
1/1 Retained Earnings—P Company		6,300
.9($96,000 − $89,000)		

Consolidated net income and consolidated retained earnings can be verified as follows:

CONSOLIDATED INCOME

P Company income from its independent operations ($118,000 − $18,000 dividends from S Company)	$100,000
P Company's share of S Company's income since acquisition (.9 × $27,000)	24,300
Consolidated Net Income	$124,300

CONSOLIDATED RETAINED EARNINGS

P Company's reported retained earnings	$282,000
P Company's share of the *undistributed* income of S Company since date of acquisition [($27,000 − $20,000) × .9]	6,300
Consolidated Retained Earnings	$288,300

Likewise, the verification of the difference between cost and book value may be made as follows:

Cost of investment		$290,000
Book value of equity acquired:		
Common stock	$200,000	
Retained earnings ($80,000 + $9,000)	89,000	
Total	$289,000 × .9	260,100
Difference between cost and book value (Assigned to land on workpaper)		$ 29,900

Note that the retained earnings of $89,000 represents the amount that would be in the retained earnings account of S Company if its books had been closed on April 1, the date of acquisition.

Interim Acquisition Under the Cost Method—Alternative Two

Another method of prorating income is to include in the consolidated income statement only the subsidiary's revenue and expenses after the date of acquisition. Thus, assuming the interim purchase situation discussed earlier, because the purchase of stock took place on April 1, only three-fourths of S Company's sales, cost

Cost Method
Interim Purchase of Stock
90% Owned Subsidiary
Alternative Two

ILLUSTRATION 3-10
Consolidated Statements Workpaper
P Company and Subsidiary
For the Year Ended December 31, 1995

	P COMPANY	S COMPANY	ELIMINATIONS DR.	ELIMINATIONS CR.	NONCONTROLLING INTEREST	CONSOLIDATED BALANCES
INCOME STATEMENT						
Sales	600,000	120,000				720,000
Dividend Income	18,000		(1) 18,000			
Total Revenue	618,000	120,000				720,000
Cost of Goods Sold	380,000	60,000				440,000
Other Expenses	120,000	33,000				153,000
Total Cost and Expense	500,000	93,000				593,000
Net/Combined Income	118,000	27,000				127,000
Noncontrolling Interest in Income .10($27,000)					2,700	(2,700)
Net Income to Retained Earnings	118,000	27,000	18,000	–0–	2,700	124,300
RETAINED EARNINGS STATEMENT						
Retained Earnings						
P Company—1/1	214,000					214,000
S Company—4/1		89,000	(2) 80,100		8,900	
Net Income from above	118,000	27,000	18,000	–0–	2,700	124,300
Dividends Declared						
P Company	(50,000)					(50,000)
S Company		(20,000)		(1) 18,000	(2,000)	
12/31 Retained Earnings to Balance Sheet	282,000	96,000	98,100	18,000	9,600	288,300
BALANCE SHEET						
Current Assets	146,000	71,000				217,000
Investments in S Company	290,000			(2) 290,000		
Property and Equipment (net)	326,000	200,000				526,000
Land	120,000	90,000	(2) 29,900			239,900
Total	882,000	361,000				982,900
Liabilities	100,000	65,000				165,000
Common Stock						
P Company	500,000					500,000
S Company		200,000	(2) 180,000		20,000	
Retained Earnings from above	282,000	96,000	98,100	18,000	9,600	288,300
Noncontrolling Interest in Net Assets					29,600	29,600
Total	882,000	361,000	308,000	308,000		982,900

(1) To eliminate intercompany dividends.
(2) To eliminate investment in S Company.

of goods sold, and other expense is included in the consolidated income statement as if S Company's books had been closed on April 1, 1995. A workpaper for the preparation of consolidated financial statements on December 31, 1995, is presented in Illustration 3-10.

The workpaper entry to eliminate the investment account is:

(2) Common Stock—S Company	180,000	
Retained Earnings—S Company (.9 × $89,000)	80,100	
Land	29,900	
Investment in S Company		290,000

Note that S Company's beginning retained earnings is $9,000 greater than it is in Illustration 3-9, reflecting the implied effect of the closing to retained earnings of income earned during the first three months. Noncontrolling interest in net income included in combined income is 10% of $27,000, or $2,700, and the noncontrolling interest's share of beginning retained earnings of S Company is $900 greater. Note, however, that consolidated net income, consolidated retained earnings, and the consolidated balance sheet are identical to those in Illustration 3-9. Only the detail included in the consolidated income statement is different.

Interim Acquisition Under the Partial Equity Method—Alternative One

The preceding discussion assumed that the parent company recorded its investment using the cost method. If the partial equity method had been used, P Company would have recognized its share of subsidiary income earned *after* acquisition. Dividends would be treated as usual as a reduction in the investment account. Thus, P Company would make the following dividend and earnings entries relative to its investment in S Company for 1995:

Cash	18,000	
Investment in S Company		18,000
To record dividends received .9($20,000)		
Investment in S Company	24,300	
Equity in Subsidiary Income .9($27,000)		24,300
To record equity in subsidiary income.		

Workpaper eliminating entries at the end of 1995 under the partial equity method would be:

(1) Equity in Subsidiary Income	24,300	
Dividends Declared—S Company		18,000
Investment in S Company		6,300
To adjust investment account to beginning of year balance and to eliminate equity in subsidiary income.		
(2) Common Stock—S Company	180,000	
1/1 Retained Earnings—S Company	72,000	
Subsidiary Income Purchased .9($9,000)	8,100	
Land	29,900	
Investment in S Company		290,000
To eliminate investment account.		

Interim Acquisition Under the Partial Equity Method—Alternative Two

If alternative two is used in conjunction with the partial equity method, P Company would recognize its share of S Company's income after acquisition (just as with alternative one). However, only three-fourths of S Company's revenue and expense items would be included in the consolidated income statement. Workpaper elimination entries are then as follows:

(1)	Equity in Subsidiary Income	24,300	
	Dividends Declared—S Company		18,000
	Investment in S Company		6,300
(2)	Common Stock—S Company	180,000	
	4/1 Retained Earnings—S Company .9($89,000)	80,100	
	Land	29,900	
	Investment in S Company		290,000

APPENDIX: CONSOLIDATED STATEMENT OF CASH FLOWS

The procedures followed in the preparation of a statement of cash flows are discussed in most intermediate accounting texts. When the company is reporting on a consolidated basis, the statement of cash flows must also be presented on a consolidated basis. Some aspects of the statement are different when consolidated statements are issued. Examples are:

1. Accounting standards require the disclosure of cash flows from operating activities for the reporting period. Cash flows from operating activities may be presented by either the direct or the indirect methods. Under the indirect method, we begin with net income for the period and add back (or deduct) any items recognized in determining that net income that did not result in an outflow (or inflow) of cash. These adjustments normally include such things as depreciation and amortization. An additional adjustment for a consolidated statement is the add-back of the noncontrolling interest in combined income (or deduction of the non-controlling interest's share of a loss) since no cash outflow or inflow was involved.

2. Because the entire amount of the noncontrolling interest in combined income (loss) is added back to (deducted from) consolidated net income in determining cash flows from operating activities, any subsidiary dividends *paid to the noncontrolling stockholders* must be included with dividends paid by the parent company when calculating cash outflow from financing activities.

3. The cost of the acquisition of additional shares in a subsidiary by the parent company may or may not constitute a cash outflow from investing activities. If the acquisition is an open market purchase, it does represent such an outflow. If it is an acquisition directly from the subsidiary, however, it represents an intercompany cash transfer that does not affect the total cash balance of the consolidated group.

As an illustration of the preparation of a consolidated statement of cash flows, a consolidated income statement and comparative consolidated balance sheets for P Company and its 90% owned subsidiary, S Company, along with other information, are presented in Illustration 3-11.

ILLUSTRATION 3-11
P Company and S Company Data
Consolidated Income Statement
For the Year Ended December 31, 1996

Sales	$540,000
Cost of goods sold	294,000
Gross profit	246,000
Operating expenses	136,000
Income from operations	110,000
Equity in income of Zorn Company	6,000
Combined income	116,000
Noncontrolling interest in combined income	(4,000)
Consolidated net income	$112,000

P Company and S Company
Comparative Consolidated Balance Sheets

	DECEMBER 31	
	1995	**1996**
ASSETS		
Cash	$ 60,000	$ 97,000
Accounts receivable (net)	92,000	120,000
Inventories	110,000	101,000
Plant and equipment (net)	245,000	406,000
Investments	152,000	158,000
Goodwill	20,000	18,000
Total assets	$679,000	$900,000
EQUITIES		
Accounts payable	$ 60,000	$ 93,000
Accrued expenses payable	99,000	89,000
Total liabilities	159,000	182,000
Noncontrolling interest in net assets	20,000	22,000
Stockholders' equity:		
Common stock, $2 par value	200,000	220,000
Other contributed capital	40,000	140,000
Retained earnings	260,000	336,000
Total stockholders' equity	500,000	696,000
Total equities	$679,000	$900,000

Other information:

1. Depreciation expense of $24,000 and amortization of goodwill of $2,000 are included in operating expenses.

2. Manufacturing equipment was acquired during 1996 for cash of $185,000.

3. Investments include a 30% common stock investment in Zorn Company on which $6,000 of equity in investee income was recognized. No dividends were received during the year.

4. Noncontrolling interest in combined income was $4,000. However, $2,000 was distributed to noncontrolling stockholders as dividends during the year. Thus noncontrolling interest in net assets on the balance sheet increased by only $2,000.

5. Ten thousand shares of common stock were issued by P Company on the open market for cash at $12 per share.

6. Dividend payments totaled $38,000, of which $36,000 were to P Company stockholders (thereby reducing consolidated retained earnings), and $2,000 were to S Company noncontrolling stockholders.

A consolidated statement of cash flows, using the indirect method of presenting cash flows from operating activities, is shown in Illustration 3-12.

ILLUSTRATION 3-12
P Company and Subsidiary
Consolidated Statement of Cash Flows
For the Year Ended December 31, 1996

Cash flows from operating activities:		
Consolidated net income		$112,000
Adjustments to convert net income to net cash		
flow from operating activities:		
Depreciation expense		24,000
Amortization expense		2,000
Noncontrolling interest in combined income		4,000
Increase in accounts receivable		(28,000)
Decrease in inventories		9,000
Increase in accounts payable		33,000
Decrease in accrued expenses payable		(10,000)
Equity in income of Zorn Company		(6,000)
Net cash flow from operating activities		140,000
Cash flows from investing activities:		
Payments for purchase of plant assets		(185,000)
Cash flows from financing activities:		
Proceeds from the issuance of common stock	$120,000	
Cash dividends declared and paid	(38,000)	
Net cash flow from financing activities		82,000
Increase in cash		$ 37,000

If the direct method is used to report cash flows from operations in Illustration 3-12, the cash flows from operating activities section of the SCF would be as follows:

Cash flows from operating activities:		
Cash received from customers (1)		$512,000
Less cash paid for:		
Purchases of merchandise (2)	$252,000	
Operating expenses (3)	120,000	372,000
Net cash flow from operating activities		$140,000

(1)	Beginning accounts receivable	$ 92,000
	Sales	540,000
	Ending accounts receivable	(120,000)
	Cash received from customers	$512,000)
(2)	Cost of goods sold	$294,000
	Beginning inventory	(110,000)
	Ending inventory	101,000
	Accrual basis purchases	285,000
	Beginning accounts payable	60,000
	Ending accounts payable	(93,000)
	Cash basis purchases	$252,000
(3)	Operating expenses	$136,000
	Amortization and depreciation expense	(26,000)
	Beginning accrued expenses	99,000
	Ending accrued expenses	(89,000)
	Cash paid for operating expenses	$120,000

Questions

1. How should nonconsolidated subsidiaries be reported in consolidated financial statements?

2. How are liquidating dividends treated on the books of an investor?

3. How are dividends declared and paid by a subsidiary during the year eliminated in the consolidated workpapers?

4. Define: Consolidated net income; consolidated retained earnings.

5. At the date of an 80% acquisition, a subsidiary had common stock of $100,000 and retained earnings of $16,250. Seven years later, at December 31, 1994, the subsidiary's retained earnings had increased to $461,430. What adjustment will be made on the consolidated workpaper at December 31, 1995, to recognize the parent's share of the cumulative undistributed profits (losses) of its subsidiary? Why?

6. On a consolidated workpaper for a parent and its partially owned subsidiary, the noncontrolling interest column accumulates the noncontrolling interests' share of several account balances. What are these accounts?

7. If a parent company elects to use the partial equity method rather than the cost method to record its investments in subsidiaries, what effect will this choice have on the consolidated financial statements?

8. How are dividends declared and paid by a subsidiary during the year eliminated in the consolidated workpapers under the partial equity method? Under the cost method?

9. Describe two methods for treating the preacquisition revenue and expense items of a subsidiary purchased during a fiscal period.

10. A principal limitation of consolidated financial statements is their lack of separate financial information about the assets, liabilities, revenues, and expenses of the individual companies included in the consolidation. Identify some problems that the reader of consolidated financial statements would encounter as a result of this limitation.

11A. In the preparation of a consolidated statement of cash flows, what adjustments are necessary because of the existence of a noncontrolling interest? *(AICPA adapted)*

Exercises

Exercise 3-1

Percy Company purchased 80% of the outstanding voting shares of Song Company at the beginning of 1995 for $387,000. At the time of purchase, Song Company's total stockholders' equity amounted to $475,000. Income and dividend distributions for Song Company from 1995 through 1997 are as follows:

	1995	1996	1997
Net income (loss)	$63,500	$52,500	($55,000)
Dividend distribution	25,000	50,000	35,000

Required:

Prepare journal entries on the books of Percy Company from the date of purchase through 1997 to account for its investment in Song Company. Percy Company uses the cost method to record its investment.

Exercise 3-2

Park Company purchased 90% of the stock of Salt Company on January 1, 1991, for $465,000, an amount equal to $15,000 in excess of the book value of equity acquired. This excess payment relates to an undervaluation of Salt Company's land. On the date of purchase, Salt Company's retained earnings balance was $50,000. The remainder of the stockholders' equity consists of no-par common stock. During 1995, Salt Company declared dividends in the amount of $10,000, and reported net income of $40,000. The retained earnings balance of Salt Company on December 31, 1994, was $160,000. Park Company uses the cost method to record its investment.

Required:

Prepare in general journal form the workpaper entries that would be made in the preparation of a consolidated statements workpaper on December 31, 1995.

Exercise 3-3

At the beginning of 1987, Presidio Company purchased 95% of the common stock of Succo Company for $494,000. On that date, Succo Company's stockholders' equity consisted of the following:

Common stock	$300,000
Other contributed capital	100,000
Retained earnings	120,000
Total	$520,000

During 1995, Succo Company reported net income of $40,000 and distributed dividends in the amount of $19,000. Succo Company's retained earnings balance at the end of 1994 amounted to $160,000. Presidio Company uses the cost method.

Required:

Prepare in general journal form the workpaper entries necessary in the compilation of consolidated financial statements on December 31, 1995.

Exercise 3-4

Poco Company purchased 85% of the outstanding common stock of Serena Company on December 31, 1992, for $310,000 cash. On that date, Serena Company's stockholders' equity consisted of the following:

Common stock	$240,000
Other contributed capital	55,000
Retained earnings	50,000
	$345,000

During 1995, Serena Company distributed a dividend in the amount of $12,000 and at year-end reported a net loss of $10,000. During the time that Poco Company has held its investment in Serena Company, Serena Company's retained earnings balance has decreased $29,500 to a net balance of $20,500 after closing on December 31, 1995. The difference between cost and book value relates to subsidiary land. Poco Company uses the cost method.

Required:

Prepare in general journal form the entries needed in the preparation of a consolidated statements workpaper on December 31, 1995.

Exercise 3-5

On January 1, 1995, Plate Company purchased a 90% interest in the common stock of Set Company for $650,000, an amount $20,000 in excess of the book value of equity acquired. The excess relates to the understatement of Set Company's land holdings.

Excerpts from the consolidated retained earnings section of the consolidated statements workpaper for the year ended December 31, 1995, follow:

	SET COMPANY	CONSOLIDATED BALANCES
1/1/95 retained earnings	190,000	880,000
Net income from above	132,000	420,000
Dividends declared	(50,000)	(88,000)
12/31/95 retained earnings to the balance sheet	272,000	1,212,000

Set Company's stockholders equity is composed of common stock and retained earnings only.

Required:

A. Prepare the eliminating entries required for the preparation of a consolidated statements workpaper on December 31, 1995. Assume use of the cost method.

B. Determine the total noncontrolling interest that will be reported on the consolidated balance sheet on December 31, 1995.

Exercise 3-6

On January 1, 1995, Pert Company purchased 85% of the outstanding common stock of Sales Company for $350,000. On that date, Sales Company's stockholders' equity consisted of common stock, $100,000; other contributed capital, $40,000; and retained earnings, $140,000. Pert Company paid more than the book value of net assets acquired because the recorded cost of Sales Company's land was significantly less than its fair value.

During 1995 Sales Company earned $148,000 and declared and paid a $50,000 dividend. Pert Company uses the partial equity method to record its investment in Sales Company.

Required:

A. Prepare the investment related entries on Pert Company's books for 1995.

B. Prepare the workpaper eliminating entries for a workpaper on December 31, 1995.

Exercise 3-7

Continue the situation in Exercise 3-6 and assume that during 1996 Sales Company earned $190,000 and declared and paid a $50,000 dividend.

Required:

A. Prepare the investment related entries on Pert Company's books for 1996.

B. Prepare the workpaper eliminating entries for a workpaper on December 31, 1996.

Exercise 3-8

On May 1, 1995, Peters Company purchased 80% of the common stock of Smith Company for $50,000. Additional data concerning these two companies for the years 1995 and 1996 are:

	1995		1996	
	PETERS	SMITH	PETERS	SMITH
Common stock	$100,000	$25,000	$100,000	$25,000
Other contributed capital	40,000	10,000	40,000	10,000
Retained earnings, 1/1	80,000	10,000	129,000	53,000
Net income (loss)	64,000	45,000	37,500	(5,000)
Cash dividends (11/30)	15,000	2,000	5,000	–0–

Any difference between cost and book value relates to Smith Company's land. Peters Company uses the cost method to record its investment.

Required:

A. Prepare the workpaper entries that would be made on a consolidated statements work-paper for the years ended December 31, 1995 and 1996 for Peters Company and its subsidiary, assuming that Smith Company's income is earned evenly throughout the year. (Use alternative one.)

B. Calculate consolidated net income and consolidated retained earnings for 1995 and 1996.

Exercise 3-9

Using the data presented in Exercise 3-8, prepare workpaper elimination entries for 1995 assuming use of alternative two.

Exercise 3-10

On October 1, 1995, Para Company purchased 90% of the outstanding common stock of Star Company for $210,000. Additional data concerning Star Company for 1995 follows:

Common stock	$70,000
Other contributed capital	30,000
Retained earnings, 1/1	70,000
Net income	60,000
Dividends declared and paid (12/15)	10,000

Any difference between cost and book value relates to Star Company land. Para Company uses the partial equity method to record its investment in Star Company.

Required:

A. Prepare on Para Company's books journal entries to record the investment related activities for 1995.

B. Prepare workpaper eliminating entries for a workpaper on December 31, 1995. Star Company's net income is earned evenly throughout the year. (Use alternative two.)

Exercise 3-11A

A consolidated income statement and selected comparative consolidated balance sheet data for Palano Company and subsidiary follow:

PALANO COMPANY AND SUBSIDIARY
Consolidated Income Statement
For the Year Ended December 31, 1995

Sales		$701,000
Cost of sales		263,000
Gross profit		438,000
Operating expenses: *(Non cash exp.)*		
Depreciation expense *(Non cash exp.)*	$ 76,000	
Selling expenses	122,000	
Administrative expenses	85,000	283,000

Combined income	155,000
Less noncontrolling interest (Non Cash exp.)	38,750
Consolidated net income	$116,250

	DECEMBER 31	
	1994	1995
Accounts receivable	$229,000	$318,000
Inventory	194,000	234,000
Prepaid selling expenses	26,000	30,000
Accounts payable	99,000 20,000	79,000
Accrued selling expenses Liability acct.	96,000 12,000	84,000
Accrued administrative expenses	56,000 17,000	39,000

Required:

Prepare the cash flow from operating activities section of a consolidated statement of cash flows assuming use of the:

A. Direct method.

B. Indirect method.

Problems

Problem 3-1

On January 1, 1995, Perelli Company purchased 90,000 of the 100,000 outstanding shares of common stock of Singer Company as a long-term investment. The purchase price of $4,972,000 was paid in cash. At the purchase date, the balance sheet of Singer Company included the following:

Current assets	$2,926,550
Long-term assets	3,894,530
Other assets	759,690
Current liabilities	1,557,542
Common stock, $20 par value	2,000,000
Other contributed capital	1,891,400
Retained earnings	1,621,000

Additional data on Singer Company for the four years following the purchase are:

	1995	1996	1997	1998
Net income (loss)	$1,997,800	$476,000	$(179,600)	$(323,800)
Cash dividends paid, 12/30	500,000	500,000	500,000	500,000

Required:

Prepare journal entries to record the purchase and all investment-related subsequent events on the books of Perelli Company for the four years assuming use of the cost method.

Problem 3-2

Parry Corporation acquired a 100% interest in Sent Company on January 1, 1995, paying $140,000. Financial statement data for the two companies for the year ended December 31, 1995 follow:

INCOME STATEMENT	PARRY	SENT
Sales	$476,000	$154,500
Cost of goods sold	285,600	121,000
Other expense	45,500	29,500
Dividend income	3,500	–0–
RETAINED EARNINGS STATEMENT		
Balance, 1/1	76,000	19,500
Net income	148,400	4,000
Dividends declared	17,500	3,500
BALANCE SHEET		
Cash	84,400	29,000
Accounts receivable	76,000	56,500
Inventory	49,500	36,500
Investment in Sent Company	140,000	–0–
Land	4,000	12,000
Accounts payable	27,000	14,000
Common stock	120,000	100,000
Retained earnings	206,900	20,000

Required:

Prepare a workpaper for the preparation of consolidated financial statements on December 31, 1995. Any difference between the cost of the investment and the book value of equity acquired relates to subsidiary land.

Problem 3-3

Perkins Company acquired 100% of Schultz Company on January 1, 1995, for $161,500. On December 31, 1995, the companies prepared the following trial balances:

	PERKINS	SCHULTZ
Cash	$ 25,000	$ 30,000
Inventory	105,000	97,500
Investment in Schultz Company	161,500	–0–
Land	111,000	97,000
Cost of Goods Sold	225,000	59,500
Other Expense	40,000	40,000
Dividends Declared	15,000	10,000
Total Debits	$682,500	$334,000
Accounts Payable	$ 72,500	$ 17,500
Capital Stock	160,000	75,000
Other Contributed Capital	35,000	17,500

Retained Earnings, 1/1	25,000	54,000
Sales	380,000	170,000
Dividend Income	10,000	–0–
Total Credits	$682,500	$334,000

Required:

Prepare a workpaper for the preparation of consolidated financial statements on December 31, 1995. Any difference between the cost of the investment and the book value of equity acquired relates to subsidiary land.

Problem 3-4

Place Company purchased 95% of the common stock of Shaw, Inc. on January 1, 1995, for $420,000. Trial balances at the end of 1995 for the companies were:

	PLACE	SHAW
Cash	$ 75,816	$ 80,774
Accounts and Notes Receivable	196,000	208,520
Inventory, 1/1	69,360	46,510
Investment in Shaw, Inc.	420,000	–0–
Plant Assets	301,604	200,500
Dividends Declared	30,000	20,000
Purchases	239,522	149,800
Selling Expenses	27,082	19,334
Other Expenses	14,888	12,796
	$1,374,272	$738,234
Accounts and Notes Payable	$ 91,000	$ 32,540
Other Liabilities	42,800	14,194
Common Stock	200,000	100,000
Premium on Common Stock	250,000	150,000
Retained Earnings	222,352	165,500
Sales	549,120	276,000
Dividend Income	19,000	–0–
	$1,374,272	$738,234

Inventory balances on December 31, 1995, were 24,380 for Place and $12,300 for Shaw, Inc. Shaw's accounts and notes payable contain a $10,000 note payable to Place.

Required:

Prepare a workpaper for the preparation of consolidated financial statements on December 31, 1995. The difference between cost and book value of equity acquired relates to subsidiary land, which is included in plant assets.

Problem 3-5

On January 1, 1991, Perez Company purchased 90% of the capital stock of Sanchez Company for $85,000. Sanchez Company had capital stock of $70,000 and retained earnings of $12,000 at that time. On December 31, 1995, the trial balances of the two companies were:

	PEREZ	SANCHEZ
Cash	$ 13,000	$ 14,000
Accounts receivable	22,000	36,000
Inventory, 1/1	14,000	8,000
Advance to Sanchez Company	8,000	–0–
Investment in Sanchez Company	85,000	–0–
Plant and equipment	50,000	44,000
Land	17,800	6,000
Dividends declared	10,000	12,000
Purchases	84,000	20,000
Other expense	10,000	16,000
Total debits	$313,800	$156,000
Accounts payable	$ 6,000	$ 6,000
Other liabilities	37,000	–0–
Advance from Perez Company	–0–	8,000
Capital stock	100,000	70,000
Retained earnings	50,000	30,000
Sales	110,000	42,000
Dividend income	10,800	–0–
Total credits	$313,800	$156,000
Inventory, 12/31	$ 40,000	$ 15,000

Any difference between cost and book value relates to subsidiary land.

Required:

Prepare a workpaper for the preparation of consolidated financial statements on December 31, 1995.

Problem 3-6

On January 1, 1991, Plank Company purchased 80% of the outstanding capital stock of Scoba Company for $53,000. At that time, Scoba's stockholders' equity consisted of capital stock, $55,000; other contributed capital, $5,000; and retained earnings, $4,000. On December 31, 1995, the two companies' trial balances were as follows:

	PLANK	SCOBA
Cash	$ 42,000	$ 22,000
Accounts Receivable	21,000	17,000
Inventory	15,000	8,000
Investment in Scoba Company	53,000	
Land	52,000	48,000
Dividends Declared	10,000	8,000
Cost of Goods Sold	85,400	20,000
Other Expense	10,000	12,000
	$288,400	$135,000

	PLANK	SCOBA
Accounts Payable	$ 12,000	$ 6,000
Other Liabilities	5,000	4,000
Capital Stock	100,000	55,000
Other Contributed Capital	20,000	5,000
Retained Earnings, 1/1	40,000	15,000
Sales	105,000	50,000
Dividend Income	6,400	
	$288,400	$135,000

The accounts payable of Scoba Company include $3,000 payable to Plank Company.

Required:

Prepare a consolidated statements workpaper at December 31, 1995. Any difference between cost and book value relates to subsidiary land.

Problem 3-7

Price Company purchased 90% of the outstanding common stock of Score Company on January 1, 1991, for $450,000. At that time, Score Company had stockholders' equity consisting of common stock, $200,000; other contributed capital, $160,000; and retained earnings, $90,000. On December 31, 1995, trial balances for Price Company and Score Company were as follows:

	PRICE	SCORE
Cash	$ 109,000	$ 78,000
Accounts Receivable	166,000	94,000
Note Receivable	75,000	–0–
Inventory	309,000	158,000
Investment in Score Company	450,000	–0–
Plant and Equipment	940,000	420,000
Land	160,000	70,000
Dividends Declared	70,000	50,000
Cost of Goods Sold	822,000	242,000
Operating Expenses	250,500	124,000
Total Debits	$3,351,500	$1,236,000
Accounts Payable	$ 132,000	$ 46,000
Notes Payable	300,000	120,000
Common Stock	500,000	200,000
Other Contributed Capital	260,000	160,000
Retained Earnings, 1/1	687,000	210,000
Sales	1,420,000	500,000
Dividend and Interest Income	52,500	–0–
Total Credits	$3,351,500	$1,236,000

Price Company's note receivable is receivable from Score Company. Interest of $7,500 was paid by Score to Price during 1995. Any difference between cost and book value relates to Score Company land.

Required:

Prepare a consolidated statements workpaper on December 31, 1995.

Problem 3-8

On January 1, 1995, Parker Company purchased 95% of the outstanding common stock of Sid Company for $160,000. At that time, Sid's stockholders' equity consisted of common stock, $120,000; other contributed capital, $10,000; and retained earnings, $23,000. On December 31, 1995, the two companies' trial balances were as follows:

	PARKER	SID
Cash	$ 62,000	$ 30,000
Accounts Receivable	32,000	29,000
Inventory	30,000	16,000
Investment in Sid Company	160,000	–0–
Plant and Equipment	105,000	82,000
Land	29,000	34,000
Dividends Declared	20,000	20,000
Cost of Goods Sold	130,000	40,000
Operating Expenses	20,000	14,000
Total Debits	$588,000	$265,000
Accounts Payable	$ 19,000	$ 12,000
Other Liabilities	10,000	20,000
Common Stock	180,000	120,000
Other Contributed Capital	60,000	10,000
Retained Earnings, 1/1	40,000	23,000
Sales	260,000	80,000
Dividend Income	19,000	–0–
Total Credits	$588,000	$265,000

Required:

A. Prepare a consolidated statements workpaper on December 31, 1995.

B. Prepare a consolidated statements workpaper on December 31, 1996, assuming trial balances for Parker and Sid on that date were:

	PARKER	SID
Cash	$ 67,000	$ 16,000
Accounts Receivable	56,000	32,000
Inventory	38,000	48,500
Investment in Sid Company	160,000	–0–
Plant and Equipment	124,000	80,000
Land	29,000	34,000
Dividends Declared	20,000	20,000
Cost of Goods Sold	155,000	52,000
Operating Expenses	30,000	18,000
Total Debits	$679,000	$300,500
Accounts Payable	$ 16,000	$ 7,000
Other Liabilities	15,000	14,500
Common Stock	180,000	120,000
Other Contributed Capital	60,000	10,000
Retained Earnings, 1/1	149,000	29,000
Sales	240,000	120,000
Dividend Income	19,000	–0–
Total Credits	$679,000	$300,500

Everything same using cost method

Problem 3-9

December 31, 1995, trial balances for Pledge Company and its subsidiary Stom Company follow:

	PLEDGE	STOM
Cash and Marketable Securities	$ 184,600	$ 72,000
Receivables (net)	182,000	180,000
Inventory	214,000	212,000
Investment in Stom Company	300,000	–0–
Plant and Equipment (net)	309,000	301,000
Land	85,000	75,000
Cost of Good Sold	460,000	185,000
Operating Expenses	225,000	65,000
Dividends Declared	50,000	30,000
Treasury Stock (10,000 shares at cost)	–0–	20,000
Total Debits	$2,009,600	$1,140,000
Accounts Payable	$ 96,000	$ 79,000
Accrued Expenses	31,000	18,000
Notes Payable	100,000	200,000
Common Stock, $1 par value	300,000	100,000
Other Contributed Capital	150,000	80,000
Retained Earnings, 1/1	422,000	320,000
Sales	880,000	340,000
Dividend and Interest Income	30,600	3,000
Total Credits	$2,009,600	$1,140,000

Pledge Company purchased 72,000 shares of Stom Company's common stock on January 1, 1990, for $300,000. On that date, Stom Company's stockholders' equity was as follows:

Common Stock, $1 par value	$100,000
Other Contributed Capital	80,000
Retained Earnings	160,000
Treasury Stock (10,000 shares at cost)	(20,000)
Total	$320,000

Other information:

1. Receivables of Pledge Company include a $55,000, 12% note receivable from Stom Company.
2. Interest amounting to $6,600 has been accrued by each company on the note payable from Stom to Pledge. Stom Company has not yet paid this interest.
3. The difference between cost and book value relates to subsidiary land.

Required:

Prepare a consolidated statements workpaper for the year ended December 31, 1995.

Problem 3-10

Poco Company purchased 80% of Solo Company's common stock on January 1, 1995, for $250,000. On December 31, 1995, the companies prepared the following trial balances:

	POCO	SOLO
Cash	$ 161,500	$125,000
Inventory	210,000	195,000
Investment in Solo Company	402,000	–0–
Land	75,000	150,000
Cost of Goods Sold	410,000	125,000
Other Expense	100,000	80,000
Dividends Declared	30,000	15,000
Total Debits	$1,388,500	$690,000
Accounts Payable	$ 154,500	$ 35,000
Common Stock	200,000	150,000
Other Contributed Capital	60,000	35,000
Retained Earnings, 1/1	50,000	60,000
Sales	760,000	410,000
Equity in Subsidiary Income	164,000	–0–
Total Credits	$1,388,500	$690,000

Required:

Prepare a consolidated statements workpaper on December 31, 1995. Any difference between cost and book value relates to subsidiary land.

Problem 3-11

(Note that this is the same problem as Problem 3-7, but assuming the use of the partial equity method.)

Price Company purchased 90% of the outstanding common stock of Score Company on January 1, 1991, for $450,000. At that time, Score Company had stockholders' equity consisting of common stock, $200,000; other contributed capital, $160,000; and retained earnings, $90,000. On December 31, 1995, trial balances for Price Company and Score Company were as follows:

	PRICE	SCORE
Cash	$ 109,000	$ 78,000
Accounts Receivable	166,000	94,000
Note Receivable	75,000	–0–
Inventory	309,000	158,000
Investment in Score Company	633,600	–0–
Plant and Equipment	940,000	420,000
Land	160,000	70,000
Dividends Declared	70,000	50,000
Cost of Goods Sold	822,000	242,000
Operating Expenses	250,500	124,000
Total Debits	$3,535,100	$1,236,000

	PRICE	SCORE
Accounts Payable	$ 132,000	$ 46,000
Notes Payable	300,000	120,000
Common Stock	500,000	200,000
Other Contributed Capital	260,000	160,000
Retained Earnings, 1/1	795,000	210,000
Sales	1,420,000	500,000
Equity in Subsidiary Income	120,600	–0–
Interest Income	7,500	–0–
Total Credits	$3,535,100	$1,236,000

Price Company's note receivable is receivable from Score Company. Interest of $7,500 was paid by Score to Price during 1995. Any difference between cost and book value relates to Score Company land.

Required:

Prepare a consolidated statements workpaper on December 31, 1995.

Problem 3-12

(Note that this is the same problem as Problem 3-8, but assuming the use of the partial equity method.)
On January 1, 1995, Parker Company purchased 95% of the outstanding common stock of Sid Company for $160,000. At that time, Sid's stockholders' equity consisted of common stock, $120,000; other contributed capital, $10,000; and retained earnings, $23,000. On December 31, 1995, the two companies' trial balances were as follows:

	PARKER	SID
Cash	$ 62,000	$ 30,000
Accounts Receivable	32,000	29,000
Inventory	30,000	16,000
Investment in Sid Company	165,700	–0–
Plant and Equipment	105,000	82,000
Land	29,000	34,000
Dividends Declared	20,000	20,000
Cost of Goods Sold	130,000	40,000
Operating Expenses	20,000	14,000
Total Debits	$593,700	$265,000
Accounts Payable	$ 19,000	$ 12,000
Other Liabilities	10,000	20,000
Common Stock	180,000	120,000
Other Contributed Capital	60,000	10,000
Retained Earnings, 1/1	40,000	23,000
Sales	260,000	80,000
Equity in Subsidiary Income	24,700	–0–
Total Credits	$593,700	$265,000

Required:

A. Prepare a consolidated statements workpaper on December 31, 1995.

B. Prepare a consolidated statements workpaper on December 31, 1996, assuming trial balances for Parker and Sid on that date were:

	PARKER	SID
Cash	$ 67,000	$ 16,000
Accounts Receivable	56,000	32,000
Inventory	38,000	48,500
Investment in Sid Company	194,200	–0–
Plant and Equipment	124,000	80,000
Land	29,000	34,000
Dividends Declared	20,000	20,000
Cost of Goods Sold	155,000	52,000
Operating Expenses	30,000	18,000
Total Debits	$713,200	$300,500
Accounts Payable	$ 16,000	$ 7,000
Other Liabilities	15,000	14,500
Common Stock	180,000	120,000
Other Contributed Capital	60,000	10,000
Retained Earnings, 1/1	154,700	29,000
Sales	240,000	120,000
Equity in Subsidiary Income	47,500	–0–
Total Credits	$713,200	$300,500

Problem 3-13

(Note that this problem is the same as Problem 3-9, but assuming the use of the partial equity method.)

December 31, 1995, trial balances for Pledge Company and its subsidiary Stom Company follow:

	PLEDGE	STOM
Cash and Marketable Securities	$ 184,600	$ 72,000
Receivables (net)	182,000	180,000
Inventory	214,000	212,000
Investment in Stom Company	478,400	–0–
Plant and Equipment (net)	309,000	301,000
Land	85,000	75,000
Cost of Goods Sold	460,000	185,000
Operating Expenses	225,000	65,000
Dividends Declared	50,000	30,000
Treasury Stock (10,000 shares at cost)	–0–	20,000
Total Debits	$2,188,000	$1,140,000
Accounts Payable	$ 96,000	$ 79,000
Accrued Expenses	31,000	18,000
Notes Payable	100,000	200,000
Common Stock, $1 par value	300,000	100,000
Other Contributed Capital	150,000	80,000
Retained Earnings, 1/1	550,000	320,000
Sales	880,000	340,000
Equity in Subsidiary Income	74,400	–0–
Interest Income	6,600	3,000
Total Credits	$2,188,000	$1,140,000

Pledge Company purchased 72,000 shares of Stom Company's common stock on January 1, 1990, for $300,000. On that date, Stom Company's stockholders' equity was as follows:

Common Stock, $1 par value	$100,000
Other Contributed Capital	80,000
Retained Earnings	160,000
Treasury Stock (10,000 shares at cost)	(20,000)
Total	$320,000

Other information:

1. Receivables of Pledge Company include a $55,000, 12% note receivable from Stom Company.
2. Interest amounting to $6,600 has been accrued by each company on the note payable from Stom to Pledge. Stom Company has not yet paid this interest.
3. The difference between cost and book value relates to subsidiary land.

Required:

Prepare a consolidated statements workpaper for the year ended December 31, 1995.

Problem 3-14

Punca Company purchased 80% of the common stock of Surrano Company on July 1, 1995, for a cash payment of $520,000. December 31, 1995, trial balances for Punca and Surrano were:

	PUNCA	SURRANO
Current Assets	$ 290,600	$ 176,200
Treasury Stock at Cost, 500 shares	–0–	32,000
Investment in Surrano Company	520,000	–0–
Property and Equipment	1,334,000	743,800
Cost of Goods Sold	1,261,000	584,000
Other Expenses	376,000	242,000
Dividends Declared	–0–	40,000
Total	$3,781,600	$1,821,000
Accounts and Notes Payable	$ 270,240	$ 144,000
Dividends Payable	–0–	40,000
Capital Stock, $10 par value	1,000,000	200,000
Other Contributed Capital	224,000	90,000
Retained Earnings	315,360	241,000
Sales	1,940,000	1,100,000
Dividend Income	32,000	6,000
Total	$3,781,600	$1,821,000

Surrano Company declared a $40,000 cash dividend on December 20, 1995, payable on January 10, 1996, to stockholders of record on December 31, 1995. Punca Company recognized the dividend on its declaration date. Any difference between cost and book value relates to subsidiary land, included in property and equipment.

Required:

Prepare a consolidated statements workpaper at December 31, 1995, assuming that revenue and expense accounts of Surrano Company for the entire year are included with those of Punca Company. (Alternative one.)

Problem 3-15

Using the data given in Problem 3-14, prepare a workpaper for the preparation of consolidated financial statements at December 31, 1995, assuming that Surrano Company's revenue and expense accounts are included in the consolidated income statement from the date of acquisition only. (Alternative two.) (Round to the nearest dollar.)

Problem 3-16

Pillow Company purchased 90% of the common stock of Satin Company on May 1, 1995, for a cash payment of $474,000. December 31, 1995, trial balances for Pillow and Satin were:

	PILLOW	SATIN
Current Assets	$ 390,600	$ 179,200
Treasury Stock at Cost, 500 shares		32,000
Investment in Satin Company	510,000	–0–
Property and Equipment	1,334,000	562,000
Cost of Goods Sold	1,261,000	584,000
Other Expenses	484,000	242,000
Dividends Declared		60,000
Total	$3,979,600	$1,659,200
Accounts and Notes Payable	$ 270,240	$ 124,000
Dividends Payable		60,000
Capital Stock, $10 par value	1,000,000	200,000
Other Contributed Capital	364,000	90,000
Retained Earnings	315,360	209,200
Sales	1,940,000	976,000
Equity in Subsidiary Income	90,000	–0–
Total	$3,979,600	$1,659,200

Satin Company declared a $60,000 cash dividend on December 20, 1995, payable on January 10, 1996, to stockholders of record on December 31, 1995. Pillow Company recognized the dividend on its declaration date. Any difference between cost and book value relates to subsidiary land, included in property and equipment.

Required:

Prepare a consolidated statements workpaper at December 31, 1995, assuming that revenue and expense accounts of Satin Company for the entire year are included with those of Pillow Company. (Alternative one.)

Problem 3-17

Using the data given in Problem 3-16, prepare a workpaper for the preparation of consolidated financial statements at December 31, 1995, assuming that Satin Company's revenue and expense accounts are included in the consolidated income statement from the date of acquisition only. (Alternative two.) (Round to the nearest dollar.)

Problem 3-18A

A consolidated income statement for 1995 and comparative consolidated balance sheets for 1994 and 1995 for P Company and its 80% owned subsidiary follow:

P COMPANY
Consolidated Income Statement
For the Year Ended December 31, 1995

Sales	$1,500,000
Cost of goods sold	800,000
Gross margin	700,000
Expenses	280,000
Operating income before tax	420,000
Investment income	60,000
Income before tax	480,000
Income taxes	199,500
Income after taxes	280,500
Less: Noncontrolling interest	56,100
Consolidated net income	$ 224,400

P COMPANY
Consolidated Balance Sheets
December 31, 1994 and 1995

ASSETS	1995	1994
Cash	$ 267,000	$ 510,000
Accounts receivable	356,000	150,000
Inventories	150,000	187,500
Equipment (net)	974,000	469,500
Long-term investments	1,132,800	1,132,800
Goodwill	120,000	150,000
Total assets	$2,999,800	$2,599,800

EQUITIES		
Accounts payable	$ 254,500	$ 925,000
Accrued expenses	120,000	300,000
Bonds payable	700,000	–0–
Premium on bonds payable	5,000	–0–
Noncontrolling interest	143,600	97,500
Common stock, $1 par value	750,000	450,000
Other contributed capital	150,000	125,000
Retained earnings	876,700	702,300
Total equities	$2,999,800	$2,599,800

Other information:

1. Equipment depreciation and goodwill amortization were $67,500 and $30,000, respectively.
2. Equipment was purchased during the year for cash, $572,000.
3. Dividends paid during 1995:
   (a) Declared and paid by S Company, $50,000.
   (b) Declared and paid by P Company, $50,000.
4. The bonds payable were issued on June 30, 1995, for $705,000.
5. Common stock issued during 1995, 300,000 shares.

Required:

Prepare a consolidated statement of cash flows for the year ended December 31, 1995, using the indirect method.

Problem 3-19A

The consolidated income statement for the year ended December 31, 1995, and comparative balance sheets for 1994 and 1995 for Parks Company and its 90% owned subsidiary SCR, Inc. are as follows:

PARKS COMPANY AND SUBSIDIARY
Consolidated Income Statement
For the Year Ended December 31, 1995

Sales		$239,000
Cost of goods sold		104,000
Gross margin		135,000
Depreciation and amortization expense	$ 27,000	
Other operating expenses	72,000	99,000
Income from operations		36,000
Investment income		4,500
Combined net income		40,500
Noncontrolling interest in net income		3,000
Consolidated net income		$ 37,500

PARKS COMPANY AND SUBSIDIARY
Consolidated Balance Sheets
December 31, 1994 and 1995

	1995	1994
Cash	$ 36,700	$ 16,000
Receivables	55,000	90,000
Inventory	126,000	92,000
Property, plant, and equipment (net of depreciation)	232,500	225,000
Long-term investment	39,000	39,000
Goodwill	58,500	60,000
Total assets	$547,700	$522,000

	1995	1994
Accounts payable	$ 67,500	$ 88,500
Accrued expenses	30,000	41,000
Bonds payable, due July 1, 2009	100,000	150,000
Total liabilities	197,500	279,500
Noncontrolling interest	32,200	30,000
Common stock	187,500	100,000
Retained earnings	130,500	112,500
Total stockholders' equity	318,000	212,500
Total equities	$547,700	$522,000

SCR Inc. declared and paid an $8,000 dividend during 1995.

Required:

Prepare a consolidated statement of cash flows using the direct method.

4

ASSIGNMENT, DEPRECIATION, AND AMORTIZATION OF THE DIFFERENCE BETWEEN COST AND BOOK VALUE

When the acquisition of a subsidiary is accounted for as a purchase, there is ordinarily a difference between the fair value of the consideration given (cost of the investment) and the book value of the equity interest acquired in the subsidiary. In most cases, the parent company's cost exceeds the book value of the stock acquired. In some instances, however, the book value of the stock acquired may exceed its cost. Circumstances that may give rise to such differences were discussed in Chapter 2.

In previous chapters it has been assumed that any difference between acquisition cost and the book value of the equity interest acquired was entirely attributable to the under- or overvaluation of land, a nonamortizable asset, on the books of the subsidiary. This chapter discusses and illustrates the assignment of this difference to assets and liabilities in the consolidated balance sheet and the amortization and depreciation of the difference in the consolidated income statement.

ASSIGNMENT OF DIFFERENCE BETWEEN COST AND BOOK VALUE TO ASSETS AND LIABILITIES OF SUBSIDIARY

When consolidated financial statements are prepared, asset and liability values must be adjusted by assigning the difference between cost and book value to specific recorded or unrecorded tangible and intangible assets and liabilities. The treatment in the consolidated financial statements of the difference between cost and book value of an investment in a wholly owned subsidiary is similar to the assignment of the cost of an acquired company to the assets acquired and liabilities assumed in a business combination as described in Chapter 1. The process is different, however, in that the book values of individual assets and liabilities must be adjusted to their fair values *in the consolidated statements workpaper each year*, as contrasted with the one-time recording of these assets and liabilities at their fair values when there is only one surviving legal and accounting entity.[1]

In the case of a wholly owned subsidiary, the difference between cost and book value is first applied to the adjustment of individual assets and liabilities to their fair values on the date of acquisition. If, after adjusting identifiable assets and liabilities to fair values, a residual amount of difference remains, it is treated as follows: When cost exceeds the aggregate fair values of identifiable assets less liabilities, the residual amounts will be positive (a debit balance). A positive residual difference is evidence of an unspecified intangible and is accounted for as goodwill and generally referred to as "consolidated goodwill." It is preferable, however, to give this positive residual difference an operational description in the consolidated financial statements such as "unamortized excess of cost over fair value of subsidiary net assets acquired."

If the total fair values of identifiable subsidiary assets less liabilities exceed acquisition cost, the residual amount of difference will be negative (credit balance). In *APB Opinion No. 16* (par. 91), the Accounting Principles Board took the position that "the value assigned to net assets acquired should not exceed the cost of an acquired company because the general presumption in historical cost based accounting is that net assets acquired should be recorded at not more than cost." Accordingly, *Opinion No. 16* (par. 91) provides that a negative residual difference should be allocated to reduce proportionately the values initially assigned to noncurrent assets (except noncurrent marketable securities) in determining their fair values. If noncurrent assets are reduced to zero by this allocation, any remaining negative difference should be classified as a deferred credit and amortized to consolidated income over a period not to exceed 40 years.

In all subsequent illustrations:

- *"Difference between cost and book value"* is used to designate the total difference between acquisition cost and the parent company's equity in the book value of the net assets of the subsidiary on the date it acquires its interest in the subsidiary.
- *"Excess of cost over fair value"* is used to designate the excess of acquisition cost over the parent company's equity in the fair value of the identifiable net assets of the subsidiary on the date the parent company acquires its interest in the subsidiary.
- *"Excess of fair value over cost"* is used to designate the excess of the parent company's equity in the fair value of the identifiable net assets of the subsidiary on the date it acquires its interest over the cost of its investment in the subsidiary.

[1]Under some circumstances, a subsidiary may adjust the recorded values of its assets and liabilities to reflect the fair values confirmed by the amount paid by the parent company for a controlling interest in its stock. The recording of such adjustments on the records of the subsidiary is referred to as "push down accounting" and is illustrated in the appendix to this chapter.

- *"Deferred excess of fair value over cost"* is used to designate that portion, if any, of the "excess of fair value over cost" that remains after the noncurrent assets of the subsidiary (excluding marketable securities) have been reduced to zero.

Acquisition Cost in Excess of Fair Value of Identifiable Net Assets of a Subsidiary

To illustrate the assignment of the difference between cost and book value to individual assets and liabilities of a subsidiary, assume that on January 1, 1995, S Company has capital stock and retained earnings of $1,500,000 and $500,000, respectively, and identifiable assets and liabilities as presented in Illustration 4-1.

ILLUSTRATION 4-1
Identifiable Assets and Liabilities
of S Company—January 1, 1995

	FAIR VALUE	BOOK VALUE	DIFFERENCE BETWEEN FAIR VALUE AND BOOK VALUE
Inventory	$ 350,000	$ 300,000	$ 50,000
Other Current Assets	450,000	450,000	–0–
Equipment (net)	600,000	300,000	300,000
Land	400,000	250,000	150,000
Other Noncurrent Assets	1,000,000	1,000,000	–0–
Liabilities	(300,000)	(300,000)	–0–
Identifiable Net Assets	$2,500,000	$2,000,000	$500,000

Adjustment of Assets and Liabilities: Wholly Owned Subsidiaries Assume further that P Company acquires a 100% interest in S Company on January 1, 1995, for $2,750,000. The consolidated statements workpaper entry to eliminate the investment balance on January 1, 1995, will result in a debit to the difference between cost and book value in the amount of $750,000 as follows:

Retained Earnings—S Company	500,000	
Capital Stock—S Company	1,500,000	
Difference Between Cost and Book Value	750,000	
Investment in S Company		2,750,000

Referring to Illustration 4-1, the workpaper entry to assign the difference between cost and book value to specific consolidated assets takes the following form:

Inventory	50,000	
Equipment (net)	300,000	
Land	150,000	
Excess of Cost over Fair Value	250,000	
Difference Between Cost and Book Value		750,000

The excess of cost over fair value is the amount of the difference between cost and book value that cannot be assigned to specifically identifiable assets and liabilities of the subsidiary. As defined earlier, it is the excess of acquisition cost over the parent company's equity in the fair value of the identifiable net assets of the subsidiary on the date the parent company acquires its interest in the subsidiary [$2,750,000 − 1.0($2,500,000) = $250,000].

Adjustment of Assets and Liabilities: Less than Wholly Owned Subsidiaries   When P Company exchanges $2,750,000 for a 100% interest in S Company, the implication is that the fair value of the net assets, including unspecified intangible assets, of S Company is $2,750,000. As was illustrated before, if the recorded book value of those net assets is $2,000,000, adjustments in the amount of $750,000 are made to specific assets and liabilities, including unspecified intangible assets (Excess of Cost over Fair Value), in the consolidated financial statements in order to recognize the total implied fair value of the subsidiary assets and liabilities.

Assume now that rather than acquiring a 100% interest for $2,750,000, P Company pays $2,200,000 for an 80% interest in S Company. The fair value of the net assets, including unspecified intangible assets, of S Company implied by this transaction is still $2,750,000 ($2,200,000/.80), and the implication remains that the net assets, including unspecified intangible assets, of S Company are understated by $750,000. In the case of a less than wholly owned subsidiary, however, current practice restricts the write-up of the net assets of S Company in the consolidated financial statements to the amount actually paid by P Company in excess of the book value of the interest it acquires, or $600,000 [$2,200,000 − .80($2,000,000) = $600,000].[2]

Thus, consolidated net assets are written up only by an amount equal to the parent company's share of the difference on the date of acquisition between the implied fair value and the book value of the subsidiary company's net assets (.80 × $750,000 = $600,000). It must be stressed, therefore, that on the date of acquisition, the amount of the difference between cost and book value that is assigned to any specific asset or liability is always equal to the *parent company's share* of the difference between the fair value and the book value of the specific asset or liability. As before, any remaining amount is assigned to excess of cost over fair value.

Referring to Illustration 4-1, and assuming that P Company acquires an 80% interest in S Company for $2,200,000 the assignment of the difference between cost and book value of $600,000 [$2,200,000 − .80($2,000,000)] is as presented in Illustration 4-2. The excess of cost over fair value is the amount of the difference between cost and book value that is not assigned to specific assets or liabilities of the subsidiary. As defined earlier, it is equal to the excess of acquisition cost over

[2]This practice is supported by the "parent company concept of consolidated financial statements" discussed in Chapter 11. Procedures for recognizing the total implied fair value of the net assets of the subsidiary in the consolidated financial statements, including the entire amount of implied goodwill, and the attendant effects on the noncontrolling interest are presented in Chapter 11 in the discussion of the "economic unit concept of consolidated financial statements."

the parent company's equity in the fair value of the identifiable net assets of the subsidiary [$2,200,000 − .80($2,500,000) = $200,000].

ILLUSTRATION 4-2
Assignment of Difference Between Cost and Book Value
Excess of Cost over Fair Value

Difference Between Cost and Book Value		$600,000
Less Amount Assigned to Specific Assets:		
Inventory (.80 × $50,000)	$ 40,000	
Equipment—net (.80 × $300,000)	240,000	
Land (.80 × $150,000)	120,000	(400,000)
Excess of Cost Over Fair Value		$200,000

Fair Value of Identifiable Net Assets of Subsidiary in Excess of Acquisition Cost Refer to Illustration 4-1 and assume that P Company acquires an 80% interest in S Company for $1,900,000. The difference between cost and book value is $300,000 [$1,900,000 − .80($2,000,000)]. However, the parent company's interest in the fair value of the identifiable net assets of the subsidiary [.80($2,500,000) = $2,000,000] exceeds acquisition cost by $100,000. An initial assignment of the difference between cost and book value is presented in Illustration 4-3. The excess of fair value over cost, (*not goodwill*) however, must be allocated to reduce proportionally the *fair values* (not book values) initially assigned to noncurrent assets (excluding marketable securities). The proportional allocation of the excess of fair value over cost in this example is summarized in Illustration 4-4.

ILLUSTRATION 4-3
Initial Assignment of Difference Between Cost and Book Value
Excess of Fair Value over Cost

820,000 − (.8 × 600,000)
820,000 − 480,000

Difference Between Cost and Book Value		$300,000 *340,000*
Less Amount Initially Assigned to Specific Assets:		
Inventory (.80 × ~~$50,000~~) *37,500*	$ 40,000 *30,000*	
Equipment—net (.80 × ~~$300,000~~) *125,000*	240,000 *180,000*	(*180,000*)
Land (.80 × ~~$150,000~~) *62,500*	120,000 *50,000*	(400,000)
Excess of Fair Value over Cost		~~($100,000)~~

.80

160,000

ILLUSTRATION 4-4
Proportional Allocation of Excess of Fair Value over Cost

	FAIR VALUE (ILLUSTRATION 4-1)	PROPORTIONAL ALLOCATION OF EXCESS OF FAIR VALUE OVER COST	
Equipment (net)	$ ~~600,000~~ *362,500*	6/20 × $100,000 =	$ 30,000
Land	~~400,000~~ *375,000*	4/20 × $100,000 =	20,000
Other Noncurrent Assets	1,000,000	10/20 × $100,000 =	50,000
Total	$2,000,000 *737,500*		$100,000

The net amount of the difference between cost and book value to be assigned to specific assets and liabilities in the consolidated financial statements can now be determined and is presented in Illustration 4-5.

ILLUSTRATION 4-5
First Assignment of Difference Between Cost and Book Value
Excess of Fair Value over Cost

	INITIAL ASSIGNMENT	ALLOCATION OF EXCESS OF FAIR VALUE OVER COST	NET AMOUNT ASSIGNED
Inventory	$ 40,000	$ –0–	$ 40,000
Equipment (net)	240,000	(30,000)	210,000
Land	120,000	(20,000)	100,000
Other Noncurrent Assets	–0–	(50,000)	(50,000)
Total	$400,000	($100,000)	$300,000
	180	160	340

The workpaper entries to eliminate the investment account and to assign the difference between cost and book value may be summarized in general journal form as follows:

Retained Earnings—S Company	400,000	
Capital Stock—S Company	1,200,000	
Difference Between Cost and Book Value	300,000	
Investment in S Company		1,900,000
Inventory	40,000	
Equipment (net)	210,000	
Land	100,000	
Other Noncurrent Assets		50,000
Difference Between Cost and Book Value		300,000

It is possible for acquisition cost to be less than the parent company's interest in the book value as well as in the fair value of the net assets of the subsidiary. In that case, the difference between cost and book value initially will be credited in the investment elimination workpaper entry. The analysis of the allocation of this credit balance, however, takes the same form as that just illustrated. For example, refer to Illustration 4-1 and assume that P Company acquired an 80% interest in S Company on January 1, 1995, for $1,500,000.

The difference between cost and book value is a negative $100,000 [$1,500,000 − (.80 × $2,000,000) = −$100,000]. An initial assignment is presented in Illustration 4-6. The allocation of the excess of fair value over cost [(.80 × $2,500,000) − $1,500,000 = $500,000] and the assignment of the credit balance of the difference between cost and book value is presented in Illustration 4-7. The workpaper entries to eliminate the investment account and to assign the difference between cost and book value are presented below in general journal form.

Capital Stock—S Company	1,200,000	
Retained Earnings—S Company	400,000	
Difference Between Cost and Book Value		100,000
Investment in S Company		1,500,000
Difference Between Cost and Book Value	100,000	
Inventory	40,000	
Equipment (net)	90,000	
Land	20,000	
Other Noncurrent Assets		250,000

ILLUSTRATION 4-6
Initial Assignment of Difference Between Cost and Book Value
Book Value of Interest Acquired Exceeds Cost

Difference Between Cost and Book Value		($100,000)
Less Amount Initially Assigned to Specific Assets:		
Inventory (.80 × $50,000)	$ 40,000	
Equipment—net (.80 × $300,000)	240,000	
Land (.80 × $150,000)	120,000	(400,000)
Excess of Fair Value over Cost		($500,000)

ILLUSTRATION 4-7
Final Assignment of Difference Between Cost and Book Value
Book Value of Interest Acquired Exceeds Cost

	INITIAL ASSIGNMENT	PROPORTIONAL ALLOCATION OF EXCESS OF FAIR VALUE OVER COST		NET AMOUNT ASSIGNED
Inventory	$ 40,000			$ 40,000
Equipment (net)	240,000	6/20 × $500,000 =	($150,000)	90,000
Land	120,000	4/20 × $500,000 =	(100,000)	20,000
Other Noncurrent Assets	–0–	10/20 × $500,000 =	(250,000)	(250,000)
Excess of Fair Value Over Cost	(500,000)		500,000	–0–
Difference Between Cost and Book Value	($100,000)		$ –0–	($100,000)

EFFECT OF ASSIGNMENT, AMORTIZATION, AND DEPRECIATION OF DIFFERENCE BETWEEN COST AND BOOK VALUE ON DETERMINATION OF CONSOLIDATED NET INCOME

Depreciation and amortization in the consolidated income statement should be based on the values assigned to depreciable and amortizable assets in the consolidated balance sheet. When any portion of the difference between cost and book value is assigned to such assets, recorded income must be adjusted in determining consolidated net income in order to reflect the difference between the amount of amortization and depreciation recorded by the subsidiary and the appropriate amount based on consolidated carrying values.

To illustrate, assume that on January 1, 1995, P Company acquires an 80% interest in S Company for $2,200,000, at which time S Company has net assets of $2,000,000 as presented in Illustration 4-1. As was previously illustrated, the difference between cost and book value in the amount of $600,000 is assigned as follows:

Inventory	$ 40,000
Equipment (net)	240,000
Land	120,000
Excess of Cost over Fair Value	200,000
Difference Between Cost and Book Value	$600,000

A comparison of the recorded and consolidated carrying values of the assets and liabilities of S Company on January 1, 1995, is presented in Illustration 4-8.

ILLUSTRATION 4-8
Comparison of Consolidated and Recorded Carrying Values of
Net Assets of S Company
January 1, 1995

	CARRYING VALUE IN S COMPANY'S RECORDS (ILLUSTRATION 4-1)	ASSIGNMENT OF DIFFERENCE BETWEEN COST AND BOOK VALUE	CONSOLIDATED CARRYING VALUE
Inventory	$ 300,000	$ 40,000	$ 340,000
Equipment (net)	300,000	240,000	540,000
Land	250,000	120,000	370,000
Excess of Cost over Fair Value	–0–	200,000	200,000
Other Assets and Liabilities (net)	1,150,000	–0–	1,150,000
Net Assets	$2,000,000	$600,000	$2,600,000

Assume now that all the inventory is sold during 1995, that the equipment has a remaining life of 10 years from January 1, 1995, and that management determines that the excess of cost over fair value should be amortized over 20 years. Adjustments in the determination of consolidated net income that result from the assignment, amortization, and depreciation of the difference between cost and book value are summarized in Illustration 4-9.

As a result of the sale of the inventory in 1995, S Company will include $300,000 in cost of goods sold, whereas from a consolidated point of view the cost of goods sold should include $340,000 (Illustration 4-8). Hence, recorded cost of goods sold must be increased by $40,000 in determining consolidated net income in 1995. This adjustment is necessary only in the year(s) the inventory is sold. S Company will record $30,000 ($300,000/10) in depreciation on the equipment each year. However, consolidated annual depreciation should be $54,000 ($540,000/10). Accordingly, depreciation expense must be increased each year by $24,000 in deter-

ILLUSTRATION 4-9
Adjustments in Determination of Consolidated Net Income
Resulting from Assignment, Amortization, and Depreciation
of Difference Between Cost and Book Value

	DIFFERENCE BETWEEN COST AND BOOK VALUE	ANNUAL ADJUSTMENTS IN DETERMINING CONSOLIDATED NET INCOME		
		1995	1996–2004	2005–2014
Inventory	$ 40,000	$40,000	$ –0–	$ –0–
Equipment (net)	240,000	24,000	24,000	–0–
Land	120,000	–0–	–0–	–0–
Excess of Cost over Fair Value	200,000	10,000	10,000	10,000
Total	$600,000	$74,000	$34,000	$10,000

mining consolidated net income. Amortization of the excess of cost over fair value is not recorded by S Company. From a consolidated point of view, however, $10,000 should be amortized each year. Thus, recorded amortization expense must be increased by $10,000 each year for 20 years in determining consolidated net income. The assignment of a portion of the difference between cost and book value to land does not require an adjustment to recorded income in determining consolidated net income, since land is not a depreciable asset.

CONSOLIDATED STATEMENTS WORKPAPER—INVESTMENT RECORDED USING THE COST METHOD

In the preparation of consolidated financial statements, the recorded balances of individual assets, liabilities, and expense accounts must be adjusted to reflect the assignment, depreciation, and amortization of the difference between cost and book value. These adjustments are accomplished through the use of *workpaper entries* in the preparation of the consolidated statements workpaper.

To illustrate, assume the following:

1. P Company acquires an 80% interest in S Company on January 1, 1995, for $2,200,000, at which time S Company has capital stock of $1,500,000 and retained earnings of $500,000. P Company uses the cost method to record its investment in S Company.

2. The assignment, amortization, and depreciation of the difference between cost and book value in the amount of $600,000 [$2,200,000 − .80($2,000,000)] is as previously presented in Illustration 4-9.

3. In 1995, S Company reported net income of $125,000 and declared and paid dividends of $20,000.

4. In 1996, S Company reported net income of $140,000 and declared and paid dividends of $60,000.

Entries on Books of P Company—1995 Entries recorded on the books of the P Company under the cost method to reflect the purchase of its interest in S Company and the receipt of dividends in 1995 are as follows:

Investment in S Company	2,200,000	
Cash		2,200,000
To record purchase of an 80% interest in S Company.		
Cash	16,000	
Dividend Income		16,000
To record receipt of dividends from S Company		
(.80 × $20,000).		

December 31,1995, Workpaper Entries (Illustration 4-10) The consolidated statements workpaper for the year ended December 31, 1995, is presented in Illustration 4-10. An analysis of the workpaper elimination entries in Illustration 4-10 is presented here:

(1) Dividend Income	16,000	
Dividends Declared		16,000
To eliminate intercompany dividends.		
(2) Beginning Retained Earnings—S Company (.80 × $500,000)	400,000	
Capital Stock—S Company (.80 × $1,500,000)	1,200,000	
Difference Between Cost and Book Value	600,000	
Investment in S Company		2,200,000
To eliminate the investment account.		
(3a)Cost of Goods Sold (Beginning Inventory)	40,000	
Equipment (net)	240,000	
Land	120,000	
Excess of Cost over Fair Value	200,000	
Difference Between Cost and Book Value		600,000
To assign the amount of difference between cost and book value at date of acquisition to specific assets and liabilities (see Illustration 4-9).		

Note that the amount of difference between cost and book value assigned to inventory on the date of acquisition is charged to cost of goods sold (beginning inventory) in the consolidated statements workpaper. The presumption implicit in this treatment is that the undervalued inventory of the subsidiary was sold in 1995. Since S Company will not have included the additional $40,000 assigned to inventory in its reported cost of goods sold, consolidated cost of goods sold must be increased by a workpaper entry. If the inventory was still on hand on December 31, 1995, the $40,000 would be assigned to ending inventory in the balance sheet rather than to cost of goods sold.

(3b)Depreciation Expense	24,000	
Equipment (net)		24,000
To depreciate the amount of difference between cost and book value assigned to equipment (see Illustration 4-9).		

ILLUSTRATION 4-10
Consolidated Statements Workpaper
P Company and Subsidiary
For Year Ended December 31, 1995

INCOME STATEMENT	P COMPANY	S COMPANY	ELIMINATIONS DR.	ELIMINATIONS CR.	NONCONTROLLING INTEREST	CONSOLIDATED BALANCES
Sales	3,100,000	2,200,000				5,300,000
Dividend Income	16,000		(1) 16,000			
Total Revenue	3,116,000	2,200,000				5,300,000
Cost of Goods Sold	1,700,000	1,360,000	(3) 40,000			3,100,000
Depreciation—Equipment	120,000	30,000	(3) 24,000			174,000
Amortization of Excess of Cost over Fair Value			(3) 10,000			10,000
Other Expenses	998,000	685,000				1,683,000
Total Cost and Expense	2,818,000	2,075,000				4,967,000
Net/Combined Income	298,000	125,000				333,000
Noncontrolling Interest in Income					25,000	(25,000)*
Net Income to Retained Earnings	298,000	125,000	90,000	–0–	25,000	308,000
RETAINED EARNINGS STATEMENT						
1/1 Retained Earnings						
P Company	1,650,000					1,650,000
S Company		500,000	(2) 400,000		100,000	
Net Income from above	298,000	125,000	90,000	–0–	25,000	308,000
Dividends Declared						
P Company	(150,000)					(150,000)
S Company		(20,000)		(1) 16,000	(4,000)	
12/31 Retained Earnings to Balance Sheet	1,798,000	605,000	490,000	16,000	121,000	1,808,000
BALANCE SHEET						
Investment in S Company	2,200,000			(2) 2,200,000		
Difference Between Cost and Book Value			(2) 600,000	(3) 600,000		
Land	1,250,000	250,000	(3) 120,000			1,620,000
Equipment (net)	1,080,000	270,000	(3) 216,000			1,566,000
Other Assets (net)	2,402,000	1,885,000				4,287,000
Excess of Cost over Fair Value			(3) 190,000			190,000
Total Assets	6,932,000	2,405,000				7,663,000
Liabilities	2,134,000	300,000				2,434,000
Capital Stock						
P Company	3,000,000					3,000,000
S Company		1,500,000	(2) 1,200,000		300,000	
Retained Earnings from above	1,798,000	605,000	490,000	16,000	121,000	1,808,000
Noncontrolling Interest in Net Assets					421,000	421,000
Total Liabilities and Equity	6,932,000	2,405,000	2,816,000	2,816,000		7,663,000

*20 × $125,000 = $25,000.

(1) To eliminate intercompany dividends.
(2) To eliminate investment account.
(3) To assign, amortize, and depreciate difference between cost and book value.

As previously noted, depreciation in the consolidated income statement should be based on the value assigned to the equipment in the consolidated balance sheet. Since the depreciation recorded by S Company is based on the book value of the equipment on its records, consolidated depreciation must be increased by a workpaper entry.

(3c) Amortization of Excess of Cost over Fair Value	10,000	
Excess of Cost over Fair Value		10,000
To amortize the amount of difference between cost and book value assigned to unspecified intangibles (see Illustration 4-9).		

The amount of the difference between cost and book value not assigned to specific identifiable assets or liabilities is treated in the consolidated financial statements as an unspecified intangible and must be amortized (the straight-line method is recommended) over an appropriate period not to exceed 40 years, in accordance with *APB Opinion No. 17*. Again, since it is not recognized on the records of S Company, no amortization of this asset is included in its income statement. Accordingly, a workpaper entry is necessary to recognize the annual charge to expense in the consolidated income statement.

It is generally more efficient to combine the workpaper entries relating to the assignment, amortization, and depreciation of the difference between cost and book value into one entry. In Illustration 4-10, for example, workpaper entries (3a), (3b), and (3c) are presented in one combined entry as follows:

(3) Cost of Goods Sold (Beginning Inventory)	40,000	
Depreciation Expense	24,000	
Amortization of Excess of Cost over Fair Value	10,000	
Equipment (net) ($240,000 − $24,000)	216,000	
Land	120,000	
Excess of Cost over Fair Value ($200,000 − $10,000)	190,000	
Difference Between Cost and Book Value		600,000

In Illustration 4-10, the calculation of noncontrolling interest is not affected by the amortization of the difference between cost and book value. Since the difference between cost and book value represents a cost incurred by the parent company in the purchase of the subsidiary stock, its amortization is properly charged in its entirety to the parent company (controlling stockholders).

Entries on Books of P Company—1996

In 1996, P Company will record dividend income as follows:

Cash	48,000	
Dividend Income		48,000
To record receipt of dividends from S Company (.8 × $60,000).		

December 31, 1996, Workpaper Entries (Illustration 4-11) The consolidated statements workpaper for the year ended December 31, 1996 is presented in Illustration 4-11. Workpaper elimination entries in Illustration 4-11 are presented in general journal form as follows:

(1)	Investment in S Company	84,000	
	Beginning Retained Earnings—P Company		84,000
	To establish reciprocity as of 1/1/96 [($605,000 − $500,000) × .80].		
(2)	Dividend Income	48,000	
	Dividends Declared		48,000
	To eliminate the intercompany dividends.		
(3)	Beginning Retained Earnings—S Company		
	(.80 × $605,000)	484,000	
	Capital Stock—S Company		
	(.80 × $1,500,000)	1,200,000	
	Difference Between Cost and Book Value	600,000	
	Investment in S Company		
	($2,200,000 + $84,000)		2,284,000
	To eliminate investment account.		

In the investment elimination entry the amount debited or credited to the Difference Between Cost and Book Value may be treated as a plug figure to balance the entry and is equal to the amount of the difference between cost and book value on the date of acquisition.

(4)	Beginning Retained Earnings—P Company		
	(Beginning Consolidated Retained Earnings)	74,000	
	Depreciation Expense ($240,000/10)	24,000	
	Amortization of Excess of Cost over Fair Value		
	($200,000/20)	10,000	
	Equipment (net) ($240,000 − $24,000 − $24,000)	192,000	
	Land	120,000	
	Excess of Cost over Fair Value		
	($200,000 − $10,000 − $10,000)	180,000	
	Difference Between Cost and Book Value		600,000
	To assign, amortize, and depreciate the difference between cost and book value.		

= 340,000

Beginning consolidated retained earnings must be adjusted each year for the cumulative amount of depreciation, amortization, and other deductions that have been made from consolidated net income because of the amortization and depreciation of the difference between cost and book value in the consolidated statements workpapers of prior years. By reducing previously reported consolidated net income, these workpaper adjustments also reduce previously reported consolidated retained earnings. The reduction of beginning consolidated retained earnings is accomplished by a debit to the beginning retained earnings of the parent company in the consolidated statements workpaper. The $74,000 debit to beginning retained

Cost Method
80% Owned Subsidiary
Subsequent to Year
of Acquisition

ILLUSTRATION 4-11
Consolidated Statements Workpaper
P Company and Subsidiary
For Year Ended December 31, 1996

INCOME STATEMENT	P COMPANY	S COMPANY	ELIMINATIONS DR.	ELIMINATIONS CR.	NONCONTROLLING INTEREST	CONSOLIDATED BALANCES
Sales	3,534,000	2,020,000				5,554,000
Dividend Income	48,000		(2) 48,000			
Total Revenue	3,582,000	2,020,000				5,554,000
Cost of Goods Sold	2,040,000	1,200,000				3,240,000
Depreciation—Equipment	120,000	30,000	(4) 24,000			174,000
Amortization of Excess of Cost over Fair Value			(4) 10,000			10,000
Other Expenses	993,000	650,000				1,643,000
Total Cost and Expense	3,153,000	1,880,000				5,067,000
Net/Combined Income	429,000	140,000				487,000
Noncontrolling Interest in Income					28,000	(28,000)*
Net Income to Retained Earnings	429,000	140,000	82,000	–0–	28,000	459,000
RETAINED EARNINGS STATEMENT						
1/1 Retained Earnings						
P Company	1,798,000		(4) 74,000	(1) 84,000		1,808,000
S Company		605,000	(3) 484,000		121,000	
Net Income from above	429,000	140,000	82,000	–0–	28,000	459,000
Dividends Declared						
P Company	(150,000)					(150,000)
S Company		(60,000)		(2) 48,000	(12,000)	
12/31 Retained Earnings to Balance Sheet	2,077,000	685,000	640,000	132,000	137,000	2,117,000
BALANCE SHEET						
Investment in S Company	2,200,000		(1) 84,000	(3) 2,284,000		
Difference Between Cost and Book Value			(3) 600,000	(4) 600,000		
Land	2,000,000	250,000	(4) 120,000			2,370,000
Equipment (net)	960,000	240,000	(4) 192,000			1,392,000
Other Assets (net)	2,137,000	2,200,000				4,337,000
Excess of Cost over Fair Value			(4) 180,000			180,000
Total Assets	7,297,000	2,690,000				8,279,000
Liabilities	2,220,000	505,000				2,725,000
Capital Stock						
P Company	3,000,000					3,000,000
S Company		1,500,000	(2) 1,200,000		300,000	
Retained Earnings from above	2,077,000	685,000	640,000	132,000	137,000	2,117,000
Noncontrolling Interest in Net Assets					437,000	437,000
Total Liabilities and Equity	7,297,000	2,690,000	3,016,000	3,016,000		8,279,000

*20 × $140,000 = $28,000.

(1) To establish reciprocity as of 1/1/96 [.80 × ($605,000 − $500,000)].
(2) To eliminate intercompany dividends.
(3) To eliminate investment account.
(3) To assign, amortize, and depreciate difference between cost and book value.

earnings is equal to the $40,000 charged to cost of goods sold plus the $24,000 charged to depreciation expense plus the $10,000 charged to amortization of the excess of cost over fair value in the 1995 consolidated statements workpaper [see entry (3) in Illustration 4-10; see also Illustration 4-9]. Where part of the difference between cost and book value is assigned to depreciable or amortizable assets, the workpaper adjustment to the beginning retained earnings of the parent company will become progressively larger each year.

The amounts charged to expense each year were calculated in Illustration 4-9. Since inventory was sold in 1995, no part of the difference between cost and book value is assigned to inventory in the years after its sale. The amounts assigned to assets and liabilities are the unamortized amounts at the end of the year. Thus, the amounts assigned to amortizable or depreciable assets and liabilities in the balance sheet will become progressively smaller each year.

In the December 31, 1997, consolidated statements workpaper, for example, the workpaper elimination entry will be as follows:

Beginning Retained Earnings—P Company		
(Beginning Consolidated Retained Earnings)		
($74,000 + $34,000)	108,000	
Depreciation Expense ($240,000/10)	24,000	
Amortization of Excess of Cost over Fair Value		
($200,000/20)	10,000	
Equipment (net)		
($240,000 − $24,000 − $24,000 − $24,000)	168,000	
Land	120,000	
Excess of Cost over Fair Value		
($200,000 − $10,000 − $10,000 − $10,000)	170,000	
Difference Between Cost and Book Value		600,000

The debit to the beginning retained earnings of the parent company in 1997 ($74,000 + $34,000 = $108,000) is equal to the amount by which consolidated net income and consolidated retained earnings have been reduced because of the assignment, amortization, and depreciation of the difference between cost and book value in the 1995 ($40,000 + $24,000 + $10,000 = $74,000) and 1996 ($24,000 + $10,000 = $34,000) consolidated statements workpapers [see entry (3) in Illustration 4-10 and entry (4) in Illustration 4-11; see also Illustration 4-9].

COST METHOD ANALYSIS OF CONSOLIDATED NET INCOME AND CONSOLIDATED RETAINED EARNINGS

In the preceding chapter an analytical approach to the calculation of consolidated net income and consolidated retained earnings was presented. These analyses must now be refined to accommodate the effect of the assignment, amortization, and depreciation of the difference between cost and book value.

Consolidated net income is the parent company's income from its independent operations plus (minus) its share of reported subsidiary income (loss) plus or minus adjustments for the period relating to the amortization of the difference between cost and book value.

The analytical calculation of consolidated net income for the year ended December 31, 1996, presented in Illustration 4-12 is based on Illustration 4-11. This, of course, is the same amount of consolidated net income as that calculated in the consolidated financial statements workpaper presented in Illustration 4-11.

ILLUSTRATION 4-12
Analytical Calculation of Consolidated Net Income
For Year Ended December 31, 1996

P Company's net income from its independent operations ($429,000 reported net income less $48,000 subsidiary dividend income included therein)		$381,000
P Company's share of the reported income of S Company (.8 × $140,000)		112,000
Less depreciation and amortization for the period of the amount of the difference between cost and book value assigned to:		
Property and Equipment (net)	$24,000	
Excess of Cost over Fair Value	10,000	(34,000)
Consolidated Net Income		$459,000

This, of course, is the same amount of consolidated retained earnings as that shown in the consolidated statements workpaper presented in Illustration 4-11.

Consolidated retained earnings is the parent company's cost basis retained earnings plus (minus) the parent company's share of the increase (decrease) in reported subsidiary retained earnings from the date of acquisition to the current date plus or minus the cumulative effect of adjustments to date relating to the amortization of the difference between cost and book value.

The analytical calculation of consolidated retained earnings on December 31, 1996, presented in Illustration 4-13 is based on Illustration 4-11. This, of course, is the same amount of consolidated retained earnings as that shown in the consolidated statements workpaper presented in Illustration 4-11.

CONSOLIDATED STATEMENTS WORKPAPER—INVESTMENT RECORDED USING PARTIAL EQUITY METHOD

The balances reported by the parent company in income, retained earnings, and the investment account differ depending on the method used by the parent company to record its investment. As illustrated in Chapter 3, however, the method used by the parent company to record its investment has no affect on the consolidated balances. To illustrate consolidation procedures when the parent company records its investment using the partial equity method, assume the following:

1. P Company acquires an 80% interest in S Company on January 1, 1995, for $2,200,000, at which time S Company has capital stock of $1,500,000 and retained earnings of $500,000.

2. The assignment, amortization, and depreciation of the difference between

ILLUSTRATION 4-13
Analytical Calculation of Consolidated Retained Earnings
December 31, 1996

P Company's retained earnings on
December 31, 1996   *215,700* $2,077,000

P Company's share of the increase in S
Company's retained earnings from date
of acquisition to December 31, 1996 [.8
× ($685,000 − $500,000)]   *.8(680-400)*   *224,000*   148,000

Less cumulative effect to December 31,
1996, of the amortization of the
difference between cost and book value:

	1995	1996	
Inventory	$40,000	$ –0–	
Equipment (net)	24,000	24,000	
Excess of Cost over Fair Value	10,000	10,000	
	$74,000	$34,000	(108,000)

Consolidated Retained Earnings on
December 31, 1996 $2,117,000

cost and book value in the amount of $600,000 [$2,200,000 − .80($2,000,000)] is as previously presented in Illustration 4-9.

3. In 1995, S Company reported net income of $125,000 and declared dividends of $20,000.

4. In 1996, S Company reported net income of $140,000 and declared dividends of $60,000.

Entries on Books of P Company

Entries recorded on the books of P Company under the partial equity method are as follows:

1995

(1) Investment in S Company	2,200,000	
Cash		2,200,000
To record purchase of 80% interest in S Company.		
(2) Cash	16,000	
Investment in S Company		16,000
To record dividends received (.80 × $20,000).		
(3) Investment in S Company	100,000	
Equity in Subsidiary Income		100,000
To record equity in subsidiary income (.80 × $125,000).		

1996

(4) Cash	48,000	
Investment in S Company		48,000
To record dividends received (.80 × $60,000).		
(5) Investment in S Company	112,000	
Equity in Subsidiary Income		112,000
To record equity in subsidiary income		
(.80 × $140,000).		

After these entries are posted, the Investment account will appear as follows:

INVESTMENT IN S COMPANY

(1) Cost	2,200,000	(2) Dividends		16,000
(3) Subsidiary Income	100,000			
12/31/95 Balance	2,284,000			
(5) Subsidiary Income	112,000	(4) Dividends		48,000
12/31/96 Balance	2,348,000			

A consolidated statements workpaper under the partial equity method for the year ended December 31, 1996, is presented in Illustration 4-14. Workpaper entries in Illustration 4-14 are presented in general journal form as follows:

(1) Equity in Subsidiary Income	112,000	
Dividends Declared		48,000
Investment in S Company		64,000
To reverse the effect of parent company entries during the year for subsidiary dividends and income.		
(2) Beginning Retained Earnings—S Company (.80 × $605,000)	484,000	
Capital Stock—S Company (.80 × $1,500,000)	1,200,000	
Difference Between Cost and Book Value	600,000	
Investment in S Company ($2,348,000 − $64,000)		2,284,000
To eliminate investment account.		

Entry (2) is the same as entry (3) in Illustration 4-11 (investment recorded at cost).

(3) Beginning Retained Earnings—P Company (Beginning Consolidated Retained Earnings)	74,000	
Depreciation Expense ($240,000/10)	24,000	
Amortization of Excess of Cost over Fair Value ($200,000/20)	10,000	
Equipment (net) ($240,000 − $24,000 − $24,000)	192,000	
Land	120,000	
Excess of Cost over Fair Value ($200,000 − $10,000 − $10,000)	180,000	
Difference Between Cost and Book Value		600,000
To assign, amortize, and depreciate the difference between cost and book value.		

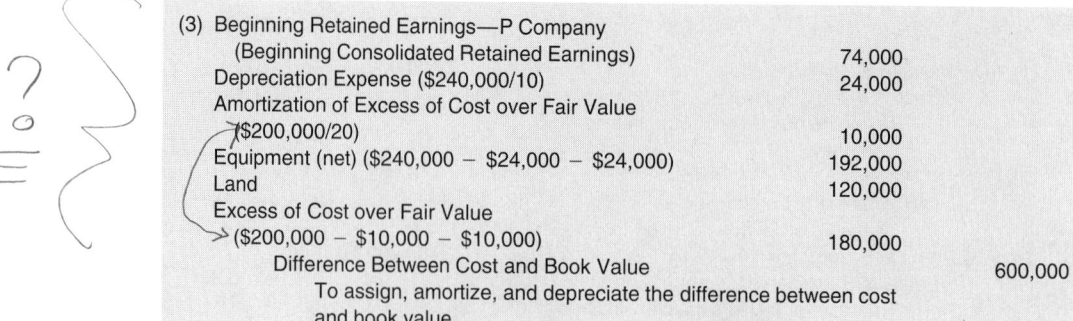

Partial Equity Method
80% Owned Subsidiary
Subsequent to Year
of Acquisition

ILLUSTRATION 4-14
Consolidated Statements Workpaper
P Company and Subsidiary
For Year Ended December 31, 1996

INCOME STATEMENT	P COMPANY	S COMPANY	ELIMINATIONS DR.		ELIMINATIONS CR.	NONCONTROLLING INTEREST	CONSOLIDATED BALANCES
Sales	3,534,000	2,020,000					5,554,000
Equity in Subsidiary Income	112,000		(1)	112,000			
Total Revenue	3,646,000	2,020,000					5,554,000
Cost of Goods Sold	2,040,000	1,200,000					3,240,000
Depreciation—Equipment	120,000	30,000	(3)	24,000			174,000
Amortization of Excess of Cost over Fair Value			(3)	10,000			10,000
Other Expenses	993,000	650,000					1,643,000
Total Cost and Expense	3,153,000	1,880,000					5,067,000
Net/Combined Income	493,000	140,000					487,000
Noncontrolling Interest in Income						28,000	(28,000)*
Net Income to Retained Earnings	493,000	140,000		146,000	–0–	28,000	459,000
RETAINED EARNINGS STATEMENT							
1/1 Retained Earnings							
P Company	1,882,000		(3)	74,000			1,808,000
S Company		605,000	(2)	484,000		121,000	
Net Income from above	493,000	140,000		146,000	–0–	28,000	459,000
Dividends Declared							
P Company	(150,000)						(150,000)
S Company		(60,000)			(1) 48,000	(12,000)	
12/31 Retained Earnings to Balance Sheet	2,225,000	685,000		704,000	48,000	137,000	2,117,000
BALANCE SHEET							
Investment in S Company	2,348,000				(1) 64,000		
					(2) 2,284,000		
Difference Between Cost and Book Value			(2)	600,000	(3) 600,000		
Land	2,000,000	250,000	(3)	120,000			2,370,000
Equipment (net)	960,000	240,000	(3)	192,000			1,392,000
Other Assets (net)	2,137,000	2,200,000					4,337,000
Excess of Cost over Fair Value			(3)	180,000			180,000
Total Assets	7,445,000	2,690,000					8,279,000
Liabilities	2,220,000	505,000					2,725,000
Capital Stock							
P Company	3,000,000						3,000,000
S Company		1,500,000	(2)	1,200,000		300,000	
Retained Earnings from above	2,225,000	685,000		704,000	48,000	137,000	2,117,000
Noncontrolling Interest in Net Assets						437,000	437,000
Total Liabilities and Equity	7,445,000	2,690,000		2,996,000	2,996,000		8,279,000

*20 × $140,000 = $28,000.

(1) To reverse the effect of parent company entries during the year for subsidiary dividends and income.
(2) To eliminate the investment account.
(3) To assign, amortize, and depreciate the difference between cost and book value.

Entry (3) is the same as entry (4) in Illustration 4-11 (investment recorded at cost).

Observe that the consolidated balances in Illustration 4-14 are the same as those in Illustration 4-11 (cost method workpaper). However, when the parent company records its investment using the partial equity method, entry (1) in Illustration 4-14 replaces the cost method entries to establish reciprocity and to eliminate dividend income [entries (1) and (2) in Illustration 4-11]. Most importantly, a comparison of entries (2) and (3) in Illustration 4-14 with entries (3) and (4) in Illustration 4-11 demonstrates that the workpaper entries to eliminate the investment account and to assign, amortize, and depreciate the difference between cost and book value are the same regardless of whether the investment is recorded using the cost method or the partial equity method.

PARTIAL EQUITY METHOD ANALYSIS OF CONSOLIDATED NET INCOME AND CONSOLIDATED RETAINED EARNINGS

The analytical calculation of consolidated net income does not depend on the method used by the parent company to record its investment. As stated earlier, *consolidated net income is the parent company's income from its independent operations plus (minus) its share of reported subsidiary income (loss) plus or minus adjustments for the period relating to the amortization of the difference between cost and book value.*

The analytical calculation of consolidated net income for the year ended December 31, 1996, presented in Illustration 4-15 is based on Illustration 4-14. This, of course, is the same amount of consolidated net income as that calculated in the consolidated statements workpaper presented in Illustration 4-14.

When the parent company uses the partial equity method to record its investment, the parent company's share of subsidiary income since acquisition is already included in the parent company's reported retained earnings. Consequently, *con-*

ILLUSTRATION 4-15
Analytical Calculation of Consolidated Net Income
For Year Ended December 31, 1996

P Company's net income from its independent operations ($493,000 reported net income less $112,000 equity in subsidiary income included therein)		$381,000
P Company's share of the reported income of S Company (.8 × $140,000)		112,000
Less depreciation and amortization for the period of the amount of the difference between cost and book value assigned to:		
Property and Equipment (net)	$24,000	
Excess of Cost over Fair Value	10,000	(34,000)
Consolidated Net Income		$459,000

solidated retained earnings is calculated as the parent company's recorded partial equity basis retained earnings plus or minus the cumulative effect of the adjustments to date relating to the amortization of the difference between cost and book value.

The analytical calculation of consolidated retained earnings on December 31, 1996, presented in Illustration 4-16 is based on Illustration 4-14. This, of course, is the same amount of consolidated retained earnings as that shown in the consolidated statements workpaper presented in Illustration 4-14.

ILLUSTRATION 4-16
Analytical Calculation of Consolidated Retained Earnings
December 31, 1996

P Company's retained earnings on
  December 31, 1996 $2,225,000

Less cumulative effect to December 31,
  1996, of the amortization of the
  difference between cost and book value:

	1995	1996	
Inventory	$40,000	$ –0–	
Equipment (net)	24,000	24,000	
Excess of Cost over Fair Value	10,000	10,000	
	$74,000	$34,000	(108,000)

Consolidated Retained Earnings on
  December 31, 1996 $2,117,000

ADDITIONAL CONSIDERATIONS RELATING TO TREATMENT OF DIFFERENCE BETWEEN COST AND BOOK VALUE

Considerations relating to the effect of the assignment of the difference between cost and book value to liabilities, and to assets with fair values less than book values, the separate disclosure of accumulated depreciation, premature disposals of long-lived assets by the subsidiary, and depreciable assets used in manufacturing are presented in the sections that follow.

Assignment of Difference Between Cost and Book Value to Long-term Debt

Notes payable, long-term debt, and other obligations of an acquired company should be valued for consolidation purposes at the present value of amounts to be paid in the future. The present value should be determined using appropriate market rates of interest at the date of acquisition.

Assume, for example, that S Company has outstanding $500,000 in 6%, 30-year bonds that were issued at par on January 1, 1970, and that interest on the bonds is paid annually. Assume further that on January 1, 1995, when P Company acquires a 100% interest in S Company, the yield rate on bonds with similar risk is

10%. The present value of S Company's bonds payable determined at the effective yield rate on the acquisition date is calculated as follows:

(1)	Interest Payments $30,000 × 3.79079 =	$113,724
(2)	Principal Payment $500,000 × .62092 =	310,460
	Present Value of Future Cash Payments Discounted at 10%	$424,184

(1) Present value of an annuity of one for five periods discounted at 10%.
(2) Present value of an amount of one received five periods hence discounted at 10%.

From the point of view of the consolidated entity, bonds payable are overstated on January 1, 1995, by $75,816 ($500,000 − $424,184), and a corresponding amount of the total difference between cost and book value on the date of acquisition must be assigned to "unamortized discount on bonds payable." In years after acquisition, interest expense reported by the subsidiary will be understated for consolidation purposes. Thus, workpaper entries must be made to amortize the discount in a manner that will reflect consolidated interest expense as a constant rate on the carrying value of the liability to the consolidated entity. An amortization schedule for this purpose is presented in Illustration 4-17. Consolidated statements workpaper entries necessary in the first five years subsequent to P Company's acquisition of S Company are summarized below (credits are shown in parentheses).

	DECEMBER 31				
	1995	1996	1997	1998	1999
Beginning Retained Earnings—P Company (Consolidated Retained Earnings)	–0–	12,418	26,078	41,104	57,633
Interest Expense	12,418	13,660	15,026	16,529	18,183
Unamortized Discount on Bonds Payable	63,398	49,738	34,712	18,183	–0–
Difference Between Cost and Book Value	(75,816)	(75,816)	(75,816)	(75,816)	(75,816)

(handwritten: $(500\,000 - PV_{BOND})$, $424\,184$)

At maturity the bonds will be redeemed at par value ($500,000), which will be also the carrying value to the consolidated entity. In all subsequent years $75,816 of the difference between cost and book value will be debited to the beginning retained earnings of the parent company in the consolidated statements workpaper in order to reduce beginning consolidated retained earnings for the cumulative amount of additional interest expense recognized in the consolidated financial statements in prior years.

The preceding example was based on the assumption that P Company owned a 100% interest in S Company. If P Company owned an 80% interest rather than a 100% interest in S Company, the amount of the difference between cost and book value assigned to unamortized discount on bonds payable on the date of acquisition

ILLUSTRATION 4-17
Bond Discount Amortization Schedule

DATE	INTEREST EXPENSE RECORDED BY S	CONSOLIDATED INTEREST EXPENSE	DISCOUNT AMORTIZATION	CONSOLIDATED CARRYING VALUE
1/1/1995	$ –0–	$–0–	$ –0–	$424,184
12/31/1995	30,000	(1) 42,418	(2) 12,418	(3) 436,602
12/31/1996	30,000	(4) 43,660	13,660	450,262
12/31/1997	30,000	45,026	15,026	465,288
12/31/1998	30,000	46,529	16,529	481,817
12/31/1999	30,000	48,183	18,183	500,000
	$150,000	$225,816	$75,816	

(1) .10 × $424,184 = $42,418.
(2) $42,418 − $30,000 = $12,418.
(3) $424,184 + $12,418 = $436,602.
(4) .10 × $436,602 = $43,660.

would be $60,653 [.80 × ($500,000 − $424,184)] and the discount amortization would be 80% of the amounts shown in column 4 of Illustration 4-17.

Assigning the Difference to Assets (Liabilities) That Have Fair Values Less (Greater) Than Book Values

Rather than being greater than its recorded value, the fair value of an asset on the date of acquisition may be less than the amount recorded in accordance with generally accepted accounting principles on the books of the subsidiary. In this case the assignment of the parent company's share of the difference between the fair value and the book value of the asset will result in a reduction of the asset. If the asset is depreciable, this difference will be amortized over the life of the asset as a reduction of depreciation expense. Likewise, the fair value of the long-term debt may be greater rather than less than its recorded value on the date of acquisition. In this case, entries are necessary to assign the parent company's share of the difference between the fair value and book value of the debt to unamortized bond premium and to amortize it over the remaining life of the debt as a reduction of interest expense.

To illustrate, assume that P Company paid $2,240,000 for 80% of the outstanding stock of S Company when S Company had identifiable net assets with a fair value of $2,600,000 and a book value of $2,150,000. The assignment of the difference between cost and book value is presented in Illustration 4-18.

Assume that the $100,000 assigned to bond premium is amortized over five years using the straight-line method,[3] that equipment has a remaining life of four years, and that the excess of cost over fair value is amortized over 10 years.

[3]The straight-line method is illustrated here as a matter of expediency. Where differences between the straight-line method and the effective interest rate method of amortization are material, the effective interest rate method as shown in Illustration 4-17 should be used.

ILLUSTRATION 4-18
Assignment of Difference between Cost and Book Value

	FAIR VALUE	BOOK VALUE	DIFFERENCE BETWEEN FAIR VALUE AND BOOK VALUE	DIFFERENCE BETWEEN COST AND BOOK VALUE
Securities	550,000	400,000	150,000	120,000
Equipment (net)	1,250,000	1,500,000	(250,000)	(200,000)
Land	1,225,000	550,000	675,000	540,000
Bonds payable	(725,000)	(600,000)	(125,000)	(100,000)
Other assets and liabilities	300,000	300,000	–0–	–0–
Total	2,600,000	2,150,000	450,000	360,000
Excess of cost over fair value				(a) 160,000
Difference between cost and book value				(b) 520,000

(a) $520,000 − $360,000 = $160,000 or $2,240,000 − .8($2,600,000) = $160,000.
(b) $2,240,000 − .8($2,150,000) = $520,000.

The workpaper entry to assign the difference between cost and book value on the date of acquisition is:

Securities	120,000	
Land	540,000	
Excess of Cost over Fair Value	160,000	
Equipment (net)		200,000
Unamortized Premium on Bonds Payable		100,000
Difference Between Cost and Book Value		520,000

At the end of the first year the workpaper entry to assign the difference between cost and book value is:

Amortization of Excess ($160,000 ÷ 10)	16,000	
Securities	120,000	
Land	540,000	
Unamortized Excess of Cost over Fair Value ($160,000 − $16,000)	144,000	
Depreciation Expense ($200,000 ÷ 4)		50,000
Interest Expense ($100,000 ÷ 5)		20,000
Equipment (net)($200,000 − $50,000)		150,000
Unamortized Premium on Bonds Payable ($100,000 − $20,000)		80,000
Difference Between Cost and Book Value		520,000

At the end of the second year the workpaper entry is:

Amortization of Excess	16,000
Securities	120,000
Land	540,000
Unamortized Excess of Cost over Fair Value	128,000
Beginning Retained Earnings—P Company ($50,000 +	
$20,000 − $16,000)	54,000
Depreciation Expense	50,000
Interest Expense	20,000
Equipment (net)	100,000
Unamortized Premium on Bonds Payable	60,000
Difference Between Cost and Book Value	520,000

In the second year a credit to the beginning retained earnings of the parent company is necessary so that consolidated retained earnings at the beginning of the second year will be equal to the consolidated retained earnings reported at the end of the first year. The credit in the amount of $54,000 is equal to the net increase in consolidated net income that resulted from the reduction of depreciation expense ($50,000), the reduction in interest expense ($20,000), and the increase in amortization expense ($16,000) in the prior year's workpaper. In this example, the credit to the beginning retained earnings of the parent company (beginning consolidated retained earnings) will become progressively larger in each subsequent year in order to account for the cumulative net increase in consolidated net income and consolidated retained earnings resulting from the treatment of the difference between cost and book value in prior years.

Reporting Accumulated Depreciation in Consolidated Financial Statements as a Separate Balance

In previous illustrations we have assumed that any particular classification of depreciable assets will be presented in the consolidated financial statements as a single balance net of accumulated depreciation. When accumulated depreciation is reported as a separate balance in the consolidated financial statements, the workpaper entry to assign and depreciate the difference between cost and book value must be slightly modified. To illustrate, assume that P Company acquires a 90% interest in S Company on January 1, 1995, and that the difference between cost and book value in the amount of $180,000 is entirely attributable to equipment with an original life of nine years and a remaining life on January 1, 1995, of six years. Pertinent information regarding the equipment is presented in Illustration 4-19.

In Illustration 4-19, the $1,200,000 fair value of the equipment (gross) is the replacement cost of the equipment if purchased *new* and is referred to as *replacement cost new*. The $400,000 in accumulated depreciation in the fair value column is the proportional amount of replacement cost new necessary to bring the net fair market value to $800,000, which is the fair market value of the subsidiary's *used* equipment. The $800,000 fair value of the used equipment is referred to in appraisal reports as the equipment's *sound value*.

If the equipment is to be presented in the consolidated financial statements as one balance net of accumulated depreciation, workpaper elimination entries to assign and depreciate the difference between cost and book value are similar to

ILLUSTRATION 4-19
Determination of Amount of Difference Between Cost and Book Value
Assigned to Equipment and to Accumulated Depreciation
January 1, 1995

	FAIR VALUE	BOOK VALUE	DIFFERENCE BETWEEN FAIR VALUE AND BOOK VALUE	P COMPANY'S 90% INTEREST THEREIN
Equipment (gross)	$1,200,000	$900,000	$300,000	$270,000
Accumulated Depreciation	400,000	300,000	100,000	90,000
Equipment (net)	$ 800,000	$600,000	$200,000	$180,000
Annual Depreciation (original life nine years, remaining life six years)		$100,000		$ 30,000

those presented in Illustrations 4-10, and 4-11 and are summarized in Illustration 4-20 for three years. However, when equipment and accumulated depreciation are reported as separate balances in the consolidated financial statements, the work-paper elimination entries must be modified as presented in Illustration 4-21. Of course, the numerical difference between the amount debited to Equipment (Gross) and the amount credited to Accumulated Depreciation in each of the work-paper entries in Illustration 4-21 is the same as the amount debited to Equipment (net) in the workpaper entries in Illustration 4-20, where equipment is presented in the consolidated financial statements net of accumulated depreciation.

ILLUSTRATION 4-20
Summary of Workpaper Entries
Equipment Presented Net of Accumulated Depreciation
(Credits are shown in parentheses.)

	1/1/95	12/31/95	12/31/96	12/31/97
Beginning Retained Earnings— Parent Company (Beginning Consolidated Retained Earnings)	–0–	–0–	30,000	60,000
Depreciation Expense	–0–	30,000	30,000	30,000
Equipment (net)	180,000	150,000	120,000	90,000
Difference Between Cost and Book Value	(180,000)	(180,000)	(180,000)	(180,000)

Allocation of the $180,000 difference assigned to Equipment (net of accu-mulated depreciation) separately to Equipment (Gross) and to Accumulated De-preciation requires knowledge of the replacement cost new and the sound value of the equipment as shown in the appraisal report, or it may be implied as follows: If the equipment is one-third depreciated on January 1, 1995, the $180,000 difference between P Company's interest in the sound value and the book value of the equip-

ILLUSTRATION 4-21
Summary of Workpaper Entries
Accumulated Depreciation Presented as Separate Balance
(Credits are shown in parentheses.)

	1/1/95	12/31/95	12/31/96	12/31/97
Beginning Retained Earnings— Parent Company (Beginning consolidated Retained Earnings)	–0–	–0–	30,000	60,000
Depreciation Expense	–0–	30,000	30,000	30,000
Equipment (Gross)	270,000	270,000	270,000	270,000
Accumulated Depreciation	(90,000)	(120,000)	(150,000)	(180,000)
Difference Between Cost and Book Value	(180,000)	(180,000)	(180,000)	(180,000)

ment is two-thirds of P Company's interest in the difference between replacement cost new and the acquisition cost of the equipment. Therefore, P Company's interest in the difference between replacement cost new and acquisition cost is $270,000 ($180,000 ÷ 2/3). Accumulated depreciation on P Company's interest in the difference between replacement cost new and acquisition cost is one-third of $270,000, or $90,000.

Premature Disposal of Depreciable Assets by Subsidiary

Assume that on January 1, 1997, two years after its acquisition by P Company, S Company sells all the equipment referred to in Illustration 4-19 for $480,000. The carrying value of the equipment on the books of the subsidiary and from a consolidated point of view on January 1, 1997 (the date of the sale), is presented in Illustration 4-22. S Company will report a gain of $80,000 on the disposal of the equipment. From the point of view of the consolidated entity, however, there is a loss of $40,000. The workpaper entry necessary to adjust the amounts in the December 31, 1997, consolidated financial statements is as follows:

Beginning Retained Earnings—Parent Company (Beginning Consolidated Retained Earnings)	60,000	
Gain on Disposal of Equipment	80,000	
Loss on Disposal of Equipment	40,000	
Difference Between Cost and Book Value		180,000

In short, in the year of sale, any gain or loss recognized by the subsidiary on the disposal of an asset to which any of the difference between cost and book value has been assigned must be adjusted in the consolidated statements workpaper by the amount of the *undepreciated* difference between cost and book value related to that asset on the date of the sale ($180,000 − $30,000 − $30,000 = $120,000). In all subsequent years, the $180,000 difference between cost and book value that was

ILLUSTRATION 4-22
Calculation of Recorded and Consolidated Gain or Loss
Premature Disposal of Equipment

	S COMPANY	UNAMORTIZED DIFFERENCE	CONSOLIDATED
Cost	$ 900,000	$270,000	$1,170,000
Accumulated depreciation	500,000	150,000	650,000
Undepreciated base	400,000	120,000	520,000
Proceeds	(480,000)		(480,000)
(Gain) loss on sale	$ (80,000)	$120,000	$ 40,000

assigned to the equipment that was disposed of will be debited to the beginning retained earnings of the parent company in the consolidated statements workpaper in order to reduce consolidated retained earnings for the cumulative amount of additional depreciation expense ($30,000 + $30,000 = $60,000) and for the amount of the adjustment to the reported gain or loss on the disposal of equipment ($80,000 + $40,000 = $120,000) recognized in the consolidated financial statements in prior years.

Depreciable Assets Used in Manufacturing

When the difference between cost and book value is assigned to depreciable assets used in manufacturing, workpaper entries necessary to reflect additional depreciation may be more complex, because the current and previous year's additional depreciation may have to be allocated among work in process, finished goods on hand at the end of the year, and cost of goods sold. In practice, such refinements are often ignored on the basis of materiality, and all the current year's additional depreciation is charged to cost of goods sold.

APPENDIX: PUSH DOWN ACCOUNTING

Push down accounting is the establishment of a new accounting and reporting basis for a subsidiary company in its separate financial statements based on the purchase price paid by the parent company to acquire a controlling interest in the outstanding voting stock of the subsidiary company. The price of the stock to the parent company is "pushed down" to the subsidiary and used to restate its assets (including goodwill) and liabilities in its separate financial statements. If all the voting stock is purchased, the assets and liabilities of the subsidiary company are restated so that the excess of the restated amounts of the assets (including goodwill) over the restated amounts of the liabilities equals the purchase price of the stock. Push down accounting is based on the notion that the basis of accounting for purchased assets and liabilities should be the same regardless of whether the acquired company continues to exist as a separate subsidiary or is merged into the parent company's operations. Thus, under push down accounting the parent company's cost of acquiring a subsidiary should be "pushed down" and used to establish a new accounting basis for the assets and liabilities of the subsidiary in the subsidiary's separate financial statements. Although the FASB has issued a discussion memorandum that addresses issues relating to push down accounting (see the next section), push down accounting has not yet been addressed in authoritative pronouncements of the FASB or its predecessors. Thus, practice has been inconsistent. Some acquired companies have used a new pushed down basis, and others, in essentially the same circumstances, have used preacquisition book values.

Proponents of push down accounting believe that a new basis of accounting should be required following a purchase transaction that results in a significant change in the ownership of a company's outstanding voting stock. In essence, they view the transaction as if the new owners had purchased an existing business and established a new company to continue that business. Consequently, they believe that, in a transaction in which a change of ownership has occurred, the parent company's basis should be imputed to the subsidiary because the new basis provides more relevant information for users of the subsidiary's separate financial statements. In addition, *APB Opinion No. 16* requires that a business purchased in a business combination be stated in consolidated statements at the basis established in the purchase transaction. To provide symmetry, the separate financial statements of the subsidiary should be presented in the same manner.

Those who oppose push down accounting believe that, under the historical cost concept, a change in ownership of an entity does not justify a new accounting basis in its financial statements. Because the subsidiary did not purchase assets or assume liabilities as a result of the transaction, the recognition of a new accounting basis based on a change in ownership, rather than on a transaction on the part of the subsidiary, represents a breach in the historical cost concept in accounting. They believe that, when changes in ownership are used to establish a new accounting basis, one or more implementation problems might arise. For example, noncontrolling stockholders may not have meaningful comparative financial statements. In addition, restatement of the financial statements may create problems in determining or maintaining compliance with various financial restrictions under debt agreements.

Push down accounting is an issue only if the subsidiary is required to issue separate financial statements for any reason, for example, because of the existence of noncontrolling interests or financial arrangements with nonaffiliates. Three important factors that must be considered in determining the acceptability of push down accounting are:

1. Whether the subsidiary has outstanding debt held by the public.

2. Whether the subsidiary has outstanding a senior class of capital stock not acquired by the parent company.

3. The level at which a major change in ownership of an entity should be deemed to have occurred, for example, 100%, 90%, 51%.

Public holders of the acquired company's debt need comparative data to assess the value and risk of their investments. These public holders generally have some expressed (or implied) rights in the subsidiary that may be adversely affected by a new basis of accounting. Similarly, holders of preferred stock, particularly if the stock includes a participation feature, may have their rights altered significantly by a new basis of accounting.

Views on the percentage level of ownership change needed to apply a new basis of accounting vary. Some believe that the purchase of substantially all the voting stock (90% or more) should be the threshold level; others believe that the percentage level of ownership change should be that needed for control, that is, more than 50%. A related problem involves the amounts to be assigned to the individual assets and liabilities, noncontrolling interest, and goodwill in the separate statements of the subsidiary. Some believe that values should be assigned on the basis of the fair value of the subsidiary as a whole imputed from the transaction. Thus, if 80% of the voting stock is acquired for $32 million, the fair value of the net assets should be imputed to be $40 million, and values assigned on that basis. Others believe that values should be assigned on the basis of the proportional interest acquired. They believe that new values should be reflected on the books of the subsidiary only to the extent of the price paid in the transaction. Thus, if 80% of a company is acquired for $32 million, the basis of the subsidiary's net assets should be adjusted by the difference between the price paid and the book value of an 80% interest. This latter approach will result in the assignment of the same values to assets and liabilities on the books of the subsidiary as that previously illustrated in the workpaper entry to assign the difference between cost and book value in the consolidated statements workpaper.

CURRENT STATUS OF PUSH DOWN ACCOUNTING

The Task Force on Consolidation Problems, Accounting Standards Division of the AICPA, released an issues paper entitled, ''Push Down Accounting'' in 1979. The paper discusses the issues related to push down accounting and cites related literature. The paper also presents the conclusions of the Accounting Standards Executive Committee on the issues discussed in the paper. The majority of the Committee recommended the use of push down accounting where there has been at least a 90% change in ownership. The AICPA sent the paper to the FASB with a recommendation that the Board consider the issue. The FASB has included push down accounting as one of the issues to be considered in its project on the reporting entity.

In 1983, the SEC released *Staff Accounting Bulletin No. 54*, which discusses the staff's position on the appropriateness of applying push down accounting in the separate financial statements of subsidiaries acquired in purchase transactions. The SEC believes that purchase transactions that result in an entity becoming substantially wholly owned (as defined in Regulation S-X)[4] should establish a new basis of accounting for the purchased assets and liabilities. When the form of ownership is within the control of the parent company, the basis of accounting for purchased assets and liabilities should be the same regardless of whether the entity continues

---

[4]The term *wholly owned subsidiary* means a subsidiary substantially all of whose outstanding voting shares are owned by its parent or the parent's other wholly owned subsidiaries.

to exist or is merged into the parent company's operations. As a general rule, the SEC requires push down accounting when the ownership change is greater than 95% and objects to push down accounting when the ownership change is less than 80%. In addition, the *Bulletin* expresses the view that the existence of outstanding public debt, preferred stock, or a significant noncontrolling interest in a subsidiary might have impact on the parent company's ability to control the form of ownership. In these circumstances, the staff encourages, but does not insist on, the application of push down accounting.

In December 1991, the FASB issued a Discussion Memorandum entitled *An Analysis of Issued Related to New Basis Accounting.* The discussion memorandum was published to solicit views on what, if any, transactions or events should result in changing the carrying amount of all, or most, of an entity's individual assets, including goodwill, and liabilities to amounts representing their current fair value. Transactions and events discussed include stock purchases that are of concern to us here. In addition to stock purchases, significant borrowing transactions, reorganizations and restructurings, and formations and sales of interests in joint ventures are also discussed as transactions or events that may justify a new basis of accounting.

PUSH DOWN ACCOUNTING ILLUSTRATION

To illustrate the application of push down accounting and show that the use of a pushed down basis by the subsidiary will not change consolidated results, we will use the same situation as that given in Illustration 4-10. We will, however, modify Illustration 4-10 slightly by assuming that the full market value of S Company, as implied by the 80% purchase transaction, was pushed down to S Company. The basic assumptions of Illustration 4-10, as modified, are restated below for the convenience of the reader:

1. P Company acquired an 80% interest in S Company on January 1, 1995 for $2,200,000, at which time S Company had capital stock of $1,500,000 and retained earnings of $500,000.

2. The difference between cost and book value ($600,000) is assigned as presented in Illustration 4-23.

In this example, it is assumed that values are assigned on the basis of the fair value of the subsidiary as a whole, imputed from the transaction.

ILLUSTRATION 4-23
Assignment of Difference Between Cost and Book Value

	COST BASIS	IMPLIED (100%) PUSH DOWN BASIS
Inventory (FIFO basis)	$ 40,000	$ 50,000
Equipment (10-year life)	240,000	300,000
Land	120,000	150,000
Goodwill (20-year life)	200,000	250,000
Total	$600,000	$750,000

3. In 1995, S Company reported net income of $32,500. Note that this is $92,500 less than in Illustration 4-10 because the effect of the amortization of the difference between cost and book value is recorded on the books of S Company under push down accounting. This difference of $92,500 consists of:

Increase in cost of goods sold	$50,000
Increase in depreciation expense	
($300,000 ÷ 10)	30,000
Amortization of Goodwill ($250,000 ÷ 20)	12,500
	$92,500

4. S Company declared a dividend of $20,000 on November 15, payable on December 1, 1995.

5. P Company uses the cost method to record its investment in S Company.

S Company Book Entries—1995

On January 1, 1995, the date of acquisition, S Company would make the following entry to record the effect of the pushed down values implied by the purchase of 80% of its stock by P Company:

Inventory, 1/1	50,000	
Equipment	300,000	
Land	150,000	
Goodwill	250,000	
Revaluation Capital		750,000

Recall the assumptions from Illustration 4-10: (1) all beginning inventory was sold during the year; (2) equipment has a remaining useful life of 10 years from 1/1/95; and (3) goodwill is amortized over 20 years. Given these assumptions, the $50,000 excess cost assigned to beginning inventory would be included in cost of goods sold when the goods were sold. Similarly, depreciation expense recorded on S Company's books would be $30,000 greater than if the increase in equipment value had not been recorded. In addition, an entry would be made on S Company's books to record amortization of goodwill, $12,500.

A workpaper for the preparation of consolidated financial statements on December 31, 1995, under push down accounting is presented in Illustration 4-24. Workpaper elimination entries in general journal form are:

(1) Dividend Income	16,000	
Dividends Declared—S Company		16,000
(2) Capital Stock—S Company	1,200,000	
Retained Earnings 1/1—S Company	400,000	
Revaluation Capital—S Company	600,000	
Investment in S Company		2,200,000

Cost Method
80% Owned Subsidiary
Push down Basis

ILLUSTRATION 4-24
Consolidated Statements Workpaper
P Company and Subsidiary
For the Year Ended December 31, 1995

INCOME STATEMENT	P COMPANY	S COMPANY	ELIMINATIONS DR.	ELIMINATIONS CR.	NONCONTROLLING INTEREST	CONSOLIDATED BALANCES
Sales	3,100,000	2,200,000				5,300,000
Dividend income	16,000		(1) 16,000			
Total Revenue	3,116,000	2,200,000				5,300,000
Cost of Goods Sold	1,700,000	1,410,000				3,110,000
Depreciation—Equipment	120,000	60,000				180,000
Amortization—Goodwill		12,500				12,500
Other Expenses	998,000	685,000				1,683,000
Total Cost and Expense	2,818,000	2,167,500				4,985,500
Net/Combined Income	298,000	32,500				314,500
Noncontrolling Interest in Income					6,500	(6,500)*
						308,000
Net Income to Retained Earnings	298,000	32,500	16,000	–0–	6,500	

RETAINED EARNINGS STATEMENT						
1/1 Retained Earnings:						
P Company	1,650,000					1,650,000
S Company		500,000	(2) 400,000		100,000	
Net Income from above	298,000	32,500	16,000	–0–	6,500	308,000
Dividends Declared:						
P Company	(150,000)					(150,000)
S Company		(20,000)		(1) 16,000	(4,000)	
12/31 Retained Earnings to the Balance Sheet	1,798,000	512,500	416,000	16,000	102,500	1,808,000

BALANCE SHEET						
Investment in S Company	2,200,000			(2) 2,200,000		
Land	1,250,000	400,000				1,650,000
Equipment (net)	1,080,000	540,000				1,620,000
Other Assets	2,402,000	1,885,000				4,287,000
Goodwill		237,500				237,500
Total	6,932,000	3,062,500				7,794,500
Liabilities	2,134,000	300,000				2,434,000
Capital Stock:						
P Company	3,000,000					3,000,000
S Company		1,500,000	(2) 1,200,000		300,000	
Revaluation Capital		750,000	(2) 600,000		150,000	
Retained Earnings from above	1,798,000	512,500	416,000	16,000	102,500	1,808,000
Noncontrolling Interest in Net Assets					552,500	552,500
Total	6,932,000	3,062,500	2,216,000	2,216,000		7,794,500

*20 × $32,500 = $6,500

(1) To eliminate intercompany dividends.
(2) To eliminate investment account.

A comparison of Illustration 4-24 with Illustration 4-10 shows that combined income is smaller as is the noncontrolling interest in combined income when push down accounting is used. Consolidated net income and consolidated retained earnings are the same. Thus, when values are assigned on the basis of fair values of the subsidiary as a whole imputed from the transaction, the use of push down accounting has no effect on these consolidated balances.[5] Note, however, that both consolidated net assets and the noncontrolling interest in consolidated net assets are $131,500 greater in Illustration 4-24, reflecting the decision to push down the full value of S Company implied by the amount paid by P Company for its 80% interest. This amount can be verified as follows:

The noncontrolling interest's share of revaluation capital .20($750,000)	$150,000
Less amortization and depreciation thereon .20($92,500)	18,500
Balance	$131,500

Note also that no workpaper entries were necessary in Illustration 4-24 to assign, amortize, and depreciate the difference between cost and book value since these have already been made on S Company's books.

Questions

1. Distinguish among the following concepts:
   (a) Difference between cost and book value.
   (b) Excess of cost over fair value.
   (c) Excess of fair value over cost.
   (d) Deferred excess of fair value over cost.

2. In what account is "the difference between cost and book value" recorded on the books of the investor? In what account is the "excess of cost over fair value" recorded?

---

[5]A slight dilemma arises if values are pushed down on the basis of the proportional interest acquired. When that alternative is elected, the calculation of the noncontrolling interest in combined income must be based, not on the reported income of the subsidiary, but on subsidiary income before the assignment, depreciation, and amortization of the difference between cost and book value (which is now recorded on the records of the subsidiary) in order for push down accounting to have no effect on the calculation of consolidated net income and consolidated retained earnings. When values are pushed down on the basis of the proportional interest acquired, combined income does not change. If the noncontrolling interest in combined income is based on the subsidiary's reported net income, the allocation of combined income to the noncontrolling interest will be smaller and to the controlling interest (consolidated net income) larger than if push down accounting, based on the proportional interest acquired, were not used. We consider this an inappropriate result and recommend that noncontrolling interest in combined income be calculated as described before when push down accounting is based on the proportional interest acquired.

If this recommendation is followed, beginning consolidated retained earnings must also be reduced and the noncontrolling interest in consolidated net assets must be increased by the cumulative amount by which the noncontrolling interest in combined income has been increased in prior years because of the application of this recommendation. As a matter of workpaper procedure, this is accomplished by a debit to the retained earnings of the parent company (beginning consolidated retained earnings) and a credit to the retained earnings of the subsidiary (noncontrolling interest).

3. How do you determine the amount of the "difference between cost and book value" to be assigned to a specific asset of a less than wholly owned subsidiary?

4. The parent company's share of the fair value of the net assets of a subsidiary may exceed acquisition cost. How must this excess be treated in the preparation of consolidated financial statements?

5. Why are marketable securities excluded from the noncurrent assets to which any excess of fair value over cost is to be allocated?

6. P Company acquired a 100% interest in S Company. On the date of acquisition the fair value of the assets and liabilities of S Company was equal to their book value except for land that had a fair value of $1,500,000 and a book value of $300,000. At what amount should the land of S Company be included in the consolidated balance sheet? At what amount should the land of S Company be included in the consolidated balance sheet if P Company acquired an 80% interest in S Company rather than a 100% interest?

7. Corporation A purchased the net assets of Corporation B for $80,000. On the date of A's purchase, Corporation B had no long-term investments in marketable securities and $10,000 (book and fair value) of liabilities. The fair values of Corporation B's assets, when acquired, were:

Current assets	$ 40,000
Noncurrent assets	60,000
Total	$100,000

How should the $10,000 difference between the fair value of the net assets acquired ($90,000) and the cost ($80,000) be accounted for by Corporation A?
(a) The $10,000 difference should be credited to retained earnings.
(b) The noncurrent assets should be recorded at $50,000.
(c) The current assets should be recorded at $36,000, and the noncurrent assets should be recorded at $54,000.
(d) A deferred credit of $10,000 should be set up and then amortized to income over a period not to exceed 40 years.

8. Assume that Corporation A paid $110,000 for Corporation B's net assets, and that all other information given in Question 7 remains the same. What is the minimum annual difference between financial accounting income and tax income because of this purchase?
(a) Zero.
(b) $500.
(c) $2,000.
(d) Cannot be determined from the information given.

9. Meredith Company and Kyle Company were combined in a purchase transaction. Meredith was able to acquire Kyle at a bargain price. The sum of the market or appraised values of identifiable assets acquired less the fair value of liabilities assumed exceeded the cost to Meredith. After reducing noncurrent assets to zero, there was still some "negative goodwill." Proper accounting treatment by Meredith is to report the amount as
(a) An extraordinary item.
(b) Part of current income in the year of combination.

(c) A deferred credit and amortize it.

(d) Paid-in capital.

10. How does the recording in the consolidated statements workpaper of the increase in depreciation that results from the assignment of a portion of the difference between cost and book value to depreciable property affect the calculation of noncontrolling interest in combined income?

11. Define consolidated net income using the analytical approach.

Exercises

Exercise 4-1

On January 1, 1995, P Company purchased an 80% interest in S Company for $500,000. On this date, S Company had common stock of $375,000 and retained earnings of $137,500.

An examination of S Company's assets and liabilities revealed that their book value was equal to their fair value except for marketable securities and equipment:

	BOOK VALUE	FAIR VALUE
Marketable securities	$ 30,000	$ 60,000
Equipment (net)	100,000	120,000

Required:

Determine the amounts that should be assigned to S Company's assets on the consolidated financial statements workpaper on January 1, 1995.

Exercise 4-2

On January 1, 1996, Payne Corporation purchased a 75% interest in Salmon Company for $585,000. A summary of Salmon Company's balance sheet on that date revealed the following:

	BOOK VALUE	FAIR VALUE
Equipment	$525,000	$705,000
Other assets	150,000	150,000
	$675,000	$855,000
Liabilities	$ 75,000	$ 75,000
Common stock	225,000	
Retained earnings	375,000	
	$675,000	

The equipment had an original life of 15 years and has a remaining useful life of 10 years. Any excess of cost over fair value will be amortized over the maximum period allowable.

Required:

For the December 31, 1996, consolidated financial statements workpaper, prepare the workpaper entry to assign, amortize, and depreciate the difference between cost and book value assuming:

A. Equipment is presented net of accumulated depreciation.

B. Accumulated depreciation is presented on a separate row in the workpaper and in the consolidated statement of financial position.

Exercise 4-3

Pace Company purchased 20,000 of the 25,000 shares of Saddler Corporation for $525,000. On January 3, 1995, the acquisition date, Saddler Corporation's capital stock and retained earnings account balances were $500,000 and $100,000, respectively.

The following values were determined for Saddler Corporation on the date of purchase:

	BOOK VALUE	FAIR VALUE
Inventory	$ 50,000	$ 70,000
Other current assets	200,000	200,000
Marketable securities	100,000	125,000
Plant and equipment	300,000	330,000

Handwritten annotations: 80% BV = 520,000 ; 80% FV = 580,000 ; +20 ; +25 ; +30 ; FAIR VALUE exceeds book ; 650,000 ; 725,000

Required:

A. Prepare the entry on the books of Pace Company to record its investment in Saddler Corporation.

B. Prepare a schedule to assign the difference between the cost and book value in the consolidated statements workpaper.

Exercise 4-4

On January 1, 1996, Porter Company purchased an 80% interest in Salem Company for $260,000. On this date, Salem Company had common stock of $207,000 and retained earnings of $130,500.

An examination of Salem Company's balance sheet revealed the following comparisons between book and fair values:

	BOOK VALUE	FAIR VALUE
Inventory	$ 30,000	$ 35,000
Other current assets	50,000	55,000
Equipment	300,000	350,000
Land	200,000	200,000

Required:

A. Determine the amounts that should be assigned to Salem Company's assets on the consolidated financial statements workpaper on January 1, 1996.

B. Prepare the January 1, 1996, consolidated financial statements workpaper entries to eliminate the investment account and to assign the difference between cost and book value.

Exercise 4-5

On January 1, 1995, P Company purchased an 80% interest in S Company for $600,000, at which time S Company had retained earnings of $300,000 and capital stock of $350,000. Any difference between cost and book value was entirely attributable to a patent with a remaining useful life of 10 years.

Assume that P and S companies reported net incomes from their independent operations of $200,000 and $100,000, respectively.

Required:

Prepare an analytical calculation of consolidated net income for the year ended December 31, 1995.

Exercise 4-6

Park Company acquires an 85% interest in Sunland Company on January 2, 1996. The resulting difference between cost and book value in the amount of $120,000 is entirely attributable to equipment with an original life of 15 years and a remaining useful life, on January 2, 1996, of 10 years.

Required:

Prepare the December 31 consolidated financial statements workpaper entries for 1996 and 1997 to assign and depreciate the difference between cost and book value, recording accumulated depreciation as a separate balance.

Exercise 4-7

On January 1, 1995, Packard Company purchased an 80% interest in Sage Company for $600,000. On this date Sage Company had common stock of $150,000 and retained earnings of $400,000.

Sage Company's equipment on the date of Packard Company's purchase had a book value of $400,000 and a fair value of $600,000. All equipment had an estimated useful life of 10 years on January 1, 1990.

Required:

Prepare the December 31 consolidated financial statements workpaper entries for 1995 and 1996 to assign and depreciate the difference between cost and book value, recording accumulated depreciation as a separate balance.

Exercise 4-8

Padilla Company purchased 80% of the common stock of Sanoma Company in the open market on January 1, 1994, paying $31,000 more than the book value of the interest acquired. The difference between cost and book value is attributable to land.

Required:

A. What workpaper entry is required each year until the land is disposed of?

B. Assume that the land is sold on 1/1/97 and that Sanoma Company recognizes a $50,000 gain on its books. What amount of gain will be reflected on the 1997 consolidated income statement?

C. In all years subsequent to the disposal of the land, what workpaper entry will be necessary?

(handwritten margin notes at top: "# Test", "Total amount of on Amt on discount or premium present")

(handwritten margin notes at right: "⅔ = 75 yrs", "Premium y", "MR < Stated rate interest")

Exercise 4-9

On January 1, 1994, Point Corporation acquired an 80% interest in Sharp Company for $2,000,000. At that time Sharp Company had capital stock of $1,500,000 and retained earnings of $700,000. The book values of Sharp Company's assets and liabilities were equal to their fair values except for land and bonds payable. The land had a fair value of $100,000 and a book value of $80,000. The outstanding bonds were issued at par value on January 1, 1989, pay 10% interest annually, and mature on January 1, 1999. The bond principal is $500,000 and the current yield rate on similar bonds is 8%.

(handwritten margin note: "→ 5yrs.")

Required:

A. Prepare a schedule to assign the difference between cost and book value in the consolidated statements workpaper on the acquisition date.

B. Prepare the workpaper entries necessary on December 31, 1994, to assign, amortize, and depreciate the difference between cost and book value.

Exercise 4-10

On January 2, 1994, Page Corporation acquired a 90% interest in Salcedo Company for $3,500,000. At that time Salcedo Company had capital stock of $2,250,000 and retained earnings of $1,250,000. The book values of Salcedo Company's assets and liabilities were equal to their fair values except for land and bonds payable. The land had a fair value of $200,000 and a book value of $120,000. The outstanding bonds were issued on January 1, 1989, at 9% and mature on January 1, 1999. The bonds' principal is $500,000 and the current yield rate on similar bonds is 6%.

Required:

A. Assuming interest is paid annually, prepare a schedule to assign the difference between cost and book value in the consolidated statements workpaper on the acquisition date.

B. Prepare the workpaper entries necessary on December 31, 1994, to assign, amortize, and depreciate the difference between cost and book value.

Exercise 4-11

On January 1, 1994, Piper Company acquired an 80% interest in Sand Company for $2,276,000. At that time the capital stock and retained earnings of Sand Company were $1,800,000 and $700,000, respectively. Differences between the fair value and the book value of the identifiable assets of Sand Company were as follows:

	FAIR VALUE IN EXCESS OF BOOK VALUE
Inventory	$45,000
Equipment (net)	50,000

The book values of all other assets and liabilities of Sand Company were equal to their fair values on January 1, 1994. The equipment had a remaining useful life of eight years, and the management of Piper Company decided that the excess of cost over fair value should be amortized over a 20-year period. Inventory is accounted for on a FIFO basis. Sand Company's reported net income and declared dividends for 1994 through 1996 are shown here:

	1994	1995	1996
Net income	$100,000	$150,000	$80,000
Dividends	20,000	30,000	15,000

Required:

Prepare the consolidated statements workpaper entries to establish reciprocity, to eliminate the investment account, and to assign, amortize, and depreciate the difference between cost and book value for the years 1994, 1995, and 1996.

Exercise 4-12

A 90% interest in Saxton Corporation was purchased by Palm Incorporated on January 2, 1995. The capital stock balance of Saxton Corporation was $3,000,000 on this date, and the balance in retained earnings was $1,000,000. The cost of the investment to Palm Incorporated was $3,750,000.

The balance sheet information available for Saxton Corporation on the acquisition date revealed these values:

	BOOK VALUE	FAIR VALUE
Inventory (FIFO)	$ 700,000	$ 800,000
Equipment (net)	2,000,000	2,000,000
Land	1,600,000	2,000,000

The equipment was determined to have a 15-year useful life when purchased at the beginning of 1990. Saxton Corporation reported net income in 1995 of $250,000 and $300,000 in 1996. No dividends were declared in either of those years.

Required:

A. Prepare the entries to establish reciprocity, to eliminate the investment account, and to assign, amortize, and depreciate the difference between cost and book value in the 1996 consolidated statements workpaper.

B. Calculate the consolidated retained earnings for the year ended December 31, 1996, assuming that the balance in Palm Incorporated's ending retained earnings on that date was $2,000,000.

Exercise 4-13A

Pascal Corporation purchased 90% of the stock of Salzer Company for $2,070,000 on January 1, 1996. On this date, the fair value of the assets and liabilities of Salzer Company was equal to their book value except for the inventory and equipment accounts. The inventory had a fair value of $725,000 and a book value of $600,000. The equipment had a book value of $900,000 and a fair value of $1,075,000.

The balances in Salzer Company's capital stock and retained earnings accounts on the date of acquisition were $1,200,000 and $600,000, respectively.

Required:

In general journal form, prepare the entries on Salzer Company's books to record the effect of the pushed down values implied by the purchase of its stock by Pascal Company assuming that:

A. Values are assigned on the basis of the fair value of Salzer Company as a whole imputed from the transaction.

B. Values are assigned on the basis of the proportional interest acquired by Pascal Company.

Problems

Problem 4-1

On January 1, 1995, Palmero Company purchased an 80% interest in Santos Company for $2,800,000, at which time Santos Company had retained earnings of $1,000,000 and capital stock of $500,000. On the date of acquisition, the fair value of the assets and liabilities of Santos Company was equal to their book value, except for property and equipment (net), which had a fair value of $1,500,000 and a book value of $600,000. The property and equipment had an estimated remaining life of 10 years. Palmero Company amortizes the excess of cost over fair value over 20 years. Palmero Company reported net income from independent operations of $400,000 in 1995 and $425,000 in 1996. Santos Company reported net income of $300,000 in 1995 and $400,000 in 1996. Neither company declared dividends in 1995 or 1996.

Required:

A. Prepare in general journal form the entries necessary in the consolidated statements workpapers for the years ended December 31, 1995 and 1996.

B. Prepare in good form a schedule showing the calculation of consolidated net income for the years ended December 31, 1995, and December 31, 1996.

Problem 4-2

On January 1, 1995, Paxton Company purchased a 70% interest in Sagon Company for $1,300,000, at which time Sagon Company had retained earnings of $500,000 and capital stock of $1,000,000. On January 1, 1995, the fair value of the assets and liabilities of Sagon Company was equal to their book value except for bonds payable. Sagon Company had outstanding a $1,000,000 issue of 6% bonds that were issued at par and that mature on January 1, 2000. Interest on the bonds is payable annually, and the yield rate on similar bonds on January 1, 1995, is 10%. Paxton Company amortizes the excess of cost over fair value over 16 years. Paxton Company reported net income from independent operations of $300,000 in 1995 and $250,000 in 1996. Sagon Company reported net income of $100,000 in 1995 and $120,000 in 1996. Neither company paid or declared dividends in 1995 or 1996.

Required:

A. Prepare in general journal form the entries necessary in the consolidated statements workpapers for the years ended December 31, 1995, and December 31, 1996.

B. Prepare in good form a schedule showing the calculation of consolidated net income for the years ended December 31, 1995, and December 31, 1996.

Problem 4-3

Perke Corporation purchased 80% of the stock of Superstition Company for $1,970,000 on January 1, 1996. On this date, the fair value of the assets and liabilities of Superstition Company was equal to their book value except for the inventory and equipment accounts. The inventory had a fair value of $725,000 and a book value of $600,000. Sixty percent of Superstition Company's inventory was sold in 1996; the remainder was sold in 1997. The equipment had a book value of $900,000 and a fair value of $1,075,000. The remaining useful life of the equipment is seven years.

The balances in Superstition Company's capital stock and retained earnings accounts on the date of acquisition were $1,200,000 and $600,000, respectively. Any excess of cost over fair value is amortized over the maximum time allowable. The following financial data are from Superstition Company's records.

	1996	1997
Net income	$750,000	$900,000
Dividends declared	150,000	225,000

Required:

A. In general journal form, prepare the entries on Perke Company's books to account for its investment in Superstition Company for 1996 and 1997.

B. Prepare the eliminating entries necessary for the consolidated statements workpapers in 1996 and 1997.

C. Assuming Perke Corporation's net income for 1996 was $1,000,000, calculate consolidated net income for 1996.

Problem 4-4

On January 1, 1993, Porter Company purchased an 80% interest in the capital stock of Salem Company for $820,000. At that time, Salem Company had capital stock of $500,000 and retained earnings of $100,000.

Differences between the fair value and the book value of the identifiable assets of Salem Company were as follows:

	FAIR VALUE IN EXCESS OF BOOK VALUE
Equipment	$125,000
Land	62,500
Inventory	37,500

The book values of all other assets and liabilities of Salem Company were equal to their fair values on January 1, 1993. The equipment had a remaining life of five years on January 1, 1993, the inventory was sold in 1993, and goodwill is amortized over 40 years.

Financial data for 1995 are presented here:

	PORTER COMPANY	SALEM COMPANY
Sales	$1,050,000	$400,000
Dividend income	40,000	
Total revenue	1,090,000	400,000
Cost of goods sold	850,000	180,000
Depreciation expense	35,000	25,000
Other expenses	65,000	45,000
Total cost and expense	950,000	250,000
Net income	$ 140,000	$150,000
1/1 Retained earnings	$ 480,000	$200,000
Net income	140,000	150,000
Dividends declared	(100,000)	(50,000)
12/31 Retained earnings	$ 520,000	$300,000
Cash	$ 80,000	$ 50,000
Accounts receivable	250,000	170,000
Inventory	230,000	150,000
Investment in Salem Company	820,000	
Land	–0–	300,000
Pland and equipment	350,000	250,000
Total assets	$1,730,000	$920,000
Accounts payable	$ 160,000	$100,000
Notes payable	50,000	20,000
Capital stock	1,000,000	500,000
Retained earnings	520,000	300,000
Total liabilities and equity	$1,730,000	$920,000

Required:

A. Prepare a consolidated financial statements workpaper for the year ended December 31, 1995.

B. Prepare a consolidated statement of financial position and a consolidated income statement for the year ended December 31, 1995.

C. Describe the effect on the consolidated balances if Salem Company uses the LIFO cost flow assumption in pricing its inventory and there has been no decrease in ending inventory quantities since 1993.

D. Prepare an analytical calculation of consolidated retained earnings for the year ended December 31, 1995.

Problem 4-5

On January 1, 1995, Palmer Company acquired a 90% interest in Stevens Company at a cost of $1,000,000. At the purchase date, Stevens Company's stockholders' equity consisted of the following:

Common stock	$500,000
Retained earnings	190,000

An examination of Stevens Company's assets and liabilities revealed the following at the date of acquisition:

	BOOK VALUE	FAIR VALUE
Cash	$ 90,726	$ 90,726
Accounts receivable	200,000	200,000
Inventories	160,000	210,000
Equipment	300,000	390,000
Accumulated depreciation—equipment	(100,000)	(130,000)
Land	190,000	290,000
Bonds payable	(205,556)	(150,000)
Other	54,830	54,830
Total	$690,000	$955,556

Additional Information—Date of Acquisition:

Stevens Company's equipment had an original life of 15 years and a remaining useful life of 10 years. All the inventory was sold in 1995. The excess of cost over fair value, if any, is amortized over 20 years. Stevens Company purchased its bonds payable on the open market on January 10, 1995, for $150,000 and recognized a gain of $55,556.

Financial statement data for 1997 are presented here:

	PALMER COMPANY	STEVENS COMPANY
Sales	$ 620,000	$340,000
Cost of sales	430,000	240,000
Gross margin	190,000	100,000
Depreciation expense	30,000	20,000
Other expenses	60,000	35,000
Income from operations	100,000	45,000
Dividend income	31,500	
Net income	$ 131,500	$ 45,000
1/1 Retained earnings	$ 297,600	$210,000
Net income	131,500	45,000
	429,100	255,000
Dividends	(120,000)	(35,000)
12/31 Retained earnings	$ 309,100	$220,000
Cash	$ 201,200	$151,000
Accounts receivable	221,000	173,000
Inventories	100,400	81,000
Investment in Stevens Company	1,000,000	
Equipment	450,000	300,000
Accumulated depreciation—equipment	(300,000)	(140,000)
Land	360,000	290,000
Total Assets	$2,032,600	$855,000

	PALMER COMPANY	STEVENS COMPANY
Accounts payable	$ 323,500	$135,000
Bonds payable	400,000	
Common stock	1,000,000	500,000
Retained earnings	309,100	220,000
Total liabilities and equity	$2,032,600	$855,000

Required:

A. Prepare in general journal form the workpaper entry to assign, amortize, and depreciate the difference between cost and book value in the December 31, 1995, consolidated statements workpaper.

B. Prepare a consolidated financial statements workpaper for the year ended December 31, 1997.

C. Prepare in good form a schedule showing the calculation of consolidated net income for the year ended December 31, 1997.

Problem 4-6

On January 1, 1995, Perini Company purchased an 85% interest in Silvas Company for $400,000. On this date, Silvas Company had common stock of $90,000 and retained earnings of $210,000. An examination of Silvas Company's assets and liabilities revealed that their book value was equal to their fair value except for the equipment.

	BOOK VALUE	FAIR VALUE
Equipment	$360,000	
Accumulated depreciation	120,000	
	$240,000	$300,000

The equipment had an expected remaining life of six years and no salvage value. Straight-line depreciation is used. Perini Company has decided to amortize any excess of cost over fair value over a period of 10 years.

During 1995 and 1996, Perini Company reported net income from its own operations of $80,000 and paid dividends of $50,000 in each year. Silvas Company had income of $40,000 each year and paid dividends of $30,000 on each December 31.

Required:

A. Prepare eliminating entries for the consolidated financial statements workpaper for the year ended December 31, 1995. Accumulated depreciation is presented on a separate row in the workpaper and in the consolidated financial statements.

B. On January 1, 1996, Silvas Company sold all its equipment for $220,000. Prepare the eliminating entries for the consolidated financial statements workpaper for the year ended December 31, 1996.

Problem 4-7

On January 1, 1995, Pueblo Corporation purchased a 75% interest in Sanchez Company for $900,000. A summary of Sanchez Company's balance sheet at date of purchase follows.

	BOOK VALUE	FAIR VALUE
Equipment	$720,000	
Accumulated depreciation	(240,000)	
Equipment (net)	480,000	$660,000
Other assets	450,000	450,000
	$930,000	
Liabilities	$255,000	$255,000
Common stock	300,000	
Retained earnings	375,000	
	$930,000	

The equipment had an original life of 15 years and a remaining useful life of 10 years. Any excess of cost over fair value will be amortized over the maximum period allowable.

During 1995 Pueblo Corporation reported income of $237,000 and paid dividends of $150,000. Sanchez Company reported net income of $123,000 and paid dividends of $120,000.

Required:

A. Prepare the elimination entries for the consolidated financial statements workpaper on December 31, 1995. Accumulated depreciation is presented on a separate row in the workpaper and in the consolidated financial statements.

B. Assume that Sanchez Company disposed of all its equipment on January 1, 1997, for $450,000.
  (1) What amount of gain (loss) will Sanchez Company report?
  (2) What is the consolidated gain (loss)?
  (3) Prepare the workpaper entry necessary to assign the amount of the difference between cost and book value that was originally assigned to the equipment that has now been sold to outsiders.
  (4) What workpaper entry will be necessary to assign this difference between cost and book value in future years?

Problem 4-8

Patten Corporation acquired an 80% interest in Savage Company for $2,720,000 on January 1, 1995. On this date, the balances in Savage Company's capital stock and retained earnings accounts were $1,900,000 and $600,000, respectively.

An examination of Savage Company's books revealed the following:

	BOOK VALUE	FAIR VALUE
Current assets	$ 700,000	$ 700,000
Inventory	500,000	625,000
Marketable securities	400,000	400,000
Plant and equipment	1,100,000	1,500,000
Land	500,000	1,000,000
Liabilities	700,000	700,000

The remaining useful life of the plant and equipment is 13 years, and all the inventory was sold in 1995. The net income from Patten Corporation's own operations was $800,000 in

1995 and $600,000 in 1996. Savage Company's net income for the respective years was $100,000 and $200,000. No dividends were declared.

Required:

A. Prepare the consolidated statements workpaper eliminating entries for 1995 and 1996 in general journal form.

B. Calculate consolidated net income for 1995 and 1996.

Problem 4-9

On January 1, 1995, Pump Company acquired all the outstanding common stock of Sound Company for $556,000 in cash. Financial data relating to Sound Company on January 1, 1995, are presented here:

	BALANCE SHEET	
	BOOK VALUE	FAIR VALUE
Cash	$104,550	$ 104,550
Receivables	123,000	112,310
Inventories	220,000	268,000
Buildings	331,000	375,000
Accumulated depreciation—buildings	(264,800)	(300,000)
Equipment	145,000	130,000
Accumulated depreciation–equipment	(108,750)	(97,500)
Land	150,000	420,000
Total assets	$700,000	$1,012,360
Current liabilities	$106,000	$ 106,000
Bonds payable, 8% due 1/1/2013		
interest payable on 6/30 and 12/31	300,000	
Common stock	200,000	
Premium on common stock	80,000	
Retained earnings	14,000	
Total equities	$700,000	

Sound Company would expect to pay 10% interest to borrow long-term funds on the date of acquisition. During 1995, Sound Company wrote its receivables down by $10,690 and recorded a corresponding loss. Sound Company accounts for its inventories at lower of FIFO cost or market. Its buildings and equipment had a remaining estimated useful life on January 1, 1995, of 10 years and 2½ years, respectively. Sound Company reported net income of $80,000 and declared no dividends in 1995.

Required:

A. Prepare in general journal form the December 31, 1995, workpaper entries necessary to eliminate the investment account and to assign, amortize, and depreciate the difference between cost and book value.

B. Assume that Pump Company's net income from independent operations in 1995 amounts to $500,000. Calculate consolidated net income for 1995.

Problem 4-10

Pearson Company purchased a 100% interest in Sanders Company and a 90% interest in Taylor Company on January 2, 1995, for $800,000 and $1,300,000, respectively. The account balances and fair values of the acquired companies on the acquisition date were as follows:

	SANDERS		TAYLOR	
	BOOK VALUE	FAIR VALUE	BOOK VALUE	FAIR VALUE
Current assets	$ 200,000	$200,000	$ 350,000	$350,000
Inventory	400,000	400,000	500,000	575,000
Plant and equipment (net)	300,000	350,000	600,000	600,000
Land	600,000	600,000	550,000	625,000
Total	$1,500,000		$2,000,000	
Current liabilities	$ 500,000	$500,000	$ 300,000	$300,000
Bonds payable	300,000	300,000	600,000	600,000
Capital stock	500,000		800,000	
Retained earnings	200,000		300,000	
Total	$1,500,000		$2,000,000	

Sanders Company's equipment has a remaining useful life of 10 years. Two-thirds of Taylor Company's inventory was sold in 1995 and the rest was sold in the following year. Any excess of cost over fair value is amortized over 20 years. In 1995, Sanders Company reported net income of $500,000 and declared dividends of $100,000. Taylor Company's net income and declared dividends for 1995 were $800,000 and $200,000, respectively.

Required:

A. Prepare in general journal form the entries on the books of Pearson Corporation to account for its investments in 1995.

B. Prepare the elimination entries necessary in the consolidated statements workpaper for the year ended December 31, 1995.

Problem 4-11

(Note that this is the same problem as Problem 4-4, but assuming the use of the partial equity method.)

On January 1, 1993, Porter Company purchased an 80% interest in the capital stock of Salem Company for $820,000. On the date of acquisition, Salem Company had capital stock of $500,000 and retained earnings of $100,000. Porter Company uses the partial equity method to record its investment in Salem Company. Differences between the fair value and the book value of the identifiable assets of Salem Company were as follows:

	FAIR VALUE IN EXCESS OF BOOK VALUE
Equipment	$125,000
Land	62,500
Inventory	37,500

The book values of all other assets and liabilities of Salem Company were equal to their fair values on January 1, 1993. The equipment had a remaining life of five years on January 1, 1993, the inventory was sold in 1993, and goodwill is amortized over 40 years.

Financial data for 1995 are presented here:

	PORTER COMPANY	SALEM COMPANY
Sales	$1,050,000	$400,000
Equity in subsidiary income	120,000	
Total revenue	1,170,000	400,000
Cost of goods sold	850,000	180,000
Depreciation expense	35,000	25,000
Other expenses	65,000	45,000
Total cost and expense	950,000	250,000
Net income	$ 220,000	$150,000
1/1 Retained earnings	$ 560,000	$200,000
Net income	220,000	150,000
Dividends declared	(100,000)	(50,000)
12/31 Retained earnings	$ 680,000	$300,000
Cash	$ 80,000	$ 50,000
Accounts receivable	250,000	170,000
Inventory	230,000	150,000
Investment in Salem Company	980,000	
Land	–0–	300,000
Plant and equipment	350,000	250,000
Total assets	$1,890,000	$920,000
Accounts payable	$ 160,000	$100,000
Notes payable	50,000	20,000
Capital stock	1,000,000	500,000
Retained earnings	680,000	300,000
Total liabilities and equity	$1,890,000	$920,000

Required:

A. Prepare a consolidated financial statements workpaper for the year ended December 31, 1995.

B. Prepare a consolidated statement of financial position and a consolidated income statement for the year ended December 31, 1995.

C. Describe the effect on the consolidated balances if Salem Company uses the LIFO cost flow assumption in pricing its inventory and there has been no decrease in ending inventory quantities since 1993.

D. Prepare an analytical calculation of consolidated retained earnings for the year ended December 31, 1995.

E. If you completed Problem 4-4, a comparison of the consolidated balances in this problem with those you obtained in Problem 4-4 will demonstrate that the method (cost or partial equity) used by the parent company to record its investment in a consolidated subsidiary has no effect on the consolidated balances.

Problem 4-12

(Note that this is the same problem as Problem 4-5, but assuming the use of the partial equity method.)

On January 1, 1995, Palmer Company acquired a 90% interest in Stevens Company at a cost of $1,000,000. At the purchase date, Stevens Company's stockholders' equity consisted of the following:

Common stock	$500,000
Retained earnings	190,000

An examination of Stevens Company's assets and liabilities revealed the following at the date of acquisition:

	BOOK VALUE	FAIR VALUE
Cash	$ 90,726	$ 90,726
Accounts receivable	200,000	200,000
Inventories	160,000	210,000
Equipment	300,000	390,000
Accumulated depreciation—equipment	(100,000)	(130,000)
Land	190,000	290,000
Bonds payable	(205,556)	(150,000)
Other	54,830	54,830
Total	$690,000	$955,556

Addition Information—Date of Acquisition:

Stevens Company's equipment had an original life of 15 years and a remaining useful life of 10 years. All the inventory was sold in 1995. The excess of cost over fair value, if any, is amortized over 20 years. Stevens Company purchased its bonds payable on the open market on January 10, 1995, for $150,000 and recognized a gain of $55,556. Palmer Company uses the partial equity method to record its investment in Stevens Company.

Financial statement data for 1997 are presented here:

	PALMER COMPANY	STEVENS COMPANY
Sales	$ 620,000	$340,000
Cost of sales	430,000	240,000
Gross margin	190,000	100,000
Depreciation expense	30,000	20,000
Other expenses	60,000	35,000
Income from operations	100,000	45,000
Equity in subsidiary income	40,500	
Net income	$ 140,500	$ 45,000
1/1 Retained earnings	$ 315,600	$210,000
Net income	140,500	45,000
	456,100	255,000
Dividends	(120,000)	(35,000)
12/31 Retained earnings	$ 336,100	$220,000

	PALMER COMPANY	STEVENS COMPANY
Cash	$ 201,200	$151,000
Accounts receivable	221,000	173,000
Inventories	100,400	81,000
Investment in Stevens Company	1,027,000	
Equipment	450,000	300,000
Accumulated depreciation—equipment	(300,000)	(140,000)
Land	360,000	290,000
Total assets	$2,059,600	$855,000
Accounts payable	$ 323,500	$135,000
Bonds payable	400,000	
Common stock	1,000,000	500,000
Retained earnings	336,100	220,000
Total liabilities and equity	$2,059,600	$855,000

Required:

A. Prepare in general journal form the workpaper entry to assign, amortize, and depreciate the difference between cost and book value in the December 31, 1995, consolidated statements workpaper.

B. Prepare a consolidated financial statements workpaper for the year ended December 31, 1997.

C. Prepare in good form a schedule showing the calculation of consolidated net income for the year ended December 31, 1997.

D. If you completed Problem 4-5, a comparison of the consolidated balances in this problem with those you obtained in Problem 4-5 will demonstrate that the method (cost or partial equity) used by the parent company to record its investment in a consolidated subsidiary has no effect on the consolidated balances.

Problem 4-13A

On January 2, 1995, Press Company purchased on the open market 90% of the outstanding common stock of Sensor Company for $800,000 cash. Balance sheets for Press Company and Sensor Company on January 1, 1995, just before the stock acquisition by Press Company, were:

	PRESS COMPANY	SENSOR COMPANY
Cash	$1,065,000	$ 38,000
Receivables	422,500	76,000
Inventory	216,500	124,000
Building (net)	465,000	322,000
Equipment (net)	229,000	185,000
Land	188,000	100,000
Patents	167,500	88,000
Total assets	$2,753,500	$933,000

	PRESS COMPANY	SENSOR COMPANY
Liabilities	$ 667,000	$249,000
Common stock	700,000	300,000
Other contributed capital	846,000	164,000
Retained earnings	540,500	220,000
Total equities	$2,753,500	$933,000

The full implied value of Sensor Company is to be "pushed down" and recorded in Sensor Company's books. The excess of the implied fair value over the book value of net assets acquired is assigned as follows: To equipment, 30%; to land, 20%; to patents, 50%.

Required:

A. Prepare the entry on Sensor Company's books on January 2, 1995, to record the values implied by the 90% stock purchase by Press Company.

B. Prepare a consolidated balance sheet workpaper on January 1, 1995.

Problem 4-14A

On January 1, 1993, Push Company purchased an 80% interest in the capital stock of WayDown Company for $820,000. At that time, WayDown Company had capital stock of $500,000 and retained earnings of $100,000. Differences between the fair value and the book value of identifiable assets of WayDown Company were as follows:

	FAIR VALUE IN EXCESS OF BOOK VALUE
Equipment	$125,000
Land	62,500
Inventory	37,500

The book values of all other assets and liabilities of WayDown Company were equal to their fair values on January 1, 1993. The equipment had a remaining life of five years on January 1, 1993, the inventory was sold in 1993, and goodwill is amortized over 40 years. WayDown Company revalued its assets on January 2, 1993. New values were assigned on the basis of the fair value on WayDown Company as a whole imputed from the transaction.
    Financial data for 1995 are presented here:

	PUSH COMPANY	WAYDOWN COMPANY
Sales	$1,050,000	$ 400,000
Dividend income	40,000	
Total revenue	1,090,000	400,000
Cost of goods sold	850,000	180,000
Depreciation expense	35,000	50,000
Other expenses	65,000	50,000
Total cost and expense	950,000	280,000
Net income	$ 140,000	$ 120,000

	PUSH COMPANY	WAYDOWN COMPANY
1/1 Retained earnings	$ 480,000	$ 102,500
Net income	140,000	120,000
Dividends declared	(100,000)	(50,000)
12/31 Retained earnings	$ 520,000	$ 172,500
Cash	$ 80,000	$ 50,000
Accounts receivable	250,000	170,000
Inventory	230,000	150,000
Investment in WayDown Company	820,000	
Goodwill	–0–	185,000
Land	–0–	362,500
Plant and equipment	350,000	300,000
Total assets	$1,730,000	$1,217,500
Accounts payable	$ 160,000	$ 100,000
Notes payable	50,000	20,000
Capital stock	1,000,000	500,000
Revaluation capital		425,000
Retained earnings	520,000	172,500
Total liabilities and equity	$1,730,000	$1,217,500

Required:

A. In general journal form, prepare the entry made by WayDown Company on January 2, 1993, to record the effect of the pushed down values implied by the purchase of its stock by Push Company assuming that values were assigned on the basis of the fair value of WayDown Company as a whole imputed from the transaction.

B. Prepare a consolidated financial statements workpaper for the year ended December 31, 1995.

C. Compare the consolidated balances in the workpaper prepared in part (B) with those in the consolidated statements workpaper prepared for Problem 4-4. What effect does the decision to apply the full push down approach have on:
   (1) Consolidated net income?
   (2) Consolidated retained earnings?
   (3) Consolidated net assets?
   (4) Noncontrolling interest in consolidated net assets?

Problem 4-15A

(Solution requires an understanding of the content of footnote 5 of this chapter.)
On January 1, 1993, Push Company purchased an 80% interest in the capital stock of Down Company for $820,000. At that time, Down Company had capital stock of $500,000 and retained earnings of $100,000. Differences between the fair value and the book value of identifiable assets of Down Company were as follows:

	FAIR VALUE IN EXCESS OF BOOK VALUE
Equipment	$125,000
Land	62,500
Inventory	37,500

The book values of all other assets and liabilities of Down Company were equal to their fair values on January 1, 1993. The equipment had a remaining life of five years on January 1, 1993, the inventory was sold in 1993, and goodwill is amortized over 40 years. Down Company revalued its assets on January 2, 1993. New values were assigned on the basis of the proportional interest acquired by Push Company.

Financial data for 1995 are presented here:

	PUSH COMPANY	DOWN COMPANY
Sales	$1,050,000	$ 400,000
Dividend income	40,000	
Total revenue	1,090,000	400,000
Cost of goods sold	850,000	180,000
Depreciation expense	35,000	45,000
Other expenses	65,000	49,000
Total cost and expense	950,000	274,000
Net income	$ 140,000	$ 126,000
1/1 Retained earnings	$ 480,000	$ 122,000
Net income	140,000	126,000
Dividends declared	(100,000)	(50,000)
12/31 Retained earnings	$ 520,000	$ 198,000
Cash	$ 80,000	$ 50,000
Accounts receivable	250,000	170,000
Inventory	230,000	150,000
Investment in Down Company	820,000	
Land	–0–	350,000
Goodwill	–0–	148,000
Plant and equipment	350,000	290,000
Total assets	$1,730,000	$1,158,000
Accounts payable	$ 160,000	$ 100,000
Notes payable	50,000	20,000
Revaluation capital		340,000
Capital stock	1,000,000	500,000
Retained earnings	520,000	198,000
Total liabilities and equity	$1,730,000	$1,158,000

Required:

A. In general journal form, prepare the entry made by Down Company on January 2, 1993, to record the effect of the pushed down values implied by the purchase of its stock by Push Company assuming that values were assigned on the basis of the proportional interest acquired by Push Company.

B. Prepare a consolidated financial statements workpaper for the year ended December 31, 1995. Review footnote 5 in this chapter before you complete the workpaper.

C. Compare the consolidated balances in the workpaper prepared in part (B) with those in the consolidated statements workpaper prepared for Problem 4-4.

5

ELIMINATION OF UNREALIZED PROFIT ON INTERCOMPANY SALES OF INVENTORY

Affiliated companies may make intercompany sales of inventory or other assets. Ordinarily, the selling affiliate will record a profit or loss on such sales. From the point of view of the consolidated entity, however, such profit or loss should not be reported until the inventory or other assets acquired by the purchasing affiliate have been used during the course of operations or sold to parties outside the affiliated group (third parties). Profit (loss) that has not been realized from the point of view of the consolidated entity through subsequent sales to third parties is defined as *unrealized intercompany profit (loss)* and must be eliminated in the preparation of consolidated financial statements. The elimination of unrealized profit resulting from intercompany sales of inventory is examined in this chapter. The elimination of unrealized profit resulting from intercompany sales of property and equipment will be examined in Chapter 6.

EFFECTS OF INTERCOMPANY SALES OF MERCHANDISE ON THE DETERMINATION OF CONSOLIDATED BALANCES

The workpaper procedures illustrated in this chapter are designed to accomplish the following financial reporting objectives in the consolidated financial statements.

- To include in consolidated sales only *sales that have been consummated in transactions with parties outside the affiliated group*.

- To present as cost of goods sold *the cost to the affiliated group* of goods that have been sold to parties outside the affiliated group.
- To present inventory at its *cost to the affiliated group*.
- To allocate combined income to the noncontrolling interest based on its share of the amount of subsidiary income that is included in combined income.

Stated another way, the objective of eliminating the effects of intercompany sales of merchandise is to present consolidated balances for sales, cost of goods sold, and inventory as if the intercompany sale had never occurred. As a result, the recognition of income or loss on the intercompany transaction, including its allocation between the noncontrolling and controlling interests, is deferred until the profit or loss is confirmed by sales of the merchandise to nonaffiliates.

Thoughtful consideration of these financial reporting objectives will indicate that they are logical and noncontroversial. However, the workpaper procedures for accomplishing these objectives are not self-evident. Thus the workpaper procedures for accomplishing these objectives are the central topic of this chapter. These procedures include workpaper entries to adjust the recorded amounts of sales, cost of sales (or components thereof), and ending inventory to amounts based on the objectives stated above. In addition, the procedures are designed to equate beginning consolidated retained earnings with the amount reported as ending consolidated retained earnings in the previous reporting period and to allocate combined income to the noncontrolling interest based on its share of adjusted subsidiary income that is included in combined income.

In order to concentrate on intercompany profit eliminations and adjustments, reporting complications relating to accounting for the difference between cost and book value are avoided in all illustrations by assuming that all acquisitions are made at the book value of the acquired interest in net assets and that the book value of the subsidiary company's net assets equals their fair value on the date the parent company's interest is acquired. It is also assumed that the affiliates file consolidated income tax returns. Deferred tax consequences that may arise in the consolidated financial statements because of the elimination of unrealized intercompany profit or because of undistributed subsidiary income are discussed in Chapter 7.

Determination of Consolidated Sales, Cost of Sales, and Inventory Balances

The basic workpaper eliminating entries required because of intercompany sales of merchandise are illustrated using the following simplifying assumptions:

1. P Company sells all goods it manufactures to its wholly owned subsidiary, S Company, at 125% of cost.

2. During the first year of this arrangement, goods that cost P Company $200,000 are sold to S Company for $250,000.

3. During the same year, S Company sold all the goods purchased by it from P Company to third parties for $270,000.

Sales, cost of sales, and inventory balances reported by the affiliated companies are

presented in Illustration 5-1. The workpaper entry in the year of the sale to eliminate intercompany sales of merchandise takes the following form:

(1) Sales	250,000	
Cost of Sales (Purchases)		250,000

ILLUSTRATION 5-1
Partial Consolidated Statements Workpaper
Elimination of Intercompany Sale of Inventory
No Unrealized Profit

	P	S	ELIMINATIONS		CONSOLIDATED
INCOME STATEMENT	COMPANY	COMPANY	DR.	CR.	BALANCES
Sales	250,000	270,000	(1) 250,000		270,000
Cost of sales	200,000	250,000		(1) 250,000	200,000
Gross profit	50,000	20,000			70,000
BALANCE SHEET					
Inventory	–0–	–0–			–0–

(1) To eliminate intercompany sales.

No unrealized intercompany profit exists, since all goods sold by P Company to
S Company have been resold to third parties. After the elimination of intercompany
sales, consolidated sales of $270,000 equals the amount of sales by the affiliated
group (S Company) to third parties, and consolidated cost of sales of $200,000
equals the cost to the affiliated group (P Company) of manufacturing the goods
sold.

Failure to eliminate intercompany sales would result in an overstatement of
sales and of cost of sales in the consolidated financial statements. Since both sales
and cost of sales would be overstated by the same amounts, consolidated net income
is not affected by the failure to eliminate intercompany sales. However, the gross
profit rate and other financial ratios would be distorted if the elimination were not
made.

Assume now that S Company sells only one-half of the goods purchased from
P Company to third parties prior to the end of the current year. Sales, cost of sales,
and inventory balances reported by each of the affiliated companies are presented
in Illustration 5-2. Entry (1) to eliminate sales and cost of sales is the same as
explained before. However, unrealized intercompany profit in the amount of
$25,000 [$125,000 − ($125,000/1.25)] resides in the ending inventory balance of
S Company. When, at the end of the accounting period, some of the merchandise
remains in the inventory of the purchasing affiliate, the intercompany profit recognized thereon must be excluded from consolidated net income and from the
inventory balance in the consolidated balance sheet. The workpaper entry to accomplish this elimination is as follows:

ILLUSTRATION 5-2
Partial Consolidated Statements Workpaper
Elimination of Intercompany Sale of Inventory
Unrealized Profit in Ending Inventory

	P	S	ELIMINATIONS		CONSOLIDATED
INCOME STATEMENT	COMPANY	COMPANY	DR.	CR.	BALANCES
Sales	250,000	135,000	(1) 250,000		135,000
Cost of sales	200,000	125,000	(2) 25,000	(1) 250,000	100,000
Gross profit	50,000	10,000			35,000
BALANCE SHEET					
Inventory	–0–	125,000		(2) 25,000	100,000

(1) To eliminate intercompany sales.
(2) To eliminate unrealized intercompany profit in ending inventory.

(2) Cost of Sales (Ending Inventory in Income Statement)	25,000	
Inventory		25,000

The form of the entry eliminating intercompany sales, Entry (1), implicitly assumes that there is no unrealized intercompany profit. Accordingly, either that entry must be adjusted, or this second entry must be made to remove the unrealized intercompany profit from the ending inventory and to reduce the excessive credit to cost of sales. The first and second eliminating entries could be combined and one entry prepared as follows:

Sales	250,000	
Cost of Sales (Purchases)		225,000
Inventory		25,000

As a practical matter, two entries are conventionally prepared as shown in Illustration 5-2. In either case, after adjustment, consolidated sales of $135,000 equals the amount of sales of the affiliated group (S Company) to third parties. Consolidated cost of sales of $100,000 equals the cost to the affiliated group (P Company) of manufacturing the goods sold ($\frac{1}{2} \times \$200,000$), and the consolidated inventory balance of $100,000 equals the cost to the affiliated group (P Company) of manufacturing the goods held by S Company at the end of the year.

Assume now that in the next period P Company sells merchandise to S Company in the amount of $500,000 (cost $400,000) and that S Company sells all its beginning inventory ($125,000) and one-half its current purchases from P Company ($250,000) to third parties for $405,000. Sales, cost of sales, and inventory balances reported by the affiliated companies are presented in Illustration 5-3.

Unrealized intercompany profit in the amount of $50,000 [$250,000 − ($250,000/1.25)] resides in the ending inventory of S Company. Workpaper eliminating entries (1) and (2) are similar to those discussed in the preceding example. Assuming a first-in, first-out (FIFO) inventory cost flow, intercompany

ILLUSTRATION 5-3
Partial Consolidated Statements Workpaper
Elimination of Intercompany Sale of Inventory
Intercompany Profit in Beginning and Ending Inventories

INCOME STATEMENT	P COMPANY	S COMPANY	ELIMINATIONS DR.	ELIMINATIONS CR.	CONSOLIDATED BALANCES
Sales	500,000	405,000	(1) 500,000		405,000
Cost of Sales	400,000	375,000	(2) 50,000	(1) 500,000 (3) 25,000	300,000
Gross Profit	100,000	30,000			105,000
RETAINED EARNINGS STATEMENT					
Beginning Retained Earnings P Company (Consolidated)	XXX		(3) 25,000		XXX
BALANCE SHEET					
Inventory	–0–	250,000		(2) 50,000	200,000

(1) To eliminate intercompany sales.
(2) To eliminate unrealized intercompany profit in ending inventory.
(3) To recognize intercompany profit in beginning inventory realized during the period and reduce beginning consolidated retained earnings for unrealized intercompany profit at the beginning of the year.

profit in inventories excluded from consolidated net income in one period will be realized by sales to third parties in the next period. The form of the workpaper entry to recognize profit in the buying affiliate's beginning inventory that is realized during the current period is as follows:

(3) Beginning Retained Earnings—Parent Company	25,000	
(Beginning Consolidated Retained Earnings)		
Cost of Sales (Beginning Inventory in Income Statement)		25,000

The credit to cost of sales (beginning inventory) in Entry (3) is necessary in order to recognize in consolidated income the amount of profit in the beginning inventory that has been confirmed by sales to third parties during the current period. S Company charged cost of sales for its cost of $125,000, whereas the cost to the affiliated group of the beginning inventory of S Company is only $100,000. Accordingly, cost of sales must be decreased by $25,000, which increased consolidated net income by $25,000.

The rationale for the debit of $25,000 to beginning retained earnings of P Company (beginning consolidated retained earnings) is as follows. In the previous year, P Company recorded $50,000 in profit on intercompany sales and transferred it to its Retained Earnings account as part of the normal accounting process. Since, at the beginning of the year, one-half of that amount has not been realized by sales to third parties, it must be eliminated from the beginning retained earnings of P Company (beginning consolidated retained earnings). The debit to beginning retained earnings may also be explained in the following manner. In determining consolidated net income and ending consolidated retained earnings in the prior year, $25,000 was deducted from the reported income and retained earnings of the affiliated group by a workpaper entry. Therefore, in the current year, the amount indicated by the beginning account balances on the books of the affiliated companies must be reduced by a workpaper entry in the amount of $25,000 in order that beginning consolidated retained earnings of the current year will be reported at an amount equal to that reported for ending consolidated retained earnings in the previous period.

Consolidated sales of $405,000 are equal to the amount of sales of the affiliated group (S Company) to third parties. Consolidated cost of sales of $300,000 equals the cost to the affiliated group (P Company) of manufacturing the goods sold and is calculated as follows:

Cost of one-half of goods transferred to S Company in prior year (½ × $200,000)	$100,000
Cost of one-half of goods transferred to S Company in current year (½ × $400,000)	200,000
Cost of goods sold to third parties during current year	$300,000

Consolidated inventory of $200,000 equals the cost to the affiliated group (P Company) of manufacturing the goods on hand at the end of the year (½ × $400,000).

Over two consecutive periods, assuming a FIFO flow of inventory costs, differences between the net income recorded on the books of the individual affiliates and consolidated net income offset each other, as does the effect of the differences on beginning retained earnings.

If an inventory cost flow assumption other than FIFO is used, unrealized intercompany profit in beginning inventory balances may continue to be included in the ending inventory. In that case, to the extent that unrealized intercompany profit at the beginning of the year remains unrealized, the increase in consolidated net income that would otherwise result from the credit to cost of sales in Entry (3) is offset by a portion of the debit to cost of sales in Entry (2). Thus, as a matter of workpaper procedure, there is no need to be concerned in formulating Entry (3) as to whether or not unrealized intercompany profit in the beginning inventory is also included in the ending inventory.

Individual components (beginning inventory, purchases, ending inventory) of cost of sales are shown parenthetically in the entries illustrated earlier. If the detail of cost of sales is to be presented in the consolidated income statement, workpaper entries must be made so as to adjust the individual components as indicated rather than aggregate cost of sales.

Determination of Amount of Intercompany Profit

In the preceding examples, the amount of intercompany profit subject to elimination was calculated on the basis of the selling affiliate's **gross profit rate**. This is the concept that is normally applied in practice. An alternative would be to determine intercompany profit on the basis of the selling affiliate's profit after deducting selling and administrative expense. The effect of this approach, as compared with the gross profit method, would be to reduce the amount of profit subject to elimination and increase consolidated inventory balances by the amount of the selling and administrative expense associated with the goods still held by the affiliated group. Support for the gross profit approach is based on the proposition that consolidated inventory balances should include manufacturing costs only and that generally accepted accounting standards normally preclude the capitalization of selling and administrative costs.

Inventory Pricing Adjustments

Assume that (1) P Company sells S Company goods costing $200,000 for $250,000; (2) at the end of the year, all these goods remain in the ending inventory of S Company and are written down from $250,000 to $215,000 on that company's books; (3) the write-down on the books of S Company results from the application of the lower of cost or market rule in pricing its ending inventory; and (4) the related loss is included in the cost of sales of S Company. What amount of intercompany profit is subject to elimination in the preparation of consolidated financial statements? Since the gross profit of $50,000 recognized by P Company is offset by the reduction of gross profit of $35,000 recognized by S Company, only the remaining $15,000 is still subject to elimination in the preparation of consolidated financial statements. The deduction of the amount of the current year's write-down of intercompany inventory from the amount of intercompany profit otherwise subject to elimination also results in the presentation of intercompany inventory at cost to the affiliated group ($215,000 − $15,000 = $200,000). In summary, the amount of intercompany profit subject to elimination should be reduced to the extent that the related goods have been written down by the purchasing affiliate.

Determination of Proportion of Intercompany Profit to Be Eliminated

It is clear that unrealized intercompany profit should not be included in consolidated net income or assets. However, two alternative views of the amount of intercompany profit that should be considered as "unrealized" exist. The elimination methods associated with these two points of view are generally referred to as *100%* (total) *elimination* and *partial elimination*.

Proponents of 100% elimination regard *all* the intercompany profit associated with assets remaining in the affiliated group to be unrealized. Proponents of partial elimination regard only the parent company's share of the profit recognized by the *selling affiliate* to be unrealized. Stated another way, they regard the noncontrolling interests' share of the *selling affiliate's* profit on intercompany sales to be realized.

Under 100% elimination, the entire amount of unconfirmed intercompany profit is eliminated from combined income and the related asset balance. Under partial elimination, only the parent company's share of the unconfirmed intercompany profit recognized by the *selling affiliate* is eliminated.

Generally accepted accounting standards *require* 100% elimination of intercompany profit *in the preparation of consolidated financial statements*. This standard was originally promulgated in paragraph 14 of *ARB No. 51* as follows:

> The amount of intercompany profit or loss to be eliminated . . . is not affected by the existence of a minority [noncontrolling] interest. The complete elimination of the intercompany profit or loss is consistent with the underlying assumption that consolidated statements represent the financial position and operating results of a single business enterprise.

Because generally accepted accounting standards currently require total elimination of intercompany profit in the preparation of consolidated financial statements, all illustrations of consolidating workpapers in this text are based on 100% elimination of intercompany profit. The reader needs to be aware, however, that there is support in the accounting literature for partial elimination of intercompany profit. The concepts underlying each of the approaches and their effects on consolidated balances are discussed in Chapter 11.

Determination of the Noncontrolling Interest in Combined Income

Sales from a parent company to one or more of its subsidiaries are referred to as *downstream sales*. Sales from subsidiaries to the parent company are referred to as *upstream sales*. Sales from one subsidiary to another subsidiary are referred to as *horizontal sales*.

When the selling affiliate is a less than wholly owned subsidiary and 100% of intercompany profit is eliminated, the amount of profit eliminated should be allocated proportionately between the controlling (consolidated net income) and noncontrolling (noncontrolling interest in combined income) interests. If the income of a less than wholly owned subsidiary is, in effect, increased or decreased by intercompany profit workpaper entries before its aggregation with the income of the parent, the calculation of the noncontrolling interest in the combined income should be based on the amount of subsidiary income included in the combined income of that period. Likewise, the calculation of the noncontrolling interest in consolidated net assets should be based on the amount of net assets of the subsidiary included in the consolidated balance sheet.

When the 100% elimination method is used to eliminate intercompany profit, the amount of the noncontrolling interest in combined income that is deducted in determining consolidated net income is based on the amount of reported subsidiary income (loss) that has been realized in transactions with third parties.

The general format for the calculation of the noncontrolling interest in combined income in the case of an upstream sale is presented in Illustration 5-4.

The calculation of the noncontrolling interest may be summarized more succinctly in Illustration 5-5.

The reader is reminded, however, that this modification of the calculation of the noncontrolling interest is applicable only when the less than wholly owned subsidiary is the *selling affiliate* (upstream or horizontal sales). Where the parent

ILLUSTRATION 5-4
Calculation of the Noncontrolling Interest in Combined Income
When Selling Affiliate Is a Less than Wholly Owned Subsidiary

Net income reported by subsidiary	$XXX,XXX
Less unrealized intercompany profit recorded by the subsidiary in the current period	(XXX)
Plus intercompany profit recognized by the subsidiary in the prior period(s) that is realized by sales to third parties during the current period	XXX
Amount of subsidiary income included in combined income	XXX,XXX
Multiplied by the noncontrolling ownership percentage interest	%
The noncontrolling interest in combined income	$ X,XXX

ILLUSTRATION 5-5
Succinct Calculation of the Noncontrolling Interest in Combined Income
When Selling Affiliate is a Less than Wholly Owned Subsidiary

Net income reported by subsidiary	$XXX,XXX
Less unrealized profit in ending inventories	(XXX)
Plus unrealized profit in beginning inventories	XXX
Amount of subsidiary income included in combined income	XXX,XXX
Multiplied by the noncontrolling ownership percentage interest	%
The noncontrolling interest in combined income	$ X,XXX

company is the selling affiliate (downstream sale), the amount of subsidiary income included in combined income is not affected by the elimination of unrealized intercompany profit and no adjustment is necessary in the calculation of the noncontrolling interest in combined income.

Although 100% elimination of intercompany profit is required in the preparation of consolidated financial statements, the adjustment in the calculation of the noncontrolling interest described before is discretionary under current generally accepted accounting standards. This position is stated in paragraph 14 of *ARB No. 51* as follows: "The elimination of intercompany profit or loss **may** be allocated proportionately between the majority [controlling] and minority [noncontrolling] interests [emphasis added]." Thus, the adjustments to the calculation of the noncontrolling interest (and as a result to consolidated net income) **may** be made but are not **required** under generally accepted accounting standards.

This position was taken more than 30 years ago, and today the reasons for permitting discretionary allocation are obscure. Since that time, however, the concept of evaluating accounting and reporting standards in terms of the objectives of financial statements has gained widespread consideration and support. The objective of eliminating the effects of intercompany transactions from consolidated balances is to report the corresponding consolidated financial position and results of operations as if those transactions had never occurred. Given this objective, the logic of proportional allocation can be demonstrated with a simple illustration.

Assume that P Company and S Company had income from their independent operations as presented in Illustration 5-6. Assume further that during the year

P Company purchased but has not yet sold to third parties merchandise from S Company on which S Company recorded a profit of $25,000. A comparison of the effects on the determination of consolidated net income of the proportional allocation between the controlling and noncontrolling interests of unrealized intercompany profit on upstream sales with no allocation to the noncontrolling interest of such unrealized profit is presented in Illustration 5-6.

ILLUSTRATION 5-6
Comparison of the Effects
of Proportional Allocation Versus No Allocation
of Intercompany Profit Eliminations

	NO ALLOCATION OF UNREALIZED INTERCOMPANY PROFIT TO THE NONCONTROLLING INTEREST	PROPORTIONAL ALLOCATION OF UNREALIZED INTERCOMPANY PROFIT BETWEEN THE CONTROLLING AND THE NONCONTROLLING INTERESTS
P Company's income from its independent operations	$ 90,000	$ 90,000
S Company's reported income	35,000	35,000
Reduction of combined income for 100% elimination of unrealized profit (accomplished by debit to Cost of Goods Sold and credit to inventory in consolidated statements workpaper)	(25,000)	(25,000)
Combined income	100,000	100,000
The noncontrolling interest in combined income		
No allocation to the noncontrolling interest [.20 × ($35,000)]	(7,000)	
Proportional allocation between controlling and noncontrolling interests [.20 × ($35,000 − $25,000)]		(2,000)
Consolidated Net Income (controlling interest)	$ 93,000	$ 98,000

If we assume that the intercompany sale had never occurred, S Company would have reported net income of $10,000 ($35,000 − $25,000), rather than $35,000 and the analytical calculation of consolidated net income would be as follows:

P Company's net income from its independent operations	$90,000
P Company's interest in the reported net income of S Company (.80 × $10,000)	8,000
Consolidated net income	$98,000

Thus, since the amount of consolidated net income reported when proportional allocation is used is the same as would be reported if the transaction giving rise to the unrealized profit had never occurred, we conclude that proportional allocation between the controlling and noncontrolling interests meets the previously stated reporting objective, whereas the alternative of no allocation fails to meet that objective. In our opinion, where the amounts are material, the allocation of intercompany profit and loss eliminations proportionately between the controlling and noncontrolling interests is necessary for fair presentation, and there is no justification other than expediency for permitting discretionary allocation. Therefore, appropriate adjustments to the calculation of the noncontrolling interest for the effects of intercompany profit will be adhered to in all consolidated statements workpaper illustrations in this text.

CONSOLIDATED STATEMENTS WORKPAPER—INVESTMENT RECORDED USING COST METHOD

To illustrate consolidation procedures when the parent company records its investment using the cost method, assume the following:

1. P Company acquires an 80% interest in S Company on January 1, 1995, for $1,360,000, at which time S Company has capital stock of $1,000,000 and retained earnings of $700,000.

2. In 1995, S Company reported net income of $125,000 and declared dividends of $20,000.

3. In 1996, S Company reported net income of $140,000 and declared dividends of $60,000.

4. P Company uses the cost method to account for its investment in S Company.

5. S Company sells merchandise to P Company as follows:

YEAR	TOTAL SALES OF S COMPANY TO P COMPANY	INTERCOMPANY MERCHANDISE IN 12/31 INVENTORY OF P COMPANY	UNREALIZED INTERCOMPANY PROFIT (25% OF SELLING PRICE)
1995	$ 700,000	$400,000	$100,000
1996	1,000,000	500,000	125,000

Consolidated statements workpapers for the years ended December 31, 1995, and December 31, 1996, are presented in Illustration 5-7 and Illustration 5-8, respectively. Entries **on the books** of P Company as well as **workpaper entries** necessary in the consolidated statements workpapers for the years ended December 31, 1995, and December 31, 1996, are summarized in general journal form below. The workpaper entries and the determination of the noncontrolling interest are explained in more detail as needed.

Cost Method
80% Owned Subsidiary
Upstream Sale of Inventory

ILLUSTRATION 5-7
Consolidated Statements Workpaper
P Company and Subsidiary
For Year Ended December 31, 1995

INCOME STATEMENT	P COMPANY	S COMPANY	ELIMINATIONS DR.	ELIMINATIONS CR.	NONCONTROLLING INTEREST	CONSOLIDATED BALANCES
Sales	3,104,000	2,200,000	(1) 700,000			4,604,000
Dividend Income	16,000		(3) 16,000			
Total Revenue	3,120,000	2,200,000				4,604,000
Inventory 1/1	500,000	300,000				800,000
Purchases	1,680,000	1,370,000		(1) 700,000		2,350,000
	2,180,000	1,670,000				3,150,000
Inventory 12/31	480,000	310,000	(2) 100,000			690,000
Cost of Goods Sold	1,700,000	1,360,000				2,460,000
Other Expenses	1,124,000	715,000				1,839,000
Total Expense	2,824,000	2,075,000				4,299,000
Net/Combined Income	296,000	125,000				305,000
Noncontrolling Interest in Income					5,000	(5,000)*
Net Income to Retained Earnings	296,000	125,000	816,000	700,000	5,000	300,000
RETAINED EARNINGS STATEMENT						
1/1 Retained Earnings						
P Company	1,650,000					1,650,000
S Company		700,000	(4) 560,000		140,000	
Net Income from above	296,000	125,000	816,000	700,000	5,000	300,000
Dividends Declared						
P Company	(150,000)					(150,000)
S Company		(20,000)		(3) 16,000	(4,000)	
12/31 Retained Earnings to Balance Sheet	1,796,000	805,000	1,376,000	716,000	141,000	1,800,000
BALANCE SHEET						
Inventory	480,000	310,000		(2) 100,000		690,000
Investment in S Company	1,360,000			(4) 1,360,000		
Other Assets (net)	5,090,000	2,310,000				7,400,000
Total	6,930,000	2,620,000				8,090,000
Liabilities	2,134,000	815,000				2,949,000
Capital Stock						
P Company	3,000,000					3,000,000
S Company		1,000,000	(4) 800,000		200,000	
Retained Earnings from above	1,796,000	805,000	1,376,000	716,000	141,000	1,800,000
Noncontrolling Interest in Net Assets					341,000	341,000
Total Liabilities and Equity	6,930,000	2,620,000	2,176,000	2,176,000		8,090,000

*.2 ($125,000 − $100,000) = $5,000.

(1) To eliminate intercompany sales.
(2) To eliminate unrealized intercompany profit in ending inventory.
(3) To eliminate intercompany dividends.
(4) To eliminate the investment account.

Entries on Books of P Company—1995

(1)	Investment in S Company	1,360,000	
	Cash		1,360,000
	To record purchase of S Company stock.		
(2)	Cash	16,000	
	Dividend Income		16,000
	To record receipt of dividends from S Company (.8 × $20,000).		

Consolidated Statements Workpaper Entries—December 31, 1995
(Illustration 5-7)

(1)	Sales	700,000	
	Purchases		700,000
	To eliminate intercompany sales.		
(2)	12/31 Inventory-Income Statement (Cost of Sales)	100,000	
	Inventory		100,000
	To eliminate unrealized intercompany profit in ending inventory.		
(3)	Dividend Income	16,000	
	Dividends Declared		16,000
	To eliminate intercompany dividends		
(4)	Beginning Retained Earnings—S Company	560,000	
	Capital Stock—S Company	800,000	
	Investment in S Company		1,360,000
	To eliminate investment account.		

Since the selling affiliate is a partially owned subsidiary, unrealized intercompany profit is subtracted from reported subsidiary income when calculating the noncontrolling interest in combined income as follows:

$$.20 \times (\$125,000 - \$100,000) = \$5,000$$

If the sale of merchandise had been downstream rather than upstream, the amount of subsidiary income included in combined income would not be affected by the elimination of unrealized intercompany profit and no adjustment would be necessary in the calculation of the noncontrolling interest in combined income.

Entry on Books of P Company—1996

Cash	48,000	
Dividend Income		48,000
To record receipt of dividends from S Company (.80 × $60,000).		

Consolidated Financial Statements Workpaper Entries—December 31, 1996
(Illustration 5-8)

(1)	Investment in S Company	84,000	
	Beginning Retained Earnings—P Company		84,000
	To establish reciprocity [.80 × ($805,000 − $700,000)]		

Cost Method
80% Owned Subsidiary
Upstream Sale of Inventory

ILLUSTRATION 5-8
Consolidated Statements Workpaper
P Company and Subsidiary
For Year Ended December 31, 1996

INCOME STATEMENT	P COMPANY	S COMPANY	ELIMINATIONS DR.	ELIMINATIONS CR.	NONCONTROLLING INTEREST	CONSOLIDATED BALANCES
Sales	3,546,000	2,020,000	(2) 1,000,000			4,566,000
Dividend Income	48,000		(5) 48,000			
Total Revenue	3,594,000	2,020,000				4,566,000
Inventory 1/1	480,000	310,000		(4) 100,000		690,000
Purchases	2,070,000	1,250,000		(2) 1,000,000		2,320,000
	2,550,000	1,560,000				3,010,000
Inventory 12/31	510,000	360,000	(3) 125,000			745,000
Cost of Goods Sold	2,040,000	1,200,000				2,265,000
Other Expenses	1,100,000	680,000				1,780,000
Total Expense	3,140,000	1,880,000				4,045,000
Net/Combined Income	454,000	140,000				521,000
Noncontrolling Interest in Income					23,000	(23,000)*
Net Income to Retained Earnings	454,000	140,000	1,173,000	1,100,000	23,000	498,000
RETAINED EARNINGS STATEMENT						
1/1 Retained Earnings						
P Company	1,796,000		(4) 80,000	(1) 84,000		1,800,000
S Company		805,000	(4) 20,000		141,000	
			(6) 644,000			
Net Income from above	454,000	140,000	1,173,000	1,100,000	23,000	498,000
Dividends Declared						
P Company	(150,000)					(150,000)
S Company		(60,000)		(5) 48,000	(12,000)	
12/31 Retained Earnings to Balance Sheet	2,100,000	885,000	1,917,000	1,232,000	152,000	2,148,000
BALANCE SHEET						
Inventory	510,000	360,000		(3) 125,000		745,000
Investment in S Company	1,360,000		(1) 84,000	(6) 1,444,000		
Other Assets	5,450,000	2,330,000				7,780,000
Total	7,320,000	2,690,000				8,525,000
Liabilities	2,220,000	805,000				3,025,000
Capital Stock						
P Company	3,000,000					3,000,000
S Company		1,000,000	(6) 800,000		200,000	
Retained Earnings from above	2,100,000	885,000	1,917,000	1,232,000	152,000	2,148,000
Noncontrolling Interest in Net Assets					352,000	352,000
Total Liabilities and Equity	7,320,000	2,690,000	2,801,000	2,801,000		8,525,000

*.20 ($140,000 − $125,000 + $100,000) = $23,000.
  (1) To establish reciprocity as of 1/1/96 [.8 × ($805,000 − $700,000)].
    (2) To eliminate intercompany sales.
    (3) To eliminate unrealized intercompany profit in ending inventory.

    (4) To recognize profit realized during year and to reduce the controlling and noncontrolling interests for their shares of unrealized intercompany profit at beginning of year.
    (5) To eliminate intercompany dividends.
    (6) To eliminate investment account.

(2) Sales	1,000,000	
Purchases (Cost of Sales)		1,000,000
To eliminate intercompany sales.		
(3) 12/31 Inventory—Income Statement (Cost of Sales)	125,000	
Inventory		125,000
To eliminate unrealized intercompany profit in ending inventory.		
(4) Beginning Retained Earnings—P Company		
(.80 × $100,000)	80,000	
Beginning Retained Earnings—S Company		
(.20 × $100,000)	20,000	
1/1 Inventory—Income Statement (Cost of Sales)		100,000
To recognize intercompany profit in beginning inventory realized during the year and to reduce the controlling and noncontrolling interests for their shares of unrealized intercompany profit at beginning of year.		
(5) Dividend Income	48,000	
Dividends Declared—S Company		48,000
To eliminate intercompany dividends (.80 × $60,000).		
(6) Beginning Retained Earnings—S Company	644,000	
(.80 × $805,000)		
Capital Stock—S Company (.80 × $1,000,000)	800,000	
Investment in S Company ($1,360,000 + $84,000)		1,444,000
To eliminate investment account.		

The unrealized profit in the current year's beginning inventory is the same as the unrealized profit in last year's ending inventory. Since the sale is upstream, the unrealized profit at the end of last year was apportioned between the controlling and noncontrolling interests by reducing the noncontrolling interest in combined income in the consolidated statements workpaper in the previous year. To be consistent, a similar apportionment of unrealized profit in beginning inventory must be made between the controlling and noncontrolling interests in the current year's workpaper. This apportionment is accomplished in workpaper Entry (4).

As a matter of workpaper procedure, adjustments to the controlling interest (consolidated retained earnings) are made by debiting (decrease) or crediting (increase) the beginning retained earnings row of the parent company. Adjustments to the noncontrolling interest are made by debiting (decrease) or crediting (increase) the beginning retained earnings row of the subsidiary company.

The noncontrolling interest in the beginning retained earnings of S Company in the amount of $141,000 is equal to the noncontrolling interest's share of the reported retained earnings of S Company (.20 × $805,000 = $161,000) *reduced* by its share of the unrealized intercompany profit included therein (.20 × $100,000 = $20,000).

The net effect of the adjustments to the noncontrolling interest in the income statement and retained earnings statement sections of the consolidated statements workpaper that are necessary in the case of *upstream sales* is to adjust the amount of the noncontrolling interest in consolidated net assets. The amount of the noncontrolling interest reported in the consolidated balance sheet is based on the net assets of the subsidiary that have been realized in transactions with third parties. In Illustration 5-8, for example, the noncontrolling interest in consolidated net assets on December 31, 1996, may be calculated as presented in Illustration 5-9.

ILLUSTRATION 5-9
Calculation of the Noncontrolling Interest
in Consolidated Net Assets

Capital stock—S Company		$1,000,000
Realized retained earnings—S Company		
Reported retained earnings	$885,000	
Unrealized intercompany profit	(125,000)	760,000
Realized net assets—S Company		$1,760,000
Noncontrolling interest in consolidated net assets (.20 × $1,760,000)		$ 352,000

The realized net assets of S Company in the amount of $1,760,000 may also be determined by subtracting unrealized intercompany profit at the end of the year on upstream sales from the reported net assets of S Company as presented in Illustration 5-10.

ILLUSTRATION 5-10
Alternate Calculation of the Noncontrolling Interest
in Consolidated Net Assets

Total assets—S Company	$2,690,000
Total liabilities—S Company	(805,000)
Reported net assets—S Company	1,885,000
End of year unrealized intercompany profit on upstream sales	(125,000)
Realized net assets—S Company	$1,760,000
Noncontrolling interest in consolidated net assets (.20 × $1,760,000)	$ 352,000

The noncontrolling interest in combined income is calculated after subtracting end-of-year unrealized intercompany profit and adding intercompany profit realized during the current year to the net income reported by the subsidiary, as presented in Illustration 5-11. If the sale of merchandise had been downstream rather than upstream, the amount of subsidiary income included in combined income would not be affected by the workpaper entries related to unrealized intercompany profit, and no adjustment would be necessary in the calculation of the noncontrolling interest in combined income.

COST BASIS ANALYSIS OF CONSOLIDATED NET INCOME AND CONSOLIDATED RETAINED EARNINGS

In Chapter 4, the analytical calculations of consolidated net income and consolidated retained earnings were refined to accommodate the effect of the amortization of the difference between cost and book value. These analyses must now be further refined to accommodate the effect of unrealized intercompany profit.

ILLUSTRATION 5-11
Calculation of the Noncontrolling Interest in Combined Income

Reported net income—S Company	$140,000
Less end-of-year unrealized profit on upstream intercompany sales	(125,000)
Add intercompany profit on upstream sales realized during the current year	100,000
Amount of S Company income included in combined income	$115,000
Noncontrolling interest in combined income (.20 × $115,000)	$ 23,000

Consolidated Net Income

Consolidated net income is the parent company's income from its independent operations that has been realized in transactions with third parties plus (minus) its share of subsidiary income (loss) that has been realized in transactions with third parties plus or minus adjustments for the period relating to the amortization of the difference between cost and book value.

On the basis of Illustration 5-8, the analytical calculation of consolidated net income for the year ended December 31, 1996, is demonstrated in Illustration 5-12.

ILLUSTRATION 5-12
Calculation of Consolidated Net Income
For Year Ended December 31, 1996

P Company's net income from its independent operations ($454,000 reported income less $48,000 in subsidiary dividend income)		$406,000
Less unrealized profit on 1996 sales to S Company		(–0–)
Plus profit on prior year's sales to S Company realized in transactions with third parties in 1996		–0–
P Company's income from its independent operations that has been realized in transactions with third parties		406,000
Reported income of S Company	$140,000	
Less unrealized profit on 1996 sales to P Company	(125,000)	
Plus profit on prior year's sales to P Company realized in transactions with third parties in 1996	100,000	
Income of S Company that has been realized in transactions with third parties	$115,000	
P Company's share thereof (.8 × $115,000)		92,000
Less amortization of the difference between cost and book value		(–0–)
Consolidated net income		$498,000

Consolidated Retained Earnings

Consolidated retained earnings is the parent company's cost basis retained earnings that have been realized in transactions with third parties plus (minus) the parent company's share of the increase (decrease) in subsidiary retained earnings that has been realized in transactions with third parties from the date of acquisition to the current date plus or minus the cumulative effect of adjustments to date relating to the amortization of the difference between cost and book value.

On the basis of Illustration 5-8, the analytical calculation of consolidated retained earnings on December 31, 1996, is demonstrated in Illustration 5-13.

ILLUSTRATION 5-13
Calculation of Consolidated Retained Earnings
December 31, 1996

P Company's retained earnings on 12/31/96		$2,100,000
Less the amount of P Company's retained earnings that has not been realized in transactions with third parties		–0–
P Company's retained earnings that have been realized in transactions with third parties		2,100,000
Increase in retained earnings of S Company from date of acquisition to 12/31/96 ($885,000 − $700,000)	$185,000	
Less unrealized profit on 1996 sales to P Company included in S Company's retained earnings on 12/31/96	(125,000)	
Increase in retained earnings of S Company since acquisition that has been realized in transactions with third parties	$ 60,000	
P Company's share thereof (.80 × $60,000)		48,000
Less cumulative amount of the amortization of the difference between cost and book value:		–0–
Consolidated retained earnings 12/31/96		$2,148,000

To illustrate all aspects of the analytical calculations of consolidated net income and consolidated retained earnings, assume that:

1. P Company acquired 80% of the voting stock of S Company on January 1, 1993, when S Company's retained earnings amounted to $150,000.

2. The difference between cost and book value on the date of acquisition was assigned as follows:

Land	$50,000
Equipment (10 year life)	20,000
Excess of cost over fair value	40,000

3. S Company reported retained earnings of $260,000 on January 1, 1996, and $320,000 on December 31, 1996.

4. S Company reported net income of $90,000 and declared dividends of $30,000 in 1996.

5. P Company reported net income in 1996 in the amount of $724,000 and retained earnings on December 31, 1996, of $3,500,000.

6. There were no intercompany sales prior to 1995 and unrealized profits on January 1 and on December 31, 1996, resulting from intercompany sales are as summarized below.

	UNREALIZED INTERCOMPANY PROFIT ON	
RESULTING FROM	1/1/96	12/31/96
Sales by S Company to P Company	$10,000	$ 5,000
Sales by P Company to S Company	15,000	20,000

Analytical calculations of consolidated net income for the year ended December 31, 1996, and consolidated retained earnings on December 31, 1996 are presented in Illustration 5-14 and Illustration 5-15 respectively.

ILLUSTRATION 5-14
Calculation of Consolidated Net Income
For Year Ended December 31, 1996

P Company's net income from independent operations [$724,000 − (.80 × $30,000)]		$700,000
Less unrealized intercompany profit on 1996 sales to S Company		(20,000)
Plus profit on 1995 sales to S Company realized in transactions with third parties in 1996		15,000
P Company's net income from independent operations that has been realized in transactions with third parties		695,000
Reported net income of S Company	$90,000	
Less unrealized intercompany profit on 1996 sales to P Company	(5,000)	
Plus profit on 1995 sales to P Company realized in transactions with third parties in 1996	10,000	
S Company's net income that has been realized in transactions with third parties	$95,000	
P Company's share thereof (.80 × $95,000)		76,000
Less current year's amortization of the difference between cost and book value:		
Depreciation ($20,000/10)	$ 2,000	
Amortization of excess of cost over fair value ($40,000/40)	1,000	(3,000)
Consolidated net income		$768,000

ILLUSTRATION 5-15
Calculation of Consolidated Retained Earnings
December 31, 1996

P Company's retained earnings on 12/31/96		$3,500,000
Less the amount of P Company's retained earnings that has not been realized in transactions with third parties		(20,000)
P Company's retained earnings that have been realized in transactions with third parties		3,480,000
Increase in retained earnings of S Company from date of acquisition to 12/31/96 ($320,000 − $150,000)	$170,000	
Less unrealized profit included in S Company's retained earnings on 12/31/96	(5,000)	
Increase in reported retained earnings of S Company since acquisition that has been realized in transactions with third parties	$165,000	
P Company's share thereof (.80 × $165,000)		132,000
Less cumulative amount of the amortization of the difference between cost and book value:		
Depreciation [4 years × ($20,000 ÷ 10)]	$ 8,000	
Amortization of excess of cost over fair value [4 years × ($40,000 ÷ 40)]	4,000	(12,000)
Consolidated retained earnings 12/31/96		$3,600,000

CONSOLIDATED STATEMENTS WORKPAPER— PARTIAL EQUITY METHOD

The balances reported by the parent company in income, retained earnings, and the investment account differ depending on the method used by the parent company to record its investment. As illustrated in Chapters 3 and 4, however, the method used by the parent company to record its investment has no affect on the consolidated balances. To illustrate consolidation procedures when the parent company records its investment using the partial equity method, assume the following:

1. P Company acquires an 80% interest in S Company on January 1, 1995, for $1,360,000, at which time S Company has capital stock of $1,000,000 and retained earnings of $700,000.

2. In 1995, S Company reported net income of $125,000 and declared dividends of $20,000.

3. In 1996, S Company reported net income of $140,000 and declared dividends of $60,000.

4. P Company uses the partial equity method to account for its investment in S Company.

5. S Company sells merchandise to P Company as follows:

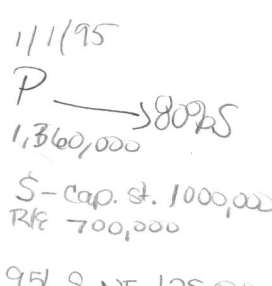

YEAR	TOTAL SALES OF S COMPANY TO P COMPANY	INTERCOMPANY MERCHANDISE IN 12/31 INVENTORY OF P COMPANY	UNREALIZED INTERCOMPANY PROFIT (25% OF SELLING PRICE)
1995	$ 700,000	$400,000	$100,000
1996	1,000,000	500,000	125,000

Entries on Books of P Company

Entries recorded on the books of P Company under the partial equity method are as follows:

1995

(1) Investment in S Company	1,360,000	
Cash		1,360,000
To record purchase of 80% interest in S Company.		
(2) Cash	16,000	
Investment in S Company		16,000
To record dividends received (.80 × $20,000).		
(3) Investment in S Company	100,000	
Equity in Subsidiary Income		100,000
To record equity in subsidiary income (.80 × $125,000).		

1996

(4) Cash	48,000	
Investment in S Company		48,000
To record dividends received (.80 × $60,000).		
(5) Investment in S Company	112,000	
Equity in Subsidiary Income		112,000
To record equity in subsidiary income (.80 × $140,000).		

After these entries are posted, the investment account will appear as follows:

INVESTMENT IN S COMPANY

(1) Cost	1,360,000	(2) Dividends	16,000
(3) Subsidiary Income	100,000		
12/31/95 Balance	1,444,000		
(5) Subsidiary Income	112,000	(4) Dividends	48,000
12/31/96 Balance	1,508,000		

A consolidated statements workpaper under the partial equity method for the year ended December 31, 1996, is presented in Illustration 5-16. Workpaper entries in Illustration 5-16 are presented in general journal form as follows:

(1) Equity in Subsidiary Income	112,000	
Dividends Declared		48,000
Investment in S Company		64,000
To reverse the effect of parent company entries during the year for subsidiary dividends and income.		
(2) Sales	1,000,000	
Purchases (Cost of Sales)		1,000,000
To eliminate intercompany sales.		
(3) 12/31 Inventory—Income Statement (Cost of Sales)	125,000	
Inventory		125,000
To eliminate unrealized intercompany profit in ending inventory.		

Partial Equity Method
80% Owned Subsidiary
Upstream Sale of Inventory

ILLUSTRATION 5-16
Consolidated Statements Workpaper
P Company and Subsidiary
For Year Ended December 31, 1996

	P COMPANY	S COMPANY	ELIMINATIONS DR.	ELIMINATIONS CR.	NONCONTROLLING INTEREST	CONSOLIDATED BALANCES
INCOME STATEMENT						
Sales	3,546,000	2,020,000	(2) 1,000,000			4,566,000
Equity in Subsidiary Income	112,000		(1) 112,000			
Total Revenue	3,658,000	2,020,000				4,566,000
Inventory 1/1	480,000	310,000		(4) 100,000		690,000
Purchases	2,070,000	1,250,000		(2) 1,000,000		2,320,000
	2,550,000	1,560,000				3,010,000
Inventory 12/31	510,000	360,000	(3) 125,000			745,000
Cost of Goods Sold	2,040,000	1,200,000				2,265,000
Other Expenses	1,100,000	680,000				1,780,000
Total Cost and Expense	3,140,000	1,880,000				4,045,000
Net/Combined Income	518,000	140,000				521,000
Noncontrolling Interest in Income					23,000	(23,000)*
Net Income to Retained Earnings	518,000	140,000	1,237,000	1,100,000	23,000	498,000
RETAINED EARNINGS STATEMENT						
1/1 Retained Earnings						
P Company	1,880,000		(4) 80,000			1,800,000
S Company		805,000	(4) 20,000		141,000	
			(5) 644,000			
Net Income from above	518,000	140,000	1,237,000	1,100,000	23,000	498,000
Dividends Declared						
P Company	(150,000)					(150,000)
S Company		(60,000)		(1) 48,000	(12,000)	
12/31 Retained Earnings to Balance Sheet	2,248,000	885,000	1,981,000	1,148,000	152,000	2,148,000
BALANCE SHEET						
Inventory	510,000	360,000		(3) 125,000		745,000
Investment in S Company	1,508,000			(1) 64,000		
				(5) 1,444,000		
Other Assets	5,450,000	2,330,000				7,780,000
Total	7,468,000	2,690,000				8,525,000
Liabilities	2,220,000	805,000				3,025,000
Capital Stock						
P Company	3,000,000					3,000,000
S Company		1,000,000	(5) 800,000		200,000	
Retained Earnings from above	2,248,000	885,000	1,981,000	1,148,000	152,000	2,148,000
Noncontrolling Interest in Net Assets					352,000	352,000
Total Liabilities and Equity	7,468,000	2,690,000	2,781,000	2,781,000		8,525,000

*.20 ($140,000 − $125,000 + $100,000) = $23,000.
　(1) To reverse the effect of parent company entries during the year for subsidiary dividends and income.
　　(2) To eliminate intercompany sales.
　　(3) To eliminate unrealized intercompany profit in ending inventory.

　(4) To recognize profit realized during year and to reduce the controlling and noncontrolling interests for their shares of unrealized intercompany profit at beginning of year.
　　(5) To eliminate investment account.

(4) Beginning Retained Earnings—P Company		
(.80 × $100,000)	80,000	
Beginning Retained Earnings—S Company	20,000	
(.20 × $100,000)		
1/1 Inventory—Income Statement (Cost of Sales)		100,000
To recognize intercompany profit in beginning inventory realized during the year and to reduce controlling and noncontrolling interest for their share of unrealized intercompany profit at beginning of year.		

Entries (2), (3), and (4) are the same as the corresponding entries in Illustration 5-8 [investment recorded at cost].

(5) Beginning Retained Earnings—S Company		
(.80 × $805,000)	644,000	
Capital Stock—S Company (.80 × $1,000,000)	800,000	
Investment in S Company ($1,508,000 − $64,000)		1,444,000
To eliminate investment account.		

This entry is the same as Entry (6) in Illustration 5-8 [investment recorded at cost].

Observe that the consolidated balances in Illustration 5-16 are the same as those in Illustration 5-8 (cost method workpaper). However, when the parent company records its investment using the partial equity method, Entry (1) in Illustration 5-16 replaces the cost method entries to establish reciprocity and to eliminate dividend income [entries (1) and (5) in Illustration 5-8]. Most importantly, a comparison of entries (2), (3), and (4) in Illustration 5-16 with entries (2), (3), and (4) in Illustration 5-8 demonstrates that the workpaper entries to eliminate intercompany sales and unrealized intercompany profit are the same regardless of whether the investment is recorded using the cost method or the partial equity method.

PARTIAL EQUITY METHOD ANALYSIS OF CONSOLIDATED NET INCOME AND CONSOLIDATED RETAINED EARNINGS

The analytical calculation of consolidated net income is independent of the method used by the parent company to record its investment. As stated earlier, *consolidated net income is the parent company's income from its independent operations that has been realized in transactions with third parties plus (minus) its share of reported subsidiary income (loss) that has been realized in transactions with third parties plus or minus adjustments for the period relating to the amortization of the difference between cost and book value.*

On the basis of Illustration 5-16, the analytical calculation of consolidated net income for the year ended December 31, 1996, is demonstrated in Illustration 5-17.

When the parent company uses the partial equity method to record its investment, the parent company's share of subsidiary income since acquisition is already included in the parent company's reported retained earnings. Consequently, *consolidated retained earnings is calculated as the parent company's recorded partial equity basis retained earnings that has been realized in transactions with third parties plus or minus the cumulative effect of the adjustments to date relating to the amortization of the difference between cost and book value.*

On the basis of Illustration 5-16, the analytical calculation of consolidated retained earnings on December 31, 1996, is demonstrated in Illustration 5-18.

ILLUSTRATION 5-17
Calculation of Consolidated Net Income
For Year Ended December 31, 1996

P Company's net income from its independent operations ($518,000 reported net income less $112,000 Equity is S Company Income included therein)		$406,000
Less unrealized profit on 1996 sales to S Company		(–0–)
Plus profit on prior year's sales to S Company realized in transactions with third parties in 1996		–0–
P Company's income from its independent operations that has been realized in transactions with third parties		406,000
Reported Income of S Company	$140,000	
Less unrealized profit on 1996 sales to P Company	(125,000)	
Plus profit on prior year's sales to P Company realized in transactions with third parties in 1996	100,000	
Income of S Company that has been realized in transactions with third parties	$115,000	
P Company's share thereof (.8 × $115,000)		92,000
Less amortization of the difference between cost and book value		(–0–)
Consolidated net income		$498,000

ILLUSTRATION 5-18
Calculation of Consolidated Retained Earnings
December 31, 1996

P Company's retained earnings on December 31, 1996	$2,248,000
Less 100% of unrealized profit on downstream sales on December 31, 1996	(–0–)
Less P Company's share of unrealized profit on upstream sales on December 31, 1996 (.80 × $125,000)	(100,000)
P Company's retained earnings on December 31, 1996, that have been realized in transactions with third parties	2,148,000
Less cumulative amortization of the difference between cost and book value	(–0–)
Consolidated retained earnings on December 31, 1996	$2,148,000

SUMMARY OF WORKPAPER ENTRIES RELATING TO INTERCOMPANY SALES OF MERCHANDISE

Consolidated statement workpaper eliminating entries for intercompany sales of merchandise are summarized in Illustration 5-19. The entries are the same whether the parent company uses the cost method or the partial equity method to record is investment. However, the form of the workpaper entry for unrealized profit in beginning inventories differs as between upstream and downstream sales.

ILLUSTRATION 5-19
Intercompany Profit—Inventories
Summary of Workpaper Elimination Entries

SELLING AFFILIATE IS PARENT OR WHOLLY OWNED SUBSIDIARY	SELLING AFFILIATE IS A LESS THAN WHOLLY OWNED SUBSIDIARY

Sales
   Cost of Sales
      To eliminate intercompany sales.
	SAME

Cost of Sales
   Inventory (Balance Sheet)
      To eliminate intercompany profit in
      ending inventory.
	SAME

Beginning Retained Earnings—P
 	
   Cost of Sales
To recognize intercompany profit in ***beginning inventory*** realized during the current year and to adjust beginning consolidated retained earnings for the amount of unrealized profit at the beginning of the year.
	Beginning Retained Earnings—P
	Beginning Retained Earnings—S
	   Cost of Sales
	To recognize the intercompany profit in ***beginning inventory*** realized during the current year and to adjust the controlling and noncontrolling interest for their shares of the unrealized profit at the beginning of the year.

INTERCOMPANY PROFIT PRIOR TO PARENT–SUBSIDIARY AFFILIATION

Generally accepted accounting standards are silent as to the appropriate treatment of unrealized profit on assets that result from sales between companies prior to affiliation (preaffiliation profit). The question is whether or not preaffiliation profit should be eliminated in consolidation. In our opinion, workpaper entries eliminating preaffiliation profit are inappropriate.

If the selling company is the new subsidiary, the profit recognized by it prior to its acquisition is implicitly considered in determining the book value of the interest acquired by the parent company. Accordingly, such profit is automatically eliminated from consolidated retained earnings in the investment elimination entry. A second elimination would therefore result in a double reduction of the amount of preaffiliation profit from consolidated retained earnings on the date of acquisition. When the assets are sold to third parties in subsequent years, consolidated net income would be increased by a corresponding amount, thus restoring the amount of the second reduction to consolidated retained earnings. The net result is to make an unwarranted reduction of consolidated retained earnings on the date of acquisition in order to report preacquisition profit in consolidated net income in years subsequent to affiliation that has already been reported by the subsidiary prior to affiliation. In our opinion such effects lack both conceptual and practical merit.

If the selling company is the parent, the preaffiliation profit will ultimately be included in consolidated retained earnings in any case. However, a reduction of such profit from consolidated retained earnings on the date of affiliation simply results in the inclusion of the profit in the consolidated net income of subsequent years. Again, the effect of the elimination would be to report the profit twice, once before affiliation and once after affiliation. Again, we perceive no conceptual or practical merit in procedures that produce such a result. Support for the elimination of preaffiliation profit is based primarily on the application of conservatism to the valuation of consolidated assets on the date of acquisition.

ALTERNATIVE WORKPAPER FORMATS

A variety of workpaper formats may be used in the preparation of consolidated financial statements. They may be classified generally into two categories, the three-division workpaper format used in this text, and the trial balance format. In the three-divisional format the account balances of the individual firms are first arranged into financial statement format. In contrast, in the trial balance format, columns are provided for the trial balances, the elimination entries, and normally, each financial statement to be prepared, except for the statement of cash flows.

The consolidated balances derived in a workpaper are the same regardless of the format selected. The statement preparer with a sound understanding of consolidation principles should be able to adapt quite easily to alternative workpaper formats. However, the reader may want to develop a familiarity with the trial balance format, since this format is sometimes preprinted on forms to be used in solving CPA examination problems. Although it would probably be acceptable to classify the trial balance into the three-divisional workpaper format, valuable examination time may be lost in doing so.

To illustrate the trial balance workpaper format, and at the same time to verify that the results are the same as they would be if the three-divisional format were used, the same facts used in the preparation of Illustration 5-8 are assumed in Illustration 5-20. The facts of the case are:

1. P Company acquired an 80% interest in S Company for $1,360,000 on January 1, 1995. On this date S Company reported a retained earnings balance of $700,000.

2. S Company sold merchandise to P Company as follows:

YEAR	TOTAL SALES OF S COMPANY TO P COMPANY	INTERCOMPANY MERCHANDISE IN 12/31 INVENTORY OF P COMPANY	UNREALIZED INTERCOMPANY PROFIT
1995	$ 700,000	$400,000	$100,000
1996	1,000,000	500,000	125,000

3. S Company declared dividends of $60,000 in 1996.

The December 31, 1996, trial balances for P Company and S Company are contained in the first two columns of Illustration 5-20. The steps in the preparation

Cost Method
80% Owned Subsidiary
Trial Balance Format

ILLUSTRATION 5-20
Consolidated Statements Workpaper
P Company and Subsidiary
For the Year Ended December 31, 1996

DEBITS	P COMPANY	S COMPANY	ELIMINATIONS DR.	ELIMINATIONS CR.	CONSOLIDATED INCOME STATEMENT	CONSOLIDATED RETAINED EARNINGS STATEMENT	NONCONTROLLING INTEREST	CONSOLIDATED BALANCE SHEET
Inventory 1/1	480,000	310,000		(4) 100,000	690,000			
Investment in S Company	1,360,000		(1) 84,000	(6) 1,444,000				–0–
Other Assets	5,450,000	2,330,000						7,780,000
Dividends Declared								
P Company	150,000					(150,000)		
S Company		60,000		(5) 48,000			(12,000)	
Purchases	2,070,000	1,250,000		(2) 1,000,000	2,320,000			
Other Expense	1,100,000	680,000			1,780,000			
Total	10,610,000	4,630,000						
Inventory 12/31 (Asset)	510,000	360,000		(3) 125,000				745,000
Total Assets								8,525,000

CREDITS	P COMPANY	S COMPANY	ELIMINATIONS DR.	ELIMINATIONS CR.	CONSOLIDATED INCOME STATEMENT	CONSOLIDATED RETAINED EARNINGS STATEMENT	NONCONTROLLING INTEREST	CONSOLIDATED BALANCE SHEET
Liabilities	2,220,000	805,000						3,025,000
Capital Stock								
P Company	3,000,000							3,000,000
S Company		1,000,000	(6) 800,000				200,000	
1/1 Retained Earnings								
P Company	1,796,000		(4) 80,000	(1) 84,000		1,800,000		
S Company		805,000	(4) 20,000				141,000	
			(6) 644,000					
Sales	3,546,000	2,020,000	(2) 1,000,000		(4,566,000)			
Dividend Income	48,000		(5) 48,000		–0–			
Totals	10,610,000	4,630,000						
Inventory 12/31 (COGS)	510,000	360,000	(3) 125,000		(745,000)			
			2,801,000	2,801,000				
Combined Income					521,000			
Noncontrolling interest in Income [.2($140,000 + $100,000 − $125,000)]					(23,000)		23,000	
Consolidated Net Income					498,000	498,000		
Consolidated Retained Earnings						2,148,000		2,148,000
Noncontrolling Interest in Net Assets							352,000	352,000
Total Liabilities and Equity								8,525,000

(1) To establish reciprocity as of 1/1/96 [($805,000 − $700,000) × .80].
(2) To eliminate intercompany sales.
(3) To eliminate unrealized intercompany profit in ending inventory.
(4) To recognize profit realized during the year and to reduce the controlling and noncontrolling interests at beginning of the year for their shares of unrealized intercompany profit at beginning of year.
(5) To eliminate intercompany dividends.
(6) To eliminate investment account.

of the workpaper are: (1) The trial balances of the individual affiliates are entered in the first two columns. In this case, the debit account balances are separated from the credit account balances. Or the accounts can be listed as they appear in the ledger. A debit column and a credit column may be provided for each firm or one column may be used and the credit balances identified by parentheses. (2) The account balances are analyzed, and the required adjustments and eliminations are entered in the next two vertical columns. (3) The net adjusted balances are extended to the appropriate columns. Separate columns are provided to accumulate the account balances needed for the preparation of the consolidated income statement, retained earnings statement, and balance sheet. In addition, an optional column is provided for the identification of the noncontrolling interest. (4) Once the accounts are extended, the combined income is computed from the income statement column and allocated between the noncontrolling and controlling interests. (5) The consolidated retained earnings balance and total noncontrolling interest can now be computed. The amounts are extended to the final column and should balance the liabilities and equities with the total assets. The reader will observe that these procedures are similar to the preparation of an eight-column worksheet developed to facilitate the preparation of financial statements for an individual firm.

A comparison of the elimination entries in Illustration 5-20 with those of Illustration 5-8 will reveal that the entries are the same, regardless of the form of workpaper used to accumulate the consolidated balances.

Questions

1. Does the elimination of the effects of intercompany sales of merchandise always affect the amount of reported consolidated net income? Explain.

2. Why is the gross profit on intercompany sales, rather than profit after deducting selling and administrative expenses, ordinarily eliminated from consolidated inventory balances?

3. P Company sells inventory costing $100,000 to its subsidiary, S Company, for $150,000. At the end of the current year, one-half of the goods remains in S Company's inventory. Applying the lower of cost or market rule, S Company writes down this inventory to $60,000. What amount of intercompany profit should be eliminated on the consolidated statements workpaper?

4. Are the adjustments to the noncontrolling interest for the effects of intercompany profit eliminations illustrated in this text necessary for fair presentation in accordance with generally accepted accounting principles? Explain.

5. Why are adjustments made to the calculation of the noncontrolling interest for the effects of intercompany profit eliminations and not for the amortization, depreciation, and assignment of the difference between cost and book value?

6. What procedure is used in the consolidated statements workpaper to adjust the noncontrolling interest in consolidated net assets at the beginning of the year for the effects of intercompany profits?

7. What is the essential procedural difference between workpaper eliminating entries for unrealized intercompany profit made when the selling affiliate is a less than wholly owned subsidiary and those made when the selling affiliate is the parent company or a wholly owned subsidiary?

8. Define consolidated net income using the analytical approach.

9. Why is it important to distinguish between upstream and downstream sales in the analysis of intercompany profit eliminations?

10. In what period and in what manner should profits relating to the intercompany sale of merchandise be recognized in the consolidated financial statements?

Exercises

Exercise 5-1

P Company owns 80% of the outstanding stock of S Company. During 1995, S Company reported net income of $525,000 and declared no dividends. At the end of the year, S Company's inventory included $487,500 in unrealized profit on purchases from P Company. Intercompany sales for 1995 totaled $2,700,000.

Required:

Prepare in general journal form all consolidated financial statement workpaper entries necessary at the end of the year to eliminate the effects of the 1995 intercompany sales.

Exercise 5-2

Refer to Exercise 5-1. Calculate the amount of the noncontrolling interest to be deducted from combined income in arriving at 1995 consolidated net income.

Exercise 5-3

Peabody Company owns 90% of the outstanding capital stock of Sloane Company. During 1995 and 1996 Sloane Company sold merchandise to Peabody Company at a markup of 25% of selling price. The selling price of the merchandise sold during the two years was $20,800 and $25,000, respectively. At the end of each year, Peabody Company had in its inventory one-fourth of the goods purchased that year from Sloane Company. Sloane Company reported net income of $30,000 in 1995 and $35,000 in 1996.

Required:

Determine the amount of the noncontrolling interest in combined income to be reported for 1995 and 1996.

Exercise 5-4

On January 1, 1995, Pearce Company purchased an 80% interest in the capital stock of Searl Company for $2,460,000. At that time, Searl Company had capital stock of $1,500,000 and retained earnings of $300,000. The difference between cost and the book value of the 80% interest acquired was attributed to specific assets of Searl Company as follows:

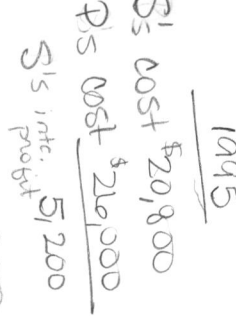

$300,000	to equipment of Searl Company with a five-year remaining life.
150,000	to land held by Searl Company.
90,000	to inventory of Searl Company. Searl uses the FIFO assumption in pricing its inventory.
480,000	that could not be assigned to specific assets or liabilities of Searl Company (amortized over 40 years).
$1,020,000	Total

At year-end 1995 and 1996, Searl had in its inventory merchandise that it had purchased from Pearce at a 25% markup on cost during each year in the following amounts:

1995	$90,000
1996	$105,000

During 1995, Pearce reported net income from independent operations (including sales to affiliates) of $1,500,000, while Searl reported net income of $600,000. In 1996, Pearce's net income from independent operations (including sales to affiliates) was $1,800,000 and Searl's was $750,000.

Required:

Calculate consolidated net income for 1995 and 1996.

Exercise 5-5

Refer to Exercise 5-4. Using the same figures, assume that the merchandise mentioned was included in Pearce's inventory, having been purchased from Searl.

Required:

Calculate consolidated net income for 1995 and 1996.

Exercise 5-6

Payne Company owns all the outstanding common stock of Sierra Company and 80% of the outstanding common stock of Santa Fe Company. The amount of intercompany profit included in the inventories of Payne Company on December 31, 1995, and December 31, 1996, is indicated here:

	INTERCOMPANY PROFIT ON GOODS PURCHASED FROM		
	SIERRA COMPANY	SANTA FE COMPANY	TOTAL
Inventory, 12/31/95	$3,800	$4,600	$8,400
Inventory, 12/31/96	4,800	2,300	7,100

The three companies reported net income from their independent operations (including sales to affiliates) for the year ended December 31, 1996, as follows:

Payne Company	$280,000
Sierra Company	172,000
Santa Fe Company	120,000

Required:

Calculate consolidated net income for the year ended December 31, 1996.

Exercise 5-7

Perkins Company owns 85% of Sheraton Company. Perkins Company sells merchandise to Sheraton Company at 20% above cost. During 1995 and 1996, such sales amounted to $450,000 and $486,000, respectively. At the end of each year, Sheraton Company had in its inventory one-third of the amount of goods purchased from Perkins during that year.

Required:

Prepare the workpaper entries necessary to eliminate the effects of the intercompany sales for 1995 and 1996.

Exercise 5-8

Refer to Exercise 5-7. Using the same figures, assume that the sales were upstream instead of downstream.

Required:

Prepare the workpaper entries necessary to eliminate the effects of the intercompany sales for 1995 and 1996.

Exercise 5-9

Peat Company owns a 90% interest in Seaton Company. The consolidated income statement drafted by the controller of Peat Company appeared as follows:

Peat Company and Subsidiary
Consolidated Income Statement
For Year Ended December 31, 1996

Sales		$14,000,000
Cost of sales	$9,200,000	
Operating expense	1,800,000	11,000,000
Combined income		3,000,000
Less noncontrolling interest in combined income		200,000
Consolidated net income		$ 2,800,000

During your audit you discover that intercompany sales transactions were not reflected in the controller's draft of the consolidated income statement. Information relating to inter-company sales and unrealized intercompany profit is as follows:

	COST	SELLING PRICE	UNSOLD AT YEAR-END
1995 Sales—Seaton to Peat	$1,500,000	$1,800,000	1/3
1996 Sales—Peat to Seaton	900,000	1,400,000	2/5

Required:

Prepare a corrected consolidated income statement for Peat Company and Seaton Company for the year ended December 31, 1996.

Problems

Problem 5-1

Peel Company owns 90% of the common stock of Seacore Company. Seacore Company sells merchandise to Peel Company at 20% above cost. During 1995 and 1996, such sales amounted to $436,000 and $532,000, respectively. At the end of each year, Peel Company had in its inventory one-fourth of the goods purchased from Seacore Company during that year.

Peel Company reported $300,000 in net income from its independent operations in 1995 and 1996. Seacore Company reported net income of $130,000 in each year and did not declare any dividends in any year. There were no intercompany sales prior to 1995.

Required:

A. Prepare in general journal form all entries necessary on the consolidated financial statements workpaper to eliminate the effects of the intercompany sales for each of the years 1995 and 1996.

B. Calculate the amount of noncontrolling interest to be deducted from combined income in the consolidated income statement for 1996.

C. Calculate consolidated net income for 1996.

Problem 5-2

Shell Company, an 85% owned subsidiary of Plaster Company, sells merchandise to Plaster Company at a markup of 20% of selling price. During 1995 and 1996, intercompany sales amounted to $442,500 and $386,250, respectively. At the end of 1995, Plaster had one-half of the goods that it purchased that year from Shell in its ending inventory. Plaster's 1996 ending inventory contained one-fifth of that year's purchases from Shell. There were no intercompany sales prior to 1995.

Plaster had net income in 1995 of $750,000 from its own operations and in 1996 its independent income was $780,000. Shell reported net income of $322,500 and $335,400 for 1995 and 1996, respectively.

Required:

A. Prepare in general journal form all entries necessary on the consolidated financial statement workpapers to eliminate the effects of the intercompany sales for each of the years 1995 and 1996.

B. Calculate the amount of noncontrolling interest to be deducted from combined income in the consolidated income statement for 1996.

C. Calculate consolidated net income for 1996.

Problem 5-3

Peer Company owns 80% of the common stock of Seacrest Company. Peer Company sells merchandise to Seacrest Company at 25% above its cost. During 1995 and 1996 such sales amounted to $265,000 and $475,000, respectively. The 1995 and 1996 ending inventories of Seacrest Company included goods purchased from Peer Company for $125,000 and $170,000, respectively.

Peer Company reported net income from its independent operations (including sales to affiliates) of $450,000 in 1995 and $480,000 in 1996. Seacrest reported net income of $225,000 in 1995 and $275,000 in 1996 and did not declare dividends in either year. There were no intercompany sales prior to 1995.

Required:

A. Prepare in general journal form all entries necessary in the consolidated financial statements workpapers to eliminate the effects of the intercompany sales for each of the years 1995 and 1996.

B. Calculate the amount of noncontrolling interest to be deducted from combined income in the consolidated income statements for 1995 and 1996.

C. Calculate consolidated net income for 1996.

Problem 5-4

Pace Company owns 85% of the outstanding common stock of Sand Company and all the outstanding common stock of Star Company. During 1996, the affiliates engaged in intercompany sales as follows:

Sales of Merchandise

Pace to Sand	$ 40,000
Sand to Pace	60,000
Sand to Star	75,000
Star to Pace	50,000
	$225,000

The following amounts of intercompany profits were included in the December 31, 1995, and December 31, 1996, inventories of the individual companies:

	INTERCOMPANY PROFIT IN DECEMBER 31, 1995, INVENTORY OF			
SELLING COMPANY	PACE	SAND	STAR	TOTAL
Pace Company		$7,000		$ 7,000
Sand Company	$ 5,000		$3,000	8,000
Star Company	8,000			8,000
Total	$13,000	$7,000	$3,000	$23,000

| SELLING COMPANY | PACE | INTERCOMPANY PROFIT IN DECEMBER 31, 1996, INVENTORY OF | | |
		SAND	STAR	TOTAL
Pace Company		$2,000		$ 2,000
Sand Company	$ 6,000		$9,000	15,000
Star Company	4,000			4,000
Total	$10,000	$2,000	$9,000	$21,000

Income from each company's independent operations (including sales to affiliates) for the year ended December 31, 1996, is presented here:

Pace Company	$200,000
Sand Company	150,000
Star Company	125,000

Required:

A. Prepare in general journal form the workpaper entries necessary to eliminate intercompany sales and intercompany profit in the December 31, 1996, consolidated financial statements workpaper.

B. Calculate the balance to be reported in the consolidated income statement for the following line items:
Combined income
Noncontrolling interest in combined income
Consolidated net income

Problem 5-5

Pruitt Corporation owns 90% of the common stock of Sedbrook Company. The stock was purchased for $540,000 on January 1, 1991, when Sedbrook Company's retained earnings were $100,000. Preclosing trial balances for the two companies at December 31, 1995, are presented here:

	PRUITT CORPORATION	SEDBROOK COMPANY
Cash	$ 83,000	$ 80,000
Accounts receivable (net)	213,000	112,500
Inventory 1/1	150,000	110,000
Investment in Sedbrook Co.	540,000	
Other assets	500,000	400,000
Dividends declared	100,000	30,000
Purchases	850,000	350,000
Other expenses	180,000	137,500
Total	$2,616,000	$1,220,000
Accounts payable	$ 70,000	$ 30,000
Other liabilities	75,000	40,000
Common stock	800,000	500,000
Retained earnings	544,000	120,000
Sales	1,100,000	530,000
Dividend income	27,000	
Total	$2,616,000	$1,220,000
Ending inventory	$ 200,000	$ 120,000

The January 1, 1995, inventory of Sedbrook Company includes $30,000 of profit re-corded by Pruitt Corporation on 1994 sales. During 1995, Pruitt Corporation made intercom-pany sales of $200,000 with a markup of 25% on cost. The ending inventory of Sedbrook Company includes goods purchased in 1995 from Pruitt for $50,000.

Required:

A. Prepare the consolidated statements workpaper for the year ended December 31, 1995.

B. Calculate consolidated retained earnings on December 31, 1995, using the analytical approach.

Problem 5-6

Using the information in Problem 5-5, prepare a consolidated statements workpaper using the trial balance format.

Problem 5-7

Paque Corporation owns 90% of the common stock of Segal Company. The stock was pur-chased for $810,000 on January 1, 1991, when Segal Company's retained earnings were $150,000.

Financial data for 1995 are presented here:

	PAQUE CORPORATION	SEGAL COMPANY
Sales	$1,650,000	$ 795,000
Dividend income	54,000	
Total revenue	1,704,000	795,000
Cost of goods sold:		
Beginning inventory	225,000	165,000
Purchases	1,275,000	525,000
Cost of goods available	1,500,000	690,000
Less: Ending inventory	210,000	172,500
Cost of goods sold	1,290,000	517,500
Other expenses	310,500	206,250
Total cost and expense	1,600,500	723,750
Net income	$ 103,500	$ 71,250
1/1 Retained earnings	811,500	180,000
Net income	103,500	71,250
Dividends declared	(150,000)	(60,000)
12/31 Retained earnings	$ 765,000	$ 191,250
Cash	$ 93,000	$ 75,000
Accounts receivable	319,500	168,750
Inventory	210,000	172,500
Investment in Segal Company	810,000	
Other assets	750,000	630,000
Total assets	$2,182,500	$1,046,250

	PAQUE CORPORATION	SEGAL COMPANY
Accounts payable	$ 105,000	$ 45,000
Other current liabilities	112,500	60,000
Capital stock	1,200,000	750,000
Retained earnings	765,000	191,250
Total liabilities and equity	$2,182,500	$1,046,250

The January 1, 1995, inventory of Paque Corporation includes $45,000 of profit recorded by Segal Company on 1994 sales. During 1995, Segal Company made intercompany sales of $300,000 with a markup of 20% of selling price. The ending inventory of Paque Corporation includes goods purchased in 1995 from Segal Company for $75,000.

Required:

A. Prepare the consolidated statements workpaper for the year ended December 31, 1995.

B. Prepare an analytical calculation of consolidated net income for the year ended December 31, 1995.

Problem 5-8

On January 2, 1995, Patten Company purchased a 90% interest in Sterling Company for $1,350,000. At that time Sterling Company had capital stock outstanding of $750,000 and retained earnings of $450,000. The difference between cost and book value was assigned to the following assets:

Inventory	$ 30,000
Plant and equipment (net)	150,000
Excess of cost over fair value	90,000

The plant and equipment had a remaining useful life of 16 years on January 2, 1995. Patten Company amortizes the excess of cost over fair value over 40 years.

During 1995 Sterling sold merchandise with a cost of $900,000 to Patten at a 25% markup above cost. At December 31, 1995, Patten still had merchandise in its inventory that it purchased from Sterling for $562,500.

In 1995, Sterling Company reported net income of $375,000 and declared no dividends.

Required:

A. Prepare in general journal form all entries necessary on the consolidated financial statements workpaper to eliminate the effects of the intercompany sales, to eliminate the investment account, and to assign the difference between cost and book value.

B. Assume that Patten Company reports net income of $1,950,000 from its independent operations. Calculate consolidated net income.

C. Calculate noncontrolling interest in combined income.

Problem 5-9

On January 1, 1994, Perry Company purchased 80% of Selby Company for $960,000. At that time Selby had capital stock outstanding of $400,000 and retained earnings of $400,000.

The fair value of Selby Company's assets and liabilities is equal to their book value except for the following:

	FAIR VALUE	BOOK VALUE
Inventory	$230,000	$155,000
Plant and equipment (10-year life)	800,000	600,000

One-half of the inventory was sold in 1994; the remainder was sold in 1995. Any excess of cost over fair value is to be amortized over a 40-year period.

At the end of 1994, Perry Company had in its ending inventory $54,000 of merchandise it had purchased from Selby Company during the year. Selby Company sold the merchandise at 20% above cost. During 1995, Perry Company sold merchandise to Selby Company for $300,000 at a markup of 20% of the selling price. At December 31, 1995, Selby still had merchandise that it purchased from Perry Company for $78,000 in its inventory.

Financial data for 1995 are presented here:

	PERRY COMPANY	SELBY COMPANY
Sales	$1,385,000	$ 720,000
Dividend income	24,000	
Total revenue	1,409,000	720,000
Cost of goods sold:		
Beginning inventory	210,000	155,000
Purchases	875,000	360,000
Cost of Goods Available	1,085,000	515,000
Less: Ending inventory	400,000	225,000
Cost of goods sold	685,000	290,000
Other expenses	225,000	170,000
Total cost and expense	910,000	460,000
Net Income	$ 499,000	$ 260,000
1/1 Retained earnings	$1,432,700	$ 450,000
Net income	499,000	260,000
Dividends declared	(40,000)	(30,000)
12/31 Retained earnings	$1,891,700	$ 680,000
Cash	$ 90,000	$ 65,000
Accounts receivable (net)	297,000	85,000
Inventory	400,000	225,000
Investment in Selby Company	960,000	
Plant and equipment (net)	880,000	540,000
Other assets (net)	384,000	230,000
Total assets	$3,011,000	$1,145,000
Accounts payable	$ 24,300	$ 25,000
Other liabilities	95,000	40,000
Common stock	1,000,000	400,000
Retained earnings	1,891,700	680,000
Total liabilities and equity	$3,011,000	$1,145,000

Required:

A. Prepare the consolidated statements workpaper for the year ended December 31, 1995.

B. Calculate consolidated retained earnings on December 31, 1995, using the analytical approach.

Problem 5-10

Penn Company owns a 90% interest in Salvador Company and an 80% interest in Sencal Company. Profit remaining in ending inventories from intercompany sales for 1995 and 1996 are indicated below.

	INTERCOMPANY PROFIT IN ENDING INVENTORY OF:			
	1995		1996	
SELLING COMPANY	SALVADOR	SENCAL	SALVADOR	SENCAL
Penn	$8,000	$4,000	$5,000	$ 9,000
Salvador		6,000		10,000
Sencal	5,000		2,000	

Salvador Company reported net income of $50,000 in 1995 and $45,000 in 1996, whereas Sencal Company's net income was $60,000 and $75,000 in 1995 and 1996, respectively.

Penn Company's net income from its own operations (including sales to affiliates) for 1995 and 1996 was $600,000 and $400,000, respectively.

Required:

A. Determine noncontrolling interest in combined income for 1995 and 1996.

B. Calculate consolidated net income for 1995 and 1996.

Problem 5-11

(Note that this is the same problem as Problem 5-5, but assuming the use of the partial equity method.) Pruitt Corporation owns 90% of the common stock of Sedbrook Company. The stock was purchased for $540,000 on January 1, 1991, when Sedbrook Company's retained earnings were $100,000. Preclosing trial balances for the two companies at December 31, 1995, are presented here:

	PRUITT CORPORATION	SEDBROOK COMPANY
Cash	$ 83,000	$ 80,000
Accounts receivable (net)	213,000	112,500
Inventory 1/1	150,000	110,000
Investment in Sedbrook Co.	578,250	
Other assets	500,000	400,000
Dividends declared	100,000	30,000
Purchases	850,000	350,000
Other expenses	180,000	137,500
	$2,654,250	$1,220,000

	PRUITT CORPORATION	SEDBROOK COMPANY
Accounts payable	$ 70,000	$ 30,000
Other liabilities	75,000	40,000
Common stock	800,000	500,000
Retained earnings	562,000	120,000
Sales	1,100,000	530,000
Equity in subsidiary income	47,250	
	$2,654,250	$1,220,000
Ending inventory	$ 200,000	$ 120,000

The January 1, 1995, inventory of Sedbrook Company includes $30,000 of profit recorded by Pruitt Corporation on 1994 sales. During 1995, Pruitt Corporation made intercompany sales of $200,000 with a markup of 25% on cost. The ending inventory of Sedbrook Company includes goods purchased in 1995 from Pruitt for $50,000. Pruitt Company uses the partial equity method to record its investment in Sedbrook Company.

Required:

A. Prepare the consolidated statements workpaper for the year ended December 31, 1995.

B. Calculate consolidated retained earnings on December 31, 1995, using the analytical approach.

C. If you completed Problem 5-5, compare the consolidated balances obtained in part (A) with those obtained in Problem 5-5.

Problem 5-12

Using the information in Problem 5-11, prepare a consolidated statements workpaper using the trial balance format.

Problem 5-13

(Note that this is the same problem as Problem 5-7, but assuming the use of the partial equity method.) Paque Corporation owns 90% of the common stock of Segal Company. The stock was purchased for $810,000 on January 1, 1991, when Segal Company's retained earnings were $150,000.
Financial data for 1995 are presented here:

	PAQUE CORPORATION	SEGAL COMPANY
Sales	$1,650,000	$ 795,000
Equity in subsidiary income	64,125	
Total revenue	1,714,125	795,000
Cost of goods sold:		
Beginning inventory	225,000	165,000
Purchases	1,275,000	525,000
Cost of goods available	1,500,000	690,000
Less: Ending inventory	210,000	172,500
Cost of goods sold	1,290,000	517,500
Other expenses	310,500	206,250
Total cost and expense	1,600,500	723,750
Net income	$ 113,625	$ 71,250

	PAQUE CORPORATION	SEGAL COMPANY
1/1 Retained earnings	838,500	180,000
Net income	113,625	71,250
Dividends declared	(150,000)	(60,000)
12/31 Retained earnings	$ 802,125	$191,250
Cash	$ 93,000	$ 75,000
Accounts receivable	319,500	168,750
Inventory	210,000	172,500
Investment in Segal Company	847,125	
Other assets	750,000	630,000
Total assets	$2,219,625	$1,046,250
Accounts payable	$ 105,000	$ 45,000
Other current liabilities	112,500	60,000
Capital stock	1,200,000	750,000
Retained earnings	802,125	191,250
Total liabilities and equity	$2,219,625	$1,046,250

The January 1, 1995, inventory of Paque Corporation includes $45,000 of profit recorded by Segal Company on 1994 sales. During 1995, Segal Company made intercompany sales of $300,000 with a markup of 20% of selling price. The ending inventory of Paque Corporation includes goods purchased in 1995 from Segal Company for $75,000. Paque Corporation uses the partial equity method to record its investment in Segal Company.

Required:

A. Prepare the consolidated statements workpaper for the year ended December 31, 1995.

B. Calculate consolidated retained earnings on December 31, 1995, using the analytical approach.

C. If you completed Problem 5-7, compare the consolidated balances obtained in part (A) with those obtained in Problem 5-7.

Problem 5-14

(Note that this is the same problem as Problem 5-9, but assuming the use of the partial equity method.) On January 1, 1994, Perry Company purchased 80% of Selby Company for $960,000. At that time Selby had capital stock outstanding of $400,000 and retained earnings of $400,000.

The fair value of Selby Company's assets and liabilities is equal to their book value except for the following:

	FAIR VALUE	BOOK VALUE
Inventory	$230,000	$155,000
Plant and equipment (10-year life)	800,000	600,000

One-half of the inventory was sold in 1994; the remainder was sold in 1995. Any excess of cost over fair value is to be amortized over a 40-year period.

At the end of 1994, Perry Company had in its ending inventory $54,000 of merchandise it had purchased from Selby Company during the year. Selby Company sold the merchandise at 20% above cost. During 1995, Perry Company sold merchandise to Selby Company for $300,000 at a markup of 20% of the selling price. At December 31, 1995, Selby still had merchandise that it purchased from Perry Company for $78,000 in its inventory.

Financial data for 1995 are presented here:

	PERRY COMPANY	SELBY COMPANY
Sales	$1,385,000	$ 720,000
Equity in subsidiary income	208,000	
Total revenue	1,593,000	720,000
Cost of goods sold:		
Beginning inventory	210,000	155,000
Purchases	875,000	360,000
Cost of goods available	1,085,000	515,000
Less: Ending inventory	400,000	225,000
Cost of goods sold	685,000	290,000
Other expenses	225,000	170,000
Total cost and expense	910,000	460,000
Net income	$ 683,000	$ 260,000
1/1 Retained earnings	$1,472,700	$ 450,000
Net income	683,000	260,000
Dividends declared	(40,000)	(30,000)
12/31 Retained earnings	$2,115,700	$ 680,000
Cash	$ 90,000	$ 65,000
Accounts receivable (net)	297,000	85,000
Inventory	400,000	225,000
Investment in Selby Company	1,184,000	
Plant and equipment (net)	880,000	540,000
Other assets (net)	384,000	230,000
Total assets	$3,235,000	$1,145,000
Accounts payable	$ 24,300	$ 25,000
Other liabilities	95,000	40,000
Common stock	1,000,000	400,000
Retained earnings	2,115,700	680,000
Total liabilities and equity	$3,235,000	$1,145,000

Required:

A. Prepare the consolidated statements workpaper for the year ended December 31, 1995.

B. Calculate consolidated retained earnings on December 31, 1995, using the analytical approach.

C. If you completed Problem 5-9, compare the consolidated balances obtained in part (A) with those obtained in Problem 5-9.

Problem 5-15

On January 1, 1993, Paul Company purchased 80% of the voting stock of Simon Company for $1,360,000 when Simon Company had retained earnings and capital stock in the amounts of $450,000 and $1,000,000, respectively. The difference between cost and book value is amortized over 25 years. Simon Company's retained earnings amount to $780,000 on January 1, 1996, and $960,000 on December 31, 1996. In 1996, Simon Company reported net income of $270,000 and declared dividends of $90,000. Paul Company reported net income from independent operations in 1996 in the amount of $700,000 and retained earnings on December 31, 1996, of $1,500,000. During 1996, intercompany sales of merchandise from Paul to Simon amounted to $70,000 and from Simon to Paul were $50,000. Unrealized profits on January 1 and on December 31, 1996, resulting from intercompany sales are as summarized here:

	UNREALIZED INTERCOMPANY PROFIT ON	
RESULTING FROM	1/1/96	12/31/96
Sales by Simon Company to Paul Company	$20,000	$10,000
Sales by Paul Company to Simon Company	30,000	5,000

There were no intercompany sales prior to 1995.

Required:

A. Prepare in general journal form the entries necessary in the December 31, 1996, consolidated statements workpaper to eliminate the effects of the intercompany sales.

B. Calculate consolidated net income for the year ended December 31, 1996.

C. Calculate consolidated retained earnings on December 31, 1996.

D. Calculate noncontrolling interest in combined income for the year ended December 31, 1996.

6

ELIMINATION OF UNREALIZED PROFIT ON INTERCOMPANY SALES OF PROPERTY AND EQUIPMENT

Affiliated companies may recognize profit or loss on intercompany sales of non-depreciable property or on intercompany sales of depreciable property or equipment. They also may recognize revenue or expense in connection with intercompany loans, intercompany service fees, or intercompany operating leases. As with intercompany sales of merchandise discussed in Chapter 5, workpaper entries are also necessary in these situations in order to present related balances in the consolidated financial statements as if the intercompany transactions had never occurred.

In this chapter, the effects on the preparation of consolidated financial statements of intercompany transactions involving property and equipment, loans, services, and operating leases are described and illustrated.

Reporting complications relating to accounting for the difference between acquisition cost and book value are avoided in all illustrations by assuming that all acquisitions are made at the book value of the acquired interest in net assets, and that the book value of the subsidiary net assets is equal to their fair value on the date the parent company's interest is acquired. It is also assumed that the affiliates file consolidated income tax returns. Deferred tax consequences that may arise in the consolidated financial statements because of the elimination of unrealized intercompany profit or because of undistributed subsidiary income are discussed in Chapter 7.

INTERCOMPANY SALES OF NONDEPRECIABLE PROPERTY

When there have been intercompany sales of nondepreciable property, workpaper entries are necessary to accomplish the following financial reporting objectives in the consolidated financial statements.

- To include gains or losses on the sale of nondepreciable property in combined income only at the time such property is **sold to parties outside the affiliated group** and in an amount equal to the difference between the cost of the property to the affiliated group and the proceeds received from outsiders.
- To present nondepreciable property in the consolidated balance sheet at **its cost to the affiliated group.**
- To allocate combined income to the noncontrolling interest based on its share of the amount of subsidiary income that is included in combined income.

Workpaper procedures to accomplish these objectives as well as to equate beginning consolidated retained earnings with the amount of consolidated retained earnings reported at the end of the prior reporting period are presented here.

Assume that S Company (an 80% owned subsidiary) sells to P Company for $500,000 a parcel of land that cost S Company $300,000. Entries made on the books of each affiliate to record this intercompany sale are presented below.

ENTRY ON BOOKS OF S COMPANY			ENTRY ON BOOKS OF P COMPANY		
Cash	500,000		Land	500,000	
Land		300,000	Cash		500,000
Gain on Sale					
of Land		200,000			

In the year of the intercompany sale, a workpaper entry is necessary to eliminate the $200,000 gain reported by S Company and to reduce the land balance from the $500,000 recorded on the books of P Company to its $300,000 cost to the affiliated group. Both objectives are accomplished in one workpaper entry as follows:

Workpaper Entry in Year of Intercompany Sale		
Gain on Sale of Land	200,000	
Land		200,000

If S Company reported $900,000 in income, the noncontrolling interest in combined income is $140,000 [.20 × ($900,000 − $200,000) = $140,000]. The noncontrolling interest in combined income is based on the amount of income of S Company that was realized in transactions with third parties ($900,000 in reported income less $200,000 unrealized gain on sale of land). Stated another way, the noncontrolling interest in combined income is based on the amount of income from the subsidiary that ended up being included in combined income. Since $200,000 of subsidiary income is excluded from combined income, the noncontrolling interest in combined income is reduced by $40,000 (.2 × $200,000).

In subsequent years, so long as P Company owns the land, it will be reported in the statements of P Company at the intercompany selling price of $500,000. However, in the consolidated balance sheet, the land should continue to be reported at its cost to the affiliated group of $300,000. In addition since, in the year of the sale combined income was reduced by $200,000, consolidated net income and consolidated retained earnings were reduced by $160,000 (.8 × $200,000). The workpaper entry necessary in all subsequent years, until the land is disposed of by P Company, is as follows:

Workpaper Entry in Subsequent Years		
Beginning Retained Earnings—P Company	160,000	
Beginning Retained Earnings—S Company	40,000	
Land		200,000

The $200,000 of unrealized profit is allocated between the controlling interest ($160,000 = .8 × $200,000) and the noncontrolling interest ($40,000 = .2 × $200,000) based on their percentage interests in the selling affiliate. As in Chapter 5, the workpaper procedure to adjust the controlling interest (consolidated retained earnings) is to debit the beginning retained earnings of the parent company and the workpaper procedure to adjust the noncontrolling interest is to debit the beginning retained earnings of the subsidiary. If the intercompany sale of the land has been downstream, the entire $200,000 would be an adjustment to the controlling interest and debited to the beginning retained earnings of the parent company.

If and when the land is sold by P Company to a nonaffiliate, P company will use the $500,000 carrying value of the land on its books to calculate any gain or loss. For example, if P Company sells the land it purchased for $500,000 from S Company to an outside party for $550,000, P company will record a gain on the sale of $50,000 ($550,000 − $500,000). However, the cost of the land to the affiliated group is $300,000, and the gain to the affiliated group confirmed by its sale for $550,000 to a nonaffiliate is $250,000 ($550,000 − $300,000). The workpaper entry to adjust the $50,000 gain reported by P Company to the $250,000 gain realized on the sale by the affiliated group is as follows:

Workpaper Entry in Year Land is Sold to Nonaffiliated Company		
Beginning Retained Earnings—P Company	160,000	
Beginning Retained Earnings—S Company	40,000	
Gain on Sale of Land		200,000

The debits to beginning retained earnings are the same as if the sale to outsiders had not occurred. In the year of the sale of the land to outsiders, it is still necessary to adjust *beginning* consolidated retained earnings (Beginning Retained Earnings—P Company) in order to equate *beginning* consolidated retained earnings in the year of sale with the consolidated retained earnings reported at the end of the prior year.

In the year of the sale of the land to outsiders, combined income is increased by $200,000 and consolidated net income, consolidated retained earnings, and non-controlling interest in combined income are increased accordingly. At the end of the year of the sale to outsiders, the amount of profit on the sale of the land recorded on the books of the affiliates and the amount of profit on the sale of the land recognized in the consolidated financial statements are equal and are calculated below.

PROFIT RECORDED ON BOOKS OF AFFILIATES

S Company on sale to P Company	$200,000
P Company on sale to nonaffiliate	50,000
Total	$250,000

PROFIT REPORTED IN CONSOLIDATED INCOME
STATEMENT IN YEAR OF SALE

Reported by P Company	$ 50,000
Workpaper adjustment	200,000
Reported in combined income	$250,000

Thus no workpaper entries relating to the intercompany sale of land are necessary in years subsequent to the sale of the land to parties outside the affiliated group.

INTERCOMPANY SALES OF DEPRECIABLE PROPERTY

A company may sell property or equipment to an affiliate for a price that differs from its book value. In the year of the sale, the amount of intercompany profit (loss) recorded by the selling affiliate must be eliminated in consolidation. After the sale, the purchasing affiliate will calculate depreciation on the basis of *its* cost. The depreciation recorded by the purchasing affiliate will, therefore, be excessive (deficient) from a consolidated point of view and will also require adjustment. From the point of view of the consolidated entity, the intercompany profit (loss) is considered to be realized as a consequence of the use of the property or equipment in the generation of revenue. Because such use is measured by depreciation, the recognition of the realization of intercompany profit (loss) is accomplished through depreciation adjustments.

When there have been intercompany sales of depreciable property, workpaper entries are necessary to accomplish the following financial reporting objectives in the consolidated financial statements.

- To report as gains or losses in the consolidated income statement only those that result from the sale of depreciable property *to parties outside the affiliated group*.

- To present property in the consolidated balance sheet at *its cost to the affiliated group*.
- To present accumulated depreciation in the consolidated balance sheet based on the *cost to the affiliated group* of the related assets.
- To present depreciation expense in the consolidated income statement based on the *cost to the affiliated group* of the related assets.
- To allocate combined income to the noncontrolling interest based on its share of the amount of subsidiary income that is included in combined income.

Workpaper procedures to accomplish these objectives as well as to equate beginning consolidated retained earnings with the amount of consolidated retained earnings reported at the end of the prior reporting period are presented here.

Illustration of Basic Workpaper Elimination Entries

The basic workpaper eliminating entries required because of intercompany sales of depreciable property are illustrated using the following simplifying assumptions.

1. On January 1, 1995, P Company sells to S Company, a 90% owned subsidiary, equipment with a book value of $750,000 (original cost $1,350,000 and accumulated depreciation of $600,000) for $900,000.

2. On the date of the sale, the equipment has an estimated remaining useful life of three years, has no residual value, and is depreciated using the straight-line method.

3. No other equipment is owned by S Company or P Company.

The entries on the books of P Company and S Company to record the intercompany sale are summarized in general journal form below.

P COMPANY

Cash	900,000	
Accumulated Depreciation	600,000	
Equipment		1,350,000
Gain on Sale of Equipment		150,000

S COMPANY

Equipment	900,000	
Cash		900,000

Year of the Intercompany Sale Balances on December 31, 1995, of the accounts of the affiliated companies affected by this transaction are presented in Illustration 6-1.

ILLUSTRATION 6-1
Partial Consolidated Statements Workpaper
Elimination of Intercompany Sale of Equipment
Year of Intercompany Sale
December 31, 1995

INCOME STATEMENT	P COMPANY	S COMPANY	ELIMINATIONS DR.	ELIMINATIONS CR.	CONSOLIDATED BALANCES
Gain on Sale of Equipment	(150,000)		(1) 150,000		
Depreciation Expense		300,000		(2) 50,000	250,000
BALANCE SHEET					
Equipment		900,000	(3) 600,000	(1) 150,000	1,350,000
Accumulated Depreciation		(300,000)	(2) 50,000	(3) 600,000	(850,000)

Workpaper entries in the year of the sale take the following form:

(1) Gain on Sale of Equipment	150,000	
Equipment		150,000

P Company will have recorded a gain of $150,000 on the intercompany sale and S Company will have recorded the equipment at $900,000. From the point of view of the consolidated entity, however, no gain should be reported on the intercompany sale, and equipment should be reported at cost to the affiliated group. Thus, both the gain and the recorded value of the equipment must be reduced by $150,000 in the determination of consolidated balances. The effect of this entry is to decrease combined net income by $150,000.

(2) Accumulated Depreciation	50,000	
Depreciation Expense		50,000

The purchasing affiliate (S Company) will record depreciation in the amount of $300,000 ($900,000 ÷ 3) each year. From the point of view of the consolidated entity, only $250,000 ($750,000 ÷ 3) in depreciation on the equipment should be recognized. The effect of this entry is to increase combined net income by $50,000 and thus treat an equivalent amount of intercompany profit as realized through the use of the equipment.

(3) Equipment	600,000	
Accumulated Depreciation		600,000

Without this entry equipment would be reported in the consolidated balance sheet at $750,000 and accumulated depreciation would be reported at $250,000. Had the intercompany sale never occurred, however, P Company would have reported equipment of $1,350,000 and accumulated depreciation of $850,000 [$600,000 + ($750,000 ÷ 3)]. In order to show equipment (gross) and accumulated depreciation in the consolidated financial statements as they would have appeared if the intercompany sale had never taken place, they must be increased by *the amount of accumulated depreciation that was removed from the books of the selling affiliate on the date of the intercompany sale.*

As a result of these adjustments, the gain of $150,000 is eliminated and consolidated depreciation ($250,000), consolidated equipment ($1,350,000), and consolidated accumulated depreciation ($850,000) are all based on the original cost of the equipment to the affiliated group.

The net effect of these adjustments is to reduce combined income by $100,000 (the original $150,000 of intercompany profit recorded by P Company less the $50,000 of intercompany profit that is considered realized during the year through the utilization of the equipment by S Company).

Years Subsequent to the Year of the Intercompany Sale Balances of the affected accounts of the affiliated companies on December 31, 1996, are presented in Illustration 6-2.

ILLUSTRATION 6-2
Partial Consolidated Statements Workpaper
Elimination of Unrealized Profit on Intercompany Sale of Equipment
Year Subsequent to Intercompany Sale
December 31, 1996

	P COMPANY	S COMPANY	ELIMINATIONS DR.	ELIMINATIONS CR.	CONSOLIDATED BALANCES
INCOME STATEMENT					
Depreciation Expense		300,000		(2) 50,000	250,000
RETAINED EARNINGS STATEMENT					
1/1 Retained Earnings P Company (Consolidated)	2,000,000		(1) 100,000		1,900,000
BALANCE SHEET					
Equipment		900,000	(3) 600,000	(1) 150,000	1,350,000
Accumulated Depreciation		(600,000)	(1) 50,000	(3) 600,000	(1,100,000)
			(2) 50,000		

In years after the year of the intercompany sale, the basic workpaper elimination entries related to the intercompany sale are as follows:

(1) Beginning Retained Earnings—P Company		
(Beginning Consolidated Retained Earnings)	100,000	
Accumulated Depreciation	50,000	
Equipment		150,000

The amount debited to the beginning retained earnings of the parent company (beginning consolidated retained earnings) is the amount of the intercompany profit recorded on the sale that is not considered realized at the beginning of the year ($150,000 − $50,000). The entry has the effect of restoring consolidated retained earnings at the beginning of the year to the same amount shown in the consolidated financial statements at the end of the prior year.

The debit to accumulated depreciation is for the cumulative amount of excessive depreciation recorded by the purchasing affiliate from the date of the intercompany sale up to the *beginning of the current year*. The credit to equipment is for the original amount of profit recorded on the sale and reduces the equipment balance to its depreciated cost to the affiliated group. The credit to the equipment account is for the same amount each year.

(2) Accumulated Depreciation	50,000	
Depreciation Expense		50,000
(3) Equipment	600,000	
Accumulated Depreciation		600,000

The explanation for Entries (2) and (3) are the same as those for the corresponding entries in Illustration 6-1.

As a result of these entries, consolidated depreciation ($250,000), consolidated equipment ($1,350,000), and consolidated accumulated depreciation ($1,100,000) are all based on the cost of the equipment to the affiliated companies. The net effect of these workpaper entries is to increase combined income by $50,000, which is the amount of profit recorded on the intercompany sale that is considered realized from a consolidated point of view through the utilization of the equipment during the current year.

The entries in the December 31, 1997, consolidated statements workpaper to eliminate the effects of the intercompany sale are as follows:

(1) Beginning Retained Earnings—P Company		
($150,000 − $50,000 − $50,000)	50,000	
Accumulated Depreciation ($50,000 + $50,000)	100,000	
Equipment		150,000
To reduce consolidated retained earnings by amount of unrealized profit at beginning of year, to reduce accumulated depreciation by amount of excess depreciation accumulated to beginning of year, and to reduce recorded value of the equipment to its book value on the date of intercompany sale.		
(2) Accumulated Depreciation ($150,000 ÷ 3)	50,000	
Depreciation Expense		50,000
To reverse amount of excess depreciation recorded during current year and to recognize an equivalent amount of intercompany profit as realized.		
(3) Equipment	600,000	
Accumulated Depreciation		600,000
To restate property and equipment at original cost to the selling affiliate.		

Over the life of the equipment, the amount of profit recognized in the consolidated income statement will be the same as the amount of gain recorded by the selling affiliate, and no further adjustments will be necessary in the consolidated statements workpaper. The recognition of the profit on the sale of the equipment on the books of the selling affiliate and in the consolidated income statement may be compared as follows:

	ON BOOKS OF SELLING AFFILIATE	IN CONSOLIDATED INCOME STATEMENT
Gain on sale of equipment—1995	$150,000	
Reduction of depreciation expense		
1995		$ 50,000
1996		50,000
1997		50,000
Total profit recognized	$150,000	$150,000

Determination of Noncontrolling Interest

In the preceding example, the selling affiliate was the parent company (downstream sale). Accordingly, even though 100% of the unrealized intercompany profit was eliminated, no modification in the calculation of the noncontrolling interest in combined income or consolidated net assets was necessary. Had the selling affiliate been a less than wholly owned subsidiary (upstream sale), however, workpaper modifications in the determination of the noncontrolling interest would have been necessary if the controlling and the noncontrolling interests were to be adjusted in proportion to their interest in the amount of unrealized intercompany profit eliminated.

Calculations of the noncontrolling interest in combined income would be modified as follows:

Year of Intercompany Sale

(Noncontrolling interest percentage) × (reported net income of subsidiary company minus the net amount of unrealized profit on the intercompany sale eliminated from combined income)

Years Subsequent to Year of Intercompany Sale

(Noncontrolling interest percentage) × (reported net income of subsidiary company plus intercompany profit considered realized in the current period)

For example, assume that S Company is 90% owned, was the selling affiliate in the previous illustration, and reports $300,000 in income in each of the years 1995, 1996, and 1997. The calculation of the noncontrolling interest in combined income in each of the respective years is presented in Illustration 6-3.

ILLUSTRATION 6-3
Calculation of the Noncontrolling Interest in Combined Income

	1995	1996	1997
Net income reported by S Company	$300,000	$300,000	$300,000
Less unrealized profit recorded on upstream sale	(150,000)		
Add profit considered realized in the current period	50,000	50,000	50,000
Amount of S Company income included in combined income	$200,000	$350,000	$350,000
Noncontrolling interest in combined income (10%)	$20,000	$35,000	$35,000

As was explained in the discussion of unrealized intercompany profit in inventory, as a matter of workpaper procedure, the noncontrolling interest in net assets is adjusted by debiting (decrease in noncontrolling interest) or crediting (increase in noncontrolling interest) the beginning retained earnings of the subsidiary company. The amount of the adjustment to the noncontrolling interest is equal to the noncontrolling interest's share (percentage) of unrealized intercompany profit at the beginning of the period. If S Company were the selling affiliate, workpaper entry (1) in Illustration 6-2 would be modified as follows in order to adjust the controlling and the noncontrolling interests in net assets at the beginning of the year.

(1) Beginning Retained Earnings—P Company		
(Beginning Consolidated Retained Earnings)		
[.90 × ($150,000 − $50,000)]	90,000	
Beginning Retained Earnings—S Company		
(Noncontrolling Interest) [.10 × ($150,000 − $50,000)]	10,000	
Accumulated Depreciation	50,000	
Equipment		150,000

To reduce the controlling and noncontrolling interests for their respective shares of unrealized intercompany profit at the beginning of the year, to reduce accumulated depreciation by the amount of excess depreciation accumulated to the beginning of the year, and to reduce the carrying value of equipment to its book value on the date of the intercompany sale.

CONSOLIDATED STATEMENTS WORKPAPER—INVESTMENT RECORDED USING COST METHOD

Assume that P Company acquires an 85% interest in S Company for $1,190,000 in 1993, when the retained earnings and capital stock of S Company amount to $400,000 and $1,000,000, respectively. The retained earnings of S Company on January 1, 1995, are $666,000. On January 1, 1995, S Company sells P Company equipment with a book value of $500,000 (original cost of $800,000 and accumulated depreciation of $300,000) for $600,000. On January 1, 1995, the equipment has an estimated remaining useful life of five years and is depreciated using the straight-line method. S Company will record a gain of $100,000 on the sale of the equipment, and each year P Company will record depreciation that is $20,000 [($600,000 − $500,000) ÷ 5] greater than depreciation based on the cost of the equipment to the consolidated group. Consolidated statements workpapers for the years ended December 31, 1995, and December 31, 1996, are presented in Illustration 6-4 and Illustration 6-5, respectively.

Consolidated Statements Workpaper Entries—December 31, 1995 (Illustration 6-4)

Workpaper entries in Illustration 6-4 are presented in general journal form as follows:

(1) Investment in S Company	226,100	
Beginning Retained Earnings—P Company		226,100
To establish reciprocity [.85 × ($666,000 − $400,000) = $226,100].		
(2) Gain on Sale of Equipment	100,000	
Property and Equipment		100,000
To eliminate unrealized profit recorded on intercompany sale of equipment and reduce carrying value of equipment to its book value on date of sale.		
(3) Accumulated Depreciation	20,000	
Depreciation Expense		20,000
To reverse amount of excess depreciation recorded during current year and to recognize an equivalent amount of intercompany profit as realized ($100,000 ÷ 5 = $20,000).		
(4) Property and Equipment	300,000	
Accumulated Depreciation		300,000
To restate property and equipment at original cost to the selling affiliate.		
(5) Beginning Retained Earnings—S Company	566,100	
Capital Stock—S Company	850,000	
Investment in S Company ($1,190,000 + $226,100)		1,416,100
To eliminate investment account.		

Since the selling affiliate is a partially owned subsidiary (upstream sale), the calculation of the noncontrolling interest in combined income is modified by subtracting the amount of the gain recognized by the subsidiary and adding the amount of the gain considered to be realized (through depreciation) to the reported net income of the subsidiary [.15 × ($144,000 − $100,000 + $20,000) = $9,600].

If the sale of the equipment had been downstream rather than upstream, the amount of subsidiary income included in combined income would not be affected by the workpaper entries related to unrealized intercompany profit and no adjust-

Cost Method
85% Owned Subsidiary
Upstream Sale of Equipment

ILLUSTRATION 6-4
Consolidated Statements Workpaper
P Company and Subsidiary
For Year Ended December 31, 1995

INCOME STATEMENT	P COMPANY	S COMPANY	ELIMINATIONS DR.	ELIMINATIONS CR.	NONCONTROLLING INTEREST	CONSOLIDATED BALANCES
Sales	3,500,000	2,000,000				5,500,000
Gain on Sale of Equipment		100,000	(2) 100,000			
Total Revenue	3,500,000	2,100,000				5,500,000
Cost of Sales	1,800,000	1,130,000				2,930,000
Depreciation Expense	380,000	330,000		(3) 20,000		690,000
Income Tax Expense	200,000	96,000				296,000
Other Expense	820,000	400,000				1,220,000
Total Cost and Expense	3,200,000	1,956,000				5,136,000
Net/Combined Income	300,000	144,000				364,000
Noncontrolling Interest in Income					9,600	(9,600)*
Net Income to Retained Earnings	300,000	144,000	100,000	20,000	9,600	354,400

RETAINED EARNINGS STATEMENT						
1/1 Retained Earnings						
P Company	1,500,000			(1) 226,100		1,726,100
S Company		663,000	(5) 566,100		99,900	
Net Income from above	300,000	144,000	100,000	20,000	9,600	354,400
12/31 Retained Earnings to Balance Sheet	1,800,000	810,000	666,100	246,100	109,500	2,080,500

BALANCE SHEET						
Current Assets	1,000,000	570,000				1,570,000
Investment in S Company	1,190,000		(1) 226,100	(5) 1,416,100		
Land	1,000,000	200,000				1,200,000
Property and Equipment	3,800,000	2,700,000	(4) 300,000	(2) 100,000		6,700,000
(Accumulated Depreciation)	(1,520,000)	(960,000)	(3) 20,000	(4) 300,000		(2,760,000)
Total Assets	5,470,000	2,510,000				6,710,000
Liabilities	670,000	700,000				1,370,000
Capital Stock						
P Company	3,000,000					3,000,000
S Company		1,000,000	(5) 850,000		150,000	
Retained Earnings from above	1,800,000	810,000	666,100	246,100	109,500	2,080,500
Noncontrolling Interest in Net Assets					259,500	259,500
Total Liabilities and Equity	5,470,000	2,510,000	2,062,200	2,062,200		6,710,000

*.15 × ($144,000 − $100,000 + $20,000) = $9,600.

(1) To establish reciprocity [.85 × ($666,000 − $400,000)].
(2) To eliminate unrealized gain on intercompany sale of equipment.
(3) To reverse amount of excess depreciation recorded during current year.
(4) To restate property and equipment at original cost to S Company.
(5) To eliminate investment account.

ment would be necessary in the calculation of the noncontrolling interest in combined income.

Consolidated Statements Workpaper Entries—December 31, 1996 (Illustration 6-5)

Workpaper entries in Illustration 6-5 are presented in general journal form as follows:

(1) Investment in S Company	348,500	
Beginning Retained Earnings—P Company		348,500
To establish reciprocity [.85 × ($810,000 − $400,000) = $348,500].		
(2) Beginning Retained Earnings—P Company	68,000	
Beginning Retained Earnings—S Company	12,000	
Accumulated Depreciation	20,000	
Property and Equipment		100,000
To reduce the controlling and noncontrolling interests at beginning of year for their shares of unrealized intercompany profit at beginning of the year, to reduce accumulated depreciation by amount of excess depreciation accumulated to beginning of year, and to reduce carrying value of the equipment to its book value on date of intercompany sale.		
(3) Accumulated Depreciation	20,000	
Depreciation Expense		20,000
To reverse amount of excess depreciation recorded during current year and to recognize an equivalent amount of intercompany profit as realized.		
(4) Property and Equipment	300,000	
Accumulated Depreciation		300,000
To restate property and equipment at original cost to selling affiliate.		
(5) Beginning Retained Earnings—S Company	688,500	
Capital Stock—S Company	850,000	
Investment in S Company ($1,190,000 + $348,500)		1,538,500
To eliminate investment account.		

The noncontrolling interest in combined income is calculated after adding profit considered realized during the year to the net income reported by the subsidiary [.15 × ($162,000 + $20,000) = $27,300].

The net effect of the adjustments to the noncontrolling interest in the income statement and retained earnings sections of the consolidated statements workpaper that are necessary in the case of upstream sales is to adjust the amount of the noncontrolling interest in consolidated net assets. The amount of the noncontrolling interest reported in the consolidated balance sheet is based on the net assets of the subsidiary that have been realized in transactions with third parties. For example, the amount of the noncontrolling interest in consolidated net assets shown in Illustration 6-5 is calculated in Illustration 6-6. The realized net assets of S Company presented in Illustration 6-6 in the amount of $1,912,000 may also be determined by subtracting unrealized intercompany profit on upstream sales at the end of the year ($60,000) from the reported net assets of S Company ($2,400,000 − $428,000 = $1,972,000).

Cost Method
85% Owned Subsidiary
Upstream Sale of Equipment

ILLUSTRATION 6-5
Consolidated Statements Workpaper
P Company and Subsidiary
For Year Ended December 31, 1996

INCOME STATEMENT	P COMPANY	S COMPANY	ELIMINATIONS DR.	ELIMINATIONS CR.	NONCONTROLLING INTEREST	CONSOLIDATED BALANCES
Sales	4,000,000	2,200,000				6,200,000
Cost of Sales	2,100,000	1,180,000				3,280,000
Depreciation Expense	380,000	330,000		(3) 20,000		690,000
Income Tax Expense	272,000	108,000				380,000
Other Expense	840,000	420,000				1,260,000
Total Cost and Expense	3,592,000	2,038,000				5,610,000
Net/Combined Income	408,000	162,000				590,000
Noncontrolling Interest in Income					27,300	(27,300)*
Net Income to Retained Earnings	408,000	162,000	–0–	20,000	27,300	562,700
RETAINED EARNINGS STATEMENT						
1/1 Retained Earnings						
P Company	1,800,000		(2) 68,000	(1) 348,500		2,080,500
S Company		810,000	(2) 12,000		109,500	
			(5) 688,500			
Net Income from above	408,000	162,000	–0–	20,000	27,300	562,700
12/31 Retained Earnings to Balance Sheet	2,208,000	972,000	768,500	368,500	136,800	2,643,200
BALANCE SHEET						
Current Assets	1,190,000	790,000				1,980,000
Investment in S Company	1,190,000		(1) 348,500	(5) 1,538,500		
Land	1,600,000	200,000				1,800,000
Property and Equipment	3,800,000	2,700,000	(4) 300,000	(2) 100,000		6,700,000
(Accumulated Depreciation)	(1,900,000)	(1,290,000)	(2) 20,000	(4) 300,000		(3,450,000)
			(3) 20,000			
Total Assets	5,880,000	2,400,000				7,030,000
Liabilities	672,000	428,000				1,100,000
Capital Stock						
P Company	3,000,000					3,000,000
S Company		1,000,000	(5) 850,000		150,000	
Retained Earnings from above	2,208,000	972,000	768,500	368,500	136,800	2,643,200
Noncontrolling Interest in Net Assets					286,800	286,800
Total Liabilities and Equity	5,880,000	2,400,000	2,307,000	2,307,000		7,030,000

*.15 × ($162,000 + $20,000) = $27,300.

(1) To establish reciprocity as of 1/1/96 [.85 × ($810,000 − $400,000)].
(2) To eliminate unrealized intercompany profit at beginning of year.
(3) To reverse amount of excess depreciation recorded during current year.
(4) To restate property and equipment at original cost to S Company.
(5) To eliminate investment account.

ILLUSTRATION 6-6
Calculation of the Noncontrolling Interest in Consolidated Net Assets

Capital stock—S Company		$1,000,000
Realized retained earnings—S Company		
Reported retained earnings	$972,000	
Unrealized intercompany profit on 12/31/96		
($100,000 − $20,000 − $20,000)	(60,000)	912,000
Realized net assets—S Company		$1,912,000
Noncontrolling interest in consolidated net		
assets (.15 × $1,912,000)		$ 286,800

Premature Disposal of Property and Equipment by Purchasing Affiliate

Assume that on January 1, 1997, P Company sells the equipment it purchased from S Company to a party outside the affiliated group for $400,000. The recorded and consolidated book values of the equipment on January 1, 1997, are calculated in Illustration 6-7. P Company will record a $40,000 gain on the sale of the equipment to the party outside the affiliated group as follows:

Cash	400,000	
Accumulated Depreciation	240,000	
Property and Equipment		600,000
Gain on Sale of Equipment		40,000

ILLUSTRATION 6-7
Calculation of Book Value of Equipment on January 1, 1997

On Books of P Company

Cost	$600,000
Accumulated Depreciation [($600,000/5) × 2]	240,000
Recorded Book Value—January 1, 1997	$360,000

Consolidated

Cost	$800,000
Accumulated Depreciation [$300,000 +	
([($800,000 − $300,000) ÷ 5] × 2)]	500,000
Consolidated Book Value—January 1, 1997	$300,000

However, the consolidated book value of the equipment on the date of the sale by P Company is only $300,000, and from the point of view of the consolidated entity a $100,000 gain on the sale ($400,000 − $300,000) should be recognized. The entry on the December 31, 1997, consolidated statements workpaper necessary to accomplish this result is as follows:

Beginning Retained Earnings—P Company		
(.85 × $60,000)	51,000	
Beginning Retained Earnings—S Company		
(.15 × $60,000)	9,000	
Gain on Sale of Equipment		60,000

To adjust reported gain on the sale of equipment by P Company to third party from $40,000 to $100,000 and to adjust the controlling and noncontrolling interests for their share of unrealized intercompany profit at beginning of year ($100,000 − $20,000 − $20,000 = $60,000).

From a consolidated point of view, the amount of gain recorded by the selling affiliate will always be understated (or the amount of loss recorded will always be overstated) by an amount that is equal to the unrealized intercompany profit associated with the equipment on the date of its premature disposal.

After December 31, 1997, no more book or workpaper entries relating to this equipment will be required, because by that date the amount of profit recorded by the affiliates is equal to the amount of profit considered realized in the consolidated financial statements. The equality of the recorded and consolidated amounts is confirmed in Illustration 6-8.

ILLUSTRATION 6-8
Reconciliation of Income Recorded on Books with Income Reported on Consolidated Financial Statements

Amount of profit recorded by affiliates	
1995—Gain on sale from S Company to P Company	$100,000
1997—Gain on sale by P Company to nonaffiliate	40,000
Total	$140,000
Amount of profit considered to be realized in the consolidated income statement	
1995—Reduction of depreciation expense	$ 20,000
1996—Reduction of depreciation expense	20,000
1997—Gain on sale of equipment to nonaffiliate	100,000
Total	$140,000

ANALYTICAL CALCULATION OF CONSOLIDATED NET INCOME AND CONSOLIDATED RETAINED EARNINGS

In Chapter 5, the analytical calculations of consolidated net income and consolidated retained earnings were refined to accommodate the effect of unrealized intercompany profit. The application of these calculations to circumstances involving unrealized profit on intercompany sales of equipment is presented next.

Consolidated Net Income

After modification for the effects of unrealized intercompany profit, consolidated net income was calculated in Chapter 5 as the parent company's income from its independent operations that has been realized in transactions with third parties plus (minus) its share of subsidiary income (loss) that has been realized in transactions with third parties plus or minus adjustments for the period relating to the amortization of the difference between cost and book value.

On the basis of Illustration 6-4, the analytical calculation of consolidated net income for the year ended December 31, 1995, is demonstrated in Illustration 6-9. The amount of consolidated net income calculated in Illustration 6-9 is, of course, the same as that shown in the consolidated statements workpaper in Illustration 6-4.

ILLUSTRATION 6-9
Calculation of Consolidated Net Income
For Year Ended December 31, 1995
Year of Intercompany Sale of Equipment

P Company's net income from its independent operations ($300,000 reported income less $–0– in subsidiary dividend income)		$300,000
Less unrealized profit on 1995 sales of equipment to S Company		(–0–)
Plus profit on prior year's sales of equipment to S Company realized through depreciation in 1995		–0–
P Company's income from its independent operations that has been realized in transactions with third parties		300,000
Reported income of S Company	$144,000	
Less profit on 1995 sale of equipment to P Company not considered realized in 1995 ($100,000 − $20,000)	(80,000)	
Income of S Company that has been realized in transactions with third parties	$ 64,000	
P Company's share thereof (.85 × $64,000)		54,400
Less amortization of the difference between cost and book value		(–0–)
Consolidated net income—1995		$354,400

On the basis of Illustration 6-5, the analytical calculation of consolidated net income for the year ended December 31, 1996, is presented in Illustration 6-10. The amount of consolidated net income calculated in Illustration 6-10 is, of course, the same as that shown in the consolidated statements workpaper in Illustration 6-5.

ILLUSTRATION 6-10
Calculation of Consolidated Net Income
For Year Ended December 31, 1996
Year Subsequent to Year of Intercompany Sale of Equipment

P Company's net income from its independent operations ($408,000 reported income less $–0– in subsidiary dividend income)		$408,000
Less unrealized profit on 1996 sales of equipment to S Company		(–0–)
Plus profit on prior year's sales of equipment to S Company realized through depreciation in 1996		–0–
P Company's income from its independent operations that has been realized in transactions with third parties		408,000
Reported income of S Company	$162,000	
Less profit on 1996 sales of equipment to P Company not considered realized in 1996	(–0–)	
Plus profit on prior year's sales of equipment to P Company realized through depreciation in 1996	20,000	
Income of S Company that has been realized in transactions with third parties	$182,000	
P Company's share thereof (.85 × $182,000)		154,700
Less amortization of the difference between cost and book value		(–0–)
Consolidated net income—1996		$562,700

ILLUSTRATION 6-11
Calculation of Consolidated Retained Earnings
December 31, 1996

P Company's retained earnings on 12/31/96		$2,208,000
Less the amount of P Company's retained earnings that has not been realized in transactions with third parties because of unrealized profit on downstream sales		(–0–)
P Company's retained earnings that have been realized in transactions with third parties		2,208,000
Increase in retained earnings of S Company from date of acquisition to 12/31/96 ($972,000 − $400,000)	$572,000	
Less unrealized profit on 1995 sale of equipment to P Company included in S Company's retained earnings on 12/31/96 ($100,000 − $20,000 − $20,000)	(60,000)	
Increase in retained earnings of S Company since acquisition that has been realized in transactions with third parties	$512,000	
P Company's share thereof (.85 × $512,000)		435,200
Less cumulative amount of the amortization of the difference between cost and book value		(–0–)
Consolidated retained earnings 12/31/96		$2,643,200

Consolidated Retained Earnings

Consolidated retained earnings was calculated in Chapter 5 as the parent company's cost method retained earnings that have been realized in transactions with third parties plus (minus) the parent company's share of the increase (decrease) in subsidiary retained earnings that has been realized in transactions with third parties from the date of acquisition to the current date plus or minus the cumulative effect of adjustments to date relating to the amortization of the difference between cost and book value.

On the basis of Illustration 6-5, the analytical calculation of consolidated retained earnings on December 31, 1996 is demonstrated in Illustration 6-11.

CONSOLIDATED STATEMENTS WORKPAPER—
PARTIAL EQUITY METHOD

The balances reported by the parent company in income, retained earnings, and the investment account differ depending on the method used by the parent company to record its investment. As illustrated in Chapters 3, 4, and 5, however, the method used by the parent company to record its investment has no effect on the consolidated balances.

As has been illustrated in Chapters 3, 4, and 5, when the parent company records its investment using the partial equity method, a workpaper entry to reverse the effect of parent company entries during the year for subsidiary dividends and income replaces the cost method entries to establish reciprocity and to eliminate dividend income. However, as demonstrated in Chapters 4 and 5, the workpaper entries to assign and amortize the difference between cost and book value, to eliminate intercompany sales, and to eliminate unrealized intercompany profit are the same regardless of whether the investment is recorded using the cost method or the partial equity method. Thus, the workpaper entries to eliminate the effects of intercompany sales of equipment are the same when the parent company records its investment using the partial equity method as those just illustrated under circumstances where the parent company used the cost method to record its investment.

SUMMARY OF WORKPAPER ENTRIES RELATING
TO INTERCOMPANY SALES OF EQUIPMENT

Consolidated statements workpaper eliminating entries for intercompany sales of equipment are summarized in Illustration 6-12. The entries are the same whether the parent company uses the cost method or the partial equity method to record its investment. However, the form of the workpaper entry to adjust for unrealized intercompany profit at the beginning of the year differs as between upstream and downstream sales.

ILLUSTRATION 6-12
Intercompany Profit—Equipment
Summary of Workpaper Elimination Entries

SELLING AFFILIATE IS PARENT OR WHOLLY OWNED SUBSIDIARY	SELLING AFFILIATE IS A LESS THAN WHOLLY OWNED SUBSIDIARY

ENTRIES IN YEAR OF INTERCOMPANY SALE

Gain on Sale   SAME
    Equipment
        To eliminate unrealized profit on intercompany sale in year of sale and to reduce carrying value of equipment to its book value on the date of the intercompany sale.

Accumulated Depreciation   SAME
    Depreciation Expense
        To reverse amount (if any) of excess depreciation recorded during current year and to recognize an equivalent amount of intercompany profit as realized.

Equipment   SAME
    Accumulated Depreciation
        To restate equipment at its original cost to the selling affiliate.

ENTRIES IN YEARS SUBSEQUENT TO THE YEAR OF INTERCOMPANY SALE

Beginning Retained Earnings—P	Beginning Retained Earnings—P
	Beginning Retained Earnings—S
Accumulated Depreciation	Accumulated Depreciation
Equipment	Equipment
To reduce consolidated retained earnings (controlling interest) for the unrealized intercompany profit at the ***beginning of the year***, to reduce accumulated depreciation by the excess depreciation accumulated to the ***beginning of the year***, and to reduce the carrying value of equipment to its book value on the date of the intercompany sale.	To reduce the controlling and noncontrolling interests for their respective shares of the unrealized intercompany profit at the ***beginning of the year***, to reduce accumulated depreciation by the excess depreciation accumulated to the ***beginning of the year***, and to reduce the carrying value of equipment to its book value on the date of the intercompany sale.

Accumulated Depreciation   SAME
    Depreciation Expense
        To reverse amount of excess depreciation recorded during current year and to recognize an equivalent amount of intercompany profit as realized.

Equipment   SAME
    Accumulated Depreciation
        To restate equipment at its original cost to the selling affiliate.

INTERCOMPANY INTEREST, RENTS, AND SERVICE FEES

Income and expenses relating to interest, fees, and rents should be reported in the consolidated income statement only when they arise from transactions with parties outside the affiliated group. In addition, as discussed in Chapter 2, only receivables and payables that are receivable from or payable to parties outside the affiliated group should be reported in the consolidated balance sheet.

Intercompany Interest

When interest is charged on intercompany loans, the intercompany interest income on the lending affiliate's books is equal to the intercompany interest expense on the borrowing affiliate's books. The workpaper entry to eliminate intercompany interest is:

Interest Income	XXX	
Interest Expense		XXX

Since equal amounts of revenue and expense are removed from combined income, the net amount of combined income is not affected by this entry. When intercompany loans or interest remain unpaid on the balance sheet date, additional entries are necessary to eliminate related intercompany payables and receivables as follows:

Notes Payable	XXX	
Notes Receivable		XXX
Interest Payable	XXX	
Interest Receivable		XXX

Intercompany Rents

When there is an intercompany operating lease, intercompany rent income on the books of the lessor will equal intercompany rent expense on the books of the lessee. The workpaper entry to eliminate intercompany rent is:

Rent Income	XXX	
Rent Expense		XXX

Since equal amounts of revenue and expense are removed from combined income the net amount of combined income is not affected by this entry.

Intercompany Service Fees

When one affiliate charges fees to another the eliminating entry will depend on how the transaction is recorded by the affiliates. If the affiliate that provides the service treats the fee as revenue and the affiliate that receives the service treats the fee as an expense, the necessary workpaper entry is simply a debit to service fee revenue and a credit to service fee expense. On the other hand, the affiliate that receives the service may treat the amount it is charged for the service as a capital addition. For example, fees for architectural services to an affiliate may be treated by the purchasing affiliate as part of the cost of a building. In this case, architectural fees should be debited for the amount recorded as revenue on the intercompany transaction, appropriate expense accounts (as recorded on the selling affiliates books) should be credited for the cost to the selling affiliate of providing the services and the building should be credited for the difference between the revenue recorded and the cost of providing the service. Additional workpaper entries will also be necessary in subsequent years to report balances for the building, accumulated depreciation, and depreciation expense at amounts based on the cost of the building to the affiliated group.

For example, assume that P Company bills its subsidiary, S Company, $400,000 for architectural services. The cost to P Company of providing the services is $250,000. S Company charges the services to the cost of a building that it opens at the beginning of the next year that has an estimated useful life of 15 years. Workpaper entries to eliminate the effects of the intercompany service fee are as follows:

In the Year the Services Are Rendered		
Architectural Fees	400,000	
Salary Expense		200,000
Travel Expense		15,000
Other Expense		35,000
Building		150,000
In the Year the Building Is Opened		
Beginning Retained Earnings—P Company	150,000	
Building		150,000
Accumulated Depreciation	10,000	
Depreciation Expense		10,000
In the Fifth Year After the Building Is Opened		
Beginning Retained Earnings—P Company	110,000	
Accumulated Depreciation	40,000	
Building		150,000
Accumulated Depreciation	10,000	
Depreciation Expense		10,000

Thus eliminating entries relating to intercompany transactions depend on how these transactions are recorded on the books of the affiliates. In all cases, however, the financial reporting objectives identified in previous sections of this chapter and in Chapter 5 apply. In the preceding example, the reporting objectives were:

- To include in revenue only the amounts that result from transactions with parties outside the affiliated group.
- To present property in the consolidated balance sheet at *its cost to the affiliated group.*
- To present accumulated depreciation in the consolidated balance sheet based on the *cost to the affiliated group* of the related assets.
- To present depreciation expense in the consolidated income statement based on the *cost to the affiliated group* of the related assets.

In order to apply the objectives identified in this chapter and in Chapter 5 to a situation that is not illustrated in this text, the student may wish to work out the workpaper entries necessary in a situation like the following. S Company is in the business of selling equipment that it manufactures. S Company treats equipment manufactured by it as finished goods inventory. S Company sells equipment manufactured by it to its parent company at a profit. The equipment is capitalized and depreciated on the books of the parent company.

Questions

1. From a consolidated point of view, when should profit be recognized on intercompany sales of depreciable assets? Nondepreciable assets?

2. In what circumstances might a consolidated gain be recognized on the sale of assets to a nonaffiliate when the selling affiliate recognizes a loss?

3. What is the essential procedural difference between workpaper eliminating entries for unrealized intercompany profit when the selling affiliate is a less than wholly owned subsidiary and such entries when the selling affiliate is the parent company or a wholly owned subsidiary?

4. Define consolidated net income using the analytical approach.

5. Why is it important to distinguish between upstream and downstream sales in the analysis of intercompany profit eliminations?

6. In what period and in what manner should profits relating to the intercompany sale of depreciable property and equipment be recognized in the consolidated financial statements?

7. Define consolidated retained earnings using the analytical approach.

Exercises

Exercise 6-1

On January 1, 1995, Sherwood Company, an 80% owned subsidiary of Paradise Company, sold to Paradise Company equipment with a book value of $600,000 for $840,000. The equipment had an estimated remaining useful life of eight years on the date of the intercompany sale.

Paradise Company reported net income from its independent operations of $550,000, and Sherwood Company reported net income of $300,000 in the years of 1995 and 1996.

Required:

Calculate consolidated net income for the years ended December 31, 1995, and December 31, 1996.

Exercise 6-2

On January 1, 1995, Polar Company, which owns an 80% interest in Superior Company, sold Superior Company equipment with a book value of $400,000 for $560,000. The equipment had an estimated remaining useful life of eight years on the date of the intercompany sale.

Polar Company reported net income from its independent operations (including sales to affiliates) of $400,000, and Superior Company reported net income of $200,000 from its independent operations in 1995 and 1996.

Required:

Calculate consolidated net income for the years ended December 31, 1995, and December 31, 1996.

Exercise 6-3

Pearson Company owns 90% of the outstanding common stock of Spring Company. On January 1, 1995, Spring Company sold equipment to Pearson Company for $200,000. Spring Company had purchased the equipment for $300,000 on January 1, 1990, and had depreciated it using a 10% straight-line rate. The management of Pearson Company estimated that the equipment had a remaining useful life of five years on January 1, 1995. In 1996, Pearson Company reported $150,000 and Spring Company reported $100,000 in net income from their independent operations (including sales to affiliates).

Required:

A. Prepare in general journal form the workpaper entries relating to the intercompany sale of equipment that are necessary in the December 31, 1995, and December 31, 1996, consolidated financial statements workpapers.

B. Calculate consolidated net income for 1996.

Exercise 6-4

Procter Company owns 90% of the outstanding stock of Silex Company. On January 1, 1995, Silex Company sold land to Procter Company for $350,000. Silex had originally purchased the land on June 30, 1991, for $200,000.

Procter Company plans to construct a building on the land bought from Silex in which it will house new production machinery. The estimated useful life of the building and the new machinery is 15 years.

Required:

A. Prepare the entries on the books of Procter related to the intercompany sale of land for the years ended December 31, 1995, and December 31, 1996.

B. Prepare in general journal form the workpaper entries necessary because of the intercompany sale of land in:
(1) The consolidated financial statements workpaper for the year ended December 31, 1995.
(2) The consolidated financial statements workpaper for the year ended December 31, 1996.

Exercise 6-5

Patterson Company owns 80% of the outstanding common stock of Stevens Company. On June 30, 1994, land costing $500,000 is sold by one affiliate to the other for $800,000.

Required:

Prepare in general journal form the workpaper entries necessary because of the intercompany sale of land in the consolidated financial statements workpaper for the year ended December 31, 1995, assuming that:

A. Patterson Company purchased the land from Stevens Company.

B. Stevens Company purchased the land from Patterson Company.

Exercise 6-6

P Company owns 90% of the outstanding common stock of S Company. On January 1, 1995, S Company sold land to P Company for $600,000. S Company originally purchased the land for $400,000.

On January 1, 1996, P Company sold the land purchased from S Company to a company outside the affiliated group for $700,000.

Required:

A. Calculate the amount of gain on the sale of the land that is recognized on the books of P Company in 1996.

B. Calculate the amount of gain on the sale of the land that should be recognized in the consolidated financial statements in 1996.

C. Prepare in general journal form the workpaper entries necessary because of the intercompany sale of land in the consolidated financial statements workpaper for the year ended December 31, 1996.

Exercise 6-7

On January 1, 1994, Price Company acquired an 80% interest in the common stock of Smith Company on the open market for $750,000, the book value at that date.

On January 1, 1995, Price Company purchased new equipment for $14,500 from Smith Company. The equipment cost $9,000 and had an estimated life of five years as of January 1, 1995.

During 1996, Price Company had merchandise sales to Smith Company of $100,000; the merchandise was priced at 25% above Price Company's cost. Smith Company still owes Price Company $17,500 on open account and has 20% of this merchandise in inventory at December 31, 1996. At the beginning of 1996, Smith Company had in inventory $25,000 of merchandise purchased in the previous period from Price Company.

Required:

A. Prepare all workpaper entries necessary to eliminate the effects of the intercompany sales on the consolidated financial statements for the year ended December 31, 1996.

B. Assume that Smith Company reports net income of $40,000 for the year ended December 31, 1996. Calculate the amount of noncontrolling interest to be deducted from combined income in the consolidated income statement for the year ended December 31, 1996.

Exercise 6-8

On January 1, 1995, P Company acquired a 90% interest in S Company. During 1996, S Company sold merchandise to P Company at 25% above cost in the amount (selling price) of $225,000. At the end of the year, P Company had in its inventory one-third of the amount of goods purchased from S Company.

On January 1, 1996, P Company sold equipment that had a book value of $80,000 to S Company for $120,000. The equipment had an estimated remaining life of four years.

S Company reported net income of $120,000, and P Company reported net income of $300,000 from their independent operations (including sales to affiliates) for the year ended December 31, 1996.

Required:

Calculate consolidated net income for the year ended December 31, 1996.

Exercise 6-9

P Company owns 80% of the outstanding stock of S Company. The 1995 sales of S Company included revenue of $390,000 consisting of consulting services billed to P Company at cost plus 30%. P Company was billed the full $390,000; of this amount $260,000 was charged to selling expenses and $130,000 was charged to administrative expense.

Required:

Prepare in general journal form the workpaper entry necessary to eliminate the effects of intercompany sales of services in the consolidated financial statements workpaper for the year ended December 31, 1995.

Exercise 6-10

During 1994, Pier One Company billed its 80% owned subsidary, Scale Company, $700,000 for architectural services. The cost to Pier One Company of providing the services was $400,000 for salaries and $150,000 for other operating expenses. Scale Company charged the architecture fees to the cost of a building that it opened on January 1, 1995. The building had an estimated useful life of 30 years.

Required:

Prepare in general journal form the workpaper entries relating to the intercompany fees that are necessary in the consolidated statements work papers for the years ended December 31, 1994, 1995, and 1996.

Exercise 6-11

Pinta Company, a forklift manufacturer, owns 80% of the voting stock of Standard Company. On January 1, 1995, Pinta Company sold forklifts to Standard Company for $400,000. The forklifts, which represented inventory to Pinta Company, had a cost to Pinta Company of $310,000. The management of Standard Company estimated that the forklifts had a useful life of nine years from the date of purchase. Standard Company uses the straight-line method to depreciate its capital assets.

In 1995, Pinta Company reported $700,000 in net income from its independent operations (including sales to affiliates), and Standard Company reported $250,000 in net income from its operations.

Required:

A. Prepare in general journal form the workpaper entries necessary because of the intercompany sales in:
   (1) The consolidated financial statements workpaper for the year ended December 31, 1995.
   (2) The consolidated financial statements workpaper for the year ended December 31, 1996.
B. Calculate consolidated net income for the year ended December 31, 1995.

Exercise 6-12

Pomeroy Corporation owns an 80% interest in Sherer Company and a 90% interest in Tampa Company. On January 2, 1995, Tampa Company sold equipment with a book value of $600,000 to Sherer Company for $780,000. This equipment has a remaining useful life of three years. Sherer Company reported $100,000 and Tampa Company reported $150,000 in net income (including sales to affiliates) in 1995.

Required:

Prepare the 1995 and 1996 consolidated statements workpaper entries to eliminate the effects of this sale of equipment.

Problems

Problem 6-1

Powell Company owns 80% of the outstanding common stock of Sullivan Company. On June 30, 1995, Sullivan Company sold equipment to Powell Company for $500,000. The equipment cost Sullivan Company $780,000 and had accumulated depreciation of $400,000 on the date of the sale. The management of Powell Company estimated that the equipment had a remaining useful life of four years from June 30, 1995. In 1996, Powell Company reported $300,000 and Sullivan Company reported $200,000 in net income from their independent operations (including sales to affiliates).

Required:

A. Prepare in general journal form the workpaper entries necessary because of the intercompany sale of equipment in:
   (1) The consolidated financial statements workpaper for the year ended December 31, 1995.
   (2) The consolidated financial statements workpaper for the year ended December 31, 1996.
B. Calculate the balances to be reported in the consolidated income statement for the year ended December 31, 1996, for the following items:
   (1) Combined income.

(2) Noncontrolling interest in combined income.

(3) Consolidated net income.

Problem 6-2

Pico Company, a truck manufacturer, owns 90% of the voting stock of Seward Company. On January 1, 1995, Pico Company sold trucks to Seward Company for $350,000. The trucks, which represented inventory to Pico Company, had a cost to Pico Company of $260,000. The management of Seward Company estimated that the trucks had a useful life of six years from the date of purchase. Seward Company uses the straight-line method to depreciate its capital assets.

In 1995, Pico Company reported $600,000 in net income from its independent operations (including sales to affiliates), and Seward Company reported $200,000 in net income from its operations.

Required:

A. Prepare in general journal form the workpaper entries necessary because of the intercompany sales in:

(1) The consolidated financial statements workpaper for the year ended December 31, 1995.

(2) The consolidated financial statements workpaper for the year ended December 31, 1996.

B. Calculate consolidated net income for the year ended December 31, 1995.

Problem 6-3

On January 1, 1995, P Company purchased equipment from its 80% owned subsidiary for $600,000. The carrying value of the equipment on the books of S Company was $450,000. The equipment had a remaining useful life of six years on January 1, 1995. On January 1, 1996, P Company sold the equipment to an outside party for $550,000.

Required:

A. Prepare in general journal form the entries necessary in 1995 and 1996 on the books of P Company to account for the purchase and sale of the equipment.

B. Determine the consolidated gain or loss on the sale of the equipment and prepare in general journal form the entry necessary on the December 31, 1996, consolidated statements workpaper to properly reflect this gain or loss.

Problem 6-4

Prout Company owns 80% of the common stock of Sexton Company. The stock was purchased for $1,600,000 on January 1, 1992, when Sexton Company's retained earnings were $800,000. On January 1, 1994, Prout Company sold fixed assets to Sexton Company for $360,000. These assets were originally purchased by Prout Company for $400,000 on January 1, 1984, at which time their estimated depreciable life was 25 years. The straight-line method of depreciation is used.

On December 31, 1995, the trial balances of the two companies were as shown here:

	PROUT COMPANY	SEXTON COMPANY
Current assets	$ 568,000	$ 271,000
Fixed assets	1,972,000	830,000
Other assets	1,000,800	1,600,000
Investment in Sexton Company	1,600,000	
Dividends declared	120,000	100,000
Cost of goods sold	942,000	795,000
Other expenses (including depreciation)	145,000	90,000
Income tax expense	187,200	90,000
Total	$6,535,000	$3,776,000
Liabilities	$ 305,000	$ 136,000
Accumulated depreciation	375,000	290,000
Sales	1,475,000	1,110,000
Dividend income	80,000	
Common stock	3,000,000	1,200,000
Retained earnings	1,300,000	1,040,000
Total	$6,535,000	$3,776,000

Required:

A. Prepare a consolidated statements workpaper for the year ended December 31, 1995.

B. Assuming that on January 1, 1996, Sexton Company sells the fixed assets purchased from Prout Company to a party outside the affiliated group for $300,000:
   (1) Prepare the entry that would have been entered on the books of Sexton Company to record the sale.
   (2) Prepare entries for the December 31, 1996, consolidated statements workpaper necessitated by the sale of the assets.
   (3) Prepare any workpaper entries that will be needed in the December 31, 1997, consolidated statements workpaper in regard to these fixed assets.

Problem 6-5

Using the information presented in Problem 6-4, prepare a consolidated financial statements workpaper for the year ended December 31, 1995, using the trial balance format.

Problem 6-6

Pitts Company owns 80% of the common stock of Shannon Company. The stock was purchased for $960,000 on January 1, 1993, when Shannon Company's retained earnings were $675,000. On January 1, 1995, Shannon Company sold fixed assets to Pitts Company for $960,000; Shannon Company had purchased these assets for $1,350,000 on January 1, 1985, at which time their estimated useful life was 25 years. The estimated remaining useful life to Pitts Company on 1/1/95 is 10 years. Both companies employ the straight-line method of depreciation.

The financial data for 1996 are presented here:

	PITTS COMPANY	SHANNON COMPANY
Sales	$1,950,000	$1,350,000
Dividend income	60,000	
Total revenue	2,010,000	1,350,000
Cost of goods sold	1,350,000	900,000
Other expenses	225,000	150,000
Total cost and expense	1,575,000	1,050,000
Net income	$ 435,000	$ 300,000
1/1 Retained earnings	$1,215,000	$1,038,000
Net income	435,000	300,000
Dividends declared	(150,000)	(75,000)
12/31 Retained earnings	$1,500,000	$1,263,000
Inventory	$ 498,000	$ 225,000
Investment in Shannon Company	960,000	
Fixed assets	2,168,100	2,625,000
Accumulated depreciation—fixed assets	(900,000)	(612,000)
Total assets	$2,726,100	$2,238,000
Liabilities	$ 465,600	$ 450,000
Common stock	760,500	525,000
Retained earnings	1,500,000	1,263,000
Total liabilities and equity	$2,726,100	$2,238,000

Required:

A. Prepare a consolidated statements workpaper for the year ended December 31, 1996.

B. Calculate consolidated retained earnings on December 31, 1996, using the analytical approach.

Problem 6-7

Parsons Company acquired 90% of the outstanding common stock of Shea Company on June 30, 1995, for $426,000. On that date, Shea Company had retained earnings in the amount of $60,000, and the fair value of its recorded assets and liabilities was equal to their book value. The excess of cost over the fair value of the recorded net assets was attributed to an unrecorded manufacturing formula held by Shea Company, which had an expected remaining useful life of five years from June 30, 1995.

Financial data for 1997 are presented here:

	PARSONS COMPANY	SHEA COMPANY
Sales	$2,555,500	$1,120,000
Dividend income	54,000	
Total revenue	2,609,500	1,120,000
Cost of goods sold	1,730,000	690,500

	PARSONS COMPANY	SHEA COMPANY
Expenses	654,500	251,000
Total cost and expense	2,384,500	941,500
Net income	$ 225,000	$ 178,500
1/1 Retained earnings	$ 595,000	$ 139,500
Net income	225,000	178,500
Dividends declared	(100,000)	(60,000)
12/31 Retained earnings	$ 720,000	$ 258,000
Cash	$ 119,500	$ 132,500
Accounts receivable	342,000	125,000
Inventory	362,000	201,000
Other current assets	40,500	13,000
Land	150,000	
Investment in Shea Company	426,000	
Property and equipment	825,000	241,000
Accumulated depreciation	(207,000)	(53,500)
Total assets	$2,058,000	$ 659,000
Accounts payable	$ 295,000	$ 32,000
Other liabilities	43,000	19,000
Capital stock	1,000,000	300,000
Additional paid-in capital		50,000
Retained earnings	720,000	258,000
Total liabilities and equity	$2,058,000	$ 659,000

On December 31, 1995, Parsons Company sold equipment to Shea Company at a profit of $47,500. This equipment has since been depreciated at an annual rate of 20% of the purchase price. During 1996 Shea Company sold land to Parsons Company at a profit of $15,000.

The inventory of Parsons Company on December 31, 1996, included goods purchased from Shea Company on which Shea Company recognized a profit of $7,500. During 1997, Shea Company sold goods to Parsons Company for $375,000, of which $60,000 was unpaid on December 31, 1997. The December 31, 1997, inventory of Parsons Company included goods acquired from Shea Company on which Shea Company recognized a profit of $10,500.

Required:

A. Prepare a consolidated financial statements workpaper for the year ended December 31, 1997.

B. Prepare a schedule to calculate consolidated retained earnings on December 31, 1997, using the analytical approach.

Problem 6-8

On January 1, 1994, Phelps Company purchased an 85% interest in Sloane Company for $955,000 when the retained earnings of Sloane Company were $150,000. The difference between cost and book value was assigned as follows:

Inventory	$40,000
Land	30,000
Discount on bonds payable	40,000
Excess of cost over fair value	80,000

One-half of the inventory was sold in 1994 and the remaining inventory was sold in 1995. The bonds mature in eight years; the excess of cost over fair value is amortized over the maximum period allowable.

On December 31, 1994, Phelps Company's inventory contained $10,000 in unrealized intercompany profit. During 1995 Phelps Company sold merchandise with a cost of $200,000 to Sloane Company at a 30% markup on cost. Only $65,000 (selling price) of this merchandise remains in Sloane Company's 1995 ending inventory. As of December 31, 1995, Sloane Company owes Phelps Company $40,000 for merchandise purchased during 1995.

Equipment with a book value of $500,000 was sold by Sloane Company on January 2, 1995, to Phelps Company for $640,000. This equipment had an estimated useful life when purchased by Sloane Company on July 1, 1992, of 10 years.

Financial data for 1995 are presented here:

	PHELPS COMPANY	SLOANE COMPANY
Sales	$1,291,500	$ 560,000
Other income		140,000
Dividend income	42,500	
Total revenue	1,334,000	700,000
Cost of goods sold	660,000	300,000
Depreciation expense	138,000	20,000
Interest expense	8,000	10,000
Other expenses	174,000	140,000
Total cost and expense	980,000	470,000
Net income	$ 354,000	$ 230,000
1/1 Retained earnings	$ 350,500	$ 250,000
Net income	354,000	230,000
Dividends declared	(100,000)	(50,000)
12/31 Retained earnings	$ 604,500	$ 430,000
Cash	$ 127,000	$ 70,000
Accounts receivable	300,000	210,000
Inventory	270,000	175,000
Investment in Sloane Company	955,000	
Land	100,000	390,000
Plant and equipment	800,000	700,000
Accumulated depreciation	(200,000)	(200,000)
Total assets	$2,352,000	$1,345,000
Accounts payable	$ 167,500	$ 65,000
Bonds payable	80,000	100,000
Capital stock	1,500,000	750,000
Retained earnings	604,500	430,000
Total liabilities and equity	$2,352,000	$1,345,000

Required:

Prepare a consolidated financial statements workpaper for the year ended December 31, 1995.

Problem 6-9

Pierce Company acquired a 90% interest in Sanders Company on January 1, 1995, for $1,480,000. At this time, Sanders Company's common stock and retained earnings balances were $1,000,000 and $500,000, respectively. An examination of the books of Sanders on the date of purchase revealed the following:

	BOOK VALUE	FAIR VALUE
Current assets	$300,000	$300,000
Marketable securities	200,000	200,000
Inventory	175,000	225,000
Plant and equipment (net)	650,000	800,000
Land	500,000	600,000

Sanders Company's equipment has a remaining life of 11 years. Eighty percent of the inventory was sold in 1995, the remainder in 1996.

During 1995, Pierce Company sold merchandise costing $400,000 to Sanders at a 25% markup on cost, and Sanders sold merchandise to Pierce Company for $100,000 (this price included $25,000 in profit). In 1996, Pierce Company sold merchandise to Sanders Company for $350,000, while Sanders Company sold merchandise to Pierce Company for $80,000. The 1995 markup percentages were also used on the 1996 sales.

The selling price of intercompany merchandise remaining in ending inventories for both years is summarized here:

MERCHANDISE FROM INTERCOMPANY SALES IN ENDING INVENTORY OF	1995	1996
Pierce Company	$40,000	$20,000
Sanders Company	50,000	30,000

In 1996, Sanders Company also sold a piece of land that had a book value of $250,000 to Pierce Company for $300,000. On December 31, 1996, Pierce Company holds a $60,000 receivable on the merchandise it sold to Sanders Company.

Adjusted trial balances for the year ended December 31, 1996 are shown here:

	PIERCE	SANDERS
Cash	$ 200,000	$ 150,000
Accounts receivable	300,000	250,000
Marketable securities	100,000	200,000
Inventory 12/31	300,000	250,000
Investment in Sanders Company	1,480,000	
Land	400,000	350,000
Plant and equipment (net)	1,000,000	800,000
Cost of goods sold	600,000	400,000
Depreciation expense	60,000	40,000
Other expenses	400,000	260,000
Dividends declared	120,000	70,000
Total	$4,960,000	$2,770,000

	PIERCE	SANDERS
Accounts payable	$ 241,000	$ 140,000
Notes payable	350,000	100,000
Common stock	1,900,000	1,000,000
1/1 Retained earnings	706,000	580,000
Sales	1,700,000	900,000
Gain on sale of land		50,000
Dividend income	63,000	
Total	$4,960,000	$2,770,000

Required:

Prepare a consolidated statements workpaper for the year ended December 31, 1996.

Problem 6-10

(Note that this is the same problem as Problem 6-4, but assuming the use of the partial equity method.) Prout Company owns 80% of the common stock of Sexton Company. The stock was purchased for $1,600,000 on January 1, 1992, when Sexton Company's retained earnings were $800,000. On January 1, 1994, Prout Company sold fixed assets to Sexton Company for $360,000. These assets were originally purchased by Prout Company for $400,000 on January 1, 1984, at which time their estimated depreciable life was 25 years. The straight-line method of depreciation is used.

On December 31, 1995, the trial balances of the two companies were as shown here:

	PROUT COMPANY	SEXTON COMPANY
Current assets	$ 568,000	$ 271,000
Fixed assets	1,972,000	830,000
Other assets	1,000,800	1,600,000
Investment in Sexton Company	1,820,000	
Dividends declared	120,000	100,000
Cost of goods sold	942,000	795,000
Other expenses (including depreciation)	145,000	90,000
Income tax expense	187,200	90,000
Total	$6,755,000	$3,776,000
Liabilities	$ 305,000	$ 136,000
Accumulated depreciation	375,000	290,000
Sales	1,475,000	1,110,000
Equity in subsidiary income	108,000	
Common stock	3,000,000	1,200,000
Retained earnings	1,492,000	1,040,000
Total	$6,755,000	$3,776,000

Required:

A. Prepare a consolidated statements workpaper for the year ended December 31, 1995.

B. Assuming that on January 1, 1996, Sexton Company sells the fixed assets purchased from Prout Company to a party outside the affiliated group for $300,000:

(1) Prepare the entry that would have been entered on the books of Sexton Company to record the sale.

(2) Prepare entries for the December 31, 1996, consolidated statements workpaper necessitated by the sale of the assets.

(3) Prepare any workpaper entries that will be needed in the December 31, 1997, consolidated statements workpaper in regard to these fixed assets.

C. If you completed Problem 6-4, compare the consolidated balance obtained in part (A) to those obtained in Problem 6-4.

Problem 6-11

Using the information presented in Problem 6-10 prepare a consolidated financial statements workpaper for the year ended December 31, 1995, using the trial balance format.

Problem 6-12

Prather Company owns 80% of the common stock of Stone Company. The stock was purchased for $960,000 on January 1, 1993, when Stone Company's retained earnings were $675,000. On January 1, 1995, Stone Company sold fixed assets to Prather Company for $960,000; Stone Company had purchased these assets for $1,350,000 on January 1, 1985, at which time their estimated useful life was 25 years. The estimated remaining useful life to Prather Company on 1/1/95 is 10 years. Both companies employ the straight-line method of depreciation.

The financial data for 1996 are presented here:

	PRATHER COMPANY	STONE COMPANY
Sales	$1,950,000	$1,350,000
Equity in subsidiary income	240,000	
Total revenue	2,190,000	1,350,000
Cost of goods sold	1,350,000	900,000
Other expenses	225,000	150,000
Total cost and expense	1,575,000	1,050,000
Net income	$ 615,000	$ 300,000
1/1 Retained earnings	$1,505,400	$1,038,000
Net income	615,000	300,000
Dividends declared	(150,000)	(75,000)
12/31 Retained earnings	$1,970,400	$1,263,000
Inventory	$ 498,000	$ 225,000
Investment in Stone Company	1,430,400	
Fixed assets	2,168,100	2,625,000
Accumulated depreciation—fixed assets	(900,000)	(612,000)
Total assets	$3,196,500	$2,238,000
Liabilities	$ 465,600	$ 450,000
Common stock	760,500	525,000
Retained earnings	1,970,400	1,263,000
Total liabilities and equity	$3,196,500	$2,238,000

Required:

A. Prepare a consolidated statements workpaper for the year ended December 31, 1996.

B. Calculate consolidated retained earnings on December 31, 1996, using the analytical approach.

Problem 6-13

Padilla Company acquired 90% of the outstanding common stock of Sanchez Company on June 30, 1995, for $426,000. On that date, Sanchez Company had retained earnings in the amount of $60,000, and the fair value of its recorded assets and liabilities was equal to their book value. The excess of cost over the fair value of the recorded net assets was attributed to an unrecorded manufacturing formula held by Sanchez Company, which had an expected remaining useful life of five years from June 30, 1995.

Financial data for 1997 are presented here:

	PADILLA COMPANY	SANCHEZ COMPANY
Sales	$2,555,500	$1,120,000
Equity in subsidiary income	160,650	
Total revenue	2,716,150	1,120,000
Cost of goods sold	1,730,000	690,500
Expenses	654,500	251,000
Total cost and expense	2,384,500	941,500
Net income	$ 331,650	$ 178,500
1/1 Retained earnings	666,550	139,500
Net income	331,650	178,500
Dividends declared	(100,000)	(60,000)
12/31 Retained earnings	$ 898,200	$ 258,000
Cash	$ 119,500	$ 132,500
Accounts receivable	342,000	125,000
Inventory	362,000	201,000
Other current assets	40,500	13,000
Land	150,000	
Investment in Sanchez Company	604,200	
Property and equipment	825,000	241,000
Accumulated depreciation	(207,000)	(53,500)
Total assets	$2,236,200	$ 659,000
Accounts payable	$ 295,000	$ 32,000
Other liabilities	43,000	19,000
Capital stock	1,000,000	300,000
Additional paid-in capital		50,000
Retained earnings	898,200	258,000
Total liabilities and equity	$2,236,200	$ 659,000

On December 31, 1995, Padilla Company sold equipment to Sanchez Company at a profit of $47,500. This equipment has since been depreciated at an annual rate of 20% of the purchase price. During 1996, Sanchez Company sold land to Padilla Company at a profit of $15,000.

The inventory of Padilla Company on December 31, 1996, included goods purchased from Sanchez Company on which Sanchez Company recognized a profit of $7,500. During 1997, Sanchez Company sold goods to Padilla Company for $375,000, of which $60,000 was unpaid on December 31, 1997. The December 31, 1997, inventory of Padilla Company included goods acquired from Sanchez Company on which Sanchez Company recognized a profit of $10,500.

Required:

A. Prepare a consolidated financial statements workpaper for the year ended December 31, 1997.

B. Prepare a schedule to calculate consolidated retained earnings on December 31, 1997, using the analytical approach.

Problem 6-14

Platt Company acquired an 80% interest in Sloane Company when the retained earnings of Sloane Company were $300,000. On January 1, 1995, Sloane Company recorded a $250,000 gain on the sale to Platt Company of equipment with a remaining life of five years. On January 1, 1996, Platt Company recorded a $180,000 gain on the sale to Sloane Company of equipment with a remaining life of six years. Sloane Company reported net income of $180,000 and declared dividends of $60,000 in 1996. It reported retained earnings of $520,000 on January 1, 1996, and $640,000 on December 31, 1996. Platt Company reported net income from independent operations of $400,000 in 1996 and retained earning of $1,800,000 on December 31, 1996.

Required:

A. Prepare in general journal form the entries necessary in the December 31, 1996, consolidated statements workpaper to eliminate the effects of the intercompany sales.

B. Calculate consolidated net income for the year ended December 31, 1996.

C. Calculate consolidated retained earnings on December 31, 1996.

D. Calculate noncontrolling interest in combined income for the year ended December 31, 1996.

7

DEFERRED INCOME TAX CONSEQUENCES IN BUSINESS COMBINATIONS AND CONSOLIDATED FINANCIAL STATEMENTS

When a business combination is accounted for by use of the purchase method, deferred tax consequences arise because of differences between the values assigned to individual assets and liabilities under the purchase method and the tax bases of the same individual assets and liabilities. These tax consequences arise without regard to whether the legal form of the business combination is a statutory merger, a statutory consolidation, or a stock acquisition. In the case of a stock acquisition, these tax consequences arise without regard to whether the affiliated companies file a consolidated income tax return or separate tax returns. Tax consequences in business combinations accounted for by the purchase method are described in the first section of this chapter.

Deferred income tax consequences may also arise when consolidated financial statements are prepared for affiliates that file separate income tax returns rather than a consolidated income tax return. Tax consequences that may arise in the preparation of consolidated financial statements when the affiliated companies file separate income tax returns are described in the second section of this chapter.

INCOME TAX CONSEQUENCES IN BUSINESS COMBINATIONS ACCOUNTED FOR BY THE PURCHASE METHOD

The market values of specific assets acquired and liabilities assumed in a business combination may differ from the income tax bases of those items. Prior to the adoption of *SFAS No. 109*, "Accounting for Income Taxes," the estimated future tax effects of differences between market values and income tax bases of those assets and liabilities were one of the variables in determining their recorded fair values. Thus, the assets acquired and liabilities assumed were recorded net of the tax effects of differences in bases, and no specific deferred tax asset or liability was recorded. *SFAS No. 109*, however, changed that procedure.

SFAS No. 109 requires that a deferred tax asset or liability be recognized for differences between the assigned values and tax bases of the assets and liabilities (except goodwill, unallocated "negative goodwill," and leveraged leases) recognized in a purchase business combination.[1] There is no tax consequence relating to goodwill since the amortization of goodwill recorded in a business combination is not deductible in determining a company's taxable income.

We will use the information in Illustration 7-1 to present the accounting for two possibilities: (1) a statutory merger and (2) a stock acquisition. (Accounting for a statutory consolidation is similar to that of a statutory merger.)

Business Combination is a Statutory Merger

Assume P Company paid $875,000 for all the common stock of S Company on January 1, 1995, in a statutory merger. A computation of the difference between cost and book value of the net assets acquired and a schedule to assign this difference is presented in Illustration 7-2.

Recall that, under a statutory merger, the acquiring company survives whereas the acquired company's stock is retired and the company ceases to exist. Thus, P Company will record the acquisition of S Company's assets and liabilities, as well as a deferred income tax liability, as follows:

Cash	82,000	
Accounts Receivable	94,000	
Inventory	FV 130,000	
Land	FV 160,000	
Plant and Equipment	FV 505,000	
Discount on Notes Payable	10,000	
Goodwill	100,100	
Current Liabilities		65,000
Notes Payable		100,000
Deferred Income Tax Liability		41,100
Cash		875,000

Assets acquired and liabilities assumed are recorded at their fair values, a deferred income tax liability is recorded equal to the tax rate times the difference between the fair values and tax bases of individual assets and liabilities [.30 × ($127,000 + $10,000) = $41,100], and the remaining cost is recorded as goodwill.

The deferred income tax liability will be eliminated in the future as the temporary differences between the fair values and tax bases of the assets acquired, and

---

[1] *Statement of Financial Accounting Standards No. 109*, "Accounting for Income Taxes," FASB (Stamford, 1992), par. 30.

ILLUSTRATION 7-1
Illustrative Data
S Company
Balance Sheet
January 1, 1995

Cash	$ 82,000
Accounts receivable (net)	94,000
Inventory (FIFO)	118,000
Land	120,000
Plant and equipment (net)	430,000
Total assets	$844,000
Current liabilities	$ 65,000
Notes payable	100,000
Common stock, $2 par value	150,000
Other contributed capital	300,000
Retained earnings	229,000
Total equities	$844,000

Other information:
1. The book values/tax bases of assets and liabilities were equal to their fair values except for the following:

ASSET/LIABILITY	FAIR VALUE	BOOK VALUE/ TAX BASIS	DIFFERENCE	REMAINING LIFE
Inventory	$130,000	$118,000	$ 12,000	N/A
Land	160,000	120,000	40,000	N/A
Plant & equipment	505,000	430,000	75,000	15 yrs.
Total			$127,000	
Note payable	90,000	100,000	$ 10,000	4 yrs.

2. P Company's effective income tax rate is 30%.
3. P Company reported pretax income for 1995 in the amount of $170,000.
4. Goodwill is amortized over 20 years.
5. Note discount is amortized using the straight-line method.

ILLUSTRATION 7-2
Assignment of Difference Between the Cost of Acquisition
and the Book Value of the Net Assets Acquired

Cost of acquisition	$875,000
Book value of net assets acquired	679,000
Difference between cost and book value	196,000
Assigned to:	
Increase inventory, land, and plant and equipment to fair value	(127,000)
Decrease note payable to fair value	(10,000)
Establish deferred income tax liability (30% × ($127,000 + $10,000))	41,100
Balance assigned to goodwill	$100,100

844-65-100 (handwritten)

liabilities assumed are realized through depreciation, amortization, or sale. Since P Company uses the FIFO inventory method, the entire $12,000 difference between the fair value and tax basis of the inventory reverses out in 1995. In addition, $5,000 ($75,000 ÷ 15 yrs.) of the difference assigned to plant and equipment and $2,500 ($10,000 ÷ 4 yrs.) of the difference assigned to discount on note payable reverses each year. Thus P Company will make the following income tax entry for 1995:

Income Tax Expense (balancing amount)	52,502	
Deferred Income Tax Liability		
[.30 × ($12,000 + $5,000 + $2,500)]	5,850	
Income Tax Payable (.30 × $194,505)		58,352

Income tax payable is based on taxable income, which is calculated as follows:

Pretax income	$170,000
Add recorded expenses not deductible in determining taxable income:	
Cost of sales	12,000
Depreciation	5,000
Discount amortization	2,500
Goodwill amortization	
($100,100 ÷ 20 yrs.)	5,005
Taxable income	$194,505

Recognition of a Deferred Tax Asset The preceding illustration involved the recognition of a deferred income tax liability only, because the temporary differences between the tax bases and recorded (fair) values of assets and liabilities all related to future taxable amounts. To illustrate the recognition of a deferred income tax asset, assume that the fair value of the note payable was $110,000 rather than $90,000, thereby requiring the recognition of a $10,000 premium on the note payable in the initial acquisition entry. Under these circumstances, the assignment of the difference between cost and book value would be as presented in Illustration 7-3:

ILLUSTRATION 7-3
Assignment of Difference Between the Cost of Acquisition
and the Book Value of the Net Assets Acquired

Difference between cost and book value	$196,000
Assigned to:	
Increase inventory, land, and plant and equipment to fair value	(127,000)
Increase note payable to fair value	10,000
Establish deferred income tax liability (30% × $127,000)	38,100
Establish deferred income tax asset (30% × $10,000)	(3,000)
Balance assigned to goodwill	$114,100

The entry to record the acquisition of S Company would then be:

Cash	82,000	
Accounts Receivable	94,000	
Inventory	130,000	
Land	160,000	
Plant and Equipment	505,000	
Deferred Income Tax Asset	3,000	
Goodwill	114,100	
Current Liabilities		65,000
Note Payable		100,000
Premium on Note Payable		10,000
Deferred Income Tax Liability		38,100
Cash		875,000

In this case, in 1995, P Company will record $5,000 less in interest expense (a $2,500 reduction in discount amortization plus a $2,500 increase in premium amortization) and $700 more in amortization of goodwill [($114,100 − $100,100) ÷ 20 yrs] and its pretax income for 1995 will be $174,300 ($170,000 + $5,000 − $700) rather than $170,000.

Assuming P Company reported $174,300 in pretax income for 1995, the book entry to record 1995 income taxes would be:

Income Tax Expense (balancing amount)	54,002	
Deferred Income Tax Liability		
[.30 × ($12,000 + $5,000)]	5,100	
Deferred Income Tax Asset (.30 × $2,500)		750
Income Tax Payable (.30 × $194,505)		58,352

Income tax payable is based on taxable income, which is calculated as follows:

Pretax income		$174,300
Add recorded expenses not deductible in		
determining taxable income:		
Cost of sales	$12,000	
Depreciation	5,000	
Goodwill amortization		
($114,100 ÷ 20 yrs.)	5,705	22,705
Deduct nontaxable amortization of		
premium on note payable		(2,500)
Taxable income		$194,505

Business Combination Is a Stock Acquisition

Rather than purchasing all the common stock of S Company, assume P Company purchased 90% of S Company's common stock for $787,500 as a stock acquisition. P Company and S Company file a consolidated income tax return. In a stock acquisition, the acquiring company records the cost of the stock required as an investment, which is then eliminated with a workpaper entry in the preparation of consolidated financial statements. Thus, P Company would make the following stock acquisition entry on January 1, 1995:

Investment in S Company	787,500	
Cash		787,500

Assuming the information presented in Illustration 7-1, the December 31, 1995, workpaper entries to eliminate the investment account, assign the difference between cost and book value, record depreciation and amortization, and report the related deferred income tax liability would be:

Common Stock—S Company (.9 × $150,000)	135,000	
Other Contributed Capital—S (.9 × $300,000)	270,000	
1/1 Retained Earning—S (.9 × $229,000)	206,100	
Difference Between Cost and Book Value	176,400	
Investment in S Company		787,500
To eliminate the investment account.		
Cost of Goods Sold (.9 × $12,000)	10,800	
Land (.9 × $40,000)	36,000	
Plant and Equipment (net) (.9 × $75,000)	67,500	
Discount on Note Payable (.9 × $10,000)	9,000	
Goodwill (balancing amount)	90,090	
Deferred Income Tax Liability		
[.9 × ($137,000 × .3)]		36,990
Difference Between Cost and Book Value		176,400
To assign the difference between cost and book value.		
Depreciation Expense ($67,500 ÷ 15 yrs.)	4,500	
Interest Expense—Note Payable ($9,000 ÷ 4 yrs.)	2,250	
Amortization of Goodwill ($90,090 ÷ 20 yrs.)	4,505	
Plant and Equipment (net)		4,500
Discount on Note Payable		2,250
Goodwill		4,505
To depreciate and amortize the difference between cost and book value.		
Deferred Income Tax Liability	5,265	
Income Tax Expense		
[.30 × ($10,800 + $4,500 + $2,250)]		5,265
To adjust tax expense as a result of the reversal of temporary differences.		

INCOME TAX CONSEQUENCES IN THE CONSOLIDATED FINANCIAL STATEMENTS WHEN THE AFFILIATES HAVE FILED SEPARATE INCOME TAX RETURNS

Internal Revenue Service rules and regulations relating to the preparation of consolidated income tax returns are beyond the scope of this text. However, when a parent company owns at least an 80% interest in a domestic subsidiary, the companies generally may elect to file a consolidated income tax return. When consolidated income tax returns are filed, temporary differences relating to the consolidation process normally do not arise in the preparation of consolidated financial statements.[2] For example, unrealized intercompany profit is generally treated in the same way in calculating consolidated taxable income as it is in calculating combined income in the consolidated income statement. Thus, when the affiliates file a consolidated income tax return, no timing differences arise because of the elimination of unrealized intercompany profit. In previous chapters we have assumed that the affiliates elected to file a consolidated income tax return.

However, many affiliated groups do not qualify to file consolidated income tax returns and must file separate tax returns. When the affiliates file separate income tax returns, deferred tax consequences may arise in the consolidated financial statements since differences usually exist between the time income is reported in the consolidated financial statements and the time such income becomes a determinate of the taxable income of the separate affiliates. Two major topics require attention in addressing the treatment in the consolidated financial statements of deferred income tax consequences when the affiliates each file separate income tax returns:

1. Deferred income tax consequences that arise in the consolidated financial statements because of undistributed subsidiary income.

2. Deferred income tax consequences that arise in the consolidated financial statements because of the elimination of unrealized intercompany profit.

Deferred Tax Consequences Arising Because of Undistributed Subsidiary Income

When separate tax returns are filed by members of an affiliated group, the parent company will include dividends received from a subsidiary in its taxable income, but the parent company's share of the entire reported income of the subsidiary is included in consolidated net income. Thus, deferred tax consequences must be accounted for, since a difference equal to the parent company's share of the undistributed income of its subsidiary will exist between the amount of pretax income reported in the consolidated income statement and the total taxable income reported on the separate income tax returns of the affiliated companies. It is a temporary difference that must be taken into consideration when calculating the deferred income tax liability of the consolidated entity.

The measurement of the deferred tax consequences of the undistributed income of a subsidiary necessarily depends on assumptions as to the nature of the transaction(s) that will result in the future taxation of the previously undistributed income. If it is expected that the parent company's equity in the undistributed income ultimately will be realized in the form of a taxable dividend, the deferred tax amount is calculated after giving effect to all available tax credits and exclusions. Federal income tax rules permit a portion of the dividends received from a domestic subsidiary to be excluded from taxable income. Under current federal income tax rules, 80% of dividends received from a less than 80% owned domestic subsidiary

---

[2]In general, when a consolidated income tax return is filed, the income tax liability of the consolidated group is determined on the basis of the relevant rules and regulations of the Internal Revenue Service. Then the total tax liability so determined is allocated to and recorded as an expense on the books of the individual affiliates in the consolidated group.

and 100% of dividends received from an 80% or more owned domestic subsidiary may be excluded from taxable income.[3] Thus, if it is expected that the undistributed income of the subsidiary will be realized in the form of future dividend distributions, the expected dividends received exclusion must be considered. On the other hand, if it is expected that the undistributed earnings of the subsidiary will not be realized until the subsidiary is sold, the dividend received exclusion does not apply.

Tax consequences relating to undistributed income are not recorded on the books of the parent company when the investment to be consolidated is recorded using the cost method or the partial equity method.[4] Thus, when investments are recorded using the cost or partial equity methods of accounting, *workpaper* entries are necessary each year to report the income tax consequences of past and current undistributed income.

To illustrate, assume that P Company owns 75% of the voting stock of S Company. The stock was acquired when S Company's retained earnings amounted to $150,000. Assume further that the affiliates file separate income tax returns and (1) S Company's retained earnings are $260,000 at the beginning of 1995, (2) it reported net income of $90,000 for the year ended December 31, 1995, (3) it declared dividends of $30,000 during 1995, (4) its retained earnings are $320,000 at the end of 1995; (5) undistributed income is expected to be received in the form of future dividends, and (6) the past, current, and estimated future marginal income tax rates are 40%. The following *workpaper entry* is needed at the end of 1995 to report the income tax consequences of past and current undistributed income.

Retained Earnings 1/1—P Company (1)	6,600	
Income Tax Expense (balancing amount) (3)	3,600	
Deferred Income Tax Liability (2)		10,200

(1) $260,000 − $150,000 = $110,000 × 75% × 20% × 40% = $6,600
(2) $320,000 − $150,000 = $170,000 × 75% × 20% × 40% = $10,200
(3) $10,200 − $6,600 = $3,600

The debit to the beginning balance of P Company's retained earnings reflects the estimated tax on P Company's share of the undistributed income of S Company from the date of acquisition to the beginning of the current year. If tax rates change, the debit to beginning retained earnings is the same as the credit made to the deferred tax liability in the prior year's workpaper. The deferred income tax liability is credited for the estimated tax on P Company's share of the undistributed income of S Company from the date of acquisition to the end of the year. If tax rates change, the credit to the deferred tax liability is based on the new tax rate. The debit to income tax expense is the difference between these two amounts, that is, the

---

[3]For less than 20% owned investees, only 70% of the dividends received from a domestic corporation may be excluded from taxable income.

[4]When an investment is *reported* using the equity method, entries to report the income tax consequences of undistributed investee income are recorded on the books of the investor. Entries necessary when an investment is reported as an investment using the equity method are described and illustrated in Chapter 12.

amount necessary to balance the entry. A similar workpaper entry must be made every year.

If it is expected that the undistributed income will not be realized until the subsidiary is sold, the workpaper entry at the end of 1995 to report the income tax consequences is:

Retained Earnings 1/1—P Company (1)	33,000	
Income Tax Expense (balancing amount) (3)	18,000	
Deferred Income Tax Liability (2)		51,000

    (1) $260,000 − $150,000 = $110,000 × 75% × 40% = $33,000
    (2) $320,000 − $150,000 = $170,000 × 75% × 40% = $51,000
    (3) $51,000 − $33,000 = $18,000

Note that the 80% dividend exclusion is ignored. In addition, the appropriate tax rate to use in the calculation is the capital gains tax rate. Under current federal income tax regulations, capital gains are taxed at the same rate as ordinary income. As mentioned earlier, a similar workpaper entry is needed every year.

Deferred Tax Consequences Arising Because of Unrealized Intercompany Profit

If the affiliated companies file consolidated income tax returns, profits from intercompany transactions are included in taxable income in the same years that they are included in the consolidated income statement. In that case, the amount at which the asset is reported in the consolidated financial statements and its tax basis are the same, and it is not necessary to consider deferred tax consequences.

However, when the affiliates file separate income tax returns, the tax basis for an asset that is transferred between affiliates is based on the price paid by the purchasing affiliate. Thus, when a gain or loss is recorded by the selling affiliate, the tax basis of the asset will differ from the amount reported for that asset in the consolidated financial statements. Assuming that the selling affiliate recognized a profit on the intercompany sale, the amount of this difference is equal to the **un-realized** profit associated with that asset on the balance sheet date. This difference is a temporary difference that will result in deductible amounts on the tax return of the **purchasing affiliate** in a future year(s) when the profit is considered realized in the consolidated financial statements through the sale or depreciation of the asset. However, under *SFAS No. 109*, "Accounting for Income Taxes," the measurement of the tax benefit for temporary differences related to unrealized profit on intercompany sales is not subject to the basic principles that apply to other temporary differences that will result in deductible amounts in future years. Rather, the provisions of *ARB No. 51*, "Consolidated Financial Statements," relating to income taxes paid on intercompany profit, are applied.

Paragraph 17 of *ARB No. 51* requires deferral of income taxes **paid by the seller** on intercompany profits on assets remaining within the consolidated group. By adopting the provisions of *ARB No. 51*, the Board in *SFAS No. 109* elected to require that deferred tax effects be calculated based on the income taxes paid by the selling affiliate rather than on the future tax benefit to the purchasing affiliate. The amounts calculated under these two approaches would be different, for example, if the affiliates had different marginal tax rates or were in different tax jurisdictions, or when expected future tax rates differ from the tax rate used to determine the tax paid or accrued by the selling affiliate. In effect, the taxes paid by the selling affiliate on unrealized intercompany profits are treated as prepaid taxes in the consolidated financial statements, and the tax expense associated with the intercompany profit is reported in the consolidated financial statements in the same period that the profit is reported as realized.[5]

Intercompany Sales of Inventory

To illustrate the treatment in the consolidated financial statements of deferred income taxes relating to intercompany sales of inventory assume that:

1. S Company is a 70% owned subsidiary of P Company.

2. The companies file separate income tax returns and the marginal income tax rates for both companies are 40%.

3. On December 31, 1995, there is $500,000 of unrealized intercompany profit in the ending inventory of the purchasing affiliate.

Workpaper eliminating entries relating to the unrealized profit included in inventory of the purchasing affiliate differ depending on whether the selling affiliate is the parent company (downstream sale) or the subsidiary (upstream or horizontal sale). Entries in the December 31, 1995, and December 31, 1996, consolidated statements workpapers under each of these conditions are illustrated below:

Consolidated Statements Workpaper Entries
December 31, 1995

DOWNSTREAM SALE				UPSTREAM SALE		
Cost of Sales	500,000			Cost of Sales	500,000	
Inventory		500,000		Inventory		500,000

To eliminate unrealized profit in ending inventory.

Deferred Tax Asset	200,000			Deferred Tax Asset	200,000	
Income Tax Expense		200,000		Income Tax Expense		200,000

To defer income tax paid or accrued by the selling affiliate on unrealized intercompany profit (.4 × $500,000 = $200,000).

---

[5]Some accountants contend that the Board's decision in *SFAS No. 109* to recognize a prepaid asset for the seller's tax payments rather than to recognize a deferred tax asset for the buyer's deductible temporary difference reflects a ***deferred approach*** that is inconsistent with the ***asset and liability approach*** to accounting for income taxes. The Board concluded that although the excess of the buyer's tax basis over the cost of transferred assets as reported in the consolidated statements ***technically*** meets the definition of a temporary difference, the ***substance*** of accounting for it as such would be to recognize income taxes related to intercompany gains that are not recognized under *ARB No. 51*. As a result, the Board left *ARB No. 51* unchanged, and the income taxes paid by the selling affiliate including the tax effect, in the selling affiliate's tax jurisdiction, of any reversing temporary differences as a result of that intercompany sale are deferred in the consolidated financial statements.

Although the workpaper entries are the same, when calculating the noncontrolling interest in combined income in the case of upstream sales, the *after-tax* unrealized intercompany profit of $300,000 [($500,000 − $200,000) or (.60 × $500,000)] must be subtracted from reported subsidiary income. For example, if the sale is upstream and S Company reports net income of $900,000 in 1995, the noncontrolling interest in combined income is $180,000 [.30 × ($900,000 − (.60 × $500,000))]. If the sale is downstream, the amount of subsidiary income included in combined income is not affected by the elimination of unrealized intercompany profit and no adjustment is necessary in the calculation of the noncontrolling interest in combined income.

Consolidated Statements Workpaper Entries
December 31, 1996

DOWNSTREAM SALE			UPSTREAM SALE		

1/1 Retained Earnings—
  P Company
  (1.0 × $500,000)
	500,000		1/1 Retained Earnings—
			  P Company
			  (.7 × $500,000)
				350,000	

			1/1 Retained Earnings—
			  S Company
			  (.3 × $500,000)
				150,000	

Cost of Sales		500,000	Cost of Sales		500,000

To recognize intercompany profit realized during the year and to reduce the controlling and the noncontrolling interests for their share of unrealized intercompany profit at the beginning of the year.

Income Tax Expense	200,000		Income Tax Expense	200,000	

1/1 Retained Earnings—
  P Company
  (1.0 × $200,000)
		200,000	1/1 Retained Earnings—
			  P Company
			  (.7 × $200,000)
					140,000

			1/1 Retained Earnings—
			  S Company
			  (.3 × $200,000)
					60,000

To recognize income tax expense on intercompany profit considered realized during the year and to adjust the controlling and noncontrolling interests for the tax consequence of unrealized intercompany profit eliminated in the previous entry.

In the case of the upstream sales the net after-tax adjustment to the noncontrolling interest at the **beginning of the year** is $90,000 ($150,000 − $60,000) which is the same amount by which the noncontrolling interest in combined income was reduced for after-tax unrealized intercompany profit at the end of the prior year [.3 × ($500,000 − $200,000) = $90,000].

If the sale is upstream, the noncontrolling interest in combined income is calculated after adding the after-tax amount of intercompany profit that is included in combined income in the current year (.60 × $500,000 = $300,000). For example, if the sale is upstream and S Company reports net income of $600,000 in 1996, the noncontrolling interest in combined income is $270,000 [.30 × ($600,000 + $300,000)].

If the sale is downstream, no adjustment is necessary in the calculation of the noncontrolling interest in combined income.

Impact of Unrealized Intercompany Profit on the Calculation of Deferred Tax Consequences Related to Undistributed Subsidiary Income

The workpaper entry necessary to report the tax consequences of past and current undistributed earnings of a subsidiary was described and illustrated earlier. The workpaper entry is necessary when there is undistributed subsidiary income and the affiliates file separate income tax returns. Now that we have discussed the effects of unrealized intercompany profits, it is important to note that the calculation of the tax consequences of undistributed income is based on the undistributed income of the subsidiary that has been *included in combined income.* Thus, before calculating the deferred tax consequences relating to undistributed subsidiary income, the amount of undistributed income of the subsidiary must be adjusted for the *after-tax amount of* unrealized intercompany profit *recorded by the subsidiary* that has been recognized in the determination of combined income.

To illustrate, assume that:

1. P Company acquired 75% of the voting stock of S Company when S Company's retained earnings amounted to $150,000.

2. S Company reported retained earnings of $260,000 on January 1, 1996, and $320,000 on December 31, 1996.

3. S Company reported net income of $90,000 and declared dividends of $30,000 in 1996.

4. P Company reported net income from independent operations in 1996 in the amount of $700,000 and retained earnings on December 31, 1996, of $3,500,000.

5. The affiliates file separate income tax returns.

6. Undistributed income is expected to be received in the form of future dividends.

7. The dividends received deduction is 80%, and past, current, and future expected marginal income tax rates are 40%.

8. There were no intercompany sales prior to 1995 and unrealized profits on January 1 and on December 31, 1996, resulting from intercompany sales are as summarized below.

	UNREALIZED INTERCOMPANY PROFIT ON	
RESULTING FROM	1/1/96	12/31/96
Sales by S Company to P Company	$10,000	$ 5,000
Sales by P Company to S Company	15,000	20,000

The calculation of the amounts of the undistributed income of S Company that have been included in combined income is presented in Illustration 7-4.

The following workpaper entry is needed in the December 31, 1996, consolidated financial statements workpaper to report the income tax consequences of past and current undistributed subsidiary income.

1/1 Retained Earnings—P Company (1)	6,240	
Income Tax Expense (balancing amount) (2)	3,780	
Deferred Income Tax Liability (3)		10,020

(1) $104,000 × 75% × 20% × 40% = $6,240
(2) $10,020 − $6,240 = $3,780
(3) $167,000 × 75% × 20% × 40% = $10,020

Note that the calculation of the deferred income tax liability on undistributed subsidiary income is not affected by unrealized intercompany profit recorded by the parent company on sales to the subsidiary (downstream sales). The calculation is also not affected by the assignment, depreciation, or amortization of any difference between cost and book value.

ILLUSTRATION 7-4
Undistributed Income of S Company
That Has Been Included in Combined Income

S COMPANY	FROM ACQUISITION TO 1/1/96	FOR CALENDAR YEAR 1996	FROM ACQUISITION TO 12/31/96
Retained earnings 1/1/96	$260,000		
Retained earnings 12/31/96			$320,000
Retained earnings date of acquisition	(150,000)		(150,000)
Increase in retained earnings	110,000		170,000
Net income 1996		$90,000	
Dividends 1996		(30,000)	
After-tax unrealized profit on 1/1/96 (.6 × $10,000)	(6,000)	6,000	
After-tax unrealized profit on 12/31/96 (.6 × $5,000)		(3,000)	(3,000)
Undistributed income that has been included in combined income	$104,000	$63,000	$167,000

Analytical Calculations of Consolidated Net Income and Consolidated Retained Earnings

When the affiliated companies file separate income tax returns, the analytical calculations of consolidated net income and consolidated retained earnings must be modified to incorporate income tax consequences. When calculating the amounts of net income or retained earnings that have been realized in transactions with third parties, adjustments must now be made for the *after-tax amounts* of unrealized intercompany profit. In addition, consolidated net income is reduced by the income tax consequences of undistributed income for the current year and consolidated retained earnings is reduced by the income tax consequences of undistributed income from the date of acquisition to the date of the calculation.

The calculation of consolidated net income in Illustration 7-5 and the calculation of consolidated retained earnings in Illustration 7-6 are based on the same assumptions as those used in the preparation of Illustration 7-4.

ILLUSTRATION 7-5
Calculation of Consolidated Net Income
For Year Ended December 31, 1996

P Company's net income from independent operations		$700,000
Less after-tax unrealized intercompany profit on 1996 sales to S Company (.6 × $20,000)		(12,000)
Plus after-tax profit on 1995 sales to S Company realized in transactions with third parties in 1996 (.6 × $15,000)		9,000
P Company's net income from independent operations that has been realized in transactions with third parties		697,000
Reported net income of S Company	$90,000	
Less after-tax unrealized intercompany profit on 1996 sales to P Company (.6 × $5,000)	(3,000)	
Plus after-tax profit on 1995 sales to P Company realized in transactions with third parties in 1996 (.6 × $10,000)	6,000	
S Company's net income that has been realized in transactions with third parties	$93,000	
P Company's share thereof (.75 × $93,000)		69,750
Less income tax consequence of undistributed income of S Company for 1996 that has been included in combined income [($93,000 − $30,000) = $63,000 × .75 × .20 × .40]		(3,780)
Less amortization of the difference between cost and book value		(−0−)
Consolidated net income		$762,970

ILLUSTRATION 7-6
Calculation of Consolidated Retained Earnings
December 31, 1996

P Company's Retained Earnings on 12/31/96		$3,500,000
Less after-tax amount of P Company's retained earnings that have not been realized in transactions with third parties (.6 × $20,000)		(12,000)
P Company's retained earnings that have been realized in transactions with third parties		3,488,000
Increase in retained earnings of S Company from date of acquisition to 12/31/96 ($320,000 − $150,000)	$170,000	
Less after-tax unrealized profit included in S Company's retained earnings on 12/31/96 (.6 × $5,000)	(3,000)	
Increase in reported retained earnings of S Company since acquisition that has been realized in transactions with third parties	$167,000	
P Company's share thereof (.75 × $167,000)		125,250
Less income tax consequence of undistributed income of S Company that has been included in combined income from date of acquisition to 12/31/96 ($167,000 × .75 × .20 × .40)		(10,020)
Less cumulative amortization of the difference between cost and book value to 12/31/96		(−0−)
Consolidated retained earnings 12/31/96		$3,603,230

Intercompany Sales of Equipment

To illustrate the treatment in the consolidated financial statements of deferred income taxes relating to intercompany sales of equipment, assume that P Company owns a 70% interest in S Company and that on January 1, 1995, S Company sells P Company equipment with a book value of $500,000 (original cost of $800,000 and accumulated depreciation of $300,000) for $600,000. On January 1, 1995, the equipment has a remaining useful life of five years and is depreciated using the straight-line method. The marginal income tax rates for both companies are 40% and separate income tax returns are filed.

S Company will record a gain of $100,000 on the sale of the equipment and each year P Company will record depreciation that is $20,000 greater than depreciation based on the cost of the equipment to the selling affiliate. Workpaper eliminating entries in the December 31, 1995, and December 31, 1996, consolidated statements workpapers relating to the unrealized profit on the intercompany sale of the equipment are illustrated below:

Consolidated Statements Workpaper Entries
December 31, 1995

(1) Gain on Sale of Equipment	100,000	
Property and Equipment		100,000
To eliminate unrealized profit recorded on intercompany sale of equipment.		
(2) Accumulated Depreciation	20,000	
Depreciation Expense		20,000
To reverse the amount of excess depreciation recorded during the current year.		
(3) Deferred Tax Asset	32,000	
Income Tax Expense		32,000
To defer the net amount of income tax paid or accrued by the affiliates on the amount of unrealized intercompany profit in equipment at the end of the year [.4 × ($100,000 − $20,000)].		
(4) Property and Equipment	300,000	
Accumulated Depreciation		300,000
To restate property and equipment at original cost to the selling affiliate.		

Since the selling affiliate is a partially owned subsidiary (upstream sale), the calculation of the noncontrolling interest in combined income requires that the *after-tax* amount of gain recorded by the subsidiary (.60 × $100,000 = $60,000) be subtracted from the reported net income of the subsidiary and that the *after-tax* amount of the gain considered to be realized through depreciation (.6 × $20,000 = $12,000) be added to the reported net income of the subsidiary before multiplying by the noncontrolling interest percentage. Assuming that S Company reported net income of $144,000 in 1995, the noncontrolling interest in combined income is $28,800 [.30 × ($144,000 − $60,000 + $12,000)].

If the sale of equipment is downstream, no adjustments to the reported net income of the subsidiary are necessary in the calculation of the noncontrolling interest in combined income.

Consolidated Statements Workpaper Entries
December 31,1996

(1) 1/1 Retained Earnings—P Company

$\quad$ [.70 × ($100,000 − $20,000)] 56,000

$\quad$ 1/1 Retained Earnings—S Company

$\quad$ [.30 × ($100,000 − $20,000)] 24,000

$\quad$ Accumulated Depreciation 20,000

$\qquad$ Equipment 100,000

$\qquad$ To reduce the controlling and the noncontrolling interests for their respective shares of unrealized intercompany profit at the beginning of the year, to reduce accumulated depreciation by the amount of excess depreciation accumulated to the beginning of the year, and to reduce the carrying value of equipment to its book value on the date of the intercompany sale.

(2) Accumulated Depreciation 20,000

$\quad$ Depreciation Expense 20,000

$\qquad$ To reverse the amount of excess depreciation recorded during the current year.

(3) Deferred Tax Asset 24,000

$\quad$ Income Tax Expense 8,000

$\qquad$ 1/1 Retained Earnings—P Company 22,400

$\qquad$ 1/1 Retained Earnings—S Company 9,600

$\qquad$ To recognize deferred taxes for taxes paid in prior years on the amount of intercompany profit still considered unrealized at the **end of the year** [.40 × ($100,000 − $20,000 − $20,000) = $24,000], to recognize income tax expense on intercompany profit considered to be realized during the current year (.40 × $20,000 = $8,000), to adjust consolidated retained earnings for the controlling interest's share of the tax consequence of unrealized profit at the beginning of the year (.70 × $32,000 = $22,400), and to adjust the noncontrolling interest for its share of the tax consequence of unrealized profit at the beginning of the year (.30 × $32,000 = $9,600).

(4) Property and Equipment 300,000

$\quad$ Accumulated Depreciation 300,000

$\qquad$ To restate property and equipment to original cost to the selling affiliate.

The noncontrolling interest in combined income is calculated after adding the *after-tax* profit considered realized during the year (.6 × $20,000 = $12,000) to the reported net income of the subsidiary. If S Company reported net income of $162,000 in 1996, the noncontrolling interest in combined income is $52,200 [.30 × ($162,000 + $12,000)].

Impact of Unrealized Intercompany Profit on the Calculation of Deferred Tax Consequences Related to Undistributed Subsidiary Income

Earlier we emphasized that the calculation of the tax consequences of undistributed income is based on the undistributed income of the subsidiary that has been *included in combined income*. Thus, before calculating the deferred tax consequences relating to undistributed subsidiary income, the amount of undistributed income must be adjusted for the *after-tax* amount of unrealized intercompany profit *recorded by the subsidiary* that has been recognized in the determination of combined income.

To illustrate, assume that

1. P Company acquired 70% of the voting stock of S Company when S Company's retained earnings amounted to $150,000.

2. On January 1, 1995, S Company recorded a $100,000 gain on the sale to P Company of equipment with a remaining life of five years.

3. On January 1, 1996, P Company recorded a $60,000 gain on the sale to S Company of equipment with a remaining life of six years.

4. S Company reported retained earnings of $260,000 on January 1, 1996, and $320,000 on December 31, 1996.

5. S Company reported net income of $90,000 and declared dividends of $30,000 in 1996.

6. P Company reported net income from independent operations in 1996 in the amount of $700,000 and retained earnings on December 31, 1996, of $3,500,000.

7. The affiliates file separate income tax returns.

8. Undistributed income is expected to be received in the form of future dividends.

9. The dividends received deduction is 80%, and the past, current, and expected future marginal income tax rates are 40%.

The calculation of the amounts of the undistributed income of S Company that have been included in combined income is presented in Illustration 7-7. The

ILLUSTRATION 7-7
Undistributed Income of S Company
That Has Been Included in Combined Income

S COMPANY	FROM ACQUISITION TO 1/1/96	FOR CALENDAR YEAR 1996	FROM ACQUISITION TO 12/31/96
Retained earnings 1/1/96	$260,000		
Retained earnings 12/31/96			$320,000
Retained earnings date of acquisition	(150,000)		(150,000)
Increase in retained earnings	110,000		170,000
Net income 1996		$90,000	
Dividends 1996		(30,000)	
After-tax unrealized profit on 1/1/96. [.6 × ($100,000 − $20,000)	(48,000)		
After-tax profit realized in 1996 (.6 × $20,000)		12,000	
After-tax unrealized profit on 12/31/96 [.6 × ($100,000 − $20,000 − $20,000)]			(36,000)
Undistributed income that has been included in combined income	$ 62,000	$72,000	$134,000

following entry is needed in the December 31, 1996, consolidated statements workpaper to report the income tax consequences of past and current undistributed subsidiary income:

9-18

A.

1/1 Retained Earnings—P Company (1)	3,472	
Income Tax Expense (balancing amount) (2)	4,032	
Deferred Income Tax Liability (3)		7,504

(1) $62,000 × 70% × 20% × 40% = $3,472
(2) $7,504 − $3,472 = $4,032
(3) $134,000 × 70% × 20% × 40% = $7,504

Note that the calculation of the deferred income tax liability on undistributed subsidiary income is not affected by unrealized intercompany profit recorded by the parent company on sales to the subsidiary (downstream sales). The calculation is also not affected by the assignment, depreciation, or amortization of any difference between cost and book value.

Analytical Calculations of Consolidated Net Income and Consolidated Retained Earnings

When the affiliated companies file separate income tax returns, the analytical calculations of consolidated net income and consolidated retained earnings must be modified to incorporate income tax consequences. When calculating the amounts of net income or retained earnings that have been realized in transactions with third parties, adjustments must now be made for the ***after-tax amounts*** of unrealized intercompany profit. In addition, consolidated net income is reduced by the income tax consequence of undistributed income for the current year and consolidated retained earnings is reduced by the income tax consequence of undistributed income from the date of acquisition to the date of the calculation.

The calculation of consolidated net income in Illustration 7-8 and the calculation of consolidated retained earnings in Illustration 7-9 are based on the same assumptions as those used in the preparation of Illustration 7-7.

Consolidated Statements Workpaper—Partial Equity Method

The balances reported by the parent company in income, retained earnings, and the investment account differ depending on the method used by the parent company to record its investment. As illustrated in previous chapters, however, the method used by the parent company to record its investment has no affect on the consolidated balances.

As has also been illustrated in previous chapters, when the parent company records its investment using the partial equity method, a workpaper entry to reverse the effect of parent company entries during the year for subsidiary dividends and income replaces the cost method entries to establish reciprocity and to eliminate dividend income. However, workpaper entries to assign and amortize the difference between cost and book value, to eliminate intercompany sales, and to eliminate

ILLUSTRATION 7-8
Calculation of Consolidated Net Income
For Year Ended December 31, 1996

P Company's net income from independent operations		$700,000
Less after-tax intercompany profit on 1/1/96 sale of equipment to S Company (.6 × $60,000)		(36,000)
Plus after-tax profit on 1/1/96 sale of equipment considered realized in current year through depreciation (.60 × $10,000)		6,000
P Company's net income from independent operations that has been realized in transactions with third parties		670,000
Reported net income of S Company	$ 90,000	
Plus after-tax profit on 1/1/95 sale of equipment considered realized in current year through depreciation (.60 × $20,000)	12,000	
S Company's net income that has been realized in transactions with third parties	$102,000	
P Company's share thereof (.70 × $102,000)		71,400
Less income tax consequence of undistributed income of S Company for 1996 that has been included in combined income [($102,000 − $30,000) = $72,000 × .70 × .20 × .40]		(4,032)
Less amortization of the difference between cost and book value		−0−
Consolidated net income		$737,368

ILLUSTRATION 7-9

Calculation of Consolidated Retained Earnings
December 31, 1996

P Company's retained earnings on 12/31/96		$3,500,000
Less the after-tax amount of P Company's retained earnings that have not been realized in transactions with third parties [.6 × ($60,000 − $10,000)]		(30,000)
P Company's retained earnings that have been realized in transactions with third parties		3,470,000
Increase in retained earnings of S Company from date of acquisition to 12/31/96 ($320,000 − $150,000)	$170,000	
Less after-tax unrealized profit included in S Company's retained earnings on 12/31/96 [.6 × ($100,000 − $20,000 − $20,000)]	(36,000)	
Increase in reported retained earnings of S Company since acquisition that has been realized in transactions with third parties	$134,000	
P Company's share thereof (.70 × $134,000)		93,800
Less income tax consequence of undistributed income of S Company that has been included in combined income from date of acquisition to 12/31/96 ($134,000 × .70 × .20 × .40)		(7,504)
Less cumulative amortization of the difference between cost and book value		−0−
Consolidated retained earnings 12/31/96		$3,556,296

unrealized intercompany profit are the same regardless of whether the investment is recorded using the cost method or the partial equity method. Workpaper entries to record deferred tax consequences of unrealized intercompany profit and undistributed subsidiary income are also the same when the parent company records its investment using the partial equity method as those just illustrated where the parent company used the cost method to record its investment.

Summary of Workpaper Entries Relating to Intercompany Sales

Consolidated statements workpaper elimination entries for intercompany sales of merchandise are summarized in Illustration 7-10. Consolidated statements work-

ILLUSTRATION 7-10
Intercompany Profit—Inventories
Summary of Workpaper Elimination Entries

SELLING AFFILIATE IS PARENT OR WHOLLY OWNED SUBSIDIARY	SELLING AFFILIATE IS A LESS THAN WHOLLY OWNED SUBSIDIARY
Sales	**SAME**
Cost of Sales	
To eliminate intercompany sales.	
Cost of Sales	**SAME**
Inventory (balance sheet)	
To eliminate intercompany profit in ending inventory.	
Beginning Retained Earnings—P	**Beginning Retained Earnings—P**
	Beginning Retained Earnings—S
Cost of Sales	**Cost of Sales**
To recognize intercompany profit in **beginning inventory** realized during the current year and to adjust beginning consolidated retained earnings for the amount of unrealized profit at the beginning of the year.	To recognize the intercompany profit in **beginning inventory** realized during the current year and to adjust the controlling and the noncontrolling interests for their shares of the unrealized profit at the beginning of the year.

If the affiliates file separate income tax returns, additional workpaper eliminating entries may be necessary as follows:

Deferred Tax Asset	**SAME**
Income Tax Expense	
To defer income tax paid or accrued by the selling affiliate on unrealized intercompany profit in ending inventory.	
Income Tax Expense	**Income Tax Expense**
Beginning Retained Earnings—P	**Beginning Retained Earnings—P**
	Beginning Retained Earnings—S
To recognize income tax expense on intercompany profit in **beginning inventory** considered to be realized during the current year and to adjust beginning consolidated retained earnings for the income tax consequences of unrealized profit at the beginning of the year.	To recognize income tax expense on intercompany profit in **beginning inventory** considered to be realized during the current year and to adjust the controlling and the noncontrolling interests for their shares of the income tax consequences of unrealized profit at the beginning of the year.

paper elimination entries for intercompany sales of equipment are summarized in Illustration 7-11. The entries are the same whether the parent company uses the cost method or the partial equity method to record its investment. However, the form of the workpaper entry to adjust for unrealized intercompany profit at the beginning of the year differs as between upstream and downstream sales.

ILLUSTRATION 7-11
Intercompany Profit—Equipment
Summary of Workpaper Elimination Entries

SELLING AFFILIATE IS PARENT OR WHOLLY OWNED SUBSIDIARY	SELLING AFFILIATE IS A LESS THAN WHOLLY OWNED SUBSIDIARY

ENTRIES IN YEAR OF INTERCOMPANY SALE

Gain on Sale   **SAME**
    Equipment
    To eliminate unrealized profit on intercompany sale in year of sale and to reduce carrying value of equipment to its book value on date of sale.

Accumulated Depreciation   **SAME**
    Depreciation Expense
    To reverse amount (if any) of excess depreciation recorded during current year and to recognize an equivalent amount of intercompany profit as realized.

Equipment   **SAME**
    Accumulated Depreciation
    To restate equipment at its original cost to the selling affiliate.

If the affiliates file separate income tax returns an additional workpaper entry may be necessary as follows:

Deferred Tax Asset   **SAME**
    Income Tax Expense
    To defer the net amount of income tax paid or accrued by the affiliates on the amount of unrealized intercompany profit in equipment at the end of the year.

ENTRIES IN YEARS SUBSEQUENT TO THE YEAR OF INTERCOMPANY SALE

Beginning Retained Earnings—P	**Beginning Retained Earnings—P**
	Beginning Retained Earnings—S
Accumulated Depreciation	**Accumulated Depreciation**
Equipment	**Equipment**
To reduce consolidated retained earnings (the controlling interest) for the unrealized intercompany profit at the ***beginning of the year***, to reduce accumulated depreciation by the excess depreciation accumulated to the ***beginning of the year***, and to reduce the carrying value of equipment to its book value on the date of the intercompany sale.	To reduce the controlling and the noncontrolling interests for their respective shares of the unrealized intercompany profit at the ***beginning of the year***, to reduce accumulated depreciation by the excess depreciation accumulated to the ***beginning of the year***, and to reduce the carrying value of equipment to its book value on the date of the intercompany sale.

Accumulated Depreciation   **SAME**
    Depreciation Expense
    To reverse amount of excess depreciation recorded during current year and to recognize an equivalent amount of intercompany profit as realized.

(Continued)

Equipment	**SAME**
Accumulated Depreciation	
To restate equipment at its original cost to the selling affiliate.	

If the affiliates file separate income tax returns an additional workpaper entry may be necessary as follows:

Deferred Tax Asset	**Deferred Tax Asset**
Income Tax Expense	**Income Tax Expense**
Beginning Retained Earnings—P	**Beginning Retained Earnings—P**
	Beginning Retained Earnings—S
To recognize deferred taxes for taxes paid in prior years on the amount of intercompany profit still considered unrealized at the **end of the year**, to recognize income tax expense on intercompany profit considered to be realized during the current year, and to adjust consolidated retained earnings (the controlling interest) for the tax consequences of unrealized profit at the **beginning of year**.	To recognize deferred taxes for taxes paid in prior years on the amount of intercompany profit still considered unrealized at the **end of the year**, to recognize income tax expense on intercompany profit considered to be realized during the current year, and to adjust the controlling and the noncontrolling interests for their respective shares of the tax consequences of unrealized profit at the **beginning of year**.

Questions

1. Did the decision in *SFAS No.109* to require that a deferred tax asset or liability be recognized for differences between the assigned values and tax bases of assets and liabilities recognized in purchase business combinations change the amount of consolidated net income reported in years subsequent to the business combination? Explain.

2. Is the recognition of a deferred tax asset or deferred tax liability when assigning the difference between cost and book value affected by whether or not the affiliates file a consolidated income tax return?

3. What assumptions must be made about the realization of undistributed subsidiary income when the affiliates file separate income tax returns? Why?

4. The FASB elected to require that deferred tax effects relating to unrealized intercompany profits be calculated based on the income tax paid by the selling affiliate rather than on the future tax benefit to the purchasing affiliate. Describe circumstances where the amounts calculated under these approaches would be different.

5. How must the analytical calculations of consolidated net income and consolidated retained earnings be adjusted when the affiliated companies file separate income tax returns?

6. Identify two types of timing differences that may arise in the consolidated financial statements when the affiliates file separate income tax returns.

7. Must unrealized profit on intercompany transactions be considered when calculating the tax consequences of undistributed subsidiary income? Explain.

Exercises

Exercise 7-1

Patel Company paid $600,000 cash for the net assets of Seely Company on January 1, 1995, in a statutory merger. Seely Company had the following assets, liabilities, and owners' equity at that time:

	BOOK VALUE TAX BASIS	FAIR VALUE	EXCESS
Cash	$ 20,000	$ 20,000	$ –0–
Accounts receivable	112,000	112,000	–0–
Inventory (LIFO)	82,000	134,000	52,000
Land	30,000	55,000	25,000
Plant assets (net)	392,000	463,000	71,000
Total assets	$636,000	$784,000	
Allowance for uncollectible accounts	$ 10,000	$ 10,000	$ –0–
Accounts payable	54,000	54,000	–0–
Bonds payable	200,000	180,000	20,000
Common stock, $1 par value	80,000		
Other contributed capital	132,000		
Retained earnings	160,000		
Total equities	$636,000		

Required:

Prepare the journal entry to record the assets acquired and liabilities assumed. Assume an income tax rate of 40%.

Exercise 7-2

Assume the situation in Exercise 7-1 except that Patel Company paid $570,000 for 95% of the common stock of Seely Company on January 1, 1995.

Required:

A. Prepare the stock acquisition entry on the books of Patel Company.

B. Prepare eliminating entries for the preparation of a consolidated balance sheet work-paper on January 1, 1995.

Exercise 7-3

P Company acquired a 75% interest in the common stock of S Company on December 31, 1993. In 1995, S Company sold $400,000 in merchandise to P Company for $500,000. On December 31, 1995, P Company has in its inventory intercompany merchandise for which it paid $100,000.

The companies file separate income tax returns, and marginal income tax rates for both companies are 35%. There were no intercompany sales prior to 1995.

Required:

Prepare the consolidated financial statements workpaper entries needed to eliminate the effect of the intercompany sale for the year ended December 31, 1995.

Exercise 7-4

Pasco Company owns 75% of Shank Company. Pasco Company sells merchandise to Shank Company at 20% above cost. During 1995 and 1996, such sales amounted to $450,000 and $486,000, respectively. At the end of each year, Shank Company had in its inventory one-third of the amount of goods purchased from Pasco during that year. Marginal income tax rates for both companies are 40%.

Required:

Assume that the companies file separate income tax returns. Prepare the workpaper entries necessary to eliminate the effects of the intercompany sales for 1995 and 1996.

Exercise 7-5

Refer to Exercise 7-4. Using the same figures, assume that the sales were upstream instead of downstream.

Required:

Assume that the companies file separate income tax returns. Prepare the workpaper entries necessary to eliminate the effects of the intercompany sales for 1995 and 1996.

Exercise 7-6

P Company acquired an 80% interest in S Company on June 30, 1992. In 1995 and 1996, S Company sold merchandise to P Company as follows:

	TOTAL SALES OF S COMPANY TO P COMPANY	INTERCOMPANY MERCHANDISE IN 12/31 INVENTORY OF P COMPANY	UNREALIZED INTERCOMPANY PROFIT (20% OF SALES)
1995	$600,000	$300,000	$60,000
1996	800,000	200,000	40,000

The companies file separate income tax returns, and the marginal income tax rates for both companies are 45%. There were no intercompany sales prior to 1995.

Required:

A. Prepare, in general journal form, the entries necessary in the consolidated statements workpapers for the years ended December 31, 1995, and December 31, 1996, to eliminate the effects of intercompany sales of merchandise.

B. Assume that all intercompany sales are downstream. Prepare, in general journal form, the entries necessary in the consolidated statements workpapers for the years ended December 31, 1995, and December 31, 1996, to eliminate the effects of intercompany sales of merchandise.

Exercise 7-7

Probe Company owns all the outstanding common stock of Space Company and 80% of the outstanding common stock of Stellar Company. The amount of intercompany profit included in the inventories of Probe Company on December 31, 1995, and December 31, 1996, is indicated here.

	INTERCOMPANY PROFIT ON GOODS PURCHASED FROM		
	SPACE COMPANY	STELLAR COMPANY	TOTAL
Inventory—12/31/95	$3,800	$4,600	$8,400
Inventory—12/31/96	4,800	2,300	7,100

The three companies reported net income from their independent operations (including sales to affiliates) for the year ended December 31, 1996, as follows:

Probe Company	$280,000
Space Company	172,000
Stellar Company	120,000

The marginal income tax rates for each company are 40%, and the companies file separate income tax returns. Ignore the income tax consequences of undistributed subsidiary income.

Required:

Calculate consolidated net income for the year ended December 31, 1996.

Exercise 7-8

Pratt Company acquired 70% of the voting stock of Shelby Company when Shelby Company's retained earnings amounted to $450,000. Shelby Company's retained earnings amount to $800,000 on January 1, 1996, and $980,000 on December 31, 1996. In 1996, Shelby Company reported net income of $270,000 and declared dividends of $90,000. Pratt Company reported net income from independent operations in 1996 in the amount of $600,000 and retained earnings on December 31, 1996, of $1,800,000. The affiliates file separate income tax returns, undistributed earnings are expected to be received in the form of future dividends, the dividends received exclusion is 80%, and the prior, current, and expected future marginal income tax rates are 40%. Unrealized profits on January 1 and on December 31, 1996, resulting from intercompany sales are as summarized here:

	UNREALIZED INTERCOMPANY PROFIT ON	
RESULTING FROM	1/1/96	12/31/96
Sales by Shelby Company to Pratt Company	$20,000	$30,000
Sales by Pratt Company to Shelby Company	10,000	40,000

There were no intercompany sales prior to 1995.

Required:

A. Prepare in general journal form the entry necessary in the December 31, 1996, consolidated statements workpaper to report the income tax consequences of past and current undistributed subsidiary income.

B. Calculate consolidated net income for the year ended December 31, 1996.

C. Calculate consolidated retained earnings on December 31, 1996.

Exercise 7-9

On January 1, 1995, Pillar Company acquires a 75% interest in Samatros Company. On that date Pillar Company sells Samatros Company equipment with a book value of $600,000 (original cost of $900,000 and accumulated depreciation of $300,000) for $700,000. On January 1, 1995, the equipment has an estimated remaining useful life of five years and is depreciated using the straight-line method.

The companies file separate income tax returns, and they have marginal income tax rates of 30%.

Required:

A. Prepare the entries to eliminate the effects of the intercompany sale of equipment in the consolidated statements workpapers for the years ended December 31, 1995, and December 31, 1996.

B. Assume that the intercompany sale is upstream rather than downstream. Prepare the entries to eliminate the effects of the intercompany sale of equipment in the consolidated statements workpapers for the years ended December 31, 1995, and December 31, 1996.

Exercise 7-10

On January 1, 1992, Peltin Company acquired a 70% interest in Seal Company when its retained earnings were $700,000. Seal Company reported retained earnings on December 31, 1995, of $850,000. During 1996 Seal Company reported net income of $300,000 and distributed $100,000 in dividends. For the year ended December 31, 1996, Peltin Company reported net income from its independent operations of $2,000,000.

On January 1, 1995, Seal Company sold Peltin Company assets with a book value of $600,000 (original cost of $900,000 and accumulated depreciation of $300,000) for $700,000. On the date of sale, the equipment has an estimated remaining useful life of 10 years and is depreciated using the straight-line method.

The companies file separate income tax returns, both companies have prior, current, and expected future marginal income tax rates of 40%, and the dividends received exclusion is 80%.

Required:

A. Prepare the entries to eliminate the effects of the intercompany sale of equipment in the consolidated statements workpapers for the years ended December 31, 1995, and December 31, 1996. Do not prepare entries to report the income tax consequence of undistributed subsidiary income as part of this requirement.

B. Prepare in general journal form the entry necessary in the December 31, 1996, consolidated statements workpaper to report the income tax consequences of past and current undistributed subsidiary income.

Exercise 7-11

On January 1, 1994, Penta Company acquired a 70% interest in the common stock of Serna Company on the open market for $750,000, the book value at that date.

On January 1, 1995, Penta Company purchased new equipment for $14,500 from Serna Company. The equipment cost $9,000 and had an estimated life of five years as of January 1, 1995.

During 1995, Penta Company had merchandise sales to Serna Company of $100,000; the merchandise was priced at 25% above Penta Company's cost. Serna Company still owes Penta Company $17,500 on open account and has 20% of this merchandise in inventory at December 31, 1995. At the beginning of 1995, Serna Company had in inventory $25,000 of merchandise purchased in the previous period from Penta Company. The companies file separate income tax returns and both companies have marginal income tax rates of 30%.

Required:

A. Prepare all workpaper entries necessary to eliminate the effects of the intercompany sales on the consolidated financial statements for the year ended December 31, 1995.

B. Assume that Serna Company reports net income of $40,000 for the year ended December 31, 1996. Calculate the amount of noncontrolling interest to be deducted from combined income in the consolidated income statement for the year ended December 31, 1996.

Exercise 7-12

Preston Company acquired a 70% interest in Stretz Company when the retained earnings of Stretz Company were $300,000. On January 1, 1995, Stretz Company recorded a $300,000 gain on the sale to Preston Company of equipment with a remaining life of five years. On January 1, 1996, Preston Company recorded a $180,000 gain on the sale to Stretz Company of equipment with a remaining life of six years. Stretz Company reported net income of $180,000 and declared dividends of $60,000 in 1996. It reported retained earnings of $620,000 on January 1, 1996, and $740,000 on December 31, 1996. Preston Company reported net income from independent operations of $700,000 in 1996 and retained earnings of $1,200,000 on December 31, 1996. The affiliates file separate income tax returns, undistributed earnings are expected to be received in the form of future dividends, the dividends received exclusion is 80%, and the prior, current, and expected future marginal income tax rates are 40%.

Required:

A. Prepare in general journal form the entry necessary in the December 31, 1996, consolidated statements workpaper to report the income tax consequences of past and current undistributed subsidiary income.

B. Calculate consolidated net income for the year ended December 31, 1996.

C. Calculate consolidated retained earnings on December 31, 1996.

Problems

Problem 7-1

On January 1, 1995, Pruitt Company issued 30,000 shares of its $2 par value common stock for the net assets of Shah Company in a statutory merger accounted for as a purchase. Pruitt's common stock had a fair value of $28 per share at that time. A schedule of the Shah Company assets acquired and liabilities assumed at book values (which are equal to their tax bases) and fair values follows.

Item	BOOK VALUE/ TAX BASIS	FAIR VALUE	EXCESS
Receivables (net)	$125,000	$ 125,000	$ –0–
Inventory	167,000	195,000	28,000
Land	86,500	120,000	33,500
Plant assets (net)	467,000	567,000	100,000
Patents	95,000	200,000	105,000
Total	$940,500	$1,207,000	$266,500
Current liabilities	$ 89,500	$ 89,500	$ –0–
Bonds payable	300,000	360,000	60,000
Common stock	120,000		
Other contributed capital	164,000		
Retained earnings	267,000		
Total	$940,000		

Additional Information:

1. Pruitt's income tax rate is 35%.

2. Shah's beginning inventory was all sold during 1995.

3. Useful lives for depreciation and amortization purposes are:

Plant assets	10 years
Patents	8 years
Bond premium	10 years
Goodwill	25 years

4. Pruitt uses the straight-line method for all depreciation and amortization purposes.

Required:

A. Prepare the entry on Pruitt Company's books to record the acquisition of the assets and assumption of the liabilities of Shah Company.

B. Assuming Pruitt Company had taxable income of $468,000 in 1995, prepare the income tax entry for 1995.

Problem 7-2

Assume the situation in Problem 7-1, except that Pruitt Company issued 25,500 shares of its common stock in exchange for 85% of the outstanding common stock of Shah Company. Pruitt Company uses the cost method to account for its investment in Shah Company and files a consolidated income tax return.

Required:

A. Prepare the stock acquisition entry on Pruitt Company's books.

B. Assuming Shah Company earned $216,000 and declared a $90,000 dividend during 1995, prepare the eliminating entries for a consolidated statements workpaper on December 31, 1995.

C. Assuming Shah Company earned $240,000 and declared a $100,000 dividend during 1996, prepare the eliminating entries for a consolidated statements workpaper on December 31, 1996.

Problem 7-3

Pearson Company owns 80% of the common stock of Sedbrook Company. Pearson Company sells merchandise to Sedbrook Company at 25% above its cost. During 1995 and 1996, such sales amounted to $265,000 and $475,000, respectively. The 1995 and 1996 ending inventories of Sedbrook Company included goods purchased from Pearson Company for $150,000 and $195,000, respectively.

Pearson Company reported net income from its independent operations (including sales to affiliates) of $450,000 in 1995 and $480,000 in 1996. Sedbrook reported net income of $225,000 in 1995 and $275,000 in 1996 and did not declare dividends in either year. There were no intercompany sales prior to 1995. The affiliated companies file separate income tax returns and have marginal income tax rates of 30%. Ignore the income tax consequences of undistributed subsidiary income.

Required:

A. Prepare in general journal form all entries necessary in the consolidated financial statements workpapers to eliminate the effects of the intercompany sales for each of the years 1995 and 1996.

B. Calculate the amount of noncontrolling interest to be deducted from combined income in the consolidated income statements for 1995 and 1996.

C. Calculate consolidated net income for 1996.

Problem 7-4

Peck Corporation owns 70% of the common stock of Seacrest Company. The stock was purchased for $420,000 on January 1, 1991, when Seacrest Company's retained earnings were $100,000. Preclosing trial balances for the two companies at December 31, 1995, are presented here:

	PECK CORPORATION	SEACREST COMPANY
Cash	$ 35,000	$ 100,000
Accounts receivable (net)	211,000	107,750
Inventory—1/1	150,000	110,000
Investment in Seacrest Company	420,000	
Other assets	500,000	400,000
Dividends declared	100,000	10,000
Purchases	850,000	350,000
Other expenses	180,000	114,000
Income tax expense	27,000	28,250
Total	$2,473,000	$1,220,000
Accounts payable	$ 70,000	$ 30,000
Other liabilities	55,000	35,000
Deferred tax liability	20,000	5,000
Common stock	680,000	500,000
Retained earnings	541,000	120,000
Sales	1,100,000	530,000
Dividend income	7,000	
Total	$2,473,000	$1,220,000
Inventory—12/31	$ 140,000	$ 115,000

The January 1, 1995, inventory of Peck Corporation includes $10,000 of profit recorded by Seacrest Company on 1994 sales. During 1995, Seacrest Company made intercompany sales of $100,000 with a markup of 25% on cost. The ending inventory of Peck Corporation includes goods purchased in 1995 from Seacrest Company for $40,000.

The affiliates file separate tax returns, and the prior, current, and expected future marginal income tax rates for both companies are 40%. Dividends received from Seacrest Company are subject to an 80% dividends received exclusion.

Required:

A. Prepare a consolidated statements workpaper for the year ended December 31, 1995.

B. Calculate consolidated net income for the year ended December 31, 1995, and consolidated retained earnings on December 31, 1995, using the analytical approach.

Problem 7-5

Using the information in Problem 7-4, prepare a consolidated statements workpaper for the year ended December 31, 1995, using the trial balance format.

Problem 7-6

Phelps Company acquired 75% of the voting stock of Stanton Company on January 1, 1993, for $1,500,000 when Stanton Company had retained earnings of $450,000 and total stockholders equity of $2,000,000. Stanton Company's retained earnings amount to $820,000 on January 1, 1996, and $1,000,000 on December 31, 1996. In 1996, Stanton Company reported net income of $270,000 and declared dividends of $90,000. Phelps Company reported net income from independent operations in 1996 in the amount of $700,000 and retained earnings on December 31, 1996, of $1,500,000. The affiliates file separate income tax returns, undistributed earnings are expected to be received in the form of future dividends, the dividends received exclusion is 80%, and prior, current, and expected future marginal income tax rates are 40%. During 1996, intercompany sales of merchandise from Phelps to Stanton amounted to $70,000 and from Stanton to Phelps were $50,000. Unrealized profits on January 1 and on December 31, 1996, resulting from intercompany sales are as summarized here:

	UNREALIZED INTERCOMPANY PROFIT ON	
RESULTING FROM	1/1/96	12/31/96
Sales by Stanton Company to Phelps Company	$40,000	$20,000
Sales by Phelps Company to Stanton Company	60,000	10,000

There were no intercompany sales prior to 1995.

Required:

A. Prepare in general journal form the entries necessary in the December 31, 1996, consolidated statements workpaper to eliminate the effects of the intercompany sales.

B. Prepare in general journal form the entry necessary in the December 31, 1996, consolidated statements workpaper to report the income tax consequences of past and current undistributed subsidiary income.

C. Calculate consolidated net income for the year ended December 31, 1996.

D. Calculate consolidated retained earnings on December 31, 1996.

E. Calculate the noncontrolling interest in combined income for the year ended December 31, 1996.

Problem 7-7

Pickett Company acquired a 75% interest in Senna Company when the retained earnings of Senna Company were $300,000. On January 1, 1995, Senna Company recorded a $250,000 gain on the sale to Pickett Company of equipment with a remaining life of five years. On January 1, 1996, Pickett Company recorded a $180,000 gain on the sale to Senna Company of equipment with a remaining life of six years. Senna Company reported net income of $180,000 and declared dividends of $60,000 in 1996. It reported retained earnings of $520,000 on January 1, 1996, and $640,000 on December 31, 1996. Pickett Company reported net income from independent operations of $400,000 in 1996 and retained earning of $1,800,000 on December 31, 1996. The affiliates file separate income tax returns, undistributed earnings are expected to be received in the form of future dividends, the dividends received exclusion is 80%, and the prior, current, and expected future marginal income tax rates are 40%.

Required:

A. Prepare in general journal form the entries necessary in the December 31, 1996, consolidated statements workpaper to eliminate the effects of the intercompany sales.

B. Prepare in general journal form the entry necessary in the December 31, 1996, consolidated statements workpaper to report the income tax consequences of past and current undistributed subsidiary income.

C. Calculate consolidated net income for the year ended December 31, 1996.

D. Calculate consolidated retained earnings on December 31, 1996.

E. Calculate the noncontrolling interest in combined income for the year ended December 31, 1996.

Problem 7-8

Peer Company acquired an 80% interest in Sells Company on January 1, 1995, for $1,600,000. On this date, the common stock and retained earnings balances were $1,500,000 and $500,000, respectively. During the year, Peer Company sold merchandise to Sells Company for $200,000. Only one-fourth of this merchandise was in Sells Company's 1995 ending inventory, and $10,000 of this amount is unrealized profit.

On January 2, 1995, Sells Company sold equipment with a book value of $300,000 to Peer Company for $400,000. The equipment has a remaining useful life of four years.

Sells Company's net income for 1995 was $300,000, while Peer Company's was $800,000. Neither company declared dividends in 1995. The affiliated companies file separate income tax returns, the dividends received exclusion is 80%, and the prior, current, and expected future marginal income tax rates for both companies are 40%.

Required:

A. Prepare in general journal form all consolidated statements workpaper entries necessary for 1995.

B. Calculate consolidated net income for the year ended December 31, 1995.

C. Calculate the noncontrolling interest in combined income for the year ended December 31, 1995.

Problem 7-9

Perez Company owns 80% of the common stock of Stratton Company. The stock was purchased for $1,600,000 on January 1, 1992, when Stratton Company's retained earnings were $800,000. On January 1, 1994, Perez Company sold fixed assets to Stratton Company for $540,000. These assets were originally purchased by Perez Company for $600,000 on January 1, 1984, at which time their estimated depreciable life was 25 years. The straight-line method of depreciation is used.

Financial data for December 31,1995, are presented here:

	PEREZ COMPANY	STRATTON COMPANY
Sales	$1,475,000	$1,110,000
Dividend income	80,000	
Total revenue	1,555,000	1,110,000
Cost of goods sold	942,000	795,000
Other expenses	145,000	90,000
Income tax expense	187,200	90,000
Total cost and expense	1,274,200	975,000
Net income	$ 280,800	$ 135,000
1/1 Retained earnings	$1,300,000	$1,040,000
Net income	280,800	135,000
Dividends declared	(120,000)	(100,000)
12/31 Retained earnings	$1,460,800	$1,075,000
Current assets	$ 568,000	$ 271,000
Investment in Stratton Company	1,600,000	
Fixed assets	1,972,000	830,000
Accumulated depreciation—fixed assets	(375,000)	(290,000)
Other assets	1,068,800	1,600,000
Total assets	$4,833,800	$2,411,000
Deferred tax liability	$ 168,000	$ 126,000
Other liabilities	205,000	10,000
Common stock	3,000,000	1,200,000
Retained earnings	1,460,800	1,075,000
Total liabilities and equity	$4,833,800	$2,411,000

The prior, current, and expected future marginal income tax rates for both companies are 40%, and Stratton Company files a separate income tax return. Dividends received from Stratton Company are subject to an 80% dividends received exclusion.

Required:

A. Prepare the consolidated statements workpaper for the year ended December 31, 1995.

B. Assuming that on January 1, 1996, Stratton Company sells the fixed assets purchased from Perez Company to a party outside the affiliated group for $400,000:
   (1) Prepare the entry that would be entered on the books of Stratton Company to record the sale.
   (2) Prepare workpaper entries for the December 31, 1996, consolidated statements workpaper necessitated by the sale of the assets.
   (3) Prepare any workpaper entries that will be needed in the December 31, 1997, consolidated statements workpaper in regard to these fixed assets.

Problem 7-10

On January 1, 1995, Pasco Company purchased a 70% interest in Shank Company for $1,000,000, when the common stock and retained earnings accounts were $900,000 and $200,000, respectively. An examination of Shank Company's balance sheet on the acquisition date revealed the following:

	TAX BASIS/ BOOK VALUE	FAIR VALUE
Inventory	$225,000	$275,000
Plant and equipment (net)		
(cost $750,000; accumulated depreciation $150,000)	600,000	680,000
Land	500,000	600,000

The book values and the tax bases of all other assets and liabilities were equal to their fair values. The plant and equipment has a remaining useful life of eight years. All the inventory had been sold by the end of 1995. Any goodwill is to be amortized over a period of 30 years.

Adjusted trial balances for the year ended December 31, 1996, are as follows:

DEBITS	PASCO COMPANY	SHANK COMPANY
Cash	$ 250,000	$ 100,000
Accounts receivable	500,000	300,000
Inventory	400,000	200,000
Investment in Shank Company	1,000,000	
Plant and equipment	1,200,000	900,000
Accumulated depreciation	(423,000)	(350,000)
Land	700,000	600,000
Cost of goods sold	1,037,000	400,000
Depreciation expense	70,000	50,000
Other expenses	322,000	100,000
Income tax expense	178,000	210,000
Dividends declared	40,000	20,000
Total	$5,274,000	$2,530,000

CREDITS	PASCO COMPANY	SHANK COMPANY
Current liabilities	$ 420,000	$ 30,000
Deferred income tax liability	100,000	60,000
Notes payable	500,000	200,000
Common stock	1,600,000	900,000
Retained earnings	780,000	260,000
Sales	1,860,000	990,000
Gain on sale of equipment		90,000
Dividend income	14,000	
Total	$5,274,000	$2,530,000

Additional Information:

1. On January 2, 1995, Shank Company sold equipment with a book value of $150,000 (original cost $175,000) to Pasco Company for $182,000. The equipment is depreciated using the straight-line method and had a remaining useful life of four years.

2. On January 2, 1996, Shank Company sold equipment with a book value of $200,000 (original cost $300,000) to Pasco Company for $290,000. The equipment is depreciated using the straight-line method and has a remaining useful life of three years.

3. Unrealized profit in the 12/31/95 inventory of Pasco Company resulting from 1995 purchases from Shank Company amounts to $15,000. During 1996, Pasco Company sold merchandise to Shank Company at a 20% markup on cost. Total sales for 1996 were $300,000, but only one-fifth of the merchandise is in the ending inventory.

4. The trial balances include a $50,000 payable from Shank Company to Pasco Company.

5. The companies file separate tax returns and the prior, current, and expected future marginal income tax rates for both companies are 40%. Dividends received from Shank Company are subject to an 80% dividends received exclusion. All undistributed income is expected to be distributed as dividends in later years.

Required:

A. Prepare the consolidated statements workpaper for the year ended December 31, 1996.

B. Calculate consolidated retained earnings on December 31, 1996, using the analytical approach.

Problem 7-11

Using the information in Problem 7-10, prepare the consolidated statements workpaper for the year ended December 31, 1996, using the trial balance format.

Problem 7-12

Piper Corporation owns 70% of the common stock of Savin Company. The stock was purchased for $420,000 on January 1, 1991, when Savin Company's retained earnings were $100,000.

Financial data for December 31, 1995, are presented here:

	PIPER CORPORATION	SAVIN COMPANY
Sales	$1,100,000	$530,000
Equity in subsidiary income	33,250	
Total revenue	1,133,250	530,000
Cost of goods sold:		
Inventory—1/1	150,000	110,000
Purchases	850,000	350,000
	1,000,000	460,000
Inventory—12/31	140,000	115,000
Cost of goods sold	860,000	345,000
Other expense	175,000	117,000
Income tax expense	32,000	20,500
Total cost and expense	1,067,000	482,500
Net income	$ 66,250	$ 47,500
1/1 Retained earnings	$ 695,000	$320,000
Net income	66,250	47,500
Dividends declared	(100,000)	(30,000)
12/31 Retained earnings	$ 661,250	$337,500
Cash	$ 80,000	$ 50,000
Accounts receivable (net)	213,000	112,500
Inventory	140,000	115,000
Investment in Savin Company	586,250	
Other assets	599,000	630,000
Total assets	$1,618,250	$907,500
Deferred tax liability	$ 52,000	$ 15,000
Accounts payable	70,000	30,000
Other liabilities	35,000	25,000
Common stock	800,000	500,000
Retained earnings	661,250	337,500
Total liabilities and equity	$1,618,250	$907,500

The January 1, 1995, inventory of Piper Corporation includes $30,000 of profit recorded by Savin Company on 1994 sales. During 1995, Savin Company made intercompany sales of $200,000 with a markup of 25% on cost. The ending inventory of Piper Corporation includes goods purchased in 1995 from Savin Company for $50,000.

The affiliates file separate tax returns, and the prior, current, and expected future marginal income tax rates for both companies are 30%. Dividends received from Savin Company are subject to an 80% dividends received exclusion.

Required:

A. Prepare the consolidated statements workpaper for the year ended December 31, 1995.

B. Calculate consolidated net income for the year ended December 31, 1995, using the analytical approach.

C. Calculate consolidated retained earnings on December 31, 1995, using the analytical approach.

Problem 7-13

Petra Corporation owns 70% of the common stock of Swain Company. The stock was purchased for $420,000 on January 1, 1991, when Swain Company's retained earnings were $100,000. Preclosing trial balances for the two companies at December 31, 1995, are presented here:

	PETRA CORPORATION	SWAIN COMPANY
Cash	$ 35,000	$ 100,000
Accounts receivable (net)	211,000	107,750
Inventory—1/1	150,000	110,000
Investment in Swain Company	456,925	
Other assets	500,000	400,000
Dividends declared	100,000	10,000
Purchases	850,000	350,000
Other expenses	180,000	114,000
Income tax expense	27,000	28,250
	$2,509,925	$1,220,000
Accounts payable	$ 70,000	$ 30,000
Other liabilities	55,000	35,000
Deferred tax liability	20,000	5,000
Common stock	680,000	500,000
Retained earnings	555,000	120,000
Sales	1,100,000	530,000
Equity in subsidiary income	29,925	
	$2,509,925	$1,220,000
Inventory—12/31	$ 140,000	$ 115,000

The January 1, 1995, inventory of Petra Corporation includes $10,000 of profit recorded by Swain Company on 1994 sales. During 1995, Swain Company made intercompany sales of $100,000 with a markup of 25% on cost. The ending inventory of Petra Corporation includes goods purchased in 1995 from Swain Company for $40,000.

The affiliates file separate tax returns, and the marginal income tax rate for both companies is 40%. Dividends received from Swain Company are subject to an 80% dividends received exclusion.

Required:

A. Prepare a consolidated statements workpaper for the year ended December 31, 1995.

B. Calculate consolidated net income for the year ended December 31, 1995, and consolidated retained earnings on December 31, 1995, using the analytical approach.

Problem 7-14

The Perez Company owns 80% of the common stock of Salars Company. The stock was purchased for $1,600,000 on January 1, 1992, when Salars Company's retained earnings were $800,000. On January 1, 1994, Perez Company sold fixed assets to Salars Company for $540,000. These assets were originally purchased by Perez Company for $600,000 on January 1, 1984, at which time their estimated depreciable life was 25 years. The straight-line method of depreciation is used. Financial data for December 31, 1995, are presented here:

	PEREZ COMPANY	SALARS COMPANY
Sales	$1,475,000	$1,110,000
Equity in subsidiary income	108,000	
Total revenue	1,583,000	1,110,000
Cost of goods sold	942,000	795,000
Other expenses	145,000	90,000
Income tax expense	187,200	90,000
Total cost and expense	1,274,200	975,000
Net income	$ 308,800	$ 135,000
1/1 Retained earnings	$1,492,000	$1,040,000
Net income	308,800	135,000
Dividends declared	(120,000)	(100,000)
12/31 Retained earnings	$1,680,800	$1,075,000
Current assets	$ 568,000	$ 271,000
Investment in Salars Company	1,820,000	
Fixed assets	1,972,000	830,000
Accumulated depreciation—fixed assets	(375,000)	(290,000)
Other assets	1,068,800	1,600,000
Total assets	$5,053,800	$2,411,000
Deferred tax liability	$ 168,000	$ 126,000
Other liabilities	205,000	10,000
Common stock	3,000,000	1,200,000
Retained earnings	1,680,800	1,075,000
Total liabilities and equity	$5,053,800	$2,411,000

The prior, current, and expected future marginal income tax rates for both companies are 40%, and Salars Company files a separate income tax return. Dividends received from Salars Company are subject to an 80% dividends received exclusion.

Required:

A. Prepare the consolidated statements workpaper for the year ended December 31, 1995.

B. Assuming that on January 1, 1996, Salars Company sells the fixed assets purchased from Perez Company to a party outside the affiliated group for $400,000:

  (1) Prepare the entry that would have been entered on the books of Salars Company to record the sale.

  (2) Prepare workpaper entries for the December 31, 1996, consolidated statements workpaper necessitated by the sale of the assets.

  (3) Prepare any workpaper entries that will be needed in the December 31, 1997, consolidated statements workpaper in regard to these fixed assets.

8

CHANGES IN OWNERSHIP INTEREST

Two assumptions regarding the equity interest acquired have been followed in previous chapters dealing with consolidated financial statements. Although not expressly stated, those assumptions were:

    1. The interest in the subsidiary was obtained through a single open-market transaction.

    2. The percentage of ownership remained constant.

Obviously, these assumptions are not always valid. For example, control of a purchased subsidiary might not be obtained until two or more stock purchases have been made. Similarly, the percentage of ownership may change for several reasons, such as (1) additional shares of the subsidiary may be purchased on the open market; (2) some of the shares held by the parent company may be sold; (3) the subsidiary may engage in capital transactions with the parent company and/or outside parties that change the parent company's percentage of ownership. A summary of those transactions and the recommended accounting treatments follow:

SITUATION	ACCOUNTING TREATMENT
1. Parent buys additional shares of subsidiary from third parties.	Purchase of additional investment with assignment of difference between cost and book value.

SITUATION	ACCOUNTING TREATMENT
2. Parent sells subsidiary shares to third parties.	Sale of investment with recognition of gain or loss.
3. Subsidiary issues additional shares (including treasury shares):	
(a) Parent buys no shares or less than its pro-rata number of shares. Percentage of ownership decreases	Sale of investment with recognition of gain or loss.
(b) Parent buys more than its pro-rata number of shares. Percentage of ownership increases.	Purchase of additional investment with assignment of difference between cost and book value.
4. Subsidiary buys treasury stock:	
(a) Parent sells no shares or less than its pro-rata number of shares. Percentage of ownership increases.	Purchase of additional investment with assignment of difference between cost and book value.
(b) Parent sells more than its pro-rata number of shares. Percentage of ownership decreases.	Sale of investment with recognition of gain or loss.

Justification for these recommended accounting treatments is based on the concept of economic substance over form. That is, a parent company can effectively increase its ownership interest in a subsidiary by either (1) buying additional subsidiary shares directly from third parties or (2) having a subsidiary purchase its (subsidiary's) shares from third parties. Similarly, the parent can effectively decrease its ownership interest by either (1) selling some of its subsidiary shares directly to third parties or (2) having a subsidiary sell additional shares (including treasury shares) to third parties. Since the economic substance is essentially the same from the parent company's point of view, the transactions should be accounted for in a consistent manner. Accounting for these changes in the parent company's percentage of ownership is discussed and illustrated in this chapter.

ACQUISITION OF STOCK THROUGH SEVERAL OPEN MARKET PURCHASES

Sometimes the controlling interest in a subsidiary is acquired through the initial stock purchase; at other times control is not achieved until two or more stock purchases have been made. When control is achieved on the first purchase, the date of acquisition is the purchase date. However, when more than one purchase is made before control is obtained, there are actually two or more acquisition dates.

Determination of the date of acquisition is important under purchase accounting because subsidiary retained earnings accumulated before that date constitute a portion of the equity acquired by the parent company, whereas the parent's share of subsidiary retained earnings accumulated after acquisition is properly included in consolidated retained earnings. If two or more purchases are made over a period of time, the retained earnings of the subsidiary at acquisition should be determined on a step-by-step basis. Interpretation No. 2 of *APB Opinion No. 17* suggests that the purchasing company should identify the cost of each investment, the fair value of the underlying assets acquired, and the difference between cost and book value for each step purchase.

To illustrate the consolidation of an investment acquired on a step-by-step basis, assume that S Company had 10,000 shares of $10 par value common stock outstanding during 1994–97 and retained earnings as follows:

	S COMPANY RETAINED EARNINGS
January 1, 1994	$ 40,000
January 1, 1995	70,000
January 1, 1996	120,000
January 1, 1997	185,000
December 31,1997	265,000

P Company purchased for cash S Company common stock on the open market as follows:

DATE	SHARES ACQUIRED	COST
January 1, 1994	1,500 (15%)	$ 24,000
January 1, 1996	7,500 (75%)	188,000
Total		$212,000

Some additional simplifying assumptions are made in order to concentrate attention on the new issues introduced and because the issues covered by the assumptions have been discussed in detail in previous chapters. The assumptions are:

1. Any difference between cost and book value of the purchases relates solely to the misvaluation of land owned by S Company and is, therefore, not subject to amortization.

2. S Company distributes no dividends during the periods under consideration.

3. Income tax deferral on the parent company's share of the undistributed income of the subsidiary is ignored.

4. P Company uses the cost method to record its investment in S Company.

The initial purchase of the 15% interest in S Company is recorded at its cost of $24,000 and reported as an investment on P Company's balance sheets on December 31, 1994 and 1995. No income on the investment is recognized for either 1994 or 1995 because no dividends were distributed by S Company. The second purchase on January 1, 1996, is also recorded in the investment account at its cost of $188,000. Again, no income is recognized on the investment during 1996 because S Company declared no dividends.

Since P Company now has controlling ownership of S Company, the investment must be consolidated. In the preparation of a consolidated workpaper on December 31, 1996, it is necessary to compute the amount of S Company equity to eliminate, as well as the difference between cost and book value. On a step-by-step basis, the computation is as follows:

| | PURCHASE | | |
	1ST	2ND	TOTAL
Cost	$24,000	$188,000	$212,000
Equity acquired:			
Common stock	15,000	75,000	90,000
Retained earnings	(1) 6,000	(2) 90,000	96,000
Total	21,000	165,000	186,000
Difference between cost and book value	$ 3,000	$ 23,000	$ 26,000

(1) 15% × $40,000.
(2) 75% × $120,000.

The workpaper entry on December 31, 1996 to establish reciprocity to the beginning of 1996 is:

Investment in S Company	12,000	
1/1 Retained Earnings—P Company [.15 × ($120,000 − $40,000)]		12,000

S Company retained earnings increased from $40,000 on January 1, 1994, to $120,000 on January 1, 1996. During that time, P Company owned 15% of S Company; thus, the reciprocity entry is made for $12,000 [15% × ($120,000 − $40,000)].

After reciprocity is established, the investment is eliminated by the following workpaper entry:

Common Stock—S Company (.90 × $100,000)	90,000	
1/1 Retained Earnings—S Company (.90 × $120,000)	108,000	
Land	26,000	
Investment in S Company ($212,000 + $12,000)		224,000

The workpaper is then completed as previously illustrated.

In subsequent periods, reciprocity is established by adding to (deducting from) the $12,000, 90% of the increase (decrease) in S Company's retained earnings between January 1, 1996, and the beginning of the year for which consolidated statements are being prepared. For example, for the preparation of a consolidated statements workpaper on December 31, 1997, reciprocity would be established as follows:

Amount from the December 31, 1996, workpaper	$12,000
Add: [.90 × ($185,000 − $120,000)]	58,500
Total	$70,500

The computation of noncontrolling interest in combined income and net assets is made by multiplying the ***end-of-year*** noncontrolling interest percentage times realized subsidiary income and subsidiary stockholders' equity amounts.

In the preceding example, the difference between cost and book value was assumed to relate to land. If the differences were assignable to depreciable or amortizable assets (and liabilities), the difference from each purchase should be separately analyzed and assigned to the appropriate assets and/or liabilities. Amortization effects of each should be determined separately from the date of each purchase, although the amounts might be combined into a single workpaper amortization entry. Although this treatment is technically correct, for expediency purposes and because the amounts are often immaterial, the difference between cost and book value on each purchase is often amortized as if each purchase had been made on the date control was achieved.

SALE OF SUBSIDIARY STOCK INVESTMENTS ON THE OPEN MARKET

The sale of all or a portion of its investment by the parent company is treated in a manner similar to that used to account for the sale of any other corporate asset. The asset received is recorded, the portion of the investment sold is written off, and gain or loss is recognized on the sale as the difference between the value of the asset received and the carrying value of the investment sold. Because the value of the asset received is generally easily measured, the amount of any gain or loss recognized hinges on the appropriate measurement of the carrying value of the investment sold. If only a portion of the investment is sold, federal tax law specifies that either specific identification or the first-in, first-out (FIFO) method must be used to determine the value of the shares sold. These methods are also acceptable for financial reporting purposes; we will use specific identification for illustration purposes.

To illustrate the procedures involved in the sale of part of an investment, refer to the preceding example and assume that P Company sold 1,500 shares of S Company stock on July 1, 1997, for $70,000. The shares were specifically identified as 20% (1,500 ÷ 7,500) of those purchased on January 1, 1996. After the sale, P Company retains control with a 75% (7,500 ÷ 10,000) interest.

To record the sale of the shares, P Company made the following entry in its books on July 1, 1997.

Cash	70,000	
Investment in S Company (20% × $188,000)		37,600
Gain on Sale of Investments		32,400

The $32,400 gain recorded by P Company contains three elements: (1) the undistributed profit of S Company from the date of acquisition by P Company to the beginning of 1997 that is associated with the shares sold, $9,750 [.2 × .75($185,000 − $120,000)]; (2) the undistributed profit of S Company from January 1, 1997, to July 1, 1997, that is associated with the shares sold, $6,000 [.2 × .75(½ × $80,000)] (assuming S Company earns its income evenly throughout the year); and (3) fluctuations in the value of the stock that was sold that come about from a variety of market factors other than accumulated earnings. Although the full gain is properly reflected in P Company's records, for consolidated statement purposes the gain must be allocated to (1) that relating to the undistributed profit on the shares sold to the beginning of the year of sale, (2) that relating to the profit for the first six months of 1997 on the shares sold, and (3) that arising from other factors. Only the latter amount of $16,650 [$32,400 − ($9,750 + $6,000)] is reported as a gain in the consolidated income statement. The first allocation is necessary because the undistributed profit to January 1, 1997, on the shares sold has already been included in consolidated income in a previous year (during 1996 in this example). Although included in consolidated retained earnings, this amount is not included in the reported beginning retained earnings of P Company. Inclusion of the full gain in consolidated income again would represent a double counting of the undistributed profit portion of the gain because it was included in S Company's income and, therefore, consolidated income in 1996. Thus, an entry is made on the consolidated statements workpaper only as follows:

(1) Gain on Sale of Investments	ΔRE 1/1/97- 1/1/96	9,750	
1/1 Retained Earnings—P Company	× 75% × 20%		9,750
(Consolidated Retained Earnings)			

During 1996 S Company's retained earnings increased by $65,000 (from $120,000 to $185,000), $48,750 (75%) of which accrues to the benefit of P Company on the second block of shares purchased. Because 20% of the investment was sold, $9,750 (20% × $48,750) represents undistributed profit to the beginning of the year of sale on the shares sold.

The second allocation is made by a workpaper entry to adjust noncontrolling interest in combined income for the portion of subsidiary income earned during the first six months of 1997 that was sold to the noncontrolling stockholders. From January 1, 1997, to July 1, 1997, S Company earned $40,000, $30,000 (75%) of which relates to the second block of shares purchased. Because 20% of those shares was sold, $6,000 (20% × $30,000) represents net income purchased by the noncontrolling stockholders. The $6,000 should be excluded from noncontrolling interest in combined income, since it was purchased by the noncontrolling stockholders rather than being earned by them. Thus, a second workpaper only entry is made as follows:

NI 1/1 → 7/1 own

| (2) Gain on Sale of Investments | 40000 ×.75 ×.20% | 6,000 | |
| Subsidiary Income Sold | | | 6,000 |

A workpaper for the preparation of consolidated financial statements on December 31, 1997, is presented in Illustration 8-1. Data necessary to complete the workpaper, other than those previously provided, are assumed. Workpaper entries, in addition to those made to adjust the gain on sale, are:

| (3) Investment in S Company | 60,750 | |
| 1/1 Retained Earnings—P Company | | 60,750 |

Cost Method
Sale of Part of Investment
75% Owned Subsidiary

ILLUSTRATION 8-1
Consolidated Statements Workpaper
P Company and Subsidiary
For the Year Ended December 31, 1997

INCOME STATEMENT	P COMPANY	S COMPANY	ELIMINATIONS DR.	ELIMINATIONS CR.	NONCONTROLLING INTEREST	CONSOLIDATED BALANCES
Net Income Before Gain on Sale of Investment	120,000	80,000				200,000
			(1) 9,750			
Gain on Sale of Investment	32,400		(2) 6,000			16,650
Net/Combined Income	152,400	80,000				216,650
Subsidiary Income Sold				(2) 6,000		6,000
Noncontrolling Interest in Income .25($80,000)					20,000	(20,000)
Net Income to Retained Earnings	152,400	80,000	15,750	6,000	20,000	202,650
RETAINED EARNINGS STATEMENT						
1/1 Retained Earnings						
			(1) 9,750			
P Company	282,000		(3) 60,750			352,500
S Company		185,000	(4) 138,750		46,250	
Net Income from Above	152,400	80,000	15,750	6,000	20,000	202,650
Dividends Declared 10/30						
P Company	(40,000)					(40,000)
12/31 Retained Earnings to Balance Sheet	394,400	265,000	154,500	76,500	66,250	515,150
BALANCE SHEET						
Current Assets	220,000	100,000				320,000
Investment in S Company	174,400		(3) 60,750	(4) 235,150		
Other Assets	512,600	300,000				812,600
Land	90,000	40,000	(4) 21,400			151,400
Total	997,000	440,000				1,284,000
Liabilities	102,600	75,000				177,600
Common Stock						
P Company	500,000					500,000
S Company		100,000	(4) 75,000		25,000	
Retained Earnings from above	394,400	265,000	154,500	76,500	66,250	515,150
Noncontrolling Interest in Net Assets					91,250	91,250
Total	997,000	440,000	311,650	311,650		1,284,000

(1) To adjust gain on sale of investment for portion included in income in prior years.
(2) To adjust for current year's income sold to noncontrolling stockholders.
(3) To recognize P Company's share of S Company's undistributed income from date of acquisition to beginning of the current year.
(4) To eliminate investment in S Company.

Entry (3) establishes reciprocity by recognizing P Company's share of the increase in S Company's retained earnings from the date of purchase to the beginning of 1997 on the **shares still held at the end of 1997**, computed as follows:

From January 1, 1994, to January 1, 1996	
.15($120,000 − $40,000)	$12,000
From January 1, 1996, to January 1, 1997	
.75($185,000 − $120,000)	48,750
Total	$60,750

After reciprocity is established, the workpaper investment elimination entry is:

(4) Common Stock—S Company .75($100,000)	75,000	
1/1 Retained Earnings—S Company .75($185,000)	138,750	
Difference Between Cost and Book Value	21,400	
Investment in S Company ($212,000 − $37,600 + $60,750)		235,150

The elimination of S Company's equity against the investment account is based on end-of-year equity owned, or 75%. The difference between cost and book value is $21,400, rather than the $26,000 original amount. This results because 20% of the $23,000 difference (or $4,600) on the second stock purchase was sold with the sale of the stock. If the difference had been assigned to depreciable assets, the undepreciated portion would have been reduced by 20%, and future adjustments to depreciation expense would be reduced accordingly. Several items on the workpaper should be specifically noted:

1. The gain on sale of investment recognized for consolidation purposes is $16,650, consisting of the $32,400 recorded gain less the portion of the gain recognized in consolidated income in prior years ($9,750) and the portion of the current year's income to the date of sale associated with the shares sold ($6,000).

2. Noncontrolling interest in combined income is represented by the December 31, 1997, noncontrolling interest percentage times reported subsidiary income (25% × $80,000), or $20,000, less the $6,000 subsidiary income that was purchased by the noncontrolling stockholders at the time of the sale of shares by the parent company to them. That is, the $6,000 represents a reduction in the $20,000 noncontrolling interest included in the consolidated balances column of the workpaper. Thus, the noncontrolling interest in combined income reported in the formal consolidated income statement is $14,000 ($20,000 − $6,000). Note, however, that the full $20,000 is reflected as a part of the noncontrolling interest on the balance sheet (the $14,000 noncontrolling interest share of combined income plus the $6,000 purchased by the noncontrolling stockholders). That is, the full $20,000 represents an appropriate claim by the noncontrolling stockholders against the consolidated net assets, although $14,000 represents assets earned during the period and $6,000 reflects assets purchased. The $20,000 is included on the balance sheet in the noncontrolling interest column of the income statement section of the

workpaper, from which it is appropriately carried forward to the retained earnings section and eventually to the balance sheet section.

3. Verification of consolidated net income is:

S Company's reported income		$ 80,000
Allocated to the noncontrolling interest:		
1st 6 months ($40,000 × 10%)	$ 4,000	
2nd 6 months ($40,000 × 25%)	10,000	14,000
Allocated to the controlling interest		66,000
P Company's income from its own operations, including gain on sale of stock realized for consolidation purposes ($120,000 + $16,650)		136,650
Consolidated net income		$202,650

In subsequent periods, the amount needed to establish reciprocity is the total of 15% of the increase in S Company's retained earnings from January 1, 1994 to January 1, 1996, plus (minus) 75% of the increase (decrease) in S Company's retained earnings thereafter. Thus, the entry needed to establish reciprocity for a workpaper on December 31, 1998, would be:

Investment in S Company	120,750	
1/1 Retained Earnings—P Company		120,750
[15% × ($120,000 − $40,000)] + [75% × ($265,000 − $120,000)]		

PARTIAL EQUITY METHOD FOR PURCHASES AND SALES OF SUBSIDIARY STOCK

Recall that under the partial equity method, the parent company adjusts its investment in subsidiary account for its share of subsidiary income or loss and dividends distributed. To illustrate the procedures followed for open-market purchases and sales of subsidiary stock under the partial equity method, the previous cost method example will be used. For convenience, the facts are repeated here:

1. S. Company had 10,000 shares of $10 par value common stock outstanding during 1994-97 and retained earnings as follows:

	S COMPANY RETAINED EARNINGS
January 1, 1994	$ 40,000
January 1, 1995	70,000
January 1, 1996	120,000
January 1, 1997	185,000
December 31, 1997	265,000

2. P Company purchased S Company common stock on the open market as follows:

DATE	SHARES ACQUIRED	COST
January 1, 1994	1,500 (15%)	$ 24,000
January 1, 1996	7,500 (75%)	188,000
Total	9,000 (90%)	$212,000

3. Any difference between cost and book value of net assets acquired relates to land.

4. S. Company distributed no dividends during the periods under consideration.

5. Deferred income taxes are ignored.

6. P Company sold 1,500 shares of S Company stock on July 1, 1997, for $70,000. The shares were identified as 20% (1,500 ÷ 7,500) of those purchased on January 1, 1996.

As with the cost method, the initial purchase of the 15% interest is recorded at its cost of $24,000 and reported as an investment on P Company's balance sheets on December 31, 1994 and 1995. The second purchase on January 1, 1996, is also recorded in the investment account at its cost of $188,000. Since P Company now has a 90% interest in S Company and intends to apply the partial equity method, the investment account must be restated to recognize P Company's share (15%) of the increase in S Company's retained earnings from January 1, 1994, to January 1, 1996. This is accomplished by a book entry on P Company's books as follows:

Investment in S Company	12,000	
Retained Earnings		12,000
[15% × ($120,000 − $40,000)]		

P Company will recognize its share of S Company income for 1996 with the following entry:

Investment in S Company	58,500	
Equity in Subsidiary Income		58,500
[90% × ($185,000 − $120,000)]		

When a sale of subsidiary shares is made during a fiscal period, the parent's share of the subsidiary's income to the date of sale is normally recorded by a book entry if the information is available. Thus, assuming P Company received a 6-month interim income statement from S Company reporting $40,000 net income, the following entry will be made by P Company on June 30, 1997:

Investment in S Company	36,000	
Equity in Subsidiary Income		36,000
(90% × $40,000)		

After this entry, the Investment in S Company account will appear as follows:

INVESTMENT IN S COMPANY		
1/1/94 Purchase	24,000	
1/1/96 Purchase	188,000	
1/1/96 Adjustment	12,000	
12/31/96 Subsidiary Income	58,500	
6/30/97 Subsidiary Income	36,000	
Balance	318,500	

To record the sale of the S Company shares on July 1, 1997, P Company will make the following entry:

Cash	70,000	
Investment in S Company*		53,350
Gain on Sale of Investment		16,650

*Carrying value of the investment sold:	
Cost of 2nd purchase — 75% interest	$188,000
1996 subsidiary income (75% × $65,000)	48,570
1997 subsidiary income to date of sale	
(75% × $40,000)	30,000
Total	266,750
Portion of 2nd purchase sold	20%
Carrying value of investment sold	$ 53,350

The gain on sale of $16,650 is appropriately reported as a gain for consolidated purposes and agrees with the amount of gain reported for consolidated purposes under the cost method (Illustration 8-1). Since the investment account was brought up to date as of the date of sale under the partial equity method, no workpaper adjustments to the gain are necessary.

After the sale of the 1,500 shares, P Company holds a 75% interest in S Company consisting of the 15% interest acquired in 1994 and the 60% unsold interest acquired in 1996. Thus, for the second six months of 1997 (and for subsequent periods), P Company will recognize 75% of the reported income and dividends received from S Company. The December 31, 1997 book entry by P Company is:

Investment in S Company	30,000	
Equity in Subsidiary Income		30,000
(75% × $40,000)		

A December 31, 1997, workpaper, using the same basic information as under the cost basis (Illustration 8-1) is presented in Illustration 8-2. Notice, again, that consolidated net income, consolidated retained earnings, and consolidated balance sheet totals are identical in Illustrations 8-1 and 8-2.

Partial Equity Method
Sale of Part of Investment
75% Owned Subsidiary

ILLUSTRATION 8-2
Consolidated Statements Workpaper
P Company and Subsidiary
For the Year Ended December 31, 1997

INCOME STATEMENT	P COMPANY	S COMPANY	ELIMINATIONS DR.	ELIMINATIONS CR.	NONCONTROLLING INTEREST	CONSOLIDATED BALANCES
Net Income Before Gain on Sale and Equity in Subsidiary Income	120,000	80,000				200,000
Equity in Subsidiary Income	66,000		(1) 66,000			
Gain on Sale of Investment	16,650					16,650
Net/Combined Income	202,650	80,000				216,650
Subsidiary Income Sold				(1) 6,000		6,000
Noncontrolling Interest in Income					20,000	(20,000)
Net Income to Retained Earnings	202,650	80,000	66,000	6,000	20,000	202,650
RETAINED EARNINGS STATEMENT						
1/1 Retained Earnings						
P Company	352,500					352,500
S Company		185,000	(2) 138,750		46,250	
Net Income from Above	202,650	80,000	66,000	6,000	20,000	202,650
Dividends Declared—						
P Company	(40,000)					(40,000)
12/31 Retained Earnings to Balance Sheet	515,150	265,000	204,750	6,000	66,250	515,150
BALANCE SHEET						
Current Assets	220,000	100,000				320,000
Investment in S Company	295,150			(1) 60,000		
				(2) 235,150		
Other Assets	512,600	300,000				812,600
Land	90,000	40,000	(2) 21,400			151,400
Total	1,117,750	440,000				1,284,000
Liabilities	102,600	75,000				177,600
Common Stock						
P Company	500,000					500,000
S Company		100,000	(2) 75,000		25,000	
Retained Earnings from Above	515,150	265,000	204,750	6,000	66,250	515,150
Noncontrolling Interest in Net Assets					91,250	91,250
Total	1,117,750	440,000	301,150	301,150		1,284,000

(1) To reverse the effect of subsidiary income for the year.
(2) To eliminate investment in S Company.

SUBSIDIARY STOCK INSURANCE AND TREASURY STOCK TRANSACTIONS

A parent company's equity interest in a subsidiary also may change as the result of the issuance of additional shares of stock by the subsidiary, or the purchase by a subsidiary of some of its outstanding shares. The effect of these subsidiary stock transactions on the parent company depends on whether the parent is a party to the transactions, as well as on the price at which the subsidiary shares are sold or treasury stock is purchased.

Issuance of Additional Shares by a Subsidiary

When a subsidiary issues additional shares of its common stock, the shares may be purchased (1) entirely by the parent company, (2) partly by the parent company and partly by the noncontrolling stockholders, or (3) entirely by the noncontrolling stockholders.

New Shares Purchased by the Parent Company Only When shares are purchased by the parent company directly from the subsidiary, care must be exercised in the determination of equity acquired and any difference between cost and book value, because the number of subsidiary shares outstanding is greater and the proceeds from the stock issue flow into the subsidiary, thereby increasing its total stockholders' equity. If the parent company holds less than a 100% interest and purchases the entire new issue of stock directly from the subsidiary, one of two situations must exist. Either (1) the preemptive right has been waived previously or (2) the noncontrolling stockholders have elected not to exercise their rights. The purchase of the entire new issue by the parent company will increase the parent company's percentage of ownership with an equal reduction in the noncontrolling interest's percentage of ownership. Since a subsidiary's stock transactions affect the balances in the subsidiary's stockholders' equity accounts, a special computational method is needed to determine the change in the parent's share of the subsidiary's equity. The change is determined by comparing the parent's share of the subsidiary's equity immediately before and immediately after the new purchase.

To illustrate, assume that P Company purchased 14,000 shares (70%) of S Company's $10 par value common stock on January 1, 1987, for $216,000, which included a $20,000 excess of cost over book value; the excess cost was assigned to land. S Company's retained earnings on January 1, 1987, were $50,000. On January 1, 1995, P Company purchased 4,000 additional shares of S Company stock directly from S Company at its current market price of $22 per share ($88,000). Noncontrolling stockholders elected not to participate in the new issue. S Company's stockholders equity on January 1, 1995, was:

	IMMEDIATELY BEFORE THE NEW ISSUE	NEW ISSUE	IMMEDIATELY AFTER THE NEW ISSUE
Common stock, $10 par value	$200,000	$40,000	$240,000
Other contributed capital	30,000	48,000	78,000
Retained earnings	120,000	–0–	120,000
Total	$350,000	$88,000	$438,000

There are 24,000 shares of S Company stock outstanding after the new issue, 18,000 of which are owned by P Company. Thus, P Company's percentage of ownership has increased to 75% (18,000 ÷ 24,000 shares). The computation of the book value of the equity interest acquired in the purchase of the new shares is:

	BOOK VALUE OF P COMPANY'S SHARE OF S COMPANY'S EQUITY		
	BEFORE NEW PURCHASE (70%)	AFTER NEW PURCHASE (75%)	BOOK VALUE OF INTEREST ACQUIRED
Common stock	(1) $140,000	(4) $180,000	$40,000
Other contributed capital	(2) 21,000	(5) 58,500	37,500
Retained earnings	(3) 84,000	(6) 90,000	6,000
Total	$245,000	$328,500	$83,500

(1) .7 × $200,000.
(2) .7 × $30,000.
(3) .7 × $120,000.
(4) .75 × $240,000.
(5) .75 × $78,000
(6) .75 × $120,000

The cost of the new shares was $88,000 and the book value of the interest acquired was $83,500, as determined above; thus, there is a $4,500 excess of cost over book value. This excess cost is assigned following the procedures described in Chapter 4. Here we assume it relates to subsidiary land. Although the noncontrolling stockholders did not participate in the new issue and their percentage of ownership decreased, the amount of their total book value interest in S Company's net assets increased by $4,500. Because the shares were purchased directly from the subsidiary, the $4,500 represents a transfer of interest from the controlling interest to the noncontrolling stockholders. This can be verified as follows:

Noncontrolling Interest

Before the new issue	.30 × $350,000 =	$105,000
After the new issue	.25 × $438,000 =	109,500
Increase in noncontrolling interest		$ 4,500

Essentially, the transaction resulted in a decrease in the controlling stockholders' book value interest with an increase in the noncontrolling stockholders' book value interest.

To record the purchase of the new shares, P Company will make the following entry:

Investment in S Company	88,000	
Cash		88,000

If a workpaper were prepared immediately after the purchase of the new shares, the workpaper entries to establish reciprocity and eliminate the investment account would be:

Investment in S Company	49,000	
1/1 Retained Earnings—P Company		49,000
[70% × ($120,000 − $50,000)]		
Common Stock—S Company .75($240,000)	180,000	
Other Contributed Capital—S Company .75($78,000)	58,500	
Retained Earnings—S Company .75($120,000)	90,000	
Land ($20,000 + $4,500)	24,500	
Investment in S Company		353,000
($216,000 + $88,000 + $49,000)		

Note that reciprocity is established based on the percentage of ownership as of the beginning of the year (70%). In later years, reciprocity is established on the basis of a 70% interest to the date of purchase of the new shares plus a 75% interest thereafter. The elimination of S Company's stockholders' equity, however, is based on the level of ownership held after the purchase of the new shares (75%).

It should be noted that the $4,500 excess cost resulted because P Company purchased the additional shares from S Company at a price of $22 per share, which exceeded the $17.50 book value of S Company's shares ($350,000 ÷ 20,000 shares). If the new shares are issued at a price equal to their book value, there is no difference between cost and book value. For example, if the shares are issued at their book value of $17.50, the computation is:

P. Company's share of S Company's net assets:		
Before the new issue	.75 × $350,000 =	$245,000
After the new issue	.75[$350,000 + (4,000 × $17.50)] =	315,000
Increase in P Company's share		70,000
Cost of the investment (4,000 × $17.50)		70,000
Difference		$ –0–

Although the noncontrolling stockholders' percentage of ownership decreases from 30% to 25%, their share of the net assets of S Company remains unchanged, as shown here:

Noncontrolling Interest

Before the new issue	.30 × $350,000 =	$105,000
After the new issue	.25 × ($350,000 + $70,000) =	105,000
Change in noncontrolling interest		$ –0–

If the new shares are issued at a price less than their book value, an excess of book value over cost results, total noncontrolling book value interest decreases, and the controlling book value interest increases. For example, assume the new shares were issued at $14 per share. The excess of book value over cost is computed as follows:

Before the new issue	.70 × $350,000 = $245,000
After the new issue	.75[$350,000 + (4,000 × $14)] = 304,500
Increase in P Company's share	59,500
Cost of the investment (4,000 × $14)	56,000
Excess of book value over cost	$ 3,500

The resulting decrease in the noncontrolling interest is verified as:

Noncontrolling Interest

Before the new issue	.30 × $350,000 = $105,000
After the new issue	.25[$350,000 + (4,000 × $14)] = 101,500
Decrease in noncontrolling interest	$ 3,500

In this case, the journal entry by P Company to record the purchase of the new shares is:

Investment in S Company	56,000	
Cash		56,000

In this case, the $3,500 excess of book value over cost is treated as a reduction in the difference between cost and book value assigned to land. Thus, the work-paper entries to establish reciprocity and eliminate the investment account in the preparation of a consolidated workpaper immediately after the purchase are:

Investment in S Company	49,000	
1/1 Retained Earnings—P Company		49,000
[70% × ($120,000—$50,000)]		
Common Stock— S Company .75 ($240,000)	180,000	
Other Contributed Capital—S Company .75($46,000)	34,500	
Retained Earnings—S Company .75($120,000)	90,000	
Land ($20,000 − $3,500)	16,500	
Investment in S Company		321,000
($216,000 + $56,000 + $49,000)		

As demonstrated in the preceding analyses, a difference between cost and book value results whenever the parent company purchases stock from the subsidiary for more or less than book value per share.

New Shares Purchased Ratably by Parent and Noncontrolling Stockholders In the previous example, noncontrolling stockholders elected not to exercise their right to purchase a ratable number of the new shares. If the noncontrolling stockholders had elected to exercise their rights, the percentage of stock owned by the parent and noncontrolling stockholders after the new issue would be the same as their respective interests prior to the new issue.

Assume, for example, that the shares are issued at $22 each, that P Company is permitted to purchase only its ratable share of the new issue, and that the remaining shares are purchased by the noncontrolling stockholders. Thus, P Company would purchase 2,800 of the 4,000 new shares and retain its 70% (16,800 ÷ 24,000 shares) interest in S Company. Comparison of cost with the book value of the interest acquired by P Company is as follows:

Cost of investment (2,800 × $22)		$61,600
Book value of equity interest acquired:		
P Company's share of S Company's net assets:		
Before the new purchase .7($350,000)	$245,000	
After the new purchase .7[$350,000 + (4,000 × $22)	306,600	
Increase in P Company's share of S Company		61,600
Difference		$ –0–

Note that the book value of the interest acquired is equal to the cost of the shares to P Company; thus, no difference between cost and book value arises. This condition will always result if the shares are purchased ratably by the existing stockholders, regardless of whether the new shares are issued at a price below, equal to, or above their book value.

New Shares Purchased Entirely by Noncontrolling Stockholders Occasionally, in order to obtain an additional capital increment for the consolidated entity or to meet the requirements of employee stock options or stock purchase plans, the subsidiary may issue new shares entirely to noncontrolling stockholders. Since any shares purchased by the parent represent a transfer of funds within the affiliated group, purchases by the parent do not provide any additional capital to the group as a whole. As long as the number of new shares issued is not so large that it reduces the parent's percentage of ownership below that needed for control, new financing can be made available and control retained.

The issuance of all the new shares to noncontrolling stockholders does, of course, reduce the parent's percentage of ownership. Thus, the economic substance of the transaction is a sale of interest by P Company. However, the book value of the parent's interest in the subsidiary may increase, decrease, or remain unchanged depending on the relationship of the issue price to book value per share of stock.

To illustrate, assume the previous example except that the 4,000 new shares were issued entirely to noncontrolling stockholders at the current market price of $22 per share. The new issue results in a decrease in P Company's percentage of ownership from 70% to 58⅓% (14,000 ÷ 24,000 shares). The change in the book value of P Company's interest in S Company is determined as before by an immediately "before" and "after" computation as follows:

[handwritten margin notes: Immed yt Issue / CS 120,000 / RE 50,500 / Oee___ / 170,500]

P Company's share of S Company's net assets:		
Before the new issue	.70 × $350,000 =	$245,000
After the new issue	58⅓% × [$350,000 + (4,000 × $22)] =	255,500
Increase		$ 10,500

[handwritten: .80 × 170,500 = 136,400]

[handwritten: (48000 ÷ 75000)]

[handwritten: .64 × [170,500 + (15000 × 3)] = 137,920]
[handwritten: 1520 increase]

Although P Company's ownership interest decreased from 70% to $58\frac{1}{3}$%, the book value of its interest in S Company after the new issue increased by $10,500. The $10,500 increase in P Company's book value interest represents a decrease in the noncontrolling book value interest and an increase in the controlling book value interest, as computed here:

Cost of new shares to noncontrolling interest		*45,000*
(4,000 × $22)		$88,000
Less equity in net assets acquired:		
Noncontrolling interest's share of net assets:	*341,0*	
Before the purchase .3($350,000)	$105,000	
After the purchase $41\frac{2}{3}$% × ($350,000 + $88,000)	182,500	
Increase in noncontrolling interest	*77580*	77,500 *4348*
Increase in controlling interest		$10,500

1520 .

Since the purchase of the shares by the noncontrolling stockholders decreased P Company's ownership percentage, the situation is analogous to a sale of shares by P Company. The transfer of the $10,500 interest in consolidated net assets from the noncontrolling stockholders to the controlling stockholders is recorded on the books of P Company as follows:

Investment in S Company	10,500	
Gain from Subsidiary Issuance of Shares		10,500

Because the shares were purchased by the noncontrolling stockholders for more then book value, P Company's percentage interest decreased, and P Company's interest in the consolidated net assets increased, the effect is the equivalent of a sale of a portion of its interest by P Company at a gain.

Note that, in this example, the new shares are purchased by the noncontrolling stockholders at a price in excess of book value, which results in an increase in P Company's share of consolidated net assets. If the new shares are issued at book value, there is no change in P Company's book value interest as shown here:

P Company's share of S Company's equity:		
Before the new issue	.70 × $350,000 =	$245,000
After the new issue	$58\frac{1}{3}$% × [$350,000 + ($17.50 × 4,000) =	245,000
Change in P Company's interest		$ –0–

If the shares are issued below book value, P Company's book value interest decreases and a book entry debiting Loss from Subsidiary Issuance of Shares and crediting Investment in S Company is made. For example, assuming the issue of the entire 4,000 shares to noncontrolling stockholders at $14 per share, the computation and journal entry are:

P Company's share of S Company's equity:

Before the new issue	.70 × $350,000 =	$245,000
After the new issue	58⅓% × [$350,000 + ($14 × 4,000)] =	236,833
Decrease in P Company's interest		$ 8,167

Loss from Subsidiary Issuance of Shares	8,167	
Investment in S Company		8,167

Subsidiary Stock Issuance Transactions—Partial Equity Method

Gains and losses resulting from subsidiary stock issuance transactions that decrease the parent company's percentage of ownership are recorded on the parent's books in the same way as under the cost method. Also like the cost method, the effects of subsidiary stock issuance transactions that change the parent's percentage of ownership are adjusted to the difference between cost and book value when the investment is eliminated on the consolidated workpaper. In either case, subsequent recognition of the parent's share of subsidiary income and dividends is based on the new percentage of ownership.

SUBSIDIARY TREASURY STOCK TRANSACTIONS AFTER ACQUISITION

The parent company's percentage of ownership and total equity interest in its subsidiary may increase or decrease as a result of its subsidiary's dealings in its own shares. The reissue (sale) of treasury stock by the subsidiary creates no new problems. The accounting is analogous to that previously discussed in relation to the issuance of new shares of subsidiary stock. However, purchases of treasury stock by the subsidiary result in a decrease in total subsidiary stockholders' equity and require some additional discussion.

Although it is possible for a subsidiary to reacquire some of its own shares entirely from noncontrolling stockholders, entirely from the parent company, or in part from both, the latter two situations are relatively rare and, therefore, are not discussed here. Subsidiary treasury stock transactions are usually open-market purchases under which the shares are acquired from noncontrolling stockholders.

The purchase by a subsidiary of some of its shares from the noncontrolling stockholders results in an increase in the parent company's percentage interest in the subsidiary. The parent company's share of the subsidiary's net assets will remain unchanged, decrease, or increase, depending on whether the shares are purchased at a price equal to, below, or above book value.

Illustrations of these possibilities are based on the following case: P Company owns 18,000 shares (75%) of the common stock of S Company on January 1, 1995, when S Company's stockholders' equity consists of the following:

Common stock, $10 par value	$240,000
Retained earnings	144,000
Total	$384,000

Book value per common share = $384,000 ÷ 24,000 = $16

The shares were purchased for $255,000 when S Company's stockholders' equity consisted of $240,000 of common stock and $60,000 of retained earnings. Thus, the difference between cost and book value was $30,000 [$255,000 — (75% × $300,000)]. The difference was assigned to undervalued subsidiary land.

On January 1, 1995, S Company purchased 1,500 shares of its common stock from noncontrolling stockholders. Thus, P Company's percentage of ownership increased from 75% to 80% (18,000 ÷ 22,500 shares). The treatment by P Company under three assumptions as to the purchase price of the treasury stock follows.

Shares Purchased at Book Value

Assuming the 1,500 shares are purchased at book value of $16 per share, there is no net effect on the dollar amount of P Company's share of S Company's equity. The decrease in P Company's share of S Company's net assets from the purchase of the treasury stock is exactly offset as a result of the increase in P Company's ownership percentage as shown here:

P Company's share of S Company's net assets:		
Before the treasury stock purchase	.75($384,000) =	$288,000
After the treasury stock purchase .8[$384,000 − (1,500 × $16)] =		288,000
Increase (decrease) in P Company's interest		$ –0–

Workpaper entries to establish reciprocity and eliminate the investment account for a workpaper prepared on December 31, 1995, are:

Investment in S Company	63,000	
1/1 Retained Earnings—P Company		63,000
.75($144,000 − $60,000)		

Reciprocity is established based on the percentage of ownership prior to the treasury stock purchase (75%). After reciprocity is established, the investment account is eliminated as follows, assuming the cost method is used to account for treasury stock.

Common Stock—S Company .8($240,000)	192,000	
1/1 Retained Earnings—S Company .8($144.000)	115,200	
Land	30,000	
Treasury Stock .80(($24,000)		19,200
Investment in S Company ($255,000 + $63,000)		318,000

In subsequent periods, reciprocity is established on the basis of a 75% interest to the date of treasury stock purchase plus an 80% interest thereafter. For example, if S Company earned $50,000 during 1995 and declared no dividends, the amount needed to establish reciprocity for a workpaper on December 31, 1996, is

To January 1, 1995—.75($144,000 − $60,000)	$ 63,000
From January 1, 1995 to January 1, 1996—	
.8($194,000 − $144,000)	40,000
Total	$103,000

Shares Purchased at More or Less Than Book Value

Accounting standards provide that the purchase of treasury stock by a subsidiary for more or less than book value per share should be treated as though the parent company purchased additional shares of the subsidiary because the transaction results in an increase in the parent's percentage interest.[1] If the shares are purchased at more than book value, the decrease in the parent company's interest in the net assets of the subsidiary will result in an increase in the difference between cost and book value when the investment is eliminated in the preparation of consolidated financial statements. Conversely, if the shares are purchased at less than book value, the increase in the parent company's interest will result in a decrease in the difference between cost and book value.

Shares Purchased for More Than Book Value   Assume the 1,500 shares are purchased at $25 per share, which is more than its book value of $16. The decrease in P Company's equity interest is computed as follows:

P Company's share of S Company's net assets:		
Before the treasury stock purchase	.75($384,000) =	$288,000
After the treasury stock purchase	.8[$384,000 − (1,500 × $25)] =	277,200
Decrease in P Company's interest		$ 10,800

The price paid implies an undervaluation of subsidiary net assets, and the decrease in P Company's equity interest is added to the difference between cost and book value (land) in the workpaper investment elimination entry as follows:

Common Stock—S Company .8($240,000)	192,000	
1/1 Retained Earnings—S Company .8($144,000)	115,200	
Land ($30,000 + $10,800)	40,800	
Treasury Stock—S Company .8($37,500)		30,000
Investment in S Company		318,000

The $10,800 increase in the difference between cost and book value is assigned following the procedures for treatment of an excess of cost over book value as described in Chapter 4. Here, we assume it relates to undervalued subsidiary land.

Shares Purchased at Less Than Book Value   Assume that the shares are purchased at $10 per share, which is less than its book value. The increase in P Company's equity interest is computed as follows:

---

[1]See *APB Opinion No. 16*, pars. 5 and 43, and *Accounting Interpretation No. 26* of *APB Opinion No. 16*.

P Company's share of S Company's net assets:

Before the treasury stock purchase	.75 ($384,000) =	$288,000
After the treasury stock purchase .80[$384,000 − (1,500 × $10)] =		295,200
Increase in P Company's interest		$ 7,200

The price paid implies the overvaluation of subsidiary net assets, and the increase in P Company's equity interest is deducted from the original difference between cost and book value in the workpaper investment elimination entry as follows:

Common Stock—S Company	192,000	
1/1 Retained Earnings—S Company	115,200	
Land ($30,000 − $7,200)	22,800	
Treasury Stock—S Company .8($15,000)		12,000
Investment in S Company		318,000

The $7,200 decrease in the difference between cost and book value is assigned following the procedures for the treatment of an excess of book value over cost as described in Chapter 4. Again, here we assume it relates to overvalued subsidiary land.

Subsidiary Treasury Stock Purchases—Partial Equity Method

When the partial equity method is used to record investments in subsidiaries, increases and decreases in the parent company's interest in the net assets of a subsidiary resulting from purchases of treasury stock by the subsidiary are treated in the same way as under the cost method. Increases are treated as additions to and decreases as subtractions from the difference between cost and book value when the workpaper investment elimination entry is made. The adjusted difference is then assigned following the procedures described in Chapter 4.

Reissuance of Treasury Shares by Subsidiary

As indicated earlier, the subsidiary may reissue some or all of its treasury shares entirely to the parent company, entirely to noncontrolling stockholders, or to both. In all these treasury stock reissuance cases, the accounting is analogous to that previously discussed in relation to the issuance of new shares of subsidiary stock. An immediately before-and-after computation of the parent's share of the net assets of the subsidiary is made in order to determine the amount of the increase or decrease in the parent company's equity interest in the subsidiary. If the parent company purchases all the treasury stock, its percentage of ownership increases and the purchase is treated as a purchase of additional investment with the appropriate assignment of any difference between cost and book value. If the treasury shares are purchased by noncontrolling stockholders, the parent's percentage of ownership decreases, and any change in the parent's equity interest is recorded as a nonoperating gain or loss.

Questions

1. Identify three types of transactions that result in a change in a parent company's ownership interest in its subsidiary.

2. Why is the date of acquisition of subsidiary stock important under the purchase method?

3. When a parent company has obtained control of a subsidiary through several purchases and subsequently sells a portion of its shares in the subsidiary, how is the carrying value of the shares sold determined?

4. A gain or loss on the sale of a portion of its investment by a parent company that records its investment using the cost method during a fiscal period consists of three elements. What are they?

5. ABC Corporation purchased 10,000 shares (80%) of EZ Company at $30 per share and sold them several years later for $35 per share. The consolidated income statement reports a loss on the sale of this investment. Explain.

6. Explain how a parent company that owns less than 100% of a subsidiary can purchase an entire new issue of common stock directly from the subsidiary.

7. When a subsidiary issues additional shares of stock to noncontrolling stockholders and such issuance results in an increase in the book value of the parent's share of the subsidiary's equity, what justification exists for treating this increase as a gain?

8. P Company holds an 80% interest in S Company. Determine the effect (that is, increase, decrease, no change, not determinable) on both the total book value of the noncontrolling interest and the noncontrolling interests's percentage of ownership in the net assets of S Company for each of the following situations:

   A. P Company acquires additional shares directly from S Company at a price equal to the book value per share of the S Company stock immediately prior to the issuance.
   B. S Company acquires its own shares on the open market. The cost of these shares is less than their book value.
   C. Assume the same situation as in (B) except that the cost of the shares is greater than their book value.
   D. P Company and a noncontrolling stockholder each acquire 100 shares directly from S Company at a price below the book value per share.

Exercises

Exercises 8-1

Peck Company purchased Sanno Company common stock in a series of open-market cash purchases from 1994 through 1996 as follows:

DATE	SHARES ACQUIRED	COST
January 1, 1994	1,800	$ 46,000
January 1, 1995	4,500	95,000
January 1, 1996	9,900	262,000

Sanno Company had 18,000 shares of $20 par value common stock outstanding during the entire period. Retained earnings balances for Sanno Company on relevant dates were:

January 1, 1994	$ 20,000
January 1, 1995	(30,000)
January 1, 1996	85,000
December 31, 1996	170,000

Dividends in the amount of $50,000 were distributed by Sano Company only in 1996. Any difference between cost and book value is assigned to subsidiary land. Peck Company uses the cost method to account for its investment in Sanno Company.

Required:

A. Prepare the journal entries that Peck Company would record on its books during 1996 to account for its investment in Sanno Company.

B. Prepare the workpaper eliminating entries necessary to prepare a consolidated statements workpaper on December 31, 1996.

Exercise 8-2

Papke Company acquired 85% of the common stock of Serbin Company in two separate cash transactions. The first purchase of 72,000 shares (60%) on January 1, 1995, cost $490,000. The second purchase, one year later, of 30,000 shares (25%) cost $220,000. Serbin Company's stockholders' equity was as follows:

	DECEMBER 31 1995	DECEMBER 31 1996
Common stock, $5 par	$600,000	$600,000
Retained earnings, 1/1	175,000	201,000
Net income	46,000	60,000
Dividends declared, 9/30	(20,000)	(25,000)
Retained earnings, 12/31	201,000	236,000
Total stockholders' equity, 12/31	$801,000	$836,000

On April 1, 1996, after a significant rise in the market price of Serbin Company's stock, Papke Company sold 21,600 of its Serbin Company shares for $260,000. Serbin Company notified Papke Company that its net income for the first three months was $15,000. The shares sold were identified as those obtained in the first purchase. Any difference between cost and book value relates to subsidiary land. Papke uses the cost method to account for its investment in Serbin Company.

Required:

Prepare the journal entries Papke Company would record on its books during 1996 to account for its investment in Serbin Company.

Exercise 8-3

Use the data provided in Exercise 8-2.

Required:

A. Prepare the workpaper eliminating entries needed for a consolidated statements workpaper on December 31, 1996.

B. Determine the amount of noncontrolling interest that would be reported on the consolidated balance sheet on December 31, 1996.

Exercise 8-4

Use the data from Exercise 8-1, but assume use of the partial equity method rather than the cost method.

Required:

A. Prepare the journal entries Peck Company will make on its books during 1995 and 1996 to account for its investment in Sanno Company.

B. Prepare workpaper eliminating entries necessary to prepare a consolidated statements workpaper on December 31, 1996.

Exercise 8-5

Use the date presented in Exercise 8-2, but assume use of the partial equity method rather than the cost method.

Required:

A. Prepare the journal entries Papke Company will make on its books during 1995 and 1996 to account for its investment in Serbin Company.

B. Prepare the workpaper eliminating entries needed for a consolidated statements workpaper on December 31, 1996.

Exercise 8-6

On January 1, 1996, Pace Company purchased 250,000 shares of common stock directly from its subsidiary, Sime Company, for $1.50 per share. Noncontrolling stockholders elected not to participate in the new issue.

Pace Company acquired its initial 92.5% interest in Sime Company by purchasing on the open market 462,500 shares of Sime's common stock for $578,125 on January 1, 1992. Sime Company's stockholders' equity just before each of the two purchases was as follows:

	DECEMBER 31 1991	DECEMBER 31 1995
Common Stock $1 par	$500,000	$500,000
Other Contributed Captial	40,000	40,000
Retained Earnings	60,000	150,000
Total	$600,000	$690,000

During 1996 Sine Company reported $90,000 net income and declared a dividend in the amount of $30,000. Any difference between cost and book value relates to subsidiary land. Pace uses the cost method to account for its investment.

Required:

A. Prepare the journal entry on Pace Company's books to record the purchase of the additional shares on January 1, 1996.

B. Prepare the eliminating entries needed for the preparation of a consolidated statements workpaper on December 31, 1996.

Exercise 8-7

Use the same data provided in Exercise 8-6, with the exception that Pace Company purchased the additional shares from Sime Company on January 1, 1996, at a price of $1.30 per share rather than $1.50.

Required:

A. Prepare the journal entry on Pace Company's books to record the purchase of the additional shares on January 1, 1996.

B. Prepare the eliminating entries needed for the preparation of a consolidated statements workpaper on December 31, 1996.

Exercise 8-8

Padilla Company acquired 80% of the outstanding common stock of Skon Company on January 1, 1994, for $132,000. At the date of purchase, Skon Company had a balance in its $2 par value common stock account of $120,000 and retained earnings of $30,000.

On January 1, 1996, Skon Company issued 15,000 shares of its previously unissued stock to noncontrolling stockholders for $3.00 per share. On this date, Skon Company had a retained earnings balance of $50,500. The difference between cost and book value relates to subsidiary land. No dividends were paid in 1996. Padilla uses the cost method.

Required:

A. Prepare the journal entry on Padilla's books to record the effect of the issuance.

B. Prepare the eliminating entries needed for the preparation of a consolidated statements workpaper on December 31, 1996.

Exercise 8-9

Pitt Company purchased 112,500 of the outstanding common shares of Simik Company on January 1, 1993, for $326,000 when Simik Company's stockholders' equity consisted of the following:

Common Stock $2 par value	$300,000
Retained Earnings	84,000
Total	$384,000

On January 1, 1996 Simik Company purchased 25,000 of its common shares from noncontrolling stockholders for $80,000. The shares will be held as treasury stock. Simik uses the cost method to account for treasury stock. Stockholders' equity for Pitt and Simik companies on the date of treasury stock purchase was:

	PITT	SIMIK
Common Stock	$500,000	$300,000
Retained Earnings	230,000	60,000
Total	$730,000	$360,000

No dividends were declared in 1996. The difference between cost and book value relates to land. Pitt uses the cost method.

Required:

Prepare the workpaper eliminating entries needed for the preparation of a consolidated statements workpaper on December 31, 1996.

Problems

Problem 8-1

Sarko Company had 300,000 shares of $10 par value common stock outstanding at all times, and retained earnings balances as indicated here:

January 1, 1995	$260,000
January 1, 1996	540,000
January 1, 1997	630,000
January 1, 1998	820,000

Pelzer Company acquired Sarko Company stock through open-market purchases as follows:

DATE	SHARES	COST
1/1/95	30,000	$ 365,000
1/1/96	75,000	960,000
1/1/97	135,000	1,860,000

Sarko Company declared no dividends during this period. The fair values of Sarko Company's assets and liabilities were approximately equal to their book values throughout this period (1995 through 1997). Pelzer Company's policy is to amortize goodwill over an estimated economic life of 10 years from the date of each stock purchase. Pelzer Company uses the cost method.

Required:

A. Prepare a schedule to compare investment cost with the book value of equity acquired for each stock purchase.

B. Prepare elimination entries for the preparation of a consolidated statements workpaper on December 31, 1997.

Problem 8-2

Trial balances for Phan Company and its subsidiary Sato Company on December 31, 1995, are as follows:

	PHAN	SATO
Current assests	$ 191,500	$ 138,000
Investment in Sato Company	600,500	
Other assets	920,000	672,000
Dividends declared	150,000	70,000
Cost of goods sold	1,100,000	325,000
Other expenses	350,000	125,000
	$3,312,000	$1,330,000
Liabilities	$ 168,000	$ 80,000
Capital stock, $10 par	700,000	400,000
1/1 Retained earnings	581,000	250,000
Sales	1,800,000	600,000
Dividend income	63,000	
	$3,312,000	$1,330,000

Phan Company acquired its investment in Sato Company through open-market purchases of stock as follows:

DATE	SHARES PURCHASED	COST	SATO COMPANY RETAINED EARNINGS BALANCE
1/1/93	9,000	$110,500	$ 46,000
1/1/94	12,500	210,000	165,000
1/1/95	14,500	280,000	250,000
Total	36,000	$600,500	

Any difference between cost and book value of the interest acquired relates to Sato Company land, which is included in Other assets.

Sato Company issued 40,000 shares of stock on July 1, 1990, its date of incorporation. No other capital stock transactions were undertaken by Sato Company after that time.

No intercompany transactions had occurred between Phan Company and Sato Company before 1995. During 1995, however, Phan Company made sales of merchandise to Sato Company in the amount of $150,000. Phan Company sells merchandise to Sato Company at a markup of 25% above cost. One-fourth of the goods purchased from Phan were still in Sato's inventory on December 31, 1995. At the end of the year, Phan owed Sato $22,000 for goods purchased during the year.

Required:

Prepare a consolidated financial statements workpaper for Phan Company and its subsidiary Sato Company on December 31, 1995.

Problem 8-3

The accounts of Pyle Company and its subsidiary, Stern Company, are summarized below as of December 31, 1995:

DEBITS	PYLE	STERN
Current assets	$ 600,000	$ 320,000
Investment in Stern Company	480,000	
Other assets	1,180,000	668,000
Dividends declared, 11/1	80,000	60,000
	$2,340,000	$1,048,000

CREDITS		
Liabilities	$ 190,000	$ 90,000
Common stock, $5 par	500,000	300,000
Other contributed capital	160,000	180,000
1/1 Retained earnings	1,200,000	292,000
Net income	290,000	186,000
	$2,340,000	$1,048,000

Pyle Company made the following open-market purchase and sale of Stern Company common stock: January 2, 1993, purchased 51,000 shares, cost $510,000; April 1, 1995, sold 3,000 shares, proceeds, $100,000.

The book value of Stern Company's net assets on January 2, 1993, $600,000, approximated the fair value of those net assets. Subsequent changes in book value of the net assets are entirely attributable to earnings of Stern Company. Stern Company earns its income evenly throughout the year.

Required:

Prepare a consolidated financial statements workpaper as of December 31, 1995. Begin the income statement section of the workpaper with "Net Income Before Dividend Income and Gain on Sale of Investment," which is $172,000 and $186,000 for Pyle Company and Stern Company, respectively.

Problem 8-4

Trial balances for Porter Company and its subsidiary, Spitz Company, as of December 31, 1995, follow:

DEBITS	PORTER	SPITZ
Cash	$ 90,000	$ 40,000
Accounts receivable (net)	62,000	38,000
Inventory	106,000	64,000
Investment in Spitz Company	121,500	
Plant assets	320,000	149,000
Land	69,000	46,000
Dividends declared, 10/1	50,000	30,000
Total	$818,500	$367,000

CREDITS	PORTER	SPITZ
Liabilities	$102,000	$ 61,000
Common stock, $2 per value	250,000	100,000
Other contributed capital	158,000	20,000
1/1 Retained earnings	206,500	126,000
Income summary	102,000	60,000
Total	$818,500	$367,000

Porter Company made the following open-market purchase and sale of Spitz Company common stock: January 1, 1991, purchased 45,000 shares for $135,000; May 1, 1995, sold 4,500 shares for $28,000.

The book value of Spitz Company's net assets on January 1, 1991, was $140,000; the excess of cost over net assets acquired relates to land. Subsequent changes in the book value of Spitz Company's net assets are entirely attributable to earnings retained in the business. Spitz Company earns its income evenly throughout the year. Porter Company uses the cost method to account for its investment.

Required:

Prepare a consolidated financial statements workpaper as of December 31, 1995. Begin the Income Statement section of the workpaper with "Net Income Before Dividend Income and Gain on Sale of Investment," which is $63,200 for Porter Company and $60,000 for Spitz Company.

Problem 8-5

(Note that this is the same problem as Problem 8-3, but assuming use of the partial equity method.)

The accounts of Pyle Company and its subsidiary, Stern Company, are summarized below as of December 31, 1995:

DEBITS	PYLE	STERN
Current assets	$ 600,000	$ 320,000
Investment in Stern Company	718,400	
Other assets	1,180,000	668,000
Dividends declared, 11/1	80,000	60,000
Total	$2,578,400	$1,048,000

CREDITS		
Liabilities	$ 190,000	$ 90,000
Common stock, $5 par value	500,000	300,000
Other contributed capital	160,000	180,000
1/1 Retained earnings	1,346,200	292,000
Net income	382,200	186,000
Total	$2,578,400	$1,048,000

Pyle Company made the following open-market purchase and sale of Stern Company common stock: January 2, 1993, purchased 51,000 shares, cost $510,000; April 1, 1995, sold 3,000 shares, proceeds, $100,000.

The book value of Stern Company's net assets on January 2, 1993, $600,000, approximated the fair value of those net assets. Subsequent changes in book value of the net assets are attributable to earnings of Stern Company. Stern Company earns its income evenly throughout the year.

Required:

Prepare a consolidated financial statements workpaper as of December 31, 1995. Begin the income statement section of the workpaper with "Income Before Equity in Subsidiary Income and Gain on Sale of Investment," which is $172,000 and $186,000 for Pyle Company and Stern Company, respectively.

Problem 8-6

(Note that this is the same problem as Problem 8-4, but assuming use of the partial equity method.)

Trial balances for Porter Company and its subsidiary, Spitz Company, as of December 31, 1955, follow:

DEBITS	PORTER	SPITZ
Cash	$ 90,000	$ 40,000
Accounts receivable (net)	62,000	38,000
Inventory	106,000	64,000
Investment in Spitz Company	231,660	
Plant assets	320,000	149,000
Land	69,000	46,000
Dividends declared, 10/1	50,000	30,000
Total	$928,660	$367,000

CREDITS		
Liabilities	$102,000	$ 61,000
Common stock, $2 par value	250,000	100,000
Other contributed capital	158,000	20,000
1/1 Retained earnings	301,900	126,000
Income summary	116,760	60,000
Total	$928,660	$367,000

Porter Company made the following open-market purchase and sale of Spitz Company common stock: January 1, 1991, purchased 45,000 shares for $135,000; May 1, 1995, sold 4,500 shares for $28,000.

The book value of Spitz Company's net assets on January 1, 1991, was $140,000; the excess of cost over net assets acquired relates to land. Subsequent changes in the book value of Spitz Company's net assets are entirely attributable to earnings retained in the business. Spitz Company earns its income evenly throughout the year.

Required:

Prepare a consolidated financial statements workpaper as of December 31, 1995. Begin the income statement section of the workpaper with "Net Income Before Equity in Subsidiary

Income and Gain on Sale of Investment,'' which is $63,200 for Porter Company and $60,000 for Spitz Company.

Problem 8-7

On January 1, 1995, Plum Company made an open-market purchase of 30,000 shares of Spivey Company common stock for $122,000. At that time, Spivey Company had common stock ($2 par) of $600,000 and retained earnings of $240,000. On July 1, 1995, an additional 210,000 shares were purchased on the open market by Plum Company at a cost of $790,000. On November 1, 1995, 3,000 of the shares purchased on January 1, 1995, were sold on the open market for $21,000.

During 1995, Plum Company earned $22,000 (excluding any gain or loss on the sale of the shares). Plum Company received income statements from Spivey Company reporting the following results:

January 1, 1995 to June 30, 1995	$ 60,000
January 1, 1995 to October 31, 1995	96,000
For the year ended December 31, 1995	130,000

Neither company declared dividends during the year. Plum Company's retained earnings were $460,000 on January 1, 1995.

Required:

A. Prepare the book entries Plum Company would make during 1995 to account for its investment in Spivey Company, assuming use of the cost method.

B. Prepare in general journal form the eliminating entries for a consolidated statements workpaper on December 31, 1995.

C. Compute consolidated net income for 1995.

Problem 8-8

Pryor Company acquired 51,000 shares of Spero Company's common stock on January 1, 1994, for $400,000 when Spero Company had common stock ($5 par) of $300,000 and retained earnings of $200,000.

On January 1, 1996, Spero Company issued 7,500 additional shares of its common stock for $8.50 per share. The new shares were purchased entirely by Pryor Company. Spero Company's retained earnings had increased to $360,000 by that date.

During 1996 Spero Company declared dividends of $40,000 and reported net income at year-end of $90,000. Pryor Company uses the cost method.

Required:

A. Prepare the journal entry on Pryor's books to record the purchase of the new shares.

B. Prepare in general journal form the workpaper entries needed for the preparation of a consolidated statements workpaper on December 31, 1996.

Problem 8-9

On January 1, 1994, Purdy Company acquired 84% of the capital stock of Sally Company for $840,000. On that date, Sally Company's stockholders' equity was:

Capital stock, $20 par	$600,000
Other contributed capital	200,000
Retained earnings	160,000
Total	$960,000

The difference between cost and book value relates to land owned by Sally Company.

On January 2, 1996, Sally Company issued 6,000 shares of its authorized capital stock, with a market value of $55 per share, to Marcy Smith in exchange for a patent. Sally Company's retained earnings balance on this date was $400,000; capital stock and other contributed capital balances had not changed during 1994 and 1995.

Required:

A. Prepare (1) the entry on Purdy's books to record the effect of the issuance, and (2) the elimination entries for the preparation of a consolidated balance sheet workpaper immediately after the new issue of shares assuming use of the cost method.

B. Assuming that the market value of the new shares issued was $34 per share, repeat requirement (A) above.

Problem 8-10

Plat Company purchased on the open market 33,750 shares of the capital stock of Sova Company for $300,000 on January 2, 1993, when Sova Company had the following stockholder's equity:

Capital stock, $5 par value	$225,000
Other contributed capital	85,000
Retained earnings	40,000
Total	$350,000

The difference between cost and book value relates to Sova Company land.

On January 1, 1996, Sova Company purchased 7,500 of its own shares from a noncontrolling stockholder for cash of $95,000. The shares are to be held as treasury stock. Sova Company's retained earnings had increased to $100,000 by January 1, 1996; capital stock and other contributed capital balances had not changed since January 2, 1993. Sova Company uses the cost method to account for its treasury shares. Plat company uses the cost method to account for its investment in Sova Company.

Required:

Prepare all determinable workpaper entries for the preparation of a consolidated statements workpaper on December 31, 1996.

Problem 8-11

On January 2, 1990, Pullen Company purchased, on the open market, 135,000 shares of Souza Company common stock for $665,000. At that time, Souza Company had common stock ($2 par value) of $300,000 and retained earnings of $400,000. On May 1, 1995, Pullen Company sold 13,500 of its Souza Company shares on the open market for $91,000. Changes in Souza Company retained earnings during 1995 follow:

Retained earnings, 1/1/95	$500,000
Net income for 1995 (earned evenly throughout the year)	270,000
Dividends declared on 11/1/95 and paid on 12/16/95	(70,000)
Retained earnings, 12/31/95	$700,000

Pullen Company, which uses the cost method to record its investment in Souza Company, reported net income for 1995 amounting to $352,500. Any difference between cost and book value relates to subsidiary land.

Required:

A. Prepare the book entries Pullen Company will make during 1995 to account for its investment in Souza Company.

B. Prepare, in general journal form, the eliminating entries needed to prepare a consolidated statements workpaper on December 31, 1995.

C. Prepare a schedule to calculate consolidated net income for 1995.

D. Prepare the workpaper entry to establish reciprocity for the 1996 consolidated statements workpaper.

9

INDIRECT OWNERSHIP AND RECIPROCAL STOCKHOLDINGS

In preceding chapters, we have dealt only with situations in which one company, the parent company, had a direct controlling interest in another company, the subsidiary. At times a parent may have an interest in a subsidiary that has an interest in a subsidiary of its own. For example, P Company may own 90% of S Company, which, in turn, owns 80% of R Company. Thus, P Company has a 90% direct interest in S Company and a 72% (90% × 80%) indirect interest in R Company. Consequently, consolidated net income should consist of P Company's income from independent operations plus 90% and 72% of S Company's and R Company's income from independent operations, respectively.

As another example, P Company may own 90% of S Company and 80% of R Company, and S Company may own a portion, say 10%, of R Company. Thus, P Company owns a direct interest in S Company of 90% and a combined direct and indirect interest in R Company of 89% [80% + (90% × 10%)]. With relationships of this type, it is often helpful to prepare an affiliation diagram identifying ownership relationships, with the direction of the arrow indicating the direction of ownership. The two situations described above may be diagrammed as follows:

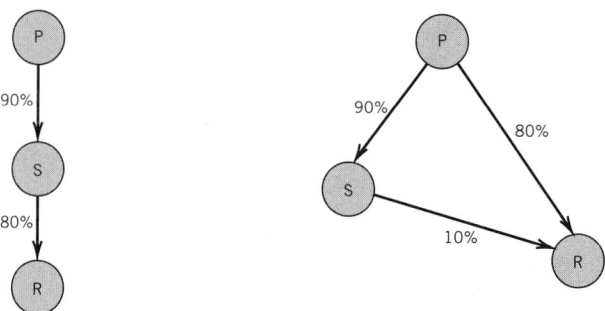

Occasionally two or more affiliates may have ownership interests in each other. For example, P Company may own 90% of S Company, which, in turn, owns 10% of P Company. Or P Company may own 90% of S Company, which owns 80% of R Company, which, in turn, owns 10% of S Company. Relationships of this type are generally termed **reciprocal stockholdings**. They may be diagrammed as follows:

Problems in preparing consolidated financial statements where there are indirect or reciprocal stockholdings are discussed in this chapter. Many indirect and reciprocal possibilities exist, and no attempt will be made to discuss them all. However, sufficient illustrations are presented to give the reader a basic understanding of the principles involved.

INDIRECT OWNERSHIP

The preparation of consolidated financial statements for a group of affiliates where there is some type of indirect ownership involves two primary determinations—earnings and total stockholders' equity. After the investment and retained earnings accounts are properly adjusted to establish reciprocity, the consolidation procedures are essentially the same for indirect ownership as they are for direct ownership situations.

Three illustrations of indirect ownership affiliations are presented, with appropriate affiliation diagrams. Since the date of acquisition of individual investments is an important consideration, the diagrams indicate both the percentage of ownership and the date of acquisition. Illustrations are based on the following investment cost and stockholders' equity information:

	P COMPANY	S COMPANY	R COMPANY
Cost of:			
P's investment in S Company	$295,000		
S's investment in R Company		$145,000	
Stockholders' equity:			
Common stock	$500,000	$200,000	$100,000
Retained earnings, 1/1/94	230,000	70,000	50,000
1994 reported income	100,000	50,000	20,000
1994 dividends declared	(30,000)	(20,000)	(10,000)
Retained earnings, 12/31/94	300,000	100,000	60,000
1995 reported income	110,000	50,000	30,000
1995 dividends declared	(30,000)	(20,000)	(10,000)
Retained earnings, 12/31/95	380,000	130,000	80,000
Stockholders' equity, 12/31/95	$880,000	$330,000	$180,000

The difference between cost and book value (computed below) relates to subsidiary land. The companies use the cost method to record their investments.

	P'S INVESTMENT IN S COMPANY ACQUIRED 1/1/94	S'S INVESTMENT IN R COMPANY ACQUIRED 1/1/95
Cost of investment	$295,000	$145,000
Book value of new assets acquired:		
.9($200,000 + $70,000)	243,000	
.8($100,000 + $60,000)		128,000
Difference between cost and book value	$ 52,000	$ 17,000

P Company's Interest in S Company Is Acquired Prior to S Company's Interest in R Company

Assume first that P Company purchased a 90% interest in S Company on January 1, 1994, and that S Company purchased an 80% interest in R Company on January 1, 1995. (This type of affiliation is often referred to as a *father–son–grandson* affiliation.) The appropriate diagram is:

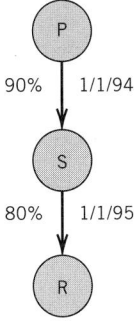

Notice that P Company has a 90% direct interest in S Company and a 72% (90% × 80%) indirect interest in R Company. Noncontrolling stockholders therefore have a 10% direct interest in S Company and a 28% [20% + (10% × 80%)] combined direct and indirect interest in R Company.

In accounting for their investments during 1995, S Company and P Company made the following book entries:

S COMPANY'S BOOKS

Cash	8,000	
Dividend Income		8,000
(80% × $10,000)		

Thus, S Company's income from independent operations for 1995 is $42,000 ($50,000 − $8,000).

P COMPANY'S BOOKS

Cash	18,000	
Dividend Income		18,000
(90% × $20,000)		

Thus, P Company's income from independent operations for 1995 is $92,000 ($110,000 − $18,000).

Consolidated net income for 1995 is $151,400, which might be computed in one of several ways as follows:

1. P Company's share of its income from the independent operations of its subsidiaries might be added to P Company's income from its own independent operations:

P Company's income from its independent operations	$ 92,000
Plus P Company's share of income from independent operations of its subsidiaries:	
S Company (90% × $42,000)	37,800
R Company (90% × 80% × $30,000)	21,600
Consolidated net income	$151,400

2. P Company's share of the undistributed income of its subsidiaries might be added to P Company's reported income:

P Company's reported income	$110,000
Plus P Company's share of its subsidiaries' undistributed income for 1995:	
S Company [90% × ($50,000 − $20,000)]	27,000
R Company [72% × ($30,000 − $10,000)]	14,400
Consolidated net income	$151,400

3. The noncontrolling stockholders' interest in income might be deducted from the combined income from independent operations of all affiliates:

Combined income from independent operations of all companies ($92,000 + $42,000 + $30,000)	$164,000
Less noncontrolling interest in the independent income of:	
S Company (10% × $42,000)	(4,200)
R Company (28% × $30,000)	(8,400)
Consolidated net income	$151,400

A *partial* workpaper for the preparation of consolidated financial statements on December 31, 1995, is presented in Illustration 9-1. The remainder of the workpaper would be completed in the same manner as presented in previous chapters. Workpaper eliminating entries in general journal form are:

(1)	Investment in S Company	27,000	
	1/1 Retained Earnings—P Company		27,000
	To establish reciprocity from 1/1/94 to 1/1/95 [90% × ($100,000 − $70,000)].		
(2)	Dividend Income	26,000	
	Dividends Declared—S Company		18,000
	Dividends Declared—R Company		8,000
	To eliminate intercompany dividends.		
(3)	Common Stock—R Company .8($100,000)	80,000	
	1/1 Retained Earnings—R Company .8($60,000)	48,000	
	Difference Between Cost and Book Value (Land)	17,000	
	Investment in R Company		145,000
	To eliminate S Company's investment in R Company.		
(4)	Common Stock—S Company .9($200,000)	180,000	
	1/1 Retained Earnings—S Company .9($100,000)	90,000	
	Difference Between Cost and Book Value (Land)	52,000	
	Investment in S Company ($295,000 + $27,000)		322,000
	To eliminate P Company's investment in S Company.		

In subsequent years, reciprocity must be established for each investment. In doing so, it is important to recognize that establishing reciprocity should proceed "up the ladder"; that is, reciprocity should be established for P Company's investment in S Company after S Company has recognized in its beginning-of-the-year retained earnings its (S Company's) share of the change in the retained earnings of R Company. For example, in the preparation of a consolidated statements workpaper on December 31, 1996, the following reciprocity entry would be made for S Company's investment in R Company:

Cost Method
Partially Owned Subsidiaries
Indirect Ownership

ILLUSTRATION 9-1
P Company and Subsidiaries
Partial Consolidated Statements Workpaper
For the Year Ended December 31, 1995

INCOME STATEMENT	P COMPANY	S COMPANY	R COMPANY	ELIMINATIONS DR.	ELIMINATIONS CR.	NON-CONTROLLING INTEREST	CONSOLIDATED BALANCES
Income before Dividend Income	92,000	42,000	30,000				164,000
Dividend Income	18,000	8,000		(2) 26,000			
Noncontrolling Interest in Income						12,600	(12,600)*
Net Income to Retained Earnings	110,000	50,000	30,000	26,000	–0–	12,600	151,400
RETAINED EARNINGS STATEMENT							
1/1 Retained Earnings							
P Company	300,000				(1) 27,000		327,000
S Company		100,000		(4) 90,000		10,000	
R Company			60,000	(3) 48,000		12,000	
Net income from above	110,000	50,000	30,000	26,000	–0–	12,600	151,400
Dividends declared							
P Company	(30,000)						(30,000)
S Company		(20,000)			(2) 18,000	(2,000)	
R Company			(10,000)		(2) 8,000	(2,000)	
12/31 Retained Earnings to the Balance Sheet	380,000	130,000	80,000	164,000	53,000	30,600	448,400
BALANCE SHEET							
Investment in S Company	295,000			(1) 27,000	(4) 322,000		
Investment in R Company		145,000			(3) 145,000		
Difference between Cost and Book Value (Land)				{ (3) 17,000 { (4) 52,000			69,000
Common Stock							
P Company	500,000						500,000
S Company		200,000		(4) 180,000		20,000	
R Company			100,000	(3) 80,000		20,000	
Retained Earnings from above	380,000	130,000	80,000	164,000	53,000	30,600	448,400
Noncontrolling Interest in Net Assets						70,600	70,600
				520,000	520,000		

*(10% × $42,000) + (28% × $30,000).

(1) To establish reciprocity for P Company's investment in S Company 90% × ($100,000 − $70,000).
(2) To eliminate intercompany dividends.
(3) To eliminate S Company's investment in R Company.
(4) To eliminate P Company's investment in S Company.

Investment in R Company	16,000	
1/1 Retained Earnings—S Company		16,000

To establish reciprocity for S Company's investment in R Company from 1/1/95 to 1/1/96 [80% × ($80,000 − $60,000)].

After this adjustment is made, reciprocity is established for P Company's investment in S Company.

Investment in S Company	68,400	
1/1 Retained Earnings—P Company		68,400

To establish reciprocity for P Company's investment in S Company from 1/1/94 to 1/1/96. [90% × ($130,000 + $16,000 − $70,000)]

Note that reciprocity is established for P Company's share of the difference between the adjusted retained earnings of S Company on January 1, 1996 ($146,000), and S Company's retained earnings on the date of acquisition by P Company ($70,000).

S Company's Interest in R Company Acquired Prior to P Company's Interest in S Company

As a second illustration, assume the same data as in the first case except that S Company purchased an 80% interest in R Company on January 1, 1994, and P Company purchased a 90% interest in S Company on January 1, 1995. The appropriate affiliation diagram is as follows:

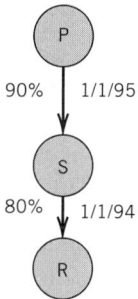

When one company (P Company) acquires a controlling interest in another company (S Company) that already owns a controlling interest in a third company (R Company), two important points must be considered. First, additional care must be exercised in determining the amount of subsidiary equity acquired by P Company, since S Company may have an equity interest in some prior years' undistributed income of R Company that is not included in S Company's retained earnings at the date of acquisition by P Company. Second, extra care must be used in determining the amount needed to establish reciprocity; that is, as explained earlier, reciprocity should be established for P Company's investment in S Company after reciprocity is established for S Company's investment in R Company.

The cost of each investment and stockholders' equity information for each company is repeated here for convenience in following the illustration.

	P COMPANY	S COMPANY	R COMPANY
Cost of:			
P's Investment in S Company	$295,000		
S's Investment in R Company		$145,000	
Stockholders' equity:			
Common stock	$500,000	$200,000	$100,000
Retained earnings, 1/1/94	230,000	70,000	50,000
1994 reported income	100,000	50,000	20,000
1994 dividends declared	(30,000)	(20,000)	(10,000)
Retained earnings, 12/31/94	300,000	100,000	60,000
1995 reported income	110,000	50,000	30,000
1995 dividends declared	(30,000)	(20,000)	(10,000)
Retained earnings, 12/31/95	380,000	130,000	80,000
Stockholders' equity, 12/31/95	$880,000	$330,000	$180,000

The difference between cost and book value for each investment may be computed as follows:

	P COMPANY'S INVESTMENT IN S		S COMPANY'S INVESTMENT IN R	
Cost of investment		$295,000		$145,000
Book value of equity acquired	(1)	277,200	(2)	120,000
Difference between cost and book value		$ 17,800		$ 25,000

(1) (90% × $308,000)
(2) (80% × $150,000)

When S Company acquired its interest in R Company, the determination of equity acquired was straightforward. On January 1, 1994, R Company had stockholders' equity of $150,000 ($100,000 common stock + $50,000 retained earnings), of which S Company acquired an 80% interest, or $120,000. When P Company acquired its interest in S Company, however the computation of equity acquired is more complex because S Company's share of R Company's undistributed income for 1994 is not reflected in S Company's retained earnings account. During 1994 R Company earned $20,000, distributed a dividend of $10,000, and, therefore, had $10,000 of undistributed income, 80% of which accrues to the benefit of S Company. On January 1, 1995, S Company's retained earnings actually consist of the $100,000 reflected on its books plus its $8,000 (80% × $10,000) share of the undistributed income of R Company, which has not been recorded on S Company's books. Thus, the equity acquired by P Company on January 1, 1995, is computed as follows:

90% × ($200,000 capital stock + $108,000 retained earnings) = $277,200

Eliminating entries for the preparation of a consolidated statements workpaper on December 31, 1995, follow. It is assumed that the difference between cost and book value relates to subsidiary land.

(1) Investment in R Company	8,000	
1/1 Retained Earnings—S Company		8,000
To establish reciprocity (80% × $10,000).		

Note that there is no reciprocity entry for P Company's investment in S Company because the investment was acquired on January 1, 1995.

(2) Dividend Income	26,000	
Dividends Declared—S Company		18,000
Dividends Declared—R Company		8,000
To eliminate intercompany dividends		
(3) Common Stock—R Company. .8($100,000)	80,000	
1/1 Retained Earnings—R Company .8($60,000)	48,000	
Difference Between Cost and Book Value (Land)	25,000	
Investment in R Company ($145,000 + $8,000)		153,000
To eliminate S Company's investment in R Company.		
(4) Common Stock—S Company .9($200,000).	180,000	
1/1 Retained Earnings—S Company .9($108,000)	97,200	
Difference Between Cost and Book Value (Land)	17,800	
Investment in S Company		295,000
To eliminate P Company's investment in S Company.		

As discussed earlier, a workpaper reciprocity entry is made to give recognition, in retained earnings as of the beginning of the year, to the investor's share of the undistributed earnings of its subsidiary from the date of acquisition to the beginning of the current year. After the reciprocity entry is made, the investment accounts are eliminated, as usual, against the related subsidiary equity. Note that in the elimination of P Company's investment in S Company, 90% of S Company's *adjusted retained earnings* of $108,000 on January 1, 1995, is eliminated.

The computation of noncontrolling interest in combined income must include the fact that S Company's income must be adjusted for its share of the undistributed income of R Company for 1995, as follows:

Noncontrolling interest in income of R Company (20% × $30,000)		$ 6,000
Noncontrolling interest in income of S Company:		
S Company's reported income	$50,000	
Add S Company's share of undistributed income		
of R Company during 1995 [80% × ($30,000 − $10,000)]	16,000	
S Company's adjusted net income	66,000	
Noncontrolling interest therein	10%	6,600
Total noncontrolling interest in combined income		$12,600

As mentioned earlier, when establishing reciprocity for subsequent years, reciprocity should be established for S Company's investment in R Company before reciprocity is established for P Company's investment in S Company. For example, in the preparation of a consolidated statements workpaper on December 31, 1996, the following reciprocity entry should be made for S Company's investment in R Company.

Investment in R Company	24,000	
1/1 Retained Earnings—S Company		24,000
[80% × ($80,000 − $50,000)]		

After this adjustment is made, reciprocity is established for P Company's investment in S Company.

Investment in S Company	41,400	
1/1 Retained Earnings—P Company		41,400
[90% × ($130,000 + $24,000 − $108,000)]		

Note that reciprocity is established for P Company's share of the difference between the *adjusted retained earnings* of S Company on January 1, 1996 ($154,000), and the *adjusted retained earnings* of S Company on the date of acquisition by P Company ($108,000). This can be verified by looking at the investment elimination entries on the 1996 workpaper as shown below. The differences between cost and book value, which relate to land, remain the same.

Common Stock—R Company	80,000	
1/1 Retained Earnings—R Company .8($80,000)	64,000	
Difference Between Cost and Book Value (Land)	25,000	
Investment in R Company ($145,000 + $24,000)		169,000
To eliminate S Company's investment in R Company.		
Common Stock—S Company	180,000	
1/1 Retained Earnings—S Company .9($154,000)	138,600	
Difference Between Cost and Book Value (Land)	17,800	
Investment in S Company ($295,000 + $41,400)		336,400
To eliminate P Company's investment in S Company.		

Connecting Affiliates

As a third illustration of indirect holdings, assume that on January 1, 1994, P Company acquired 90% and 70% of the common stock of S Company and R Company for $295,000 and $145,000 respectively. One year later, on January 1, 1995, S Company acquired 20% of the common stock of R Company for $35,000. (These affiliations are often referred to as *connecting affiliates*.) The relationships are diagrammed as follows:

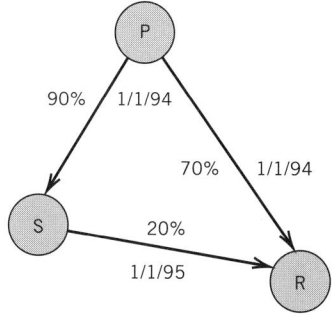

Notice that P Company has a 90% direct interest in S Company and an 88% combined direct and indirect interest in R Company [70% + (90% × 20%)]. Consequently, noncontrolling stockholders have a 10% interest in S Company and a 12% interest in R Company.

Stockholders' equity of the three companies is the same as in prior illustrations, as summarized here:

	P COMPANY	S COMPANY	R COMPANY
Cost of:			
P's investment in S Company	$295,000		
P's investment in R Company	145,000		
S's investment in R Company		$ 35,000	
Stockholders' equity:			
Common stock	$500,000	$200,000	$100,000
Retained earnings, 1/1/94	230,000	70,000	50,000
1994 Reported income	100,000	50,000	20,000
1994 Dividends declared	(30,000)	(20,000)	(10,000)
Retained earnings, 12/31/94	300,000	100,000	60,000
1995 Reported income	110,000	50,000	30,000
1995 Dividends declared	(30,000)	(20,000)	(10,000)
Retained earnings, 12/31/95	380,000	130,000	80,000
Stockholders' equity, 12/31/95	$880,000	$330,000	$180,000

The difference between cost and book value, which, as before, relates to land, is computed as follows:

	P COMPANY'S INVESTMENT IN S COMPANY	P COMPANY INVESTMENT IN R COMPANY	S COMPANY'S INVESTMENT IN R COMPANY
Investment cost	$295,000	$145,000	$35,000
Equity acquired	(1) 243,000	(2) 105,000	(3) 32,000
Difference between cost and book value	$ 52,000	$ 40,000	$ 3,000

(1) 90% × $270,000
(2) 70% × $150,000
(3) 20% × $160,000

The companies record their investments using the cost method. Net income from independent operations for each company for 1995 is:

	P COMPANY	S COMPANY	R COMPANY
Reported income	$110,000	$50,000	$30,000
Less intercompany dividends:			
P Company from S Company	(18,000)		
P Company from R Company	(7,000)		
S Company from R Company		(2,000)	
Income from independent operations	$ 85,000	$48,000	$30,000

A partial workpaper for the preparation of consolidated financial statements on December 31, 1995, is given in Illustration 9-2. Workpaper entries, in general journal form, are presented below for the convenience of the reader.

(1) Investment in S Company	27,000	
1/1 Retained Earnings—P Company		27,000
To establish reciprocity [90% × ($100,000 − $70,000)].		
(2) Investment in R Company	7,000	
1/1 Retained Earnings—P Company		7,000
To establish reciprocity [70% × ($60,000 − $50,000)].		
(3) Dividend Income	27,000	
Dividends Declared—S Company		18,000
Dividends Declared—R Company		9,000
To eliminate intercompany dividends.		
(4) Common Stock—R Company .2($100,000)	20,000	
1/1 Retained Earnings—R Company .2($60,000)	12,000	
Difference Between Cost and Book Value (Land)	3,000	
Investment in R Company		35,000
To eliminate S Company's investment in R Company.		
(5) Common Stock—S Company .9($200,000)	180,000	
1/1 Retained Earnings—S Company .9($100,000)	90,000	
Difference Between Cost and Book Value (Land)	52,000	
Investment in S Company ($295,000 + $27,000)		322,000
To eliminate P Company's investment in S Company.		
(6) Common Stock—R Company .7($100,000)	70,000	
1/1 Retained Earnings—R Company .7($60,000)	42,000	
Difference Between Cost and Book Value (Land)	40,000	
Investment in R Company ($145,000 + $7,000)		152,000
To eliminate P Company's investment in R Company.		

Consolidated net income of $154,600 can be verified as follows:

P Company's income from independent operations	$ 85,000
P Company's share of its subsidiaries' income	
from independent operations:	
S Company (90% × $48,000)	43,200
R Company (88% × $30,000)	26,400
Consolidated net income	$154,600

Cost Method
Partially Owned Subsidiaries
Indirect Ownership

ILLUSTRATION 9-2
P Company and Subsidiaries
Partial Consolidated Statements Workpaper
For the Year Ended December 31, 1995

INCOME STATEMENT	P COMPANY	S COMPANY	R COMPANY	ELIMINATIONS DR.	ELIMINATIONS CR.	NON-CONTROLLING INTEREST	CONSOLIDATED BALANCES
Income before Dividend Income	85,000	48,000	30,000				163,000
Dividend Income	25,000	2,000		(3) 27,000			
Noncontrolling Interest in Income						8,400	(8,400)*
Net Income to Retained Earnings	110,000	50,000	30,000	27,000	–0–	8,400	154,600
RETAINED EARNINGS STATEMENT							
1/1 Retained Earnings P Company	300,000				(1) 27,000 / (2) 7,000		334,000
S Company		100,000		(5) 90,000 / (4) 12,000		10,000	
R Company			60,000	(6) 42,000		6,000	
Net Income from above	110,000	50,000	30,000	27,000	–0–	8,400	154,600
Dividends Declared P Company	(30,000)						(30,000)
S Company		(20,000)			(3) 18,000	(2,000)	
R Company			(10,000)		(3) 9,000	(1,000)	
12/31 Retained Earnings to the Balance Sheet	380,000	130,000	80,000	171,000	61,000	21,400	458,600
BALANCE SHEET							
Investment in S Company	295,000			(1) 27,000	(5) 322,000		
Investment in R Company	145,000			(2) 7,000	(6) 152,000		
Investment in R Company		35,000			(4) 35,000		
Difference between Cost and Book Value (Land)				(4) 3,000 / (5) 52,000 / (6) 40,000			95,000
Common Stock P Company	500,000						500,000
S Company		200,000		(5) 180,000 / (4) 20,000		20,000	
R Company			100,000	(6) 70,000		10,000	
Retained Earnings from above	380,000	130,000	80,000	171,000	61,000	21,400	458,600
Noncontrolling Interest in Net Assets						51,400	51,400
				570,000	570,000		

*(12% × $30,000) + (10% × $48,000).

(1) To establish reciprocity for P Company's investment in S Company.
(2) To establish reciprocity for P Company's investment in R Company.
(3) To eliminate intercompany dividends.
(4) To eliminate S Company's investment in R Company.
(5) To eliminate P Company's investment in S Company.
(6) To eliminate P Company's investment in R Company.

As an alternative, consolidated net income can be verified by adding P Company's share of the undistributed reported income of its subsidiaries to P Company's reported income:

P Company's reported income	$110,000
P Company's share of the undistributed reported	
income of its subsidiaries:	
S Company 90% × [$30,000 + (20% × $20,000)]	30,600
R Company 70% × $20,000	14,000
Consolidated net income	$154,600

Indirect Ownership—Several Levels

In some situations, a chain of ownership may exist in which the "primary" parent company actually has an indirect interest of less than 50% in one or more of the affiliates. Assume, for example, the following affiliation:

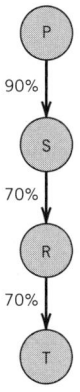

P Company has an indirect interest in T Company of only 44.1% (90% × 70% × 70%). Nonetheless, T Company is properly included in the consolidated group, because P Company effectively controls the operations of T Company through its ability to elect boards of directors of all three subsidiaries. Of course, only 44.1% of T Company's income will be included in consolidated net income. The remainder represents noncontrolling interest.

Partial Equity Method

If the partial equity method is used to record the investments, P Company should record its share of S Company's income *after* S Company has recorded its share of R Company's income. Workpaper elimination entries are then prepared following the procedures illustrated earlier for the partial equity method. To illustrate, assume the same data used in Illustration 9-2. Basic data as it would appear under the partial equity method is given below for the convenience of the reader.

On January 1, 1994, P Company acquired 90% and 70% of the common stock of S Company and R Company for $295,000 and $145,000, respectively. One year later, on January 1, 1995, S Company acquired 20% of the common stock of R Company for $35,000. Investment account balances and stockholders' equity amounts at various dates follow:

	P COMPANY	S COMPANY	R COMPANY
Investment balances, 1/1/95:			
P's Investment in S Company	$322,000		
P's Investment in R Company	152,000		
S's Investment in R Company		$ 35,000	
Stockholders' equity:			
Common stock	$500,000	$200,000	$100,000
Retained earnings, 1/1/94	230,000	70,000	50,000
1994 Reported income	134,000	50,000	20,000
1994 Dividends declared	(30,000)	(20,000)	(10,000)
Retained earnings, 12/31/94	334,000	100,000	60,000
1995 Reported income	154,600	54,000	30,000
1995 Dividends declared	(30,000)	(20,000)	(10,000)
Retained earnings, 12/31/95	458,600	134,000	80,000
Stockholders' equity, 12/31/95	$958,600	$334,000	$180,000

Book entries for 1995 and eliminating entries for a consolidated statements workpaper on December 31, 1995 are:

S Company Books

Cash	2,000	
Investment in R Company		2,000
Dividends received .2($10,000)		
Investment in R Company	6,000	
Equity in Subsidiary Income		6,000
Share of R Company income .2($30,000)		

P Company Books

Cash	7,000	
Investment in R Company		7,000
Dividends received .7($10,000)		
Investment in R Company	21,000	
Equity in Subsidiary Income		21,000
Share of R Company income .7($30,000)		
Cash	18,000	
Investment in S Company		18,000
Dividends received .9($20,000)		
Investment in S Company	48,600	
Equity in Subsidiary Income		48,600
Share of S Company income .9($54,000)		

Workpaper Entries

Equity in Subsidiary Income	6,000	
Dividends Declared—R		2,000
Investment in R Company		4,000
To eliminate intercompany income and dividends for S Company's investment in R Company.		
Equity in Subsidiary Income	21,000	
Dividends Declared—R Company		7,000
Investment in R Company		14,000
To eliminate intercompany income and dividends for P Company's investment in R Company.		
Equity in Subsidiary Income	48,600	
Dividends Declared—S Company		18,000
Investment in S Company		30,600
To eliminate intercompany income and dividends for P Company's investment in S Company.		
Common Stock—R Company .2($100,000)	20,000	
1/1 Retained Earnings—R Company .2($60,000)	12,000	
Land	3,000	
Investment in R Company		35,000
To eliminate S Company's investment in R Company.		
Common Stock—S Company .9($200,000)	180,000	
1/1 Retained Earnings—S Company .9($100,000)	90,000	
Land	52,000	
Investment in S Company		322,000
To eliminate P Company's investment in S Company.		
Common Stock—R Company .7($100,000)	70,000	
1/1 Retained Earnings—R Company .7($60,000)	42,000	
Land	40,000	
Investment in R Company		152,000
To eliminate P Company's investment in R Company.		

RECIPROCAL STOCKHOLDINGS

Indirect ownership situations are relatively common; reciprocal stockholdings are not. Occasionally a subsidiary owns a small equity interest in its parent company, or subsidiaries of the same parent own equity interests in one another. Where these reciprocal stockholdings exist, the reciprocal effect is often immaterial. The infrequency of occurrence of reciprocal stockholdings, and the often relatively immaterial effect where they do exist suggests that this topic may not require as much attention as others. Nevertheless, some familiarity with the problems created may be useful.

Two general approaches are used to treat the effect of reciprocal stockholdings—a mathematical approach and a treasury stock approach. The mathematical approach gives explicit recognition to the effect of the reciprocal stockholding, whereas the treasury stock approach simply treats the reciprocal stockholding as treasury stock on the consolidated balance sheet. Surveys of practice show that this treasury stock approach is the approach most often used in practice.[1] Because the

[1]Accountants International Study Group, *Consolidated Financial Statements*, 1973, par. 67.

treasury stock approach is generally used in practice, it is discussed and illustrated in the following section. The mathematical approach is presented in the appendix for those who may be interested in its application.

Treasury Stock Approach

Subsidiary stockholdings in the parent company are generally treated the same as treasury stock, because the parent company is considered to have reacquired some of its own shares by using subsidiary resources. Under this approach, the reciprocal relationship is ignored, and the cost of the subsidiary's investment in the stock of the parent company is deducted from total stockholders' equity on the consolidated balance sheet. Dividends distributed to the subsidiary by the parent company are recognized by the subsidiary as dividend income.[2]

To illustrate, assume that P Company acquired 90% of the common stock of S Company on January 1, 1995. On the same date, S Company acquired 10% of the common stock of P Company. P Company records its investment in S Company using the cost method. An affiliation diagram, along with relevant investment cost, stockholders' equity, income, and dividend data follows:

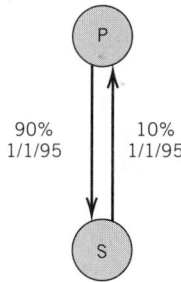

	P COMPANY	S COMPANY
Cost of investment in S Company	$240,000	
Cost of investment in P Company		$ 70,000
Common stock	$500,000	$200,000
Retained earnings, 1/1/95	150,000	50,000
1995 Reported income	105,000	60,000
1995 Dividends declared	(20,000)	(10,000)
Retained earnings, 12/31/95	235,000	100,000
1996 Reported income	140,000	60,000
1996 Dividends declared	(30,000)	(10,000)
Retained earnings, 12/31/96	$345,000	$150,000

[2]If the subsidiary owned 20% or more of the common stock of the parent company, its investment in the parent would have to be adjusted to the equity method when reporting to parties outside the affiliated group. In the event the subsidiary elected to use the equity method on its books to account for its investment in the stock of its parent, a workpaper entry to return the investment account to its cost would be required so that the investment account could be deducted at its cost from stockholders' equity on the consolidated balance sheet.

Because S Company's investment in P Company is treated as treasury stock, any difference between cost and book value acquired on the investment is irrelevant in the preparation of consolidated financial statements. However, there is a $15,000 difference between cost and book value [$240,000 − .9($200,000 + $50,000)] relating to P Company's investment in S Company; we assume it relates to subsidiary land.

A *partial* consolidated statement workpaper is presented in Illustration 9-3. Several items should be specifically noted:

1. Because the cost of S Company's investment in P Company is treated as treasury stock, there is no reciprocity entry for this investment.

2. In the computation of the amount needed to establish reciprocity for P Company's investment in S Company, the reciprocal nature of S Company's investment in P Company is ignored. Thus, the reciprocity amount is [90% × ($100,000 − $50,000)].

3. S Company's investment in P Company is not eliminated, but is extended to the consolidated balances column and identified as treasury stock. It will be deducted on the consolidated balance sheet just as though it were held by P Company, as shown in Illustration 9-4.

4. Noncontrolling interest in combined income is based on the noncontrolling stockholders' share of the *reported* income of S Company. That is, the noncontrolling stockholders' share of combined income includes their share of dividend income received from P Company. If the noncontrolling stockholders' share of this dividend income were excluded, total noncontrolling interest on the consolidated balance sheet would be less than the noncontrolling stockholders' share of the reported net assets of S Company. The authors believe that the noncontrolling interest on the consolidated balance sheet should reflect the noncontrolling stockholders' full share of the net assets of S Company that are included in the consolidated balance sheet, .1($200,000 + $150,000), since the reciprocal relationship is ignored.

5. Only $27,000 of P Company dividends declared are deducted from consolidated retained earnings, since that is the amount that was distributed to outside stockholders. The other $3,000 is eliminated because it represents an interaffiliate dividend distribution.

The consolidated balance sheet, in condensed form, that results from the data in Illustration 9-3 is presented in Illustration 9-4. (The "liabilities" amount is an assumed amount.)

Cost Method
Reciprocal Stockholdings
Treasury Stock Method

ILLUSTRATION 9-3
P Company and Subsidiary
Partial Consolidated Statements Workpaper
For the Year Ended December 31, 1996

INCOME STATEMENT	P COMPANY	S COMPANY	ELIMINATIONS DR.	ELIMINATIONS CR.	NON-CONTROLLING INTEREST	CONSOLIDATED BALANCES
Income before Dividend Income	131,000	57,000				188,000
Dividend Income	9,000	3,000	(2) 12,000			
Noncontrolling Interest in Income .1($60,000)					6,000	(6,000)
Net Income to Retained Earnings	140,000	60,000	12,000	–0–	6,000	182,000
RETAINED EARNINGS STATEMENT						
1/1 Retained Earnings						
P Company	235,000			(1) 45,000		280,000
S Company		100,000	(3) 90,000		10,000	
Net Income from above	140,000	60,000	12,000	–0–	6,000	182,000
Dividends Declared						
P Company	(30,000)			(2) 3,000		(27,000)
S Company		(10,000)		(2) 9,000	(1,000)	
12/31 Retained Earnings to the Balance Sheet	345,000	150,000	102,000	57,000	15,000	435,000
BALANCE SHEET						
Investment in S Company	240,000		(1) 45,000	(3) 285,000		
Investment in P Company		70,000				70,000 T/S
Difference between Cost and Book Value (Land)			(3) 15,000			15,000
Common Stock						
P Company	500,000					500,000
S Company		200,000	(3) 180,000		20,000	
Retained Earnings from above	345,000	150,000	102,000	57,000	15,000	435,000
Noncontrolling Interest in Net Assets					35,000	35,000
			342,000	342,000		

(1) To establish reciprocity—P Company's investment in S Company .9($100,000 − $50,000).
(2) To eliminate intercompany dividends.
(3) To eliminate P Company's investment in S Company.

ILLUSTRATION 9-4
P Company and Subsidiary
Consolidated Balance Sheet
For the Year Ended December 31, 1996

Assets		$1,467,000
Liabilities		$ 567,000
Noncontrolling Interest		35,000
Stockholders' Equity		
Common Stock	$500,000	
Retained Earnings	435,000	
Less P Company shares held by subsidiary (at cost)	(70,000)	865,000
Total Liabilities and Stockholders' Equity		$1,467,000

December 31, 1996, workpaper entries to eliminate intercompany equity in subsidiary income and dividend income are:

Equity in Subsidiary Income	51,300	
Dividends Declared—S Company		9,000
Investment in S Company		42,300
Dividend Income	3,000	
Dividends Declared—P Company		3,000

After these workpaper entries are prepared, the remainder of the workpaper is completed as illustrated for the cost method (Illustration 9-3).

Partial Equity Method

Under the partial equity method, P Company recognizes its share of S Company's income, but *ignoring the reciprocal relationship.* Thus, during 1996, P Company will recognize $51,300 [.9 × ($60,000 − $3,000 dividend income from P Company)] of subsidiary income and reduce the Investment in S Company for the $9,000 dividends received, through the following book entries:

Investment in S Company	51,300	
Equity in Subsidiary Income		51,300
Cash	9,000	
Investment in S Company		9,000

APPENDIX: MATHEMATICAL APPROACH TO RECIPROCAL STOCKHOLDINGS

When reciprocal stockholdings exist and the mathematical approach is used, the allocation of the total income of the affiliates between consolidated income and the noncontrolling interest must consider the interdependency of the relationship. In the situation that follows (the same as that presented earlier under the treasury stock approach), consolidated net income consists of P Company's income from its independent operations plus P Company's share of S Company's reciprocally determined income. Conversely, the noncontrolling stockholders share of the total affiliated income is based on S Company's reciprocally determined income. The mathematical approach uses simultaneous equations to determine the allocation of total affiliated income.

To illustrate, assume that P Company acquired 90% of the common stock of S Company on January 1, 1995. On the same date, S Company acquired 10% of the common stock of P Company. P Company records its investment in S Company using the cost method. Investment cost, stockholders' equity, income, and dividend data are the same as those in the previous example. The difference between cost and book value on P Company's investment in S Company is $15,000, the same as in the previous example. Since the cost of S Company's investment in P Company was treated as consolidated treasury stock under the treasury stock approach, there was no reported difference between cost and book value on that investment. Under the mathematical approach, however, S Company's investment in P Company is treated as an intercompany investment that must be eliminated on the consolidated statements workpaper. When the investment is eliminated, a $5,000 difference between cost and book value will be reported, computed as follows:

Investment cost	$70,000
Book value of P Company's equity acquired:	
.1($500,000 capital stock + $150,000 retained earnings)	65,000
Difference between cost and book value	$ 5,000

Consolidated net income and noncontrolling interest in combined income must be determined giving effect to the reciprocal nature of the investments. The computation begins with the income from independent operations of P Company and S Company, which for 1995 are:

	P COMPANY	S COMPANY
Reported income	$105,000	$60,000
Less intercompany dividend income	9,000	2,000
Income from independent operations	$ 96,000	$58,000

Thus, the 1995 reciprocally based incomes of P Company and S Company, and the noncontrolling interest in combined income can be determined as follows:

Let P = P Company's reciprocally based income
S = S Company's reciprocally based income

The algebraic formulation and solution become:

$$
\begin{aligned}
P &= \$\ 96{,}000 + .9S \\
S &= \ \ \ \ 58{,}000 + .1P \\
P &= \ \ \ \ 96{,}000 + .9(58{,}000 + .1P) \\
P &= \ \ \ \ 96{,}000 + 52{,}200 + .09P \\
.91P &= \ \ \ 148{,}200 \\
P &= \ \ \ 162{,}857 \\
S &= \ \ \ \ 58{,}000 + .1(162{,}857) \\
S &= \ \ \ \ 58{,}000 + 16{,}286 \\
S &= \ \ \ \ 74{,}286
\end{aligned}
$$

Thus, P Company's reciprocal income is $162,857, S Company's reciprocal income is $74,286, and noncontrolling interest in combined income is $7,429 (10% × $74,286). Consolidated net income is 90% of P Company's reciprocal income of $162,857, or $146,571. The remaining 10% of P Company's reciprocal income represents intercompany income on shares held by S Company. The combined income is, therefore, $154,000 ($146,571 + $7,429), which is equal to the actual income of both companies from their independent operations ($96,000 + $58,000). A partial consolidated statements workpaper for this situation is presented in Illustration 9-5. Workpaper entries are presented also in general journal form for the convenience of the reader:

Cost Method
Reciprocal Stockholdings
Mathematical Approach

ILLUSTRATION 9-5
P Company and Subsidiary
Partial Consolidated Statements Workpaper
For the Year Ended December 31, 1995

	P COMPANY	S COMPANY	ELIMINATIONS DR.	ELIMINATIONS CR.	NON-CONTROLLING INTEREST	CONSOLIDATED BALANCES
INCOME STATEMENT						
Income before Dividend Income	96,000	58,000				154,000
Dividend Income	9,000	2,000	(1) 11,000			
Noncontrolling Interest in Income					7,429	(7,429)
Net Income to Retained Earnings	105,000	60,000	11,000	–0–	7,429	146,571
RETAINED EARNINGS STATEMENT						
1/1 Retained Earnings						
P Company	150,000		(3) 15,000			135,000
S Company		50,000	(2) 45,000		5,000	
Net Income from above	105,000	60,000	11,000	–0–	7,429	146,571
Dividends Declared						
P Company	(20,000)			(1) 2,000		(18,000)
S Company		(10,000)		(1) 9,000	(1,000)	
12/31 Retained Earnings to the Balance Sheet	235,000	100,000	71,000	11,000	11,429	263,571
BALANCE SHEET						
Investment in S Company	240,000			(2) 240,000		
Investment in P Company		70,000		(3) 70,000		
Difference between Cost and Book Value (Land)			{(2) 15,000 {(3) 5,000			20,000
Common Stock						
P Company	500,000		(3) 50,000			450,000
S Company		200,000	(2) 180,000		20,000	
Retained Earnings from above	235,000	100,000	71,000	11,000	11,429	263,571
Noncontrolling Interest in Net Assets					31,429	31,429
			321,000	321,000		

(1) To eliminate intercompany dividends.
(2) To eliminate P Company's investment in S Company.
(3) To eliminate S Company's investment in P Company.

(1) Dividend Income	11,000	
Dividends Declared—P Company		2,000
Dividends Declared—S Company		9,000
To eliminate intercompany dividends.		
(2) Common Stock—S Company	180,000	
1/1 Retained Earnings—S Company	45,000	
Difference Between Cost and Book Value (Land)	15,000	
Investment in S Company		240,000
To eliminate P Company's investment in S Company.		
(3) Common Stock—P Company	50,000	
1/1 Retained Earnings—P Company	15,000	
Difference Between Cost and Book Value (Land)	5,000	
Investment in P Company		70,000
To eliminate S Company's investment in P Company.		

The previous example treated the preparation of a consolidated statements workpaper at the end of the year of acquisition. In subsequent periods, an additional computation must be made, on a reciprocal basis, to determine the amount needed to establish reciprocity for each of the investments. For example, the computation of the amounts needed to establish reciprocity for a workpaper at the end of 1996 would be:

Let P = Increase in P Company's retained earnings since date of acquisition of
P Company stock by S Company ($235,000 − $150,000 = $85,000)
Let S = Increase in S Company's retained earnings since date of acquisition of
S Company stock by P Company ($100,000 − $50,000 = $50,000)

Then:

$$
\begin{aligned}
P &= \$\ 85,000 + .9S \\
S &= \ \ \ 50,000 + .1P \\
S &= \ \ \ 50,000 + .1(85,000 + .9S) \\
S &= \ \ \ 50,000 + 8,500 + .09S \\
.91S &= \ \ \ 58,500 \\
S &= \ \ \ 64,286 \\
P &= \ \ \ 85,000 + .9(64,286) \\
P &= \ \ \ 85,000 + 57,857 \\
P &= \ \ \ 142,857
\end{aligned}
$$

Based on these computations, the workpaper entries to establish reciprocity in the preparation of a consolidated statements workpaper on December 31, 1996, are:

Investment in P Company	14,286	
1/1 Retained Earnings—S Company		14,286
To establish reciprocity for S Company's investment in P Company (10% × $142,857).		
Investment in S Company	57,857	
1/1 Retained Earnings—P Company		57,857
To establish reciprocity for P Company's investment in S Company (90% × $64,286).		

In all other respects, the workpaper at December 31, 1996, is completed as in previous illustrations.

Questions

1. Distinguish among direct, indirect, and reciprocal stockholder interests.

2. What is meant by "up-the-ladder" eliminations?

3. X Company owns 70% of Y Company, and Y Company owns 60% of Z Company. Are consolidated financial statements for X, Y, and Z companies appropriate? Justify your answer.

4. A Company owns 90% of B Company, 80% of C Company, and 70% of E Company. B Company owns 75% of D Company, which, in turn, owns 60% of F Company. C Company owns 15% of E Company. E Company owns 5% of F Company. What percent of each company's income should be included in consoldiated net income?

5. Describe two approaches to the treatment of reciprocal stockholdings in the preparation of consolidated financial statements.

6. How does the determination of noncontrolling interests differ in the two approaches to the treatment of reciprocal stockholdings?

Exercises

Exercise 9-1

Alto Company purchased 80% of the outstanding common stock of Bat Company on January 1, 1995, and Bat Company purchased a 90% interest in the capital stock of Curt Company on January 1, 1996. Income from the independent operations of the three companies and dividends declared during 1995 and 1996 were:

	ALTO	BAT	CURT
INCOME FROM INDEPENDENT OPERATIONS			
1995	$300,000	$150,000	$105,000
1996	350,000	180,000	126,000
DIVIDENDS DECLARED			
1995	50,000	40,000	36,000
1996	90,000	45,000	46,000

Required

A. Prepare entries on the books of Alto and Bat Companies during 1995 and 1996 to recognize the effect of dividends declared by affiliates. Investments are accounted for by the cost method.

B. Prepare a schedule to compute the amount of consolidated net income for 1996.

Exercise 9-2

On January 1, 1994, Prill Company purchased 90% of the outstanding common stock of Speer Company and 30% of the outstanding common stock of Rack Company. One year later, on January 1, 1995, Speer Company purchased 60% of the oustanding common stock of Rack Company. Income from independent operations and dividends declared during 1995 were:

	PRILL	SPEER	RACK
Income from Independent Operations	$150,000	$60,000	$40,000
Dividends Declared	60,000	20,000	15,000

Required:

A. Prepare an affiliation diagram.

B. Prepare entries on the books of Prill and Speer to recognize the effects of dividends declared by affiliates during 1995, assuming use of the cost method to record investments.

C. Prepare a schedule to compute the amount of consolidated net income for 1995.

Exercise 9-3

On January 1, 1995, Bill Company purchased 90% of the capital stock of Chris Company. On January 1, 1995, Allen Company purchased 80% of the capital stock of Bill Company. On January 1, 1996, Allen Company purchased 10% of the capital stock of Chris Company. The following data are relevant to the affiliates:

	ALLEN	BILL	CHRIS
Retained earnings, 1/1/94	$300,000	$180,000	$120,000
Income from independent operations:			
1994	190,000	70,000	70,000
1995	200,000	80,000	50,000
1996	230,000	90,000	80,000
Dividends declared:			
1994	60,000	30,000	25,000
1995	80,000	50,000	30,000
1996	85,000	40,000	30,000

Required:

A. Calculate consolidated retained earnings on December 31, 1995.

B. Calculate consolidated retained earnings on December 31, 1996.

C. Calculate noncontrolling interest in combined income for 1995 and 1996.

Exercise 9-4

A Company owns 80% of B Company, 70% of C Company, 90% of D Company, and 50% of E Company. In addition, D Company owns 20% of C Company, and B Company owns 90% of F Company. During 1996 the companies had the following incomes from their independent operations:

A Company	$140,000
B Company	90,000
C Company	100,000
D Company	60,000
E Company	70,000
F Company	40,000
Total	$500,000

Required:

A. Draw an affiliation diagram.

B. Calculate consolidated net income for 1996.

C. Calculate noncontrolling interest in combined income for 1996.

Exercise 9-5

The following investments were all made on January 1, 1996:

ACQUIRING COMPANY	ACQUIRED COMPANY	% INTEREST ACQUIRED	COST
P	S	90%	$306,000
S	T	80%	154,880
T	U	70%	80,000

Stockholders' equity, earnings, and dividend data for the affiliated companies at the end of 1996 were:

	P	S	T	U
Capital stock	$250,000	$200,000	$100,000	$50,000
Retained earnings, 1/1	174,250	108,000	93,600	53,250
Reported net income	120,404	83,560	54,250	30,250
Dividends declared	20,000	15,000	10,000	10,000
Retained earnings, 12/31	274,654	176,560	137,850	73,500

Investments are recorded using the cost method.

Required:

Prepare the workpaper eliminating entries for the preparation of a consolidated statements workpaper on December 31, 1996. Assume that any difference between cost and book value pertains to subsidiary land.

Exercise 9-6A

P Company owns 80% of S Company, and S Company owns 10% of P Company. During 1996, the companies earned net income from their independent operations of:

P Company	$300,000
S Company	100,000

Required:

Using the mathematical approach of treating reciprocal stockholdings:

A. Compute consolidated net income.

B. Compute noncontrolling interest in combined income.

Exercise 9-7A

A Company owns 80% of B Company and 90% of G Company. B Company owns 20% of A Company. G Company owns 10% of B Company. The companies earned the following amounts from their independent operations during the current year:

A Company	$400,000
B Company	270,000
G Company	140,000
Total	$810,000

Required:

Using the mathematical approach of treating reciprocal stockholdings:

A. Compute the noncontrolling interest in the net income of B Company and G Company.

B. Compute consolidated net income.

C. Prepare a schedule to reconcile the amounts above with the total combined income of the three companies.

Problems

Problem 9-1

Adel Company made an open-market purchase of 85% of the common stock of Bell Company on January 1, 1995, at a cost of $188,000. On that date, Bell Company had common stock of $180,000 and retained earnings of $50,000. On January 1, 1996, Bell Company made an open-market purchase of 90% of the common stock of Camp Company for $96,000. Camp Company's equity on January 1, 1996, consisted of common stock of $80,000 and retained earnings of $25,000. Stockholders' equity accounts for the three companies on December 31, 1996, were:

	ADEL COMPANY	BELL COMPANY	CAMP COMPANY
Common stock	$400,000	$180,000	$80,000
Retained earnings, 1/1	240,000	90,000	25,000
Net income before			
dividend income	90,000	40,000	27,000
Dividends declared	38,000	17,500	9,000

Any difference between cost and book value of equity acquired represents an over (under)-valuation of land. Investments are recorded using the cost method.

Required:

A. Prepare journal entries on the books of Adel Company and Bell Company to recognize subsidiary dividends for 1996.

B. Prepare eliminating entries in general journal form for the preparation of a consolidated statements workpaper on December 31, 1996.

C. Compute:
  (1) Noncontrolling interest in combined income.
  (2) Consolidated net income for 1996.

Problem 9-2

Blue Company purchased an 80% interest in Green Company on the open market for $128,750 on January 1, 1995. On that date, Green Company had capital stock of $100,000 and retained earnings of $50,000. One year later, on January 1, 1996, Dean Company purchased a 90% interest in Blue Company on the open market for $310,000. Relevant account balances for the three companies on December 31, 1996, were:

	DEAN	BLUE	GREEN
Capital stock	$350,000	$200,000	$100,000
Retained earnings, 1/1	240,000	140,000	70,000
Net income from independent operations	74,000	36,000	25,000
Dividends declared	30,000	15,000	10,000

Any difference between cost and book value acquired is assignable to subsidiary land.

Required:

A. Prepare a schedule to compute the difference between cost and book value acquired for each investment.

B. Prepare in general journal form the eliminating entries necessary for the preparation of a consolidated statements workpaper on December 31, 1996.

C. Compute:
  (1) Noncontrolling interest in combined income for 1996.
  (2) Consolidated net income for 1996.
  (3) Consolidated retained earnings at December 31, 1996.

Problem 9-3

On January 1, 1994, A Company purchased an 80% interest in the common stock of B Company for $400,000 and a 70% interest in the common stock of C Company for $175,000. One year later, on January 1, 1995, B Company purchased a 15% interest in the common stock of C Company for $49,500. Stockholders' equity for the three companies on January 1, 1994, was:

	A	B	C
Common stock	$ 800,000	$400,000	$200,000
Retained earnings	320,000	80,000	40,000
Total	$1,120,000	$480,000	$240,000

Each company had income from independent operations of $60,000 for each of 1994 and 1995. No dividends were declared by any of the companies. Any difference between cost and book value pertains to subsidiary land. Investments are recorded using the cost method.

Required:

Prepare a partial workpaper for the preparation of consolidated financial statements for A, B, and C Companies on December 31, 1995. Start your workpaper with "Income from Independent Operations" in the Income Statement section.

Problem 9-4

Phung Company purchased 70% of the outstanding common stock of Soto Company on January 2, 1996. On that date Sato Company held a 10% interest in common stock of Phung Company. Summary account data for Phung Company and Soto Company on December 31, 1996 are as follows:

DEBITS	PHUNG	SOTO
Assets	$282,000	$121,250
Investment in Soto Company	68,000	
Investment in Phung Company		12,500
Cost of goods sold and expenses	220,000	95,000
Dividends declared	25,000	15,000
Total	$595,000	$243,750

CREDITS		
Liabilities	$ 43,000	$ 31,250
Common stock, $10 par value	100,000	25,000
Retained earnings	140,000	60,000
Sales	301,500	125,000
Dividend income	10,500	2,500
Total	$595,000	$243,750

Required:

Prepare a consolidated statements workpaper on December 31, 1996, using the treasury stock approach for the reciprocal investment in Phung Company. Any difference between cost and book value relates to land.

Problem 9-5

B Company purchased an 80% interest in C Company on the open market for $125,000 on January 1, 1995. On that date, C Company had capital stock of $100,000 and retained earnings of $42,500. One year later, on January 1, 1996, A Company purchased a 90% interest in B Company on the open market for $330,000. Relevant account balances for the three companies on December 31, 1996, were:

	A	B	C
Capital stock	$350,000	$200,000	$100,000
Retained earnings, 1/1	240,000	130,000	55,000
Net income reported for 1996	87,500	43,000	25,000
Dividends declared during 1996	30,000	15,000	10,000

The difference between cost and book value is assignable to land. Investments are recorded using the cost method.

Required:

A. Prepare a schedule to compute the difference between cost and book value for each investment.

B. Prepare in general journal form reciprocity and elimination entries for the preparation of a consolidated statements workpaper on December 31, 1996.

C. Compute:
  (1) Noncontrolling interest in combined income for 1996.
  (2) Consolidated net income for 1996.
  (3) Consolidated retained earnings at December 31, 1996.

Problem 9-6

The following investments were all made on January 1, 1996:

ACQUIRING COMPANY	ACQUIRED COMPANY	% INTEREST ACQUIRED	COST
Allen	Barry	85%	$310,000
Barry	Candy	80%	148,000
Candy	Dandy	70%	68,000

Stockholders' equity, earnings, and dividend data for the affiliated companies at the end of 1996 were:

	ALLEN	BARRY	CANDY	DANDY
Capital stock	$250,000	$200,000	$100,000	$50,000
Retained earnings, 1/1	174,250	108,000	93,600	53,250
1996 Net income reported	58,700	48,160	42,100	30,250
1996 Dividends declared	20,000	15,000	10,000	10,000
Retained earnings, 12/31	212,950	141,160	125,700	73,500

Investments are recorded using the cost method.

Required:

A. Compute consolidated net income for 1996.

B. Compute consolidated retained earnings at December 31, 1996.

C. Compute noncontrolling interest in combined income for 1996.

Problem 9-7

Condensed balance sheets for A Company, B Company, and C Company on December 31, 1995, are as follows:

	A COMPANY	B COMPANY	C COMPANY
Curent assets	$ 693,600	$ 440,200	$ 420,600
Investment in B Company	1,135,000		
Investment in C Company	75,000	590,000	
Other assets	1,441,400	680,200	785,000
Total assets	$3,345,000	$1,710,400	$1,205,600
Liabilities	$ 988,800	$ 494,400	$ 413,800
Capital stock	1,200,000	600,000	400,000
Other contributed capital	381,200	174,800	205,000
Retained earnings	775,000	441,200	186,800
Total equities	$3,345,00	$1,710,400	$1,205,600

B Company purchased an 80% interest in C Company for $590,000 on January 1, 1991, when C Company had stockholders' equity consisting of Capital Stock, $400,000; Other Contributed Capital, $205,000; and Retained Earnings, $82,400.

On January 1, 1995, A Company purchased an 85% interest in B Company for $1,135,000 and a 10% interest in C Company for $75,000. Stockholders' equity for B and C Companies on January 1, 1995 was:

	B COMPANY	C COMPANY
Capital stock	$ 600,000	$400,000
Other contributed capital	174,800	205,000
Retained earnings	480,000	124,600
Total	$1,254,800	$729,600

Required:

Prepare a workpaper for a consolidated balance sheet on December 31, 1995. Include a schedule to verify the difference between cost and book value, which is assignable to land (included in Other assets).

Problem 9-8

Pagone Company acquired 90% of the outstanding stock of Suter Company on January 2, 1995. On that date, Suter Company held a 15% interest in Pagone Company. Summary account data for Pagone Company and Suter Company on December 31, 1995, were:

DEBITS	PAGONE	SUTER
Assets	$284,750	$116,250
Investment in Suter Company	72,250	
Investment in Pagone Company		15,000
Cost of sales and expenses	220,000	95,000
Dividends declared	25,000	15,000
Total	$602,000	$241,250

CREDITS

Liabilities	$ 49,250	$ 27,500
Capital stock, $10 par value	100,000	25,000
Retained earnings	140,000	60,000
Sales	299,250	125,000
Dividend income	13,500	3,750
Total	$602,000	$241,250

Required:

Prepare a consolidated statements workpaper on December 31, 1995, using the treasury stock approach for the reciprocal investment in Pagone Company.

Problem 9-9

On January 1, 1994, B Company purchased 90% of the capital stock of C Company. On January 1, 1995, A Company purchased 80% of the capital stock of B Company. On January 1, 1996, A Company purchased 10% of the capital stock of C Company. The following data relate to the affiliated companies:

	A	B	C
Capital stock	$200,000	$125,000	$50,000
Retained earnings, 1/1/94	60,000	40,000	25,000
Reported net income			
1994	35,000	20,000	15,000
1995	45,000	25,000	10,000
1996	50,000	25,000	15,000
Dividends declared and paid			
1994	15,000	5,000	5,000
1995	20,000	10,000	5,000
1996	20,000	10,000	5,000

Investments are recorded using the cost method.

Required:

A. Calculate consolidated retained earings on January 1, 1996.

B. Calculate consolidated retained earnings on January 1, 1997.

C. Calculate consolidated net income for 1996.

Problem 9-10 (This is the same problem as Problem 9-1, but assuming use of the partial equity method.)

Adel Company made an open-market purchase of 85% of the common stock of Bell Company on January 1, 1995, at a cost of $188,000. On that date, Bell Company had common stock of $180,000 and retained earnings of $50,000. On January 1, 1996, Bell Company made an open-market purchase of 90% of the common stock of Camp Company for $96,000. Camp Company's equity on January 1, 1996, consisted of common stock of $80,000 and retained earnings of $25,000. Stockholders' equity accounts for the three companies on December 31, 1996, were:

	ADEL COMPANY	BELL COMPANY	CAMP COMPANY
Common stock	$400,000	$180,000	$80,000
Retained earnings, 1/1	240,000	90,000	25,000
Net income from			
independent operations	90,000	40,000	27,000
Dividends declared	38,000	17,500	9,000

Any difference between cost and book value of equity acquired represents an over (under)-valuation of land.

Required:

A. Prepare journal entries on the books of Bell Company and Adel Company to recognize subsidiary income and dividends received for 1996.

B. Prepare eliminating entries in general journal form for the preparation of a consolidated statements workpaper on December 31, 1996.

C. Compute:
   (1) Noncontrolling interest in combined income for 1996.
   (2) Consolidated net income for 1996.

Problem 9-11

(This is the same problem as Problem 9-4, but assuming use of the partial equity method.) Phung Company purchased 70% of the outstanding common stock of Soto Company on January 2, 1996. On that date Soto Company held a 10% interest in common stock of Phung Company. Summary account data for Phung Company and Soto Company on December 31, 1996, follows:

DEBITS	PHUNG	SOTO
Assets	$282,000	$121,250
Investment in Soto Company	78,500	
Investment in Phung Company		12,500
Cost of goods sold and expenses	220,000	95,000
Dividends declared	25,000	15,000
Total	$605,500	$243,750

CREDITS		
Liabilities	$ 43,000	$ 31,250
Common stock, $10 par value	100,000	25,000
Retained earnings	140,000	60,000
Sales	301,500	125,000
Dividend income		2,500
Equity in subsidiary income	21,000	
Total	$605,500	$243,750

Required:

Prepare a consolidated statements workpaper on December 31, 1996, using the treasury stock approach for the reciprocal investment in Phung Company.

Problem 9-12A

On January 1, 1993, the date of incorporation of S Company, P Company purchased 32,000 shares of S Company capital stock at par value of $320,000. On January 1, 1994, S Company purchased 10,000 shares of P Company capital stock on the open market at $22 per share.

The capital stock of each company is $400,000, consisting of 40,000 shares with a par value of $10 per share. Retained earnings balances on January 1, 1993, and earnings and dividends declared for each company for 1993, 1994, and 1995 were:

	PAR COMPANY	SUB COMPANY
Retained earnings, 1/1/93	$160,000	$ –0–
Net income, 1993	60,000	40,000
Dividends declared, 1993	(20,000)	(20,000)
Net income, 1994	80,000	20,000
Net income, 1995	100,000	40,000
Retained earnings, 12/31/95	$380,000	$80,000

Required:

Assuming the use of the mathematical approach of treating reciprocal stockholdings, prepare workpaper entries to establish reciprocity and eliminate the investment accounts for the preparation of consolidated financial statements on December 31, 1995.

10

CONSOLIDATED FINANCIAL STATEMENTS—MISCELLANEOUS TOPICS

In this chapter, we discuss several areas related to the preparation of consolidated financial statements, including:

1. Intercompany bond holdings.
2. Intercompany notes receivable discounted.
3. Stock dividends issued by a subsidiary company.
4. Cash dividends from preacquisition earnings.
5. Preferred stock of a subsidiary.

Illustrations in this chapter are based on the assumption that investments are recorded using the cost method. Reporting complications relating to accounting for the difference between the cost of a common stock investment and the book value interest acquired are avoided by assuming that all acquisitions of common stock are made at the book value of the acquired interest in net assets, and that the book values of the subsidiary's assets and liabilities are equal to their fair values on the date of acquisition. Also, deferred tax consequences are avoided by assuming the affiliates file consolidated tax returns.

INTERCOMPANY BOND HOLDINGS

An affiliate company may purchase bonds issued by another affiliate directly from the issuing company or from outsiders after the original issue. In either case, because the bonds are held within the affiliated group, the intercompany bond investment (a receivable) and the bonds payable (a liability), along with any related intercompany interest expense and interest income, must be eliminated. In other words, because the bonds are not held by external parties, they are viewed as being *constructively retired* in the consolidated financial statements. Constructively retired means that the bonds are considered retired from a consolidated entity point of view, but legally the bonds are still outstanding as far as the issuing company is concerned. Since this is viewed as an early retirement of debt, a gain or loss on the constructive retirement is computed and allocated to the affiliated companies. A brief review of accounting for bond transactions is presented in the next section before the preparation of a consolidated statements workpaper involving intercompany bond holdings is illustrated.

ACCOUNTING FOR BONDS—A REVIEW

To review accounting for bonds, assume that a company issued $100,000 par value bonds on January 2, 1995, for $90,000. The bonds mature 10 years later and pay 12% interest each December 31. The bonds were all acquired by one investor, and the fiscal year-end of both entities is December 31. The journal entries for the first year of operations, assuming straight-line amortization of the discount, are:[1]

ISSUING COMPANY

1995				
Jan. 2	Cash		90,000	
	Discount on Bonds Payable		10,000	
	Bonds Payable			100,000
Dec. 31	Interest Expense		12,000	
	Cash			12,000
31	Interest Expense		1,000	
	Discount on Bonds Payable			1,000

INVESTOR COMPANY

1995				
Jan. 2	Investment in Bonds		90,000	
	Cash			90,000
Dec. 31	Cash		12,000	
	Interest Income			12,000
31	Investment in Bonds		1,000	
	Interest Income			1,000

From the point of view of the issuing company, $90,000 was received, but the company must pay $100,000 to the bondholders when the bonds mature 10 years later.

---

[1]For simplicity, it is assumed in this chapter that straight-line amortization policies are adopted by the reporting entities. However, the reader is reminded that the interest rate method is required unless the straight-line amortization method does not result in a material difference. *Opinions of the Accounting Principles Board No. 21,* "Interest on Receivables and Payables" (New York: AICPA; 1971), par. 15.

Instead of deferring the $10,000 discount to be reported as a reduction in income in the year that the bonds mature, one-tenth of the discount ($1,000) is amortized each year as an increase in interest expense. The increase in expense results in a reduction of $1,000 in net income each year, which also reduces the retained earnings balance. At the end of 10 years, the issuing company's retained earnings is reduced $120,000 for the cash interest paid and $10,000 for the discount amortization. In effect, the $10,000 discount is recognized as additional interest expense over the life of the bonds. From the investor's point of view, $90,000 is paid for the bonds, but if the bonds are held to maturity, $100,000 will be received. One-tenth of this $10,000 is added to interest income each period, which results in an increase in reported income. As a result of acquiring the bond investment at a discount, retained earnings is increased $1,000 each year for a cumulative total of $10,000 over the life of the bonds.

If, in the foregoing example, the bonds had been issued for $110,000, the issuing company receives $10,000 more on the date of issue than must be paid when the bonds mature, while the investor will receive $10,000 less than the purchase price when the bonds mature. The investor (issuing) company, rather than re-porting a reduction (increase) in income when the bonds mature, records one-tenth of the reduction (increase) each year as the premium on the bonds is am-ortized to interest income (expense) over the remaining life of the bonds. The effect is that the net income of the investor (issuing) company is $1,000 less (greater) each year as a result of amortizing the premium. The effect on income is, of course, also reflected in the reported retained earnings balance.

CONSTRUCTIVE GAIN OR LOSS ON INTERCOMPANY BOND HOLDINGS

The purchase of an affiliate's bonds does not alter the accounting in the books of the individual companies. As noted in the preceding section, the issuing company and the purchasing company recognize a gain or loss on the bond transaction indirectly as the related premium or discount is amortized to interest expense and interest income over the remaining life of the bonds. Thus, on the books of the individual companies, the bonds are accounted for as if the transactions were with independent parties. In the preparation of consolidated statements, however, the acquisition of an affiliate's outstanding bonds from outsiders is considered *a con-structive retirement* of the bond obligation by the consolidated entity.[2] The generally accepted practice of accounting for the early extinguishment of debt is to report an extraordinary gain (loss) if the carrying value of the bonds is greater than (less than) the purchase price.[3] Thus, as with the intercompany sale of inventory or other

[2]When one affiliate purchases bonds directly from another affiliate, the purchase price of the bond investment will be equal to the issue price of the bonds. Therefore, there is no constructive gain or loss reported in the consolidated income statement. However, under the approach used in this text, if the issue price is greater than or less than par value, one company will be allocated a gain and the other allocated a loss of an equal amount.

[3]A gain or loss on the early extinguishment of debt is reported as an extraordinary item net of related income tax consequences. *Statement of Financial Accounting Standards No. 4,* "Reporting Gains or Losses from Extinguishment of Debt" (Stamford, Conn.: Financial Accounting Standards Board, March, 1975), par. 8.

assets, the constructive gain or loss is eventually recognized both on the books of the individual companies and the consolidated financial statements but in different periods.

Observe, however, that the constructive gain or loss on the bond retirement *is recognized in the consolidated income statement prior to the recognition of the gain or loss on the books of the individual companies.* In contrast (see Chapter 5), a gain or loss on the intercompany sale of inventory or other assets *is recognized currently on the books of the selling company, but the gain or loss is deferred for consolidation purposes* until the profit or loss is confirmed by an arm's-length transaction with an independent party. Thus, the objectives of the intercompany bond workpaper entries are essentially opposite the objectives of making workpaper entries for the intercompany sale of inventory or other assets. That is to say, in the period the bonds are purchased, workpaper entries are made to accelerate the recognition of the constructive gain or loss. After the bonds are purchased, workpaper entries are then needed to eliminate the portion of the constructive gain or loss recorded during the period on the books of the individual companies. In the case of the intercompany sale of inventory or other assets, workpaper entries are made in the year of the sale to eliminate or defer the profit or loss recorded on the books of the individual companies. In subsequent periods when the asset is sold to a third party and the profit or loss realized from a consolidated point of view, workpaper entries are made to recognize the profit or loss.

As noted in a preceding paragraph, the gain or loss on the bond retirement is computed as the difference between the carrying value (book value) of the liability and the purchase price of the bonds. There is general agreement on the amount of the gain or loss to be reported, but not on how the gain or loss should be allocated between the affiliated companies involved in the bond transaction for purposes of calculating consolidated net income and the noncontrolling interest in combined income.

Allocation of Constructive Gain or Loss

Four methods for allocating the constructive gain or loss between the parent and subsidiary are supported in practice and in the accounting literature.

1. The constructive gain or loss is allocated entirely to the issuing company. Support for this method is based on the contention that the purchasing affiliate, as a member of the consolidated group operating under the control of common management, was simply acting as an agent for the issuing company. Thus, any gain or loss on the constructive retirement is allocated entirely to the issuing company.

2. The constructive gain or loss is allocated entirely to the purchasing company. Support for this method rests on the contention that the purchasing company initiated the transaction and should be assigned the full amount of the gain or loss.

3. The constructive gain or loss is allocated entirely to the parent company. Under this approach, it is maintained that the management of the parent company controls the financing decisions of the consolidated affiliates. Since management directed or permitted the purchase of the bonds, any gain or loss is allocated entirely to the parent company.

4. The constructive gain or loss is allocated between the purchasing and issuing companies. This method recognizes that a discount or premium will often be associated with both the issuance and purchase of the bonds on the open market. A gain or loss will be recognized over the remaining life of the bonds as each company amortizes the related discount or premium to interest expense and interest income. If the bonds are held to maturity, the full amount of the gain or loss will be recognized by the two entities.

The authors consider the fourth method to be the soundest conceptually. The method is consistent with the allocation of a gain or loss between the noncontrolling and controlling interest on other types of intercompany transactions. It also recognizes that if the purchasing company holds the bonds to maturity, the maturity value is paid by the issuing company. In such cases, each company realizes a gain or loss on the bond issuance or purchase that has been recognized on the books of the individual companies over the life of the bonds. Thus, if one of the companies is a partially owned subsidiary, the noncontrolling shareholders have an interest in the portion of the gain or loss allocated to and recorded by the subsidiary. It should be noted, however, that although consolidated net income each year may vary depending on the method used to allocate the gain or loss, over the life of the issue, *use of any of the methods will result in the same total consolidated net income* and the same total noncontrolling interest in combined income.

Computing the Constructive Gain or Loss

On the date that bonds of an affiliate are purchased, a constructive gain or loss is computed and this total gain or loss is allocated between the issuing and purchasing companies. The portion of the gain or loss allocated to the issuing company is the difference between the book value (carrying value) of the bonds issued and their par value; the portion allocated to the purchasing company is the difference between the par value of the bonds and their cost. There is no constructive gain or loss to the issuing company if the bonds are issued at par value, nor is there a constructive gain or loss to the purchasing company if the bonds are purchased at par value. If the issue price and the purchase price of the bonds were not equal to par value, there are four possible combinations that can result when a constructive gain or loss to the consolidated entity is allocated between two affiliated companies. The combinations are shown below assuming two different book values of $110,000 and $90,000 and two different purchase prices of $115,000 and $85,000. The bonds have a par value of $100,000 in all situations.

ISSUING COMPANY		PURCHASING COMPANY
1. Book value >	Par value >	Purchase price
$110,000	$100,000	$ 85,000
2. Book value <	Par value <	Purchase price
$ 90,000	$100,000	$115,000
3. Book value >	Par value <	Purchase price
$110,000	$100,000	$115,000

	ISSUING COMPANY		PURCHASING COMPANY

4. Book value < Par value > Purchase price
   $ 90,000 $100,000 $ 85,000

The constructive gain or loss for combination 3 is illustrated below. To compute the gain or loss allocated to each affiliate, the par value is subtracted from the book value and then the purchase price is subtracted from the par value. If the number is positive, it is a gain, if it is negative, it is a loss.

Issuing company	Book value	$110,000	+$10,000	Constructive gain
Purchasing company	Par value	$100,000	−$15,000	Constructive loss
	Purchase price	$115,000		
	Net constructive gain (loss)		($5,000)	

There is a net constructive loss of $5,000 to the consolidated entity because the purchase price of the bonds on the open market exceeded the carrying value of the debt.

To illustrate another situation, assume that the $100,000 par value bonds with a book value of $90,000 were purchased by an affiliated company for $85,000 (combination 4 above).

Issuing company	Book value	$ 90,000	−$10,000	Constructive loss
Purchasing company	Par value	$100,000	+$15,000	Constructive gain
	Purchase price	$ 85,000		
	Net constructive gain (loss)		$5,000	

In this case there is a favorable settlement of debt (carrying value > purchase price) and a constructive gain of $5,000 is reported in the consolidated income statement, of which a $10,000 loss is allocated to the issuing company and a $15,000 gain is allocated to the purchasing company.

In the year that the bonds are constructively retired, if either the issuing company or the purchasing company is a partially owned subsidiary, the noncontrolling interest in combined income is reduced (increased) by a loss (gain). In subsequent periods, the income of the subsidiary will be decreased or increased as the related discount or premium is amortized. The noncontrolling interest is also affected by this increase or decrease in income.

ACCOUNTING FOR INTERCOMPANY BONDS ILLUSTRATED

To illustrate entries that are necessary on the books of the affiliated companies and in the consolidated statements workpaper when one affiliate holds bonds of another affiliate, the following are assumed:

1. P Company acquired an 80% interest in S Company for $1,200,000 on January 2, 1992, when the retained earnings and common stock accounts of S Company were $500,000 and $1,000,000, respectively.

2. On December 31, 1995, P Company acquired $300,000 of S Company's par value bonds on the open market for $310,000 after the semiannual interest payment had been made. At the time of purchase there were $500,000 par value bonds outstanding with a book value of $480,000. The bonds mature in four years on December 31, 1999, and carry a nominal interest rate of 9%. Interest is paid semiannually on June 30 and December 31.

3. Both companies use the straight-line method to amortize bond discounts and premiums because the results obtained do not materially differ from those that would be obtained if the effective-interest method were used.

4. The fiscal year-end of both companies is December 31.

In this illustration, bonds of the subsidiary are purchased by the parent company. Book entries, as well as consolidated statements workpaper entries and procedures, would be similar if the parent company bonds were purchased by a subsidiary company except that the Investment in Bonds account is carried on the books of the subsidiary and the bond liability is carried on the parent company's books.

BOOK ENTRY RELATED TO BOND INVESTMENT

P Company will prepare the following entry to record the bond investment:

Dec. 31	Investment in S Company Bonds	310,000	
	Cash		310,000

Note that the usual practice of recording a bond investment does not separate the discount or premium. Since the bonds were purchased on the open market, there is no entry made on the issuing company's books.

In this illustration, the bonds were purchased on the last day of the fiscal period after the semiannual interest had been paid. Thus, there is no accrued interest to be recorded in the current period.

Consolidated Statements Workpaper—1995

The total gain or loss on the constructive retirement to be reported in the 1995 consolidated income statement and the constructive gain or loss allocated to each company is computed as follows:

S Company (issuing company)	Book value*	$288,000	−$12,000 Constructive loss
	Par value	$300,000	
P Company (purchasing company)	Purchase price	$310,000	−$10,000 Constructive loss
	Net constructive gain (loss)	($22,000)	

*Book value of bonds outstanding	$480,000
Percentage purchase ($300,000 ÷ $500,000)	.60
Book value of bonds purchased	$288,000

A total constructive gain would be computed if the purchase price was less than the book value of $288,000.

On the books of the individual companies, the constructive loss is not recorded in the year that the bonds are purchased on the open market. From a consolidated entity point of view, however, the purchase is a constructive retirement of debt. Thus, the constructive loss is recognized in the determination of combined income in the year of the purchase.

Workpaper entries necessary in the consolidated statements workpaper for the year ended December 31, 1995, are presented in general journal from below. The consolidated statements workpaper for 1995 is presented in Illustration 10-1.

**Consolidated Statements Workpaper Entries—1995
(From Illustration 10-1)**

(1) Investment in S Company Stock	160,000	
Beginning Retained Earnings—P Company		160,000
To establish reciprocity.		

The amount of the reciprocity entry is computed as follows:

Retained earnings balance—January 1, 1995	$700,000
Retained earnings balance—date of acquisition	500,000
Increase in retained earnings	200,000
Percentage interest held by P Company	.80
Amount to establish reciprocity	$160,000

(2) Loss on Constructive Retirement of Bonds	10,000	
Investment in S Company Bonds		10,000
To recognize the constructive loss not recorded by P Company and adjust the bond investment to par value.		
(3) Loss on Constructive Retirement of Bonds	12,000	
Discount on Bonds Payable		12,000
To recognize the constructive loss not recorded by the subsidiary and adjust the intercompany bonds to par value.		

Entries (2) and (3) recognize the constructive loss allocated to each company and adjust the bond investment and carrying value of the intercompany debt to par value in preparation for the elimination of the intercompany receivable and payable.

(4) Bonds Payable	300,000	
Investment in S Company Bonds		300,000
To eliminate intercompany bond investment and liability.		
(5) Dividend Income	16,000	
Dividends Declared—S Company		16,000
To eliminate intercompany dividends		

Cost Method
80% Owned Subsidiary
Constructive Retirement of
  Subsidiary's Bonds—
  Year of Retirement

ILLUSTRATION 10-1
Consolidated Statements Workpaper
P Company and Subsidiary
For the Year Ended December 31, 1995

INCOME STATEMENT	P COMPANY	S COMPANY	ELIMINATIONS DR.	ELIMINATIONS CR.	NONCONTROLLING INTEREST	CONSOLIDATED BALANCES
Sales	3,104,000	2,200,000				5,304,000
Dividend Income	16,000		(5) 16,000			–0–
Total Revenue	3,120,000	2,200,000				5,304,000
Cost of Goods Sold	1,700,000	1,360,000				3,060,000
Interest Expense		50,000				50,000
Other Expense	1,124,000	665,000				1,789,000
Loss on Constructive Retirement			(2) 10,000			
of Bonds			(3) 12,000			22,000
Total Cost and Expense	2,824,000	2,075,000				4,921,000
Net/Combined Income	296,000	125,000				383,000
Noncontrolling Interest in						
Income*					22,600	(22,600)
Net Income to Retained Earnings	296,000	125,000	38,000	—	22,600	360,400
RETAINED EARNINGS STATEMENT						
1/1 Retained Earnings						
P Company	1,650,000		(1) 160,000			1,810,000
S Company		700,000	(6) 560,000		140,000	
Net Income from above	296,000	125,000	38,000		22,600	360,400
Dividends Declared						
P Company	(150,000)					(150,000)
S Company		(20,000)		(5) 16,000	(4,000)	
12/31 Retained Earnings to						
Balance Sheet	1,796,000	805,000	598,000	176,000	158,600	2,020,400
BALANCE SHEET						
			(2) 10,000			
Investment in S Company Bonds	310,000			(4) 300,000		–0–
Investment in S Company Stock	1,200,000		(1) 160,000	(6) 1,360,000		–0–
Other Assets	5,420,000	2,620,000				8,040,000
Total Assets	6,930,000	2,620,000				8,040,000
9% Bonds Payable		500,000	(4) 300,000			200,000
Discount on Bonds Payable		(20,000)		(3) 12,000		(8,000)
Other Liabilities	2,134,000	335,000				2,469,000
Capital Stock						
P Company	3,000,000					3,000,000
S Company		1,000,000	(6) 800,000		200,000	
Retained Earnings from above	1,796,000	805,000	598,000	176,000	158,600	2,020,400
Noncontrolling Interest in Net						
Assets					358,600	358,600
Total Liabilities and Equity	6,930,000	2,620,000	1,858,000	1,858,000		8,040,000

*Noncontrolling interest in income computation: ($125,000 − $12,000) × .20 = $22,600

(1) To establish reciprocity as of 1/1/1995 [($700,000 − $500,000) × .80 = $160,000].
(2) To recognize constructive loss not recorded by P Company and adjust the bond investment to par value.
(3) To recognize the constructive loss not recorded by S Company and adjust the intercompany bonds payable to par value.
(4) To eliminate intercompany bond investment and liability.
(5) To eliminate intercompany dividends.
(6) To eliminate investment account.

(6) Beginning Retained Earnings—S Company	560,000	
Common Stock—S Company	800,000	
Investment in S Company Stock		1,360,000
To eliminate investment account.		

Workpaper entries (2), (3), and (4) could be combined into one entry as follows:

Loss on Constructive Retirement of Bonds	22,000	
Bonds Payable	300,000	
Discount on Bonds Payable		12,000
Investment in S Company Bonds		310,000

Since the bonds were purchased on the open market on the last day of the fiscal period, there is no intercompany interest reported in the 1995 income statement. Accordingly, no elimination of intercompany interest income and expense is required in the 1995 consolidated statements workpaper. Since the amount of net income reported by S Company that is included in combined income is reduced by the constructive loss allocated to S Company, noncontrolling interest in combined income is 20% of the income reported by S Company reduced by the constructive loss of $12,000 allocated to the subsidiary [.20 × ($125,000 − $12,000) = $22,600].

A careful review of Illustration 10-1 will reveal these important points concerning the objectives of the bond elimination entries:

1. Since the bonds were purchased this year, the constructive loss is reported in full in the determination of combined income.

2. Interest expense is the amortized interest paid to outside parties during the fiscal period. In this illustration, the intercompany portion was purchased on December 31. Therefore, the bonds were held by outside parties for the full 12 months. Interest expense reported in the consolidated income statement is for the full year, which is equal to the cash interest paid of $45,000 plus discount amortization of $5,000. As shown in the next illustration, if the bonds are held by P Company during the period, interest expense, net of amortization, is eliminated. Thus, for a 12-month period, $30,000 in interest expense is eliminated, resulting in consolidated interest expense of $20,000 ($50,000 times the 40% held by outside parties).

3. The book value of the debt is the amount held by outside parties on the balance sheet date, which is $192,000 [($500,000 − $20,000) × .40]. The 60% held by the parent is eliminated by workpaper entries (3) and (4).

Analytical Definition of Consolidated Net Income and Retained Earnings

As has been indicated in previous chapters, an analytical approach to the calculation of consolidated net income and retained earnings may be useful. As shown here, consolidated net income in 1995 includes 100% of the $10,000 loss allocated to the parent company but only 80% of the $12,000 loss allocated to the subsidiary company. Consolidated net income for 1995 and consolidated retained earnings as of December 31, 1995 are computed in Illustration 10-2. Note the similarity between

ILLUSTRATION 10-2
Calculations to Compute Consolidated
Net Income and Retained Earnings

CONSOLIDATED NET INCOME

Reported net income of P Company		$ 296,000
Less: Dividend income		16,000
Net income from independent operations		280,000
Less: Constructive loss not recorded by P Company		10,000
P Company's contribution to combined income		270,000
Reported net income of S Company	$125,000	
Less: Constructive loss not recorded by S Company	12,000	
S Company's contribution to combined income	113,000	
Percentage interest in S Company	.80	90,400
Consolidated net income		$ 360,400

CONSOLIDATED RETAINED EARNINGS

Ending retained earnings—P Company		$1,796,000
Less: Constructive loss on bond retirement not recorded by P Company		10,000
Retained earnings adjusted for unrecorded constructive loss		1,786,000
Ending retained earnings—S Company	$805,000	
Less: Retained earnings—date of acquisition	500,000	
Increase in recorded retained earnings	305,000	
Less: Constructive loss on bond retirement not recorded by S Company	12,000	
Adjusted increase in recorded retained earnings	293,000	
Percentage interest in S Company	.80	234,400
Consolidated retained earnings on December 31, 1995		$2,020,400

these analytical computations and those made for intercompany sales of fixed assets. As discussed earlier, a gain or loss on the constructive retirement of intercompany bonds is not recorded on the books of the affiliated companies at the time of purchase, but is reported in the consolidated income statement for that period. After the date of purchase, the constructive gain or loss is recorded on the books of the affiliated companies via the periodic amortization adjustment to interest expense or interest income. In the case of intercompany sales of fixed assets, however, a gain or loss on the sale is recorded on the books of the selling affiliate, but is deferred for consolidation purposes until the gain or loss is realized.

Entries on the Books of Affiliated Companies—1996

During 1996 the two companies record on their individual books the following entries related to the bond transaction:

<u>P COMPANY</u>

JUNE 30 AND DECEMBER 31

Cash	13,500	
Interest Income		13,500
To record receipt of interest ($300,000 × .09 × 6/12)		
Interest Income	1,250	
Investment in S Company Bonds		1,250
To amortize premium on bond investment ($10,000 ÷ 8 periods).		

<u>S COMPANY</u>

JUNE 30 AND DECEMBER 31

Interest Expense	22,500	
Cash		22,500
To record payment of interest ($500,000 × .09 × 6/12).		
Interest Expense	2,500	
Discount on Bonds Payable		2,500
To amortize discount on outstanding bonds ($20,000 ÷ 8 periods).		

For the full year (1996), $2,500 ($1,250 × 2) of the total constructive loss was recognized on the books of P Company as a result of amortizing the premium on the investment. S Company recognized $3,000 [($2,500 × 2) × .60] of its share of the loss through the amortization of the discount.

The account balances related to the intercompany bond holdings at the end of 1996 are:

P Company

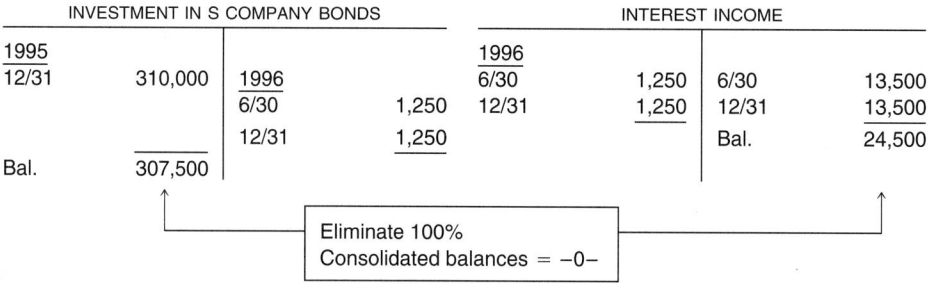

S Company

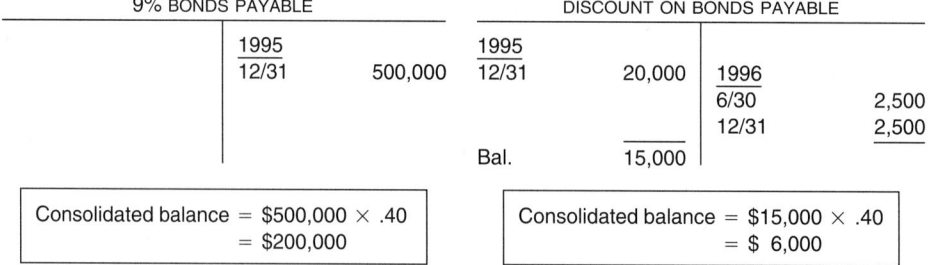

INTEREST EXPENSE

1996		
6/30	22,500	
6/30	2,500	
12/31	22,500	
12/31	2,500	
Bal.	50,000	

Consolidated balance = $50,000 × .40
= $20,000

Rationale: For consolidated balances must eliminate 60% held by affiliated company. Remaining 40% held by outside parties is reported in consolidated financial statement. See Illustration 10-3.

Consolidated Statements Workpaper Entries—December 31,1996 (Illustration 10-3)

Workpaper entries necessary in the consolidated statements workpaper for the year ended December 31, 1996, are presented in general journal form below. The consolidated statements workpaper for 1996 is presented in Illustration 10-3.

**Consolidated Statements Workpaper Entries—1996
(From Illustration 10-3)**

(1)	Investment in S Company Stock	244,000	
	Beginning Retained Earnings—P Company		244,000
	To establish reciprocity [($805,000 − $500,000) × .80 = $244,000].		
(2)	Beginning Retained Earnings—P Company	10,000	
	Interest Income ($1,250 + $1,250)		2,500
	Investment in S Company Bonds		7,500
	To adjust beginning retained earnings for unrecorded constructive loss at the beginning of the year, adjust interest income for the loss recorded this period, and adjust bond investment to par value.		
(3)	Beginning Retained Earnings—P Company ($12,000 × .80)	9,600	
	Beginning Retained Earnings—S Company ($12,000 × .20)	2,400	
	Interest Expense ($5,000 × .60)		3,000
	Discount on Bonds Payable ($15,000 × .60)		9,000
	To adjust beginning retained earnings balances for unrecorded constructive loss at beginning of the year, adjust interest expense for the loss recorded this period, and adjust intercompany bonds to par value.		

A constructive loss of $22,000 was recognized last year in the consolidated income statement. On the books of the individual companies a portion of the loss ($5,500 in total) was recorded this year as the discount ($5,000 × .60 = $3,000) and premium ($2,500) were amortized. Workpaper entries are necessary to add back this portion of the loss reported as a reduction in the current income of the individual companies because the entire loss was reported in the consolidated income statement in the year that the bonds were acquired by P Company. Failure to do so will result in reporting the constructive loss twice, once in the year of acquisition and again in subsequent periods when the companies record the loss. The credit to

Cost Method
80% Owned Subsidiary
Constructive Retirement of
   Subsidiary's Bonds—
   One Year After Retirement

ILLUSTRATION 10-3
Consolidated Statements Workpaper
P Company and Subsidiary
For the Year Ended December 31, 1996

INCOME STATEMENT	P COMPANY	S COMPANY	ELIMINATIONS DR.		ELIMINATIONS CR.		NON-CONTROLLING INTEREST	CONSOLIDATED BALANCES
Sales	3,546,000	2,020,000						5,566,000
Dividend Income	48,000		(6)	48,000				–0–
Interest Income	24,500		(4)	27,000	(2)	2,500		–0–
Total Revenue	3,618,500	2,020,000						5,566,000
Cost of Goods Sold	2,040,000	1,200,000						3,240,000
Interest Expense		50,000			(3)	3,000		20,000
					(4)	27,000		
Other Expense	1,124,500	630,000						1,754,500
Total Cost and Expense	3,164,500	1,880,000						5,014,500
Net/Combined Income	454,000	140,000						551,500
Noncontrolling Interest in Income*							28,600	(28,600)
Net Income to Retained Earnings	454,000	140,000		75,000		32,500	28,600	522,900

RETAINED EARNINGS STATEMENT								
1/1 Retained Earnings								
P Company	1,796,000		(2)	10,000	(1)	244,000		2,020,400
			(3)	9,600				
S Company		805,000	(3)	2,400			158,600	
			(7)	644,000				
Net Income from above	454,000	140,000		75,000		32,500	28,600	522,900
Dividends Declared								
P Company	(150,000)							(150,000)
S Company		(60,000)			(6)	48,000	(12,000)	
12/31 Retained Earnings to Balance Sheet	2,100,000	885,000		741,000		324,500	175,200	2,393,300

BALANCE SHEET								
Investment in S Company Bonds	307,500				(2)	7,500		–0–
					(5)	300,000		
Investment in S Company Stock	1,200,000		(1)	244,000	(7)	1,444,000		–0–
Other Assets	5,812,500	2,690,000						8,502,500
Total Assets	7,320,000	2,690,000						8,502,500
9% Bonds Payable		500,000	(5)	300,000				200,000
Discount on Bonds Payable		(15,000)			(3)	9,000		(6,000)
Other Liabilities	2,220,000	320,000						2,540,000
Capital Stock								
P Company	3,000,000							3,000,000
S Company		1,000,000	(7)	800,000			200,000	
Retained Earnings from above	2,100,000	885,000		741,000		324,500	175,200	2,393,300
Noncontrolling Interest in Net Assets							375,200	375,200
Total Liabilities and Equity	7,320,000	2,690,000		2,085,000		2,085,000		8,502,500

*Noncontrolling interest in income computation: ($140,000 + $3,000)
  × .20 = $28,600

(1) To establish reciprocity as of 1/1/1996 [($805,000 − $500,000)
  × .80 = $244,000].
(2) To adjust beginning retained earnings for unrecorded
  constructive loss at beginning of year, adjust interest income for the
  loss recorded this period, and adjust bond investment to par value.

(3) To adjust beginning retained earnings for unrecorded
  constructive loss at the beginning of year, adjust interest expense
  for the loss recorded this period, and adjust intercompany bond
  payable to par value.
(4) To eliminate intercompany interest.
(5) To eliminate intercompany bond investment and bonds
  payable.
(6) To eliminate intercompany dividends.
(7) To eliminate investment account.

interest income for $2,500 [entry (2)] and the credit to interest expense for $3,000 [entry (3)] increase combined income by $5,500.

(4) Interest Income ($45,000 × .60) or ($13,500 + $13,500)	27,000	
Interest Expense		27,000
To eliminate intercompany interest.		
(5) Bonds Payable ($500,000 × .60)	300,000	
Investment in S Company Bonds		300,000
To eliminate intercompany bond investment and bonds payable.		
(6) Dividend Income	48,000	
Dividends Declared		48,000
To eliminate intercompany dividends.		
(7) Beginning Retained Earnings—S Company	644,000	
Common Stock—S Company	800,000	
Investment in S Company Stock		1,444,000
To eliminate investment account.		

Workpaper entries (2), (3), (4), and (5) could be combined into one entry as follows:

Beginning Retained Earnings—P Company	19,600	
Beginning Retained Earnings—S Company	2,400	
Interest Income	24,500	
Bonds Payable	300,000	
Interest Expense		30,000
Discount on Bonds Payable		9,000
Investment in S Company Bonds		307,500

Noncontrolling interest in combined income is 20% of the income reported by S Company plus the portion of the loss recorded by S during 1996, but fully reported in the 1995 consolidated income statement, the year the bonds were constructively retired [.20 × ($140,000 + $3,000) = $28,600].

Whether a single entry or a series of entries are made, the eliminating entries must accomplish the following:

1. The parent company's beginning retained earnings is reduced by:
   (a) 100% of the constructive loss allocated to P Company that has not been recorded in prior periods as a decrease in interest income via the periodic amortization of premium ($10,000).
   (b) 80% of the constructive loss allocated to S Company that has not been recorded in prior periods as an increase in interest expense via the periodic discount amortization ($9,600).

The sum of these two components is the controlling interest share of the constructive loss not recorded on the books of the affiliated companies as of the beginning of the current period. This sum is also equal to (a) 100% of the unamortized premium on the books of the parent ($10,000) plus (b) the parent's share of the unamortized discount related to the intercompany bonds on the subsidiary's books (.80 × $12,000 = $9,600) at the beginning of the year.

2. The beginning retained earnings balance of the subsidiary is reduced by the noncontrolling interest share of the constructive loss allocated to the subsidiary that has not been recorded in prior periods through periodic amortization of the discount related to the intercompany bonds.

3. The interest expense and interest income related to the intercompany bonds and reported by the respective companies are eliminated from the income statement.

4. The bond investment and the carrying value of the intercompany bonds are eliminated from the balance sheet.

Analytical Definition of Consolidated Net Income and Retained Earnings—1996

Consolidated net income and retained earnings are computed in Illustration 10-4. Note that consolidated net income is increased by the premium amortization on the books of the parent company and 80% of the discount amortization recorded in the current year on the subsidiary's books.

ILLUSTRATION 10-4
Calculations to Compute Consolidated
Net Income and Retained Earnings

CONSOLIDATED NET INCOME

Reported net income of P Company		$ 454,000
Less: Dividend income		48,000
Net income from independent operations		406,000
Add: Constructive loss recorded by P Company in current year (premium amortization)		2,500
P Company's contribution to combined income		408,500
Reported net income of S Company	$140,000	
Add: Constructive loss recorded by S Company in current year (discount amortization)	3,000	
S Company's contribution to combined income	143,000	
Percentage interest in S Company	.80	114,400
Consolidated net income		$522,900

CONSOLIDATED RETAINED EARNINGS

Ending retained earnings—P Company		$2,100,000
Less: Constructive loss on bond retirement not recorded by P Company ($10,000 − $2,500)		7,500
Retained earnings adjusted for unrecorded constructive loss		2,092,500
Ending retained earnings—S Company	$885,000	
Less: Retained earnings—date of acquisition	500,000	
Increase in recorded retained earnings	385,000	
Less: Constructive loss on bond retirement not recorded by S Company ($12,000 − $3,000)	9,000	
Adjusted increase in recorded retained earnings	376,000	
Percentage interest in S Company	.80	300,800
Consolidated retained earnings on December 31, 1996		$2,393,300

In subsequent years until the bonds mature, the companies will continue to recognize a portion of the loss each year as the discount and premium are amortized on their separate books. The consolidated statements workpaper entries are similar to those illustrated for 1996. Workpaper entries in general journal form related to the intercompany bondholdings in the 1997 consolidated statements workpaper are:

Beginning Retained Earnings—P Company	7,500	
Interest Income		2,500
Investment in S Company Bonds		5,000
To adjust beginning retained earnings for unrecorded constructive loss at the beginning of the year, adjust interest income for the loss recorded this period, and adjust bond investment to par value.		
Beginning Retained Earnings—P Company	7,200	
Beginning Retained Earnings—S Company	1,800	
Interest Expense		3,000
Discount on Bonds Payable		6,000
To adjust beginning retained earnings balances for unrecorded constructive loss at beginning of the year, adjust interest expense for the loss recorded this period, and adjust intercompany bonds to par value ($10,000 discount balance × .60 = $6,000).		
Interest Income	27,000	
Interest Expense		27,000
To eliminate intercompany interest.		
Bonds Payable	300,000	
Investment in S Company Bonds		300,000
To eliminate intercompany bond investment and bonds payable.		

INTERIM PURCHASE OF INTERCOMPANY BONDS

In the preceding illustration, the intercompany bonds were initially purchased on December 31, the fiscal year-end of both affiliates. Had the bonds been held during 1995, P Company would have amortized a portion of the premium and S Company would have amortized a part of the discount that was related to the intercompany bonds. Thus, a part of the constructive loss would have been recorded in 1995 by the individual companies. Assuming that P Company amortized $500 and S Company amortized $600 during 1995, workpaper entries (2) and (3) on page 370 are modified as follows:

(2)	Loss on Constructive Retirement of Bonds	10,000	
	Interest Income		500
	Investment in S Company Bonds		9,500
(3)	Loss on Constructive Retirement of Bonds	12,000	
	Interest Expense		600
	Discount on Bonds Payable		11,400

The consolidated income statement will still show a total loss on the constructive retirement of $22,000. The credits to interest income and interest expense add back the portion of the loss that was recorded by the individual companies, but which is reported in total in 1995, the year the bonds were constructively retired. Failure to add back the $1,100 ($500 + $600) to the reported income of the individual companies will result in reporting this portion of the loss twice, as part of the $22,000 and again as a reduction in interest income and as an increase in interest expense, both of which have reduced reported income.

NOTES RECEIVABLE DISCOUNTED

Occasionally a company may issue a note to an affiliated company that may then discount the note with an outside party, or a company holding a note receivable from an outside party may discount the note with an affiliated company. The affiliate acquiring the note may discount the note again with an outside party. From a consolidation point of view, a receivable held by one of the affiliated companies should be reported in the consolidated balance sheet only if the note is due from an outside party. A contingent liability should be disclosed if a note has been discounted with an outside party and the endorsement was with recourse.

To illustrate the workpaper elimination that may be required, assume that P Company issued a $100,000 note to its subsidiary, S Company, for cash. The two companies record the transaction as normal on their own books, that is, P Company debits cash and establishes a note payable account and S Company credits cash and records a note receivable. Assume further that S Company discounted the note at a nonaffiliated bank before maturity. Ignoring interest for simplicity, two methods are used commonly to record the discounting of a note. These methods are:

Method 1: Cash	100,000	
Notes Receivable		100,000
Method 2: Cash	100,000	
Notes Receivable Discounted		100,000

If consolidated statements are prepared before the note matures, an elimination entry may be required, depending on the method used by S Company to record the discounting of the note. If Method 1 was used, the credit to notes receivable would cancel the debit made to notes receivable when the note was received. The consolidated balance sheet would appropriately report the $100,000 note held by the bank and still reported on the books of P Company as a liability. If the second method was used, the notes receivable and the notes receivable discounted accounts would have to be eliminated, because the consolidated group is not contingently liable for the note, but is the primary maker of the note held by an outside party.

Now assume that P Company discounts with S Company a note that had originally been received from one of its customers. Here it is P Company that may record the transfer in one of two ways. Again, if the first method was used, no elimination would be required, for the reasons discussed in the preceding paragraph. However, if the second method was used, both companies would report the same note receivable as an asset, and P Company would show a contingent liability for a note receivable discounted. In the consolidating workpaper, one note receivable must be eliminated, along with the note receivable discounted account, as shown below in the partial balance sheet section of a consolidated statements work-paper:

DEBITS	P COMPANY	S COMPANY	ELIMINATIONS DR.	ELIMINATIONS CR.	CONOLIDATED BALANCES
Notes Receivable	100,000	100,000		(1) 100,000	100,000
CREDITS					
Notes Receivable Discounted	100,000		(1) 100,000		–0–

The consolidated balance sheet would report one receivable from an outside party. The note was discounted to an affiliated company and, therefore, there is no contingent liability to an outside party.

Next, assume that S Company discounted the customer's note with an outside firm. If both companies used Method 1 to record the two discounting transactions, no elimination entry would be required. If the second method was used, the accounts would appear as follows in the trial balances of the two companies:

	P COMPANY	S COMPANY
DEBITS		
Notes Receivable	100,000	100,000
CREDITS		
Notes Receivable Discounted	100,000	100,000

In this case, one of the notes receivable and one of the notes receivable discounted should be eliminated. The consolidated balance sheet would report:

Notes Receivable	$100,000	
Less: Notes Receivable Discounted	100,000	–0–

Alternatively, both notes receivable and both discount accounts could be eliminated and the contingent liability disclosed in a footnote to the consolidated statement.

In the foregoing examples the notes were always transferred from the parent to the subsidiary. The same analysis is appropriate if the notes were transferred from the subsidiary to the parent.

STOCK DIVIDENDS ISSUED BY A SUBSIDIARY COMPANY

A subsidiary may issue stock dividends in the same class of stock that is held by the parent company. The parent company records the receipt of the shares in a memorandum entry only, since a dividend in like stock is not considered income to the recipient. An important fact to recognize in consolidation is that the stock dividend does not alter the investor's proportionate interest in the subsidiary. On the books of the subsidiary, the declaration of a stock dividend is recorded as a transfer from the retained earnings account to one or more paid-in capital accounts. The amount transferred is dependent on whether the dividend is a large or small stock dividend. (Recall from intermediate accounting that a large stock dividend is one in which the number of shares issued is greater than 20–25% of the outstanding shares.) Also, the source of a stock dividend is the earliest earnings accumulated in the retained earnings balance. Conversely, a cash dividend is considered to be a distribution of the most recent profits.

To illustrate the effects of a stock dividend on the preparation of the consolidated statements workpaper, assume that P Company purchased 4,000 shares of S Company's $100 par value common stock on January 2, 1995, for $560,000. At the time of purchase, S Company reported common stock and retained earnings balances of $500,000 and $200,000, respectively. If consolidated statements were prepared on January 2, 1995, the investment eliminating entry would be:

Capital Stock—S Company	400,000	
1/1 Retained Earnings—S Company	160,000	
Investment in S Company		560,000

Now assume that S Company reports net income of $50,000 and declares a 30% stock dividend (1,500 shares) on December 31, 1995. S Company would record the dividend as follows, assuming that the company capitalized the par value of the stock issued:

Stock Dividend Declared (or Retained Earnings)	150,000	
Capital Stock (1,500 shares × $100)		150,000

Note that this entry has no effect on the total stockholders' equity. It changes only the composition of the account balances as shown here:

	S COMPANY'S CAPITAL ACCOUNT BALANCES	
ACCOUNTS	BEFORE THE STOCK DIVIDEND	AFTER THE STOCK DIVIDEND
Capital Stock	$500,000	$650,000
Retained Earnings	250,000*	100,000
Totals	$750,000	$750,000

*$200,000 + $50,000

If the dividend had been considered a small stock dividend, the totals in the schedule above would not change. To record a small stock dividend, the retained earnings account is normally reduced by an amount equal to the number of shares to be issued times the fair market value per share; capital stock and other paid-in capital accounts are increased by the same amount.

The only book entry made by P Company in 1995 is the following memorandum entry to record the receipt of the 1,200 shares from S Company, since no cash dividends were declared during the period.

Memorandum entry—Received 1,200 shares (1,500 × .80) of S Company common stock based on the declaration of a 30% stock dividend.

A condensed consolidated statements workpaper for the year ended December 31, 1995, is presented in Illustration 10-5. In the year that the stock dividend is declared, one additional workpaper eliminating entry is made to eliminate the effects of the dividend on the parent's interest in the capital accounts of the subsidiary. This entry is necessary because the capital stock account has been increased

Cost Method
80% Owned Subsidiary
Subsidiary Issued
Stock Dividend

ILLUSTRATION 10-5
Consolidated Statements Workpaper
P Company and Subsidiary
For the Year Ended December 31, 1995

	P COMPANY	S COMPANY	ELIMINATIONS DR.	ELIMINATIONS CR.	NONCONTROLLING INTEREST	CONSOLIDATED BALANCES
INCOME STATEMENT						
Net/Combined Income	240,000	50,000				290,000
Noncontrolling Interest in Income ($50,000 × .20)					10,000	(10,000)
Net Income to Retained Earnings	240,000	50,000			10,000	280,000
RETAINED EARNINGS STATEMENT						
1/1 Retained Earnings						
P Company	460,000					460,000
S Company		200,000	(2) 160,000		40,000	
Net Income from above	240,000	50,000			10,000	280,000
Dividends Declared S Company—Stock Dividend		(150,000)		(1) 120,000	(30,000)	
12/31 Retained Earnings to Balance Sheet	700,000	100,000	160,000	120,000	20,000	740,000
BALANCE SHEET						
Investment in S Company	560,000			(2) 560,000		–0–
Net Assets	1,040,000	750,000				1,790,000
Total Assets	1,600,000	750,000				1,790,000
Capital Stock						
P Company	900,000					900,000
S Company		650,000	(1) 120,000			
			(2) 400,000		130,000	
Retained Earnings from above	700,000	100,000	160,000	120,000	20,000	740,000
Noncontrolling Interest in Net Assets					150,000	150,000
Total Liabilities and Equity	1,600,000	750,000	680,000	680,000		1,790,000

(1) To reverse effects of the stock dividend.
(2) To eliminate investment account.

by $150,000, but the stock dividend declared account has not been closed to retained earnings. In other words, the balance in the capital stock account is the ending balance and needs to be restored to the beginning of year balance before elimination of the investment account. The workpaper entries in general journal form are:

(1) Capital Stock—S Company	120,000	
Stock Dividends Declared—S Company		120,000
To reverse effects of stock dividend ($150,000 × .80).		
(2) 1/1 Retained Earnings—S Company (.8 × $200,000)	160,000	
Capital Stock—S Company (.8 × $500,000)	400,000	
Investment in S Company		560,000
To eliminate investment account.		

In the closing process the stock dividends declared account is closed to the retained earnings account. In subsequent periods the two workpaper entries are combined: $40,000 ($160,000 — $120,000) is included in the debit to the beginning retained earnings balance, and the capital stock is debited for $520,000 ($400,000 + $120,000). The result is that the debit to capital stock is increased $120,000, and a corresponding decrease is made in the debit to the retained earnings balance.

In the consolidated workpapers the entry to establish reciprocity is based on the undistributed income earned by the subsidiary since the date of acquisition. A cash dividend declared by the subsidiary is generally considered to be a distribution of the most recent profits, which, of course, reduces undistributed profits of the subsidiary accumulated after the date the parent obtained control of the subsidiary. Conversely, the source of a stock dividend is the earliest earnings accumulated in the retained earnings balance.

In this illustration the procedures to compute the amount of the entry to establish reciprocity must be modified to recognize that the retained earnings balance at the date of acquisition has been reduced to $50,000 as a result of the stock dividend. The December 31, 1996, workpaper entries are as follows:

(1) Investment in S Company		40,000	
Beginning Retained Earnings—P Company			40,000
To establish reciprocity as of 1/1/96 ($50,000 × .80).			
1/1 Retained earnings balance			
($200,000 − $150,000 + $50,000)			$100,000
Retained earnings balance—			
date of acquisition		$200,000	
Less: Stock dividend		150,000	
Adjusted retained earnings balance—			
date of acquisition			50,000
Increase in retained earnings since			
date of acquisition			$ 50,000

(2) Beginning Retained Earnings—S Company ($100,000 × .80)	80,000		
Common Stock—S Company ($650,000 × .80)	520,000		
Investment in S Company ($560,000 + $40,000)		600,000
To eliminate investment account.		

A portion of the retained earnings section of the December 31, 1996 workpaper is presented here:

	P COMPANY	S COMPANY	ELIMINATIONS DR.	ELIMINATIONS CR.	NONCONTROLLING INTEREST	CONSOLIDATED BALANCES
1/1 Retained earnings						
P Company	700,000			(1) 40,000		740,000
S Company		100,000	(2) 80,000		20,000	

Observe that the foregoing entries result in beginning retained earnings balances that are equal to the ending retained earnings balances reported for the noncontrolling interest and the consolidated retained earnings in the December 31, 1995, workpaper (see Illustration 10-5).

The issuance of a stock dividend does not affect the computation of consolidated retained earnings. As proof, the consolidated retained earnings balance as of December 31, 1995, is computed using the analytical approach as follows:

P Company's retained earnings balance at December 31, 1995	$700,000
P Company's share of the change in the subsidiary's adjusted retained earnings since the date of acquisition ($50,000 × .80)	40,000
Consolidated retained earnings—December 31, 1995	$740,000

Stock Dividends Issued from Postacquisition Earnings

In the foregoing illustration, the retained earnings transferred to paid-in capital ($150,000) was less than the retained earnings balance ($200,000) at the date of acquisition. If the stock dividend had been more than $200,000, some of the postacquisition earnings of the subsidiary would have been capitalized. For example, assume that S Company made the following entry to record the stock dividend:

Stock Dividends Declared (or Retained Earnings)	220,000	
Capital Stock		220,000

The entry capitalized $200,000 of the retained earnings that existed at the date of acquisition plus $20,000 of the net income reported after the date of acquisition. The capitalization of the current earnings does not affect consolidated retained earnings, which is still $740,000 as determined in Illustration 10-5, but it does result in the inclusion of earnings in the consolidated retained earnings balance that have been capitalized and are not available for the payment of dividends. The amount of the subsidiary's postacquisition earnings that have been capitalized and included in the consolidated retained earnings should be disclosed in the consolidated financial statements. Some may contend that the portion of the retained earnings that has been capitalized should be reported as contributed capital in the consolidated balance sheet. In response to this contention, the Committee on Accounting Procedure of the American Institute of Certified Public Accountants made the following comment:

> Occasionally, subsidiary companies capitalize earned surplus [retained earnings] arising since acquisition, by means of a stock dividend or otherwise. This does not require a transfer to capital surplus on consolidation, inasmuch as the retained earnings in the consolidated financial statements should reflect the accumulated earnings of the consolidated group not distributed to the shareholders of, or capitalized by, the parent company.[4]

DIVIDENDS FROM PREACQUISITION EARNINGS

The nature of a liquidating dividend (dividend from preacquisition earnings) and the entries to record a liquidating dividend were discussed in Chapter 3. The objective of this section is to illustrate the effects of a liquidating dividend on the consolidated statements workpaper entries.

To illustrate the adjustment required in the workpaper when a liquidating dividend is involved, assume that P Company acquired an 80% interest in S Company on January 2, 1995, for $560,000. At the time of purchase, S Company had capital stock and retained earnings in the amounts of $500,000 and $200,000, respectively. During the first year that the investment was held, S Company reported net income of $200,000. On December 31, 1995, the subsidiary declared and paid a cash dividend of $250,000. In this case, $50,000 of the dividend is a distribution of earnings accumulated before the controlling interest was obtained in the subsidiary. As discussed in Chapter 3, there is general agreement that a liquidating dividend should be accounted for as a return of part of the original investment rather than income to the parent company.

Recall that the source of a cash dividend is considered to be the most recent earnings. Under the cost method the following entry is made on the books of P Company to recognize that $200,000 of the dividend is based on the current earnings and $50,000 is a distribution of preacquisition earnings:

Cash	200,000	
Dividend Income ($200,000 × .80)		160,000
Investment in S Company ($50,000 × .80)		40,000
To record receipt of a cash dividend from S Company.		

This entry reduces the investment account balance to $520,000. In the year of the liquidating dividend, one additional workpaper entry must be made to reverse the effects of the liquidating dividend, since the dividend has been adjusted to the

---

[4]Committee on Accounting Procedure, American Institute of Certified Public Accountants, *Accounting Research and Terminology Bulletin, Final Edition* (New York: AICPA, 1961), *Bulletin No. 51,* par. 18.

investment account, but the dividends declared are still shown as a separate amount in the trial balance of S Company. Although the consolidated statements workpaper is not presented, the December 31, 1995, eliminating entries are:

(1)	Dividend Income	160,000	
	Dividends Declared—S Company		160,000
	To eliminate intercompany dividends.		
(2)	Investment in S Company	40,000	
	Dividends Declared—S Company		40,000
	To reverse the liquidating dividend.		
(3)	Beginning Retained Earnings—S Company ($200,000 × .80)	160,000	
	Capital Stock—S Company ($500,000 × .80)	400,000	
	Investment in S Company		560,000
	To eliminate investment account.		

In the workpapers prepared in subsequent years, the amount of the entry made to establish reciprocity is based on the difference between the current year's beginning retained earnings balance and the retained earnings balance at the date of acquisition reduced by the $50,000 liquidating dividend. The investment elimination entry is a combination of entry (2) and entry (3) above. The December 31, 1996, workpaper entry would be:

(1)	Beginning Retained Earnings—S Company ($150,000 × .80)	120,000	
	Capital Stock—S Company ($500,000 × .80)	400,000	
	Investment in S Company		520,000
	To eliminate investment account.		

No entry is needed to establish reciprocity, because all the earnings of the subsidiary since acquisition have been distributed, and the parent's share thereof was recorded by and is reported in the retained earnings balance of P Company.

SUBSIDIARY WITH BOTH PREFERRED AND COMMON STOCK OUTSTANDING

A subsidiary company may have both common and preferred stock outstanding. To justify consolidation, the parent must hold a controlling interest in the outstanding voting stock. At the same time, the parent may or may not hold shares of the preferred stock. In either case, in the preparation of consolidated financial statements, the shares of the preferred stock not held by the parent company are considered part of the noncontrolling interest.

Determining Equity Interest of Each Class of Stockholders

The existence of preferred stock creates special problems in the preparation of consolidated financial statements because each class of stockholders has an interest in the net assets of the firm. To determine the equity interest of each class of stockholders on a certain date, it is necessary to allocate the subsidiary's stockholders' equity between the preferred and common stock interests. In doing so, the provisions of the preferred stock issue, in particular the *call price*, sometimes called the *redemption price*, and dividend provisions, must be analyzed and provided for in making the allocation. After the date of acquiring the controlling interest, the operating results of the subsidiary must also be allocated to determine the interest of the two classes of stockholders in the changes in the retained earnings balance. The dividend preference of the preferred stock issue will determine the amounts allocated to each class of stockholders.

The effects that the various rights and priorities granted to the preferred stockholders have on the determination of the book value interests and the claim to earnings are discussed in intermediate accounting texts. The procedures and the steps indicated numerically for determining such allocations for some of the more common alternatives are summarized in Illustration 10-6.

Illustration 10-6 does not include the steps to be taken in the allocation of a deficit balance in the retained earnings account or a subsidiary reporting a net loss during an operating period. If the preferred stock is noncumulative, nonparticipating, and has a call price equal to par value, the full deficit in the retained earnings account or net loss is allocated totally to the common stock interest. If the preferred stock is cumulative and nonparticipating, a deficit balance in retained earnings is assigned to the common stock, unless there are dividends in arrears, in which case the amount of the preferred dividends in arrears increases the book value interest of the preferred stockholders and is added to the deficit assigned to the common equity. In the case of a net loss, the current year's dividends on the preferred stock are added to the preferred interest and added to the net loss (which reduces the common interest) to determine the interest of the common stockholders in current operations. In the case of deficit operations, the participating provision can be ignored.

Allocation of Difference Between Cost of Preferred Stock Investment and Book Value Interest Acquired

In the case of a common stock investment, the difference between the cost of the investment and the book value of the interest acquired is assigned to undervalued or overvalued assets and liabilities. However, because holders of cumulative/nonparticipating preferred stock do not have a residual interest in the firm's net assets, the excess paid for a preferred stock interest is generally not related to the market value of the firm's net assets. If the preferred stock is nonconvertible and nonparticipating, the market price is more closely associated with the preferred dividend return related to the market rate of return on investments of similar risk. In essence, the market factors that cause movements in the market value of the preferred stock are similar to the market factors that cause movements in the market value of the firm's bonds. Thus, the difference between the cost of preferred stock and the book value of the interest acquired is similar to a discount or premium on a bond issue. One of the major differences between preferred stock and debt is that a preferred stock issue does not normally have a maturity date.

ILLUSTRATION 10-6
Allocation of Retained Earnings Balance and Net Income
When Subsidiary Has Both Common and Preferred Stock Outstanding

	ACCUMULATED RETAINED EARNINGS BALANCE		ALLOCATION OF NET INCOME	
	PREFERRED STOCK*	COMMON STOCK	PREFERRED STOCK	COMMON STOCK
Noncumulative/ nonparticipating	1. Zero.	2. Balance in retained earnings account.	1. Current year's dividend if one was declared.	2. Net income in excess of preferred dividend.
Cumulative/ nonparticipating	1. Dividends in arrears.	2 Balance after subtracting dividend in arrears.	1. Current year's dividend whether declared or not.	2. Net income in excess of preferred dividend.
Noncumulative/ fully participating	1. Allocated between preferred and common stock.[†]		1. Current year's dividend if one was declared.	2. Current year's dividend if declared on common, but not to exceed the amount to match the percentage on preferred.
			3. Remaining net income is allocated between preferred and common stock.[†]	
Cumulative/fully participating[‡]	1. Dividends in arrears. 2. Balance after subtracting any dividend in arrears is allocated between preferred and common stock.[†]		1. Current year's dividend whether declared or not.	2. Current year's dividend if declared on common, but not to exceed the amount to match the percentage on preferred.
			3. Remaining net income is allocated between preferred and common stock.[†]	

*It is assumed that the call price of the preferred stock is equal to the stock's par value. If the call price is greater, the preferred stock interest in retained earnings is increased by the amount of the call premium and a corresponding reduction is made in the common stock interest.

[†]It is assumed that the allocation is based on the ratio of the par values of each class of stock.

[‡]It is assumed that a common stock dividend is lost if not declared in any one year to match the preference rate on the preferred stock. In other words, before the participation feature is effective, the common stockholders normally receive a dividend equal to the same percentage paid to the preferred stockholders. However, if an equal percentage is not declared on the common stock during the period, it is lost to the common stockholders and will not be paid in subsequent periods. Since the preferred stock is cumulative, a passed dividend on preferred stock is considered in arrears in the determination of dividend payments in future periods. Such a dividend agreement with the preferred stockholders could be detrimental to the interest of the common stockholders. Alternative agreements could be negotiated, and this is only one possibility.

Because the preferred stock does not normally have a maturity date, the period selected to amortize the difference would be arbitrary. One approach is to recognize the difference as a loss in the consolidated income statement in the year of the purchase. However, in our view, the acquisition of outstanding preferred stock by the consolidated entity reflects a constructive retirement of the stock and should be accounted for as an equity transaction. Thus, the difference between cost and the book value interest acquired (a debit difference) is accounted for as a reduction in consolidated other contributed capital, or if none exists, is recorded as a reduction in consolidated retained earnings. If the book value of the interest acquired is greater than the cost of the preferred stock, the credit difference is carried to other contributed capital.

Most preferred stock agreements contain the cumulative feature and are non-participating. For this reason, the preparation of consolidated financial statements when cumulative/nonparticipating preferred stock is outstanding is illustrated in the next section. The reader must recognize, however, that the illustration is only one of many possibilities, since the rights and priorities granted to the preferred stockholders may take numerous forms. When there is preferred stock outstanding, the stock agreement should be carefully reviewed to assess the rights and priorities of each class of stock. Allocations of the stockholders' equity and net income should be made in accordance with the agreement.

CONSOLIDATING A SUBSIDIARY WITH PREFERRED STOCK OUTSTANDING

To illustrate the accounting for a subsidiary and the consolidated statements workpaper procedures to be followed when the subsidiary has both preferred stock and common stock outstanding, the following information concerning the capital accounts of S Company as of January 2, 1995, is assumed.

8%, $100 par value preferred stock, cumulative, nonparticipating, dividends in arrears for 1994, call price is $103	$ 500,000
$10 par value common stock	1,000,000
Other contributed capital—premium on issue of common stock	305,000
Retained earnings	200,000
Total stockholders' equity	$2,005,000

On January 2, 1995, P Company acquired 80% of the outstanding common stock for $1,160,000 and 30% of the outstanding preferred stock for $180,000. The entry to record the purchase is:

Investment in S Company Preferred Stock	180,000	
Investment in S Company Common Stock	1,160,000	
Cash		1,340,000

During the year, S Company reported net income of $200,000 and declared no cash dividends.

The stockholders' equity accounts of S Company must be allocated to determine the book value interest in the net assets of the preferred and common stockholders. The allocation on the date of acquisition would be made as shown in Illustration 10-7.[5] In this illustration, if the preferred shares were called, a payment

---

[5]Another approach to determine the allocation of equity interest is:

Book value of net assets		$2,005,000
Less: Allocated to preferred stock		
Par value of preferred stock	$500,000	
Call premium (5,000 shares $\times$ $3)	15,000	
Dividends in arrears (5,000 shares $\times$ $8)	40,000	
Total allocated to preferred stock		555,000
Residual allocated to common stock		$1,450,000

ILLUSTRATION 10-7
Allocation of Difference Between Cost and Book Value

ACCOUNT	ACCOUNT BALANCE	BOOK VALUE INTEREST PREFERRED STOCK	BOOK VALUE INTEREST COMMON STOCK
$100 par preferred stock—8%	$ 500,000	$500,000	—
$10 par common stock	1,000,000		$1,000,000
Other contributed capital— common stock	305,000		305,000
Retained earnings	200,000	55,000	145,000
Totals	$2,005,000	555,000	1,450,000
Percentage interest acquired		30%	80%
Book value interest acquired		166,500	1,160,000
Cost		180,000	1,160,000
Difference between cost and book value interest		$ 13,500	$ –0–

of $111 ($103 call price + $8 dividend in arrears) must be made to acquire each share of stock. Accordingly, retained earnings of $55,000 (5,000 shares outstanding × $11 per share) is allocated to the preferred stockholders' interest. Thus, on the date of acquisition the preferred stock interest in the net assets ($555,000) is equal to the call price of $515,000 plus the $40,000 dividends in arrears.

Consolidated Statements Workpaper—1995 (Illustration 10-8)

Workpaper procedures are similar to those illustrated in earlier sections of this text. The only difference is that an additional workpaper entry must be made to eliminate the preferred stock investment account. The consolidating statements workpaper at December 31, 1995, is contained in Illustration 10-8. The balances are assumed except for the ones previously given. Note that the beginning retained earnings balance of S Company is allocated between the two classes of stock. Making the allocation in the workpaper facilitates preparing the elimination entries and is necessary because dividends in arrears are not recorded in the accounts of S Company.

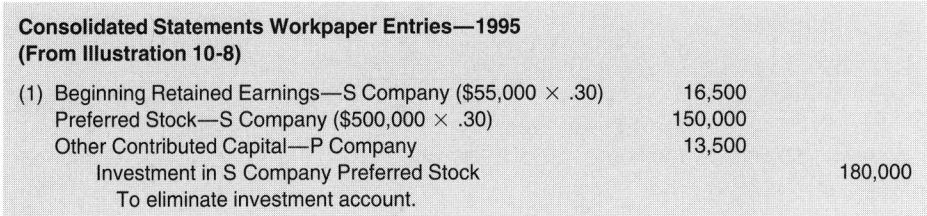

Consolidated Statements Workpaper Entries—1995
(From Illustration 10-8)

(1) Beginning Retained Earnings—S Company ($55,000 × .30)	16,500	
Preferred Stock—S Company ($500,000 × .30)	150,000	
Other Contributed Capital—P Company	13,500	
Investment in S Company Preferred Stock		180,000
To eliminate investment account.		

As discussed earlier, the $13,500 difference between the cost of the preferred stock investment and the book value interest acquired is not allocated to specific assets or liabilities, but rather is accounted for as an equity transaction and debited to other contributed capital.

Cost Method
80% Owned Subsidiary
Subsidiary Has Preferred
Stock Outstanding

ILLUSTRATION 10-8
Condensed Consolidated Statements Workpaper
P Company and Subsidiary
For the Year Ended December 31, 1995

INCOME STATEMENT	P COMPANY	S COMPANY	ELIMINATIONS DR.	ELIMINATIONS CR.	NON-CONTROLLING INTEREST	CONSOLIDATED BALANCES
Net/Combined Income	800,000	200,000				1,000,000
Noncontrolling Interest in Income						
Preferred Stock ($40,000 × .70)					28,000	
Common Stock [($200,000 − $40,000) × .20]					32,000	(60,000)
Net Income to Retained Earnings	800,000	200,000	—	—	60,000	940,000
RETAINED EARNINGS STATEMENT						
1/1 Retained Earnings						
P Company	1,450,000					1,450,000
S Company						
Preferred Stock		55,000	(1) 16,500		38,500	
Common Stock		145,000	(2) 116,000		29,000	
Net Income from above	800,000	200,000			60,000	940,000
Dividends Declared						
P Company	(500,000)					(500,000)
12/31 Retained Earnings to Balance Sheet	1,750,000	400,000	132,500	—	127,500	1,890,000
BALANCE SHEET						
Investment in S Company Preferred Stock	180,000			(1) 180,000		–0–
Investment in S Company Common Stock	1,160,000			(2) 1,160,000		–0–
Other Assets	5,410,000	2,805,000				8,215,000
Total Assets	6,750,000	2,805,000				8,215,000
Liabilities	1,600,000	600,000				2,200,000
Preferred Stock						
S Company		500,000	(1) 150,000		350,000	
Common Stock						
P Company	3,000,000					3,000,000
S Company		1,000,000	(2) 800,000		200,000	
Other Contributed Capital						
P Company	400,000		(1) 13,500			386,500
S Company		305,000	(2) 244,000		61,000	
Retained earnings from above	1,750,000	400,000	132,500		127,500	1,890,000
Noncontrolling Interest in Net Assets*					738,500	738,500
Total Liabilities and Equity	6,750,000	2,805,000	1,340,000	1,340,000		8,215,000

(1) To eliminate the preferred stock investment account.
(2) To eliminate the common stock investment account.

*Noncontrolling interest in net assets can be verified as follows:

	$	NONCONTROLLING PERCENTAGE	TOTAL
Total stockholders' equity	$2,205,000		
Allocated to the preferred:			
Par value	$500,000		
Call premium	15,000		
Dividends in arrears	80,000		
Book value of preferred stock	595,000	.70	$416,500
Book value of common stock	$1,610,000	.20	322,000
Noncontrolling interest—12/31			$738,500

(2) Beginning Retained Earnings—S Company ($145,000 × .80)	116,000		
Common Stock—S Company ($1,000,000 × .80)	800,000		
Other Contributed Capital—S Company ($305,000 × .80)	244,000		
Investment in S Company Common Stock			1,160,000
To eliminate investment account.			

In computing the noncontrolling interest in combined income, S Company's contribution to combined income is first allocated between the two classes of stock. Because of the cumulative feature of the preferred stock, $40,000 of S Company's net income is first allocated to the cumulative preferred stock even though no cash dividends were declared in this period. This, of course reduces the amount of income available for distribution to the common stockholders. The residual net income of $160,000 is allocated to the common stockholders' interest since the preferred stock is nonparticipating. Noncontrolling interest in the 1995 combined income is computed as follows:

	CONTRIBUTION TO COMBINED INCOME	NONCONTROLLING PERCENTAGE	NONCONTROLLING INTEREST
Reported net income of S Company	$200,000		
Income allocated to preferred stock	40,000	.70	$28,000
Income allocated to common stock	$160,000	.20	32,000
Noncontrolling interest in combined income			$60,000

Such an allocation is necessary whether or not P Company holds any of the preferred stock.

Note that the allocation of net income is unaffected by dividends in arrears on preferred stock at the beginning of the year. The allocation of net income reflects the increase in the book value interest of each class of stock due to operations of the current period only. Dividends in arrears at the beginning of the year are recognized as an allocation of the beginning retained earnings balance.

Consolidated net income for 1995 and consolidated retained earnings as of December 31, 1995, can be verified as shown in Illustration 10-9.

ILLUSTRATION 10-9
Calculations of Consolidated Net
Income and Retained Earnings

CONSOLIDATED NET INCOME

P Company's net income from independent operations— 1995		$ 800,000
P Company's share of S Company's reported net income:		
Allocated to preferred stock interest:		
$40,000 × .30 =	$ 12,000	
Allocated to common stock interest:		
$160,000 × .80 =	128,000	140,000
Consolidated net income—1995		$ 940,000

CONSOLIDATED RETAINED EARNINGS ON DECEMBER 31, 1995

P Company's December 31, 1995, retained earnings balance			$1,750,000
Undistributed net income earned since date of acquisition:			
Preferred stock	$ 40,000 × .30 =	$ 12,000	
Common stock	160,000 × .80 =	128,000	140,000*
Consolidated retained earnings—December 31, 1995			$1,890,000

*Undistributed net income can be computed as follows when income statements of prior years are not available.

	RETAINED EARNINGS ALLOCATION		
	PREFERRED STOCK	COMMON STOCK	TOTAL
Retained earnings balance			
End of current year	$95,000	$305,000	$400,000
Date of acquisition	55,000	145,000	200,000
Increase in retained earnings	40,000	160,000	$200,000
Percentage interest	.30	.80	
Share of undistributed income	$12,000	$128,000	$140,000

Accounting Subsequent to the Year of Acquisition

Now assume that S Company reported net income of $300,000 in 1996 and paid cash dividends of $120,000 to the preferred stockholders ($80,000 for the arrearages of 1994 and 1995 + $40,000 for the current year) and $50,000 to the common stockholders.

Entries on the Books of P Company—1996   P Company would record receipt of the cash dividends as follows:

Cash	36,000	
Dividend Income		24,000
Investment in S Company Preferred Stock		12,000
To record receipt of dividends on preferred stock investment ($120,000 × .30 = $36,000).		

Note that the distribution of $40,000 for dividends in arrears at the date of acquisition is a liquidating dividend and is accounted for as a reduction in the investment account.

Cash	40,000	
Dividend Income		40,000
To record receipt of dividends on common stock investment		
($50,000 × .80 = $40,000).		

Consolidated Statements Workpaper—1996 (Illustration 10-10)

A consolidated statements workpaper for December 31, 1996 is presented in Illustration 10-10. To facilitate making the eliminating entries, the beginning retained earnings balance of $400,000 of S Company is allocated between the two classes of stock as follows:

Retained earnings balance—1/1		$400,000
Allocated to preferred stock:		
Undistributed income allocated to preferred stock		
interest—1994 and 1995—$40,000 × 2 years =	$80,000	
Call premium	15,000	95,000
Residual allocated to common stock		$305,000

The December 31, 1996, workpaper elimination entries in journal form are:

Consolidated Statements Workpaper Entries—1996 (From Illustration 10-10)		
(1) Investment in S Company Preferred Stock	12,000	
Investment in S Company Common Stock	128,000	
Beginning Retained Earnings—P Company		140,000
To establish reciprocity as of 1/1/96.		
($95,000 − $55,000) × .3 = $12,000		
($305,000 − $145,000) × .80 = $128,000		
(2) Dividend Income	64,000	
Dividends Declared—S Company (Preferred)		24,000
Dividends Declared—S Company (Common)		40,000
To eliminate intercompany dividends.		
(3) Investment in S Company Preferred Stock	12,000	
Dividends Declared—S Company		12,000
To reverse the liquidating dividend.		
(4) Beginning Retained Earnings—S Company	28,500	
Preferred Stock—S Company	150,000	
Other Contributed Capital—P Company	13,500	
Investment in S Company Preferred Stock		192,000
To eliminate preferred stock investment account.		
(5) Beginning Retained Earnings—S Company	244,000	
Common Stock—S Company	800,000	
Other Contributed Capital—S Company	244,000	
Investment in S Company Common Stock		1,288,000
To eliminate common stock investment account.		

Cost Method
80% Owned Subsidiary
Subsidiary Has Preferred
Stock Outstanding

ILLUSTRATION 10-10
Consolidated Statements Workpaper
P Company and Subsidiary
For the Year Ended December 31, 1996

	P COMPANY	S COMPANY	ELIMINATIONS DR.	ELIMINATIONS CR.	NONCONTROLLING INTEREST	CONSOLIDATED BALANCES
INCOME STATEMENT						
Net/Income Before Dividend Income	636,000	300,000				936,000
Dividend Income						
($24,000 + $40,000)	64,000		(2) 64,000			–0–
Net/Combined Income	700,000	300,000				936,000
Noncontrolling Interest in Income						
Preferred Stock						
($40,000 + .70)					28,000	
Common Stock						
($260,000 + .20)					52,000	(80,000)
Net Income to Retained Earnings	700,000	300,000	64,000	—	80,000	856,000
RETAINED EARNINGS STATEMENT						
1/1 Retained Earnings						
P Company	1,750,000			(1) 140,000		1,890,000
S Company						
Preferred Stock		95,000	(4) 28,500		66,500	
Common Stock		305,000	(5) 244,000		61,000	
Net Income from above	700,000	300,000	64,000		80,000	856,000
Dividends Declared						
P Company	(500,000)					(500,000)
S Company		(120,000)		(2) 24,000	(84,000)	
Preferred Stock				(3) 12,000		
Common Stock		(50,000)		(2) 40,000	(10,000)	
12/31 Retained Earnings to						
Balance Sheet	1,950,000	530,000	336,500	216,000	113,500	2,246,000
BALANCE SHEET						
Investment in S Company						
Preferred Stock			(1) 12,000	(4) 192,000		–0–
($180,000 − $12,000)	168,000		(3) 12,000			
Investment in S Company						
Common Stock	1,160,000		(1) 128,000	(5) 1,288,000		–0–
Other Assets	5,322,000	2,785,000				8,107,000
Total Assets	6,650,000	2,785,000				8,107,000
Liabilities	1,300,000	450,000				1,750,000
Preferred Stock						
S Company		500,000	(4) 150,000		350,000	
Common Stock						
P Company	3,000,000					3,000,000
S Company		1,000,000	(5) 800,000		200,000	
Other Contributed Capital						
P Company	400,000		(4) 13,500			386,500
S Company		305,000	(5) 244,000		61,000	
Retained Earnings from above	1,950,000	530,000	336,500	216,000	113,500	2,246,000
Noncontrolling Interest in Net Assets					724,500	724,500
Total Liabilities and Equity	6,650,000	2,785,000	1,696,000	1,696,000		8,107,000

(1) To establish reciprocity as of 1/1/96
(2) To eliminate intercompany dividends.
(3) To reverse liquidating dividend.
(4) To eliminate preferred stock investment account.
(5) To eliminate common stock investment account.

At the end of the year, there are no dividends in arrears on the preferred stock. This means that all income allocated to the preferred stock interest since the date of acquisition has been distributed. Thus, at the end of the period, $15,000 of the ending retained earnings balance is allocated to the preferred stock for the call premium. The residual balance of $515,000 is allocated to the common stock interest.

Consolidated net income and retained earnings for the year ended December 31, 1996, using the analytical approach, are computed as follows:

Consolidated Net Income

P Company's net income from independent operations		
($700,000 − $64,000 dividends)		$636,000
P Company's share of S Company's net income:		
Allocated to preferred stock	$40,000 × .30 = $ 12,000	
Allocated to common stock	$260,000 × .80 = 208,000	220,000
Consolidated net income		$856,000

Consolidated Retained Earnings   P Company's interest in the undistributed net income at the end of 1996 is computed as follows:

RETAINED EARNINGS—S COMPANY	PREFERRED STOCK	COMMON STOCK	TOTAL
End of current year	$15,000	$515,000	$530,000
Date of acquisition	15,000*	145,000	160,000*
Undistributed income	−0−	370,000	$370,000
Percentage interest	.30	.80	
Share of undistributed income	$ −0−	$296,000	$296,000

*Dividends in arrears of $40,000 were paid and accounted for as a liquidating divided.

Consolidated Retained Earnings

P Company's ending retained earnings balance	$1,950,000
P Company's share of undistributed income of S Company earned	
since date of acquisition	
Preferred stock	−0−
Common stock	296,000
Consolidated retained earnings, December 31, 1996	$2,246,000

The entry to establish reciprocity in the December 31, 1997, consolidated statements workpaper is:

Investment in S Company Common Stock	296,000	
Beginning Retained Earnings—P Company		296,000

A reciprocity entry is not needed for the preferred stock interest because there is no undistributed income relating to the preferred stock at the end of 1996.

CONSOLIDATED STATEMENTS WORKPAPER—PARTIAL EQUITY METHOD

The balances reported by the parent company in income, retained earnings, and the investment account differ depending on the method used by the parent company to record its investment. As illustrated in previous chapters, however, the method used by the parent company to record its investment has no effect on the consolidated balances.

As has been illustrated in previous chapters, when the parent company records its investment using the partial equity method, a workpaper entry to reverse the effect of the parent company entries during the year for subsidiary dividends and income replaces the cost method entries to establish reciprocity and to eliminate divided income. However, the workpaper entries to eliminate the effects of intercompany transactions discussed in this chapter are the same when the parent company records its investment using the partial equity method as those illustrated where the parent company used the cost method to record its investment.

Questions

1. Define "constructive retirement of debt." How is the total constructive gain or loss computed?

2. The gain or loss on the constructive retirement of debt is recognized subsequently by the individual companies. Explain.

3. Allocating the gain or loss on constructive bond retirement between the purchasing and issuing companies is preferred conceptually. Describe how this allocation would be made.

4. Give the primary argument(s) in favor of assigning the *total* gain or loss on constructive bond retirement to the company that issued the bonds.

5. Under the allocation method followed in this text, how is the noncontrolling interest in combined income affected by intercompany bondholdings?

6. Investor Company purchased 70% of the $500,000 par value outstanding bonds of Investee Company, a 70% owned subsidiary. The bonds cost $338,000 and had a carrying value of $360,000 on the date of purchase.
   (a) What portion of the gain or loss resulting from the constructive bond retirement should be allocated to Investor Company?
   (b) What portion of the constructive gain or loss should be allocated to Investee Company?

7. An outside party issued a note to Affiliate X, who then sold the note to Affiliate Y. Y discounted the note at an unaffiliated bank, endorsing it with recourse. Which party is primarily liable and which party is contingently liable for the note?

8. Cash dividends are viewed as a distribution of the most recent earnings. How are stock dividends viewed?

9. Explain how the reciprocity calculation is modified in periods after the declaration of a stock dividend.

10. What journal entry, if any, would the parent company make to record the receipt of a stock dividend?

11. What effect does a stock dividend have on the consolidated statements workpaper in the year of declaration? In subsequent periods?

12. How does the existence of preferred stock affect the calculation of noncontrolling interest?

13. Explain how to account for the difference between cost and book value interest of an investment in preferred stock of a subsidiary.

14. What effect would cumulative preferred stock have on the allocation of a net loss to the common stockholders?

Exercises

Exercise 10-1

Pacelli Company issued 10-year, 10% bonds with a par value of $1,000,000 on January 2, 1994, for $940,000. Interest is paid semiannually on June 30 and December 31. On December 31, 1995, $800,000 of the par value bonds were purchased by Salez Company for $820,000. Salez Company is an 80% owned subsidiary of Pacelli Company. Both companies use the straight-line method to amortize bond discounts and premiums.

Salez Company declared cash dividends of $60,000 each year during the period 1995–1996.

Required:

A. Compute the total gain or loss on the constructive retirement of debt.

B. Allocate the total gain or loss between Pacelli Company and Salez Company.

C. Prepare the book entries related to the bonds made by the individual companies during 1996.

D. Assume that the two companies reported net income as follows:

	PACELLI COMPANY	SALEZ COMPANY
1995	$260,000	$140,000
1996	280,000	190,000

Compute consolidated net income and the noncontrolling interest in combined income for 1995 and 1996.

Exercise 10-2

Refer to the data provided in Exercise 10-1.

Required:

Prepare in general journal form the intercompany bond elimination entries required in the preparation of the December 31, 1995, December 31, 1996, and December 31, 1997, consolidated statements workpapers.

Exercise 10-3

Weber Company issued five-year, 10% bonds on January 2, 1995, for 105. Par value is $850,000. Interest is paid semiannually on June 30 and December 31. Weber Company is a 90% owned subsidiary of Fairfield Company. On December 31, 1995, Fairfield Company purchased $510,000 of Weber Company's par value bonds at 90 after the semiannual interest payment had been made. Weber Company declared dividends of $60,000 in 1995 and $80,000 in 1996. Both companies use the straight-line method to amortize bond discount and premium.

Required:

A. Compute the total gain or loss on the constructive retirement of the debt.

B. Allocate the total gain or loss between Weber Company and Fairfield Company.

C. Prepare the book entries related to the bonds made by the individual companies in 1996.

D. Assume that the two companies reported net income as follows:

	FAIRFIELD COMPANY	WEBER COMPANY
1995	$275,000	$190,000
1996	350,000	225,000

Compute consolidated net income and the noncontrolling interest in combined income for 1995 and 1996.

Exercise 10-4

Use the information relating to Weber Company and Fairfield Company in Exercise 10-3.

Required:

Prepare in general journal form the intercompany bond elimination entries for the consolidated statements workpapers prepared on December 31, 1995, December 31, 1996, and December 31, 1997.

Exercise 10-5

On January 2, 1995, Peoples, Inc. acquired an 80% interest in Schmidt Corporation for $900,000. Schmidt reported total stockholders' equity of $1,000,000 on this date. An examination of Schmidt's books revealed that book value was equal to fair value for all assets and liabilities except for inventory, which was undervalued by $60,000. All of the undervalued inventory was sold during 1995. Any excess of cost over fair value will be amortized over 10 years.

Peoples also purchased 30% of the $500,000 par value outstanding bonds of Schmidt Corporation for $140,000 on January 2, 1995. The bonds mature in 10 years, carry an 11% annual interest rate payable on June 30 and December 31, and had a carrying value of $505,000 on the date of purchase. Both companies use the straight-line method to amortize bond discounts and premiums.

Peoples reported net income of $300,000 for 1995 and paid dividends of $130,000 during 1995. Schmidt Corporation reported net income of $320,000 for 1995 and paid dividends of $90,000 during the year.

Required:

Compute the following items at December 31, 1995:

1. Carrying value of the debt.
2. Interest revenue reported by Peoples, Inc.
3. Interest expense reported by Schmidt Corporation
4. Balance in the Investment in Schmidt Bonds account.
5. Consolidated net income for 1995 using the analytical approach.
6. Noncontrolling interest in combined income for 1995.

Exercise 10-6

Wyatt Corporation, an 80% owned subsidiary, accepted a $60,000, 12%, 90-day note from a customer for services performed. On that same date, because Wyatt Corporation was in need of cash for operations, the subsidiary endorsed the note over to its parent company in exchange for $60,000. After holding the note for 30 days, the parent discounted the note with an independent bank. The discount rate was 13%. Both companies record discounted notes in a Discounted Notes Receivable account.

Required:

A. Compute the proceeds received by the parent company from discounting the note.

B. Prepare the workpaper entry, if any, needed to eliminate the note. If none is needed, explain why.

Exercise 10-7

Perez, Inc. owns 7,000 shares (70% interest) of Salata Company's $100 par value common stock. The stock was purchased for $1,250,000 on January 2, 1994, when Salata reported a common stock balance of $1,000,000, a retained earnings balance of $400,000, and other contributed capital balance of $100,000. Any difference between cost and book value interest acquired is attributable to the under- or overvalaution of land. During 1995, Salata reported net income of $80,000. Because the company was short of liquid assets, dividends have not been paid since 1990. During 1995, however, the company declared and issued a 15% stock dividend (market price of common stock on the date of issue, $160 per share). The retained earnings balance at the beginning of 1995 was $500,000.

Required:

A. Prepare the journal entries required in the books of Perez, Inc. during 1995.

B. Prepare in general journal form the workpaper entries necessary in the consolidated statements workpaper for the year ended December 31, 1995.

C. Prepare the workpaper entry to establish reciprocity to be made in the 1996 consolidated statements workpaper.

Exercise 10-8

On January 1, 1995, Pacelli Company acquired a 90% interest in Swartz Corporation for $720,000. On this date, Swartz Corporation reported common stock of $500,000 and retained earnings of $200,000. Any difference between cost and book value interest acquired is attributable to the under- or overvaluation of land.

Other information pertaining to Swartz Corporation follows:

1995 Net income	$65,000
1995 Cash dividends	90,000
1996 Net income	80,000
1996 Cash dividends	40,000

Pacelli Company uses the cost method to account for its investment in Swartz Corporation.

Required:

A. Prepare the general journal entries for 1995 and 1996 to record the receipt of the cash dividends.

B. Prepare all determinable workpaper entries that would be made in the preparation of the 1995 consolidated statements workpaper.

C. Prepare all determinable workpaper entries that would be made in the preparation of consolidated statements for 1997.

Exercise 10-9

On January 2, 1995, Pasqual Corporation purchased 80% of the outstanding common stock and 30% of the outstanding cumulative, nonparticipating, preferred stock of Sung Company for $400,000 and $70,000, respectively. At this date, Sung Company reported account balances of $400,000 in common stock, $200,000 in preferred stock, and $100,000 in retained earnings. No other contributed capital accounts exist. The difference between cost and book value of the common stock is attributable to under- or overvalued land. Dividends on the 12% cumulative preferred stock (par $10) were not paid during 1994.
Other information:

	PASQUAL CORPORATION	SUNG COMPANY
1/2/1995 Retained earnings	$45,000	$100,000
1995 Reported net income	84,600	90,000
1995 Dividends declared	25,000	50,000

Required:

A. Prepare the journal entries made by Pasqual Corporation in 1995 to account for the investments.

B. Compute the noncontrolling interest in Sung Company's net income.

C. Prepare the 1995 workpaper entries related to the foregoing investments.

Exercise 10-10

Sam's Company reported the following stockholders' equity account balances on December 31, 1995.

Preferred stock (12%, $100 par value, call price is $105)	$100,000
Common stock, $10 par value	500,000
Other contributed capital—premium on issue of common stock	160,000
Retained earnings	110,000
Total	$870,000

On December 31, 1995, Peterson, Inc. acquired 60% of Sam Company's common stock for $550,000 and 40% of its preferred stock for $55,000.

The difference between the cost of the common stock (preferred stock) and the book value interest acquired is assignable to land (other contributed capital).

Required:

Prepare in general journal form the December 31, 1995, workpaper entries to eliminate the investment in common and preferred stock for each of the following independent cases:

Case 1: The preferred stock is noncumulative and nonparticipating.

Case 2: The preferred stock is cumulative and nonparticipating, and dividends were not paid in 1994 and 1995.

Case 3: The preferred stock is noncumulative and fully participating.

Exercise 10-11

On January 1, 1995, Perez Company acquired 80% of Serrano Company's $300,000 par value common stock for $200,000 and 40% of Serrano Company's 8%, $100,000 par value preferred stock for $86,000. During 1995, Serrano Company reported net income of $80,000 and declared cash dividends of $45,000. Perez Company reported net income (including dividends from subsidiary) of $200,000 in 1995.

Required:

In each of the following independent cases, compute consolidated net income for 1995.

Case 1: The preferred stock is noncumulative and nonparticipating.

Case 2: The preferred stock is cumulative and nonparticipating. Dividends were in arrears two years as of January 1, 1995.

Case 3: The preferred stock is noncumulative and fully participating.

Case 4: The preferred stock is cumulative and fully participating. Dividends were in arrears one year as of January 1, 1995.

Problems

Problem 10-1

On January 1, 1992, Pace Corporation issued $500,000 par value, 10-year, 15% bonds. Interest is payable each June 30 and December 31. On January 1, 1995, Supra Corporation, a 90% owned subsidiary, purchased on the open market all of the parent company bonds. Both companies have a December 31 year-end. For this problem, assume the following four independent cases.

	ISSUE PRICE BY PACE CORPORATION ON JANUARY 1, 1992	PURCHASE PRICE BY SUPRA CORPORATION ON JANUARY 1, 1995
Case 1	$512,000	$514,000
Case 2	488,000	486,000
Case 3	512,000	486,000
Case 4	488,000	514,000

Required:

A. For cases 1 and 2, compute the total constructive gain or loss and the portion allocated to each company.

B. For cases 1 and 2 prepare the journal entry or entries to be made by Pace Corporation and Supra Corporation on June 30, 1995. Both companies amortize discounts and premiums each interest payment date and use the straight-line method of amortization.

C. Complete the following schedules as of December 31, 1995, after the December 31 interest payment (receipt) and amortization of discount or premium have been recorded.

	ISSUE PRICE	
PACE CORPORATION	$512,000	$488,000
Bonds payable	_____	_____
Unamortized premium (discount)	_____	_____
Carrying value of bonds	_____	_____
1995 Cash payment for interest	_____	_____
(Premium) discount amortization	_____	_____
1995 Bond interest expense	_____	_____
Increase (decrease) in net income from amortization	_____	_____

	PURCHASE PRICE	
SUPRA CORPORATION	$514,000	$486,000
Investment in Pace Corp. bonds	————	————
1995 Cash receipts for interest	————	————
(Premium) discount amortization	————	————
1995 Bond interest income	————	————
Increase (decrease) in net income from amortization	————	————

	CASE			
	1	2	3	4
Amount of constructive gain (loss) recognized by Pace Corporation	————	————	————	————
Amount of constructive gain (loss) recognized by Supra Corporation	————	————	————	————

D. For cases 1 and 2, prepare in general journal form the intercompany bond elimination entries required in the December 31, 1995, consolidated statements workpaper.

Problem 10-2

Prezo Company purchased 80% of Satz Company's common stock for $880,000 on January 2, 1995. Condensed financial information for the Prezo Company and Satz Company is given below.

Balance Sheet
December 31, 1995

	PREZO CO.	SATZ CO.
Current assets	$ 920,000	$ 580,000
Investment in Satz Company common stock	880,000	
Investment in Satz Company bonds	227,143	
Other assets	2,345,457	1,320,000
	$4,372,600	$1,900,000
Bonds payable (10%)	$ 700,000	$ 400,000
Premium on bonds payable	20,000	9,000
Other liabilities	1,434,600	141,000
Common stock	1,600,000	800,000
Retained earnings	618,000	550,000
	$4,372,600	$1,900,000

Retained Earnings Statement
For the Year Ended December 31, 1995

	PREZO CO.	SATZ CO.
1/1 Balance	$480,000	$300,000
Net income	388,000	400,000
Dividends	(250,000)	(150,000)
12/31 Balance	618,000	$550,000

Income Statement
For the Year Ended December 31, 1995

	PREZO CO.	SATZ CO.
Sales	$2,680,000	$1,860,000
Dividend income	120,000	
Other income	266,000	120,000
Total revenue	3,066,000	1,980,000
Expenses	2,678,000	1,580,000
Net income	$ 388,000	$ 400,000

On July 1, 1995, Prezo Company purchased 60% of Satz Company's bonds for $225,000. The bonds mature on December 31, 1998. Interest of 10% per annum is paid on June 30 and December 31 each year. Both companies use the straight-line method to amortize bond discounts and premiums.

Required:

A. Compute the gain or loss on the constructive retirement of the bonds allocated to each of the affiliated companies.

B. Prepare a consolidated financial statements workpaper on December 31, 1995.

C. Prepare in good form a schedule showing the calculation of consolidated net income for the year ended December 31, 1995.

Problem 10-3

On January 1, 1994, Pasta Company purchased an 80% interest in Salsa Company for $152,000. On this date, Salsa Company reported capital stock and retained earnings of $100,000 and $90,000, respectively. During 1994, Salsa Company reported net income of $30,000 and declared a cash dividend of $35,000. At the end of 1995, Salsa Company was facing a cash shortage. Rather than distributing a cash dividend to the common stockholders, the board of directors elected to issue a 30% stock dividend. Salsa Company's accountant recorded the stock dividend as follows.

Stock Dividend Declared	30,000	
Common Stock		30,000

On December 31, 1995, Pasta Company purchased on the open market bonds of Salsa Company with a par value of $100,000 for $94,000. Financial data for the two companies as of December 31, 1995, follows:

INCOME STATEMENT	PASTA COMPANY	SALSA COMPANY
Sales	$370,000	$200,000
Other revenues	15,000	2,000
	385,000	202,000
Cost of good sold	180,000	110,000
Other expenses	80,000	30,000
Net Income	$125,000	$ 62,000

RETAINED EARNINGS	PASTA COMPANY	SALSA COMPANY
1/1 Retained earnings	$ 96,000	$ 85,000
Net income	125,000	62,000
Less: Dividends declared		
Stock dividend declared	(30,000)	(30,000)
12/31 Retained earnings	$191,000	$117,000

BALANCE SHEET		
Current assets	$171,000	$169,000
Investment in Salsa Company stock	148,000	
Investment in Salsa Company bonds	94,000	
Other assets	300,000	315,000
Totals	$713,000	$484,000
Accounts payable	$ 72,000	$ 40,000
Long-term bonds payable	250,000	200,000*
Discount on bonds payable	—	(3,000)
Common stock ($10 par value)	200,000	130,000
Retained earnings	191,000	117,000
Totals	$713,000	$484,000

*8%, maturity date December 31, 1998.

Required:

A. Prepare a consolidated statements workpaper on December 31, 1995.

B. Prepare in general journal form the entry that would be made in the December 31, 1996, workpaper to establish reciprocity as of January 1, 1996.

Problem 10-4

Condensed financial information for the Prince Company and South Company follows:

Balance Sheet
December 31, 1995

	PRINCE COMPANY	SOUTH COMPANY
Current assets	$ 826,000	$ 700,000
Investment in South Company stock	1,120,000	
Investment in South Company bonds	312,000	
Other assets	1,252,000	1,400,000
Totals	$3,510,000	$2,100,000

	PRINCE COMPANY	SOUTH COMPANY
Bonds payable	$ 300,000	$ 500,000
Premium on bonds payable	20,000	40,000
Other liabilities	380,000	160,000
Common stock	2,000,000	1,000,000
Retained earnings	810,000	400,000
Totals	$3,510,000	$2,100,000

Combined Statement of Income and Retained Earnings
For the Year Ended December 31, 1995

	PRINCE COMPANY	SOUTH COMPANY
Sales	$3,000,000	$2,000,000
Equity in subsidiary income	160,000	
Other income	100,000	200,000
Total revenues	3,260,000	2,200,000
Expenses	2,800,000	2,000,000
Net income	460,000	200,000
1/1 Retained earnings balance	600,000	300,000
	1,060,000	500,000
Dividends	(250,000)	(100,000)
12/31 Retained earnings balance	$ 810,000	$ 400,000

Prince Company purchased 80% of South Company's common stock for $1,000,000 at the beginning of 1994 and uses the partial equity method to account for the investment. At the time of purchase, South Company reported a common stock balance of $1,000,000 and a retained earnings balance of $250,000.

On July 1, 1995, Prince Company purchased 60% of South Company's 10% bonds for $315,000. The bonds mature on December 31, 1997. Interest is paid on June 30 and December 31.

Required:

A. Prepare the entries made on the books of Prince Company during 1995 to record its interest in South Company and account for the bond investment.

B. Prepare a consolidated financial statements workpaper on December 31, 1995.

Problem 10-5

On January 1, 1990, Pabst Company acquired 80% of Secor Company's common stock and 30% of Secor Company's 10% preferred stock. Papst Company paid $680,000 for the common stock and $135,000 for the preferred stock. The preferred stock is cumulative and nonparticipating and has a call price of $104. On the date of acquisition, there were no dividends in arrears. On January 1, 1990, Secor Company reported the following account balances:

10% Preferred stock ($100 par value)	$ 400,000
Common stock ($10 par value)	500,000
Other contributed capital (Sale of common stock in excess of par value)	100,000
Retained Earnings	230,000
Total	$1,230,000

Condensed preclosing trial balances for the two companies at December 31, 1995 are presented below.

INCOME STATEMENT	PABST COMPANY	SECOR COMPANY
Sales	$700,000	$450,000
Expenses	(580,000)	(350,000)
Net income	$120,000	$100,000
RETAINED EARNINGS		
1/1 Balance	$507,000	$430,000
Net income	120,000	100,000
Less: Dividends declared	(100,000)	
12/31 Balance	$527,000	$530,000
BALANCE SHEET		
Current assets	$1,618,000	$ 890,000
Investment in Secor Company common stock	680,000	
Investment in Secor Company preferred stock	135,000	
Other assets	1,025,000	1,000,000
Totals	$3,458,000	$1,890,000
Liabilities	$ 931,000	$ 360,000
Preferred stock	400,000	400,000
Common stock	1,000,000	500,000
Other contributed capital	600,000	100,000
Retained earnings	527,000	530,000
Totals	$3,458,000	$1,890,000

On December 31, 1995, dividends on the preferred stock were in arrears for 1994 and 1995.

Required:

Prepare a consolidated statements workpaper for the year ended December 31, 1995. Assume that any difference between cost and book value interest acquired is attributable to an undervaluation in the land of Secor Company in the case of common stock, and any difference between the cost of preferred stock and the book value interest acquired is assignable to other contributed capital.

Problem 10-6

PAL Corporation acquired 40% of the outstanding preferred stock of Saltz, Inc. for $60,000 and 90% of that firm's outstanding common stock for $600,000 on January 1, 1994. On the date that the controlling interest was acquired, the stockholders' equity section of Saltz, Inc. was as follows.

Preferred stock—10%, cumulative, fully participating, liquidation value is equal to par value	$100,000
Common stock—$10 par value	400,000
Retained earnings	200,000
Total	$700,000

There were no dividends in arrears on January 1, 1994. For the fiscal year ended December 31, 1994, Saltz, Inc. reported net income of $130,000. No cash or stock dividends were declared by the company during 1994.

The difference between cost and the book value of the equity interest acquired in the common stock relates to the land owned by Saltz, Inc. Condensed financial information for the two companies at December 31, 1995, are presented below.

	PAL CORP.	SALTZ INC.
INCOME STATEMENT DATE		
Sales	$890,000	$750,000
Interest, dividends, and other revenues	91,000	50,000
Cost of goods sold	(500,000)	(400,000)
Selling administrative, and other expenses	(330,000)	(280,000)
Net income	$151,000	$120,000
RETAINED EARNINGS		
1/1 Balance	$560,000	$330,000
Net income	151,000	120,000
Less: Dividends declared		(90,000)
12/31 Balance	$711,000	$360,000
BALANCE SHEET		
Current assets	$ 810,000	$380,000
Investment in common stock	600,000	
Investment in preferred stock	60,000	
Other assets	1,276,000	600,000
Totals	$2,746,000	$980,000
Liabilities	$1,335,000	$120,000
Preferred stock		100,000
Common Stock	700,000	400,000
Retained earnings	711,000	360,000
Totals	$2,746,000	$980,000

Required:

A. Prepare a schedule to compute the difference between the cost of the common stock and the book value interest acquired.

B. Prepare consolidated statements workpapers for the year ended December 31, 1995.

Problem 10-7

P Company owns 80% of S Company's common stock (cost $650,000) and 20% of its preferred stock (cost $50,000). Both interests were acquired on January 1, 1993. On the date of purchase, S Company's stockholders' equity consisted of the following accounts.

Preferred stock	$200,000
Common stock	500,000
Retained earnings	160,000

The preferred stock is $25 par value, 9% cumulative, and nonparticipating. The call price is $27 per share. Dividends have been declared in all years except for 1994.

An examination of S Company's assets and liabilities revealed that their book values were equal to fair values except for the inventory and equipment.

	BOOK VALUE	FAIR VALUE
Inventory	$120,000	$150,000
Equipment (net)	560,000	640,000

The equipment had a remaining life of five years at the date of the equity purchase, and the FIFO cost flow assumption is used in costing inventory. The excess of cost over fair value, if any, is to be amortized over 40 years.

S Company sells inventory to P Company at 25% above cost. During 1994 and 1995, such sales amounted to $350,000 and $390,000, respectively. The 1994 and 1995 ending inventories of P Company included goods purchased from S Company for $77,500 and $54,000, respectively.

The companies file consolidated tax returns. Ignore deferred income taxes when assigning the difference between cost and book value.

Selected data for the 1995 December 31 fiscal year-end is given below.

	P COMPANY	S COMPANY
Net income (including dividend income and sales to affiliates)	$234,500	$100,000
1/1/95 Retained earnings	430,000	310,000
Dividends declared and paid	80,000	50,000

Required:

A. Prepare a schedule to compute the book value interest acquired for each equity investment.

B. Prepare a schedule to assign the difference between the cost of the common stock investment and the book value interest acquired.

C. Compute the following items
   (1) Dividends received during 1995 by P Company from S Company for each equity interest held.
   (2) Noncontrolling interest in 1995 combined income.
   (3) Consolidated net income for 1995.
   (4) Consolidated retained earnings on January 1, 1995.

Problem 10-8

Parson Industries purchased 80% of the common stock of Succo Company on January 1, 1988, for $300,000 when Succo Company's capital consisted of common stock of $200,000, preferred stock of $100,000, other contributed capital of $50,000, and retained earnings of $62,000.

The $100 par value preferred is 15%, cumulative and nonparticipating, and has a call price of $104 per share. Dividends on the preferred stock were not paid in 1987.

Trial balances for the parent and subsidiary for the December 31, 1995, year-end are presented below.

	PARSON INDUSTRIES	SUCCO COMPANY
INCOME STATEMENT		
Sales	$ 404,000	$300,000
Dividend income	4,000	
Cost of goods sold	(200,000)	(160,000)
Operating expenses	(36,400)	(50,000)
Income Taxes	(40,200)	(27,000)
Net Income	$ 131,400	$ 63,000
RETAINED EARNINGS		
1/1 Retained earnings	$ 157,400	$107,000
Net income	131,400	63,000
Less: dividends declared	(65,000)	(50,000)
12/31 Retained earnings	$ 223,800	$120,000
BALANCE SHEET		
Cash and receivables	$ 396,800	$205,000
Inventories	200,000	170,000
Land	300,000	120,000
Buildings and equipment	697,000	245,000
Accumulated depreciation	(100,000)	(70,000)
Investment in Succo Company	300,000	
Totals	$1,793,800	$670,000
Current liabilities	$ 370,000	$100,000
Bonds payable	400,000	100,000
Preferred stock		100,000
Common stock, $10 par value	600,000	200,000
Other contributed capital	200,000	50,000
Retained earnings	223,800	120,000
Totals	$1,793,800	$670,000

Additional information:

1. At the beginning of 1995, dividends on the preferred stock were in arrears for 1993 and 1994.
2. Succo Company owed Parson Industries $10,000 for purchases of inventory on account.

3. At the date of acquisition, the portion of the difference between cost and the book value interest acquired that was attributed to tangible assets of Succo Company was allocated as follows:

Equipment (net)	$10,000
Inventories	5,000
Land	5,000

The amount not allocated to tangible assets was allocated to goodwill (excess of cost over fair value). The equipment had a remaining life of 20 years at the date of acquisition. Succo Company uses the FIFO cost flow assumption in pricing inventory. The amount not assignable to tangible assets is to be amortized over a period of 20 years.

4. The building and equipment account of Parson Industries includes $50,000 of equipment acquired from Succo Company on July 1, 1994. When sold to Parson Industries, the asset was carried on the books of Succo Company at a cost of $100,000 and accumulated depreciation of $20,000. The asset is being depreciated by Parson Industries over a remaining life of five years. Parson Industries uses the straight-line method of depreciation.

5. The 1994 and 1995 ending inventories of Succo Company included goods purchased from Parson Industries for $15,000 and $25,000, respectively. Parson Industries sells merchandise to Succo Company at 20% above cost. During 1995, such sales amounted to $100,000.

6. The affiliates file consolidated tax returns. Ignore deferred income taxes in the assignment of the difference between cost and book value.

Required:

A. Compute the book value interest acquired by Parson Industries at the date of acquisition and allocate the difference to undervalued assets of Succo Company.

B. Prepare a consolidated statements workpaper for the year ended December 31, 1995.

C. Prepare a schedule showing the calculation of consolidated net income for the year ended December 31, 1995.

♡
Rick
♥u

11

POOLING OF INTERESTS AND ALTERNATIVE CONCEPTS OF CONSOLIDATED FINANCIAL STATEMENTS

POOLING OF INTERESTS IN A PARENT–SUBSIDIARY RELATIONSHIP

The pooling of interests method of accounting for a business combination representing a merger or consolidation was discussed and illustrated in Chapter 1. Recall that in a merger or consolidation, the assets and liabilities of the acquired company are recorded on the books of the acquiring company, and the acquired company (or companies) ceases to exist as a separate legal entity, that is, the acquired company is dissolved. But, as indicated in *APB Opinion No. 16*, dissolution of the acquired company is not a necessary condition for use of the pooling method.

> Dissolution of a combining company is not a condition for applying the pooling of interests method of accounting for a business combination. One or more combining companies may be subsidiaries of the issuing corporation after the combination is consummated if the other conditions are met.[1]

One requirement of the pooling method is that the acquiring company issue common stock for substantially all (at least 90%) of the voting common stock of the acquired company. Thus, a *stock acquisition* accomplished through an exchange of

---

[1] *Opinions of the Accounting Principles Board No. 16*, "Business Combinations" (New York: AICPA, 1970), par. 49.

voting stock for at least 90% of the voting stock of the acquired company must be accounted for as a pooling of interests if all other pooling requirements are met. This section will cover accounting and consolidation procedures followed for stock acquisitions treated as poolings of interests.

Accounting for a Pooled Subsidiary at Date of Acquisition

The discussion and illustrations in this section are based on the following preacquisition balance sheets for P Company and S Company on December 31, 1994:

	P COMPANY	S COMPANY
Cash	$100,000	$ 20,000
Other current assets	140,000	50,000
Property and equipment (net)	120,000	40,000
Land	40,000	20,000
Total assets	$400,000	$130,000
Liabilities	$ 60,000	$ 50,000
Common stock, $10 par value	40,000	50,000
Other contributed capital	200,000	10,000
Retained earnings	100,000	20,000
Total equities	$400,000	$130,000

Wholly Owned Subsidiary To illustrate the pooling method for a wholly owned subsidiary, assume that, on January 1, 1995, P Company exchanged 6,000 shares of its common stock for all the shares (5,000) of the common stock of S Company. The exchange of stock is recorded by P Company by the following entry:

Investment in S Company		80,000
Common Stock (6,000 × $10)		60,000
Retained Earnings		20,000

Where a stock acquisition is treated as a pooling and a parent–subsidiary relationship is established, the acquired stock is recorded as an investment in subsidiary on the parent company's books at an amount equal to the book value of the equity (net assets) acquired. The debit to the investment account is equal to the subsidiary's stockholders' equity acquired, 100%. The credit to common stock reflects the par value of P Company stock issued, which is $10,000 more than the par value of S Company stock acquired. Where the amount of the par or stated value of the stock issued ($60,000) exceeds the total of the par or stated value of the stock acquired ($50,000), the excess should be deducted first from the combined other contributed capital and then from combined retained earnings. Since the par value of the stock issued exceeds the par value of the stock acquired by $10,000, the excess serves to reduce S Company's other contributed capital to zero, and the entire amount of S Company's retained earnings is carried forward.

A workpaper for the preparation of a consolidated balance sheet on the date of acquisition is presented in Illustration 11-1.

Pooling Accounting
Par Value Issued Exceeds
  Par Value Acquired
Wholly Owned Subsidiary
Date of Acquisition

ILLUSTRATION 11-1
Consolidated Balance Sheet Workpaper
P Company and Subsidiary
January 1, 1995

	P COMPANY	S COMPANY	ELIMINATIONS DR.	ELIMINATIONS CR.	CONSOLIDATED BALANCES
Cash	100,000	20,000			120,000
Other Current Assets	140,000	50,000			190,000
Plant and Equipment	120,000	40,000			160,000
Land	40,000	20,000			60,000
Investment in S Company	80,000			(1) 80,000	
Total Assets	480,000	130,000			530,000
Liabilities	60,000	50,000			110,000
Common Stock					
P Company	260,000				260,000
S Company		50,000	(1) 50,000		
Other Contributed Capital					
P Company	40,000				40,000
S Company		10,000	(1) 10,000		
Retained Earnings					
P Company	120,000				120,000
S Company		20,000	(1) 20,000		
Total Equities	480,000	130,000	80,000	80,000	530,000

(1) To eliminate investment in S Company.

The workpaper investment elimination entry is:

(1) Common Stock—S Company	50,000	
Other Contributed Capital—S Company	10,000	
Retained Earnings—S Company	20,000	
Investment in S Company		80,000

In this entry, the investment account is eliminated against S Company's common stock, other contributed capital, and retained earnings.

  In recording the exchange of stock, the excess of the par value of the shares issued over the par value of the shares acquired is deducted first from **combined** other contributed capital. If combined other contributed capital is reduced to zero, retained earnings is reduced. For example, if P Company exchanged 9,000 of its shares for all of those of S Company, the following analysis and acquisition entry would be made:

Par value of P Company stock issued (9,000 × $10)	$90,000	190,000
Par value of S Company stock acquired	50,000	140,000
Increase in par value	40,000	50,000
Reduce S Company other contributed capital	(10,000)	(20,000)
Reduce P Company other contributed capital	$30,000	30,000

Investment in S Company	80,000	
Other Contributed Capital	30,000	
Common Stock (9,000 × $10)		90,000
Retained Earnings		20,000

After the appropriate eliminating entry [the same as entry (1) above] is prepared on the workpaper, consolidated stockholders' equity on the consolidated balance sheet would be reported as

Common Stock, $10 par ($200,000 + $90,000)	$290,000
Other Contributed Capital ($40,000 − $30,000)	10,000
Retained Earnings ($100,000 + $20,000)	120,000
Total	$420,000

The point at which combined retained earnings would be reduced in this case is reached when the par value of the shares issued is more than $50,000 greater than the par value of the shares acquired. For example, if P Company exchanged 11,000 shares for all the shares of S Company, the analysis and acquisition entry would be

Par value of P Company stock issued (11,000 × $10)	$110,000
Par value of S Company stock acquired	50,000
Increase in par value	60,000
Reduce S Company other contributed capital	(10,000)
Reduce P Company other contributed capital	(40,000)
Reduce S Company retained earnings recorded	$ 10,000

Investment in S Company	80,000	
Other Contributed Capital	40,000	
Common Stock (11,000 × $10)		110,000
Retained Earnings ($20,000 − $10,000)		10,000

Only $10,000 of S Company's retained earnings is carried forward to be combined with P Company's retained earnings for a total consolidated retained earnings of $110,000. If the par value of the shares issued is *more* than $70,000 greater than the par value of the shares acquired, P Company's retained earnings would be reduced in the acquisition entry.

In the event that the par value of P Company stock issued is *less* than the par value of S Company stock acquired, other contributed capital is increased. Assume, for example, that P Company gave only 4,000 of its shares for all those of S Company. In this case, P Company would make the following analysis and acquisition entry:

Par value of P Company stock issued (4,000 × $10)	$40,000
Par value of S Company stock acquired	50,000
Decrease in par value	(10,000)
Increase combined other contributed capital	$10,000

Investment in S Company	80,000	
Common Stock (4,000 × $10)		40,000
Other Contributed Capital ($10,000 + $10,000)		20,000
Retained Earnings		20,000

Partially Owned Subsidiary Acquisition of less than 100% of the subsidiary's stock does not change the basic concept of pooling. The investment account is debited on the parent company's books for the equity acquired, which is less than 100%; the common stock account is credited for the par value of the stock issued; and other equity accounts are adjusted to reflect any reclassification of equity.

Assume the preceding case except that P Company exchanges 5,000 of its shares of common stock for 95% (4,750 shares) of the common stock of S Company. P Company would make the following analysis and acquisition entry:

Par value of P Company stock issued (5,000 × $10)	$50,000
Par value of S Company stock acquired (4,750 × $10)	47,500
Increase in par value	2,500
Reduce S Company other contributed capital recorded	$(2,500)

Investment in S Company ($80,000 × .95)	76,000	
Common Stock (5,000 × $10)		50,000
Other Contributed Capital [.95($10,000) − $2,500]		7,000
Retained Earnings ($20,000 × .95)		19,000

The noncontrolling interest in S Company's other contributed capital is $500 (5% × $10,000), and the remaining $9,500 represents P Company's interest. Since the par value of the stock given ($50,000) exceeds the par value of the stock acquired ($47,500), the $2,500 increase in par value serves to reduce P Company's interest to $7,000 ($9,500 − $2,500). P Company's share of S Company's reported retained earnings (95% × $20,000) is carried forward. A date of acquisition workpaper in this case is presented in Illustration 11-2.

Elimination of 95% of S Company's equity against the investment account is accomplished by the following workpaper entry:

(1) Common Stock—S Company	47,500	
Other Contributed Capital—S Company	9,500	
Retained Earnings—S Company	19,000	
Investment in S Company		76,000

Accounting for a Pooled Subsidiary after Acquisition

Just as two methods—the cost method and the partial equity method—may be used to account for an investment after acquisition under the purchase approach, two methods—the book value method and the partial equity method—may be used to account for an investment after acquisition under the pooling approach.

Pooling Accounting
Par Value Issued Exceeds
  Par Value Acquired
95% Owned Subsidiary
Date of Acquisition

ILLUSTRATION 11-2
Consolidated Balance Sheet Workpaper
P Company and Subsidiary
January 1, 1995

	P COMPANY	S COMPANY	ELIMINATIONS DR.	ELIMINATIONS CR.	NONCONTROLLING INTEREST	CONSOLIDATED BALANCES
Cash	100,000	20,000				120,000
Other Current Assets	140,000	50,000				190,000
Plant and Equipment	120,000	40,000				160,000
Land	40,000	20,000				60,000
Investment in S Company	76,000			(1) 76,000		
Total Assets	476,000	130,000				530,000
Liabilities	60,000	50,000				110,000
Common Stock						
P Company	250,000					250,000
S Company		50,000	(1) 47,500		2,500	
Other Contributed Capital						
P Company	47,000					47,000
S Company		10,000	(1) 9,500		500	
Retained Earnings						
P Company	119,000					119,000
S Company		20,000	(1) 19,000		1,000	
Noncontrolling Interest					4,000	4,000
Total Equities	476,000	130,000	76,000	76,000		530,000

(1) To eliminate investment in S Company.

The Book Value Method The book value method is used to record a pooled subsidiary on the books of the parent company. The method is applied in the same way as the cost method under the purchase approach, except that the investment is recorded initially at an amount equal to the book value of the subsidiary equity acquired, as illustrated earlier. Subsidiary earnings are not recorded until dividends are declared, at which time the parent company recognizes dividend income. Thus, the investment account remains at an amount equal to the initial book value of the subsidiary equity acquired unless the parent company acquires additional subsidiary shares or disposes of a part of its investment.

To illustrate, assume that, on January 1, 1995, P Company issued 8,100 of its $10 par value common shares for 90% (9,000 shares) of the outstanding common stock of S Company when S Company's stockholders' equity was as follows:

Common stock, $10 par value	$100,000
Other contributed capital	50,000
Retained earnings	40,000
Total	$190,000

P Company made the following analysis and book entry to record its investment in S Company:

Par value of P Company stock issued (8,100 × $10)	$81,000
Par value of S Company stock acquired (9,000 × $10)	90,000
Decrease in par value	(9,000)
Increase combined other contributed capital	$ 9,000

Investment in S Company .9($190,000)	171,000	
Common Stock (8,100 × $10)		81,000
Other Contributed Capital [.9($50,000) + $9,000]		54,000
Retained Earnings .9($40,000)		36,000

Because the par value of S Company's stock acquired ($90,000) exceeds the par value of P Company's stock issued ($81,000) by $9,000, the $9,000 is recorded as an increase in other contributed capital.

Assume further that during 1995, S Company reported earnings of $30,000 and declared a $15,000 dividend. Trial balances for P and S Companies on December 31, 1996, are presented in Illustration 11-3. (Note that S Company's retained earnings on January 1, 1996 are $55,000, reflecting the $15,000 excess of earnings over dividends during 1995. Note also that P Company recognized dividend income of $9,000 in 1996.)

ILLUSTRATION 11-3
Trial Balances for P Company and S Company
December 31, 1996

	P COMPANY		S COMPANY	
	DR.	CR.	DR.	CR.
Cash	$ 261,500		$ 36,000	
Accounts Receivable (net)	68,000		32,000	
Inventory, 12/31	82,000		39,000	
Investment in S Company	171,000			
Property and Equipment (net)	220,000		185,000	
Other Assets	38,000		18,000	
Accounts Payable		$ 52,000		$ 30,000
Other Liabilities		70,000		45,000
Common Stock, $10 par value		281,000		100,000
Other Contributed Capital		94,000		50,000
1/1 Retained Earnings		294,500		55,000
Dividends Declared	30,000		10,000	
Sales		350,000		190,000
Dividend Income		9,000		
Cost of Goods Sold	200,000		94,000	
Other Expense	80,000		56,000	
	$1,150,500	$1,150,500	$470,000	$470,000

A workpaper for the preparation of consolidated financial statements on December 31, 1996, is presented in Illustration 11-4.

The method of preparing consolidated workpapers for years subsequent to acquisition under the book value method is similar to the cost method. A workpaper entry is made to establish reciprocity for the parent's share of the undistributed earnings of the subsidiary from the date of acquisition (which is always the beginning of the year of acquisition under pooling) to the beginning of the current year as follows:

(1) Investment in S Company	13,500	
1/1 Retained Earnings—P Company		13,500
.9($30,000 − $15,000)		

After reciprocity is established, intercompany dividends and the parent's share of the subsidiary's equity are eliminated:

(2) Dividend Income	9,000	
Dividends Declared—S Company		9,000
(3) 1/1 Retained Earnings—S Company	49,500	
Common Stock—S Company	90,000	
Other Contributed Capital—S Company	45,000	
Investment in S Company		184,500

Workpaper balances are then either combined in the consolidated column or identified as part of the noncontrolling interest.

The Partial Equity Method   Under the partial equity method, the investment is recorded initially at an amount equal to the book value of subsidiary stockholders' equity acquired. Accounting after acquisition follows the same procedures as those used under the partial equity method with a purchase approach, with the parent company recording its share of subsidiary earnings as reported by the subsidiary and treating dividends received as reductions in the investment account.

Interim Acquisition Under the Pooling Method

Under the pooling of interests method, the revenue and expense accounts of the subsidiary are combined with those of the parent company for the entire year in which the pooling takes place. As a result, the investment is recorded as if the pooling had taken place at the beginning of the year of acquisition. Because consolidated net income includes the parent's share of the subsidiary's net income for the entire year in which the acquisition occurs, a deduction for "net income purchased," which was required under the purchase method, is not needed. (See Chapter 3.)

Pooling Accounting
Book Value Method
90% Owned Subsidiary
After Year of Acquisition

ILLUSTRATION 11-4
Consolidated Statements Workpaper
P Company and Subsidiary
For the Year Ended December 31, 1996

	P COMPANY	S COMPANY	ELIMINATIONS DR.	ELIMINATIONS CR.	NONCONTROLLING INTEREST	CONSOLIDATED BALANCES
INCOME STATEMENT						
Sales	350,000	190,000				540,000
Dividend Income	9,000		(2) 9,000			
Total Revenue	359,000	190,000				540,000
Cost of Goods Sold	200,000	94,000				294,000
Other Expense	80,000	56,000				136,000
Total Cost and Expense	280,000	150,000				430,000
Net/Combined Income	79,000	40,000				110,000
Noncontrolling Interest in Income .10($40,000)					4,000	(4,000)
Net Income to Retained Earnings	79,000	40,000	9,000	–0–	4,000	106,000
RETAINED EARNINGS STATEMENT						
1/1 Retained Earnings						
P Company	294,500			(1) 13,500		308,000
S Company		55,000	(3) 49,500		5,500	
Net Income from Above	79,000	40,000	9,000	–0–	4,000	106,000
Dividends Declared						
P Company	(30,000)					(30,000)
S Company		(10,000)		(2) 9,000	(1,000)	
12/31 Retained Earnings to Balance Sheet	343,500	85,000	58,500	22,500	8,500	384,000
BALANCE SHEET						
Cash	261,500	36,000				297,500
Accounts Receivable (net)	68,000	32,000				100,000
Inventory, 12/31	82,000	39,000				121,000
Investment in S Company	171,000		(1) 13,500	(3) 184,500		
Property and Equipment (net)	220,000	185,000				405,000
Other Assets	38,000	18,000				56,000
Total	840,500	310,000				979,500
Accounts Payable	52,000	30,000				82,000
Other Liabilities	70,000	45,000				115,000
Common Stock						
P Company	281,000					281,000
S Company		100,000	(3) 90,000		10,000	
Other Contributed Capital						
P Company	94,000					94,000
S Company		50,000	(3) 45,000		5,000	
Retained Earnings from Above	343,500	85,000	58,500	22,500	8,500	384,000
Noncontrolling Interest in Net Assets					23,500	23,500
Total	840,500	310,000	207,000	207,000		979,500

(1) To establish reciprocity as of 1/1/96 [($55,000 − $40,000) × .9].
(2) To eliminate intercompany dividends.
(3) To eliminate investment in S Company.

Unrealized Profits on Intercompany Sales of Assets

The practice of recognizing in the consolidated financial statements only profits resulting from the sale of goods and services to parties outside the affiliated group is the same under pooling of interests as under purchase accounting. Therefore, workpaper entries for the elimination of unrealized profit are the same whether the consolidation is accounted for as a purchase or as a pooling of interests.

Acquisition of a Noncontrolling Interest

Accounting standards specifically provide that the acquisition of some or all of the shares held by noncontrolling stockholders of a subsidiary should be accounted for by the purchase method, rather than by the pooling of interests method. This requirement holds whether the shares are acquired by the parent company, the subsidiary itself, or another affiliate.[2] This provision is consistent with the basic notion that a pooling should take place in a single transaction, but it appears to be somewhat inconsistent with the prohibition of the use of the "part-purchase, part-pooling" approach discussed in Chapter 1.

ALTERNATIVE CONCEPTS OF CONSOLIDATED FINANCIAL STATEMENTS

In previous chapters, we have presented the principles currently followed in the preparation of consolidated financial statements. Current practice essentially reflects a compromise between two general concepts of consolidation given various designations in the accounting literature. For our purposes, we will refer to them as the *parent company concept* and the *economic unit concept* (sometimes called the *entity concept.*) The concepts are described by the Financial Accounting Standards Board as follows:[3]

Parent Company Concept:

> The parent company concept emphasizes the interests of the parent's shareholders. As a result, the consolidated financial statements reflect those stockholder interests in the parent itself, plus their undivided interests in the net assets of the parent's subsidiaries. The consolidated balance sheet is essentially a modification of the parent's balance sheet with the assets and liabilities of all subsidiaries substituted for the parent's investment in subsidiaries. The stockholders' equity of the parent company is also the stockholders' equity of the consolidated entity. Similarly, the consolidated income statement is essentially a modification of the parent's income statement with the revenues, expenses, gains, and losses of subsidiaries substituted for the parent's income from investment in subsidiaries. These multiline substitutions for single lines in the parent's balance sheet and income statement are intended to make the parent's financial statements more informative about the parent's total ownership holdings.

---

[2] *Opinions of the Accounting Principles Board No. 16,* op. cit., par. 43.

[3] *FASB Discussion Memorandum,* "Consolidation Policy and Procedures" (Norwalk, CT: FASB, September 10, 1991), pars. 63 and 64.

Economic Unit Concept:

The economic unit concept emphasizes control of the whole by a single management. As a result, under this concept, consolidated financial statements are intended to provide information about a group of legal entities—a parent company and its subsidiaries—operating as a single unit. The assets, liabilities, revenues, expenses, gains, and losses of the various component entities are the assets, liabilities, revenues, expenses, gains, and losses of the consolidated entity. Unless all subsidiaries are wholly owned, the business enterprise's proprietary interest (assets less liabilities) is divided into the controlling interest (stockholders or other owners of the parent company) and one or more noncontrolling interests in subsidiaries. Both the controlling and the noncontrolling interests are part of the proprietary group of the consolidated entity, even though the noncontrolling stockholders' ownership interests relate only to the affiliates whose shares they own.

The parent company concept represents the view that the primary purpose of consolidated financial statements is to provide information relevant to the controlling stockholders. The parent company effectively controls the assets and operations of the subsidiary. Noncontrolling stockholders do not exercise any ownership control over the subsidiary company or the parent company. Thus, the parent company concept places emphasis on the needs of the controlling stockholders, and the noncontrolling interest is essentially relegated to the position of a claim against the consolidated entity.

The economic unit concept represents the view that the affiliated companies are a separate, identifiable economic entity. Meaningful evaluation by any interested party of the financial position and results of operations of the economic entity is possible only if the individual assets, liabilities, revenues, and expenses of the affiliated companies making up the economic entity are combined. Strictly interpreted, the economic unit concept denies the primacy of the interest of the parent company stockholders and treats both controlling and noncontrolling stockholders as contributors to the economic unit's capital.

Differences between the concepts are relevant only to less than wholly owned subsidiaries; they center around conflicting views concerning answers to three basic questions:

1. What is the nature of a noncontrolling interest?
2. What income figure constitutes consolidated net income?
3. What values should be reported in the consolidated balance sheet?

An additional issue involving all these questions concerns the percentage (total or partial) of unrealized intercompany profit to be eliminated in the determination of consolidated balances.

Noncontrolling Interest

Under the economic unit concept, a noncontrolling interest is a part of the ownership equity in the entire economic unit. Thus, a noncontrolling interest is of the same general nature and is accounted for in essentially the same way as the controlling interest. Under the parent company concept, the nature and classification of a noncontrolling interest are unclear. The parent company concept views the consolidated financial statements as those of the parent company. From that perspective, the noncontrolling interest is not a liability because the parent does not have a present obligation to pay cash or release other assets. Nor is it a component of owners' equity since the noncontrolling investors in a subsidiary do not have an ownership interest in the subsidiary's parent. Consequently, the parent company concept generally reports the noncontrolling interest below liabilities but above stockholders' equity in the consolidated balance sheet.

Consolidated Net Income

Under the *parent company* concept, consolidated net income consists of the realized combined income of the parent company and its subsidiaries after deducting noncontrolling interest in income; that is, the noncontrolling interest in income is deducted as an expense item in determining consolidated net income. Identification of noncontrolling interest in income as an expense is based on the theory that the noncontrolling interest in net assets represents a liability, and noncontrolling interest in income represents an accrued addition to that liability for the use of assets "borrowed" from the noncontrolling stockholders. Dividends distributed by the subsidiary to the noncontrolling stockholders reflect a decrease in the liability to them. This view emphasizes that the parent company stockholders are directly interested in their share of the results of operations as a measure of earnings in relation to their investment and dividend expectations.

Under the *economic unit* concept, consolidated net income consists of the total realized combined income of the parent company and its subsidiaries. The total combined income is then allocated proportionately to the noncontrolling interest and the controlling interest. Noncontrolling interest in income is considered an allocated portion of consolidated net income, rather than an element in the determination of consolidated net income. The concept emphasizes the view that the consolidated financial statements represent those of a single economic unit with several classes of stockholder interest. Thus, noncontrolling interest in net assets is considered a separate element of stockholders' equity, and the noncontrolling interest in net income reflects the share of consolidated net income allocated to the noncontrolling stockholders.

Consolidated Balance Sheet Values

As indicated in Chapter 4, in the case of less than wholly owned subsidiaries, the question arises as to whether to value the subsidiary assets and liabilities at the *total* fair value implied by the price paid for the controlling interest, or at their book value adjusted only for the excess of cost over book value paid by the parent company. For example, assume that P Company acquires a 60% interest in S Company for $960,000 when the book value of the net assets and of the stockholders' equity of S Company is $1,000,000. The implied fair value of the net assets of S Company is $1,600,000 ($960,000 ÷ .6), and the difference between the implied fair value and the book value is $600,000 ($1,600,000 − $1,000,000). For presentation in the consolidated financial statements, should the net assets of S Company be written up by $600,000 or by 60% of $600,000?

Application of the *parent company* concept in this situation restricts the write-up of the net assets of S Company to $360,000 (.6 × $600,000) on the theory that the write-up should be restricted to the amount actually paid by P Company in excess of the book value of the interest it acquires [$960,000 − (.6 × $1,000,000) = $360,000]. In other words, the value assigned to the net assets should not exceed cost to the parent company. Thus, the net assets of the subsidiary are included in the consolidated financial statements at their book value ($1,000,000) plus *the parent company's share* of the difference between fair value and book value (.6 × $600,000 = $360,000), or at a total of $1,360,000 on the date of acquisition. Noncontrolling interest is reported at its percentage interest in the *reported book value* of the net assets of S Company, or $400,000 (.4 × $1,000,000).

Application of the *economic unit* concept results in a write-up of the net assets of S Company in the consolidated statements workpaper by $600,000 to $1,600,000 on the theory that the consolidated financial statements should reflect 100% of the net asset values of the affiliated companies. On the date of acquisition, the net assets of the subsidiary are included in the consolidated financial statements at their book value ($1,000,000) plus *the entire difference* between their fair value and their book value ($600,000), or a total of $1,600,000. Noncontrolling interest is reported at its percentage interest in the *fair value* of the net assets of S Company, or $640,000 (.4 × $1,600,000).

Regardless of the concept followed, the controlling interest in the net assets of the subsidiary reported in the consolidated financial statements is the same and is equal to P Company's cost, as demonstrated here:

	PARENT COMPANY CONCEPT	ECONOMIC UNIT CONCEPT
Net assets of S Company included in consolidation	$1,360,000	$1,600,000
Less noncontrolling interest	400,000	640,000
Controlling interest (cost)	$ 960,000	$ 960,000

Elimination of Unrealized Intercompany Profit

As discussed in Chapter 5, there are two alternative points of view as to the amount of intercompany profit that should be considered unrealized in the determination of consolidated income. The elimination methods associated with these two points of view are generally referred to as *total* (100%) *elimination* and *partial elimination.*

Proponents of total elimination regard all the intercompany profit associated with assets remaining in the affiliated group to be unrealized. Proponents of partial elimination regard only the parent company's share of the profit recognized by the selling affiliate to be unrealized. Under total elimination, the entire amount of unconfirmed intercompany profit is eliminated from combined income and the related asset balance. Under partial elimination, only the parent company's share of the unconfirmed intercompany profit recognized by the selling affiliate is eliminated.

In the case of all downstream sales and in the case of upstream or horizontal sales *where the selling affiliate is a wholly owned subsidiary*, the amount of intercompany profit eliminated is the same under total elimination and partial elimination. In those cases, 100% of the intercompany profit is eliminated, since the parent company's interest in the profits of the selling affiliate (the parent company itself or its wholly owned subsidiary) is 100%. The two approaches give different results, however, in the case of upstream or horizontal sales *where the selling affiliate is a less than wholly owned subsidiary.*

Partial elimination is consistent with the *parent company* concept. Because the noncontrolling interest is viewed as a claim or liability of the consolidated entity under the parent company concept, any intercompany profit in an affiliate company's assets acquired from a partially owned subsidiary is considered to be realized to the extent of the noncontrolling stockholders' interest in the selling subsidiary. Thus, under the parent company view, the noncontrolling interest is deemed to be entitled to its share of the reported profit of the subsidiary regardless of whether the profit results from sales to affiliates or to third parties.

Total elimination is consistent with the *economic unit* concept. Because the noncontrolling interest is considered to be a part of consolidated stockholders' equity under the economic unit concept, the noncontrolling stockholders are not considered to be outside parties. Thus, their share of intercompany profit in an affiliate company's assets acquired from a partially owned subsidiary is considered to be unrealized.

As an illustration of the difference between the parent company concept and the economic unit concept, assume that, on January 1, 1995, P Company acquired a 60% interest in S Company for $960,000 when the book value of the net assets of S Company was $1,000,000. P Company records its investment in S Company using the cost method. In addition, assume the following:

1. The book values and the fair values of individual assets and liabilities of S Company on the date of acquisition are the same, except for the fair value of a depreciable asset with a remaining life of 20 years, which is $600,000 greater than its book value.

2. Intercompany sales from S Company to P Company during 1995 amount to $1,000,000, on which S Company recognized a gross profit of $300,000, or 30%.

3. On December 31, 1995, P Company has on hand goods it purchased from S Company for $500,000.

4. Income tax consequences are ignored.

5. S Company declared and paid a $40,000 dividend in 1995.

6. S Company reported net income of $200,000 for 1995.

Entries on the books of P Company during 1995 are:

Investment in S Company	960,000	
Cash		960,000
To record purchase of a 60% interest in S Company.		
Cash	24,000	
Dividend income		24,000
To record receipt of dividends (.6 × $40,000).		

Book entries made to account for an investment are not affected by the concepts (parent company or economic unit) used in the preparation of consolidated financial statements. The differences between the parent company concept and the economic unit concept are reflected by different workpaper elimination entries. The application of the parent company concept and the economic unit concept in the preparation of consolidated financial statements workpapers is presented in Illustration 11-5 and Illustration 11-6, respectively. The effects of the two methods on consolidated balances are compared in Illustration 11-7. The workpaper entries in Illustration 11-5 and 11-6 are presented here in general journal form.

	PARENT COMPANY CONCEPT ILLUSTRATION 11-5		ECONOMIC UNIT CONCEPT ILLUSTRATION 11-6	
(1) Sales	1,000,000		1,000,000	
Cost of Goods Sold		1,000,000		1,000,000
To eliminate intercompany sales.				
(2) Cost of Goods Sold	90,000		15,000	
Inventory, 12/31		90,000		150,000
To eliminate unrealized intercompany profit in ending inventory.				
(3) Dividend Income	24,000		24,000	
Dividends Declared		24,000		24,000
To eliminate intercompany dividends.				
(4) Capital Stock—S Company	420,000		420,000	
Retained Earnings—S Company	180,000		180,000	
Difference between Cost				
and Book Value	360,000		360,000	
Investment in S Company		960,000		960,000
To eliminate investment account.				
(5) Property, Plant, and Equipment	360,000		600,000	
Difference between Cost				
and Book Value		360,000		360,000
Noncontrolling Interest		–0–		240,000
To assign difference between cost and book value (Parent Company), and to write up assets to their fair value (Economic Unit).				
(6) Other Expenses	18,000		30,000	
Property, Plant, and Equipment		18,000		30,000
To recognize depreciation on difference between cost and book value (Parent Company) or fair value (Economic Unit)				

A comparison of the consolidated balances presented in Illustration 11-7 demonstrates that the concept followed in the preparation of consolidated financial statements has no effect on the amount of consolidated net income. Application of the economic unit concept decreases the amount of combined income and the amount of noncontrolling interest in combined income by the same amount, $72,000. In a similar manner, application of the economic unit concept increases combined net assets and noncontrolling interest in combined net assets by the same amount, $168,000, on the consolidated balance sheet. Thus, the noncontrolling interest in combined net assets is unaffected. Note also that, because consolidated net income is unaffected by the concept followed, consolidated retained earnings is also unaffected.

Cost Method
60% Owned Subsidiary
Parent Company Concept

ILLUSTRATION 11-5
P Company and Subsidiary
Consolidated Statements Workpaper
For the Year Ended December 31, 1995

INCOME STATEMENT	P COMPANY	S COMPANY	ELIMINATIONS DR.	ELIMINATIONS CR.	NON-CONTROLLING INTEREST	CONSOLIDATED BALANCES
Sales	3,400,000	2,000,000	(1) 1,000,000			4,400,000
Cost of Goods Sold	2,380,000	1,400,000	(2) 90,000	(1) 1,000,000		2,870,000
Gross Profit	1,020,000	600,000				1,530,000
Other Expense	(670,000)	(400,000)	(6) 18,000			(1,088,000)
Dividend Income	24,000		(3) 24,000			
Net/Combined Income	374,000	200,000				442,000
Noncontrolling Interest in Income .4($200,000)					80,000	(80,000)
Net Income to Retained Earnings	374,000	200,000	1,132,000	1,000,000	80,000	362,000
RETAINED EARNINGS STATEMENT						
1/1 Retained Earnings						
P Company	768,000					768,000
S Company		300,000	(4) 180,000		120,000	
Net Income from Above	374,000	200,000	1,132,000	1,000,000	80,000	362,000
Dividends Declared	—0—	(40,000)		(3) 24,000	(16,000)	
12/31 Retained Earnings to the Balance Sheet	1,142,000	460,000	1,312,000	1,024,000	184,000	1,130,000
BALANCE SHEET						
Inventory	510,000	260,000		(2) 90,000		680,000
Investment in S Company	960,000			(4) 960,000		
Property, Plant, and Equipment	2,000,000	1,000,000	(5) 360,000	(6) 18,000		3,342,000
Other Assets	172,000	60,000				232,000
Difference Between Cost and Book Value			(4) 360,000	(5) 360,000		
Total	3,642,000	1,320,000				4,254,000
Liabilities	500,000	160,000				660,000
Capital Stock						
P Company	2,000,000					2,000,000
S Company		700,000	(4) 420,000		280,000	
Retained Earnings from above	1,142,000	460,000	1,312,000	1,024,000	184,000	1,130,000
Noncontrolling Interest in Net Assets					464,000	464,000
Total	3,624,000	1,320,000	2,452,000	2,452,000		4,254,000

(1) To eliminate intercompany sales.
(2) To eliminate unrealized intercompany profit in ending inventory.
(3) To eliminate intercompany dividends.
(4) To eliminate the investment account.
(5) To assign difference between cost and book value to depreciable assets.
(6) To recognize depreciation on the difference between cost and book value.

Cost Method
60% Owned Subsidiary
Economic Unit Concept

ILLUSTRATION 11-6
P Company and Subsidiary
Consolidated Statements Workpaper
For the Year Ended December 31, 1995

INCOME STATEMENT	P COMPANY	S COMPANY	ELIMINATIONS DR.	ELIMINATIONS CR.	NON-CONTROLLING INTEREST	CONSOLIDATED BALANCES
Sales	3,400,000	2,000,000	(1) 1,000,000			4,400,000
Cost of Goods Sold	2,380,000	1,400,000	(2) 150,000	(1) 1,000,000		2,930,000
Gross Profit	1,020,000	600,000				1,470,000
Other Expense	(670,000)	(400,000)	(6) 30,000			(1,100,000)
Dividend Income	24,000		(3) 24,000			
Net/Combined Income	374,000	200,000				370,000
Noncontrolling Interest in Income .4($200,000 − $150,000 − $30,000)					8,000	(8,000)
Net Income to Retained Earnings	374,000	200,000	1,204,000	1,000,000	8,000	362,000
RETAINED EARNINGS STATEMENT						
1/1 Retained Earnings						
P Company	768,000					768,000
S Company		300,000	(4) 180,000		120,000	
Net Income from Above	374,000	200,000	1,204,000	1,000,000	8,000	362,000
Dividends Declared	−0−	(40,000)		(3) 24,000	(16,000)	
12/31 Retained Earnings to the Balance Sheet	1,142,000	460,000	1,384,000	1,024,000	112,000	1,130,000
BALANCE SHEET						
Inventory	510,000	260,000		(2) 150,000		620,000
Investment in S Company	960,000			(4) 960,000		
Property, Plant, and Equipment	2,000,000	1,000,000	(5) 600,000	(6) 30,000		3,570,000
Other Assets	172,000	60,000				232,000
Difference Between Cost and Book Value			(4) 360,000	(5) 360,000		
Total	3,642,000	1,320,000				4,422,000
Liabilities	500,000	160,000				660,000
Capital Stock						
P Company	2,000,000					2,000,000
S Company		700,000	(4) 420,000		280,000	
Retained Earnings from above	1,142,000	460,000	1,384,000	1,024,000	112,000	1,130,000
Noncontrolling Interest in Net Assets				(5) 240,000	392,000	632,000
Total	3,642,000	1,320,000	2,764,000	2,764,000		4,422,000

(1) To eliminate intercompany sales.
(2) To eliminate unrealized intercompany profit in ending inventory.
(3) To eliminate intercompany dividends.
(4) To eliminate the investment account.
(5) To write up depreciable assets to reflect fair values implied by investment cost.
(6) To depreciate the write-up of depreciable assets.

ILLUSTRATION 11-7
Comparison of Consolidated Financial Statements
Parent Company Concept vs. Economic Unit Concept

	(000 OMITTED)		
	PARENT COMPANY CONCEPT	ECONOMIC UNIT CONCEPT	
CONSOLIDATED INCOME STATEMENT	(ILLUSTRATION 11-5)	(ILLUSTRATION 11-6)	DIFFERENCE
Sales	$4,400	$4,400	$–0–
Cost of Goods Sold	2,870	2,930	60
Gross Profit	1,530	1,470	60
Other Expense	1,088	1,100	12
Combined Income	442	370	72
Less: Noncontrolling Interest	(80)	(8)	(72)
Net Income	$ 362	$ 362	$–0–
CONSOLIDATED BALANCE SHEET			
Inventory	$ 680	$ 620	$ (60)
Property, Plant and Equipment	3,342	3,570	228
Other Assets	232	232	–0–
Total	$4,254	$4,422	$168
Liabilities	$ 660	$ 660	$–0–
Noncontrolling Interest	464	632	168
Capital Stock	2,000	2,000	–0–
Retained Earnings	1,130	1,130	–0–
Total	$4,254	$4,422	$168

Current Practice

Current practice follows neither the parent company nor the economic unit concept entirely. The differences in practice relate primarily to the classification of noncontrolling interest and the total elimination of unrealized intercompany profits in assets acquired from an affiliate. Current practice views noncontrolling interest in income neither as an expense nor as an allocation of consolidated net income, but as a special equity interest in the consolidated entity's combined income that must be recognized when all the earnings of a less than wholly owned subsidiary are combined with the earnings of the parent company. Noncontrolling interest in net assets is viewed neither as a liability nor as stockholders' equity. Rather, it is viewed as a special interest in the combined net assets that must be recognized when all the assets and liabilities of a less than wholly owned subsidiary are combined with those of the parent company.

Current accounting standards require the total elimination of unrealized intercompany profit in assets acquired from affiliated companies, regardless of the percentage of ownership. This procedure is basically consistent with the economic unit concept view, as discussed earlier. The primary issue, however, in the elimination of intercompany profits is not whether the economic unit concept or parent company concept should prevail, but that of compliance with the cost principle in accounting that the reported value of assets should not exceed cost to the reporting entity. Total elimination of unrealized intercompany profits complies with this principle by reporting consolidated balances as if intercompany transactions between consolidated affiliates had never occurred.

Author's View

We believe the economic unit concept more clearly meets the primary objective of consolidated financial statements, which is to present to the stockholders and creditors of the parent company the financial condition and results of operations of a parent company and its subsidiaries as if they were a single company. Both the parent company concept and current practice include, in the consolidated balance sheet, the parent company's share of the *fair value* of S Company's net assets, but the noncontrolling interest's share of the *book value* of those net assets. We believe that users view the consolidated financial statements as those of a single economic unit. Consequently, for consistency purposes, the entire fair value of the subsidiary's net assets, as well as the effects of the use of those net assets, should be included in the consolidated financial statements.

Questions

1. Describe the accounting treatment of a difference between the par value of common stock issued and the par value of common stock acquired in a pooling of interests if:
   (a) The par value of the common stock issued exceeds the par value of the common stock acquired.
   (b) The par value of the common stock acquired exceeds the par value of the common stock issued.

2. In general terms, how does the balance in a parent company's retained earnings account differ after a subsidiary is acquired through a pooling of interests from the balance in the same account after a subsidiary is acquired through a purchase?

3. How are the preacquisition revenue and expense items of a subsidiary acquired during a fiscal period treated under the pooling of interests method?

4. Identify and briefly describe the alternatives for accounting for a subsidiary on the books of a parent company subsequent to acquisition under the pooling of interests method as explained in this chapter.

5. Describe the difference between the economic unit concept and parent company concept approaches to the reporting of subsidiary assets and liabilities in the consolidated financial statements on the date of acquisition.

6. What arguments might be used to support partial elimination as opposed to 100% elimination of intercompany profit in the preparation of consolidated financial statements?

7. What are the effects on the consolidated balance sheet if the partial elimination method, rather than the 100% elimination method, is used in the preparation of consolidated financial statements? Be specific.

8. Contrast the consolidation effects of the parent company concept and the economic unit concept in terms of:
   (a) The treatment of noncontrolling interests.
   (b) The elimination of intercompany profit.
   (c) The valuation of subsidiary net assets in the consolidated financial statements.
   (d) The definition of consolidated net income.

9. Under the economic unit concept, the net assets of the subsidiary are included in the consolidated financial statements at the total fair value that is implied by the price paid by the parent company for its controlling interest. What practical or conceptual problems do you see in this approach to valuation?

10. Compare the effects of partial elimination and 100% elimination of unrealized intercompany profit on the determination of:
    (a) Combined income.
    (b) Noncontrolling interest in combined income.
    (c) Consolidated net income.
    (d) Consolidated net assets.
    (e) Noncontrolling interest in consolidated net assets.
    (f) Controlling interest in consolidated net assets.

Exercises

Exercise 11-1

Page Company intends to issue common stock in exchange for the common stock of Sime Company. Four possibilities follow:

				SIME COMPANY EQUITY BALANCES	
	PERCENT	PAGE		OTHER	
	OF	SHARES	COMMON	CONTRIBUTED	RETAINED
CASE	OWNERSHIP	ISSUED	STOCK	CAPITAL	EARNINGS
a.	100%	6,000	$200,000	$110,000	$140,000
b.	100%	10,500	200,000	120,000	140,000
c.	90%	7,500	200,000	90,000	30,000
d.	95%	6,000	200,000	60,000	(35,000)

Page Company common stock is $40 par value; Page has total other contributed capital of $50,000.

Required:

Assuming the use of pooling of interests accounting, prepare in general journal form for each case (1) the investment acquisition entry, and (2) the workpaper entry to eliminate the investment account in the preparation of a consolidated balance sheet workpaper on the date of acquisition.

Exercise 11-2

On February 1, 1995, Paag Company acquired 100% of the outstanding common stock of Santee Company in a pooling of interests. Paag Company exchanged 19,000 shares of its $10 par value common stock with a market value of $20 per share for all Santee Company's common stock. Immediately before the acquisition, the two companies had the following balance sheets:

	PAAG COMPANY	SANTEE COMPANY
Current assets	$ 386,500	$106,200
Property, plant, and equipment	704,000	108,000
Total assets	$1,090,500	$214,200
Liabilities	$ 192,500	$ 36,000
Common stock, $10 par	400,000	
Common stock, $12 par		140,000
Other contributed capital	250,000	20,000
Retained earnings	248,000	18,200
Total equities	$1,090,500	$214,200

Required:

A. Prepare the entry on the books of Paag Company to record the exchange of shares.

B. Prepare a consolidated balance sheet workpaper immediately after the exchange of shares.

Exercise 11-3

Pack and Sims companies had the following balance sheets just before a pooling of interests:

	PACK	SIMS
Current assets	$346,000	$122,000
Property, plant, and equipment	589,000	244,000
Total assets	$935,000	$366,000
Liabilities	$197,000	$ 82,000
Common stock, $4 par	500,000	
Common stock, $2 par		90,000
Other contributed capital	120,000	83,000
Retained earnings	118,000	111,000
Total equities	$935,000	$366,000

Pack Company will exchange shares of its authorized but unissued stock for the outstanding shares of Sims Company.

Required:

Record the exchange of shares on the books of Pack Company for each of the following cases:

CASE	PACK SHARES ISSUED	SIMS SHARES ACQUIRED
a.	24,000	45,000
b.	22,500	45,000
c.	27,000	40,500
d.	50,000	40,500

Exercise 11-4

On February 1, 1995, Pogue Company issued 55,000 shares of its $5 par value common stock for 90% of the outstanding common stock of Singh Company in a business combination meeting all criteria for a pooling of interests. Singh Company's general ledger accounts showed the following stockholders' equity amounts on that date:

Common stock, $10 par value	$200,000
Other contributed capital	110,000
Retained earnings, 1/1	80,000

During 1995 Singh Company reported net income of $250,000 and declared and paid a $70,000 cash dividend.

Required:

A. Prepare journal entries on the books of Pogue Company to record the investment-related events for 1995 assuming:
   (1) Pogue Company uses the book value method.
   (2) Pogue Company uses the partial equity method.

B. Prepare eliminating entries for the preparation of a consolidated statements workpaper on December 31, 1995, assuming:
   (1) Pogue Company uses the book value method.
   (2) Pogue Company uses the partial equity method.

Exercise 11-5

Assume the situation presented in Exercise 11-4, and that Singh Company reported net income of $240,000 and declared and paid a $80,000 cash dividend during 1996.

Required:

Prepare eliminating entries for the preparation of a consolidated statements workpaper on December 31, 1996, assuming:

A. Pogue Company uses the book value method.

B. Pogue Company uses the partial equity method.

Exercise 11-6

Pippin Company acquired on 80% interest in the capital stock of Stein Company on January 1, 1995, for $360,000. The trial balances for each company on December 31, 1995, follow:

	PIPPIN COMPANY	STEIN COMPANY
Current assets	$ 210,000	$249,000
Investment in Stein Company	360,000	
Equipment (net)	290,500	141,000
Land	61,000	125,000
Dividends declared		35,000
Cost of goods sold	188,000	125,000
Expenses	63,000	52,500
	$1,172,500	$727,500

	PIPPIN COMPANY	STEIN COMPANY
Liabilities	$ 46,000	$ 37,500
Capital stock	350,00	210,000
Retained earnings	298,500	140,000
Sales	450,000	340,000
Dividend income	28,000	
	$1,172,500	$727,500

The entire difference between cost and book value is assigned to land.

Required:

Prepare a consolidated balance sheet as of December 31, 1995, and a consolidated income statement for the year then ended:

A. Using the economic unit concept.

B. Using the parent company concept.

Exercise 11-7

Paar Company purchased 90% of the outstanding common stock of Star Company for $446,500 on March 1, 1995. On that date, Star Company had stockholders' equity as follows:

Common stock, $2 par value	$200,000
Other contributed capital	110,000
Retained earnings	75,000
Total	$385,000

The book values of Star Company's assets and liabilities are equal to their fair values except for the following:

	BOOK VALUE	FAIR VALUE
Equipment	$ 60,000	$ 85,000
Land	140,000	200,000

Ignore income tax consequences.

Required:

A. Prepare in general journal form the workpaper entries needed to eliminate the investment account in the preparation of a consolidated balance sheet workpaper on the date of acquisition:
   (1) Following the economic unit concept.
   (2) Following the parent company concept.

B. Compute the total noncontrolling interest that would be reported in the consolidated balance sheet:
   (1) Following the economic unit concept.
   (2) Following the parent company concept.

Problems

Problem 11-1

On March 1, 1995, Perry Company acquired 36,000 of the 40,000 outstanding common shares of Sands Company (par $10) by issuing 35,000 shares of its own common stock (par $15).

Before the acquisition, balance sheets of the two companies were as follows:

	PERRY COMPANY	SANDS COMPANY
Cash	$ 200,000	$ 72,000
Receivables	190,000	84,500
Inventories	270,000	175,000
Property, plant, and equipment	600,000	350,000
Patents	70,500	
Total	$1,330,500	$681,500
Current liabilities	$ 47,000	$ 57,500
Long-term liabilities	207,500	100,000
Common stock	600,000	400,000
Other contributed capital	172,000	85,000
Retained earnings	304,000	39,000
Total	$1,330,500	$681,500

Required:

Assuming that the acquisition meets all the criteria for a pooling of interests:

A. Prepare the entry to record the stock exchange on the books of Perry Company.

B. Prepare a consolidated balance sheet workpaper immediately after the acquisition.

Problem 11-2

On January 1, 1995, Phan Company acquired 171,000 of the outstanding common shares of Scali Company (par $2) by issuing 110,000 shares of its own common stock (par $5). The balance sheets of the two companies were as follows just before the acquisition:

	PHAN COMPANY	SCALI COMPANY
Cash	$ 195,000	$170,000
Other current assets	625,000	240,000
Long-term assets	1,580,000	410,000
Other assets	140,000	
Total	$2,540,000	$820,000
Current liabilities	$ 325,000	$ 85,000
Bonds payable	400,000	
Common stock	1,000,000	400,000
Treasury stock at par		(40,000)
Other contributed capital	320,000	120,000
Retained earnings	495,000	255,000
Total	$2,540,000	$820,000

Required:

Assume that the acquisition meets all the criteria for a pooling of interests:

A. Give the entry to record the stock exchange in the accounts of Phan Company.

B. Prepare a consolidated balance sheet workpaper immediately after the acquisition.

Problem 11-3

On January 2, 1991, Paine Company exchanged 20,000 shares of its $10 par value common stock for 95% of the outstanding common stock of Sato Company in a business combination meeting all conditions for a pooling of interests. On that date, Sato Company's stockholders' equity consisted of common stock of $180,000 and retained earnings of $65,000. Trial balances for Paine Company and Sato Company on December 31, 1995, follow:

	PAINE COMPANY	SATO COMPANY
Current assets	$ 218,750	$132,000
Investment in Sato Company	232,750	–0–
Plant assets	426,000	360,000
Dividends declared	90,000	50,000
Cost of goods sold	321,000	220,000
Other expenses	120,000	87,000
Total debits	$1,408,500	$849,000
Liabilities	$ 102,000	$ 71,000
Common stock	300,000	180,000
1/1 Retained earnings	397,000	198,000
Sales	562,000	400,000
Dividend income	47,500	–0–
Total credits	$1,408,500	$849,000

Required:

Prepare a consolidated statements workpaper at December 31, 1995.

Problem 11-4

(Note that this problem is the same as Problem 11-3, but assuming the use of the partial equity method.)

On January 2, 1991, Paine Company exchanged 20,000 shares of its $10 par value common stock for 95% of the outstanding common stock of Sato Company in a business combination meeting all conditions for a pooling of interests. On that date, Sato Company's stockholders' equity consisted of common stock of $180,000 and retained earnings of $65,000. Trial balances for Paine Company and Sato Company on December 31, 1995, follow:

	PAINE COMPANY	SATO COMPANY
Current assets	$ 218,750	$132,000
Investment in Sato Company	399,950	–0–
Plant assets	426,000	360,000
Dividends declared	90,000	50,000
Cost of goods sold	321,000	220,000
Other expenses	120,000	87,000
Total debits	$1,575,700	$849,000
Liabilities	$ 102,000	$ 71,000
Common stock	300,000	180,000
1/1 Retained earnings	523,350	198,000
Sales	562,000	400,000
Equity in subsidiary income	88,350	–0–
Total credits	$1,575,700	$849,000

Required:

Prepare a consolidated statements workpaper at December 31, 1995.

Problem 11-5

The following account balances were taken from the December 31, 1995 trail balance of Sun Company:

Common Stock—$5 par	$100,000
1/1 Retained earnings	32,000
Sales	393,000
Cost of sales	236,000
Expenses	105,500
Dividends declared	12,500

Prime Company acquired 80% of the common stock of Sun Company on January 1, 1995, for $156,000. The difference between cost and book value was attributable to several small computers owned by Sun, which, anticipating a faster than experienced advance in computer technology, had depreciated the computers too rapidly. The computers had been acquired by Sun on January 1, 1992, and were being depreciated over a six-year estimated life by the straight-line method. Ignore income tax consequences.

Required:

Applying the entity concept, compute:

A. The noncontrolling interest in the net income of Sun Company for 1995.

B. The noncontrolling interest in the net assets of Sun Company on December 31, 1995.

Problem 11-6

On January 1, 1995, P Company purchased 90% of the common stock of S Company. At that time the retained earnings of S Company were $120,000. Selected financial information for the affiliated companies on December 31, 1996, follows:

	DECEMBER 31, 1996	
	P COMPANY	S COMPANY
Sales	$400,000	$200,000
Purchases	200,000	104,000
Expenses	16,000	8,000
Inventory, January 1	72,000	32,000
Inventory, December 31	96,000	48,000
Retained earnings, January 1	365,900	172,000
Dividends declared	40,000	10,000
Dividend income	9,000	–0–

During 1996 P Company purchased merchandise from S Company for $60,000. S Company sells merchandise to P Company at cost plus 25% of cost. On December 31, 1996, merchandise purchased from S Company for $30,000 remains in the inventory of P Company. On January 1, 1996, P Company's inventory contained merchandise purchased from S Company for $10,000. The affiliated companies file a consolidated income tax return. There was no difference between cost and book value and no excess of cost over fair value on the date of acquisition. P Company uses the cost method to record its investment in S Company.

Required:

A. Prepare the income statement and retained earnings statement sections of the consolidated financial statements workpaper for the year ended December 31, 1996, under each of the following assumptions:
   (1) Intercompany profits are eliminated using the 100% elimination method.
   (2) Intercompany profits are eliminated using the partial elimination method.

B. List and compare the balances obtained using each method in part (A) for:
   (1) Combined income.
   (2) Noncontrolling interest in combined income.
   (3) Consolidated net income.
   (4) Consolidated retained earnings—December 31, 1996.
   (5) Consolidated inventories—December 31, 1996.

Problem 11-7

On January 1, 1993, Peak Company purchased an 80% interest in the capital stock of Stull Company for $450,000. At that time, Stull Company had capital stock of $250,000 and retained earnings of $50,000. The difference between fair value and book value of the net assets acquired was attributed to specific assets of Stull Company as follows:

To equipment with five-year remaining life on 1/1/93 (original life of 10 years)	$ 80,000
To land	100,000
To inventory. Stull Company uses the FIFO inventory method	30,000
To goodwill (amortized over 20 years)	52,500
Total	$262,500

The adjusted trial balances of Peak Company and Stull Company follow:

December 31, 1995
Adjusted Trial Balances

	PEAK COMPANY	STULL COMPANY
Cash	$ 40,000	$ 25,000
Accounts receivable	85,000	85,000
12/31 Inventory	115,000	75,000
Investment in Stull Company	450,000	
Land		150,000
Property and equipment (net)	175,000	125,000
Cost of goods sold	425,000	90,000
Other expense	50,000	35,000
Dividends declared	50,000	25,000
Total	$1,390,000	$610,000

	PEAK COMPANY	STULL COMPANY
Accounts payable	$ 83,000	$ 50,000
Notes payable	25,000	10,000
Capital stock	500,000	250,000
1/1 Retained earnings	240,000	100,000
Sales	522,000	200,000
Dividend income	20,000	
Total	$1,390,000	$610,000

Required:

A. Prepare in general journal form the entries required on the books of Peak Company during 1995 to account for its investment in Stull Company.

B. Prepare a consolidated financial statements workpaper for the year ended December 31, 1995 using the economic unit concept.

C. Repeat requirement (B) using the parent company concept; list and compare the consolidated balances with those in part (B).

Problem 11-8

Pinney Company owns 80% of the common stock of Star Company. The stock was purchased for $240,000 on January 1, 1991, when Star Company's retained earnings were $50,000. Pre-closing trail balances for the two companies at December 31, 1995, are:

	PINNEY COMPANY	STAR COMPANY
Cash	$ 40,000	$ 25,000
Accounts receivable (net)	106,500	56,250
Inventory, 1/1	85,000	55,000
Investment in Star Co.	240,000	
Other assets	250,000	200,000
Dividends declared	50,000	30,000
Purchases	425,000	175,000
Other expenses	60,000	45,000
Income tax expense	43,500	23,750
	$1,300,000	$610,000
Accounts payable	$ 28,000	$ 15,000
Other liabilities	27,500	20,000
Common stock	350,000	250,000
Retained earnings	270,500	60,000
Sales	600,000	265,000
Dividend income	24,000	
	$1,300,000	$610,000
Inventory, 12/31	$ 70,000	$ 57,500

The January 1, 1995 inventory of Pinney Company includes $20,000 of profit recorded by Star Company on 1994 sales. During 1995 Star Company made intercompany sales of

$100,000 with a markup of 20% on cost. The ending inventory of Star Company includes goods purchased in 1995 from Star Company for $30,000.

The affiliates file a consolidated income tax return.

Required:

A. Prepare the entries made on the books of Pinney Company during 1995 to record its interest in Star Company.

B. Prepare a consolidated statements workpaper for the year ended December 31, 1995, using the parent company concept (partial elimination).

C. Repeat requirement (B) using the economic unit concept (100% elimination); list and compare the consolidated balances with those in part (B).

12

THE EQUITY METHOD OF REPORTING INVESTMENTS IN COMMON STOCK

METHODS OF REPORTING INVESTMENTS IN COMMON STOCK

Investments in the voting stock of other companies may be consolidated, or they may be separately reported as investments in the financial statements of the investor at cost, at fair value, or at equity. *Investor* refers to a business entity that holds an investment in the voting stock of another company. *Investee* refers to a corporation that has outstanding voting stock that is held by an investor. The method of reporting an investment depends on several factors including the degree of influence exercised by the investor over the investee and the marketability of the stock.

When an investor owns more than 50% of the common stock of an investee, the investee is a *majority owned subsidiary*. The investor must consolidate majority owned subsidiaries unless control is temporary or does not rest with the investor. A majority owned subsidiary that is not consolidated is reported as a separate investment using the cost method.

Investments in *less than 50% owned investees* where the investor has the ability to significantly influence the operating and financial policies of an investee are reported using the equity method. If the equity method is not appropriate and the investment is in *common stock with a readily determinable fair value*, the investment is reported at fair value. If the equity method is not appropriate and the common stock does not have a readily determinable fair value, the investment is reported using the cost method.

The Equity Method of Reporting Investments in Common Stock

The use of the equity method for reporting certain investees was introduced by the Accounting Principles Board in 1971 when it issued *APB Opinion No. 18*.[1] In that opinion the board concluded that the equity method of accounting should be used to report on investments in voting stock when the investor has the ability to exercise significant influence over the operating and financial policies of the investee.

The concept of "significant influence" was elaborated on in paragraph 17 of *Opinion No. 18* as follows:

> Ability to exercise that influence may be indicated in several ways, such as representation on the board of directors, participation in policy making processes, material intercompany transactions, interchange of managerial personnel, or technological dependency. Another important consideration is the extent of ownership by an investor in relation to the concentration of other shareholdings, but substantial or majority ownership of the voting stock of an investee by another investor does not necessarily preclude the ability to exercise significant influence by the investor. The Board recognizes that determining the ability of an investor to exercise such influence is not always clear and applying judgment is necessary to assess the status of each investment.

To assist in the application of such judgments, the Board established the presumption that, in the absence of evidence to the contrary, an investor has the ability to exercise significant influence over an investee if it owns 20% or more of the voting stock of the investee and, conversely, that an investor does not have the ability to exercise significant influence if it owns less than 20% of the voting stock of an investee unless such ability can be demonstrated. Examples of circumstances that may provide evidence contrary to the presumption that an investor has significant influence over the operating and financial policies of an investee in which it owns 20% or more of the voting stock are identified in *FASB Interpretation No. 35*. They include:

a) Opposition by the investee, such as litigation or complaints to governmental regulatory authorities . . .

b) The investor and investee sign an agreement under which the investor surrenders significant rights as a shareholder.

c) Majority ownership of the investee is concentrated among a small group of shareholders who operate the investee without regard to the views of the investor.

---

[1] *Opinions of the Accounting Principles Board No. 18*, "The Equity Method of Accounting for Investments in Common Stock" (New York: AICPA, 1971).

d) The investor needs or wants more financial information to apply the equity method than is available to the investee's other shareholders (for example, the investor wants quarterly financial information from an investee that publicly reports only annually), tries to obtain that information, and fails.

e) The investor tries and fails to obtain representation to the investee's board of directors.

The equity method of reporting an investment is often referred to as a one-line consolidation and is intended to have the same effect on the reported net income and retained earnings of the investor as if the investment were consolidated. Thus, a complete understanding of the application of the equity method of reporting requires an understanding of concepts developed in prior chapters dealing with consolidated financial statements such as the amortization of the difference between cost and book value, the elimination of unrealized intercompany profit, and the income tax consequences of unrealized intercompany profit and undistributed income. The purpose of this chapter is to compare income recognition under the cost and equity methods of reporting an investment and to describe and illustrate the equity method of recording and reporting an investment.

COMPARISON OF THE COST METHOD AND THE EQUITY METHOD

On the date stock is purchased, the investor records the investment at cost under both the cost method and the equity method. The major difference between the methods pertains to the period in which investee income is recorded on the books of the investor and the amount of income recognized.

Under the equity method, income is recorded on the books of the investor in the same accounting period that it is reported by the investee, whether or not such income is distributed to the investor. Under the cost method, no income is recorded by the investor until it becomes available in the form of a dividend. Under the equity method, the amount of income reported is the investor's share of the investee's reported income that has been realized in transactions with third parties. Under the cost method the amount of income reported is the amount of dividends received from the investee or, stated another way, it is the investor's share of the income or accumulated income distributed by the investee.

Illustration of the Basic Difference Between the Cost and Equity Methods

Assume that A Company acquired 40% of the outstanding voting stock of B Company at the beginning of year 1 for $800,000. The reported net income (loss) and dividend distributions of B Company are summarized in Illustration 12-1.

Under the equity method, A Company records its share of B Company's reported income, which amounts to $72,000 (40% of $180,000) in year 1 and $48,000 (40% of $120,000) in year 2, whereas under the cost method, it records its share of the income distributed by B Company, which amounts to $32,000 (40% of $80,000) in both year 1 and year 2.

ILLUSTRATION 12-1
Net Income and Dividends Reported by B Company
End of Years (1 Through 4)

END OF YEAR	REPORTED INCOME (LOSS)*	DIVIDENDS DISTRIBUTED*	INCOME OVER (UNDER) DIVIDENDS	UNDISTRIBUTED INCOME SINCE STOCK WAS ACQUIRED BY A COMPANY
1	$180,000 (2)	$ 80,000 (3)	$100,000	$100,000
2	120,000 (4)	80,000 (5)	40,000	140,000
3	(40,000) (6)	80,000 (7)	(120,000)	20,000
4	37,500 (8)	80,000 (9)	(42,500)	0 *(22,500)*
Total	$297,500	$320,000	$ (22,500)	

*Numbers in parentheses refer to the corresponding journal entries.

Journal entries required on the books of A Company to account for its investment in B Company under the cost method and under the equity method of accounting are illustrated and explained next.

Entries in Year 1—Income Exceeds Dividends

	COST METHOD		EQUITY METHOD	
(1)	Investment in B 800,000		Investment in B 800,000	
	Cash	800,000	Cash	800,000
	To record investment in B Company stock.			
(2)	No Entry		Investment in B 72,000 *(40% × 180,000)*	
			Equity in Investee Income	72,000
	To record equity in reported income of B Company in year 1.			
(3)	Cash 32,000 *(40% × 80,000)*		Cash 32,000	
	Dividend Income	32,000	Investment in B	32,000
	To record dividends received from B Company in year 1.			

Entries in Year 2—Income Exceeds Dividends

(4)	No Entry		Investment in B 48,000 *(40% × 120,000)*	
			Equity in Investee Income	48,000
	To record equity in reported income of B Company in Year 2.			
(5)	Cash 32,000		Cash 32,000	
	Dividend Income	32,000	Investment in B	32,000
	To record dividends received from B Company in year 2.			

Entries in Year 3—Investee Reports a Loss

(6)	No Entry		Equity in Investee Loss 16,000 *(40% × 40,000)*	
			Investment in B	16,000
	To record equity in reported loss of B Company in year 3.			
(7)	Cash 32,000		Cash 32,000	
	Dividend Income	32,000	Investment in B	32,000
	To record dividends received from B Company in year 3.			

Under the equity method the investor records its share of the investee's loss in the period in which it is reported. Under the cost method, reported losses of the investee are ordinarily not recorded or recognized by the investor.

Entries in Year 4—Liquidating Dividend

COST METHOD		EQUITY METHOD	
(8) No Entry		Investment in B 15,000 *(40% × 37500)*	
		Equity in Investee Income	15,000

To record equity in reported income of B Company in year 4.

COST METHOD		EQUITY METHOD	
(9) Cash	32,000	Cash	32,000
Dividend Income	23,000	Investment in B	32,000
Investment in B	9,000 *(40% × (320000 − 297,500))*		

To record (liquidating) dividend received from B Company in year 4.

From the point of view of an investor, a liquidating dividend is received when, subsequent to the investor's purchase of the investee's stock, the investee's cumulative dividends exceed the investee's cumulative net income. Since, under the equity method, the investor treats its share of the investee's reported income as an increase in its investment, all dividend distributions are routinely treated as a return of its investment and are deducted from the investment account. Therefore, under the equity method, liquidating dividends require no special treatment. Under the cost method, however, liquidating dividends must be recorded as a reduction of the investment account rather than as dividend income.

In this example, net income of B Company in years 1 through 4 totals $297,500, whereas dividends distributed by B Company during the same period amount to $320,000 (see Illustration 12-1). Hence, from A Company's point of view, a portion of the $32,000 dividend received from B Company in year 4 is a liquidating dividend. The amount of the liquidating dividend is equal to A Company's share of the excess of cumulative dividends over cumulative income or $9,000 [.40 × ($320,000 − $297,500)].

Illustration 12-2 shows the amount of income recorded each year and the end-of-year balances in the investment account under both the cost and equity methods.

ILLUSTRATION 12-2
Comparison of Investment Account Balances and
Income Recorded by A Company
(Based on Assumptions in Illustration 12-1)

END OF YEAR	INVESTMENT ACCOUNT BALANCE			INCOME (LOSS) RECORDED			
	COST METHOD	EQUITY METHOD	DIFFERENCE	COST METHOD	EQUITY METHOD	DIFFERENCE	CUMULATIVE DIFFERENCE
1	$800,000	$840,000	$40,000	$ 32,000	$ 72,000	$ 40,000	$40,000
2	800,000	856,000	56,000	32,000	48,000	16,000	56,000
3	800,000	808,000	8,000	32,000	(16,000)	(48,000)	8,000
4	791,000	791,000	–0–	23,000	15,000	(8,000)	–0–
				$119,000	$119,000	$ –0–	

After the recording of a liquidating dividend, the balance in the investment account and the total amount of investee income recorded on the books of the investor from the date the stock was purchased to the date the liquidating dividend is recorded will be the same under both the cost and the equity methods. The amounts of income recorded in individual accounting periods, however, vary substantially.

Comparison of Cost and Equity Methods

Differences in the balances in the investment account and in the cumulative amount of recorded income that result from applying the equity method and the cost method are shown in Illustration 12-2. The difference in the investment account balances is equal to the cumulative differences in recorded income. Both differences can be defined as and are equal to the investor's share of the undistributed income of the investee from the date the stock was purchased to the date of the calculation. For example, the $56,000 difference between balances under the cost and the equity methods at the end of year 2 (see Illustration 12-2) is 40% of the $140,000 undistributed income of B Company at the end of year 2 (see Illustration 12-1). The difference between the cost and equity method balances is the same as the amount calculated to establish reciprocity in the consolidated statements workpaper when the investment in a subsidiary is recorded at cost.

The differences illustrated in this basic example do not take into consideration adjustments to equity in investee income and to the investment balance that are necessary under the equity method because of deferred income tax consequences or (1) when there is a difference between the cost of the investment and the book value of the equity interest purchased, (2) when there is unrealized intercompany profit or loss on intercompany transactions, or (3) when there is a change in the percentage of investee common stock owned by the investor. Adjustments to equity in investee income and the investment balance for these items are considered in the next section of this chapter.

APPLICATION OF THE EQUITY METHOD OF REPORTING AN INVESTMENT

In this section, additional considerations in recording and reporting an investment using the equity method of accounting are described and illustrated.

Determining Ownership Percentage and Share of Earnings

For purposes of the 20% presumption, the investor, in determining its percentage of *voting stock interest* in an investee, should consider *all currently outstanding voting securities* of the investee. For purposes of income determination, the investor's share of earnings or loss of the investee should be based on the number of shares of *common stock* it holds. Securities that are defined as "common stock equivalents" under *APB Opinion No. 15* should not be considered as outstanding common stock in this calculation. The investor should compute its share of earnings after deducting the amount of the current year's preferred dividends that is declared or paid by the investee or that will require declaration and payment by the investee in the future, such as dividends on cumulative preferred stock.

Classification of Investment Income

The investor's share of income or loss from its investment is normally reported in the income statement as a single amount. However, if prior-period adjustments or extraordinary items reported by the inves*tee* are material in the income statement of the invest*or*, they should be separately classified by the investor in the same manner as they were classified by the investee. For example, the investor's share of an investee's extraordinary item would also be set out as an extraordinary item in the investor's financial statements. Similarly, if the amounts reported by the investee are material to the investor, the investor's share of the investee's cumulative effect of an accounting change (*APB Opinion No. 20*) and the investor's share of the effect of the disposal of a segment of the investee's business (*APB Opinion No. 30*) should be reported in the investor's financial statements in the same manner as those items are reported in the investee's financial statements.

Amortization of the Difference Between Cost and Book Value

The assignment, depreciation, and amortization of the difference between cost and book value in the consolidated statements workpaper was described in Chapter 4. Since the equity method is intended to have the same effect on reported income and retained earnings as if the investment were consolidated, under the equity method entries must be made on the books of the investor to amortize the difference between cost and book value.

Assume for example that A Company acquired a 30% interest in the voting stock of B Company for $825,000 on January 1, 1995, when the book value of the net assets of B Company is $2,000,000. The identifiable assets and liabilities of B Company on January 1, 1995, and the assignment of the difference between cost and book value are presented in Illustration 12-3.

For the moment, ignore the last column of Illustration 12-3. As explained in Chapter 4, the amount of difference between cost and book value assigned to a specific asset or liability is equal to the investor's percentage ownership interest in the investee times the difference between the fair value and the book value of the specific asset or liability. In addition, as explained in Chapter 7, a deferred tax liability and/or deferred tax asset must be recognized for the tax consequences of the differences between the fair values and tax bases of individual assets and liabilities. The assignment of the difference between cost and book value using these procedures is presented in the next to the last column of Illustration 12-3.

Now assume that the inventory was sold by B Company in 1995, the equipment had a remaining life on January 1, 1995, of nine years, and goodwill is amortized over 10 years. An amortization schedule is presented in Illustration 12-4.

ILLUSTRATION 12-3
Identifiable Assets and Liabilities of B Company — January 1, 1995,
and Assignment of Difference Between Cost and Book Value

$(1 - .4) = .6$

	FAIR VALUE	TAX BASIS/ BOOK VALUE	DIFFERENCE BETWEEN FAIR VALUE AND TAX BASIS/BOOK VALUE	ASSIGNMENT OF THE DIFFERENCE BETWEEN COST AND BOOK VALUE	ASSIGNMENT OF THE DIFFERENCE BETWEEN COST AND BOOK VALUE (NET OF 40% TAX)
Inventory	$ 350,000	$ 300,000	$ 50,000	$ 15,000 × .6 = $ 9,000 (2)	
Other current assets	450,000	450,000	–0–	–0–	–0–
Equipment (net)	600,000	300,000	300,000	90,000 × .6 = 54,000 (3)	
Land	400,000	250,000	150,000	45,000 × .6 = 27,000 (4)	
Other noncurrent assets	1,000,000	1,000,000	–0–	–0–	–0–
Liabilities	(300,000)	(300,000)	–0–	–0–	–0–
Deferred tax liability (1)	–0–	–0–	–0–	(60,000)	–0–
Identifiable net assets	$2,500,000	$2,000,000	$500,000	90,000	90,000
Difference between cost and book value [$825,000 − (.3 × $2,000,000)]				(225,000)	(225,000)
Goodwill				$135,000	$135,000

(1) .4 × ($15,000 + 90,000 + $45,000) = $60,000 $(1 - .4)$
(2) $15,000 − .4($15,000) = $9,000; or $15,000 × .6 = $9,000; or $50,000 × .6 × .3 = $9,000
(3) $90,000 − .4($90,000) = $54,000; or $90,000 × .6 = $54,000; or $300,000 × .6 × .3 = $54,000
(4) $45,000 − .4($45,000) = $27,000; or $45,000 × .6 = $27,000; or $150,000 × .6 × .3 = $27,000

ILLUSTRATION 12-4
Adjustment in Determining Equity in Investee Income
Resulting from the Amortization of the
Difference Between Cost and Book Value

	ASSIGNMENT OF DIFFERENCE BETWEEN COST AND BOOK VALUE	ANNUAL AMORTIZATION		
		1995	1996	1997
Inventory	$ 15,000	$15,000	$ –0–	$ –0–
Equipment (net)	90,000	10,000	10,000	10,000
Land	45,000	–0–	–0–	–0–
Deferred tax liability	(60,000)	(10,000) (1)	(4,000) (2)	(4,000) (2)
Goodwill	135,000	13,500	13,500	13,500
Total	$225,000	$28,500	$19,500	$19,500

(1) .4 × ($15,000 + $10,000) = $10,000
(2) .4 × $10,000 = $4,000

If the investee reports net income of $200,000 in 1995 and $220,000 in 1996, A Company's equity in the income of B Company would be recorded as follows:

	1995		1996	
(1) Investment in B Company	60,000		66,000	
Equity in Investee Income		60,000		66,000
To record equity in reported income of B Company.				
(2) Equity in Investee Income	28,500		19,500	
Investment in B Company		28,500		19,500
To record adjustment to equity in investee income for the amortization of the difference between cost and book value.				

The two entries could of course be combined each year into a single entry. In either case, A company will report equity in investee income of $31,500 ($60,000 − $28,500) in 1995 and $46,500 ($66,000 − $19,500) in 1996.

For purposes of applying the equity method, we are interested in determining only the ***net amount*** of the amortization of the difference between cost and book value. Since we need to determine only the net amount, that amount may be calculated more efficiently by using the net of tax amounts calculated in the last column of Illustration 12-3. The calculation of the amortization of the difference between cost and book value using the net of tax amounts from Illustration 12-3 is presented in Illustration 12-5.

ILLUSTRATION 12-5
Adjustment in Determining Equity in Investee Income
Resulting from the Amortization of the
Difference Between Cost and Book Value

	ASSIGNMENT OF DIFFERENCE BETWEEN COST AND BOOK VALUE (NET OF TAX)	ANNUAL AMORTIZATION		
		1995	1996	1997
Inventory	$ 9,000	$ 9,000	$ −0−	$ −0−
Equipment (net)	54,000 ÷ 9 yrs =	6,000	6,000	6,000
Land	27,000	−0−	−0−	−0−
Goodwill	135,000 ÷ 10 yrs =	13,500	13,500	13,500
Total	$225,000	$28,500	$19,500	$19,500

An investor in a less than majority-owned investee may find that it is impractical to determine, on the day it acquires its investment, the fair values of the investee's assets and liabilities as a basis for determining the appropriate assignment of the difference between cost and book value and the related adjustments to reported investee income. Generally accepted accounting standards require that a reasonable effort at such a determination be made. As a practical matter, however, the investor may elect to amortize the total amount of the difference between cost and book value as an adjustment to income in equal amounts over a reasonable period not to exceed 40 years. Frequently, the selection of a reasonable amortization period is based on an estimate of the average remaining life of the depreciable assets of the investee.

Elimination of Unrealized Intercompany Profit Including Income Tax Consequences

Intercompany Sales of Merchandise In order for the equity method of reporting an investee to have the same effect on reported net income and retained earnings as would result from the application of the consolidation procedures described in Chapter 5, the investor's net income must be reduced by the investor's share of the after-tax amounts of unrealized intercompany profit.[2] Consolidated income tax returns can be filed only with investees in which the investor owns 80% or more of the voting stock. Thus, the investor and less than 80% owned investee will always file separate income tax returns and it will always be necessary to treat the income tax consequences of unrealized intercompany profit when applying the equity method of accounting to less than 80% owned investees.

To illustrate the entries necessary on the books of the investor to treat the effects of unrealized intercompany profit under the equity method, assume that (1) A Company owns 30% of the voting stock of B Company and there is no unamortized difference between cost and book value, (2) merchandise with a cost to the selling affiliate of $300,000 is sold in 1995 to the purchasing affiliate for $750,000, (3) two-thirds of the merchandise was sold to third parties in 1995 and the remaining one-third was sold to third parties in 1996, (4) B Company reports net income of $200,000 in 1995 and $220,000 in 1996, and (5) the marginal income tax rate for both companies is 40%.

Upstream sales If B Company is the selling affiliate and A Company is the purchasing affiliate, the intercompany sale is an upstream sale and A Company will record its equity in investee income as follows:

1995

(1) Investment in B Company	(30% of 200,000) =	60,000	
Equity in Investee Income			60,000
To record equity in reported income of B Company.			
(2) Equity in Investee Income		27,000	
Investment in B Company			27,000
To record adjustment to 1995 equity in investee income for A Company's share of the after-tax unrealized profit included in the reported net income of B Company {.30 × [.6 × 1/3 × ($750,000 − $300,000)]}.			

---

[2]Although required by the provisions of *APB Opinion No. 18*, your authors see no benefit from nor need for the elimination of profit on intercompany sales from the reported income of the investor. Most such transactions are consummated at market prices. For transactions with investees that are not consummated at market prices, current reporting standards regarding transactions with related parties provide for sufficient disclosure.

These entries could, of course, be combined into a single entry. In either case, A Company will report equity in investee income of $33,000 ($60,000 − $27,000) in 1995. Adjustment of equity in investee income for the after-tax unrealized intercompany profit on upstream sales is appropriate since the intercompany profit is included in the after-tax net income reported by the investee. In the case of upstream sales, elimination of an amount equal to the *investor's percentage interest* in the after-tax unrealized profit [entry (2)] is appropriate, since only the *investor's percentage interest* in the reported net income of the investee was recorded in entry (1).

1996

(1) Investment in B Company	66,000	
Equity in Investee Income		66,000
To record equity in reported income of B Company.		
(2) Investment in B Company	27,000	
Equity in Investee Income		27,000
To record adjustment to 1996 equity in investee income for A Company's share of the after-tax intercompany profit recorded by B Company in 1995 and realized in sales to third parties in 1996.		

These entries could, of course, be combined into a single entry. In either case, A Company will report equity in investee income of $93,000 ($66,000 + $27,000) in 1996.

Downstream sales If the selling affiliate is A Company and the purchasing affiliate is B Company, the intercompany sale is a downstream sale. In that case the $250,000 in sales (1/3 × $750,000), the $100,000 in cost of sales (1/3 × $300,000), and the $150,000 in gross profit on intercompany sales that has not been confirmed in transactions with third parties ($250,000 − $100,000) are recorded on the books of A Company, as is the income tax related thereto of $60,000 (.40 × $150,000). Since the profit was recognized on the books of A Company, it would not be appropriate for A Company to adjust its equity in investee income. Rather, intercompany profit on downstream sales is eliminated on the investor's books as follows:

1995

(1) Sales	250,000	
Cost of Sales		100,000
Deferred Gross Profit on Sales to Affiliates		150,000
To eliminate unrealized profit on downstream sales to affiliates.		
(2) Deferred Tax Asset	60,000	
Income Tax Expense		60,000
To recognize the tax consequence of the temporary difference related to deferred gross profit that will result in a deductible amount in future years (.40 × $150,000 = $60,000).		

Deferred gross profit on sales to affiliates is presented in the investor's balance sheet as a current or noncurrent liability depending on the period in which the profit is expected to be confirmed in transactions with third parties. Since the tax basis of the deferred gross profit is zero, the deferred tax consequences resulting from the elimination of unrealized intercompany profit on downstream sales must also be recognized.

In the year(s) in which the merchandise is sold by the investee to third parties, the following entries are recorded on the books of the investor.

1996

(1) Deferred Gross Profit on Sales to Affiliates	150,000	
Cost of Sales	100,000	
Sales		250,000
To recognize profit on 1995 downstream sales to affiliates realized in 1996.		
(2) Income Tax Expense	60,000	
Deferred Tax Asset		60,000
To recognize the tax consequence of the reversal of the temporary difference related to deferred gross profit.		

Intercompany Sales of Equipment Similar entries on the books of the investor are required under the equity method to treat the effects of unrealized intercompany profit on the sale of equipment. To illustrate assume that (1) A Company owns 30% of the voting stock of B Company, (2) on January 1, 1995, one of the affiliates sells the other affiliate equipment with a remaining life of six years and records a gain on the sale of $120,000, (3) B Company reports net income of $200,000 in 1995 and $220,000 in 1996, and (4) the marginal income tax rate for both companies is 40%.

Upstream sale If B Company is the selling affiliate, the sale is an upstream sale and the gain will be included in its 1995 net income. As discussed in Chapter 6, the gain is realized through the utilization of the equipment in the production of goods or services, and the amount of the gain considered to be realized each year is measured by the amount of excess depreciation. Assuming straight-line depreciation, annual excess depreciation in this example is $20,000 ($120,000 ÷ 6). A Company will record its equity in investee income as follows:

1995

(1) Investment in B Company	60,000	
Equity in Investee Income		60,000
To record equity in reported income of B Company.		
(2) Equity in Investee Income	18,000	
Investment in B Company		18,000
To record adjustment to 1995 equity in investee income for A Company's share of the net amount of the after-tax unrealized profit resulting from the intercompany sale of equipment [.30 × (.6 × ($120,000 − $20,000))].		

These entries could, of course, be combined into a single entry.

1996

(1) Investment in B Company		66,000	
Equity in Investee Income			66,000
To record equity in reported income of B Company.			
(2) Investment in B Company		3,600	
Equity in Investee Income			3,600

To record adjustment to 1996 equity in investee income for A Company's share of the after-tax intercompany profit recorded by B Company in 1995 that is considered realized through depreciation in 1996 [.30 × (.6 × $20,000)].

Downstream sales If the selling affiliate is A Company and the purchasing affiliate is B Company, the intercompany sale is a downstream sale. In that case the $120,000 gain on the sale of the equipment is recorded on the books of A Company. Entries on the books of the investor to treat the effects of unrealized intercompany profit on downstream sales of equipment in the year of the sale are as follows:

YEAR OF INTERCOMPANY SALE

(1) Gain on Sale of Equipment		120,000	
Realized Profit on Current Year's Sales to Affiliates			20,000
Deferred Profit on Sales to Affiliates			100,000

To eliminate gain recorded on intercompany sale and to recognized profit realized in current year.

(2) Deferred Tax Asset		40,000	
Income Tax Expense			40,000

To recognize the tax consequence of the temporary difference related to deferred gross profit that will result in a deductible amount in future years (.40 × $100,000).

Entries on the books of the investor in years subsequent to the sale are as follows:

YEARS SUBSEQUENT TO INTERCOMPANY SALE

(1) Deferred Profit on Sales to Affiliates		20,000	
Realized Profit on Prior Year's Sales to Affiliates			20,000

To recognize profit on prior year sale of equipment realized in the current year.

(2) Income Tax Expense		8,000	
Deferred Tax Asset			8,000

To recognize the tax consequence of the reversal of the temporary difference related to deferred gross profit (.40 × $20,000).

Income Tax Consequences Related to Undistributed Investee Income

When the investor records its investment in its investee using the equity method, there is usually a difference between the pretax accounting income recorded by the investor and the investor's taxable income. This difference is equal to the investor's interest in the realized undistributed income of the investee; it arises because the investee's income is not taxable to the investor until it is distributed. This difference is a temporary difference and must be taken into consideration when calculating the deferred income tax liability of the investor.

To illustrate, assume that A Company acquired a 30% interest in B Company for $360,000 when the book value of the stock of B Company was $1,000,000. The $60,000 difference between cost and book value is being amortized over 10 years. In 1995, B Company distributed $10,000 in dividends and reported net income of $80,000. The marginal income tax rate is 40%. Eighty percent of dividends received from more than 20% owned domestic corporations are excluded from taxable income. Entries, using the equity method, to record A Company's interest in B Company are as follows:

(1)	Investment in B Company	24,000	
	Equity in Investee Income		24,000
	To record equity in the reported net income of B Company (.30 × $80,000).		
(2)	Equity in Investee Income	6,000	
	Investment in B Company		6,000
	To record amortization of the difference between cost and book value ($60,000 ÷ 10).		
(3)	Cash	3,000	
	Investment in B Company		3,000
	To record receipt of dividend from B Company (.30 × $10,000).		

The entry to record the tax consequence of undistributed investee income is dependent on assumptions as to the manner in which A Company ultimately expects to realize its equity therein. Assume that A Company ultimately expects to realize its equity in undistributed income through the sale of its investment in B Company. The entry to provide for income tax expense on recorded investee income is as follows:

(4a)	Income Tax Expense	8,640	
	Income Tax Payable [.4 × .2 × (.3 × $10,000)]		240
	Deferred Tax Liability [.4 × (.3 × ($80,000 − $10,000))]		8,400

Since A Company ultimately expects to realize its equity in undistributed income through the sale of its investment in B Company, the dividends received exclusion is ignored when calculating the deferred tax liability on undistributed income. However, the dividends received exclusion is considered when calculating income tax payable on dividends received in the current year.

If A Company expects to realize its equity in the undistributed income of B Company through future dividend receipts, the entry to provide for income tax expense on recorded investee income would be as follows:

(4b)	Income Tax Expense	1,920	
	Income Tax Payable [.4 × .2 × (.3 × $10,000)]		240
	Deferred Tax Liability		
	[.4 × .2 × (.3 × $80,000 − $10,000))]		1,680

Since A Company expects to realize its equity in undistributed income through future dividend receipts, the 80% dividends received exclusion is considered when calculating both income tax payable and the deferred tax liability.

If the investee has recorded profits on sales to the investor, the calculation of the deferred tax consequences should be based on the undistributed *income of the investee that has been realized in transactions with third parties.* Note that the amortization of the difference between cost and book value is not considered in determining these tax consequences. If the investee does not intend to distribute its undistributed income and the investor does not intend to dispose of its investment, a question arises as to what assumption should be made regarding the realization of undistributed income. In that case, deferred tax consequences should be calculated assuming that the undistributed income will ultimately be realized by the investor in the form of a dividend.

Changes in Equity Interest Arising from the Transactions of an Investee in Its Own Shares

The concepts underlying adjustments to the investment account and the controlling interest's equity in the consolidated financial statements necessitated by transactions in which a subsidiary sells or purchases its own shares of stock directly to or from controlling or noncontrolling stockholders on a non-pro-rata basis were discussed in Chapter 8. The same concepts apply to the effects of transactions by an investee in its own shares and an entry on the books of the investor may be required. To illustrate, assume that on January 1, 1995, A Company owns 3,000 of the 10,000 outstanding shares of B Company and that the book value of the net assets of B Company is $1,000,000. Assume further that on January 1, 1995, B Company issues an additional 2,000 shares of stock to third parties in exchange for $240,000. The percentage and dollar amount of A Company's interest in B Company's net assets, immediately before and immediately after the issue of the 2,000 additional shares is:

	BEFORE	AFTER
Net Assets of B Company	$1,000,000	$1,240,000
A Company's ownership interest in B Company	.30 (3,000 ÷ 10,000)	.25 (3,000 ÷ 12,000)
Dollar amount of A Company's interest in B Company	$ 300,000	$ 310,000

The following entry is recorded on the books of A Company to record the change in its interest in B Company resulting from B Company's issue of all the additional shares to third parties at a price in excess of the book value per share.

Investment in B Company	10,000	
Gain on Investee Stock Transactions		10,000

This is the same as the entry illustrated in Chapter 8. An analysis similar to that presented here could be made for each of the types of investee stock transactions described in Chapter 8.

Other Than Temporary Declines in Value

An other than temporary decline in the value of an investment that is reported under the equity method should be recognized by the investor. Evidence of a permanent loss in value includes the absence of an ability to recover the carrying amount of an investment; a series of operating losses that brings into question the ability of the investee to sustain an earnings capacity that justifies the carrying amount of the investment; or a decline in the market value of the stock of an investee that can be attributed to specific adverse conditions for that particular company or industry. Except in the case of marketable securities, it is difficult to measure the "value" of an investment and changes in it. In the case of marketable securities, changes in value may be easily measured, but judgments as to whether or not declines in market value are temporary or other than temporary are still difficult to make. If an other than temporary decline in value is determined to have occurred and if the estimated value of the investment is lower than its carrying value under the equity method, the investment account is written down to the lower value, and a realized loss in the amount of the necessary write-down is recognized in the current year's income statement.

To illustrate, assume that A Company purchased 30% of the outstanding common stock of B Company for $800,000, and that undistributed earnings of B Company since A Company purchased its stock amount to $100,000. Near the end of the current year, the total market value of B Company's outstanding common stock declines precipitously to $1,800,000, after the announcement by federal regulatory authorities of a permanent injunction against the production, use, or sale of Blue Dye #4 because of the environmental and health hazards associated with the product. Blue Dye #4 previously constituted about 50% of the production and sales of B Company.

In this illustration, the decline in the market value of the outstanding stock of B Company is considered to be other than temporary because of the specific adverse circumstances that precipitated the decline in value. Since the carrying value of the investment under the equity method [$800,000 + (.30 × $100,000) = $830,000] exceeds the market value of the investment (.30 × $1,800,000 = $540,000)], the investment account must be written down to $540,000 and a $290,000 realized loss (before income tax effects) recognized in the current year's income statement. Income (loss) reported and dividends received from an investee subsequent to the write-down of the investment accounts are recorded under the equity method in the manner previously illustrated. Subsequent recoveries in the market value of the investment, however, are not recorded on the investor's books or recognized in the investor's income statement.

Reduction of Carrying Value Below Zero

Under the equity method of reporting, the investor's share of reported investee loss is recorded as a charge to income and a reduction in the carrying amount of the investment. What happens if the point is reached where the investor's share of the current year's loss exceeds the carrying amount of the investment? Ordinarily, when the investment is reduced to zero, the investor would discontinue the application of the equity method and no additional loss would be provided for. The investor would then resume application of the equity method only after its share of net income subsequently reported by the investee equaled its share of the net loss that was not recognized during the period the equity method was suspended.

However, if the investor has guaranteed obligations of the investee or is otherwise committed to provide further financial support for the investee, the equity method should not be suspended and the investor should continue to recognize its share of reported investee losses even when the investment account has been reduced to zero. In circumstances where the investment account has been reduced to zero, additional losses should also be provided for if the imminent return of the investee to profitable operations seems assured. The equity method would not be suspended if, for example, a material nonrecurring loss of an isolated nature reduced the investment below zero but the underlying profitable operating pattern of the investee remained unimpaired.

If the investment account is reduced below zero, the resulting credit balance may be reported as a liability or as a deduction from other investments (that is, as a contra asset). We recommend reporting the credit balance as a liability, particularly when the investor has guaranteed obligations of the investee or is otherwise committed to provide further financial support to the investee.

CHANGE IN THE METHOD OF ACCOUNTING FOR AN INVESTEE

A change in the ability of an investor to significantly influence an investee may require a change from the cost to the equity method of reporting or vice versa.

Change from Cost Method to Equity Method

An investment accounted for using the cost method may become qualified for the use of the equity method because of a change in the ability of the investor to influence the policies of an investee. This may result, for example, because of the purchase of additional shares of investee stock by the investor. In this case the investment should be converted from cost to the balance that it would have had if the equity method of accounting had been used since the first purchase of stock in the investee. This adjustment also requires retroactive adjustment of the retained earnings of the investor.

To illustrate, assume that A Company purchased 15% of the voting stock of B Company for $190,000 when the capital stock and retained earnings of B Company were $800,000 and $200,000, respectively. Under the cost method, the balance in the investment account remains unchanged at $190,000 and dividend income is recognized as received. Assume that four years after the first purchase, A Company purchases an additional 20% of the voting stock for $300,000 when the retained earnings of B Company are $400,000. Assume also that any difference between cost and book value is to be amortized over the average life of the depreciable assets of B Company, which is 20 years.

The difference between cost and book value for each purchase is:

	1ST PURCHASE	2ND PURCHASE
Cost	$190,000	$300,000
Book value acquired	150,000 (1)	240,000 (2)
Difference between cost and book value	$ 40,000	$ 60,000

(1) .15 × ($800,000 + $200,000)
(2) .20 × ($800,000 + $400,000)

The entry to convert from the cost to the equity method on the date of the second purchase is:

Investment in B Company	22,000	
Retained Earnings		22,000

The $22,000 adjustment is calculated as follows:

A Company's share of the undistributed income of B Company from the date of the first purchase to the date of the second purchase [.15 × ($400,000 − $200,000)]	$30,000
Less amortization for four years of the difference between cost and book value associated with the first purchase [4 × ($40,000 ÷ 20)]	(8,000)
Adjustment to convert from cost method to equtiy method of accounting for the first purchase	$22,000

The second purchase will be recorded at its cost of $300,000, and, subsequent to the second purchase, 35% of the investee's income less the $5,000 amortization of the difference between cost and book value ($2,000 per year from the first purchase and $3,000 per year from the second purchase) will be recorded as equity in investee income.

Change from Equity Method to Cost Method

Alternatively, the investor's interest in an investee that has been accounted for using the equity method or its influence over such an investee may be reduced to a point where it no longer qualifies for reporting under the equity method. If this occurs, the investor should discontinue use of the equity method and account for investee income using the cost method. The earnings or losses that relate to the stock retained by the investor and that were previously accrued should remain a part of the carrying amount of the investment; that is, the investment account *should not* be adjusted retroactively. However, dividends received by the investor in subsequent periods that exceed its share of earnings for such periods should be applied to reduce the carrying amount of the investment.

WORKPAPER ELIMINATION ENTRIES WHEN A SUBSIDIARY IS RECORDED USING THE EQUITY METHOD OF ACCOUNTING

In prior chapters we have illustrated consolidated financial statements workpaper entries for subsidiaries that were recorded on the books of the parent company using the cost method or the partial equity method. In some instances, a parent company may record an investment in a majority owned subsidiary using the equity method. As illustrated in prior chapters, the method used by the parent company to record its investment in a subsidiary that is consolidated has no effect on the balances that appear in the consolidated financial statements. Eliminating entries in the consolidated financial statements workpaper do, however, differ depending on the method used by the parent company to record its investment. In this section, workpaper procedures to consolidate investments in subsidiaries that have been recorded on the books of the parent company using the equity method are reviewed and illustated.

Workpaper Elimination Entries

The modifications necessary in the workpaper entries to eliminate an investment in a subsidiary that is recorded using the equity method rather than the cost method or the partial equity method are summarized as follows:

1. The entry to establish reciprocity and the entry to eliminate intercompany dividends that were illustrated for the cost method in Chapter 3 are replaced with a single workpaper entry that takes the same form as when an investment is recorded using the partial equity method as follows:

Equity in Subsidiary Income	xxx	
Dividends Declared		x
Investment in Subsidiary		xx

The debit to equity in subsidiary income (credit if a loss is recorded) is for the amount recorded on the books of the parent company for the current year. The credit to dividends declared is for the parent company's share of the dividends declared by the subsidiary in the current year. Investment in subsidiary is debited or credited for the amount necessary to balance the entry.

2. The investment elimination takes the same form as that illustrated in Chapter 3 for the cost and partial equity methods. However, the amount debited to the difference between cost and book value will be for the ***unamortized*** difference between cost and book value at the beginning of the year and will become progressively smaller each year.

3. The entry to assign, depreciate, and amortize the difference between cost and book value takes the same form as that illustrated in Chapter 4. However, the debit to the beginning retained earnings of the parent company for amounts amortized in prior years that is made when the investment is recorded using the cost

or partial equity methods is not necessary when the investment is recorded using the equity method.

4. Entries to treat the effects of intercompany profit and intercompany bond holdings take the same form as those illustrated in Chapters 5, 6, 7, and 10. However, under the equity method, *investment in subsidiary* rather than *beginning retained earnings of the parent company* is debited or credited for the controlling interest's share of unrealized profit or loss on intercompany sales or for its share of constructive gain or loss on intercompany bonds.

To illustrate, assume that P Company owns a 70% interest in S Company and that on January 1, 1995, S Company sells P Company equipment with a book value of $500,000 (original cost of $800,000 and accumulated depreciation of $300,000) for $600,000. On January 1, 1995, the equipment has a remaining useful life of five years and is depreciated using the straight-line method. The marginal income tax rate for both companies is 40% and separate income tax returns are filed. P Company records its investment in S Company using the equity method.

Workpaper eliminating entries in December 31, 1996, consolidated statements workpaper relating to the unrealized profit on the intercompany sale of the equipment are illustrated here:

(1)	**Investment in S Company**		
	[.70 × ($100,000 − $20,000)]	56,000	
	1/1 Retained Earnings—S Company		
	[.30 × ($100,000 − $20,000)]	24,000	
	Accumulated Depreciation	20,000	
	Equipment		100,000
	To reduce the controlling and noncontrolling interests for their respective shares of unrealized intercompany profit at the beginning of the year, to reduce accumulated depreciation by the amount of excess depreciation accumulated to the beginning of the year, and to reduce the carrying value of equipment to its book value on the date of the intercompany sale.		
(2)	Accumulated Depreciation	20,000	
	Depreciation Expense		20,000
	To reverse the amount of excess depreciation recorded during the period and to recognize an equivalent amount of intercompany profit as realized.		
(3)	Deferred Tax Asset	24,000	
	Income Tax Expense	8,000	
	Investment in S Company		22,400
	1/1 Retained Earnings—S Company		9,600
	To recognize deferred taxes for taxes paid in prior years on the amount of intercompany profit still considered unrealized at the **end of the year** [.40 × ($100,000 − $20,000 − $20,000) = $24,000], to recognize income tax expense on intercompany profit considered to be realized during the current year (.40 × $20,000 = $8,000), to adjust the controlling interest for its share of the tax consequence of unrealized profit at the beginning of the year (.70 × $32,000 = $22,400), and to adjust the noncontrolling interest for its share of the tax consequence of unrealized profit at the beginning of the year (.30 × $32,000 = $9,600).		
(4)	Property and Equipment	300,000	
	Accumulated Depreciation		300,000
	To restate property and equipment to original cost to the selling affiliate.		

Noncontrolling Interest, Consolidated Net Income, and Consolidated Retained Earnings

The calculation of the noncontrolling interest in combined income and the calculation of the noncontrolling interest in consolidated net assets are not affected by the method used by the parent company to record its investment in its subsidiaries. In the analytical calculation of consolidated net income, equity in subsidiary income rather than dividend income is subtracted from the parent company's reported net income to calculate the income from its independent operations. Other than that, the calculation of consolidated net income is not affected by the method used by the parent company to record its investment in its subsidiaries. When the parent company uses the equity method of accounting to record its investment in its subsidiaries, consolidated net income and consolidated retained earnings are identical to the recorded net income and retained earnings of the parent company.

Consolidated Statements Workpaper: Investment Recorded at Equity

To illustrate, we use the same example as that used in Illustration 5-8 except that, rather than P Company recording its investment in S Company using the cost method, it is assumed here that P Company records its investment in S Company using the equity method.

Assume that P Company purchases an 80% interest in S Company for $1,360,000 on January 1, 1995, when the retained earnings and capital stock of S Company are $700,000 and $1,000,000, respectively. The reported net income of S Company is $125,000 in 1995 and $140,000 in 1996. The companies file a consolidated income tax return. S Company pays dividends of $20,000 in 1995 and $60,000 in 1996. S Company sells merchandise to P Company as follows:

YEAR	TOTAL SALES OF S COMPANY TO P COMPANY	INTERCOMPANY MERCHANDISE IN 12/31 INVENTORY OF P COMPANY	UNREALIZED INTERCOMPANY PROFIT (25% OF SELLING PRICE)
1995	$ 700,000	$400,000	$100,000
1996	1,000,000	500,000	125,000

A consolidated statements workpaper for the year ended December 31, 1996, is presented in Illustration 12-6. Entries on the books of P Company during 1995 and 1996 to record its interest in S Company using the equity method as well as workpaper entries necessary in the consolidated statements workpaper for the year ended December 31, 1996, are presented in general journal form here:

Entries on Books of P Company—1995 and 1996

1995

(1) Investment in S Company	1,360,000	
Cash		1,360,000
To record purchase of 80% interest in S Company.		

Entries on Books of P Company—1995 and 1996

1995

(2) Cash	16,000	
Investment in S Company		16,000
To record receipt of dividends from S Company (.80 × $20,000).		
(3) Investment in S Company	100,000	
Equity in Subsidiary Income		100,000
To record P Company's share of the reported net income of S Company (.80 × $125,000).		
(4) Equity in Subsidiary Income	80,000	
Investment in S Company		80,000
To eliminate P Company's share of unrealized intercompany profit in ending inventory (.80 × $100,000).		

Entries (3) and (4) could be combined into one entry as follows:

Investment in S Company	20,000	
Equity in Subsidiary Income		20,000

In either case, the net amount of equity in subsidiary income recorded by P Company in 1995 is $20,000.

1996

(1) Cash	48,000	
Investment in S Company		48,000
To record receipt of dividends from S Company (.8 × $60,000).		
(2) Investment in S Company	112,000	
Equity in Subsidiary Income		112,000
To record P Company's share of reported net income of S Company (.80 × $140,000).		
(3) Investment in S Company	80,000	
Equity in Subsidiary Income		80,000
To record intercompany profit in beginning inventory realized during 1996 (.80 × $100,000).		
(4) Equity in Subsidiary Income	100,000	
Investment in S Company		100,000
To eliminate P Company's share of unrealized intercompany profit in ending inventory (.80 × $125,000).		

Entries (2), (3), and (4) may be combined into one entry as follows:

Investment in S Company	92,000	
Equity in Subsidiary Income		92,000

In either case the net amount of equity in subsidiary income recorded by P Company in 1996 is $92,000. The balance in the investment account on the books of P Company on December 31, 1996, is $1,408,000 as indicated in the following T account.

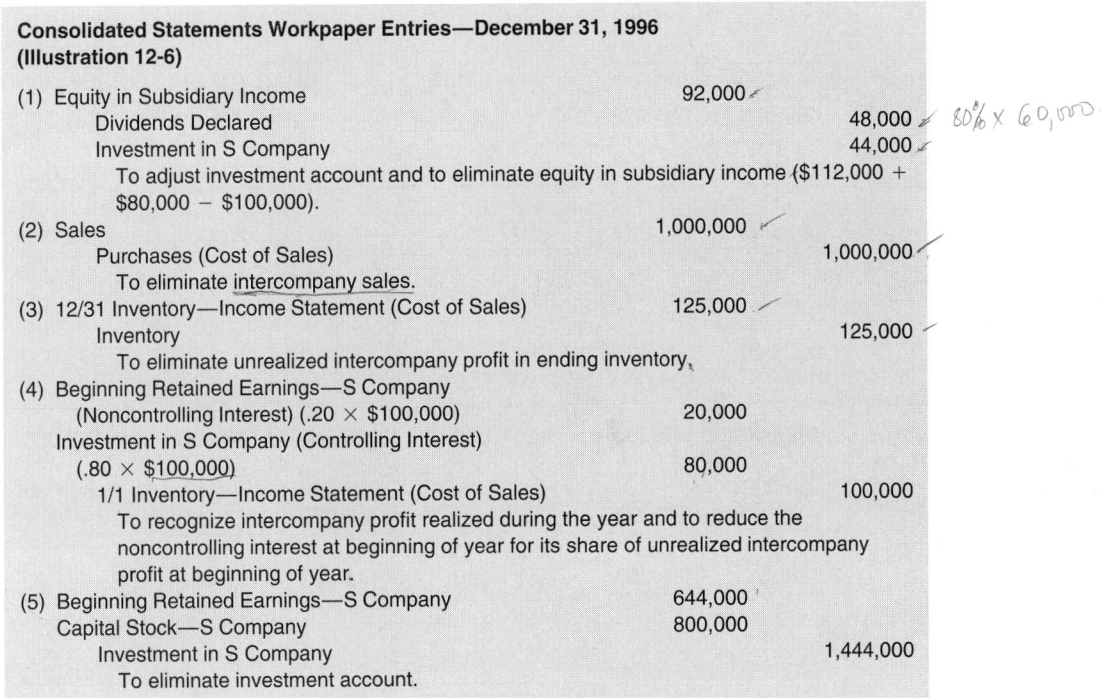

INVESTMENT IN S COMPANY

(A)	1,360,000		
(C)	20,000	(B)	16,000
(E)	92,000	(D)	48,000
Balance	1,408,000		

(A) To record purchase of 80% interest on January 1, 1995.
(B) To record dividends received in 1995.
(C) To record equity in realized income of S Company for 1995 ($100,000 − $80,000).
(D) To record dividends received in 1996.
(E) To record equity in realized income of S Company for 1996 ($112,000 + $80,000 − $100,000).

Consolidated Statements Workpaper Entries—December 31, 1996 (Illustration 12-6)

(1) Equity in Subsidiary Income   92,000
     Dividends Declared   48,000   80% × 60,000.
     Investment in S Company   44,000
       To adjust investment account and to eliminate equity in subsidiary income ($112,000 + $80,000 − $100,000).

(2) Sales   1,000,000
     Purchases (Cost of Sales)   1,000,000
       To eliminate intercompany sales.

(3) 12/31 Inventory—Income Statement (Cost of Sales)   125,000
     Inventory   125,000
       To eliminate unrealized intercompany profit in ending inventory.

(4) Beginning Retained Earnings—S Company
     (Noncontrolling Interest) (.20 × $100,000)   20,000
     Investment in S Company (Controlling Interest)
     (.80 × $100,000)   80,000
       1/1 Inventory—Income Statement (Cost of Sales)   100,000
       To recognize intercompany profit realized during the year and to reduce the noncontrolling interest at beginning of year for its share of unrealized intercompany profit at beginning of year.

(5) Beginning Retained Earnings—S Company   644,000
     Capital Stock—S Company   800,000
       Investment in S Company   1,444,000
       To eliminate investment account.

By comparing the consolidated balances in Illustration 12-6 with those in Illustrations 5-8 and 5-16, you can satisfy yourself that consolidated balances are not affected by the method used by a parent company to record its investment in a subsidiary. By comparing recorded net income and retained earnings of P Company in Illustration 12-6 with consolidated net income and consolidated retained earnings in the same illustration, you can satisfy yourself that, when the equity method of accounting is used to record an investment in a subsidiary, the recorded net income and retained earnings of the parent company are equal to consolidated net income and consolidated retained earnings.

ILLUSTRATION 12-6
Consolidated Statements Workpaper
P Company and Subsidiary
For Year Ended December 31, 1996

INCOME STATEMENT	P COMPANY	S COMPANY	ELIMINATIONS DR.	ELIMINATIONS CR.	NON-CONTROLLING INTERESTS	CONSOLIDATED BALANCES
Sales	3,546,000	2,020,000	(2) 1,000,000			4,566,000
Equity in Subsidiary Income	92,000		(1) 92,000			
Total Revenue	3,638,000	2,020,000				4,566,000
Inventory 1/1	480,000	310,000		(4) 100,000		690,000
Purchases	2,070,000	1,250,000		(2) 1,000,000		2,320,000
	2,550,000	1,560,000				3,010,000
Inventory 12/31	510,000	360,000	(3) 125,000			745,000
Cost of Goods Sold	2,040,000	1,200,000				2,265,000
Other Expense	1,100,000	680,000				1,780,000
Total Cost and Expense	3,140,000	1,880,000				4,045,000
Net/Combined Income	498,000	140,000				521,000
Noncontrolling Interest in Income					23,000	(23,000)*
Net Income to Retained Earnings	498,000	140,000	1,217,000	1,100,000	23,000	498,000
RETAINED EARNINGS STATEMENT						
1/1 Retained Earnings						
P Company	1,800,000					1,800,000
S Company		805,000	(5) 644,000			
			(4) 20,000		141,000	
Net Income from above	498,000	140,000	1,217,000	1,100,000	23,000	498,000
Dividends Declared						
P Company	(150,000)					(150,000)
S Company		(60,000)		(1) 48,000	(12,000)	
12/31 Retained Earnings to Balance Sheet	2,148,000	885,000	1,881,000	1,148,000	152,000	2,148,000
BALANCE SHEET						
Inventory	510,000	360,000		(3) 125,000		745,000
Investment in S Company	1,408,000		(4) 80,000	(1) 44,000		
				(5) 1,444,000		
Other Assets	5,450,000	2,330,000				7,780,000
Total	7,368,000	2,690,000				8,525,000
Liabilities	2,220,000	805,000				3,025,000
Capital Stock						
P Company	3,000,000					3,000,000
S Company		1,000,000	(5) 800,000		200,000	
Retained Earnings from above	2,148,000	885,000	1,881,000	1,148,000	152,000	2,148,000
Noncontrolling Interest in Net Assets					352,000	352,000
Total Liabilities and Equity	7,368,000	2,690,000	2,761,000	2,761,000		8,525,000

*.20 ($140,000 − $125,000 + $100,000) = $23,000.

(1) To adjust investment account and to eliminate equity in subsidiary income.
(2) To eliminate intercompany sales.
(3) To eliminate unrealized intercompany profit.
(4) To recognize profit realized during the year and to reduce the noncontrolling interest at beginning of year for its share of unrealized intercompany profit at beginning of year.
(5) To eliminate investment account.

Questions

1. How does the treatment of a liquidating dividend differ under the cost and equity methods of accounting?

2. Describe the calculation necessary to adjust an investment balance from the cost basis to the equity basis.

3. Describe the circumstances that may require the treatment of tax consequences when using the equity method of accounting for an investee.

4. Distinguish between the treatment of (a) amortization of the difference between cost and book value, (b) unrealized intercompany profit on upstream sales, and (c) unrealized intercompany profit on downstream sales in calculating the tax consequences of undistributed investee income.

5. Was the adoption of the equity method as the required method of reporting on investments in investees over which the investor has significant influence a relaxation or a constriction of revenue-recognition criteria for investment revenue?

6. What are the guidelines for evaluating significant influence for purposes of the application of the equity method of accounting?

7. During an era of continually improving business operations, would one expect the equity method of accounting for investments to produce a larger or a smaller amount of investment revenue than the cost method? Explain.

8. What problems might confront auditors in verifying investment income reported under the equity method of accounting?

9. Explain how the equity method of accounting is applied when the investment is acquired through a series of stock acquisitions and the initial acquisition was accounted for by the cost method.

10. Explain the required accounting treatment when the sale of part of an investment reduces the investor's percentage of ownership to less than 20%.

Exercises

Exercise 12-1

On January 1, 1995, Adams Company purchased 30% of the 25,000 shares of common stock of Talley Company for $36 per share. At that date, the following data were available:

	TALLEY COMPANY
Assets	$1,500,000
Liabilities	300,000
Preferred stock, 8%	300,000
Common stock, $20 par	750,000
Retained earnings	150,000

During 1995, Talley Company earned $525,000 and declared a $24,000 dividend on preferred stock and a $187,500 dividend on common stock. The difference between cost and book value is attributed to land.

Required:

Prepare entries to account for Adams Company's investment in Talley Company during 1995 assuming that:

A. The cost method is used.

B. The equity method is used.

Exercise 12-2

On January 1, 1995, Alonzo Company acquired a 25% interest in the common stock of Terrell Company for $152,500, when Terrell Company had capital stock in the amount of $300,000 and retained earnings in the amount of $150,000. The marginal tax rate for both companies is 40%. On January 1, 1995, the average remaining life of the depreciable assets of Terrell Company was 10 years. Although it was not practicable for Alonzo Company to determine the fair values of the specific noncurrent assets of Terrell Company on January 1, 1995, it was determined that the book value of the current assets and liabilities of Terrell Company was equal to their fair value except for inventory that had a book value of $150,000 and a fair value of $190,000. Terrell Company prices its inventory using the FIFO method and reported net income of $250,000 in 1995 and $200,000 in 1996. Terrell Company also distributed dividends of $100,000 in each year. Ignore the income tax consequences of undistributed investee income.

Required:

A. Calculate the amount of equity in investee income to be reported by Alonzo Company in 1995 and 1996. Justify the assumptions (if any) that you must make.

B. Calculate the balance in the investment in Terrell Company account reported by Alonzo Company on December 31, 1995, and December 31, 1996.

Exercise 12-3

On January 1, 1995, Aldrich Company acquired 30% of the outstanding common stock of Thomas Company for $468,000. At that time, Thomas Company had total stockholders' equity in the amount of $1,000,000. The marginal tax rate for both companies is 40%. On January 1, 1995, the average remaining life of the depreciable assets of Thomas Company was 15 years. Although it was not practicable for Aldrich Company to determine the fair value of the specific noncurrent assets of Thomas Company on January 1, 1995, it was determined that fair value of the current assets and liabilities of Thomas Company was equal to their book value, except for inventory that had a fair value of $260,000 and a book value of

$200,000. Thomas Company prices its inventory at the lower of FIFO cost or market and reported net income of $280,000 in 1995 and $220,000 in 1996. Ignore the income tax consequences of undistributed investee income.

Required:

Calculate the amount of equity in investee income to be reported by Aldrich Company in 1995 and 1996. Justify the assumptions (if any) that you must make.

Exercise 12-4

On January 1, 1995, Allan Company acquired a 40% interest in Toro Company. For the year ended December 31, 1995, Allan Company reported pretax accounting income from its independent operations of $1,000,000. During the same period, Toro Company reported net income of $300,000 and distributed no dividends. Allan Company had no temporary differences other than that relating to its use of the equity method. Each company has a marginal income tax rate of 35%.

Required:

Calculate the amount of deferred income tax liability to be recorded on the books of Allan Company under each of the following assumptions:

A. Allan Company does not intend to liquidate or otherwise dispose of its investment in Toro Company in the foreseeable future.

B. Allan Company intends to dispose of its investment in Toro Company at an undefined future date.

Exercise 12-5

A Company acquired a 40% interest in T Company on June 30, 1992. In 1995 and 1996, T Company sold merchandise to A Company as follows:

YEAR	TOTAL SALES OF T COMPANY TO A COMPANY	INTERCOMPANY MERCHANDISE IN 12/31 INVENTORY OF A COMPANY	UNREALIZED INTERCOMPANY PROFIT (20% OF SALES PRICE)
1995	$600,000	$300,000	$60,000
1996	800,000	200,000	40,000

Each company has a marginal income tax rate of 45%. There were no intercompany sales prior to 1995. Ignore the income tax consequences of undistributed income.

Required:

A. Prepare the entries on the books of A Company to record the effects of intercompany sales of merchandise for the years ended December 31, 1995, and December 31, 1996.

B. Assume that all intercompany sales are downstream. Prepare the entries on the books of A Company to record the effects of the intercompany sales of merchandise for the years ended December 31, 1995, and December 31, 1996.

Exercise 12-6

On January 1, 1995, Alpert Company acquires a 40% interest in Thompson Company. On that date, Alpert Company sells Thompson Company equipment with a book value of $600,000 (original cost of $900,000 and accumulated depreciation of $300,000) for $700,000. On January 1, 1995, the equipment has an estimated remaining useful life of five years and is depreciated using the straight-line method.

Each company has a marginal income tax rate of 30%. Ignore the income tax consequences of undistributed income.

Required:

A. Prepare the entries to record the effects of the intercompany sale of equipment on the books of Alpert Company for the years ended December 31, 1995, and December 31, 1996.

B. Assume that the intercompany sale is upstream rather than downstream. Prepare the entries to record the effects of the intercompany sale of equipment on the books of Alpert Company for the years ended December 31, 1995, and December 31, 1996.

Exercise 12-7

On January 1, 1992, Alcorn Company acquired a 30% interest in Thorn Company. For the year ended December 31, 1995, Thorn Company reported net income of $300,000 and distributed $100,000 in dividends.

On January 1, 1995, Thorn Company sells Alcorn Company assets with a book value of $600,000 for $700,000. On the date of sale the equipment has an estimated remaining useful life of 10 years and is depreciated using the straight-line method.

Each company has a marginal income tax rate of 40%. Ignore the income tax consequences of undistributed income.

Required:

A. Calculate Alcorn Company's equity in the income of Thorn Company for the year ended December 31, 1995.

B. Assume that the sale of equipment was downstream rather than upstream. Prepare the entry(s) on the books of Alcorn Company for the year ended December 31, 1995, to eliminate the effects of the intercompany sale.

Exercise 12-8

Alexandar Company purchased 30% of the outstanding common stock of Teller Company on June 1, 1991, for $450,000, when Teller Company had stockholders' equity of $1,500,000. Alexandar Company records and reports its investment in Teller Company using the equity method. The marginal income tax rate for Alexandar Company is 40%. Eighty percent of dividends received from domestic corporations may be excluded from taxable income. In 1996, Teller Company reported net income of $200,000 and distributed dividends in the amount of $40,000.

Required:

Prepare in general journal form the necessary entries, including tax consequences, that should be recorded by Alexandar Company during 1996 to account for its investment in Teller Company, assuming that:

A. Alexandar Company never intends to dispose of its investment and expects to recover its interest in the undistributed income of Teller Company in future dividend distributions.

B. Alexandar Company expects to recover its interest in the undistributed income of Teller Company through the future sale of its investment in Teller Company.

Exercise 12-9

Abram Company owns 30% of the voting stock of Todd Company. In 1995, Todd Company reported net income of $400,000 and paid dividends of $200,000. Abram Company's marginal income tax rate is 40%. Abram Company can deduct from its taxable income 80% of any dividends received from Todd Company.

Required:

Prepare the entry(s) on Abram Company's books in 1995 to record income tax expense on the income recognized by it on its investment in Todd Company, assuming that:

A. Abram Company expects to realize its interest in the undistributed income of Todd Company through the sale of its investment in Todd Company.

B. Abram Company never intends to dispose of its investment in Todd Company.

Exercise 12-10

Amato Company purchased Trujillo Company common stock in two open-market cash purchases as follows:

DATE	SHARES ACQUIRED	COST
January 1, 1994	1,000	$18,000
January 1, 1995	3,000	55,000

Trujillo Company had 10,000 shares of $10 par value common stock outstanding during the entire period. Retained earnings balances for Trujillo Company on relevant dates were:

January 1, 1994	$ 5,000
January 1, 1995	(10,000)
January 1, 1996	20,000
December 31, 1996	100,000

Dividends in the amount of $20,000 were distributed by Trujillo Company only in 1996. Any difference between cost and book value is attributed in its entirety to the net of tax difference between the fair value and the book value of land owned by Trujillo Company.

Required:

Prepare the journal entries that Amato Company would record on its books during 1994, 1995, and 1996 to account for its investment in Trujillo Company.

Exercise 12-11

Akin Company acquired 40% of the outstanding common stock of Tanner Company on January 1, 1994, for $90,000. At the date of purchase, Tanner Company had a balance in its $75 par value common stock account of $150,000 and retained earnings of $30,000.

On January 1, 1996, Tanner Company issued 500 shares of its previously unissued stock to nonaffiliated stockholders for $90 per share. On this date, Tanner Company had a retained earnings balance of $60,000. The difference between cost and book value is attributable in its entirety to the net of tax difference between the fair value and the book value of land owned by Tanner Company.

Required:

Prepare the entry on Akin Company's books to reflect the effect of the new issue of shares by Tanner Company.

Exercise 12-12

Almond Company purchased 3,000 of the outstanding common shares of Tag Company on January 1, 1993, for $80,000 when Tag Company's stockholders' equity consisted of the following:

Common stock, $20 par value	$240,000
Retained earnings	80,000
Total	$320,000

On January 1, 1996, Tag Company reacquired 2,000 of its common shares from stockholders other than Almond Company for $40,000. The shares will be held as treasury stock. Stockholders' equity for Almond and Tag companies on the date of reacquisition was:

	ALMOND	TAG
Common stock	$ 800,000	$240,000
Retained earnings	340,000	40,000
Total	$1,140,000	$280,000

Required:

Describe any adjustments to Almond Company's books necessitated by Tag Company's reacquisition of its stock.

Problems

Problem 12-1

On December 31, 1995, Alex Industries acquired 20% of the outstanding stock of Tipton Machinery through a cash purchase for $475,000. The difference between cost and book value was entirely attributable to land. Income and dividend information for Tipton Machinery for six years following the acquisition is as follows:

YEAR	REPORTED INCOME	DIVIDENDS DISTRIBUTED
1996	$174,000	$50,000
1997	139,000	50,000
1998	71,000	75,000
1999	47,000	75,000
2000	(59,500)	75,000
2001	(9,400)	75,000

362,100   400,000   = 37,900

Required:

A. Prepare journal entries for 2000 and 2001 under both the cost and equity methods of accounting for investments.

B. Immediately after a liquidating dividend is recorded, the balance in the investment account and the total amount of investee income recorded on the books of the investor from date of acquisition to date of the liquidating dividend is the same under both the cost and equity methods. Prepare a schedule for Alex Industries and its investee to reconcile the income totals and investment account balances under the two accounting methods at the end of 2001.

Problem 12-2

On January 1, 1990, Akers Company acquired 40% of the common stock of Tang Company for $360,000 when the common stock and retained earnings of Tang Company were $750,000 CS and $150,000, respectively. The following information is also available:

RE

	TANG COMPANY	
YEAR	DIVIDEND DISTRIBUTIONS	NET INCOME (LOSS)
1995	$90,000	$292,500
1996	90,000	(75,000)
1997	90,000	120,000

270,000   337,500

40% of 292,500.

The retained earnings balance of Tang Company on January 1, 1995, was $375,000.

Required:

A. Calculate the balance in the investment account on the books of Akers Company on January 1, 1995.

B. Prepare the journal entries necessary to account for the investment on the books of Akers Company for the years 1995 through 1997.   Ask, cost or equity

Problem 12-3

Akin Company owns 40% of the common stock of Tanner Company. Tanner Company's ending inventory included $80,000 in 1995 and $60,000 in 1996 of unrealized intercompany profit on merchandise it had purchased from Akin Company. Akin Company's sales to Tanner Company were made at 25% above cost. The companies have a marginal income tax rate of 40%. Ignore the tax consequences of undistributed investee income.   Downstream

Required:

Prepare in general journal form the entries on the books of Akin Company in 1995 and 1996 to adjust for the effects of the intercompany transactions recorded by Akin Company in 1995 and 1996.

Problem 12-4

Abott Company acquired a 40% interest in Trent Company on January 1, 1995. On this date, Abott Company sold equipment to Trent Company with a book value of $900,000 (original cost $1,200,000 and accumulated depreciation of $300,000) for $1,050,000. On the date of sale, Trent Company executives estimated that the equipment had a remaining useful life of eight years and established that it would be depreciated using the straight-line method. During 1995 and 1996, Trent Company made the following merchandise sales to Abott Company:

YEAR	SALES	MERCHANDISE IN ENDING INVENTORY 12/31	UNREALIZED PROFIT IN ENDING INVENTORY
1995	$400,000	$200,000	$100,000
1996	750,000	450,000	225,000

Each company has a marginal income tax rate of 30%. Ignore the income tax consequences of undistributed investee income.

Required:

A. Prepare the journal entries necessary on the books of Abott Company to account for unrealized profit on intercompany transactions in 1995 and 1996.

B. Repeat part (A) assuming that the intercompany sale of equipment was upstream and the intercompany sale of merchandise was downstream.

Problem 12-5

Agnew Company purchased 30% of the common stock of Tandy Company on January 1, 1995, for $340,000. On this date, Tandy Company had common stock of $400,000 and retained earnings of $200,000. The difference between cost and book value was attributed in its entirety to the net of tax difference between the fair value and book value of assets with an average remaining useful life of five years. Assets of Tandy Company are depreciated using the straight-line method.

For the year ended December 31, 1995, Agnew Company reported pretax accounting income from its own operations of $2,000,000. During the same period, Tandy Company had net income of $300,000 and declared no dividends. Each company has a marginal income tax rate of 40%.

Required:

Prepare in general journal form the necessary entries, including tax consequences, that should be recorded by Agnew Company during 1995 to account for its investment in Tandy Company, assuming that:

chuyển nhường

A. Agnew Company does not intend to dispose of its investment in Tandy Company and has established that Tandy Company will divert all undistributed income into a plant expansion fund to build additional facilities.

B. Agnew Company has established that Tandy Company intends to permanently reinvest all undistributed income and expects to recover its investment through the future sale of Tandy Company stock.

C. Tandy Company distributed $100,000 in dividends in 1995 and that the assumptions in part (A) apply.

Problem 12-6

Alcorn Company owns 30% of the voting stock of Tibbs Company. The investment in Tibbs company was made at the beginning of 1991 and is accounted for by use of the equity method. On the date the investment was made, the cost of the investment exceeded the book value of the equity interest acquired by $160,000. Alcorn Company is amortizing this difference over 25 years, the average remaining life of the property and equipment of Tibbs Company on January 1, 1991.

The January 1, 1995, inventory of Alcorn Company included merchandise in the amount of $400,000 that cost Tibbs Company $320,000. During 1995, Alcorn Company purchased merchandise from Tibbs Company in the amount of $800,000. The December 31, 1995, inventory of Alcorn Company includes merchandise in the amount of $550,000 that cost Tibbs Company $375,000. Tibbs Company reported net income of $250,000 in 1995. The marginal income tax rate for both companies is 40%. Ignore the income tax consequences of undistributed investee income.

Required:

A. Prepare a schedule to compute Alcorn Company's equity in Tibbs Company's income for 1995.

B. Assume that the intercompany sale of merchandise was downstream rather than up-stream. Prepare a schedule to compute Alcorn Company's equity in Tibbs Company's income for 1995.

C. Using the information from part (B), prepare in general journal form the entries recorded by Alcorn Company to record any necessary adjustments resulting from the intercompany sales for the year ended December 31, 1995.

Problem 12-7

Acosta Company owns 30% of the voting stock of Tate Company. On January 1, 1995, Tate Company sold equipment to Acosta Company for $500,000. The equipment had a book value to Tate Company of $430,000 on the date of sale. The management of Acosta Company estimated that the equipment had a seven-year remaining useful life on January 1, 1995.

In 1995, Acosta Company's ending inventory included merchandise purchased from Tate Company for $180,000 that cost Tate Company $120,000 to produce. In 1996, Acosta Company's ending inventory included merchandise purchased from Tate Company for $120,000 that cost Tate Company $80,000 to produce.

Tate Company reported net income of $300,000 in 1995 and $250,000 in 1996. The marginal income tax rate for both companies is 40%. Ignore the income tax consequences of undistributed investee income.

Required:

A. Prepare a schedule to determine the amount to be recorded by Acosta Company to recognize its equity in the net income of Tate Company for the years ended December 31, 1995, and December 31, 1996.

B. Assume that the intercompany sales of merchandise and equipment were downstream rather than upstream. Prepare in general journal form the entries recorded by Acosta Company to record its equity in the net income of Tate Company and to adjust for the effects of intercompany sales for the years ended December 31, 1995, and December 31, 1996.

Problem 12-8

Adair Company owns a 30% interest in the voting stock of Tong Company. Tong Company reported net income after taxes of $200,000 in 1995 and $300,000 in 1996. In addition, Tong Company's ending inventories included $40,000 in 1995 and $60,000 in 1996 of unrealized profit on intercompany sales of merchandise that cost Adair Company $60,000 and $90,000, respectively.

An intercompany sale of land took place in 1995. Tong Company had originally purchased the land in 1989 for $50,000 and sold the land to Adair Company for a bargain price of $65,000. In 1996, Adair Company sold the land in an arm's-length transaction for $70,000.

The marginal income tax rate for both companies is 40%. Ignore the income tax consequences of undistributed investee income.

Required:

A. Prepare the entries made by Adair Company during 1995 and 1996 relating to its investment in Tong Company.

B. Assuming that the intercompany merchandise sales were upstream instead of downstream, and that the land sale was downstream instead of upstream, prepare the entires that Adair Company would have made during 1995 and 1996 relating to its investment in Tong Company.

Problem 12-9

Taft Company had 100,000 shares of $10 par value common stock outstanding at all times and retained earnings balances as indicated here:

January 1, 1995	$160,000
January 1, 1996	240,000
December 31, 1996	300,000

Arron Company acquired Taft Company stock through open-market purchases as follows:

DATE	SHARES	COST
1/1/95	10,000	$130,000
1/1/96	20,000	300,000

Taft Company declared no dividends during this period. The fair value of Taft Company's assets and liabilities was approximately equal to their book value throughout this period (1995 through 1996). Arron Company's policy is to amortize goodwill over an estimated economic life of 10 years from the date of each stock purchase.

Required:

A. Prepare a schedule to compare investment cost with the book value of equity acquired for each stock purchase.

B. Prepare book entries on Arron Company's books for 1995 and 1996.

Problem 12-10

On January 1, 1994, Aguilar Company acquired 42% of the capital stock of Thorn Company for $180,000. On that date, Thorn Company's stockholders' equity was:

Capital stock, $20 par	$200,000
Other contributed capital	80,000
Retained earnings	120,000
Total	$400,000

The difference between cost and book value is attributed in its entirety to the net of tax difference between the fair value and the book value of land owned by Thorn Company.

On January 2, 1996, Thorn Company issued 2,000 shares of its authorized capital stock, with a market value of $65 per share, to Jason Still in exchange for a patent. Thorn Company's retained earnings balance on this date was $190,000; capital stock and other contributed capital balances had not changed during 1994 and 1995.

Required:

A. Prepare the journal entry on Aguilar Company's books to reflect the effect of the issue of the additional shares by Thorn Company.

B. Assuming that the market value of the new shares issued was $45 per share, repeat requirement (A).

Problem 12-11

Arron Company purchased on the open market 21,000 shares of the capital stock of Taft Company for $210,000 on January 2, 1993, when Taft Company had the following stockholders' equity:

Capital stock, $5 par value	$300,000
Other contributed capital	120,000
Retained earnings	88,000
Total	$508,000

The difference between cost and book value is attributed in its entirety to the net of tax difference between the fair value and the book value of Taft Company land.

On January 1, 1996, Taft Company reacquired 10,000 of its own shares by direct purchase from another stockholder for cash of $140,000. The shares are to be held as treasury stock. Taft Company's retained earnings had increased to $180,000 by January 1, 1996; capital stock and other contributed capital balances had not changed since January 2, 1993.

Required:

Describe the adjustments on Arron Company's books necessitated by the reacquisition of shares by Taft Company.

Problem 12-12

On January 1, 1995, Alcott Enterprises purchased 2,500 of the 10,000 outstanding shares of common stock of Temple Company, paying an amount equal to the book value of the shares acquired. Relevant income statement data for the two firms for 1995 follow:

	ALCOTT ENTERPRISES	TEMPLE COMPANY
Gross revenues	$4,162,755	$755,436
Cost of goods sold	2,986,754	485,618
Miscellaneous operating expense	374,932	52,784
Administrative expense	166,693	23,347
Retained earnings, 1/1/95	864,279	137,482

In addition to the foregoing data, the following items are relevant to the financial operations of the two companies for 1995:

1. Temple Company suffered a $275,500 uninsured loss when one of its plants was demolished by a flash flood. Management had not carried flood insurance on the plant because of its location in a semi-arid region where no such natural disasters had ever been recorded.

2. Temple Company embarked on a plan to dispose of all its chemical manufacturing facilities on June 30, 1995. The chemical operations accounted for 20% of Temple's revenue and 30% of costs and expenses during 1994, spread evenly throughout the year. The final disposal date was December 31, 1995, and the facilities were sold at a loss of $180,000.

3. Temple changed from the double-declining balance method to the straight-line method of depreciating its manufacturing equipment. The cumulative effect of the change on prior years was to increase income by $104,103. (The new method became effective on January 2, 1995.)

4. In previous years, Temple Company had recorded royalty income on the cash basis. Starting with 1995, royalty income was recorded when earned. The effect of this change was the recognition of additional income for prior periods in the amount of $47,565. (This change was made to comply with generally accepted accounting principles.)

5. In 1995, Alcott Enterprises had additional income of $135,400 resulting from changes in accounting principles, and an extraordinary fire loss of $452,875. (The additional income represents the cumulative effect on prior years of the changes in accounting principles.)

Required:

Assuming that all amounts are material (ignore income taxes):

A. Prepare an income statement and statement of retained earnings for Temple Company.

B. Prepare an income statement and statement of retained earnings for Alcott Enterprises in which its investment income is recognized by use of the equity method.

Problem 12-13

Thomas Laboratories, a drug company, manufactures and distributes a variety of nonprescription drugs and sundry cosmetic products. Altman Company, realizing the excellent profit potential in the nonprescription drug and cosmetics business, purchased 30% of the outstanding voting common stock shares of Thomas Laboratories in 1989 for $700,000, an amount equal to the equity acquired. Undistributed income for Thomas Laboratories from the date of acquisition to January 1, 1995, amounted to $645,000.

More than 45% of Thomas Laboratories' revenues for the previous five years had come from the sale of its facial cleanser products. During 1995, a federal agency found one of the ingredients of this product line to be a cancer-causing agent and banned its use in products manufactured in the United States. Stockholders witnessed a precipitous decline in their common stockholdings during the remainder of 1995, and as of December 31, 1995, the total market value of Thomas Laboratories' outstanding common stock had decreased to $1,500,000.

Additional information related to Thomas Laboratories' performance during 1995 and 1996 is as follows:

	1995	1996
Net income	$255,545	$395,500
Dividends paid	150,000	150,000

Required:

Ignore income tax consequences

A. Prepare the journal entries that would be required on the books of Altman Company during 1995. Management considers the decline in the market value of the Thomas Laboratories common stock to be permanent.

B. Early in 1996, an outstanding scientist working for Thomas Laboratories found an effective replacement for the banned ingredient, and the market responded with an increase in the total market value for the common stock of Thomas Laboratories to $2,200,000. Prepare the journal entries required on the books of Altman Company during 1996.

Problem 12-14

On January 1, 1993, Porter Company purchased an 80% interest in the capital stock of Salem Company for $820,000. At that time, Salem Company had capital stock of $500,000 and retained earnings of $100,000.

Differences between the fair value and the book value of the identifiable assets of Salem Company were as follows:

	FAIR VALUE IN EXCESS OF BOOK VALUES
Equipment	$125,000
Land	62,500
Inventory	37,500

The book values of all other assets and liabilities of Salem Company were equal to their fair values on January 1, 1993. The equipment had a remaining life of five years on January 1,

1993, the inventory was sold in 1993, and goodwill is amortized over 40 years. Ignore deferred income tax considerations in the assignment of the difference between cost and book value.

Porter Company accounts for its investment in Salem Company using the equity method of accounting. The affiliated companies file consolidated income tax returns. Financial data for 1995 are presented here:

	PORTER COMPANY	SALEM COMPANY
Sales	$1,050,000	$400,000
Equity in subsidiary income	96,000	
Total revenue	1,146,000	400,000
Cost of goods sold	850,000	180,000
Depreciation expense	35,000	25,000
Other expenses	65,000	45,000
Total cost and expense	950,000	250,000
Net income	$ 196,000	$150,000
1/1 Retained earnings	$ 482,000	$200,000
Net income	196,000	150,000
Dividends declared	(100,000)	(50,000)
12/31 Retained earnings	$ 578,000	$300,000
Cash	$ 80,000	$ 50,000
Accounts receivable	250,000	170,000
Inventory	230,000	150,000
Investment in Salem Company	878,000	
Land		300,000
Plant and equipment	350,000	250,000
Total assets	$1,788,000	$920,000
Accounts payable	$ 160,000	$100,000
Notes payable	50,000	20,000
Capital stock	1,000,000	500,000
Retained earnings	578,000	300,000
Total liabilities and equity	$1,788,000	$920,000

Required:

A. Prepare in general journal form the entries required on the books of Porter Company during 1995 to account for its investment in Salem Company.

B. Prepare a consolidated financial statements workpaper for the year ended December 31, 1995.

C. Calculate consolidated net income using the analytical approach.

D. To satisfy yourself that, under the equity method, the net income and retained earnings reported by the parent company are the same as consolidated net income and consolidated retained earnings, compare consolidated net income and consolidated retained earnings to the net income and retained earnings reported by Porter Company.

E. If you have previously completed the consolidated statements workpaper for Problem 4-4, compare the consolidated balances in the consolidated statements workpaper prepared in part (B) with the consolidated balances in the consolidated statements workpaper prepared for Problem 4-4 to satisfy yourself that the method, cost or equity, used by the parent company to record its investment does not affect balances reported in the consolidated financial statements.

Problem 12-15

Paque Corporation owns 90% of the common stock of Segal Company. The stock was purchased for $810,000 on January 1, 1991, when Segal Company's retained earnings were $150,000. Paque Company uses the equity method to account for its investment in Segal Company. The affiliated companies file consolidated income tax returns. Financial data for 1995 are presented here:

	PAQUE CORPORATION	SEGAL COMPANY
Sales	$1,650,000	$ 795,000
Equity in subsidiary income	91,125	
Total revenue	1,741,125	795,000
Cost of goods sold		
Beginning inventory	225,000	165,000
Purchases	1,275,000	525,000
Cost of goods available	1,500,000	690,000
Less: Ending inventory	210,000	172,500
Cost of goods sold	1,290,000	517,500
Other expenses	310,500	206,250
Total cost and expense	1,600,500	723,750
Net income	$ 140,625	$ 71,250
1/1 Retained earnings	$ 798,000	$ 180,000
Net income	140,625	71,250
Dividends declared	(150,000)	(60,000)
12/31 Retained earnings	$ 788,625	$191,250
Cash	$ 93,000	$ 75,000
Accounts receivable	319,500	168,750
Inventory	210,000	172,500
Investment in Segal Company	833,625	
Other assets	750,000	630,000
Total assets	$2,206,125	$1,046,250
Accounts payable	$ 105,000	$ 45,000
Other current liabilities	112,500	60,000
Capital stock	1,200,000	750,000
Retained earnings	788,625	191,250
Total liabilities and equity	$2,206,125	$1,046,250

The January 1, 1995, inventory of Paque Corporation includes $45,000 of profit recorded by Segal Company on 1994 sales. During 1995, Segal Company made intercompany sales of $300,000 with a markup of 20% of selling price. The ending inventory of Paque Corporation includes goods purchased in 1995 from Segal Company for $75,000.

Required:

A. Recalculate the amount of equity in subsidiary earnings reported by Paque Corporation.

B. Prepare the entries made on the books of Paque Corporation during 1995 to record its interest in Segal Company.

C.   Prepare the consolidated statements workpaper for the year ended December 31, 1995.

D.   Calculate consolidated net income using the analytical approach.

E.   To satisfy yourself that, under the equity method, the net income and retained earnings reported by the parent company are the same as consolidated net income and consolidated retained earning, compare consolidated net income and consolidated retained earnings to the net income and retained earnings reported by Paque Corporation.

F.   If you have previously completed the consolidated statements workpaper for Problem 5-7, compare the consolidated balances in the consolidated statements workpaper prepared in part (C) with the consolidated balances in the consolidated statements workpaper prepared for Problem 5-7 to satisfy yourself that the method, cost or equity, used by the parent company to record its investment does not affect balances reported in the consolidated financial statements.

Problem 12-16

Pitts Company owns 80% of the common stock of Shannon Company. The stock was purchased for $960,000 on January 1, 1993, when Shannon Company's retained earnings were $675,000. On January 1, 1995, Shannon Company sold fixed assets to Pitts Company for $960,000; Shannon Company had purchased these assets for $1,350,000 on January 1, 1985, at which time their estimated useful life was 25 years. The estimated remaining useful life to Pitts Company on 1/1/95 is 10 years. Both companies employ the straight-line method of depreciation. Pitts Company uses the equity method to record its investment in Shannon Company and the affiliated companies file consolidated income tax returns. The financial data for 1996 are presented here:

	PITTS COMPANY	SHANNON COMPANY
Sales	$1,950,000	$1,350,000
Equity in subsidiary income	252,000	
Total revenue	2,202,000	1,350,000
Cost of goods sold	1,350,000	900,000
Other expenses	225,000	150,000
Total cost and expense	1,575,000	1,050,000
Net income	$ 627,000	$ 300,000
1/1 Retained earnings	$1,397,400	$1,038,000
Net income	627,000	300,000
Dividends declared	(150,000)	(75,000)
12/31 Retained earnings	$1,874,400	$1,263,000
Inventory	$ 498,000	$ 225,000
Investment in Shannon Company	1,334,400	
Fixed assets	2,168,100	2,625,000
Accumulated depreciation—fixed assets	(900,000)	(612,000)
Total assets	$3,100,500	$2,238,000
Liabilities	$ 465,600	$ 450,000
Common stock	760,500	525,000
Retained earnings	1,874,400	1,263,000
Total liabilities and equity	$3,100,500	$2,238,000

Required:

A. Recalculate the balance recorded in the equity in subsidiary income account.

B. Prepare the entries Pitts Company makes on its books during 1996 to record its interest in Shannon Company.

C. Prepare a consolidated statements workpaper for the year ended December 31, 1996.

D. Calculate consolidated net income using the analytical approach.

E. To satisfy yourself that, under the equity method, the net income and retained earnings reported by the parent company are the same as consolidated net income and consolidated retained earnings, compare consolidated net income and consolidated retained earnings to the net income and retained earnings reported by Pitts Company.

F. If you have previously completed the consolidated statements workpaper for Problem 6-6, compare the consolidated balances in the consolidated statements workpaper prepared in part (C) with the consolidated balances in the consolidated statements workpaper prepared for Problem 6-6 to satisfy yourself that the method, cost or equity, used by the parent company to record its investment does not affect balances reported in the consolidated financial statements.

Problem 12-17

On January 1, 1995, Pasquel Company purchased a 70% interest in Santosa Company for $1,000,000, when the common stock and retained earnings accounts were $900,000 and $200,000, respectively. An examination of Santosa Company's balance sheet on the acquisition date revealed the following:

	TAX BASIS/ BOOK VALUE	FAIR VALUE
Inventory	$225,000	$275,000
Plant and equipment (net) (cost $750,000; accumulated depreciation $150,000)	600,000	680,000
Land	500,000	600,000

The plant and equipment has a remaining useful life of eight years. All the inventory had been sold by the end of 1995. Goodwill is amortized over a period of 20 years. Pasquel Company records its investment in Santosa Company using the equity method.

Adjusted trial balances for 1995 are as follows:

DEBITS	PASQUEL COMPANY	SANTOSA COMPANY
Cash	$ 250,000	$ 100,000
Accounts receivable	500,000	300,000
Inventory	400,000	200,000
Investment in Santosa Company	1,148,730	
Plant and equipment	1,200,000	900,000
Accumulated depreciation	(423,000)	(350,000)
Land	700,000	600,000
Cost of goods sold	1,037,000	500,000
Depreciation expense	70,000	50,000
Other expenses	300,000	130,000

DEBITS	PASQUEL COMPANY	SANTOSA COMPANY
Tax expense	121,200	80,000
Dividends declared	40,000	20,000
Total	$5,343,930	$2,530,000

CREDITS		
Income taxes payable	$ 106,700	$ 40,000
Accounts payable	300,000	50,000
Deferred tax liability	114,500	60,000
Notes payable	500,000	200,000
Common stock	1,600,000	900,000
Retained earnings	700,000	200,000
Sales	1,860,000	990,000
Gain on sale of equipment		90,000
Equity in Santosa Company income	162,730	
Total	$5,343,930	$2,530,000

The companies file separate tax returns and the marginal income tax rate for both companies is 40%.

Additional Information:

1. On January 2, 1995, Santosa Company sold equipment with a book value of $200,000 to Pasquel Company for $290,000. The equipment is depreciated using the straight-line method and has a remaining useful life of three years.
2. Santosa Company sells merchandise to Pasquel Company at a 20% markup on cost. Total sales for 1995 were $300,000, but only one-fifth of the merchandise is in the ending inventory.
3. The trial balances include a $50,000 payable from Pasquel Company to Santosa Company.
4. Dividends received from Santosa Company are subject to the 80% dividends received exclusion. All undistributed income is expected to be distributed as dividends in later years.

Required:

A. Recalculate the balance recorded in the Equity in Santosa Company Income account.

B. Prepare the entry necessary on the books of Pasquel Company to record the current year's income tax expense relating to its equity in subsidiary income, including the tax consequences of undistributed subsidiary income.

C. Prepare the consolidated statements workpaper for 1995.

13

ACCOUNTING FOR HOME OFFICE AND BRANCH ACTIVITIES

A company seeking to grow or to diversify can do so by acquiring an interest in an established company or by acquiring a controlling interest in the common stock of a newly created entity. The preceding chapters on consolidated financial statements focused on the accounting issues related to consolidating the financial statements of two or more separate entities. The purpose of preparing consolidated financial statements is to provide information about the total performance of separate legal entities that are controlled and operated under common management.

As an alternative to growth by acquisition, companies often expand into new marketing territories through internal growth by establishing branch offices that operate within the firm. In other words, a branch office operates at a location separate from the firm's principal office, called the *home office*, but a branch is not a separate legal entity. The rise of national and regional chain-store operations and suburban shopping centers has contributed significantly to the number of branch operations.

The manager of a branch office is normally given some degree of autonomy in order to provide better service to the branch customers. The amount of autonomy that the branch manager is granted by the home office will vary from firm to firm, but regardless of the responsibility granted, he or she is subject to the control of the home office and is governed by general corporate policies. To provide the home office management with the information needed to evaluate the performance of the branch manager, the branch is normally accounted for as a separate segment or responsibility center for internal purposes. However, for external reporting purposes, combined financial statements for the home office and branch operations are prepared in order to evaluate the financial position and operating performance of the firm as a whole. In this chapter, we consider the problems associated with accounting for a branch office and the preparation of combined financial statements.

SALES AGENCY AND BRANCH CONTRASTED

When a separate office is established to provide a sales outlet, it most often takes the organizational form of either a sales agency or a branch office. Factors such as the needs of the clientele, competition in the new territory, and the type of product being marketed dictate which form will best accomplish the objectives established by management.

The term *sales agency* is commonly applied to an office that maintains samples of the firm's products. Staff members of the sales agency take orders for merchandise, but the home office normally grants credit, ships the merchandise, and collects accounts receivable. Ordinarily, transactions of the agency are recorded on the books of the home office. The agency normally maintains a petty cash system containing standard control procedures.

In contrast, the term *branch* is used to describe a facility that maintains and sells its own merchandise. All the merchandise may be obtained from the home office, or some of it may be purchased from outsiders. A branch normally maintains its own accounting system as a basis for preparing financial statements and reports. The branch management may have the authority to grant credit and collect outstanding receivables, or these functions may be centralized.

ACCOUNTING FOR A SALES AGENCY

As noted above, the manager of a sales agency does not keep a financial accounting system; operations of the agency are recorded on the books of the home office. To provide information on each agency, revenue and expense transactions of a particular agency are recorded in accounts identified with that agency. For control purposes, assets other than cash transferred to an agency are recorded in accounts identified with the agency. A petty cash fund is established for the purpose of paying small expenditures that can be settled more conveniently by the agency.

To illustrate the accounting for an agency, assume that Vella Corporation, a manufacturer of home furniture, established a sales agency in Atlanta. The entries to record the typical transactions of the agency are as follows:

Land—Atlanta Agency	20,000	
Building—Atlanta Agency	35,000	
Furniture and Equipment—Atlanta Agency	15,000	
Cash		70,000
To record acquisition of facilities and equipment for Atlanta sales agency.		

Petty Cash Fund—Atlanta Agency	5,000	
Cash		5,000

      To establish a petty cash fund.

Sample Inventory—Atlanta Agency	18,000	
Inventory		18,000

      To record transfer of sample merchandise. (If a periodic inventory system is used, an account such as Merchandise Shipments—Atlanta Agency is credited. In the income statement, this account reduces the cost of goods available for sale at the home office.)

Accounts Receivable	80,000	
Sales—Atlanta Agency		80,000

      To record the shipment of orders submitted by the agency and approved by the home office.

Cost of Goods Sold—Atlanta Agency	45,000	
Inventory		45,000

      To record cost of goods identified with sales of the agency.

Operating Expenses*—Atlanta Agency	15,000	
Cash		12,500
Accumulated Depreciation—Atlanta Agency		2,500

      To record expenses incurred by the agency.

Operating Expenses*—Atlanta Agency	4,000	
Cash		4,000

      To replenish petty cash fund.

*Individual expense accounts are debited in practice.

ACCOUNTING FOR A BRANCH OPERATION

Accounting System Used to Account for a Branch

The accounting system created to account for the transactions of a branch can be centralized as described above for a sales agency. A centralized system is used by many small merchandising firms. In a centralized system, most of the accounting records are maintained by the home office. The branch provides basic source documents such as sales invoices and payroll time cards to the home office as a basis for the recording of the branch transactions. It may be useful for the home office to separate the activities of the branch from the activities of the home office by establishing separate accounts for branch transactions. The branch manager may operate a cash fund to pay some items that are paid more conveniently by the branch. Such a cash fund is similar to a petty cash fund operation, and no special accounting problems are involved.

As the system of branch operations grows and the volume of transactions between the branch and the home office increases, the associated accounting problems support the use of a decentralized accounting system. In such a system, each branch maintains a self-contained accounting system including books of original entry and a fully self-balancing set of accounts. Often an on-site computer is used to maintain the accounting records and to accumulate other data. Transactions between the branch and independent parties are recorded as if the branch were an autonomous store. Although the branch is not a separate legal entity, internal transactions between the branch and home office are recorded on both sets of books in reciprocal accounts. (Reciprocal accounts measure the same thing on different sets of books. The accounts will have equal but opposite balances when all the accounting is complete. That is, if the account on one set of books has a debit balance, the reciprocal account on the other set of books will have an equal credit balance.) As in the preparation of consolidated financial statements, reciprocal accounts are eliminated before the combined financial statements are prepared for use by external parties.

Because a decentralized system is more complex than a centralized system, it will be illustrated in the remainder of this chapter. After a typical branch accounting system is reviewed, the preparation of combined financial statements for the home office and branch will be illustrated.

Recording Transactions Between Home Office and Branch

In a decentralized system, transactions between the home office and the branch are recorded on both the home office and the branch books. On the home office books, a reciprocal account, ***Investment in Branch***, is opened for each branch established. If there are a number of branches, a control account in the general ledger may be used with supporting detail for each branch maintained in a subsidiary ledger. Investment in Branch is debited when assets are transferred to the branch or if the branch reports a net income. The account is credited when the branch transfers assets to the home office or reports a net loss. The account serves as a record of the investment in the branch and also as a controlling account over the branch ledger; that is, the amount of net assets reported on the branch books should equal the balance in the Investment in Branch account.

In the branch ledger, a reciprocal ***Home Office*** account is created to record transactions between the home office and the branch. When the home office transfers cash or other assets to the branch, Home Office is credited to offset the equal amount of debits made to the asset accounts. Conversely, the account is debited when assets are returned to the home office. The account is also credited (debited) for the amount of reported profit (loss) of the branch. As can be seen, the Home Office account is necessary if the branch is to use a double-entry accounting system and is a substitute for the equity section of the balance sheet. Thus, the balance in the account reflects the home office's equity in the net assets of the branch.

The nature of the reciprocal relationship between the two accounts is emphasized below in T-account format.

Home Office Books

INVESTMENT IN BRANCH

Assets transferred to the branch	Assets received from the branch
Branch net income	Branch net loss

Branch Books

HOME OFFICE

Assets transferred to the home office	Assets received from the home office
Branch net loss	Branch net income

Note that the type of transactions debited (credited) to Investment in Branch are recorded as credits (debits) in the Home Office account. The balance in the reciprocal accounts should be equal unless, as is often the case, some transactions between the home office and branch are unrecorded on one set of books because of items in transit.

Merchandise Inventory Shipments to a Branch

A branch may acquire all its inventory from the home office, or some of it may be acquired from independent parties. When the branch is authorized to purchase goods for resale from outsiders, the normal journal entry is made to record the purchase. The Purchases account is debited if a periodic inventory system is used; the Inventory account is debited when a perpetual inventory system is used. Inventory purchased by the home office and shipped to the branch for resale is normally billed to the branch at cost or some amount above cost. The approach used to bill the branch affects the journal entries to account for the shipments as well as the preparation of workpapers to combine the trial balances of the home office and branch.

Inventory Shipments Billed to the Branch at Cost The journal entry to record a shipment of inventory to the branch that is billed at cost depends on whether the firm uses a periodic or perpetual inventory system. To illustrate both systems, assume that the home office shipped goods that cost $5,000 to the branch.

Periodic Inventory System

HOME OFFICE			BRANCH		
Investment in Branch	5,000		Shipments from Home Office	5,000	
Shipments to Branch		5,000	Home Office		5,000

Perpetual Inventory System

Investment in Branch	5,000		Inventory—Home Office	5,000	
Inventory		5,000	Home Office		5,000

In both cases, the transfer of assets from the home office to the branch increases the accountability of the branch to the home office. Also note that the transaction does not affect revenue, since this is not an arm's-length transaction, but is merely the transfer of goods within the same firm. Any profit or loss on the sale of the inventory is deferred until it is sold to an independent party by the branch.

When a periodic inventory system is used by the firm, two additional reciprocal accounts are opened to record the transfer. The home office credits a reciprocal account, Shipments to Branch. On the income statement of the home office, this account is subtracted from the sum of the beginning inventory and purchases to reflect the fact that the shipment of goods to the branch reduces the goods available for sale by the home office. On the books of the branch, the reciprocal account,

Shipments from Home Office, is equivalent to a purchases account. A different account title is used to distinguish goods received from the home office from goods purchased from outsiders. For the purpose of preparing combined financial statements, this distinction is not necessary when the goods are billed at cost. However, as will be demonstrated in a later section of this chapter, differentiation facilitates development of worksheet entries that are necessary to eliminate mark-ups above cost on inventories acquired from the home office.

The inventory acquired from the home office is also recorded in a separate account, Inventory—Home Office, when the perpetual system is used. The entries made under the perpetual system are otherwise self-explanatory.

Freight charges incurred on the shipment of goods from the home office to the branch are considered normal inventoriable costs. The freight is an added cost of inventory, since the goods are presumably more valuable to the firm at the branch facility than in the home office warehouse. However, excessive freight that results from inefficiencies should be expensed. For example, if because of an error, a mode of transportation must be used that is more expensive than the mode normally used, only the normal freight charges should be recognized as an addition to the cost of inventory. The excessive freight charges should be expensed currently. From a practical point of view, however, immaterial freight charges are sometimes expensed currently as a debit to a Freight-in account on the branch books rather than added to the cost of inventory.

Billing the branch for shipments at cost has limitations for internal uses, such as evaluating the performance of the branch management, because all the gross profit realized from the sale is reported by the branch. Such a policy does not recognize the cost incurred by the home office in acquiring the goods or other services provided by the home office on behalf of the branch. In particular, if the home office manufactures the goods, any manufacturing profit is included in the gross profit of the branch. Thus, a portion of the gross profit attributable to the branch should properly be included in the books of the home office.

Inventory Shipments Billed to the Branch in Excess of Cost   The home office may follow the practice of pricing inventory shipped to the branch at some percentage above its cost. Examples of policies followed in practice are

1. Cost plus a selected percentage mark-up.
2. Sales price charged to independent parties (wholesale price).
3. Retail price.

The first approach is used to charge the branch for services performed by the home office. The second approach permits separating the gross profit earned by the home office from the gross profit of the branch. Because they provide a more equitable allocation of gross profit, both methods provide more useful information for performance evaluation than billing the shipments to the branch at home office cost.

Sometimes inventory is billed to the branch at its retail price. The procedures to operate such a billing system are similar to the retail inventory method. This procedure eliminates the need for a dual pricing system, one for billings to the branches and one for normal sales. The primary objective of the system is to provide information to management on the unsold inventory held by the branch, without the branch taking a physical count, and to improve internal control over the inventory. With such a system, management can approximate the ending inventory at retail by subtracting the sales of the branch from the goods available (beginning inventory at retail plus shipments from home office during the current period) for sale at retail. Management can then approximate the ending inventory at cost by multiplying the ending inventory at retail by 1.0 minus a mark-up percentage of sales. A physical count of the inventory should be taken at least once a year to check on the reliability of the estimating procedure. The system will require more detailed records if the branch is permitted to alter the retail price and if goods are acquired from outside parties. Obviously, under this approach, the amount of sales reported by the branch will be equal to the cost of goods sold, and the branch will show a net loss equal to its operating expenses. In this form, the income statement of the branch has limited direct use in evaluating the branch manager's performance.

Regardless of the policy followed by the home office, the mark-up on the inventory shipped to the branch is not realized until the goods are sold by the branch. To facilitate accounting for the mark-up and to maintain the cost of inventory shipped to the branch, the home office usually separates the unrealized profit from the cost of the goods. This may be done either by memorandum entry or by incorporation in the home office ledger. To illustrate the latter approach, assume that inventory costing the home office $30,000 is shipped and billed to the branch for $36,000 (120% of cost). The journal entry is

$$\frac{36,000}{30,000} = 120\%$$

Home Office Books

Investment in Branch (billed price)	36,000	
Shipments to Branch (cost)*		30,000
Unrealized Profit in Shipments to Branch		6,000

*Inventory is credited if a perpetual inventory system is used.

Accounting on the branch books when the inventory is billed to the branch in excess of cost to the home office is essentially the same as accounting procedures discussed earlier. However, since the ending inventory must be adjusted to cost on the combined financial statements, it is necessary for the branch to maintain sufficiently detailed inventory records to permit differentiating the ending inventory acquired from the home office from the ending inventory acquired from outsiders.[1] The branch records the $36,000 inventory shipment from the home office as follows:

---

[1]To avoid the necessity of maintaining separate inventory records, the ending inventory acquired from the home office is sometimes estimated by multiplying the ending inventory by a ratio of the goods acquired from the home office over total inventory purchases (from home office and outsiders).

Branch Books

II a

Shipments from Home Office*	36,000	
Home Office		36,000

*Inventory—Home Office is debited if a perpetual system is maintained.

The two accounts credited on the home office books are reciprocal to the Shipments from Home Office account on the branch books, and all three are eliminated in the preparation of combined statements.

The branch recognizes revenue on inventory acquired for resale when there is an arm's-length transaction with an outside party. The portion of the unrealized profit carried on the books of the home office that is related to the goods sold by the branch is considered earned. Generally, the home office defers recognition of the realized profit on individual sales until a periodic report is received from the branch. For example, assume that the only transaction of the branch during the year was the sale for $30,000 of three-fourths of the inventory acquired from the home office for $36,000. The branch would recognize $3,000 profit on the sale and report to the home office that one-fourth of the goods acquired from the home office is still on hand. The home office would record the net income reported by the branch and adjust Unrealized Profit in Shipments to Branch as follows:

Home Office Books

Investment in Branch	3,000	
Branch Net Income		3,000

The net income is computed as follows:

Sales	$30,000
Cost of sales ($36,000 × .75)	27,000
Net income reported by branch	$ 3,000

Unrealized Profit in Shipments to Branch	4,500	
Branch Net Income ($6,000 × .75)		4,500

The debit in the last entry reduces the $6,000 credit balance in the unrealized profit account on the home office books to $1,500, which is equal to the unrealized profit in the inventory still held by the branch. This $1,500 will be recognized as income when the remaining one-fourth of the goods is sold by the branch. The $4,500 credit increases the $3,000 net income reported by the branch to $7,500 so as to reflect the total confirmed profit on the sale.[2] The required adjustment to the accounts can be verified as follows:

[2]The $7,500 gross profit can be verified as follows:

Sales price	$30,000
Cost of goods sold: $30,000 cost × .75	22,500
Gross profit	$ 7,500

Balance in unrealized profit account		$6,000
Ending inventory reported by branch	$9,000	
Cost of the ending inventory: $9,000 ÷ 1.2	7,500	
Unrealized profit in ending inventory		1,500
Realized profit—Adjustment required		$4,500

At the end of the period, the $9,000 ending inventory balance reported by the branch includes the $1,500 intracompany mark-up. The shipments from home office and ending inventory reported in the income statement of the branch are also overstated by the amount of the mark-up. Before combining the trial balances of the branch and home office, it is necessary to reduce the inventory-related accounts to cost by eliminating the intracompany mark-up. The procedures for doing so are described in a subsequent illustration.

Acquisition of Fixed Assets for Use by a Branch In some branch operations, the home office maintains the records for all fixed assets even though the fixed assets are located at branch facilities. For control purposes, the home office may establish an individual fixed asset account for each branch. Thus, the journal entry to record the home office purchase of $10,000 of equipment for Branch #8 would be as follows:

Home Office Books

Equipment—Branch #8	10,000	
Cash		10,000

Note that the journal entry does not affect the branch books, since the equipment is to be carried on the home office books. A journal entry must be made on both sets of books if the branch acquires equipment, but the asset is to be recorded on the home office books. The journal entries for both sets of books are as follows:

HOME OFFICE BOOKS			BRANCH BOOKS		
Equipment—Branch #8	10,000		Home Office	10,000	
Investment in Branch #8		10,000	Cash		10,000

In this latter case, the payment by the branch to acquire an asset to be carried on the home office books reduces the amount for which the branch is responsible to the home office. The result is the same as if the branch transferred assets to the home office. The reduction in the Home Office account by the branch requires a corresponding reduction in the Investment in Branch account by the home office and the concurrent recognition by the home office of the fixed asset.

The procedure for accounting for fixed assets described above facilitates computing depreciation charges when the company seeks to apply company-wide uniform depreciation policies. In particular, group depreciation rates can be computed more conveniently when the company follows the practice of grouping like assets for depreciation purposes or uses a composite depreciation method. The branch may or may not be informed of the amount of the depreciation charges on the fixed assets used by the branch.

Normal journal entries are made if the assets are to be recorded on the branch books. Purchases of equipment by the home office for the branch are recorded on both sets of books. The home office records the equipment purchase and then recognizes the transfer of the asset to the branch; upon receipt of the equipment, the branch records the asset with a corresponding increase in the Home Office account. Direct acquisitions of equipment by the branch are recorded on the branch books as asset purchases.

Assignment of Expenses Incurred by the Home Office The manager of the branch normally is granted the authority to engage in most functions necessary for the conduct of branch operations. It may be more efficient and economical, however, for the home office to maintain a large, highly qualified staff centralized in one location to perform certain functions than to duplicate the functions at each branch. For example: (1) It may be more effective for the home office to conduct a national or regional advertising program than for branches to conduct individual advertising campaigns. (2) The company may obtain a lower insurance rate and receive better service if the contract is negotiated for company-wide coverage. (3) A central purchasing department acquiring items of equipment, inventory, and supplies for all branches may receive discounts on quantity purchases. Of course, branches may still be granted authority to acquire some of these goods and services from their own sources.

The services provided by the home office for the branch and expenses paid directly by the home office for the branch are factors that affect the profitability of the branch. The home office may adjust the financial statements provided by the branch when they are received, or the branch may be notified by the home office of the charges to be reflected on the branch financial statements. In the latter case, the home office debits the Investment in Branch account and credits the appropriate accounts to reduce the accounts for the amounts allocated to the branch. For example, if the home office has charged advertising to an expense account, a credit is made to that account for the portion assigned to a particular branch. When notified of the charges, the branch enters the expenses by a debit to the appropriate expense accounts and a credit to the Home Office account.

Some costs, such as property taxes, may be identified specifically with each branch. Other costs incurred by the home office may benefit a number of branches. In such cases the home office must allocate joint costs to its branches. Problems involved in allocating joint costs are discussed in most managerial accounting textbooks.

Preparation of Combined Financial Statements

At the end of the reporting period, the branch will provide the home office with a complete set of financial statements and any supplementary information required by management. The financial statements prepared by the branch may take various forms, since they are prepared for internal use and therefore need not be presented in accordance with generally accepted accounting principles. The statements, however, generally do follow the format of a publicly traded manufacturing or merchandising firm with a few differences, such as reporting the Home Office account in place of the owners' equity section on the balance sheet. These statements are used as the basis for performing the usual kinds of managerial evaluations, as for example, evaluating the financial position and the operating performance of the branch during the reporting period. Also, separate financial statements provide information that can be used to compare branches. Without separate statements, an unprofitable branch operation may be concealed by profitable operations of other branches. When evaluating the performance of the branch for the period under review, management should recognize that the net income probably does not accurately reflect the operations of a completely independent entity, because services performed by the home office may not be charged to the branch, or if they are charged, the services may be billed on some arbitrary basis.

The home office also prepares a balance sheet and income statement based on the results of the home office operations. The additional ledger accounts required to account for transactions with the branch may be reported separately. If so, the Investment in Branch is reported on the home office balance sheet as an asset. Shipments to Branch is reported as a subtraction from goods available for sale. The net income reported by the branches is reported as a separate line item on the income statement. Separate home office statements provide a periodic record of the home office activities and also provide information for management to use in evaluating the performance of the home office without the inclusion of the branch activities. Again, one must recognize that some costs incurred by the home office may also benefit branch operations. The failure to allocate such costs results in an understatement in the home office operations and an overstatement in the branch net income.

Before issuing financial statements to users outside the firm, it is necessary to combine the assets, liabilities, revenues, and expenses of the individual branches with like accounts of the home office. Before the accounts are combined, however, transactions between the branch and home office must be eliminated. The presumption is that information provided to external statement readers should disclose the financial position and results of operations for the firm as a whole (that is, as if the branches and home office had operated as one combined business entity).

Procedurally, it is easy to eliminate the intracompany transactions that occur during the period if the transactions are accounted for in reciprocal accounts. More specifically, most transactions between the home office and the branch are accounted for in the Home Office account and Investment in Branch account. These two accounts should have equal but opposite balances that are eliminated before the balance sheet accounts are combined. The result is that the assets and liabilities of the branch are substituted for the Investment in Branch account, which is reported as an asset in the trial balance of the home office. In other words, as noted earlier, the Investment in Branch account can be viewed as a control account, the balance of which equals the net assets of the branch. On the combined balance sheet, the individual assets and liabilities of the branch are included after being added to the like accounts of the home office.

On the income statement, the debit balance in Shipments from Home Office is eliminated by a credit; the offsetting debit is made against the credit balance in Shipments to Branch and the Unrealized Profit in Shipments to Branch accounts. In addition, any intracompany mark-up is removed from the amounts reported for the beginning and ending inventories. Finally, the revenue and expense accounts of the branch are added to the respective home office accounts.

Accounting for a Branch Illustrated—Inventory Billed to Branch in Excess of Home Office Cost

Journal Entries on Books of Home Office and Branch   To illustrate the accounting for a branch that maintains a complete set of books, assume the following:

1. The branch files financial statements at the end of each fiscal year with the home office.

2. The branch has the authority to purchase inventory and fixed assets from the home office or from other sources.

3. Inventory acquired from the home office is billed to the branch at 20% above its cost to the home office.

4. All goods purchased from outsiders were sold during the year.

5. Accounting records for fixed assets of the branch are maintained by the home office.

6. The home office and branch use a periodic inventory system.

7. The branch is billed by the home office for services rendered and certain expenses incurred by the home office. These charges are to be reflected on the branch financial statements.

8. The branch began the current fiscal period with a $1,000 cash balance and $8,400 in inventory, all acquired from the home office. The cost of the inventory to the home office was $7,000 ($8,400 ÷ 1.20).[3]

9. The branch ended the current fiscal year with an inventory balance of $7,200 all acquired from the home office. The cost to the home office was $6,000 ($7,200 ÷ 1.20 = $6,000).

Transactions and journal entries related to the year's operations are shown in Illustration 13-1 for both the home office (ABC Company) and its Branch #1. The two most active ledger accounts (Investment in Branch #1 and Home Office) are reproduced in Illustration 13-2.

---

[3]The home office will show a beginning balance of $1,400 in Unrealized Profit in Shipments to Branch.

ILLUSTRATION 13-1
Journal Entries to Record Branch Transactions on Books of Home Office and Branch

TRANSACTION	HOME OFFICE			BRANCH #1		

(1) Home office transferred $10,000 in cash and $20,000 of display equipment.	Investment in Branch
	  Cash
	Equipment—Branch
	  Equipment
		10,000
		
		20,000
			
			10,000
			
			20,000
				Cash
				  Home Office
				
				(NO ENTRY)
					10,000	
						10,000

(2) Home office ships inventory that cost $30,000 to branch; billing price is $36,000.	Investment in Branch
	  Shipments to Branch
	  Unrealized Profit in
	    Shipments to
	    Branch
		36,000	
			30,000
			
			6,000
				Shipments from Home
				  Office
				  Home Office
					36,000	
						
						36,000

(3) Branch purchases equipment costing $5,000.	Equipment—Branch
	  Investment in Branch
		5,000	
			5,000
				Home Office
				  Cash
					5,000	
						5,000

(4) Branch makes $40,000 in credit sales and $20,000 in cash sales.	(NO ENTRY)			Accounts Receivable
				  Sales
				Cash
				  Sales
					40,000
					
					20,000
						
						40,000
						
						20,000

(5) Expenses of $7,000 are incurred and paid by the branch.	(NO ENTRY)			Operating Expenses Cash	7,000	 7,000
(6) Branch purchases $6,000 of inventory on account from an outside company.	(NO ENTRY)			Purchases Accounts Payable	6,000	 6,000
(7) Branch collects $15,000 of accounts receivable.	(NO ENTRY)			Cash Accounts Receivable	15,000	 15,000

(8) Cash of $20,000 is remitted to home office.	Cash
	  Investment in Branch
		20,000	
			20,000
				Home Office
				  Cash
					20,000	
						20,000

(9) Home office bills branch $2,000 for services performed and for depreciation.	Investment in Branch
	  Operating Expenses
		2,000	
			2,000
				Operating Expenses
				  Home Office
					2,000	
						2,000

(10) At the end of the year, the branch had $1,000 of accrued expenses.	(NO ENTRY)			Operating Expenses Accrued Liabilities	1,000	 1,000

ILLUSTRATION 13-2
Transactions Recorded in Reciprocal Accounts

INVESTMENT IN BRANCH #1

TRANSACTIONS	DEBIT	CREDIT	BALANCE
Beginning balance			
(Inventory, $8,400; Cash, $1,000)	9,400		9,400
Entry (1) Home office transferred cash	10,000		19,400
(2) Shipment of inventory	36,000		55,400
(3) Branch purchased equipment		5,000	50,400
(8) Branch remitted cash to home office		20,000	30,400
(9) Expenses billed by home office	2,000		32,400
(11) Closing entry (See next section.)	6,800		39,200

HOME OFFICE

TRANSACTIONS	DEBIT	CREDIT	BALANCE
Beginning balance			
(Inventory, $8,400; Cash, $1,000)		9,400	9,400
Entry (1) Home office transferred cash		10,000	19,400
(2) Shipment of inventory		36,000	55,400
(3) Branch purchased equipment	5,000		50,400
(8) Branch remitted cash to home office	20,000		30,400
(9) Expenses billed by home office		2,000	32,400
(11) Closing entry (See next section.)		6,800	39,200

Closing Entries In this illustration, since the branch maintains a complete set of books, closing entries are made on both the branch and home office books. The normal closing entries are made except that the home office recognizes the net income or loss of the branch as reported in the income statement submitted by the branch management. In addition, the unrealized profit account is adjusted to record the portion that was realized during the period. The adjustment is computed as follows, based on the branch ending inventory of $7,200.

Beginning balance	$1,400
Additions during the year	6,000
Balance before adjustment	7,400
(1) Balance needed	1,200
Adjustment	$6,200

(1) $7,200 − ($7,200 ÷ 1.2) = $1,200 or
($7,200 ÷ $36,000) = .20; .20 × $6,000 = $1,200

The closing entries for this illustration are

TRANSACTION	HOME OFFICE		BRANCH		
(11) Closing entries— Ending inventory balance is $7,200.	(The home office would follow the normal procedures to close other nominal accounts.)		Income Summary	8,400	
			Inventory, 1/1		8,400
			Inventory, 12/31	7,200	
			Income Summary		7,200
			Sales	60,000	
			Income Summary		60,000
			Income Summary	52,000	
			Purchases		6,000
			Shipments from Home Office		36,000
			Operating Expenses		10,000
	Investment in Branch	6,800	Income Summary	6,800	
	Branch Net Income		6,800	Home Office		6,800
	Unrealized Profit in Shipments to Branch	6,200			
	Branch Net Income		6,200		
	Branch Net Income	13,000			
	Income Summary		13,000		

Combined Statements Workpaper Illustrated   Although the process of combining the financial statements of the branch and home office is normally not difficult, the use of a workpaper will facilitate the accumulation of the needed account balances. An example of one workpaper format, which takes the three-divisional format used in the consolidated financial statements workpaper, is presented in Illustration 13-3. The branch preclosing trial balance is developed from the journal entries presented in Illustration 13-1. The home office account balances are assumed except for the reciprocal account balances. Also note that within the retained earnings section of the workpaper, the branch reports no beginning retained earnings balance. The beginning balance will always be zero, because the net income or loss reported by the branch in prior years is closed to the Home Office account.

Workpaper eliminating entries are summarized below in general journal form for the convenience of the reader.

December 31, 1995 Workpaper Entries in General Journal Form

(1) Unrealized Profit in Shipments to Branch 1,400
    Inventory, 1/1 (Income Statement) 1,400
      To eliminate intracompany profit in beginning inventory. This reduces branch beginning inventory to cost ($7,000)

(2) Shipments to Branch 30,000
    Unrealized Profit in Shipments to Branch 6,000
      Shipments from Home Office 36,000
      To eliminate intracompany transfer of inventory and unrealized profit recorded on books of home office.

(3) Inventory, 12/31 (Income Statement) 1,200
    Inventory (Balance Sheet) 1,200
      To eliminate unrealized profit in branch ending inventory. This reduces ending inventory to cost in both the balance sheet and the income statement.

(4) Home Office 32,400
    Investment in Branch 32,400
      To eliminate Investment in Branch and Home Office accounts.

Note that the balance in Unrealized Profit in Shipments to Branch is eliminated in full in the workpaper, although the mark-up in the ending inventory ($1,200) is carried forward on the home office books.

The purpose of the eliminating entries is to reflect the operations of one firm as if all the transactions had been recorded on one set of books. In this case the eliminating entries result in a combined net income of $28,000, which is equal to the $15,000 reported by the home office plus the adjusted branch net income of $13,000 ($6,800 reported + $6,200 adjustment to the unrealized profit account).

Financial statements for ABC Company are prepared (see Illustration 13-4) from the combined balances column of the workpaper.

INTERBRANCH TRANSFER OF ASSETS

In the preceding illustration, the home office established only one branch facility. Frequently, however, the home office may operate with a number of branch offices. To improve the operating efficiency of the firm, the home office may authorize the

ILLUSTRATION 13-3
Combined Statements Workpaper
ABC Company and Branch #1
December 31, 1995

	TRIAL BALANCES		ELIMINATIONS		
	ABC COMPANY	BRANCH #1	DR.	CR.	COMBINED BALANCES
INCOME STATEMENT					
Sales	100,000	60,000			160,000
Inventory, 1/1	20,000	8,400		(1) 1,400	27,000
Purchases	95,000	6,000			101,000
Shipments from Home Office	—	36,000		(2) 36,000	—
	115,000	50,400			128,000
Shipments to Branch	30,000	—	(2) 30,000		—
Inventory, 12/31	25,000	7,200	(3) 1,200		31,000
Cost of Goods Sold	60,000	43,200			97,000
Other Expenses	25,000	10,000			35,000
Net Income to Retained Earnings	15,000	6,800	31,200	37,400	28,000
RETAINED EARNINGS STATEMENT					
1/1 Retained Earnings	57,000	—			57,000
Net Income from above	15,000	6,800	31,200	37,400	28,000
Dividends Declared	(10,000)	—			(10,000)
12/31 Retained Earnings to Balance Sheet	62,000	6,800	31,200	37,400	75,000
BALANCE SHEET					
Cash	33,000	14,000			47,000
Accounts Receivable	20,000	25,000			45,000
Inventory	25,000	7,200		(3) 1,200	31,000
Investment in Branch	32,400	—		(4) 32,400	—
Plant and Equipment—Home Office (net of accumulated depreciation)	75,000	—			75,000
Plant and Equipment—Branch (net of accumulated depreciation)	24,000	—			24,000
Other Assets	30,000	—			30,000
Total	239,400	46,200			252,000
Current Liabilities	20,000	7,000			27,000
Long-term Notes Payable	50,000	—			50,000
Home Office	—	32,400	(4) 32,400		—
Unrealized Profit in Shipments to Branch	7,400*		(1) 1,400 (2) 6,000		—
Capital Stock	100,000				100,000
Retained Earnings from above	62,000	6,800	31,200	37,400	75,000
Total Liabilities and Equity	239,400	46,200	71,000	71,000	252,000

(1) To eliminate unrealized profit in branch beginning inventory.
(2) To eliminate intracompany shipment of inventory and unrealized profit thereon.
(3) To eliminate unrealized profit in branch ending inventory.
(4) To eliminate investment account.
*$1,400 mark-up on branch beginning inventory + $6,000 mark-up on shipments during the year.

ILLUSTRATION 13-4
Combined Financial Statements for ABC Company and Branch # 1

ABC Company
Income Statement
For the Year Ended December 31, 1995

Sales		$160,000
Cost of Goods Sold:		
Beginning Inventory	$ 27,000	
Purchases	101,000	
Goods Available for Sale	128,000	
Less: Ending Inventory	31,000	97,000
Gross Profit on Sales		63,000
Operating Expenses		35,000
Net Income		$ 28,000

ABC Company
Retained Earnings Statement
For the Year Ended December 31, 1995

Beginning Retained Earnings Balance	$ 57,000
Add: Net Income	28,000
Less: Dividends	10,000
Ending Retained Earnings Balance	$ 75,000

ABC Company
Balance Sheet
December 31, 1995

Cash	$ 47,000	Liabilities:		
Accounts Receivable	45,000	Current Liabilities		$ 27,000
Inventory	31,000	Long-term Notes Payable		50,000
Plant and Equipment (net		Total Liabilities		77,000
of accumulated		Stockholders' Equity:		
depreciation)	99,000	Capital Stock	$100,000	
Other Assets	30,000	Retained Earnings	75,000	
		Total Stockholders' Equity		175,000
		Total Liabilities and		
Total Assets	$252,000	Stockholders' Equity		$252,000

transfer of cash or other assets between branches. For example, one branch may transfer excessive inventory to another branch that has an inventory shortage. The branch that transfers the asset will recognize a decrease in the appropriate asset account. Instead of recording a receivable from another branch, the branch typically recognizes the transfer as a reduction in the accountability to the home office. The branch that receives the asset records the asset and increases the Home Office account. To maintain equal reciprocal balances, the home office must record appropriate adjustments to the investment accounts of the two branches involved in the transfer.

ESTABLISHING RECIPROCAL BALANCES

In the preceding illustration, it was assumed that the balance in Investment in Branch was equal to the balance in the Home Office account. However, these accounts may not be in balance because of a delay in recording a transaction on one set of books. The two most common causes of differences in the accounts are errors that have been made in recording reciprocal transactions, or transactions that have been recorded by either the home office or the branch, but not both. For example, the branch records cash payments to the home office at the time the check is written and mailed to the home office. The home office will not record an entry until the check is received, which may be several days later. In the case of inventory, the home office will record inventory shipments to the branch when the goods are shipped. Depending on the mode of transportation and distance shipped, it may be a matter of weeks before the branch receives the goods and records the transaction. Between financial reports, there is no problem if the accounts are not in agreement. However, before combined financial statements are prepared, the full effect of the transaction should be recognized on both sets of books. Failure to do so will result in the assets of the firm being understated. In other words, cash and inventory in transit at the end of the period are not recorded on either set of books. The transaction will eventually be recorded on both sets of books; however, to bring the accounts up to date at year-end, the unrecorded side of the transaction should be entered in the elimination columns of the workpaper.

To illustrate reconciling the two reciprocal accounts, assume the following account balances were reported in the preclosing trial balances:

Home office books: Investment in Branch #1, $26,850.

Branch books: Home Office, $15,850.

Before the reciprocal accounts can be eliminated in the workpaper, the cause(s) of the discrepancy between the two accounts must be determined and proper adjusting entries made to bring the accounts into balance. A review of the year-end transactions reveals that the following transactions have not been recorded in one reciprocal account by either the home office or the branch:

1. Inventory at a billed price of $5,000 was shipped by the home office to Branch #1 on December 27 and received by the branch on January 10.

2. Branch #1 transferred cash of $6,000 to the home office on December 30. The payment was received by the home office on January 4.

The workpaper adjusting entries and explanation for each entry follow:

(a) Shipments from Home Office	5,000	
Inventory (Balance Sheet)	5,000	
Home Office		5,000
Inventory, 12/31 (Income Statement)		5,000
To record shipment of inventory to Branch #1 in transit at year-end and not included in ending inventory count.		
(b) Cash	6,000	
Investment in Branch #1		6,000
To recognize transfer of cash by Branch #1 that was not recorded by the home office.		

The two accounts in T-account form are shown below after the adjustments are posted:

INVESTMENT IN BRANCH #1					HOME OFFICE		
Preclosing		(b)	6,000		Preclosing		
balance	26,850				balance	15,850	
Balance	20,850				(a)	5,000	
					Balance	20,850	

Note in entry (a) that with the use of the periodic inventory system, the ending inventory as reported in both the balance sheet and income statement is adjusted to reflect the unrecorded shipments in transit at year-end.

Questions

1. What is the difference between a sales agency and a branch?

2. What is a decentralized accounting system?

3. Why would a home office establish a decentralized branch accounting system?

4. What type of an account is the Home Office account on the books of the branch?

5. Investment in Branch can be thought of as a control account. What accounts does it control?

6. How would you record the following transactions between a home office and its branch? (a) cash transfer; (b) inventory transfer (periodic inventory system); and (c) branch billed for services rendered by home office.

7. What type of transactions are recorded in the branch books but not on the home office books?

8. What type of an account is Unrealized Profit in Shipments to Branch? What does its balance represent?

9. How does Shipments to Branch affect determination of the cost of goods sold by the home office?

10. Home office instructs Branch A to transfer $XXX of inventory to Branch B. Give the entries to be made on the books of both branches and the home office. (Assume periodic inventory system and inventory billed at cost.)

11. Reciprocal accounts on the home office and branch books may not always be equal. Why?

12. What eliminations are necessary for the preparation of combined financial statements?

13. What closing entries peculiar to branch accounting are made on the books of the home office?

Exercises

Exercise 13-1

Rent a Movie rents and sells videotapes through 12 branch stores. During the past year, the following transactions took place between the home office and Branch #6. The company uses a periodic inventory system.

1. Cash of $26,000 was transferred to the branch.
2. Merchandise to be held for sale that cost $24,000 was shipped to the branch at a billed price of $24,000. The branch paid the freight-in of $750.
3. Movies to be held for rentals with a cost of $20,000 were shipped to the branch. The branch records such shipments in an account called Movie Rentals Inventory.
4. Home office expenses charged to the branch: depreciation, $2,000; advertising $450; rent, $550. The home office had recorded these items in expense accounts.
5. Cash of $8,000 was remitted to the home office.
6. The branch recorded an amortization of movie rental inventory in the amount of $10,000.

Required:

Prepare journal entries to record the transactions above on the books of both the home office and the branch.

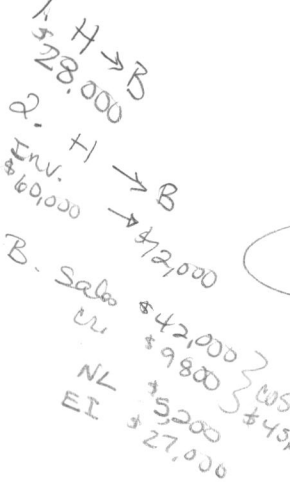

Exercise 13-2

Valenza Company entered into the following transactions with its Chicago branch.

1. The home office transferred $28,000 to the checking account of the branch.
2. Inventory that cost the home office $60,000 was shipped to the branch. Inventory is billed to the branch at 20% above cost. (Assume the use of a periodic inventory system.)
3. The branch reported cash sales of $42,000 and credit sales of $9,800. The goods were all received from the home office and were carried on the branch books at a cost of $45,000.
4. The branch reported a net loss of $5,200 for the period.
5. The branch reported $27,000 of ending inventory acquired from the home office.

Required:

Prepare the general journal entries to record the transactions on the books of the home office and branch.

Exercise 13-3

The Hotz Company was organized in 1994 to sell solar hot-water heaters. Shortly after opening its doors to the public at the main store, Hotz Company established a branch in another city. At the end of the second year of operations, the home office received the following condensed income statement from the branch.

Revenues	$180,000
Cost of goods sold	140,000
Gross margin	40,000
Selling and administrative expenses	25,000
Net income	$ 15,000

The management at the home office questioned the accuracy of these figures and assigned you the task of verifying the branch data. Your review of the records uncovered the following facts:

1. The beginning-of-year balance in Unrealized Profit in Shipments to Branch was $6,000.
2. During the period, the home office shipped goods to the branch that had cost the main store $75,000. However, your review of the branch receiving reports revealed that a number of shipments from the home office had been recorded twice by the branch accountant.
3. The branch is billed a uniform 20% above cost and receives inventory only from the home office.
4. The branch ending inventory was correctly reported by the branch at a billed price of $20,880.
5. When reconciling reciprocal accounts, you found that the branch had not recorded $2,600 of services performed by the home office and billed to the branch. All other selling and administrative expenses were correctly reported by the branch.

Required:

A. Prepare a corrected cost of goods sold section of the branch income statement based, first, on cost as billed to the branch by the home office and, second, on the original cost of the inventory to the home office.

B. Prepare the correcting entry (entries) necessary on the books of the branch. Assume that the branch books have not been closed.

C. Compute the amount of net income (loss) that should have been reported by the branch.

D. Prepare the entries on the books of the home office to record the correct branch net income (loss) and adjust Unrealized Profit in Shipments to Branch.

Exercise 13-4

Select the best answer for each of the following.

1. The Investment in Branch account is credited when
   (a) The branch reports a net loss or the branch transfers assets to the home office.
   (b) Assets are transferred to the branch or when the branch reports a net loss.
   (c) The branch transfers assets to the home office or the branch reports a net income.
   (d) None of the above.

2. The Home Office account is debited when
   (a) The branch reports a net profit.
   (b) Assets are returned to the home office.
   (c) The home office transfers cash or other assets to the branch.
   (d) Both (a) and (c) above.
3. The Shipments to Branch account is reported on the home office's books as
   (a) A subtraction from goods available for sale.
   (b) An expense.
   (c) An offset against the Investment in Branch account.
   (d) A reduction in the inventory account.
4. The failure to allocate costs incurred by the home office that benefit the branch operations causes
   (a) Both (b) and (d) below.
   (b) An overstatement in the branch net income.
   (c) An understatement in the branch net income.
   (d) An understatement in the home office net income.
5. Which of the following would cause the balance in the Home Office account to be greater than the balance in the Investment in Branch account?
   (a) Cash transferred from the branch to the home office is in transit and is not recorded on the home office books.
   (b) Inventory transferred to the branch from the home office is in transit and is not recorded on the branch books.
   (c) Both (a) and (b) above.
   (d) None of the above.

Exercise 13-5

Just before the books are closed for the December 31 fiscal year-end, the trial balances for the home office and branch contained the following account balances:

	TRIAL BALANCE	
	HOME OFFICE	BRANCH
Investment in Branch	$42,400 Dr.	
Home Office		$25,120 Cr.

Your examination of the accounts revealed the following information:

1. On December 26, the branch remitted $10,400 in cash to the home office, which was not received until January 3.
2. Inventory that was billed to the branch at $7,280 was in transit at December 31.
3. A cash payment of $400 on an open accounts receivable was received by the home office. The account, however, was carried on the books of the branch. The home office did not notify the branch of the cash collection.

Required:

Prepare a statement to reconcile to a correct balance the Home Office and Investment in Branch accounts.

Exercise 13-6

Silly Saw, Inc., of Chicago, Illinois, established a branch store in Peoria to distribute goods purchased by the home office. The home office prices inventory shipped to the branch at

25% above cost. The following account balances were taken from the ledgers maintained by the home office and the branch as of December 31, 1995.

ACCOUNT	SILLY SAW, INC.	PEORIA BRANCH
Revenues	$962,000	$272,000
Beginning inventory	120,000	50,000
Purchases	500,000	28,000
Shipments to Peoria branch	114,000	–0–
Shipments from home office	–0–	142,500
Operating expenses	272,000	36,000
Ending inventory	98,000	48,000

The branch ending inventory contains $32,000 of inventories acquired from the home office. All the branch beginning inventory was acquired from the home office.

Required:

On the basis of these account balances, prepare the income statement section of a combined workpaper to determine the net income of the home office (excluding the branch net income), the net income reported by the branch, and the combined net income of the home office and branch.

Exercise 13-7

Draft Company sells merchandise to its branch at a mark-up approximating 15% of billed prices. A periodic inventory system is used. Certain account balances are given below.

Ending inventory, branch (at billed prices)	$ 84,000
Shipments to branch	300,000
Unrealized profits in shipments to branch	60,000

Required:

A. Prepare the entries made by the home office during the year relative to merchandise transactions with the branch, including closing entries.

B. Compute the beginning inventory of the branch (at billed prices).

C. Prepare the related eliminating entries appearing on a combined financial statements workpaper.

Problems

Problem 13-1

On January 1, Sunrise Company, a recreational products manufacturer, opened a sales outlet in Monmouth, Oregon. The following home office–branch transactions took place during the year:

1. The Sunrise Company transferred $48,000 in cash to its Monmouth branch.
2. Merchandise costing the home office $46,600 was shipped to the branch at an invoice price of $55,920. The home office and branch use a perpetual inventory system.

3. The Monmouth branch received office equipment costing $42,000, purchased by the home office. The home office maintains all fixed asset accounts.

4. The Monmouth branch purchased additional merchandise from an outside wholesaler for cash at a cost of $34,000.

5. Branch sales for the first six months: cash—$19,200; charge—$44,600. A portion of the goods sold were purchased from the outside wholesaler and had an original cost to the Monmouth branch of $8,680. The remaining goods sold were from the home office shipment and were inventoried in the branch books at $21,420.

6. Branch collections on credit sales—$26,700.

7. Cash remitted to home office—$40,000.

8. Branch sales for the last six months: cash—$20,100; charge—$38,580. Part of the goods sold were purchased from the outside wholesaler and had an original cost to the Monmouth branch of $13,460. The remaining goods sold were from the home office shipment and were inventoried in the branch books at $22,800.

9. Branch collection of credit sales—$45,400.

10. Branch cash expenses for the year.

Advertising	$ 4,280
Maintenance	750
Miscellaneous	125
Utilities	1,800
Salaries	30,480

11. Depreciation expense for the year recorded by Sunrise Company on assets used by the Monmouth outlet totaled $1,600. The branch is notified of the depreciation charge to be reflected on its branch financial statements.

Required:

A. Record the journal entries to be made by the home office and by its branch in regard to the transactions above.

B. The branch files financial statements at the end of each year with the home office. Prepare the necessary closing entries on the branch books.

C. Compute the branch ending inventory purchased from the home office. Prepare the entry to be made on the home office books to adjust the Unrealized Profit in Shipment to Branch account for the amount realized in the current year.

Problem 13-2

The home office of Surplus, Inc. purchases blenders from a supplier at a cost of $15 a unit and retails these same units at $30 in both its home office and Rutgers branch retail outlet. During 1995, the home office purchased 10,000 units, of which 4,000 were sold at the home office outlet and 3,000 were shipped to the branch. During 1996, the home office purchased 12,000 units. During the year 9,000 were sold at the home office outlet and 4,500 were shipped to the branch.

The Rutgers branch sold 2,600 units in 1995 and 4,000 units in 1996. Both the home office and the branch office use a periodic inventory system. Beginning inventories were as follows (in units):

	HOME OFFICE	BRANCH
1/1/95	–0–	–0–
1/1/96	3,000	400
1/1/97	1,500	900

All purchases and sales are on account.

Required:

Prepare journal entries, including closing entries, for the books of the home office and its Rutgers branch for 1995 and 1996. Inventory is billed to the branch at cost. In completing the closing process, assume operating expenses were incurred as follows:

	SURPLUS, INC.	RUTGERS BRANCH
1995	$62,000	$12,000
1996	83,400	18,900

Problem 13-3

Use the information relating to Surplus, Inc. and its Rutgers branch in Problem 13-2, except assume that the inventory is billed to the branch at a mark-up of 20% above cost.

Required:

Prepare the journal entries, including closing entries, for the books of the Surplus, Inc. Company and its branch for 1995 and 1996.

Problem 13-4

As you begin to audit the books of the Applebee Company, you notice a discrepancy between the balance in the Investment in Branch ($141,020 Dr.) and the Home Office ($108,900 Cr.) accounts. The following information is available:

1. The home office bills goods shipped to the branch at 125% of cost. At the beginning of the year, branch inventory was stated at $62,500 after the annual physical count, and the home office unrealized profit account had a credit balance of $8,000. You find that a shipment made toward the end of the prior year had not been recorded by the home office. (*Hint*: You need to compute the billed amount of the shipment.)
2. On December 31 of the year under review, the branch mailed to the home office a check for $25,000 and a notice that the branch had collected $4,380 on a home office customer's account receivable. These items had not been recorded by the home office.
3. At the end of the current period, you find that a shipment billed at $34,000 to the branch had not been recorded by the branch.
4. The branch was opened during the preceding year and its operating loss of $42,800 for that year was capitalized by the branch as a start-up expense by the following entry:

Start-up Costs (Intangible Asset)	42,800	
Income Summary		42,800

The account is not being amortized by the branch, and no entry was made by the home office to record the net loss.

Required:

Prepare a schedule to reconcile to the correct reciprocal account balances at December 31 of the current year.

Problem 13-5

On July 1, 1995, Pratt Company established a branch office in a nearby city. To establish the branch, the home office sent the branch management $35,000 cash, furniture and fixtures that were carried on the home office books at a book value of $40,000, and 600 units of inventory that had cost $40 per unit. The home office bills inventory to the branch at 20% above cost. The management decided that furniture and fixtures are to be carried on the branch books and a periodic inventory system is to be used by the branch.

The branch transactions for the six-month period ending December 31, 1995 are summarized below.

Sales:	
Cash	$36,000
On account	60,400
Operating expenses paid by the branch	
(lease, salaries, utilities)	21,300
Purchase of inventory on account from	
outsiders—190 units	9,120
Collection of accounts receivable	48,200
Operating expenses paid by the home office	
and charged to the branch	8,000
Payment on accounts payable	8,200
Cash remittance to home office	25,000
Year-end data:	
Unpaid operating expenses	1,500
Depreciation expense	4,600
Inventory per physical count—160 units (45 of these	
units were purchased from outsiders)	

Required:

A. Prepare the journal entries on the branch books to record the transactions above.

B. Prepare adjusting and closing entries at year-end on the branch books.

C. Prepare a balance sheet for the branch as of December 31, 1995, after all closing entries have been posted to the ledger.

D. Prepare the journal entries needed on the home office books to record the branch transactions including the entry to record the branch net income (loss) and the entry to adjust the unrealized profit account and correct the branch reported net income (loss).

Problem 13-6

On January 1, 1995, Host Company opened a branch office, its first, in St. Paul, Minnesota. The branch was given the responsibilities for granting credit and collecting receivables on its sales. The branch pays its own operating expenses. All merchandise was purchased from the home office at cost. Preclosing trial balances for the home office and branch at the end of the first year of operation are as follows:

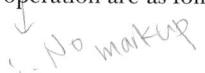

ACCOUNT TITLE	HOME OFFICE		BRANCH	
	DEBIT	CREDIT	DEBIT	CREDIT
Cash	$ 408,000		$ 414,000	
Accounts receivable (net)	970,000		263,000	
Inventory, 1/1/95	906,000			
Property and equipment— home office (net)	300,000			
Property and equipment— branch (net)	72,000			
Investment in branch	777,000			
Other assets	120,000			
Accounts payable		$ 410,000		$ 20,000
Other liabilities		349,000		
Common stock		1,000,000		
Home office				587,000
Retained earnings		660,000		
Sales		4,100,000		1,210,000
Purchases	2,860,000			
Expenses	1,196,000		200,000	
Shipments to branch		1,090,000		
Shipments from home office			940,000	
	$7,609,000	$7,609,000	$1,817,000	$1,817,000
Inventory, 12/31/95	$ 524,000		$ 189,000	

(handwritten: → not include 150,000)

A portion of the difference between the Home Office account and the Investment in Branch account is due to a transfer of $40,000 of cash by the branch on December 30 that was not received by the home office until the next fiscal year. The remainder is due to inventory in transit at year-end.

Required:

A. Prepare the closing entries at December 31, 1995, for the branch books.

B. Prepare the closing entries at December 31, 1995, for the home office books.

C. Prepare in journal form year-end adjustments to the trial balance that pertains to the branch operations that will be made in the combined statements workpaper.

D. Prepare a combined statements workpaper at December 31, 1995.

Problem 13-7

Picadilly Company has a branch located in Billings. The branch purchases 100% of its inventory for resale from Picadilly at billed prices representing a mark-up equal to 20% of cost to Picadilly. Trial balances for both businesses at December 31, 1995, follow:

	HOME OFFICE	BRANCH
Cash	$ 22,000	$ 5,500
Accounts receivable	40,000	17,000
1/1 Inventory	36,000	
Investment in branch	57,000	

	HOME OFFICE	BRANCH
Plant and equipment	150,000	
Accumulated depreciation	(10,000)	
Accounts payable	(20,000)	
Home office		(30,500)
Common stock	(150,000)	
1/1 Retained earnings	(70,000)	
Sales	(388,000)	(112,000)
Purchases	306,000	
Shipments to branch	(80,000)	
Shipments from home office		81,000
Operating expenses	83,000	39,000
Dividends declared	40,000	
Unrealized profit on shipments	(16,000)	
	$ –0–	$ –0–

The following information has been gathered by Picadilly's controller:

1. On December 31, 1995, the branch mailed a check for $3,000 to the home office.
2. Expenses incurred by Picadilly on behalf of the branch and allocated to the branch amounted to $8,500. The branch was never notified.
3. The final merchandise shipment to the branch left Picadilly on December 28; invoice amount was $15,000.
4. Ending inventories of the home office and branch, excluding shipments in transit on December 31, amounted to $50,000 and $22,000, respectively.

Required:

Prepare a combined statements workpaper for Picadilly Company and its branch at December 31, 1995. Adjusting and eliminating entries in journal form and combined financial statements are not required.

Problem 13-8

The home office for Salsbury Company is located in Los Angeles. In 1993, the company opened a branch in Norfolk. Although the branch is allowed to purchase locally from suppliers, the majority of its merchandise is acquired from the home office and billed to the branch at 125% of cost. Financial information for the home office and its Norfolk branch at December 31, 1995, is presented below.

INCOME STATEMENT	SALSBURY COMPANY	NORFOLK BRANCH
Sales	$16,870,000	$10,103,000
Cost of goods sold	(10,826,000)	(8,171,000)
Expenses	(2,436,100)	(1,324,200)
Net income	$ 3,607,900	$ 607,800

RETAINED EARNINGS STATEMENT		
1/1 Retained earnings	$ 1,238,000	$
Net income	3,607,900	607,800
Dividends declared	(450,000)	
12/31 Retained earnings	$ 4,395,900	$ 607,800

BALANCE SHEET

Cash	$ 258,175	$ 304,000
Short-term securities	280,300	
Accounts receivable (net)	543,200	291,000
Inventory	1,870,000	700,000*
Investment in branch	830,300	
Property and equipment (net)	8,208,200	
Totals	$11,990,175	$ 1,295,000
Accounts payable	$ 748,600	$ 87,300
Notes payable	1,522,500	
Common stock	4,000,000	
Retained earnings	4,395,900	607,800
Home office		599,900
Unrealized profit in shipments to branch	1,323,175	
Totals	$11,990,175	$ 1,295,000

*Purchased from the home office	$652,200
Purchased from outsiders	47,800
Total ending inventory of branch	$700,000

Additional information:

1. Both the home office and the branch use the FIFO cost flow assumption.

2. The branch, owing to unexptectedly heavy post-Christmas sales, made three cash transfers to the home office within a one-week period.

DATE FORWARDED BY BRANCH	DATE RECORDED BY HOME OFFICE	AMOUNT
12/28	12/29	$ 60,000
12/30	1/3	125,000
1/3	1/5	63,000

3. The branch beginning inventory contained goods acquired from the home office at a billed price of $532,000.

4. During the year, the home office shipped goods costing $4,867,100 to the branch. The following entry is made by the home office to record such shipments, assuming a shipment of goods that had cost $100.

Investment in Branch	125	
Inventory		100
Unrealized Profit in Shipments to Branch		25

5. A shipment of merchandise from the home office, billed at $105,400, was in transit to the branch at December 31, 1995.

Required:

Prepare a combined statements workpaper at December 31, 1995.

Problem 13-9

The trial balances of the home office and branch office of the Peabody Company are given below:

The Peabody Company
Trial Balance
For the Year Ended December 31, 1995

DEBITS	HOME OFFICE	BRANCH
Cash	$ 33,140	$ 2,115
Inventory—home office	23,000	
Inventory—branch		13,860
Other assets	200,200	48,700
Investment in branch	60,325	
Purchases	190,000	
Shipments from home office		119,500
Freight-in from home office		5,250
Other operating expenses	42,000	24,300
	$548,665	$213,725

CREDITS		
Liabilities	$ 35,000	$ 3,500
Home office		51,225
Sales	155,000	159,000
Shipments to branch	100,000	
Unrealized profit in shipments to branch	27,665	
Capital stock	200,000	
Retained earnings	31,000	
	$548,665	$213,725

The audit at December 31, 1995, disclosed the following:

1. The branch office deposits all cash receipts in a local bank for the account of the home office. The audit worksheet for the cash cut-off revealed:

AMOUNT	DEPOSITED BY BRANCH	RECORDED BY HOME OFFICE
$1,050	December 27, 1995	December 31, 1995
$1,100	December 30, 1995	January 1, 1996
$ 900	December 31, 1995	January 3, 1996
$ 300	January 2, 1996	January 6, 1996

2. The branch office pays expenses incurred locally from an imprest bank account that is maintained with a balance of $2,000. Checks are drawn once a week on this imprest account, and the home office is notified of the amount needed to replenish the account. At December 31, a $1,600 reimbursement check was mailed to the branch office.

3. The branch office receives all its goods from the home office. The home office bills the goods at cost plus a mark-up of 25% of cost. At December 31, a shipment with a billing value of $5,500 was in transit to the branch. Freight costs are typically 4% of billed values. Freight costs are considered inventoriable costs.

4. The trial balance opening inventories are shown at their respective costs to the home office and to the branch office. The inventories at December 31, excluding the shipment in transit, are

Home office, at cost	$30,000
Branch office, at billing value (i.e., excludes freight costs)	10,400

Required:

Prepare a three-divisional workpaper to combine the Peabody Company and its branch. (Formal journal entries are not required. Supporting computations must be in good form.)

(AICPA adapted)

14

ACCOUNTING FOR FOREIGN CURRENCY TRANSACTIONS

Many companies in the United States engage in international activities such as exporting or importing goods, establishing a foreign branch, or holding an equity investment in a foreign company. Recording and reporting problems are encountered when transactions with a foreign company or the financial statements of a foreign branch or investee are measured in a currency other than U.S. currency. Transactions to be settled in a foreign currency must be translated—that is, expressed in dollars—before they can be aggregated with the domestic transactions of the U.S. firm. When a foreign branch or investee maintains its accounts and prepares its financial statements in terms of the currency of the country in which it is domiciled, the accounts must be translated from the foreign currency into dollars before financial statements for the combined entity are prepared. Translation is necessary because useful financial reports cannot be prepared until all transactions and account balances are stated in a common unit of currency.

Because of the widespread involvement of U.S. companies in foreign activities, accountants must be familiar with the problems associated with accounting for those activities. This chapter includes a discussion of the nature and use of exchange rates in the translation process, as well as the accounting standards applied in the translation of transactions measured in a foreign currency. The translation of accounts maintained in terms of a foreign currency is discussed in the next chapter.

The expansion of international business has been of particular concern to accountants because of developments in the worldwide monetary system. These developments, coupled with the existence of a number of acceptable methods of translating foreign financial statements and reporting gains or losses on foreign currency fluctuations, led the FASB to place the topic on its agenda in 1973. The final result was the issuance in 1981 of *Statement of Financial Accounting Standards (SFAS) No. 52*, "Foreign Currency Translation."[1] The discussion in this chapter focuses on the accounting prescribed in *SFAS No. 52*.

EXCHANGE RATES—MEANS OF TRANSLATION

Transactions that are to be settled in a foreign currency and financial statements of an affiliate maintained in terms of a foreign currency are translated into dollars by multiplying the number of units of the foreign currency by a direct exchange rate. Thus, *translation* is the process of expressing monetary amounts that are stated in terms of a foreign currency in the currency of the reporting entity by using an appropriate exchange rate. An *exchange rate* "is the ratio between a unit of one currency and the amount of another currency for which that unit can be exchanged at a particular time."[2]

A *direct exchange quotation* is one in which the exchange rate is quoted in terms of how many units of the domestic currency can be converted into *one unit of foreign currency*. For example, a direct quotation of U.S. dollars for one British pound of 1.517 means that $1.517 could be exchanged for one British pound. To translate pounds into dollars, the number of pounds is multiplied by the direct exchange rate. Exchange rates are also stated in terms of converting *one unit of the domestic currency* into units of a foreign currency, which is called an *indirect quotation*. In the example above, one U.S. dollar could be converted into .6592 pounds ($1.00 ÷ 1.517). To translate pounds into dollars, the number of pounds could also be divided by the indirect exchange rate.

Exchange rates may be quoted for the immediate delivery of currencies exchanged (*spot rate*), or for future delivery (*forward* or *future rate*) of currencies exchanged. The forward rate is an exchange rate established at the time a forward exchange contract is negotiated. A *forward exchange contract* is a contract to exchange at a specified rate (the *forward rate*) currencies of different countries on a stipulated future date. Before the currencies are exchanged, the spot rate may move above or below the contracted forward exchange rate, but this has no effect on the forward rate established when the forward exchange contract was negotiated. In both the spot and forward markets, a foreign exchange trader provides a quotation for buying (the *bid rate*) and a quotation for selling (the *offer rate*) foreign currency. The trader's buying rate will be lower than the quoted selling rate, and the spread between the two rates is profit for the trader. Exchange rates are reported daily in terms of both direct and indirect quotations (see Illustration 14-1) in the financial section of many newspapers.

---

[1] *Statement of Financial Accounting Standards No. 52*, "Foreign Currency Translation" (Norwalk, Conn.: FASB, 1981).

[2] Ibid., par. 26.

EXCHANGE RATES

Tuesday, August 24, 1993

The New York foreign exchange selling rates below apply to trading among banks in amounts of $1 million and more, as quoted at 3 p.m. Eastern time by Bankers Trust Co., Telerate and other sources. Retail transactions provide fewer units of foreign currency per dollar.

Country	U.S. $ equiv. Tues.	U.S. $ equiv. Mon.	Currency per U.S. $ Tues.	Currency per U.S. $ Mon.
Argentina (Peso)	1.01	1.01	.99	.99
Australia (Dollar)	.6689	.6692	1.4950	1.4943
Austria (Schilling)	.08459	.08429	11.82	11.86
Bahrain (Dinar)	2.6518	2.6518	.3771	.3771
Belgium (Franc)	.02825	.02812	35.40	35.56
Brazil (Cruzeiro real)	.0120934	.0121065	82.69	82.60
Britain (Pound)	1.4985	1.5040	.6673	.6649
30-Day Forward	1.4950	1.5003	.6689	.6665
90-Day Forward	1.4887	1.4939	.6717	.6694
180-Day Forward	1.4814	1.4869	.6750	.6725
Canada (Dollar)	.7590	.7575	1.3176	1.3202
30-Day Forward	.7580	.7565	1.3193	1.3219
90-Day Forward	.7560	.7544	1.3228	1.3255
180-Day Forward	.7534	.7518	1.3273	1.3301
Czech. Rep. (Koruna)				
Commercial rate	.0345304	.0347464	28.9600	28.7800
Chile (Peso)	.002522	.002528	396.48	395.64
China (Renminbi)	.174856	.174856	5.7190	5.7190
Colombia (Peso)	.001458	.001459	685.71	685.23
Denmark (Krone)	.1453	.1442	6.8834	6.9333
Ecuador (Sucre)				
Floating rate	.000527	.000527	1899.01	1899.01
Finland (Markka)	.17268	.17222	5.7909	5.8065
France (Franc)	.17112	.17023	5.8438	5.8745
30-Day Forward	.17038	.16955	5.8693	5.8980
90-Day Forward	.16933	.16848	5.9055	5.9355
180-Day Forward	.16821	.16738	5.9448	5.9745
Germany (Mark)	.5954	.5933	1.6795	1.6855
30-Day Forward	.5935	.5913	1.6850	1.6912
90-Day Forward	.5904	.5882	1.6939	1.7001
180-Day Forward	.5865	.5845	1.7050	1.7110
Greece (Drachma)	.004247	.004232	235.45	236.30
Hong Kong (Dollar)	.12907	.12907	7.7475	7.7477
Hungary (Forint)	.0107550	.0107388	92.9800	93.1200
India (Rupee)	.03212	.03212	31.13	31.13
Indonesia (Rupiah)	.0004768	.0004768	2097.54	2097.54
Ireland (Punt)	1.4091	1.4028	.7097	.7129
Israel (Shekel)	.3584	.3580	2.7905	2.7935
Italy (Lira)	.0006284	.0006268	1591.34	1595.33
Japan (Yen)	.009643	.009685	103.70	103.25
30-Day Forward	.009645	.009687	103.68	103.23
90-Day Forward	.009652	.009693	103.61	103.16
180-Day Forward	.009670	.009711	103.41	102.97
Jordan (Dinar)	1.4767	1.4767	.6772	.6772
Kuwait (Dinar)	3.3261	3.3261	.3007	.3007
Lebanon (Pound)	.000579	.000579	1726.50	1726.50
Malaysia (Ringgit)	.3923	.3922	2.5490	2.5495
Malta (Lira)	2.5873	2.5873	.3865	.3865
Mexico (Peso)				
Floating rate	.3215434	.3215434	3.1100	3.1100
Netherland (Guilder)	.5296	.5275	1.8884	1.8958
New Zealand (Dollar)	.5527	.5511	1.8093	1.8146
Norway (Krone)	.1373	.1368	7.2848	7.3075
Pakistan (Rupee)	.0336	.0336	29.75	29.75
Peru (New Sol)	.4991	.4991	2.00	2.00
Philippines (Peso)	.03676	.03676	27.20	27.20
Poland (Zloty)	.00005716	.00005736	17494.00	17433.00
Portugal (Escudo)	.005866	.005812	170.47	172.06
Saudi Arabia (Riyal)	.26665	.26665	3.7503	3.7503
Singapore (Dollar)	.6219	.6220	1.6080	1.6078
Slovak Rep. (Koruna)	.0306185	.0306185	32.6600	32.6600
South Africa (Rand)				
Commercial rate	.2975	.2971	3.3613	3.3658
Financial rate	.2149	.2146	4.6525	4.6600
South Korea (Won)	.0012335	.0012332	810.70	810.90
Spain (Peseta)	.007410	.007319	134.95	136.63
Sweden (Krona)	.1245	.1237	8.0305	8.0828
Switzerland (Franc)	.6784	.6748	1.4740	1.4820
30-Day Forward	.6774	.6737	1.4762	1.4843
90-Day Forward	.6758	.6722	1.4797	1.4877
180-Day Forward	.6744	.6708	1.4828	1.4908
Taiwan (Dollar)	.037481	.037100	26.68	26.95
Thailand (Baht)	.03976	.03976	25.15	25.15
Turkey (Lira)	.0000862	.0000863	11595.00	11581.00
United Arab (Dirham)	.2723	.2723	3.6725	3.6725
Uruguay (New Peso)				
Financial	.237699	.237699	4.21	4.21
Venezuela (Bolivar)				
Floating rate	.01076	.01060	92.98	94.30
			- - -	
SDR	1.40392	1.40784	.71229	.71031
ECU	1.13910	1.13500	....	....

Special Drawing Rights (SDR) are based on exchange rates for the U.S., German, British, French and Japanese currencies. Source: International Monetary Fund.

European Currency Unit (ECU) is based on a basket of community currencies.

ILLUSTRATION 14-1

Before the 1970s, rates of exchange of free market countries were controlled to some extent by member countries of the International Monetary Fund. Most of the member countries agreed to establish exchange rates in terms of U.S. dollars and gold. Although the actual rate was free to fluctuate, the countries that established *official* or *fixed* rates agreed to maintain the actual rate within 1% ($2\frac{1}{4}$% after 1971) of the official rate by buying or selling U.S. dollars or gold. Because of pressure on the dollar, the United States in 1971 suspended its commitment to convert dollars into gold at $35 per ounce. The relationship between major currencies is now determined largely by supply and demand factors, called *floating rates*. As a result, significant realignments have occurred between the currencies of various countries over a relatively short period of time.

Floating rates increase the risk to companies doing business with a foreign company.[3] After a rate change occurs, all transactions are conducted at the new rate until the next change occurs. Because the amount to be received or paid is affected by a change in exchange rates, there is a direct economic impact on a company's operations. For example, a payable to be settled in 100,000 yen has a dollar equivalent value of $434 when the direct exchange rate is $.00434. An increase in the value of the yen to $.00625 would result in an increase in the payable to $625.

The selection of an exchange rate to be used in the translation process is complicated by the fact that some countries maintain multiple exchange rates. The government of a country may maintain official rates that differ from the market-determined rate, depending on the nature of the transaction. For example, a government may establish a set exchange rate for "essential goods and services" and allow the exchange rate for nonessential goods and services to float.

MEASURED VERSUS DENOMINATED

Transactions are normally *measured* and recorded in terms of the currency in which the reporting entity prepares its financial statements. This currency is usually the domestic currency of the country in which the company is domiciled and is called the *reporting currency*. In subsequent illustrations the U.S. dollar is assumed to be the reporting currency of U.S.-based firms. Assets and liabilities are *denominated* in a currency if their amounts are fixed in terms of that currency. Thus, a transaction between two U.S. companies requiring payment of a fixed number of dollars is both measured and denominated in dollars. In a transaction between a U.S. firm and a foreign company, the two parties usually negotiate whether the settlement is to be made in dollars or in the domestic currency of the foreign company. If the trans-

---

[3]Exposure to currency fluctuations may be defined in terms of economic exposure or accounting exposure. A company's *economic exposure* can be defined broadly as the uncertainty associated with the effect of exchange rate changes on the expected cash flow of the reporting entity. Alternatively, an entity's *accounting exposure* is related to accounts that are translated at the current exchange rate. Thus, as will be shown in the next chapter, in balance sheets prepared on two different dates, those accounts translated at the current rate will be reported at different amounts when the exchange rate changes, resulting in a translation gain or loss to the entity. Accounting exposure may not be a good surrogate for economic exposure.

action is to be settled by the payment of a fixed amount of foreign currency, the U.S. firm measures the receivable or payable in dollars, but the transaction is denominated in the specified foreign currency. To the foreign company, the transaction is both measured and denominated in its domestic currency.

FOREIGN CURRENCY TRANSACTIONS

A transaction that requires settlement in a foreign currency is called a *foreign currency transaction*. A transaction with a foreign company that is to be settled in dollars is not a foreign currency transaction to a U.S. firm because the number of dollars to be received or paid to settle the account is fixed and remains unaffected by subsequent changes in the exchange rate. Thus, a transaction of a U.S. firm with a foreign entity to be settled in dollars is accounted for in the same manner as if the transaction had been with a U.S. company.

A foreign currency transaction will be settled in a foreign currency, and the U.S. firm is exposed to the risk of unfavorable changes in the exchange rate that may occur between the date the transaction is entered into and the date the account is settled. For example, assume that a U.S. firm purchased goods from a French firm and the U.S. firm is to settle the liability by the payment of 20,000 francs. The French firm would measure and record the transaction as normal because the billing is in its reporting currency. Because the billing is in a foreign currency (denominated in francs), the U.S. firm must translate the amount of the foreign currency payable into dollars before the transaction is entered in its accounts. An increase (decrease) in the direct exchange rate will increase (decrease) the number of dollars required to buy the fixed number of francs needed to settle the foreign currency liability.[4] In the case of a foreign currency receivable, a change in the exchange rate between dollars and the foreign currency in which the transaction is denominated increases or decreases the number of dollars that will be obtained when the foreign currency received to settle the receivable is converted into dollars. As will be shown later, the U.S. firm may *hedge*, that is, protect itself against an unfavorable change in the exchange rate.

Some of the more common foreign currency transactions are:

1. Importing or exporting goods or services on credit with the receivable or payable denominated in a foreign currency.

2. Borrowing from or lending to a foreign company with the amount payable or receivable denominated in a foreign currency.

3. Engaging in a transaction with the intention of hedging a net investment in a foreign entity.

4. Entering into a forward contract to buy or sell foreign currency.

Accounting for each of these types of transactions is discussed below.

[4]If more dollars are needed to acquire the francs, the franc is sometimes said to be *strengthening* in relation to the U.S. dollar. Another way to look at this is that the direct exchange rate is increasing. If fewer dollars are needed to obtain the needed francs, then the franc is *weakening* or depreciating in relation to the dollar. Accordingly, the direct exchange rate is decreasing.

Importing or Exporting of Goods or Services

Probably the most common form of foreign currency transaction is the exporting or importing of goods or services. In each unsettled foreign currency transaction, there are three stages of concern to the accountant. These stages and the appropriate exchange rate to use in translating accounts denominated in units of foreign currency (except for forward exchange contracts) are as follows:

1. *At the date the transaction is first recognized in conformity with GAAP.* Each asset, liability, revenue, expense, gain, or loss arising from the transaction is measured and recorded in dollars by multiplying the units of foreign currency by the current exchange rate.[5] (The *current exchange rate* is the spot rate in effect on a given date.)

2. *At each balance sheet date that occurs between the transaction date and the settlement date.* Recorded balances that are denominated in a foreign currency are adjusted to reflect the current exchange rate in effect at the balance sheet date.[6]

3. *At the settlement date.* In the case of a foreign currency payable, a U.S. firm must convert U.S. dollars into foreign currency units to settle the account, whereas foreign currency units received to settle a foreign currency receivable will be converted into dollars. Although translation is not required, a transaction gain or loss is recognized if the number of dollars paid or received upon conversion does not equal the carrying value of the related payable or receivable.

Application of these rules results in accounting for a change in the exchange rate that occurs during a reporting period as a change in estimate. In other words, using the current exchange rate to translate foreign currency receivables and payable at each measurement date *provides an estimate of the number of dollars to be received or to be paid to settle the amount.* Note that both gains and losses are adjusted to the receivable or payable, resulting in a form of current value accounting. The increase or decrease in the expected cash flow is generally reported as a foreign currency *transaction gain or loss*, sometimes referred to as an *exchange gain or loss*, in determining net income for the current period. Exceptions to this treatment of transaction gains and losses are:

1. Intercompany transactions that are of a long-term financing or capital nature between an investor and an investee that is consolidated, combined, or accounted for by the equity method.

2. Transactions that are designated as, and are effective as, economic hedges of a net investment in a foreign entity.

3. Transactions that are designated as, and are effective as, economic hedges of an identifiable foreign currency commitment.

Transaction gains and losses that result from the first two exceptions are reported as a component of stockholders' equity; gains and losses for exception number 3 are generally deferred and included in the measurement of the related foreign currency transaction.

---

[5] *Statement of Financial Accounting Standards No. 52*, par. 16(a).
[6] Ibid., par. 16(b).

Importing Transaction   To illustrate an importing transaction, assume that on December 1, 1995, a U.S. firm purchased 100 units of inventory from a French firm for 500,000 francs to be paid on March 1, 1996. The firm's fiscal year-end is December 31. Assume further that the U.S. firm did not engage in any form of hedging activity. The spot rate for francs at various times is as follows:

Transaction date—December 1, 1995	$.20
Balance sheet date—December 31, 1995	.23
Settlement date—March 1, 1996	.22

The U.S. firm would prepare the following journal entry on December 1, 1995:

Dec. 1	Purchases	100,000	
	Accounts Payable (500,000 francs × $.20)		100,000

At the balance sheet date, the payable denominated in foreign currency is adjusted using the exchange rate in effect at the balance sheet date. The entry is

Dec. 31	Transaction Loss	15,000	
	Accounts Payable		15,000

Commitment at 12/31 (500,000 francs × $.23)	$115,000
Recorded liability	100,000
Adjustment needed	$ 15,000

or

[500,000 francs × ($.23 − $.20) = $15,000]

If the exchange rate had declined below $.20, for example to $.18, the U.S. firm would have recognized a gain of $10,000 since it would have taken only $90,000 (500,000 francs × $.18) to settle the $100,000 recorded liability.

Before the settlement date, the U.S. firm must buy francs in order to satisfy the liability. With a change in the exchange rate to $.22, the firm must pay $110,000 on March 1, 1996, to acquire the 500,000 francs. The journal entry to record the settlement is:

Mar. 1	Accounts Payable	115,000	
	Transaction Gain		5,000
	Cash		110,000

Over the three-month period, the decision to delay making payment cost the firm $10,000. This net amount was recognized as a loss of $15,000 in 1995 and a gain of $5,000 in 1996.

Note in the example above that at December 31, the balance sheet date, a transaction loss was recognized on the open account payable. Such a loss is considered unrealized because the account has not yet been settled or closed. When an account payable (or receivable) is settled or closed, a transaction gain or loss on the settlement is considered realized. The FASB reasoned that users of financial statements are best served by reporting the effects of exchange rate changes on a firm's financial position in the accounting period in which they occur, even though they are unrealized and may reverse or partially reverse in a subsequent period, as in the illustration above. This procedure is criticized, however, because under GAAP, gains are not ordinarily reported until realized and because the recognition of unrealized gains and losses results in increased earnings volatility.

Exporting Transaction   Now assume that the U.S. firm sold 100 units of inventory for 500,000 francs to a French firm. All other facts are the same as those for the importing transaction. The journal entries to record this exporting transaction on the books of the U.S. Company are

December 1, 1995—Date of Transaction

Accounts Receivable (500,000 francs × $.20)	100,000	
Sales		100,000

December 31, 1995—Balance Sheet Date

Accounts Receivable	15,000	
Transaction Gain		15,000
(500,000 francs × $.23 = $115,000 − $100,000)		

March 1, 1996—Settlement Date

Cash (500,000 francs × $.22)	110,000	
Transaction Loss	5,000	
Accounts Receivable		115,000

A comparison of the entries to record the exporting transaction with those prepared to record an importing transaction reveals that a movement in the exchange rate has an opposite effect on the company's reported income. That is, the increase in the exchange rate from $.20 to $.23 resulted in a transaction gain in the case of a foreign currency receivable, whereas a transaction loss was reported in the case of a foreign currency payable. When the exchange rate decreased from $.23 to $.22, a transaction loss was reported on the exposed receivable, whereas a transaction gain was reported on the exposed payable. Thus, one tool available to management to hedge a potential loss on a foreign currency receivable is to enter into a transaction to establish a liability to be settled in the same foreign currency. Similarly, a liability to be settled in units of a foreign currency can be hedged by entering into a receivable transaction denominated in the same foreign currency.

These relationships are summarized below.

	BALANCE SHEET		
	EXPOSED ACCOUNT	EFFECT ON BALANCE REPORTED	INCOME STATEMENT EFFECT
Increase in direct exchange rate			
Importing transaction	Liability	Increase	Transaction loss
Exporting transaction	Receivable	Increase	Transaction gain
Decrease in direct exchange rate			
Importing transaction	Liability	Decrease	Transaction gain
Exporting transaction	Receivable	Decrease	Transaction loss

How should a transaction gain or loss be reported?   In the previous examples, the dollar amount recorded in the Sales account and the Purchases account was determined by the exchange rate prevailing at the transaction date. Adjustments to the foreign currency denominated receivable or payable were recorded directly to transaction gain or loss. Under this approach, referred to as the *two-transaction approach*, the sale or purchase is viewed as a transaction separate and distinct from the financing arrangement. Thus, the transaction gain or loss does not result from an operating decision to buy or sell goods or services in a foreign market, but from a financial decision to delay the payment or receipt of foreign currency and not to hedge the exposed receivable or payable against possible unfavorable currency rate changes.

An alternative view that was rejected by the FASB considers the initial transaction and settlement to be one transaction. Supporters of this method contend that the initial transaction is incomplete and the amounts recorded are estimates until such time as the total sacrifice from the purchase (units of domestic currency paid) or the total benefits from the sale (units of domestic currency received) are known. Under this view, transaction gains or losses should be accounted for as an adjustment to the cost of the asset purchased or to the revenue recorded in a sales transaction. There is an obvious implementation problem with this method when the sale or purchase is recorded in one fiscal period and the receipt or payment occurs in another period.

Other Forms of Foreign Borrowing or Lending

In the preceding section, the exporting or importing of inventory was illustrated. Accounting for other types of foreign borrowing or lending transactions is similar; that is, the two-transaction approach is followed in which the cost of an asset acquired or revenue recognized is accounted for independently from the method of settlement. For example, if a fixed asset is acquired from a foreign company on credit, the cost of the asset is the number of foreign currency units that would be paid in a cash transaction multiplied by the exchange rate at the transaction date. The cost of the asset is not adjusted for subsequent changes in the exchange rate, but the liability is adjusted at each balance sheet date on the basis of the exchange rate in effect at that date. The adjustment to the liability is reported currently in income. The amount recorded for interest expense is the equivalent number of U.S. dollars needed to make the interest payment.

Economic Hedge of a Net Investment in a Foreign Entity

A U.S. firm that maintains an equity investment in a foreign company may enter into a foreign currency transaction in an effort to minimize or offset the effects of currency fluctuations on the net investment. A foreign currency transaction is considered a hedge of a net investment in a foreign entity if both of the following conditions are met:

(1) The forward contract is designated as, and is effective as, a hedge of the net investment.

(2) The foreign currency commitment is firm.[7]

For example, assume that a U.S. firm holds an investment in the net assets of a French company that conducts its business primarily in francs. As will be shown in Chapter 15, the investor company applying the equity method to a less than 50% owned investee will record its share of the effect of a change in the exchange rate on the net assets of the foreign investee. To hedge against the exposure to exchange rate changes, the U.S. firm may enter into an agreement to borrow francs from a French bank. Assume further that the loan is designated as, and is effective as, a hedge of the net investment in the French company. On subsequent balance sheet dates, both the net assets of the foreign company and the loan denominated in francs are adjusted to reflect the current exchange rate. A gain (loss) from the adjustment of the liability will offset a loss (gain) from the adjustment of the net investment in the foreign company, and a hedge results. Both adjustments are reported as a component of stockholders' equity rather than reported currently in income. However, if the adjustment to the loan balance exceeds the adjustment of the balance of the net investment, the excess is reported in the determination of net income as a transaction gain or loss. The gains or losses accumulated in a separate component of stockholders' equity remain there until part or all of the investment in the foreign company is sold.

Forward Exchange Contracts

A forward exchange contract (forward contract) is an agreement to exchange currencies of two different countries at a specified rate (the forward rate) on a stipulated future date. At the inception of the contract, the forward rate normally varies from the spot rate. *The difference between the two rates is referred to as a discount (premium) if the forward rate is less than (greater than) the spot rate*, as shown here.

	EXCHANGE RATE	
Forward rate	$.175	.007 premium
Spot rate	.168	.006 discount
Forward rate	.162	

Although there are several reasons why the forward and spot rates may not be the same, the FASB considered the difference normally to reflect the interest rate differential between the two countries.

There are a number of business situations in which a firm may desire to acquire a forward exchange contract. Forward contracts may be classified as follows:

1. Hedges
   (a) To hedge a foreign currency exposed receivable or payable position.
   (b) To hedge a net investment in a foreign entity.[8]

---

[7]Ibid., par. 21.

[8]The analysis of a forward contract to hedge a net investment in a foreign entity is similar to the analysis in the preceding section on "Economic Hedge of a Net Investment in a Foreign Entity"; it is summarized in Illustration 14-2.

(c) To hedge an identifiable foreign currency commitment on an after-tax basis.

2. Speculation
   (a) To speculate in foreign currency in anticipation of a gain.

The classification above is important because the accounting for a particular type of forward contract depends on the purpose for which it was obtained. The difference in accounting relates primarily to two questions.

1. How is a transaction gain or loss on the forward contract computed and when should the gain or loss be reported?

2. How is the discount or premium on a forward contract accounted for over the life of the contract?

Hedge of a Foreign Currency Exposed Asset or Exposed Liability Position It has been demonstrated that a U.S. firm buying goods on account from a foreign company or selling goods on credit to a foreign customer in a transaction denominated in a foreign currency is exposed to an added risk that the exchange rate will change unfavorably before the receivable or payable is settled. To eliminate or reduce this risk, the firm may enter into a forward contract to buy or sell foreign currency. For example, assume that a U.S. firm purchased inventory on account for 500,000 francs, payable in 90 days. If the exchange rate is $.20 on the settlement date, the U.S. firm could acquire 500,000 francs for $100,000 to settle the account payable. However, if the exchange rate is $.25, it would require $125,000 (500,000 francs × $.25) to satisfy the firm's obligation. To eliminate the risk, the firm could acquire 500,000 francs when the goods were purchased, but by doing so, it would lose the use of the money for 90 days and the effect would be the same as that of a cash purchase.

Another approach that the firm can take is to shift the risk of a possible unfavorable rate change by negotiating a forward contract to buy a specific number of francs with dollars in 90 days at a specified exchange rate. Conversely, assume that the firm sold goods to a foreign customer for 500,000 francs to be received in 90 days. A decrease in the exchange rate of $.05 would reduce the value of the francs received upon settlement of the receivable balance by $25,000 (500,000 francs × $.05). To hedge this exposed asset position, the firm may negotiate a forward contract to sell the foreign currency for a fixed number of U.S. dollars on the date payment is received. In either case, by obtaining a forward contract, a firm is able to eliminate or reduce the risk of exchange rate fluctuations and fix the number of dollars that are to be received or paid at the settlement date.

Hedge of a foreign currency exposed liability To illustrate the accounting for a forward contract that is a hedge of an exposed liability position, we will use the same set of assumptions that was used in the section on exporting and importing of goods so that the reader can compare the effects on the operations of the firm from acquiring a forward contract. The assumptions were as follows:

1. On December 1, 1995, a U.S. firm purchased inventory for 500,000 francs payable on March 1, 1996.

2. Spot rates were as follows:
   Date of purchase (12/1/95)—$.20
   Balance sheet date (12/31/95)—$.23
   Settlement date (3/1/96)—$.22

3. The transaction is denominated in francs.

Now assume that on the date of purchase, the U.S. firm entered into a forward contract to buy 500,000 francs on March 1, 1996, for $.205. It should be noted that in the series of journal entries that follow, the purchase transaction and the forward contract are accounted for as separate transactions. The entries to record the purchase transaction, which were discussed earlier, will not be elaborated on in the discussion that follows.

The entries to record the purchase and forward exchange contract are:

December 1, 1995—Transaction Date

(1) Purchases	100,000	
Accounts Payable (500,000 francs × $.20)		100,000
To record purchase of goods on account.		
(2) Foreign Currency (FC) Receivable from Exchange		
Dealer (500,000 francs × $.20)	100,000	
Premium on Forward Contract*	2,500	
Dollars Payable to Exchange Dealer		
(500,000 francs × $.205)		102,500
To record forward contract to buy 500,000 francs.		

*A premium is recorded because the forward rate ($.205) is greater than the spot rate ($.20). In the entry the total premium is a balancing amount, but it can be computed directly by multiplying the number of foreign currency units by the difference between the forward rate and the spot rate [($.205 − $.20) × 500,000 francs = $2,500].

At the date of the transaction, the U.S. firm records the forward contract by recognizing an obligation of $102,500 for the number of dollars to be paid (units of foreign currency to be purchased multiplied by forward rate) to the exchange dealer when the forward contract matures.[9] At the same time, the foreign currency contracted for in the forward contract is recorded. The 500,000 francs to be re-

[9]In practice, a journal entry may not be made to record a forward contract when the contract was negotiated because it represents an executory contract. Although the contract was negotiated on the transaction date, payment is not made to the exchange dealer until the contract matures and the foreign currency is received from the dealer. If one party to a forward contract does not perform, the other party to the contract does not have to perform. Within the framework of GAAP, an agreement to exchange resources in the future that at present are unfulfilled commitments on both sides are not normally recorded until such time as one party to the contract performs part of the agreement.

Some accountants contend, however, that a forward contract is both an economic resource (that is, the firm has a claim to either dollars or foreign currency) and an economic liability (that is, the firm must deliver either dollars or units of foreign currency). This position is supported by the fact that the unperformed forward contract may have a market value, and the rights and the related obligation can normally be assigned. See Leonard Lorensen, "Reporting Foreign Operations of U.S. Companies in U.S. Dollars," *Accounting Research Study No. 12*, (New York: AICPA, 1972), pp. 65–66. In this chapter, forward contracts are recorded because it is easier to analyze the subsequent adjustments required to report the effects of a forward contract on the firm's reported income.

ceived are translated into $100,000 using the spot rate ($.20) in effect at the date of the transaction. Note that the obligation is for a fixed amount of dollars ($102,500), and that it is based on the contracted forward rate, while the right to receive 500,000 francs reflects the units to be received at the current spot rate. In future periods the obligation is not adjusted since it represents a commitment to pay a fixed number of dollars and is unaffected by future changes in the exchange rate. However, because the currency to be received is a foreign currency, fluctuations in the exchange rate are recognized in the reporting period in which a change occurs. The premium is accounted for separately from any transaction gain or loss on the forward contract and is amortized to income over the life of the forward contract using the straight-line method of amortization.

December 31, 1995—Balance Sheet Date

(3) Transaction Loss 15,000
    Accounts Payable 15,000
      To record a loss on the liability denominated in foreign currency (500,000
      francs × $.23 = $115,000 − $100,000) or [500,000 francs × ($.23 − $.20)].
(4) FC Receivable from Exchange Dealer 15,000
    Transaction Gain 15,000
      To record a gain on foreign currency to be received from exchange dealer
      (500,000 francs × $.23 = $115,000 − $100,000).

(As will be discussed later, the transaction loss in entry (3) and the transaction gain in entry (4) are offset, producing no income statement effect since the exposed position is fully hedged.)

(5) Amortization Expense 833
    Premium on Forward Contract 833
      To record amortization of premium on forward contract for one month
      [(1 month expired ÷ 3 month life of forward contract) × $2,500].

At December 31, the account payable is adjusted [entry (3)] to reflect the current spot rate since it is denominated in francs. Entries (4) and (5) recognize the two components of the forward contract. In entry (4) a gain or loss on the number of francs contracted for in the forward contract is recorded. Since the forward contract is for the same number of foreign currency units and is for the same period of time as the original purchase contract, the transaction loss on the exposed liability position is offset by the transaction gain on the foreign currency receivable from the exchange broker. In entry (5) the premium on the forward contract is amortized using the straight-line method.

March 1, 1996—Settlement Date

(6) Accounts Payable 5,000
    Transaction Gain 5,000
      To record a gain from 12/31/95 to 3/1/96 on liability denominated in foreign
      currency (500,000 francs × $.22 = $110,000 − $115,000).

(7) Transaction Loss   5,000
    FC Receivable from Exchange Dealer   5,000
        To record a loss from 12/31/95 to 3/1/96 on foreign currency to be received
        from exchange dealer.

(8) Dollars Payable to Exchange Dealer   102,500
    Investment in FC   110,000
        FC Receivable from Exchange Dealer   110,000
        Cash   102,500
        To record payment to exchange dealer and receipt of 500,000 francs (500,000
        francs $\times$ \$.22 = \$110,000).

(9) Accounts Payable   110,000
    Investment in FC   110,000
        To record payment of liability upon transfer of 500,000 francs.

(10) Amortization Expense   1,667
     Premium on Forward Contract   1,667
        To record amortization of premium on forward contract for two months
        [(2 $\div$ 3) $\times$ \$2,500].

At the settlement date, the exposed liability position and the foreign currency receivable related to the forward contract are both adjusted to reflect the current spot rate [entries (6) and (7)]. Other entries are needed to record payment to the exchange dealer in exchange for the 500,000 francs [entry (8)], the delivery of the 500,000 francs to settle the liability related to the original inventory purchase [entry (9)], and amortization of the premium on the forward contract [entry (10)].

By obtaining the forward contract, the firm was able to establish at the transaction date the number of dollars (\$102,500) that it would take to acquire the 500,000 francs needed to settle the account with the foreign firm. Note, however, that the cost of the inventory of \$100,000 was established on December 1 [entry (1)]. The \$2,500 difference between these two numbers is expensed over the life of the contract. If the forward contract had not been obtained, the firm would have had to pay \$110,000 to settle the account and would have reported a net loss of \$10,000 (\$15,000 loss − \$5,000 gain) on the exposed liability position. The net gain from entering into the forward contract, however, canceled out the net loss on the exposed liability position.

Hedge of a foreign currency exposed asset   In the example above, the U.S. firm entered into a forward purchase contract to hedge an exposed liability position at a time when the forward rate was at a premium. Accounting for a forward contract entered into as a hedge of an exposed receivable position is based on similar analysis. However, because the U.S. firm will be receiving foreign currency in settlement of the exposed receivable balance, it would enter into a forward contract to sell foreign currency for U.S. dollars. In this case, the receivable from the dealer is denominated in a fixed number of dollars, the amount of which is based on the contracted forward rate, whereas the obligation to the dealer is denominated in a foreign currency, which is translated into dollars using the current spot rate. The difference between the receivable and liability is accounted for as a discount or premium on a forward contract.

Illustration 14-2 compares the entries to record a forward contract to either purchase or sell foreign currency at the transaction date, when the forward rate is at a premium or at a discount. On intervening balance sheet dates, the foreign currency receivable from or payable to the exchange dealer is adjusted to reflect the current spot rate resulting in a gain or loss being recorded in the period that the exchange rate changes. Note that the dollars payable or receivable are recorded at the forward rate and are not adjusted because they represent a fixed obligation or receivable. The discount or premium is amortized to income over the life of the forward contract using the straight-line method.

ILLUSTRATION 14-2
Recording a Forward Contract

Importing Transaction

Exposed payable for 500,000 francs.
Forward contract to buy 500,000 francs for $.205 per franc.

	SPOT RATE—$.20		SPOT RATE—$.21	
FC Receivable from Exchange Dealer	100,000		105,000	
Premium on Forward Contract*	2,500		–0–	
Discount on Forward Contract**		–0–		2,500
Dollars Payable to				
Exchange Dealer		102,500		102,500

Exporting Transaction

Exposed receivable for 500,000 francs.
Forward contract to sell 500,000 francs for $.205 per franc.

	SPOT RATE—$.20		SPOT RATE—$.21	
Dollars Receivable from Exchange				
Dealer	102,500		102,500	
Discount on Forward Contract**	–0–		2,500	
Premium on Forward Contract**		2,500		–0–
FC Payable to Exchange Dealer		100,000		105,000

*Forward rate > spot rate ($.205 − $.20) × 500,000 francs = $2,500
**Forward rate < spot rate ($.21 − $.205) × 500,000 francs = $2,500

Disclosure Requirements   Although a loss or gain on an exposed liability or receivable position is offset by a gain or loss on a forward contract entered into to hedge the exposed position, the two are accounted for separately, since they are considered independent transactions (i.e., the decision to buy or sell in a foreign market is separate from the decision to hedge the transaction). For reporting purposes, however, the gains or losses may be combined. The firm is required to disclose the aggregate transaction gain or loss included in the determination of net income for the period. A gain or loss on a forward contract is considered a transaction gain or loss.[10] Firms are also required to disclose changes in the exchange rate that occur after the balance sheet date and their effect on unsettled foreign currency transactions, if significant,[11] and the fair value of contractual obligations to deliver cash for which it is practicable to estimate that value.[12]

Hedging an Identifiable Foreign Currency Commitment   In the preceding discussion of the importing and exporting of goods, the purchase or sale of an asset was recorded on the transaction date. This date is considered the point at which title to the goods is transferred, which is consistent with the recording of a transaction with another domestic company. However, if the U.S. firm at a date earlier than the transaction date made a commitment to a foreign company to sell goods or buy goods, and the price was established in foreign currency at the commitment date, changes in the exchange rate between the commitment date and transaction date would be reflected in the cost or sales price of the asset. For example, assume that a U.S. firm made an agreement on June 1 to buy goods from a French company for 500,000 francs. At this date, the spot rate was $.20, but on the transaction date, when title to the goods transferred and a journal entry was recorded, the spot rate was $.22. The entry to record the purchase is

Purchases (500,000 francs × $.22)	110,000	
Accounts Payable		110,000

Thus, the change in the exchange rate that occurred between the commitment and the transaction date becomes a part of the cost of inventory, rather than being reported as a separate gain or loss item. The company, however, may still acquire a forward contract to hedge against unfavorable rate changes that may occur after the commitment date.

A forward contract is considered a hedge of an identifiable foreign currency commitment if the forward contract is designated as, and is effective as, a hedge of a foreign currency commitment, and the foreign currency commitment is firm.[13] A gain or loss on a forward contract that meets both conditions is deferred and included in the measurement of the related foreign currency transaction when recorded.[14] Thus, the effect of this treatment is to account for the forward contract as an integral part of the importing or exporting transaction. For example, a gain or loss on a forward contract used to hedge a commitment to buy equipment that is to be paid for with foreign currency would be included in the cost of the equipment when it is recorded.

---

[10]*Statement of Financial Accounting Standards No. 52*, par. 31.

[11]Ibid., par. 32.

[12]*Statement of Financial Accounting Standards No. 107*, "Disclosure about Fair Value of Financial Instruments" (Norwalk, Conn.: FASB, 1991) par. 10.

[13]*Statement of Financial Accounting Standards No. 52*, par. 21.

[14]Losses on a forward contract "shall not be deferred, however, if it is estimated that deferral would lead to recognizing losses in later periods." For example, a loss on a forward contract shall not be deferred if future revenue from the sale or other disposition of an asset is estimated to be less than the sum of (a) the asset's cost, including the deferred loss on the related forward contract, and (b) reasonably predictable costs of sale or disposal. Ibid., par. 21.

The forward contract, to be a hedge of an identifiable foreign currency commitment, need not be equal to the commitment nor must there be a linkage between the contract dates. However, if the contract is intended as a hedge of a particular foreign currency commitment, management must designate it as such. To the extent that the amount of the forward contract exceeds the amount of the commitment on an after-tax basis, the gain or loss pertaining to that part of the forward contract in excess of the after-tax commitment should not be deferred.[15] Likewise, if the life of the forward contract extends beyond the transaction date, a gain or loss pertaining to the extended period should not be deferred, but should be included in net income currently.[16]

To illustrate the accounting for a forward contract acquired to hedge an identifiable foreign currency commitment, the following facts are assumed:

1. On March 1, 1995, a U.S. firm contracts to sell equipment to a foreign customer for 200,000 German marks. The equipment is expected to cost $60,000 to manufacture and is to be delivered and the account is to be settled on March 1, 1996.

2. On March 1, 1995, the U.S. firm enters into a forward contract to sell 200,000 German marks in 12 months at the forward rate of $.41.

3. Spot rates for German marks on selected dates are

DATE	EXCHANGE RATE
March 1, 1995	$.40
December 31, 1995	.395
March 1, 1996	.38

The journal entries to record the forward contract during 1995 are:

March 1, 1995

(1) Dollars Receivable from Exchange Dealer		
(200,000 marks × $.41)	82,000	
Deferred Transaction Adjustment		2,000
FC Payable to Exchange Dealer (200,000 marks × $.40)		80,000
To record the forward contract to sell 200,000 German marks.		

December 31, 1995

(2) FC Payable to Exchange Dealer	1,000	
Deferred Transaction Adjustment		1,000
To record gain on foreign currency to be delivered to exchange dealer [$80,000 − (200,000 marks × $.395)].		

There are two major differences between accounting for a contract to hedge an identifiable foreign currency commitment and a contract to hedge a foreign cur-

---

[15]The amount of the gain or loss pertaining to the portion of the forward contract in excess of the commitment and related to the tax impact should be deferred and "included as an offset to the related tax effects in the period in which such tax effects are recognized." Ibid., par. 21.

[16]Ibid., par. 21.

rency exposed asset or liability position. First, the discount or premium on the forward contract "that relates to the commitment period may be included in the measurement of the basis of the related foreign currency transaction when recorded."[17] Second, the transaction gain (or loss if the spot rate was greater than $.40) is deferred rather than reported currently in income. As will be seen in a March 1, 1996, entry [see entry (7) below], these elements are included in the determination of the dollar basis of the foreign currency transaction on the transaction date. Since both the discount or premium and transaction gains or losses are eventually closed into the same account, both are accumulated in one account called "Deferred Transaction Adjustment."

On March 1, 1996 (the transaction date), the journal entries are:

(3) FC Payable to Exchange Dealer	3,000	
Deferred Transaction Adjustment		3,000
To record gain on forward contract from 12/31/95 to 3/1/96		
[$79,000 − (200,000 marks × $.38)].		
(4) Investment in FC	76,000	
Sales (200,000 marks × $.38)		76,000
To record sale of equipment to foreign customer.		
(5) Cost of Goods Sold	60,000	
Inventory		60,000
To record cost of equipment sold.		
(6) Cash	82,000	
FC Payable to Exchange Dealer	76,000	
Investment in FC		76,000
Dollars Receivable from Exchange Dealer		82,000
To record settlement of forward contract.		
(7) Deferred Transaction Adjustment	6,000	
Sales		6,000
To close the deferred transaction adjustment account to revenue.		

Most of the entries on March 1, 1996 are self-explanatory. It should be emphasized that the transaction gain or loss on a forward contract acquired to hedge a specific commitment or an exposed asset or liability position is computed on the basis of changes in the spot rates that occurred during the current operating period. In this case the spot rate for German marks decreased from $.395 at the last balance sheet date to $.38 at the transaction date. The transaction gain of $3,000 plus the $1,000 gain from 1995, along with the $2,000 premium on the forward contract, are included as an adjustment to the sales account.

The effect of these transactions on the firm's profitability is as follows:

Sales ($76,000 + $6,000)	$82,000
Cost of goods sold	60,000
Gross profit	$22,000

[17]Ibid., par. 18. As an alternative, a company may amortize a premium or discount on the forward contract to income over the life of the contract.

The number of dollars to be received was locked in by the forward contract at $82,000 and the equipment was expected to cost $60,000. Thus, the forward contract permitted the U.S. firm to lock in an expected profit of $22,000 on the sales contract. If the forward contract had not been obtained, the profit on the contract would have been affected by the exchange rate in effect when payment was received from the German customer. An exchange rate of $.30 would have eliminated any gross profit on the contract (200,000 marks × $.30 = $60,000).

Forward Contracts Acquired to Speculate in the Movement of Foreign Currencies A forward contract may be acquired for speculative purposes in anticipation of realizing a gain. For example, assume that on December 1, 1995, the spot rate for the British pound is $2.35 and that the 90-day futures rate is $2.36. Further assume that a company expecting the exchange rate to increase to, say, $2.43, enters into a contract on December 1 to acquire £100,000 on March 1, 1996. (A forward contract to sell foreign currency would be negotiated if the firm expected the future spot rate to be lower than the forward rate.) The firm's fiscal year ends on December 31, and on that date the futures rate for pounds to be purchased on March 1, 1996 is $2.37. The spot rate is $2.42 on March 1, 1996. The journal entries to record the transactions are:

December 1, 1995

(1) FC Receivable from the Exchange Dealer		236,000	
Dollars Payable to Exchange Dealer			236,000
To record the forward contract (£100,000 × $2.36).			

This entry recognizes that the U.S. firm has contracted to buy £100,000 in 90 days when the payment of $236,000 is made to the exchange dealer. Both the debit and credit related to a forward contract are measured by multiplying the £100,000 by the forward rate of $2.36. The FASB reasoned that the forward rate should be used because a firm speculating in foreign currency changes is exposed to the risk of movements in the forward rate. Since both accounts are based on the forward rate, there is no separate accounting for any discount or premium on the forward contract.

December 31, 1995

(2) FC Receivable from Exchange Dealer		1,000	
Transaction Gain			1,000
To record gain on foreign currency to be received from exchange dealer (£100,000 × $2.37 = $237,000 − $236,000) or [£100,000 × ($2.37 − $2.36)].			

The foreign currency receivable is adjusted at the financial statement date since it is denominated in foreign currency units. The amount of the adjustment is computed by multiplying the units of foreign currency to be received by the difference between the forward rate available for the remaining life of the forward contract and the rate last used to value the contract.[18] The transaction gain (or loss) is reported currently in income.

---

[18]*Statement of Financial Accounting Standards No. 52*, par. 19.

March 1, 1996

(3) FC Receivable from Exchange Dealer	5,000	
Transaction Gain		5,000
To record gain on foreign currency to be received from exchange dealer (£100,000 × $2.42 = $242,000 − $237,000).		
(4) Dollars Payable to Exchange Dealer	236,000	
Investment in FC	242,000	
Cash		236,000
FC Receivable from Exchange Dealer		242,000
To record payment to exchange dealer and receipt of foreign currency.		
(5) Cash	242,000	
Investment in FC		242,000
To record conversion of pounds into cash.		

On March 1, the firm records any gain or loss as a result of changes in the exchange rate from the last valuation date to the date of the transaction. Upon payment of $236,000 to the exchange dealer, the firm will receive £100,000, which can be converted into $242,000. The total gain of $6,000 recognized over the life of the contract is the difference between the value of the foreign currency received ($242,000) when the forward contract was exercised and the amount paid ($236,000) to the exchange dealer.

If the firm had entered into a forward contract to sell foreign currency, the accounting would be similar to that above, except the debit in entry (1) is for a fixed amount of dollars to be received; the credit records the obligation to buy foreign currency units for delivery to the exchange dealer. The estimated cost of units to be delivered will vary as the exchange rate fluctuates.

Accounting for forward contracts in accordance with the provisions of *SFAS No. 52* is summarized in Illustration 14-3.

ILLUSTRATION 14-3
Summary of Accounting for Forward Contracts

PURPOSE OF THE FORWARD CONTRACT	BASIS FOR VALUATION OF FORWARD CONTRACT AT BALANCE SHEET DATE	REPORTING TRANSACTION GAIN OR LOSS	ACCOUNTING FOR DISCOUNT OR PREMIUM ON FORWARD CONTRACT
1. Hedge of net investment in a foreign entity.	Spot rate at balance sheet date.	Included with translation adjustments in a separate component of stockholders' equity.	Included with translation adjustments in a separate component of stockholders' equity.
2. Hedge of an exposed asset or liability position.	Spot rate at balance sheet date.	Reported currently in determination of income.	Amortized over the life of the forward contract as a component of net income.
3. Hedge of an identifiable foreign currency commitment.	Spot rate at balance sheet date.	Deferred and included in the measurement of the related foreign currency transaction.	Deferred and included in the measurement of related foreign currency transaction or amortized to income over life of contract.
4. Speculation.	Forward rate at balance sheet date available over remaining life of forward contract.	Reported currently in determination of income.	Not accounted for separately.

Questions

1. Define currency exchange rates and distinguish between "direct" and "indirect" quotations.

2. Explain why a firm is exposed to an added risk when it enters into a transaction that is to be settled in a foreign currency.

3. Name the three stages of concern to the accountant in accounting for import–export transactions. Briefly explain the accounting for each stage.

4. How should a transaction gain or loss be reported that is related to an unsettled receivable recorded when the firm's inventory was exported?

5. A U.S. firm carried a receivable for 100,000 yen. Assuming that the direct exchange rate declined from $.009 at the date of the transaction to $.006 at the balance sheet date, compute the transaction gain or loss. What balance would be reported for the receivable in the firm's balance sheet?

6. Explain what is meant by the "two-transaction method" in recording exporting or importing transactions. What support is given for this method?

7. Describe a forward exchange contract.

8. Explain the effects on income from hedging a foreign currency exposed net asset position or net liability position.

9. What criteria must be satisfied for a foreign currency transaction to be considered a hedge of an identifiable foreign currency commitment?

10. The FASB classifies forward contracts as those acquired for the purpose of hedging and those acquired for the purpose of speculation. What main differences are there in accounting for these two classifications?

11. How are unrealized transaction gains and losses from hedging an identifiable foreign currency commitment reported?

Exercises

Exercise 14-1

Selco, a U.S. Company, imports and exports tools, shop equipment, and industrial construction supplies. The company uses a periodic inventory system. During April the company entered into the following transactions. All rate quotations are direct exchange rates.

April 3   Purchased power tools from a wholesaler in Japan, on account, at an invoice cost of 1,600,000 yen. On this date the exchange rate for the yen was $.0072.

5   Sold hand tools on credit that were manufactured in the U.S. to a retail outlet located in West Germany. The invoice price was $2,800. The exchange rate for marks was $.5829.

9   Sold electric drills on account to a retailer in New Zealand. The invoice price was 16,800 U.S. dollars and the exchange rate for the New Zealand dollar was $.576.

11   Purchased drill bits on account from a manufacturer located in Belgium. The billing was for 801,282 francs. The exchange rate for francs was $.0312.

16   Paid 1,000,000 yen on account to the wholesaler for purchases made on April 3. The exchange rate on this date was $.0067.

18   Settled the accounts payable with the Belgium manufacturer. The exchange rate was $.0368.

22 Received full payment from the New Zealand retailer. The exchange rate was $.568.

30 Completed payment on the April 3 purchase. The exchange rate was $.0078.

Required:

Prepare journal entries on the books of Selco to record the transactions listed above.

Exercise 14-2

During December of the current year, Teletex Systems, Inc., a company based in Seattle, Washington, entered into the following transactions:

Dec. 10 Sold seven office computers to a company located in Colombia for 8,541,000 pesos. On this date, the spot rate was 365 pesos per U.S. dollar.

12 Purchased computer chips from a company domiciled in Taiwan. The contract was denominated in 500,000 Taiwan dollars. The direct exchange spot rate on this date was $.0391.

Required:

A. Prepare journal entries to record the transactions above on the books of Teletex Systems, Inc. The company uses a periodic inventory system.

B. Prepare journal entries necessary to adjust the accounts as of December 31. Assume that on December 31 the direct exchange rates were as follows:

Colombia peso	$.00268
Taiwan dollar	$.0351

C. Prepare journal entries to record settlement of both open accounts on January 10. Assume that the direct exchange rates on the settlement dates were as follows:

Colombia peso	$.00320
Taiwan dollar	$.0398

D. Prepare journal entries to record the December 10 transaction, adjust the accounts on December 31, and record settlement of the account on January 10, assuming that the transaction was denominated in dollars rather than pesos. Assume the same exchange rates as those given.

Exercise 14-3

On December 1, 1995, Tuscano Corp. entered into a transaction to import raw materials from a foreign company. The account is to be settled on February 1 with the payment of 60,000 foreign currency units (FCU). On December 1, Tuscano also entered into a forward contract to hedge the exposed position resulting from the import transaction. The forward rate is $.71 per unit of foreign currency. Tuscano Corp. has a December 31 fiscal year-end. Spot rates on relevant dates were:

DATE	PER UNIT OF FOREIGN CURRENCY
December 1	$.69
December 31	.72
February 1	.73

Required:

Use the data given to select the best answer to each question.

1. The forward contract entered into on December 1 is an example of
   (a) A hedge of an exposed receivable position.
   (b) A hedge of a foreign currency commitment.
   (c) A contract entered into for speculation.
   (d) A hedge of an exposed payable position.

2. The entry to record the forward contract is

(a)	Dollars Receivable	42,600	
	Premium on Forward Contract		1,200
	FCU Payable		41,400
(b)	FCU Receivable	42,600	
	Premium on Forward Contract		1,200
	Dollars Receivable		41,400
(c)	Dollars Receivable	42,600	
	Discount on Forward Contract		1,200
	FCU Payable		41,400
(d)	FCU Receivable	41,400	
	Premium on Forward Contract	1,200	
	Dollars Payable		42,600

   (e) None of the above.

3. On December 31, what will be the adjusted balance in the Accounts Payable account and how much gain or loss was recorded as a result of the adjustment?

	PAYABLE BALANCE	GAIN OR LOSS RECORDED
(a)	$43,200	$1,800 gain
(b)	40,800	2,400 loss
(c)	40,800	2,400 gain
(d)	43,200	1,800 loss

4. What amount of transaction gain or loss from the transaction should be included in the determination of the 1995 net income?
   (a) $2,400 loss.
   (b) $1,800 loss.
   (c) $–0– Because a gain or loss on the forward contract is offset by a loss or gain on the exposed position.
   (d) $2,400 gain.

5. Which of the following statements is *not* true?
   (a) Assuming the account payable is to be settled on February 1, Tuscano Corp. was able to reduce its cash outflow for the purchases as a result of entering into the forward contract.
   (b) During 1996, a transaction loss of $600 was recorded on the forward contract.
   (c) Tuscano Corp. paid $42,600 to complete the forward contract.
   (d) During 1996 a transaction loss of $600 was recorded on the exposed payable.

Exercise 14-4

Select the best answer for each of the following.

1. The discount or premium on a forward contract entered into as a hedge of an identifiable foreign currency commitment should be
   (a) Included in net income in the period that the forward contract is entered into.

(b) Deferred and amortized over a period not to exceed 40 years.

(c) Deferred and included in the measurement of the related foreign currency transaction when recorded.

(d) Included as a separate item in the equity section of the balance sheet.

2. A forward contract is a hedge of an identifiable foreign currency commitment if

(a) The forward contract is designated as, and is effective as, a hedge of a foreign currency commitment.

(b) The foreign currency commitment is firm.

(c) The amount of the forward contract is equal to the amount of the commitment.

(d) Both (a) and (b).

(e) Both (a) and (c).

3. The Carnival Company has a receivable from a foreign customer that is payable in the local currency of the foreign customer. The account receivable for 800,000 local currency units (LCU), has been translated into $280,000 on Carnival's December 31, 1995 balance sheet. On January 15, 1996, the receivable was collected in full when the exchange rate was 4 LCU to $1. What journal entry should Carnival make to record the collection of this receivable?

(a)	Cash	200,000	
	Accounts receivable		200,000
(b)	Cash	200,000	
	Transaction Loss	80,000	
	Accounts Receivable		280,000
(c)	Cash	200,000	
	Deferred Transaction Loss	80,000	
	Accounts Receivable		280,000
(d)	Cash	280,000	
	Accounts receivable		280,000

4. A foreign currency transaction to a company domiciled in the United States is a transaction in which the amount is

(a) Measured in a foreign currency.

(b) Denominated in U.S. dollars.

(c) Denominated in a foreign currency.

(d) Measured in U.S. dollars.

5. A direct exchange quotation is one in which the exchange rate is quoted

(a) In terms of how many units of the domestic currency can be converted into one unit of foreign currency.

(b) In terms of how many units of the foreign currency can be converted into one unit of the domestic currency.

(c) For the future delivery of currencies exchanged.

(d) For the immediate delivery of currencies exchanged.

Exercise 14-5

Select the best answer for each of the following.

1. A sale of goods by a U.S. company was denominated in a foreign currency. The sale resulted in a receivable that was fixed in terms of the amount of foreign currency that would be received. Exchange rates between the dollar and the currency in which the transaction was denominated changed so that a loss was incurred. This loss should be included as a(n)

(a) Extraordinary item in the income statement.

(b) Component of income from continuing operations.

(c) Separate component of stockholders' equity.

(d) Deferred item in the balance sheet.

2. A discount or premium on a forward contract is required to be amortized over the life of the forward contract if the contract is classified as a

(a) Contract to speculate in the movement of exchange rates.

(b) Hedge of a net investment in a foreign entity.

(c) Hedge of an exposed asset or liability position.

(d) Hedge of an identifiable foreign currency commitment.

3. On September 1, 1995, Change Corp. received an order for equipment from a foreign customer for 300,000 units of foreign currency when the U.S. dollar equivalent was $96,000. Change shipped the equipment on October 15, 1995, and billed the customer for 300,000 units of foreign currency when the U.S. dollar equivalent was $110,000. Change received the customer's remittance in full on November 16, 1995, and sold the 300,000 foreign currency units for $105,000. In its income statement for the year ended December 31, 1995, Change should report a foreign exchange loss of

(a) $9,000

(b) $5,000

(c) $14,000

(d) $ –0–

4. McNeil, a U.S. corporation, bought inventory items from a supplier in West Germany on November 5, 1995 for 100,000 marks, when the spot rate was $.4395. At McNeil's December 31, 1995 year-end, the spot rate was $.4345. On January 15, 1996, McNeil's bought 100,000 marks at the spot rate of $.4445 and paid the invoice. How much should McNeil report in its income statement for 1995 and 1996 as transaction gain or loss?

	1995	1996
(a)	$–0–	$ 500 loss
(b)	$500 loss	$ –0–
(c)	$500 loss	$1,000 gain
(d)	$500 gain	$1,000 loss

5. During 1995 a U.S. firm sold inventory to a foreign customer. The transaction was denominated in the local currency of the buyer. The direct exchange rate decreased from the date of the transaction to the end of the fiscal period; the rate increased from the end of the fiscal year to the date the account was settled in 1996. A transaction gain or loss should be recognized

	1995	1996
(a)	Loss	Loss
(b)	Gain	Loss
(c)	Loss	Gain
(d)	Gain	Gain

(AICPA adapted)

Exercise 14-6

Agentel Corporation is a U.S.-based importing–exporting company. The company entered into the following transactions during the month of November.

Nov. 6 Purchased merchandise from AGT, a Swiss firm, for 600,000 francs.

15 Sold merchandise to SLS, Inc. a firm located in Berlin, for $200,000.

18 Sold merchandise to TNT, Ltd., a British firm, for 130,000 pounds.
20 Purchased merchandise from SDS, Ltd., a British firm, for $160,000.

All the transactions were unsettled at December 31, Agentel's fiscal year-end. Spot rates are as follows:

	CURRENCY		
DATE	FRANC	MARK	POUND
November 6	$.490	$.412	$1.520
November 15	.487	.409	1.509
November 18	.476	.414	1.506
November 20	.468	.405	1.498
December 31	.460	.398	1.482

Required:

A. Compute the amount that Agentel would report for each unsettled receivable and payable in its balance sheet prepared at December 31.

B. Compute the transaction gain or loss on each unsettled receivable and payable that would be reported in the income statement prepared for the year ended December 31.

Exercise 14-7

ASI recently completed the development and installation of an accounting information system for a company located in Munich, Germany. The company considered that all revenue realization criteria were satisfied and accordingly recorded on October 2, 1995, a receivable from the foreign company. The receivable is to be settled in 120 days on February 1 by the delivery of 300,000 German marks. To hedge against an unfavorable change in the foreign exchange rate, ASI acquired a forward contract to sell 300,000 German marks on February 1 for $.4730 per mark. The following exchange rates were quoted:

DATE	SPOT RATE	FORWARD RATE (DELIVERY ON 2/1)
October 2	$.4737	$.4730
December 31	.4895	.4810
February 1	.4950	—

ASI is a calendar-year company.

Required:

A. Prepare the journal entries to record the transactions, adjust the accounts on December 31, and settle the receivable and forward contract on February 1.

B. (1) Based on the data given above, complete the following table.

	1995	1996
Revenue	_____	_____
Transaction gain (loss) related to the exposed receivable balance	_____	_____

	1995	1996
Transaction gain (loss) related to the forward contract	_____	_____
Increase (decrease) in net income from amortization of the discount or premium related to the forward contract	_____	_____
Effect on net income	_____	_____

(2) What was the cumulative effect on net income (i.e., 1995 plus 1996)?

(3) How much cash was received when the account was settled?

Exercise 14-8

Vanderbilt Clothing Company placed a clothing order with a company located in Taiwan. The order was placed on November 1, 1995, for delivery on May 1, 1996. Vanderbilt agreed to pay for the goods on May 1, 1996 with the delivery of 5,000,000 Taiwan dollars. To protect against fluctuations in the exchange rate, the company entered into a forward contract on November 1, 1995, to buy 5,000,000 Taiwan dollars on May 1, 1996, for $.02634 per unit.

Direct exchange rates per Taiwan dollar on specific dates are as follows:

DATE	SPOT RATE	FORWARD RATE— MATURITY MAY 1
November 1, 1995	$.02631	$.02634
December 31, 1995	.02740	.02735
May 1, 1996	.02591	—

Required:

Prepare the journal entries to be made by Vanderbilt Clothing Company during 1995 and 1996 to account for the transactions described above.

Exercise 14-9

Sharon Myers, chief finance officer for Sitco Products, convinced the president of the company to enter into a 90-day forward contract to sell 900,000 West German marks as a speculative venture. When the forward contract was acquired on November 1, 1995, the spot rate for the mark was $.5045 and the 90-day future rate was $.5085. At December 31, 1995, the end of the firm's fiscal year, the spot rate was $.4981 and the future rate for marks to be sold on January 30, 1996 was $.4996. On January 30, 1996, the spot rate was $.4826.

Required:

Prepare all necessary journal entries in regard to the forward contract.

Exercise 14-10

Use the data given in Exercise 14-9, except assume that on November 1, Sitco Products entered into a 90-day forward contract to buy 900,000 West German marks on January 30 for $.5085 per mark.

Required:

Prepare all necessary journal entries in regard to the forward contract.

Exercise 14-11

Roland Brothers, Inc. purchased equipment from a British firm for £120,000 on April 1, 1995. To finance the purchase of the equipment, the president of the company signed a note for £120,000 with a British bank. The loan is denominated in pounds, matures on March 31, 1996, and bears interest at 12% per annum payable on June 30, September 30, December 31, and March 31. Spot rates for the British pound are as follows:

April 1, 1995	$1.574
June 30, 1995	1.560
September 30, 1995	1.526
December 31, 1995	1.498
March 31, 1996	1.538

Required:

Prepare journal entries to record the purchase of the equipment, the interest payments, the adjustment of the accounts on December 31 (the fiscal year-end), and the payment of the note at maturity.

Exercise 14-12

On November 15, 1995, Solanski Inc. imported 500,000 barrels of oil from an oil company in Venezuela. Solanski agreed to pay 50,000,000 bolivars on January 15, 1996. To ensure that the dollar outlay for the purchase will not fluctuate, the company entered into a forward contract to buy 50,000,000 bolivars on January 15 at the forward rate of $.0269. Direct exchange rates on various dates were:

November 15	$.0239
December 31	.0224
January 15	.0291

Solanski Inc. is a calendar-year company.

Required:

Compute the following:

1. The dollars to be paid on January 15, 1996, to acquire the 50,000,000 bolivars from the exchange dealer.

2. The dollars that would have been paid to settle the account payable had Solanski not hedged the purchased contract with the forward contract.

3. The discount or premium on the forward contract.

4. The transaction gain or loss on the exposed liability related to the oil purchase in 1995 and 1996.

5. The transaction gain or loss on the forward contract in 1995 and 1996.

6. The total transaction gain or loss to be reported in 1995 and 1996.

7. The amount of the discount or premium on the forward contract amortized in 1995 and 1996.

Problems

Problem 14-1

GAF manufactures electrical cells at its St. Louis facility. The company's fiscal year-end is September 30. It has adopted the perpetual inventory cost flow method to control inventory costs. The company entered into the following transactions during the month of September. All exchange rates are direct quotations.

DATE	TRANSACTION	BILLING AMOUNT	RATE OF EXCHANGE
1995			
Sept. 5	Exported 10 electrical cells to a company located in Argentina. Cost per unit, $950.	17,341 Australs	$1.1291
9	Received raw materials ordered from a British company. The goods were shipped FOB destination and had not been recorded on the books of GAF, Inc.	12,200 pounds	1.6821
14	Exported 12 electrical cells to a company domiciled in Paris. Cost per unit, $970.	160,274 francs	.1450
30	End of fiscal year-end.		
	Austral		1.1091
	British pound		1.6911
	Franc		.1530
Oct. 5	Received full payment for the 10 units sold on September 5.		1.1190
9	Paid British company in full for raw materials purchased September 9.		1.5948
30	Received full payment for 12 units sold on September 14.		.1440

Required:

A. Prepare the journal entries required on the books of GAF to record the transactions and year-end adjustments. Round all computations to the nearest dollar.

B. Based on the two exporting transactions listed above, complete the following table.

	TRANSACTION	
	SEPT. 5	SEPT. 14
September 30, 1995 year-end:		
1. Sales	_____	_____
2. Transaction gain (loss)	_____	_____
September 30, 1996 year-end:		
3. Sales	_____	_____
4. Transaction gain (loss)	_____	_____
5. Net effect on income for both years (Sum lines 1–4)	_____	_____
6. Cash received on settlement date	_____	_____

Problem 14-2

Crystal Exporting Co. is a U.S. wholesaler engaged in foreign trade. The following transactions are representative of its business dealings. The company uses a periodic inventory system and is on a calendar-year basis. All exchange rates are direct quotations.

Dec. 1   Crystal Exporting purchased merchandise from Chang's, Ltd., a Hong Kong manufacturer. The invoice was for 210,000 Hong Kong dollars, payable on April 1.
On this same date, Crystal Exporting acquired a forward contract to buy 210,000 Hong Kong dollars on April 1 for $.1314.

Dec. 29   Crystal Exporting sold merchandise to Zintel Retailers for 120,000 Hong Kong dollars, receivable in 90 days. No hedging was involved.

April 1   Crystal Exporting received 120,000 Hong Kong dollars from Zintel Retailers.

1   Crystal Exporting submitted full payment of 210,000 Hong Kong dollars to Chang's, Ltd., after obtaining the 210,000 Hong Kong dollars on its forward contract.

Spot rates for the Hong Kong dollar were as follows:

Dec. 1	$.1265
Dec. 29	.1240
Dec. 31	.1259
April 1	.1430

Required:

A. Prepare journal entries for the transactions including the necessary adjustments on December 31.

B. Explain the income statement treatment given to any transaction gains and losses recognized at December 31.

Problem 14-3

On December 1, 1995, King Company exported equipment that had cost $210,000 to a Netherlands company for 1,000,000 guilders. The account is to be settled on January 31, 1996. King Company is a calendar-year company and uses a perpetual inventory system. Direct exchange rates were:

December 1	$.4441
December 31	.3690
January 31	.4421

Required:

A. Prepare journal entries to record the exporting transaction, adjust the accounts on December 31, and settle the account on January 31.

B. What effect did changes in the exchange rate have on income in 1995 and 1996?

C. Assume the facts given above, except that on December 1, King Company entered into a forward contract to sell 1,000,000 guilders on January 31 for $.4451 per guilder. Prepare the journal entries needed in 1995 and 1996 to record the forward contract and settle the accounts.

D. What is the combined effect on income in 1995 and 1996 from the exporting transaction and the forward contract?

Problem 14-4

Centennial Exchange of St. Louis, Missouri, imports and exports grains. The company has a September 30 fiscal year-end. The periodic inventory system and the weighted-average cost flow method are used by the company to account for inventory cost. The company negotiated the following transactions during 1995.

Sept. 1 Sold 1,000,000 bushels of wheat to a Paris company for 16,500,000 francs. The account is to be settled on October 30.

Sept. 1 The management of Centennial was concerned that the franc would decline in value. They therefore entered into a forward contract to sell 16,500,000 francs on October 30 for $.1442 per franc.

Sept. 5 Sold 1,000,000 bushels of wheat to a Madrid company for $5,300,000. The account is to be settled on November 5.

Sept. 15 Purchased rice from an exporting company that operates in Japan. The contract provides for the payment of 20,000,000 yen on October 15.

Sept. 15 Entered into a forward contract to buy 20,000,000 yen on October 15 for $.006490 per yen.

Sept. 18 Sold 500 tons of soybean meal to Able & Born, Ltd., a Toronto company, for 48,000 Canadian dollars. The account is to be settled on December 17.

Oct. 15 Completed the forward contract to buy 20,000,000 yen and then submitted payment to pay for the rice purchased on September 15.

Oct. 30 Received 16,500,000 francs from the Paris customer and settled forward contract.

Nov. 5 Received payment in full for the wheat sold on September 5 to the Madrid company.

Dec. 17 Received payment from Able & Born, Ltd. for the September 18 sale.

Direct exchange quotations for specific dates are presented below:

	FRANCE— FRANC	SPAIN— PESETA	JAPAN— YEN	CANADA— DOLLAR
September 1	$.1480	$.00738	$.006427	$.8250
September 5	.1458	.00740	.006428	.8248
September 15	.1456	.00741	.006430	.8246
September 18	.1456	.00737	.006431	.8245
September 30	.1455	.00736	.006433	.8243
October 15	.1458	.00734	.006435	.8241
October 30	.1457	.00732	.006370	.8241
November 5	.1456	.00730	.006439	.8244
December 17	.1453	.00731	.006438	.8250

Required:

Prepare journal entries, including year-end adjustments, to record the above transactions.

Problem 14-5

Apple Company was incorporated in Delaware in 1993. On November 2, 1995, the controller of the company entered into a forward contract to sell 50,000 British pounds for $1.5920 on March 1, 1996. The following exchange rates were quoted on the indicated dates:

November 2, 1995	Spot rate	$1.6021
December 31, 1995	Spot rate	1.5820
Future delivery on March 1		1.5800
March 1, 1996	Spot rate	1.6543

Apple Company's fiscal year-end is December 31.

Required:

A. Assume that the forward contract was entered into as a hedge against an exposed foreign currency receivable balance in the amount of £50,000. Prepare the journal entries that would be made by Apple Company on

    (1) November 2—to record the sale of the goods on account for £50,000 and to record the forward contract.

    (2) December 31—to adjust the accounts related to the exposed asset and forward contract at fiscal year-end.

    (3) March 1—to adjust the accounts related to the exposed asset and forward contract and to record the settlement of the receivable and delivery of the pounds to the exchange dealer.

B. Assume that the controller indicated on November 2 that the forward contract was acquired as a hedge of a future foreign currency transaction that is a commitment of Apple to sell inventory for £50,000 on March 1. Apple Company follows the practice of including discounts and premiums and transaction gains or losses related to the forward contract in the dollar basis of the related transaction. Prepare the journal entries related to the forward contract and commitment to sell inventory that would be made by Apple Company on November 2, December 31, and March 1.

C. Assume that the contract was entered into to speculate in future exchange rate fluctuations. Prepare the journal entries that would be made by Apple Company on November 2, December 31, and March 1.

D. Compute the effect of the transactions in (A), (B), and (C) on the net income for the fiscal years ended December 31, 1995, and December 31, 1996. Indicate how the balance sheet accounts related to the forward contract would be reported in the December 31, 1995, balance sheet.

Problem 14-6

Citron Company is a U.S.-based citrus grower. On October 1, 1995, the company entered into a contract to ship 25,000 boxes of grapefruit on January 28 to Japan. Payment of 50,100,000 yen is to be received on March 29, 1996. On October 1, Citron also entered into a forward contract to sell 50,100,000 yen on March 29 at the forward rate of $.007412. The forward contract is considered a hedge of the foreign currency commitment. The direct exchange rate and forward rate for the yen were as follows:

	OCTOBER 1	DECEMBER 31	JANUARY 29	MARCH 29
Spot rate	$.007235	$.007879	$.007623	$.007640
Forward rate available for the remaining period of the forward contract	.007412	.007910	.007674	Not appl.

Required:

A. Prepare the necessary journal entries to record the following transactions and events:

   Oct. 1 Entered into the contract to sell the grapefruit and negotiated the forward contract.
   Dec. 31 Fiscal year-end of Citron Company.
   Jan. 28 The grapefruit were shipped FOB shipping point. The grapefruit cost Citron $7.50 per box. Citron uses a perpetual inventory system.
   Mar. 29 Received the payment and delivered the yen to the exchange broker to settle the forward contract.

B. Compute the increase or decrease in income for each fiscal year as a result of the transactions above.

C. Compute the increase or decrease in income each period that would have occurred if Citron had not entered into the forward contract.

Problem 14-7

During her first quarter review of the financial statements, Debra Bell, the CFO of HAL Computer Corporation, was distressed to notice the company's transaction loss had been steadily increasing each month. HAL is a publicly held manufacturer of "PC clone" personal computers. Like most manufacturers of its kind, HAL does not manufacture domestically but utilizes lower cost offshore suppliers for components and subcontractors for assembly. As it is HAL's policy to denominate foreign contracts in U.S. dollars whenever possible, the increase in transaction losses was particularly puzzling.

Subsequent conversations with HAL's controller, Tom Stewart, revealed all new contracts had been denominated in foreign currencies (primarily the South Korean won and Taiwanese dollar) in order to obtain more favorable purchase terms. Further, Mr. Stewart believed that the U.S. dollar would strengthen due to it being an election year. Since these contracts specify delivery and payment at various dates over the next 12 months, tremendous potential for exposure exists for the company if the dollar continues to decline against the major foreign currencies.

Required:

A. Mr. Stewart executed all new foreign contracts in foreign currencies in the belief it would help the company.
   (1) Do you think he was justified in his actions given the company policy?
   (2) On what basis did you decide if the controller was justified or not?
   (3) Was the loss a factor in your decision? Is this appropriate?

B. A substantial amount of foreign denominated contracts already exist for goods and services not yet received.
   (1) What actions may HAL take to minimize potential losses?
   (2) What are the advantages and disadvantages of these actions?
   (3) What implication does each of these scenarios have for financial statement disclosure?

C. Assume that you are Ms. Bell, and you are concerned about how the Board of Directors and the stockholders may react. Additionally, you are about to purchase a new home and are planning to sell some HAL stock for the down payment.

(1) After carefully considering all of your options, what action do you decide to take?

(2) Did concern over the Board, stockholders, or HAL's stock price enter into your decision? Why or why not?

15

THE TRANSLATION OF FINANCIAL STATEMENTS OF FOREIGN AFFILIATES

In the preceding chapter, the translation of various types of foreign currency transactions entered into by a U.S. company was described. A U.S. company also may be involved in foreign activities through the operations of a branch, a subsidiary, or an investee company in a foreign country. If the foreign entity maintains its books in a foreign currency, its accounts must be restated into dollars, called translation, so that the accounts of the U.S. company and the foreign entity are stated in a common currency before the accounts are combined or consolidated or the equity method of accounting is applied. The concepts underlying the restatement of the accounts of a foreign entity are discussed in this chapter.

ACCOUNTING FOR OPERATIONS IN FOREIGN COUNTRIES

A U.S. firm may maintain branch offices or hold equity interests in companies that are domiciled in foreign countries. As a general rule, a foreign subsidiary is consolidated if the parent company owns, directly or indirectly, more than 50% of the voting stock of the subsidiary. The exceptions to the general rule are as follows:

1. The intent to control is likely to be temporary.

2. Control does not rest with the parent company. For example, some governments restrict the withdrawal of assets from the country or impose exchange restrictions. Thus, a foreign entity may operate under conditions of foreign exchange restrictions, controls, or other government-imposed regulations that are of a

type that raise significant doubt as to the parent company's ability to control the subsidiary.[1]

A majority-owned subsidiary that is not consolidated is accounted for by use of the cost method. Disclosures discussed in earlier chapters also apply to foreign subsidiaries.

APB Opinion No. 18 extended the equity method of accounting to an investment in common stock of a foreign company in which the investor can exert significant influence (that is, holds a 20–50% interest in the voting stock) over the investee, unless the investee operates under conditions of exchange restrictions, controls, or other uncertainties that would affect the ability to influence the policies of the foreign investee.[2] In other words, the APB considered it misleading to include in operations the investor's equity interest in the investee's net income if the income might not be distributed because of government restrictions. Investments, in common stock not accounted for using the equity method are reported at fair value or at cost.

Accounting for a foreign entity is further complicated when there are significant differences between accounting principles in the U.S. and those in the other country. For example, long-term leases are not capitalized and the pooling of interests method of accounting for a business combination is not used in France or Germany. When such differences in accounting concepts exist, it is difficult to compare the results of operations and the financial position of companies operating in different countries. To aid statement users in making comparisons, foreign statements that are not in conformity with generally accepted accounting standards in the U.S. must be adjusted to conform to U.S. standards before translation into U.S. dollars.

TRANSLATING FINANCIAL STATEMENTS OF FOREIGN AFFILIATES

A foreign entity will generally measure and record its transactions in terms of the currency of the country in which it is located, called the *local currency*. A U.S. company maintaining a branch office in a foreign country or holding an equity interest in a foreign company must translate the account data expressed in a foreign currency into dollars before the financial statements can be combined or consolidated. Furthermore, if the equity method of accounting is used to account for an investment in a foreign investee company, the financial statements of the affiliate must be translated into dollars before the investor's share of the investee's reported net income or loss is properly determinable.

In the process of translation, all accounts of the foreign entity stated in units of foreign currency are translated into the reporting currency by multiplying the

---

[1]The threat of expropriation of assets is a contingency and should be accounted for and disclosed in accordance with the provisions of *Statement of Financial Accounting Standards No. 5*, "Accounting for Contingencies" (FASB, 1975), par. 32.

[2]*Opinions of the Accounting Principles Board No. 18*, "The Equity Method of Accounting for Investments in Common Stock" (New York: AICPA, 1971), par. 17.

foreign currency amounts by an exchange rate.[3] The development of translation procedures is complicated by the fact that the rate of exchange between two currencies is not stable. There has been considerable controversy as to which foreign currency accounts should be translated using the current exchange rate and which accounts should be translated using historical exchange rates. The ***current exchange rate*** is the spot rate in effect at the end of the accounting period (i.e., the balance sheet date). The ***historical exchange rate*** is the spot rate in effect on the date a transaction takes place. Another controversial area relates to how to report the adjustment that is needed to balance the accounts that results when there are changes in the exchange rate.

Translation Adjustment or Translation Gain or Loss

The translation of some accounts using the current exchange rate and others using the historical exchange rate will result in an inequality between the total of the debit account balances and the total of the credit account balances. This difference is called a ***translation adjustment*** or ***translation gain or loss***. As will be shown in a later section of this chapter, the amount of the translation adjustment is affected by an entity's accounting exposure to changes in the exchange rate. In an accounting sense, an entity's exposure to exchange risk is related to the set of accounts translated at the current rate. Current accounting standards require that the translation adjustment (gain or loss) be reported currently in income or deferred as a component of stockholders' equity, depending on the method used to translate the accounts.

OBJECTIVES OF TRANSLATION—*SFAS NO. 52*

Functional Currency Concept

In *Statement of Financial Accounting Standards (SFAS) No. 52*, the board determined that the objectives of translation are to[4]:

1. Provide information the is generally compatible with the exposed economic effects of an exchange rate change on an enterprise's cash flows and equity (par. 4(a)].

2. Reflect in consolidated statements the financial results and relationships of the individual consolidated entities as measured in their ***functional currencies*** in conformity with U.S. generally accepted accounting principles [par. 4(b)].

With respect to the first objective, compatibility in terms of effect on equity is achieved if, for example, an entity is in an exposed asset position and the translation process results in an increase in stockholders' equity when there is a favorable change in the exchange rate. (An entity's exposed asset position is the excess of

---

[3]The ***reporting currency*** is the currency in which a company prepares its financial statements. The U.S. dollar is assumed to be the reporting currency in this chapter.

[4]*Statement of Financial Accounting Standards No. 52*, "Foreign Currency Translation" (Norwalk, Conn.: FASB, 1981).

assets that are translated at the current exchange rate over liabilities that are translated at the current exchange rate.) An unfavorable change in the exchange rate should result in a reduction in stockholders' equity. Compatibility in terms of cash flow consequences is achieved if favorable (unfavorable) rate changes that are reasonably expected to affect cash flows are reflected as gains (losses) in determining net income for the period and the effect of rate changes that have only remote and uncertain implications for realization are excluded from determining net income for the period.

In objective 2, the Board moved from a single-enterprise perspective of consolidation of a foreign entity to a multiple enterprise perspective. The Board reasoned that foreign operations are often conducted in economic and currency environments that differ from those of the U.S. parent. Thus, a foreign entity is viewed as a separate business entity that generates its earnings in its local economic, legal, and political environment. The Board believes that the operating performance and financial condition of a foreign entity are best measured by expressing its accounts in the currency of the economic environment in which it primarily conducts its operations and generates and expends its cash, its *functional currency*.[5] (The determination of an entity's functional currency is discussed in a later section of this chapter.) Under this view of a foreign entity, the translation of accounts expressed in the functional currency should retain the financial results and relationships that were created in the economic environment of the foreign operations rather than as if the operations had been conducted in the economic environment of the reporting currency.

TRANSLATION METHODS

To accomplish the objectives of translation, two translation methods are used depending on the functional currency of the foreign entity. The two methods are:[6]

Current rate method. When using the current rate method, all assets and liabilities are translated using the current exchange rate. Revenue and expense transactions are translated at the exchange rate prevailing on the date each underlying transaction occurred. Since separate translation of each transaction is usually impractical, an appropriate average rate can be used to approximate the results that would be obtained from translation of each transaction.

Temporal method. Under this method, monetary assets such as cash, receivables,

---

[5] *Statement of Financial Accounting Standards No. 52*, par. 5.

[6] Two other methods described below were considered acceptable at various times in the past.

Current–noncurrent method. Under this method, all current assets and liabilities were translated at the current exchange rate. Noncurrent assets and liabilities were translated at historical rates. Revenues and expenses were translated using procedures similar to those set forth for the temporal method.

Monetary–nonmonetary method. Under this method, monetary assets and liabilities were translated at the current exchange rate, and other accounts were translated at historical exchange rates. Revenues and expenses were translated using procedures similar to those set forth for the temporal method.

These two methods were rejected by the Board on the basis that the measurement bases used to account for items classified with the current, noncurrent, monetary, or nonmonetary classifications did not measure the same attributes.

and payables are translated at the current exchange rate. Assets and liabilities carried at historical cost are translated at historical exchange rates. Assets and liabilities carried at current values (such as inventory carried at market when applying the lower of cost or market rule) are translated at the current exchange rate. Thus, the temporal method places emphasis on whether an account is measured in terms of historical cost or current values.

Revenue and expense transactions, except those related to assets and liabilities translated at historical rates, are translated at exchange rates in effect on the dates the underlying transaction occurred. An appropriate average rate can be used to approximate the results that would be obtained from translation of each transaction. Revenues and expenses that relate to assets and liabilities translated at historical rates are translated at the historical rates used to translate the related assets and liabilities.

IDENTIFYING THE FUNCTIONAL CURRENCY

The functional currency may be (1) the currency of the country in which the foreign entity is located (the local currency), (2) the U.S. dollar, or (3) the currency of another foreign country. Generally, the functional currency is the local currency of the country in which the entity is located and in which the accounting records are maintained. For example, a French subsidiary with operations that are relatively self-contained and integrated in France would have the French franc as its functional currency. In this example, the French subsidiary primarily generates and expends francs.

In other cases, the dollar may be identified as the functional currency when a foreign subsidiary is a direct extension or an integral component of the reporting U.S. parent company. For example, the dollar would ordinarily be the functional currency for a subsidiary domiciled in Mexico that is financed by a U.S. parent company, that acquires significant assets by expending dollars, and whose only business is to assemble components that are manufactured in the United States and are returned to the United States to be sold by the parent company. In this case, the dollar may be the functional currency even though transactions of the subsidiary are recorded in pesos in the subsidiary's books.

In still other cases, the identification of the functional currency will not be as clear as in these two examples. For example, a Mexico City subsidiary might manufacture a component for a product, a significant number of which are sold in Mexico or to companies domiciled in other foreign countries, in addition to providing some units for the U.S. parent, or a foreign entity might conduct significant amounts of business in two or more currencies. In such situations the functional currency could be a currency other than the dollar, such as the local currency of the foreign entity or the currency of a third country. To provide some guidance in selecting the functional currency, the FASB identified six economic indicators for management to consider. These indicators are listed in Illustration 15-1. The order in which the indicators are listed does not suggest any priority; rather, the indicators are to be considered both individually and collectively. When the indicators are mixed and the functional currency cannot be clearly identified, *SFAS No. 52* indi-

ILLUSTRATION 15-1
Functional Currency Indicators

ECONOMIC INDICATOR	INDICATORS POINTING TO LOCAL CURRENCY AS FUNCTIONAL CURRENCY	INDICATORS POINTING TO U.S. DOLLAR AS FUNCTIONAL CURRENCY
Cash flows	Primarily in the local currency and do not directly affect parent's cash flows.	Directly affect the parent's cash flows on a current basis and are readily available for remittance to the parent.
Sales prices	Are not primarily responsive in the short term to exchange rate changes; determined primarily by local conditions.	Are primarily responsive in the short term to exchange rate changes; determined primarily by worldwide competition.
Sales market	Active local market although there may be significant amounts of exports.	Sales are mostly in the United States, or sales contracts are denominated in dollars.
Expenses	Production costs and operating expenses are determined primarily by local conditions.	Production costs and operating expenses are obtained primarily from U.S. sources.
Financing	Primarily denominated in the local currency, and foreign entity's cash flow from operations is sufficient to service existing and normally expected obligations.	Primarily from parent or other dollar-denominated obligations, or parent company is expected to service the debt.
Intercompany transactions	Low volume of intercompany transactions and there is not an extensive interrelationship between operations of the foreign entity and those of the parent. However, foreign entity may rely on parent's or affiliates' competitive advantages such as patents and trademarks.	High volume of intercompany transactions; there is an extensive interrelationship between operations of the parent and those of the foreign entity, or the foreign entity is an investment or financing device for the parent.

SOURCE: *Statement of Financial Accounting Standards No. 52*, par. 42

cates that management's judgment is required to assess the facts and circumstances in identifying the functional currency.

A foreign entity may operate and generate cash flows through more than one distinct and separable operation. Each of these operations may be identified as an entity and may have a different functional currency if conducted in different economic environments.

TRANSLATION OF FOREIGN CURRENCY FINANCIAL STATEMENTS

The method used to translate a foreign entity's financial statements and the disposition of the resulting translation adjustment depend on the determination of the functional currency. As indicated earlier, the functional currency of the foreign entity might be (1) the local currency of the foreign entity, (2) the U.S. dollar, or (3) the currency of a third country (i.e., a country other than the country in which the subsidiary is located or the United States). The translation process and the disposition of the translation adjustment for these three situations, assuming that the books are kept in the local currency of the foreign entity and that the accounting conforms to U.S. generally accepted accounting principles, are summarized in a flow chart in Illustration 15-2. If the books of the foreign entity are kept in dollars,

ILLUSTRATION 15-2
Summary of Translation Process and Disposition of Translation Gain or Loss

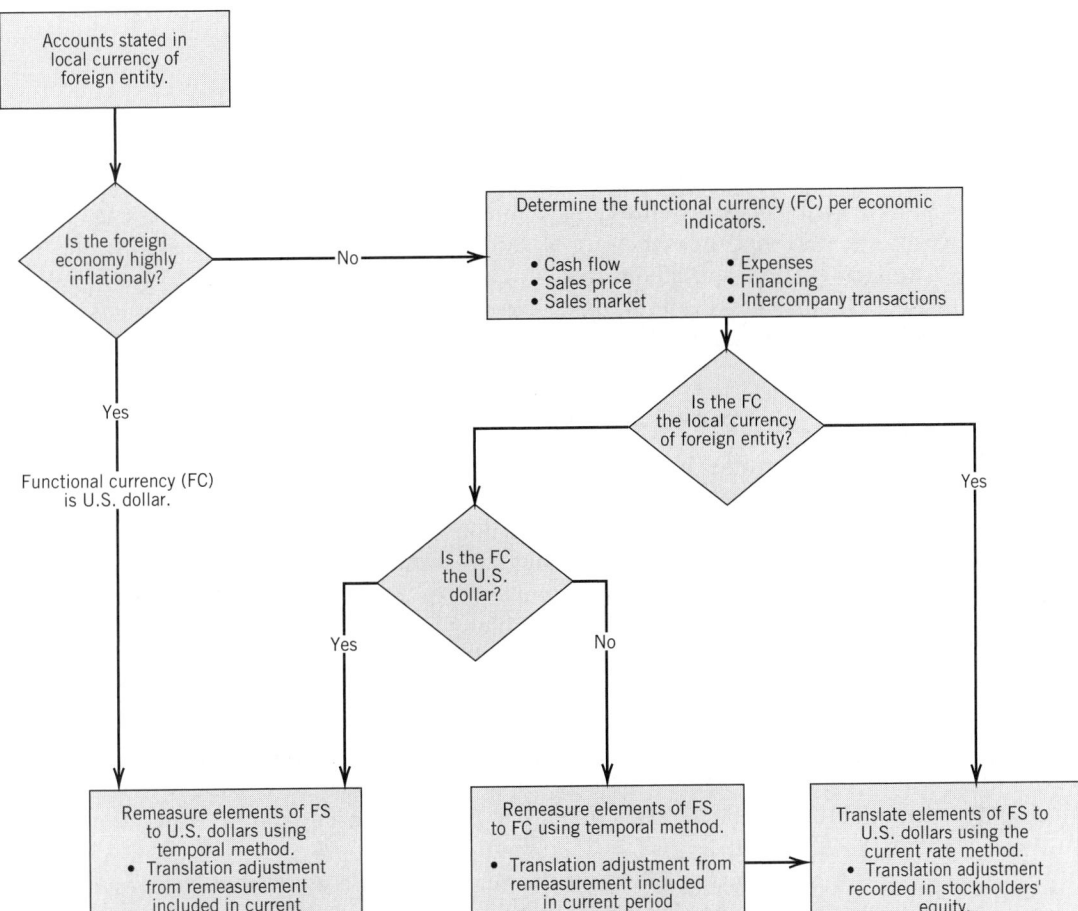

SOURCE: Adapted from Dahli Gray, "Functional Currency Concept-Flexibility, and Comparability Effects," *The Woman CPA*, January, 1983, p. 22.

translation is not necessary. Also, if the books of the foreign entity are not kept in accordance with U.S. generally accepted accounting principles, the accounts must be adjusted to conform before translating the account balances.

Note in Illustration 15-2 that the terms ***remeasurement*** and ***translation*** are used when the accounts stated in one currency are translated into another currency. The distinction between the two is as follows:

Remeasurement. If a foreign entity does not maintain its records in its functional currency, the local currency accounts are remeasured into the functional currency using the temporal method. ***Remeasurement*** is the process of translating the accounts of a foreign entity into its functional currency when they are stated in another currency.[7]

Translation. Accounts measured in the functional currency are translated into the reporting currency using the current rate method.[8]

As explained later remeasurement is a change in the unit of measure, whereas translation retains the functional currency as the unit of measure and simply changes the form in which the accounts are stated. (Note that the term ***translation*** is used in two different ways: (1) as a generic term to apply to any restatement of foreign currency units into dollars and (2) more specifically, to the restatement of foreign currency units that are already measured in the functional currency into dollars (current rate method).)

The first step in the translation process is to determine if the foreign entity is operating in a highly inflationary economy.

Foreign Entity Operates in a Highly Inflationary Economy

The relative rate of inflation between two countries is an important contributing factor to changes in exchange rates. Often, the currency of a country experiencing high inflation will weaken (i.e., one unit of that country's currency can be purchased with less domestic currency) substantially against the currency of a more stable economy. Thus, using the current rate method to translate inventories and fixed assets of foreign operations in highly inflationary economies often results in a substantial reduction in the translated amounts.

To illustrate, assume that a foreign subsidiary acquired land for 100,000 foreign currency units (FCU) when the exchange rate was $1 per FCU. In subsequent years, the foreign country experienced significant inflation and the exchange rate decreased to $.20 per FCU. If the current exchange rate is used, the land would translate to $20,000 (100,000 FCU × $.20) and a cumulative translation loss of $80,000 is reported.

It is the Board's belief that the currency of a country that has a highly inflationary economy has lost its utility as a store of value and cannot be a functional measuring unit.[9] As a practical solution to the problem, the Board prescribed that the financial statements of a foreign entity operating in a highly inflationary economy shall be remeasured as if the functional currency were the reporting currency (U.S. dollar). For such entities this means that the foreign financial statements should be translated using the ***temporal method.*** According to the foregoing illustration, the land account would be translated to $100,000 (100,000 FCU × $1.00) using the historical exchange rate when the land was purchased.

---

[7] *FASB Statement No. 52,* par. 10.

[8] Ibid., par. 12.

[9] A highly inflationary economy is defined as one having cumulative inflation of approximately 100% or more over a three-year period. *Statement of Financial Accounting Standards No. 52,* par. 11.

Foreign Entity Operates in an Economy That Is Not Highly Inflationary

If the foreign entity does not operate in a highly inflationary economy, the functional currency must be identified.[10] The translation process for the three possibilities follows:

1. The local currency is the functional currency. The accounts are translated into dollars using the current rate method. Since the functional currency is the local currency, the accounts are already measured in the functional currency, and remeasurement is unnecessary. The resulting translation adjustment is recorded as a separate component of stockholders' equity.[11]

2. The U.S. dollar is the functional currency. When the foreign entity does not maintain its records in its functional currency, the accounts are remeasured into the functional currency, in this case dollars, using the temporal method. Since the U.S. dollar is the functional currency, remeasurement translates the accounts into dollars and no further translation is necessary. The resulting translation adjustment is reported in the current period's income statement.

3. The functional currency is the currency of a third country. The local currency accounts are first (a) remeasured in the functional currency (the currency of the third country) using the temporal approach, and then (b) the remeasured functional currency amounts are translated into dollars using the current rate approach. The translation gain or loss from using the temporal method is reported in income, while the adjustment resulting from use of the current rate approach is reported in a separate component of owners' equity.

The steps in the translation process may be diagrammed as shown in Illustration 15-3. As can be seen, identification of the functional currency is the key step in the translation process as it determines the method to be used to translate the foreign currency accounts.

[10]In a survey of the 1981 annual reports of 158 companies, Coopers & Lybrand reported the following results as to the identification of the functional currency:

FUNCTIONAL CURRENCY DESIGNATION	NUMBER
Local currencies	57
Both local currencies and U.S. dollar	66
U.S. dollar	4
Not disclosed	31
Total	158

Coopers & Lybrand, *Foreign Currency Translation—An Implementation Study* (National Office of Coopers & Lybrand, 1982), pp. 29–30.

[11]The term **translation adjustment** is defined in *SFAS No. 52* (par. 162) as the amount that results "from the process of translating financial statements from the entity's functional currency into the reporting currency." The current rate method is used to accomplish this translation, and the balancing amount is reported as a component of stockholders' equity. When the temporal method is used to translate the local currency of a foreign entity into its functional currency, the balancing amount is reported in the income statement and is often identified as a "translation or exchange gain or loss." The distinction described here is maintained in this chapter, but for convenience the term **translation adjustment** is often used as a generic term referring to both categories of balancing amounts.

ILLUSTRATION 15-3
Diagram of Translation Process

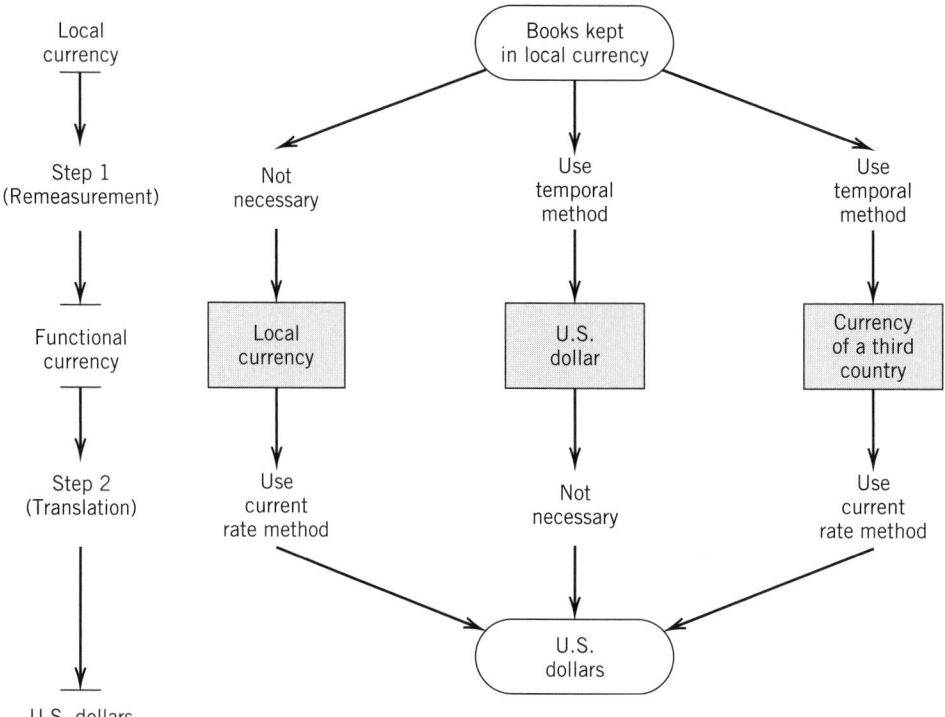

The approach outlined is consistent with the objective of preserving the financial results and relationships of an individual consolidated entity as measured in its functional currency. That is, when the local currency is identified as the functional currency, use of the current rate method retains the local currency as the unit of measure. A translation method preserves the financial results if a net income or loss reported in the functional currency statements is retained in the translated income statement. Maintaining relationships as measured in their functional currency is achieved when, for example, the current ratio is 2 : 1 when computed from the functional currency balance sheet and the ratio is also 2 : 1 when computed from the translated statements. The current rate method retains the financial results and relationships as measured in their functional currency by translating the assets and liabilities at one constant rate (the current rate) and the income statement items at one constant rate (the average rate).

Remeasurement using the temporal method when the functional currency is the U.S. dollar is consistent with a single-enterprise perspective of consolidation. In this case, the operations of the foreign entity are viewed as a direct extension or an integral component of the parent's domestic operations. That is, the parent and subsidiary are viewed as if they were a single company. The objective of translation is to change the unit of measure from that of the local currency to the reporting currency of the parent company, the functional currency. The translation process should then reflect all transactions of the subsidiary as if they were conducted or measured in one currency only, the parent's reporting currency. The use of historical exchange rates to translate accounts carried at historical cost preserves the original cost of the accounts in conformity with the historical cost concept. In effect, the accounts are restated as if dollars had been used to measure and record the assets and liabilities on the transaction dates.

When the functional currency is that of a third country, the accounts of the foreign entity maintained in its local currency are remeasured (translated) into the functional currency using the temporal method. The relationships as measured in the functional currency are retained by translating the functional currency balances into the reporting currency using the current rate method.

The reporting of the translation adjustment is also dependent on the selection of the functional currency. When the foreign entity's accounts are remeasured (temporal method) to the functional currency, either the U.S. dollar or the currency of a third country, the resulting adjustment is reported in the current period's income statement. When translating the accounts from the functional currency into dollars (current rate method), translation adjustments are accumulated and reported as a separate component of stockholders' equity. In the latter case, the Board regarded translation adjustments associated with a foreign investment as unrealized and considered their effect on cash flow to be uncertain and remote. As discussed earlier, one objective of translation is to provide information that is compatible with the expected economic effects of rate changes on cash flow. Compatibility is achieved when the effect of rate changes that have uncertain and remote implications for realization are excluded from income.

The cumulative translation adjustment is carried in the accounts until sale of the foreign entity. At that time, the amount attributable to that entity is removed from the separate component of equity and reported as part of the gain or loss on the sale.

TRANSLATION OF FOREIGN FINANCIAL STATEMENTS ILLUSTRATED

To illustrate the translation process, assume that on January 2, 1995, P Company, a U.S.-based company, acquired for 2,000,000 francs an 80% interest in SFr Company, a French company. SFr maintains its books in francs, and they are in conformity with GAAP in the United States. The translation process will be illustrated under two different assumptions: (1) the French franc is the functional currency, and (2) the U.S. dollar is the functional currency.

Exchange rates for the franc for the 1995 fiscal year are as follows:

DATE	SPOT RATE
January 2 (date of acquisition)	$.150
September 1	.160
December 31	.170
Average for the 4th quarter	.165
Average for the year	.156

In translating the income statement accounts, it is assumed that revenues were generated and expenses were incurred evenly during the year. It is also assumed that the company uses the FIFO cost flow assumption, and that the ending inventory was acquired during the last quarter.

Entries made on the books of P Company to account for the investment and the preparation of a consolidated statements workpaper based on the translated account balances are illustrated in the appendix to this chapter.

Functional Currency Is the Local Currency—Current Rate Method

Year-end financial statements at December 31 in francs for the subsidiary and the translation of the account balances into dollars using the current rate method are presented in Illustration 15-4. The translation rules are as follows:

1. All assets and liabilities are translated from the local currency into the reporting currency using the current exchange rate (i.e., the spot rate on the balance sheet date).

2. Paid-in capital accounts are translated using the historical rate, but the date to which the historical rate pertains depends on whether the acquisition was accounted for as a purchase or a pooling of interests. In a **purchase transaction**, the accounts are translated using the historical rate on the date the acquisition of the equity interest occurred. In the case of a **pooling of interests**, these accounts are translated using the historical rate(s) that existed on the date(s) that the foreign entity's capital transaction(s) occurred.

3. Components of the ending retained earnings are translated as follows:
   (a) The beginning retained earnings balance is set equal to the ending balance of last year. In this case, since this is the first year of acquisition, the balance is set equal to the January 2 balance of $72,000 (480,000 francs × $.15).
   (b) As a component of equity, dividends are translated into dollars using the exchange rate in effect when the dividend was declared.
   (c) Net income or loss is carried forward from the translated income statement as discussed later.
   (d) The cumulative translation adjustment is a balancing amount in the balance sheet. (The adjustment is discussed in more detail in the next section.)

4. Revenue and expense accounts (including cost of goods sold and depreciation), gains, and losses are translated using the exchange rate when the elements were recognized during the period. Because separate translation of numerous transactions is usually impractical, the use of an appropriate average to translate revenue and expense accounts is permitted.

An Analysis of the Translation Adjustment   When some accounts in a trial balance are translated using one rate and other accounts are translated using a different rate, an inequality will result between the total of the debit account balances and the total of the credit account balances. For example, in Illustration 15-4 the 608,000

Functional Currency
Is Local Currency
(Franc)—Current
Rate Method

ILLUSTRATION 15-4
SFr Company
Workpaper to Translate Account
Balances of Foreign Subsidiary
December 31, 1995

COMBINED STATEMENT OF INCOME AND RETAINED EARNINGS	ADJUSTED TRIAL BALANCE (FRANCS)	CURRENT RATE METHOD		
		TRANSLATION RATE		ADJUSTED TRIAL BALANCE (DOLLARS)
Sales	3,020,000	(A)	$.156	471,120
Cost of Goods Sold	1,850,000	(A)	.156	288,600
Depreciation Expense	100,000	(A)	.156	15,600
Other Expenses	655,000	(A)	.156	102,180
Income Tax Expense	82,000	(A)	.156	12,792
Net Income	333,000			51,948
1/2 Retained Earnings	480,000	(1)		72,000
	813,000			123,948
Less: 9/1 Dividends Declared	300,000	(H)	.16	48,000
12/31 Retained Earnings	513,000			75,948
BALANCE SHEET				
Cash	930,000	(C)	.17	158,100
Accounts Receivable (net)	608,000	(C)	.17	103,360
Inventories (FIFO cost)	830,000	(C)	.17	141,100
Land	500,000	(C)	.17	85,000
Buildings (net)	650,000	(C)	.17	110,500
Equipment (net)	430,000	(C)	.17	73,100
Total	3,948,000			671,160
Accounts Payable	640,000	(C)	.17	108,800
Short-term Notes Payable	635,000	(C)	.17	107,950
Bonds Payable	900,000	(C)	.17	153,000
Common Stock	960,000	(H)	.15	144,000
Additional Paid-in Capital	300,000	(H)	.15	45,000
Retained Earnings	513,000			75,948
Total	3,948,000			634,698
Cumulative Translation Adjustment— Credit Balance*		(B/A)		36,462
Total				671,160

*Included as a component of stockholders' equity.

(1) Retained earnings in dollars on January 2.
(A) Average exchange rate used to approximate the rate on the date these elements were recognized.
(H) Historical exchange rate.
(C) Current exchange rate.
(B/A) Balancing amount.

franc debit balance in the accounts receivable account is translated to $103,360 using the current exchange rate of $.17, and the 608,000 franc credit included in the sales account balance is translated to $94,848 (608,000 francs × $.156) using the average exchange rate for the period. On these transactions there is a translation adjustment credit of $8,512, since the accounts receivable could be converted into $103,360 at the balance sheet date, as opposed to $94,848 at the time of the sale. A translation adjustment will also result when items that are translated at the current rate are included in two successive trial balances and the exchange rate changes.

In Illustration 15-4 the translation adjustment is a balancing amount that reconciles the total debit balances with the total credit balances after the individual accounts have been translated and is reported as a component of stockholders' equity. The translation adjustment for the period results from an entity's accounting exposure to exchange risk, which in an accounting sense is related to the set of accounts that are translated at the current rate. Fluctuations in the exchange rate have no effect on the translated amount of an account translated at an historical rate on two balance sheets.

The translation adjustment under the current rate method may be verified by a direct computation as in Illustration 15-5. Since all assets and liabilities are translated at the current rate under the current rate method, only net assets (assets minus liabilities) are exposed to currency fluctuations and thus result in a translation gain or loss. This net investment view of the firm recognizes that functional currency assets produce revenues in a foreign currency and can be an effective hedge of liabilities that require payment in the same foreign currency. Thus, equal amounts of functional currency assets and liabilities hedge one another and only net assets are exposed to exchange risk. Most firms will be in a net asset position, which results in a transaction gain (loss), when the direct exchange rate increases (decreases).

The first column in Illustration 15-5 reconciles the net asset position at the beginning of the year to the net asset position at the end of the year. Note that only the transactions that affected stockholders' equity will cause a change in the net asset position. The franc balances in column 1 are translated into dollars using different exchange rates as follows. The beginning exposed net asset position is translated using the exchange rate in effect at the beginning of the period. The increases and decreases in the net asset position are translated using the exchange rate at the date the transactions were assumed to occur. The ending exposed net asset position is translated using the current exchange rate.

Interpretation of Results   In the preceding illustration, the current rate method was used to translate the foreign currency financial statements when the franc, as opposed to the dollar, was identified as the functional currency. As noted earlier, one of the objectives of translation is to retain in the translated statements the financial results and relationships of the financial statements as measured in the functional currency. With respect to financial results, a net income is reported in both the functional currency statements and the translated statements. A few selected financial ratios are computed here to show that the current rate method retains the financial relationships:

	FRANCS		DOLLARS	
Current ratio	$\dfrac{2,368,000}{1,275,000}$	= 1.86	$\dfrac{402,560}{216,750}$	= 1.86
Debt to equity	$\dfrac{2,175,000}{1,773,000}$	= 1.23	$\dfrac{369,750}{301,410}$	= 1.23
Gross profit percentage	$\dfrac{1,170,000}{3,020,000}$	= 38.7%	$\dfrac{182,520}{471,120}$	= 38.7%
Net income to sales	$\dfrac{333,000}{3,020,000}$	= 11.0%	$\dfrac{51,948}{471,120}$	= 11.0%

The other objective of translation is to provide information that is generally compatible with the expected economic effects of a change in exchange rates. In the illustration, the exchange rate increased from $.15 to $.17 during the period, a favorable change for a U.S. parent company holding an investment in an exposed net asset position. Translation of the foreign currency financial statements using the current rate approach resulted in a $36,462 increase in stockholders' equity.

ILLUSTRATION 15-5
Verification of the Translation Adjustment
Current Rate Method
Functional Currency—Franc

	FRANCS	TRANSLATION RATE	REPORTING CURRENCY (DOLLARS)
1/1 Exposed net asset position	1,740,000*	$.15	261,000
Adjustments for changes in net asset position during year			
Net income for year	333,000	.156	51,948
Dividends declared	(300,000)	.16	(48,000)
Net asset position translated using rate in effect at date of each transaction	—		264,948
12/31 Exposed net asset position	1,773,000	.17	301,410
Change in cumulative translation adjustment during year—net increase			36,462
1/1 Cumulative translation adjustment[†]			–0–
12/31 Cumulative translation adjustment			36,462

*A condensed balance sheet for SFr Company on January 2, 1995 was as follows:

	FRANCS		FRANCS
Monetary assets	1,100,000	Monetary liabilities	1,800,000
Nonmonetary assets:		Common stock	960,000
Inventory	760,000	Additional paid-in capital	300,000
Fixed assets	1,680,000	Retained earnings	480,000
Total	3,540,000	Total	3,540,000

1/1 Net assets = 3,540,000 francs − 1,800,000 francs = 1,740,000 francs.
[†]The beginning balance is zero since this was the first year the investment was held.

Functional Currency Is the U.S. Dollar—Temporal Method

The temporal method is used to remeasure the accounts of a foreign entity when the entity operates in a highly inflationary economy or its books are maintained in a currency other than its functional currency. The objective of the remeasurement process is to produce the same results as if the transactions of the foreign entity had been recorded initially in its functional currency.[12] To accomplish this, the historical exchange rate is used to translate accounts carried at historical cost, while the current exchange rate is used to translate other accounts. The remeasurement process is as follows:

1. Monetary assets and liabilities (for example, cash, receivables, and most liabilities) that are expressed in the balance sheet at current values are translated using the current rate. (An asset or a liability is monetary if it represents a claim to a fixed amount of dollars. All other assets and liabilities are nonmonetary.)

2. Nonmonetary assets and liabilities carried at past exchange prices (historical cost) are translated at historical exchange rates, which results in translating these amounts to the equivalent number of dollars on the date the transaction took place.

3. Nonmonetary assets and liabilities carried at current or future exchange prices (for example, marketable securities or inventory carried at replacement cost) are translated at the current exchange rate.

4. Paid-in capital accounts are translated using the historical exchange rate at the date of acquisition if a purchase transaction and at the date the original capital transaction(s) occurred if the acquisition is a pooling of interests.

5. The components that make up the ending retained earnings balance are translated as follows:
   (a) The beginning balance is set equal to the ending balance of the last period.
   (b) Dividends are translated at the rate existing on the date of the declaration.
   (c) Net income or loss is carried forward from the translated income statement.

6. Revenues and expenses related to assets and liabilities translated at historical rates (primarily inventory cost and depreciation) are translated at the respective historical rates used to translate the related asset or liability.

7. Other revenue and expense accounts are translated in a manner that produces approximately the same results as if the individual transactions were translated at the rate in effect when the transaction occurred.

8. The translation gain or loss is reported in the income statement.

A list of some common nonmonetary items that should be remeasured using the historical rate is presented in Illustration 15-6. Remeasurement of the nonmonetary accounts using historical exchange rates normally requires that the foreign entity maintain detailed records identifying the purchase date and the exchange rate.

---

[12]*Statement of Financial Accounting Standards No. 52*, par. 10.

ILLUSTRATION 15-6
Nonmonetary Items Remeasured Using the
Historical Rate

Balance Sheet Items
   Equity securities carried at cost
✳Inventories carried at cost
   Prepaid expenses such as insurance, advertising, and rent
   Property, plant, and equipment
   Accumulated depreciation on property, plant, and equipment
   Patents, trademarks, licenses, and formulas
   Goodwill
   Other intangible assets
   Deferred charges and credits, except deferred income taxes and policy acquisition
     costs for life insurance companies
   Deferred income
   Common stock
   Preferred stock carried at issuance price
Income Statement Items
   Cost of goods sold
   Depreciation of property, plant, and equipment
   Amortization of intangible items such as goodwill, patents, licenses, etc.
   Amortization of policy acquisition costs for life insurance companies

SOURCE: *Statement of Financial Accounting Standards No. 52*, par. 48.

The December 31 trial balance of SFr Company in francs and the remeasurement of the accounts using the temporal method are shown in Illustration 15-7. The first step is to translate the individual accounts, except for the ending retained earnings balance of 513,000 francs, using the appropriate exchange rate. The ending retained earnings balance of $76,660 is computed as a balancing amount required to equate the firm's liabilities and stockholders' equity with the total assets. Next, the ending retained earnings is carried to the combined statement of income and retained earnings where the translation loss of $11,918 is the balancing amount in the combined statement.

An Analysis of the Translation Gain or Loss   The translation loss in the temporal method of translation is derived by a direct calculation in Illustration 15-8. Procedurally, the approach is based on the same underlying concept as that used to verify the translation adjustment reported when the current rate method was used. That is, the translation loss is related to those accounts translated at the current exchange rate. However, in applying the temporal method, in general, monetary items only are translated at the current rate while most nonmonetary items are translated at historical rates. Accordingly, the dollar value of monetary items is affected by variations in the exchange rate, giving rise to a gain or loss. On the other hand, nonmonetary items will not result in a gain or loss because each item is translated in successive balance sheets using its respective historical exchange rate. As a result,

Functional Currency
Is U.S. Dollar—
Temporal Method

ILLUSTRATION 15-7
SFr Company
Workpaper to Remeasure Account
Balances of Foreign Subsidiary
December 31, 1995

	ADJUSTED	TEMPORAL METHOD	
			ADJUSTED
	TRIAL BALANCE	TRANSLATION	TRIAL BALANCE
BALANCE SHEET	(FRANCS)	RATE	(DOLLARS)
Cash	930,000	(C) .17	158,100
Accounts Receivable (net)	608,000	(C) .17	103,360
Inventories (FIFO cost)	830,000	Sch. 1	136,950
Land	500,000	(H) .15	75,000
Buildings (net)	650,000	(H) .15	97,500
Equipment (net)	430,000	(H) .15	64,500
Total	3,948,000		635,410
Accounts Payable	640,000	(C) .17	108,800
Short-term Notes Payable	635,000	(C) .17	107,950
Bonds Payable	900,000	(C) .17	153,000
Common Stock	960,000	(H) .15	144,000
Additional Paid-in Capital	300,000	(H) .15	45,000
Retained Earnings	513,000	(B/A)	76,660 ⌐
Total	3,948,000		635,410

COMBINED STATEMENT OF
INCOME AND RETAINED EARNINGS

Sales	3,020,000	(A) .156	⌐ 471,120
Cost of Goods Sold	1,850,000	Sch. 1	276,570	① Carry
Depreciation Expense	100,000	(H) .15 ②	15,000	down
Other Expenses	655,000	(A) .156	102,180	retained
Income Tax Expense	82,000	(A) .156 ∟	12,792	earnings
Translation Loss	—	(B/A) ④	11,918
Net Income	333,000		⌐ 52,660
1/2 Retained Earnings	480,000	(1)	72,000
	813,000	③	124,660
Less: 9/1 Dividends Declared	300,000	(H) .16	48,000
12/31 Retained Earnings	513,000		∟ 76,660 ←

(1) Retained earnings in dollars on January 2.
(A) Average exchange rate used to approximate the rate on the date these elements were recognized.
(H) Historical exchange rate.
(C) Current exchange rate.
(B/A) Balancing amount.

Schedule 1
Translation of cost of goods sold

	FRANCS	TRANS. RATE	DOLLARS
Beginning inventory (assumed)	760,000	.15	114,000
Purchases (assumed)	1,920,000	.156	299,520
	2,680,000		413,520
Less: Ending inventory	830,000	.165	136,950
Cost of goods sold	1,850,000		276,570

① Carry down retained earnings.
② Complete income statement down to translation gain or loss.
③ Beginning with ending retained earnings, work back to net income.

$$\underset{\$76,660}{\underset{\text{earnings}}{\text{Ending retained}}} + \underset{+\ \$48,000}{\text{Dividends}} - \underset{\$72,000}{\underset{\text{earnings}}{\text{Beginning retained}}} = \underset{=\ \$52,660}{\underset{\text{income}}{\text{Net}}}$$

④ Compute translation gain or loss.

ILLUSTRATION 15-8
Verification of the Translation Loss
Temporal Method
Functional Currency—U.S. Dollar

	FRANCS	TRANSLATION RATE	REPORTING CURRENCY (U.S. DOLLAR)
1/1 Exposed net monetary liability position	700,000*	$.15	105,000
Adjustments for changes in net monetary position during the year:			
Less: Increase in cash and receivables from sales	(3,020,000)	.156	(471,120)
Add: Decrease in monetary assets or increase in monetary liabilities:			
Purchases	1,920,000	.156	299,520
Other expenses	655,000	.156	102,180
Income taxes	82,000	.156	12,792
Dividends declared	300,000	.16	48,000
Net monetary liability position translated using rate in effect at date of each transaction	—		96,372
12/31 Exposed net monetary liability position	637,000†	.17	108,290
Translation gain (loss)			(11,918)

*The January 2, 1995, condensed balance sheet is given in Illustration 15-5.

	FRANCS
Monetary liabilities	1,800,000
Less: Monetary assets	1,100,000
Net monetary liability position	700,000

†See Illustration 15-7.

	FRANCS
Monetary liabilities (640,000 + 635,000 + 900,000)	2,175,000
Less: Monetary assets (930,000 + 608,000)	1,538,000
Net monetary liability position	637,000

as long as these items are reported in the balance sheet, they will retain their original translated dollar amounts (less accumulated amortization), even though the exchange rate may have changed.

A translation loss results from application of the temporal method, as opposed to the credit translation adjustment calculated on the exposed assets using the current rate method, because SFr Company maintained a net monetary liability position throughout the year. An increasing exchange rate will produce a translation loss on an exposed net monetary liability position.

Comparison of the Two Methods

In translating the balance sheet, the differences and similarities between the temporal and current rate methods are highlighted in the following schedule:

	BALANCE SHEET TRANSLATION RATES	
	CURRENT RATE METHOD	TEMPORAL METHOD
Monetary asset	Current	Current
Nonmonetary asset carried at historical cost	Current	Historical
Nonmonetary asset carried at market value	Current	Current
Monetary liability	Current	Current
Nonmonetary liability	Current	Historical

As can be seen, the two methods differ primarily in terms of the appropriate rate to use for nonmonetary items carried at historical cost.

In the income statement, a net income of $51,948 resulted when the franc was the functional currency (Illustration 15-4), whereas a net income of $52,660 was reported when the U.S. dollar was the functional currency (Illustration 15-7). There are two reasons for this difference. First, when the foreign currency is strengthening against the dollar, cost of goods sold and depreciation expense generally are greater when the current rate method of translation is used. Second, a translation loss of $11,918 is reported in the dollar functional currency income statement, whereas a credit adjustment of $36,462 is reported in stockholders' equity in the franc functional currency statement.

TRANSLATING STATEMENTS OF FOREIGN BRANCHES

Accounting for a domestic branch when both branch and home office maintain their accounting records in the same currency was discussed in an earlier chapter. The home office may adopt a similar accounting system to record the transactions of a foreign branch. Although the branch records the transactions in terms of the local currency of the country in which it is domiciled, the home office measures the branch transactions in terms of the domestic currency. Before combined financial statements are prepared, or before the home office can record the income or loss of the foreign branch, the trial balance of the branch must be translated into the reporting currency of the home office. The exchange rates prescribed in *SFAS No. 52* for translating the accounts of a foreign subsidiary are also applicable for translating nonreciprocal accounts of a foreign branch.

A reciprocal account on the books of the branch is not translated but is restated to the dollar amount in the reciprocal account on the books of the home office. The reciprocal accounts can then be eliminated in the combined workpaper. To facilitate this procedure and to provide information to management concerning the value of the foreign currency and dollars transferred between the home office and branch, separate reciprocal accounts typically are created to record the transfers. In other words, instead of using one single reciprocal account on each set of books (Investment in Branch and Home Office), two separate sets of reciprocal accounts are used to record remittances to and from the branch on the books of the home office and the branch. The various remittance accounts in the home office books are closed at the end of the period to Investment in Branch, and the remittance accounts on the branch books are closed to Home Office.

In the case of a domestic branch, a disparity between the balance in the Home Office account and the balance in the Investment in Branch account would indicate that there were errors or unrecorded transaction(s) between the home office and the branch on one set of books at year-end. If the reciprocal account balances on the branch books are set to equal the related reciprocal account balance on the home office books, this automatic check is not available. Therefore, transactions between the home office and the branch must be reconciled to ensure that there are no unrecorded transactions on one set of books at year-end. In order to perform the reconciliation, the branch must provide the home office with a summary of transactions recorded in the reciprocal accounts.

FINANCIAL STATEMENT DISCLOSURE

Companies are required to disclose certain items, as follows:

1. The aggregate transaction gain or loss included in the determination of net income for the period, including gains or losses related to forward contracts, should be disclosed in either the financial statements or notes thereto.

2. An analysis of the cumulative translation adjustment equity account should be provided in a separate statement or note or as part of a statement of changes in equity. The analysis should include:
   (a) The beginning and ending cumulative translation adjustment amounts.
   (b) The aggregate adjustment for the period resulting from the translation of foreign currency statements and gains and losses from certain hedging activities and intercompany long-term investment transactions.
   (c) The amount of income taxes for the period allocated to the cumulative translation adjustment equity account.
   (d) The amounts transferred from the cumulative translation adjustment equity account and included in the determination of net income for the period as a result of the sale of part or all of an investment in a foreign entity.

3. Exchange rate changes that occur after the balance sheet date and their effect on unsettled foreign currency transactions, if significant.

U.S. companies must also comply with the provisions of the Foreign Corrupt Practices Act (FCPA). The FCPA was enacted in 1977 in response to disclosures by more than 400 U.S. corporations of questionable or improper payments made to foreign officials to elicit their support for business arrangements with the U.S. firms.

An extensive investigation by the SEC revealed that in a significant number of cases, the foreign payments had been made to appear in the corporate records as a normal operating expense and that inadequate documentation precluded the verification of the purpose of the payment.

The FCPA contains two major sections: an antibribery section and an accounting standards section. The antibribery provision makes it a criminal offense to offer a bribe to a foreign government official or foreign political official. The accounting standards section of the Act is intended to help prevent the concealment of foreign corrupt payments.

In February 1978 the SEC issued *Accounting Series Release No. 242*, which emphasized the importance of the provisions of the Act and the need to comply with its requirements. In the release the SEC stated that although the Act imposed new requirements with respect to the maintenance of internal accounting controls and outlawed certain foreign corrupt practices, it did not alter the existing obligation to adequately disclose questionable and illegal corporate payments and practices. The SEC went on to state that "registrants have a continuing obligation to disclose all material information and all information necessary to prevent other disclosures made from being misleading with respect to such transactions."

HARMONIZATION OF WORLDWIDE ACCOUNTING STANDARDS

Financial accounting practices, required disclosures, and auditing requirements are not uniform among individual countries. Not only are there differences in broad principles, but there are many variations in the everyday application of these principles. An extensive list of differences is not necessary here, but the following provides evidence of the wide variations that exist in accounting practices:

1. In some countries, goodwill is not amortized until it is apparent that is has diminished in value. Companies in England are able to write off goodwill against stockholders' equity.

2. Outside the United States the pooling of interests method of recording a business combination is permitted in only a few countries.

3. Only a limited number of countries require comprehensive tax allocation.

4. LIFO inventory costing is not permitted in some countries.

As noted earlier, accounting reports of a foreign entity must be made to conform to U.S. generally accepted accounting standards before consolidation or the equity method is applied. An accountant working with the financial statements of a foreign company must therefore be familiar with the differences between accounting practices in the United States and those in the foreign country in which it is domiciled and be prepared to deal with them.

With the growth of international trade, multinational firms, and a global financial marketplace, significant resources have been devoted to the "harmonization" of accounting principles and auditing standards. Harmonization is an approach to international accounting standard setting in which the focus is on the communication of information in a form that could be interpreted and understood internationally, rather than standardization of procedures to be used in all countries. Under this approach, international standards were drafted in broad terms and permitted acceptable alternatives adopted by rulemakers in various developed countries. However, to a growing number of preparers and users of financial statements, harmonization means the narrowing of differences between generally accepted accounting procedures of different countries.[13]

The organization that has done the most for international standard setting is the International Accounting Standards Committee (IASC). The IASC was established in 1973 by the leading accountancy bodies of Australia, Canada, France, Germany, Japan, Mexico, the Netherlands, the United Kingdom and Ireland, and the United States. The IASC now has a membership representing more than 70 countries. The objective of the IASC is to formulate and publish standards to be followed in the preparation of financial statements, promote worldwide acceptance of the standards, and work generally for improvements in international accounting. The first international accounting standard was issued in January 1975; 31 standards have been issued up to December 31, 1992. Members of the IASC have agreed to make their best efforts to ensure that financial statements issued in their respective countries conform to the standards issued by the IASC and that noncompliance with those standards be disclosed in the financial reports.[14] For example, General Electric included the following excerpt in the Management's Discussion of Financial Responsibility section of its 1989 annual report:

> The financial information in this report, including the audited financial statements, has been prepared by management. Preparation of financial statements and related data involves estimates and the use of judgment. Accounting principles used in preparing the financial statements are those that are generally accepted in the United States. These principles are consistent in most important respects with standards issued by the International Accounting Standards Committee.

It is now recognized that a global financial marketplace exists and that the use of different accounting standards works against the efficiency of international cap-

---

[13]Bernard R. Doyle and Sidney D. Spencer, "International Accounting Standards: Why They Merit Support," *Management Accounting* (October 1986), p. 28.

[14]The AICPA, not the FASB, is the U.S. member on the IASC. The AICPA has strongly encouraged its members to support the IASC, but has stated that standards issued by the IASC do not establish standards enforceable under the Code of Professional Ethics. The FASB does consider international accounting standards in its deliberations. For example, in paragraph 24 of the *Proposed Standard on Foreign Currency Translations*, the Board states:

> The Board also believes that, to the extent practicable, the accounting for the translation of foreign currency transactions and financial statements in the United States should harmonize with related accounting practices followed in other countries of the world. The Board maintained close liaison with representatives of the IASC and the accounting standards-setting bodies in Canada and the United Kingdom and Ireland as this Statement was developed. Representatives from each of those groups were active participants with the Board's foreign currency task force. The Accounting Standards Committee in the United Kingdom and Ireland has issued a proposed standard for foreign currency translation that is similar in all material respects to the standards set forth in this Statement.

ital markets. With the emergence of significant global corporate operations and markets, the IASC is attempting to improve the quality of its standards. The IASC issued Exposure Draft no. 32, **Comparability of Financial Statements**, in January 1989 that is designed to make its standards less general and eliminate many alternative choices that now exist. There were 29 proposals in the exposure draft. Most of them are to be incorporated in revised international accounting standards.

HISTORICAL DEVELOPMENTS OF ACCOUNTING STANDARDS

The expansion of international business has been of particular concern to accountants because of developments in the worldwide monetary system during the 1970s. These developments, coupled with the existence of a number of acceptable methods of translating foreign financial statements and reporting gains or losses on foreign currency fluctuations, led the FASB to place the topic on its agenda in 1973. The result was the issuance in October 1975 of *Statement of Financial Accounting Standards No. 8*, "Accounting for the Translation of Foreign Currency Transactions and Foreign Currency Financial Statements."[15]

One objective of *Statement No. 8* was to provide uniform accounting standards for the translation of foreign financial statements. A second objective was to fill the gap in authoritative literature on accounting for transactions with foreign companies. The *Statement* was not well received; it proved to be one of the most controversial statements issued by the FASB. Major criticism of the statement focused on the following points:[16]

1. Reporting translation gains and losses in current income often resulted in unnecessary fluctuations in reported income.

2. Translation required by the statement sometimes resulted in reporting a loss when the economic effects of a rate change were expected to be favorable, and a gain when the economic effects were expected to be unfavorable.

3. Certain effective hedges of foreign exchange risk were ignored.

Concerned with the increasing criticism leveled against *Statement No. 8*, the Board added to its agenda a project to reconsider it in January 1979. As a result of this project, an exposure draft entitled "Foreign Currency Translation" was issued in August 1980. On the basis of more than 360 comment letters and views expressed in a public hearing, the Board issued a revised exposure draft.[17] These series of developments culminated in the issuance of *SFAS No. 52*, which was discussed in this and the previous chapter.

---

[15] *Statement of Financial Accounting Standards No. 8*, "Accounting for the Translation of Foreign Currency Transactions and Foreign Currency Financial Statements" (Norwalk, Conn.: FASB, October 1975).

[16] For an excellent bibliography of the literature related to *FASB Statement No. 8*, see John K. Shank, Jesse F. Dillard, and Richard J. Murdock, *Assessing the Economic Impact of FASB No. 8* (New York: Financial Executives Research Foundation, 1979).

[17] *Proposed Statement of Financial Accounting Standards*, "Foreign Currency Translation" (Norwalk, Conn.: FASB, June 1981).

APPENDIX: ACCOUNTING FOR A FOREIGN AFFILIATE AND PREPARATION OF CONSOLIDATED STATEMENTS WORKPAPER ILLUSTRATED

To illustrate the accounting for a foreign affiliate and the preparation of a consolidated statements workpaper, the illustration of the 80% interest in SFr Company will be continued. Since SFr Company maintains its books in francs, the trial balance in dollars is based on the translated balances contained in Illustrations 15-4 and 15-7.

DATE OF ACQUISITION

The direct exchange rate for francs on January 2, 1995, was $.15. Thus it would have taken $300,000 (2,000,000 francs × $.15) to buy the 2,000,000 francs needed for the purchase price. The entry to record the acquisition is

Investment in SFr Company	300,000	
Cash		300,000

On the date of acquisition, since the business combination must be accounted for using the purchase method of accounting (cash was used to acquire the voting stock), assets, liabilities, and stockholders' equity accounts are translated from francs into dollars using the spot rate of $.15. Any difference between cost and book value interest acquired is allocated to individual assets and liabilities of a foreign subsidiary using essentially the same approach as that illustrated in Chapter 4. On January 2, SFr Company reported common stock of 960,000 francs, additional paid-in capital of 300,000 francs, and retained earnings of 480,000 francs for a net asset balance of 1,740,000 francs. The difference between cost and book value in francs and dollars is allocated to land and buildings in Illustration 15-9. When an acquisition qualifies as a purchase transaction, all accounts of the subsidiary are translated at the date of acquisition using the then current exchange rate whether the current rate method or the temporal method is used in the translation process. Thus, the computation of the difference and its allocation is the same for both methods.

ILLUSTRATION 15-9
Allocation of Difference
Between Cost and Book Value

	FRANCS	TRANSLATION RATE	DOLLARS
Cost	2,000,000	$.15	300,000
Book value interest acquired:			
(1,740,000 francs × .80)	1,392,000	.15	208,800
Difference between cost and book value interest acquired	608,000		91,200
Allocated to:			
Land	(308,000)*	.15	(46,200)
Buildings—10-year remaining life	(300,000)*	.15	(45,000)
Unallocated balance	–0–		–0–

*Amounts are assumed.

ACCOUNTING FOR AN INVESTMENT IN A FOREIGN AFFILIATE—AFTER ACQUISITION

After the initial entry to record the purchase of the equity interest in SFr Company, P Company will make a book entry to record the declaration and receipt of cash dividends. P Company accounts for its investment by the cost method. In this case, SFr Company declared and paid a 300,000 franc dividend on September 1 when the direct exchange rate was $.16. The book entry to record the dividend receipt is:

Cash	38,400	
Dividend Income		38,400
300,000 francs × $.16 = $48,000 × .80 = $38,400		

Before consolidated financial statements are prepared, the subsidiary's financial statements must be translated into dollars using either the current rate method (Illustration 15-4) or the temporal method (Illustration 15-7). A workpaper to consolidate P Company and SFr Company is presented in Illustration 15-10 assuming

Cost Method
80% Owned Foreign Subsidiary
Current Rate Method
  of Translation
Year of Acquisition

ILLUSTRATION 15-10
Consolidated Statements Workpaper
P Company and Foreign Subsidiary
For the Year Ended December 31, 1995

INCOME STATEMENT	P COMPANY	SFr COMPANY	ELIMINATIONS DR.	ELIMINATIONS CR.	NON-CONTROLLING INTEREST	CONSOLIDATED BALANCES
Sales and Other Revenue	4,200,000	471,120				4,671,120
Dividend Income	38,400		(1) 38,400			—
Total Revenues	4,238,400	471,120				4,671,120
Cost of Goods Sold	2,720,000	288,600				3,008,600
Depreciation Expense	210,000	15,600	(4) 4,680			230,280
Other Expenses	914,000	102,180				1,016,180
Income Tax Expense	100,000	12,792				112,792
Total Cost and Expense	3,944,000	419,172				4,367,852
Net/Combined Income	294,400	51,948				303,268
Noncontrolling Interest in Net Income ($51,948 × .20)					10,390	(10,390)
Net Income to Retained Earnings	294,400	51,948	43,080	—	10,390	292,878
RETAINED EARNINGS STATEMENT						
1/1 Retained Earnings						
P Company	450,000					450,000
SFr Company		72,000	(2) 57,600		14,400	
Net Income from above	294,400	51,948	43,080		10,390	292,878
Dividends Declared						
P Company	(200,000)					(200,000)
SFr Company		(48,000)		(1) 38,400	(9,600)	
12/31 Retained Earnings to Balance Sheet	544,400	75,948	100,680	38,400	15,190	542,878

BALANCE SHEET	P COMPANY	SFr COMPANY	ELIMINATIONS DR.	ELIMINATIONS CR.	NON-CONTROLLING INTEREST	CONSOLIDATED BALANCES
Current Assets	1,324,400	402,560				1,726,960
Investment in SFr Company	300,000			(2) 300,000		—
Land	450,000	85,000	(4) 52,360			587,360
Buildings (net)	720,000	110,500	(4) 45,900			876,400
Equipment (net)	390,000	73,100				463,100
Difference Between Cost and Book Value	—		(2) 91,200	(4) 91,200		—
Total Assets	3,184,400	671,160				3,653,820
Current Liabilities	840,000	216,750				1,056,750
Bonds Payable	700,000	153,000				853,000
Common Stock						
P Company	800,000					800,000
SFr Company		144,000	(2) 115,200		28,800	
Additional Paid-in Capital						
P Company	300,000					300,000
SFr Company		45,000	(2) 36,000		9,000	
Cumulative Translation Adjustment						
P Company	—			{(3) 29,170 {(4) 11,740		40,910
SFr Company		36,462	(3) 29,170		7,292	
Retained Earnings from above	544,400	75,948	100,680	38,400	15,190	542,878
Noncontrolling Interest in Net Assets					60,282	60,282
Total Liabilities and Owners' Equity	3,184,400	671,160	470,510	470,510		3,653,820

(1) To eliminate intercompany dividends.
(2) To eliminate the investment account.
(3) To recognize interest in cumulative translation adjustment.
(4) To assign difference between cost and book value.

that the current rate method was appropriate for translating the subsidiary's accounts (i.e., the functional currency of the subsidiary was its local currency). Workpaper entries in general journal form are given here.

**Consolidated Statements Workpaper Entries—December 31, 1995
(From Illustration 15-10)**

(1) Dividend Income	38,400	
Dividends Declared—SFr Company		38,400
To eliminate intercompany dividends.		
(2) Beginning Retained Earnings—SFr Company	57,600	
Common Stock—SFr Company	115,200	
Additional Paid-in Capital—SFr Company	36,000	
Difference Between Cost and Book Value	91,200	
Investment in SFr Company		300,000
To eliminate the investment account.		

| (3) Cumulative Translation Adjustment—SFr Company | 29,170 | |
| Cumulative Translation Adjustment—P Company | | 29,170 |

To recognize P Company's interest in the increase in stockholders' equity resulting from a change in exchange rates.

(4) Depreciation Expense	4,680	
Land	52,360	
Buildings	45,900	
Cumulative Translation Adjustment—P Company		11,740
Difference Between Cost and Book Value		91,200

To allocate the difference between cost and book value and to recognize the related translation adjustment.

The major differences between the foregoing entries for the current rate method and those prepared in Chapter 4 are as follows:

1. Using the current rate method to translate the accounts of the subsidiary resulted in a cumulative translation adjustment of $36,462. The $36,462 increases stockholders' equity and translated net assets of the subsidiary. Since this amount is not reported in the income statement, a workpaper entry [entry (3)] is made to recognize the parent's interest therein ($36,462 × .80 = $29,170). The remaining portion ($36,462 × .20 = $7,292) is extended to the noncontrolling interest column.

2. The difference between cost and book value at the date of acquisition was assigned to specific assets and translated into dollars using the exchange rate in effect on the purchase date. However, with a change in the exchange rate, the amortization expense in the income statement is translated using the average exchange rate, and the unamortized ending balances in the balance sheet are translated using the current exchange rate at the balance sheet date. As a result, there will be a translation adjustment related to the translation of these accounts. The amount of the adjustment balances the sum of the debits and the credits in entry (4), and can be verified as shown in Illustration 15-11.

ILLUSTRATION 15-11
Verification of Cumulative Translation Adjustment

	FRANCS	TRANSLATION RATE	DOLLARS
Undervalued net assets at beginning of year	608,000	$.15	91,200
Amortization this period	(30,000)	.156	(4,680)
Net asset position translated using rate in effect at date of transaction	—		86,520
Unamortized balance at end of year*	578,000	.17	98,260
Cumulative translation adjustment			11,740

	FRANCS		DOLLARS
*Land	308,000	.17	52,360
Buildings	270,000	.17	45,900
Totals	578,000		98,260

Subsequent to the Year of Acquisition

In years after the year of acquisition, an entry to establish reciprocity is made based on the undistributed net income. In this case the entry for the next year is:

Investment in SFr Company	3,158	
Beginning Retained Earnings—P Company		3,158
Retained earnings—12/31/1995		$75,948
Retained earnings—Date of acquisition		72,000
Undistributed net income		$ 3,948

$3,948 × .80 = $3,158

The other workpaper entries are similar to those illustrated before.

CONSOLIDATION WHEN THE TEMPORAL METHOD OF TRANSLATION IS USED

In completing the remeasurement process using the temporal method, a consolidated statements workpaper would be similar to the one illustrated previously for the current rate method. The major differences between the workpapers are as follows:

1. Under the temporal method, the translation gain or loss is included in the subsidiary's income statement and becomes a part of its ending retained earnings balance. The controlling interest in the gain or loss is recognized as part of consolidated net income in the current period. In subsequent periods the gain or loss is included in consolidated retained earnings as part of the reciprocity entry. Thus, a separate entry is not needed to recognize the parent's share of the translation gain or loss such as was done in entry (3) when the current rate method of translation was used.

2. The unamortized portion of the difference assigned to land and buildings and the amortization for the current period retain their historical dollar values since such nonmonetary assets are translated using historical rates.

REMEASUREMENT AND TRANSLATION OF FOREIGN CURRENCY TRANSACTIONS

SFAS No. 52 defines a foreign currency transaction as one that is denominated in a currency other than the entity's functional currency. As discussed in Chapter 14, at the transaction date, the current exchange rate is used to measure and record a foreign currency transaction in the functional currency of the recording entity. At subsequent balance sheet dates, recorded balances that are denominated in a currency other than the functional currency are adjusted to the functional currency using the current exchange rate. Any transaction gain or loss resulting from this procedure is recognized currently in income. Although a thorough discussion and illustration of the effects on the financial statements of affiliated companies and on consolidated statements is beyond the scope of this text, two examples are presented to illustrate the procedures.

Assume that a French subsidiary has a $100,000 loan payable to a U.S. bank. The loan is denominated in dollars and the franc is the functional currency of the subsidiary. Thus, this is a foreign currency transaction to the subsidiary but not to the U.S. bank. The current exchange rate was $.20 on the transaction date and $.16 on the balance sheet date. The subsidiary would compute a gain or loss as follows at the balance sheet date:

		FRANCS
Transaction date	$100,000 ÷ .20 =	500,000
Balance sheet date	$100,000 ÷ .16 =	625,000
Transaction loss reported in income		125,000

The U.S. bank would not record a gain or loss on its books because the payable is denominated in dollars.

Before consolidation, the accounts of the subsidiary are translated into dollars (the reporting currency) using the current rate method. In this illustration the payable of 625,000 francs as measured in the functional currency is translated to $100,000 (625,000 francs × $.16) to reflect the dollar denominated amount of the loan. In the income statement, the transaction loss of 125,000 francs is translated using the average exchange rate. When the current rate method is used, the adjustment resulting from translating the accounts into dollars is made to stockholders' equity.

If, in the foregoing illustration, the loan were denominated in francs (the functional currency of the subsidiary), the translation would not be a foreign currency transaction to the subsidiary. The loan is a foreign currency transaction, however, to the U.S. bank. The bank will measure the 500,000 franc receivable into dollars at the transaction and balance sheet dates using the current rate. A transaction loss is computed at the balance sheet date as follows:

Transaction date	500,000 francs × $.20 =	$100,000
Balance sheet date	500,000 francs × $.16 =	$ 80,000
Transaction loss reported in income		$ 20,000

In the trial balance of the subsidiary, the payable is already measured in francs. Thus, a transaction gain or loss is not recognized currently in income. Note, however, that the payable is a component of the subsidiary's net asset position and will affect the translation gain or loss reported in the stockholders' equity section of the balance sheet when the payable is translated into U.S. dollars for consolidation purposes.

If the dollar is identified as the foreign entity's functional currency, then a dollar denominated transaction is not a foreign currency transaction to either party. In the dollar trial balance of the subsidiary, the payable is restated to $100,000 at both the transaction date and the balance sheet date. Finally, if the functional currency is the dollar and the loan is denominated in francs, it is a foreign currency transaction to both parties, and the 500,000 franc loan is remeasured to $80,000 at the balance sheet date by both.

INTERCOMPANY RECEIVABLES AND PAYABLES

SFAS No. 52 requires that transaction gains and losses on intercompany receivables and payables be recognized in the period that the exchange rate changes. The procedures for doing so are similar to those discussed in the preceding section. However, a company is required to distinguish between transactions that are of a long-term investment nature and other transactions. Intercompany transactions for which settlement is not planned or intended in the foreseeable future are considered a part of the net investment in the foreign entity. Accordingly, transaction gains or losses on the receivable or payable, whether denominated in dollars or in the local currency of the foreign entity, are deferred and accumulated with the translation adjustment in a separate component of stockholders' equity. A transaction gain or loss attributable to other intercompany accounts is reported currently in the determination of net income because it is expected to affect functional currency cash flows.

ELIMINATION OF INTERCOMPANY PROFIT

Profits and losses attributable to intercompany sales or transfers are eliminated on the basis of the exchange rate at the date of each sale or transfer. Here again, the use of averages or reasonable approximations of specific rates in effect on the due date of each transaction is permitted. To illustrate, the following assumptions are made:

1. Exchange rates: date of sale, $.14; balance sheet date, $.17.
2. The intercompany sale and profit in dollars and francs is:

	DOLLARS	FRANCS
Sales price to foreign subsidiary	14,000	100,000
Cost to parent company	10,500	75,000
Intercompany profit	3,500	25,000

3. None of the inventory was sold by the subsidiary during the current period.
4. The franc is the functional currency of the foreign entity.

At year-end, the inventory balance of 100,000 francs is translated to $17,000 using the current rate at the balance sheet date. In the consolidated balance sheet, the intercompany profit of $3,500 is eliminated from the inventory, which results in a carrying value for the inventory of $13,500. As shown below, this process includes $750 in the inventory carrying value that is related to the effect of the exchange rate change on the intercompany profit element.

	FRANCS	TRANSLATION RATE	DOLLARS
Inventory cost	75,000	.17	12,750
Intercompany profit	25,000	(.17 − .14)	750
Carrying value of ending inventory	100,000		13,500

The Board reasoned that intercompany profit occurs at the date of sale and that is the amount that should be eliminated. The $750 results from a subsequent change in the exchange rate, an event considered independent from the sale.

LIQUIDATION OF A FOREIGN INVESTMENT

Upon the sale of part or all of an investment in a foreign entity, a pro-rata share of the amount included in the accumulated translation adjustment equity account associated with that foreign investment is removed and reported as part of the gain or loss from the disposition of the investment.[18] For example, if a company disposed of 50% of its interest in a foreign entity, 50% of the related accumulated translation adjustment would be removed from stockholders' equity and recognized in measuring the gain or loss on the sale.

Questions

1. What requirements must be satisfied if a foreign subsidiary is to be consolidated?

2. What is meant by an entity's functional currency and what are the economic indicators identified by the FASB to provide guidance in selecting the functional currency?

3. The _____ is the functional currency of a foreign subsidiary with operations that are relatively self-contained and integrated within the country in which it is located. In such cases, the _____ method of translation would be used to translate the accounts into dollars.

4. The _____ is the functional currency of a foreign subsidiary that is a direct and integral component or extention of a U.S. parent company. In such cases, the _____ method of translation is used to translate (remeasure) the accounts into dollars.

5. Which method of translation is used to remeasure the financial statements when a foreign subsidiary operates in a highly inflationary economy?

6. Define remeasurement.

7. Under the current rate method, how are assets and liabilities that are stated in a foreign currency translated?

8. How does the method of accounting for a business combination (purchase or pooling of interests) affect the translation of a foreign affiliate's financial statements when the current rate method is used to translate the accounts?

[18]*FASB Interpretation No. 37*, "Accounting for Translation Adjustment Upon Sale of Part of an Investment in a Foreign Entity" (Norwalk, Conn., FASB, 1983), par. 2.

9. What is the objective of the temporal method of translation?

10. Assuming that the temporal method is used, how are revenue and expense items in foreign currency financial statements translated?

11. A translation adjustment results from the process of translating financial statements of a foreign subsidiary from its functional currency into dollars. Where is the translation adjustment reported in the financial statements if the current rate method is used to translate the accounts?

Exercises

Exercise 15-1

Accounts are listed below for a foreign subsidiary that maintains its books in its local currency. The equity interest in the subsidiary was acquired in a purchase transaction. In the space provided, indicate the exchange rate that would be used to translate the accounts into dollars assuming that the functional currency was identified (a) as the U.S. dollar and (b) as the foreign entity's local currency. Use the following letters to identify the exchange rate:

H—historical exchange rate
C—current exchange rate
A—average exchange rate for the current period.

ACCOUNT	EXCHANGE RATE IF THE FUNCTIONAL CURRENCY IS:	
	U.S. DOLLAR	LOCAL CURRENCY
Cash		
Accounts receivable		
Inventory carried at cost		
Inventory carried at market		
Prepaid rent		
Property, plant, and equipment		
Goodwill		
Accounts payable		
Bonds payable		
Unamortized premium on bonds payable		
Preferred stock carried at issuance price		
Common stock		
Sales		
Cost of goods sold		
Depreciation expense		

Exercise 15-2

Select the best answer for each of the following items:

1. Golf Company acquired 80% of the outstanding stock of Ping Company, a foreign company, in an acquisition accounted for as a purchase transaction. In preparing consolidated statements, the paid-in capital of Ping Company should be translated into dollars at the
(a) Current exchange rate in effect at the balance sheet date.
(b) Exchange rate in effect at the date the capital transactions of the subsidiary took place.

(c) Exchange rate in effect at the date Golf Company purchased the Ping Company stock.

(d) Exchange rate effective when Ping Company was organized.

2. The account balances of a foreign entity are required by *SFAS No. 52* to be measured using that entity's functional currency. The functional currency of an entity is defined as
   (a) The currency in which the entity's transactions are recorded.
   (b) The currency of the primary economic environment in which the entity operates.
   (c) The U.S. dollar.
   (d) The local currency of the country in which the entity is physically located.

3. When translating foreign currency financial statements for an entity whose functional currency is the local currency of the country in which it is physically located, which of the following accounts is translated using current exchange rates?

	BONDS PAYABLE	INVENTORIES CARRIED AT MARKET
(a)	No	No
(b)	Yes	No
(c)	No	Yes
(d)	Yes	Yes

4. A translation adjustment (or translation gain) that is a consequence of translation of a functional currency that is different from the reporting currency should be
   (a) Deferred and amortized over a period not to exceed 40 years.
   (b) Deferred until a subsequent year when a loss occurs and offset it against that loss.
   (c) Included as a separate item in the equity section of the balance sheet.
   (d) Included in net income in the period in which it occurs.

5. A wholly owned foreign subsidiary of Import Corporation has certain expense accounts for the year ended December 31, 1995, stated in local currency units (LCU) as follows:

	LCU
Amortization of patent (patent was acquired January 1, 1993)	40,000
Provision for doubtful accounts	40,000
Rent	120,000

The exchange rates at various dates are as follows:

	DOLLAR EQUIVALENT OF 1 LCU
December 31, 1995	$.20
Average for the year ended December 31, 1995	.24
January 1, 1993	.25

The subsidiary's operations were an extension of the parent company's operations. What total dollar amount should be included in Import's income statement to reflect the foregoing expenses for the year ended December 31, 1995?
   (a) $48,000.
   (b) $40,000.
   (c) $48,400.
   (d) $42,000.

(AICPA adapted)

Exercise 15-3

Select the best answer choice for each of the following items.

1. Perez Company's operations are unrelated to the operations of its subsidiary. Certain balance sheet accounts of the foreign subsidiary at December 31, 1995, have been translated into U.S. dollars as follows:

	TRANSLATED AT:	
	CURRENT RATES	HISTORICAL RATES
Accounts receivable, current	$200,000	$220,000
Accounts receivable, long-term	130,000	140,000
Prepaid insurance	50,000	55,000
Goodwill	100,000	110,000

   If the accounting is in accordance with *SFAS No. 52*, what total should be included in Perez's balance sheet at December 31, 1995, for the foregoing items?
   (a) $480,000.
   (b) $490,000.
   (c) $495,000.
   (d) $580,000.

2. When the functional currency of a foreign operation is the U.S. dollar, translation gains and losses resulting from translating (remeasuring) foreign currency financial statements into U.S. dollars should be included as
   (a) An extraordinary item in the income statement for the period in which the rate changes.
   (b) An ordinary item in the income statement for losses but deferred for gains in accordance with the conservatism convention.
   (c) An ordinary item in the income statement for the period in which the rate changes.
   (d) A deferred item in the balance sheet.

3. Pal Company is translating account balances of its foreign subsidiary into dollars for its December 31, 1995, balance sheet and its 1995 income statement. The functional currency was identified as the local currency of the foreign subsidiary. The average exchange rate for 1995 should be used to translate
   (a) Retained earnings at January 1, 1995.
   (b) Equipment purchased in 1995.
   (c) Sales for 1995.
   (d) Cash at December 31, 1995.

4. One of the first steps in translating the financial statements of a foreign subsidiary is the identification of the functional currency of that entity. Which of the following indicates that the functional currency is the local currency of the foreign entity?
   (a) There is a high volume of intercompany transactions.
   (b) Financing is primarily denominated in the local currency.
   (c) Sales are mostly in the United States, or sales contracts are denominated in dollars.
   (d) Sales prices are primarily responsive in the short term to exchange rate changes.

5. When the foreign operations are conducted in a highly inflationary economy, at what translation rates should the goodwill and accounts receivable accounts in foreign statements be translated into U.S. dollars?

	GOODWILL	ACCOUNTS RECEIVABLE
(a)	Current	Average for year
(b)	Historical	Current
(c)	Historical	Historical
(d)	Current	Current

(AICPA adapted)

Exercise 15-4

On January 1, 1995, Trenten Systems, a U.S.-based company, purchased a controlling interest in Grant Management Consultants located in Zurich, Switzerland. The acquisition was treated as a purchase transaction. The 1995 financial statements stated in Swiss francs are given below.

GRANT MANAGEMENT CONSULTANTS
Comparative Balance Sheets
January 1 and December 31, 1995

	JAN. 1	DEC. 31
Cash and receivables	20,000	55,000
Net property, plant, and equipment	40,000	37,000
Totals	60,000	92,000
Accounts and notes payable	30,000	32,000
Common stock	20,000	20,000
Retained earnings	10,000	40,000
Totals	60,000	92,000

GRANT MANAGEMENT CONSULTANTS
Combined Income and Retained Earnings Statement
For the Year Ended December 31, 1995

Revenues	75,000
Operating expenses including depreciation of 3,000 francs	30,000
Net income	45,000
Dividends declared and paid	15,000
Increase in retained earnings	30,000

Direct exchange rates for the Swiss franc are:

	DOLLARS PER FRANC
January 1, 1995	$.5987
December 31, 1995	.5321
Average for 1995	.5654
Dividend declaration and payment date	.5810

Required:

A. Translate the year-end balance sheet and income statement of the foreign subsidiary using the current rate method of translation.

B. Prepare a schedule to verify the translation adjustment.

Exercise 15-5

Use the information provided in Exercise 15-4.

Required:

A. Translate (remeasure) the financial statements of the foreign subsidiary using the temporal method of translation.

B. Prepare a schedule to verify the translation gain or loss.

Exercise 15-6

Refer to Exercise 15-4. Using the same information, assume that the West German mark is identified as the functional currency of the subsidiary.

Required:

A. Remeasure the account balances that are expressed in Swiss francs in West German marks. Direct exchange rates for the West German mark are:

	MARKS PER FRANC
Beginning of current year	1.3940
End of current year	1.2899
Average for current year	1.3445
Dividend payment date	1.2438

B. Translate the remeasured accounts that are now stated in West German marks into dollars using the current rate method. Direct exchange rates for the West German mark are:

	DOLLARS PER MARK
Beginning of current year	$.4891
End of current year	.4630
Average for current year	.4751
Dividend payment date	.4740

Exercise 15-7

Dorsey Corporation purchased 90% of the common stock of Lansing Company on January 1, 1989. The cost of the investment was equal to the book value interest acquired. Dorsey Corporation accounted for the acquisition as a purchase transaction. Lansing Company operates two retail stores and an exporting business in London that specializes in buying and selling British tweeds. The subsidiary provided the following financial statements in pounds to the parent company:

LANSING COMPANY
Combined Income and Retained Earnings Statement
For the Year Ended December 31, 1995

Sales	2,900,000
Cost of goods sold	(1,400,000)
Depreciation expense	(300,000)
Other expenses	(400,000)
Net income	800,000
1/1 Retained earnings	900,000
	1,700,000
Less: Dividends declared and paid, December 31	(325,000)
12/31 Retained earnings	1,375,000

LANSING COMPANY
Balance Sheet
December 31, 1995

Cash and receivables	1,275,000
Merchandise inventory	490,000
Property, plant, and equipment	3,450,000
Total	5,215,000
Current liabilities	640,000
Long-term notes payable	1,200,000
Capital stock	2,000,000
Retained earnings	1,375,000
Total	5,215,000

Lansing Company was incorporated on January 1, 1987, at which time all the property, plant, and equipment was purchased. The long-term notes were issued to partially finance the purchase of the fixed assets.

Direct exchange rates for the British pound are as follows:

January 1, 1987	$1.8996
January 1, 1989	1.8365
Average for the last quarter 1994	1.5300
January 1, 1995	1.4919
December 31, 1995	1.4730
Average for 1995	1.4788
Average for August–December 1995	1.4950

The January 1, 1995, retained earnings balance of Lansing in dollars was $1,593,408, and the cumulative translation adjustment was a debit balance of $939,898. The beginning inventory of £420,000 was acquired during the last quarter of 1994 and the ending inventory was acquired during the last five months of 1995. Sales were made and purchases and other expenses were incurred evenly during the year.

Required:

Translate the December 31, 1995, account balances of Lansing Company into dollars assuming that the pound is the functional currency of Lansing Company.

Exercise 15-8

Refer to the data provided in Exercise 15-7 for Dorsey Corporation and Lansing Company.

Required:

Translate (remeasure) the account balances of Lansing into dollars assuming that the dollar is the functional currency of Lansing Company. The beginning retained earnings balance of Lansing Company in dollars was $1,791,324.

Exercise 15-9

Slocome Travel owns a travel agency that operates in London. Account balances in pounds for the subsidiary are summarized below:

	1995	
	JANUARY 1	DECEMBER 31
Cash and receivables	32,000	35,000
Office supplies	1,500	900
Land, building, and equipment	70,000	65,000
Accounts payable	(15,500)	(6,900)
Long-term note payable	(25,000)	(15,000)
Common stock	(40,000)	(40,000)
Retained earnings	(23,000)	(23,000)
Dividends—declared and paid		
on December 31	—	4,000
Revenues	—	(40,000)
Operating expenses	—	20,000
Totals	–0–	–0–

Exchange rates for 1995 were as follows:

January 1	$1.5403
December 31	1.5961
Average for year	1.5532

The subsidiary did not make any purchases of office supplies or plant assets during the year. Revenues were earned and operating expenses, other than depreciation and supplies used, were incurred evenly throughout the year.

Required:

A. Prepare a schedule to compute the translation adjustment for the year, assuming the foreign entity's functional currency is the pound.

B. Prepare a schedule to compute the translation gain or loss, assuming the foreign entity's functional currency is the U.S. dollar.

C. Explain why your results differ under the two methods.

Exercise 15-10A

A U.S. company owns an 80% interest in a company located in West Germany. During the year the parent company sold inventory that had cost $24,000 to the subsidiary on account for $30,000 when the exchange rate was $.5192. The subsidiary still held one-half of the inventory and had not paid the parent company for the purchase at the end of the fiscal period. The unsettled account is denominated in dollars. The exchange rate at the fiscal year-end was $.4994.

Required:

A. (1) Compute the amounts that would be reported for the inventory and accounts payable in the subsidiary's translated balance sheet. The entity's functional currency is the mark.

(2) Compute the subsidiary's transaction gain or loss on the accounts payable denominated in dollars.

(3) How is the transaction gain or loss reported in the foreign entity's financial statements?

B. Compute the amount of the intercompany profit to be eliminated in the consolidated statements workpaper prepared for the current year.

C. (1) Assuming that the transaction had been denominated in 50,204 West German marks rather than dollars, compute the transaction gain or loss that would be reported by the parent company.

(2) How is the gain or loss reported in the consolidated financial statements?

(3) How would your answer differ if the loan to the foreign subsidiary was considered to be of a long-term investment nature?

Problems

Problem 15-1

On January 1, 1995, a U.S. company purchased 100% of the outstanding stock of Ventana Grains, a company located in Latz City, New Zealand. Ventana Grains was organized on January 1, 1981. All the property, plant, and equipment held on January 1, 1995, was acquired when the company was organized. The business combination was accounted for as a purchase transaction. The 1995 financial statements for Ventana Grains, prepared in its local currency, the New Zealand dollar, are given here.

VENTANA GRAINS
Comparative Balance Sheets
January 1 and December 31, 1995

	JAN. 1	DEC. 31
Cash and receivables	500,000	880,000
Inventories	600,000	500,000
Land	400,000	400,000
Buildings (net)	650,000	605,000
Equipment (net)	465,000	470,000
Totals	2,615,000	2,855,000

	JAN. 1	DEC. 31
Short-term accounts and notes	295,000	210,000
Long-term notes (600,000 issued September 1, 1991, 80,000 issued July 1, 1995)	600,000	680,000
Common stock	800,000	800,000
Additional paid-in capital	200,000	200,000
Retained earnings	720,000	965,000
Total	2,615,000	2,855,000

VENTANA GRAINS
Combined Income and Retained Earnings Statement
For the Year Ended December 31, 1995

Revenues		3,225,000
Cost of goods sold:		
Beginning inventory	600,000 .7480	
Purchases	2,100,000 .7480	
Goods available for sale	2,700,000	
Less: Ending inventory	500,000 .7476	
Cost of goods sold		2,200,000
Gross profit on sales		1,025,000
Depreciation expense	140,000	
Other expenses	540,000	680,000
Net income		345,000
Jan. 1 Retained earnings		720,000
Total		1,065,000
Less: Dividends paid 50,000 × .7412 50000 × .7298		100,000
Dec. 31 Retained earnings		965,000

The account balances are computed in conformity with U.S. generally accepted accounting standards.

Other information is as follows:

1. Direct exchange rates for the New Zealand dollar on various dates were:

DATE	EXCHANGE RATE
January 1, 1981	$.8011
September 1, 1991	.5813
January 1, 1995	.7924
July 1, 1995	.7412
December 31, 1995	.7298
Average for 1995	.7480
Average for the last four months of 1995	.7476

2. Ventana Grains purchased additional equipment for 100,000 New Zealand dollars on July 1, 1995, by issuing a note for 80,000 New Zealand dollars and paying the balance in cash.
3. Sales were made and purchases and "Other expenses" were incurred evenly throughout the year.

4. Depreciation for the period in New Zealand dollars was computed as follows:

Building	45,000
Equipment—purchased before 1/1/1995	85,000
—purchased July 1, 1995	10,000

5. The inventory is valued on a FIFO basis. The beginning inventory was acquired when the exchange rate was $.7480. The ending inventory was acquired during the last four months of 1995.

6. Dividends of 50,000 New Zealand dollars were paid on July 1 and December 31.

Required:

A. Translate the financial statements into dollars assuming that the local currency of the foreign subsidiary was identified as its functional currency.

B. Prepare a schedule to verify the translation adjustment determined in part (A). Describe how the translation adjustment would be reported in the financial statements.

Problem 15-2

Refer to the information given in Problem 15-1.

Required:

A. Remeasure the financial statements into dollars assuming that the U.S. dollar was identified as the functional currency of the foreign subsidiary.

B. Prepare a schedule to verify the translation gain or loss determined in part (A). Describe how the translation gain or loss would be reported in the financial statements.

Problem 15-3

(This problem is a continuation of the illustration presented in the chapter.)

On January 2, 1995, P Company, a U.S.-based company, acquired for 2,000,000 francs an 80% interest in SFr Company, a French company. On January 2, 1995, SFr Company reported a retained earnings balance of 480,000 francs. SFr's books are maintained in francs and are in conformity with U.S. generally accepted accounting principles. Trial balances of the two companies as of December 31, 1996, are presented here:

DEBITS	P COMPANY (DOLLARS)	SFr COMPANY (FRANCS)
Cash	500,200	962,500
Accounts receivable	516,400	660,000
Inventories (FIFO cost)	627,800	1,037,500
Investment in SFr Company	300,000	—
Land	450,000	500,000
Buildings (net)	610,000	550,000
Equipment (net)	290,000	405,000
Dividends declared	200,000	375,000
Cost of goods sold	2,720,000	2,312,500
Depreciation expense	210,000	125,000
Other expense	914,000	818,750
Income tax expense	100,000	102,500
Totals	7,438,400	7,848,750

CREDITS

Accounts payable	540,000	800,000
Short-term notes payable	300,000	650,750
Bonds payable	700,000	850,000
Common stock	800,000	960,000
Additional paid-in capital	300,000	300,000
Retained earnings	544,400	513,000
Sales	4,200,000	3,775,000
Dividend income	54,000	—
Totals	7,438,400	7,848,750

Other information related to the subsidiary follows:

1. Beginning inventory of 830,000 francs was acquired when the exchange rate was $.165.
2. Purchases made uniformly throughout 1996 were 2,520,000 francs.
3. The franc is identified as the subsidiary's functional currency.
4. The subsidiary's beginning (1/1/96) retained earnings and cumulative translation adjustment (credit) in dollars were $75,948 and $36,462, respectively.
5. All plant assets were acquired before the parent obtained a controlling interest in the subsidiary.
6. Sales are made and all expenses are incurred uniformly throughout the year.
7. The ending inventory was acquired during the last quarter.
8. The subsidiary declared and paid dividends of 375,000 francs on September 2.
9. The following direct exchange rate quotations were available:

Date of subsidiary acquisition	$.15
Average for 1995	.156
January 1, 1996	.17
September 2, 1996	.18
December 31, 1996	.19
Average for the 4th quarter, 1996	.185
Average for 1996	.176

Required:

A. Prepare a translated balance sheet and combined statement of income and retained earnings for the subsidiary.

B. Prepare a schedule to verify the translation adjustment.

C. Compute the following ratios based on the franc and the U.S. dollar financial statements.
   (1) Current ratio.
   (2) Debt to equity.
   (3) Gross profit percentage.
   (4) Net income to sales.

Problem 15-4

Use the information provided in Problem 15-3 for P Company and SFr Company.

Required:

A. Translate the accounts of the foreign subsidiary, assuming that the U.S. dollar is the functional currency of both companies. For this problem assume that the subsidiary's beginning (1/1/96) retained earnings balance in the translated balance sheet is $76,660.

B. Prepare a schedule to verify the translation gain or loss, assuming a 637,000 franc net exposed liability position at the beginning of the year.

Problem 15-5

Pasquale Company is a manufacturer of oil drilling equipment located in Canada. The company is 90% owned by a U.S. parent company. The accounting department of Pasquale Company accumulated the following 1995 information for the company's auditor.

EQUIPMENT

1. The equipment account contained the following items:

DESCRIPTION	COST (CAN. $)	USEFUL LIFE	ACQUISITION DATE	EXCHANGE RATE ON ACQUISITION DATE
Drill press	30,000	5 years	July 15, 1991	$.8430
Stamping press	80,000	4 years	January 2, 1993	.7360
Fork lift	42,000	6 years	September 1, 1994	.6998

2. Pasquale Company depreciates assets by the straight-line method and assumes a zero residual value.
3. Its policy is to take a full year's depreciation on all depreciable assets acquired before July 1 and no depreciation on all depreciable assets acquired after July 1.

INVENTORY

1. The beginning inventory of 60,000 Canadian dollars was acquired during the last quarter of 1994.
2. Inventory purchases of 400,000 Canadian dollars were made uniformly during the year.
3. The ending inventory of 60,000 Canadian dollars was acquired during November and December, 1995.

MARKETABLE SECURITIES

1. Marketable securities, carried at cost, were acquired for 30,000 Canadian dollars when the direct exchange rate was $.9320.

DIRECT EXCHANGE RATES

Average for the last quarter of 1994, $.7322

January 1, 1995, $.7080

Average for November and December, 1995, $.6845

Average for 1995, $.7140

December 31, 1995, $.6960

Required:

A. Compute the account balances that would be reported for equipment, inventory, and marketable securities in the December 31, 1995, balance sheet expressed in U.S. dollars, assuming that the temporal method was used to translate the accounts.

B. Compute the depreciation expense and cost of goods sold for 1995 in U.S. dollars, assuming that the temporal method was used to translate the accounts.

C. Repeat parts (A) and (B), assuming that the current rate method was used to translate the accounts.

D. Contrast the effects on income from using the current rate method and the temporal method to translate cost of goods sold and depreciation expense. Explain why net income is increased or decreased when the accounts were translated using the current rate method.

Problem 15-6A

For this problem, refer to the information provided in Problem 15-3 for P Company and SFr Company. Ignore deferred income taxes in the assignment of the difference between cost and book value.

Required:

A. If you have not already done so, prepare a workpaper to translate the trial balance of the subsidiary into dollars using the current rate method.

B. Prepare the journal entries made on the books of P Company during 1996 to account for its investment in SFr Company. P Company uses the cost method to record its investment in SFr Company. At the date of acquisition, the 608,000 franc difference between cost and book value interest acquired was allocated as follows:

ASSET	FRANCS	TRANSLATION RATE	DOLLARS
Land	308,000	$.15	46,200
Building	300,000	.15	45,000
Total	608,000		91,200

The building is depreciated over a 10-year remaining life using the straight-line method of amortization.

C. Prepare a consolidated statements workpaper at December 31, 1996.

Problem 15-7A

P Company holds an 80% interest in SFr Company, a French company. A trial balance for P Company and SFr Company at December 31, 1996, and other data are given in Problems 15-3 and 15-4. Ignore deferred income taxes in the assignment of the difference between cost and book value.

Required:

A. If you have not already done so (Problem 15-4), prepare a workpaper to translate the trial balance of the subsidiary into dollars using the temporal method of translation. The subsidiary's beginning retained earnings balance in the translated balance sheet is $76,660.

B. Prepare the journal entries made on the books of P Company during 1996 to account for the investment in SFr Company. P Company uses the cost method to record its investment in SFr Company. At the date of acquisition, the 608,000 franc difference between cost and book value interest acquired was allocated as follows:

ASSET	FRANCS	TRANSLATION RATE	DOLLARS
Land	308,000	$.15	46,200
Building	300,000	.15	45,000
Total	608,000		91,200

The building is depreciated over a 10-year remaining life using the straight-line method of amortization.

C. Prepare a consolidated statements workpaper at December 31, 1996.

Problem 15-8A

Babbit, Inc., a multinational corporation based in the United States, owns an 80% interest in Nakima Company, which is located in Sydney, Australia. The acquisition, which was made on January 1, 1995, was accounted for using the purchase method of accounting. The difference between cost of 648,500 Australian dollars and the book value of the 80% interest acquired was attributed to specific assets of Nakima Company as follows:

	80% OF DIFFERENCE (AUSTRALIAN DOLLARS)
Equipment that has a 5-year remaining life	59,100
Land	43,250
Inventories—Nakima uses the FIFO cost flow assumption in pricing its inventory	21,750
Amount that could not be assigned to specific assets or liabilities (amortize over 10 years)	120,000
Total difference in Australian dollars	244,100

Ignore deferred income taxes in the assignment of the difference between cost and book value. The adjusted trial balances for the two companies on December 31, 1995 are presented here:

DEBITS	BABBIT INC. (U.S. DOLLARS)	NAKIMA COMPANY (AUSTRALIAN DOLLARS)
Cash	65,885	95,250
Accounts receivable	150,116	106,250
12/31 Inventory	115,000	83,250
Investment in Nakima Company	514,585	–0–
Land	59,400	187,500
Buildings and equipment	200,000	250,000
Cost of goods sold	425,000	121,500
Other expenses	75,000	51,750
Dividends declared	50,000	31,250
Totals	1,654,986	926,750

CREDITS

Accumulated depreciation	125,000	93,750
Accounts payable	14,750	62,500
Notes payable	25,000	15,000
Capital stock	600,000	340,500
1/1 Retained earnings	325,000	165,000
Sales	545,475	250,000
Dividend income	19,761	–0–
Totals	1,654,986	926,750

Other information:

1. Sales, purchases, and other expenses were incurred evenly during the year.
2. Dividends of 15,625 Australian dollars were paid on April 30 and October 31.
3. The accounts are presented in conformity with U.S. generally accepted accounting principles.
4. Direct rates of exchange:

1/1/95	$.7935
4/30/95	.7899
10/31/95	.7910
12/31/95	.7575
Average for 1995	.7962

5. The Australian dollar is identified as the functional currency of Nakima Company.

Required:

A. Prepare a workpaper to translate the trial balance of the subsidiary into U.S. dollars.

B. Prepare a schedule to verify the translation adjustment.

C. Prepare journal entries on the books of the parent company to record the purchase of the 80% interest in the subsidiary and to apply the cost method of accounting.

D. Prepare a consolidated statements workpaper at December 31, 1995. Journal entries made in part (C) that are not reflected in the trial balance of Babbit, Inc. are to be made as adjusting entries in the elimination columns of the workpaper.

16

REPORTING FOR SEGMENTS AND INTERIM FINANCIAL PERIODS

REPORTING FOR SEGMENTS

In previous chapters we have dealt with the process of aggregating the financial data relating to the activities of an affiliated group of companies. Investors and lenders holding equity or creditor interests are aware of the importance of consolidated statements in reporting the financial position and results of operations of a group of companies under common control. At the same time, investors, creditors, and other users of financial statements also need disaggregated data that provide information about the various segments of an enterprise or affiliated group of companies.

NEED FOR DISAGGREGATED FINANCIAL DATA

Research studies conducted by various organizations such as the Financial Executives Research Foundation, the Financial Analysts Federation, and the National Association of Accountants concluded that financial statement users want information to aid them in evaluating prospective investments. If return on investment is computed on the basis of expected cash flows, the evaluation of risk requires an assessment of the uncertainty surrounding both the timing and the amount of these expected cash flows. Major uncertainty results from (1) factors unique to individual companies, (2) factors related to the industries and geographical areas in which those companies operate, and (3) related national and international economic and political factors.

Statement users use financial statement information to determine conditions, trends, and ratios that assist them in predicting cash flows of firms. These factors are often compared with those of other firms, as well as with industry-wide data, and general national and international economic information is considered in making an overall evaluation of the risk involved. When a firm engages in activities in several industries or geographic areas, analysis and the process used to predict future cash flows become more complex. Different industries or geographic areas may have different rates of profitability, opportunities for growth, and types of risk. Thus, many statement users reported that, although consolidated financial information is important, it is more useful if supplemented with disaggregated information to assist them in analyzing the uncertainties surrounding the timing and amount of expected cash flows.

STANDARDS OF FINANCIAL ACCOUNTING AND REPORTING

Recognizing the importance of "segment" data and the necessity of establishing standards for disclosure, the Financial Accounting Standards Board issued *Statement of Financial Accounting Standards (SFAS) No. 14*, "Financial Reporting for Segments of a Business Enterprise." *SFAS No. 14*, as amended by *SFAS No. 21*, requires that information concerning (1) the enterprise's operations in different industries (segments), (2) its foreign operations and export sales, and (3) its major customers be included in its financial statements when a complete set of financial statements is issued in conformity with generally accepted accounting principles for a fiscal period.[1] If statements are presented for more than one period, the required information must be presented for each period. The information required should be a disaggregation of **consolidated financial information** where the firm has consolidated subsidiaries, and a disaggregation of the individual firm data if it has no consolidated subsidiaries.

Although transactions among affiliates are eliminated in the preparation of consolidated financial statements, intersegment transactions are **included** in the segment information for purposes of the application of *SFAS No. 14*. Thus, revenue reported for a segment includes sales to outside parties and sales or transfers to other segments. The same principle applies to intersegment expenses. A reconciliation of segment information with amounts reported in consolidated financial statements is then required.

Disaggregation by Segment   *SFAS No. 14* requires that financial statements include certain information about the industry segments of the firm. Before discussing procedures for determining (1) the types of information required, (2) appropriate segments, and (3) methods of presentation, some terms must be defined because

---

enterprise other than (1) one whose debt or equity securities are traded in a public market on a foreign or domestic stock exchange or in the over-the-counter market (including securities quoted only locally or regionally), or (2) one that is required to file financial statements with the Securities and Exchange Commission. In addition, the disclosures are not required in interim reports.

they have been given specific definitions for purposes of reporting on industry segments. The terms and their definitions are:

a) *Industry segment.* A component of an enterprise engaged in providing a product or service or a group of related products and services primarily to unaffiliated customers for a profit. Because an industry segment is defined in terms of products and services that are sold primarily to unaffiliated customers, the disaggregation of the vertically integrated operations of an enterprise is not required.

b) *Reportable segment.* An industry segment (or, in certain cases, a group of two or more closely related industry segments) for which information is required to be reported.

c) *Revenue.* The revenue of an industry segment includes revenue both from sales to unaffiliated customers and from intersegment sales or transfers, if any, of products and services similar to those sold to unaffiliated customers. (Intersegment billings for the cost of shared facilities or other jointly incurred costs do **not** represent intersegment sales or transfers.) Interest from sources outside the enterprise and interest earned on intersegment trade receivables is included in revenue if the asset on which the interest is earned is included among the industry segment's identifiable assets, but interest earned on advances or loans to other industry segments generally is not included unless the advances or loans are made by a segment whose primary function is of a financial nature (bank, finance company, etc.). Revenue from intersegment sales or transfers is accounted for on the basis used by the enterprise to price the intersegment sales or transfers.

d) *Operating profit or loss.* The operating profit or loss of an industry segment is its revenue as defined above minus all operating expenses. Operating expenses include expenses that relate to both revenue from sales to unaffiliated customers and revenue from intersegment sales or transfers. Those operating expenses incurred by an enterprise that are not directly traceable to an industry segment must be allocated on a reasonable basis among those segments for whose benefit the expenses were incurred. Intersegment purchases are accounted for on the same basis as intersegment sales or transfers. The following items are **excluded** in computing the operating profit or loss of the segment:
   1) Revenue earned at the corporate level (e.g., investment income) and not derived from the operations of an industry segment.
   2) General corporate expenses.
   3) Interest expense (unless the segment is a financial organization).
   4) Income taxes.
   5) Equity in income or loss of equity method investees.
   6) Gain or loss on discontinued operations.
   7) Extraordinary items.
   8) Noncontrolling interest.
   9) The cumulative effect of a change in accounting principle.

e) *Identifiable assets.* Those tangible and intangible assets that are used by the industry segment, including (1) assets that are used exclusively by that segment and (2) an allocated portion of assets used jointly by two or more segments. Assets used jointly are allocated among the segments on a reasonable basis. Because the assets of a segment that transfers products or services to another segment are not used in the operations of the receiving segment, no amount of those assets is allocated to the receiving segment. Assets that represent part of an enterprise's investment in a segment, such as goodwill, are included in the industry segment's identifiable assets. Assets maintained for general corporate purposes (those not used in the operations of any segment) are not allocated. Advances or loans to or investments in another segment are not included unless they represent advances or loans from a financial segment to other segments. (Advances or loans from a financial segment are included because the income therefrom is included in computing the financial segment's operating profit or loss.) Asset valuation allowances are deducted in computing the amount of a segment's identifiable assets.[2]

Two of the most difficult tasks in applying the segment disclosure requirements are those of determining (1) an appropriate basis for the allocation of joint operating expenses and (2) appropriate industry segments.

Joint Operating Expense Allocation *SFAS No. 14* provides that, to compute operating profit or loss of segments, operating expenses that are not directly traceable to an industry segment must be allocated on a reasonable basis among those segments for whose benefit the expenses were incurred. Emphasis is on *operating* expenses; general corporate expenses are not allocated. Unfortunately, no guidelines as to appropriate bases for allocation are provided; thus, the allocation process must depend to a large extent on the judgment of management.

Although judgment must be used, research mentioned earlier contains recommendations concerning common cost allocation methods. Probably the most extensive study on appropriate allocation methods was conducted by the Cost Accounting Standards Board, and its recommendations were issued in *Cost Accounting Standard No. 403*. Although *Standard No. 403* concerns the problem of allocating joint home office expenses to segments of an organization involved in defense contracts, the general guidelines developed should be useful in applying the allocation provisions of *SFAS No. 14*. In essence, *Cost Accounting Standard No. 403* suggests that, where possible, joint costs should be accumulated into logical and relatively homogeneous expense pools. The pools are then allocated to segments on the basis of beneficial or casual relationships as measured by activity or output of the segments.

For example, joint data-processing expenses might be allocated on the basis of machine time or number of reports, joint personnel administration expenses on the basis of number of personnel or total labor hours, and joint centralized warehouse expenses on the basis of square footage, value of materials, or volume of transactions. Any remaining expenses that cannot be logically included in any of the homogeneous expense pools are allocated proportionately under a three-factor formula based on payroll costs, revenue, and assets of the segments. That is, the

---

[2] *Statement of Financial Accounting Standards No. 14*, "Financial Reporting for Segments of a Business Enterprise" (Norwalk, Conn.: FASB, 1976), par. 10.

percentage of the residual expenses to be allocated to any segment is the arithmetical average of the following three percentages:

1. The segment's payroll dollars to the total payroll dollars of all segments.

2. The segment's operating revenue to the total operating revenue of all segments.

3. The average net book value of the sum of the segment's tangible capital assets plus inventories to the total average net book value of such assets of all segments.

Determining Reportable Segments   *SFAS No. 14* provides that reportable segments of the firm are to be determined by identifying the products and services from which the firm obtains its revenues, grouping those products and services by industry lines into industry segments, and selecting those segments that are significant with respect to the firm as a whole.

Determination of the firm's industry segments must depend to a large extent on the judgment of management. Many firms maintain profit centers for individual products and services, or groups of related products and services, to accumulate information about revenue and profitability. These profit centers represent a starting point for the determination of the firm's industry segments. If a profit center crosses industry lines, it is, of course, necessary to disaggregate that profit center into smaller groups of related products and services. If a firm operates in more than one industry, but does not maintain profit centers, it must disaggregate its operations along industry lines.

If the firm accumulates data along industry lines for its foreign operations, or if it is practicable to do so, segments should be determined on a worldwide basis. If it is impracticable to disaggregate part or all of its foreign operations, the firm should disaggregate its domestic operations and foreign operations for which disaggregation is practicable along industry lines and treat the remainder of its foreign operations as a single industry segment. Disclosure should be made of the types of industries included in the foreign operations that have not been disaggregated. In addition, as discussed in a later section, data concerning significant foreign operations and export sales must also be disclosed.

Each segment that is significant to the enterprise as a whole must be identified as a reportable segment. A segment is considered to be significant if it meets **one or more** of the following tests, the tests being applied separately for each fiscal year for which financial statements are prepared:

a) Its revenue, as defined earlier, is 10% or more of the combined revenue of all of the enterprise's industry segments.

b) The absolute amount of its operating profit or operating loss is 10% or more of the greater, in absolute amount, of:
  1) The combined operating profit of all industry segments that did not incur an operating loss, or
  2) The combined operating loss of all industry segments that did incur an operating loss.

c) Its identifiable assets are 10% or more of the combined identifiable assets of all industry segments.[3]

Revenue, operating profit or loss, and identifiable assets relating to those foreign operations that have not been disaggregated along industry lines on grounds of impracticability are included in computing the combined revenue, combined operating profit or loss, and combined identifiable assets of the firm's segments.

An example of the application of these tests for Papco, Inc. is presented in Illustration 16-1.

ILLUSTRATION 16-1
Significance Tests
(Thousands of Dollars)
Papco, Inc.

			SEGMENTS			
REVENUE TEST	LUMBER	PAPER	PRINTING	FURNITURE	LEATHER	COMBINED
Sales to Unaffiliated Customers	$16,000	$3,000	$2,000	$1,500	$1,000	$23,500
Intersegment Sales	5,000	2,000	500	500	–0–	8,000
Total Revenue	$21,000	$5,000	$2,500	$2,000	$1,000	$31,500

The lumber and paper segments are reportable segments under the revenue test because their total revenues are at least 10% of combined total revenue of $31,500, whereas the other segments are not reportable segments under this test.

OPERATING PROFIT TEST

Operating Profit (Loss)	$2,500	$600	$(300)	$150	$(100)	$2,850

The lumber and paper segments are reportable segments under the operating profit test because the absolute amounts of their operating profit or loss are each **at least 10% of the greater of** (1) the combined profit of all industry segments that did not incur a loss ($2,500 + $600 + $150 = $3,250), or (2) the combined loss of all industry segments that incurred a loss ($300 + $100 = $400). The other segments are not reportable segments under this test.

IDENTIFIABLE ASSETS TEST

Identifiable Assets	$25,000	$12,000	$8,000	$3,000	$4,000	$52,000

The lumber, paper, and printing segments are reportable segments because their identifiable assets are at least 10% of combined identifiable assets of $52,000. The furniture and leather segments are not reportable segments under this test.

Thus, the lumber, paper, and printing segments are all reportable (subject to one further test discussed later) because they meet one or more of the three tests. The furniture and leather segments would be reported in combined form.

The results of the tests should be evaluated from the standpoint of comparability. Thus, a segment that has been significant in the past and is expected to be significant in the future should be treated as a reportable segment even though it fails to meet a test in the current year. Conversely, a segment that has been insig-

---

[3]Ibid., par. 15.

nificant in the past and is expected to be insignificant in the future should be excluded as a reportable segment even though it may meet one of the tests in the current period because of abnormally high revenues or because the combined revenue or operating profit or loss of all segments is abnormally low.

In addition to the tests described above, the reportable segments taken together must represent a substantial portion of the firm's total operations. To determine whether a substantial portion of a firm's operations are explained by its segment information, the combined revenue from sales to unaffiliated customers of all reportable segments must constitute at least 75% of the combined revenue from sales to unaffiliated customers of all industry segments. The test is applied separately for each fiscal period for which financial statements are prepared. Revenue relating to those foreign operations that have not been disaggregated along industry lines on grounds of impracticability is included in the denominator of the computation and is included in the numerator if those operations have been identified as a reportable segment.

Application of this 75% test to the situation presented in Illustration 16-1 produces the following:

$$\frac{\text{Combined sales to unaffiliated customers by the lumber, paper, and printing segments}}{\text{Combined sales to unaffiliated customers by all segments}} = \frac{(\$16,000 + \$3,000 + \$2,000)}{\$23,500} = 89\%$$

Thus, the 75% test is met, and the lumber, paper, and printing segments will be reported individually and the furniture and leather segments combined into one unit. If the 75% test had not been met, one or more of the segments that did not qualify as reportable segments under the previous tests would have to be included as reportable segments.

A firm may operate in only one industry or a major portion of its operations may be in a single industry segment and the remaining portion in one or more other segments. In this case the segment information disclosures described in the next section need *not* be made, but financial statements should identify the industry in which the major portion of the firm's operations take place. A major portion of its operations is considered to take place in a given industry segment if its revenue, operating profit or loss, and identifiable assets each constitute more than 90% of related combined totals for all industry segments.

Information to Be Presented   The following types of information must be presented for each of a firm's reportable segments, and in the aggregate for the segments that are not separately reported.

a) *Revenue.* Sales to unaffiliated customers and sales or transfers to other segments must be separately disclosed in presenting revenue of a reportable segment. The basis of accounting for intersegment sales or transfers must be disclosed. If the basis is changed, disclosure must be made of the nature of the change and its effect on the reportable segments' operating profit or loss in the period of change.

b) *Profitability.* Operating profit or loss as defined earlier must be presented for each reportable segment along with an explanation of the nature and amount of any unusual or infrequently occurring items reported in the consolidated income statement that have been added or deducted in computing operating profit or loss of the segment. In addition, a firm may elect to present some other measure of profitability for some or all segments, i.e., contribution margin, net income, or some measure of profitability between operating profit and net income. If presenting contribution margin, the firm must describe the difference between contribution margin and operating profit or loss. If presenting other measures of profitability, the nature and amount of each category of revenue or expense that was added to or deducted from operating income or loss should be disclosed.

c) *Identifiable assets.* The aggregate amount of identifiable assets as defined earlier must be presented for each segment.

d) *Other related disclosures.* Other disclosures relating to each reportable segment must be made as follows:
   1) The aggregate amount of depreciation, depletion, and amortization expense.
   2) The amount of capital expenditures for the period, i.e., additions to property, plant and equipment.
   3) The firm's equity in the net income from and investment in equity method investees whose operations are vertically integrated with the operations of that segment, and the geographic areas in which those vertically integrated equity method investees operate.
   4) The effect on the operating profit of a change in accounting principle in the period in which the change is made. (Pro forma effects of retroactive application on segments need not be disclosed.)[4]

Methods of Presentation Information about the reportable segments of a firm may be included in its financial statements in any of the following ways:

a) Within the body of the financial statements, with appropriate explanatory disclosures in the footnotes to the financial statements.

b) Entirely in the footnotes to the financial statements.

c) In a separate schedule that is included as an integral part of the financial statements. If, in a report to securityholders, that schedule is located on a page that is not clearly a part of the financial statements, the schedule must be referenced in the financial statements as an integral part thereof and covered by the auditor's opinion.[5]

Financial information such as revenue, operating profit or loss, and identifiable assets must be presented in dollar amounts; related percentages may be shown if desired.

The information required to be presented for individual reportable segments, and in the aggregate for industry segments not deemed separately reportable, must

[4]Ibid., pars. 23–27.
[5]Ibid., par. 28.

be reconciled to related amounts in the financial statements for the enterprise as a whole as follows:

a) Revenue to revenue reported in the consolidated income statement.

b) Operating profit or loss to pretax income from continuing operations in the consolidated income statement.

c) Identifiable assets to consolidated total assets, with assets maintained for general corporate purposes separately identified in the reconciliation.[6]

As an illustration of segment reporting, assume the segment data presented in Illustration 16-1. In addition, assume that the consolidated income statements and balance sheets for 1995 and 1996 for Papco, Inc. are as shown in Illustration 16-2.

Disclosure of industry segment information might take the form of the supporting schedules and footnotes as shown in Illustration 16-3 (page 611).

Foreign Operations and Export Sales

Foreign Operations *SFAS No. 14* also requires that companies distinguish between domestic and significant foreign operations, and that foreign operations be reported by country or groups of countries (geographic areas). Foreign operations are defined as those located outside the United States (or other "home country") that produce revenue from sales to unaffiliated customers or from intra-enterprise sales or transfers between countries or geographic areas. Foreign operations do *not*, however, include unconsolidated subsidiaries and investees. If operations are conducted in two or more foreign countries or geographic areas, information must be presented separately for each significant foreign country or geographic area and in the aggregate for all other foreign operations. Where the operations of some foreign countries are grouped into geographic areas, the groupings should be made on the basis of a consideration of (1) proximity, (2) economic affinity, (3) similarities of business environments, and (4) the nature, scale, and degree of interrelationship of the operations in the various countries.

"Significant" foreign operations are determined in a way similar to that used in determining reportable industry segments, except that the operating profit test is not applied. Thus, foreign operations are considered to be significant if *either* of the following tests is met:

1. Revenue generated by the foreign operations from sales to unaffiliated companies is 10% or more of consolidated revenue.

2. Identifiable assets of the firm's foreign operations are 10% or more of consolidated assets.[7]

Information to be disclosed is similar to that reported for industry segments and

[6]Ibid., par. 30.
[7]Ibid., par. 32.

ILLUSTRATION 16-2
Papco Inc.
Consolidated Income Statement
(Thousands of Dollars)

	YEAR END DECEMBER 31	
	1996	1995
Sales	$23,500	$22,100
Cost of goods sold	16,400	15,300
Selling, general, and administrative expense	4,530	4,380
Interest expense	600	570
Total cost and expense	21,530	20,250
Net	1,970	1,850
Equity in income of B Company	150	120
Income before income taxes	2,120	1,970
Income taxes	1,020	980
Net Income	$ 1,100	$ 990

Papco Inc.
Consolidated Balance Sheet
(Thousands of Dollars)

	DECEMBER 31	
	1996	1995
Cash	$ 1,870	$ 1,785
Receivables	2,640	2,860
Inventories	6,400	6,345
Investment in B Company	700	600
Plant and equipment (net of accumulated depreciation of $17,500 in 1996 and $16,200 in 1995)	41,500	40,400
Other assets	690	970
Total Assets	$53,800	$52,960
Current liabilities	$ 2,400	$ 2,320
Bonds payable	12,000	12,000
Common stock, $50 par value	30,000	30,000
Additional paid-in capital	3,000	3,000
Retained earnings	6,400	5,640
Total Liabilities and Stockholders' Equity	$53,800	$52,960

includes, for domestic operations and for each foreign country or geographic area, the following:

Revenue, with separate disclosure of sales to nonaffiliates and intracompany sales or transfers. The basis of accounting for intracompany sales and transfers and the nature and effect of any change in method should be disclosed.

Operating profit or loss, or some other measure of profitability. A common measure of profitability must be used for all countries and/or geographic areas presented.

	YEAR ENDED DECEMBER 31	
REVENUE	1996	1995
Lumber		
Sales to nonaffiliates	$16,000	$15,200
Intersegment sales	5,000	4,800
	21,000	20,000
Paper		
Sales to nonaffiliates	3,000	2,800
Intersegment sales	2,000	1,700
	5,000	4,500
Printing		
Sales to nonaffiliates	2,000	2,100
Intersegment sales	500	300
	2,500	2,400
Other		
Sales to nonaffiliates	2,500	2,000
Intersegment sales	500	460
	3,000	2,460
Total sales	31,500	29,360
Elimination of intersegment sales	8,000	7,260
Total Consolidated Revenue	$23,500	$22,100
OPERATING PROFIT OR LOSS		
Lumber	$ 2,500	$ 2,460
Paper	600	580
Printing	(300)	(430)
Other	50	70
Total Operating Profit	2,850	2,680
Corporate expense	(280)	(260)
Interest expense	(600)	(570)
Equity in net income of B Company	150	120
Income Before Income Tax	$ 2,120	$ 1,970
IDENTIFIABLE ASSETS		
Lumber	$25,000	$24,460
Paper	12,000	11,500
Printing	8,000	7,900
Other	7,000	7,520
General corporate assets	1,100	980
Investment in net assets of B Company	700	600
Total Consolidated Assets	$53,800	$52,960
DEPRECIATION AND AMORTIZATION EXPENSE		
Lumber	$ 1,300	$ 1,200
Paper	600	560
Printing	350	325
Other	240	225

	YEAR ENDED DECEMBER 31	
CAPITAL EXPENDITURES	1996	1995
Lumber	$ 1,740	$ 1,280
Paper	420	360
Printing	30	20
Other	210	240
EQUITY IN B COMPANY		
Equity in earnings	$ 150	$ 120
Investment in net assets	700	600

Note D—Industry Segments

The Company operates in three main areas, lumber products, paper products, and printing. The principal products of these operations are described in the "Business Operations" section of this report.

Intersegment sales are made at the same prices as sales to nonaffiliates. Operating profit consists of total revenue less all operating expenses except interest and general corporate expense. Identifiable assets include those directly identified with the operations of each segment plus an allocated portion of assets used jointly. Corporate assets consist primarily of cash and investments.

The Company has a 30% interest in B Company, a domestic cattle-feeding venture.

Identifiable assets, using the same procedures for presenting industry segment information.

To illustrate, foreign operations information for Papco, Inc. might be presented as shown in Illustration 16-4, assuming that the company conducts operations in the United States, Canada and Mexico.

Export Sales In addition to the foregoing disclosures concerning foreign operations, if sales by a company's *domestic* operations to *unaffiliated* foreign customers are 10% or more of consolidated revenues, the amount of those export sales should be disclosed and, where appropriate, reported by foreign country or geographic area. Although *SFAS No. 14* gives no guidance as to when it is appropriate to disclose by foreign country or geographic area, the prevalent use of the 10% or more guide throughout the *Statement* suggests that disclosure of export sales by individual foreign country or geographic area would be appropriate if the export sales to those countries or geographic areas are 10% or more of total consolidated revenues. Export sales disclosure is often presented in a separate footnote, or another section might be added to the disclosure as shown in Illustration 16-4.

Information About Major Customers

To provide information about the potential effects of dependency on one or more major customers, if 10% or more of the revenue of a firm is derived from sales to any single customer, that fact and the amount of revenue from each such customer must be disclosed. (A group of customers under common control is considered to be a single customer.) Also, if 10% or more of the revenue is derived from sales to the federal government, a state government, a local government or a foreign government, that fact and the amount of revenue must be disclosed. Disclosure should include the amount of sales to each customer and the industry segment making the sales. Customer's names, however, need not be disclosed. These disclosures are

ILLUSTRATION 16-4
Papco Inc.
Data on Operations in Different Geographic Areas
(Thousands of Dollars)

	YEAR ENDED DECEMBER 31	
REVENUE	1996	1995
United States		
Sales to nonaffiliates	$18,000	$17,500
Intracompany sales and transfers	500	600
	18,500	18,100
Canada		
Sales to nonaffiliates	4,000	3,500
Intracompany sales and tranfers	200	300
	4,200	3,800
Mexico		
Sales to nonaffiliates	1,500	1,100
Total Sales	24,200	23,000
Elimination of intracompany sales and transfers	700	900
Total Consolidated Revenue	$23,500	$22,100

Intracompany sales and transfers are made at the same prices charged for sales to nonaffiliates.

OPERATING PROFIT OR LOSS		
United States	$ 2,080	$ 2,000
Canada	570	530
Mexico	200	150
Total Operating Profit	2,850	2,680
Corporate expense	(280)	(260)
Interest expense	(600)	(570)
Equity in income of B Company	150	120
Net Income Before Tax	$ 2,120	$ 1,970

IDENTIFIABLE ASSETS		
United States	$34,000	$33,600
Canada	12,200	12,000
Mexico	5,800	5,780
General corporate assets	1,100	980
Investment in net assets of B Company	700	600
Total Consolidated Assets	$53,800	$52,960

UNITED STATES OPERATIONS EXPORT SALES	1996	1995
To japan	$2,600	$2,300
Other	300	250

required even though the firm may not be required to report information about operations in different industries or foreign operations.[8]

[8] *Statement of Financial Accounting Standards No. 30,* "Disclosure of Information about Major Customers" (Norwalk, Conn.: FASB, 1979), par. 6.

SEC RULES ON REPORTING BUSINESS SEGMENTS

The SEC, in *Release No. 236*, December 23, 1977, adopted the industry segment reporting guidelines established in *SFAS No. 14*, with a few exceptions to be discussed later. The SEC also adopted *SFAS No. 14* requirements concerning disclosure of foreign and domestic operations, major customers, and export sales. In general, the required disclosures are to be made in annual reports to stockholders, although any information required by the SEC, but not by *SFAS No. 14*, can be presented outside of the audited financial statements.

Disclosures required include all the data required by *SFAS No. 14* with the following exceptions:

1. *Major customers.* If a material part of an industry segment is dependent on a major customer or customers, and the loss of such customer or customers would have a materially adverse effect on the enterprise, the customer or customers must be *identified* and described for each segment. *SFAS No. 14* does not require identification of major customers.

2. *Intra-enterprise sales.* The basis of accounting for intra-enterprise transfers (that is, between industry segments and geographic areas) and the effect of such transfers on the revenue and/or profit or loss of the segment or geographic area must be disclosed if (a) transfers are made at prices substantially higher or lower than prevailing market prices for similar products or services or at prices substantially higher or lower than those charged to unaffiliated parties for similar products or services, and (b) the effect of the pricing practice on the revenue and/or profit or loss of a segment or geographic area is quantitatively or qualitatively material to an understanding of the business as a whole.

3. *Dominant segment.* *Release No 236* does not include a requirement relating to financial information about a dominant segment because other SEC provisions already require appropriate disclosure.

SEC rules are compared with *SFAS No. 14* requirements in Illustration 16-5.

INTERIM FINANCIAL REPORTING

In a dynamic business environment, financial information must be available on a timely basis if sound investment decisions are to be made. Although businesses have historically considered the fiscal year to be the primary reporting period, interim financial statements have been presented frequently to provide information concerning financial status and progress for time periods of less than one year. The normal time period for interim reporting is a quarter of a year (such reports are generally called quarterly reports), but other periods such as a month might be used. These interim statements are generally prepared for the most recent interim period, as well as on a cumulative or year-to-date basis; they may consist of statements of financial position, income, and cash flows. The primary focus, however, has been on the presentation of interim income information, and some companies present only interim income statements.

ILLUSTRATION 16-5
Significant Disclosure Requirements of
***SFAS No. 14* and SEC Rules**

	DISCLOSURES REQUIRED?	
REQUIREMENT	SFAS NO. *14*	SEC RULES
Applicability to annual statements	Years for which a complete set of financial statements is presented.	Most recent 5 years.
Applicability to interim statements	Voluntary	Only if, in the opinion of management, the 5-year segment data may not be indicative of current or future operations of the segment.
Industry segment data		
Revenue	Yes	Yes
Operating profit (loss)	Yes	Yes
Identifiable assets	Yes	Yes
Depreciation expense	Yes	No
Capital expenditures	Yes	No
Reconciliation of segment data to consolidated amounts	Yes	Yes
Foreign and domestic operations:		
Revenue	Yes	Yes
Operating profit, net profit, or other	Yes	Yes
Identifiable assets	Yes	Yes
Reconciliation of area data to consolidated amounts	Yes	Yes
Export sales	Yes	Yes
Major customers		
Applicability	Disclose if amounts are at least 10% of total revenue.	Disclose if a material part of the industry.
Disclosures	Amount and segment.	Customer name, relationship, and material facts.
Intersegment or interarea transfers		
Revenue by segment or area	Yes	Yes
Purchases by segment or area	No	No*
Comparative pricing data	No	No*
Other Disclosures		
Description of segment accounting policies	Identify major policies.	No
Description of segment products and services	Briefly identify.	Lengthy description of major business factors.
Effect, by segment or area, of change in accounting method or allocation method	Amount and nature of change.	No
Unusual or infrequently occurring items by segment	Amount and nature.	No

*Unless transfers are made at prices substantially higher or lower than prevailing market prices for similar products or services or at prices substantially higher or lower than those charged to unaffiliated parties for similar products or services, and the effect of the pricing practice on the revenue and/or profit or loss of a segment or geographic area is quantitatively or qualitatively material to an understanding of the business as a whole.

Publicly owned companies are generally required to file some type of quarterly report as part of the agreement with the stock exchanges that list their stock. In addition, the SEC requires public companies to file Form 10-Q with the Commission within 45 days after the end of each of the first three quarters of the fiscal year. The financial information disclosure portion of Form 10-Q requires that condensed financial statements include (1) comparative income statements for the quarter and year-to-date for the current and preceding year, (2) comparative statements of financial position at the end of the most recent quarter for the current and preceding year, and (3) comparative statements of cash flows for the current and preceding year. Most public companies also issue these reports required by the SEC to their stockholders and to other interested parties.

Problems in Interim Reporting

Although the SEC established disclosure requirements for the financial information included in Form 10-Q, the development of accounting practices to be followed in preparing interim financial reports for external reporting purposes was left to the accounting profession. No official guide or pronouncement on the practices to be used was issued until the Accounting Principles Board issued *Opinion No. 28*, "Interim Financial Reporting," in May 1973. Thus, before *APB Opinion No. 28* was issued, the form and content of interim reports and the accounting practices to be used in their preparation were left to the discretion of the reporting companies. In addition, interim reports are essentially unaudited reports. As a result, several problems evolved in the preparation of interim reports.

The seasonal nature of operations in many industries can cause wide fluctuations in revenues, expenses, and net income from one interim period to another. The relatively short time period available to determine interim results and the added cost of determining accurate figures for accruals, deferrals, and inventories encouraged the use of a variety of estimation techniques, some of which proved to be highly inaccurate. In fact, many firms used a wider variety of accounting practices and estimation procedures for interim reports than they did for year-end reports. In addition, two essentially conflicting views of the nature of interim periods exist among accountants. Some accountants hold that each interim period should stand alone as a basic accounting period; they conclude, therefore, that the results of operations for each interim period should be determined in the same manner as if the interim period were an annual period. Under this view, deferrals, accruals, and estimations at the end of each interim period are determined by following essentially the same principles and judgments that apply to annual periods.

Other accountants view each interim period as essentially an integral part of the annual period. Under this view, deferrals, accruals, and estimations at the end of each interim period are affected by judgments made at the interim date as to results of operations for the balance of the annual period. Thus, an expense item that might be considered as falling wholly within an annual accounting period could be allocated among interim periods on the basis of estimated time, sales volume, productive activity, or some other basis.[9]

---

[9] *Opinions of the Accounting Principles Board No. 28,* "Interim Financial Reporting" (New York: AICPA, May, 1973), par. 5.

As a result of the problems just described, some companies issued interim financial statements reporting significant quarterly and year-to-date income for the first three quarters, but full-year statements that reported substantial net losses. The SEC filed complaints against several companies for failure to make adequate adjustments for accruals and deferrals of revenue and expenses on an interim basis and for failing to make appropriate adjustments on an interim basis for amortization, depreciation, and inventory obsolescence. In response to SEC complaints and general pressure from the financial and investing community, the APB issued *APB Opinion No. 28* in May 1973.

APB Opinion No. 28

In *Opinion No. 28*, the Board indicated that its basic objective was "to clarify the application of accounting principles and reporting practices to interim financial information, including interim financial statements and summarized interim financial data of publicly traded companies issued for external reporting purposes."[10] The Board also concluded that "each interim period should be viewed primarily as an integral part of an annual period."[11] The Board also took the position that financial statements for each interim period should be based on the same accounting practices that are used for the preparation of annual financial statements. The *Opinion* presents guidelines for the presentation of revenue, costs associated with revenue, all other costs and expenses, and income tax provisions.

Revenue   Revenue from products sold or services performed should be recognized as earned during an interim period on the same basis as that used for the full year. In addition, business with material seasonal variations should disclose the seasonal nature of their activities.[12]

Costs Associated with Revenue   Costs and expenses that are associated directly with or allocated to the products sold or to the services rendered for annual reporting purposes should be similarly treated for interim reporting purposes. However, the following are acceptable alternatives for inventory costing.

1. Estimated gross profit rates may be used by some companies to determine the cost of goods sold during interim periods, or they may use methods other than those used for year-end inventories. Companies using these methods should disclose the method used in the interim report and any significant adjustments that result from reconciliations with the annual physical inventory.

2. Companies using the LIFO method may encounter a liquidation of base period inventories at an interim date that is expected to be replaced by the end of the annual period. In these cases, cost of goods sold should be charged with the expected replacement cost of the liquidated LIFO base.

3. Inventory losses from market declines should be recognized in the interim period in which the decline occurs. Subsequent recoveries of these losses in interim

---

[10]Ibid., par. 1.
[11]Ibid., par. 7.
[12]Ibid., par. 11.

periods should be recognized as gains to the extent of losses previously recognized in interim periods of the same fiscal period. However, market declines that are expected to be temporary within the fiscal year need not be recognized.

To illustrate, assume that Drex Company, which uses the FIFO inventory method, had 18,000 units in inventory at the beginning of the year at a FIFO cost per unit of $6. No purchases were made during the year. Information concerning quarterly sales and end-of-quarter replacement cost follows:

QUARTER	SALES IN UNITS	UNITS ON HAND	END-OF-QUARTER REPLACEMENT COST
1	3,000	15,000	$6.30
2	3,500	11,500	5.80
3	2,500	9,000	6.10
4	5,000	4,000	5.50
Total	14,000		

Assuming that the market decline in the second quarter was not expected to be temporary, cost of sales for the four quarters would be:

QUARTER	COMPUTATION OF COST OF GOODS SOLD		COST OF GOODS SOLD QUARTER	CUMULATIVE
1	Sold 3,000 units @ $6		$18,000	$18,000
2	Sold 3,500 units @ $6	$21,000		
	Plus write-down of ending inventory of 11,500 units to market			
	[11,500 × ($6.00 − $5.80)]	2,300	23,300	41,300
3	Sold 2,500 units @ $5.80	14,500		
	Less write-down recovery on ending inventory of 9,000 units			
	[9,000 × ($6.00 − $5.80)]	1,800	12,700	54,000
4	Sold 5,000 units @ $6	30,000		
	Plus write-down of ending inventory of 4,000 units to market			
	[4,000 × ($6.00 − $5.50)]	2,000	32,000	86,000

Because each interim period is considered an integral part of an annual period, the cumulative cost of goods sold ($86,000) should equal the amount that would be computed if the lower-of-cost-or-market method was applied on an annual basis. Thus, we can verify as follows:

UNITS SOLD DURING YEAR		FIFO COST/UNIT	AMOUNT
14,000	×	$6.00	$84,000
Add: Write-down of ending inventory to the lower of cost or market (4,000 × $.50)			2,000
Total cost of goods sold for the year			$86,000

4. Companies that use standard cost for determining inventory and product cost should generally follow the procedures in reporting variances that are used for the fiscal year. Purchase price and volume variances that are expected to be absorbed by the end of the annual period should ordinarily be deferred at interim reporting dates. Unplanned purchase price and volume variances, however, should be reported at the end of the interim period by the procedures used at the end of the fiscal year.[13]

All Other Costs and Expenses The Board concluded that, in accounting for costs and expenses that are not allocated to products sold or to services rendered, the following standards should apply:

1. Cost and expenses other than product costs should be charged to income in interim periods as incurred, or be allocated among interim periods based on an estimate of time expired, benefit received or activity associated with the periods. Procedures adopted for assigning specific cost and expense items to an interim period should be consistent with the bases followed by the company in reporting results of operations at annual reporting dates. However, when a specific cost or expense item charged to expense for annual reporting purposes benefits more than one interim period, the cost or expense item may be allocated to those interim periods.

2. Some costs and expenses incurred in an interim period cannot be readily identified with the activities or benefits of other interim periods and should be charged to the interim period in which incurred. Disclosure should be made as to the nature and amount of such costs unless items of a comparable nature are included in both the current interim period and in the corresponding interim period of the preceding year.

3. Arbitrary assignment of the amount of such costs to an interim period should not be made.

4. Gains and losses that arise in any interim period similar to those that would not be deferred at year-end should not be deferred to later interim periods within the same fiscal year.[14]

Provision for Income Taxes Accounting for income taxes in interim financial statements can be very complex for a company with such items as operating loss carrybacks or carryforwards, extraordinary gains and losses, capital gains and losses, and other similar items. Our treatment here will cover the basic issue of interim provision of income taxes. The reader is referred to *FASB Interpretation No. 18*, "Account-

---

[13]Ibid., par. 14.
[14]Ibid., par. 15.

ing for Income Taxes in Interim Periods,'' which discusses complicating issues in detail and presents numerous examples of appropriate treatment.

The basic technique for computing income tax provisions for interim financial statements is described in *APB Opinion No. 28* as follows:

> In reporting interim financial information, income tax provisions should be determined under the procedures set forth in *APB Opinion Nos. 11,* * *23,* and *24.* *At the end of each interim period the company should make its best estimate of the effective tax rate expected to be applicable for the full fiscal year. The rate so determined should be used in providing for income taxes on a current year-to-date basis. The effective rate should reflect anticipated tax credits, foreign tax rates, percentage depletion, and other available tax planning alternatives. However, in arriving at this effective tax rate no effect should be included for the tax related to significant unusual or extraordinary items that will be separately reported or reported net of their related tax effect in reports for the interim period or for the fiscal year.[15]
>
> *Superseded by SFAS No. 109.

To illustrate the basic procedures, assume that during 1995 Drex Company had actual first-quarter earnings of $150,000 and expected to have full-year earnings of about $500,000. On the basis of its full-year earnings projection, Drex Company estimated that its combined state and federal tax rate would be 30%. Assume further that Drex Company estimated that it would have permanent differences between accounting income and taxable income during the year of $20,000 for amortization of goodwill, and a dividend exclusion of $50,000. On the basis of this information, Drex Company would compute its estimated effective income tax rate for the year as follows:

Estimated income before taxes	$500,000
Add: Goodwill amortization	20,000
Less: Dividends exclusion	(50,000)
Estimated taxable income	$470,000
Estimated combined income tax payable	
($470,000 × 30%)	$141,000
Estimated effective combined tax rate	
($141,000 ÷ $500,000)	28.2%

This estimated rate is used to determine the income tax provision for the first quarter. Drex Company would, therefore, make the following entry:

Income Tax Expense ($150,000 × 28.2%)	42,300	
Income Tax Payable		42,300

Now assume that during the second quarter of 1995 Drex Company had actual earnings of $170,000, and that estimated total income for the year is $600,000. Estimated permanent differences remain the same as projected during the first

[15]Ibid., par. 19.

quarter. Using this new information, Drex Company would again compute an estimated combined federal and state tax rate for the year.

Estimated income before taxes	$600,000
Less: Net permanent differences	
($50,000 − $20,000)	(30,000)
Estimated taxable income	$570,000
Estimated combined income tax payable	
($570,000 × 30%)	$171,000
Estimated effective combined tax rate	
($171,000 ÷ $600,000)	28.5%

The new estimated tax rate is used to compute the estimated year-to-date income tax provision, and the provision required for the second quarter as indicated here:

Cumulative income for the first two quarters	
($150,000 + $170,000)	$320,000
Estimated effective tax rate	28.5%
Cumulative tax provision needed	91,200
Less: Tax provided in first quarter	42,300
Tax provision for second quarter	$ 48,900

Drex Company would make the following tax provision entry for the second quarter:

Income tax expense	48,900	
Income Tax Payable		48,900

Note that the new estimated effective tax rate is **not** applied retroactively; that is, the first-quarter results are not restated. Tax expense reported in the second-quarter interim income statement would be $48,900, and the year-to-date tax expense and tax payable would be reported in the year-to-date income statement and statement of financial position at $91,200. The procedures for the third-quarter would duplicate those followed for the second quarter, taking new information and estimates into consideration. It should also be noted that the treatment provided in *APB Opinion No. 28*, and just illustrated, is entirely consistent with the normal treatment afforded a change in estimate under the provisions of *APB Opinion No. 20*, "Accounting Changes"; that is, changes in estimates are treated currently and prospectively, not retroactively.

The preceding illustration assumed that there were no temporary differences. If temporary differences existed, they would have no effect on the computation of the combined effective tax rate, but would affect the tax expense and the tax liability recorded. For example, if there were an excess of tax depreciation over book depreciation during the first quarter amounting to $40,000, the first-quarter tax entry would be modified as follows:

Income Tax Expense	42,300	
Income Tax Payable [.282($150,000 − $40,000)]		31,020
Deferred Income Tax Liability (.282 × $40,000)		11,280

Accounting Changes in Interim Periods

Change in Estimate A change in estimate should be accounted for in the interim period in which the change is made. No restatement of previously reported interim information should be made, but the effect on earnings of a change in estimate made in a current interim period should be reported in the current and subsequent interim periods, if material in relation to any period presented, and should continue to be reported as long as necessary to avoid misleading comparisons.

Changes in Principle Changes in principle are of two types: those that require retroactive restatement and those that require a cumulative effect adjustment in the income statement of the period of change. These changes should be accounted for in interim financial statements in accordance with the provisions of *APB Opinion No. 20*, ''Accounting Changes,'' with the following exception:

> If a cumulative effect type accounting change is made during the first interim period of an enterprise's fiscal year, the cumulative effect of the change on retained earnings at the beginning of that fiscal year shall be included in net income of the first interim period (and in last-twelve-months-to-date financial reports that include that first interim period).
>
> If a cumulative effect type accounting change is made in other than the first interim period of an enterprise's fiscal year, no cumulative effect of the change shall be included in net income of the period of change. Instead, financial information for the pre-change interim periods of the fiscal year in which the change is made shall be restated by applying the newly adopted accounting principle to those pre-change interim periods. The cumulative effect of the change on retained earnings at the beginning of that fiscal year shall be included in restated net income of the first interim period of the fiscal year in which the change is made (and in any year-to-date or last-twelve-months-to-date financial reports that include the first interim period). Whenever financial information that includes those pre-change interim periods is presented, it shall be presented on the restated basis.[16]

Minimum Disclosures in Interim Reports

Because the amount of financial information disclosed in interim reports varied widely, the APB established minimum disclosure standards relating to the following:

---

[16]*Statement of Financial Accounting Standards No. 3*, ''Reporting Accounting Changes in Interim Financial Statements'' (Conn.: FASB, 1974), par. 9, 10.

a. Sales or gross revenues, provision for income taxes, extraordinary items (including related income tax effects), cumulative effect of a change in accounting principles or practices, and net income.

b. Primary and fully diluted earnings per share data for each period presented determined in accordance with the provisions of *APB Opinion No. 15*, "Earnings Per Share."

c. Seasonal revenue, costs or expenses.

d. Significant changes in estimates or provisions for income taxes.

e. Disposal of a segment of a business and extraordinary, unusual or infrequently occurring items.

f. Contingent items.

g. Changes in accounting principles or estimates.

h. Significant changes in financial position.[17]

Overall, the APB and FASB have made a significant effort to improve the quality of interim financial reports. However, considerable controversy still exists and appears to center around the APB's assumption that an interim period should be accounted for as an integral part of the annual period.

Questions

1. For what types of companies would segmented financial reports have the most significance? Why?

2. Why do financial statement users (financial analysts, for example) need information about segments of a firm?

3. List the three major types of information disclosures required by *SFAS No. 14*.

4. Define the following:
   (a) Industry segment.
   (b) Reportable industry segment.

5. Describe the guidelines to be used in determining whether a specific industry segment is a significant segment.

6. How does one determine whether a major portion of a company's operations occur within a single industry?

7. What type of disclosure is required of a firm when the major portion of its operations takes place within a single industry?

8. List the types of information that must be presented for each reportable segment of a company under the rules of *SFAS No. 14*.

9. Describe the methods that might be used to disclose reportable industry segment information.

---

[17] *Opinion of the Accounting Principles Board No. 28*, par. 30.

10. How does one determine whether foreign operations constitute a significant portion of total enterprise operations?

11. What types of information must be disclosed about foreign operations under *SFAS No. 14.?*

12. What factors should be considered in grouping foreign operations into "geographic area" operations?

13. What are the major differences between the requirements for industry segment disclosures under *SFAS No. 14.* and SEC regulations?

14. What is the purpose of interim financial reporting?

15. Some accountants hold the view that each interim period should stand alone as a basic accounting period, whereas others view each interim period as essentially an integral part of the annual period. Distinguish between these views.

16. Describe the basic procedure for computing income tax provisions for interim financial statements.

17. Describe how changes in estimates should be treated in interim financial statements.

18. What are the minimum disclosure requirements established by the APB for interim financial reports?

19. What is the general rule regarding the treatment of costs and expenses associated directly with revenues for interim reporting purposes?

Exercises

Exercise 16-1

Pong Industries' operations involve four industry segments, A, B, C, and D. During the past year, the operating profit (loss) of each segment was

SEGMENT	OPERATING PROFIT (LOSS)
A	$(600)
B	100
C	900
D	(700)

Required:

Applying the operating profit or loss test, determine which of the segments are reportable segments.

Exercise 16-2

Mane Company operates in five identifiable industries, V, W, X, Y, and Z. During the past year, sales to unaffiliated customers and intersegment sales for each segment were as follows:

SEGMENT	SALES TO NONAFFILIATES	INTERSEGMENT SALES	TOTAL SALES
V	$2,000	$ 400	$2,400
W	280	20	300
X	100	600	700
Y	1,100	–0–	1,100
Z	350	25	375
Total	$3,830	$1,045	$4,875

Required:

Applying the revenue test, determine which of the segments are reportable segments.

Exercise 16-3

Twodor Company is involved in four separate industries. Selected financial information concerning Twodor's involvement in each of the four industries is presented below:

	INDUSTRY SEGMENT				
	A	B	C	D	TOTAL
Sales to nonaffiliates	$ 80,000	$20,000	$24,000	$12,200	$136,200
Intersegment sales	130,000	84,000	12,000	3,800	229,800
Total revenue	210,000	104,000	36,000	16,000	366,000
Operating profit (loss)	(17,400)	12,000	1,500	(600)	(4,500)
Identifiable assets	222,000	110,500	28,000	26,000	386,500

Required:

Using all tests, determine which of the industry segments are reportable segments and explain how nonreportable segments (if any) should be reported.

Exercise 16-4

The following information concerns the operations of Blane Company for the year ended December 31, 1995.

	(IN THOUSANDS OF DOLLARS)		
	GENERAL OFFICE	SEGMENT A	SEGMENT B
Net sales (operating revenue)		$60,000	$99,000
Cost of goods sold		27,200	35,600
Allocable expenses		12,600	10,800
Joint expenses	$15,000		
Payroll dollars	9,200	34,800	18,200
Average net book value of tangible capital assets and inventories	5,200	70,000	54,500

Required:

Determine the operating profit (loss) for each of Blane's two segments for 1995.

Exercise: 16-5

LAX Inc. has the following income before income tax and estimated effective annual income tax rates for the first three quarters of 1995:

QUARTER	INCOME BEFORE INCOME TAX PROVISION	ESTIMATED EFFECTIVE ANNUAL TAX RATE AT END OF QUARTER
1st	$70,000	32%
2nd	50,000	32%
3rd	40,600	38%

Required:

What should be LAX's income tax provision in the third-quarter income statement?

(AICPA adapted)

Exercise 16-6

The following information is available for Bailey Company for 1995:

1. On January 2, 1995, Bailey paid property taxes amounting to $60,000 on its plant and equipment for the calendar year 1995. In late March 1995 Bailey made major repairs to its machinery amounting to $66,000. These repairs will benefit the remainder of the calendar year's operations.
2. An inventory loss of $150,000 from market decline occurred in August 1995. Bailey recorded this loss in August 1995 after its June 30 quarterly report was issued. None of this loss had been recovered by the end of 1995.
3. At the end of July 1995, Bailey sold some equipment with a book value of $22,000 for $32,500.

Required:

State the dollar amounts that should appear in Bailey Company's March 31, June 30, September 30, and December 31, 1995 quarterly financial statements to report:

A. Property taxes.

B. Major repairs to machinery.

C. Inventory loss from market decline.

D. The gain or loss on sale of equipment.

(AICPA adapted)

Exercise 16-7

Day Company, which uses the FIFO inventory method, had 254,000 units in inventory at the beginning of the year at a FIFO cost per unit of $30. No purchases were made during the year. Quarterly sales information and two sets of end-of-quarter replacement cost figures follow:

		END-OF-QUARTER REPLACEMENT COST	
QUARTER	UNIT SALES	CASE A	CASE B
1	100,000	$29	$25
2	30,000	22	27
3	42,500	18	19
4	30,500	22	27

The market decline in the first quarter under Case A was expected to be temporary, whereas under Case B the decline was expected to be nontemporary. Declines in other quarters were expected to be permanent.

Required:

Determine cost of goods sold for the four quarters under each case and verify the amounts by computing cost of goods sold using the lower-of-cost-or-market method applied on an annual basis.

Exercise 16-8

Spur Company's actual earnings for the first two quarters of 1995 and its estimate during each quarter of its annual earnings are:

Actual first-quarter earnings	$ 400,000
Actual second-quarter earnings	510,000
First-quarter estimate of annual earnings	1,350,000
Second-quarter estimate of annual earnings	1,420,000

Spur Company estimated its permanent differences between accounting income and taxable income for 1995 as:

Goodwill amortization	$ 25,000
Dividend income exclusion	180,000

These estimates did not change during the second quarter. The combined state and federal tax rate for Spur Company for 1995 is 42%.

Required:

Prepare journal entries to record Spur Company's provision for income taxes for each of the first two quarters of 1995.

Exercise 16-9

Select the best answer for each of the following.

1. Which of the following is *not* a consideration in segment reporting for diversified companies?
   (a) Consolidation policy.
   (b) Defining the segments.
   (c) Transfer pricing.
   (d) Allocation of joint costs.

2. Cream Company operates in three different industries, each of which is appropriately regarded as a reportable segment. Segment No. 1 contributed 60% of Cream Company's total sales. Sales for Segment No. 1 were $450,000 and traceable costs were $200,000. Total common costs for Cream were $300,000. Cream allocates common costs on the basis of the ratio of a segment's sales to total sales, an appropriate method of allocation. What should be the operating profit presented for Segment No. 1 for the year?
   (a) $270,000.
   (b) $70,000.
   (c) $180,000.
   (d) $250,000.

3. The profitability information that should be reported for each reportable segment of a business enterprise consists of
   (a) An operating profit or loss figure consisting of segment revenues less traceable costs but *not* allocated common costs.
   (b) An operating profit or loss figure consisting of segment revenues less allocated common costs but *not* traceable costs.
   (c) An operating profit or loss figure consisting of segment revenues less traceable costs and allocated common costs.
   (d) Segment revenues only.

4. In financial reporting for segments of a business enterprise, the operating profit or loss of a segment should include
   (a) Revenue earned at the corporate level.
   (b) Federal income taxes.
   (c) Interest expense even though the segment's operations are *not* principally of a financial nature.
   (d) Common costs allocated on a reasonable basis.

5. A company that uses the LIFO method of inventory pricing finds at an interim reporting date that there has been a partial liquidation of the base period inventory level. The decline is considered temporary and the partial liquidation will be replaced before year-end. The amount shown as inventory at the interim reporting date should
   (a) Be shown at the actual level, and cost of sales for the interim reporting period should reflect the decrease in the LIFO base period inventory level.
   (b) *Not* give effect to the LIFO liquidation, and cost of sales for the interim reporting period should reflect the decrease in the LIFO base period inventory level.
   (c) *Not* give effect to the LIFO liquidation, and cost of sales for the interim reporting period should include the expected cost of replacement of the liquidated LIFO base.
   (d) Be shown at the actual level, and the decrease in inventory level should *not* be reflected in the cost of sales for the interim reporting period.

6. Which of the following is an inherent difficulty in determination of the results of operations on an interim basis?
   (a) Costs expended in one interim period may benefit other periods.
   (b) Depreciation on an interim basis is a partial estimate of the actual annual amount.
   (c) Cost of sales reflects only the amount of product expense allocable to revenue recognized as of the interim date.
   (d) Revenues from long-term construction contracts accounted for by the percentage-of-completion method are based on annual completion, and interim estimates may be incorrect.

7. In considering interim financial reporting, how did the Accounting Principles Board conclude that such reporting should be viewed?

(a) As useful only if activity is evenly spread throughout the year so that estimates are unnecessary.

(b) As a "special" type of reporting that need *not* follow generally accepted accounting principles.

(c) As reporting of an integral part of an annual period.

(d) As reporting for a basic accounting period.

8. Which of the following methods of inventory valuation is allowable at interim dates but *not* at year-end?

(a) Estimated gross profit rates.

(b) Retail method.

(c) Specific identification.

(d) Weighted average.

(AICPA adapted)

Problems

Problem 16-1

Bacon Industries operates in seven different industries. Information concerning the operations of these industries for the most recent fiscal period follows:

INDUSTRY SEGMENT	REVENUE TOTAL	REVENUE INTERSEGMENT	OPERATING PROFIT (LOSS)	IDENTIFIABLE ASSETS
1	$ 4,200	$ 800	$ (600)	$ 7,000
2	6,000	1,200	2,000	8,800
3	51,000	7,000	2,100	35,400
4	48,000	-0-	8,800	37,600
5	13,000	-0-	3,200	14,000
6	64,500	3,400	4,000	52,000
7	12,000	2,000	(3,000)	16,400

Required:

Determine which of the segments must be treated as reportable segments.

Problem 16-2

Pacheco Industries is comprised of four separate profit centers, which are distributed throughout the United States. Relevant data for each profit center are summarized for 1995:

	PROFIT CENTER (IN THOUSANDS)				
	A	B	C	D	TOTAL
Sales to nonaffiliates	$3,600	$ 8,700	$1,500	$1,200	$15,000
Intersegment sales	1,500	2,400	300	3,000	7,200
Operating profit (loss) before joint expense allocation	840	1,500	240	(60)	2,520
Identifiable assets	7,200	18,000	2,400	2,400	30,000
Labor hours worked	2,700	5,700	1,500	2,100	12,000

You determine that intersegment sales are distributed as follows:

			BUYER		
SELLER	A	B	C	D	TOTAL
A	$ –0–	$1,200	$150	$150	$1,500
B	1,200	–0–	600	600	2,400
C	150	150	–0–	–0–	300
D	1,800	1,050	150	–0–	3,000
Total	$3,150	$2,400	$900	$750	$7,200

Administrative expenses of $2,400,000 were incurred at the corporate level during 1995. Management believes that total labor hours worked during the year provides a reasonable basis for allocation of these costs.

In each situation described below, an industry segment is comprised of different combinations of profit centers. Thus, the "AB" industry segment consists of profit centers "A" and "B." Consider the following five combinations of industry segments:

1. AB, CD
2. AB, C, D
3. A, B, CD
4. A, B, C, D
5. A, BD, C

Required:

A. For each combination listed, determine which industry segments are reportable segments. Apply all required tests and indicate the results of each test separately.

B. For each combination given, indicate if the reportable segments determined in (A) above collectively represent a "substantial portion" of Pacheco Industries' total operations, applying the 75% revenue test.

Problem 16-3

Perez Industries, a publicly held corporation, consists of several companies, each of which provides a diverse array of products and services to unaffiliated customers. In your opinion, each of these companies qualifies as a separate industry segment.

The corporation is in the process of completing its first-year financial statements. Although the directors of Perez Industries wish to comply with the provisions of *SFAS No. 14*, they believe that disclosing each individual industry segment would result in an unwieldy and cumbersome set of financial statements. For this reason, they request that when you prepare these statements, you keep the identified segments to the minimum number that would ensure compliance with *SFAS No. 14*.

Required:

A. To what extent does the management of Perez Industries have a choice in deciding whether an industry segment must be reported?

B. The directors of Perez Industries presumably feel that too much disclosure of financial information will impair the overall utility of the financial statements. What flexibility does the FASB allow that could invalidate this criticism? Explain.

C. Explain the needs for segment reporting. Why do consolidated financial statements fail to meet these needs?

D. Relate the concept of comparability to the required accounting treatment for intersegment transactions. What arguments would favor *excluding* the effect of intersegment transfers?

Problem 16-4

Branson Industries conducts operations in five major industries, A, B, C, D, and E. Financial data relevant to each industry for the year ending December 31, 1995, are as follows:

	(IN THOUSANDS)				
	A	B	C	D	E
Sales	$57,000	$120,000	$880,000	$50,000	$ 83,000
Cost of goods sold	20,000	75,000	400,000	9,400	46,000
Administrative expenses	18,000	26,000	152,000	12,000	8,000
Selling expenses	7,000	44,000	172,000	12,600	20,000
Total cost and expense	45,000	145,000	724,000	34,000	74,000
Operating profit	$12,000	$(25,000)	$156,000	$16,000	$ 6,000
Identifiable assets	$50,000	$ 95,000	$600,000	$98,000	$240,000
Depreciation and amortization expense	6,400	10,700	76,000	12,200	26,400
Captial expenditures	5,600	8,000	39,000	20,000	25,000

Included in the sales of segments C and E are intersegment sales of $120,000 and $40,000, respectively. Corporate offices have assets of $95,000 and incurred general corporate expenses of $76,000.

Required:

A. Which industry segments should be separately reported in the segment report? Justify your answer.

B. Prepare a report to disclose required industry segment information under *SFAS No. 14.*

Problem 16-5

Bismac Industries is a diversified company whose operations are conducted in five industries, L, M, N, O, and P. Segmented financial information is to be included with the December 31, 1995 annual report. Financial information pertaining to each segment for 1995 is as follows:

	L	M	N	O	P
Sales	$40,000	$ 85,000	$600,000	$50,000	$48,000
Cost of sales	15,000	45,000	275,000	22,000	29,000
General and administrative expense	9,000	19,000	104,000	10,000	6,000
Selling expense	8,000	32,000	140,000	9,000	10,000
Total cost and expense	32,000	96,000	519,000	41,000	45,000
Operating profit (loss)	$ 8,000	$(11,000)	$ 81,000	$ 9,000	$ 3,000
Identifiable assets	$30,000	$ 48,000	$320,000	$45,000	$95,000

Other information:

1. In addition to the identifiable assets listed, the general corporate office has assets of $90,000 on December 31, 1995.
2. Included in the sales of segment P are $15,000 of sales made to segment N during the year. None of these goods remains in the ending inventory of segment N on December 31, 1995.
3. Income tax amounts to 30% of operating profit.

Required:

A. Determine which of the five segments must be treated as reportable segments and indicate the basis for your decision.

B. Prepare a financial report by segments that is reconciled to consolidated data.

Problem 16-6

Actual quarterly earnings and quarterly estimates of annual earnings for Sloan Company for the year ended December 31, 1995 are as follows:

QUARTER	ACTUAL QUARTERLY EARNINGS	QUARTERLY ESTIMATES OF ANNUAL EARNINGS
1	$95,000	$400,000
2	85,000	370,000
3	92,000	370,000
4	96,000	N/A

The combined state and federal tax rate for 1995 is 30%. Sloan Company estimated it would have permanent differences between accounting income and taxable income during 1995. Each quarter's estimate of these annual differences is provided in the following table:

	ESTIMATED PERMANENT DIFFERENCES	
ESTIMATE AT END OF QUARTER	GOODWILL AMORTIZATION	DIVIDEND EXCLUSION
1	$14,000	$40,000
2	14,000	40,000
3	14,000	50,000

The actual amount of permanent differences for 1995 were goodwill amortization, $14,000 dividend exclusion, $55,000.

Required

Prepare journal entries to record Sloan Company's 1995 quarterly income tax provisions.

Problem 16-7

The following statement is an excerpt from paragraphs 9 and 10 of *APB Opinion No. 28*, "Interim Financial Reporting":

Interim financial information is essential to provide investors and others with timely information as to the progress of the enterprise. The usefulness of such information rests on the relationship that it has to the annual results of operations. Accordingly, the Board has concluded that each interim period should be viewed primarily as an integral part of an annual period.

In general, the results for each interim period should be based on the accounting principles and practices used by an enterprise in the preparation of its latest annual financial statements unless a change in an accounting practice or policy has been adopted in the current year. The Board has concluded, however, that certain accounting principles and practices followed for annual reporting purposes may require modification at interim reporting dates so that the reported results for the interim period may better relate to the results of operations for the annual period.

Required:

Listed below are six independent cases on how accounting facts might be reported on an individual company's interim financial reports. For each case, state whether the method proposed to be used for interim reporting would be acceptable under generally accepted accounting principles applicable to interim financial data. Support each answer with a brief explanation.

A. Reed Company wrote inventory down to reflect lower of cost or market in the first quarter of 1995. At year-end the market value exceeds the original acquisition cost of this inventory. Consequently, management plans to write the inventory back up to its original cost as a year-end adjustment.

B. Greenfield Company realized a large gain on the sale of investments at the beginning of the second quarter. The company wants to report one-third of the gain in each of the remaining quarters.

C. Dole Company has estimated its annual audit fee. They plan to prorate this expense equally over all four quarters.

D. Fur Company was reasonably certain they would have an employee strike in the third quarter. As a result, they shipped heavily during the second quarter but plan to defer the recognition of the sales in excess of the normal sales volume. The deferred sales will be recognized as sales in the third quarter when the strike is in progress. Fur Company management thinks this is more nearly representative of normal second- and third-quarter operations.

E. Rexx Company takes a physical inventory at year-end for annual financial statement purposes. Inventory and cost of sales reported in the interim quarterly statements are based on estimated gross profit rates, because a physical inventory would result in a cessation of operations. Rexx Company does have reliable perpetual inventory records.

F. Shelly Company is planning to report one-fourth of its pension expense in each quarter.
(CMA adapted)

17

INSOLVENCY—LIQUIDATION AND REORGANIZATION

Previous chapters have treated problems relating to the expansion of business activity through mergers, stock acquisitions, and branch operations, as well as the procedures followed in reporting the effects of the expanded operations. But just as some companies expand, others face financial circumstances that cause contraction or cessation of business activities. Every year many businesses, small and large, encounter financial difficulties, and many are forced to seek relief through accommodations with creditors or some form of reorganization in order to survive. Those that are unable to obtain such relief generally terminate operations by liquidating the business unit.

This chapter deals with the various relief procedures available to an insolvent debtor. *Insolvency* refers to the inability of a debtor to pay its obligations as they become due. Our discussion includes relief procedures not requiring court actions, as well as the legal procedures available under the Bankruptcy Reform Act of 1978, relevant provisions of which are discussed in later sections of this chapter. Although the Bankruptcy Reform Act provides for relief of all types of insolvent debtors, including individuals, our discussion will concentrate on the provisions of the act dealing with insolvent business entities.

When a business becomes insolvent, it generally has three possible courses of action: (1) the debtor and its creditors may enter into a contractual agreement, outside of formal bankruptcy proceedings; (2) the debtor or its creditors may file a bankruptcy petition, after which the debtor is liquidated under Chapter 7 of the

Bankruptcy Reform Act; or (3) the debtor or its creditors may file a petition for reorganization under Chapter 11 of the Bankruptcy Reform Act.

CONTRACTUAL AGREEMENTS

A business that is unable to pay its obligations as they mature may attempt to reach an accommodation with its creditors without recourse to legal action. The procedures are relatively simple. The debtor and its creditors meet and develop a voluntary agreement or plan for settlement of obligations. The possibilities generally include (1) an extension of payment periods, (2) composition agreements, (3) formation of a creditors' committee, or (4) a voluntary assignment of assets.

Extension of Payment Periods

When the insolvency results from temporary financial difficulties and the debtor is expected to operate profitably in the future if it receives some minor relief, its creditors may find it advantageous in the long run to extend the period of payment of outstanding debts. In this situation, the debtor continues to manage the business with the expectation of obtaining sufficient profitability and financial strength to settle existing debts in full. Such an agreement is often effective for a business with few creditors. No particular accounting problem is encountered, in that interest on the debt normally continues at the originally contracted rate(s) and is paid or accrued periodically. No accounting entries are needed to reflect the extension of the payment period(s), although the nature of the new agreement should be disclosed in notes to the financial statements. *Statement of Financial Accounting Standards (SFAS) No. 15* provides that where a debt restructuring involves only a modification of terms of payment, the debtor should account for the effects of the restructuring prospectively from the time of restructuring, and should not change the carrying amount of the payable, unless the carrying amount exceeds the total future cash payments of principal and interest specified by the new terms.[1] Thus, no gain is recognized when the restructuring involves an extension of the payment period only.

Although this approach to accounting for debt restructuring is simple to apply, it lacks conceptual support because it ignores the time value of money. Many accountants support a present value approach under which the debt would be restated to its current value by discounting it at the current rate of interest and recognizing a gain from debt restructuring. This approach would permit a more accurate reflection of actual interest expense in future accounting periods. On the other hand, the recognition of a substantial gain on debt restructuring would increase current income or decrease a current loss, which may give the impression of an improvement in the general financial condition of the debtor. One solution would be to report the gain as a direct adjustment to owners' equity.

---

[1] *Statement of Financial Accounting Standards No. 15*, "Accounting by Debtors and Creditors for Troubled Debt Restructurings" (Norwalk, Conn.: FASB, June, 1977), par. 16.

Composition Agreements

A composition agreement is an agreement between the debtor and its creditors under which the creditors agree to accept less than the full amount to their claims. In addition, accrued interest is sometimes canceled or the interest rate lowered. Creditors are often given some immediate cash payment, and the amount of the remaining debts and their interest rates are renegotiated. If a few creditors with small claims refuse to enter into the agreement, they may be paid in full and the remaining creditors may grant relief to the debtor. The benefit to the creditors is that they receive an immediate cash payment and expect to receive eventually more than they would receive if the debtor were forced to liquidate. The benefit to the debtor, of course, is that it can continue to operate with the expectation of returning to profitable operations, and, therefore, survive. As with extension of payment agreements, composition agreements are usually used only where there is a relatively small group of creditors. In addition, as with an extension of payment agreement, no gain or loss is recognized by either party to the restructuring unless the carrying amount of the remaining payable exceeds the total future cash payments of principal and interest required by the new terms.

Formation of a Creditors' Committee

The debtor and its creditors may agree to the formation of a creditors' committee that is responsible for managing the debtor's business affairs for the period during which plans are developed to rehabilitate, reorganize, or liquidate the business. Often, an extension of payment periods for debtor obligations is agreed to while the committee deliberates the ultimate disposition of the business. If the decision is to rehabilitate the business, the agreement may include the cancelation or restructuring of existing debts and possible infusion of new capital by the creditors. When the rehabilitation plan is completed, operating control of the business is generally returned to the debtor. If the decision is to reorganize or liquidate the business, the debtor's property may be turned over to a trustee who is responsible for conducting the affairs of the business during the period of reorganization or liquidation.

Voluntary Assignment of Assets

A debtor may elect to place its property under the control of a trustee for the benefit of its creditors. The purpose of the assignment is to permit the trustee to sell the property and distribute the proceeds among the creditors. If the creditors agree, the assignment results in the full discharge of the debtor's obligations to them. If there are proceeds remaining after payment of the creditors, they are returned to the debtor.

BANKRUPTCY

Article I, Section 8 of the U.S. Constitution gives the Congress authority to enact uniform bankruptcy laws. Congress passed the first bankruptcy law in 1800 and has repealed and enacted new laws on several occasions since that time. The most recent revision is the Bankruptcy Reform Act of 1978 (hereafter referred to as the Reform Act), which became effective in October 1979. The Reform Act consists of eight chapters as follows:

Chapter 1   General Provisions

Chapter 3   Case Administration

Chapter 5   Creditors, the Debtor, and the Estate

Chapter 7   Liquidation

Chapter 9   Adjustment of Debts of a Municipality

Chapter 11   Reorganization

Chapter 13   Adjustment of Debts of an Individual with Regular Income

Chapter 15   United States Trustees[2]

Chapters 1, 3, and 5 deal with general issues, a description of the administrative process, and definitions of various terms that apply to bankruptcy proceedings. The Reform Act provides that a bankruptcy petition may be filed under one of Chapters 7, 9, 11, or 13. Chapter 9, which applies to municipalities seeking voluntary relief, and Chapter 13, which applies to bankruptcy petitions by individuals, will not be discussed here. We will concentrate on petitions by business entities under Chapter 7 (Liquidation) and Chapter 11 (Reorganization). Chapter 15 is a special chapter establishing an experiment designed to relieve bankruptcy judges of many administrative duties, thereby permitting them to concentrate on substantive matters. Chapter 15 provides for the appointment of U.S. trustees under the supervision of the U.S. Assistant Attorney General. The U.S. trustees' duties are to (1) monitor the performance of the private trustees that they appoint in bankruptcy cases, (2) act as trustees when private trustees are unwilling to serve, and (3) oversee the general administration of bankruptcy cases. The results of the experiment will be used by Congress in establishing the bankruptcy courts that will be created at the end of the experiment. Until the new courts are established, the present bankruptcy courts have been given authority to apply the provisions of the Reform Act.

Provisions of the Reform Act apply to individuals, corporations, and partnerships, all of which are referred to as *persons*, as well as to municipalities seeking voluntary relief from their creditors (municipalities cannot be forced into bankruptcy proceedings). Insurance companies and most financial institutions are excluded because they are covered by other specific statutes.

As mentioned earlier, when a business is unable to pay its obligations as they mature, it may attempt to negotiate some type of contractual agreement with its

---

[2]Several revisions to the bankruptcy statute over time have resulted in the elimination of some chapters by consolidating them with others. For example, Chapters VIII, X, XI, and XII (before the Reform Act, Roman numerals were used) were consolidated into Chapter 11 of the Reform Act. Because of these revisions the act contains only uneven chapter numbers.

creditors without initiating a bankruptcy proceeding. If a satisfactory agreement cannot be reached, a legal petition for bankruptcy will be initiated by either the debtor (a voluntary petition) or its creditors (an involuntary petition). The Reform Act uses the single term *debtor* to refer to the subject of a bankruptcy proceeding.

Voluntary Petitions

A debtor may file a voluntary petition with a bankruptcy court for liquidation under Chapter 7 or for reorganization under Chapter 11. Filing of a voluntary or involuntary petition constitutes an *order for relief*, which prohibits the start or continuation of legal action against the debtor by its creditors. The bankruptcy judge, however, may refuse a voluntary petition if refusal is considered to be in the best interest of the creditors.

The bankruptcy petition (either voluntary or involuntary) is an official form that initiates bankruptcy proceedings and establishes an *estate* consisting of the debtor's assets. The debtor must file a form listing all its property (at current market values) and its debts. This form, called a Statement of Assets and Liabilities, consists of the following separate schedules:

Schedule A. Statement of All Liabilities of Debtor
    Schedule A-1. Creditors Having Priority (with amount of claims)
          A-2. Creditors Holding Security (with market value of security and amount of claims)
          A-3. Creditors Having Unsecured Claims Without Priority (with amount of claims)
Schedule B. Statement of All Property of Debtor.
    Schedule B-1. Real Property (with market values)
          B-2. Personal Property (with market values)
          B-3. Property Not Otherwise Scheduled (property discovered later)
          B-4. Property Claimed as Exempt (pertains to individuals only)

In addition, the debtor must complete a questionnaire, called a Statement of Affairs, containing questions concerning all aspects of its financial condition and operations.

Involuntary Petitions

In an involuntary proceeding, creditors initiate the action by filing a petition for liquidation or reorganization with the bankruptcy court. If there are 12 or more creditors, the petition must be signed by three or more of such creditors whose claims aggregate at least $5,000 more than the value of any liens on the property of the debtor. If there are fewer than 12 creditors, the petition may be filed by one or more of such creditors whose claims aggregate at least $5,000 more than the value of any liens on the debtor's property. Involuntary petitions may be filed under either Chapter 7 or Chapter 11 of the Reform Act. The bankruptcy court will generally enter an order for relief against the debtor only if evidence indicates that the debtor, in fact, has not been paying its debts as they become due.

Secured and Unsecured Creditors

Creditors are classified by law as *secured* or *unsecured*. Secured creditors are those whose claims are secured by liens or pledges of specific assets. If the proceeds from the sale of a pledged asset(s) exceeds the secured claim, the excess proceeds are available for distribution to unsecured creditors. If the secured claim exceeds the proceeds from the sale of a pledged asset(s), the remaining claim constitutes an unsecured claim. Unsecured creditors do not have claims to proceeds received from the sale of specific assets, but are paid from whatever total money remains after secured creditors have been satisfied. That is, secured creditors are paid first with the proceeds from the sale of specific assets upon which they have liens. Thereafter, unsecured creditors, including those having priority, are paid from whatever proceeds remain from the realization process. Thus, it is probably better to classify claims as fully secured, partially secured, and unsecured. Fully secured claims are those with liens against assets whose realizable value is equal to or in excess of the claim. Partially secured claims are those with liens against assets whose realizable value is less than the amount of the claim.

The Reform Act assigns priorities to certain claims, and each rank must be satisfied in full before the next lower rank is paid. The following order of priority for *unsecured* creditors is specified:

1. Administration expenses, fees, and charges incurred in administering the bankrupt's estate.

2. Unsecured claims for wages, salaries, or commissions earned by an employee within 90 days before the date of filing of the petition, but limited to the extent of $2,000 per employee.

3. Unsecured claims for contributions to employee benefit plans from services rendered within 180 days before the date of the filing of the petition, but limited to the extent of $2,000 per employee.

4. Unsecured claims of individuals, to the extent of $900 for each such individual, arising from the deposit of money in connection with the purchase, lease, or rental of property or services that were not delivered or performed.

5. Unsecured claims of governmental units for unpaid taxes.

After all these priorities have been satisfied, any remaining unsecured creditors participate pro rata in any remaining realization proceeds. The distribution to unsecured creditors is termed a *dividend* and is generally expressed in terms of the percentage of the total unsecured claims that will be paid. For example, if $100,000 of proceeds remains after all secured claims and claims having priority have been paid, and total unsecured claims amount to $400,000, each unsecured creditor will receive a 25% dividend.

LIQUIDATION

In addition to a voluntary assignment of assets, which constitutes a liquidation without bankruptcy proceedings, a voluntary or involuntary petition for liquidation may be filed under Chapter 7 of the Reform Act. Upon filing, the bankruptcy court must decide whether to accept or dismiss the petition. Although dismissals occur infrequently, the debtor may dispute an *involuntary petition*, in which case a trial will be held to determine whether the petition should be dismissed.

If the petition is accepted, an order for relief is entered and the bankruptcy court will appoint an interim trustee to oversee activities until a permanent trustee is selected. In addition, the court must call a meeting of the debtor's creditors, who will select a trustee and elect a creditors' committee to assist the trustee in the administration of the estate. If the creditors cannot agree on a trustee, the interim trustee becomes the trustee. Only creditors who have filed a claim at or before the meeting are entitled to vote. The interim trustee examines the claims and accepts them or, if improper, disallows them. The debtor must attend the creditors' meeting to answer questions by the creditors and the trustee, to clarify the contents of the statement of affairs included with the petition, and to generally assist the trustee in the preparation of an inventory of property and the examination of claims.

Duties of the Trustee

The duties of the trustee in liquidation are specified in the Reform Act. The trustee shall

1. Collect and reduce to money the property of the estate.
2. Account for all money and property received.
3. Investigate the financial affairs of the debtor.
4. Examine claims and disallow any that are improper.
5. Furnish reasonable requests for information about the estate and its administration to parties of interest.
6. Operate the business of the debtor during the liquidation period if authorized by the court, and file periodic reports and summaries of operations.
7. Pay creditors as promptly as possible, giving due regard to secured claims and priorities.
8. File a final report on the administration of the estate including a statement of receipts and disbursements.

In addition, the trustee has the authority to hire attorneys, accountants, appraisers, and other professionals to assist in carrying out his or her duties.

REORGANIZATION UNDER THE REFORM ACT

Creditors of an insolvent debtor may believe that their long-range interests would be better served by rehabilitating or reorganizing the debtor than by having it liquidated. In such a case, the creditors and debtor may agree to a plan for reorganization without recourse to the judicial process by employing one or more of the contractual agreements discussed earlier in this chapter. Alternatively, the debtor or creditors may prefer to file with the bankruptcy court a petition for reorganization under Chapter 11 of the Reform Act.

The Reform Act provides that, as soon as practicable after the acceptance of a petition for reorganization, the court shall appoint a committee of creditors holding unsecured claims, ordinarily consisting of those holding the seven largest claims against the debtor. The court may appoint additional committees of creditors or of stockholders if necessary to assure adequate representation of creditors and stockholders. If a committee of stockholders is appointed, it will normally consist of the persons who hold the seven largest amounts of equity securities.

The committee appointed by the court has the following powers and duties:

1. Select and authorize the appointment of one or more attorneys, accountants, or other agents, to represent or perform services for the committee.

2. Consult with the trustee or debtor concerning the administration of the case.

3. Investigate the acts, conduct, assets, liabilities, and financial condition of the debtor, the operation of the debtor's business and the desirability of the continuance of such business, and any other matter relevant to the case or to the formulation of a plan.

4. Participate in the formulation of a plan, advise those represented by the committee of the committee's recommendations as to any plan formulated, and collect and file with the court acceptances of a plan.

5. Request the appointment of a trustee if a trustee has not previously been appointed in the case.[3]

6. Perform such other services as are in the interest of those represented.

The court may permit the debtor to maintain possession of its assets and conduct the affairs of the business, or it may appoint a trustee. If a trustee is appointed, his or her primary duties in a reorganization are:

1. To be accountable for all property received.

2. To examine claims and object to the allowance of any claim that is improper.

3. To furnish such information concerning the estate and the estate's administration as is requested by a party in interest.

4. If the business of the debtor is authorized to be operated, file with the court and with any governmental unit charged with responsibility for collection of any tax arising out of such operation, periodic reports and summaries of the operation of the business.

---

[3]A trustee must be appointed if the debtor's debts (other than debts for goods, services, or taxes) exceed $5,000,000.

5. If the debtor has not done so, file with the court a list of creditors, a schedule of assets and liabilities, and a statement of the debtor's financial affairs.

6. File a plan of reorganization.

7. After confirmation of a plan, file such reports as are required by the court.

The reorganization plan may propose the alteration of legal, contractual, and equity interests of any class of creditors or equity security holders. Unsecured creditors will generally accept payment of a portion of their claims and cancelation of the remainder of their claims. The plan must be equitable to all parties by providing for the same treatment for each claim or interest of a particular class. The plan must also contain adequate means for its own execution; that is, it must contain specific provisions for such things as (1) the retention of any property by the debtor, (2) the transfer of property to other entities, (3) the merger or consolidation of the debtor with another company, (4) the sale of property or the distribution of property to parties of interest, and (5) the issuance of securities of the debtor for cash, property, or existing securities of the debtor. After the plan is filed with the court, it must be accepted by two-thirds in amount and one-half in number of the allowed claims of each class of creditors, and by two-thirds in amount of the allowed interests of each class of stockholders. In addition, the court must approve of the overall fairness of the plan before it will be accepted.

Accounting for Reorganizations—Troubled Debt Restructurings

Standards followed in accounting for reorganizations are contained in *SFAS No. 15*, "Accounting by Debtors and Creditors for Troubled Debt Restructurings." The standards deal primarily with valuation problems, the recognition of gain or loss on restructuring, and general disclosure requirements. Debt may be restructured in any one (or a combination) of the following methods:

1. The debtor may transfer assets in full settlement of the payable.

2. The debtor may give an equity interest in its firm in full settlement of the payable.

3. The creditor may modify terms of the payable.

Transfer of Assets A debtor that transfers assets to a creditor in full settlement of a payable recognizes a gain on the restructuring. The gain is measured by the excess of the carrying value of the payable settled over the fair value of the assets transferred. The *carrying value* of the payable is the face amount increased or decreased by applicable accrued interest and applicable unamortized premium, discount, finance charges, or issue costs. The *fair value* of the assets transferred is the amount that the debtor could reasonably expect to receive in a current sale between a willing buyer and a willing seller, that is, other than in a forced sale.[4] The difference

---

[4]*Statement of Financial Accounting Standards No. 15*, par. 13.

between the fair value and the carrying amount of the assets transferred is a gain or loss on the transfer of assets and is reported as a component of net income for the period of transfer according to the provisions of *APB Opinion No. 30,* "Reporting the Results of Operations."[5] The gain on restructuring is included in net income in the period of restructuring and, if material, classified as an extraordinary item, net of related income tax effect.[6] Assume, for example, that a debtor transferred land with a cost of $20,000 and a fair value of $15,000 to a creditor in full settlement of a $25,000 payable. Ignoring income tax effects, the debtor would report a $5,000 loss ($20,000 − $15,000) from the transfer of assets and a $10,000 extraordinary gain ($25,000 − $15,000) from debt restructuring.

Grant of an Equity Interest   A debtor that issues an equity interest in its firm to a creditor in full settlement of a payable shall account for the equity interest at its fair value. The difference between the fair value of the equity interest issued and the carrying amount of the payable is reported as an extraordinary gain on restructuring.[7]

Modification of Terms   A debtor in a troubled debt restructuring involving only modification of terms of a payable accounts for the effects of the restructuring prospectively from the time of restructuring. The carrying value of the payable is not changed at the time of restructuring unless the carrying value exceeds the total future cash payments specified by the new terms. That is, the effects of changes in the amounts or timing (or both) of future cash payments designated as either interest or face amount are reflected in future periods. Interest expense is computed in such a way that a constant effective interest rate is applied to the carrying value of the payable at the beginning of each period between restructuring and maturity. The new effective interest rate is the discount rate that equates the present value of the future cash payments specified by the new terms with the carrying value of the payable.[8]

If, however, the total future cash payments specified by the new terms, including both payments designated as interest and those designated as face amount, are less than the carrying value of the payable, the debtor should reduce the carrying value to an amount equal to the total future cash payments specified by the new terms and recognize a gain on restructuring. Thereafter, all cash payments under the terms of the payable should be accounted for as reductions of the carrying value of the payable, and no interest expense should be recognized on the payable for any period between the restructuring and maturity.[9]

A restructuring may involve a combination of asset transfer, grant of an equity interest, and modification of terms. In those cases, assets transferred or the equity

---

[5]Ibid., par. 14.
[6]Ibid., par. 21.
[7]Ibid., par. 15.
[8]Ibid., par. 16.
[9]Ibid., par. 17.

interest given are treated first and measured as described earlier. The carrying value of the payable is reduced by the total fair value of the assets transferred or equity interest given, and a gain or loss on the transfer of assets is recognized for the difference between the fair value and carrying value of the assets transferred. A gain on restructuring is then recognized only if the remaining carrying value of the payable exceeds the total future cash payments specified by the terms of the debt remaining unsettled.[10]

Restructuring Illustration

To illustrate the accounting process, assume that Box Company filed a petition for reorganization with the bankruptcy court. The reorganization plan has been approved by the parties of interest and the court. Box Company's balance sheet on April 30, 1995, prior to reorganization, is shown in Illustration 17-1.

ILLUSTRATION 17-1
Box Company
Balance Sheet
April 30, 1995

Current Assets		
Cash		$ 86,000
Accounts receivable	$120,000	
Less: Allowance for uncollectibles	13,000	107,000
Inventories		142,000
Total current assets		335,000
Plant and equipment	680,000	
Less: Accumulated depreciation	275,000	405,000
Land held as an investment		80,000
Total Assets		$820,000
Current Liabilities		
Accounts payable—secured by inventory		$ 60,000
Accounts payable—unsecured		134,000
Notes payable—unsecured		200,000
Accrued expenses—with priority		24,000
Accrued interest payable		50,000
Total current liabilities		468,000
Bonds payable—unsecured		450,000
Total Liabilities		918,000
Stockholders' Equity		
Common stock, $1 par value	$500,000	
Retained earnings (deficit)	(598,000)	
Total Stockholders' Deficiency		(98,000)
Excess of Liabilities over Stockholders' Deficiency		$820,000

---

[10]Ibid., par. 19.

Provisions of the reorganization plan and the appropriate journal entries to account for the restructuring follow:

1. Creditors represented by the unsecured accounts payable agree to accept the accounts receivable of Box Company in full settlement of their claims. The fair value of the receivables, which is not guaranteed by Box Company, is $100,000.

Allowance for Uncollectibles	13,000	
Loss on Transfer of Assets	7,000	
Accounts Receivable		20,000
Accounts Payable—Unsecured	134,000	
Accounts Receivable		100,000
Gain on Restructuring of Debt		34,000

Notice that a loss on transfer of assets is recognized for the difference between the book value of the receivables ($107,000) and their fair value ($100,000). A gain on restructuring is then recognized for the difference between the carrying value of the payable ($134,000) and the fair value of the receivables ($100,000).

2. Accrued expenses with priority are paid in full.

Accrued Expenses	24,000	
Cash		24,000

3. A creditor holding a $120,000 note from Box Company agrees to accept the land held as an investment in full settlement of the note plus accrued interest of $8,000. The land has a fair value of $95,000.

Land	15,000	
Gain on Transfer of Assets		15,000
Notes Payable	120,000	
Accrued Interest Payable	8,000	
Land		95,000
Gain on Restructuring of Debt		33,000

The land is increased to its fair value and a gain on transfer of assets is recognized in the amount of $15,000. The land and payable are then written off and a gain on restructuring is recognized for the difference between the carrying value of the payable ($128,000) and the fair value of the land ($95,000).

4. A creditor holding a 14%, $80,000 note from Box Company (on which $4,000 interest has accrued) agrees to extend the maturity date of the note for two years (until April 30, 1997) and reduce the interest rate to 8%.

Note Payable	80,000	
Accrued Interest Payable	4,000	
Restructured Debt		84,000

Since the total future cash payments of $92,800 (principal of $80,000 and interest of $12,800) exceed the carrying value of the debt ($84,000), no gain on restructuring is recognized. Interest expense is recorded in the future by computing the effective interest rate that, when applied to the carrying amount of the payable at the beginning of the period, will amortize the debt over the period to maturity.

5. Bondholders agree to accept an equity interest in Box Company of 150,000 shares of common stock in exchange for the par value of the bonds. Accrued interest of $38,000 is to be paid in cash by January 1, 1996. The market value of the common stock is $1.25 per share.

Bonds Payable	450,000	
Common Stock (150,000 × $1)		150,000
Other Contributed Capital (150,000 × $.25)		37,500
Gain on Restructuring of Debt		262,500

Since the carrying value of the bonds payable exceeds the fair value of the equity interest given, a gain on restructuring is recognized.

6. Bankruptcy administration expenses totaling $16,000 are paid in cash.

Bankruptcy Administration Expenses	16,000	
Cash		16,000

The net gain on transfer of assets ($15,000 − $7,000) will be reported as a part of operations on the income statement, and the gain on restructuring of debt of $329,500 ($34,000 + $33,000 + $262,500) is reported as an extraordinary item. After giving effect to the reorganization entries, Box Company's balance sheet will be as shown in Illustration 17-2.

Notice that, although the stockholders' deficiency has been eliminated, there is still a retained earnings deficit. If desired by the parties of interest, the reorganization plan could have included a provision to decrease the par value of the common stock and eliminate the accumulated deficit.

The Statement of Affairs[11]

The Reform Act provides that a plan for reorganization will not be approved by the court unless it can be shown that creditors will receive at least as much as they would receive if the debtor were liquidated. Consequently, it is important that the estimated amounts to be received by all parties be determined before filing either a liquidation or reorganization petition with the court. The *Statement of Affairs* is a report designed to show the estimated amount that would be received by each class of claim in the event of liquidation. It is essentially a balance sheet prepared on the basis of an assumption of liquidation rather than on the going-concern assumption. The appropriate emphasis is no longer one of reporting residual costs, but one of reporting on the legal status of resources and claims against those resources. Thus, assets are reported at their expected realizable values, rather than at book values.

---

[11]This statement is an accounting report and should not be confused with the statement of affairs the Bankruptcy Reform Act requires from the debtor company, which is simply a series of questions concerning the debtor company's financial position.

ILLUSTRATION 17-2
Box Company
Balance Sheet
May 1, 1995

Current Assets		
Cash		$ 46,000
Inventories		142,000
Total current assets		188,000
Plant and equipment	$680,000	
Less: Accumulated depreciation	275,000	405,000
Total Assets		$593,000
Current Liabilities		
Accounts payable		$ 60,000
Accrued interest payable		38,000
Total Current Liabilities		98,000
Restructured debt—due 4/30/97		84,000
Total Liabilities		182,000
Stockholders' Equity		
Common stock, $1 par value	$650,000	
Other contributed capital	37,500	
Retained earnings (deficit)	(276,500)	
Total Stockholders' Equity		411,000
Total Liabilities and Stockholders' Equity		$593,000

In addition, the current/noncurrent distinction is set aside, and assets are segregated into those that are pledged with fully secured creditors, those pledged with partially secured creditors, and those that are essentially "free" and therefore available to settle unsecured claims. Likewise, the current/noncurrent distinction for liabilities is meaningless; that is, if the company liquidates, all liabilities are current. Thus, liabilities are classified on the basis of their legal status as those having priority, those that are fully secured, those that are partially secured, and those that are unsecured.

In summary, the statement of affairs is an accounting report that is designed to permit the user to determine the total expected amounts that could be realized on the disposition of the assets, the priorities in the use of the realization proceeds in satisfying claims, and the potential net deficiency that would result if the assets were realized and claims liquidated. In that respect, stockholders' or owners' equity balances have no significance.

Illustration of a Statement of Affairs As an illustration of a statement of affairs, assume that the Preston Company had the following balance sheet on April 30, 1995, at which time the company is contemplating filing a petition for liquidation or reorganization.

PRESTON COMPANY
Balance Sheet
April 30, 1995

ASSETS

Cash	$ 8,200
Notes receivable	24,000
Accounts receivable (net)	47,000
Inventories	
Finished goods	56,000
Work in process	24,000
Raw materials	39,000
Prepaid expenses	1,200
Investment in Beta Company stock, 1,000 shares at market value	26,500
Land	42,000
Buildings (net)	198,000
Machinery and equipment (net)	93,000
Total Assets	$558,900

LIABILITIES AND STOCKHOLDERS' EQUITY

Bank notes payable	$ 32,000
Accounts payable	195,000
Accrued salaries and wages	13,500
Accrued interest	
On bank notes	1,100
On mortgage note	8,500
Mortgage note payable	200,000
Capital stock	250,000
Retained earnings (deficit)	(141,200)
Total Liabilities and Stockholders' Equity	$558,900

Additional information concerning estimated realizable values and other balance sheet relationships follows:

1. The notes receivable are expected to be fully realized, and they have been pledged as collateral on a bank note in the principal amount of $20,000 plus accrued interest of $600.

2. Accounts receivable have an estimated collectible value of $28,000.

3. Finished-goods inventory can be sold at a mark-up of 20% over cost, with selling expenses estimated at 10% of selling price. Work-in-process inventory has no value unless completed. The estimated cost to complete totals $12,000, of which $5,000 represents the cost of raw materials. The estimated selling price of the work-in-process inventory when completed (after allowing for selling expenses) is $25,000. The remaining raw materials inventory has an estimated selling price of 70% of its cost.

4. The recovery value of prepaid expenses is $600.

5. The Beta Company stock is pledged as collateral on a bank note payable in the principal amount of $12,000 plus accrued interest of $500.

6. Land and buildings have appraised values of $40,000 and $100,000, respectively, and serve as collateral on the mortgage note payable.

7. The machinery and equipment have an estimated disposal value of $38,000.

The statement of affairs for Preston Company, along with a *deficiency account* summarizing estimated gains and losses on the realization of assets, is presented in Illustration 17-3.

ILLUSTRATION 17-3
Preston Company
Statements of Affairs
April 30, 1995

BOOK VALUE	ASSETS			REALIZABLE VALUE
	ASSETS PLEDGED WITH FULLY SECURED CREDITORS			
$ 24,000	Notes receivable		$ 24,000	
	Bank note payable	$ 20,000		
	Accrued interest	600	20,600	$ 3,400
26,500	Investment in stock of Beta Company		26,500	
	Bank note payable	$ 12,000		
	Accrued interest	500	12,500	14,000
	ASSETS PLEDGED WITH PARTIALLY SECURED CREDITORS			
42,000	Land	$ 40,000		
198,000	Buildings	100,000	140,000	
	Mortgage note payable	200,000		
	Accrued interest	8,500	208,500	
	FREE ASSETS			
8,200	Cash			8,200
47,000	Accounts receivable			28,000
1,200	Prepaid expenses			600
	Inventories			
56,000	(1) Finished goods			60,480
24,000	(2) Work in process			18,000
39,000	(3) Raw material			23,800
93,000	Machinery and equipment			38,000
	Total net realizable value			194,480
	Liabilities having priority— Salaries and wages			13,500
	Net free assets			180,980
	Estimated deficiency to unsecured creditors (balancing amount)			82,520
$558,900				$263,500

BOOK VALUE	EQUITIES		UNSECURED
	LIABILITIES HAVING PRIORITY		
$ 13,500	Accrued salaries and wages	$ 13,500	
	FULLY SECURED CREDITORS		
32,000	Notes payable	32,000	
1,100	Accrued interest	1,100	
	PARTIALLY SECURED CREDITORS		
200,000	Mortgage note payable	200,000	
8,500	Accrued interest	8,500	
	Total	208,500	
	Land and buildings	140,000	$ 68,500
	UNSECURED CREDITORS		
195,000	Accounts payable		195,000
	STOCKHOLDERS' EQUITY		
250,000	Capital stock		
(141,200)	Retained earnings (deficit)		
$558,900			$263,500

(1) $56,000 \times 1.20 = \$67,200 \times .9 = \$60,480$.

(2) Estimated Selling Price $25,000
Less: Estimated completion costs other than raw materials ... 7,000
Realizable Value $18,000

(3) $39,000 - \$5,000 = \$34,000 \times .70 = \$23,800$.

Preston Company
Deficiency Account
April 30, 1995

ESTIMATED LOSSES		ESTIMATED GAINS	
Accounts receivable	$ 19,000	Capital stock	$250,000
Inventory	16,720	Retained earnings	(141,200)
Prepaid expenses	600	Estimated deficiency to	
Land	2,000	unsecured creditors	82,520
Buildings	98,000		
Machinery and equipment	55,000		
Total	$191,320	Total	$191,320

Several comments concerning Illustration 17-3 should be noted:

1. Assets pledged with fully secured creditors—notes receivable, and the investment in stock of Beta Company—have realizable values in excess of the secured debts in an amount of $17,400, which becomes available for distribution to unsecured creditors.

2. Assets pledged with partially secured creditors—land and buildings—have a realizable value that is $68,500 less than the total related debt. Thus, mortgage holders have a $68,500 remaining claim that ranks as an unsecured one.

3. Free assets are those that have not been pledged with specific liabilities and are, therefore, available to satisfy general unsecured creditors. Note that the "free" assets include the excess of the realizable value of pledged assets over the related debts of fully secured creditors.

4. In the Deficiency Account, the capital stock and retained earnings deficit are included in the estimated gains column only to indicate the extent to which total potential deficiency is covered by stockholders' equity.

5. The final settlement with the unsecured creditors can be computed by dividing the "net free assets" by the total amount owed to unsecured creditors:

$$\frac{\$180,980}{\$263,500} = 68.7\%$$

Thus, it is estimated that each unsecured creditor will receive approximately 69% of the amount due under the claim.

TRUSTEE ACCOUNTING AND REPORTING

As indicated earlier, a trustee is often appointed to assume the responsibility of managing the debtor's business for the period during which a reorganization plan is developed or the business is liquidated. The trustee takes title to the debtor's assets and is accountable to the court, the creditors, and other parties of interest for the subsequent utilization or realization of the assets. From an accounting standpoint, two main approaches are available to the trustee. He or she may continue to use the debtor's accounting records, which is the approach often used when it is expected that the business will be rehabilitated and returned to the control of the debtor at some future date or when the business is expected to be sold as an operating unit. Or the trustee may open a new set of books, the approach frequently used when the assets are to be realized and liabilities liquidated. In either case, the better approach is probably to open a new set of books, because it will make it easier to distinguish between the assets and liabilities of the debtor that existed before the appointment of the trustee and those arising after his or her appointment.

When new books are opened, the trustee records, at their book values, the assets (as well as any related valuation accounts) that have been placed under trustee control. The net credit in the entry is to an account normally entitled with the name of the debtor company and the term "in receivership," for example, "Axon Company—In Receivership." No existing liabilities are recorded by the trustee, but liabilities incurred later are recorded. Although liabilities existing at the date the trustee takes control are not recorded, the trustee may pay these liabilities in the course of operating the company or as part of the realization and liquidation process. This payment of preexisting debts, of course, reduces the assets for which the trustee is accountable.

The transfer of the assets to the trustee is recorded on the debtor's books by crediting the various asset accounts (with debits to related valuation accounts) and debiting an account in the name of the trustee. Subsequent activities engaged in by the trustee are recorded on the trustee's books with entries on the debtor's books where appropriate, for example, to record the payment of preexisting debts by the trustee.

As an example of the accounting procedures used where the trustee opens a new set of books, assume that Axon Company has the following account balances on October 1, 1995, at which time Gary Trent was appointed trustee.

Cash	$ 6,400
Receivables	32,000
Inventory	48,600
Property and equipment	120,000
Total	$207,000
Allowance for uncollectibles	$ 2,900
Accumulated depreciation	44,100
Accounts payable	75,000
Capital stock	180,000
Retained earnings (deficit)	(95,000)
Total	$207,000

During the period from October 1, 1995, through December 31, 1995, the following transactions occurred:

(1) All Axon Company's assets were transferred to the trustee.
(2) Additional merchandise inventory was purchased by the trustee on account in the amount of $26,000.
(3) Sales for the period were: on account, $52,000; cash, $7,000.
(4) Cash was collected by the trustee on

Accounts receivable (old)	$18,000
Accounts receivable (new)	46,000

(5) Payments were made by the trustee for

Accounts payable (old)	$43,000
Accounts payable (new)	14,000
Operating expenses	10,500
Trustee's expenses	2,000

(6) Adjusting entries recorded by the trustee on December 31, 1995 were:

Estimated uncollectibles on	
Accounts receivable (old)	$ 3,500
Accounts receivable (new)	400
Accounts receivable written off	
On accounts receivable (old)	4,500
Depreciation expense	7,600

(7) The merchandise inventory balance on December 31 was $42,000.

Entries to record the effect of these transactions on the trustee's and the debtor's books are presented in Illustration 17-4. In order to prepare financial statements for Axon Company on December 31, 1995, the trustee's accounts must be combined

ILLUSTRATION 17-4
Journal Entries

TRUSTEE'S BOOKS			AXON COMPANY'S BOOKS		
(1) Cash	6,400		Gary Trent, Trustee	160,000	
Receivables (old)	32,000		Allowance for Uncollectibles	2,900	
Inventory	48,600		Accumulated Depreciation	44,100	
Property and Equipment	120,000		Cash		6,400
Allowance for			Receivables		32,000
Uncollectibles		2,900	Inventory		48,600
Accumulated Depreciation		44,100	Property and Equipment		120,000
Axon Company—					
in Receivership		160,000			
(2) Purchases	26,000		No entry		
Accounts Payable (new)		26,000			
(3) Cash	7,000				
Accounts Receivable (new)	52,000		No entry		
Sales		59,000			
(4) Cash	64,000				
Accounts Receivable (old)		18,000	No entry		
Accounts Receivable (new)		46,000			
(5) Axon Company—					
in Receivership	43,000		Accounts Payable	43,000	
Accounts Payable (new)	14,000		Gary Trent, Trustee		43,000
Operating Expenses	10,500				
Trustee's Expenses	2,000				
Cash		69,500			
(6) Bad Debts Expense	3,900				
Depreciation Expense	7,600				
Allowance for					
Uncollectibles (old)		3,500	No entry		
Allowance for					
Uncollectibles (new)		400			
Accumulated Depreciation		7,600			
Allowance for Uncollectibles (old)	4,500		No entry		
Accounts Receivable (old)		4,500			
(7) Sales	59,000		Gary Trent, Trustee	2,400	
Inventory		6,600	Income Summary		2,400
Purchases		26,000	Income Summary	2,400	
Operating Expenses		10,500	Retained Earnings		2,400
Trustee's Expenses		2,000			
Bad Debts Expense		3,900			
Depreciation Expense		7,600			
Income Summary		2,400			
Income Summary	2,400				
Axon Company—					
in Receivership		2,400			

with Axon Company's accounts. A combining workpaper for this purpose is presented in Illustration 17-5.

REALIZATION AND LIQUIDATION ACCOUNT

When a trustee is appointed to handle the affairs of a company in financial difficulty, the court expects to receive periodic reports summarizing the realization and

ILLUSTRATION 17-5
Axon Company—in Receivership
Combining Workpaper
December 31, 1995

DEBITS	TRIAL BALANCES TRUSTEE	AXON COMPANY	ADJUSTMENTS AND ELIMINATIONS DR.	CR.	COMBINED INCOME STATEMENT	BALANCE SHEET
Cash	7,900					7,900
Accounts receivable (old)	9,500					9,500
Accounts receivable (new)	6,000					6,000
Inventory	48,600			(1) 6,600		42,000
Property and equipment	120,000					120,000
Purchases	26,000			(1) 26,000		
Operating expenses	10,500				10,500	
Trustee expenses	2,000				2,000	
Bad debts expense	3,900				3,900	
Depreciation expense	7,600				7,600	
Cost of goods sold			(1) 32,600		32,600	
Gary Trent, trustee		117,000		(2) 117,000		
Total	242,000	117,000			56,600	185,400
CREDITS						
Allowance for uncollectibles (old)	1,900					1,900
Allowance for uncollectibles (new)	400					400
Accumulated depreciation	51,700					51,700
Accounts payable (old)		32,000				32,000
Accounts payable (new)	12,000					12,000
Capital stock		180,000				180,000
Retained earnings (deficit)		(95,000)				(95,000)
Sales	59,000				59,000	
Axon Company, in receivership	117,000		(2) 117,000			
Total	242,000	117,000	149,600	149,600	59,000	
Net Income					2,400	2,400
Total					56,600	185,400

(1) To adjust inventory and set up cost of goods sold.
(2) To eliminate reciprocal accounts.

distribution activities of the fiduciary.[12] Although the traditional financial statements may be prepared by the fiduciary, court officials are interested primarily in the changes that have occurred in the monetary items during a period. The legal form used to report these activities is termed a ***realization and liquidation account***. The report has three main sections—assets, liabilities, and revenues and expenses. The asset section consists of four parts, illustrated, as follows:

[12]A fiduciary is a person to whom property is entrusted to hold, control, or manage for another.

ASSETS	
Assets to be realized	Assets realized
Assets acquired	Assets not realized

The *assets to be realized* part identifies the individual assets to which the trustee has taken title from the debtor. Cash is not included in the report because it is already realized. Although cash is excluded, the court is given a copy of the cash account of the trustee, which shows the beginning amount received from the debtor, as well as all the individual receipts and disbursements for the period covered. The *assets acquired* part itemizes the assets either discovered or received from operating activities during the period. The *assets realized* part identifies proceeds received from the conversion of specific assets. The *assets not realized* part identifies the assets remaining with the trustee at the end of the reporting period.

In a similar manner, the liabilities section consists of four parts, as indicated below:

LIABILITIES	
Liabilities liquidated	Liabilities to be liquidated
Liabilities not liquidated	Liabilities incurred

The *liabilities to be liquidated* part identifies the liabilities that the trustee took responsibility for at the date of appointment. *Liabilities incurred* reflect the liabilities incurred by the trustee for operating activities during the period. *Liabilities liquidated* identify specific liabilities paid by the trustee, and *liabilities not liquidated* reflect those that remain to be paid by the trustee.

The revenues and expenses section of the report lists the supplementary expenses incurred and revenues received by the trustee during the period, as follows:

REVENUES AND EXPENSES	
Supplementary charges	Supplementary credits

The realization and liquidation account is prepared in the typical account form with debits on the left side and credits on the right side of the account. Any figure needed to balance the account reflects a gain or loss for the period reported on.

As an example of a realization and liquidation account, assume the previous illustration concerning the receivership of Gary Trent for Axon Company. The realization and liquidation account is presented in Illustration 17-6.

A copy of the Cash account of the trustee that would be included with the report is presented below:

CASH			
Balance, 10/1	6,400	Accounts payable (old)	43,000
Sales	7,000	Accounts payable (new)	14,000
Accounts receivable (old)	18,000	Operating expenses	10,500
Accounts receivable (new)	46,000	Trustee's expenses	2,000
Balance, 12/31	7,900		

ILLUSTRATION 17-6
Axon Company
Gary Trent, Trustee
Realization and Liquidation Account
October 1, 1995 to December 31, 1995

ASSETS TO BE REALIZED			ASSETS REALIZED		
Receivables (old)	$ 32,000		Accounts receivable (old)		$ 18,000
Less: Allowance for uncollectibles	2,900	$ 29,100	Accounts receivable (new)		46,000
Inventory		48,600	**ASSETS NOT REALIZED**		
Property and equipment	120,000		Accounts receivable (old)	$ 9,500	
Less: Accumulated depreciation	44,100	75,900	Less: Allowance for uncollectibles	1,900	7,600
ASSETS ACQUIRED			Accounts receivable (new)	6,000	
Accounts receivable (new)		52,000	Less: Allowance for uncollectibles	400	5,600
SUPPLEMENTARY CHARGES			Inventory		42,000
			Property and equipment	120,000	
Purchases		26,000	Less: Accumulated depreciation	51,700	68,300
Operating expenses		10,500			
Trustee's expenses		2,000	**SUPPLEMENTARY CREDITS**		
LIABILITIES LIQUIDATED			Sales		59,000
Accounts payable (old)		43,000	**LIABILITIES TO BE LIQUIDATED**		
Accounts payable (new)		14,000	Accounts payable (old)		75,000
LIABILITIES NOT LIQUIDATED			**LIABILITIES INCURRED**		
Accounts payable (old)		32,000	Accounts payable (new)		26,000
Accounts payable (new)		12,000			
Net gain		2,400			
Total		$347,500	Total		$347,500

Note that the balancing figure (labeled "net gain") in the realization and liquidation account is the same as the $2,400 net income reported for the period October 1 to December 31, 1995, in Illustration 17-5. This is as it should be, since no assets were realized during the period except through normal operating activities. If assets had been realized by other than normal operating activities (for example, the sale of land), any gain or loss would increase or decrease the net gain reported in the Realization and Liquidation account. The transaction could be treated in one of two ways. Assets realized could be reported at the amount received from the sale of the asset (the traditional approach), or they might be reported at the book value of the asset sold and any gain or loss on the sale reported as a supplemental credit or supplemental charge. For example, assume that the property and equipment account of Axon Company included a parcel of land that cost $25,000, and that the parcel was sold by the trustee for $35,000. The traditional approach would report assets realized at $35,000 with a decrease in assets not realized of $25,000. The $10,000 difference between the two would be reflected as part of a net gain of $12,400, rather than the $2,400 in Illustration 17-6. The items that would be different in Illustration 17-6 are:

ASSETS REALIZED		
Property and equipment		$35,000
ASSETS NOT REALIZED		
Property and equipment ($120,000 − $25,000)	$95,000	
Less: Accumulated depreciation	51,700	43,300
Net gain		12,400

The basic weakness in this approach is that the components of the "net gain" or "net loss" are not disclosed.

An alternative is to report the sale of the land as assets realized at book value, $25,000, a decrease in assets not realized of $25,000, and a supplementary credit "Gain on sale of land" of $10,000. Although the net gain needed to balance the account is still $12,400, the reader of the report is able to identify the components of the net gain. The items that would be different in Illustration 17-6 under this approach are:

ASSETS REALIZED		
Property and equipment		$25,000
ASSETS NOT REALIZED		
Property and equipment	$95,000	
Less: Accumulated depreciation	51,700	43,300
SUPPLEMENTARY CREDITS		
Gain on sale of land		10,000
Net gain		12,400

Similar alternative treatments could be afforded the favorable or unfavorable liquidation of liabilities.

Other items on the realization and liquidation account deserve comment:

1. Note that we have elected to show sales of merchandise as supplementary credits and purchases of merchandise as supplementary charges. As an alternative, the trustee might report sales of merchandise as *assets realized* and purchases of merchandise as *assets acquired*. We believe our treatment is more informative because it separates operating effects from nonoperating effects, although the latter treatment is more common in practice.

2. Expenses representing cost allocations (such as depreciation), and estimated bad debts expense are not reported separately. These expenses are reflected in the report, however, as increases in accumulated depreciation and allowance for uncollectibles in the *assets not realized* part of the report. Thus, because the net gain (loss) for the period is a balancing figure, these expenses are factors in the determination of that net gain (loss).

Questions

1. List the primary types of contractual agreements between a debtor company and its creditors and briefly explain what is involved in each of them.

2. Distinguish between a voluntary and involuntary bankruptcy petition.

3. Distinguish among fully secured, partially secured, and unsecured claims of creditors.

4. Five priority categories of unsecured claims must be paid before general unsecured creditors are paid. Briefly describe what makes up each category.

5. What are "dividends" in a bankruptcy proceeding?

6. For each of the following debt restructurings, indicate whether a gain is recognized and, if so, how the gain is measured and reported.
   (a) Transfer of assets by the debtor to the creditor.
   (b) Grant of an equity interest by the debtor to the creditor.
   (c) Modification of the terms of the payable.

7. What is the purpose of a statement of affairs?

8. One of the officers of a corporation that had just received a discharge in bankruptcy said, "Good, now we don't owe anyone." Is he correct?

9. What are the duties of a trustee in a liquidation proceeding?

10. What is the purpose of a combining workpaper prepared by a trustee?

11. What is the purpose of a realization and liquidation account?

Exercises

Exercise 17-1

Select the best answer choice for each of the following:

1. Johnson joined other creditors of Alpha Company in a composition agreement seeking to avoid the necessity of a bankruptcy proceeding against Alpha. Which statement describes the composition agreement?
   (a) It provides that the creditors will receive less than the full amount of their claims.
   (b) It provides a temporary delay, not to exceed six months, insofar as the debtor's obligation to repay the debts included in the composition is concerned.
   (c) It must be approved by all creditors.
   (d) It provides for the appointment of a receiver to take over and operate the debtor's business.

2. Freeman Company ceased doing business and is in bankruptcy. Among the claimants are employees seeking unpaid wages. The following statements describe the possible status of such claims in a bankruptcy proceeding or legal limitations placed upon them. Which one is an **incorrect** statement?
   (a) The amounts of excess wages not entitled to a priority are mere unsecured claims.
   (b) Such claims include wages earned within 180 days before the filing of the bankruptcy petition, but not to exceed $2,000 in amount.
   (c) They are entitled to priority.
   (d) If a priority is afforded such claims, it cannot exceed $2,000 per wage earner.

3. Which of the entities listed is not subject to an involuntary bankruptcy petition?
   (a) A municipality.
   (b) A partnership.
   (c) A wholesaler company.
   (d) A retailing corporation.

4. The highest priority for payment of unsecured claims in a bankruptcy proceeding is
   (a) Wages up to $2,000 earned within three months before the petition.
   (b) Unpaid federal income taxes.
   (c) Administrative expenses of the bankruptcy.
   (d) Wages owed to an insolvent employee.

5. Which of the following situations that arise because of a debtor's financial difficulties and would not otherwise be acceptable to the creditor must be accounted for as a troubled debt restructuring?
   (a) As part of a negotiated settlement designed to maintain a relationship with a debtor, a creditor reduces the effective interest rate on debt outstanding to reflect the lower market interest rate currently applicable to debt of that risk class.
   (b) Because of a court order, a creditor reduces the stated interest rate for the remaining original life of the debt.
   (c) Because of a court order, a creditor accepts as full satisfaction of its receivable a building the fair value of which equals the creditor's recorded investment in the receivable.
   (d) As part of a negotiated settlement, a creditor accepts as full satisfaction of its receivable a building the fair value of which equals the debtor's carrying amount of the payable.

Exercise 17-2

Indicate whether each of the following is true or false. If an answer is false, explain why.

——— 1. Insolvency means that a debtor has more current liabilities than current assets.

——— 2. Voluntary bankruptcy petitions may be filed under either Chapter 7 or Chapter 11 of the Reform Act.

——— 3. If an insolvent debtor has more than 12 creditors, an involuntary petition must be signed by at least three of those creditors.

——— 4. Unsecured creditors with priority will receive full satisfaction before secured creditors are paid.

——— 5. Either a debtor or its creditors may file a petition for reorganization under Chapter 11 of the Reform Act.

——— 6. In a reorganization involving a transfer of assets, the debtor will recognize a gain on restructuring measured by the excess of the carrying value of the payable settled over the book value of the assets transferred.

——— 7. Restructuring gains that arise from troubled debt restructurings are reported by the debtor as extraordinary gains.

——— 8. The statement of affairs is a report designed to estimate the amount expected to be earned by a debtor company during the time period needed to complete a reorganization.

Exercise 17-3

Bar Company, which is in financial difficulty and in the process of a voluntary reorganization, has agreed to transfer to a creditor a copyright it owns in full settlement of a $150,000 note payable and $15,000 in accrued interest. The copyright, which originally cost $100,000, has an accumulated amortization balance of $55,000 and a current fair value of $95,000.

Required:

A. Prepare the journal entries on Bar Company's books to record the transfer of the copyright.

B. Explain the proper treatment of any gain or loss recognized in (A).

C. Assuming the fair value of the copyright was $30,000, repeat the requirement in (A).

Exercise 17-4

Lake Company, a major creditor of financially troubled Spain Company, has agreed to modify the terms of a debt owed to Lake Company. The debt consists of a $900,000, 12% note that is due currently along with accrued interest of $95,000. Lake Company agreed to extend the due date of the note and accrued interest for three years and to reduce the interest rate to 5% per annum (on both maturity value and accrued interest), with interest to be paid annually.

Required:

A. Should a gain on restructuring be recognized by Spain Company? Explain.

B. Prepare the entry that should be made on Spain Company's books on the date of restructure.

Exercise 17-5

Assume the same situation described in Exercise 17-4 except that the terms of modification of the debt are

1. Accrued interest of $95,000 is to be canceled.
2. The face value of the note is reduced to $600,000, payable at the end of three years. Interest on the new face value at 8% is to be paid annually.

Required:

A. Should a gain on restructuring be recognized? Explain.

B. Prepare entries on the books of Spain Company to record the restructuring.

C. Prepare the entry on Spain Company's books to record the interest payment at the end of the first year after restructuring.

Exercise 17-6

The following data are taken from the statement of affairs of the Monroe Company. (Assume that the realizable values of assets are accurate.)

Assets pledged with fully secured creditors (realizable value, $190,000)	$240,000
Assets pledged with partially secured creditors (realizable value, $90,000)	110,000
Free assets (realizable value, $102,000)	160,000
Fully secured creditor claims	91,000
Partially secured creditor claims	120,000
Unsecured creditor claims with priority	30,000
General unsecured creditor claims	350,000

Required

Compute the amount that will be paid to each class of creditor.

Exercise 17-7

Ball Company is facing bankruptcy proceedings. A balance sheet dated June 30, 1995, and other information are presented below:

Ball Company
Balance Sheet
June 30, 1995

Cash	$ 20,400
Accounts receivable (net)	170,000
Inventory	180,000
Property and equipment (net)	430,000
Total assets	$800,400
Accounts payable	$350,000
Accrued wages	120,000
Notes payable	200,000
Common stock	400,000
Retained earnings (deficit)	(269,600)
Total equities	$800,400

Extimated realizable values of the company's assets are:

Accounts receivable	$ 95,000
Inventory	110,000
Property and equipment	320,000

Accounts receivable and inventory are each pledged as security on individual notes payable in the amount of $100,000 each.

Required:

Prepare a statement of affairs and determine the estimated settlement per dollar for general unsecured creditors. (Assume that all accrued wages are priority items.)

Exercise 17-8

The following balance sheet was prepared for Crane Company on December 31, 1995:

Crane Company
Balance Sheet
December 31, 1995

Cash		$ 33,000
Accounts receivable	$52,500	
Less: Allowance for uncollectibles	3,800	48,700
Inventory		71,000
Property and equipment (net)		142,000
Goodwill		20,000
Total assets		$314,700
Accounts payable		$ 66,000
10% Bonds payable, due 6/30/98		130,000
Common stock, $20 par, 10,000 shares outstanding		200,000
Retained earnings (deficit)		(81,300)
Total equities		$314,700

Crane Company has had operating difficulties, accumulating a deficit over several years before 1995. During 1995, however, Crane reported a significantly lower operating loss, and prospects for the future are relatively bright. Although management and stockholders are optimistic about the future, it is almost certain that the company will lack the necessary working capital to handle existing obligations and expected future growth. In light of these facts, Crane has filed for reorganization under Chapter 11 of the Bankruptcy Reform Act of 1978. The reorganization plan, the provisions of which are set out below, has received the approval of stockholders, creditors, and the court. Provisions of the reorganization plan are as follows:

1. Accounts receivable are to be written down to $40,000 to reflect their current expected realizable value.
2. Inventory is fairly valued, but goodwill is to be written off, and property and equipment is to be written down to its fair value of $118,000.
3. The $20 par value common stock is to be replaced with $4 par value common stock on a share-for-share basis in order to create some reorganization capital, which will be used to eliminate the deficit.
4. The bondholders agree to exchange their bonds for new 8% bonds in the same maturity amount, but with a due date of June 30, 2002, and 6,000 share of $4 par value common stock. The stock will be divided ratably among the bondholders. The fair value of the common stock is equal to its par value.
5. Accounts payable are expected to be paid in full, although creditors have agreed to extend due dates by as much as six months.
6. Any accumulated deficit is to be eliminated.

Required:

A. Prepare journal entries to record the effects of the reorganization plan.

B. Prepare a balance sheet as it would appear immediately after the reorganization.

Exercise 17-9

TRX Company has been forced into receivership, and you have been appointed trustee. You decide to open your own set of books in order to distinguish more clearly between transactions occurring before and after your appointment. The following account balances were reported on September 1, 1995:

Cash	$ 26,700
Accounts receivable	130,400
Inventory	191,900
Property and equipment	590,400
Total	$939,400

Allowance for uncollectibles	$ 16,000
Accumulated depreciation	211,500
Accounts payable	308,400
Capital stock	800,000
Retained earnings (deficit)	(396,500)
Total	$939,400

In the four months immediately after your appointment, the following transaction occurred:

1. Sales were made in the amount of $296,000, of which $31,500 were cash sales.
2. Receivables were collected in the following amounts:

Old receivables	$ 76,800
New receivables	242,200

3. Additional inventory was purchased on account in the amount of $127,500.
4. Cash payments were made as follows:

On old accounts payable	$206,500
On new accounts payable	61,600
For operating expenses	46,000
For trustee fees	13,000

5. Journal entries were made to record
    (a) Bad debt expense of $21,600, of which $8,600 related to new accounts receivable.
    (b) Depreciation expense of $32,400.
    (c) Write off old accounts receivable of $21,000.

The inventory balance at the end of your first four months as trustee (the end of the fiscal year for TRX Company) was $149,700.

Required:

Prepare journal entries to record the foregoing on your set of books. Include appropriate closing entries.

Exercise 17-10

Use the data provided in Exercise 17-9.

Required:

Prepare a combining workpaper for TRX Company as of the end of the first four months of receivership (December 31, 1995).

Problems

Problem 17-1

On February 1, 1995, Clover Company filed a petition for reorganization under the bankruptcy statutes. The court approved the plan on September 1, 1995, including the following provisions:

1. Unsecured creditors of open accounts amounting to $71,600 are paid 42 cents on the dollar in full settlement.
2. Clover Company is to exchange accounts receivable in the face amount of $92,000 and an allowance for uncollectible accounts of $19,450 for the full settlement of $132,400 owed on open account to one of its major unsecured creditors. The estimated fair value of the receivables is $69,000.
3. Accrued expenses of $14,620, representing priority items, are to be paid in full.
4. Clover Company's only other major unsecured creditor agreed to a five-year extension of the $300,000 principal owed him on a 10% note payable. Accrued interest on the note on September 1, 1995, amounts to $27,000, one-third of which is to be paid in cash and the remainder canceled. In addition, no interest is to be charged during the remaining five years to maturity of the note.

Required:

Prepare journal entries on the books of Clover Company to give effect to the foregoing provisions.

Problem 17-2

On September 30, 1994, SRP Company filed a petition for reorganization with a bankruptcy court. The plan was approved by the court and all parties of interest on January 2, 1995, when SRP Company's balance sheet was as follows:

SRP Company
Balance Sheet
January 2, 1995

Cash		$ 32,200
Accounts receivable	$ 71,450	
Less: Allowance for uncollectibles	16,750	54,700
Inventories		126,600
Plant and equipment	322,000	
Less: Accumulated depreciation	180,700	141,300
Land		20,800
Patents		92,000
Total assets		$467,600
Current liabilities		
Accounts payable—unsecured		$142,700
12% Notes payable—unsecured		57,000
Accrued wages—with priority		11,900
Accrued interest payable		38,400
Total current liabilities		250,000
10% Note payable—unsecured		54,400
9% Mortgage note payable—secured by equipment		80,000
Stockholders' equity		
Common stock, $.50 par value, 2,500,000		
shares authorized, 480,000 shares issued		
and outstanding		240,000
Retained earnings (deficit)		(156,800)
Total equities		$467,600

The terms of the reorganization plan are as follows:

1. Creditors represented by $69,000 of the unsecured accounts payable agree to accept the accounts receivable of SRP Company in full settlement of their claims. The fair value of the receivables is $51,000.

2. Creditors represented by $54,000 of the unsecured accounts payable agree to accept a patent with a book value of $42,000 and a fair value of $50,000 in full settlement of their claims.

3. Creditors of the remaining unsecured accounts payable agree to accept $.60 on the dollar. Cash is paid to these creditors and to the creditors with priority.

4. The creditor holding the 12%, $57,000 note (on which there is $6,000 accrued interest) agreed to extend the due date for two years from January 3, 1995, and to reduce the interest rate to 6% on the current carrying value of the debt ($63,000), payable annually.

5. The holder of the 10%, $54,400 unsecured note (on which there is $11,900 accrued interest) agreed to cancel the accrued interest and $14,400 of the principal; interest on the new note at 10% is due annually with the principal due on January 3, 1998.

6. The holder of the 9%, $80,000 mortgage note (on which there is $20,500 accrued interest) agreed to accept 100,000 shares of common stock in exchange for full satisfaction of the debt. The common stock has a fair value of $.59 per share.

7. The par value of the common stock is reduced to $.10 per share and any remaining accumulated deficit is eliminated.

Required:

A. Prepare journal entries to give effect to the reorganization.

B. Prepare a post-reorganization balance sheet dated January 2, 1995.

C. Prepare journal entries to accrue interest on December 31, 1995, and to record the payment of interest on January 2, 1996.

Problem 17-3

Prost Company has filed a bankruptcy petition. Its account balances at December 31, 1995 are presented here:

Cash	$ 2,500
Notes receivable	60,000
Accounts receivable (net)	76,000
Inventories	
Finished goods	43,000
Work in process	60,000
Raw materials	51,000
Prepaid expenses	4,000
Investment in stock	12,000
Land	140,000
Plant and equipment (net)	400,000
Goodwill	10,000
Total	$858,500
Accounts payable	$220,000
Accrued wages (all with priority)	45,000
Bank notes payable	225,000
Mortgage payable	350,000
Common stock	380,000
Retained earnings (deficit)	(361,500)
Total	$858,500

The following additional information is available:

1. All notes receivable with the exception of one for $2,500 are expected to be collected. The notes receivable are pledged as security on the bank notes payable.
2. Of the total accounts receivable, $55,000 is expected to be collected. The accounts receivable are also pledged as security on the bank notes payable.
3. Finished goods can be sold at 30% above cost. Selling expenses will be approximately 15% of selling price. Work in process is to be completed at an additional cost of $30,000, of which $19,000 represents the cost of raw materials. The expected selling price of the work in process (after completion) is 10% above cost, with selling expenses of 15% of selling price. Unused raw materials can be sold for $18,000.
4. Prepaid expenses are fully recoverable.
5. The investment in stock consists of 100 shares of MBI Company with a current market value of $19,000.
6. Land is appraised at $200,000, and plant and equipment is appraised at $205,000. The land and plant and equipment serve as collateral on the mortgage payable. Accrued but unrecorded interest on the mortgage payable amounts to $3,000.

Required

A. Prepare a statement of affairs, including a deficiency account.

B. Compute the estimated dividend to be paid general unsecured creditors.

Problem 17-4

A balance sheet for Bran Company on June 30, 1995, the date Jim Brown was appointed trustee, is presented here:

Bran Company
Balance Sheet
June 30, 1995

Cash		$ 15,000
Accounts receivable	$ 45,000	
Less: Allowance for uncollectibles	6,000	39,000
Inventory		104,000
Plant and equipment	215,000	
Less: Accumulated depreciation	70,000	145,000
Total assets		$303,000
Accounts payable		$145,000
Common stock		225,000
Retained earnings (deficit)		(67,000)
Total equities		$303,000

The following information concerning the period from June 30, 1995, to December 31, 1995, is also available:

1. All Bran Company's assets were transferred to the trustee.
2. Sales for the period were $130,000, of which $30,000 were cash sales.
3. Receivables collected by the trustee in cash were:

Old receivables	$38,000
New receivables	85,000

4. Merchandise inventory was purchased on account by the trustee in the amount of $35,000.

5. Cash payments were made by the trustee for
(a) Accounts payable (old)	$110,000
(b) Accounts payable (new)	30,000
(c) Operating expenses	47,000
(d) Trustee expense	2,000

6. Adjusting entries recorded by the trustee on December 31, 1995, were:
(a) Estimated uncollectibles	
Accounts receivable (old)	$ 1,000
Accounts receivable (new)	2,000
(b) Accounts receivable written off (old)	7,000
(c) Depreciation expense	10,000

7. The merchandise inventory balance on December 31 was $75,000.

8. The plant and equipment included a parcel of land and a piece of equipment, both of which were sold by the trustee for cash. The land cost $14,000 and was sold for $25,000. The equipment, which had a book value of $25,000 (cost, $50,000; accumulated depreciation, $25,000), was sold for $13,000.

Required:

Prepare a realization and liquidation account, including a copy of the cash account, for the period June 30, 1995 to December 31, 1995. Use the alternate approach for reporting the components of the net gain or loss on the sale of land and equipment.

Problem 17-5

Plum Company has been in receivership for the past five months. At the beginning of this period, the following trial balance was taken from Plum Company's books.

Cash	$ 4,500
Accounts receivable	15,000
Inventory	142,650
Property and equipment	90,600
	$252,750
Allowance for uncollectibles	$ 3,750
Accumulated depreciation	36,825
Accounts payable	143,175
Capital stock	135,000
Retained earnings (deficit)	(66,000)
	$252,750

The trustee, P. Smith, who was appointed to manage the debtor's business during the period of liquidation, opened a new set of books and took title to Plum Company's assets on June 1, 1995. The activities of the trustee during the five-month period ended October 31, 1995 are as follows:

1. The trustee sold all Plum Company's inventory for $153,000, of which $75,000 represented credit sales.

2. Cash was collected on old receivables, $11,250, and on new receivables, $64,500.

3. Expenses paid during the period were
Operating expenses	$11,850
Trustee expenses	3,200

4. The trustee recorded depreciation expense of $5,250.
5. The trustee paid off all the accounts payable.
6. Estimated uncollectibles on the new accounts receivable were $2,250; the trustee wrote off all the remaining old accounts receivable.
7. The trustee sold all the property and equipment for $43,500.

Required:

A. Prepare journal entries to record the effects of these transactions on the books of both the trustee and Plum Company.

B. Prepare a combining workpaper at the end of the five-month period, October 31, 1995.

Problem 17-6

Use the data provided in Problem 17-5.

Required:

Prepare a realization and liquidation account for Plum Company to cover the five-month period of receivership (June 1, 1995, to October 31, 1995). Use the alternate approach to present the components of the net gain or net loss, and include a copy of the trustee's cash account for the period.

Problem 17-7

Miner Company is being forced into bankruptcy. The company's creditors and stockholders have requested an estimate of the results of a liquidation of the company. Miner's trial balance follows:

Miner Company
Trial Balance
May 31, 1995

	DEBIT	CREDIT
Cash	$ 6,000	
Accounts receivable	63,000	
Allowance for bad debts		$ 2,000
Notes receivable	50,000	
Accrued interest on notes receivable	1,200	
Inventory	60,000	
Buildings	182,000	
Accumulated depreciation—buildings		63,000
Equipment	14,600	
Accumulated depreciation—equipment		1,400
Prepaid insurance	1,100	
Goodwill	8,500	
Accrued wages—with priority		6,000
Taxes payable—with priority		2,400
Accounts payable		170,000
Notes payable		80,000
Accrued interest payable		1,600
Common stock		110,000
Retained earnings (deficit)	50,000	
	$436,400	$436,400

The assets are expected to bring cash on conversion in the following amounts:

Accounts receivable	$50,000
Notes receivable including $1,000 accrued interest	40,800
Inventory	30,000
Building	75,000
Equipment	4,200
Prepaid insurance	400

The notes receivable are pledged as security on a note payable of $40,000. A note payable of $20,000 is secured by a lien on the building, and the equipment is pledged as security on a note payable of $10,000. One-half of the interest payable relates to the $40,000 note payable; the other half of the interest payable relates to the $20,000 note payable. There is no accrued interest on the other notes payable.

Required:

Prepare a statement of affairs as of May 31, 1995. Include a deficiency account, and determine the estimated dividend rate to the general unsecured creditors.

Problem 17-8

A receiver was appointed by the court to manage the affairs of Davis Manufacturing Company on March 31, 1995. On this date, the following balance sheet applied:

Davis Manufacturing Company
Balance Sheet
March 31, 1995

Cash	$ 22,500
Accounts receivable	115,500
Notes receivable	60,000
Accrued interest on notes receivable	1,375
Inventories	
Finished goods	140,000
Work in process	97,500
Raw materials	60,000
Supplies	7,750
Prepaid expenses	3,000
Investment in stock	66,250
Land	105,000
Buildings (net)	495,000
Equipment (net)	232,500
Total	$1,406,375
Notes payable	$ 196,000
Accounts payable	587,500
Wages payable (all with priority)	33,750
Payroll taxes payable (all with priority)	5,250
Accrued interest payable	
On notes payable	2,750
On mortgage note payable	21,250
Mortgage note payable	440,000
Common stock	469,000
Retained earnings (deficit)	(349,125)
Total	$1,406,375

Additional Information:

1. The cash account includes a $500 travel advance that has been spent.
2. Of the total accounts receivable, $75,000 are believed to be collectible. The remaining accounts are doubtful, but it is believed that about one-third of these will be realized eventually. The accounts receivable are pledged as security on a $10,000 note payable.
3. Notes receivable of $50,000 have been pledged as security on a note payable of $45,000. This portion of the notes receivable has an estimated realizable value of $35,000. The remaining notes receivable, including the accrued interest, are expected to be fully collected. The $45,000 note payable has accrued interest due of $1,000.
4. The finished-goods inventory is expected to sell at 20% above its cost, with expenses involved in its disposition approximating 10% of selling price. The work in process inventory can be completed at an additional cost of $55,000, of which $40,000 represents materials used from the present raw materials inventory. The completed work in process should then sell for $145,000; the remaining raw materials should sell for one-half their cost. Supplies are expected to realize $1,300.
5. The investment in stock consists of 2,000 shares of Monelli Vineyards. The stock has a current market value of $50 per share and is pledged as security on a note payable of $41,000. Interest accrued on the note payable amounts to $1,750.
6. The land and buildings have been appraised at $165,000 and $240,000, respectively. They are pledged as collateral on the mortgage note payable.
7. The equipment is expected to realize $100,000.
8. Prepaid expenses are nonrealizable.

Required:

A. Prepare a statement of affairs.

B. Prepare a deficiency account detailing estimated gains and losses.

C. Calculate the dividend rate per dollar of unsecured liabilities.

18

PARTNERSHIPS: FORMATION, OPERATION, AND OWNERSHIP CHANGES

The next two chapters deal exclusively with accounting and reporting problems associated with the partnership form of business organization. These chapters cover the complete life cycle of a partnership from its formation and operation to its liquidation. Partnerships are covered in this text because they are a common form of business organization. They are popular because they permit the pooling of limited resources, are easy to form (no special governmental approval is required), and may have certain tax advantages. Because partnerships are common, accountants are often called upon to account for and serve in an advisory capacity to partnerships. Although many of the accounting concepts applicable to a sole proprietorship or a corporation are also applicable to partnerships, some aspects of partnership formation, operation, and liquidation require additional consideration. The unique aspects of accounting for a partnership are the focus of these chapters.

Accounting for a partnership is influenced by the agreement made between the partners and the appropriate state statutes. Partnerships operate within the legal framework of the state in which they are organized and the statutes may vary from state to state. In order to illustrate statutory provisions, the Uniform Partnership Act (UPA) is integrated throughout the partnership chapters because it, or some modification thereof, is the partnership law that has been adopted by the majority of the states. An in-depth study of the legal aspects of partnerships is generally contained in the typical business law course.

PARTNERSHIP DEFINED

A partnership is defined by the UPA as "an association of two or more persons to carry on as co-owners a business for profit."[1] Persons in this definition include individuals, partnerships, corporations, and other associations. In some cases, it may be difficult to determine whether a partnership has been formed or whether an individual is a partner in a business arrangement. To determine the existence of a partnership, it may be helpful to look for the following three attributes: (1) there must be an agreement, either expressed or implied, between two or more persons; (2) the business must be operated for the purpose of making a profit; and (3) members of the firm must be co-owners of the business. Co-ownership involves the right of each partner to share in the profits of the business, to participate in the management of the business, and to hold an interest in properties conveyed to the partnership. These rights are shared equally unless agreed to otherwise in the partnership agreement.

REASONS FOR FORMING A PARTNERSHIP

The prospective owner(s) of a business should consider the various attributes of the different forms of business organizations before selecting the one that they believe best meets their organizational objectives and personal goals. A form suitable for one set of business objectives may not be appropriate for another. It is possible for a firm to start as a proprietorship and, as the business and personal environments change, to move to a partnership form, and ultimately, to incorporate.

One of the major advantages of a partnership is that it permits the pooling of capital and other resources without the complexities and formalities of a corporation. A partnership is easier and less costly to establish than a corporation and is generally not subject to as much governmental regulation. Furthermore, the partners may be able to operate with more flexibility because they are not subject to the control of a board of directors. There may also be certain tax advantages to a partnership, as discussed later.

CHARACTERISTICS OF A PARTNERSHIP

The principal types of partnerships are general partnerships, limited partnerships, and joint ventures. The characteristics of these types of business organization are discussed in this section. Some partnership characteristics may make it more difficult for a partnership to raise capital than for a corporation. Partnerships are thus most common in comparatively small businesses, professional organizations, such as medical clinics or an accounting practice, and some limited projects undertaken to accomplish a single goal, such as an oil and gas exploration project or the purchase of a parcel of real estate for investment purposes. However, there is no limit to the size or number of partners in a firm. For example, in the large international

---

[1] UPA, Section 6.

CPA firms, the number of partners is in the hundreds and revenue is in the millions of dollars.

General Partnership

In a general partnership, each member is a general partner within the firm. That is, there is no "limited partner" in the organization. The following are characteristics of a general partnership.

Mutual Agency   Every general partner is an agent of both the partnership and every other partner. Thus, a partner can bind the other partners to a contract if he or she is acting within the apparent scope of the business. Outside parties transacting business with a partner can assume the partner has the power to bind the partnership unless they are informed otherwise. Outside parties should be aware, however, that for certain acts, such as the assignment of partnership property, unanimous consent of the partners is required.

Right to Dispose of a Partnership Interest   A capital interest in a general partnership is a personal asset of the individual partner that can be sold or disposed of in any legal way. However, the UPA, recognizing the highly personal relationship of the partners, provides that a purchaser of another partner's interest does not have the right to participate in management unless he or she is accepted by all the partners. The new partner is entitled to the profit allocation acquired and, in the event of liquidation, to receive whatever assets the selling partner would have received had he or she continued in the partnership.

Unlimited Liability   In a ***general partnership***, each partner is jointly and severally liable for the debts and obligations of the partnership. This means that in the case of liquidation, the creditors of the partnership, if not satisfied from assets of the partnership, can look to each partner's personal resources for recovery of unsatisfied claims. Jointly and severally means that a creditor can seek recovery from all the partners or can proceed against one or more of them separately.

Limited or Uncertain Life   A general partnership may be dissolved for a number of reasons, including the death of a partner, the bankruptcy of an individual partner, the withdrawal of a partner from the partnership or a judgment by a court that a partner is unsound of mind and incapable of performing his or her partnership duties.

Tax Implications   A general partnership is not subject to income tax, but it must file an information return. The income or loss of the partnership is allocated to the individual partners, and their respective share of the income or loss is reported on their individual income tax returns whether distributed by the partnership or not. Also, a partner's capital interest in a partnership for tax purposes is the amount of cash invested. If noncash assets are invested, his or her tax basis is the adjusted basis of the asset at the date of investment reduced by any related indebtedness assumed by the partnership, regardless of the fair value of the asset invested. For example, if a partner invests land with a tax basis of $50,000 and a fair value of $80,000, the partner's tax basis in the partnership is $50,000. Of course, for tax purposes, no gain or loss is recognized by the partner in the year the land was transferred to the partnership.

The characteristics just discussed underline the importance of careful selection of the individuals to be associated with in a general partnership. In particular, mutual agency and unlimited liability are distinctive features of a general partnership that could result in extensive personal liability resulting from the acts of other partners.

Limited Partnership

In a *limited partnership*, one or more of the partners are general partners and one or more are limited partners. General partners manage the firm and are personally liable for obligations of the partnership. Limited partners invest capital only and limit their liability for partnership obligations to the amount of investment they have agreed to make. In return, limited partners give up the right to participate in the management of the firm.

The limited partnership form of organization is selected when the general partners want to raise capital without giving up management control of the business. It is also an attractive form when the tax benefits associated with a partnership are desired, but the investors do not want to assume personal liability for the obligations of the partnership. For these reasons, the limited partnership form is often used for professional sports franchises and offerings of partnership interests made to the public for the purpose of carrying out a specific business plan, such as real estate ventures or oil and gas exploration projects.

Laws relating to a limited partnership are codified in the Uniform Limited Partnership Act (ULPA). The ULPA provides that in forming a limited partnership, a certificate required by state statute must be signed and filed with the appropriate government official. The certificate is generally drafted and filed by the general partners. Among other things, it should describe the nature of the business, state the firm's name, location, and term of its existence, and identify all partners and their capital contributions. Although the general partners must obtain the consent of the limited partners for certain actions, in general, partnership law applies to limited partnerships. The accounting procedures described in this and the following chapter are applicable to both general and limited partnerships.

Joint Ventures

A *joint venture* is an arrangement entered into by two or more parties to accomplish a single or limited purpose for the mutual benefit of the members of the group, often to earn a profit. For example, a firm in one country may enter into an agreement with the firm of another country to pool their resources to construct an automobile manufacturing plant, or two or more firms may enter into an arrangement to develop a new product that requires complementary technological knowledge. Thus, the life of the joint venture is limited to that of the undertaking, which may be of short- or long-term duration.

The relationship between the parties in the arrangement is generally governed by a written agreement. A distinguishing characteristic of the agreement is that each joint venturer participates directly or indirectly in the overall management of the resources. Accordingly, major decisions require the consent of the ownership group.

Joint ventures are commonly organized as corporations or partnerships. If organized as a corporation, the investment in the joint venture generally must be accounted for using the equity method in accordance with the provisions of *Accounting Principles Board Opinion No. 18.*[2] As a corporation, a joint venture is governed by corporate law. If the arrangement is a partnership joint venture, interpretations of *Opinion No. 18* indicate that many of the provisions of that opinion are appropriate in accounting for the investment.[3] In general, partnership law applies to a partnership joint venture, but the authority of a joint venturer is limited to a greater extent than that of a general partner. For example, as a general rule, one party to the arrangement is not an agent of the other parties.

PARTNERSHIP AGREEMENT

A partnership is a voluntary association based on the contractual agreement between or among legally competent persons. The contract between the parties is called the ***partnership agreement, partnership contract,*** or ***articles of partnership.*** The partnership agreement generally contains provisions related to the nature of the business, operating policies, and the relations between the partners in operating and terminating the business. In the contract, the partners should clearly express their intention, and the document should cover all aspects of operating the partnership. If there are subsequent disputes and the partners are unable to reach a satisfactory agreement, it may be necessary to resort to litigation.

The partnership agreement should reflect fully the precise intentions of the parties and be as unambiguous as possible. The agreement should include the following important points:

1. The name of the firm and identity of the partners.
2. The nature, purpose, and scope of the business.
3. The effective date of organization.
4. The length of time the partnership is to operate.
5. Location of the place of business.

---

[2]*Opinions of the Accounting Principles Board No. 18*, "The Equity Method of Accounting for Investments in Common Stock" (New York: AICPA, 1971).

[3]*Accounting Interpretations of APB Opinion No. 18* (New York: AICPA, 1972), par. 2.

6. Provision for the allocation of profit and loss.

7. Provision for salaries and withdrawals of assets by partners.

8. The rights, duties, and obligations of each partner such as the amount of time each partner will spend on business activities, and whether each partner is a general or limited partner.

9. Authority of each partner in contract situations.

10. Procedures for admitting a new partner.

11. Provisions that specify how operations are to be conducted and how the various partners' interests are to be satisfied on the withdrawal or the death of a partner.

12. Procedures for the arbitration of disputes.

13. Fiscal period of the partnership.

14. Identification and valuation of initial asset investments and the specification of capital interest that each partner is to receive.

15. Situations that may cause the dissolution of the partnership and provisions for terminating or continuing the business.

16. Accounting practices to be followed, such as depreciation policies, the sequence of closing procedures, and whether the cash or accrual basis is to be used in measuring net income.

17. Whether or not an audit is to be performed.

Some of the items listed will be discussed in more detail in later sections.

The law does not specify the form of the agreement. Although it may be oral, it is good business practice to have the agreement in writing for the protection of the individual partners. A written agreement tends to reduce the number of disagreements resulting from misunderstandings and "loss of memory."

Legally, the partners have a great deal of flexibility in drafting an agreement among themselves, but they must recognize that the UPA specifies certain rights of and obligations to outside parties that may not be avoided by the individual partners. For example, as noted previously, the UPA (Section 15) imposes unlimited liability on each general partner for partnership debts and obligations. A provision in a partnership agreement that exempts a general partner from this obligation would be superseded by the provision in the UPA.

In drafting the agreement, the partners should seek both legal and accounting assistance to assure that their rights are protected and to help anticipate and avoid as many points of conflict as possible. If there are later disputes related to the relations between the partners, most provisions set out in the UPA control only if the partners have failed to make an express agreement, or if the partners are unable to reach a mutually satisfying agreement. For example, in the absence of an agreement concerning how to share profits, the UPA provides that profits are to be shared equally. Differences arising from ordinary matters may be decided by a majority vote of the partners [UPA, Section 18(H)].

Capital Interest Versus Profit Interest

In preparing the partnership agreement, the partners must recognize that there is a distinction between a partner's capital interest and his or her interest in income and losses subsequently reported by the partnership. A partner's *capital interest* is a claim against the net assets of the partnership as shown by the balance in the partner's capital account; an *interest in income and loss* determines how the partner's capital interest will increase or decrease as a result of subsequent operations. The partners may agree that an individual partner is to receive a one-third capital interest in the partnership, but the same partner's interest in income and loss may be equal to, greater than, or less than one-third.

ACCOUNTING FOR A PARTNERSHIP

For accounting purposes, a partnership is considered a separate economic and accounting entity. The assets, liabilities, and residual capital interest, as well as the transactions and events that affect the accounts of the partnership, are areas of interest that require a separate accounting to provide information to the partners and other interested parties. Separation of these activities from the personal transactions of the individual partners is necessary in order to evaluate the performance of the partnership. This does not mean that other forms of statements cannot be prepared for other purposes. For example, a general partner has unlimited liability to the creditors of the partnership. Accordingly, the creditors may require information concerning the personal assets and debt position of individual partners, as well as the financial statements of the firm.

Accounting for a partnership basically follows the same procedures and adheres to the same generally accepted accounting principles as accounting for a proprietorship or a corporation. The primary difference in accounting for the different forms of organization is in the recording and reporting of capital transactions. A corporation's equity section purports to report the different sources of capital (for example, the issue of capital stock, additional paid-in capital from various sources, and retained earnings). Because each share of common stock has the same proportional interest in net income, dividends, voting rights, and assets in liquidation as any other share of the same class of stock, a separate capital account for each shareholder is not needed. However, in the case of a partnership, the capital interest in assets of each partner can vary. In addition, the partners' interest in net income or loss can vary and may not be proportional to their respective capital interests. As a result, the relationship of the partners' capital interest will change over time. To report the interest of each partner, a partnership's equity section normally consists of one capital account and one drawing account for each partner.

Practice varies as to which of the two accounts is changed by capital transactions. Generally, investments and withdrawals of assets considered to be other than temporary are recorded in the capital account. The drawing account is typically debited to record withdrawals of assets in anticipation of profitable operations or payments of personal expenses of a partner from partnership assets. It is common practice to close the income summary account to either the drawing account or the capital account. The drawing account may be closed periodically to the capital account. The various sources of capital may thus be combined into one account. In this text, the income summary account and each partner's drawing account will be closed to the appropriate partners' capital accounts.

To illustrate the entries, assume that Ed Bell and Jane Peters operate a partnership in which income of $60,000 is to be allocated equally and each partner withdraws $1,000 per month. The entries follow:

Each month to record the withdrawals.

Bell, Drawing	1,000	
Peters, Drawing	1,000	
Cash		2,000
To record monthly withdrawals.		

At the end of the period.

Income Summary	60,000	
Bell, Capital		30,000
Peters, Capital		30,000
To close the income summary account.		
Bell, Capital	12,000	
Peters, Capital	12,000	
Bell, Drawing		12,000
Peters, Drawing		12,000
To close the partners' drawing accounts.		

The determination of partnership net income is usually based on the same accounting concepts as those used for a corporation. There are, however, several differences that should be noted. First, as noted earlier, a partnership is not subject to income tax. Thus, no income tax expense is reported in the income statement of a partnership. Second, interest on capital investment and salaries to partners for personal services have traditionally been treated as components in the allocation of net income, rather than as expenses of the business. This practice is considered appropriate under the proprietary theory view of the firm in which all transactions with the owners are viewed as capital transactions. In other words, no revenue or expense should be recognized in transactions with the partners. Also, since the partners are owners of the business, the interest and salaries may not represent objectively determined amounts.

In addition to the transactions discussed before that affect a partner's capital interest, an individual partner may also lend cash to the partnership that may be accounted for as a liability of the partnership. A partner may also borrow cash from the partnership with the intention of repaying the loan to the partnership. In contrast to capital transactions, such as the withdrawal of assets as part of a profit allocation, an advance to a partner is accounted for as a receivable of the partnership, provided that the receivable satisfies the normal tests of collectibility. Generally accepted accounting standards should also be followed in accounting for and disclosing receivables from officers or members of a firm.

Recording the Formation of a Partnership

Assets invested in the partnership, any debts assumed by the partnership, and the capital interest each partner is to receive should be specified in the partnership agreement. A listing of partnership assets is important, because creditors of the partnership must satisfy their claims from partnership assets before seeking recovery of unpaid claims from the personal assets of individual partners.

Assets invested in the partnership can be either cash or noncash assets, such as a patent, land, or equipment. Noncash assets invested in the partnership are properly recorded at fair values on the date of investment.[4] Liabilities assumed by the partnership should also be recorded at their fair values.

Once the partners agree as to the identification and valuation of assets being invested, liabilities being assumed by the partnership, and the capital interest that each partner is to receive, the assets, liabilities, and equities are recorded on the books of the partnership. To illustrate, assume that the following items are being invested to form WY Partnership:

	AGREED FAIR VALUES	
	INVESTMENT BY WRIGHT	INVESTMENT BY YOUNG
Cash	$10,000	$10,000
Inventory	10,000	—
Land	—	20,000
Building	—	40,000
Equipment	20,000	—
Totals	40,000	70,000
Mortgage on building assumed by the partnership	—	20,000
Net assets invested	$40,000	$50,000

The journal entry to record the <u>initial investment</u>, assuming that Wright and Young agree that each partner is to receive a capital credit equal to the fair value of the net assets each partner invested is:

Cash	20,000	
Inventory	10,000	
Land	20,000	
Building	40,000	
Equipment	20,000	
Mortgage Payable		20,000
Wright, Capital		40,000
Young, Capital		50,000

A problem results if the sum of the agreed net asset values does not equal the

---

[4]*Accounting Principles Board Opinion No. 29*, "Accounting for Nonmonetary Transactions" (New York: AICPA, 1973), par. 18.

negotiated capital interest or if the agreement is unclear. For example, there are several possible interpretations of an agreement that each partner is to receive an equal capital interest. Two possible entries to record the formation, assuming the facts in the preceding paragraph, are as follows:

	I		II	
	BONUS METHOD		GOODWILL METHOD	
Cash	20,000		20,000	
Inventory	10,000		10,000	
Land	20,000		20,000	
Building	40,000		40,000	
Equipment	20,000		20,000	
Intangible Asset*	—		10,000	
Mortgage Payable		20,000		20,000
Wright, Capital		45,000		50,000
Young, Capital		45,000		50,000

*Generally referred to as partnership goodwill.

Under the first method, there is a capital interest transfer of $5,000 from Young to Wright to equalize the capital balances. Such an entry is made if Young recognizes that Wright is contributing something to the firm other than tangible assets, but the partners are reluctant to recognize an intangible asset, or a value for it cannot be determined objectively. The transfer is frequently referred to as a *bonus*. Under the second method, the equalization is accomplished by recognizing an intangible asset of $10,000 with a corresponding increase in the credit to the capital account of Wright. It is assumed that the partners agree that Wright is contributing something of value to the partnership that is intangible in nature, and which could not be specifically identified. The value assigned to the intangible asset could have been more than $10,000. Young may also be contributing an intangible asset to the partnership in addition to the tangible assets identified and valued. Unless the intangible is specifically identifiable, such as a patent, it should probably not be recognized. It is difficult to justify the recognition of an unspecified intangible such as goodwill on the books of a *new* partnership that does not have an established earnings record.

Allocation of Net Income or Net Loss

The partners should include in the articles of partnership a provision indicating how income and losses are to be allocated. The profit and loss agreement determines how much each partner's interest in the firm increases or decreases as a result of operations. Often one of the major problems of accounting for a partnership is to determine the intent of the partners as indicated in the partnership agreement. The partners have much flexibility in the area; however, if the intent of the partners is unclear, it may be necessary to settle the disagreement by litigation. To avoid disagreement and potential litigation, the profit and loss agreement should be explicitly stated, even to the extent of including examples of application of the allocation agreement in the articles of partnership. In the absence of an agreement, courts have generally concluded that the intent of the parties was to allocate profits and losses equally. If a provision for profits, but not losses, is included in the agreement, the courts have generally concluded that losses should be allocated in the same ratio that profits are allocated. Therefore, if losses are to be allocated differently than profits, the agreement should so state.

The objective of the profit and loss agreement should be to reward the individual partners for their contributions of resources to the partnership. Some of the more common agreements are based on some combination of the following:

1. Fixed ratio.

2. A ratio based on capital balances.

3. Interest on capital investment.

4. An allocation for time or managerial talent devoted to the partnership operation, either in the form of a fixed allocation or a bonus as a percentage of income.

There are a number of possibilities, some of which will be illustrated in the following sections. Unless stated otherwise, income for the period of $20,000 is assumed.

Fixed Ratio One of the simplest agreements is for each partner to be allocated profit or loss on the basis of an equal percentage or some other specified ratio each period. For example, Adams and Brown may agree that profit and loss are to be allocated in the ratio 7 : 3. A profit of $20,000 would be allocated $14,000 to Adams and $6,000 to Brown. The entry to close the Income Summary account would take the following form:

Income Summary	20,000	
Adams, Capital		14,000
Brown, Capital		6,000

Note that the allocation determines the increase in each partner's interest in net assets resulting from operations. It has nothing to do with the withdrawals of assets by a partner, which are recorded as debits to the capital or drawing accounts.

Unless stated otherwise, a loss of $20,000 would also be allocated using a 7 : 3 ratio. If this is not the intent of the partners, a separate loss agreement should be stipulated.

Capital Balances Assets invested in the partnership are important resources. The allocation of profits on the basis of the ratio of capital balances may result in an equitable allocation of profits where operation of the partnership requires little of the partners' time, for example, the operation of an apartment building in which there is a hired manager. To avoid conflicts, the capital ratio to be used should be clearly stated as, for example, original investment, beginning-of-year balances, average, or end-of-year balances. The partners should recognize that allocations based on beginning and ending balances could be inequitable. For example, if the allocation ratio is based on ending balances, a partner could make a large capital investment at the end of the year. To avoid such abuse, partners may want to provide for restrictions on investments and withdrawals.

Assuming that the ratio is based on beginning capital balances and that Adams and Brown had balances of $60,000 and $40,000, respectively, the net income of $20,000 would be allocated as follows:

CAPITAL INVESTMENT		NET INCOME ALLOCATION
Adams	$ 60,000	($60,000/$100,000) × $20,000 = $12,000
Brown	40,000	($40,000/$100,000) × $20,000 = 8,000
	$100,000	$20,000

Sometimes net income allocation is based on a ratio of the weighted-average capital investment as computed in Illustration 18-1. The weighted average is computed by multiplying the various capital balances that each partner maintained during the year by the fraction of the year that a particular capital balance was maintained. The $20,000 net income is allocated on the basis of the ratio of the weighted-average capital investment.

The allocation of a loss on the basis of the ratio of capital balances would mean that Adams, who has invested the most capital, would absorb the greatest amount of the loss, which may be considered an unreasonable allocation. If this is the case, the partners may want to stipulate a different ratio for the allocation of losses.

Interest on Capital Investment Using the ratio of capital balances as the basis for allocation of profit assumes that invested capital is the most important resource of the partnership. However, in many profit-making organizations, it is only one resource, and other factors should be recognized. To recognize other factors and still

ILLUSTRATION 18-1
Computation of Weighted-Average Capital Balances

	(A) INCREASE (DECREASE) IN CAPITAL	(B) CUMULATIVE BALANCE	(C) FRACTION OF YEAR IN MONTHS	(D) WEIGHTED AVERAGE (B) × (C)
ADAMS, CAPITAL				
January 1 Beginning balance		$60,000	3/12	$15,000
April 1 Added investment	$30,000	90,000	3/12	22,500
July 1 Withdrawal	(10,000)	80,000	6/12	40,000
				$77,500
BROWN, CAPITAL				
January 1 Beginning balance		$40,000	9/12	$30,000
October 1 Withdrawal	$(10,000)	30,000	3/12	7,500
				$37,500

AVERAGE INVESTMENT		NET INCOME ALLOCATION
Adams	$ 77,500	($77,500/$115,000) × $20,000 = $13,478
Brown	37,500	($37,500/$115,000) × $20,000 = 6,522
Total	$115,000	$20,000

provide an equitable allocation, the partners may want to provide for interest on capital investment and allocate the remaining income on some other basis. Such a provision may also provide an incentive for capital to be invested, if the firm has a use for added investment. Again the key is to be as explicit as possible to avoid problems in applying the agreement. The agreement should specify at least:

1. The interest rate,
2. Which capital balance is to be used (beginning, ending, or average),
3. How remaining profits should be allocated, and
4. Whether or not interest should still be allocated in case of loss or in case profits are less than the agreed interest allocation.

It is easy to overlook provision No. 4 but, as will be shown, in the event of disagreement between the partners, the lack of such an express provision would result in an allocation of interest when there is a reported loss or when profits are insufficient to cover the interest allocation.

If interest is part of the profit allocation formula, the partners must be careful to distinguish between capital investments and loans made by a partner to the partnership. The UPA [Section 18(d)] provides that unless otherwise stated, a partner is entitled to receive interest on capital investment only from the date when repayment should be made. Then the partner is entitled to the legal rate in the absence of a specific provision. However, an advance made in excess of the agreed investment is considered a liability of the firm and subject to repayment with interest. Accountants also recognize this distinction and record accrued interest on a loan balance as an expense, whereas an interest allowance on capital is not an expense but rather is one element in the allocation of profit and loss. Thus, the manner in which a partner's investment is classified will affect the profit or loss allocation and the amount reported as net income.

Frequently, the interest allocation is based on weighted-average capital investment. To illustrate, assume the average investment in Illustration 18-1. Interest is then computed on this amount. Assuming a net income of $20,000, an 8% rate of interest, and that any remaining profit is to be divided equally, the profit is allocated as follows:

INTEREST ALLOCATION	ADAMS	BROWN	TOTAL
$77,500 × .08 =	$ 6,200		$ 6,200
37,500 × .08 =		$3,000	3,000
Total interest allocated	6,200	3,000	9,200
Remainder shared equally	5,400	5,400	10,800
Total to be allocated	$11,600	$8,400	$20,000

Salary The UPA [Section 18(f)] provides that a partner is not entitled to remuneration for services performed for the partnership unless such remuneration is provided for by the partners in their profit and loss agreement. The partners may provide, as part of the profit and loss formula, a salary allowance in recognition of personal services rendered by a partner. The amount by which net income exceeds the salary allowances may then be divided in any ratio agreed on by the partners. For example, if Adams devotes full time to the business activity and Brown spends a limited amount of time, the partnership agreement may provide that Adams is allowed a salary of $1,000 per month and that the remaining income is to be divided on the basis of the ratio of the beginning capital balances ($60,000 and $40,000, respectively). The allocation would be as follows:

	ADAMS		BROWN	TOTAL
Salary allowance	$12,000		$-0-	$12,000
Remainder $60,000 ÷ $100,000	4,800	$40,000 ÷ $100,000	3,200	8,000
	$16,800		$3,200	$20,000

A salary agreement is considered part of the profit and loss allocation formula and may be made independent of the agreement between the partners as to the right to withdraw cash or other assets from the partnership. The withdrawal of cash reduces the partner's capital interest (debit to the drawing account) but plays no part in the allocation of net income. Since the term *salary* is normally understood to mean a cash payment for services received, it is important that the partners specify their intentions as to an allocation of profit or permission to withdraw assets.

Bonus Instead of basing the salary allocation on a fixed amount, the partners may provide for a bonus arrangement as a percentage of income or some other basis. Since a number of interpretations can result, the partners should explicitly state the basis to be used in calculating the bonus. Some possibilities based on net income are

1. Net income before any allocation of income to partners (for example, before interest on capital, salaries to partners, and any bonus).

2. Net income after other income allocations, but before subtracting the bonus.

3. Net income after subtracting the bonus, but before subtracting the other allocations.

4. Net income after subtracting the bonus and other allocations from net income.

Calculation of the bonus in the first two alternatives is straightforward. To illustrate alternatives 3 and 4, assume that net income is $24,000, and a bonus of 20% is to be paid to Adams. Also, interest of $4,000 and $2,000 is to be allocated to Adams and Brown, respectively, and any remainder is to be allocated equally. The bonus and a proof of the calculation are as follows:

ALTERNATIVE 3	ALTERNATIVE 4
Bonus = .2($24,000 − Bonus)	Bonus = .2($24,000 − $6,000 − Bonus)
Bonus = $4,800 − .2Bonus	Bonus = .2($18,000 − Bonus)
1.2 Bonus = $4,800	Bonus = $3,600 − .2Bonus
Bonus = $4,000	1.2 Bonus = $3,600
	Bonus = $3,000

Proof:

	ALTERNATIVE 3	ALTERNATIVE 4
Net income	$24,000	$24,000
Bonus	4,000	3,000
Interest	—	6,000
Income subject to bonus	$20,000	$15,000
	Bonus = .2($20,000)	Bonus = .2($15,000)
	Bonus = $4,000	Bonus = $3,000

Insufficient Income to Cover Allocation

In some cases, the partnership net income may be less than the interest and/or salary provided for in the partnership agreement. If the partners fail to provide for such an occurrence in the profit and loss formula, the established practice is to allocate the interest and/or salary as if sufficient income had been earned. The amount by which the salary and/or interest exceeds the net income is allocated to the individual partners in their agreed ratio for allocating residual income. For example, assume that Adams and Brown agree to divide profits as follows:

1. Salary: Adams, $4,000; Brown, $2,000.
2. Interest: 8% on average capital balances (see Illustration 18-1).
3. Remainder: To be divided equally.

A net income of $11,000 would be allocated as follows:

	ADAMS	BROWN	TOTAL
Salary	$ 4,000	$2,000	$ 6,000
Interest	6,200	3,000	9,200
	10,200	5,000	15,200
Excess allocation ($11,000 − $15,200)	(2,100)	(2,100)	(4,200)
Income allocation	$ 8,100	$2,900	$11,000

The entry to close the Income Summary account is:

Income Summary	11,000	
Adams, Capital		8,100
Brown, Capital		2,900

As will be shown in the next section, this procedure produces the same results as if each partner's salary and interest had been treated as an expense in the determination of the partnership net income or loss.

In the case of a loss of $20,000, the allocation would be as follows:

	ADAMS	BROWN	TOTAL
Salary	$ 4,000	$ 2,000	$ 6,000
Interest	6,200	3,000	9,200
	10,200	5,000	15,200
Excess allocation (− $20,000 − $15,200)	(17,600)	(17,600)	(35,200)
Loss allocation	$ (7,400)	$(12,600)	$(20,000)

To avoid such an allocation, the partners may elect to state an alternative allocation in the articles of partnership. Once again, this situation indicates the need for careful planning in drafting the partnership agreement.

SPECIAL PROBLEMS IN ALLOCATION OF INCOME AND LOSS

Salaries and Interest as an Expense

In the foregoing illustrations, salaries and interest were accounted for as an allocation of net income, rather than as an expense in the determination of net income. However, the partners may find the income statement more useful for evaluating the operating performance of the partnership if either or both salary and interest allocations were treated as an expense in the determination of net income. If the salary levels and interest rates are reasonable for the resources provided, the income statement for the partnership may be more comparable to income statements of nonpartnership forms of organization. To illustrate, assume that the partnership reported net income of $11,000 before the interest and salaries of the partners. The partners are to be allocated salaries and interest as follows:

	ADAMS	BROWN
Salary	$4,000	$2,000
Interest	6,200	3,000

The partners agree to allocate residual income and loss evenly. Journal entries to record the salaries and interest would be:

Salary Expense	6,000	
Adams, Capital		4,000
Brown, Capital		2,000
Interest Expense	9,200	
Adams, Capital		6,200
Brown, Capital		3,000

Net loss for the period after salaries and interest would be $4,200, computed as follows:

Net income before salaries and interest		$11,000
Less: Salary expense	$6,000	
Interest expense	9,200	15,200
Net loss		$ 4,200

After the revenue and expense accounts are closed, the Income Summary would have a debit balance of $4,200, which would be allocated evenly to the partners as agreed. The following entry would be recorded to close the income summary account:

Adams, Capital	2,100	
Brown, Capital	2,100	
Income Summary		4,200

Changes in the capital accounts are presented here:

ADAMS, CAPITAL

From Income Summary	2,100	Salary entry	4,000
		Interest entry	6,200
		Net change in capital	8,100

BROWN, CAPITAL

From Income Summary	2,100	Salary entry	2,000
		Interest entry	3,000
		Net change in capital	2,900

This procedure results in the same change in the capital accounts as if the salaries and interest were considered an allocation of profit. (See the illustration on page 687 when profits were insufficient to cover salary and interest allocations.) The method of reporting that is selected should be the one that provides the most useful information to the partners. Since the normal practice is to recognize salaries and interest as an allocation of profit, any such amounts treated as an expense should be adequately disclosed so the statement reader can properly evaluate the operating performance of the firm.

Adjustment of Income of Prior Years

Errors may occur in accounting for partnership operations, such as failure to accrue or defer expenses or revenue, errors in the inventory count or pricing, or errors in the calculation or amortization of fixed assets. Problems in the allocation of profit and loss can result if (1) errors are discovered that occurred in specific prior years, and (2) the partners have altered the profit and loss agreement since the period in which the error occurred. In a corporation, an error correction is accounted for as an adjustment to the beginning retained earnings balance. However, in a partnership the correction is allocated to the individual partners' capital accounts. The allocation should be based on the profit and loss agreement in effect during the period of the error.

Other allocation problems may arise, such as market changes in assets being held for investment purposes that occur before a change in the allocation formula, or an adjustment for bad debts that cannot be attributed to any specific period. There is no clear-cut answer to such problems. Litigation can be avoided by providing for the treatment of such potential problems in the partnership agreement.

FINANCIAL STATEMENT PRESENTATION

The income statement, balance sheet, and statement of cash flows for a partnership presented in conformity with GAAP are prepared in much the same manner as they are for a corporation. The following is a list of some of the differences in partnership reporting:

1. On the balance sheet or in a supplementary schedule, changes in partner's equity during the year should be disclosed.[5]

2. Partners' salary allowances are generally recognized as an allocation of net income, not as an expense in the determination of net income.

3. There is no income tax expense. The partners report their share of the partnership income or loss for the period on their individual income tax returns.

4. Interest paid to a partner on a loan balance is recognized as an expense. Interest allowance on capital investment is considered an allocation of profit.

A statement of changes in partners' capital is prepared to disclose changes in the interest of each partner during the year as shown in Illustration 18-2. For some external reporting purposes, such detail may not be considered necessary. The partnership capital, for example, may be reported as one amount, and the capital balance of each partner may be disclosed in a supplementary schedule or not disclosed at all.

ILLUSTRATION 18-2

AB Partnership
Statement of Partners' Capital
For the Year Ended December 31, 1995

	ADAMS	BROWN	TOTAL
Capital balance, January 1	$ 60,000	$40,000	$100,000
Add: Additional investment	30,000	–0–	30,000
Net income allocation	16,800	3,200	20,000
	106,800	43,200	150,000
Less: Withdrawals	10,000	10,000	20,000
Capital balance, December 31	$ 96,800	$33,200	$130,000

[5]This disclosure is usually not made when the number of partners is very large. For example, some accounting firms have hundreds of partners.

CHANGES IN THE OWNERSHIP OF THE PARTNERSHIP

The UPA (Section 29) defines *dissolution* as ''the change in the relation of the partners caused by any partner ceasing to be associated in the carrying on as distinguished from the winding up of the business.'' The partnership dissolution may be voluntary (for example, mutual agreement by the partners) or involuntary (for example, bankruptcy of an individual partner or the partnership itself).[6] Although dissolution means the end of a specific relationship between the partners, it does not automatically result in the termination of business activity. For example, in some forms of dissolution, such as the bankruptcy of the partnership, the partnership operations are eventually terminated and the partnership ceases to exist. In other cases of dissolution the partnership may be dissolved, but the remaining partners may continue the normal operations of the partnership without any visible interruptions of the firm's operations.

In this chapter we consider the accounting problems associated with changes in the ownership of a continuing partnership. The changes that will be considered result from (1) admission of a new partner by the purchase of an interest directly from one or more current partners, which is frequently referred to as an assignment of a partnership interest, (2) admission of a new partner by investing assets in the partnership, and (3) withdrawal of a partner as a result of retirement or death. Unless precluded from doing so in the partnership agreement, generally a partner may insist on liquidation of the partnership in these forms of dissolutions. Because the going-concern value of the business is usually greater than its liquidation value, the partners may provide in the partnership agreement that such changes in the relations of the partners does not dissolve the partnership. Dissolution of the partnership in which operations are eventually terminated will be covered in the next chapter.

VALUATION—A CENTRAL ISSUE

When there is a change in the membership of the partnership, the problem of assigning a fair value to the firm arises. For example, if a partner withdraws from the partnership and there are no express provisions in the partnership agreement for determining the settlement, an equitable payment for his or her interest must be negotiated between the existing partners. Similarly, before admission, an incoming partner must negotiate with the existing partners an equitable purchase price for the interest he or she acquires. The settlement or purchase price is based on a number of factors, one of which is the fair values of the partnership assets. However, the fair values of the partnership assets are generally not reflected on the partnership books. In accordance with generally accepted accounting standards, partner-

---

[6]Sections 31 and 32 of the UPA identify other circumstances that may constitute a dissolution of a partnership. Examples are

1. *The death of a partner.*
2. *A partner is judged to be unsound of mind.*
3. *A partner becomes incapable of performing his/her part of the partnership contract.*
4. *Termination of a definite term specified in the partnership agreement.*

ship assets are recorded at cost, and subsequent increases in their market value are not recognized.

One approach is to first revalue assets and liabilities to their fair values and record any identifiable unrecorded assets and liabilities before recording the admission or withdrawal of a partner. In addition, the settlement price paid to a withdrawing partner or the purchase price paid by a new partner may be used to infer a value for the firm as a whole. Any difference between the value of the firm implied by the payment and the fair value of the net assets may be assigned to an intangible asset frequently referred to as partnership goodwill. An increase or decrease in net assets is allocated to the appropriate partners in their profit or loss ratio. Under this approach, the use of fair values provides an equitable measure of each partner's capital interest in the partnership. Furthermore, when a new partner is admitted, failure to recognize fair values will result in unrecorded value changes realized later being allocated in the profit- and loss-sharing ratio unless a separate provision is made. An unrecorded increase in value would benefit the new partner, whereas an unrecorded decrease would be a detriment. Revaluation of assets and liabilities is supported on the basis that, in dissolution, the old partnership is dissolved and a new entity is formed.

In practice, some accountants are reluctant to recognize a change in the value of an asset, even though there may be objective evidence that a specific asset is undervalued. They argue that recording an increase in fair value for external reporting purposes is not in accordance with generally accepted accounting practice and that economic substance should take precedence over legal form. That is, even though the partnership may be legally dissolved, the economic substance of some types of dissolution is that the business activity continues without interruption. Proponents of this method would retain the historical cost carrying value, and either prescribe in the agreement that unrecorded changes in value will not be shared with a new partner when realized, or will require a disproportionately high capital investment in relation to the new partner's income-sharing percentage.[7] In this chapter, the revaluation of assets is shown as one of the approaches to recording changes in ownership because it is commonly advocated as an acceptable alternative and its use has some merit.

METHODS OF RECORDING CHANGES IN THE MEMBERSHIP OF THE PARTNERSHIP

Two methods are frequently used to record changes in partnership membership. The two methods are:

1. *The bonus method.* When this method is used, the assets of the partnership are increased by the amount of the assets invested by the partner being admitted. Any difference between the assets invested and the credit to the new partner's capital account is adjusted to the capital accounts of the other partners involved in

[7]John C. Burton, Russel E. Palmer, and Robert S. Kay, *Handbook of Accounting and Auditing* (Boston: Warren, Gorham, & Lamont, Inc., 1981), pp. 27–28.

the negotiations. If a partner withdraws from a partnership, the partners may agree to settle his capital interest by permitting the withdrawal of partnership assets. If the bonus method is used to record the withdrawal, the difference between the recorded value of the assets withdrawn and the debit to the withdrawing partner's capital account is adjusted to the capital accounts of the remaining partners.

2. *The goodwill method.* When this method is used, a new asset is recorded that is based on the difference between the value implied by the amount of consideration negotiated in the admission or withdrawal of a partner and the values reported in the partnership books.

Whether the bonus method or goodwill method is used, unrecorded changes in the value of existing assets and liabilities that are objectively determinable may be recorded before the change in membership is recorded.

As will be demonstrated, if certain limited conditions related to the profit and loss agreement are satisfied, the bonus and goodwill methods will produce the same result. If these conditions are met, the use of the bonus method precludes the problem of recording an intangible asset.

ADMISSION OF A NEW PARTNER

An individual may acquire an interest in a partnership (1) by purchasing all or part of an interest directly from one or more existing partners, that is, the transaction is conducted by the individuals outside the partnership and represents a transfer of assets between individuals, or (2) by being admitted as an additional partner on the investment of assets in the firm. Generally, the individual invests cash and/or other assets (for example, land, patent rights, equipment, marketable securities). A new partner could be admitted, however, by contributing a resource such as managerial talent. Because accountants ordinarily do not record such assets, unless the partners agree to transfer capital to the new partner's account, he or she will begin with a zero capital balance.

Assignment of an Interest by an Existing Partner

A partner is entitled to sell his or her interest in the firm, but no partner can be forced to accept a new member to the partnership. The UPA (Section 27) provides that the purchasing party acquires only the right to receive profits and assets in the event of liquidation to which the selling partner would otherwise be entitled. The purchaser does not acquire the right to participate in management unless all remaining partners agree to grant this right. The mere act of selling an interest does not dissolve the partnership, because the overall relation of the partners is not changed.

In the following illustrations, it is assumed that the partnership currently consists of two partners, Alan Adams and Bill Brown, with respective capital interests of $60,000 and $40,000. Adams and Brown share income and losses in the ratio of 6 : 4. Both partners agree to the admission of a new partner.

Acquisition of Interest by Payment to One Partner   If an individual acquires an interest in a partnership by making payment directly to an existing partner, the interest acquired is recorded in a new capital account by transferring a corresponding amount equal to the percentage interest acquired from the selling partner's capital account. For example, assume that Adams sold one-half of his interest in the firm to Carol Call for $36,000. The only entry necessary on the partnership books is to record the transfer of capital interest from the selling partner to the capital account established for the new partner. The entry is:

Adams, Capital	30,000	
Call, Capital		30,000

The following should be noted:

1. Since this is a personal transaction between the two individuals, the entry is the same regardless of the amount paid by Call directly to Adams.

2. Net assets and equities of the firm are not changed as a direct result of the transaction, since the sale was negotiated outside the partnership. However, as noted earlier, the partners may choose to revalue assets and liabilities.

3. The amount of capital transferred to Call is equal to Adams' recorded capital multiplied by the percentage interest in Adams' capital acquired by Call.

4. Call now has a capital interest of 30% ($30,000 of total interest of $100,000), but her profit interest does not have to equal this percentage.

A simplified balance sheet after the admission of Call would be as follows:

Net assets	$100,000	Adams, capital	$ 30,000
		Brown, capital	40,000
		Call, capital	30,000
Total	$100,000	Total	$100,000

Acquisition of an Interest by Payment to More Than One Partner   If Call had purchased a 30% interest from each partner for $36,000, the entry would be:

Adams, Capital (.30 × $60,000)	18,000	
Brown, Capital (.30 × $40,000)	12,000	
Call, Capital (.30 × $100,000)		30,000

The observations outlined before when the purchase was made from one partner apply in this case as well. Furthermore, this entry has no effect on how the cash payment made by Call is to be distributed to Adams and Brown outside the partnership. The amount and distribution of cash is a negotiated transaction between individuals and does not affect the partnership accounts unless the amount is used as a basis for the revaluation of the firm.

Goodwill Implied from the Purchase Price   In the foregoing examples, the amount paid by Call to gain admission to the firm was ignored in recording the transfer of interest. This procedure is often referred to as the bonus method. Some argue that the payment of $36,000 for a $30,000 interest in the partnership indicates that the firm has assets that are unrecorded or undervalued. The assumption is that the negotiated purchase price took into consideration such factors as the fair values of the firm's assets, the present value of the firm's liabilities, and the valuation of the firm on the basis of future prospects. Thus, the payment can be used to approximate the value of the firm. If Call is willing to pay $36,000 for a 30% interest in the firm, then the implied value of the partnership net assets is $120,000 ($36,000 ÷ .30). Net assets and capital should be increased $20,000 from the recorded amounts of $100,000. Since this represents an unrecorded increase in the value of the firm's assets, the increase in assets of $20,000 is allocated to Adams and Brown in their profit-sharing ratio. To the extent that the excess cannot be assigned to specific identifiable recorded assets, the remaining amount is recorded as partnership goodwill. Assuming that the book values of assets and liabilities equal their fair values, the entries to record the increase in assets and admission of Call are:

Goodwill	20,000	
Adams, Capital (.60 × $20,000)		12,000
Brown, Capital (.40 × $20,000)		8,000
Adams, Capital (.30 × $72,000)	21,600	
Brown, Capital (.30 × $48,000)	14,400	
Call, Capital (.30 × $120,000)		36,000

This results in account balances as presented in Illustration 18-3.

The goodwill must be amortized over an appropriate period not to exceed 40 years, in accordance with *APB Opinion No. 17*.

Comparison of Bonus and Goodwill Methods   In the illustration, Call is credited with a 30% interest in the firm under the bonus and the goodwill methods. To assist the partners in making a decision between the two methods, it may be helpful to demonstrate the effects of the two methods on their respective capital balances. To compare the two methods, the goodwill is initially recorded in the accounts and is

ILLUSTRATION 18-3
Schedule of Account Balances

	NET ASSETS	+	GOODWILL	=	CAPITAL ADAMS	+	BROWN	+	CALL
Book values	$100,000	+	$ –0–	=	$(60,000)	+	$(40,000)	+	$ –0–
Record goodwill			20,000		(12,000)		(8,000)		–0–
	100,000	+	20,000	=	(72,000)	+	(48,000)	+	–0–
Transfer of capital					21,600		14,400		(36,000)
Balance after admission of Call	$100,000	+	$20,000	=	$(50,400)	+	$(33,600)	+	$(36,000)

*In this and the following chapter, ( ) means that an account has a credit balance or a credit is posted to an account.

amortized in future periods. If the firm were forced to liquidate, the unamortized goodwill would probably be of no value and, therefore, would represent a loss to the partnership. In either case, the amortization of the goodwill reduces the partners' capital accounts by their agreed profit- and loss-sharing ratio.

In order to isolate the effect of the goodwill amortization, all other capital changes are ignored. The bonus and goodwill methods will yield the same result if two conditions related to the new profit and loss agreement are met. These are:

1. The new partner's profit-sharing percentage must be equal to his or her initial percentage interest in capital. In this illustration, Call received a capital interest of 30%. Her profit-sharing ratio must be 30%.

2. The old partner's profit-sharing ratio in the new partnership must be the same relatively as it was in the old partnership. Thus, if Call is to receive 30% of the profit in the new partnership, Adams and Brown must receive the remaining 70%. To be in the same relative ratio of 6:4, Adams must receive 42% (.6 × .70) of profits, and Brown must receive 28% (.4 × .70). The two methods are equivalent if, after amortizing goodwill, the account balances are the same as they would be under the bonus method. The balances for each method are presented in Illustration 18-4.

The two methods will also yield the same results if the bonus method is used and the unrecorded assets ($20,000) are ultimately realized and allocated to the partners in the ratio of 42:28:30.

Acquisition of an Interest by Investing Assets

An individual may obtain a partnership interest in capital and future income by investing something of value in the firm. If assets are invested, the admission is recorded by debiting the assets invested and adjusting the net capital interest in

ILLUSTRATION 18-4
Schedule of Account Balances

GOODWILL METHOD	NET ASSETS	+	GOODWILL	=	ADAMS	+	BROWN	+	CALL
Balances after recording goodwill and admitting Call	$100,000	+	$20,000	=	$(50,400)	+	$(33,600)	+	$(36,000)
Amortize goodwill									
$20,000 × .42			(20,000)		8,400				
20,000 × .28							5,600		
20,000 × .30									6,000
Totals	$100,000	+	$ –0–	=	$(42,000)	+	$(28,000)	+	$(30,000)

BONUS METHOD									
Balances after recording admission of Call	$100,000	+	$ –0–	=	$(42,000)	+	$(28,000)	+	$(30,000)

the firm by a corresponding amount. It is important that the assets invested be fairly valued. Any gain or loss recognized on sales subsequent to recording the admission will be allocated on the basis of the new profit and loss formula.

Three situations can exist when an individual invests assets in a firm:

1. Book value of the capital interest acquired is equal to the fair value of the assets invested.

2. Book value of the capital interest acquired is less than the fair value of the assets invested.

3. Book value of the capital interest acquired is greater than the fair value of the assets invested.

The book value of the capital interest acquired is computed as follows:

$$\left(\begin{array}{l}\text{Capital balances of} \\ \text{existing partners}\end{array} + \begin{array}{l}\text{Investment of} \\ \text{new partner}\end{array}\right) \times \begin{array}{l}\text{Percentage} \\ \text{interest acquired} \\ \text{by new partner}\end{array} = \begin{array}{l}\text{Book value of capital} \\ \text{interest acquired}\end{array}$$

To illustrate the three situations, assume that Adams and Brown have capital interests of $40,000 and $30,000, respectively. Assume further that, unless stated otherwise, the book values of the recorded assets and liabilities of the firm equal their fair values. Profits are shared in the ratio of $6:4$. Call is to be admitted to the partnership, after which the profit ratio is to be $4:4:2$. For simplicity, we will assume in all cases that Call invests cash.

Case 1: Book Value Acquired Is Equal to Assets Invested   Assume that Adams, Brown, and Call agree that Call is to invest $35,000 for a one-third capital interest in the partnership. The book value of Call's interest is equal to the assets invested and is computed as follows:

$$(\$70,000 + \$35,000) = \$105,000 \times \tfrac{1}{3} = \$35,000$$

The entry to record the admission of Call is simply:

Cash	35,000	
Call, Capital		35,000

Adams' and Brown's capital accounts remain unchanged at $70,000, which represents the remaining two-thirds interest in the firm. Call's capital account properly reflects a one-third interest of $35,000.

It should be noted that the ratio of the capital balance of $40:30:35$ does not equal the agreed profit and loss ratio $4:4:2$.

Case 2: Book Value Acquired Is Less Than Assets Invested   Assume now that Call is to invest $50,000 for a one-third capital interest in the firm. Book value of the interest acquired is:

$$(\$70,000 + \$50,000) = \$120,000 \times \tfrac{1}{3} = \$40,000$$

In this case, the amount invested exceeds the book value interest acquired by

$10,000. There could be a number of explanations for Call's willingness to pay this $10,000 excess. It could be that, as a result of a profitable and favorable outlook for the firm's operations, Adams and Brown are in a strong bargaining position.

The accounting problem is to record the admission of Call in accordance with the negotiated intentions of the parties involved. Obviously, if Call's capital account is credited with $50,000, her interest would exceed one-third of the partnership's total capital. Either the bonus method or the goodwill method can be used to record the admission so that Call will end up with a one-third capital interest.

Bonus method   When the bonus method is used, the excess of the amount invested over the book value interest received is considered a bonus to the existing partners. In this example, Call invested $10,000 more than the capital interest received. The $10,000 bonus is allocated to the old partners on the basis of their profit and loss ratio, since this is an increase in partnership assets. The entry to admit Call is:

Cash	50,000	
Adams, Capital		6,000
Brown, Capital		4,000
Call, Capital		40,000

Adams and Brown now have capital balances of $46,000 and $34,000 for a total capital interest of $80,000, which is a two-thirds interest in total capital of $120,000. Call has the remaining one-third interest of $40,000.

The assets of the partnership may have been revalued before the admission of a new partner was recorded. The bonus method is frequently used when the parties do not want to record an intangible asset. Notice in the entry to record the admission that the assets are increased only by the amount invested. Any difference between the capital credit for Call and the cash invested is an adjustment to the capital accounts of Adams and Brown.

Goodwill method   Call may negotiate that she is to receive a capital credit equal to her investment. If Call is to receive a capital credit of $50,000 for a one-third interest, the total capital interest implied by this contract is $150,000. Adams and Brown must have the remaining two-thirds interest, or $100,000. Since their current balances of $70,000 represent their interest in the net assets, assets and capital appear to be understated by $30,000.[8] Assuming that the specific assets and liabilities are fairly valued, this understatement is recognized as goodwill attributable to the old partners and is allocated to Adams and Brown on the basis of their current profit and loss ratios. The journal entry is:

[8]An alternate way to calculate goodwill is as follows:

Net value of firm implied by contract	$150,000
Minus: Adams' and Brown's capital balance + Call's investment	120,000
Goodwill	$ 30,000

Goodwill	30,000	
Adams, Capital (.60 × $30,000)		18,000
Brown, Capital (.40 × $30,000)		12,000

The entry to record the admission of Call is:

| Cash | 50,000 | |
| Call, Capital | | 50,000 |

Net assets undervalued   Had the net assets not been fairly valued as assumed here, the excess payment by Call could mean that specific assets of the firm are undervalued, or that partnership liabilities are overstated. If so, the specific assets (whether tangible or identifiable intangible assets) and liabilities of the partnership could be adjusted instead of creating a goodwill account. However, the specific accounts should not be adjusted in the absence of objective evidence that there are unrecorded changes in value.

Case 3: Book Value Acquired Is Greater Than Assets Invested   Assume that Call is to invest $20,000 for a one-third capital interest in the firm. Book value of the interest acquired is:

$$(\$70,000 + \$20,000) = \$90,000 \times \tfrac{1}{3} = \$30,000$$

In this case, the book value interest acquired exceeds the value of the assets invested by Call, which could imply that assets are overvalued ($\tfrac{1}{3}$ X = $20,000; X = $60,000) or that for some reason, Adams and Brown are willing to grant Call a capital credit greater than the amount of assets she is investing. In some cases, for example, a partnership may be in need of operating capital and the partners may be willing to sacrifice their interest in existing assets to acquire the cash; or it could be that Call is bringing some particularly needed talent or reputation to the partnership.

In this case, as in Case 2, the admission could be recorded either by the bonus method or by the goodwill method. Under either method, Call will end up with a one-third interest in the net assets of the firm.

Bonus method   When the bonus method is used, assets are not increased above what the new partner is investing. If Call is to receive a $30,000 capital credit on investment of $20,000, then a bonus of $10,000 is being granted to Call. This bonus is allocated to reduce Adams' and Brown's capital in their agreed profit and loss ratio. The following entry reflects the bonus to Call and a resulting one-third interest in the total capital of $90,000:

Cash	20,000	
Adams, Capital (.60 × $10,000)	6,000	
Brown, Capital (.40 × $10,000)	4,000	
Call, Capital		30,000

Adams and Brown now have capital balances of $34,000 and $26,000, respectively, for a total of $60,000, or a two-thirds interest.

Goodwill method If Adams and Brown are unwilling to reduce their capital accounts on the admission of Call, then an alternative to the bonus method is to compute and record the goodwill implicit in the agreement. Since Adams' and Brown's capital interests are to remain unchanged, the old partners' capital balances are used as the base to compute the value of the firm. If their interest represents a two-thirds interest in the net assets of the new partnership, then a three-thirds interest in the firm is $105,000, of which Call is to receive a capital credit of $35,000 ($\frac{1}{3} \times$ $105,000).[9] The $15,000 difference between the capital credit of $35,000 and Call's investment of $20,000 is goodwill. The entry to record the admission of Call is:

Cash	20,000	
Goodwill	15,000	
Call, Capital		35,000

The entry recognizes that the new partner is investing cash and is bringing an intangible asset to the partnership. The amount recorded is based on the value implied by the partners' agreement.

Net assets overvalued The payment of $20,000 by Call for a $30,000 capital interest may provide evidence that the recorded value of the firm's net assets does not reflect fair values and that the use of the bonus method or the creation of a goodwill account is an effort to avoid a reduction in net assets. The $20,000 invested by Call for a one-third interest could be used to impute a value for the partnership net assets after the admission of Call of only $60,000.[10] The journal entries to revalue the assets and admit Call are as follows:

[9]An alternate way to calculate goodwill is as follows:

a. First compute the capital interest implied from the capital interest of existing partners:

$$X = \text{total capital of the new partnership}$$
$$\tfrac{2}{3}X = \$70,000$$
$$X = \$105,000$$

b. Compute the goodwill amount:

Implied value of net assets including Call's investment	$105,000
Recorded value of net assets plus Call's investment ($70,000 + $20,000)	90,000
Goodwill	$ 15,000

[10]The amount of asset overstatement is calculated as follows:

$$\tfrac{1}{3}X = \$20,000$$
$$X = \$60,000$$

Implied value of net assets including Call's investment	$60,000
Recorded value of net assets including Call's investment ($40,000 + $30,000 + $20,000)	90,000
Overvalued assets	$30,000

Adams, Capital		18,000	
Brown, Capital		12,000	
Assets			30,000
Cash		20,000	
Call, Capital			20,000

Account balances that result from the admission of Call for the three alternatives discussed are given in Illustration 18-5. Subsequent events alone can indicate which method should have been used to record the admission. An examination of one of a number of events that could result will emphasize the importance of the initial asset valuation. Assume that the bonus method was used to record the admission of Call and that the assets were overvalued and subsequently sold at a loss of $30,000. The agreed profit and loss ratio is 4 : 4 : 2. After this transaction, the partners' capital balances are as follows:

	ADAMS	BROWN	CALL
Balance after admission of Call	$(34,000)	$(26,000)	$(30,000)
Share of $30,000 loss	12,000	12,000	6,000
	$(22,000)	$(14,000)	$(24,000)

The selection of the bonus method as opposed to reducing overvalued assets results in a gain in Call's capital relative to Brown's. Additional comparisons of the three methods assuming various other subsequent events could be developed.

ILLUSTRATION 18-5
Schedule of Account Balances

	BONUS METHOD	GOODWILL METHOD	OVERVALUED NET ASSETS
DEBIT			
Net Assets	$90,000	$105,000	$60,000
CREDITS			
Adams, Capital	$34,000	$ 40,000	$22,000
Brown, Capital	26,000	30,000	18,000
Call, Capital	30,000	35,000	20,000
Totals	$90,000	$105,000	$60,000

WITHDRAWAL OF A PARTNER

A partner cannot be prevented from withdrawing from a partnership by the other partners. Although some complex legal issues are involved, the partnership agreement may specify conditions for withdrawal and provisions for computing the settlement. If a settlement is not specifically provided for in the partnership agreement, Section 42 of the UPA states that "he or his legal representative . . . may have the value of his interest ascertained and shall receive as an ordinary creditor an amount equal to the value of this interest."

If a partner withdraws in violation of the partnership agreement and without approval of the remaining partners, he is entitled only to his interest in the firm without consideration of goodwill. In such a case, the withdrawing partner is liable for damages sustained by the remaining parties for his breach of the partnership agreement. A partner who is forced to withdraw from a partnership is entitled to compensation for his full interest including goodwill.

In the following examples, it is assumed that the partners mutually agree to the withdrawal: (1) the withdrawing partner may elect to sell his interest to an outside party; (2) the withdrawing partner may elect to sell his interest to one or more of the remaining partners; or (3) the partners may mutually agree to transfer partnership assets to the withdrawing partner for his interest in the firm. Case 1 has been discussed earlier and need not be reviewed again. The same considerations apply to Case 2, if negotiated outside the partnership. In Case 3 the partnership agreement may include requirements for determining the settlement price. In most cases the capital account does not reflect the current value of the partner's interest. To be equitable the fair values of the assets and liabilities need to be determined. It may be necessary to recognize unrecorded assets, correct the accounts for errors, or reflect changes in estimates such as the book value of depreciable assets. In the absence of a specific agreement, the partners may have to negotiate a settlement price at the date of withdrawal. Determination of an equitable value may be very difficult. The agreed settlement price may be equal to, greater than, or less than the book value interests of the withdrawing partner.

To illustrate the accounting for the withdrawal of a partner by transferring firm assets, assume a partnership consisting of three patterns, Adams, Brown, and Call, with capital balances of $30,000, $40,000, $30,000, and a profit and loss ratio of 5 : 3 : 2. Any agreed asset and liability revaluations have already been recorded.

Payment to a Retiring Partner

Payment in Excess of Book Value to a Withdrawing Partner

Assume now that Adams is withdrawing from the partnership and the partners have mutually agreed that he is to receive payment of $40,000. The partners may agree to use the bonus method or the goodwill method to record the withdrawal.

Bonus method If the bonus method is used, the remaining partners are charged with the amount of the payment that exceeds the book value of the retiring partner's capital balance. The amount of the bonus paid to the retiring partner is commonly allocated to the remaining partners on the basis of their relative profit and loss ratio (in this case the relative ratio of Brown to Call is 3 : 2). Support for this method is based on the cost principle. The bonus method may also be justified when the remaining partners are simply anxious to get rid of a partner for various reasons. Any recognition of goodwill is difficult to justify in the absence of an arm's-length transaction. The entry to record the withdrawal would be as follows:

Adams, Capital	30,000	
Brown, Capital	6,000	
Call, Capital	4,000	
Liability to Adams		40,000

Goodwill method The goodwill method is used if (1) Brown and Call will not agree to a reduction in their capital balances; (2) the partners made specific provisions in the partnership agreement on how the withdrawal is to be recorded; or (3) the partners agree that an intangible asset should be recognized. If the partnership has been profitable, the firm as a whole may be worth more than the fair value of the net assets. Once again, the goodwill method is supported on the basis that a new entity is being formed and the accounts of the new entity should be based on fair values. One alternative is to calculate the implied goodwill from the price paid to the retiring partner. In our example, Adams receives a $10,000 excess payment over his capital balance. Since Adams' capital account is increased by 50% of any increase in assets, then a $10,000 excess payment implies a total goodwill of $20,000. The entries are:

Goodwill	20,000	
Adams, Capital		10,000
Brown, Capital		6,000
Call, Capital		4,000
Adams, Capital	40,000	
Liability to Adams		40,000

Some argue that, in accordance with the cost basis, only the goodwill of $10,000 that has been purchased should be recorded (called the partial goodwill method) and the entry should be:

Goodwill	10,000	
Adams, Capital		10,000
Adams, Capital	40,000	
Liability to Adams		40,000

Others would contend that the basis for recognizing goodwill should be "all or nothing at all."

It is probably difficult to justify recognition of any goodwill. If the goodwill is related to Adams, it will not exist if he withdraws. However, as discussed before, if the goodwill is based on past operations, the withdrawal may provide the objective evidence necessary to recognize it in the partnership accounts.

Comparison of the bonus and goodwill methods Once again, it may be helpful to the partners to see under what conditions the two methods will yield the same results. The only condition that must be met is that the remaining partners' profit and loss ratio must be in the same ratio as it was before the withdrawal of Adams. In the preceding illustration, this condition would be met if, after the withdrawal of Adams, Brown and Call share profits 3 : 2 as shown as Illustration 18-6.

ILLUSTRATION 18-6
Schedule of Account Balances

	ADAMS	BROWN	CALL
Capital balances before withdrawal	$(30,000)	$(40,000)	$(30,000)
Allocate goodwill	(10,000)	(6,000)	(4,000)
	(40,000)	(46,000)	(34,000)
Withdraw Adams	40,000	—	—
	–0–	(46,000)	(34,000)
Amortize goodwill			
$20,000 × .60		12,000	
$20,000 × .40			8,000
	$ –0–	$(34,000)	$(26,000)
Capital balances using bonus method	$ –0–	$(34,000)	$(26,000)

Payment of Less Than Book Value to a Withdrawing Partner   A partner who is anxious to dispose of his interest in the partnership may agree to accept less than his book value interest in the partnership. He may do so for a number of reasons, such as (1) he may view the future of the company negatively, (2) he may need operating capital for personal reasons, or (3) the business association may no longer be acceptable to him and, in his opinion, a forced liquidation of the firm might be detrimental to his interest. In such cases, use of the bonus method is justified, since the settlement may not be based on the economic value of the firm.

To illustrate, assume that Adams withdraws from the ABC Partnership and agrees to settle his $30,000 interest for $25,000. A bonus of $5,000 accrues to the remaining partners. The common practice is to allocate the bonus on the basis of their relative profit and loss ratio of 3 : 2. The entry would be:

Adams, Capital	30,000	
Brown, Capital		3,000
Call, Capital		2,000
Liability to Adams		25,000

A payment to Adams that is less than his capital interest may be an indication that assets are overvalued. Assets should be written down to fair values if it is determined that they are overvalued and that the settlement price is based on the net assets' fair value. In particular, if goodwill was previously recorded, an agreement to accept a payment that is less than the partner's book value interest may provide evidence that the intangible is overstated. Accordingly, the intangible should be reduced by the difference between the settlement price and the capital interest being retired. Assuming that assets are overvalued by $10,000, the sequence of entries becomes:

Adams, Capital	5,000	
Brown, Capital	3,000	
Call, Capital	2,000	
Asset		10,000
Adams, Capital	25,000	
Liability to Adams		25,000

Reducing the assets to fair value provides an equitable starting point for the new partnership formed by Brown and Call. As long as Brown and Call share profits in the same relative ratio, they will be indifferent as to the method used. However, it is more informative and conceptually preferred for the recorded asset values to reflect fair values if such values can be determined.

Death of a Partner

Under the UPA [Section 31(4)], a partnership is dissolved by the death of a partner. Historically, if the surviving partners continued to operate the partnership, a new partnership was considered formed (that is, the old partnership was terminated), even though the partners may have provided for the continuation of the business in the partnership agreement. Under this interpretation, the surviving partners should enter into a new agreement. More recent court cases—and some state statutes—now permit the partnership to continue operating in accordance with terms provided for in the partnership agreement.

A deceased partner's estate is entitled to receive the partner's current equity in the partnership. Determining a partner's equity interest in the firm can result in disagreements between the surviving partners and the executor of the estate. To avoid litigation, the articles of partnership should contain procedures for determining a deceased partner's current equity in the partnership and the method of settlement. In the absence of specific provisions, the surviving partners and the executor of the estate must negotiate a settlement. To determine a partner's equity interest at the time of death, the assets and liabilities normally are adjusted to current values and the accounts are closed to determine the net income or loss earned since the end of the last fiscal period.

The partnership agreement may provide that the interest is to be settled by distributing partnership assets to the estate or the estate may receive payment by selling the interest to an outside party or to one or more of the surviving partners as individuals. Entries to record both types of settlements were presented in earlier sections of this chapter.

Questions

1. Describe the tax treatment of partnership income.

2. Distinguish between a partner's interest in capital and his interest in the partnership's income and losses. Also, make a general distinction between a partner's capital account and his drawing account.

3. Explain why a partnership is viewed in accounting as a "separate economic entity."

4. What are some of the methods commonly used in allocating income and losses to the partners?

5. Explain the distinction between the terms "withdrawals" and "salaries."

6. List some of the alternative methods of calculating a bonus that may appear in a partnership agreement.

7. What is meant by dissolution and what are its causes?

8. Discuss the methods used to record changes in partnership membership.

9. Differentiate between the admission of a new partner through assignment of an interest and through investment in the partnership.

10. Under what two conditions will the bonus and goodwill methods of recording the admission of a partner yield the same result?

11. Describe the circumstances where neither the goodwill nor the bonus method should be used to record the admission of a new partner.

12. How might a partner withdrawing in violation of the partnership agreement and without the consent of the other partners be treated? What about a partner who is forced to withdraw?

Exercises

Exercise 18-1

John, Jeff, and Jane decided to engage in a real estate venture as a partnership. John invested $100,000 cash and Jeff provided office equipment that is carried on his books at $82,000. The partners agree that the equipment has a fair value of $110,000. There is a $30,000 note payable remaining on the equipment to be assumed by the partnership. Although Jane has no physical assets to invest in the partnership, both John and Jeff believe that her experience as a real estate appraiser is a valuable skill needed by the partnership and is a basis for granting her a capital interest in the partnership.

Required:

Assuming that each partner is to receive an equal capital interest in the partnership,

A. Record the partnership formation under the bonus method.

B. Record the partnership formation under the goodwill method, and assume a total goodwill of $90,000

C. Discuss the appropriateness of using either the bonus or goodwill methods to record the formation of the partnership.

Exercise 18-2

Tom and Julie formed a management consulting partnership on January 1, 1995. The fair value of the net assets invested by each partner follows:

	TOM	JULIE
Cash	$13,000	$12,000
Accounts receivable	8,000	6,000
Office supplies	2,000	800
Office equipment	30,000	—
Land	—	30,000
Accounts payable	2,000	5,000
Mortgage payable	—	18,800

During the year, Tom withdrew $15,000 and Julie withdrew $12,000 in anticipation of operating profits. Net profit for 1995 was $50,000, which is to be allocated based on the original net capital investment.

Required:

A. Prepare journal entries to:
   (1) Record the initial investment in the partnership.
   (2) Record the withdrawals.
   (3) Close the Income Summary and Drawing accounts.

B. Prepare a statement of changes in partners' capital for the year ended December 31, 1995.

Exercise 18-3

Jones, Silva, and Thompson form a partnership and agree to allocate income equally after recognition of 10% interest on beginning capital balances and monthly salary allowances of $2,000 to Jones and $1,500 to Thompson. Capital balances on January 1 were as follows:

Jones	$40,000
Silva	25,000
Thompson	30,000

Required:

Calculate the net income (loss) allocation to each partner under each of the following independent situations.

1. Net income for the year is $99,500.
2. Net income for the year is $38,300.
3. Net loss for the year is $15,100.

Exercise 18-4

Mary and Nancy invested $80,000 each to form a partnership. Mary has been authorized a salary of $20,000, while Nancy's salary is $25,000. Each partner is to receive 10% on the original capital investment. The profit and loss agreement stipulates that any remaining income or loss is to be divided equally. The partnership had a net loss of $20,000 this year.

Required:

Prepare the journal entry to record the allocation of the net loss for the year. Show supporting computations.

Exercise 18-5

On January 1, 1995, Tony and Jon formed T&J Personal Financial Planning with capital investments of $480,000 and $340,000, respectively. The partners wanted to draft a profit and loss agreement that would reward each individual for the resources invested in the partnership. Accordingly, the partnership agreement provides that profits are to be allocated as follows:

1. Annual salaries of $42,000 and $66,000 are granted to Tony and Jon, respectively.

2. In addition to the salary, Jon is entitled to a bonus of 10% of net income after salaries and bonus but before interest on capital investments is subtracted.
3. Each partner is to receive an interest credit of 8% on the original capital investment.
4. Remaining profits are to be allocated 40% to Tony and 60% to Jon.

On December 31, 1995, the partnership reported net income before salaries, interest, and bonus of $188,000.

Required:

Calculate the 1995 allocation of partnership profit.

Exercise 18-6

Hill, Jones, and Vose have been partners throughout 1995. Their average balances for the year and their balances at the end of the year before closing the nominal accounts are as follows:

PARTNER	AVERAGE BALANCES	BALANCES 12/31/95
Hill	$97,500	$70,000
Jones	27,300	21,800
Vose	14,250	11,700*

*Debit balance.

The income for 1995 is $108,000 before charging partners' salary allowances and before payment of interest on average balances at the agreed rate of 5% per annum. Annual salary allocations are $12,000 to Hill, $9,600 to Jones, and $8,800 to Vose. The balance of income is to be allocated at the rate of 60% to Hill, 10% to Jones, and 30% to Vose.

It is intended to distribute cash to the partners so that, after credits and allocations have been made as indicated in the preceding paragraph, the balances in the partners' accounts will be proportionate to their residual profit-sharing ratios. None of the partners is to invest additional cash, but they wish to distribute the lowest possible amount of cash.

Required:

Prepare a schedule of partners' accounts, showing balances at the end of 1995 before closing, the allocations of the net income for 1995, the cash distributed, and the closing balances.

(AICPA adapted)

Exercise 18-7

Phil Phoenix and Tim Tucson are partners in an electrical repair business. Their respective capital balances are $90,000 and $50,000, and they share profits and losses equally. Because the partners are confronted with personal financial problems, they decided to admit a new partner to the partnership. After an extensive interviewing process they elect to admit Don Dallas into the partnership.

Required:

Prepare the journal entry to record the admission of Don Dallas into the partnership under each of the following conditions:

1. Don acquires one-fourth of Phil's capital interest by paying $30,000 directly to him.

2. Don acquires one-fifth of each of Phil's and Tim's capital interests. Phil receives $25,000 and Tim receives $15,000 directly from Don.

3. Don acquires a one-fifth capital interest for a $60,000 cash investment in the partnership. Total capital after the admission is to be $200,000.

4. Don invests $40,000 for a one-fifth interest in partnership capital. Implicit goodwill is to be recorded.

Exercise 18-8

Bill and Jane share profits and losses in a 70:30 ratio. Mike is to be admitted into a partnership upon the investment of $14,000 for a one-third capital interest. Account balances for Bill and Jane on June 30, 1995 just before the admission of Mike are as follows:

	DEBIT	CREDIT
Cash	$ 6,000	
Accounts receivable	9,000	
Notes receivable	2,000	
Merchandise inventory	12,000	
Prepaid insurance	500	
Accounts payable		$ 9,500
Bill, capital		12,000
Jane, capital		8,000
	$29,500	$29,500

It is agreed that for purposes of establishing the interests of the former partners, the following adjustments shall be made:

1. An allowance for doubtful accounts of 2% of the accounts receivable is to be established.
2. The merchandise inventory is to be valued at $10,000.
3. Accrued expenses of $600 are to be recognized.
4. Prepaid insurance is to be valued at $300.
5. The goodwill method is to be used to record the admission of Mike.

Required:

Prepare the entries to adjust the account balances in establishing the interests of Bill and Jane and to record the investment by Mike.

Exercise 18-9

Beth, Steph, and Linda have been operating a small gift shop for several years. After an extensive review of their past operating performance, the partners concluded that the business needed to expand in order to provide an adequate return to the partners. The following balance sheet is for the partnership prior to the admission of a new partner, Mary.

Cash	$160,000
Other assets	640,000
	$800,000
Liabilities	$200,000
Beth, capital (40%)	265,000
Steph, capital (40%)	215,000
Linda, capital (20%)	120,000
	$800,000

Figures shown parenthetically reflect agreed profit-and-loss sharing percentages.

Required:

Prepare the necessary journal entries to record the admission of Mary in each of the following independent situations. Some situations may be recorded in more than one way.

1. Mary is to invest sufficient cash to receive a one-sixth capital interest. The parties agree that the admission is to be recorded without recognizing goodwill or bonus.

2. Mary is to invest $160,000 for a one-fifth capital interest.

3. Mary is to invest $160,000 for a one-fourth capital interest.

4. Mary is to invest $160,000 for a 40% capital interest.

Exercise 18-10

Select the best answer for each of the following.

1. Jon and Joe formed a partnership on July 1, 1995, and invested the following assets:

	JON	JOE
Cash	$65,000	$125,000
Realty		250,000

The realty was subject to a mortgage of $25,000, which was assumed by the partnership. The partnership agreement provides that Jon and Joe will share profits and losses in the ratio of one-third and two-thirds, respectively. Joe's capital account at July 1, 1995, should be

(a) $375,000
(b) $366,667
(c) $285,000
(d) $350,000

2. On July 1, 1995, Mary and Jane formed a partnership, agreeing to share profits and losses in the ratio of 4:6, respectively. Mary invested a parcel of land that cost her $40,000. Jane invested $50,000 cash. The land was sold for $60,000 on July 1, 1995, four hours after formation of the partnership. How much should be recorded in Mary's capital account on formation of the partnership?

(a) $8,000
(b) $24,000
(c) $60,000
(d) $20,000

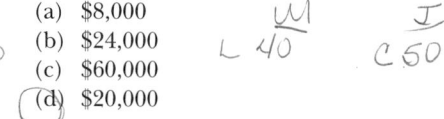

3. The partnership agreement of Tami, Julie, and Kim provides for annual distribution of profit or loss in the following order:

Tami, the managing partner, receives a bonus of 15% of profit.

Each partner receives 10% interest on average capital investment.

Residual profit or loss is divided equally.

The average capital investments for 1995 were:

Tami	$100,000
Julie	200,000
Kim	300,000

How much of the $94,500 partnership profit for 1995 should be allocated to Tami?
(a) $10,000
(b) $20,000
(c) $30,950
(d) $14,175

4. Tom and Jim are partners who share profits and losses in the ratio of 3:2, respectively. On August 31, 1995, their capital accounts were as follows:

Tom	$ 80,000
Jim	50,000
	$130,000

On that date they agreed to admit John as a partner with a one-third interest in the capital and profits and losses, for an investment of $50,000. The new partnership will begin with a total capital of $180,000. Immediately after John's admission, what are the capital balances of the partners?

	TOM	JIM	JOHN
(a)	$60,000	$60,000	$60,000
(b)	$73,333	$46,667	$60,000
(c)	$74,000	$46,000	$60,000
(d)	$80,000	$50,000	$50,000

pg. 697

5. On June 30, 1995, the balance sheet for the partnership of Al, Carl, and Paul, together with their respective profit and loss ratios, were as follows:

Assets, at cost	$180,000
Al, loan	$ 9,000
Al, capital (20%)	42,000
Carl, capital (20%)	39,000
Paul, capital (60%)	90,000
Total	$180,000

Al has decided to retire from the partnership. By mutual agreement, the assets are to be adjusted to their fair value of $220,000 at June 30, 1995. It was agreed that the partnership would pay Al $61,200 cash for Al's partnership interest, including Al's loan, which is to be repaid in full. No goodwill is to be recorded. After Al's retirement, what is the balance of Carl's capital account?
(a) $36,450.
(b) $39,000.
(c) $46,450.
(d) $47,000.

(AICPA adapted)

Exercise 18-11

Select the best answer for each of the following.

1. Which of the following is *not* a characteristic of a partnership?
   (a) Limited life.
   (b) Mutual agency.
   (c) Limited liability.
   (d) Right to dispose of partnership interest.
2. The articles of partnership need not include which of the following?
   (a) Location of the place of business.
   (b) Allocation of profit/loss.
   (c) Procedures for admitting a new partner.
   (d) Fiscal period of the partnership.
   (e) All of the above should be included.
3. The High and Low partnership agreement provides special compensation to High for managing the business. High receives a bonus of 15% of partnership net income before salary and bonus, and also receives a salary of $45,000. Any remaining profit or loss is to be allocated equally. During 1995, the partnership had net income of $50,000 before the bonus and salary allowance. As a result of these distributions, Low's equity in the partnership would
   (a) Increase.
   (b) Not change.
   (c) Decrease the same as High's.
   (d) Decrease.
4. The allocation of an error correction should be based on the profit and loss agreement in effect when
   (a) The error was made.
   (b) The error was corrected.
   (c) The error was discovered.
   (d) The allocation should always be made equally.
5. If there is a provision for allocation of profits but not losses in the partnership agreement, courts have generally concluded that
   (a) Losses should not be allocated to the capital accounts, but matched against future earnings.
   (b) Losses should be allocated using the same approach as allocation of profits.
   (c) Losses should be allocated equally.
   (d) Losses should be allocated according to the ratio of balances in the capital accounts.
6. Partners E and F share profits and losses equally after each has been credited in all circumstances with annual salary allowances of $15,000 and $12,000, respectively. Under this agreement, E will benefit by $3,000 more than F in which of the following circumstances?
   (a) Only if the partnership has earnings of $27,000 or more for the year.
   (b) Only if the partnership does not incur a loss for the year.
   (c) In all earnings or loss situations.
   (d) Only if the partnership has earnings of at least $3,000 for the year.

Exercise 18-12

The partnership agreement of ABC Associates provides that income should be allocated in the following manner:

1. Each partner receives interest of 20% of beginning capital.
2. Sue receives a salary of $25,000 and Josh receives a salary of $21,000.
3. Josh also receives a bonus of 10%.
4. Residual—divided equally.

The partnership's net income for 1995 was $90,000. Beginning capital balances were Sue, $30,000; Josh, $40,000.

Required:

Prepare a schedule to allocate the net income under each of the following independent situations:

A. Bonus is to be based on income before any profit allocation to partners for interest and salary.

B. Bonus is to be based on income after subtracting the bonus, but before allocation to partners for interest and salary.

C. Bonus is to be based on income after subtracting the bonus, interest, and salary.

Exercise 18-13

Kazma, Folkert, and Tucker are partners with capital account balances of $30,000, $75,000, and $45,000, respectively. Income and losses are divided in a 4:4:2 ratio. When Tucker decided to withdraw, the partnership revalued its assets from $225,000 to $252,000, which represented an increase in the value of inventory of $8,000 and an increase in the value of land of $19,000. Tucker was then given $15,000 cash and a note for $40,000 for his withdrawal from the partnership.

Required:

A. Prepare the journal entry to record the revaluation of the partnership's assets.

B. Prepare the journal entry to record the withdrawal using the following independent methods.
    (1) Bonus.
    (2) Partial goodwill.
    (3) Full goodwill amount.

Problems

Problem 18-1

Day and Night formed an accounting partnership in 1995. Capital transactions for Day and Night during 1995 are as follows:

DATE	TRANSACTION	AMOUNT
DAY		
1/1	Beginning balance	$75,000
4/1	Withdrawal	18,750
6/1	Investment	37,500
11/1	Investment	18,750

DATE	TRANSACTION	AMOUNT
NIGHT		
1/1	Beginning balance	$37,500
7/1	Investment	18,750
10/1	Withdrawal	9,375

Partnership net income for the year ended December 31, 1995, is $68,400 before considering salaries or interest.

Required:

Determine the amount of profit that is to be allocated to Day and Night in accordance with each of the following independent profit-sharing agreements:

1. Day and Night failed to provide a profit-sharing arrangement in the articles of partnership and fail to compromise on an agreement.

2. Net income is to be allocated 60% to Day and 40% to Night.

3. Net income is to be allocated in the ratio of ending capital balances.

4. Net income is to be allocated in the ratio of average capital balances.

5. Interest of 15% is to be granted on average capital balances, salaries of $15,000 and $8,250 are to be allocated to Day and Night, respectively, and the remainder is to be divided equally.

Problem 18-2

Dave, Brian, and Paul are partners in a retail appliance store. The partnership was formed January 1, 1995, with each partner investing $45,000. They agreed that profits and losses are to be shared as follows:

1. Divided in the ratio of 40:30:30 if net income is not sufficient to cover salaries, bonus, and interest.
2. A net loss is to be allocated equally.
3. Net income is to be allocated as follows if net income is in excess of salaries, bonus, and interest.
    (a) Monthly salary allowances are:

Dave	$3,500
Brian	2,500
Paul	1,500

    (b) Brian is to receive a bonus of 8% of net income before subtracting salaries and interest, but after subtracting the bonus.
    (c) Interest of 10% is allocated based on the beginning-of-year capital balances.
    (d) Any remainder is to be allocated equally.

Operating performance and other capital transactions were as follows.

		CAPITAL TRANSACTIONS					
	NET INCOME	DAVE		BRIAN		PAUL	
YEAR-END	(LOSS)	INVESTMENT	WITHDRAWALS	INVESTMENT	WITHDRAWALS	INVESTMENT	WITHDRAWALS
12/31/95	$ (5,400)	$15,000	$17,000	$15,000	$7,000	$6,000	$3,200
12/31/96	27,000	–0–	17,000	–0–	7,000	6,000	3,200
12/31/97	120,000	–0–	19,000	–0–	9,000	6,000	3,200

Required:

A. Prepare a schedule of changes in partners' capital accounts for each of the three years.

B. Prepare the journal entry to close the income summary account to the partners' capital accounts at the end of each year.

Problem 18-3

The partnership of Cain, Gallo, and Hamm engaged you to adjust its accounting records and convert them uniformly to the accrual basis in anticipation of admitting Kerns as a new partner. Some accounts are on the accrual basis and some are on the cash basis. The partnership's books were closed at December 31, 1995, by the bookkeeper, who prepared the general ledger trial balance that appears below.

Cain, Gallo, and Hamm
General Ledger Trial Balance
December 31, 1995

	DEBIT	CREDIT
Cash	$ 15,000	
Accounts receivable	40,000	
Inventory	30,000	
Land	9,000	
Buildings	50,000	
Allowance for depreciation of buildings		$ 6,000
Equipment	56,000	
Allowance for depreciation of equipment		6,000
Goodwill	5,000	
Accounts payable		56,000
Allowance for future inventory losses		8,000
Cain, capital		37,000
Gallo, capital		60,000
Hamm, capital		32,000
Totals	$205,000	$205,000

Your inquiries disclose the following:

1. The partnership was organized on January 1, 1994. No provision was made in the partnership agreement for the allocation of partnership profits and losses. During 1994, profits were allocated equally among the partners. The partnership agreement was amended, effective January 1, 1995, to provide for the following profit and loss ratio: Cain, 40%; Gallo, 40%; and Hamm, 20%. The amended partnership agreement also stated that the accounting records were to be maintained on the accrual basis and that any adjustments necessary for 1994 should be allocated according to the 1994 profit allocation agreement.

2. The following amounts were not recorded as prepayments or accruals.

	DECEMBER 31	
	1995	1994
Prepaid insurance	$700	$ 800
Advances from customers	900	1,500
Accrued interest expense	—	450

The advances from customes were recorded as sales in the year the cash was received.

3. In 1995, the partnership recorded a provision of $8,000 for anticipated declines in inventory prices. You convinced the partners that the provision was unnecessary and should be removed from the books.

4. The partnership charged equipment purchased for $4,400 on January 1, 1995, to expense. This equipment has an estimated life of 10 years and an estimated salvage value of $400. The partnership depreciates its capitalized equipment using the declining balance method at twice the straight-line deprecition rate.

5. The partners agreed to establish an allowance for doubtful accounts at 2% of current accounts receivable and 5% of past-due accounts. At December 31, 1994, the partnership had $54,000 of accounts receivable, of which only $4,000 was past due. At December 31, 1995, 20% of accounts receivable was past due, of which $4,000 represented sales made in 1994 and was considered collectible. The partnership had written off uncollectible accounts in the year the accounts became worthless as follows:

	ACCOUNTS WRITTEN OFF IN	
	1995	1994
1995 accounts	$ 800	—
1994 accounts	1,000	$250

6. Goodwill was recorded on the books in 1995 and credited to the partners' capital accounts in the profit and loss ratio in recognition of an increase in the value of the business resulting from improved sales volume. The partners agreed to write off the goodwill before admitting the new partner.

Required:

Prepare a worksheet showing the adjustments and the adjusted trial balance for the partnership on the accrual basis at December 31, 1995. All adjustments affecting income should be made directly to partners' capital accounts. Supporting computations should be in good form. (Do not prepare formal financial statements or formal journal entries.)

(AICPA adapted)

Problem 18-4

Brown and Coss have been operating a tax accounting service as a partnership for five years. Their current capital balances are $92,000 and $88,000, respectively, and they share profits in a 60:40 ratio. Because of the growth in their tax business, they decide that they need a new partner. Moore is admitted to the partnership, after which the partners agree to share profits 40% to Brown, 35% to Coss, and 25% to Moore.

Required:

Prepare the necessary journal entries to admit Moore in each of the following independent conditions. If the information is such that both the bonus and goodwill methods are appropriate, record the admission using both methods.

1. Moore invests $90,000 in cash and receives a one-third capital interest.

2. Moore invests $120,000 cash for a 45% capital interest. Total capital after his admission is to be $300,000.

3. Moore agrees to invest $120,000 cash for a one-third capital interest, but will not accept a capital credit for less than his investment.

4. Moore invests $40,000 cash for a one-fourth capital interest. The partners agree that assets and the firm as a whole should not be revalued.

5. Moore invests $35,000 cash for a one-fifth capital interest. The partners agree that total capital after the admission of Moore should be $225,000.

6. Moore invests land in the partnership as a site for a new office building. The land, which originally cost Moore $90,000, now has a current market value of $150,000. Moore is admitted with a one-third capital interest. → Irrelevant

7. Moore is admitted to the partnership by purchasing a 30% capital interest from each partner. A payment of $35,000 is made outside the partnership and is split between Brown and Coss.

Problem 18-5

The CAB Partnership, although operating profitably, has had a cash flow problem. Unable to meet its current commitments, the firm borrowed $34,000 from a bank giving a long-term note. During a recent meeting, the partners decided to obtain additional cash by admitting a new partner to the firm. They feel that the firm is an attractive investment, but that proper management of their liquid assets will be required. Meyers agrees to invest cash in the firm if her chief accountant can review the accounting records of the partnership.

The balance sheet for CAB Partnership as of December 31, 1995, is as follows:

ASSETS

Cash	$ 8,000
Accounts receivable	33,600
Inventory (at cost)	35,750
Land	27,000
Building (net of depreciation)	41,600
Equipment (net of depreciation)	27,250
Total	$173,200

LIABILITIES AND CAPITAL

Accounts payable	$ 32,450
Other current liabilities	6,750
Long-term note (8% due 1999)	34,000
Cox, capital	37,500
Andrews, capital	25,000
Bennet, capital	37,500
Total	$173,200

The review of the accounts resulted in the accumulation of the following information:

1. Approximately 5% of the accounts receivable are uncollectible. The old partnership had been using the direct write-off method of accounting for bad debts.
2. Current replacement cost of the inventory is $41,250.
3. The market value of the land based on a current appraisal is $65,000.

4. The partners had been using an unreasonably long estimated life in establishing a depreciation policy for the building. On the basis of sound value (current replacement cost adjusted for use), the value of the building is $32,750.
5. There are unrecorded accrued liabilities of $3,275.

The partners agree to recognize the foregoing adjustments to the accounts. Cox, Andrews, and Bennet share profits 40:30:30. After the admission of Meyers, the new profit agreement is to be 30:20:30:20. Meyers is to receive a 25% capital interest in the partnership after she invests sufficient cash to increase the total capital interest to $150,000. Because of the uncertainty of the business, no goodwill is to be recognized before or after Meyers is admitted.

Required:

A. Prepare the necessary journal entries on the books of the old partnership to adjust the accounts.

B. Record the admission of Meyers.

C. Prepare a new balance sheet giving effect to the foregoing requirements.

Problem 18-6

The December 31, 1995, balance sheet of the Datamation Partnership is shown below.

Datamation Partnership
Balance Sheet
December 31, 1995

ASSETS

Cash	$ 80,000
Accounts receivable	80,000
Inventory	62,000
Equipment	290,000
Total Assets	$512,000

LIABILITIES AND PARTNERS' EQUITY

Accounts payable	$ 60,000
Notes payable to Dave, 8% dated September 1, 1995	22,000
Dave, capital	220,000
Allen, capital	110,000
Matt, capital	100,000
Total liabilities and partners' equity	$512,000

Dave, Allen, and Matt share profits and losses in the ratio of 50:30:20. The inventory on December 31 has a fair value of $68,000; accrued interest on the note payable to Dave is to be recognized as of December 31. The book values of all the other accounts are equal to their fair values. Allen withdrew from the partnership on December 31, 1995.

Required:

Prepare the journal entry or entries to record the withdrawal of Allen, given each of the following situations. Assume that the *bonus* method is used to account for the withdrawal.

1. Allen receives $36,624 cash and a $75,000 note from the partnership for his interest.

2. Matt purchases Allen's interest for $110,000.

3. The partnership gives Allen $35,000 cash and equipment with a book value and a fair value of $90,000 for his interest.

4. The partnership gives Allen $100,000 cash for his interest.

5. Allen sells one-fourth of his interest to Dave for $40,000 and three-fourths to Matt for $90,000.

Problem 18-7

Neal, Palmer, and Ruppe are partners in a real estate company. Their respective capital balances and profit-sharing ratios are as follows:

AS OF DECEMBER 31, 1995

PARTNERS	CAPITAL BALANCE	PROFIT-SHARING RATIO
Neal	$250,000	4
Palmer	150,000	3
Ruppe	100,000	3

Neal wishes to withdraw from the partnership on January 1, 1996, Palmer and Ruppe have agreed to pay Neal $300,000 from the partnership assets for his 50% capital interest. This settlement price was based on such factors as capital investments, sales performance, and earning capacity.

Palmer and Ruppe must decide whether to use the bonus method or the goodwill method (recognize total goodwill implied by the payment) to record the withdrawal, and they wish to compare the results of using the two methods.

Required:

Prepare a comparison of capital balances using the bonus and goodwill methods (and amortizing goodwill implied from the payment to Neal), assuming that

1. The new profit and loss ratio is in the same relative ratio as that existing before Neal's withdrawal.

2. The profit and loss ratio is changed to 3:2. Palmer is particularly interested in these results, because he feels that his present contribution of time and capital is better reflected by this new profit and loss ratio.

Problem 18-8

Brian Snow and Wendy Waite formed a partnership on July 1, 1994. Brian invested $20,000 cash, inventory valued at $15,000, and equipment valued at $67,000. Wendy invested $50,000 cash and land valued at $120,000. The partnership assumed the $40,000 mortgage on the land.

On June 30, 1995, the partnership reported a net loss of $24,000. The partnership contract specified that income and losses were to be allocated by allowing 10% interest on the original capital investment, salaries of $15,000 to Brian and $20,000 to Wendy, and the remainder to be divided in the ratio of 40:60.

On July 1, 1995, Alan Young was admitted into the partnership with a $70,000 cash investment. Alan was given a 30% interest in the partnership because of his special skills.

The partners elect to use the bonus method to record the admission. Any bonus should be divided in the old ratio of 40:60.

On June 30, 1996, the partnership reported a net income of $150,000. The new partnership contract stipulated that income and losses were to be divided in a fixed ratio of 20:50:30.

On July 2, 1996, Brian withdrew from the partnership for personal reasons. Brian was given $40,000 cash and a $60,000 note for his capital interest.

Required:

Prepare journal entries for each of the following events. Show computations.

1. Formation of the partnership.

2. Distribution of the net loss for the first year.

3. Admission of Alan into the partnership.

4. Distribution of the net income for the second year.

5. Withdrawal of Brian from the partnership.

Problem 18-9

The partnerships of Up & Down and Back & Forth started in business on July 1, 1992; each partnership owns one retail appliance store. It was agreed as of June 30, 1995, to combine the partnerships to form a new partnership to be known as Discount Partnership. Trial balances of the two original partnerships as of June 30, 1995 follow.

	UP & DOWN TRIAL BALANCE JUNE 30, 1995		BACK & FORTH TRIAL BALANCE JUNE 30, 1995	
Cash	$ 25,000		$ 20,000	
Accounts receivable	90,000		140,000	
Allowance for doubtful accounts		$ 2,000		$ 6,000
Merchandise inventory	180,000		115,000	
Land	25,000		35,000	
Buildings and equipment	80,000		125,000	
Allowance for depreciation		24,000		61,000
Prepaid expenses	6,000		8,000	
Accounts payable		42,000		54,000
Notes payable		65,000		74,000
Accrued expenses		34,000		44,000
Up, capital		95,000		
Down, capital		144,000		
Back, capital				65,000
Forth, capital				139,000
Totals	$406,000	$406,000	$443,000	$443,000

The following additional information is available.

1. The profit- and loss-sharing ratios for the former partnerships were 40% to Up and 60% to Down; 30% to Back and 70% to Forth. The profit- and loss-sharing ratio for the new partnership will be Up, 20%; Down, 30%; Back, 15%; and Forth, 35%.

2. The opening capital ratios for the new partnership are to be the same as the profit- and loss-sharing ratios for the new partnership. The capital assigned to Up & Down will total $225,000. Any cash settlements among the partners arising from capital account adjustments will be a private matter and will not be recorded on the partnership books.

3. The partners agreed that the allowance for bad debts for the new partnership is to be 4% of the accounts receivable balances.

4. The opening inventory of the new partnership is to be valued by the FIFO method. The inventory of Up & Down was valued by the FIFO method and the Back & Forth inventory was valued by the LIFO method. The LIFO inventory represents 80% of its FIFO value.

5. Depreciation is to be computed by the double-declining balance method with a 10-year life for the depreciable assets. Depreciation for three years is to be accumulated in the opening balance of the Allowance for Depreciation account. Up & Down computed depreciation by the straight-line method, and Back & Forth used the double-declining balance method. All assets were obtained on July 1, 1992.

6. After the books were closed, an unrecorded merchandise purchase of $4,000 by Back & Forth was discovered. The merchandise had been sold by June 30, 1995.

7. The accounts of Up & Down include a vacation pay accrual. It was agreed that Back & Forth should make a similar accrual for their 10 employees, who will receive a two-week vacation of $200 per employee per week.

Required:

A. Prepare a worksheet to determine the opening balances of a new partnership after giving effect to the information above. Formal journal entries are not required. Supporting computations, including the computation of goodwill, should be in good form.

B. Prepare a schedule computing the cash to be exchanged between Up & Down and between Back & Forth, in settlement of the affairs of each original partnership.

(AICPA adapted)

19

PARTNERSHIP LIQUIDATION

In the preceding chapter, dissolution of a partnership in which the business affairs were continued without interruption was discussed. In this chapter, we will consider dissolutions in which the partnership is terminated. The phase of partnership operations that begins after dissolution and ends with the termination of partnership activities is referred to as "winding up the affairs." During this period the partnership's unfinished business is completed, some of the firm's noncash assets may be converted into cash (realization), liabilities are settled to the extent possible, and any remaining assets are distributed to the partners in settlement of their residual interest. These events may occur over a relatively short period of time (for example, there may be a lump-sum sale of the assets, and the liabilities may be assumed by the purchaser or discharged with the cash received), or over a period of several years if the assets are sold individually as the business affairs are gradually terminated.

In the first part of this chapter, we will assume that all noncash assets are converted into cash before any assets are distributed to creditors and partners; this procedure is referred to as *simple liquidation*. In the second part of the chapter, we assume instead that noncash assets are sold in installments and cash is distributed to the various equity interests as it becomes available.

During the liquidation process, the accountant can provide service to the partners in a number of areas. He or she may assist in preparing financial statements and providing guidance to the partners to ensure that the liquidation proceeds in accordance with legal requirements and the partnership agreement. Much of the accounting for partnership liquidations depends on interpretation of the partnership agreement and the legal provisions governing partnership liquidation. The accountant needs to be familiar with pertinent statutory provisions, which may include the UPA and federal and state bankruptcy laws (see Chapter 17). In addition, for the protection of all parties concerned, it may be advisable to seek legal counsel.

STEPS IN THE LIQUIDATION PROCESS

The first step in the liquidation process is to compute any net income or loss up to the date of dissolution. The closing process should be completed and, as part of it, any net income or loss should be allocated to the partners in accordance with their profit and loss agreement.

In the next step of the liquidation process, assets that are not acceptable for distribution in their present form are converted into cash. If the sales price of an asset is greater than (less than) the recorded book value, there is a gain (loss) from the sale. Procedurally, gains and losses on the realization of assets may be collected in one account and then closed to the capital accounts of the individual partners. The allocation of realization gains or losses should be based on the residual profit and loss ratio, unless specific provisions for such allocation are made in the partnership agreement.[1] The rationale for this procedure is that since the changes in asset values are the result of risk assumed by the partnership, the gain or loss should be shared in the agreed profit and loss ratio. In addition, it may be difficult to separate gains and losses that result from liquidation from the under- or overstatement of book values that results from accounting policies followed in prior years. For example, a gain on the sale of an item of equipment could reflect the fact that the firm had used a conservative depreciation policy and recorded excessive depreciation in prior years. Other adjustments could result from the failure to recognize changes in market values in the appropriate year. Furthermore, any agreement as to interest and salaries in the income allocation formula is ignored when allocating realization gains and losses. The use of the residual ratio is justified, since interest and salaries are income allocations for time and resources devoted to the normal operating activities of a going concern and are not directly associated with changes in fair values of assets.

The last step is to distribute the available assets to creditors and partners. Section 40(b) of the UPA provides that

The liabilities of the partnership shall rank in order of payment, as follows:

    (I)   Those owing to creditors other than partners,

    (II)   Those owing to partners other than for capital and profits,

---

[1]Section 18 of the UPA provides a list of rights and duties of partners, "subject to any agreement between them." Section 18(a) provides that "each partner . . . must contribute towards the losses, whether of capital or otherwise, sustained by the partnership according to his share in the profits."

(III)   Those owing to partners in respect of capital,

(IV)   Those owing to partners in respect of profits.

According to this ranking, firm creditors are the first to be paid from partnership assets. In determining the rights of various creditors to payment, liabilities are classified as those that are secured, partially secured, and unsecured, with some unsecured having priority. Bankruptcy laws (see Chapter 17) dictate which of the partnership creditors are to be paid as cash becomes available. However, since this decision would have no impact on the total unpaid claims of the partnership, we will view the pool of creditors as if it were one unsecured obligation and will treat any cash payment as a reduction in total liabilities.

The UPA then provides for an order of payment that ranks partnership obligations to a partner ahead of asset distribution to a partner for capital investment. However, in practice it is legally permissible to offset a partner's loan balance against his debit capital balance. The courts have recognized that this "right of offset" is necessary in order to avoid the potential inequity of distributing cash to a partner to satisfy an outstanding loan balance when the partner has either a debit capital balance, or potential for a debit capital balance. A debit capital balance is considered an asset of the partnership.[2] If the partner is unable to honor this obligation to the partnership, and for some reason cannot be forced to do so, the debit capital balance is allocated as a realization loss to the remaining partners in their relative profit and loss ratio. The residual claims of the remaining partners are reduced, as is the amount of cash they will receive. Thus, without the right of offset, the order of payment established by the UPA may result in a payment to a partner who may eventually owe cash to the partnership as a result of a debit capital balance.

Items III and IV are generally combined into one balance because of the practical problem of separating them. In other words, after several years of operation, a partner's capital investments, withdrawals, and income and loss elements may become combined into one balance and difficult to separate if the income summary account is closed to the capital accounts of each partner. In settlement of a partner's claim against the partnership, the partners may agree to the distribution of noncash assets. If so, the carrying value of the asset should be adjusted to fair value and the amount of the adjustment allocated to all the partners in accordance with the partnership agreement. The fair value of the distributed asset is then charged against the proper capital account.

---

[2]Section 40(a) of the UPA defines the assets of the partnership as:

(I) The partnership property,

(II) The contributions of partners necessary for the payment of all the liabilities specified in clause (b) of this paragraph.

Section 40(b), referred to before, specifies that amounts owing to creditors and to partners for loans, capital, and profits are liabilities of a partnership. Thus, if a partner has a debit balance, there must be unsatisfied claims against the partnership. The amount due from the deficit partner to settle the unsatisfied claim is an asset as defined in Section 40(a).

PRIORITIES OF PARTNERSHIP AND PERSONAL CREDITORS

The UPA (Section 15) provides that partners are jointly liable for all contracts and other obligations of the partnership. This means that creditors of a partnership that are not paid in full from distribution of partnership assets must bring legal action against all the partners together to enforce their unsettled claims. Partners are jointly and severally liable for obligations that arise out of a tort and breach of trust committed by a partner while acting within the scope of the partnership business. *Joint and several* means that legal action may be brought against all the partners together or against any one or more of the partners in separate suits. A number of states have enacted legislation eliminating the distinction, and in those jurisdictions both contract and tort actions are joint and several. This latter approach, which permits suits against all (joint) or less than all (several) of the partners, is followed in this chapter. Conversely, personal creditors of an individual partner can seek recovery of payment from personal assets of the respective partner, and under certain conditions from partnership assets. Recognition of the rights of these two groups of creditors and the classification of assets into personal and partnership categories is referred to as *marshaling of assets*. The order of priority concerning the availability of assets for each class of creditors in states that have adopted the UPA is as follows:

    A. Partnership assets
        1. Partnership creditors.
        2. Personal creditors that did not recover their claims in full from personal assets. Recovery from partnership assets is limited to the extent that the partner has a credit interest in the partnership assets.
    B. Personal assets
        1. Personal creditors.
        2. Partnership creditors who were not satisfied from partnership assets. Such claims may be made against an individual partner regardless of whether the partner has a debit or credit equity interest in the partnership.
        3. Claims of the partnership against the partner by nature of a deficit equity interest.

Because of the foregoing rules, the reader should recognize the importance of properly recording all partnership assets, liabilities, and capital interest of each partner.

To illustrate the marshaling of assets rules, assume that ABCD Partnership reports the following balance sheet after the sale of all noncash assets:

DEBITS		CREDITS	
Cash	$ 50,000	Liabilities	$ 75,000
Bill Baker, capital	15,000	Alice Amos, capital	15,000
Carol Carter, capital	35,000	Don Davis, capital	10,000
Total	$100,000	Total	$100,000

The partners share profits and losses equally.

The personal status of each partner, excluding their claims against the partnership or claims of unsettled partnership creditors and other partners against them, is as follows:

PARTNER	PERSONAL ASSETS	PERSONAL LIABILITIES	ASSETS GREATER THAN (LESS THAN) LIABILITIES
Alice Amos	$20,000	$50,000	$(30,000)
Bill Baker	33,000	30,000	3,000
Carol Carter	90,000	40,000	50,000
Don Davis	40,000	10,000	30,000

The personal assets of each partner must be applied to the settlement of his or her personal liabilities before personal assets can be used to satisfy any partnership claims. Thus, the maximum amount that the partnership creditors and other partners could recover from the personal assets is $83,000 ($3,000 + $50,000 + $30,000). Because the personal liabilities of Amos exceed her personal assets, partnership claims cannot be enforced against her personal assets even though she has a credit interest in the partnership. However, her unsettled personal creditors in the amount of $30,000 can look for full or partial settlement of their claims from final distribution of partnership assets in settlement of her capital interest. At this time, the partnership has a claim of $15,000 and $35,000 against Baker and Carter, respectively. Baker, however, will have only $3,000 left for investment in the partnership to reduce his capital deficit.[3] Carter has sufficient personal assets to satisfy her personal liabilities and invest in the partnership to cover her share of partnership losses. Davis is personally solvent and has a credit capital interest in the partnership.

The liquidation of the partnership is summarized in Illustration 19-1. Although formal journal entries are not shown, they would be recorded in a journal in accordance with the tabular arrangement summarized in the liquidation schedule. The steps in the liquidation process may proceed in any order as long as the rights of the partners, partnership creditors, and personal creditors are recognized. Here it is assumed that Baker invested $3,000 in the partnership and his remaining deficit of $12,000 is a liquidation loss that is allocated to the remaining partners in their relative profit and loss ratio, one-third each. Note that because Carter has sufficient assets to cover her share of additional losses, $4,000 is allocated, even though she currently has a deficit capital balance. After cash of $53,000 is distributed to the

---

[3]In states in which the common law or federal bankruptcy laws are controlling, the personal assets of a partner are allocated between the personal creditors and the amount owed to the partnership. In this illustration, the personal assets of Baker would be allocated as follows:

Total liabilities	
Personal liabilities	$30,000
Amount owed to partnership	15,000
Total obligations of Baker	$45,000
Allocation	
To personal creditors ($30,000 ÷ $45,000) × $33,000 =	$22,000
To partnership ($15,000 ÷ $45,000) × $33,000 =	11,000
Total personal assets of Baker	$33,000

Marshaling of Assets

ILLUSTRATION 19-1
Schedule of Partnership Liquidation

			CAPITAL AND LOAN BALANCES			
			AMOS	BAKER	CARTER	DAVIS
	CASH	LIABILITIES	¼	¼	¼	¼
Balance before cash distributions	50,000	(75,000)*	(15,000)	15,000	35,000	(10,000)
Investment by Baker	3,000			(3,000)		
	53,000	(75,000)	(15,000)	12,000	35,000	(10,000)
Allocation of Baker's deficit			4,000	(12,000)	4,000	4,000
	53,000	(75,000)	(11,000)	–0–	39,000	(6,000)
Payment to creditors	(53,000)	53,000				
	–0–	(22,000)	(11,000)	–0–	39,000	(6,000)
Investment by Carter	39,000				(39,000)	
	39,000	(22,000)	(11,000)	–0–	–0–	(6,000)
Payment to creditors	(22,000)	22,000				
	17,000	–0–	(11,000)	–0–	–0–	(6,000)
Payment to partners	(17,000)		11,000			6,000
	–0–	–0–	–0–	–0–	–0–	–0–

*In this chapter ( ) means that an account has a credit balance or a credit is posted to an account.

creditors, the partnership has unpaid obligations of $22,000. It is assumed that the partnership creditors obtained judgment against Carter. (The creditors could have proceeded to recover their claims from any solvent partner individually, including Davis, who has a credit capital interest, or from the partners jointly.) Since Carter has a personal net asset position of $50,000, she will invest an additional $39,000 in the partnership; $22,000 to cover the amount owed to partnership creditors plus $17,000 for the amount owed to the other partners to cover her deficit. The cash is distributed first to liquidate partnership liabilities and then to satisfy partners' capital interest. Observe that the cash distribution to partners is based on their capital balances, not their profit and loss ratio. The unpaid personal creditors of Amos have a claim against her $11,000 partnership distribution.

If, in the illustration above, Carter was able to invest only $20,000 from her personal assets and Davis was personally insolvent, then the creditors and partners Amos and Davis would have unrecoverable losses of $19,000 as shown next.

	CASH	LIABILITIES	AMOS	BAKER	CARTER	DAVIS
From Illustration 19-1	–0–	(22,000)	(11,000)	–0–	39,000	(6,000)
Investment by Carter	20,000				(20,000)	
Payment to creditors	(20,000)	20,000				
	–0–	(2,000)	(11,000)	–0–	19,000	(6,000)

SIMPLE LIQUIDATION ILLUSTRATED

To illustrate the accounting for a simple liquidation, assume that the condensed balance sheet of ABC Partnership that follows was prepared just before the liquidation:

ASSETS		LIABILITIES AND CAPITAL	
Cash	$ 20,000	Liabilities	$ 70,000
Noncash Assets	180,000	Carter, Loan	10,000
		Alice Amos, capital (50%)	80,000
		Bill Baker, capital (30%)	30,000
		Carol Carter, capital (20%)	10,000
Total	$200,000	Total	$200,000

The profit and loss ratio is in parentheses. Personal assets and liabilities of the partners are

	ASSETS	LIABILITIES
Amos	$50,000	$30,000
Baker	40,000	12,000
Carter	20,000	25,000

The liquidation of the ABC Partnership is summarized in the schedule presented in Illustration 19-2.

ILLUSTRATION 19-2

Simple Liquidation

Schedule of Partnership Realization and Liquidation

	CASH	NONCASH ASSETS	LIABILITIES	CARTER LOAN	CAPITAL BALANCES AMOS .5	BAKER .3	CARTER .2
Account balances before realization	20,000	180,000	(70,000)	(10,000)	(80,000)	(30,000)	(10,000)
(1) Sale of assets and allocation of $128,000 loss	52,000	(180,000)			64,000	38,400	25,600
	72,000	–0–	(70,000)	(10,000)	(16,000)	8,400	15,600
(2) Payment to creditors	(70,000)		70,000				
	2,000	–0–	–0–	(10,000)	(16,000)	8,400	15,600
(3) Offset loan against debit capital balance				10,000			(10,000)
	2,000	–0–	–0–	–0–	(16,000)	8,400	5,600
(4) Allocate debit capital balance of insolvent partner					3,500	2,100	(5,600)
	2,000	–0–	–0–	–0–	(12,500)	10,500	–0–
(5) Investment by Baker	10,500					(10,500)	
	12,500	–0–	–0–	–0–	(12,500)	–0–	–0–
(6) Payment to Amos	(12,500)				12,500		
	–0–	–0–	–0–	–0–	–0–	–0–	–0–

The sequence of events recorded in Illustration 19-2 is based on the concepts that were discussed earlier:

1. Noncash assets of $180,000 are sold for $52,000 and the resulting realization loss of $128,000 is allocated to the partners according to their profit and loss ratio.

2. Partnership liabilities, other than to partners, are paid before assets are distributed to partners.

3. The right of offset is exercised where a partner with an outstanding loan has a debit capital balance.

4. In transactions (4) and (5), the principles concerning the marshaling of assets are applied to determine if additional investments can be expected. In this case, Carter with a deficit capital interest is also personally insolvent. Thus, her deficit is allocated to the other partners on the basis of their relative loss-sharing ratio: ⅝ to Amos, ⅜ to Baker.

5. Baker invests $10,500 in the partnership to eliminate his deficit after his personal assets were applied to the settlement of his personal liabilities.

6. Cash is distributed to Amos to satisfy her capital claim against the partnership assets.

INSTALLMENT LIQUIDATION

In the preceding section, all the noncash assets were converted into cash and the resulting gain or loss allocated before any distribution was made to the creditors and to the partners. It could be an advantage to the partnership, however, if conversion of noncash assets into cash were extended over several months. For example, in certain types of businesses, such as land development, more cash may be generated if the company completes construction projects it has started, or, as is frequently the case, the partnership may receive a greater cash price for the noncash assets if they are not sold at a forced liquidation. If the liquidation extends over a period of time, the partners will probably prefer that cash be distributed as it becomes available. If partners are to receive cash in installments before the total liquidation losses and the total cash available are known, safeguards must be taken to protect the interests of the creditors and the respective interest of each partner. In addition, the individual in charge of the liquidation must use safeguards to avoid potential liability for wrongful distributions.

The remainder of this chapter focuses on the problems associated with a liquidation in installments and the general rules governing such liquidations. Once again, many of the procedures followed are necessary to satisfy legal requirements and for the protection of the person in charge of the liquidation and the residual partners' interests.

Safe Payment Approach

In computing how cash is to be distributed to the partners before all assets are disposed of, care must be taken to ensure that the partners' remaining capital balances will be adequate to absorb any potential loss. However, at this point, the amount of cash to be generated from the sale of noncash assets and the resulting gain or loss is not known. Therefore, the partners should view each cash distribution as if it were the final distribution.

One approach used to calculate a safe cash distribution is based on three assumptions:

1. A loan to or from an individual partner will be combined with the respective partner's capital account to determine his or her net interest in the partnership assets.

2. The remaining noncash assets will not provide any additional cash. In other words, the maximum potential loss is equal to the book value of noncash assets. (This assumption will be modified later in the chapter.)

3. A partner with a debit balance in his or her capital account will be unable to pay amounts owed to the partnership (that is, each partner is personally insolvent).

The result of applying these assumptions is that cash will not be distributed to a partner whose capital account balance (including loan balance and drawing account) is insufficient to absorb his or her share of potential losses either from the write-off of assets or from the failure of a deficit partner to cover a debit capital balance. Of course, no partner should receive cash until the liabilities have been liquidated or provided for through the retention of adequate cash.

Computation of Safe Payment Before Each Distribution To illustrate the safe payment approach when a partnership is liquidated in installments, assume that the following condensed balance sheet was prepared before the partners' agreement to liquidate the partnership.

Cash	$ 10,000	Liabilities	$ 28,000
Noncash assets	100,000	Alice Amos, capital (30%)	34,000
		Bill Baker, capital (50%)	30,000
		Carol Carter, capital (20%)	18,000
Total	$110,000	Total	$110,000

The partners' income- and loss-sharing percentages are stated in parentheses. The noncash assets were converted into cash over a period of time as follows:

	SALES PRICE	BOOK VALUE
Sale No. 1	$20,000	$30,000
Sale No. 2	15,000	25,000
Sale No. 3	10,000	30,000
Sale No. 4	2,000	10,000
Sale No. 5	–0–	5,000

The realization of the partnership assets and liquidation of the partnership are summarized in Illustration 19-3. After the first sale of assets and payment to creditors, $2,000 remains to be distributed to partners. In this case, the assumption that the remaining noncash assets of $70,000 (Schedule 1) are worthless results in a debit balance in Baker's capital account. Another assumption is that all partners are personally insolvent. Therefore, the hypothetical deficit is allocated to the re-

ILLUSTRATION 19-3
Schedule of Partnership Realization and Liquidation
Installment Liquidation

	CASH	OTHER ASSETS	LIABILITIES	AMOS .3	BAKER .5	CARTER .2
				CAPITAL AND LOAN BALANCES		
Balance before realization	10,000	100,000	(28,000)	(34,000)	(30,000)	(18,000)
Sale of assets	20,000	(30,000)		3,000	5,000	2,000
	30,000	70,000	(28,000)	(31,000)	(25,000)	(16,000)
Payment to creditors	(28,000)	—	28,000			
	2,000	70,000	–0–	(31,000)	(25,000)	(16,000)
Payment to partners						
Safe payment Schedule I	(2,000)			2,000		
	–0–	70,000	–0–	(29,000)	(25,000)	(16,000)
Sale of assets	15,000	(25,000)		3,000	5,000	2,000
	15,000	45,000	–0–	(26,000)	(20,000)	(14,000)
Payment to partners						
Safe payment Schedule II	(15,000)			11,000		4,000
	–0–	45,000	–0–	(15,000)	(20,000)	(10,000)
Sale of assets	10,000	(30,000)		6,000	10,000	4,000
	10,000	15,000	–0–	(9,000)	(10,000)	(6,000)
Payment to partners						
Safe payment Schedule III	(10,000)			4,500	2,500	3,000
	–0–	15,000	–0–	(4,500)	(7,500)	(3,000)
Sale of assets	2,000	(10,000)		2,400	4,000	1,600
	2,000	5,000	–0–	(2,100)	(3,500)	(1,400)
Payment to partners	(2,000)			600	1,000	400
	–0–	5,000	–0–	(1,500)	(2,500)	(1,000)
Write-off of assets		(5,000)		1,500	2,500	1,000
	–0–	–0–	–0–	–0–	–0–	–0–

SCHEDULE I
COMPUTATION OF SAFE PAYMENTS

	AMOS .3	BAKER .5	CARTER .2
Capital and loan balances	(31,000)	(25,000)	(16,000)
Allocation of potential loss—$70,000	21,000	35,000	14,000
	(10,000)	10,000	(2,000)
Allocation of Baker's potential deficit	6,000	(10,000)	4,000
	(4,000)	–0–	2,000
Allocation of Carter's potential deficit	2,000		(2,000)
Safe payment	(2,000)	–0–	–0–

SCHEDULE II
COMPUTATION OF SAFE PAYMENTS

	AMOS .3	BAKER .5	CARTER .2
Capital and loan balances	(26,000)	(20,000)	(14,000)
Allocation of potential loss—$45,000	13,500	22,500	9,000
	(12,500)	2,500	(5,000)
Allocation of Baker's potential deficit	1,500	(2,500)	1,000
Safe payment	(11,000)	–0–	(4,000)

SCHEDULE III
COMPUTATION OF SAFE PAYMENTS

	AMOS	BAKER	CARTER
	.3	.5	.2
Capital and loan balances	(9,000)	(10,000)	(6,000)
Allocation of potential loss—$15,000	4,500	7,500	3,000
Safe payment	(4,500)	(2,500)	(3,000)

maining partners with credit balances on the basis of their relative profit and loss ratio: ⅗ to Amos, ⅖ to Carter. This allocation results in a hypothetical debit balance in the capital account of Carter, which is assigned to Amos. Thus, if $2,000 is paid to Amos, this will leave her with a capital balance sufficient to absorb her share of the potential remaining losses. Amos will not be required to make an additional investment in the partnership unless significant amounts of unrecorded liabilities are discovered or significant amounts of liquidation expenses are incurred. But if it became necessary for Amos to make an additional investment, the other two partners would also be required to do so.

A safe payment schedule is prepared each time cash is to be distributed. The second payment to Amos and Carter brings their capital balances into a ratio of 3:2. The two partners now have capital balances sufficient to absorb their share of future losses up to $50,000, which is greater than the book value of the remaining noncash assets of $45,000. However, if the fair value of the remaining assets is zero, Baker's capital balance of $20,000 would be inadequate to absorb his share of the losses, which would be $22,500 ($45,000 × .50). Accordingly, at this time, Baker does not receive any of the cash to be distributed, since he could end up with a debit capital balance. After the third cash distribution, the partner's capital balances are in their profit and loss ratio of 3:5:2. Once their capital interests are in the profit and loss ratio, any subsequent distribution of assets will be based on the profit and loss ratio. Note that each partner's capital account is now sufficient to absorb the final potential loss of $5,000.

A safe payment schedule is prepared to compute the amount of cash to be distributed and to determine which partner(s) will receive cash. The series of computations is not recorded in the accounts, since they are based on certain assumed events that have not yet occurred. Only the actual transactions as they occur, such as the sale of assets and distribution of cash, are recorded in the accounts.

Additional Losses, Discovery of Liabilities, and Liquidation Expense Up to this point in this chapter, all available cash was distributed to (1) the partnership's creditors who were recorded on the partnership books or (2) the partners. In the calculation of a safe payment, it was assumed that the potential loss was equal to the book value of the remaining noncash assets. In addition, no liquidation expenses were incurred. As the liquidation proceeds, some liabilities that had not been recorded previously may be reported. These creditors have claims that must be satisfied from the available cash before payments are made to partners for their capital interest.

Certain expenses, such as the reasonable cost of carrying out the liquidation, have priority over payments to creditors. Furthermore, the disposal cost of assets may exceed the proceeds from the sale of the assets so that the resulting loss is greater than the assets' recorded book value. Such items can be considered in the safe payment schedule by adding the estimated liquidation expenses, disposal cost, and unrecorded liabilities to the book value of noncash assets. To illustrate, assume the facts presented in Illustration 19-3 except that it is estimated that added expenses of $1,000 will be incurred in completing the liquidation. The safe payment calculation for the first cash distribution would be modified as follows:

	AMOS	BAKER	CARTER
Capital and loan balances	(31,000)	(25,000)	(16,000)
Allocation of potential losses ($70,000 + $1,000)	21,300	35,500	14,200
Balances	(9,700)	10,500	(1,800)
Allocation of Baker's potential deficit	6,300	(10,500)	4,200
Balances	(3,400)	–0–	(2,400)
Allocation of Carter's potential deficit	2,400		(2,400)
Safe payment	(1,000)	–0–	–0–

As can be seen, the effect of the adjustment is to hold back cash equal to the estimated expenses, which results in a corresponding reduction in the cash distributed to Amos.

Advance Plan for the Distribution of Cash

In the preceding illustration, a safe payment to each partner was calculated before each cash distribution. This process was necessary until the capital accounts were in the profit- and loss-sharing ratio. Although this method is feasible, it is more informative and efficient to prepare an advance schedule that specifies the order in which each partner will participate and the amount of cash each partner will receive as it becomes available for distribution. For example, from such a schedule, the personal creditors of an insolvent partner would be able to compute how much cash would have to be generated from the sale of the partnership assets before any cash is distributed to the insolvent partner.

To illustrate the procedures for the preparation of an advance cash distribution plan, assume the set of facts employed in Illustration 19-3. The objective of the procedure is to derive the order and the amount of cash that should be distributed to each partner such that no partner receiving a cash distribution will have to make an additional investment in the firm. Such a distribution plan will bring the balances of the partners' capital accounts into their profit and loss ratio as soon as possible. The rationale for this procedure is that once the capital balances are in the profit and loss ratio, no one partner is in any better position than any other partner to absorb losses.

Steps in the development of an advance cash distribution plan are presented in Illustration 19-4 and explained below.

Step 1 Determine the net capital interest of each partner by combining the balance in the partner's capital account with obligations to or receivables from the partner.

	AMOS	BAKER	CARTER
Capital balance	$34,000	$30,000	$18,000
Loan balance	–0–	–0–	–0–
Net capital interest	$34,000	$30,000	$18,000

Step 2 Determine the order in which the partners are to participate in cash distributions. The objective of this step is to provide an order of cash distribution in which the ratio of the partners' capital interest will eventually be equal to their

ILLUSTRATION 19-4
Preparation of an Advance Plan for the Distribution of Cash

STEP 1	AMOS	BAKER	CARTER
Capital balances	$34,000	$30,000	$18,000
Loan balances	—	—	—
Net capital interest	$34,000	$30,000	$18,000
Profit and loss ratio	.30	.50	.20

STEP 2			
Loss necessary to reduce net capital balance to zero	$113,333	$60,000	$90,000
Order of cash distribution	1	3	2

	LOSS ABSORPTION POTENTIAL			ASSET DISTRIBUTION		
STEP 3	AMOS	BAKER	CARTER	AMOS	BAKER	CARTER
Profit and loss ratio	.30	.50	.20	.30	.50	.20
Loss absorption potential	$113,333	$60,000	$90,000			
Net capital interest				$34,000	$30,000	$18,000
Distribution to Amos to reduce her capital interest so that her loss absorption potential is the same as Carter's ($113,333 − $90,000 = $23,333 × .30)	23,333			7,000		
Balances after distribution to Amos	90,000	60,000	90,000	27,000	30,000	18,000
Distribution to Amos and Carter to reduce their capital interest so that their loss absorption potential is the same as Baker's ($90,000 − $60,000 = $30,000 × .30) ($90,000 − $60,000 = $30,000 × .20)	30,000		30,000	9,000		6,000
Balances after distribution to Amos and Carter	$ 60,000	$60,000	$60,000	$18,000	$30,000	$12,000
Remainder of asset distributions				.30	.50	.20

STEP 4

	CASH DISTRIBUTION PLAN			
ORDER OF CASH DISTRIBUTION	LIABILITIES	AMOS .3	BAKER .5	CARTER .2
1. First $28,000	100%			
2. Next $7,000		100%		
3. Next $15,000		60%		40%
4. Remainder		30%	50%	20%

profit and loss ratio. Once this is accomplished, all partners will have an equal ability to absorb their share of partnership losses. Several approaches can be used to accomplish this objective. One systematic approach is to determine the loss absorption potential of each partner by dividing the net capital interest of each partner by his or her respective profit and loss ratio.

	AMOS	BAKER	CARTER
Net capital interest	$ 34,000	$30,000	$18,000
Profit and loss ratio	.30	.50	.20
Loss absorption potential	$113,333	$60,000	$90,000
Order of cash distribution	1	3	2

This computation determines the maximum amount of loss each partner is capable of absorbing and provides a basis for ranking the partners in terms of each partner's capital interest relative to his or her loss ratio. The partner with the largest loss absorption potential has the ability to absorb a greater share of losses before his or her capital account would be reduced to a zero balance. Thus, Amos will receive the first distribution of assets after the creditors' claims have been satisfied. The partner with the lowest loss absorption potential (Baker) will be the last partner to participate in the distribution of assets from the partnership.

Step 3 In Step 2, the order in which each partner is to participate in cash distributions was determined. The next step is to compute the amount of cash each partner is to receive as it becomes available for distribution. The objective is to determine the *amount* of cash to distribute to each partner to bring the ratios of their capital interests in the partnership into alignment with their profit and loss ratios. One way to compute this is to bring the loss absorption potential of each partner computed in Step 2 into balance. It was determined in Step 2 that Amos is in the strongest position relative to the other partners and is to receive the first cash distribution. Amos is capable of absorbing her share of $113,333 in losses, which is $23,333 greater than that of Carter ($113,333 − $90,000), who is the next partner to participate in cash distributions. However, Amos must absorb only 30% or $7,000 ($23,333 × .30) of such potential losses. Thus, a payment to Amos of $7,000 would reduce her loss absorption potential to $90,000 ($34,000 − $7,000 = $27,000 ÷ .30 = $90,000). Amos and Carter are now in the same relative position with respect to their ability to absorb their share of partnership losses. Also, note that a payment of $7,000 to Amos brings her capital interest into a ratio of 3:2 to that of Carter ($27,000:$18,000).

The next step in the process is to bring the loss absorption potential of Amos and Carter into balance with that of Baker, who is the last partner to participate in the distribution of cash. Using the same rationale, Amos and Carter are now capable of absorbing losses of $30,000 ($90,000 − $60,000) greater than Baker. Since they must absorb 30% and 20% of the losses, respectively, the distribution to each partner is computed as follows:

To Amos: $30,000 × .30 = $9,000
To Carter: $30,000 × .20 = $6,000

Of the next $15,000, Amos is to receive $9,000 and Carter is to receive $6,000. Distributions of these amounts will bring the ratio of the partners' capital balances into their agreed profit and loss ratio of 3:5:2 ($18,000:$30,000:$12,000).[4]

Step 4 A cash distribution plan is then prepared as follows:

ORDER OF CASH DISTRIBUTION	LIABILITIES	AMOS	BAKER	CARTER
1. First $28,000	100%			
2. Next $7,000		100%		
3. Next $15,000		60%		40%
4. Remainder		30%	50%	20%

The first $28,000 available is, of course, paid to the creditors. Cash may be held back from distribution if it is anticipated that unrecorded liabilities will be discovered or if additional liquidation expenses will be incurred. The distribution of cash in excess of this reserve amount proceeds as determined. Amos will receive all of any additional cash up to $7,000. Additional cash in excess of $7,000 and up to $22,000 is distributed 60:40 to Amos and Carter. After $22,000 ($15,000 + $7,000) has been distributed to the partners, the capital accounts are in the desired profit and loss ratio of 3:5:2. Any further distributions to the partners are made in the profit and loss ratio.

The advance distribution plan developed before will yield the same cash dis-

---

[4]An alternative method of determining the amount to be distributed at each level is to compute the capital account balances needed by each partner so as to bring the partners' capital balances into their agreed profit- and loss-sharing ratio. This is accomplished by bringing the ratio of the partners' capital account balances into their profit- and loss-sharing ratio in the order in which the partners are to participate in the distribution. In this case, the first step is to compute what the capital account balance of Amos should be so that her capital balance is in the profit- and loss-sharing ratio with that of Carter (3:2). This can be computed as follows:

$$\text{Let } X = \text{the desired capital balance}$$

$$\frac{\text{Loss ratio of Amos}}{\text{Loss ratio of Carter}} = \frac{X}{\text{Capital balance of Carter}}$$

$$\frac{3}{2} = \frac{X}{\$18,000}$$

$$2X = \$54,000$$

$$X = \$27,000$$

Since Amos has a capital balance of $34,000, it would take a distribution of $7,000 to reduce the balance to $27,000. The next level of payments should reduce the capital balances of Amos and Carter in such a way that their capital balances will be in the loss ratio to that of Baker, which is 3:5 and 2:5, respectively.

$$\frac{3}{5} = \frac{X}{\$30,000} \qquad \frac{2}{5} = \frac{X}{\$30,000}$$

$$5X = \$90,000 \qquad 5X = \$60,000$$

$$X = \$18,000 \qquad X = \$12,000$$

A distribution of $9,000 to Amos ($27,000 − $18,000) and $6,000 to Carter ($18,000 − $12,000) will produce capital balances in the ratio of 3:5:2 ($18,000:$30,000:$12,000). Although this method may be simple to use in some limited cases, the suggested approach may be more systematic when there are numerous partners.

tribution as will the process of computing a safe payment each time cash is available. As proof, in Illustration 19-5, the advance plan for distributing cash as developed in Illustration 19-4 is applied to determine the cash distribution in Illustration 19-3. Even though both methods produce the same results, the advance plan is more informative to creditors, both personal and partnership, and to the partners, because the interested parties now know the order in which individual partners will receive cash and the amounts that each may receive at each stage of the distribution process.

One requirement that must be satisfied in the development of the advance plan is that the partners must share income in the same ratio that they share losses. If this were not the case, the allocation of liquidation gains could alter the order of cash distribution computed in the advance plan. To illustrate, assume that Amos, Baker, and Carter, with capital balances of $45,000, $24,000, and $20,000, respectively, share losses in the ratio of 5:3:2, but share income in the ratio of 3:5:2. The order of cash distribution based on the ratio of losses would be as follows:

	AMOS	BAKER	CARTER
Net capital interest	$45,000	$24,000	$ 20,000
Loss ratios	.50	.30	.20
Loss absorption potential	$90,000	$80,000	$100,000
Order of cash distribution	2	3	1

ILLUSTRATION 19-5
Cash Distribution per Advance Plan

	LIABILITIES	AMOS	BAKER	CARTER	TOTAL
First Distribution: $30,000					
First—$28,000	$28,000				$28,000
Next—$2,000		$ 2,000			2,000
	$28,000	$ 2,000	—	—	$30,000
Second Distribution: $15,000					
First—$5,000					
(Remainder of $7,000 level)		$ 5,000			$ 5,000
Next—$10,000		6,000		$4,000	10,000
	—	$11,000	—	$4,000	$15,000
Third Distribution: $10,000					
First—$5,000					
(Remainder of $15,000 level)		$ 3,000		$2,000	$ 5,000
Next—$5,000		1,500	$2,500	1,000	5,000
	—	$ 4,500	$2,500	$3,000	$10,000
Last Distribution: $2,000					
First—$2,000	—	$ 600	$1,000	$ 400	$ 2,000

Now assume that the partnership realizes a $50,000 gain. The allocation of the gain in the ratio of $3:5:2$ and computation of the order of cash distribution follow:

	AMOS	BAKER	CARTER
Net capital interest	$(45,000)	$(24,000)	$(20,000)
Allocation of $50,000 gain	(15,000)	(25,000)	(10,000)
Net capital interest	$(60,000)	$(49,000)	$(30,000)
Loss ratios	.50	.30	.20
New loss absorption potential	$120,000	$163,333	$150,000
New order of cash distribution	3	1	2

In this illustration an allocation of the $50,000 gain moved Baker from being the last partner to receive cash to being the first partner to receive cash.

It is also necessary to recompute an advance plan if a certain classification of losses is shared in a different ratio from the one used in preparing the advance plan, or if adjustments are made to the capital balances in other than the loss ratio. For example, assume that it has been discovered that a cash withdrawal by a partner had been expensed instead of debited to his drawing account. The correction of the error would modify the loss absorption potential of that partner. If such adjustments occur frequently, then the computation of a safe payment may be less time-consuming and easier to use than the development of an advance cash distribution plan.

INCORPORATION OF A PARTNERSHIP

After a partnership has been operating for a period of time, the partners may find that the partnership form of business is no longer satisfactory. The corporation, with its limited liability, continuity of existence, and ability to raise needed resources, may become more attractive. Upon incorporation, the assets and liabilities are transferred to the corporation and the partners receive capital stock in settlement of their interests. The partnership accounts should be restated to fair values to assure that the partners receive an equitable distribution of stock for their interests.

The partnership books may be retained for use by the corporation, or a new set of books may be established.

Retention of Partnership Books by Corporation

Assuming that the partnership books are used by the corporation, the steps to record the incorporation are as follows:

1. Assets and liabilities are adjusted to fair value. Frequently, a valuation adjustment account is created to accumulate the gains and losses.

2. The valuation adjustment account is closed to the partner's capital accounts in accordance with their profit and loss ratio.

3. The partners' capital accounts are closed upon the transfer of capital stock. Since the books are retained, offsetting credits are made to Capital Stock at par

value for the number of shares issued. If the debit to partners' capital accounts exceeds the credit to Capital Stock, the difference is a credit to Additional Paid-in Capital.

To illustrate, assume that AB Partnership is to incorporate. The new corporation is authorized to issue 5,000 shares of $10 par value stock. Book values of the partnership accounts and fair values for the assets are determined to be:

	BOOK VALUE		FAIR VALUES
	DEBIT	CREDIT	
Cash	$ 5,000		$ 5,000
Accounts receivable	4,000		3,600
Inventory	5,000		7,000
Land	10,000		15,000
Equipment (net of depreciation)	6,000		5,000
Accounts payable		$ 7,000	
Notes payable		10,000	
Art, capital		8,000	
Beck, capital		5,000	
Total	$30,000	$30,000	

Other facts are: (1) Liabilities are assumed to be fairly valued; (2) Art and Beck share profits equally; (3) Art and Beck are to receive par value stock equal to their adjusted ending capital balances. The journal entries to incorporate are:

(1) Inventory	2,000	
Land	5,000	
Equipment		1,000
Accounts Receivable		400
Valuation Adjustment		5,600
(2) Valuation Adjustment	5,600	
Art, Capital		2,800
Beck, Capital		2,800
(3) Art, Capital	10,800	
Beck, Capital	7,800	
Capital Stock—$10 par		18,600

New Books Established by Corporation

If the corporation establishes a new set of books, then all accounts on the partnership books will end with a zero balance. The only difference as compared to the illustration above is that on receipt of the stock, asset and liability accounts are closed on the partnership books and transferred to the corporation. To balance the entry, an asset account is created for the capital stock received in the amount of $18,600. This balance should also equal the sum of the balances in the remaining capital accounts. The entry to record the distribution of the capital stock is:

Art, Capital	10,800	
Beck, Capital	7,800	
Capital Stock from Corporation		18,600

The corporation records the assets received and the liabilities assumed on the new books at the net cost of the stock issued ($18,600), which is also equal to the adjusted value of the net assets on the partnership books. A credit of $18,600 to balance the entry is made to capital stock issued.

Questions

1. Why are realization gains or losses allocated to partners in their profit and loss ratios?

2. In what manner should the final cash distribution be made in a partnership liquidation?

3. Why does a debit balance in a partners' capital account create problems in the UPA order of payment for a partnership liquidation?

4. Is it important to maintain separate accounts for a partner's outstanding loan and capital accounts? Explain why or why not.

5. Discuss the possible outcomes in the situation where the equity interest of one partner is inadequate to absorb realization losses.

6. During a liquidation, at which point may cash be distributed to any of the partners?

7. What is "marshaling of assets"?

8. To what extent can personal creditors seek recovery from partnership assets?

9. In an installment liquidation, why should the partners view each cash distribution as if it were the final distribution?

10. Discuss the three basic assumptions necessary for calculating a safe cash distribution. How is this safe cash distribution computed?

11. How are unexpected costs such as liquidation expenses, disposal costs, or unrecorded liabilities covered in the safe distribution schedule?

12. What is the objective of the procedures used for the preparation of an advance cash distribution plan?

13. What is the "loss absorption potential"?

14. In what order must partnership assets be distributed?

Exercises

Exercise 19-1

The CPA Partnership operated by Cook, Parks, and Argo is being liquidated. A balance sheet prepared at this stage in their liquidation process is presented below.

Cash	$40,000	Liabilities	$25,000
Other assets	50,000	Parks, loan	10,000
		Cook, capital	30,000
		Parks, capital	10,000
		Argo, capital	15,000
Total	$90,000	Total	$90,000

The partners share profits and losses 30% (Cook), 50% (Parks), and 20% (Argo). The partners are all personally insolvent.

Required:

A. The partners wish to distribute the $40,000 in cash. Record in journal entry form the distribution of the available cash.

B. Record in journal entry form the completion of the liquidation process, assuming that the other assets of $50,000 are sold for $15,000.

Exercise 19-2

John, Jake, and Joe are partners with capital accounts of $90,000, $78,000, and $64,000 respectively. They share profits and losses in the ratio of 30:40:30. When the partners decide to liquidate, the business has $70,000 in cash, noncash assets totaling $260,000, and $98,000 in liabilities. The noncash assets are sold for $270,000, and the creditors are paid.

Required:

A. Prepare a schedule of partnership liquidation.

B. Prepare journal entries to record each of the following transactions.
   1. The sale of the noncash assets.
   2. The payment to the creditors.
   3. The distribution of cash to the partners.

Exercise 19-3

The unsuccessful partnership of the Jones Brothers is about to undergo liquidation. They have asked you to estimate the amount of cash that each brother will receive. They share profits and losses equally.

Cash	$ 22,000	Liabilities	$ 35,000
Noncash assets	110,000	Doug, capital	55,000
		Dave, capital	50,000
		Dan, capital	(8,000)
	$132,000		$132,000

Both Doug and Dave are personally solvent, but Dan is not. They estimate that they will receive $65,000 from the sale of the noncash assets.

Required:

Prepare a schedule to estimate the amount of cash each brother will receive.

Exercise 19-4

The ABC Partnership is in the process of liquidation. The account balances prior to liquidation are given below:

DEBITS		CREDITS	
Cash	$ 72,000	Liabilities	$ 40,000
Amos, drawing	10,000	Boone, loan	8,000
Boone, drawing	15,000	Childs, loan	25,000
Childs, drawing	20,000	Amos, capital	49,000
Operating loss	21,000	Boone, capital	18,000
Liquidation loss	12,000	Childs, capital	10,000
	$150,000		$150,000

The partners share profits in the following ratio: Amos, 1/5; Boone, 2/5; Childs, 2/5.

Required:

Prepare a schedule showing the calculations of the distribution of cash under the Uniform Partnership Act, assuming that all three partners have personal liabilities in excess of their personal assets.

Exercise 19-5

Following is the balance sheet of the BDO Partnership:

Cash	$ 10,000	Liabilities	$ 18,000
Accounts receivable	40,000	Brink, capital	45,000
Inventory	30,000	Davis, capital	27,000
Equipment	60,000	Olsen, capital	50,000
	$140,000		$140,000

The partners share income 40:40:20, respectively. Assume that 70% of the receivables are collected and that inventory with a book value of $15,000 is sold for $10,000. All cash available at this time is to be distributed.

Required:

Determine the proper distribution of cash, using the safe payment approach.

Exercise 19-6

Pete, Tom, and Zack have operated a laundromat for 10 years. The partners, who share profits 4:3:3, respectively, decide to liquidate the partnership. The firm's balance sheet just before the partners sell the other assets for $30,000 is as follows:

ASSETS		LIABILITIES AND CAPITAL	
Cash	$ 15,000	Liabilities	$ 42,000
Other assets	110,000	Pete, capital	55,000
		Tom, capital	14,000
		Zack, capital	14,000
	$125,000		$125,000

The personal status of each partner just before liquidation is as follows:

	PERSONAL ASSETS	PERSONAL LIABILITIES
Pete	$55,000	$80,000
Tom	30,000	10,000
Zack	30,000	50,000

The partnership operates in a state that has adopted the Uniform Partnership Act.

Required:

A. Determine the amount of cash each partner will receive in liquidation and how much cash each partner must invest in the firm, given their personal positions.

B. Determine the amounts that the personal creditors will receive from personal assets and any distribution from the partnership.

Exercise 19-7

Select the best answer for each of the following items:

1. In accordance with the marshaling of assets provision of the Uniform Partnership Act, rank the following liabilities of a partnership in order of payment.
   (1) $20,000 loan from B. Barry who is a partner.
   (2) $30,000 of profits from the last year of operations.
   (3) $3,000 payable to a supplier.
   (4) $100,000 in capital balances of the partners.
   (a) 2,3,4,1.
   (b) 4,2,1,3.
   (c) 3,1,4,2.
   (d) 3,1,2,4.
2. Personal assets are first allocated to partnership creditors and then to personal creditors.
   (a) This statement is true.
   (b) True if partner has debit balance in his/her capital account.
   (c) This statement is false.
3. The following condensed balance sheet is presented for the partnership of Lisa, Lori, and Lucy, who share profits and losses in the ratio of 5:3:2, respectively:

Cash	$ 80,000	Liabilities	$140,000
Other assets	280,000	Lisa, capital	100,000
		Lori, capital	100,000
		Lucy, capital	20,000
Total	$360,000	Total	$360,000

The partners agreed to liquidate the partnership after selling the other assets. If the other assets are sold for $160,000, how much should Lisa receive upon liquidation?
   (a) $37,500
   (b) $38,500
   (c) $40,000
   (d) $100,000.

Questions 4 and 5 are based on the following balance sheet for the partnership of Allen, Bob, and Cecil:

Cash	$ 20,000	Liabilities	$ 50,000
Other assets	180,000	Allen, capital (40%)	37,000
		Bob, capital (30%)	65,000
		Cecil, capital (30%)	48,000
	$200,000		$200,00

Figures shown parenthetically reflect agreed profit and loss sharing percentages.

4. If the firm, as shown on the original balance sheet, is dissolved and liquidated by selling assets in installments, the first sale of noncash assets having a book value of $90,000 realizes $50,000, and all cash available after settlement with creditors is distributed; the respective partners would receive (to the nearest dollar)
   (a) Allen, $8,000; Bob, $6,000; Cecil, $6,000.
   (b) Allen, $6,667; Bob, $6,667; Cecil, $6,666.
   (c) Allen, $0; Bob, $10,000; Cecil, $10,000.
   (d) Allen, $0; Bob, $18,500; Cecil, $1,500.
5. If the facts are as in item 4 above except that $3,000 cash is to be withheld, the respective partners would then receive (to the nearest dollar)
   (a) Allen, $6,800; Bob, $5,100, Cecil, $5,100.
   (b) Allen, $5,667; Bob, $5,667; Cecil, $5,666.
   (c) Allen, $0; Bob, $8,500; Cecil, $8,500.
   (d) Allen, $0; Bob, $17,000; Cecil, $0.

(AICPA adapted)

Exercise 19-8

Select the best answer for each of the following items. Questions 1 and 2 are based on the following condensed balance sheet for the partnership of Caine, Davis, and Jones.

Cash	$ 90,000	Accounts payable	$220,000
Other assets	820,000	Jones, loan	40,000
Caine, receivable	40,000	Caine, capital	300,000
		Davis, capital	200,000
		Jones, capital	190,000
Total	$950,000	Total	$950,000

The partners share income and loss in the ratio of 5:3:2, respectively.

1. Assume that the assets and liabilities are fairly valued in the balance sheet and the partnership decides to admit Kuman as a new partner with a one-fourth capital interest. No goodwill or bonus is to be recorded. How much should Kuman invest in cash or other assets?
   (a) $172,500.
   (b) $175,000.
   (c) $230,000.
   (d) $233,333.
2. Assume that instead of admitting a new partner, the partners decide to liquidate the partnership. If the other assets are sold for $600,000, how much of the available cash should be distributed to Caine?
   (a) $170,000.
   (b) $150,000.
   (c) $190,000.
   (d) $300,000.

3. A, B, C, and D are partners sharing profits and losses equally. The partnership is insolvent and is to be liquidated. The status of the partnership and each partner is as follows:

		PARTNERSHIP CAPITAL BALANCE	PERSONAL ASSETS (EXCLUSIVE OF PARTNERSHIP INTEREST)	PERSONAL LIABILITIES (EXCLUSIVE OF PARTNERSHIP INTEREST)
	A	$15,000 Credit	$100,000	$40,000
	B	10,000 Credit	30,000	60,000
	C	20,000 Debit	80,000	5,000
	D	30,000 Debit	1,000	28,000

Assuming the Uniform Partnership Act applies, the partnership creditors
   (a) Must first seek recovery against C because he is solvent personally and he has a negative capital balance.
   (b) Will not be paid in full regardless of how they proceed legally because the partnership assets are less than the claims of the partnership creditors.
   (c) Will have to share B's interest in the partnership on a pro-rata basis with B's personal creditors.
   (d) Have first claim to the partnership assets before any partner's personal creditors have rights to the partnership assets.

4. If a partner with a debit capital balance during liquidation is insolvent, the following results:
   (a) The partner must borrow money to invest in the partnership.
   (b) The partnership will give the partner cash to the extent of the partners' debit balance.
   (c) The partner's debit balance will be allocated to the other partners.
   (d) None of the above.

5. If a partnership is undergoing a transformation to a corporation, which of the following is a result?
   (a) Assets and liabilities are adjusted to fair value.
   (b) The net assets are distributed to the partners in their profit and loss ratio.
   (c) The partners receive stock in the new corporation.
   (d) Both (a) and (c) are correct.

Exercise 19-9

Q, R, S, and T are partners, sharing profits and losses 40%:20%:20%:20%; respectively. After sale of firm assets and payment of the available cash to the partnership creditors, a partnership trial balance and the personal status of each partner are as follows:

	PARTNERSHIP TRIAL BALANCE			PERSONAL STATUS EXCLUSIVE OF PARTNERSHIP INTEREST		
	DEBIT	CREDIT		PARTNER	ASSETS	LIABILITIES
Creditors		$ 2,000				
Q, capital		500		Q	$15,000	$10,000
R, capital		7,500		R	8,000	20,000
S, capital	$ 6,000			S	15,000	4,000
T, capital	4,000			T	6,000	8,000
	$10,000	$10,000				

The partnership operates in a state that has adopted the Uniform Partnership Act.

Required:

A. What are the rights of the partnership creditors on the unpaid balance of $2,000?

B. What are the rights of the individual creditors of each partner?

C. Assuming that Q pays the partnership creditors, prepare a schedule to show how the settlement by the partners will be completed.

D. Indicate the amount of assets that will be available to the personal creditors of R after the settlement by the partners.

E. Indicate the amount of assets that will be available to the personal creditors of T after the settlement by the partners.

Exercise 19-10

The trial balance for the MAD Partnership is as follows just before declaring bankruptcy.

CASH	OTHER ASSETS		LIABILITIES	MATT LOAN	MATT CAPITAL	ALLEN CAPITAL	DAVE CAPITAL
$20,000	$100,000	=	$18,000	$10,000	$44,000	$30,000	$18,000

Partners share profits in the ratio 45:30:25.

Required:

A. Prepare a schedule to show how available cash would be distributed to the partners after creditors are paid in full. State which partner would receive the first cash available and at what point and to what degree each of the remaining partners would participate in cash distributions.

B. Cash of $30,000 is available to partners after the creditors have been paid in full. Prepare the general journal entry to record the distribution of $30,000.

Problems

Problem 19-1

The Discount Partnership is being liquidated. The current balance sheet is shown here.

Discount Partnership
Balance Sheet
January 14, 1995

ASSETS

Cash	$ 25,000
Other assets	120,000
Total assets	$145,000

LIABILITIES AND PARTNERS' EQUITY

Accounts payable	$ 40,000
Dawson, capital	31,000
Feeney, capital	65,000
Hardin, capital	9,000
Total liabilities and partners' equity	$145,000

Dawson, Feeney, and Hardin share profits and losses in a 30:40:30 ratio.

Required:

A. Prepare a schedule of partnership liquidation for each of the following three independent cases.

    (1) The noncash assets are sold for $60,000, and any partner with a deficit is unable to eliminate any of the deficit.

    (2) The noncash assets are sold for $60,000, and any partner with a deficit is able to invest cash equal to the amount of the deficit.

    (3) The noncash assets are sold for $50,000, and any partner with a deficit is able to invest up to $8,000 cash in the partnership.

B. Prepare all necessary journal entries for case 2 above.

Problem 19-2

Nelson, Parker, and Rice are partners who share profits 4:3:3, respectively. Parker decides that it would be more profitable for him to operate as a sole proprietor. Nelson and Rice are in agreement that life would be more rewarding if Parker were to enter into direct competition with them. Nelson and Rice make repeated attempts to acquire Parker's interest in the partnership. Unable to reach an agreement, the partners mutually agree that their association should be dissolved. A condensed balance sheet before realization of assets shows the following balances:

ASSETS		LIABILITIES AND CAPITAL	
Cash	$ 5,000	Liabilities	$20,000
Other assets	60,000	Nelson, capital	20,000
		Parker, capital	12,000
		Rice, capital	13,000
Total	$65,000	Total	$65,000

Asset realization is accomplished in four stages as follows:

STAGE	SALES PRICE	BOOK VALUE
1	$16,000	$12,000
2	12,000	10,000
3	10,000	20,000
4	2,000	18,000

The partners prefer that cash be distributed as soon as it is available.

Required:

Prepare a summary in columnar form of the partnership realization and liquidation. You should prepare supporting schedules of safe payments before each cash distribution.

Problem 19-3

Hann, Murphey, and Ryan have operated a retail furniture store for the past 30 years. Their business has been unprofitable for several years, since several large discount furniture stores opened in their sales territory. The partners recognize that they will be unable to compete with the larger chain stores and decide that since all the partners are near retirement, they should liquidate their business before it is necessary to declare bankruptcy. Account balances just before the liquidation process began were as follows:

Cash	$ 10,000	Liabilities	$110,000
Other assets	218,000	Hann, capital	50,000
		Murphey, capital	42,000
		Ryan, capital	26,000
	$228,000		$228,000

The partners share profits in the ratio of 5:3:2, respectively.

Rather than selling all the assets in a forced liquidation and incurring selling expenses, the partners agree that some of the noncash assets may be withdrawn in partial settlement of their capital interest. The partners agree that if the market value of a withdrawn asset is less than book value, the difference should be allocated to all partners in their loss ratio. If market value is greater than book value, the asset is to be adjusted to its market value before recording the withdrawal. All the partners are personally solvent and can make additional cash investment in the partnership up to $20,000 each. The following is a schedule of transactions that occurred in the liquidation process.

March 15, 1995	During liquidation sale, noncash assets with a book value of $90,000 were sold for $80,000
March 16, 1995	Sold accounts receivable with a book value of $30,000 to a factor for $26,000.
March 16, 1995	Paid all recorded partnership creditors.
March 18, 1995	Distributed all but $1,000 of available cash to partners.
March 19, 1995	Murphey withdrew from inventory furniture with a book value of $10,000 and a market value of $13,000 to satisfy part of his capital interest.
March 21, 1995	Sold remainder of inventory with a book value of $50,000 to a discount furniture store for $30,000 cash.
March 25, 1995	Assigned for $12,000 cash the remaining term of the lease on the warehouse. The lease was accounted for as an operating lease.
March 25, 1995	Distributed all available cash to partners.
April 1, 1995	Hann agreed to accept two vehicles with a book value of $10,000 and a market value of $8,000 in partial settlement of his capital interest.
April 5, 1995	All remaining assets were sold for $4,000.
April 6, 1995	Received additional cash from partners with debit capital balances.
April 6, 1995	Distributed available cash to partners.

Required:

Prepare a schedule of partnership realization and liquidation in accordance with the sequence of the foregoing events. Compute a safe payment to support your cash distribution to partners.

Problem 19-4

Mary, Paula, and Ray have operated a retail store for 20 years. The partners share profits and losses in the ratio of 4:3:3, respectively. The partnership is unable to meet its obligations and the partners decide to liquidate the partnership. The firm's balance sheet just before the partners sell the other assets for $20,000 is as follows.

ASSETS		LIABILITIES AND PARTNERS' EQUITIES	
Cash	$ 10,000	Liabilities	$ 40,000
Other assets	100,000	Mary, capital	50,000
		Paula, capital	10,000
		Ray, capital	10,000
	$110,000		$110,000

After the sale of the noncash assets, the personal assets and liabilities of each partner are determined to be the following:

	PERSONAL ASSETS	PERSONAL LIABILITIES
Mary	$50,000	$80,000
Paula	30,000	10,000
Ray	30,000	50,000

The partnership operates in a state that has adopted the Uniform Partnership Act.

Required:

A.   Determine the amount of cash each partner will receive in liquidation and how much cash each partner must contribute to the firm, given their personal positions.

B.   Determine the amounts that the personal creditors will receive from personal assets and any distribution from the partnership.

Problem 19-5

Part A

Baker, Strong, and Weak have called on you to assist them in winding up the affairs of their partnership. You are able to gather the following information.

1.   The trial balance of the partnership at June 30, 1995, is as follows.

	DEBIT	CREDIT
Cash	$ 6,000	
Accounts receivable	22,000	
Inventory	14,000	
Plant and equipment (net)	99,000	
Baker, advance	12,000	
Weak, advance	7,500	
Accounts payable		$ 17,000
Baker, capital		67,000
Strong, capital		45,000
Weak, capital		31,500
Total	$160,500	$160,500

2. The partners share profits and losses as follows: Baker, 40%; Strong, 40%; and Weak, 20%.
3. The partners are considering an offer of $100,000 for the accounts receivable, inventory, and plant and equipment as of June 30. The $100,000 would be paid to the partners in installments, the number and amounts of which are to be negotiated.

Required:

Prepare an advance cash distribution plan as of June 30, 1995. Prepare a schedule to show how the potential cash ($106,000) would be distributed as it becomes available.

Part B

Assume the facts in Part A except that the partners liquidate in stages instead of accepting the offer of $100,000. Cash is distributed to the partners at the end of each month.
    A summary of the liquidation transactions follows.

JULY

$16,500—collected on accounts receivable; balance is uncollectible.

$10,000—received for the entire inventory.

$ 1,000—liquidation expenses paid.

$ 8,000—cash retained in the business at the end of the month.

AUGUST

$ 1,500—liquidation expenses paid.
        As part payment of his capital interest, Weak accepted a piece of special equipment that he developed that had a book value of $4,000. The partners agreed that a value of $10,000 should be placed on the machine for liquidation purposes.

$ 2,500—cash retained in the business at the end of the month.

SEPTEMBER

$75,000—received on sale of remaining plant and equipment.

$ 1,000—liquidation expenses paid.
        No cash retained in the business.

Required:

Prepare a schedule of cash payments as of September 30, 1995, showing how the cash was actually distributed. Use the advance cash distribution plan developed in Part A where appropriate.

(AICPA adapted)

Problem 19-6

Mark Malone, Pete Patton, and Sally Spencer formed a partnership on January 1, 1995. Their original capital investments (all cash) were $140,000, $160,000, and $100,000, respectively. During the first year of operations, Mark withdrew $30,000, and the partnership reported a net income of $60,000. The partnership agreement stipulates that all income and losses are to be divided in the ratio of the original capital investments.

At the beginning of the second year, the partners decided to liquidate the business because of a disagreement. The assets and liabilities on January 2, 1996, were as follows: Cash, $37,000; Accounts Receivable, $129,000; Inventory, $188,000; Land, $85,000; Building (net), $180,000; Furniture and Fixtures (net), $30,000; Accounts Payable, $74,000; and Mortgage Payable, $145,000. The inventory was sold for three-quarters of its book value, the furniture and fixtures brought in $10,000, and $92,000 of the accounts receivable were collected. The remaining receivables were uncollectible. After the losses were allocated according to the partnership agreement and the accounts payable were paid in full, Pete accepted the land and building at book value and assumed the mortgage payable at book value as partial settlement of his capital interest. The cash balance was then distributed to the partners.

Required:

A Prepare a statement of changes in partners' capital for the year ended December 31, 1995.

B. Prepare the journal entries to close the Drawing and Income Summary accounts for 1995.

C. Prepare a schedule of partnership liquidation.

D. Prepare the journal entries to record the liquidation activities.

Problem 19-7

Jan and Sue have engaged successfully as partners in their law firm for a number of years. Soon after their state's incorporation laws are changed to allow professionals to incorporate, the partners decide to organize a corporation to take over the business of the partnership.

The after-closing trial balance for the partnership is as follows:

After-Closing Trial Balance
December 31, 1995

	DEBIT	CREDIT
Cash	$15,000	
Accounts receivable	32,400	
Allowance for uncollectibles		$ 2,000
Prepaid insurance	800	
Office equipment	30,200	
Accumulated depreciation		12,600
Jan, loan (outstanding since 1987, at 5%)		6,400
Jan, capital (50%)		29,400
Sue, capital (50%)		28,000
	$78,400	$78,400

Figures shown parenthetically reflect agreed profit- and loss-sharing ratios.

The partners have hired you as an accountant to adjust the recorded assets and liabilities to their market values and to close the partners' capital accounts to the new corporate capital stock. The corporation is to retain the partnership's books, and the assets of the partnership should be taken over by the corporation in the following amounts:

Cash	$15,000
Accounts receivable	32,400
Allowance for uncollectibles	2,900
Office equipment	16,000
Prepaid insurance	800

Jan's loan is to be transferred to her capital account in the amount of $6,600.

Required:

A. Prepare the necessary journal entries to express the agreement described.

B. Prepare the entries to record the issuance of shares to Jan and Sue, assuming the issuance of 400 shares (par value $100) of stock to Jan and Sue.

Problem 19-8

Alan Norwood is currently a senior associate with the law firm of Butler, Starns, and Madden (BSM). His compensation currently includes a salary of $155,000, and benefits valued at $5,000. BSM is considered among the strongest of local firms, with assets of $10 million (cash $2,000,000, and accounts receivable $8,000,000), liabilities of $7.5 million, and 11 partners.

Alan anticipates admission to the partnership on July 1 of this year. The senior managing partner, Jane Butler, has had preliminary discussions with Alan in which the senior partner proposed the following:

1. A 5% interest in BSM capital and profits in recognition of Alan's commitment to the firm and in exchange for a capital investment by Alan of $150,000. This 5% interest would be acquired from the other partners.
2. Alan's compensation will consist of a monthly withdrawal of $18,000 and benefits valued at $5,000 annually. Monthly withdrawals approximate firm profits, but any unpaid profits will be distributed as a bonus to Alan after the end of each partnership year.

On March 1, only one month prior to Alan's final negotiation meeting for entry into the partnership, Mary, one of the junior associates, discreetly informed Alan that the firm was drawing up documents for Hugh Starns' retirement. Hugh has a 5% interest in the firm's capital and profits with a book value of $125,000. The partners have agreed upon a $75,000 cash settlement of the interest held by Mr. Starns. (Of the other 10 partners, numbers 1 through 9 hold 10% interests, and number 10 holds a 5% interest).

Required:

A. Assume Mr. Starns retires with his $75,000 settlement, and Alan is admitted to the partnership as proposed.
   (1) Prepare journal entries to record the retirement and admission.
   (2) Discuss the factors Alan needs to consider in evaluating whether he has improved his annual compensation from the firm. Although this is not a tax course, include a discussion of the various tax issues.
   (3) Should Alan be concerned regarding the impending retirement and settlement of Mr. Starns' capital account assuming Alan is confident that he will be able to match the revenue-generating ability of Mr. Starns?

B. Assume instead that Alan is so disturbed by the impending departure of Mr. Starns that he decides to join Mary, the junior associate, in leaving the firm to form their own law partnership. Both Alan and Mary feel confident that during their tenures at BSM they have developed such good working relationships with their clients that the majority of their clients will follow them to the new firm.

    (1) Should Alan and Mary have any hesitation in quietly recruiting BSM clients to "follow them" to the new law firm?

    (2) Can the partners of BSM prevent such recruiting of clients based on the claim that these clients are BSM "property"?

C. Assume instead that the firm encounters difficulties from which it is unable to recover, and in April, the decision is made to liquidate the firm. It is discovered that Mr. Starns has (in violation of the partnership agreement) taken draws which reduced firm cash and his capital account by $130,000. However, BSM owes Mr. Starns $10,000 for a separate loan made to the firm some 10 years ago. As of May 1, the firm had unallocated profits of $25,000, and cash had also increased by $25,000.

    (1) Assuming that if the provisions of UPA Section 40(b) are adhered to strictly, prepare entries to record the distributions. Assume that Mr. Starns is insolvent.

    (2) If the other 10 partners are aware that Starns' capital account will take on a debit balance, can they rightfully hold repayment of the balance due to Starns for the $10,000 loan contingent on his reimbursement of his capital account's debit balance? Does this violate UPA Section 40(b)? On what basis can the partners justify their action (if challenged)?

20

INTRODUCTION TO FUND ACCOUNTING

Fund accounting concepts are generally associated with accounting for nonbusiness organizations. Nonbusiness organizations are economic entities that are organized to provide a socially desirable service without regard to financial gain. In contrast to business enterprises, nonbusiness organizations are not operated for the *financial* benefit of any specific individual or group of individuals.

The purpose of this chapter is to introduce the reader to fund accounting concepts and procedures. In order to do this, however, it is necessary first to present a brief introduction to the types and characteristics of organizations that use fund accounting concepts.

CLASSIFICATIONS OF NONBUSINESS ORGANIZATIONS

There are five major classifications of nonbusiness organizations.

1. *Governmental Units.* Governmental units include federal, state, and local governmental units. Local governmental units include counties, townships, municipalities, school districts, and special districts. Special districts include organizational units such as port authorities, industrial development districts, sanitation districts, and soil and water conservation districts.

2. *Hospitals and Other Health Care Providers.*

3. *Colleges and Universities.*

4. *Voluntary Health and Welfare Organizations.* Voluntary health and welfare

organizations are organizations that derive their revenue from voluntary contributions of the general public to be used for purposes connected with health, welfare, or community services. Examples of such organizations include heart associations, family planning councils, mental health associations, and foundations for the blind.

5. *All Other Nonbusiness Organizations.* Other nonbusiness organizations take a variety of forms. They include such organizations as trade associations (Electrical Contractors Association), professional associations (State Society of Certified Public Accountants), performing arts organizations (the Charlotte Symphony Society), museums, religious organizations, and research and scientific organizations.

DISTINCTIONS BETWEEN NONBUSINESS ORGANIZATIONS AND PROFIT-ORIENTED ENTERPRISES

The most obvious characteristic that distinguishes a nonbusiness organization from a profit-oriented enterprise is the absence of a deliberate or conscious effort to derive a profit. The performance of services by nonbusiness organizations is based on social need rather than on the profit motive. Other characteristics of nonbusiness organizations distinguish them from profit-oriented enterprises. For example, persons who contribute resources to a nonbusiness organization receive no equity interest in the net assets of the organization, and there is no equity interest therein that can be sold or exchanged. Nonbusiness organizations do not often finance their operations through adequate charges to the direct beneficiaries of their services. Thus, they must rely on political action (for example, tax levies) or fund-raising campaigns to sustain their activities and replenish their financial resources.

In addition, tax levies and voluntary contributions cannot ordinarily be justified on the basis of the value of the nonbusiness organization's services to the individuals from whom such contributions come. Those who contribute resources to nonbusiness organizations do not necessarily benefit proportionately or at all from the services provided by such organizations. Because of the characteristics identified, the net income concept cannot be used to measure the effectiveness of the management of resources dedicated to nonbusiness objectives. Therefore, the income determination model of accounting is generally not applicable to such organizations.

In profit-oriented enterprises, net income functions as an implicit regulator in the sense that (1) in the long run the organization must operate profitably to survive and (2) in the short run, failure to operate profitably will affect management's decisions and actions and perhaps the constituency of management itself. In the absence of this implicit regulator, regulation of the allocation and utilization of the financial resources of nonbusiness organizations is often achieved by the imposition of stringent controls. Such controls may be legally imposed (as in the case of governmental activities) or they may be imposed through formal action of the governing board.

Restrictions or limitations on the use of resources may also be directly imposed by the individuals or groups that contribute such resources. For example, most nonbusiness organizations receive gifts, grants, or endowments that are to be used only for specific purposes designated by the donor, such as construction of buildings, research activities, scholarships, operation of parks, recreation programs, or the acquisition of land. In addition, the donor may stipulate that the principal of the gift is to remain intact and that only the income on the invested principal is to be used for the purposes designated by the donor.

In order to account for these legally imposed, externally imposed, and self-imposed restrictions or limitations on the utilization of their resources, nonbusiness organizations have generally adopted the concepts of fund accounting. A fund has been defined by the National Council of Governmental Accounting as

> a fiscal and accounting entity with a self-balancing set of accounts recording cash and other financial resources, together with all related liabilities and residual equities or balances, and changes therein, which are segregated for the purpose of carrying on specific activities or attaining certain objectives in accordance with special regulations, restrictions, or limitations.[1]

In fund accounting, each fund consist of assets, liabilities, and a fund balance and constitutes a *separate accounting entity* created and maintained for a specific purpose. The inflow and outflow of resources of each fund must be accounted for in such a way that they can be compared with the approved or stipulated resource flows for that fund.

FINANCIAL ACCOUNTING AND REPORTING STANDARDS FOR NONBUSINESS ORGANIZATIONS

The potential users of the financial reports of nonbusiness organizations include taxpayers, contributors, grantors, creditors, employees, managers, directors and trustees, service beneficiaries, financial analysts and advisers, brokers, underwriters, economists, taxing authorities, regulatory authorities, legislators, the financial press and reporting agencies, labor unions, trade associations, researchers, teachers, and students.

Until 1980, the Financial Accounting Standards Board (FASB) and its predecessor bodies gave little if any attention to standards of reporting for nonbusiness organizations. In 1980, however, the FASB issued *Statement of Financial Accounting Concepts No. 4*, "Objectives of Financial Reporting by Nonbusiness Organizations." In that statement, the Board identified providers such as members, taxpayers, contributors, and creditors as the most important users for purposes of establishing external financial reporting objectives for nonbusiness organizations.

In 1984, the Governmental Accounting Standards Board (GASB) was created. Like those of the FASB, the operations and financing of the GASB are overseen by the Financial Accounting Foundation. The GASB is responsible for establishing financial accounting standards for all state and local governmental bodies, and the

---

[1]National Council on Governmental Accounting, *Statement 1: Governmental Accounting and Financial Reporting Principles* (Chicago: Municipal Finance Officers Association of the United States and Canada, 1979), p. 2.

FASB is responsible for establishing financial accounting standards for all other nonbusiness organizations. Accounting and reporting standards for governmental units are described and illustrated in this chapter and in Chapter 21. Accounting and reporting standards for nongovernment nonbusiness organizations are described and illustrated in Chapter 22.

FUND ACCOUNTING

Fund accounting is designed primarily to meet internal reporting and control objectives; it is not sufficient in itself to meet the objectives of financial reporting by nonbusiness organizations. Nevertheless, it does provide a basis for determining the fiscal responsibility and status of the organization and the compliance of administrators with the approved or stipulated receipt and utilization of financial resources. Thus, fund accounting is an important means of meeting several of the accounting, control, and reporting objectives of most nonbusiness organizations.

Fund entities may be classified in a number of different ways. For example, they may be classified as expendable fund entities and proprietary fund entities. Expendable fund entities are the funds most closely associated with basic fund accounting concepts.

Expendable Fund Entities

Expendable fund entities consist of net *financial resources* that are dedicated to a specified use. Thus, separate expendable fund entities are established based on the purpose for which financial resources may or must be used. Financial resources consist of cash and claims to cash such as receivables and investments in marketable securities. The difference between the financial resources of an expendable fund entity and claims against those resources is referred to as the fund balance. Thus, the statement of financial position for an expendable fund entity reflects the financial resources of the fund, the claims against those resources, and the fund balance. At a particular time the fund balance represents the net financial resources that are available for expenditure for the specified purposes or objectives for which the fund was created.

The financial resources of an expendable fund entity are not intended to be maintained intact. Ordinarily it is intended that they will be expended annually or over some other specified time period in order to carry out the objectives for which the fund was created.

The relevant measures of the operations of expendable fund entities are not, therefore, revenue, expense, and net income but rather increases in fund resources, decreases in fund resources, and the change in the fund balance. The accounting model for the operating statement of an expendable fund entity is

Financial resources inflows (by source) − Financial resource
outflows (by function) = Change in fund balance

Increases in fund resources may be classified as revenues, debt issue proceeds, or transfers from other funds. Decreases in fund resources may be classified as expenditures or as transfers to other funds. Thus, the operating results of expendable fund entities is measured in terms of inflow, outflow, and balances of net current financial resources assigned to the fund, and the appropriate operating statement for such entities is essentially a statement of changes in net financial resources. To provide a basis for comparison, both budgeted and actual resource flows may be presented in the operating statement or in related schedules.

In summary, in accounting for expendable funds, the emphasis is changed from matching revenue and expense to the comparison of the actual inflow and outflow of financial resources with stipulated or approved resource flows. Thus, rather than attempting to measure the efficiency with which management has utilized resources, accounting for expendable fund entities is designed to measure the extent to which management has complied with the regulations or restrictions that govern the utilization of expendable fund resources and to assist management with such compliance.

Proprietary Fund Entities

Proprietary (nonexpendable) fund entities are used to account for the activities of nonbusiness organizations that are similar to those of business enterprises. Many nonbusiness organizations engage in quasi-commercial activities. The operation of an electric or water utility by a municipality and the rental of real estate by a religious organization are examples of such activities. Accordingly, even though these activities are accounted for in separate fund entities, relevant accounting measurements and reports are similar to those applicable to profit-oriented enterprises and focus on the determination of net income, financial position, and cash flows.

The accounting model for the statement of financial position of a proprietary fund entity is

Current assets + Noncurrent assets = Current liabilities + Long-term liabilities + Nonbusiness organization equity

The accounting model for the operating statement of a proprietary fund entity is

Revenue − Expense = Net income (loss)

Net income plus (minus) transfers from (to) other funds = Change in nonbusiness organization equity

Budgetary Fund Entities

In the traditional compliance model of reporting on the operations of governmental units, actual resource inflows and outflows are compared with stipulated or approved inflows and outflows of resources. Approved resource flows are incorporated into annual budgets. In some instances the budget for an expendable fund entity is so important to management control of fund resources that the budget is formally incorporated into the accounting records within the framework of the double-entry system. Fund entities in which the budget is formally incorporated into the accounting records are sometimes referred to as *budgetary funds.*

The preparation, use, and importance of such budgets for governmental units cannot be overemphasized. The annual budget for a governmental unit is usually prepared by the executive branch of the governmental unit. It is then presented to the legislative branch for consideration and enactment. In the case of annually levied taxes such as property taxes, adoption of budgeted revenue amounts may require the enactment of enabling legislation. In the case of continually levied taxes such as sales taxes and income taxes, no new legislation authorizing the tax is ordinarily required for the adoption of the budgeted amounts of revenue.

When budgeted expenditures are enacted into law, they are referred to as *appropriations.* Appropriations represent the maximum expenditures that are authorized by the legislature. As such, they represent (by budget category) amounts that cannot be legally exceeded. Accordingly, the accounting system must provide administrators of governmental units with timely information as to actual expenditures and allowable expenditures (appropriations) by budget category. In addition, financial reports must be prepared in such a way that the legislature or its representative can determine that the spending limits authorized by it have not been exceeded. The approved budget may, therefore, be formally recorded in the accounting records of the appropriate fund(s). Such formal budgetary account integration is for purposes of assisting in the control and administration of fund resources.

Restricted and Unrestricted Fund Entities

Expendable fund entities may be further classified as restricted and unrestricted. This classification is usually applicable to nonbusiness organizations other than governmental units. The unrestricted expendable fund entity includes the net current financial resources of the nonbusiness organization that are available to carry out the primary or general activities of the organization at the discretion of the governing board. Current financial resources that are restricted by donors or other outside agencies for specific current operating purposes are included in restricted expendable fund entities. The word *restricted* refers to resources that bear a legal restriction as to use imposed by parties outside the organization. The primary purpose of this distinction is to assist in the determination of the current financial resources that are available for use at the discretion of the governing board and those over which the governing board has little if any discretion as to use because of *externally* imposed restrictions. As illustrated in Chapter 22, most nonbusiness organizations other than governmental units have one unrestricted fund and one or more restricted funds.

General Accounting and Reporting Considerations

Within the framework of expendable fund entities, revenues are defined as inflows of net current financial resources, and expenditures are defined as outflows of net current financial resources. Because different types of nonbusiness organizations have different sources of revenues and different purposes and objectives, the recognition and classification of fund entity revenues and expenditures vary between nonbusiness organizations. However, there is general agreement in the authoritative literature that for financial reporting purposes

1. Fund revenues should be classified by source, and transfers from other funds within the organization should be distinguished from and classified separately from revenue.

2. Fund expenditures should be classified by function or activity, and transfers to other funds within the organization should be distinguished from and classified separately from expenditures.

3. Fund revenues and expenditures should, where possible, be recognized using the accrual basis of accounting.

In this chapter, fund accounting concepts relating to expendable fund entities are developed within the framework of state and local governmental units.

Basis of Accounting

To the extent practicable, the accrual method should be used in accounting for fund entities. The cash basis of accounting is not appropriate. There are, however, some special considerations in the application of accrual accounting to expendable fund entities.

Financial resources of an expendable fund entity include cash, receivables, and securities that can be converted into cash. If an increase in net financial resources (revenue) is recorded when a valid receivable is established, rather than when the cash is ultimately collected, and if a decrease in net financial resources (expenditure) is recorded when a liability is incurred, rather than when cash is ultimately disbursed, then the accrual basis rather than the cash basis of accounting is being applied to the fund entity.

Because governments generally make no attempt to allocate costs to periods benefited and because some expenditures of the expendable fund entities of governmental units are not recognized in the period in which they are incurred, the term *modified accrual accounting* is used to describe the application of accrual accounting to expendable fund entities of governmental units.

Before proceeding further, it may be useful to distinguish among the concepts of revenue, expense, and expenditure as they are used in relation to profit-oriented entities and expendable fund entities.

Profit-Oriented Entities (Income Determination)

Revenue—   increase in net assets resulting from the sale of goods or services.

Expense—   expired costs consumed in the production of revenues (as defined above).

Expendable Fund Entities

Revenue— increase in (source of) net current financial resources other than an increase resulting from debt issue proceeds or from the transfer of financial resources from another fund within the organization.

Expenditure—decrease in (use of) net current financial resources other than a decrease resulting from a transfer of financial resources to another fund within the organization. Expenditures represent the amount of financial resources expended during the period to carry out the operations and activities of the fund entity.

Classification of Revenue and Other Resource Inflows

Revenues are classified by source. Major sources of revenue for state and local governmental units are summarized in Illustration 20-1. As is demonstrated therein, the number of sources of revenue available to governmental units is impressive when compared with those available to business enterprises.

Debt Issue Proceeds   Governmental units may finance their operations through the issuance of bonds or other debt instruments. Although debt issue proceeds are sometimes classified as revenue of a particular fund entity, *they are not revenue* from the point of view of the issuing governmental unit because of the offsetting debt. Accordingly, debt issue proceeds should be classified separately from revenue for purposes of financial reporting.

Transfers of Resources from Other Funds   Transfers of resources from other fund entities within an organization do not represent an increase in the expendable financial resources of the organization as a whole. Accordingly, even though they represent an increase in the financial resources of the recipient fund entity, they should ordinarily *be classified separately from revenue* for financial reporting purposes.

ILLUSTRATION 20-1
Major Sources of Revenue for
State and Local Governmental Units

Property Taxes	Grants from Federal, State, or
Income Taxes	Local Government Units
Sales and Excise Taxes	Shared Revenues from Federal, State,
Gift and Inheritance Taxes	or Local Government Units
Fines and Penalties	Payments in Lieu of Taxes from
Gifts and Donations	Federal, State, or Local
Forfeits	Government Units
Licenses and Permits	Interest Earned on Loans and
Sales of Property	Investments

Recognition of Revenue

In accounting for profit-oriented enterprises, revenue is ordinarily not recognized until (1) a transaction has taken place (that is, the amount of revenue can be objectively measured) and (2) the earnings process is complete or substantially complete. Criterion 2 is not applicable to expendable fund entities. The revenue-recognition criteria for expendable fund entities can be stated as follows: In accounting for expendable fund entities, revenue is ordinarily not recognized until (1) it can be objectively measured and (2) it is available to finance expenditures of the current period.

Many sources of fund revenue do not meet the criteria of measurability and availability until they are received in cash. On the other hand, significant amounts of revenue (for example, property taxes, pledges, regularly billed charges for routine services, and some types of grants) meet both criteria and are recognized as revenue prior to the receipt of cash. The application of these criteria to several significant sources of revenue of governmental units may be illustrated as follows.

Property Taxes   Property taxes usually meet both criteria when levied. The amount of property tax is precisely determinable when levied and the amount of uncollectible taxes ordinarily can be reasonably estimated on the basis of previous experience. Thus, the amount of property tax revenue is objectively determinable at the time the taxes are levied. Ordinarily, taxes are also considered to be *available* in the period levied, even though they are collectible in a period subsequent to the levy, because (1) they provide a basis for obtaining cash resources through the issuance of tax anticipation notes[2] and (2) they are usually collectible early in the subsequent period and thus are available to finance current period operations.

Income Tax and Sales Tax   Self-assessed taxes such as the income tax and the sales tax usually are not objectively measurable or available until the tax returns are filed with payment. Where the tax returns have been filed but payment is delayed, revenue should be recognized when the returns are filed, assuming that a reasonable estimate can be made of noncollectible amounts, if any. In addition, sales taxes held by merchants may be recognized as revenue before they are received by the fund entity if the measurability and availability criteria are met.

Fines and Forfeits   The amounts of fines, forfeits, inspection charges, parking meter receipts, and so on, are not objectively determinable or available until assessed or collected and are, therefore, not normally recognized as revenue until collected.

Sales of Property   The entire amount of proceeds from the sale of property is treated as revenue at the time of sale because expendable assets are increased and are available to finance current expenditures in the same manner as any other revenues would be.

---

[2]Tax anticipation notes are notes or warrants issued in anticipation of the collection of taxes and are usually retirable only from the proceeds of the tax levy whose collection they anticipate.

Pledges and Grants A pledge to contribute resources is considered revenue at the time it is made, so long as a reasonable estimate of uncollectible pledges can be made and there is no restriction on the time period in which the pledged resources can be expended. Grants may or may not be recognized as revenue at the time the grant is authorized. If the grant is dependent on the performance of services, or if the expenditure of funds is the prime factor for determining the eligibility for the grant funds, revenue should not be recognized until the time the services are performed or the expenditures are made. Grants that are not dependent on performance or expenditure of funds should be recognized in the period in which they are authorized.

Classification of Expenditures and Other Resource Outflows

Expenditures may be classified by function, by activity, by organizational unit, or by object. Since different classifications serve different purposes, multiple classification of expenditures is usually recommended.

Classification by Function and Activity Typical functional classifications of expenditures for state and local governmental units are presented in Illustration 20-2. Classification by function refers to the broad purposes for which expenditures are made. Classification by activity refers to the specific types of work performed to accomplish such purposes. For example, public safety is a major function of a municipality. The ***function*** of public safety may be divided into ***subfunctions*** such as police protection, fire protection, and protective inspection. The subfunction of police protection can be classified into ***activities*** such as criminal investigation, vice control, patrol, custody of prisoners, and crime laboratory.

Functional and activity classifications are particularly important and are the classifications ordinarily recommended for published financial reports. In addition, as noted by the National Council on Governmental Accounting:

> *Activity* classification is particularly significant because it facilitates evaluation of the economy and efficiency of operations by providing data for calculating expenditures per unit of activity. That is, the expenditure requirements of performing a given unit of work can be determined by classifying expenditures by activities and providing for performance measurement where such techniques are practicable. These expenditure data, in turn, can be used in preparing future budgets and in setting standards against which future expenditure levels can be evaluated. Further, activity expenditure data provide a convenient starting point for calculating total and/or unit expenses of activities where that is desired, e.g., for ''make or buy'' and ''do or contract out'' decisions. Current operating expenditures (total expenditures less those for capital outlay and debt service) may be adjusted by depreciation and amortization data . . . to determine activity expense.[3]

Classification by Organizational Unit Classification of expenditures by organizational unit is important for management, control, and internal reporting purposes including responsibility accounting. Classification of expenditures by organizational

ILLUSTRATION 20-2
Functional Classification of Expenditures for
State and Local Governmental Units

General Government
    Legislative
    Judicial
    Executive
    Elections
    Financial Administration
Public Safety
    Police
    Fire
    Inspection
Public Works
    Highways and Streets
    Sanitation

Health and Welfare
Recreation—Cultural
    Playgrounds
    Swimming Pools
    Golf Courses
    Parks
    Libraries
Urban Redevelopment and
    Housing
Economic Development and
    Assistance

unit is based on the departments, divisions, bureaus, or other administrative units that make expenditures to carry out their designated functions. Examples include police department, attorney general's office, corporation commission, city planning, and the like. Each organizational unit may have responsibility for several functions or activities. In some instances a function or activity may cross organizational unit lines.

Classification by Object Classification of expenditures by object identifies what is acquired in return for the expenditure. Typical object classifications are presented in Illustration 20-3. Classification by object is useful primarily for internal management and may be omitted from published financial reports.

It is generally recommended that excessively detailed object classifications be avoided, since they may unnecessarily complicate accounting procedures and reports and because the control and reporting emphasis of the organization should be on functions, activities, and organizational units, rather than on the object of expenditures per se.

With modern data-processing techniques, multiple classification of expenditures is easily accomplished. Multiple classification of expenditures by function, activity, organizational unit, and object factilitates the aggregation and analysis of data in different ways for different purposes.

Transfers to Other Funds Transfers of resources to other fund entities within an organization do not represent decreases in the expendable financial resources of the organization as a whole. Accordingly, even though they represent a decrease in the financial resources of a particular fund, they ordinarily should be classified separately from expenditures for financial reporting purposes.

[3]National Council on Governmental Accounting, *Statement 1: Governmental Accounting and Financial Reporting Principles,* op. cit. pp. 16 and 17.

ILLUSTRATION 20-3
Classification of Expenditures by Object

Personal Services
   Salaries
   Employee health and retirement benefits
   Payroll taxes, etc.
Supplies
   Office supplies
   Operating supplies
   Small tools
Other
   Professional services
   Telephone and telegraph
   Travel
   Rental (equipment, buildings, machinery)
   Postage and shipping
   Printing and publications
   Repairs and maintenance
   Insurance
   Miscellaneous
Capital Expenditures
   Land
   Buildings
   Improvements
   Machinery and equipment
   Motor vehicles
   Furniture and furnishings
   Office machines

Recognition of Expenditures

An expenditure is one of four critical events in the use of the financial resources of an expendable fund entity. The sequence of events is as follows:

Appropriation or authorization → Encumbrance → Expenditure → Disbursement

Appropriation   The appropriation process in governmental units has already been described. The necessity for giving accounting recognition to the next event, encumbrance, can be more clearly presented, however, if one recalls that it is the responsibility of administrators to use fund resources only in the amounts and for the purposes prescribed in the appropriations act. In the case of governmental units, administrators are held strictly accountable for the provisions of the appropriation act, and stiff penalties are provided by law for those who fail to adhere to them. Thus, it is of great concern to administrators to know how they stand relative to their appropriation authority and to have accounting safeguards to prevent the utilization of fund resources in excess of that authority.

Encumbrance   Since the amount of an appropriation cannot be legally exceeded, the placing of purchase orders and the signing of contracts are critical events in controlling the expenditures of expendable fund entities. The financial resources of a fund are said to be encumbered when a transaction is entered into that requires performance on the part of another party before the governmental unit becomes liable to perform (expend financial resources) its part of the transaction. An encumbrance reduces appropriation authority and is formally recorded in the accounting records. Thus, at any particular time the accounting records will reflect management's remaining available appropriation authority as follows:

$$\text{Appropriations} - (\text{Encumbrances} + \text{Expenditures}) = \text{Unencumbered balance}$$

The unencumbered balance is the amount of resources that can still be obligated or expended without exceeding the legal or authorized limit.

Encumbrances are recorded as follows:

(1) Encumbrance (appropriately classified)	10,000	
Reserve for Encumbrance		10,000
To record an order for goods in the amount of $10,000.		

Expenditures   When the vendor or supplier performs on a contract or purchase order and goods or services are received, an expenditure has taken place. Expenditures are recognized in the accounting period in which the fund liability is incurred, except for unmatured interest on long-term debt, which is recognized when due. Thus, an expenditure and a corresponding liability or cash disbursement will be recorded at the time goods or services are received or at the time funds are granted to an authorized recipient. When the goods ordered in (1) above are received, the following entries are made:

(2) Expenditures (appropriately classified)	12,000	
Vouchers Payable		12,000
To record the receipt of goods invoiced at $12,000.		
(3) Reserve for Encumbrance	10,000	
Encumbrance		10,000
To remove the encumbrance recorded in (1) for goods received and recorded as an expenditure in (2).		

In this case, the goods cost $2,000 more than was estimated when the order was placed.

Disbursements   Disbursements represent the payment of cash for expenditures. Such payments may precede the expenditure (an advance), coincide with the expenditure (a direct payment), or follow the expenditure (the payment of a liability). The payment for the goods purchased in (2) above is recorded as follows:

(4) Vouchers Payable	12,000	
Cash		12,000
To record payment of vouchers payable.		

Encumbrances and expenditures are classified on the same basis (by function, activity, object, or organizational unit) as appropriations. The effect on appropriation control of incorporating appropriations, encumbrances, and expenditures into the accounting records is demonstrated in Illustration 20-4.

In this illustration it is assumed that the appropriation for budget category 103 is $50,000 and that the amount of expenditures in this category prior to the entries illustrated above was $15,000. The effects of entries (1), (2), (3), and (4) above on the subsidiary ledger card for budget category 103 are as indicated. The most important thing to note is that at any particular time information is available to administrators as to their unexpended and uncommitted appropriation authority.

Capital Expenditures In accounting for profit-oriented enterprises, capital expenditures are recorded as assets and are distinguished from revenue expenditures. The cost of such assets is recognized in the operating statements (income statement) of such enterprises through the process of depreciation. *Neither fixed assets nor depreciation are recognized in the accounting records of an expendable fund entity.*

In accounting for an expendable fund entity, capital expenditures (see Illustration 20-3), like other expenditures, are treated as an outflow of financial resources. The assets acquired do not represent expendable financial resources but rather reflect the purposes for which financial resources have been used. Thus, they are not recorded or reported as assets of the fund entity. This treatment is consistent with the primary purpose of fund accounting, which is to provide accounting control over the collection and expenditure of financial resources and to assure that no violations of authorized limits on expenditures occur. The operating statements of expendable fund entities are therefore designed to reflect *all* the sources and uses of its financial resources. The position statement of the expendable fund entity is designed to present the status of its *financial resources*, the related liabilities, and the net financial resources available for subsequent appropriation and expenditure. This emphasis on the status and flow of net *financial resources* requires that capital expenditures be treated the same as any other classification of expenditures and that they not be reflected as assets of the fund entity. This is not to say that controls are not maintained over fixed assets acquired by means of expendable fund re-

ILLUSTRATION 20-4
Subsidiary Ledger Control Card for One Budget Category
Function: Sanitation; Activity: Sanitary Sewer Cleaning; Object: Operating Supplies

BUDGET LINE 103	(A) APPROPRIATION	(B) ENCUMBRANCE	(C) EXPENDITURE	(D) TOTAL (B) + (C)	(E) UNENCUMBERED BALANCE (A) − (D)
Prior Balance	$50,000	$ −0−	$15,000	$15,000	$35,000
Purchase Order [entry (1)]		10,000		10,000	(10,000)
Balance	50,000	10,000	$15,000	25,000	25,000
Expenditure [entries (2) & (3)]		(10,000)	12,000	2,000	(2,000)
Balance	50,000	−0−	27,000	27,000	23,000
Disbursement [entry (4)]		−0−	−0−	−0−	−0−
Balance	$50,000	$ −0−	$27,000	$27,000	$23,000

sources. The organization will establish records and controls outside of the records of the expendable fund entity. Accounting for and reporting on fixed assets is illustrated in Chapter 21 for governmental units and Chapter 22 for nongovernment nonbusiness organizations.

Depreciation is not accounted for in the records of an expendable fund entity for the same reason that fixed assets are excluded from the records of such entities. Expenditures, not expenses, are measured in accounting for expendable fund entities. Acquisitions of fixed assets require the *use* of financial resources and are accounted for as expenditures. Proceeds from the sale of fixed assets *provide* financial resources and are accounted for as revenues. Depreciation expense is neither a source nor a use of the financial resources of an expendable fund entity, and thus is not properly recorded in the accounts of such entities. Inclusion of depreciation expense in the operating statement of an expendable fund entity would confuse two fundamentally different measurements—expenditures and expense—and would result in misleading inferences relative to the operating activities of the expendable fund entity. This does not mean that the concept or measurement of depreciation is not important from the point of view of the organization as a whole. Indeed, if meaningful cost/benefit analysis is to be attempted for a particular activity, the operating expenditures of the activity must be adjusted by depreciation to determine total activity cost. However, the objective of fund accounting is not to provide information relative to the costs and benefits of activities but to control the collection and expenditure of financial resources. Accounting for and reporting on depreciation are further discussed in Chapter 21 for state and local governmental units and in Chapter 22 for nongovernment nonbusiness organizations.

Recording Budgeted and Actual Revenue and Expenditures

Condensed financial statements for an expendable fund entity are presented in Illustration 20-5. Entries that were recorded in the records of the expendable fund entity during 1995 are presented in summary form as follows:

(1) Estimated Revenue (classified)	800,000	
Appropriations (classified)		780,000
Unreserved Fund Balance		20,000
To record budgeted revenues and expenditures adopted by legislative body or governing board.		

The excess of budgeted revenue over (under) budgeted expenditures is recorded as an increase (decrease) in the unreserved fund balance. In addition to this entry, postings would be made to subsidiary accounts for each source of revenue and each appropriation expenditure category.

(2) Receivables or Cash	850,000	
Revenue (classified)		850,000
To record revenues recognized during the year.		
(3) Encumbrances (classified)	775,000	
Reserve for Encumbrances		775,000
To record encumbrances *($775,000 is an assumed amount).*		

ILLUSTRATION 20-5
Condensed Financial Statements of Expendable Fund Entity

BALANCE SHEET — JANUARY 1, 1995

Net Financial Resources (Assets − Liabilities)	$100,000
Fund Balance (Unreserved)	$100,000

STATEMENT OF CHANGES IN UNRESERVED FUND BALANCE FOR PERIOD ENDED DECEMBER 31, 1995	BUDGET	ACTUAL	ACTUAL OVER (UNDER) BUDGET
Unreserved Fund Balance—1/1	$100,000	$100,000	$ –0–
Revenue	800,000	850,000	50,000
Total Resources Available	900,000	950,000	50,000
Appropriation-Expenditures	780,000	600,000	
Encumbrances	–0–	170,000	
Total Resources Expended or Committed	780,000	770,000	(10,000)
Unreserved Fund Balance — 12/31	$120,000	$180,000	$ 60,000

BALANCE SHEET — DECEMBER 31, 1995

Net Financial Resources (Assets − Liabilities)		$350,000
Fund Balance		
Unreserved	$180,000	
Reserved for Commitments (Encumbrances)	170,000	$350,000

As encumbrances are recorded, they are also posted to the appropriate appropriation expenditure subsidiary account, thereby providing information as to the amount of each appropriation category that remains available for encumbrance or expenditure (see Illustration 20-4).

(4a) Expenditures (classified)	600,000	
Vouchers Payable or Cash		600,000
To record receipt of encumbered goods and services.		
(4b) Reserve for Encumbrances	605,000	
Encumbrances		605,000
To remove encumbrances on goods and services that have been recorded as expenditures *($605,000 is an assumed figure).*		

Two entries are required to record expenditures for goods or services that have been previously encumbered. Since the amount expended will not necessarily equal the amount encumbered, the dollar amounts in the two entries may not be the same. The reversal of the encumbrance is for the amount of the original encumbrance, which is assumed to be $605,000 in this example. The amount of expenditure is for the approved invoice price of the goods or services received.

(5)	Revenue	850,000	
	Estimated Revenue		800,000
	Unreserved Fund Balance		50,000
	To close budgeted and actual revenue accounts.		

The excess of actual revenue over (under) budgeted revenue is recorded as an increase (decrease) in the unreserved fund balance. Postings would also be made to close out each subsidiary revenue account.

(6)	Appropriations	*↗ assume amount*	780,000	
	Expenditures			600,000
	Encumbrances ($775,000 − $605,000)			170,000
	Unreserved fund balance			10,000
	To close appropriations, expenditures, and encumbrances accounts.			

The excess of appropriations over (under) expenditures plus encumbrances is recorded as an increase (decrease) in the unreserved fund balance. The balance of encumbrances at year-end is matched against appropriations because, although they are not expenditures, encumbrances do represent commitments made against the current year's appropriations and therefore represent the use of the appropriation authority of the current year. Postings would also be made to close each subsidiary appropriation expenditure account.

After entries (5) and (6) are posted, all account balances except assets, liabilities, the unreserved fund balance, and the reserve for encumbrances have been closed. The balances in the unreserved fund balance and reserve for encumbrances accounts may be calculated as follows:

Reserve for encumbrances—January 1, 1995	$ –0–
Total amounts encumbered during 1995—entry (3)	775,000
Total encumbrances expended—entry (4b)	(605,000)
Reserve for encumbrances—December 31, 1995	$170,000

Unreserved fund balance—January 1, 1995	$100,000
Excess of estimated revenue over appropriations—entry (1)	20,000
Excess of actual revenue over estimated revenue—entry (5)	50,000
Excess of Appropriations over expenditures and encumbrances—entry (6)	10,000
Unreserved fund balance—December 31, 1995	$180,000

The balance in the reserve for encumbrances account at December 31, 1995, represents the estimated amount of the net financial resources of the fund entity that will be needed in the subsequent year to liquidate obligations entered into under the authority of the current year's appropriation. As such, it represents a restriction on the availability of fund resources for future appropriation rather than a liability and is properly considered as a portion (reserved) of the total fund balance. The concept that the year-end balance in the Reserve for Encumbrance account is in reality a reserved fund balance would perhaps be clearer if an analysis of the change in the total fund balance were presented in the following form:

Total fund balance—January 1	$100,000
Add actual revenue	850,000
Deduct actual expenditures	(600,000)
Total fund balance—December 31	350,000
Less amount reserved for commitments	(170,000)
Unreserved fund balance—December 31	$180,000

It is also instructive to note that the increase in the *total* fund balance is always equal to the excess of *actual* revenues (inflows of net financial resources) over *actual* expenditures (outflows of net financial resources).

In the next year, the balance of the reserve for encumbrances will be charged by means of a separate expenditures account with the actual expenditures arising from the year-end commitments that are incurred in the subsequent year. A difference between the amount encumbered at the end of the year and the actual amount of the related expenditures that are incurred in the subsequent year is debited or credited to the unreserved fund balance.

Comprehensive Illustration—General Fund

The General Fund of Model City will now be used to illustrate the principles of fund accounting developed in this chapter.

The general fund of a municipality is used to account for all externally unrestricted financial resources of the municipality other than those required to be accounted for in another fund. It is established at the inception of the municipality and is continued as long as the municipality exists. Most of the current operations of a municipality are financed by the resources of this fund. The general ledger trial balance of the General Fund of Model City on January 1, 1995, is as follows:

Model City
The General Fund
General Ledger Trial Balance
January 1, 1995

Cash	$ 45,000
Certificates of deposit	100,000
Property tax receivable	190,000
Total debits	$335,000
Estimated uncollectible taxes	$ 20,000
Vouchers payable	65,000
Unreserved fund balance	95,000
Reserve for encumbrances—1994	155,000
Total credits	$335,000

The budget adopted by the City Council for the General Fund for the fiscal year ending December 31, 1995 is presented in summary form below.

Model City
The General Fund
1995 Fiscal-Year Budget

Estimated revenue	
Licenses and permits	$ 188,250
Property tax	1,158,750
State grant—education	300,000
Charges for services	135,000
Proceeds from sales of equipment	78,000
Total	1,860,000
Appropriations	
Public safety	416,000
General government	193,500
Highways and streets	135,500
Sanitation	75,000
Health	148,500
Cultural—recreation	88,500
Education	687,000
Total	1,744,000
Excess of estimated revenue over appropriations	116,000
Transfer from enterprise fund	150,000
Less transfers to: Debt service fund	(96,000)
Internal service fund	(200,000)
Excess (deficiency) of revenue and transfers from other funds over appropriations and transfers to other funds	$ (30,000)

Summary entries to record the activities and transactions of the General Fund during 1995 are presented below. The assignment to specific subsidiary accounts of amounts credited to revenue or appropriations and of amounts debited to encumbrances, expenditures, or estimated revenue is not shown in these summary entries. Remember, however, that each entry to these general ledger control accounts also requires detailed postings by appropriate classifications to the related subsidiary accounts.

(1)	Estimated revenue	1,860,000	
	Appropriations		1,744,000
	Unreserved fund balance		116,000
	To record budgeted revenue and expenditures.		
(2)	Due from enterprise fund	150,000	
	Transfers from other funds		150,000
	To record authorization for transfer of resources from other fund entities incorporated in budget adopted by City Council.		

For financial reporting purposes, transfers of resources from other fund entities of the same organization are distinguished from revenue of the recipient fund entity. Interfund transfers are properly recognized (accrued) in the period in which they are authorized. Control over authorized transfers from other fund entities may be achieved by recording them as a receivable at the beginning of the year for which they are authorized (budgeted).

(3) Transfers to other funds	296,000	
Due to debt service fund		96,000
Due to internal service fund		200,000
To record authorization for transfer of resources to other fund entities incorporated in budget adopted by city council.		

Although authorized transfers to other fund entities may be viewed as appropriation expenditures from the point of view of the General Fund entity, for purposes of financial reporting they are distinguished from expenditures. Control over authorized transfers to other fund entities may be achieved by recording them as liabilities at the beginning of the period for which they are authorized (budgeted).

(4) Property tax receivable	1,287,500	
Estimated uncollectible taxes		128,750
Revenue		1,158,750
To record property taxes at time they are levied.		

The estimate for uncollectible taxes is determined on the basis of collection policy and prior years' experience. It is recorded as a direct reduction of revenue, however, rather than as an expenditure, since the failure to collect taxes is not an outflow of net financial resources. Accordingly, there is no appropriation for the amount of estimated uncollectible taxes and it is, therefore, properly accounted for as a reduction of revenue rather than as an expenditure.

(5) Other Receivables	80,000	
Revenue		80,000
To record billings for routine services.		
(6) Expenditures—1994	148,000	
Vouchers Payable		148,000
To record receipt of goods and services ordered in 1994.		

A separate expenditure control account (and subsidiary ledger) is used to record expenditures during the current year that were encumbered (authorized) in the prior year. At the end of the year, this expenditure account will be closed out against Reserve for Encumbrance—1994 and any difference taken to the unreserved fund balance [see entry (25) below].

(7) Encumbrances	1,291,000	
Reserve for Encumbrances		1,291,000
To record encumbrances on goods and services ordered during current year.		
(8) Cash	1,281,000	
Property Tax Receivable		1,201,000
Other Receivables		80,000
To record collection of $170,500 of property taxes levied in 1994 and $1,030,500 of property taxes levied in 1995, and to record collection of $80,000 in other receivables.		

(9) Estimated Uncollectible Taxes   19,500
          Property Tax Receivable   19,500
              To record write-off of uncollected 1994 property taxes authorized by City
              Council ($190,000 − $170,500 = $19,500).
(10) Cash   221,000
          Revenue   221,000
              To record collection of licenses, permits, fees, service charges, etc.
(11) Expenditures   1,050,000
          Vouchers Payable   1,050,000
          Reserve for Encumbrances   1,100,000
          Encumbrances   1,100,000
              To record receipt of goods and services that had been previously encumbered
              [entry (7) above] in amount of $1,100,00.
(12) Expenditures   210,000
          Vouchers Payable   210,000
              To record receipt of goods and services that had **not** been previously
              encumbered.

Not all expenditures go through the encumbrance process. Encumbrances are formally recognized in the accounts only when there is an extended period of time between the date the commitment is made and the date the expenditure is encurred. For example, routine payroll expenditures are not encumbered.

(13) Receivable from State Government   275,000
          Revenue   275,000
              To record municipal education grant authorized by state legislature.

The amount of revenue recognized is based on an approved grant application filed with the Department of Education and is not dependent on the future performance of specific services or specified expenditures of financial resources.

(14) Encumbrances   250,000
          Reserve for Encumbrances   250,000
              To record a contract to acquire office furnishings and equipment.

(15) Cash   100,000
          Due from Enterprise Fund   100,000
              To record receipt of a cash transfer from the Enterprise Fund.

(16) Expenditures   250,000
          Vouchers Payable   250,000
          Reserve for Encumbrances   250,000
          Encumbrances   250,000
              To record receipt of office equipment and furnishings and to remove
              encumbrance.

Capital expenditures, like other expenditures, represent the approved utilization of the financial resources of the General Fund and therefore are recorded as expenditures and not as assets in the records of the General Fund.

(17) Vouchers Payable   1,650,000
          Cash   1,650,000
              To record payment of liabilities.

(18) Cash	87,250	
Revenue		87,250
To record proceeds from sale of used furniture and equipment.		

Since the proceeds from the sale of Model City assets constitute expendable financial resources, they are recorded as revenue by the recipient general fund.

(19) Cash	275,000	
Receivable from State Government		275,000
To record collection of grant from state government.		

(20) Due to Debt Service Fund	96,000	
Due to Internal Service Fund	200,000	
Cash		296,000
To record authorized transfers of cash to other Model City fund entities.		

(21) Certificates of Deposit	6,000	
Revenue		6,000
To record interest earned on certificates of deposit that has been or will be credited thereto.		

(22) Estimated Uncollectible Taxes	76,000	
Property Tax Receivable		76,000
To record write-off of 1995 property taxes authorized by City Council.		

Preclosing Trial Balance The transactions summarized in the journal entries above are reflected in the December 31, 1995, general ledger trial balance for the General Fund of Model City presented below.

Model City
The General Fund
General Ledger Trial Balance
December 31, 1995

	DR.	CR.
Cash	$ 63,250	
Certificates of deposit	106,000	
Property taxes receivable	181,000	
Due from enterprise fund	50,000	
Estimated revenue	1,860,000	
Expenditures	1,510,000	
Encumbrances	191,000	
Transfers to other funds	296,000	
Expenditures—1994	148,000	
Estimated uncollectible taxes		$ 53,250
Vouchers payable		73,000
Unreserved fund balance		211,000
Reserve for encumbrances		191,000
Reserve for encumbrances—1994		155,000
Appropriations		1,744,000
Revenue		1,828,000
Transfers from other funds		150,000
Total	$4,405,250	$4,405,250

Closing Entries December 31, 1995, closing entries for the General Fund are as follows:

(23)	Unreserved Fund Balance	32,000	
	Revenue	1,828,000	
	Estimated Revenue		1,860,000
	To close out actual and budgeted revenue accounts.		
(24)	Appropriations	1,744,000	
	Expenditures		1,510,000
	Encumbrances		191,000
	Unreserved Fund Balance		43,000
	To close out appropriations and current year's expenditures and encumbrances accounts.		
(25)	Reserve for Encumbrances—1994	155,000	
	Expenditures—1994		148,000
	Unreserved Fund Balance		7,000
	To close out expenditures for goods and services ***ordered*** and encumbered in prior year.		
(26)	Unreserved Fund Balance	146,000	
	Transfers from Other Funds	150,000	
	Transfers to Other Funds		296,000
	To close out interfund transfers to unreserved fund balance		

Financial Statements

The two basic statements prepared for expendable fund entities are (1) a balance sheet and (2) a statement of revenue, expenditures, and other changes in fund balance.

Revenue should be classified by major sources and expenditures by major functions in the statement of revenue, expenditures, and other changes in fund balance. In addition, comparative information for the prior year should be presented both in that statement and in the balance sheet.

For budgetary fund entities, a financial statement that compares budgeted and actual operating results should also be prepared. Since amounts encumbered (encumbrances) against the current year's appropriation authority (budget) must be treated in the same manner as expenditures in such a statement, the "actual" data may be different from those presented in accordance with generally accepted accounting principles in the statement of revenue, expenditures, and other changes in fund balance. In that case, the difference between the budgetary basis and generally accepted accounting principles should be explained in the notes to the financial statements.

Examples of statements and schedules for the General Fund of Model City for the year ended December 31, 1995, are presented in the following illustrations.

Illustration 20-6 Comparative Balance Sheets

Illustration 20-7 Comparative Statement of Revenue, Expenditures, and Other Changes in Fund Balance

ILLUSTRATION 20-6
Model City
The General Fund
Balance Sheet December 31, 1995 and 1994

ASSETS	1995	1994
Cash	$ 63,250	$ 45,000
Certificates of Deposit	106,000	100,000
Property Tax Receivable (less allowance for uncollectible amounts, 1995—$53,250; 1994—$20,000)	127,750	170,000
Due from Other Funds	50,000	–0–
Total	$347,000	$315,000

LIABILITIES AND FUND BALANCE	1995	1994
Vouchers Payable	$ 73,000	$ 65,000
Fund Balance		
Unreserved	83,000	95,000
Reserved for Encumbrances	191,000	155,000
Total Fund Balance	274,000	250,000
Total	$347,000	$315,000

ILLUSTRATION 20-7
Model City
The General Fund
Statement of Revenue, Expenditures, and Other Changes in Fund Balance
For Years Ended December 31, 1995, and December 31, 1994

	1995	1994
Revenue		
Licenses and Permits	$ 170,500	$ 175,000
Property Tax	1,158,750	1,105,000
State Grant—Education	275,000	250,000
Charges for Services	136,500	130,000
Proceeds from Sales of Equipment	87,250	–0–
Total Revenue	1,828,000	1,660,000
Transfer from Enterprise Fund	150,000	–0–
Total Revenue and Transfers from Other Funds	1,978,000	1,660,000

Expenditures		
Public Safety	380,000	360,000
General Government	189,000	175,000
Highways and Streets	128,000	130,000
Sanitation	70,000	71,000
Health	141,000	132,000
Cultural—Recreation	80,000	82,000
Education	670,000	640,000
Total	1,658,000	1,590,000
Transfers to Other Funds		
To Debt Service Fund	96,000	60,000
To Internal Service Fund	200,000	–0–
Total	296,000	60,000
Total Expenditures and Transfers to Other Funds	1,954,000	1,650,000
Excess (Deficiency) of Revenues and Transfers from Other Funds over Expenditures and Transfers to Other Funds	24,000	10,000
Fund Balance—January 1	250,000	240,000
Fund Balance—December 31	$ 274,000	$ 250,000

ILLUSTRATION 20-8
Model City
The General Fund
Statement of Revenue, Expenditures, and Other Changes
in Fund Balance—Budget and Actual
For Year Ended December 31, 1995

	BUDGET	ACTUAL	VARIANCE— FAVORABLE (UNFAVORABLE)
Revenue (Illustration 20-9)	$1,860,000	$1,828,000	$(32,000)
Transfers from Other Funds	150,000	150,000	–0–
Total Revenue and Transfers from Other Funds	2,010,000	1,978,000	(32,000)
Expenditures and Encumbrances under Current Year's Appropriation Authority (Illustration 20-10)	1,744,000	1,701,000	43,000
Transfers to Other Funds	296,000	296,000	–0–
Total Expenditures, Encumbrances, and Transfers to Other Funds under Current Year's Appropriation Authority	2,040,000	1,997,000	43,000
Excess (Deficiency) of Revenues and Transfers from Other Funds over Expenditures, Encumbrances, and Transfers to Other Funds under Current Year's Appropriation Authority	(30,000)	(19,000)	11,000
Expenditures under Prior Year's Appropriation Authority (Illustration 20-10)	155,000	148,000	7,000
Net Decrease in Fund Balance	185,000	167,000	18,000
Fund Balance, January 1	250,000	250,000	–0–
Unreserved Fund Balance, December 31	$ 65,000	$ 83,000	$ 18,000

ILLUSTRATION 20-9
Model City
Schedule of Revenue—Budget and Actual
For Year Ended December 31, 1995

	BUDGET	ACTUAL	VARIANCE— FAVORABLE (UNFAVORABLE)
Licenses and Permits			
Motor Vehicles	$ 103,000	$ 94,000	$ (9,000)
Hunting and Fishing	16,250	15,000	(1,250)
Marriage Licenses	24,000	27,500	3,500
Burial Permits	9,000	7,000	(2,000)
Animal Licenses	14,000	8,000	(6,000)
Other	22,000	19,000	(3,000)
Total	188,250	170,500	(17,750)
Property Tax	1,158,750	1,158,750	–0–
Intergovernmental Revenue*	300,000	275,000	(25,000)
Charges for Services*	135,000	136,500	1,500
Proceeds from Sale of Equipment*	78,000	87,250	9,250
Total	$1,860,000	$1,828,000	$(32,000)

*Detail omitted for illustrative purposes. In practice, subcategories of these major revenue sources would also be presented as under Licenses and Permits in this illustration.

ILLUSTRATION 20-10
Model City
The General Fund
Schedule of Expenditures and Encumbrances Compared with Authorizations
For Year Ended December 31, 1995

	PRIOR YEAR'S APPROPRIATION AUTHORITY			CURRENT YEAR'S APPROPRIATION AUTHORITY					
			VARIANCE— FAVORABLE		ACTUAL				VARIANCE— FAVORABLE
	BUDGET	ACTUAL	(UNFAVORABLE)	BUDGET	EXPENDITURES	ENCUMBRANCES	TOTAL		(UNFAVORABLE)
Public Safety									
Police									
Criminal Investigation	$ –0–	$ –0–	$ –0–	$ 24,000	$ 22,500	$ 750	$ 23,250		$ 750
Vice Control	–0–	–0–	–0–	6,000	–0–	–0–	–0–		6,000
Patrol	–0–	–0–	–0–	80,000	75,000	1,500	76,500		3,500
Records	–0–	–0–	–0–	35,000	32,700	50	32,750		2,250
Custody of Prisoners	–0–	–0–	–0–	16,000	15,250	500	15,750		250
Crime Laboratory	3,500	3,000	500	31,000	26,000	2,500	28,500		2,500
Traffic Control	2,500	1,000	1,500	40,000	31,300	3,700	35,000		5,000
Training	–0–	–0–	–0–	15,000	14,250	–0–	14,250		750
Other	–0–	–0–	–0–	3,000	3,000	–0–	3,000		–0–
Total Police	6,000	4,000	2,000	250,000	220,000	9,000	229,000		21,000
Fire	–0–	–0–	–0–	126,000	120,000	4,000	124,000		2,000
Inspection	–0–	–0–	–0–	40,000	36,000	–0–	36,000		4,000
Total Public Safety	6,000	4,000	2,000	416,000	376,000	13,000	389,000		27,000
General Government*	5,000	5,000	–0–	193,500	184,000	8,000	192,000		1,500
Highways and Streets*	20,000	18,000	2,000	135,500	110,000	24,250	134,250		1,250
Sanitation*	8,000	10,000	(2,000)	75,000	60,000	12,500	72,500		2,500
Health*	6,000	6,000	–0–	148,500	135,000	8,250	143,250		5,250
Cultural—Recreation*	–0–	–0–	–0–	88,500	80,000	8,000	88,000		500
Education*	110,000	105,000	5,000	687,000	565,000	117,000	682,000		5,000
Total	$155,000	$148,000	$7,000	$1,744,000	$1,510,000	$191,000	$1,701,000		$43,000

*For illustrative purposes, only major functions are presented in this schedule. In practice, each major function whould be broken down by subfunctions and activities as was done for Public Safety (function); Police (subfunction); Criminal Investigation (activity).

REPORTING INVENTORY AND PREPAYMENTS IN THE FINANCIAL STATEMENTS

Inventory

There are two acceptable methods, the ***consumption method*** and the ***purchase method,*** of accounting for and reporting inventory in the financial statements of expendable fund entities. Under the consumption method, inventory is considered to be a financial resource and expenditures for inventory are reported in the period in which the inventory is consumed. Under the purchase method, inventory is not considered to be a financial resource and expenditures are recognized in the period in which the inventory is purchased without regard to when it is consumed.

To illustrate, assume that $20,000 in inventory is on hand at the beginning of the period, that $50,000 in inventory is purchased during the period, and that inventory at the end of the period is $24,000. Entries under each method are as follows:

CONSUMPTION METHOD			PURCHASE METHOD		
WHEN PURCHASED:			**WHEN PURCHASED:**		
Expenditures	50,000		Expenditures	50,000	
Cash		50,000	Cash		50,000
END OF YEAR			**END OF YEAR**		
Inventory	4,000		NO ENTRY		
Expenditures		4,000			

The entry at the end of the year under the consumption method is to record the $4,000 increase in inventory. If inventory decreases, expenditures would be debited and inventory credited. Under the consumption method, inventories are automatically reported as an asset in the financial statements. As compared to the purchse method, financial statements prepared under the consumption method will reflect $4,000 fewer expenditures and a similarly larger fund balance.

Reserve for Inventory

Purchase Method   Although reported as an expenditure when purchased, some accountants believe that, even if the purchase method is used, material amounts of inventory should be disclosed in the financial statements either by footnote or by reporting an asset in the balance sheet with a contra account, "Reserve for Inventory," reported as part of the total fund balance. To illustrate the reporting of inventory as both an asset and an expenditure under the purchase method, assume that the balance sheet at the beginning of the period was as shown here:

Inventory	$ 20,000
Other Financial Resources (net)	400,000
Net Assets	$420,000
Fund Balance	
Reserve for Inventory	$ 20,000
Unreserved Fund Balance	400,000
Total Fund Balance	$420,000

In addition to the purchase method entry illustrated above, another entry is necessary at the end of the year to record the $4,000 increase in inventory as follows:

PURCHASE METHOD

END OF YEAR

Inventory	4,000	
Reserve for Inventory		4,000

If inventory decreases, Reserve for Inventory is debited and Inventory is credited. Assuming net financial resources (excluding inventory) increase by $100,000 during the period, the amounts that would be reported in the balance sheet at the end of the period are as follows:

Inventory	$ 24,000
Other Financial Resources (net)	500,000
Net Assets	$524,000
Fund Balance	
Reserve for Inventory	$ 24,000
Unreserved Fund Balance	500,000
Total Fund Balance	$520,000

When a reserve for inventory is created under the purchase method, the amounts reported for inventory and the *total* fund balance are the same as those reported under the consumption method. However, the amount of expenditures reported in the operating statement will still differ (in this case by $4,000).

Consumption Method In some cases it is considered desirable to both (1) use the consumption method and (2) report a reserve for inventory. If the consumption method is used, the reserve for inventory is created and adjusted by debiting or crediting the "unreserved fund balance." For example, using the above illustration and assuming the balance in Reserve for Inventory was $20,000 at the beginning of the year, another entry in addition to those illustrated under the consumption method above would be made at the end of the year as follows:

<u>CONSUMPTION METHOD</u>

END OF YEAR

Unreserved Fund Balance	4,000	
Reserve for Inventory		4,000

Prepayments

Prepayments for items such as insurance or rent that cover more than one accounting period may also be reported using the consumption or purchase methods. Under the purchase method the cost is reported as an expenditure in the period when the insurance premium or rent is paid without regard to the period benefited. Under the consumption method, a prepaid asset would be recorded and expenditures reduced to the extent that the premium or rent payment is for a subsequent period.

Lapsing of Appropriations

The treatment illustrated in this chapter for encumbrances outstanding at the end of the period was based on the assumption (and generally followed practice) that encumbered appropriations do not lapse at the end of the fiscal year. It is possible, however, for the legislative body or governing board to impose a provision that causes unexpended appropriations to lapse at the end of the year. In this case, the reserve for encumbrances must be closed out at the end of the year, and if the encumbered items are to be purchased in the next year, the appropriation for the next year must contain authority for such expenditures.

If appropriations lapse, the closing entry for appropriations at the end of the year takes the following form.

Reserve for Encumbrances	191,000	
Appropriations	1,744,000	
Expenditures		1,510,000
Encumbrances		191,000
Unreserved Fund Balance		234,000

The subsequent year's appropriation should include authorization for the purchase of the encumbered items. Therefore, the reserve for encumbrances would be reestablished at the beginning of the next year by a debit to encumbrances, and subsequent expenditures for the items would be accounted for the same as any other expenditures of that year.

Current Developments

The preceding discussion is based on existing GASB accounting and reporting standards. The GASB is currently completing a reexamination of the financial reporting model for governmental entities that may result in significant changes to the existing model. For example, it is likely that supplies inventory and prepaid expenses will be treated as financial resources, in which case the consumption method of accounting for supplies and prepaid expenses will be required rather than discretionary. The financial reporting project of the GASB is described at the end of Chapter 21.

Questions

1. What characteristics distinguish nonbusiness organizations from profit-oriented enterprises?

2. Define a fund as the term is applied in accounting for the activities of governmental units and other nonbusiness organizations.

3. What is the significance of the "unreserved fund balance" of an expendable fund entity?

4. What are the major classifications of increases and decreases in expendable fund resources?

5. What are the revenue-recognition criteria for expendable fund entities? How do these criteria differ from revenue-recognition criteria for profit-oriented enterprises?

6. Expenditures may be classified by function, activity, object, or organizational unit. Give an example of each classification for a municipality. Which classification is the most appropriate for external financial reporting?

7. Distinguish between an appropriation, an encumbrance, an expenditure, and a disbursement.

8. Distinguish between an expense and an expenditure.

9. Explain and justify the difference between the treatment of estimated uncollectible taxes in fund accounting and the treatment of estimated bad debts in commercial accounting.

10. Explain the purpose of encumbrance accounting. Might encumbrance accounting be used by commercial enterprises?

11. Is the year-end balance in the Reserve for Encumbrances account a liability? Explain.

12. What columns would you suggest for a subsidiary ledger account in order that it might be a subsidiary not only to the "appropriations" control account but also the "encumbrances" and the "expenditures" control accounts?

13. Why is depreciation on fixed assets not recorded in the records of expendable fund entities?

14. How does the adoption of a budget for a general fund entity differ from the adoption of a budget by a commercial unit?

15. Describe the principal financial statements used to report on the activities and status of expendable fund entities.

16. Why may it be difficult or impossible for a governmental unit to determine the total cost of performing a particular activity or function?

Exercises

Exercise 20-1

Several independent financial activities of a governmental unit are given below.

1. Revenue from the sale of licenses and permits for the first two months totaled $15,000.
2. Land that had been donated previously was sold for $100,000.
3. An order was placed for the purchase of a new fire engine at a price of $130,000.
4. Bonds with a face value of $500,000 were issued at par value to finance a new park.
5. A $250,000 grant was received from the federal government to help improve the local schools.
6. The new fire engine was received and accepted. The approved price, however, was $140,000 rather than $130,000.

Required:

Prepare the journal entries needed to account for each transaction in the General Fund.

Exercise 20-2

Listed are typical financial activities of a local governmental unit.

1. The legislative unit approved the budget for the general operating fund. Estimated revenues are $4,000,000, and appropriations for expenditures are $3,800,000.
2. Statements of property tax assessments totaling $3,000,000 were mailed to property owners. It is estimated that 4% of the assessed taxes will be uncollectible.
3. Notification was received from the state that this unit's share of sales tax revenues from the fourth quarter of the previous year will be $500,000.
4. The manager signed a contract to purchase equipment costing $250,000.
5. The equipment ordered above was received and paid for.
6. Employees were paid their biweekly wages of $36,000.
7. Property taxes in the amount of $2,050,000 were collected.

Required:

Prepare the necessary journal entries to record the transactions listed above in the records of the General Fund.

Exercise 20-3

Listed are transactions of the Town of Jackson.

1. A budget consisting of estimated revenues of $1,950,000 and appropriations for expenditures of $1,800,000 was passed by the town council.
2. Property taxes of $1,150,000 were assessed; $1,115,000 are expected to be collectible.
3. Property taxes in the amount of $1,080,000 were collected.
4. Equipment costing $200,000 was purchased, and the old equipment was sold at the end of its estimated useful life for $24,000.
5. A contract was signed with an independent company to do the trash collecting for the year. The contract price was $96,000.
6. The first monthly bill of $8,000 was received from the trash collector.
7. The $8,000 bill was paid.

Required:

Prepare the journal entries needed in the records of the General Fund to account for these transactions.

Exercise 20-4

Following is the preclosing trial balance for the General Fund of the City of Doyle.

Doyle City
The General Fund
General Ledger Trial Balance
December 31, 1996

Cash	$ 400,000	
Certificates of deposit	350,000	
Due from state government	112,000	
Due from other funds	30,000	
Taxes receivable	774,000	
Estimated revenue	3,110,000	
Expenditures	1,960,000	
Encumbrances	734,000	
Transfers to other funds	90,000	
Expenditures—1995	55,000	
Estimated uncollectible taxes		$ 30,000
Vouchers payable		64,000
Due to other funds		27,000
Unreserved fund balance		760,000
Reserve for encumbrances		734,000
Reserve for encumbrances—1995		50,000
Appropriations		2,700,000
Revenue		3,210,000
Transfers from other funds		40,000
	$7,615,000	$7,615,000

Required:

Prepare in general journal form the closing entries for the General Fund of Doyle City.

Exercise 20-5

The preclosing trial balance for the General Fund of the City of Springfield is presented below.

City of Springfield
The General Fund
General Ledger Trial Balance
December 31, 1995

Cash	$ 90,000
Certificates of deposit	120,000
Property taxes receivable	175,000
Estimated revenue	1,690,000

Expenditures	1,310,000	
Expenditures—1994	32,000	
Encumbrances	165,000	
Estimated uncollectible taxes		$ 51,000
Vouchers payable		65,000
Unreserved fund balance		41,000
Reserve for encumbrances		165,000
Reserve for encumbrances—1994		35,000
Appropriations		1,550,000
Revenue		1,675,000
	$3,582,000	$3,582,000

Required:

Prepare the closing entries for the General Fund.

Exercise 20-6

In 1995, Bay City purchased supplies valued at $350,000. At the end of the year, $65,000 of the supplies were still in the inventory. No supplies were on hand at the beginning of the year. The city uses the purchase method to account for supplies.

Required:

A. Prepare the journal entry necessary to report the supplies as an asset in the balance sheet of Bay City.

B. What amount of expenditures for supplies will be shown in the statement of revenue, expenditures, and other changes in fund balance?

Exercise 20-7

At the beginning of 1995, the City of Fairview reported an Unreserved Fund Balance of $555,000 and a supplies inventory balance of $175,000. During the year, Fairview purchased $225,000 in supplies and used $220,000 worth. The city will report a reserve for supplies inventory.

Required:

A. Prepare the necessary journal entries under the purchase method.

B. Prepare the journal entries needed to account for the supplies under the consumption method.

C. What would the 12/31/95 balance in the Unreserved Fund Balance be under each method, assuming that the only transactions of the fund are those involving the supplies?

Exercise 20-8

During 1995, the City of Greenfield engaged in the following financial activities:

1. The City Council approved the budget for the general operating fund. The budget

shows estimated revenues of $1,900,000 and appropriations for expenditures of $1,850,000.

2. Property tax assessments for 1995 were compiled and statements mailed to property owners. Assessments total $955,000. Past collection experience indicates that approximately 5% of assessed property taxes are delinquent or uncollectible during the year of billing.

3. A low bid of $15,000 was accepted for a new vehicle for the fire chief. A purchase order was issued providing for additional costs for painting and ancillary equipment (negotiated after the bid) prior to delivery. The estimate of additional costs is $1,400.

4. Additional purchase orders placed during the year amount to $140,000.

5. City employees are issued paychecks for the month of April. The total payroll amounts to $90,000.

6. The City received a statement from the State Treasurer that the City's portion of the state sales tax for the first half-year is $375,000.

7. Vouchers for expenditures totaling $135,000 are approved for payment. Encumbrances against these vouchers were recorded at a total of $137,000.

8. The vehicle for the fire chief was delivered and accepted. The invoice in the amount of $16,200 was approved for payment.

9. Property tax collections for the month of June amounted to $450,000.

10. The City Treasurer issued checks in payment of the vouchers totaling $135,000 and for the invoice for the fire chief's vehicle.

11. A purchase order previously issued for an electric typewriter (estimated price $650) was canceled when the vendor indicated a three-month delay in delivery.

Required:

Prepare journal entries to record and account for the foregoing transactions.

Exercise 20-9

The following events relate typical activities in a municipality that affect the General Fund.

1. The Meadville City Council passed an ordinance approving a general operating budget of $580,000 for fiscal year 1995. The city's only source of revenue is from property taxes. For 1995, these revenues are estimated at $565,000.

2. A property tax levy of $1 per $100 assessed valuation (total assessed valuation equals $60,000,000) is billed to property owners. Taxes are due in the current fiscal year. Experience indicates that 3% of taxes billed will be uncollectible.

3. A motorcycle for the Department of Public Safety is ordered by the purchasing department on the basis of a low bid of $4,200.

4. The motorcycle in (3) above is received and the invoice is approved for payment. Extra accessories not included in the bid price amount to $425.

5. Salaries and wages in the amount of $20,000 are paid by check to city employees for the two-week period ending on May 15.

6. The property division sold used typewriters and other office equipment at a public auction. Total receipts were $8,225.

7. Property taxes in the amount of $540,000 were collected.

Required:

Prepare the necessary journal entries to record each event in the accounts of the General Fund.

Exercise 20-10

Select the best answer for each of the following items:

1. When used in fund accounting, the term "fund" usually refers to
   (a) A sum of money designated for a special purpose.
   (b) A liability to other governmental units.
   (c) The equity of a municipality in its own assets.
   (d) A fiscal and accounting entity having a set of self-balancing accounts.
2. Authority granted by a legislative body to make expenditures and to incur obligations during a fiscal year is the definition of an
   (a) Appropriation.
   (b) Authorization.
   (c) Encumbrance.
   (d) Expenditure.
3. What type of account is used to earmark the fund balance to liquidate the contingent obligations of goods ordered but not yet received?
   (a) Appropriations.
   (b) Encumbrances.
   (c) Obligations.
   (d) Reserve for encumbrances.
4. A city's General Fund budget for the forthcoming fiscal year shows estimated revenues in excess of appropriations. The initial effect of recording this will result in an increase in
   (a) Taxes receivable.
   (b) Fund balance.
   (c) Reserve for encumbrances.
   (d) Encumbrances.
5. The Reserve for Encumbrances account is properly considered to be a
   (a) Current liability if payable within a year; otherwise, a long-term debt.
   (b) Fixed liability.
   (c) Floating debt.
   (d) Reservation of the fund's equity.
6. In preparing the General Fund budget of Dover City for the forthcoming fiscal year, the City Council appropriated a sum greater than expected revenues. This action of the Council will result in
   (a) A cash overdraft during that fiscal year.
   (b) An increase in encumbrances by the end of that fiscal year.
   (c) A decrease in the fund balance.
   (d) A necessity for compensatory offsetting action in the Debt Service Fund.
7. What would be the effect on the General Fund balance in the current fiscal year of recording a $150,000 purchase for a new fire truck out of General Fund resources, for

which a $146,000 encumbrance had been recorded in the General Fund in the previous fiscal year?

(a) Reduce the General Fund balance by $150,000.

(b) Reduce the General Fund balance by $146,000.

(c) Reduce the General Fund balance by $4,000.

(d) Have no effect on the General Fund balance.

(AICPA adapted)

Problems

Problem 20-1

The general ledger trial balance of the General Fund of the City of Bedford on January 1, 1995, shows the following:

	DR.	CR.
Cash	$100,000	
Taxes receivable	75,000	
Allowance for uncollectible taxes		$ 35,000
Unreserved fund balance		110,000
Reserve for encumbrances—1994		30,000
Total	$175,000	$175,000

A summary of activities and transactions for the General Fund during 1995 is presented here:

1. The City Council adopted a budget for the General Fund with estimated revenues of $1,560,000 and authorization for appropriated expenditures of $1,400,000. The budget authorized the transfer of $50,000 from the Water Fund to the General Fund for operating expenses as a payment in lieu of taxes. Cash for the payment of interest due for the year on the $1,000,000, 8% bond issue for the Civic Center is approved for transfer from the General Fund to the Debt Service Fund.

2. The annual property tax levy of 10% on assessed valuation ($11,000,000) is billed to property owners. Two percent is estimated to be uncollectible.

3. Goods and services amounting to $1,150,000 were ordered during the year.

4. Invoices for all goods ordered in 1994 amounting to $29,000 were approved for payment.

5. Funds for bond interest on Civic Center bonds were transferred to the Debt Service Fund.

6. Invoices for goods and services received during the year totaling $1,155,000 were recorded. These were encumbered previously [see (3) above].

7. Transfer of funds from the Water Company was received in lieu of taxes.

8. Taxes were collected from property owners in the amount of $1,050,000.

9. Past-due tax bills of $17,000 were charged off as uncollectible.

10. Checks in payment of invoices for goods and services ordered in 1994 and 1995 were issued [see items (4) and (6) above].

11. Revenues received from miscellaneous sources, other than property taxes, of $455,000 were recorded.

12. Purchase order for two trash collection vehicle systems complete with residence trash containers for automatic pickup of trash was issued. Bid price per system was $120,000.

Required:

A. Prepare journal entries to record the summary transactions. You may find it necessary or convenient to post journal entries to ledger T accounts before the preparation of the required trial balances.

B. Prepare a preclosing trial balance.

C. Prepare closing entries.

D. Prepare a postclosing trial balance.

Problem 20-2

The following account balances, among others, were included in the preclosing trial balance of the General Fund of the City of Lynchburg on December 31, 1996.

Estimated revenue	$630,000
Expenditures	468,000
Encumbrances	120,000
Expenditures—1995	43,000
Reserve for encumbrances (Note 1)	162,000
Appropriations	672,000
Revenue	696,000
Reserve for supplies inventory (Note 2)	72,000
Supplies inventory (Note 2)	72,000
Unreserved fund balance	24,000

Note 1: The balance in this account was $42,000 on January 1, 1996. Purchase orders outstanding on December 31, 1996, total $120,000.
Note 2: Supplies on hand on December 31, 1996, amount to $60,000.

Required:

A. What was the balance in the Unreserved Fund Balance account on December 31, 1995? What was the total Fund Balance on December 31, 1995?

B. Prepare the necessary adjusting and closing entries for the year ended December 31, 1996. Supplies inventory is accounted for using the purchase method.

C. Prepare a schedule to calculate the Unreserved Fund Balance and the total Fund Balance on December 31, 1996.

Problem 20-3

The following account balances, among others, were included in the preclosing trial balance of the General Fund of the City of Madison on December 31, 1996.

Appropriations	$3,488,000
Cash	270,000
Due to other funds	100,000
Due from other funds	250,000
Encumbrances	382,000

Estimated revenue	3,720,000
Expenditures	3,020,000
Expenditures—1995	296,000
Reserve for encumbrances	382,000
Reserve for encumbrances—1995	310,000
Revenue	3,656,000
Taxes receivable	600,000
Transfers from other funds	300,000
Transfers to other funds	520,000
Unreserved fund balance	422,000
Vouchers payable	400,000

Required:

A. Prepare the necessary closing entries on December 31, 1996.

B. Calculate the amount of both the unreserved fund balance and the total fund balance in the balance sheet (1) on December 31, 1995 and (2) on December 31, 1996.

C. Prepare a schedule reconciling the December 31, 1995, total fund balance with the December 31, 1996, total fund balance by reference to actual inflows and outflows of financial resources.

Problem 20-4

The trial balance for the General Fund of the City of Monte Vista as of December 31, 1995, is presented here:

	DEBIT	CREDIT
Cash	$300,000	
Supplies inventory	75,000	
Unreserved fund balance		$300,000
Reserve for supplies inventory		75,000
	$375,000	$375,000

Transactions of the General Fund for the year ended December 31, 1996, are summarized as follows:

1. The City Council adopted the following budget for 1996:

Estimated revenue	$1,600,000
Transfer from trust fund	50,000
Appropriations	1,530,000
Transfer to debt service fund	80,000

2. Property taxes of $1,500,000 were levied, of which it is estimated that $30,000 will not be collected.

3. Purchase orders in the amount of $1,400,000 were placed with suppliers and other vendors.

4. Property taxes in the amount of $1,450,000 were collected.

5. Cash was received from the Trust Fund in the amount of $50,000.

6. Invoices in the amount of $1,380,000 were approved for payment. The amount originally encumbered for these invoices was $1,360,000. The invoices included $25,000 net of trade-in allowance for the purchase of a new minicomputer and $400,000 for supplies.

The City received a trade-in allowance of $4,000 on its old minicomputer, which had been purchased three years earlier for $16,000. At the time the old minicomputer was purchased, it was estimated that it would have a useful life of four years. The new minicomputer is expected to last at least six years. The City of Monte Vista uses the purchase method to account for supplies inventory.

7. Licenses and fees in the amount of $48,000 were collected.
8. Vouchers in the amount of $1,300,000 were paid.
9. Cash in the amount of $80,000 was transferred to the Debt Service Fund.
10. Supplies on hand at the end of the year amount to $100,000.

Required:

A. Prepare entries in general journal form to record the transactions of the General Fund for the year ended December 31, 1996.

B. Prepare a preclosing trial balance for the General Fund as of December 31, 1996.

C. Prepare the necessary closing entries for the General Fund for the year ended December 31, 1996.

D. Prepare a balance sheet and a statement of revenue, expenditures, and other changes in fund balance for the General Fund for the year ended December 31, 1996.

Problem 20-5

The trial balance for the General Fund of the City of Fairfield as of December 31, 1995, is presented here:

City of Fairfield
The General Fund
Adjusted Trial Balance
December 31, 1995

	DEBIT	CREDIT
Cash	$430,000	
Property tax receivable	45,000	
Estimated uncollectible taxes		$ 20,000
Due from trust fund	50,000	
Vouchers payable		60,000
Reserve for encumbrances		30,000
Unreserved fund balance		415,000
	$525,000	$525,000

Transactions for the year ended December 31, 1996, are summarized as follows:

1. The City Council adopted a budget for the year with estimated revenue of $735,000 and appropriations of $700,000.
2. Property taxes in the amount of $590,000 were levied for the current year. It is estimated that $24,000 of the taxes levied will prove to be uncollectible.
3. Proceeds from the sale of equipment in the amount of $35,000 were received by the General Fund. The equipment was purchased 10 years ago with resources of the General

Fund at a cost of $150,000. On the date of purchase, it was estimated that the equipment had a useful life of 15 years.

4. Licenses and fees in the amount of $110,000 were collected.

5. The total amount of encumbrances against fund resources for the year was $642,500.

6. Vouchers in the amount of $455,000 were authorized for payment. This was $15,000 less than the amount originally encumbered for these purchases.

7. An invoice in the amount of $28,000 was received for goods ordered in 1995. The invoice was approved for payment.

8. Property taxes in the amount of $570,000 were collected.

9. Vouchers in the amount of $475,000 were paid.

10. Fifty thousand dollars was transferred to the General Fund from the Trust Fund.

11. The City Council authorized the write-off of $30,000 in uncollected property taxes.

Required:

A. Prepare entries in general journal form to record the transactions for the year ended December 31, 1996.

B. Prepare a preclosing trial balance for the General Fund as of December 31, 1996.

C. Prepare the necessary closing entries for the year ended December 31, 1996.

D. Prepare a balance sheet and a statement of revenue, expenditures, and other changes in fund balance for the General Fund for the year ended December 31, 1996.

Problem 20-6

Hunnington Township's adjusted trial balance for the General Fund at the close of its fiscal year ended June 30, 1996, is presented here:

Hunnington Township
General Fund Trial Balance
June 30, 1996

Cash	$ 11,000	
Property tax receivable—current (Note 1)	82,000	
Estimated uncollectible taxes—current		$ 1,500
Property tax receivable—delinquent	25,000	
Estimated uncollectible taxes—delinquent		16,500
Accounts receivable (Note 1)	40,000	
Allowance for uncollectible accounts		4,000
Due from internal service fund (Note 5)	50,000	
Expenditures (Note 2)	755,000	
Encumbrances	37,000	
Revenue (Note 3)		60,000
Due to enterprise fund (Note 5)		10,000
Vouchers payable		20,000
Reserve for encumbrances—prior year		44,000
Reserve for encumbrances		37,000
Surplus receipts (Note 4)		7,000
Appropriations		720,000
Unreserved fund balance		80,000
	$1,000,000	$1,000,000

Note 1: The current tax roll and accounts receivable, recorded on the accrual basis as sources of revenue, amounted to $500,000 and $200,000, respectively.

Note 2: Includes $42,500 paid during the fiscal year in settlement of all purchase orders outstanding at the beginning of the fiscal year.

Note 3: Represents the difference between the budgeted (estimated) revenue of $700,000 and the actual revenue realized during the fiscal year.

Note 4: Represents the proceeds from the sale of equipment damaged by fire. The equipment originally cost $40,000 and had been held for 80% of its useful life prior to the fire.

Note 5: The interfund payable and receivable resulted from cash advances (loans) to and from the respective funds.

Required:

A. Prepare a statement of revenue, expenditures, and other changes in fund balance.

B. Prepare a balance sheet for the General Fund at June 30, 1996.

(AICPA adapted)

Problem 20-7

The January 1, 1995, trial balance, the calendar-year 1995 budget, and the 1995 transactions of the City of Roseburg are presented here:

City of Roseburg
Trial Balance
January 1, 1995

	DEBIT	CREDIT
Cash	$155,450	
Certificates of deposit	200,000	
Accounts receivable	28,675	
Supplies inventory	37,600	
Due from federal government	58,000	
Property taxes receivable	75,600	
Allowance for uncollectible taxes		$ 32,150
Vouchers payable		181,000
Unreserved fund balance		226,075
Reserve for inventory		37,600
Reserve for encumbrances		78,500
	$555,325	$555,325

City of Roseburg
Budget for General Fund
Calendar Year 1995

Estimated revenue	
City vehicle and retail license fees	$ 252,000
Property taxes	1,448,000
City sales tax	327,000
Collections for trash service	153,000
Sale of city-owned property	88,000
Total estimated revenue	2,268,000

Appropriations	
General government	261,000
Public safety and security	875,000
Health and welfare	434,000
Recreation and parks	126,000
Street maintenance	367,000
Sanitation	162,000
Total appropriations	2,225,000
Excess of revenues over appropriations	43,000
Transfer from Water and Sewer Fund	118,000
Less payments (transfers) to Debt Service Funds	(55,000)
Excess of revenue and fund transfers to General Fund over appropriations and fund transfers out of General Fund	$ 106,000

Transactions of the City of Roseburg that affected the General Fund during the year are summarized below:

1. The City Council approved the budget and it was recorded.
2. Orders for goods and services were issued for a total of $1,202,000 during the year.
3. Goods and services were delivered against all orders placed with a total invoice amount of $1,165,600. Of this, $80,000 was for orders placed in the prior year.
4. The City accepted a low bid of $78,000 for a new street sweeper for the sanitation department. A purchase order was issued.
5. The City received $92,500 from the sale of an old street sweeper and one obsolete fire engine at public auction. The street sweeper cost $60,000 7 years ago, at which time it was estimated to have a useful life of 10 years. The fire engine cost $200,000 8 years ago, at which time it was estimated to have a useful life of 12 years.
6. Property tax statements were issued. The tax levy was 8% of the assessed valuation of $18,500,000. An estimated 2% of the tax levy will be uncollectible.
7. Payment was received from the federal government. This was a grant to be used for upgrading sanitation department equipment.
8. The amount of $55,000 was transferred to the Debt Service Fund for the payment of interest on the outstanding bond issue.
9. The city billed residents for trash service. Total billings amounted to $155,675.
10. Property taxes totaling $1,438,455 were collected, of which $34,200 was past-due collections from the prior year; $18,250 of past-due taxes was charged off as uncollectible.
11. Wages paid to employees during the year amounted to $998,765.
12. City retail establishments remitted a total of $333,650 in sales tax collections for the year.
13. Other cash receipts during the year were:

Vehicle license fees and parking fines	$ 98,682
Retail license fees	130,000
For trash services (including $28,675 due at end of prior year)	148,720
Transfer from Water and Sewer Fund	118,000

14. Cash purchases of printed forms and other office supplies for the year amounted to $57,680.
15. The street sweeper was delivered and an invoice for $78,000 plus freight charges of $1,280 was received. The invoice was approved for payment and a check issued.

16. Checks were issued in payment of outstanding vouchers totaling $1,207,100.
17. End-of-year activities: (adjustments)
    Supplies Inventory 12/31/95: $38,250
    Accrued interest on CDs at 5%

The city uses the purchase method to account for supplies expenditures.

Required:

A. Enter the opening trial balance data in T accounts.

B. Prepare journal entries for the year's transactions. Do not include entries for year-end adjustments. Post entries to T accounts.

C. Prepare a preclosing trial balance.

D. Prepare journal entries to adjust the Supplies Inventory and record the interest on the CDs.

E. Prepare journal entries to close the revenue, expenditures, and encumbrance accounts.

F. Prepare a comparative balance sheet for 1994–1995.

G. Prepare a statement of revenue, expenditures, and other changes in fund balance for 1995.

Problem 20-8

The following summary of transactions was taken from the accounts of the Madras School District General Fund before the books were closed for the fiscal year ended June 30, 1996:

	POSTCLOSING BALANCES JUNE 30, 1995	PRECLOSING BALANCES JUNE 30, 1996
Cash	$400,000	$ 700,000
Property tax receivable	150,000	170,000
Estimated uncollectible taxes	(40,000)	(70,000)
Estimated revenue		3,000,000
Expenditures		2,842,000
Expenditures—prior year		
Encumbrances		91,000
	$510,000	$6,733,000
Vouchers payable	$ 80,000	$ 408,000
Due to other funds	210,000	142,000
Reserve for encumbrances	60,000	91,000
Unreserved fund balance	160,000	182,000
Revenue from taxes		2,800,000
Miscellaneous revenue		130,000
Appropriations		2,980,000
	$510,000	$6,733,000

Additional information:

1. Property taxes in the amount of $2,870,000 were assessed for the year. Taxes collected during the year totaled $2,810,000.

2. An analysis of the transactions in the vouchers payable account for the year ended June 30, 1996, follows:

	DEBIT (CREDIT)
Current expenditures	$(2,700,000)
Expenditures for prior year	(58,000)
Vouchers for payment to other funds	(210,000)
Cash payments during year	2,640,000
Net change	$ (328,000)

3. During the year the General Fund was billed $142,000 for services performed on its behalf by other city funds.

4. On May 2, 1996, commitment documents were issued for the purchase of new textbooks at a cost of $91,000.

Required:

On the basis of the data presented, reconstruct the original detailed journal entries that were required to record all transactions for the fiscal year ended June 30, 1996, including the recording of the current year's budget. Do not prepare closing entries at June 30, 1996.

(AICPA adapted)

21

INTRODUCTION TO ACCOUNTING FOR STATE AND LOCAL GOVERNMENTAL UNITS

The lifestyles and well-being of all people are significantly affected by the activities of both profit-oriented enterprises and nonbusiness organizations. Of these, probably none is more important and pervasive in its impact on our daily lives than government. Today there are more than 70 thousand state and local governmental units, which employ more than 20 million people and collect annual revenues in excess of 500 billion dollars. The well-publicized problems of some city governments have attracted great interest and concern in the past. These problems focused attention on the need for (among other things) adequate accounting and financial reporting practices by cities and other governmental units as a basis for evaluating the extent of and the suggested solutions for such problems.

GENERALLY ACCEPTED GOVERNMENTAL ACCOUNTING STANDARDS

Like generally accepted accounting standards for profit-oriented enterprises, standards of accounting and reporting for governmental units are in a constant state of evolution and change. The pioneer organization in promulgating standards of accounting and reporting for state and local governmental units was the Municipal Finance Officers Association (MFOA). Such standards were formulated by its National Committee on Governmental Accounting, which in 1974 was reconstituted as the National Council on Governmental Accounting (NCGA). In 1979 the NCGA issued *Statement 1: Government and Financial Reporting Principles*. Until 1984 this and subsequent statements and interpretations of the NCGA along with the AICPA Industry Audit Guide: *Audits of State and Local Governmental Units* (1974) as amended by subsequently issued AICPA Statements of Position constituted the primary sources of generally accepted governmental accounting standards.

In 1984 a separate Governmental Accounting Standards Board (GASB) was established under the oversight of the Financial Accounting Foundation, which is the same foundation that oversees the activities of the Financial Accounting Standards Board (FASB). The GASB is composed of two full-time and three part-time members supported by an administrative, technical, and research staff. Funding for the GASB is separate from that of the FASB.

The GASB is the body responsible for establishing financial accounting and reporting standards for governments. With its first pronouncement, *Authoritative Status of NCGA Pronouncements and AICPA Industry Audit Guide,* the GASB endorsed prior statements and interpretations of the NCGA as well as the accounting and financial reporting standards embodied in the 1974 *AICPA Industry Audit Guide* as amended. Pronouncements of the GASB include GASB Statements (GASBS), GASB Interpretations (GASBI), GASB Concept Statements (GASBCS), and GASB Technical Bulletins (GASBTB). Pronouncements of the GASB are codified in the GASB's *Codification of Governmental Accounting and Financial Reporting Standards* (cited as *GASB Cod.*). This codification is now updated annually.

Hierarchy of Generally Accepted Reporting Standards for Governmental Entities

The hierarchy used to establish generally accepted reporting standards for all state and local governmental-owned entities, including governmental owned colleges and universities, healthcare providers, and utilities, is included in *Statement of Auditing Standards No. 68,* "The Meaning of 'Presents Fairly in Accordance with Generally Accepted Accounting Principles' in the Independent Auditors Report." The Hierarchy lists the priority sequence of pronouncements that an entity should look to for accounting and reporting guidance and may be summarized as follows:

1. First level of priority
   A. GASB Statements and Interpretations.
   B. AICPA and FASB pronouncements that have *specifically been made applicable* to state and local governmental entities *by GASB Statements or Interpretations.*
2. Second level of priority
   A. GASB Technical Bulletins.
   B. AICPA Industry Audit and Accounting Guides made applicable to state and local governmental entities by the AICPA *and cleared by the GASB.*
3. Third level of priority
   A. AICPA AcSec Practice bulletins if specifically made applicable to state and local governmental entities *and cleared by the GASB.*
4. Fourth level of priority
   A. Implementation Guides (Q & A's) published by the GASB staff.
   B. Practices widely prevalent in state and local government.

5. Fifth level of priority
    A. Other accounting literature including
        1. GASB Concepts Statements
        2. AICPA and FASB pronouncements when not made specifically applicable to state and local governmental entities.

This hierarchy distinguishes the authority of the GASB and the FASB with regard to state and local governmental entities and implements the jurisdictional determination of the FAF trustees that the GASB and the FASB should each have primary responsibility for setting standards for entities under their jurisdiction but that pronouncements of one Board should not be mandatory for entities under the jurisdiction of the other Board *unless designated as such by the primary Board.*

Current Developments

The discussion that follows is based on existing GASB accounting and reporting standards. The GASB is currently completing a reexamination of the financial reporting model for governmental entities that may result in significant changes to the existing model. The financial reporting project of the GASB is described at the end of this chapter.

THE STRUCTURE OF GOVERNMENTAL ACCOUNTING

A governmental unit, although a separate *legal* entity, consists of a number of separate fund and other *accounting* entities. The GASB recommends the use of seven different types of fund entities and two different account group entities for accounting and reporting purposes as follows:[1]

Fund Entities
Governmental Funds
(1) *The General Fund*—to account for all financial resources except those required to be accounted for in another fund.
(2) *Special Revenue Funds*—to account for the proceeds of specific revenue sources (other than expendable trusts, or for major capital projects) that are legally restricted to expenditure for specified purposes.
(3) *Capital Projects Funds*—to account for financial resources to be used for the acquisition or construction of major capital facilities (other than those financed by proprietary funds and trust funds).
(4) *Debt Service Funds*—to account for the accumulation of resources for, and the payment of, general long-term debt principal and interest.

Proprietary Funds
(5) *Enterprise Funds*—to account for operations (a) that are financed and operated in a manner similar to private business enterprises—where the intent of the governing body is that the costs (expenses, including depreciation) of

---

[1] *GASB Cod.* Sections 1300–1500.

providing goods or services to the general public on a continuing basis be financed or recovered primarily through user charges; or (b) where the governing body has decided that periodic determination of revenues earned, expenses incurred, and/or net income is appropriate for capital maintenance, public policy, management control, accountability, or other purposes.

(6) *Internal Service Funds*—to account for the financing of goods or services provided by one department or agency to other departments or agencies of the governmental unit, or to other governmental units, on a cost-reimbursement basis.

Fiduciary Funds

(7) *Trust and Agency Funds*—to account for assets held by a governmental unit in a trustee capacity or as an agent for individuals, private organizations, other governmental units, and/or other funds. These include (a) Expendable Trust Funds, (b) Nonexpendable Trust Funds, (c) Pension Trust Funds, and (d) Agency Funds. Expendable trust funds and agency funds are accounted for in essentially the same manner as governmental funds. Nonexpendable trust funds and pension trust funds are accounted for in essentially the same manner as proprietary funds.

Account Group Entities

(1) *The General Fixed Assets Account Group*—to account for all fixed assets of a governmental unit other than those fixed assets related to specific proprietary funds or trust funds. Fixed assets related to specific proprietary funds or trust funds should be accounted for through those funds. All other fixed assets of a governmental unit should be accounted for through the General Fixed Assets Account Group.

(2) *The General Long-term Obligation Account Group*—to account for all unmatured general obligation liabilities of a governmental unit other than long-term liabilities of proprietary funds and trust funds. Long-term liabilities of proprietary funds and trust funds should be accounted for through those funds. All other unmatured general obligation long-term liabilities of the governmental unit, including special assessment debt for which the government is obligated in some manner, should be accounted for through the General Long-term Obligation Account Group.

As indicated, the three major classifications of accounting entities utilized in governmental accounting and reporting are (1) Governmental (Expendable) Fund Entities, (2) Proprietary (Nonexpendable) Fund Entities, and (3) Account Group Entities. Fiduciary funds are classified either as governmental (expendable) funds or as proprietary (nonexpendable) funds.

Expendable fund entities (see Chapter 20) of a governmental unit are designated as Governmental Funds. The accounting and reporting emphasis for these types of funds is on the inflow, outflow, and unexpended balance of net financial resources and on compliance with detailed legal provisions that specify the types of revenue to be raised and the purposes for which financial resources may be expended. The different types of governmental funds are distinguished by the sources of their financial resources or the types of activities financed by the resources of the fund.

Government operations that are similar to commercial business operations such as a water utility, an electric utility, or a central garage or central computer facility are accounted for in proprietary fund entities. Financial accounting and reporting for these entities closely parallel accounting and reporting for profit-oriented enterprises. Thus both current and fixed assets and current and noncurrent liabilities are accounted for in the records of proprietary fund entities. In addition, revenue, expenses (including depreciation and amortization expense), and net income are determined and reported for these fund entities.

The third classification of accounting entity used in accounting for governmental units is the account group entity. The two account group entities are not fund entities because they do not involve financial resources. Rather they represent self-balancing sets of accounts that are used to account for the general fixed assets and the unmatured general long-term obligations of the governmental unit, the accounting for which is excluded from the governmental (expendable) fund entities. These self-balancing account groups are maintained for financial reporting and control purposes.

Each different type of fund entity and account group entity will now be discussed in more detail.

GOVERNMENTAL FUND ENTITIES

The General Fund

All revenues and expenditures of a governmental unit not accounted for in other governmental or proprietary funds are accounted for in the General Fund. The variety of revenue sources available to the General Fund and the variety of functions and activities financed by the resources of the General Fund are ordinarily more numerous than are those for any other fund entity. Accounting entries and reports for the General Fund of a governmental unit were illustrated in Chapter 20.

Special Revenue Funds

Special Revenue Funds are used to account for the proceeds of specific revenue sources that are required by statute, charter provisions, or local ordinance to be used to finance particular functions or activities of the governmental unit. Examples of Special Revenue Funds are those established to finance the operations of special facilities, such as parks or museums, or of particular activities, such as the licensing and regulation of professions. Although the sources of revenue for Special Revenue Funds in general are similar to those for the General Fund, a typical Special Revenue Fund will have only a single revenue source such as a single tax, or specified portion thereof, or a license fee, the proceeds of which must be used for a specific purpose, function, or activity.

Accounting entries and financial reports for Special Revenue Funds are analogous in all respects to the accounting entries and financial reports for the General Fund illustrated in Chapter 20, and no further illustration will be presented here.

In Special Revenue Funds, as in the General Fund, (1) a budget is established and recorded in the accounts, (2) the encumbrance process is used to control budgeted expenditures, (3) fixed assets acquired by the expenditure of Special Revenue Fund resources are not reported as assets of the Special Revenue Fund but rather are recorded and reported in the General Fixed Assets Account Group, (4) depreciation of such assets is not recorded or reported by the Special Revenue Fund, and (5) the liability for long-term debt, the proceeds of which have been received and recorded by a Special Revenue Fund, is not recorded or reported as a liability of the Special Revenue Fund but is recorded and reported in the General Long-term Obligation Account Group.

Capital Projects Funds

Capital Projects Funds are established to account for the resources used by a governmental unit to acquire major capital facilities. Major capital facilities are permanent facilities such as buildings, streets and highways, storm drain systems, and sewer systems that have relatively long lives. The primary purpose of accounting for the acquisition of major capital facilities in a separate Capital Projects Fund is to be able to show that the resources designated for such purposes were used for authorized purposes only and that any unexpended balances of such resources or resource deficits have been treated properly. Resources for the acquisition of major capital facilities include (1) proceeds of long-term debt issues, (2) grants or payments from other governmental units and agencies, (3) funds from private sources, (4) transfers of current revenues from other governmental funds, (5) special assessments (to be discussed later), and (6) other sources.

Not all major capital facilities acquisitions are accounted for in Capital Project Funds. Construction and acquisition of capital facilities financed by Enterprise Funds are accounted for in the records of those funds. In addition, in some instances the resources of the General Fund or a Special Revenue Fund are appropriated for the acquisition of a major capital facility. So long as such acquisitions do not involve the issuance of general obligation long-term debt securities, they may be accounted for in the fund that appropriates the resources rather than in a separate Capital Projects Fund.

The Operations of a Capital Projects Fund may extend over several accounting periods. Separate Capital Projects Funds are ordinarily created for each major capital project. When the project is completed, the associated Capital Projects Fund is closed out.

To illustrate accounting and reporting procedures for a Capital Projects Fund, assume that Model City authorizes the construction of a combination library and civic center that will be financed from the following sources:

General obligation bonds	$2,000,000
State government grant	1,000,000
Total authorized for construction	$3,000,000

Construction is to begin on September 1, 1995, and the bonds are to be issued on October 1, 1995.

Entries—1995 Entries to record the transactions of the Capital Projects Fund during 1995 are summarized and explained as follows:

(1) Due from State Government   1,000,000
   Revenue   1,000,000
     To open Capital Projects Fund.

There is no budget entry to incorporate estimated revenue and appropriations into the formal accounting records. Sources of estimated revenues for a capital project are few and predictable in amount. Thus, it would serve no useful purpose to incorporate budgeted revenue into the formal accounting system. Likewise, an appropriation account is not required as a formal control device, since the resources of the fund can be expended only for the single authorized project for which it was created. Thus, the fund balance itself serves as an adequate measure of and control over unexpended appropriation authority.

(2) Cash   2,100,000
   Bond Issue Proceeds   2,100,000
     To record receipt of proceeds from issuance of long-term debt securities.

When bonds are issued at a premium, the difference between the bond issue proceeds and the par value of the bonds represents an interest adjustment and is usually transferred to the Debt Service Fund that is used to service the principal and interest on the debt.

(3) Transfer to Debt Service Fund   100,000
   Cash   100,000
     To record transfer of cash in amount of bond premium to Debt Service Fund.
(4) Certificates of Deposit   1,000,000
   Cash   1,000,000
     To record investment of excess cash in temporary investments.
(5) Encumbrances   2,500,000
   Reserve for Encumbrances   2,500,000
     To record encumbrance created by signing construction contract with Lloyd-
     Jones Construction Company.
(6) Cash   750,000
   Due from State Government   750,000
     To record collection of part of grant from State Government
(7) Expenditures   200,000
   Vouchers Payable   200,000
     To record unencumbered expenditures for architect and legal fees.
(8) Reserve for Encumbrances   1,300,000
   Encumbrances   1,300,000
  Expenditures   1,300,000
   Contacts Payable   1,300,000
     To record approved contract billings on construction completed to date and to
     remove encumbrance thereon.
(9) Vouchers Payable   150,000
  Contracts Payable   1,300,000
   Cash   1,450,000
     To record payment of liabilities.
(10) Interest Receivable   12,500
   Revenue   12,500
     To record interest earned on certificate of deposit to December 31, 1995.

The treatment of interest earnings on temporary investments depends on legal provisions or established policy. One alternative would be to transfer such earnings to the Debt Service Fund. A second alternative is to treat such earnings as revenue of the Capital Projects Fund. The latter treatment is justified on the grounds that resources allocated to the project are restricted exclusively to that project and, accordingly, any earnings on such resources are also restricted resources and should not be diverted to any other use.

December 31, 1995, Trial Balance The December 31, 1995, trial balance for the Capital Projects Fund presented below reflects the transactions recorded in 1995.

	DEBIT	CREDIT
Cash	$ 300,000	
Interest receivable	12,500	
Certificates of deposit	1,000,000	
Due from state government	250,00	
Encumbrances	1,200,000	
Expenditures	1,500,000	
Vouchers payable		$ 50,000
Contracts payable		–0–
Reserve for encumbrances		1,200,000
Unreserved fund balance		–0–
Revenue		1,012,500
Bond issue proceeds		2,100,000
Transfer to debt service fund	100,000	
	$4,362,500	$4,362,500

CLOSING ENTRIES—DECEMBER 31, 1995

(11) Bond Issue Proceeds	2,100,000	
Revenue	1,012,500	
Transfer to Debt Service Fund		100,000
Unreserved Fund Balance		3,012,500
To close revenue and related accounts to unreserved fund balance.		
(12) Unreserved Fund Balance	2,700,000	
Encumbrances		1,200,000
Expenditures		1,500,000
To close expenditures and encumbrances accounts to unreserved fund balance.		

Since no budget accounts were formally recorded in the accounting records, there are no budget accounts to be closed at year-end. Hence, the nominal accounts are closed directly to the unreserved fund balance. As was true in the General Fund, the closing of the balance of the encumbrances account against the unreserved fund balance has the same effect as if an entry were made at year-end to reclassify an equal amount of the unreserved fund balance to a reserve for encumbrances.

At the end of each year, entries will also be made in the General Fixed Asset Account Group to record the cost of construction in progress represented by expenditures incurred by the Capital Projects Fund during the year.

Financial Statements At the end of the first year, a balance sheet and a statement of revenue, expenditures, and changes in fund balance would be prepared. In addition, a schedule comparing budgeted and actual revenues may be prepared if useful information is provided thereby. A schedule of expenditures and encumbrances compared with appropriations is not necessary, since all expenditures of a Capital Projects Fund are for capital outlays that relate to a single appropriation or authorization.

Completion of Project   Entries in 1996 to record the completion of the project are presented and explained below.

(13)	Encumbrances	1,200,000	
	Unreserved Fund Balance		1,200,000
	To reestablish the contract encumbrance closed out at end of previous year.		

Since Capital Projects Funds are project-oriented rather than period-oriented, there is no need, as there is in accounting for the General Fund or a Special Revenue Fund, to identify expenditures with appropriation authority of a particular year. Thus, expenditures for amounts encumbered in prior years are not segregated from other expenditures of the current year. The effect of this entry is the same as if the amount in the reserve for encumbrance account was restored to the reserved fund balance and encumbrances were then reestablished for outstanding commitments at the beginning of the year, that is, as if the following two entries were recorded:

	Reserve for Encumbrances	1,200,000	
	Unreserved Fund Balance		1,200,000
	Encumbrances	1,200,000	
	Reserve for Encumbrances		1,200,000
(14)	Expenditures	225,000	
	Vouchers Payable		225,000
	To record unencumbered expenditures.		
(15)	Cash	250,000	
	Due from State Government		250,000
	To record receipt of cash payment from State Government.		
(16)	Cash	1,020,000	
	Certificate of Deposit		1,000,000
	Interest Receivable		12,500
	Revenue		7,500
	To record redemption of certificate of deposit.		
(17)	Reserve for Encumbrances	1,200,000	
	Encumbrances		1,200,000
	Expenditures	1,200,000	
	Contracts Payable		1,200,000
	To record approved final contract billings on completed construction and to remove remaining contract encumbrance.		
(18)	Contracts Payable	1,200,000	
	Contracts Payable—Retained Percentage		125,000
	Cash		1,075,000
	To record payment of contract except for retention of 5% of the contract price pending inspection of completed project.		
(19)	Vouchers Payable	275,000	
	Cash		275,000
	To record payment of liabilities.		

December 31, 1996, Trial Balance The preclosing trial balance of the Capital Projects Fund on December 31, 1996, is presented below:

	DEBIT	CREDIT
Cash	$ 220,00	
Expenditures	1,425,000	
Contracts payable—retained percentage		$ 125,000
Unreserved fund balance		1,512,500
Revenue		7,500
	$1,645,000	$1,645,000

CLOSING ENTRY—DECEMBER 31,1996

(20)	Unreserved Fund Balance	1,417,500	
	Revenue	7,500	
	Expenditures		1,425,000
	To close nominal accounts to unreserved fund balance.		

Financial Statements A comparative balance sheet and a comparative statement of revenue, expenditures, and other changes in fund balance for the years ended December 31, 1996, and December 31, 1995, are presented in Illustration 21-1 and Illustration 21-2.

Closing Out a Capital Projects Fund Although the cost of a capital project should equal the resources provided for its acquisition, actual expenditures normally are less than, or they exceed, the project authorization. If an unexpended fund balance

ILLUSTRATION 21-1
Model City
Library and Civic Center Capital Projects Fund
Balance Sheet December 31, 1996, and December 31, 1995

ASSETS	1996	1995
Cash	$220,000	$ 300,000
Interest Receivable	–0–	12,500
Certificates of Deposit	–0–	1,000,000
Due from State Government	–0–	250,000
Total Assets	$220,000	$1,562,500
LIABILITIES AND FUND BALANCE		
Vouchers Payable	$ –0–	$ 50,000
Contracts Payable—Retained Percentage	125,000	–0–
Total Liabilities	125,000	50,000
Fund Balance		
Unreserved	95,000	312,500
Reserve for Encumbrances	–0–	1,200,000
Total Fund Balance	95,000	1,512,500
Total	$220,000	$1,562,500

ILLUSTRATION 21-2
Model City
Library and Civic Center Capital Projects Fund
Statement of Revenue, Expenditures, and Other Changes
in Fund Balance for Years Ended December 31, 1996, and December 31, 1995

	1996	1995	CUMULATIVE
Fund Balance—January 1	$1,512,500	$ –0–	$ –0–
Revenue	7,500	1,012,500	1,020,000
Debt Issue Proceeds	–0–	2,100,000	2,100,000
Total Resources Available	1,520,000	3,112,500	3,120,000
Expenditures	1,425,000	1,500,000	2,925,000
Operating Transfers Out	–0–	100,000	100,000
Total	1,425,000	1,600,000	3,025,000
Fund Balance—December 31	$ 95,000	$1,512,500	$ 95,000

remains after the completion of the project, it should be distributed to the contributors of project resources in proportion to their contribution. For example, unless legal or policy decisions dictate otherwise, the capital projects fund of Model City illustrated above would be closed out as follows:

(21) Contracts Payable—Retained Percentage	125,000	
Cash		125,000
To record final payment on contract.		
(22) Transfer to Debt Service Fund	(1) 63,333	
Expenditures	(2) 31,667	
Cash		95,000
To record distribution of Fund Balance.		

(1) ($2,000,000 ÷ $3,000,000) × $95,000 = $63,333
(2) ($1,000,000 ÷ $3,000,000) × $95,000 = $31,667

For financial reporting purposes, transfers to other funds within a governmental unit are distinguished from expenditures. The return of $31,667 to the state government is treated as an expenditure because it reduces the financial resources of Model City.

When construction is completed, the assets acquired with Capital Projects Fund resources are recorded at cost in the appropriate accounts (land, building, etc.) of the General Fixed Asset Account Group.

Debt Service Funds

Debt Service Funds are created to account for the accumulation of financial resources that will be utilized to make interest and principal payments on general obligation long-term debt. General obligation long-term debt consists of bonds, notes, or warrants that are secured by the general credit and revenue-raising powers of the governmental unit as a whole, rather than by the resources of a specific fund entity. Long-term debt that is the specific obligation and that will be paid out of the resources of an Enterprise Fund is a liability of that fund, and the accumulation of resources for its payment will be accounted for in that fund, rather than in a Debt Service Fund. Unmatured long-term debt that will be redeemed with the resources of the Debt Service Fund is not recorded or reported as a liability of the Debt Service Fund. Rather, the liability for general obligation long-term debt is recorded and reported in the General Long-term Obligation Account Group. Payments of bond principal and interest are expenditures of (rather than reduction of liabilities of) the Debt Service Fund.

General obligation bonds may be serial bonds or term bonds. The principal of a term bond is repaid in one lump sum at a specified maturity date. The total principal of serial bonds is repaid in a specified number of annual (and usually equal) installments.

Debt Service Funds are usually financed by one or more of the following sources of revenue:

General property tax

Sales tax or other specified tax revenues

Transfers of general fund revenues

Special assessments (to be discussed later)

Revenue from the investment of debt service fund resources

It is generally recommended that the debt service for general obligation long-term debt be accounted for in as few Debt Service Funds as possible. However, for purposes of illustrating the difference between the debt service for serial bonds and for term bonds, two Debt Service Funds—Land Acquisition Serial Bonds Debt Service Fund and Library and Civic Center Term Bonds Debt Service Fund—will be illustrated for Model City.

Serial Bonds Accounting for the accumulation of resources and payment of annual installments of principal and interest on serial bonds is relatively simple. To illustrate, assume that in 1992, Model City issued $1,800,000 in 8% serial bonds, $300,000 of which come due on July 1 of each year beginning July 1, 1993. On January 1, 1995, there is $1,200,000 in principal on these bonds outstanding, and $300,000 in principal and $96,000 in interest will come due on July 1, 1995. Annual installments of principal are financed from general property tax revenues, and annual interest payments are financed by the appropriation of resources of the General Fund. The trial balance of the Land Acquisition Serial Bonds Debt Service Fund on January 1, 1995, is as follows:

	DEBIT	CREDIT
Cash	$3,000	
Taxes receivable	2,000	
Fund balance		$5,000
Total	$5,000	$5,000

Transactions of the fund for 1995 are summarized in general journal form below.

(1)	Estimated Revenue	315,000	
	Authorized transfer from the General Fund	96,000	
	Appropriations		396,000
	Fund Balance		15,000
	To record budgeted revenue, transfers, and appropriations for current year.		
(2)	Property tax receivable	320,000	
	Estimated Uncollectible Tax		4,000
	Revenue		316,000
	To record general property tax levy earmarked for debt service on serial bonds.		
(3)	Due from the General Fund	96,000	
	Transfer from General Fund		96,000
	To record amount of resources authorized for transfer from General Fund during current period.		
(4)	Cash	318,000	
	Property Tax Receivable		318,000
	To record collection of property taxes.		
(5)	Cash	96,000	
	Due from the General Fund		96,000
	To record receipt of cash transfer from General Fund.		
(6)	Expenditures—Principal	300,000	
	Expenditures—Interest	96,000	
	Cash		396,000
	To record payment of interest and principal.		
(7)	Revenue	316,000	
	Estimated Revenue		315,000
	Fund Balance		1,000
	Transfer from General Fund	96,000	
	Authorized Transfer from General Fund		96,000
	Appropriations	396,000	
	Expenditures—Principal		300,000
	Expenditures—Interest		96,000
	To close nominal and budget account balances at year-end.		
(8)	Estimated Uncollectible Taxes	4,000	
	Property Tax Receivable		4,000
	To record write-off of taxes authorized by City Council.		

The postclosing trial balance for this fund on December 31, 1995, is as follows:

	DEBIT	CREDIT
Cash	$21,000	
Fund balance		$21,000
Total	$21,000	$21,000

A statement of revenue, expenditures, and other changes in fund balance is presented in Illustration 21-3.

Terms Bonds Accounting for the debt service of term bonds is more complicated than accounting for serial bonds. Debt Service Funds for term bonds require annual

ILLUSTRATION 21-3
Model City
Land Acquisition Serial Bonds Debt Service Fund
Statement of Revenue, Expenditures, and Other
Changes in Fund Balance for
Year Ended December 31, 1995

Revenue—General Property Tax	$316,000
Transfer from General Fund	96,000
Total Revenue and Transfers from Other Funds	412,000
Expenditures	
Redemption of Serial Bonds	300,000
Interest on Bonds	96,000
Total Expenditures	396,000
Excess (Deficiency) to Fund Balance	16,000
Fund Balance—January 1	5,000
Fund Balance—December 31	$ 21,000

additions to fund resources that, with compound interest, will provide the total amount of bond principal by the maturity date of the bonds. In addition, the Debt Service Fund for a term bond issue must provide for the payment of periodic interest on the bonds.

To illustrate, assume that the $2,000,000 in bonds issued on October 1, 1995, to finance the construction of the Library and Civic Center of Model City were 8% bonds that mature five years after their issue date. The calculation of the required annual additions to the Debt Service Fund presented in Illustration 21-4 is based on the assumption that fund resources can be invested at an average annual return of 10%. The required annual principal addition of $327,595 is calculated by dividing the term bond principal of $2,000,000 by the amount of an ordinary annuity of $1.00 for five periods at 10% ($2,000,000 ÷ 6.1051 = $327,595). Required annual earnings are based on the planned 10% return on invested fund resources.

The calculation in Illustration 21-4 does not take into account the $100,000 premium on the issue of the bonds that is transferred by the Capital Projects Fund to the Debt Service Fund in 1995. However, if the fund balance of a Debt Service Fund exceeds actuarial requirements, the excess is ordinarily carried forward without adjustment until the final addition to the fund is made. It is assumed that annual additions to the Library and Civic Center Term Bonds Debt Service Fund are derived from an earmarked portion of the general property tax assessment.

Transactions—1995 Transactions of the fund in 1995 are summarized in general journal form as follows:

(1) Cash	100,000	
Transfer from Capital Projects Fund		100,000
To record transfer of cash from Capital Projects Fund in amount of premium received on bond issue proceeds.		

ILLUSTRATION 21-4
Debt Service Fund—Term Bonds
Calculation of Annual Required Additions and Annual
Required Earnings for $2,000,000 Library and Civic Center Bond Issue

YEAR	REQUIRED PRINCIPAL ADDITIONS	REQUIRED EARNINGS	REQUIRED INCREASE IN FUND BALANCE	REQUIRED FUND BALANCE
1996	(1) $ 327,595		$ 327,595	$ 327,595
1997	327,595	(2) $ 32,760	(3) 360,355	(4) 687,950
1998	327,595	(5) 68,795	396,390	1,084,340
1999	327,595	108,434	436,029	1,520,369
2000	327,595	152,036	479,631	2,000,000
	$1,637,975	$362,025	$2,000,000	

Required Principal Addition	$ 327,595
Required Interest Addition (.08 × $2,000,000)	160,000
Required Annual Addition	$ 487,595

(1) $2,000,000 ÷ 6.10510 = $327,595.
(2) $327,595 × .10 = $32,759.50.
(3) $327,595 + $32,760 = $360,355.
(4) $327,595 + $360,355 = $687,950.
(5) $687,950 × .10 = $68,795.

Had there been no transfer of cash to the Debt Service Fund by the Capital Projects Fund, no entries would have been required in the Debt Service Fund until the 1996 fiscal year.

(2)	Investments	100,000	
	Cash		100,000
	To record investment of cash in a certificate of deposit.		
(3)	Interest Receivable	4,000	
	Interest Income		4,000
	To accrue interest receivable on December 31, 1995.		
(4)	Interest Income	4,000	
	Transfer from Capital Projects Fund	100,000	
	Fund Balance		104,000
	To close nominal accounts to fund balance.		

The postclosing trial balance on December 31, 1995, is as follows:

	DEBIT	CREDIT
Investments	$100,000	
Interest receivable	4,000	
Fund balance		$104,000
Total	$104,000	$104,000

Transactions—1996 Revenue and expenditure transactions for 1996 are summarized in Illustration 21-6. At the end of 1996, the postclosing trial balance for the fund is as follows:

	DEBIT	CREDIT
Cash	$ 33,000	
Interest receivable	4,000	
Property taxes receivable	6,000	
Investments	400,000	
Estimated uncollectable taxes		$ 1,000
Fund balance		442,000
Total	$443,000	$443,000

Transactions—1997 Transactions for 1997 are summarized in general journal form as follows.

(1) Required Additions 487,595
    Required Earnings 32,760
        Fund Balance   520,355
        To record budgeted additions and budgeted income on invested resources of fund for current year (see Illustration 21-4).

(2) Fund Balance 160,000
    Appropriations   160,000
        To record budgeted expenditures for bond interest for current year.

(3) Property Tax Receivable 503,000
    Estimated Uncollectible Taxes   15,000
    Revenue   488,000
        To record property tax levy earmarked for debt service on Library and Civic Center Term Bonds.

(4) Cash 485,000
    Property Tax Receivable   485,000
        To record collection of property taxes.

(5) Investments 360,000
    Premium on Investments 15,000
        Cash   375,000
        To record investment of fund resources.

Debt service fund investments are closely regulated by law and are usually restricted to quality government and municipal securities. When such investments are expected to be held to maturity, they are recorded at their par value and premium or discount is recorded in a ***separate*** account and amortized by reducing or increasing investment income over the remaining life of the investment.

(6) Cash 26,000
    Interest Receivable   4,000
    Interest Income   22,000
        To record receipt of interest on investments.

(7) Expenditures 160,000
    Interest Payable   160,000
        To record expenditures for current year's interest on bonds.

(8) Estimated Uncollectible Taxes 13,000
    Property Tax Receivable   13,000
        To record write-off of property taxes authorized by City Council.

(9) Interest Payable		160,000	
Cash			160,000
To record payment of interest.			
(10) Interest Receivable		21,000	
Interest Income			21,000
To record interest accrued on investments to December 31, 1997.			
(11) Interest Income		1,200	
Premium on Investments			1,200
To record current year's amortization of premium on investments.			
(12) Revenue		488,000	
Required Additions			487,595
Fund Balance			405
Interest Income		41,800	
Required Earnings			32,760
Fund Balance			9,040
Appropriations		160,000	
Expenditures			160,000
To close budget and nominal account balances at year-end.			

Comparative financial statements for the Library and Civic Center Term Bonds Debt Service Fund are presented in Illustrations 21-5 and 21-6. Two things should be noted about these statements as follows:

No Interest Payable Accrual on General Obligation Long-term Debt   The perceptive reader may already have noted that there were no entries to record the accrual of interest payable on the bonds from the last interest payment date (July 1 for the serial bonds and October 1 for the term bonds) to the end of the fiscal year. This significant exception to expenditure accrual is justified, because financial resources that are appropriated in other funds or from general tax levies for transfer to or receipt by Debt Service Funds are usually appropriated in the period the interest on the debt must be paid. To accrue the Debt Service Fund expenditure and liability

ILLUSTRATION 21-5
Model City
Library and Civic Center Term Bonds Debt Service Fund
Balance Sheet December 31, 1997, and December 31, 1996

ASSETS	1997	1996
Cash	$ 9,000	$ 33,000
Interest Receivable	21,000	4,000
Taxes Receivable (less allowance for uncollectible taxes, 1997—$3,000; 1996—$1,000)	8,000	5,000
Investments (at maturity value)	760,000	400,000
Unamortized Premium on Investments	13,800	–0–
Total	$811,800	$442,000

LIABILITIES AND FUND BALANCE		
Fund Balance	(1) $811,800	(2) $442,000

(1) Actuarial requirement $687,950.
(2) Actuarial requirement $327,595.

ILLUSTRATION 21-6
Model City
Library and Civic Center Term Bonds Debt Service Fund
Statement of Revenue, Expenditures, and Other Changes
in Fund Balance for Years Ended December 31, 1997, 1996, and 1995

	1997	1996	1995
Revenue			
General Property Tax	$488,000	$488,000	$ –0–
Interest on Investments			
(net of amortization)	41,800	10,000	4,000
Total Revenue	529,800	498,000	4,000
Operating Transfers in	–0–	–0–	100,000
Total Revenue and			
Operating Transfers in	529,800	498,000	104,000
Expenditures			
Redemption of Term Bonds	–0–	–0–	–0–
Interest on Bonds	160,000	160,000	–0–
Excess (Deficiency) to Fund			
Balance	369,800	338,000	104,000
Fund Balance—January 1	442,000	104,000	–0–
Fund Balance—December 31	(1) $811,800	(2) $442,000	(3) $104,000

(1) Actuarial requirement $687,950.
(2) Actuarial requirement $327,595.
(3) Actuarial requirement $–0–.

in one year, but record the transfer or collection of the financial resources appropriated for this purpose in a later year, would be confusing and would result in an overstatement of fund liabilities and expenditures and an understatement of the fund balance. Thus, it is considered appropriate and more informative to treat interest payable on general obligation long-term debt at the end of the year as an expenditure in the year of payment.

Actuarial Requirement An essential disclosure in the financial statements of Debt Service Funds for term bonds is the amount, actuarially determined, of resources that is necessary on the financial statement date for the accumulation of sufficient resources to redeem the debt on its maturity date. The actuarial requirements shown in Illustrations 21-5 and 21-6 are those determined in the "Required Fund Balance" column of Illustration 21-4.

Closing Out the Debt Service Fund Assume the following trial balance for the Library and Civic Center Term Bonds Debt Service Fund on September 15, 2000.

	DEBIT	CREDIT
Cash	$2,220,000	
Fund balance		$2,220,000
Total	$2,220,000	$2,220,000

Entries to close the fund are as follows:

(1) Expenditures—Principal   2,000,000
    Expenditures—Interest   160,000
       Cash   2,160,000
         To record redemption of matured bonds and payment of interest.
(2) Transfer to X Fund   60,000
       Cash   60,000
         To record transfer of unexpended fund resources to another governmental
         fund.

The unexpended balance of the fund after the final payment of interest and principal on the matured bonds should be disposed of in accordance with legal or bond indenture requirements. Usually the unexpended balance is transferred to another Debt Service Fund, but legal requirements may specify an alternative disposition. The accounts of the fund being terminated should be closed in such a way as to reflect compliance with applicable legal requirements.

(3) Fund Balance   2,220,000
      Expenditures—Principal   2,000,000
      Expenditures—Interest   160,000
      Transfer to X Fund   60,000
        To close out Debt Service Fund.

After these entries have been posted, the balance of all accounts would be zero and the Debt Service Fund would effectively cease to exist.

Expendable Trust and Agency Funds

Trust and Agency Funds are established to account for assets received and held by the governmental unit in the capacity of a trustee or agent for individuals, private organizations, or other governmental units. Trust Funds are classified as expendable or nonexpendable, depending on whether or not their resources must be maintained intact. All of the principal and income of an expendable trust fund may be expended to carry out its designated activities. The principal (and in some cases the income) of a nonexpendable trust fund must be maintained intact. Expendable Trust Funds and Agency Funds are classified as Governmental Funds; they are briefly illustrated in this section. Nonexpendable Trust Funds, which are classified as Proprietary Funds, are discussed in the next section.

    Accounting procedures for Agency Funds and most Expendable Trust Funds are virtually the same and are relatively simple.

Agency Funds   For example, assume that Model City collects property taxes on behalf of a legally separate governmental unit such as a water improvement district. The following entries are made to record the amount of taxes to be collected and their remittance to the water improvement district.

(1) Property Tax Receivable   250,000
      Due to Water Improvement District   250,000
        To record levy of taxes earmarked for Valley Water Improvement District.

| (2) Cash | 250,000 | |
| Property Tax Receivable | | 250,000 |

To record collection of taxes earmarked for Valley Water Improvement District.

| (3) Due to Water Improvement District | 250,000 | |
| Cash | | 250,000 |

To record remittance to Valley Water Improvement District of taxes collected on its behalf.

Agency funds are purely custodial and assets always equal liabilities (no fund balance exists or if a fund balance is recorded, it is reported as a liability). These funds do not involve revenues or expenditures, nor do they require the preparation of a statement of revenue, expenditures, and other changes in fund balance.

Expendable Trust Fund   Assume that Model City has an ordinance that requires all licensed contractors to deposit funds with the city to guarantee performance on their contracts. The deposits must be returned to the contractors when they relinquish their licenses. When a deposit is received, cash is debited and the fund balance is credited. When deposits are refunded, the fund balance is debited and cash is credited. Since the deposits may be held by the city for substantial periods of time, the resources of the trust fund are usually invested, and modest amounts of revenue may be earned thereon.

PROPRIETARY FUND ENTITIES

Proprietary Funds employed in governmental accounting are described as follows:

> Proprietary Funds—sometimes referred to as "income-determination," "nonexpendable," or "commercial-type" funds—are used to account for a government's ongoing organizations and activities which are similar to those often found in the private sector (Enterprise and Internal Services Funds). All assets, liabilities, equities, revenues, expenses, and transfers relating to the government's business and quasi-business activities—where *net income and capital maintenance are measured*—are accounted for through proprietary funds. The generally accepted accounting principles here are those applicable to similar businesses in the private sector; and the measurement focus is upon determination of *net income, financial position, and changes in financial position.*[2]

Thus, financial accounting and reporting for proprietary funds closely parallels commercial accounting and reporting. All assets (*including fixed assets*) and liabilities (*including long-term debt*) involved in the activities financed through the fund are accounted for therein. The normal commercial accounting distinction between capital and revenue expenditures is maintained, and depreciation is recorded. The operating results of Proprietary Funds are measured in terms of net income by applying the same accounting standards as those used to determine the net income of profit-oriented enterprises. In addition, the corporate accounting distinction between contributed capital and retained earnings is maintained.

[2] *GASB Cod.* Section 1300.102b.

Enterprise Funds

Enterprise Funds are used to account for the provision of goods or services to the *general public* on a continuing basis where all or most of the costs incurred are recovered from charges to users. The most common examples of governmental enterprises are public utilities that provide such services as water or electricity. Other activities of governmental units that are accounted for in Enterprise Funds include airports, transportation systems, parking lots and garages, and recreational facilities such as swimming pools.

The resources to establish an enterprise fund may come from contributions or from the proceeds of long-term debt issues or both. Contributions may be obtained from other governmental units, resources of the General Fund of the same governmental unit, property owners, subdivision developers, or customers.

Since accounting for the operations of Enterprise Funds closely parallels accounting for profit-oriented enterprises, a detailed illustration will not be presented. Instead, a condensed balance sheet of a typical Enterprise Fund is presented in Illustration 21-7, and several features of the Enterprise Fund are pointed out.

Restrictions on Enterprise Fund assets required by bond provisions or other arrangements are complied with through the use of restricted asset accounts, which represent earmarked portions of specified assets comprising "funds" in the narrow

ILLUSTRATION 21-7
Model City
Enterprise Fund
Condensed Balance Sheet—December 31, 1995

ASSETS

Current Assets		$ 551,000
Restricted Assets		509,000
Utility Plant in Service (net of accumulated depreciation)		10,000,000
Construction in Progress		40,000
Total Assets		$11,100,000

LIABILITIES, CONTRIBUTIONS, AND RETAINED EARNINGS

Current Liabilities (payable from current assets)		$ 361,000
Current Liabilities (payable from restricted assets)		282,000
Revenue Bonds Payable		4,200,000
Total Liabilities		4,843,000
Contributions		
From Municipality	$ 800,000	
From Customers	126,000	
From Subdividers	1,500,000	2,426,000
Retained Earnings		
Unappropriated	3,331,000	
Reserve for Revenue Bond Retirement	500,000	3,831,000
Total Liabilities, Contributions, and Retained Earnings		$11,100,000

private-sector usage of that term (for example, sinking fund). To avoid the confusion that may result from the use of the term *fund* in this context in the financial statements of a Fund Entity, the use of the term **restricted asset account group,** rather than "fund," is recommended.

In Illustration 21-7, the Restricted Assets consist of assets segregated in compliance with the sinking fund requirements of the revenue bonds,[3] and the Current Liabilities (Payable from Restricted Assets) consist of the current interest and principal installments due on the revenue bonds.

Contributions are classified by source and are segregated from retained earnings. Retained earnings are reserved in the same manner as in commercial accounting to indicate that assets in an amount equal to the reserve are not available for other purposes. Finally, both fixed assets and long-term debt are accounted for and reported as specific assets and liabilities of the Enterprise Fund, rather than in the General Fixed Asset Account Group and the General Long-term Obligation Account Group, respectively.

Internal Service Funds

Internal Service Funds (formerly referred to as Working Capital Funds and then as Intragovernmental Service Funds) are created to account for the financing of goods and services provided by one department or agency to other departments or agencies of the same governmental unit on a cost reimbursement basis.

Typical examples of activities accounted for in Internal Service Funds include the operations of central computer facilities, central garages and motor pools, central purchasing and stores departments, and central printing departments.

Internal Service Funds are established with resources obtained from contributions from other funds, proceeds from the sale of general obligation bonds, or long-term advances from other funds. If an Internal Service Fund obtains resources from the proceeds of the issuance of general obligation bonds, the bond liability is **not** accounted for in the records of the Internal Service Fund. Rather a Debt Service Fund is established, and the bond liability is accounted for in the General Long-term Obligation Account Group. Upon the receipt of the bond issue proceeds, the entry in the records of the Internal Service Fund is a debit to Cash and a credit to Contributions—General Obligation Bonds.

Since accounting for the operations of Internal Service Funds closely parallels that for profit-oriented enterprises, a detailed illustration is not presented. A condensed balance sheet for an Internal Service Fund is presented in Illustration 21-8. As indicated, fixed assets acquired with the resources of the Internal Service Fund and depreciation thereon are recorded in the accounting records of that fund. As in the financial statements of Enterprise Funds, the contributed capital of Internal Service Funds is accounted for by source and is distinguished from retained earnings.

---

[3]Revenue bonds are long-term obligations, the principal and interest of which are paid from the earnings of self-supporting enterprises on which the bond proceeds were spent.

ILLUSTRATION 21-8
Model City
Internal Service Fund
Condensed Balance Sheet—December 31, 1995

ASSETS

Current Assets		$122,500
Property and Equipment	$560,000	
Less Accumulated Depreciation	(140,000)	420,000
Total Assets		$542,500

LIABILITIES, CONTRIBUTIONS, AND RETAINED EARNINGS

Current Liabilities		$ 27,500
Contributions		
From General Fund	$150,000	
From General Obligation Bonds	350,000	500,000
Retained Earnings		15,000
Total Liabilities, Contributions, and Retained Earnings		$542,500

Nonexpendable Trust Funds

There are two types of Nonexpendable Trust Funds: those in which the principal must be retained intact but earnings may be expended, and those in which both the principal and the earnings of the fund must be retained intact. An example of the latter type of Nonexpendable Trust Fund is the Revolving Loan Fund in which interest collected on loans outstanding increases the funds available for subsequent loans.

Nonexpendable Trust Funds may be established as a result of a gift, a bequest, or some other action that requires the governmental unit to act in a fiduciary capacity and to maintain and conserve cash or other assets that it does not own. Trust funds must be accounted for in accordance with the terms of the trust agreement or the applicable provisions of statutory and common law. Accounting procedures must result in a clear distinction between nonexpendable fund resources and expendable resources resulting from the earnings of the fund. Appropriate procedures are also necessary to ensure that the expenditure of expendable resources is made in accordance with the trust agreement or other applicable legal provisions.

Where the earnings of a trust fund may be expended, they may be transferred to the General Fund (no restriction on expenditures) or to a Special Revenue or an Expendable Trust Fund (expenditures restricted to specified use). To illustrate, assume that a private donor granted Model City $300,000 for the purpose of financing the purchase of rare editions of the classics for the public library. As a result of this grant, two funds were created: The Classics Endowment Fund to account for the nonexpendable fund principal and the investment thereof, and the Classics Acquisition Fund to account for the expenditure of the earnings of the endowment fund.

The general ledger trial balances for each fund on January 1, 1995, are presented below.

CLASSICS ENDOWMENT FUND	DEBIT	CREDIT
Cash	$ 2,000	
Certificates of deposit	300,000	
Interest receivable	7,500	
Due to classics acquisition fund		$ 9,500
Fund balance		300,000
Total	$309,500	$309,500

CLASSICS ACQUISITION FUND		
Cash	$ 8,000	
Due from classics endowment fund	9,500	
Fund balance		$ 17,500
Total	$ 17,500	$ 17,500

Transactions for 1995 for each fund are summarized below in general journal form.

CLASSICS ENDOWMENT FUND

(1) Cash   30,000
     Interest Receivable   7,500
     Interest Income   22,500
       To record interest collected on certificate of deposit.

(2) Interest Receivable   7,500
     Interest Income   7,500
       To accrue interest on certificate of deposit.

(3) Interest Income   30,000
     Due to Classics Acquisition Fund   30,000
       To record amount of 1995 income transferable to Classics Acquisition Fund.

(4) Due to Classics Acquisition Fund   32,000
     Cash   32,000
       To record cash payment to Classics Acquisition Fund.

For purposes of simplification it is assumed that the trust agreement requires that the entire endowment principal be invested in a savings account earning 10% interest. Usually, the principal of an endowment fund is invested in various securities. If the securities are purchased at a premium or discount, such amounts should ordinarily be amortized to interest income, and only the net amount of investment income would accrue to the recipient Expendable Trust Fund. Accounting procedures for an endowment fund are complicated further if the endowment includes depreciable income-producing assets such as rental properties. In that case, earnings accruing to the recipient expendable fund must also be reduced by depreciation if the trust principal is to be maintained "intact."

CLASSICS ACQUISITION FUND

(1)	Due from Classics Endowment Fund	30,000	
	Fund Balance		30,000
	To record expendable earnings due from endowment fund.		
(2)	Cash	32,000	
	Due from Classics Endowment Fund		32,000
	To record receipt of cash from endowment fund.		
(3)	Fund Balance	18,000	
	Cash		18,000
	To record acquisition of rare books.		

In funds having few transactions, revenues, transfers, and expenditures may be debited or credited directly to the fund balance.

Financial statements for these trust funds are presented in Illustrations 21-9 and 21-10.

ILLUSTRATION 21-9
Model City
Classics Endowment Fund
Balance Sheet
December 31, 1995, and December 31, 1994

ASSETS	1995	1994
Cash	$ –0–	$ 2,000
Interest Receivable	7,500	7,500
Investments	300,000	300,000
Total	$307,500	$309,500

LIABILITIES & FUND BALANCE		
Due to Classics Acquisition Fund	$ 7,500	$ 9,500
Fund Balance	300,000	300,000
Total	$307,500	$309,500

Statement of Revenue, Expenditures, and Other Changes
in Fund Balance for Years Ended
December 31, 1995, and December 31, 1994

	1995	1994
Revenue—Interest Income	$ 30,000	$ 30,000
Transfers to Expendable Trust Fund	(30,000)	(30,000)
Excess (Deficiency) to Fund Balance	–0–	–0–
Fund Balance—January 1	300,000	300,000
Fund Balance—December 31	$300,000	$300,000

ILLUSTRATION 21-10
Model City
Classics Acquisition Fund
Balance Sheet
December 31, 1995, and December 31, 1994

ASSETS	1995	1994
Cash	$22,000	$ 8,000
Due from Classics Endowment Fund	7,500	9,500
Total	$29,500	$17,500
LIABILITIES AND FUND BALANCE		
Fund Balance	$29,500	$17,500

Statement of Revenue Expenditures, and Other Changes
in Fund Balance for Year Ended
December 31, 1995, and December 31, 1994

Transfers from Endowment Trust Fund	$30,000	$30,000
Expenditures	(18,000)	(20,000)
Excess (Deficiency) to Fund Balance	12,000	10,000
Fund Balance—January 1	17,500	7,500
Fund Balance—December 31	$29,500	$17,500

ACCOUNT GROUP ENTITIES

General fixed assets and general long-term debt of a governmental unit are accounted for and reported in the financial statements of the two account group entities: The General Fixed Asset Account Group and the General Long-term Obligation Account Group.

General fixed assets of a governmental unit are the fixed assets owned by it that are not accounted for in its proprietary (enterprise, internal service, and nonexpendable trust) funds. These assets are accounted for in the General Fixed Asset Account Group, which is essentially an "inventory" of the general fixed assets owned by the governmental unit balanced by accounts listing the sources of the resources used to acquire them.

General long-term debt of a governmental unit is the unmatured principal of general obligation indebtedness that is not properly accounted for in a Proprietary Fund or Trust Fund. Such debt is accounted for in the General Long-term Obligation Account Group, which is essentially a listing of the amounts of unmatured long-term debt principal balanced by accounts that reflect the amount of resources available in Debt Service Funds for debt principal payments and the amount of resources that must be provided in future years for the payment of debt principal.

The General Fixed Assets Account Group

General fixed assets may be acquired through ~~gift or foreclosure, or they may be acquired through~~ the expenditure of resources of the General Fund, Special Revenue Funds, or Capital Project Funds.

The cost of constructed or purchased general fixed assets is determined using the same measurement standards as those applicable to commercial enterprises. Donated assets are recorded at their estimated fair value at the time they are received.

The position of the GASB is that

> Depreciation of general fixed assets should not be recorded in the accounts of governmental funds. Depreciation of general fixed assets may be recorded in cost accounting systems or calculated for cost finding analyses; and accumulated depreciation may be recorded in the General Fixed Assets Account Group.[4]

The rationale for this position was discussed in Chapter 20.

The classification of general fixed assets is similar to that followed by commercial enterprises. The following classifications of general fixed assets and sources of general fixed assets are recommended for purposes of financial reporting.

CLASSIFICATION OF ASSETS	CLASSIFICATION OF SOURCES OF ASSETS
Land	Investments in general fixed assets from
Buildings	Capital projects funds
Improvements other than buildings	General obligation bonds
Machinery and equipment	Special assessment debt with
Construction in progress	government commitment
	Federal grants
	State grants
	Local grants
	General fund revenues
	Special revenue fund revenues
	Contributions from property owners
	Private gifts

Accounting events in 1995 that affect the General Fixed Assets Account Group of Model City are summarized below in general journal form.

```
(1)  Machinery and Equipment                              250,000
          Investment from General Fund Revenues                        250,000
              To record expenditure for office equipment made by General Fund in 1995
              (see Chapter 20).
(2)  Investment from General Fund Revenues                 225,000
          Machinery and Equipment                                      225,000
              To record sale of used office equipment.
```

---

[4]*GASB Cod.* Section 1400.113a.

Equipment, which was purchased five years ago for $225,000, was sold for $87,250. The proceeds of the sale were accounted for as revenue of the General Fund (see Chapter 20). When a general fixed asset is sold, its original cost is simply removed from the records of the General Fixed Asset Account Group [see also entry (5) below].

(3) Construction in Progress	1,500,000	
Investment from General Obligation Bonds		1,000,000
Investment from State Grant		500,000
To record expenditures incurred during 1995 for construction of Model City Library and Civic Center.		

The investment in general fixed assets is allocated between general obligation bonds and state grants in relation to the relative contribution of each to the authorized project (Bonds—$2,000,000, State Grant—$1,000,000). When construction is completed in 1996, the following entry would be made in the records of the General Fixed Assets Account Group.

Land	200,000	
Buildings	2,725,000	
Construction in Progress		1,500,000
Investment from General Obligation Bonds		950,000
Investment from State Grant		475,000

Expenditures incurred in 1996 amount to $1,425,000 and are allocated to investment from general obligation bonds and state grants in the same manner as they were in 1995. The total cost of the completed project is $2,925,000 ($1,500,000 + $1,425,000); it is allocated to Land and Buildings in accordance with information supplied from the records of the Capital Projects Fund.

(4) Reduction in Investment in General Fixed Assets		
Due to Accumulated Depreciation	306,000	
Accumulated Depreciation—Buildings		120,000
Accumulated Depreciation—Machinery and Equipment		55,000
Accumulated Depreciation—Improvements		131,000
To record accumulated depreciation on general fixed assets.		

As was previously explained, depreciation of general fixed assets is not measured or reported in the accounts of governmental (expendable) funds. However, if desired, depreciation may be measured and an allowance for accumulated depreciation may be deducted from the related assets in the General Fixed Asset Account Group with a contra reduction from the total investments in general fixed assets balance. Notice that the recognition of accumulated depreciation does *not* result in the recording or reporting of depreciation expense. It is assumed that Model City has elected to reflect accumulated depreciation on general fixed assets.

(5) Accumulated Depreciation—Machinery and Equipment	140,000	
Reduction in Investment in General Fixed Assets		
Due to Accumulated Depreciation		140,000
To adjust accumulated depreciation and contra accounts for amount of accumulated depreciation recorded on equipment sold during the year.		

This entry would ordinarily be made in conjunction with entry (2) above. It was presented last here because it would not be required unless the governmental unit elects to reflect accumulated depreciation, as discussed in connection with entry (4) above.

A comparative Statement of General Fixed Assets for the General Fixed Assets Account Group is presented in Illustration 21-11. Balances for 1994 in this illustration are assumed amounts. A Statement of Changes in General Fixed Assets should also be prepared, as may schedules detailing assets, depreciation, and accumulated depreciation by the activities in which the assets are utilized. The latter schedules would be of particular importance if any reasonable attempt were to be made to compare the benefits of governmental activities with their *cost.* Such statements and schedules are not illustrated here.

ILLUSTRATION 21-11
Model City
Statement of General Fixed Assets
December 31, 1995, and December 31, 1994

GENERAL FIXED ASSETS NET OF ACCUMULATED DEPRECIATION	1995	1994
Land	$ 500,000	$ 500,000
(1) Buildings	2,880,000	3,000,000
(2) Improvements	6,064,000	6,195,000
(3) Machinery and Equipment	660,000	550,000
Construction in Progress	1,500,000	–0–
Total	$11,604,000	$10,245,000

NET INVESTMENT IN GENERAL FIXED ASSETS		
Investments from:		
Capital Project Funds	$ 8,195,000	$ 7,195,000
State Grants	500,000	–0–
General Fund Revenues	5,775,000	5,750,000
Special Revenue Fund Revenues	500,000	500,000
Total	14,970,000	13,445,000
Less Reduction of Investment in General Fixed Assets Due to Accumulated Depreciation	(3,366,000)	(3,200,000)
Net Investment	$11,604,000	$10,245,000

(1) Less accumulated depreciation of $1,520,000 in 1995 and $1,400,000 in 1994.
(2) Less accumulated depreciation of $1,731,000 in 1995 and $1,600,000 in 1994.
(3) Less accumulated depreciation of $115,000 in 1995 and $200,000 in 1994.

The General Long-term Obligation Account Group

General long-term obligations of a governmental unit include the unmatured principal on bonds, warrants, notes, and other long-term general obligations of the governmental unit, including special assessment debt for which the government is obligated in some manner. It is not limited to liabilities arising from debt issues, but may include noncurrent liabilities arising from lease agreements and similar commitments. It does not include long-term debt that is the specific liability of Proprietary Funds. However, where the full faith and credit of the governmental unit is pledged as additional assurance that specific proprietary fund liabilities will be paid, the contingent liability should be disclosed in the notes to the Statement of General Long-term Obligations.

Major credit account balances in the General Long-term Obligation Account Group are Serial Bonds Payable, Term Bonds Payable, and Other General Long-term Liabilities. The two major divisions of the offsetting debit account balances are Resources to be Provided in Future Years for Payment of Long-term Debt and Resources Available in Debt Service Funds for Payment of Long-term Debt.

The use of these accounts can be illustrated by summarizing in general journal form the accounting events in 1995 that affect the General Long-term Debt Obligation Group of Model City.

(1) Resources to be Provided in Future Years for
          Payment of Term Bonds   2,000,000
              Term Bonds Payable   2,000,000
                  To record issuance of $2,000,000 in par value of term bonds for construction of
                  Model City Library and Civic Center.
(2) Resources Available in Debt Service
          Fund—Term Bonds   104,000
              Resources to be Provided in Future Years for Payment
                  of Term Bonds   104,000
                  To record increase in balance of Library and Civic Center Term Bonds Debt
                  Service Fund available for payment of principal.
(3) Serial Bonds Payable   300,000
              Resources to be Provided in Future Years for Payment
                  of Serial Bonds   300,000
                  To record payment by Land Acquisition Serial Bonds Debt Service Fund of
                  current year's installment of principal on Land Acquisition Serial Bonds.
(4) Resources Available in Debt Service
          Fund—Serial Bonds   16,000
              Resources to be Provided in Future Years for Payment
                  of Serial Bonds   16,000
                  To record increase in balance of Land Acquisition Serial Bonds Debt Service
                  Fund during 1995.

Changes in the fund balances of serial bond debt service funds are often minimal. If the change is insignificant in relation to the outstanding liability, it need not be recorded in the accounts of the General Long-term Obligation Account Group. A comparative Statement of General Long-term Obligations is presented in Illustration 21-12.

SPECIAL ASSESSMENTS

Some capital improvements or services provided by a municipality are undertaken for the primary benefit of a particular property owner or groups of property owners rather than for the general public. In such cases, the costs of providing the capital improvements or services are often charged in whole or in part to the property

ILLUSTRATION 21-12
Model City
Statement of General Long-term Obligations
December 31, 1995 and 1994

AMOUNT AVAILABLE AND TO BE PROVIDED FOR PAYMENT OF GENERAL LONG-TERM OBLIGATIONS	1995	1994
Term Bonds		
Resources Available in Debt Service Fund	$ 104,000	$ –0–
Resources to Be Provided in Future Years	1,896,000	–0–
Total	2,000,000	–0–
Serial Bonds		
Resources Available in Debt Service Fund	21,000	5,000
Resources to Be Provided in Future Years	879,000	1,195,000
Total	900,000	1,200,000
Total Available and to be Provided	$2,900,000	$1,200,000
GENERAL LONG-TERM DEBT PAYABLE		
Term Bonds Payable	$2,000,000	$ –0–
Serial Bonds Payable	900,000	1,200,000
Total General Long-term Debt Payable	$2,900,000	$1,200,000

owners who receive the benefit. In some cases, the municipality may share in the cost of an improvement in recognition of the public benefits that result from the project. Special assessments that are levied against the benefited property owners for services are referred to as *service-type* special assessments. Special assessments that are levied against the benefited property owners for capital improvements are referred to as *capital improvement* special assessments.

Examples of service-type special assessment projects include street lighting, street cleaning, and snow plowing. Although financing for the routine provision of such services usually comes from general revenues, when such services are extended or provided at more frequent intervals, special assessments are sometimes levied. In such cases only the affected property owners are charged for the additional services.

More frequently special assessments are levied for capital improvement projects. Examples of such improvements include the paving or widening of residential streets or the construction of sidewalks or storm sewers. Although the affected property owners may be deemed the primary beneficiary of such projects, the projects often improve or add to the general fixed assets or infrastructure of the municipality as well. In some cases, such as the construction of water or sewer mains, such projects may provide capital assets that become an integral part of the government's enterprise activities.

Unlike service-type special assessment projects, capital improvement special assessment projects have two distinct and functionally different phases. The first phase consists of financing and constructing the project. Generally, this phase is completed over a period of two months to two years depending on the nature of the project.

The second phase consists of collecting the assessment principal and interest levied against the benefited properties and repaying the cost of financing the construction. Typically, capital improvement special assessment projects are financed by the issuance of long-term debt in the form of serial bonds, the principal and interest of which is repaid from the installment collection of special assessments. Thus, the collection of special assessment principal and interest and the repayment of the special assessment debt usually extend over a substantially longer period than the period it takes to complete the construction of the related project.

Prior to 1987, *capital improvement* special assessments were accounted for in a separate governmental fund type referred to as a special assessments fund. In essence this fund combined the functions of (1) a capital projects fund (by accounting for the proceeds from the issuance of debt and related construction expenditures), (2) a debt service fund (by accounting for the collection of special assessments and the interest payments on the redemption of outstanding long-term debt), and (3) the general long-term obligation account group (by accounting for unmatured long-term debt as a liability of the special assessment fund). Some governments accounted for *service-type* special assessment activities in special assessment funds, while others accounted for those activities in the general, enterprise, or special revenue funds.

In 1987 the GASB issued *Statement No. 6,* ''Accounting and Financial Reporting for Special Assessments.'' In that Statement the GASB discontinued its recognition of the special assessment fund type and indicated that it should no longer be used in general-purpose financial statements to report the construction of public improvements or the provision of services financed by special assessments.

Reporting Service-type Special Assessments

Under *GASB Statement No. 6,* transactions of a service-type special assessment are reported in the general fund, a special revenue fund, or an enterprise fund as best reflects the nature of the transactions. Service-type special assessments are recognized as revenue in the period the services are provided regardless of when the assessment is billed or collected. Expenditures (or expenses) for which the assessments are levied are recognized on the same basis as other expenditures or expenses of the fund type used to account for the service assessment.

Reporting Capital Improvement Special Assessments

Where capital improvements are financed by special assessments, the transactions are recorded differently depending on whether or not the government is obligated in some way to assume the payment of related debt service in the event of default by property owners. The extent of the government's liability for debt related to a special assessment capital improvement can vary significantly. However, for purposes of financial reporting, a government is considered to be obligated in some manner for the repayment of special assessment debt unless (1) the government is prohibited by constitution, charter, statute, ordinance, or contract from assuming the debt in the event of default by the property owner, or (2) the government is not legally liable for assuming the debt and makes no statement, or gives no indication, that it will, or may, honor the debt in the event of default.

Where the government is obligated in some manner for the repayment of special assessment debt, all transactions related to capital improvements financed by special assessments are recorded like any other capital improvement and financing transactions. Transactions of the construction phase of the project are accounted for in a capital projects fund. Transactions of the debt service phase are accounted for in a debt service fund. The fixed assets constructed or acquired (other than those related to an enterprise fund) are accounted for in the general fixed assets account group, and the outstanding long-term debt is accounted for in the general long-term obligations account group.

In capital improvement special assessment projects where special assessment debt is issued for which the government is not obligated in any manner, the debt is not reported in the general long-term obligations account group. Furthermore, the debt service transactions for such debt is reported in an agency fund rather than a debt service fund, to reflect the fact that the goverment's duties are limited to acting as an agent for the assessed property owners and the bondholders. The construction phase is still accounted for in a capital projects fund but the source of revenue is described as "contribution from property owners." The fixed assets constructed or acquired are recorded in the general fixed assets account group or an enterprise fund as appropriate. Recording this type of capital improvement special assessment project in this manner recognizes that the construction or acquisition is a governmental activity that results in the addition of a governmental asset but that the acquired asset is not financed by government debt.

To illustrate, assume that a municipality undertakes a street-widening project that will provide additional shop-front parking. Cash for the project will be provided by the proceeds of a $10 million issue of 8% special assessment debt and $2 million in general fund revenues. One-tenth of the debt plus interest is payable each July 1. A $10 million 8% special assessment levy against the benefiting property owners will provide most of the funds to service the debt and retire the bonds. However, since special assessments will be due on June 1, the city will make a one-time payment out of general fund revenues of one month's interest on the entire special assessment debt on June 1 of the first year.

FINANCED BY BONDS FOR WHICH GOVERNMENT IS OBLIGATED IN SOME MANNER	FINANCED BY BONDS FOR WHICH GOVERNMENT IS NOT OBLIGATED IN ANY MANNER

TRANSACTIONS

(1) $10 million in 8% special assessment serial bonds are issued and $2 million is transferred to the capital projects fund from the general fund:

CAPITAL PROJECTS FUND	CAPITAL PROJECTS FUND
Cash 10,000,000	Cash 10,000,000
Bond Issue Proceeds 10,000,000	Contributions from
	Property Owners 10,000,000
To record proceeds from bond Issue.	

GENERAL FUND | GENERAL FUND

Transfer to Capital			
Projects Fund	2,000,000		Same entry
Cash		2,000,000	

CAPITAL PROJECTS FUND | CAPITAL PROJECTS FUND

Cash	2,000,000		
Transfer from			Same entry
General Fund		2,000,000	

To record transfer of funds from general fund to capital projects fund.

GENERAL LONG-TERM OBLIGATION ACCOUNT GROUP | GENERAL LONG-TERM OBLIGATION ACCOUNT GROUP

Amount to Be Provided		No entry is made in the General Long-term
by Special		Obligation Account Group. The notes to the
Assessments	10,000,000	financial statements should show the
Special Assessment		amount of the debt and the fact that the
Debt with Government		government is in no way liable for
Commitment	10,000,000	repayment but is only acting as an agent.

To recognize the government's obligation for special assessment debt.

(2) Construction is completed at a cost of $12 million:

CAPITAL PROJECTS FUND | CAPITAL PROJECTS FUND

Expenditures	12,000,000		Same entry
Cash		12,000,000	

GENERAL FIXED ASSETS ACCOUNT GROUP | GENERAL FIXED ASSETS ACCOUNT GROUP

Improvements	12,000,000		Improvements	12,000,000	
Investment from Special					
Assessment Debt					
with Government			Contributed by Property		
Commitment		10,000,000	Owners		10,000,000
Investment from General			Investment from General		
Fund Revenues		2,000,000	Fund Revenues		2,000,000

To record completion of project.

(3) The first installment of the special assessment levy is billed and collected (11 months' interest is included in the billing) and an amount equal to one month's interest is transferred to the debt service fund or an agency fund from general fund revenues:

DEBT SERVICE FUND

Special Assessments		No entry
Receivable	1,733,333	
Special Assessment		
Revenue	1,733,333	

To record billing of special assessment due June 1.

GENERAL FUND

Transfer to Debt		
Service Fund	66,667	
Cash		66,667

GENERAL FUND

Expenditures	66,667	
Cash		66,667

DEBT SERVICE FUND

Cash	66,667	
Transfer from General		
Fund		66,667
Cash	1,733,333	
Special Assessments		
Receivable		1,733,333

AGENCY FUND

Cash	66,667	
Amount Held for		
Debt Service		66,667
Cash	1,733,333	
Amount Held for		
Debt Service		1,733,333

To record cash collections from general fund revenues and from property owners.

(4) Twelve months' interest and principal is paid on the special assessment bonds on July 1:

DEBT SERVICE FUND

Expenditure—		
Principal	1,000,000	
Expenditure—		
Interest	800,000	
Cash		1,800,000

AGENCY FUND

Amount Held for		
Debt Service	1,800,000	
Cash		1,800,000

GENERAL LONG-TERM OBLIGATION ACCOUNT GROUP

Special Assessment		
Debt with Government		
Commitment	1,000,000	
Amount to Be Provided		
by Special Assessments		1,000,000

GENERAL LONG-TERM OBLIGATION ACCOUNT GROUP

No entry

To record the payment of interest and principal on special assessment debt.

Special assessment levies including interest are not recognized as revenue until the period in which payment is due from the assessed property owners. In particular, no revenue is recognized for unbilled but accrued interest on special assignments. Special assessment debt service expenditures for principal and interest are recognized in the period that the debt service payments are due. In particular, no expenditure is recognized for interest accrued, but not yet due, on special assessment debt. Nonrecognition of accrued interest receivable or payable on special assessments is based on the conclusion that the effect on the debt service fund balance would represent merely a timing difference rather than a true fund equity.

INTERFUND TRANSACTIONS

Entries in the records of the Account Group Entities are initiated by transactions that are also recorded in the records of Governmental Fund Entities. In addition to this type of "reciprocal" transaction, fund entities may engage in interfund transactions. Interfund transactions are classified as quasi-external transactions, reimbursements, loans or advances, and interfund transfers.

Quasi-External Transactions

Quasi-external transactions are interfund transactions that would be treated as revenue, expense, or expenditures if they were consummated with organizations external to the governmental unit. Contributions in lieu of taxes from an Enterprise Fund to the General Fund and Internal Service Fund billings to government departments for services rendered are examples of quasi-external transactions. Quasi-external transactions are accounted for as revenue, expense, or expenditures of the funds involved. Accounting for quasi-external transactions in this manner is necessary for the determination of the operating results (net income) of Proprietary Funds.

To illustrate, assume that the Internal Service Fund bills the Police Department for $3,000 for services rendered. The corresponding entries to record this billing are

INTERNAL SERVICE FUND

Due from General Fund	3,000	
Revenue		3,000

GENERAL FUND

Expenditures	3,000	
Due to Internal Service Fund		3,000

Reimbursements

Reimbursements are transactions that involve the transfer of resources from one fund to another in order to reimburse the recipient fund for expenditures made by it that are properly expenditures of the reimbursing fund. The recipient fund should record the transaction as a credit to expenditures, and the reimbursing fund should record the transaction as a debit to expenditures.

For example, assume that the General Fund performs services in the amount of $10,000 for a Special Revenue Fund. The corresponding entries to record the reimbursement are

SPECIAL REVENUE FUND

Expenditures	10,000	
Due to General Fund (or cash)		10,000

THE GENERAL FUND

Due from Special Revenue Fund (or cash)	10,000	
Expenditures		10,000

Loans or Advances

Interfund loans or advances are self-explanatory. Assume that the General Fund advances $4,000 as a temporary loan to a Special Revenue Fund. Corresponding entries to record the advance are

THE GENERAL FUND

Due from Special Revenue Fund	4,000	
Cash		4,000

SPECIAL REVENUE FUND

Cash	4,000	
Due to General Fund		4,000

Interfund Transfers

All interfund transactions other than quasi-external transactions, reimbursements, and loans or advances are interfund transfers. The importance of distinguishing interfund transfers from revenue and expenditures has already been explained. Interfund transfers may be classified and reported as residual equity transfers or as operating transfers.

Residual Equity Transfers   Residual equity transfers represent a transfer of equity of the funds involved. Examples include nonrecurring contributions from the General Fund to Proprietary Funds, the return of part or all of such contributions to the General Fund, and transfers of the residual balances of discontinued funds to the General Fund or to Debt Service Funds.

To illustrate, assume that an Enterprise Fund transfers $150,000 of excess resources to the General Fund. Corresponding entries to record the transfer are

ENTERPRISE FUND

Transfer to General Fund	150,000	
Cash		150,000

THE GENERAL FUND

Cash	150,000	
Transfer from Enterprise Fund		150,000

Residual equity transfers should be reported as direct additions to or reductions from the beginning fund balance of Governmental Funds. Residual equity transfers to Proprietary Funds should be reported as additions to contributed capital; those from Proprietary Funds should be reported as reductions of retained earnings or contributed capital, depending on the circumstances.

Operating Transfers   Operating transfers consist of recurring transfers between funds for the purpose of shifting resources from the fund legally required to record the revenue to the fund legally required to expend the revenue. An example of this type of transfer is the annual transfer of revenue from an Endowment Trust Fund to an Expendable Trust Fund. To illustrate, the net effect of the entries to record the transfer of revenue from the Classics Acquisition Endowment Trust Fund of Model City to the Classics Acquisition Expendable Trust Fund may be summarized as follows.

<u>ENDOWMENT TRUST FUND</u>

Transfer to Expendable Trust Fund	30,000	
Cash		30,000

<u>EXPENDABLE TRUST FUND</u>

Cash	30,000	
Transfer from Endowment Trust Fund		30,000

Operating transfers should be reported as separate items in the statement of revenue, expenditures, and changes in fund balance. Operating transfers affect the results of operations in both Governmental and Proprietary Funds.

FINANCIAL REPORTING

The development of financial reporting standards for state and local governmental units is currently in a state of flux. In 1987 the GASB published a Statement of Governmental Concepts entitled *Objectives of Financial Reporting.* Unlike other Board statements, this concepts statement does not establish standards of governmental accounting and financial reporting. Rather, the purpose of the statement is to establish a framework within which the Board will develop financial reporting standards for governmental agencies. The reader can expect to see significant changes in the financial reports of governmental units as the GASB develops such standards as a means of enhancing public understanding of government activities and their financial implications. The discussion that follows is based on existing governmental financial reporting standards as embodied in the GASB *Codification of Governmental Accounting and Financial Reporting Standards* and the underlying documents on which that codification is based.

The Reporting Entity

Thus far in this chapter, we have concentrated on appropriate financial reports for each separate fund entity. However, the governmental unit itself may be viewed as a separate reporting entity. A major reporting problem for state and local governments is finding a suitable way to aggregate the reports of the separate fund entities into a single set of integrated financial statements.

In the private sector, affiliated companies (separate legal entities) maintain separate records and may prepare separate financial statements, but the primary reporting entity is the consolidated group (economic entity), and the ***primary*** general purpose financial statements are the consolidated financial statements. If included in such reports, the financial statements of the individual affiliates are considered supplementary information.

The traditional reporting emphasis in the public sector was just the opposite. The separate funds (legal entities) were considered the ***primary*** reporting entities. Statements or schedules presenting combined or consolidated information for the fund entities were considered supplemental information rather than the primary financial statements. However, in the late 1970s, the presumption that the individual fund and account group entities should be the sole governmental financial reporting focus was challenged in the face of a persistent demand for state and local governments to produce an understandable and meaningful set of integrated, overall financial statements.

The NCGA responded to this challenge in *Statement 1* by distinguishing General Purpose Financial Statements (GPFS) from the Comprehensive Annual Financial Report (CAFR). The Council concluded that the individual funds and account groups should continue to be the basic entity reported on in the CAFR, but that the primary focus on the GPFS should be on combined fund type and account group information. In addition, requiring that interfund transfers and debt issue proceeds be reported separately from revenues and expenditures makes it easier to distinguish revenues and expenditures of the governmental unit as a whole from revenue and expenditures of the individual fund entities.

The Pyramid Concept

The NCGA recommended and the GASB endorsed a pyramid approach to financial reporting. The levels of the pyramid are identified in Illustration 21-13.[5]

The levels of the pyramid are:

(1) ***General Purpose Financial Statements (Combined Statements—Overview).*** These basic financial statements provide a summary overview of the financial position of all funds and account groups and of the operating results of all funds. They also serve as an introduction to the more detailed statements and schedules that follow. Separate columns should be used for each fund type and account group.

(2) ***Combining Statements—By Fund Type.*** Where a governmental unit has more than one fund of a given type (e.g., Special Revenue Funds), combining statements for all funds of that type should be presented in a columnar format. The total columns of these combining statements should agree with the amounts presented in the GPFS. (In some instances, disclosure sufficient to meet CAFR reporting objectives may be achieved at this level; in other cases, these statements "link" the GPFS and the individual fund statements.)

(3) ***Individual Fund and Account Group Statements.*** These statements present information

---

[5] The source for Illustration 21-13 is NCGA, *Statement 1*, "Governmental Accounting and Financial Reporting Principles," p. 20.

ILLUSTRATION 21-13
The Financial Reporting "Pyramid"

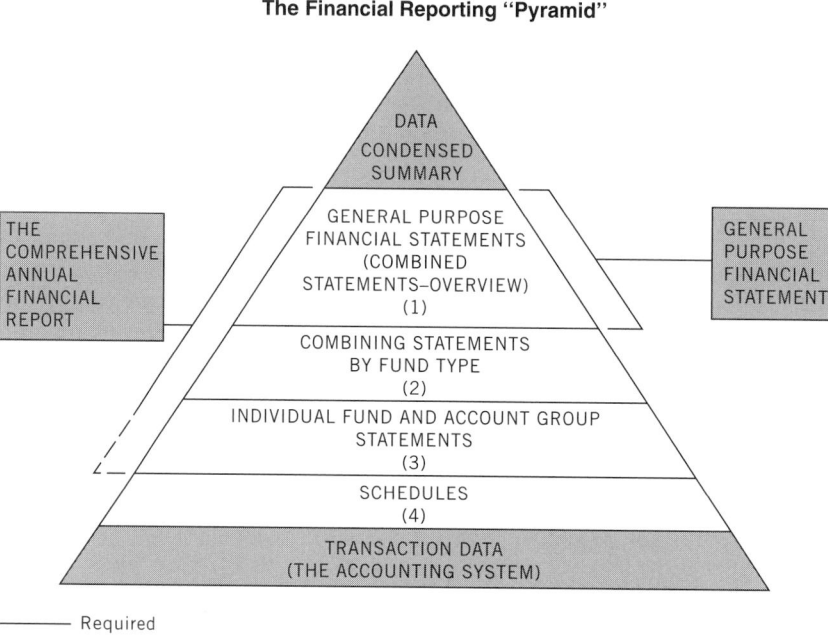

——— Required

— — — May be necessary

on the individual funds and account groups where (a) a governmental unit has only one fund of a specific type, or (b) detail to assure disclosure sufficient to meet CAFR reporting objectives is not presented in the combining statements. These statements may also be used to present budgetary data and prior year comparative data.

(4) *Schedule.* Data presented in schedules are not necessary for fair presentation in conformity with GAAP unless referenced in the notes to the financial statements. Schedules are used: (a) to demonstrate finance-related legal and contractual compliance (e.g., where bond indentures require specific data to be presented); (b) to present other information deemed useful (e.g., combined and combining schedules that encompass more than one fund or account group, such as a Combined Schedule of Cash Receipts, Disbursements, and Balances—All Funds); and (c) to provide details of data summarized in the financial statements (e.g., schedules of revenues, expenditures, transfers).

All four pyramid levels of detail may be required in some circumstances. On the other hand, adequate disclosure may require only one or two levels. Determination of the appropriate level of detail—and the distinction as to what is presented in a statement as opposed to a schedule—is a matter of professional judgment.[6]

---

[6] *GASB Cod.* Section 2200.

Recommended Financial Statements

The financial position and operating statements recommended within the framework of the pyramid approach are:

1. *Balance Sheets*
   (a) A Combined Balance Sheet—All Fund Types and Account Groups.
   (b) Combining balance sheets for all funds of each type.
   (c) Individual balance sheets for each fund and account group—where necessary to present the financial position of each fund and account group—and schedules necessary to demonstrate compliance with finance-related legal and contractual provisions.

2. *Operating Statements*
   (a) Governmental Funds
      (1) A Combined Statement of Revenues, Expenditures, and Changes in Fund Balances—All Governmental Fund Types.
      (2) Combined Statement of Revenues, Expenditures, and Changes in Fund Balances—Budget and Actual—General and Special Revenue Fund Types (and similar governmental fund types for which annual budgets have been legally adopted).
      (3) Combining statements of governmental fund revenues, expenditures, and changes in fund balances by fund type.
      (4) Individual statements of revenues, expenditures, and changes in fund balance for each fund—where necessary to present fund operating results—and schedules necessary to demonstrate compliance with finance-related legal and contractual provisions.

   (b) Proprietary Funds
      (1) A Combined Statement of Revenues, Expenses, and Changes in Retained Earnings (or Equity)—All Proprietary Fund Types.
      (2) A Combined Statement of Cash Flows—All Proprietary Fund Types.
      (3) Combining statements of proprietary fund revenues, expenses, and changes in retained earnings (or equity) by fund type.
      (4) Combining statements of proprietary fund cash flows by fund type.
      (5) Individual statements of revenues, expenses, and changes in retained earnings (or equity) and of cash flows for each proprietary fund—where necessary to present fund operating results and cash flows—and schedules necessary to demonstrate compliance with finance-related legal and contractual provisions.

   (c) Fiduciary Funds
      (1) Expendable Trust Funds are similar to governmental funds (modified accrual basis) and should be reported as indicated at 2(a) above; Non-expendable Trust and Pension Trust Funds are similar to proprietary funds (accrual basis) and should be reported as indicated at 2(b) above.
      (2) At the GPFS (Combined Statements—Overview) level, Trust Fund op-

erating statements may be presented (a) separately or (b) within the combined operating statements of the governmental funds and the proprietary funds, as appropriate.

(3) A Combining Statement of Changes in Assets and Liabilities—All Agency Funds.

(d) Account Groups

(1) Statement of Changes in General Fixed Assets (unless sufficiently disclosed in the notes to the financial statements).

(2) Statement of Changes in General Long-term Obligations (unless sufficiently disclosed in the notes to the financial statements). . . .

Combined balance sheets show the data for each fund type and account group, whereas combining balance sheets present data for each fund of a given type. Both are usually presented in columnar format. The Combined Balance Sheet—All Fund Types and Account Groups may contain a total, with or without interfund and similar eliminations. The total column of each combining balance sheet by fund type should agree with the column for that fund type of the Combined Balance Sheet—All Fund Types and Account Groups. . . .

As in the case of the Combined Balance Sheet—All Fund Types and Account Groups, the separate fund type data in the Combined Statements of Revenues, Expenditures, and Changes in Fund Balances—All Governmental Fund Types should be displayed in a series of columns and may contain a total column, with or without interfund and similar eliminations. Total columns of combining statements of governmental fund revenues, expenditures, and changes in fund balances by fund types should agree with the column for that fund type in the Combined Statement of Revenues, Expenditures, and Changes in Fund Balances—All Governmental Fund Types. Likewise, any interfund and similar eliminations should be made apparent from the headings or disclosed in the notes to the financial statements. Similar guidelines apply to the proprietary fund operating statements. . . .

The Combined Statement of Revenues, Expenditures, and Changes in Fund Balance—Budget and Actual—General and Special Revenue Fund Types, as the name implies, presents budget and actual data for the General Fund and all Special Revenue Funds. This statement should also include budget and actual data for other governmental fund types for which annual budgets have been adopted. Only the total budget and total actual data for all Special Revenue Funds (and for every other budgeted governmental fund type) are required.

If the budget is prepared on a basis consistent with GAAP, the actual data in this budgetary comparison statement is the same as in the Combined Statement of Revenues, Expenditures, and Changes in Fund Balances—All Governmental Fund Types. However, if the legally prescribed budgetary basis differs materially from GAAP, budgetary data should not be compared with GAAP-based operating data since these comparisons would not be meaningful. Rather, the Combined Statement of Revenues, Expenditures, and Changes in Fund Balances—Budget and Actual—General and Special Revenue

Fund Types should present *comparisons of the legally adopted budget with actual data on the budgetary basis* (which may include encumbrances). In such cases, this "actual" data would be different from the GAAP presentations in the Combined Statement of Revenues, Expenditures, and Changes in Fund Balances—All Governmental Fund Types. The difference between the budgetary basis and GAAP should be explained in the notes to the financial statements.[7]

A combined statement of revenue, expenditures, and changes in fund balances for all the governmental funds of Model City is presented in Illustration 21-14. A combining statement of revenue, expenditures, and changes in fund balances for all debt service funds of Model City is presented in Illustration 21-15. A statement of revenues, expenditures, and changes in fund balances—budget and actual—general fund was presented in Illustration 20-8. Recommended financial statements

ILLUSTRATION 21-14
Model City
All Governmental Funds
Combined Statement of Revenue, Expenditures, and Other Changes
in Fund Balance for Year Ended December 31, 1995

	GENERAL FUND (20-7)*	CAPITAL PROJECTS FUND (21-2)*	DEBT SERVICE FUNDS (21-15)*	EXPENDABLE TRUST FUND (21-10)*	TOTAL[†] (MEMORANDUM ONLY)
Revenue					
Property Tax	$1,158,750	$	$316,000	$	$1,474,750
State Grants	275,000	1,000,000			1,275,000
Charges for Services	136,500				136,500
Licenses and Permits	170,500				170,500
Proceeds from Sales of Property	87,250				87,250
Investment Income		12,500	4,000		16,500
Total Revenue	1,828,000	1,012,500	320,000	–0–	3,160,500
Debt Issue Proceeds	–0–	2,100,000	–0–	–0–	2,100,000
Operating Transfers from Other Funds					
From Proprietary Funds	–0–			30,000	30,000
From Other Governmental Funds			196,000		196,000
Total Operating Transfers from Other Funds	–0–	–0–	196,000	30,000	226,000
Total Revenue, Debt Issue Proceeds, and Operating Transfers from Other Funds	1,828,000	3,112,500	516,000	30,000	5,486,500

[7]*GASB Cod.* Section 2200.

ILLUSTRATION 21-14 (continued)
Model City
All Governmental Funds
Combined Statement of Revenue, Expenditures, and Other Changes
in Fund Balance for Year Ended December 31, 1995

	GENERAL FUND (20-7)*	CAPITAL PROJECTS FUND (21-2)*	DEBT SERVICE FUNDS (21-15)*	EXPENDABLE TRUST FUND (21-10)*	TOTAL[†] (MEMORANDUM ONLY)
Expenditures					
General Government	$ 189,000	$	$	$	$ 189,000
Public Safety	380,000				380,000
Highways and Streets	128,000				128,000
Sanitation	70,000				70,000
Health	141,000				141,000
Cultural—Recreation	80,000			18,000	98,000
Education	670,000				670,000
Capital Outlays		1,500,000			1,500,000
Redemption of Principal of General Long-term Debt			300,000		300,000
Interest on Debt			96,000		96,000
Total Expenditures	1,658,000	1,500,000	396,000	18,000	3,572,000
Operating Transfers to Other Funds					
To Proprietary Funds	200,000	–0–	–0–	–0–	200,000
To Other Governmental Funds	96,000	100,000			196,000
Total Operating Transfers to Other Funds	296,000	100,000	–0–	–0–	396,000
Total Expenditures and Operating Transfers to Other Funds	1,954,000	1,600,000	396,000	18,000	3,968,000
Excess (Deficiency) of Revenues, Debt Issue Proceeds, and Operating Transfers from Other Funds over Expenditures and Operating Transfers to Other Funds	(126,000)	1,512,500	120,000	12,000	1,518,500
Fund Balances—January 1	250,000	–0–	5,000	17,500	272,500
	124,000	1,512,500	125,000	29,500	1,791,000
Residual Equity Transfer from Proprietary Funds	150,000				150,000
Fund Balances—December 31	$ 274,000	$1,512,500	$125,000	$29,500	$1,941,000

*Illustration number for the source of information in this column.
[†]Generally accepted accounting standards require comparative totals for the preceding year (omitted here).

for individual governmental fund entities and proprietary fund entities have been presented throughout this chapter in connection with the discussion of each fund entity.

ILLUSTRATION 21-15
Model City
All Debt Service Funds
Combining Statement of Revenue, Expenditures, and Other Changes
in Fund Balance for Year Ended December 31, 1995

	LAND ACQUISITION SERIAL BONDS (21-3)*	LIBRARY AND CIVIC CENTER TERM BONDS (21-6)*	TOTAL[†]
Revenue			
General Property Tax	$316,000	$ −0−	$316,000
Investment Income	−0−	4,000	4,000
Total Revenue	316,000	4,000	320,000
Operating Transfers from Other Governmental Funds	96,000	100,000	196,000
Total	412,000	104,000	516,000
Expenditures			
Redemption of Bonds	300,000	−0−	300,000
Interest on Bonds	96,000	−0−	96,000
Total	396,000	−0−	396,000
Excess (Deficiency) of Revenue, Bond Issues Proceeds, and Operating Transfers from Other Funds over Expenditures	16,000	104,000	120,000
Fund Balances—January 1	5,000	−0−	5,000
Fund Balances—December 31	$ 21,000	$104,000	$125,000

*Illustration number for the source of information in this column.
[†]Generally accepted accounting standards require comparative totals for the preceding year (omitted here).

REPORTING ON SERVICE EFFORTS AND ACCOMPLISHMENTS

One objective established by the GASB is that financial reporting should provide information to assist users in assessing the service efforts and accomplishments of the governmental entity.[8] Recognizing that traditional governmental reports provide scant information or measurements relating to accomplishment, the Board undertook a research project to gather information on the measurement and reporting of service efforts and accomplishment (SEA) indicators. Based on that research the Board, in December 1992, issued a document that presented background information on the reporting of performance information as part of general purpose external financial reporting.[9] The characteristics of SEA information and several different categories of SEA indicators are described in that document. In addition, the Board concluded that, although useful SEA indicators exist, additional experimentation with and analysis of SEA indicators needs to be undertaken before

---

[8]*GASB Cod.* 100.177c
[9]"Preliminary Views of the Governmental Accounting Standards Board on Concepts Relating to Service Efforts and Accomplishment Reporting," GASB, 1992.

requiring their inclusion in financial reports. Such experimentation is ongoing, and it is likely that such measures someday will become a commonplace component of reports by governmental entities.

SEA indicators are classified as follows:[10]

Input indicators	Report the amount of resources that have been used for a specific service or program.
Output indicators	Report units produced or services provided by a service or program.
Outcome indicators	Report the results (including quality) of the service.
Efficiency (and cost-effectiveness) indicators	Measure the cost (whether in dollars or employee hours) per unit of output or outcome.
Explanatory information	Information about the environment or other factors that might affect an organization's performance on SEA indicators.

Examples of each type of indicator are presented in Illustration 21-16.

Illustration 21-16 illustrates a single SEA indicator for each SEA category. To be reasonably informative, several different SEA indicators in each category need to be measured and reported. Indicators that relate inputs to outcomes also need to be developed. This is because indicators that relate efforts to accomplishment help answer some of the fundamental questions of governments. How much better off might the public be as a result of a specific increase in resources for a specific activity? What are the trade-offs in terms of likely outcomes from cutting resources in one activity as compared to another? Designing and measuring such indicators is difficult and sometimes subjective. Examples might include cost per student achieving a prespecified test score gain or cost per mile of road maintained at some satisfactory level of condition.

ILLUSTRATION 21-16
Examples of SEA Indicators

CATEGORY OF INDICATOR	SECONDARY EDUCATION	ACTIVITY FIRE SUPPRESSION	SOLID-WASTE COLLECTION
Input	Number of personnel (by categories)	Total operating expenditures	Number of vehicles
Output	Number of student days	Number of fire calls answered	Tons of waste collected
Outcome	Standardized test score results	Response time	Percentage of collections missed
Efficiency	Cost per student graduated	Operating expenditure per $100,000 of property protected	Tons of solid waste collected per employee
Explanatory information	Percentage of students needing special remedial programs	Area served in square miles	Types of vehicle Crew size of vehicle Climatic conditions Terrain

[10]"Service Efforts and Accomplishments: Its Time Has Come," *GASB Research Report*, GASB, 1990.

THE GASB'S FINANCIAL REPORTING PROJECT

In 1984 the GASB placed on its agenda a project designed as a broad reexamination of all aspects of governmental financial reporting. It is expected that the project may result in significant changes in government reporting standards. Completed portions of the project include the *GASB Research Report,* "The Needs of Users of Governmental Financial Reports" (1985); *GASB Concepts Statement No. 1,* "Objectives of Financial Reporting" (1987); and *GASB Statement No. 14,* "The Financial Reporting Entity" (1991).

The fourth phase of the Financial Reporting project is the reexamination of the financial reporting model. A first step in that phase was the adoption in 1990 of *GASB Statement No. 11,* "Measurement Focus and Basis of Accounting—Governmental Fund Operating Statements." The financial reporting model project also includes consideration of the types of financial statements necessary for external financial reporting including levels of aggregation, budgetary reporting, cash flows reporting, and note disclosures. It also includes consideration of issues relating to capital debt service recognition and measurement and the display of capital transactions. Further, the project encompasses various detailed issues including reporting interfund transactions, fiduciary funds, and internal service funds.

In *Statement No. 11,* the GASB determined that flow of financial resources should be the measurement focus for governmental funds. Operating statements using this focus should show the extent to which financial resources obtained during a period are sufficient to cover claims against financial resources incurred during the period. This measurement focus considers financial resources only and uses an accrual basis of accounting. Taxes are recognized as revenues if the underlying transaction or event has taken place and the government has demanded the taxes, regardless of when cash is received. Revenues from other nonexchange transactions such as fines or fees are recognized when the underlying event takes place and the government has a legal claim to the amounts, regardless of when received. Revenues from exchange transactions such as charges for services or investment income are recognized when earned. Operating expenditures generally are recognized when the transactions that result in a claim against financial resources take place, regardless of when cash is paid. This includes recognizing expenditures for prepaid expenses and supplies using the consumption method. Compensated absences are recognized when the benefits are earned by the employees. The statement distinguished between general long-term capital debt and operating debt. The issuance and repayment of general long-term capital debt has an operating statement effect in a flow of financial resources measurement focus. The issuance and repayment of operating debt does not.

In relating *Statement No. 11* to *Concepts Statement No. 1,* the Board noted that the financial resources measurement focus

- Is responsive to the government environment and the needs of users.
- Is based on the concept of accountability, which includes measuring interperiod equity—whether current-year revenues were sufficient to pay for current-year services.
- Considers the performance goals and measures of governmental-type activities.

- Considers the intent and effect of budgets and other financing controls.
- Considers the use of fund accounting to achieve and demonstrate legal compliance and to enhance financial administration.

The effective date of *Statement No. 11* was originally delayed to June 1994 so that the Board would have time to develop criteria for distinguishing operating debt from general long-term capital debt and to resolve, among other things, issues relating to how to report operating debt as well as long-term accruals of revenues and expenditures.

In April 1992 the Board issued a preliminary views document on major display issues relating to the implementation of *Statement No. 11*. That document presented a preliminary view that was supported by three members of the Board and an alternative view that was supported by two members of the Board. Rather than supporting one view or the other, the overwhelming majority of respondents to the preliminary views document recommended that the GASB defer the effective date of *Statement No. 11* until the completion of all major aspects of the financial reporting model project.

In 1993 the Board deferred the effective date of *Statement No. 11* and decided to approach the financial reporting model project using a broader perspective. To do this the Board initiated a process that will take six categories of data—financial resources, interperiod equity, budgetary resources, cash flows, capital resources, and service efforts and accomplishments data—and seek answers to four basic questions.

1. What are the basic reporting alternatives for each category?

2. What objectives do these alternatives meet, or what information do the alternatives provide to financial statement users?

3. What elements of financial reporting are necessary to achieve those objectives?

4. What definitions are necessary to achieve a common understanding of the financial reporting objectives and elements?

The Board expects answers to these questions to provide it with a framework that can be used in its deliberations on *Statement No. 11* implementation issues and other important reporting model issues that have not been addressed.

Although slow and not without pitfalls, the progress of the GASB toward the development of an improved model for reporting on governmental entities continues and will likely be completed in the not-so-distant future.

Questions

1. Seven separate fund entities are recommended to account for the various activities and resources of a governmental unit. Identify these funds by title and type and briefly state (in two sentences or less) the basic purpose of each fund.

2. In addition to fund entities, two nonfund "self-balancing" account group entities are recommended for use by governmental units. Identify these account groups and state

the purpose of each. Prepare in general journal form an entry to record a typical "transaction" in the records of each.

3. What is the difference between a fund and an account group?

4. What is the difference between a governmental fund and a proprietary fund?

5. Are fiduciary funds governmental funds or proprietary funds? Explain.

6. A disbursement by the General Fund to another fund may be recorded as a receivable, an expenditure, or a fund transfer. Explain the circumstances that would result in each of these different treatments.

7. In what funds or account groups would you expect bonds payable to be included?

8. In what funds or account groups might property and other nonfinancial resources be recorded?

9. Why are budgeted revenues and expenditures formally recorded in the records of the General Fund but not in the records of a Capital Projects Fund?

10. Are all major capital facilities acquisitions accounted for in a Capital Projects Fund? Explain.

11. Describe the reporting for service-type special assessments.

12. Describe the manner in which special assessment debt for which the government is not obligated in any manner is reported in the financial statements.

13. What exception to the normal expenditure recognition criteria is associated with Debt Service Funds and what is the justification for this exception?

14. Identify and describe four types of interfund transactions. Are interfund transactions the equivalent of intercompany transactions? Explain.

15. The following funds and account groups are recommended for use in accounting for state and municipal governmental financial operations:
    A. General Fund.
    B. Special Revenue Fund.
    C. Debt Service Fund.
    D. Capital Projects Fund.
    E. Agency Fund.
    F. Enterprise Fund.
    G. Internal Service Fund.
    H. Trust Fund.
    I. General Fixed Asset Account Group.
    J. General Long-term Obligation Account Group.

    Identify, by the letters given above, the funds and account groups in which each of the account titles below might properly appear.
    1. Bonds Payable.
    2. Reserve for Encumbrances.
    3. Equipment.
    4. Appropriations.
    5. Estimated Revenue.
    6. Property Taxes Receivable.
    7. Construction Work in Progress.

8. Accumulated Depreciation.
9. Depreciation Expense.
10. Required Earnings.

Exercises

Exercise 21-1

The following transactions take place:

1. A cement mixer was purchased with resources of the General Fund.
2. A contract was signed for the construction of a new civic center.
3. Bonds were issued to finance the construction of the new civic center.
4. Construction of the civic center was completed.

Required:

Indicate the name of the fund(s) and/or account group(s) in which each of the transactions or events should be recorded.

Exercise 21-2

The following transactions take place:

1. A commitment was made to transfer general revenues to the entity in charge of providing transportation for all government agencies.
2. Construction bonds were issued at a premium. The premium is to be included in funds accumulated to retire the debt.
3. Police salaries were paid.
4. Interest and principal were paid on general obligation serial bonds.

Required:

Indicate the name of the fund(s) and/or account group(s) in which each of the transactions or events should be recorded.

Exercise 12-3

The following transactions take place:

1. The Special Revenue Fund transfers $8,000 to the Internal Service Fund as a temporary loan.
2. The Internal Service Fund bills the Special Revenue Fund $20,000 for services performed.
3. Interest payments in the amount of $14,000 that are the responsibility of the Debt Service Fund are paid by the General Fund.
4. The unexpended balance of the Capital Projects Fund, which is $65,000, is transferred to the General Fund.
5. Current expendable revenues of the Trust Fund in the amount of $35,000 are transferred to the Special Revenue Fund.
6. The General Fund transfers $100,000 to start an Internal Service Fund.

Required:

A. Identify the transactions as a quasi-external transaction, a reimbursement, a loan or advance, a residual equity transfer, or an operating transfer and prepare entries in general journal form to record the transactions on the records of the funds involved.

B. Why is it important to distinguish residual equity transfers from operating transfers?

Exercise 21-4

The following events take place:

1. Hector Madras died and left 100 acres of undeveloped land to the city for a future park. He acquired the land at $100 an acre, but at the date of his death the land was appraised at $8,000 an acre.
2. The city authorized the transfer of $100,000 of general revenues and the issuance of $1,000,000 in general obligation bonds to construct improvements on the donated land. The bonds were sold at par.
3. The improvements were completed at a cost of $1,100,000, and the operation of the park was turned over to the City Parks Department.

Required:

Prepare entries in general journal form to record these transactions in the proper fund(s) or account group(s). Designate the fund or account group in which each transaction is recorded.

Exercise 21-5

The following transactions take place:

1. The General Fund repaid the Special Revenue Fund a loan of $10,000 plus $900 in interest on the loan.
2. On January 1, the city issued 9% general obligation bonds with a face value of $2,000,000 payable in 10 years to finance the construction of city offices. Total proceeds were $2,300,000.
3. On December 20, construction was completed and occupancy taken of the city offices. The full cost of $1,960,000 was paid to the contractor, and appropriate closing entries were made with regard to the project.

Required:

Prepare entries in general journal form to record these transactions in the proper fund(s) and/or account group(s). Designate the fund or account group in which each entry is recorded

Exercise 21-6

On January 1, 1995, Allentown issued $800,000 of 9% serial bonds at par. Semiannual interest is payable on January 1 and July 1 and principal of $80,000 matures each January 1 starting in 1996. The debt will be serviced through a special tax levy designed especially for this purpose. Therefore, transfers will be provided as needed from the Special Revenue Fund.

The following transactions occurred relating to the Debt Service Fund.

1995

June 29	A transfer of $36,000 was received from the Special Revenue Fund.
July 1	The semiannual interest payment was made.
Dec. 18	A Special Revenue Fund transfer of $120,000 was received.

1996

Jan. 1	A payment on bond principal and semiannual interest was made.

2005

Jan. 2	Accumulations in the Debt Service Fund amounted to $55,000 in investments and $40,000 in cash. The investments were liquidated at face value and the final interest and principal payment was made.
Jan. 4	Having served its purpose, the Debt Service Fund's remaining assets were transferred to the Special Revenue Fund.

Required:

Prepare the journal entries necessary to record the foregoing transactions.

Exercise 21-7

Select the best answer for each of the following:

1. The City of Apache should use a Capital Projects Fund to account for
    (a) Structures and improvements constructed with the proceeds of a special assessment.
    (b) Special Revenue funds set aside to acquire land for city parks.
    (c) Construction in progress on the city-owned electric utility plant, financed by an issue of revenue bonds.
    (d) Assets to be used to retire bonds issued to finance an addition to the City Hall.
2. Activities of a central print shop offering printing services at cost to various city departments should be accounted for in
    (a) The General Fund.
    (b) An Internal Service Fund.
    (c) A Special Revenue Fund.
    (d) An Agency Fund.
3. Adams County collects property taxes for the benefit of the state government and the local school districts and periodically remits collections to these units. These activities should be accounted for in
    (a) An Agency Fund.
    (b) The General Fund.
    (c) An Internal Service Fund.
    (d) A Special Revenue Fund.
4. In order to provide for the retirement of general obligation bonds, the City of Globe invests a portion of its receipts from general property taxes in marketable securities. This investment activity should be accounted for in
    (a) A Capital Projects Fund.
    (b) A Debt Service Fund.
    (c) A Trust Fund.
    (d) The General Fund.

5. The transactions of a municipal police retirement system should be recorded in
   (a) The General Fund.
   (b) A Special Revenue Fund.
   (c) A Trust Fund.
   (d) An Internal Service Fund.

(AICPA adapted)

Exercise 21-8

Select the best answer for each of the following:

1. The activities of a municipal golf course that receives three-fourths of its total revenue from a special tax levy should be accounted for in
   (a) An Enterprise Fund.
   (b) The General Fund.
   (c) A Trust Fund.
   (d) A Special Revenue Fund.
2. Equipment in general governmental service that had been constructed 10 years before with resources of a Capital Projects Fund was sold. The receipts were accounted for as unrestricted revenue. Entries are necessary in the
   (a) General Fund and Capital Projects Fund.
   (b) General Fund and General Fixed Assets Account Group.
   (c) General Fund, Capital Projects Fund, and Enterprise Fund.
   (d) General Fund, Capital Projects Fund, and General Fixed Assets Account Group.
3. An account for expenditures does not appear in which fund?
   (a) Capital Projects.
   (b) Enterprise.
   (c) General.
   (d) Special Revenue.
4. Part of the general obligation bond proceeds from a new issuance was used to pay for the cost of a new City Hall as soon as construction was completed. The remainder of the proceeds was transferred to repay the debt. Entries are needed to record these transactions in the
   (a) General Fund and General Long-term Obligation Account Group.
   (b) General Fund, General Long-term Obligation Account Group, and Debt Service Fund.
   (c) Trust Fund, Debt Service Fund, and General Fixed Assets Account Group.
   (d) General Long-term Obligation Account Group, Debt Service Fund, General Fixed Assets Account Group, and Capital Projects Fund.
5. Cash secured from property tax revenue was transferred for the eventual payment of principal and interest on general obligation bonds. The bonds had been issued when land was acquired several years ago for a city park. Upon the transfer, an entry would **not** be made in which of the following?
   (a) Debt Service Fund.
   (b) General Fixed Assets Account Group.
   (c) General Long-term Obligation Account Group.
   (d) General Fund.

(AICPA adapted)

Exercise 21-9

Select the best answer for each of the following:

1. Premiums received on general obligation bonds are generally transferred to what fund or group of accounts?
   (a) Debt Service.
   (b) General Long-term Obligation.
   (c) General.
   (d) Special Revenue.
2. Of the items listed below, those most likely to have parallel accounting procedures, account titles, and financial statements are
   (a) Special Revenue Funds and Internal Service Funds.
   (b) Internal Service Funds and Debt Service Funds.
   (c) The General Fixed Assets Account Group and the General Long-term Obligation Account Group.
   (d) The General Fund and Special Revenue Funds.
3. Recreational facilities run by a governmental unit and financed on a user-charge basis would be accounted for in which fund?
   (a) General.
   (b) Trust.
   (c) Enterprise.
   (d) Capital Projects.
4. Taylor City should record depreciation as an expense in its
   (a) Enterprise Fund and Internal Service Fund.
   (b) Internal Service Fund and General Fixed Assets Account Group.
   (c) General Fund and Enterprise Fund.
   (d) Enterprise Fund and Capital Projects Fund.
5. A performance budget relates a governmental unit's expenditures to
   (a) Objects of Expenditure.
   (b) Expenditures of the preceding fiscal year.
   (c) Individual months within the fiscal year.
   (d) Activities and programs.

(AICPA adapted)

Exercise 21-10

Select the best answer for each of the following:

1. The City of Milford authorized the building of facilities through capital improvement special assessments. Bonds are issued that will be paid out of special assessments, and the municipality has no obligation whatsoever to the bondholders for the repayment of the debt. The proceeds from the bond issue will be reported in the special assessments capital project fund as
   (a) Transfer from Debt Service Fund.
   (b) Contributions from property owners.
   (c) Debt issue proceeds.
   (d) Special assessment revenue.
2. A fund of a municipality that rarely reports a fund balance is the
   (a) General Fund.
   (b) Agency Fund.
   (c) Special Revenue Fund.
   (d) Expendable Trust Fund.

3. When special assessment debt is issued for which the municipality is not obligated in any manner, the appropriate account to debit in the general long-term obligation account group is
   (a) Contributions from property owners.
   (b) Amount to be provided by special assessments.
   (c) Amounts available in debt service fund.
   (d) None of the above.

4. When the proceeds from special assessment debt for which the municipality is not obligated in any way is used to complete a special assessment capital project involving general improvements, the appropriate account to debit in the general fixed asset account group on the completion of the project is
   (a) Improvements.
   (b) Investment from special assessment debt with government commitment.
   (c) Contributions by property owners.
   (d) Expenditures.

5. The payment of principal and interest on special assessment debt for which a municipality is not obligated in any way is accounted for in
   (a) A special assessments debt service fund.
   (b) The General Long-term Obligation Account Group.
   (c) A capital projects fund.
   (d) An agency fund.

Exercise 21-11

Write the name of the fund(s) and/or account group(s) in which each of the following transactions or events would be recorded.

1. Bonds, the proceeds of which were to be used for the construction of a new City Hall, were issued.
2. A sum of money was appropriated, to be advanced from monies on hand, to finance the establishment of a City Garage for servicing city-owned transportation equipment.
3. A contribution was received from a private source. The use of the income earned on the investment of this sum of money was specifically designated by the donor.
4. Proceeds received from a bond issue were used for the purchase of the privately owned water utility in the city.
5. Property taxes designated to be set aside for the eventual retirement of the City Hall building bonds were collected.
6. Real estate and personal property taxes, which had not been assessed or levied for any specific purpose, were collected.
7. Payment was made to the contractor for progress made in the construction of the new City Hall.
8. Interest was paid on the bonds issued for the purchase of the water utility.
9. Bonds, the proceeds of which are to be used to pay for the improvement of streets in the residential district, were issued. The debt is to be serviced by assessments on the property benefited. The government is obligated to the bondholders to assure the timely payment of principal and interest on the debt.
10. Salaries of personnel in the office of the mayor were paid.
11. Interest was paid on the City Hall building bonds.
12. Installment payments were received from the property owners assessed for the street improvement project.
13. Interest was paid on bonds issued for the payment of the improvement of streets in the residential district.

14. Interest was received on the investment of moneys set aside for the retirement of the City Hall building bonds.
15. Sums of money were received from employees by payroll deductions to be used for the purchase of United States government bonds for those employees individually.
16. City motor vehicle license fees, to be used for general street expenditures, were collected.
17. Materials to be used for the general repair of the streets were purchased.
18. The City Garage was reimbursed for services on the equipment of the fire and police departments.
19. Excess funds were transferred from the water utility to the General Fund.

(AICPA adapted)

Exercise 21-12

On June 1, 1995, the City of Cape May authorized the construction of a police station at an expected cost of $250,000. Financing will be provided through transfers from a Special Revenue Fund.

The following transactions occurred during the fiscal year beginning June 1, 1995, relating to the Capital Project Fund.

1. The $250,000 receivable from the Special Revenue Fund was recorded.
2. The Special Revenue Fund transferred $125,000 to the Capital Project Fund to begin construction on the police station.
3. The Capital Project Fund invested the transfer of monies in a six-month certificate, at 5%.
4. A contract in the amount of $250,000 was let to the lowest bidder.
5. Architect and legal fees in the amount of $3,125 were approved for payment. There was no encumbrance for these expenditures.
6. Contract billings in the amount of $250,000 were approved for payment on the completion of the police station and the encumbrance was removed.
7. The six-month certificate was redeemed at maturity with interest revenue.
8. The Special Revenue Fund transferred the final amount of $125,000 to the Capital Projects Fund.
9. All liabilities except for the retention of 5% of the contract price were paid.
10. All requirements and obligations were completed; the final payment of the contract price was made and all nominal accounts were closed.

Required:

Prepare the journal entries necessary in the Capital Projects Fund to record the transactions and events described above.

Exercise 21-13

The town of Aberdeen authorized a fire station to be built at an estimated cost of $150,000. On January 1, 1995, 6% bonds with a par value of $150,000 were authorized and issued. Any difference between the par value of the bonds and the proceeds from their sale is transferred to the Debt Service Fund.

The following transactions relating to the Capital Project Fund occurred during 1995.

1. Encumbrances were recorded on signing contracts in the amount of $150,000.
2. Proceeds from the bond issue were received in the amount of $155,000.

3. The premium on the bond issue was transferred to the Debt Service Fund.
4. Contract billings in the amount of $150,000 were approved for payment on the completion of the fire station.
5. The contractor was paid except for retention of 5% of the contract price.
6. The final contract price was paid on the completion of the requirements and obligations of the contract. The nominal accounts were closed.

Required:

Prepare the journal entries necessary in the Capital Projects Fund to record the transactions and events described above.

Exercise 21-14

The Town of Aberdeen authorizes the construction of a Town Hall. The Town Hall is to be financed by a transfer from the General Fund in the amount of $15,000 and by the issuance of 6%, 10-year term bonds with a par value of $150,000.

The following transactions transpired relating to the General Long-term Obligation Account Group:

1. On January 1, 1995, the 6%, 10-year term bonds were issued for $162,000. The premium was transferred to the Debt Service Fund.
2. The General Fund transferred $25,000 to the Debt Service Fund on December 20, 2004.
3. The $150,000 par value term bonds were redeemed when they matured on December 31, 2004.

Required:

Prepare the journal entries necessary in the General Long-term Obligation Account Group to record the transactions and events described above.

Problems

Problem 21-1

On January 1, 1995, the City of Cape May authorized and issued $200,000 of 5%, three-year term bonds. Interest is payable annually on December 31. A debt service fund is established to accumulate the necessary resources to pay the annual interest on the bonds and to redeem the bonds when they mature. The required annual addition for principal and interest will be transferred annually to the debt service fund from the general fund. It is assumed that amounts received by the debt service fund for the payment of principal can be invested at an annual return of 8%.

Required:

A. Prepare a schedule to calculate the annual required additions and annual required earnings to repay the principal on the bonds assuming that the first installment for principal and interest is transferred to the debt service fund from the general fund on December 30, 1995.
B. Prepare the entries to be recorded by the debt service fund as follows:
   1. The 1996 budget entry.

2. The entry to record the annual transfer from the general fund.
3. The entry to record the annual payment of interest.
4. The entry to record $4,929 in interest income for 1996.
5. The entry(s) to close the accounts at the end of 1996.

Problem 21-2

The Town of Green River authorized a municipal building to be constructed at a cost of $175,000. The construction will be financed from the proceeds from the issue of $175,000 of 6% bonds. Any difference between the par value of the bonds and the proceeds from their sale is transferred to the Debt Service Fund.

Transactions and events relating to this project include the following:

1. The proceeds from the sale of the bonds were received and included a premium on the bond issue in the amount of $15,000. The premium was transferred to Debt Service Fund.
2. Encumbrances were recorded on signing of the construction contract in the amount of $175,000.
3. Contract billings in the amount of $85,000 were approved for payment.
4. Contract billings were paid in the amount of $85,000.
5. All nominal accounts were closed and construction in progress was recorded in the appropriate account group in anticipation of the preparation of financial statements.
6. Encumbrances that were closed in anticipation of the preparation of financial statements are reestablished in the Capital Projects Fund.
7. Contract billings in the amount of $90,000 were approved on the completion of the municipal building.
8. Contract billings of $90,000 less a retention of 5% were paid.
9. The building was accepted, all construction liabilities were paid, and the building was recorded as an asset in the appropriate account group.

Required:

Prepare the journal entries relating to the Capital Projects Fund and corresponding entries, if any, relating to the General Fixed Assets Account Group, the General Long-term Obligation Account Group, and the Debt Service Fund for the transactions and events described above. Clearly identify the fund or account group in which each entry is recorded.

Problem 21-3

The City of Dayville has undertaken a sidewalk construction project. The project is being financed by the proceeds from the issue on July 1, 1995, of $500,000 of 7% special assessment debt. One quarter of the principal plus interest is payable on June 30 of each year beginning June 30, 1996. Property owners are assessed to provide the funds to pay the principal and interest on the debt.

The following transactions occurred during the period July 1, 1995, through June 30, 1996.

1. The bonds for the construction of the sidewalks were issued at par value.
2. The sidewalks were completed at a cost of $500,000.

3. Property owners were assessed and billed for the first installment of principal and interest on the special assessment debt.
4. Assessments for the first installment of principal and interest on the special assessment debt were collected and the June 30, 1996, payment of principal and interest on the special assessment debt was made.

Required:

Prepare all journal entries for the above transactions that are necessary in the funds and account groups of City of Dayville assuming that

A. The City of Dayville has made a commitment to the holders of the special assessment debt to assure the timely and full payment of principal and interest on the appropriate due dates.

B. The City of Dayville has not obligated itself in any manner on the special assessment debt that was issued for the construction of the sidewalks.

Problem 21-4

The administrators of the City of Lyons have obtained approval from the City Council to centralize the computer facility as of January 1, 1995. An internal service fund is created to account for the activities of the computer facility. The City Council has approved a contribution of $25,000 from the General Fund for use as working capital and an advance from the Electric Utility Fund of $355,000 for the purchase of equipment and facilities. The $355,000 advance will be repaid by the internal service fund in 20 equal annual installments.

The following transactions relate to the establishment and operation of the Internal Service Fund.

January 1	The computer facility received the contribution from the General Fund and the advance from the Electric Utility Fund.
January 4	Land and a building were purchased for $175,000 of which $25,000 was assigned to land. Hardware was purchased for $125,000 and equipment to protect the hardware was purchased for $55,000.
April 10	The computer facility billed the Electric Utility Fund for service provided. The service cost $200,000 and was billed at a mark-up of 25% on cost. (Direct costs of providing computer services are accumulated in the "Computer Service" account. When services are billed to departments, this account is credited and the "Cost of Service" account is debited for the cost of services billed.)
April 29	Administrative expenses totaling $10,000 were approved for payment.
May 1	Payment of $37,750 was received from the Electric Utility in partial payment of the April 10 billing.
May 1	The administrative expense was paid.
December 2	The first of 20 equal annual installments to the Electric Utility Fund was paid.
December 30	Depreciation expense was recorded for the year as administration expense. The building was estimated to have a remaining useful life of 25 years; the hardware was estimated to have a useful life of 5 years; the equipment to protect the hardware was estimated to have a useful life of 10 years.
December 31	The nominal accounts of the internal service fund were closed through a closing account, "Excess of Billings to Departments over Costs," which in turn was closed to retained earnings.

Required:

Prepare the journal entries necessary in the Internal Service Fund to record the transactions and events described above. The chart of accounts presented below may be used as an aid.

CURRENT ASSETS:

Cash
Due from general fund
Due from electric utility fund
Computer service

FIXED ASSETS:

Land
Building
Equipment—hardware
Equipment—protection
Accumulated depreciation

LIABILITIES:

Vouchers payable
Advance from electric utility

FUND EQUITY:

Contribution from general fund
Retained earnings

REVENUE:

Billing to departments

COSTS AND EXPENSE:

Cost of computer service
Administrative expense

The closing account, "Excess of Billings to Departments over Costs," is similar to the "Income Summary" account of a corporation.

Problem 21-5

An administrative section of the County Assessor's Office of Mecklenburg County serves as the billing and collection agency for all property taxes assessed in Mechlenburg County. A charge of 1% of taxes and penalties collected is apportioned among recipients of the taxes for this service. All property tax records—current and delinquent—are maintained in this administrative unit. The 1% charge is included as revenue in the General Fund budget of the county government.

Information relative to the collection of property taxes for fiscal year 1995 is as follows:

Assessed valuation	$5,826,300
Tax rates per $100 assessed:	
County government	$1.20
State government	.80
City of Midvale	2.80
Unified school district	3.20

Tax bills are issued on January 1; taxes are payable without penalty by April 30; taxes paid after April 30 are subject to a 5% penalty for late payment. Taxes not paid by June 30 are considered delinquent.

No delinquent taxes remain uncollected for years prior to 1995.

An estimated 3% of billed taxes for 1995 will be uncollectible.

A summary of the activities of the Tax Agency Fund for the period January 1, 1995, to June 30, 1995, includes the following:

January 1   Tax bills are mailed to property owners. Accounts are opened by the tax collection unit.

April 30   Taxes collected and deposited during first four months total $372,883.
Distribution of taxes collected is made to the applicable governmental units.

June 30   Taxes collected and deposited during May and June including the 5% penalty total $73,412.
Distribution of taxes and penalties collected is made to the applicable governmental units.

Required:

A. Prepare in general journal form entries to record the activities of the Tax Agency Fund from January 1 to June 30. Establish a Delinquent Account for taxes not collected.

B. Prepare a balance sheet for the Tax Agency Fund after adjusting the accounts on June 30.

Problem 21-6

The following activities and transactions are typical of those that may affect the various funds used by a typical municipal government.

Required:

Prepare journal entries to record each transaction and identify the fund or group of accounts in which each entry is recorded.

A. The Greenville City Council passed a resolution approving a general operating budget of $5,000,000 for the fiscal year 1995. Total revenues are estimated at $4,900,000.

B. The Greenville City Council passed an ordinance providing a property tax levy of $6.25 per $100 of assessed valuation for the fiscal year 1995. Total property valuation in Greenville City is $204,800,000. Property is assessed at 25% of current property valuation. Property tax bills are mailed to property owners. An estimated 3% will be uncollectible.

C. Reed City sold a general obligation term bond issue for $1,000,000 at 105 to a major brokerage firm. The stated interest rate is 5%. Proceeds are to be used for construction of a new Central Law Enforcement Building. (*Note:* Entries are required in the Capital Project Fund and the General Long-term Obligation Accounts.)

D. The premium on bond sale in (C) above is transferred to the Debt Service Fund.

E. At the end of fiscal year 1995, the Greenville City Council approves the write-off of $52,550 of uncollected 1994 taxes because of inability to locate the property owners. The tax bills have been referred to the legal department for further action.

F. The Reed City Central Law Enforcement Building [(C) above] is completed. Contracts and expenses total $989,000, and all have been paid and recorded in the Capital Projects Fund. Prepare entries to close this project and record the completion of the project in all other funds or account groups affected. Any balance in the Capital Project Fund is to be applied to payment of interest and principal of the bond issue.

G. On May 1, 1995, Hopi City supervised the issue of 6% serial bonds at par to finance street curbing in an area recently incorporated in the city limits. The face amount of the bonds is $600,000; interest is payable annually, and bonds are to be retired in equal amounts over five years from collections from assessments against property owners. The

City acts as a collection agent and has given assurances to the debt holders that it will guarantee payment of principal and interest even though it is not obligated to do so.

(1) Record the issuance of the bonds on May 1, 1995.

(2) Record the payment to bondholders on May 1, 1996.

H. The curbing project in (G) above was completed on November 30 at a total cost of $590,000. Record summary entries for expenditure transactions May 1–November 30, 1995, and on completion of the project.

Problem 21-7

The following transactions take place.

1. Bond proceeds of $1,000,000 were received to be used in constructing a firehouse. An equal amount is contributed from general revenues.

2. $800,000 of serial bonds matured. Interest of $120,000 was paid on these and other serial bonds outstanding.

3. $8,000 was received as insurance proceeds from the accidental destruction of a four-year-old police car costing $24,000.

4. $120,000 in expendable funds was transferred from the City Parks Endowment Fund to the City Parks Special Revenue Fund.

5. Equipment purchased from general revenues at a cost of $200,000 was sold for $40,000

6. The City Water Company (an enterprise fund) issued a bill for $800 for water provided to the street department's street cleaner.

7. The City Water Company transferred $400,000 in excess funds to the General Fund.

8. A central motor pool was established by a contribution of $120,000 from the General Fund, a long-term loan of $80,000 from the City Park Special Revenue Fund, and general obligation bond issue proceeds of $200,000.

9. The Motor Pool Fund billed the General Fund $10,000 and the City Park Fund $4,000 for the use of motor vehicles.

10 Special Assessment Bonds in the amount of $400,000 were retired. The city has indicated a willingness to guarantee the payment of principal even though it was not obligated to do so.

11. Customers' deposits of $8,000 for water meters were received by the City Water Company during the year. The monies are to be held in trust until the customers request that their services be disconnected and the final bills are collected.

12. It is determined that the Debt Service Fund will require an annual contribution of $60,000 and earnings of $6,000 in the current year to accumulate the amounts necessary to retire general obligation term bonds.

Required:

Prepare entries in general journal form to record these transactions in the proper fund(s) or account group(s). Designate the fund or account group in which each entry is recorded.

Problem 21-8

You have been engaged to examine the financial statements of the Town of Bridgeport for the year ended June 30, 1995. Your examination disclosed that, because of the inexperience of the town's bookkeeper, all transactions were recorded in the General Fund. The following General Fund trial balance as of June 30, 1995, was furnished to you.

General Fund Trial Balance
Town of Bridgeport
June 30, 1995

	DEBIT	CREDIT
Cash	$ 16,800	
Short-term investments	40,000	
Accounts receivable	11,500	
Taxes receivable—current year	30,000	
Tax anticipation notes payable		$ 50,000
Appropriations		400,000
Expenditures	382,000	
Estimated revenue	320,000	
Revenues		360,000
General property	85,400	
Bonds payable	52,000	
Fund balance		127,700
	$937,700	$937,700

Your audit disclosed the following additional information:

1. The accounts receivable of $11,500 includes $1,500 due from the town's water utility for the sale of scrap sold on its behalf. Accounts for the municipal water utility are maintained in a separate fund.

2. The balance in Taxes Receivable—Current Year is now considered delinquent, and the town estimates that $24,000 will be uncollectible.

3. On June 30, 1995, the town retired, at par value, 6% general obligation serial bonds totaling $40,000. The bonds were issued on July 1, 1990, at a face value of $200,000. Interest paid during the year ended June 30, 1995, was charged to Bonds Payable.

4. Expenditures for the year ended June 30, 1995, included $11,200 applicable to purchase orders issued to the prior year. Outstanding purchase orders at June 30, 1995, not recorded in the accounts amounted to $17,500.

5. On June 28, 1995, the State Revenue Department informed the town that its share of a state-collected, locally shared tax would be $34,000.

6. During the year, equipment with a book value of $7,900 was removed from service and sold for $4,600. In addition, new equipment costing $90,000 was purchased. The transactions were recorded in General Property.

7. During the year, 100 acres of land were donated to the town for use as an industrial park. The land had a value of $400,000. This donation has not been recorded.

Required:

A. Prepare the formal reclassification, adjusting, and closing journal entries for the General Fund as of June 30, 1995.

B. Prepare the formal adjusting journal entries for any other fund or group of accounts as of June 30, 1995.

(AICPA adapted)

Problem 21-9

The Village of Oakridge, which was incorporated recently, began financial operations on July 1, 1995, the beginning of its fiscal year. The following transactions occurred during this first fiscal year, July 1, 1995, to June 30, 1996:

1. The Village Council adopted a budget for general operations during the fiscal year ended June 30, 1996. Revenues were estimated at $400,000. Legal authorizations for budgeted expenditures were $394,000.
2. Property taxes were levied in the amount of $390,000; it was estimated that 2% of this amount would prove to be uncollectible. These taxes are available as of the date of levy to finance current expenditures.
3. During the year, a resident of the village donated marketable securities valued at $50,000 to the village under the terms of a trust agreement. The terms of the trust agreement stipulated that the principal amount is to be kept intact; use of revenue generated by the securities is restricted to financing college scholarships for needy students. Revenue earned and received on these marketable securities amounted to $5,500 through June 30, 1996.
4. A General Fund transfer of $5,000 was made to establish an Internal Service Fund to provide for a permanent investment in inventory.
5. During the year the Internal Service Fund purchased various supplies at a cost of $1,900.
6. Cash collections recorded by the General Fund during the year were as follows:

Property taxes	$386,000
Licenses and permits	7,000

7. The Village Council decided to build a village hall at an estimated cost of $500,000 to replace space occupied in rented facilities. The village does not record project authorizations. It was decided that general obligation bonds bearing interest at 6.5% would be issued. On June 30, 1996, the bonds were issued at their face value of $500,000, payable June 30, 2013. No contracts have been signed for this project, and no expenditures have been made.
8. A fire truck was purchased for $150,000 and the voucher approved and paid by the General Fund. This expenditure was previously encumbered for $150,000.

Required:

Prepare journal entries to record each of the transactions above in the appropriate fund(s) or group of accounts of Oakridge Village for the fiscal year ended June 30, 1996. Use the following funds and account groups:

General Fund

Capital Projects Fund

Internal Service Fund

Trust Fund

General Long-term Obligation Group of Accounts

General Fixed Assets Group of Accounts

Each journal entry should be numbered to correspond with the transactions described above. Do *not* prepare closing entries for any fund. Present your answer in the following format:

TRANSACTION NUMBER	FUND OR GROUP OF ACCOUNTS	ACCOUNT TITLE AND EXPLANATION	DEBIT	CREDIT

(AICPA adapted)

Problem 21-10

The following transactions represent practical situations frequently encountered in accounting for municipal governments. Each transaction is independent of the others.

1. The City Council of Bernardville adopted a budget for the general operations of the government during the new fiscal year. Revenues were estimated at $695,000. Legal authorizations for budgeted expenditures were $650,000.
2. Taxes of $160,000 were levied for the special revenue fund of Millstown. One percent was estimated to be uncollectible.
3. (a) On July 25, 1996, office supplies estimated to cost $2,390 were ordered for the city manager's office of Bullersville. Bullersville, which operates on the calendar year, does not maintain an inventory of such supplies.
   (b) The supplies ordered July 25 were received on August 9, 1996, accompanied by an invoice for $2,500.
4. On October 10, 1996, the general fund of Washingtonville repaid to the utility fund a loan of $1,000 plus $40 interest. The loan had been made earlier in the fiscal year.
5. A prominent citizen died and left 10 acres of undeveloped land to Harper City for a future school site. The donor's cost of the land was $55,000. The fair value of the land was $85,000.
6. (a) On March 6, 1996, Dahlstrom City supervised the issue of 6% special assessment bonds payable March 6, 2001, at face value of $90,000. Interest is payable annually. Dahlstrom City, which operates on the calendar year, will supervise the use of the proceeds to finance a curbing project. The City has made no commitments and has not obligated itself in any manner with respect to the payment of principal and interest on the debt.
   (b) On October 26, 1996, the full $84,000 cost of the completed curbing project was recorded. Also, appropriate closing entries were made with regard to the project.
7. (a) Conrad Thamm, a citizen of Basking Knoll, donated common stock valued at $22,000 to the City under a trust agreement. Under the terms of the agreement, the principal amount is to be kept intact; use of revenue from the stock is restricted to financing college scholarships for needy students.
   (b) On December 14, 1996, dividends of $1,100 were received on the stock donated by Mr. Thamm.
8. (a) On February 23, 1996, the Town of Lincoln, which operates on the calendar year, issued 5% general obligation bonds with a face value of $300,000 payable February 23, 2006, to finance the construction of an addition to the City Hall. Total proceeds were $308,000.
   (b) On December 31, 1996, the addition to the City Hall was officially approved, the full cost of $297,000 was paid to the contractor, and appropriate closing entries were made with regard to the project. (Assume that no entries have been made with regard to the project since February 23, 1996.)

Required:

For each transaction, prepare the necessary journal entries for all the funds and groups of accounts involved. No explanation of the journal entries is required. Use the following headings for your workpaper.

TRANSACTION NUMBER	JOURNAL ENTRIES	DR.	CR.	FUND OR GROUP OF ACCOUNTS

In the far right column, indicate in which fund or group of accounts each entry is to be made, using the coding below:

Funds

General	G
Special revenue	SR
Capital projects	CP
Debt service	DS
Enterprise	E
Internal service	IS
Trust and agency (governmental)	TAG
Trust and agency (proprietary)	TAP

Groups of accounts

General fixed assets	GFA
General long-term obligation	LTO

(AICPA adapted)

Problem 21-11

The City of Minden entered into the following transactions during the year 1996.

1. A bond issue was authorized by vote to provide funds for the construction of a new municipal building, which it was estimated would cost $1,000,000. The bonds are to be paid in 10 equal installments from a Debt Service Fund, and payments are due March 1 of each year. Any premium on the bond issue, as well as any balance of the Capital Projects Fund, is to be transferred directly to the Debt Service Fund.
2. An advance of $80,000 was received from the General Fund to underwrite a deposit on the land contract of $120,000. The deposit was made.
3. Bonds of $900,000 were sold for cash at 102. It was decided not to sell all the bonds because the cost of the land was less than expected.
4. Contracts amounting to $780,000 were let to Sandstone and Company, the low bidder, for construction of the municipal building.
5. The temporary advance from the General Fund was repaid and the balance on the land contract was paid.
6. On the basis of the architect's certificate, contract billings were approved for $640,000 for the work completed to date.
7. Contract billings paid in cash by the treasurer amounted to $620,000.
8. Because of changes in the plans, the contract with Sandstone and Company was revised to $880,000; the remainder of the bonds were sold at 101.
9. Before the end of the year, the building had been completed, and additional contract billings amounting to $230,000 approved. All contract billings were paid by the treasurer to the contractor in final payment for the work.

Required:

A. Prepare entries to record the foregoing transactions (excluding the entries necessary to close out the fund) of the Capital Projects Fund.

B. Prepare a preclosing trial balance for the Capital Projects Fund.

C. Prepare entries necessary to close out the Capital Projects Fund on the completion of construction.

D. Prepare a statement of revenue, expenditures, and other changes in fund balance for the Capital Projects Fund.

E. Prepare preclosing trial balances at December 31, 1996, for the Debt Service Fund, General Fixed Assets Account Group, and General Long-term Obligation Account Group, considering only the proceeds, expenditures, and transfers resulting from transactions of the Capital Projects Fund.

(AICPA adapted)

22

INTRODUCTION TO ACCOUNTING FOR NONGOVERNMENT NONBUSINESS ORGANIZATIONS

Nonbusiness Organizations other than Governmental Units are referred to in this text as Nongovernment Nonbusiness Organizations or NNOs. There are four major classifications of NNOs.

1. Nonprofit institutions of higher education including colleges, universities, and community colleges.

2. Hospitals and other health care providers.

3. Voluntary Health and Welfare Organizations (VHWOs) are organizations that derive their revenue from voluntary contributions of the general public to be used for purposes connected with health, welfare, or community services. Examples of such organizations include heart associations, family planning councils, mental health associations, and foundations for the blind.

4. Other Nongovernment Nonbusiness Organizations (ONNOs) take a variety of forms and include cemetery organizations, civic organizations, fraternal organizations, labor unions, libraries, museums, other cultural institutions, performing arts organizations, political parties, private and community foundations, private elementary and secondary schools, professional associations, public broadcasting stations, religious organizations, social and country clubs, trade associations and zoological and botanical societies.

SOURCES OF GENERALLY ACCEPTED ACCOUNTING STANDARDS FOR NONGOVERNMENT NONBUSINESS ORGANIZATIONS

Until the early 1970s, accounting and reporting practices for NNOs were developed under the auspices of different interested professional associations such as the American Hospital Association, the Hospital Financial Management Association, the American Council on Education, and the National Association of College and University Business Officers. In the early 1970s, the AICPA exhibited an interest in financial reporting problems in this area that resulted in the issuance of separate *Industry Audit Guides for Hospitals, Colleges and Universities,* and *Voluntary Health and Welfare Organizations.* These *Audit Guides* were developed by different committees over approximately the same time period.

Inevitably, there were differences in the practices and reporting standards recommended in the different *Audit Guides* as well as differences between those recommended in the *Audit Guides* and those recommended in the publications of the professional associations. Later, several *Statements of Position* issued by the Accounting Standards Division of the AICPA resulted in amendments to each of the *Audit Guides.* In addition, a *Statement of Position* was issued containing the recommendations of the AICPA on accounting and reporting standards for NNOs not covered under the three *Industry Audit Guides.* By the late 1970s, all significant differences between the financial accounting and reporting standards recommended in the *Audit Guides* and those recommended in the publications of the professional associations relating to hospitals and to colleges and universities had been resolved and the various professional association publications, and *Audit Guides* had been amended accordingly. Unfortunately, there continue to be significant differences among the *Audit Guides* (as amended) themselves with regard to recommended accounting and reporting practices for different types of NNOs.

In 1979 the Financial Accounting Standards Board assumed responsibility for setting accounting and reporting standards for all nonbusiness organizations except governmental units. In preparation for addressing specific standards for NNOs, the Board first undertook to incorporate NNOs into its *Statements of Financial Accounting Concepts.* In 1980 the Board issued *FASB Concepts Statement No. 4,* "Objectives of Financial Reporting by Nonbusiness Organizations." In 1985 the Board amended *FASB Concepts Statement No. 2,* "Qualitative Characteristics of Accounting Information," to apply to NNOs as well as to business enterprises and issued *Concepts Statement No. 6,* "Elements of Financial Statements," which encompasses NNOs as well as business enterprises. Until recently the Board has issued only one *Statement of Financial Accounting Standards, SFAS No. 93,* "Recognition of Depreciation by Not for Profit Organizations" (1987), relating to NNOs. The Board recently completed projects on contributions and financial statement display.

Hierarchy of Generally Accepted Reporting Standards for Nongovernment Nonbusiness Organizations

Not-for-profit organizations (such as colleges and universities, and health care providers) that may be either government owned or privately owned are referred to herein as *special entities.* Government-owned special entities come under the jurisdiction of the GASB. The hierarchy used to establish generally accepted reporting standards for all state and local governmental-owned entities was presented in Chapter 21. Government-owned special entities come under that hierarchy. The hierarchy used to establish generally accepted reporting standards for NNOs other than government owned special entities is the same as that for business organizations and may be summarized as follows.

1. First level of priority
   A. FASB Statements and interpretations.
2. Second level of priority
   A. FASB Technical Bulletins.
   B. AICPA Industry Audit and Accounting Guides and AICPA Statements of Position, *if cleared by the FASB*.
3. Third level of priority
   A. Consensus positions of the FASB Emerging Issues Task Force.
   B. AICPA AcSec Practice bulletins *if cleared by the FASB*.
4. Fourth level of priority
   A. AICPA accounting interpretations.
   B. Implementation Guides (Q & As) published by the FASB staff.
   C. Widely recognized and prevalent industry practices.
5. Fifth level of priority
   A. Other accounting literature including
      1. FASB Concepts Statements.
      2. Pronouncements of other professional associations or regulatory agencies.

This hierarchy lists the priority sequence of pronouncements that NNOs in the private sector should look to for accounting and reporting guidance.

With different hierarchies for entities under the jurisdiction of the FASB and entities under the jurisdiction of the GASB, different accounting standards may apply to special entities depending on whether they are privately owned or government owned. For example, *SFAS No. 93* requires that all privately owned not-for-profit organizations record depreciation. *GASB Statement No. 8* states that governmental entities including government-owned special entities need not record depreciation. As a result private-sector special entities (such as hospitals) will record depreciation, whereas many similar government-owned special entities will not.

With the exception of *SFAS No. 93*, No. 116, and No. 117, most of the guidance for NNOs other than government-owned special entities is found in *Audit and Accounting Guides* of the AICPA and in publications of industry associations. Such sources include:

Colleges and Universities
Audits of Colleges and Universities, second edition (AICPA, 1975)
Financial Accounting and Reporting Manual for Higher Education [National Association of College and University Business Officers (NACUBO), Loose Leaf]
Hospitals and Other Health Care Providers
Audits of Providers of Health Care Services (AICPA, 1989)

Voluntary Health and Welfare Organizations
  Audits of Voluntary Health and Welfare Organizations (AICPA, 1988)
Other Nongovernment Nonbusiness Organizations
  Audits of Certain Nonprofit Organizations, second edition (AICPA, 1987).

GASB Statement No. 15 allows public colleges and universities to use either the AICPA/NACUBO model (described in this chapter) or the government model (described in Chapter 21). In the discussion which follows, all illustrations, including those for colleges and universities, are based on the hierarchy previously described in this chapter.

Current Developments

The FASB recently issued two Statements of Financial Accounting Standards relating to NNOs. The standards deal with accounting for contributions and with financial statement display; they will have a significant impact on annual financial statements distributed beginning in 1996 by larger NNOs and in 1997 by smaller NNOs. Major changes required by these standards are discussed later in this chapter.

FUND ACCOUNTING

While in some instances the total resources of an NNO may be available to finance its functions and operating activities, in most cases restrictions are placed on certain of the organization's resources by donors, by law or contract, or by other external authorities. Donors, for example, often specify the specific purpose or program to which their contributions are to be applied, and in some instances the time period in which the resources contributed by them may be expended. To facilitate the observance of such restrictions, most NNOs use fund accounting for record-keeping and reporting purposes.

The fund structure of different nonbusiness organizations is summarized in Illustration 22-1. Although similar, the fund structure and terminology differ among NNOs primarily because of the separate development of accounting and reporting standards for the different organizations.

ACCRUAL BASIS OF ACCOUNTING

Generally accepted accounting standards require that financial statements for NNOs be prepared using the accrual basis of accounting. Thus, revenues are reported when earned and expenditures are reported when materials or services are received. Expenses incurred at the reporting date are accrued and expenses applicable to future periods are deferred. Although accrual accounting is used, the primary emphasis in reporting on NNOs is generally on disclosing the sources of the entity's resources and how they were used to accomplish the objectives of the organization rather than on the determination of net income.

ILLUSTRATION 22-1
Comparison of Fund Structures of Different Nonbusiness Organizations

NAMES OF THE FUNDS USED BY DIFFERENT NONBUSINESS ORGANIZATIONS

PRIMARY PURPOSE OF FUNDS AND ACCOUNT GROUPS	STATE AND LOCAL GOVERNMENTAL UNITS	COLLEGES AND UNIVERSITIES	HOSPITALS	VOLUNTARY HEALTH AND WELFARE ORGANIZATIONS AND OTHER NONGOVERNMENT NONBUSINESS ORGANIZATIONS (1)
Financing of Current Operations	General Special Revenue Expendable Trust	Unrestricted Current Restricted Current	General Specific Purpose	Current Unrestricted Current Restricted
Acquisition of and Accountability for Major Capital Assets and Related Long-term Obligations	Capital Projects (2) Debt Service General Fixed Assets Account Group General Long-term Obligation Account Group	Plant: Unexpended For Renewals and Replacements For Retirement of Indebtedness Investment in Plant	Plant Replacement and Expansion (3)	Land, Buildings, and Equipment (Plant)
Fiduciary Responsibilities	Nonexpendable Trust Agency	Endowment Quasi-endowment Loan Agency Annuity Life Income	Endowment Loan Agency (4)	Endowment Loan Custodial Annuity Life Income

(1) Although the authoritative literature does not set forth a required fund structure for Voluntary Health and Welfare Organizations and for Other Nongovernment Nonbusiness Organizations (ONNOs), the funds listed are those that are most commonly used.

(2) Under some circumstances, funds for the acquisition of capital assets by state and local government units may be accounted for in the General Fund, Special Revenue Funds, Nonexpendable Trust Funds, or Proprietary Funds (see Chapter 21).

(3) Capital assets and long-term obligations of hospitals are accounted for in the General Fund.

(4) Rather than setting up separate agency funds, hospitals often account for agency relationships in the General Fund.

CLASSIFICATION OF REVENUE AND EXPENSE

For reporting purposes, revenues are classified by source, and expenses and expenditures are classified by function or activity. Major sources of revenue for different types of NNOs are presented in Illustration 22-2. As indicated, hospitals distinguish between operating revenue and nonoperating revenue, and VHWOs and ONNOs distinguish between support and revenue. Typical functional classifications of expenditures and expenses for different types of NNOs are presented in Illustration 22-3.

ILLUSTRATION 22-2
Major Sources of Revenue for Different Classifications of
Nongovernment Nonbusiness Organizations

COLLEGES AND UNIVERSITIES	HOSPITALS	VOLUNTARY HEALTH AND WELFARE ORGANIZATIONS AND OTHER NONGOVERNMENT NONBUSINESS ORGANIZATIONS

Tuition and Fees
Federal, State, or Local
  Appropriations
Federal, State, or Local Grants
  and Contracts
Private Gifts, Grants, and
  Contracts
Endowment Income
Sales and Services of Educational
  Activities (film rentals, testing
  services, etc.)
Sales and Services of Auxiliary
  Enterprises (residence halls,
  food services, etc.)
	OPERATING REVENUE
	  Patient Service Revenue (Gross)
	    Less Deductions (charity
	    allowances, courtesy allowances
	    or policy discounts, contractual
	    adjustments, etc.)
	  Net Patient Service Revenue
	  Other Operating Revenue (tuition
	    from schools, specific-purpose
	    grants, revenue from auxiliary
	    enterprises, etc.)
	NONOPERATING REVENUE
	  Unrestricted Gifts and Grants
	  Unrestricted Income from
	    Endowment Funds
	  Donated Services
	  Income from Board Designated
	    Funds
		PUBLIC SUPPORT
		  Public Contributions
		  Special Events
		  Legacies and Bequests
		  Federated and Nonfederated
		    Campaigns
		REVENUE
		  Membership Dues
		  Investment Income
		  Realized Gains on
		    Investment Activities

ACCOUNTING FOR CURRENT FUNDS

As shown in Illustration 22-1, in accounting for the current operations of NNOs, a distinction is maintained between Unrestricted Funds and Restricted (Specific Purpose) Funds. Unrestricted funds of hospitals are accounted for in the General Fund.

Current Unrestricted Funds

Current Unrestricted Funds include financial resources of the organization that may be expended at the discretion of the governing board to carry out the operations of the organization and to accomplish its objectives. The resources and operations of Current Unrestricted Funds of NNOs are similar in many ways to the resources and operations of the General Fund of a municipality.

Current Restricted Funds

In a sense, all resources of an NNO that are not accounted for as Current Unrestricted Funds (that is, Endowment, Annuity, Loan, Plant, etc.) are restricted in that there are legal, contractual, or external restrictions on their use. Current Re-

ILLUSTRATION 22-3
Functional Classification of Expenditures and Expenses for
Different Types of Nongovernment Nonbusiness Organizations

COLLEGES AND UNIVERSITIES	HOSPITALS	VOLUNTARY HEALTH AND WELFARE ORGANIZATIONS AND OTHER NONGOVERNMENT NONBUSINESS ORGANIZATIONS
Instruction	Professional Care of	PROGRAM SERVICES
Academic Instruction	Patients	Research
Community Education	Dietary Services	Public Education
Research	General Services	Professional Education
Institutes and Centers	Administrative Services	and Training
Project Research	Employee Health and	Community Service
Public Service	Welfare	Other (1)
Community Service	Medical Malpractice Costs	SUPPORT SERVICES
Conferences and Institutes	Depreciation and	Management and General
Extension Service	Amortization	Fund Raising
Academic Support	Interest	
Computer Services	Provision for Bad Debts	
Libraries		
Student Services		
Admissions		
Counseling		
Financial Aid		
Health and Infirmary		
Intramural Athletics		
Student Organizations		
Registrar		
Remedial Instruction		
Institutional Support		
Operation and Maintenance		
of Plant		
Scholarships and Fellowships		
Auxiliary Enterprises		

(1) The functional classification of program services varies in accordance with the activities of different types of Other Nongovernment Nonbusiness Organizations.

stricted Funds are distinguished from other funds in that Current Restricted Funds consist of financial resources that are *currently available* for use in *operations,* but which may be expended only for purposes specified by the donor, grantor, or other *external* party.

Thus, the resources of both Current Funds—Restricted and Unrestricted— may be used by the organization to carry out its current operations and activities. Current unrestricted resources may be expended at the discretion of the governing board, whereas current restricted resources may be expended only in accordance with externally imposed restrictions.

Accounting for Board Designated Funds

The governing board of a NNO may designate resources of the Current Unrestricted Fund (General Fund of hospitals) for specific purposes (research), projects (additions to or replacements of plant), or investment (endowments). Such designations are intended to facilitate the planning and control of expenditures and to limit the discretion of management (as distinguished from the governing board) over the expenditure of the designated resources. However, these designations do not constitute and should not be confused with donor or external restrictions on the use of resources. The governing board has the authority to reverse or modify such designations at will. Accordingly, Board Designated Funds should be accounted for as Unrestricted Funds and the term "restricted" should not be used in connection with them. Such funds should never be included in the Current Restricted (Specific Purpose) Funds.

Assets set aside by the governing board of a hospital for board designated purposes are reported separately in the general funds portion of the balance sheet as **_Assets Whose Use Is Limited_**. Other NNOs report the amounts and purposes of Board Designated Funds either in the footnotes to the financial statements or by reclassification of an equivalent portion of the Current Unrestricted Fund Balance similar to an appropriation of retained earnings.

To illustrate, assume that the governing board designated $200,000 of Current Unrestricted Funds for future research grants and $50,000 for financing an addition to plant and equipment. Hospitals would report these designations in the assets section in the general funds section of the balance sheet as follows:

General Funds

Assets whose use is limited	
By board for research grants	$200,000
By board for acquisition of equipment	50,000
Total assets whose use is limited	$250,000

Assets whose use is limited under terms of debt indentures, trust agreements, third-party reimbursement arrangements, or other similar arrangements are also presented in the balance sheet as Assets Whose Use is Limited (see Illustration 22-5A).

NNOs other than health care providers or colleges and universities may simply report these designations in the footnotes to the financial statements, or they may reclassify a portion of the Current Unrestricted Fund Balance by recording an entry as follows:

Current Unrestricted Fund

(1) Fund Balance	250,000	
Board Designated Reserve for Research Grants		200,000
Board Designated Reserve for Plant Expansion		50,000
To record designation of reserves by action of governing board.		

The reserves would be reported as part of the total Current Unrestricted Fund Balance as follows:

Fund balance	
Available for current expenditures	$1,500,000*
Board designated reserve for research grants	200,000
Board designated reserve for plant expansion	50,000
Total current unrestricted fund balance	$1,750,000

*This is an assumed figure.

Generally accepted accounting standards for colleges and universities permit the transfer of unrestricted current resources that have been designated by the governing boards for loans, investments, or plant expansion to Loan Funds, Endowment Funds, and Plant Funds, respectively. Such designated amounts are distinguished from restricted portions of the recipient funds by using "Unrestricted" and "Restricted" Fund Balance accounts. Unrestricted Current Funds of colleges and universities that are designated by the board for specific current operating purposes are accounted for in the same manner that other NNOs account for Board Designated Funds (by footnote or by reclassification of the Unrestricted Current Fund Balance).

If in the preceding example the governing board had been the Board of Regents of a university, the entries recorded on the books of the university would be as follows:

Unrestricted Current Funds

(1) Fund Balance—Unallocated	200,000	
Fund Balance—Allocated		200,000
To establish fund balance reserve for research grants.		
(2) Nonmandatory Transfer to Plant Funds	50,000	
Cash		50,000
To record the transfer to plant funds for purposes of making additions to plant.		

Unexpended Plant Fund

(1) Cash	50,000	
Fund Balance—Unrestricted		50,000
To record the receipt of cash from the Unrestricted Current Fund for the purpose of financing additions to plant.		

Mandatory and Nonmandatory Transfers

The terms *Mandatory Transfer* and *Nonmandatory Transfer*, which are unique to accounting and reporting for colleges and universities, are described in the *Industry Audit Guide* as follows:[1]

---

[1] *Audits of Colleges and Universities*, second edition (New York: AICPA, 1975), p. 104.

Mandatory Transfers. This category should include transfers from the Current Funds group to other fund groups arising out of (1) binding legal agreements related to the financing of educational plant, such as amounts for debt retirement, interest, and required provisions for renewals and replacements of plant not financed from other sources and (2) grant agreements with agencies of the federal government, donors, and other organizations to match gifts and grants to loan and other funds. Mandatory transfers may be required to be made from unrestricted or restricted current funds.

Nonmandatory Transfers. This category should include those transfers from the Current Funds group to other fund groups made at the discretion of the governing board to serve a variety of objectives, such as additions to loan funds, additions to quasi-endowment funds, general or specific plant additions, voluntary renewals and replacements of plant, and prepayments on debt principal. It also may include the retransfer of resources back to current funds.

The recording of a nonmandatory (board designated) transfer was illustrated in the preceding section. To illustrate a mandatory transfer, assume that a university is required by the terms of a mortgage agreement to transfer $340,000 of tuition and fees that have been recorded as revenue in the Unrestricted Current Funds to pay principal and interst on long-term debt that is carried as a liability in the Plant Fund accounts. The transfer of funds is recorded as follows:

Unrestricted Current Funds

Mandatory Transfer to Plant Funds	340,000	
Cash		340,000
To record transfer of funds for payment of principal and interest on mortgage note carried as a liability in Plant Fund.		

Plant Fund (For Retirement of Indebtedness)

Cash	340,000	
Fund Balance—Restricted		340,000
To record receipt of Mandatory Transfer from Unrestricted Current Funds.		

Mandatory and nonmandatory transfers are shown separately in both the Statement of Changes in Fund Balances (Illustration 22-4B) and in the Statement of Current Funds Revenues, Expenditures, and Other Changes (Illustration 22-4C). Model financial statements for the four types of NNOs discussed in this chapter are presented in the appendix to this chapter in Illustrations 22-4A through 22-7B.

Deferral of Revenue Recognition in Current Restricted (Specific Purpose) Funds

In general, the receipt of assets for operating activities that have external restrictions as to the purposes for which they can be used is not recognized as revenue or support by NNOs until the restricted assets have been expended for their restricted purposes. On receipt of such assets, a Deferred Revenue or a Deferred Support account (VHWOs and ONNOs) or a Restricted Fund Balance account (universities and hopsitals) is credited. At the time the expenditure of the restricted assets is recorded (or before the preparation of the financial statements), additional entries are made that have the effect of reducing Deferred Revenue or Deferred Support or the Restricted Fund Balance and recording an amount of revenue equal to the amount of restricted assets expended. Reasons for delaying the recognition of revenue until the related assets are expended are (1) externally restricted resources are not considered "earned" until they are used for their designated purposes, and (2) it permits the recognition of revenue in the same period in which the expenditures that are directly related to the revenue are recognized.

The procedures for accomplishing this objective vary among NNOs. To illustrate, assume that an NNO received $109,000 in contributions that were restricted for specified current operating purposes and that during the period $82,000 of these resources were expended for the specified current operating purposes. Entries to account for these resources and their expenditure on the records of Universities, ONNOs, and Hospitals are summarized and compared here:

UNIVERSITIES

Restricted Current Funds

(1) Cash   109,000

       Fund Balance—Gifts Restricted for Operating Purposes   109,000

          To record contributions received that are restricted to specific operating purposes.

(2) Expenditures—Educational   82,000

       Cash   82,000

          To record expenditure of restricted assets for specified purposes.

(3) Fund Balance—Gifts Restricted for Operating Purposes   82,000

       Revenue—Educational   82,000

          To record revenue in amount of restricted assets expended during the period.

The same transactions would be recorded by ONNOs as follows:

OTHER NONGOVERNMENT NONBUSINESS ORGANIZATIONS

Current Restricted Fund

(1) Cash   109,000

       Deferred Support—Education (Liability)   109,000

          To record contributions received that are restricted to specific operating purposes.

(2) Public Education (Expense)   82,000

       Cash   82,000

          To record expenditure of restricted assets for specified purposes.

(3) Deferred Support—Education   82,000

       Public Contributions (Revenue)   82,000

          To record support in amount of restricted assets expended during the period.

The only difference between university and ONNO accounting for current restricted resources and the recognition of related revenue or support is that unexpended restricted resources are reported as part of the Restricted Fund Balances of a university, whereas such resources are reported as liabilities (deferred support) by ONNOs. The financial statement effects of the deferral of the recognition of restricted revenue or support by universities and ONNOs is that restricted revenue and support will always be equal to restricted expenses in the operating statements of these organizations (see Illustration 22-4C and Illustration 22-7B).

Revenues and expenses of hospitals are recorded only in the accounts of the General Fund. Changes in the resources of Specific Purpose Funds are recorded as direct debits or credits to the Fund Balance accounts. Therefore, the procedures for recording the recognition of revenue from restricted sources for hospitals are different from those for other NNOs. The transactions described before would be recorded by a hospital as follows:

HOSPITALS

Specific Purpose Fund

(1) Cash	109,000	
Fund Balance		109,000
To record receipt of grant for specified operating purposes.		
(2) Fund Balance	82,000	
Cash		82,000
To record use of restricted assets for specified purposes.		

General Fund

(3) Expenditures	82,000	
Specific Purpose Grants (Other Operating revenue)		82,000
To record expenditure of restricted assets and an equal amount of revenue.		

Like universities and ONNOs, hospitals recognize revenue in an amount exactly equal to the amount of assets expended for restricted purposes. Unlike universities and ONNOs, this result is not explicitly evident in the operating statement of hospitals, since hospitals combine revenues recognized from unrestricted and restricted resources into the accounts and financial statements of the General Fund (see Illustration 22-5B).

Deferral of Revenue Recognition in Current Unrestricted Funds

Unrestricted assets that are intended by the donor to finance the operations of future years or that represent the prepayment of service fees or other revenue sources are reported as deferred revenue or deferred support in the Current Unrestricted Fund (General Fund of hospitals).

Recognition of Service Fee Revenue

The full amount of university tuition and fees is recorded as revenue at standard rates even though the university does not intend to collect the full amount because of remissions or waivers for scholarships and fellowships. Amounts of tuition and fees that are waived are recorded as expenditures for scholarships and fellowships.

Hospital patient service revenue is also recorded at established rates, regardless of whether the hospital expects to collect the full amount. Charity allowances and other arrangements for providing services at less than established rates [because of special rates given to staff or because of the terms of contracts with third-party (insurance companies) payors] are reported separately as deductions from gross patient service revenue in the financial statements (see Illustration 22-5B).

Revenue and Support from Fund-Raising Events

The costs incurred by VHWOs and ONNOs in carrying out public support fund-raising events such as dinners, dances, theater parties, auctions, and so on, are deducted from gross contributions received and only the net funds provided by the event are reported as support in the financial statements.

CONTRIBUTIONS

Contributions include gifts of cash, pledges (promises to give cash), donated services, and gifts of noncash assets.

Pledges

Pledges are signed commitments to contribute specific amounts of money to an organization on a future date or in installments. Although resembling promissory notes, pledges generally are not enforceable contracts.

Hospitals and Voluntary Health and Welfare Organizations are required to record pledges receivable in their accounts and to establish an allowance for uncollectible pledges. Colleges and universities may record pledges or they may simply disclose pledges receivable in the footnotes to the financial statements. ONNOs record only pledges that can be legally enforced.

Recording of pledges may be illustrated by assuming that, as a result of a fund-raising campaign, an organization receives written and signed pledges to contribute $300,000 for unrestricted use by the organization in the current or future years. Experience indicates that about 15% of pledges from similar past campaigns were never collected. Entries to record the pledges using the accrual basis of accounting are as follows.

Current Unrestricted Fund

(1) Pledges Receivable	300,000	
Revenue—Contributions		300,000
To record gross amount of campaign pledges.		
(2) Provision for Uncollectible Pledges	45,000	
Allowance for Uncollectible Pledges		45,000
To record provision for estimated uncollectible pledges.		

Contributions are shown net of the Provision for Uncollectible Pledges in the operating statement (see Illustration 22-6B), and Pledges Receivable are shown net of the Allowance for Uncollectible Pledges in the balance sheet (see Illustration 22-6A). If the amounts pledged contain restrictions on their use, entries similar to those made in the Current Unrestricted Fund (above) would be made in the Current Restricted Fund or in a loan, endowment, or plant fund as appropriate.

Donated Services

Some of the operations and activities of NNOs may be carried out by volunteers who donate their time and expertise. Donated services may range from the limited participation of large numbers of volunteers in fund-raising activities to active and sustained involvement in the organization by a few dedicated individuals. Because it is difficult to place a market value on such services, their values are usually not recorded by NNOs. When certain conditions are met, however, NNOs record and report the value of the services received (net of incidental expenses reimbursed to the contributing personnel) as revenue or support in the Current Unrestricted Fund (General Fund of hospitals). In the same entry, an amount equal to the revenue or support recognized is recorded as an expense.

The circumstances under which donated services are recorded and reported differ among NNOs. Under existing generally accepted accounting standards

1. Colleges operated by religious groups should report the monetary value of services contributed by members of the religious group.

2. Hospitals should record donated services only if (a) the organization controls the employment and duties of the persons donating the service and (b) the organization has a clearly measurable basis for determining the amount of revenue and expense to be recorded. The organization should be able to influence the activities of the persons donating the services in a way comparable to the control it would exercise over employees with similar responsibilities. This includes control over time, location, nature, and performance of donated services.

3. Voluntary Health and Welfare Organizations should record donated services only if both conditions in (2) above are met, and the services performed are significant and form an integral part of the efforts of the organization and they would be performed by salaried personnel if the donated services were not available.

4. ONNOs should record donated services only if the conditions in (2) and (3) above are met and the program or activity in which the services are being performed will be continued by the organization and the services of the reporting organization are not principally intended for the benefit of its members.

The conditions in (2) generally prohibit organizations from recording the value of the services of volunteer solicitors. Condition (3) generally prohibits the recording of the value of donated services received on a casual or intermittent basis. Condition (4) effectively prohibits ONNOs such as religious communities, professional and trade associations, labor unions, political parties, fraternal organizations, and social and country clubs from recording the value of donated services.

Assume that the necessary conditions are met and that the services of a CPA who audited the records of a heart association at no cost had a value of $15,000 and those of an attorney who provided necessary legal services to the organization at no cost had a value of $6,000. The entry to record the revenue and expense resulting from the donated services would be as follows:

Current Unrestricted Fund

(1)	Management and General Expense	21,000	
	Donated Services Support		21,000
	To record value of donated services.		

Had the organization incurred any costs for incidental expenses of the CPA or attorney, the value of the services recorded would be reduced by the amount of the costs incurred.

Current Developments

In SFAS No. 116, *Accounting for Contributions Received and Contributions Made,* the FASB adopted standards that will require all NNOs subject to its jurisdiction to recognize contributions, including unconditional promises to give, in the period received. Conditional promises to give would be recognized when they become unconditional, that is, when the conditions are substantially met. Donor restricted contributions would be reported as an increase in restricted net assets. Other contributions would be reported as increases in unrestricted net assets. Expiration of donor restrictions would be recognized in the period they expire.

Contributions of services would be recognized only if the services received (1) create or enhance nonfinancial assets or (2) require professional skills, are provided by individuals possessing those skills, and typically would need to be purchased if not provided by donation.

Contributions of works of art, historical treasures, and similar assets do not have to be capitalized if (a) the donated items are added to collections held for public exhibition, education, or research in furtherance of public service rather than financial gain and (b) are protected, cared for, and preserved and (c) organization policy requires proceeds from any future sale of the items be used to acquire other items for collections.

The provisions of SFAS 116 are effective for financial statements issued by larger NNOs for years *beginning* after December 15, 1994. Thus, in terms of annual financial statements, these changes will appear in financial statements distributed beginning in 1996 by larger NNOs and in 1997 by smaller NNOs. The implementation of these standards will bring much needed uniformity to the manner in which NNOs report contributions, including pledges and donated services.

ACCOUNTING FOR PLANT FUNDS

Most transactions involving property and equipment are accounted for by NNOs other than hospitals in a Plant Fund. The Plant Fund is used to account for (1) the property and equipment owned by the organization and the net investment (Expended Fund Balance) therein, (2) the accumulation of financial resources for the acquisition or replacement of property and equipment, (3) the acquisition and disposal of property and equipment, (4) liabilities relating to the acquisition of property and equipment, and (5) depreciation expense and accumulated depreciation. Colleges and universities also account for the accumulation of financial resources to service-related indebtedness in the Plant Fund. Unlike municipalities, all types of NNOs are required by generally accepted accounting standards to record depreciation expense.

The Plant Fund of colleges and universities is divided into four separate self-balancing subgroups:

1. Unexpended Plant Fund: to account for resources to be used for the acquisition of property and equipment (similar to a Capital Projects Fund of a municipality).

2. Funds for Renewals and Replacements: to account for resources to be used for the renovation or replacement of existing property and equipment (also similar to a Capital Projects Fund of a municipality).

3. Funds for Retirement of Indebtedness: to account for resources to be used to retire or pay interest on obligations incurred related to the acquisition or replacement of property and equipment (similar to the Debt Service Fund of a municipality).

4. Investment in Plant: to account for the institution's property and equipment, related indebtedness, and net investment in plant (analogous to a combination of the General Fixed Assets and General Long-term Obligation Account Groups of a municipality).

Because board designated funds as well as externally restricted funds are accounted for in the Plant Fund of colleges and universities, a distinction is maintained between Restricted and Unrestricted Fund Balances.

Most transactions of hospitals relating to property and equipment are accounted for in the General Fund and not in a Plant Fund. However, contributed resources that may be used only to acquire property and equipment are accounted for in a Plant Replacement and Expansion (Restricted) Fund until the expenditures that satisfy the donor's terms are made. At that time, the assets acquired and the related fund balance are recorded in (transferred to) the General Fund.

Voluntary Health and Welfare Organizations and ONNOs use a single Plant Fund and report the fund balance in two classifications as "expended" or "unexpended." The Expended Fund Balance is equal to the organization's net investment in property and equipment (gross assets less related liabilities and accumulated depreciation). The Unexpended Fund Balance represents the amount of resources available to replace or acquire additional property and equipment.

To illustrate the funds and the procedures used to account for transactions relating to property and equipment by different NNOs, assume that

1. During the year, resources are obtained for the acquisition of property and equipment as follows:

Loan proceeds	$500,000
Contributions	200,000
Board designation of unrestricted funds	50,000
	$750,000

2. The organization acquires land for a building site for $750,000.

3. Principal and interest of $200,000 and $20,000, respectively, are paid on long-term obligations relating to property and equipment.

4. The amount of depreciation expense for the year is $235,000.

Colleges and Universities

The transactions described above would be recorded by colleges and universities as follows:

Unrestricted Current Fund

(1A) Nonmandatory Transfer to Plant Funds	50,000	
Cash		50,000
To record transfer of board designated unrestricted funds to Plant Fund.		

Unexpended Plant Fund

(1B) Cash	750,000	
Notes Payable		500,000
Fund Balance—Restricted		200,000
Fund Balance—Unrestricted		50,000
To record receipt of resources to be used for additions to property and equipment.		
(2A) Land	750,000	
Cash		750,000
To record acquisition of land.		
(2B) Fund Balance—Restricted	200,000	
Fund Balance—Unrestricted	50,000	
Notes Payable	500,000	
Land		750,000
to transfer assets and related liabilities to Investment in Plant Fund.		

Investment In Plant Fund

(2C) Land	750,000	
Notes Payable		500,000
Net Investment in Plant		250,000
To record acquisition of land and related indebtedness.		

The construction of assets and related debt is accounted for in the Unexpended Plant Fund until the construction is completed. On the completion of construction, the assets and related liabilities are transferred from the Unexpended Plant Fund to the Investment in Plant Fund using entries similar to those presented in (2B) and (2C) above.

Funds For Retirement of Indebtedness

(3A) Fund Balance—Restricted   220,000
      Cash   220,000
          To record payment of principal and interest on obligations related to property
          and equipment.

Investment In Plant Fund

(3B) Notes Payable   200,000
          Net Investment in Plant   200,000
          To record reduction in indebtedness related to property and equipment.
(4)   Depreciation Expense   235,000
          Accumulated Depreciation   235,000
          To record annual depreciation on property and equipment that is included in
          the assets of the Investment in Plant Fund.

Prior to 1990 depreciation of assets was not required for colleges and universities (except in endowment funds and nonexpendable trust funds). *SFAS No. 93,* "Recognition of Depreciation by Not-for-Profit Organizations," as amended by *SFAS No. 99,* requires that all NNOs including colleges and universities measure and report depreciation and accumulated depreciation on all depreciable property and equipment.

Hospitals

These same transactions would be recorded by hospitals as follows:

Plant Replacement and Expansion Fund

(1A) Cash   200,000
          Fund Balance   200,000
          To record receipt of contributions that may be used only to acquire property
          and equipment.

General Fund

(1B) Cash   500,000
          Notes Payable   500,000
          To record proceeds from note authorized by governing board to be used for
          acquisition of property and equipment.

The hospital may also record a reclassification of the General Fund Balance and establish a Board Designated Reserve for Plant Expansion in an amount of unrestricted funds designated by the governing board for additions to property and equipment. It is assumed here that such designations are simply disclosed in the footnotes to the financial statements.

Plant Replacement and Expansion Fund

(2A) Fund Balance   200,000
          Cash   200,000

General Fund

(2B)	Land	750,000	
	Cash		550,000
	Fund Balance		200,000

Taken together, entries (2A) and (2B) record the acquisition of land with $200,000 in externally restricted funds and $550,000 in unrestricted board designated funds.

Interestingly, the $200,000 in restricted contributions is never recognized as revenue in the operating statement of a hospital. Rather, these and similar contributions end up being recorded as a direct increase in the General Fund Balance.

General Fund

(3)	Interest Expense	20,000	
	Notes Payable	200,000	
	Cash		220,000
	To record payment of principal and interest.		
(4)	Depreciation Expense	235,000	
	Accumulated Depreciation		235,000
	To record annual depreciation expense on property and equipment that is included in assets of the General Fund.		

Voluntary Health and Welfare Organizations and Other Nongovernment Nonbusiness Organizations

These same transactions would be accounted for by VHWOs and ONNOs as follows:

Current Unrestricted Fund

(1A)	Transfer to Plant Funds	50,000	
	Cash		50,000
	To record transfer of cash to Plant Fund.		

Plant Fund

(1B)	Cash	750,000	
	Notes Payable		500,000
	Deferred Contributions		200,000
	Transfer from Current Unrestricted Fund		50,000
	To record receipt of resources to be used for additions to property and equipment.		

While VHWOs classify contributions that are restricted for the acquisition of plant assets as Support, ONNOs classify such contributions in a separate section of the operating statement entitled Capital Additions (see Illustration 22-7B). In addition, such contributions are not recognized as Support or as Capital Additions in the operating statements of either organization until they have been expended for their intended purpose. Until that occurs, such contributions are recorded and reported as Deferred (Capital) Support.

Plant Fund

(2A)	Land	750,000	
	Cash		750,000
	To record acquisition of land.		
(2B)	Deferred Contributions	200,000	
	Contributions		200,000
	To recognize previously deferred (Capital) Support as Support (Capital Additions) in amount of restricted funds expended for their intended purpose.		
(3)	Notes Payable	200,000	
	Interest Expense	20,000	
	Cash		220,000
	To record payment of principal and interest on obligations related to property and equipment.		
(4)	Depreciation Expense	235,000	
	Accumulated Depreciation		235,000
	To record annual depreciation expense on property and equipment that is included in assets of the Plant Fund.		

As noted earlier, the Plant Fund Balance is classified as Expended Fund Balance and Unexpended Fund Balance. The Expended Fund Balance is analogous to the Net Investment in Plant recorded in the Plant Funds of a university. Before the financial statements are prepared, the Expended Fund Balance must be adjusted to reflect the change in the organization's net investment in plant resulting from the transactions above. The change in the net investment in plant is calculated as follows:

Increases:			
Purchase of land	$750,000		
Reduction of Indebtedness	200,000	$950,000	
Decreases:			
Notes Payable	500,000		
Depreciation Expense	235,000	(735,000)	
Net Increase in Investment in Plant		$215,000	

Plant Fund

(5)	Unexpended Fund Balance	215,000	
	Expended Fund Balance		215,000
	To recognize the effect on the Fund Balances of the increase in the organization's net investment in property and equipment.		

Nonexhaustible Assets of Other Nongovernment Nonbusiness Organizations

Prior to 1990 ONNOs were not required to recognize depreciation expense and accumulated depreciation on "nonexhaustible" assets such as landmarks, monuments, cathedrals, and historical treasures or on structures used primarily as houses of worship. In *SFAS No. 93*, the Board considered and rejected the assertion that such assets are nonexhaustible and that those assets and structures used primarily as houses of worship need not be depreciated. Thus depreciation concepts and measurement are applied to these as well as other depreciable assets of ONNOs. However, depreciation need not be recognized on historical treasures and works of art that have estimated useful lives that are extraordinarily long. To qualify, such assets must have cultural, historical, or esthetic value that is worth preserving perpetually, and the holder must have the financial and technological ability to protect and preserve the asset.

ACCOUNTING FOR ENDOWMENT FUNDS

Endowment Funds are similar to the Nonexpendable Trust Funds of Governmental Units described in Chapter 21. When the donated funds have been given in perpetuity, the Endowment Fund is referred to as a Pure Endowment Fund. When the donor has specified a particular date or event after which the principal of the Endowment Fund may be expended, the Endowment Fund is referred to as a Term Endowment Fund. Resources of an Unrestricted Fund that are designated by the governing board for endowment purposes are accounted for in the Unrestricted Fund by all NNOs except colleges and universities. Colleges and universities may transfer such resources from the Unrestricted Current Fund to a separate fund referred to as a Quasi-Endowment Fund. Since the establishment of a Quasi-Endowment Fund may be rescinded at the discretion of the governing board, it is recorded as a Nonmandatory Transfer in the Unrestricted Current Fund and as a credit to Fund Balance—Unrestricted in the Quasi-Endowment Fund.

The income from Endowment Funds generally may be expended as earned either for specified purposes or at the discretion of the governing board. If there are no restrictions on the use of the Endowment Fund income, it is recognized as revenue in the organization's Unrestricted or General Fund. Otherwise, Endowment Fund income is recognized as a resource addition to Current Restricted (Specific Purpose) Funds, Loan Funds, Plant Funds, or other funds as appropriate to the use of the endowment income specified by the donor.

Gains and losses on Endowment Fund investments are accounted for as increases or decreases in the Fund Balance (Principal) and *not* as Endowment Fund income unless otherwise specified by the donor.

To illustrate the recording of Endowment Fund income that may be used for restricted and unrestricted purposes, assume that dividends and interest on Endowment Fund investments amount to $400,000, of which $150,000 is restricted for research grants and the remainder is unrestricted. Entries to record the income on Endowment Fund investments are summarized here:

Endowment Fund

(1) Cash	400,000		
Due to Unrestricted Fund (General Fund of Hospital)		250,000	
Due to Specific Purpose (Restricted) Fund		150,000	
To record receipt of dividends and interest.			

Unrestricted Fund (General Fund of Hospitals)

(2)	Due from Endowment Fund	250,000	
	Unrestricted Income from Endowment Fund		
	(Investment Income)		250,000
	To record unrestricted Endowment Fund income.		

Specific Purpose (Restricted) Fund

(3)	Due from Endowment Fund	150,000	
	Fund Balance (Deferred Revenue)		150,000
	To record availability of restricted Endowment Fund income.		

Restricted Endowment Fund income is not reported as revenue until it is expended for the restricted purposes. Assuming that $100,000 in research grants is awarded during the period from these funds, income is recorded as follows:

HOSPITALS

Specific Purpose Fund

(4)	Fund Balance	100,000	
	Cash		100,000
	To record payment of $100,000 in research grants.		

General Fund

(5)	Expenditures	100,000	
	Other Operating Revenue		100,000
	To record expenditure of restricted assets for awarding of research grants and		
	to recognize an equal amount of revenue.		

NNOS OTHER THAN HOSPITALS

Restricted (Current) Fund

(4)	Expenditures	100,000	
	Cash		100,000
	To record awarding of $100,000 in research grants.		
(5)	Fund Balance (Deferred Revenue)	100,000	
	Income from Endowment Fund (Investment Income)		100,000
	To record revenue in amount of restricted assets expended during period.		

ACCOUNTING FOR INVESTMENTS

Investments may be reported by NNOs at cost or at market. However, once selected, the same method should be used to report on all investments in all funds. When investments are reported at market, unrealized gains and losses are accounted for in a manner similar to realized gains and losses.

To improve effectiveness and flexibility in investing, NNOs often pool the investments of different funds into a single investment portfolio. Once placed in the pooled investment portfolio, individual securities are no longer identified with the contributing fund. Rather, they are pooled with all other investments and gains and losses and income of the investment portfolio pool are allocated by maintaining a record of the percentage interest (equity) of each fund in the investment pool.

To illustrate, assume that on January 1, 1995, the investments of three different funds of an NNO are placed in an investment pool as follows:

	COST	MARKET VALUE	PROPORTIONAL INTEREST IN POOLED INVESTMENTS
Restricted Fund	$15,000	$ 20,000	20%
Plant Fund	25,000	30,000	30%
Endowment Fund	45,000	50,000	50%
Total	$85,000	$100,000	100%

The equity interest of each fund in the investment pool may be expressed as a percentage; it is based on the relative *market value* of the investments contributed.

Assume that in 1995, interest and dividend income amounts to $10,000 and is distributed to the appropriate funds and that realized gains on investment transactions amount to $40,000 and are retained in the investment pool and reinvested. The allocation of these amounts to the participating funds is as follows:

	PROPORTIONAL INTEREST	INTEREST AND DIVIDENDS	REALIZED GAIN
Restricted Fund	20%	$ 2,000	$ 8,000
Plant Fund	30%	3,000	12,000
Endowment Fund	50%	5,000	20,000
Total	100%	$10,000	$40,000

Each participating fund debits its share of the $10,000 in interest and dividend income to cash and its share of the $40,000 gain to investments. The appropriate accounts to be credited depend on the type of NNO. In the case of ONNOs, for example, only unrestricted investment income is recognized as revenue immediately, whereas investment income that is restricted to specific operating or capital uses is recorded as deferred support or deferred capital contributions until the related conditions or restrictions have been met.

Now assume that on December 31, 1995, the market value of the investment pool is $160,000 and that $40,000 in resources of the Unrestricted Fund are added to the investment pool. The percentage (equity) interest of the participating funds in subsequent transactions of the investment pool is calculated as follows:

	INITIAL PROPORTIONAL INTEREST IN POOLED INVESTMENTS	MARKET VALUE OF EQUITY INTEREST	REVISED PROPORTIONAL INTEREST IN POOLED INVESTMENTS
Restricted Fund	20%	.2($160,000) = $ 32,000	16%
Plant Fund	30%	.3($160,000) = 48,000	24%
Endowment Fund	50%	.5($160,000) = 80,000	40%
Subtotal	100%	160,000	
Unrestricted Fund	–0–	40,000	20%
Total	100%	$200,000	100%

The market value of the equity interest in the pooled investments associated with the originally participating funds is based on each fund's percentage (equity) interest in the total market value of the pooled investments on the date additional investments are placed in the fund ($160,000 in this example). As before, the revised percentage (equity) interest is based on the relative *market values* of the contributed investments.

Revised percentage (equity) interests in the investment pool must also be calculated when individual participating funds place additional resources in the investment pool. At the time securities are brought into or removed from the investment pool, it is considered appropriate to adjust the carrying value of the securities on the records of the participating funds to their fair market value. Differences between the fair market value and the carrying value of the securities are treated as gains or losses of the individual funds.

ACCOUNTING FOR LOAN FUNDS

Loan Funds are used to account for resources that are used to provide loans to students and staff of colleges and universities, to hospitals, and to beneficiaries of the interests of certain ONNOs (loans to music students by symphony orchestra societies). Loan Funds are generally revolving (repayments of loan balances and interest are in turn lent to other individuals). Entries to record the basic transactions of a revolving Loan Fund are presented here:

(1)	Cash	200,000	
	Fund Balance		200,000
	To record contribution received for establishment of a Loan Fund.		
(2)	Loans Receivable	125,000	
	Cash		125,000
	To record loans to students.		
(3)	Fund Balance	2,500	
	Allowance for Uncollectible Loans		2,500
	To record estimated allowance for uncollectible loans.		
(4)	Investments	75,000	
	Cash		75,000
	To record investment of excess funds in money market account.		
(5)	Allowance for Uncollectible Loans	500	
	Loans Receivable		500
	To record write-off of a loan to student severely disabled in automobile accident.		
(6)	Investments	5,000	
	Fund Balance		5,000
	To record income on money market account.		

ACCOUNTING FOR AGENCY (CUSTODIAL) FUNDS

An Agency (Custodial) Fund is the same as its counterpart in a Governmental Unit. It is used to account for the assets held by an NNO as a custodian for others. Unless significant amounts are involved, resources held by an NNO as an agent for others are often accounted for as assets and liabilities in the Unrestricted or General Fund rather than in a separate Agency Fund. When a separate Agency Fund is used, the balance in the fund is reported as a liability since the organization does not have any equity in the fund.

Assume that resources in the amount of $15,000 that belong to the Association of Volunteer Aids are deposited with an NNO. Entries to account for this agency relationship in the Unrestricted Fund are as follows:

Unrestricted Fund

(1)	Cash	15,000	
	Due to Volunteer Aids		15,000
	To record deposit of assets belonging to Association of Volunteer Aids.		

(2)	Due to Volunteer Aids	15,000	
	Cash		15,000
	To record distribution of assets to Association of Volunteer Aids.		

Similar entries would be made in an Agency Fund if such a fund were used.

ACCOUNTING FOR ANNUITY AND LIFE INCOME FUNDS

An NNO may accept the contribution of assets to the organization on the condition that the organization make annuity payments to a specified recipient for a specified period of time (Annuity Fund) or that the organization pay the income earned on the contributed assets to a specified recipient during his or her lifetime (Life Income Fund). The major distinction between the two funds is that the beneficiary of an Annuity Fund is assured of periodic payments of a ***stated amount***, whereas Life Income Fund beneficiaries receive periodic payments of ***varying amounts*** depending on the earnings of the fund. At the end of the annuity or on the death of the life income beneficiary, the unexpended assets of the fund are transferred to the Unrestricted Fund or to an Endowment Fund, Loan Fund, Plant Fund, or other fund specified by the donor.

To illustrate transactions recorded in an Annuity Fund, assume that on January 1, 1995, an individual donated securities with a market value of $325,000 to an NNO on the condition that she be paid $40,000 a year for 10 years beginning December 31, 1995. At the end of the 10-year period, unexpended assets are to be placed in an Endowment Fund. It is estimated that the investments in the Annuity Fund will yield at least 8% annually. Entries to account for the basic transactions of the Annuity Fund are presented here:

Annuity Fund

(1)	Investments	325,000	
	Annuity Payable		268,400
	Annuity Fund Balance		56,600
	To record establishment of an Annuity Fund with an Annuity Payable equal to present value of an annuity of $40,000 discounted over 10 periods at 8% (6.71008 × $40,000 = $268,400).		

(2) Cash	26,000	
Investment Income		26,000
To record investment income for year.		
(3) Annuity Payable	40,000	
Cash		40,000
To record annual annuity payment.		
(4) Investment Income	26,000	
Annuity Payable		26,000
To close investment income account.		

Each year the Annuity Payable balance is reduced by annuity payments and by losses on investments and is increased by investment income and gains on investments. The reasoning is that if actual investment earnings equal expected investment earnings, the net decrease in the Annuity Payable balance each year will be equal to the decrease in its present value.

FINANCIAL STATEMENTS

Statements of NNOs that present revenue, support, expenses, and expenditures are referred to as *statements of activity*. All NNOs include the following financial statements in their annual reports.

1. A balance sheet.

2. A statement of activity.

3. A statement of changes in fund balances (sometimes presented as part of the statement of activity).

In addition, Voluntary Health and Welfare Organizations present a statement of functional expenses.

Model financial statements for the four types of NNOs discussed in this chapter are presented in the Appendix to this chapter. The statements illustrated are taken from those presented in the relevant *Industry Audit Guide* or *Statement of Position* and are summarized below.

SAMPLE EDUCATIONAL INSTITUTION	
Illustration 22-4A	Balance Sheet
Illustration 22-4B	Statement of Changes in Fund Balances
Illustration 22-4C	Statement of Current Funds Revenues, Expenditures, and Other Changes

SAMPLE HOSPITAL	
Illustration 22-5A	Balance Sheet
Illustration 22-5B	Statement of Revenue and Expenses
Illustration 22-5C	Statement of Changes in Fund Balance

VOLUNTARY HEALTH AND WELFARE SERVICE	
Illustration 22-6A	Balance Sheets
Illustration 22-6B	Statement of Support, Revenue, and Expenses and Changes in Fund Balances

SAMPLE LIBRARY

| Illustration 22-7A | Balance Sheet |
| Illustration 22-7B | Statement of Support, Revenue, and Expenses and Changes in Fund Balances |

Careful study of the statements presented in these illustrations will reinforce many of the concepts and reporting considerations discussed in this chapter.

PROPOSED CHANGES BY THE FASB

In SFAS No. 117, *Financial Statements of Not-for-Profit Organizations*, the FASB adopted standards that will bring dramatic changes to the financial reports of private, non-for-profit organizations. Reporting will be in three categories: (1) permanently restricted, (2) temporarily restricted, and (3) unrestricted. All NNOs will be required to provide (1) a statement of financial position, (2) a statement of activities, and (3) a statement of cash flows. The total assets, liabilities, and net assets of the organization will be reported in the statement of financial position. In addition, amounts will be presented for each of the three classes of net assets: permanently restricted, temporarily restricted, and unrestricted. The statement of activities will include all revenues, expenses, gains and losses for the period. The change in the organization's net assets and the amount of change in permanently restricted net assets, temporarily restricted net assets, and unrestricted net assets also will be reported in the statement of activities. The provisions of SFAS No. 95, *Statement of Cash Flows*, will apply to all NNOs with an expansion of the description of cash flows from financing activities to include certain donor restricted cash that must be used for long-term purposes.

The Board has not proposed a prescribed format for the three financial statements. The degree of aggregation and order or presentation of assets and liabilities in the statements of financial position or of revenue and expenses in statements of activities generally will be flexible; similar to that permitted for business enterprises. For example, a statement of financial position need not be divided into fund groups. Alternate formats for a statement of activities will be permitted. They might include a single-column statement format, a multi-column statement format, or a two statement approach (e.g., a statement of unrestricted revenues, expenses, and other changes in unrestricted net assets that articulates to a statement of changes in net assets).

The provisions of SFAS 117 are effective for annual financial statements issued by larger NNOs for years *beginning* after December 15, 1994. Thus, these changes will appear in financial statements distributed in 1996 by larger NNOs and in 1997 by smaller NNOs.

ILLUSTRATION 22-4A
Sample Educational Institution
Balance Sheet
June 30, 1995
With Comparative Figures at June 30, 1994

ASSETS	CURRENT YEAR	PRIOR YEAR	LIABILITIES AND FUND BALANCES	CURRENT YEAR	PRIOR YEAR
Current funds			Current funds		
Unrestricted			Unrestricted		
Cash	$ 210,000	$ 110,000	Accounts payable	$ 125,000	$ 100,000
Investments	450,000	360,000	Accrued liabilities	20,000	15,000
Accounts receivable,			Students' deposits	30,000	35,000
less allowance of			Due to other funds	158,000	120,000
$18,000 both years	228,000	175,000	Deferred credits	30,000	20,000
Inventories, at lower of			Fund balance	643,000	455,000
cost (first-in, first-out					
basis) or market	90,000	80,000			
Prepaid expenses and					
deferred charges	28,000	20,000			
Total unrestricted	1,006,000	745,000	Total unrestricted	1,006,000	745,000
Restricted			Restricted		
Cash	145,000	101,000	Accounts payable	14,000	5,000
Investments	175,000	165,000	Fund balances	446,000	421,000
Accounts receivable,					
less allowance of					
$8,000 both years	68,000	160,000			
Unbilled charges	72,000	—			
Total restricted	460,000	426,000	Total restricted	460,000	426,000
Total current funds	$ 1,466,000	$ 1,171,000	Total current funds	$ 1,466,000	$ 1,171,000
Loan funds			Loan funds		
Cash	$ 30,000	$ 20,000	Fund balances		
Investments	100,000	100,000	U.S. government grants		
Loans to students, faculty,			refundable	$ 50,000	$ 33,000
and staff, less			University funds		
alllowance of $10,000			Restricted	483,000	369,000
current year and $9,000			Unrestricted	150,000	100,000
prior year	550,000	382,000			
Due from unrestricted					
funds	3,000	—			
Total loan funds	$ 683,000	$ 502,000	Total loan funds	$ 683,000	$ 502,000
Endowment and similar			Endowment and similar		
funds			funds		
Cash	$ 100,000	$ 101,000	Fund balances		
Investments	13,900,000	11,800,000	Endowment	$ 7,800,000	$ 6,740,000
			Term endowment	3,840,000	3,420,000
			Quasi-endowment—		
			unrestricted	1,000,000	800,000
			Quasi-endowment—		
			restricted	1,360,000	941,000
Total endowment and similar funds	$14,000,000	$11,901,000	Total endowment and similar funds	$14,000,000	$11,901,000
Annuity and life income funds			Annuity and life income funds		
Annuity funds			Annuity funds		
Cash	$ 55,000	$ 45,000	Annuities payable	$ 2,150,000	$ 2,300,000
Investments	3,260,000	3,010,000	Fund balances	1,165,000	755,000
Total annuity funds	3,315,000	3,055,000	Total annuity funds	3,315,000	3,055,000

(Continued on next page)

ILLUSTRATION 22-4A (continued)
Sample Educational Institution
Balance Sheet

ASSETS	CURRENT YEAR	PRIOR YEAR	LIABILITIES AND FUND BALANCES	CURRENT YEAR	PRIOR YEAR
Life income funds			Life income funds		
Cash	15,000	15,000	Income payable	5,000	5,000
Investments	2,045,000	1,740,000	Fund balances	2,055,000	1,750,000
Total life income funds	2,060,000	1,755,000	Total life income funds	2,060,000	1,755,000
Total annuity and life income funds	$ 5,375,000	$ 4,810,000	Total annuity and life income funds	$ 5,375,000	$ 4,810,000
Plant funds			Plant funds		
Unexpended			Unexpended		
Cash	$ 275,000	$ 410,000	Accounts payable	$ 10,000	$ —
Investments	1,285,000	1,590,000	Notes payable	100,000	—
Due from unrestricted current funds	150,000	120,000	Bond payable	400,000	—
			Fund balances		
			Restricted	1,000,000	1,860,000
			Unrestricted	200,000	260,000
Total unexpended	1,710,000	2,120,000	Total unexpended	1,710,000	2,120,000
Renewals and replacements			Renewals and replacements		
Cash	$ 5,000	4,000	Fund balances		
Investments	150,000	286,000	Restricted	25,000	180,000
Deposits with trustees	100,000	90,000	Unrestricted	235,000	200,000
Due from unrestricted current funds	5,000	—			
Total renewals and replacements	260,000	380,000	Total renewals and replacements	260,000	380,000
Retirement of indebtedness			Retirement of indebtedness		
Cash	50,000	40,000	Fund balances		
Deposits with trustees	250,000	253,000	Restricted	185,000	125,000
			Unrestricted	115,000	168,000
Total retirement of indebtedness	300,000	293,000	Total retirement of indebtedness	300,000	293,000
Investment in plant			Investment in plant		
Land	500,000	500,000	Notes payable	790,000	810,000
Land improvements	1,000,000	1,110,000	Bonds payable	2,200,000	2,400,000
Buildings[1]	20,000,000	19,560,000	Mortgages payable	400,000	200,000
Equipment[2]	12,500,000	12,200,000	Net investment in plant	30,680,000	30,020,000
Library books[3]	70,000	60,000			
Total investment in plant	34,070,000	33,430,000	Total investment in plant	34,070,000	33,430,000
Total plant funds	$36,340,000	$36,223,000	Total plant funds	$36,340,000	$36,223,000
Agency funds			Agency funds		
Cash	$ 50,000	$ 70,000	Deposits held in custody for others	$ 110,000	$ 90,000
Investments	60,000	20,000			
Total agency funds	$ 110,000	$ 90,000	Total agency funds	$ 110,000	$ 90,000

[1]Net of accumulated depreciation of $5,000,000 in current year and $4,500,000 in prior year.
[2]Net of accumulated depreciation of $2,500,000 in current year and $2,000,000 in prior year.
[3]Net of accumulated depreciation of $30,000 in current year and $20,000 in prior year.
See accompanying Summary of Significant Accounting Policies and Notes to Financial Statements.
Source: Audits of Colleges and Universities.

ILLUSTRATION 22-4B
Sample Educational Institution
Statement of Changes in Fund Balances
Year Ended June 30, 1995

	CURRENT FUNDS		LOAN FUNDS	ENDOWMENT AND SIMILAR FUNDS	ANNUITY AND LIFE INCOME FUNDS	PLANT FUNDS			
	UNRESTRICTED	RESTRICTED				UNEXPENDED	RENEWAL AND REPLACE-MENTS	RETIRE-MENT OF INDEBTED-NESS	INVESTMENT IN PLANT
Revenues and other additions									
Unrestricted current fund revenues	$7,540,000								
Expired term endowment—restricted						50,000			
State appropriations—restricted						50,000			
Federal grants and contracts—restricted		500,000							
Private gifts, grants, and contracts—restricted		370,000	100,000	1,500,000	800,000	115,000		65,000	15,000
Investment income—restricted		224,000	12,000	10,000		5,000	5,000	5,000	
Realized gains on investments—unrestricted				109,000					
Realized gains on investments—restricted			4,000	50,000		10,000	5,000	5,000	
Interest on loans receivable			7,000						
U.S. government advances			18,000						
Expended for plant facilities (including $100,000 charged to current funds expenditures)									1,550,000
Retirement of indebtedness									220,000
Accrued interest on sale of bonds								3,000	
Matured annuity and life income restricted to endowment				10,000					
Total revenues and other additions	7,540,000	1,094,000	141,000	1,679,000	800,000	230,000	10,000	78,000	1,785,000
Expenditures and other deductions									
Educational and general expenditures	4,400,000	1,014,000							
Auxiliary enterprises expenditures	1,830,000								
Indirect costs recovered		35,000							
Refunded to grantors		20,000	10,000						
Loan cancellations and write-offs			1,000						

(Continued on next page)

ILLUSTRATION 22-4B (continued)
Sample Educational Institution
Statement of Changes in Fund Balances
Year Ended June 30, 1995

	CURRENT FUNDS		LOAN FUNDS	ENDOWMENT AND SIMILAR FUNDS	ANNUITY AND LIFE INCOME FUNDS	PLANT FUNDS			
	UNRESTRICTED	RESTRICTED				UNEXPENDED	RENEWAL AND REPLACE-MENTS	RETIRE-MENT OF INDEBTED-NESS	INVESTMENT IN PLANT
Administrative and collection costs			1,000					1,000	
Adjustment of actuarial liability for annuities payable					75,000				
Expended for plant facilities (including noncapitalized expenditures of $50,000)						1,200,000	300,000		
Retirement of indebtedness								220,000	
Interest on indebtedness								190,000	
Disposal of plant facilities									115,000
Depreciation expense									1,010,000
Expired term endowments ($40,000 unrestricted, $50,000 restricted to plant)				90,000					
Matured annuity and life income funds restricted to endowment					10,000				
Total expenditures and other deductions	6,230,000	1,069,000	12,000	90,000	85,000	1,200,000	300,000	411,000	1,125,000
Transfers among funds—additions/(deductions):									
Mandatory									
Principal and interest	(340,000)							340,000	
Renewals and replacements	(170,000)						170,000		
Loan fund matching grant	(2,000)		2,000						
Nonmandatory									
Unrestricted gifts allocated	(650,000)		50,000	550,000		50,000			
Portion of unrestricted quasi-endowment funds investment gains appropriated	40,000			(40,000)					
Total transfers	(1,122,000)		52,000	510,000		50,000	170,000	340,000	
Net increase/(decrease) For the year	188,000	25,000	181,000	2,099,000	715,000	(920,000)	(120,000)	7,000	660,000
Beginning of year	455,000	421,000	502,000	11,901,000	2,505,000	2,120,000	380,000	293,000	30,020,000
End of year	$ 643,000	446,000	683,000	14,000,000	3,220,000	1,200,000	260,000	300,000	30,680,000

See accompanying Summary of Significant Accounting Policies and Notes to Financial Statements.
Source: Audits of Colleges and Universities.

ILLUSTRATION 22-4C
Sample Educational Institution
Statement of Current Funds Revenues, Expenditures, and Other Changes
Year Ended June 30, 1995

	CURRENT YEAR			PRIOR YEAR
	UNRESTRICTED	RESTRICTED	TOTAL	TOTAL
Revenues				
Tuition and fees	$2,600,000		$2,600,000	$2,300,000
Federal appropriations	500,000		500,000	500,000
State appropriations	700,000		700,000	700,000
Local appropriations	100,000		100,000	100,000
Federal grants and contracts	20,000	$ 375,000	395,000	350,000
State grants and contracts	10,000	25,000	35,000	200,000
Local grants and contracts	5,000	25,000	30,000	45,000
Private gifts, grants, and contracts	850,000	380,000	1,230,000	1,190,000
Endowment income	325,000	209,000	534,000	500,000
Sales and services of educational departments	190,000		190,000	195,000
Sales and services of auxiliary enterprises	2,200,000		2,200,000	2,100,000
Expired term endowment	40,000		40,000	
Other sources (if any)				
Total current revenues	7,540,000	1,014,000	8,554,000	8,180,000
Expenditures and mandatory transfers				
Educational and general				
Instruction	2,960,000	489,000	3,449,000	3,300,000
Research	100,000	400,000	500,000	650,000
Public service	130,000	25,000	155,000	175,000
Academic support	250,000		250,000	225,000
Student services	200,000		200,000	195,000
Institutional support	450,000		450,000	445,000
Operation and maintenance of plant	220,000		220,000	200,000
Scholarships and fellowships	90,000	100,000	190,000	180,000
Educational and general expenditures	4,400,000	1,014,000	5,414,000	5,370,000
Mandatory transfers for				
Principal and interest	90,000		90,000	50,000
Renewals and replacements	100,000		100,000	80,000
Loan fund matching grant	2,000		2,000	
Total educational and general	4,592,000	1,014,000	5,606,000	5,500,000
Auxiliary enterprises				
Expenditures	1,830,000		1,830,000	1,730,000
Mandatory transfers for				
Principal and interest	250,000		250,000	250,000
Renewals and replacements	70,000		70,000	70,000
Total auxiliary enterprises	2,150,000		2,150,000	2,050,000
Total expenditures and mandatory transfers	6,742,000	1,014,000	7,756,000	7,550,000
Other transfers and additions/(deductions)				
Excess of restricted receipts over transfers to revenues		45,000	45,000	40,000
Refunded to grantors		(20,000)	(20,000)	
Nonmandatory transfers to other funds	(650,000)		(650,000)	(510,000)
Portion of quasi-endowment gains appropriated	40,000		40,000	
Net increase in fund balances	$ 188,000	$ 25,000	$ 213,000	$ 160,000

See accompanying Summary of Significant Accounting Policies and Notes to Financial Statements.

Source: Audits of Colleges and Universities.

ILLUSTRATION 22-5A
Sample Hospital
Balance Sheets
December 31, 1995 and 1994

General Funds

ASSETS	1995	1994	LIABILITIES AND FUND BALANCES	1995	1994
General Funds					
Current assets			Current liabilities		
Cash and cash equivalents	$ 3,103,000	$ 4,525,000	Current installments of long-term debt (note 7)	$ 970,000	$ 1,200,000
Assets whose use is limited—required for current liabilities (notes 5, 7, and 8)	970,000	1,300,000	Current portion of capital lease obligations (note 7)	500,000	550,000
Patient accounts receivable, net of estimated uncollectibles of $2,500,000 in 1995 and $2,400,000 in 1994	15,100,000	14,194,000	Accounts payable	2,217,000	2,085,000
			Accrued expenses	3,396,000	3,225,000
			Estimated third-party payor settlements—Medicaid (note 2)	2,143,000	1,942,000
Estimated third-party payor settlements—Medicare (note 3)	441,000	600,000	Deferred third-party reimbursement	200,000	210,000
			Advances from third-party payors	122,000	632,000
Supplies, at lower of cost (first-in, first-out) or market	1,163,000	938,000	Current portion of estimated malpractice costs (note 8)	600,000	500,000
Other current assets	321,000	403,000	Retainage and construction accounts payable	955,000	772,000
Due from donor-restricted funds, net	—	500,000	Due to donor-restricted funds	300,000	—
Total current assets	21,098,000	22,460,000	Total current liabilities	11,403,000	11,116,000
Assets whose use is limited (notes 5, 7, and 8)			Deferred third-party reimbursement	746,000	984,000
By board for capital improvements	11,000,000	10,000,000	Estimated malpractice costs, net of current portion (note 8)	3,207,000	2,182,000
By agreements with third-party payors for funded depreciation	9,234,000	6,151,000	Long-term debt, excluding current installments (note 7)	22,644,000	23,614,000
Under malpractice funding arrangement—held by trustee	3,007,000	2,682,000	Capital lease obligations, excluding current portion (note 7)	500,000	400,000
Under indenture agreement—held by trustee	11,708,000	11,008,000	Fund balance	69,310,000	64,567,000
Total assets whose use is limited	34,949,000	29,841,000	Commitments and contingent liabilities (notes 3, 6, 8, 12, and 13)	—	—
Less assets whose use is limited and that are required for current liabilities	970,000	1,300,000			
Noncurrent assets whose use is limited	33,979,000	28,541,000			
Property and equipment, net (notes 6 and 7)	51,038,000	50,492,000			
Other assets					
Prepaid pension cost (note 12)	85,000	35,000			
Deferred financing costs	693,000	759,000			
Investment in affiliated company (note 4)	917,000	576,000			
Total other assets	1,695,000	1,370,000			
	$107,810,000	$102,863,000		$107,810,000	$102,863,000

(Continued on next page)

ILLUSTRATION 22-5A (continued)
Sample Hospital
Balance Sheets
December 31, 1995 and 1994

ASSETS	1995	1994	LIABILITIES AND FUND BALANCES	1995	1994
Donor-Restricted Funds					
Specific-purpose funds					
Cash	378,000	378,000	Accounts payable	$ 205,000	$ 72,000
Investments, at cost that			Deferred grant revenue	92,000	—
approximates market	728,000	455,000			
Grants receivable	613,000	535,000	Due to general funds	—	255,000
			Fund balance	1,422,000	1,041,000
	$ 1,719,000	$ 1,368,000		$ 1,719,000	$ 1,368,000
Plant replacement and expansion funds					
Cash	24,000	321,000			
Investments, at cost that approximates market	252,000	165,000			
Pledges receivable, net of estimated uncollectibles of $60,000 in 1995 and $120,000 in 1994	132,000	380,000	Due to general funds	$ —	$ 345,000
Due from general funds	150,000	—	Fund balance	558,000	521,000
	$ 558,000	$ 866,000		$ 558,000	$ 866,000
Endowment funds					
Cash	1,253,000	653,000			
Investments, net of $175,000 valuation allowance in 1995, market value $3,798,000 in 1995 and $5,013,000 in 1994 (note 9)	3,856,000	5,320,000			
Due from general funds	150,000	100,000	Fund balance	$ 5,259,000	$ 6,073,000
	$ 5,259,000	$ 6,073,000		$ 5,259,000	$ 6,073,000

Source: Audits of Providers of Health Care Services

ILLUSTRATION 22-5B
Sample Hospital
Statement of Revenue and Expenses of General Funds
Years Ended December 31, 1995 and 1994

	1995	1994
Net patient service revenue (notes 3 and 7)	$92,656,000	$88,942,000
Other revenue	6,010,000	5,380,000
Total revenue	98,666,000	94,322,000
Expenses (notes 7, 8, 12, and 13)		
Professional care of patients	53,016,000	48,342,000
Dietary services	4,407,000	4,087,000
General services	10,888,000	9,973,000
Administrative services	11,075,000	10,145,000
Employee health and welfare	10,000,000	9,335,000
Medical malpractice costs	1,125,000	200,000
Depreciation and amortization	4,782,000	4,280,000
Interest	1,752,000	1,825,000
Provision for bad debts	1,010,000	1,103,000
Total expenses	98,055,000	89,290,000
Income from operations	611,000	5,032,000
Nonoperating gains (losses)		
Unrestricted gifts and bequests (note 11)	822,000	926,000
Loss on investment in affiliated company (note 4)	(37,000)	(16,000)
Income on investments of endowment funds	750,000	650,000
Income on investments whose use is limited		
By board for capital improvements	1,120,000	1,050,000
By agreements with third-party payors for funded depreciation	850,000	675,000
Under indenture agreement	100,000	90,000
Other investment income	284,000	226,000
Nonoperating gains, net	3,889,000	3,601,000
Revenue and gains in excess of expenses and losses	$ 4,500,000	$ 8,633,000

Source: Audits of Providers of Health Care Services.

ILLUSTRATION 22-5C
Sample Hospital
Statements of Changes in Fund Balances
Years Ended December 31, 1995 and 1994

| | 1995 | | | | 1994 | | | |
| | | Donor-Restricted Funds | | | | Donor-Restricted Funds | | |
	General Funds	Specific-Purpose Funds	Plant Replacement and Expansion Funds	Endowment Funds	General Funds	Specific-Purpose Funds	Plant Replacement and Expansion Funds	Endowment Funds
Balances at beginning of year	$64,567,000	$1,041,000	$521,000	$6,073,000	$56,679,000	$ 933,000	$501,000	$5,973,000
Additions								
Revenue and gains in excess of expenses and losses	4,500,000	—	—	—	8,633,000	—	—	—
Gifts, grants, and bequests (notes 10 and 11)	—	869,000	220,000	—	—	558,000	290,000	—
Investment income	—	62,000	20,000	—	—	50,000	15,000	—
Net realized gain on sale of investments	—	—	100,000	—	—	—	20,000	—
Transfer to finance property and equipment additions	243,000	—	(243,000)	—	255,000	—	(255,000)	100,000
	4,743,000	931,000	97,000	—	8,888,000	608,000	70,000	100,000
Deductions								
Provision for uncollectible pledges	—	—	(60,000)	—	—	—	—	—
Capital contribution to Sample Health System (note 11)	—	—	—	—	—	—	(50,000)	—
Net realized loss on sale of investments	—	—	—	(639,000)	(1,000,000)	—	—	—
Unrealized loss on marketable equity securities (note 9)	—	—	—	(175,000)	—	—	—	—
Transfer to other revenue	—	(550,000)	—	—	—	(500,000)	—	—
	—	(550,000)	(60,000)	(814,000)	(1,000,000)	(500,000)	(50,000)	—
Balances at end of year	$69,310,000	$1,422,000	$558,000	$5,259,000	$64,567,000	$1,041,000	$521,000	$6,073,000

Source: Audits of Providers of Health Care Services.

ILLUSTRATION 22-6A
Voluntary Health and Welfare Service
Balance Sheets
December 31, 1995 and 1994

ASSETS	1995	1994	LIABILITIES AND FUND BALANCES	1995	1994
			Current Funds		
			Unrestricted		
Cash	$2,207,000	$2,530,000	Accounts payable	$ 148,000	$ 139,000
Investments (Note 2)			Research grants payable	596,000	616,000
For long-term purposes	2,727,000	2,245,000	Contributions designated for		
Other	1,075,000	950,000	future periods	245,000	219,000
Pledges receivable less			Total liabilities and		
allowance for uncollectibles			deferred revenues	989,000	974,000
of $105,000 and $92,000	475,000	363,000	Fund balances		
Inventories of educational			Designated by the		
materials, at cost	70,000	61,000	governing board for		
Accrued interest, other			long-term investments	2,800,000	2,300,000
receivables and prepaid			Purchases of new		
expenses	286,000	186,000	equipment	100,000	—
			Research purposes		
			(Note 3)	1,152,000	1,748,000
			Undesignated, available		
			for general activities		
			(Note 4)	1,799,000	1,313,000
			Total fund balance	5,851,000	5,361,000
Total	$6,840,000	$6,335,000	Total	$6,840,000	$6,335,000
			Current Funds		
			Restricted		
Cash	$ 3,000	$ 5,000	Fund balances		
Investments (Note 2)	71,000	72,000	Professional education	$ 84,000	$ —
Grants receivable	58,000	46,000	Research grants	48,000	123,000
Total	$ 132,000	$ 123,000	Total	$ 132,000	$ 123,000
			Land, Building, and Equipment Fund		
Cash	$ 3,000	$ 2,000	Mortgage payable, 8% due		
Investments (Note 2)	177,000	145,000	19XX	$ 32,000	$ 36,000
Pledges receivable less			Fund balances		
allowance for uncollectibles			Expended	484,000	477,000
of $7,500 and $5,000	32,000	25,000	Unexpended—restricted	212,000	172,000
Land, buildings, and					
equipment, at cost less					
accumulated depreciation					
of $296,000 and $262,000					
(Note 5)	516,000	513,000	Total fund balance	696,000	649,000
Total	$ 728,000	$ 685,000	Total	$ 728,000	$ 685,000
			Endowment Funds		
Cash	$ 4,000	$ 10,000	Fund balance	$1,948,000	$2,017,000
Investments (Note 2)	1,944,000	2,007,000			
Total	$1,948,000	$2,017,000	Total	$1,948,000	$2,017,000

See accompanying Notes to Financial Statements.

Source: Audits of Voluntary Health and Welfare Organizations.

ILLUSTRATION 22-6B
Voluntary Health and Welfare Service
Statement of Support, Revenue, and Expenses and Changes in Fund Balances
Year Ended December 31, 1995
With Comparative Totals for 1994

| | 1995 | | | | | |
| | CURRENT FUNDS | | LAND, BUILDING, AND EQUIPMENT FUND | ENDOWMENT FUND | TOTAL ALL FUNDS | |
	UNRESTRICTED	RESTRICTED			1995	1994
Public support and revenue						
Public support						
Contributions (net of estimated uncollectible pledges of $195,000 in 1995 and $150,000 in 1994)	$3,764,000	$162,000	$ —	$ 2,000	$3,928,000	$3,976,000
Contributions to building fund	—	—	72,000	—	72,000	150,000
Special events (net of direct costs of $181,000 in 1995 and $163,000 in 1994)	104,000	—	—	—	104,000	92,000
Legacies and bequests	92,000	—	—	4,000	96,000	129,000
Received from federated and nonfederated campaigns (which incurred related fund-raising expenses of $38,000 in 1995 and $29,000 in 1994)	275,000	—	—	—	275,000	308,000
Total public support	4,235,000	162,000	72,000	6,000	4,475,000	4,655,000
Revenue						
Membership dues	17,000	—	—	—	17,000	12,000
Investment income	98,000	10,000	—	—	108,000	94,000
Realized gain on investment transactions	200,000	—	—	25,000	225,000	275,000
Miscellaneous	42,000	—	—	—	42,000	47,000
Total revenue	357,000	10,000	—	25,000	392,000	428,000
Total support and revenue	4,592,000	172,000	72,000	31,000	4,867,000	5,083,000
Expenses						
Program services						
Research	1,257,000	155,000	2,000	—	$1,414,000	$1,365,000
Public health education	539,000	—	5,000	—	544,000	485,000
Professional education and training	612,000	—	6,000	—	618,000	516,000
Community services	568,000	—	10,000	—	578,000	486,000
Total program services	2,976,000	155,000	23,000	—	3,154,000	2,852,000
Supporting services						
Management and general	567,000	—	7,000	—	574,000	638,000
Fund raising	642,000	—	12,000	—	654,000	546,000
Total supporting services	1,209,000	—	19,000	—	1,228,000	1,184,000
Total expenses	4,185,000	155,000	42,000	—	$4,382,000	$4,036,000
Excess (deficiency) of public support and revenue over expenses	407,000	17,000	30,000	31,000		
Other changes in fund balances						
Property and equipment acquisitions from unrestricted funds	(17,000)	—	17,000	—		
Transfer of realized endowment fund appreciation	100,000	—	—	(100,000)		
Returned to donor	—	(8,000)	—	—		
Fund balances, beginning of year	5,361,000	123,000	649,000	2,017,000		
Fund balances, end of year	$5,851,000	$132,000	$696,000	$1,948,000		

See accompanying Notes to Financial Statements.

Source: Audits of Voluntary Health and Welfare Organizations.

ILLUSTRATION 22-7A
Sample Library
Balance Sheet
December 31, 1995
With Comparative Totals for 1994

| ASSETS | DECEMBER 31, 1995 | | | | | | | DECEMBER 31, 1994 |
| | UNRESTRICTED | | | CURRENT RESTRICTED | PLANT | ENDOWMENT | TOTAL | TOTAL |
	OPERATING	INVESTMENT	TOTAL					
Current assets								
Cash, including interest-bearing accounts of $600,000 in 1995, and $400,000 in 1994	$ 690,000	—	$ 690,000	$ 3,000	$ 7,000	—	$ 700,000	$ 411,000
Certificates of deposit	375,000	—	375,000	75,000	—	—	450,000	525,000
Grants receivable (Note 1)								
Governments	120,000	—	120,000	—	—	—	120,000	161,000
Other	30,000	—	30,000	27,000	8,000	—	65,000	35,000
Pledges receivable, at estimated net realizable value (Note 1)	15,000	—	15,000	—	—	—	15,000	15,000
Prepaid expenses and other current assets	70,000	—	70,000	—	—	—	70,000	85,000
Total current assets	1,300,000	—	1,300,000	105,000	15,000	—	1,420,000	1,232,000
Investments—at market (Note 2)	—	$920,000	920,000	—	165,000	985,000	2,070,000	2,172,000
Land, buildings, and equipment—at cost, less accumulated depreciation of $90,000 and $79,000 respectively (Note 3)	—	—	—	—	1,525,000	—	1,525,000	1,491,000
Total assets	$1,300,000	$920,000	$2,220,000	$105,000	$1,705,000	$985,000	$5,015,000	$4,895,000

(Continued on next page)

ILLUSTRATION 22-7A (continued)
Sample Library
Balance Sheet
December 31, 1995
With Comparative Totals for 1994

LIABILITIES AND FUND BALANCES	UNRESTRICTED OPERATING	UNRESTRICTED INVESTMENT	UNRESTRICTED TOTAL	CURRENT RESTRICTED	PLANT	ENDOWMENT	TOTAL	DECEMBER 31, 1994 TOTAL
Current liabilities								
Accounts payable, accrued expenses, and current portion of long-term debt	$ 200,000	—	$ 200,000	—	$ 10,000	—	$ 210,000	$ 130,000
Deferred restricted contributions, etc. (Note 6)	—	—	—	$105,000	5,000	—	110,000	100,000
Total current liabilities	200,000	—	200,000	105,000	15,000	—	320,000	230,000
Long-term debt (Note 4)	—	—	—	—	180,000	—	180,000	190,000
Total liabilities	200,000	—	200,000	105,000	195,000	—	500,000	420,000
Fund balances								
Unrestricted								
Designated by the board for								
Investment	—	$920,000	920,000	—	—	—	920,000	740,000
Purchase of equipment	50,000	—	50,000	—	—	—	50,000	35,000
Undesignated	1,050,000	—	1,050,000	—	1,510,000	—	2,560,000	2,725,000
Restricted	—	—	—	—	—	$985,000	985,000	975,000
Total fund balances	1,100,000	920,000	2,020,000	—	1,510,000	985,000	4,515,000	4,475,000
Total liabilities and fund balances	$1,300,000	$920,000	$2,220,000	$105,000	$1,705,000	$985,000	$5,015,000	$4,895,000

Source: Statement of Position 78-10.

ILLUSTRATION 22-7B
Sample Library
Statement of Support, Revenue, and Expenses and Changes in Fund Balances
Year Ended December 31, 1995
With Comparative Totals for 1994

| | YEAR ENDED DECEMBER 31, 1995 | | | | | | | YEAR ENDED DECEMBER 31, 1994 |
| | UNRESTRICTED | | | CURRENT | | | | |
	OPERATING	INVESTMENT	TOTAL	RESTRICTED	PLANT	ENDOWMENT	TOTAL	TOTAL
Support and revenue								
Support								
Grants (Note 1)								
Governments	$ 150,000	—	$ 150,000	—	—	—	$ 150,000	$ 150,000
Other	25,000	—	25,000	—	—	—	25,000	—
Contributions, legacies, and bequests (Note 1)	350,000	$ 90,000	440,000	$75,000	—	—	515,000	490,000
Contributed services of volunteers (Note 1)	75,000	—	75,000	—	—	—	75,000	50,000
Use of contributed facilities (Note 1)	47,000	—	47,000	—	—	—	47,000	50,000
Total support	647,000	90,000	737,000	75,000	—	—	812,000	740,000
Revenue								
Fees for services	50,000	—	50,000	—	—	—	50,000	45,000
Book rentals and fines	320,000	—	320,000	—	—	—	320,000	250,000
Investment income including net gains	25,000	93,000	118,000	10,000	—	—	128,000	103,000
Total revenue	395,000	93,000	488,000	10,000	—	—	498,000	398,000
Total support and revenue	1,042,000	183,000	1,225,000	85,000	—	—	1,310,000	1,138,000
Expenses (Note 7)								
Program services								
Circulating library	390,000	—	390,000	75,000	$5,000	—	470,000	430,000
Research library	169,000	—	169,000	—	1,000	—	170,000	155,000
Collections and exhibits	49,000	—	49,000	10,000	1,000	—	60,000	50,000
Educational services	49,000	—	49,000	—	1,000	—	50,000	55,000
Community services	29,500	—	29,500	—	500	—	30,000	20,000
Total program services	686,500	—	686,500	85,000	8,500	—	780,000	710,000

(Continued on next page)

ILLUSTRATION 22-7B (continued)
Sample Library
Statement of Support, Revenue, and Expenses and Changes in Fund Balances
Year Ended December 31, 1995
With Comparative Totals for 1994

| | YEAR ENDED DECEMBER 31, 1995 | | | | | | | YEAR ENDED DECEMBER 31, 1994 |
| | UNRESTRICTED | | | CURRENT RESTRICTED | PLANT | ENDOWMENT | TOTAL | TOTAL |
	OPERATING	INVESTMENT	TOTAL					
Supporting services General administration	315,500	3,000	318,500	—	21,500	—	340,000	290,000
Fund raising	200,000	—	200,000	—	5,000	—	205,000	200,000
Total supporting services	515,500	3,000	518,500	—	26,500	—	545,000	490,000
Total expenses	1,202,000	3,000	1,205,000	85,000	35,000	—	1,325,000	1,200,000
Excess (deficiency) of support and revenue over expenses before capital additions	(160,000)	180,000	20,000	—	(35,000)	—	(15,000)	(62,000)
Capital additions Contributions	—	—	—	—	40,000	—	40,000	95,000
Investment income including net gains	—	—	—	—	5,000	—	5,000	17,000
Contributed materials, equipment, etc. (Note 1)	—	—	—	—	10,000	—	10,000	—
	—	—	—	—	55,000	—	55,000	112,000
Excess (deficiency) of support and revenue over expenses after capital additions	(160,000)	180,000	20,000	—	20,000	—	40,000	50,000
Fund balances at beginning of year	1,270,000	740,000	2,010,000	—	1,480,000	$985,000	4,475,000	4,425,000
Required transfers— principal of indebtedness	(10,000)	—	(10,000)	—	10,000	—	—	—
Fund balances at end of year	$1,100,000	$920,000	$2,020,000	—	$1,510,000	$985,000	$4,515,000	$4,475,000

Source: Statement of Position 78-10.

Questions

1. What authoritative body(s) is (are) responsible for establishing financial accounting standards for NNOs?

2. Why do most NNOs use fund accounting?

3. NNOs distinguish between restricted and unrestricted funds. Why is this distinction important?

4. What is the major difference in accounting for the General Fund of a hospital and the Unrestricted Fund of other NNOs?

5. What is the rationale for deferring the recognition of restricted revenue until the related expenditure has been incurred?

6. What is the relationship (if any) between board designated funds and nonmandatory transfers?

7. May board designated funds ever be accounted for in the Unrestricted Current Fund? Explain.

8. When should an NNO record donated services in its accounting records?

9. The donated services of volunteer workers on fund-raising campaigns are usually not given accounting recognition. Why?

10. Universities and hospitals often reduce their standard service charge to students or patients. How are these reductions reflected in the Statements of Revenue and Expenses of these organizations? Explain.

11. What fund is used to account for the library books owned by a university? How should depreciation of the library books be reflected in the Financial Statements of the University?

12. In which fund of a hospital are medical equipment and related long-term obligations recorded? Would your answer be the same for a Voluntary Health and Welfare Organization? Explain.

13. What capital assets (if any) of ONNOs need not be depreciated?

14. Identify three different types of endowment funds and explain how they differ.

15. Distinguish an Annuity Fund from a Life Income Fund.

Exercises

Exercise 22-1

A $36,000 cash gift was received by a college during the year.

Required:

A. In which fund should the gift be recorded if there were no restrictions on the use of the cash?

B. In which fund should the gift be recorded if the donor specified that the cash was to be used to replace obsolete and damaged equipment?

Exercise 22-2

During 1995 volunteer pinstripers donated their services to General Hospital at no cost. The staff at General Hospital was in control of the pinstripers' duties. If regular employees had provided the services rendered by the volunteers, their salaries would have totaled $6,000.

While working for the hospital, the pinstripers received complimentary meals from the cafeteria, which normally would have cost $500.

Required:

Prepare the journal entry necessary in the General Fund to record the donated services on the books of General Hospital.

Exercise 22-3

The Franklin Public Library received a restricted contribution of $300,000 in 1995. The donor specified that the money must be used to acquire books of poetry written in the sixteenth century. As of December 31, 1995, only $100,000 of the restricted resources had been expended.

Required:

Prepare the journal entries necessary to record these events during 1995. Indicate the fund in which each journal entry is recorded.

Exercise 22-4

The following events relate to Grearson University Loan Fund:

1. $100,000 is received from an estate to establish a faculty and student loan fund. Annual interest rates range from 8% for students to 10% for faculty.
2. Loans to students totaled $60,000, and $40,000 was disbursed to faculty members (of the total loans made, 10% are estimated to be uncollectible).
3. Grearson wrote off a $1,000 student loan as uncollectible.
4. The following loans were repaid.

	PRINCIPAL	INTEREST
Faculty	$ 5,000	$500
Student	10,000	800

Required:

Prepare the journal entries necessary to record these transactions and indicate the fund(s) in which the transactions are recorded.

Exercise 22-5

Hastings College pooled the individual investments of three of its funds on December 31, 1994. The recorded value and the fair market value of the investments on December 31, 1994, are presented here:

	RECORDED VALUE	FAIR VALUE
Loan fund	$121,000	$105,000
Quasi-endowment fund	128,000	147,000
Life income fund	151,000	168,000
Total	$400,000	$420,000

During 1995 the investment pool earned dividends of $12,000 and interest of $18,000 and distributed cash in these amounts to the respective funds. Realized gains on transactions of the investment pool amounted to $20,000 and were reinvested in securities held in the pool.

Required:

Prepare the journal entries that are necessary in the records of each of the funds to account for the earnings of the investment pool during 1995.

Exercise 22-6

A well-known celebrity sponsored a telethon for the Help for the Blind Foundation on November 1, 1995. Pledges in the amount of $1,000,000 were called in. Using similar telethon campaigns as a basis, it is estimated that 25% of the pledges will be uncollectible.

During 1996, $700,000 of contributions from these pledges were collected. The remainder were uncollectible.

Required:

Identify the appropriate fund(s) and prepare the journal entries necessary in 1995 and 1996 to record these transactions.

Exercise 22-7

Jefferson Hospital received money from a donor to set up an endowment fund. The following information pertains to this contribution:

1995

1. $2,000,000 was received to establish the fund. The requirements were
   (a) $100,000 of the Endowment Fund's income must be used for research grants each year.
   (b) The remainder of income is under the discretion of the governing board.
   (c) The principal is expendable after the donor's death. It shall be used to purchase equipment.

2. The cash received was invested in a number of securities.

1996

3. Dividends of $100,000 and interest of $300,000 were received.
4. The income was transferred to the appropriate funds.
5. Of the restricted income, only $80,000 was expended for its specified purpose during 1996.
6. The governing board specified that $200,000 of the income would be used for loans for deserving medical students.

1997

7. $180,000 was lent to medical students.
8. The donor died of cancer.

Required:

Set up headings for the following funds: Endowment, General, Specific Purpose, and Plant Replacement and Expansion. Prepare the entries necessary in each fund to record the events listed above.

Exercise 22-8

After the election of a prominent political figure, the principal from a term endowment fund was expendable by Crandall University. The official was elected this year. The fund was restricted to the construction of a Political Science building annex. The following transactions occurred because of this event:

1. A transfer of $3,000,000 is made from the Endowment Fund (Term) to the Unexpended Plant Fund.
2. Construction is begun on the Political Science annex. Costs of construction during the year amounted to $1,000,000, of which $30,000 remained unpaid at the end of the year. (The financial controller does not record transfers to the Investment in Plant subgroup until a project has been completed.)
3. By the end of the following year, the annex is completed at an additional cost of $2,100,000. All costs have been paid.
4. The completed building is recorded in the Investment in Plant subgroup.

Required:

Record the journal entries for each transaction and identify the fund or fund subgroup in which each entry is recorded.

Exercise 22-9

Select the best answer for each of the following items:

1. Which of the following should be included in the current funds revenue of a not-for-profit private university?

	TUITION WAIVERS	UNRESTRICTED BEQUESTS
(a)	Yes	No
(b)	Yes	Yes
(c)	No	Yes
(d)	No	No

2. The current funds group of a not-for-profit private university includes which of the following subgroups?

	TERM-ENDOWMENT FUNDS	LIFE-INCOME FUNDS
(a)	No	No
(b)	No	Yes
(c)	Yes	Yes
(d)	Yes	No

3. Tuition waivers for which there is *no* intention of collection from the student should be classified by a not-for-profit university as

	REVENUE	EXPENDITURES
(a)	No	No
(b)	No	Yes
(c)	Yes	Yes
(d)	Yes	No

4. Which of the following is utilized for current expenditures by a not-for-profit university?

	UNRESTRICTED CURRENT FUNDS	RESTRICTED CURRENT FUNDS
(a)	No	No
(b)	No	Yes
(c)	Yes	No
(d)	Yes	Yes

5. In the loan fund of a college or university, each of the following types of loans would be found except
   (a) Student.
   (b) Staff.
   (c) Building.
   (d) Faculty.

(AICPA adapted)

Exercise 22-10

Select the best answer choice for each of the following items:

1. Which of the following receipts is properly recorded as unrestricted current funds on the books of a university?
   (a) Tuition.
   (b) Student laboratory fees.
   (c) Housing fees.
   (d) Research grants.

2. The current funds group of a not-for-profit private university includes which of the following?

	ANNUITY FUNDS	LOAN FUNDS
(a)	Yes	Yes
(b)	Yes	No
(c)	No	No
(d)	No	Yes

3. On January 2, 1995, John Reynolds established a $500,000 trust, the income from which is to be paid to Mansfield University for general operating purposes. The Wyndham National Bank was appointed by Reynolds as trustee of the fund. What journal entry is required on Mansfield's books?

(a)	Memo entry only		
(b)	Cash	500,000	
	Endowment Fund Balance		500,000
(c)	Nonexpendable Endowment Fund	500,000	
	Endowment Fund Balance		500,000
(d)	Expendable Funds	500,000	
	Endowment Fund Balance		500,000

4. For the fall semester of 1995, Cherry College assessed its students $2,300,000 for tuition and fees. The net amount realized was only $2,100,000 because of the following revenue reductions:

Refunds occasioned by class cancellations and student withdrawals	$ 50,000
Tuition remissions granted to faculty members' families	10,000
Scholarships and fellowships	140,000

How much should Cherry College report for the period for unrestricted current funds revenues from tuition and fees?
(a) $2,100,000.
(b) $2,150,000.
(c) $2,250,000.
(d) $2,300,000.

5. During the years ending June 30, 1994 and June 30, 1995, Schafer University conducted a cancer research project financed by a $2,000,000 gift from an alumnus. This entire amount was pledged by the donor on July 10, 1993, although he paid only $500,000 at that date. The gift was restricted to the financing of this particular research project. During the two-year research period, Schafer's related gift receipts and research expenditures were as follows:

	YEAR ENDED JUNE 30	
	1994	1995
Gift receipts	$700,000	$ 800,000
Cancer research restricted expenditures	900,000	1,100,000

How much gift revenue should Schafer University report in the restricted column of its Statement of Current Funds Revenues, Expenditures, and Other Changes for the year ended June 30, 1995?
(a) $0.
(b) $800,000.

(c) $1,100,000.
(d) $2,000,000.

(AICPA adapted)

Exercise 22-11

Select the best answer for each of the following items:

1. Cura Foundation, a voluntary health and welfare organization, supported by contributions from the general public, included the following costs in its statement of functional expenses for the year ended December 31, 1996.

Fund raising	$500,000
Administrative	300,000
Research	100,000

Cura's functional expenses for 1996 program services included
(a) $900,000.
(b) $500,000.
(c) $300,000.
(d) $100,000.

2. Community Service Center is a voluntary welfare organization funded by contributions from the general public. During 1995 unrestricted pledges of $900,000 were received, half of which were payable in 1995 with the other half payable in 1996 for use in 1996. It was estimated that 10% of these pledges would be uncollectible. How much should Community report as net contribution revenue for 1995 with respect to the pledges?
(a) $0.
(b) $405,000.
(c) $810,000.
(d) $900,000.

3. Theresa Plato is a social worker on the staff of Community Service Center, a voluntary welfare organization. She earns $30,000 annually for a normal workload of 2,000 hours. During 1995 she contributed an additional 800 hours of her time to Community at no extra charge. How much should Community record in 1995 as contributed service expense?
(a) $12,000.
(b) $6,000.
(c) $1,200.
(d) $0.

4. The basis of accounting used by nonprofit organizations is the
(a) Cash basis.
(b) Modified accrual basis.
(c) Accrual basis.
(d) Modified cash basis.

(AICPA adapted)

Exercise 22-12

Select the best answer for each of the following items:

1. Which NNOs must record depreciation on exhaustible assets?
(a) Hospitals.
(b) VHWOs.
(c) ONNOs.
(d) All of the above.

2. Which statement relating to VHWOs is most nearly correct?
   (a) Use modified accrual accounting practices.
   (b) Report expenditures on a functional basis.
   (c) Record pledges when they are received.
   (d) Recognize donated services as revenue if measurable.

3. Which of the following funds of a VHWO does not have a counterpart fund in governmental accounting?
   (a) Current Unrestricted Fund.
   (b) Land, Building, and Equipment Fund.
   (c) Agency Fund.
   (d) Endowment Fund.

4. A voluntary health and welfare organization received a pledge in 1994 from a donor specifying that the amount pledged be used in 1996. The donor paid the pledge in cash in 1995. The pledge should be accounted for as
   (a) A deferred credit in the balance sheet at the end of 1994, and as support in 1995.
   (b) A deferred credit in the balance sheet at the end of 1994 and 1995, and as support in 1996.
   (c) Support in 1996.
   (d) Support in 1995, and no deferred credit in the balance sheet at the end of 1994.

5. Which of the following should be used in accounting for nonprofit health agencies?
   (a) Fund accounting and accrual accounting.
   (b) Fund accounting but not accrual accounting.
   (c) Accrual accounting but not fund accounting.
   (d) Neither accrual accounting nor fund accounting.

(AICPA adapted)

Exercise 22-13

Select the best answer for each of the following items:

1. Depreciation should be recognized in the financial statements of
   (a) Private sector proprietary (for profit) hospitals only.
   (b) Both private sector proprietary (for profit) hospitals and not-for-profit hospitals
   (c) Both private sector proprietary (for profit) hospitals and not-for-profit hospitals, only when they are affiliated with a university.
   (d) All private sector hospitals, as a memorandum entry not affecting the statement of revenue and expenses.

2. Securities donated to a nonbusiness organization should be recorded at the
   (a) Donor's recorded amount.
   (b) Fair market value at the date of the gift.
   (c) Fair market value at the date of the gift or the donor's recorded value, whichever is lower.
   (d) Fair market value at the date of the gift or the donor's recorded value, whichever is higher.

3. The Charity Services ledger account of a nonprofit hospital is a(an)
   (a) Contra-asset account.
   (b) Expense account.
   (c) Contra-revenue account.
   (d) Loss account.

4. The restricted fund groupings recommended for hospitals do not include
   (a) Specific purpose funds.

(b) Endowment funds.

(c) Plant funds.

(d) Plant replacement and expansion funds.

(AICPA adapted)

Exercise 22-14

Select the best answer for each of the following items:

1. An unrestricted pledge from an annual contributor to a not-for-profit hospital made in December 1994 and paid in cash in March 1995 would generally be credited to

    (a) Nonoperating revenue in 1994.

    (b) Nonoperating revenue in 1995.

    (c) Operating revenue in 1994.

    (d) Operating revenue in 1995.

2. A gift to a not-for-profit hospital that is not restricted by the donor should be credited directly to

    (a) Fund balance.

    (b) Deferred revenue.

    (c) Operating revenue.

    (d) Nonoperating revenue.

3. During the year ended December 31, 1995, Melford Hospital received the following donations, stated at their respective fair values:

Employee services from members of a religious group.	$100,000
Medical supplies from an association of physicians. These supplies were restricted for indigent care and were used for such purposes in 1995.	30,000

    How much revenue (both operating and nonoperating) from donations should Melford report in its 1995 statement of revenues and expenses?

    (a) $0.

    (b) $30,000.

    (c) $100,000.

    (d) $130,000.

4. On July 1, 1994, Lilydale Hospital's Board of Trustees designated $200,000 for expansion of outpatient facilities. The $200,000 is expected to be expended in the fiscal year ending June 30, 1997. In Lilydale's balance sheet at June 30, 1995, this cash should be classified as a $200,000

    (a) Restricted current asset.

    (b) Restricted noncurrent asset.

    (c) Unrestricted current asset.

    (d) Asset whose use is limited.

(AICPA adapted)

Problems

Problem 22-1

The following events were recorded on the books of Mercy Hospital for the year ended December 31, 1995:

1. Revenue from patient services totaled $16,000,000. The allowance for uncollectibles was established at $3,400,000. Of the $16,000,000 revenue, $6,000,000 was recognized under cost reimbursement agreements. This revenue is subject to audit and retroactive adjustment by third-party payors (estimated adjustments are included in the allowance account).
2. Patient service revenue is accounted for at established rates on the accrual basis.
3. Other operating revenue totaled $346,000, of which $160,000 was from specific purpose funds.
4. Mercy received $410,000 in unrestricted gifts and bequests. They are recorded at fair market value when received.
5. Endowment funds earned $160,000 in unrestricted income.
6. Board designated funds earned $82,000 in income.
7. Mercy's operating expenses for the year amounted to $13,370,000. This included $500,000 in straight-line depreciation.

Required:

Prepare a statement of revenues and expenses for Mercy Hospital for the year ended December 31, 1995.

(AICPA adapted)

Problem 22-2

On January 1, 1995, a new Board of Directors was elected for Bradley Hospital. The new board switched to a different accountant. After reviewing the hospital's books, the accountant decided that the accounts should be adjusted. Effective January 1, 1995, the board decided that

1. Separate funds should be established for the General Fund, the Bradley Fund, and the Plant Replacement and Expansion Fund (the old balances will be reversed to eliminate them).
2. The accounts should be maintained in accordance with fund accounting principles. The balances in the general ledger at January 1, 1995, are presented here:

Cash	$ 50,000	
Investment in U.S. treasury bills	105,000	
Investment in common stock	417,000	
Interest receivable	4,000	
Accounts receivable	40,000	
Inventory	25,000	
Land	407,000	
Building	245,000	
Equipment	283,000	
Allowance for depreciation		$ 376,000
Accounts payable		70,000
Bank loan		150,000
Endowment fund balance		119,500
Other fund balances		860,500
Total	$1,576,000	$1,576,000

The following additional information is available:

1. Under the terms of the will of J. Ethington, founder of the hospital, "The principal of the bequest is to be fully invested in trust forevermore in mortgages secured by productive

real estate in Central City and/or in U.S. Government securities . . . and the income therefrom is to be used to defray current expenses.''

2. The Endowment Fund consists of the following:

Cash received in 1891 by bequest from Ethington	$ 81,500
Net gains realized from 1949 through 1982 from the sale of real estate acquired in mortgage foreclosures	23,500
Income received from 1983 through 1994 from 90-day U.S. treasury bill investments	14,500
Balance per general ledger on January 1, 1995	$119,500

3. The land account balance is composed of

1897 appraisal of land at $10,000 and building at $5,000, received by donation at that time. The building was demolished in 1927.	$ 15,000
Appraisal increase based on insured value in land title policies issued in 1947.	380,000
Landscaping costs for trees planted.	12,000
Balance per general ledger on January 1, 1995	$407,000

4. The building balance is composed of

Cost of present hospital building completed in January 1954, when the hospital commenced operations	$300,000
Adjustment to record appraised value of building in 1964.	(100,000)
Cost of elevator installed in hospital building in January 1980.	45,000
Balance per general ledger on January 1, 1995	$245,000

The estimated useful lives of the hospital building and the elevator when new were 50 years and 20 years, respectively.

5. The hospital's equipment was inventoried on January 1, 1995. The costs shown in the inventory agreed with the equipment account balance in the general ledger. The allowance for depreciation account at January 1, 1995, included $158,250 applicable to equipment, and that amount was determined to be accurate. All depreciation is computed on a straight-line basis.

6. A bank loan was obtained to finance the cost of new operating room equipment purchased in 1991. Interest was paid to December 31, 1994.

7. Common stock with a market value of $417,000 was donated to Bradley Hospital with the stipulation that the proceeds from the sale of the stock must be used for facilities expansion. The hospital plans to undertake expansion of its facilities next year and to sell these securities at that time.

Required:

Using the worksheet form below, prepare the entries necessary to establish the correct balances as of January 1, 1995.

	TRIAL BALANCE		ADJUSTMENTS		GENERAL FUND		ENDOWMENT FUND		PLANT REPLACEMENT FUND	
ACCOUNT DESCRIPTION	DEBIT	CREDIT	DEBIT	CREDIT	DEBIT	CREDIT	DEBIT	CREDIT	DEBIT	CREDIT

(AICPA adapted)

Problem 22-3

A partial balance sheet of Century University is shown below.

Century University
Partial Balance Sheet
June 30, 1994

ASSETS

Current funds
  Unrestricted
    Cash | $210,000
    Accounts receivable (less allowance for doubtful accounts, $9,000) | 341,000
    State appropriations receivable | 75,000
      Total unrestricted | 626,000
  Restricted
    Cash | 7,000
    Investments | 60,000
      Total restricted | 67,000
    Total current | $693,000

Current funds	
Unrestricted	
Cash	$210,000
Accounts receivable (less allowance for doubtful accounts, $9,000)	341,000
State appropriations receivable	75,000
Total unrestricted	626,000
Restricted	
Cash	7,000
Investments	60,000
Total restricted	67,000
Total current	$693,000

LIABILITIES AND FUND BALANCES

Current funds	
Unrestricted	
Accounts payable	$ 45,000
Deferred revenues	66,000
Fund balance	515,000
Total unrestricted	626,000
Restricted	
Fund balance	67,000
Total restricted	67,000
Total current	$693,000

During the fiscal year ended June 30, 1995, the following transactions occurred:

1. A gift of $100,000 was received from an alumnus on July 7, 1994. One-half of the gift was to be used for the purchase of books for the university's library and the rest was to be used to establish a scholarship fund per the alumnus's request. It was also requested that the income generated by the scholarship fund be awarded annually as a scholarship for a qualified disadvantaged student. The board decided that the funds for the new scholarship should be invested in savings certificates on July 20, 1994. These savings certificates were purchased on July 21, 1994.

2. Revenue for the fiscal period from student tuition and fees amounted to $1,900,000. During the fiscal year, $1,686,000 of this amount was collected; $66,000 had been collected in the prior year. The university had also received $158,000 by June 30, 1995, for fees for the session beginning July 1, 1995.

3. During the year ended June 30, 1995, the university collected $349,000 of the outstanding accounts receivable at the beginning of the year. The balance was determined to be uncollectible and was written off against the allowance account. At June 30, 1995, the allowance account was increased by $3,000.

4. Because of late student fee payments, $6,000 in interest charges were earned and collected.
5. The state appropriation was received. Another unrestricted appropriation of $50,000 was made by the state. This had not been paid to the university by the fiscal year-end.
6. An unrestricted gift of $25,000 cash was received from alumni of the university.
7. During the year, investments of $21,000 were sold for $26,000. Investment income amounting to $1,900 was received.
8. Unrestricted operating expenses were recorded at $1,777,000, $59,000 of which remains unpaid.
9. Restricted current funds of $13,000 were spent for authorized purposes during the year.
10. The accounts payable at June 30, 1994, were paid during the year.
11. During the year, $7,000 interest was earned and received on the savings certificates purchased in accordance with the board's resolution [in item (1)].

Required:

A. Prepare journal entries to record in summary form the transactions above for the year ended June 30, 1995. Each journal entry should be numbered to correspond with the transaction described above. Set up the following headings:

	CURRENT FUNDS				ENDOWMENT FUND	
	UNRESTRICTED		RESTRICTED			
ACCOUNTS	DR.	CR.	DR.	CR.	DR.	CR.

B. Prepare a statement of changes in fund balances for the year ended June 30, 1995.

C. Prepare a Statement of Current Funds Revenues, Expenditures, and Other Changes for the year ended June 30, 1995.

Problem 22-4

The following transactions of Beltville College transpired during 1995. The funds necessary are the Endowment Fund, the Annuity Fund, the Plant Fund—Unexpended, the Plant Fund—Investment in Plant, the Loan Fund, the Unrestricted Current Fund, and the Restricted Current Fund.

January 1

1. A gift of $10,000 was received from Carl Brown. The principal was to be held intact and the income to be used for any purpose designated by the governing board.
2. David Gross donated $20,000. The principal was to be held intact and the income to be used for scholarships for worthy students.
3. Roxanne Norton donated $30,000, of which the principal was to remain intact while the interest was to be used for student loans. All income is to be relent; all losses from loans are to be charged against income.
4. A gift of $205,000 was received from Brian Carr. Semiannual payments of $10,000 are to be made to the donor during his lifetime. On his death the fund is to be used to purchase or construct a students' residence. Mr. Carr has a life expectancy of five years and investments are expected to earn 8% annually.
5. Kathy Jackson donated 1,000 shares of BIM stock, which had a market value of $150 per share on that date. All income received from the shares is to be held intact and the

shares cannot be held for more than five years. Once the board sells the shares, all the proceeds are to be used to build a student hospital.

6. The assets of the Brown and Gross funds were consolidated into a pooled investment account by the governing board (in proportion to the principal accounts). Electric Power Bonds worth $30,000 were purchased. The 12% interest was payable on January 1 and July 1.

7. The Norton Fund cash is used to purchase Cravit Company 10% bonds at par for $30,000. January 1 and July 1 are the interest dates.

8. With the cash from the Carr Fund, $200,000 of 8% U.S. Treasury notes was purchased at par. The interest dates are January 1 and July 1.

July 1

9. The interest has been received on all bonds and notes and has been transferred to the proper funds. Dividends of $4,000 were received from BIM stock.

10. The stipulated payment is made to Mr. Carr from the Endowment Fund.

11. Electric Power Company bonds bought at par value for $20,000 are sold at 102. The gain is added to the principal.

12. A $300 student loan was made from the Norton Fund.

October 1

13. A notice of Brian Carr's death is received. There is no liability to his estate.

14. The Gross Scholarship Fund awards a $200 scholarship.

15. $200,000 par of U.S. Treasury notes are sold for $206,000.

December 31

16. Interest on bonds is received.

17. $100 of principal and $5 of interest were repaid on the student loan.

18. A building was purchased for $250,000 using the funds available from the Carr gift. The residence hall will have a 20-year mortgage payable to account for the balance.

Required:

Using the following format, record the journal entries necessary for each event.

EVENT FUND JOURNAL ENTRY

(AICPA adapted)

Problem 22-5

Preston Library, a nonprofit organization, presented the following balance sheet and statement of support, revenue, expenses, and changes in fund balances for its fiscal year ended February 28, 1994.

Preston Library
Balance Sheet
February 28, 1994

ASSETS

Current assets	
Cash	$ 365,000
Grants receivable	80,000
Prepaid expenses	65,000
Total	510,000
Investments (at market)	1,020,000
Land, building, and equipment	
(less accumulated depreciation of $50,000)	530,000
Total assets	$2,060,000

LIABILITIES AND FUND BALANCES

Current liabilities	
Accounts payable and accrued expenses	$ 150,000
Deferred support—contributions	80,000
Total	230,000
Long-term debt	200,000
Fund balances	1,630,000
Total liabilities and fund balances	$2,060,000

Preston Library
Statement of Support, Revenue, Expenses,
and Changes in Fund Balances
For Year Ended February 28, 1994

SUPPORT AND REVENUE

Support	
Grants	$ 70,000
Gifts	300,000
Total	370,000
Revenue	
Service fees	22,000
Book rentals and fines	107,000
Investment income	71,000
Total	200,000
Total support and revenue	$ 570,000

EXPENSES

Program services	
Circulating library	$ 212,000
Research library	86,000
Exhibits	20,000
Community services	10,000
Total	328,000
Supporting services	
General and administrative	175,000
Fund raising	111,000
Total	286,000
Total expenses	614,000
Excess (deficit) of support and revenue over expenses	(44,000)
Fund balances—beginning of year	1,674,000
Fund balances—end of year	$1,630,000

The following transactions occurred during the fiscal year ended February 28, 1995.

1. Fees were billed as follows:

Service fees	$ 30,000
Book rentals	43,000
Book fines	78,000

2. $40,000 of the Grant Receivable was received. Another grant in the amount of $20,000 was promised.

3. Contributions in the amounts summarized below were received:

Unrestricted	$215,000
Restricted	108,000

4. Investment income totaled $75,000 for the year.

5. Vouchers for the year were approved as follows:

Circulating library	$189,000
Research library	74,000
Exhibits	15,000
Community services	12,000
General and administrative	166,000
Fund raising	103,000
Total	$559,000

6. During the year, $500,000 worth of vouchers were paid.

ADJUSTMENT DATA

7. Accounts Payable and Accrued Expenses at February 28, 1995, should be $217,000. The difference should be allocated to the following expenses:

Research library	$5,000
General and administrative	3,000

8. Additions to the research library in the amount of $68,000 that were approved in (5) above were made in accordance with the terms of a contribution that had been received earlier and that was restricted for that purpose.

9. The current market value of the investments is $1,035,000 (no investment transactions occurred).

10. Depreciation amounted to $9,000 for the year. It should be allocated as follows:

Circulating library	$3,500
Research library	2,900
General and administrative	2,600

11. Prepaid Expenses should be $60,000. The difference should be allocated to:

Exhibits	$3,700
General and administrative	1,300

Required:

A. Prepare journal entries to record the transactions.

B. Prepare the balance sheet and the statement of support, revenue, expenses, and changes in fund balance for the year ended February 28, 1995.

(AICPA adapted)

Problem 22-6

The December 31, 1995, balance sheet for the Blood Donors of America Foundation is presented below.

Balance Sheet
December 31, 1995

ASSETS

Cash	$ 470,000
Accounts receivable	160,000
Allowance for doubtful accounts	(30,000)
Pledges receivable	930,000
Allowance for doubtful pledges	(130,000)
Inventories	400,000
Investments	19,300,000
Land	1,300,000
Buildings and improvements	46,500,000
Equipment	2,700,000
Accumulated depreciation	(13,500,000)
Other assets	200,000
Total assets	$58,300,000

LIABILITIES

Accounts payable	$ 700,000
Accrued expenses	130,000
Deferred revenue—unrestricted	100,000
Deferred support—restricted	6,000,000
Deferred capital addition	1,600,000
Long-term debt	7,350,000
Total liabilities	15,880,000

FUND BALANCES

Plant	29,000,000
Endowment	3,850,000
Restricted	1,300,000
Unrestricted	8,270,000
Total fund balances	42,420,000
Total liabilities and fund balances	$58,300,000

Additional information concerning the balance sheet is as follows:

1. Except for $70,000 of cash, the Endowment Fund is made up of investments only. There are no liabilities.
2. The Plant Fund has no current liabilities and includes some investments and $15,000 in cash.
3. In addition to investments, the Current Restricted Fund consists of the pledges receivable, $35,000 of accounts payable, and cash of $155,000.

Required:

Prepare a corrected balance sheet for the Blood Donors of America Foundation at December 31, 1995, using the following columnar format:

	CURRENT UNRESTRICTED	CURRENT RESTRICTED	PLANT	ENDOWMENT	TOTAL
(Account Titles)	$	$	$	$	$

(AICPA adapted)

Problem 22-7

Three funds of the Leukemia Foundation, a nonprofit welfare organization, began an investment pool on January 1, 1996. The cost and fair market value on this date were as follows:

	COST	MARKET VALUE
Restricted fund	$ 55,000	$ 70,000
Lambert endowment fund	215,000	210,000
Plant fund	200,000	220,000
Total	$470,000	$500,000

During 1996 the investment pool reinvested $20,000 in realized gains and received interest of $15,000 and dividends of $10,000. Interest and dividend income was distributed to the respective funds. The Plant Fund withdrew from the investment pool on December 31, 1996, when the total current market value was $540,000. It was distributed securities in the amount of its percentage share.

On January 3, 1997, the Fargot Annuity Fund entered the investment pool with investments costing $100,000 and having a current market value of $117,600. During 1997 the pool received interest of $25,000 and dividends of $15,000, which were distributed to the participating funds. Realized gains of $30,000 were reinvested in the pool.

Required:

A. Calculate the equity percentages of the contributing funds in the investment pool at January 1, 1996, and at January 3, 1997.

B. Using the format shown below, prepare entries necessary on the records of the funds that contributed securities to the investment pool to account for the earnings of the investment pool in 1996 and 1997.

<u>DATE</u>   <u>FUND</u>   <u>JOURNAL ENTRY</u>

23

ACCOUNTING FOR ESTATES AND TRUSTS

The term *estate* is sometimes used to denote a legal entity that holds title to the property of a deceased person, the *decedent*, for the purpose of managing and making appropriate disposition of the property. A *trust* is formed when the legal title to property is transferred to one party (the *trustee*) to be used for the benefit of another party or parties (the *beneficiary*). Frequently a trust is established because the creator of the trust does not want the beneficiary to take possession of the property until some future time.

An individual or corporation entrusted with the management and disposition of the properties on behalf of others is accountable for such activities and is called a *fiduciary*. The power and duties of the fiduciary are derived from provisions of the decedent's will or the document establishing the trust arrangement. In addition, a fiduciary comes under the jurisdiction of a state court. Thus, to understand the accounting for an estate or trust, one must be familiar with the powers and duties of a fiduciary and have some knowledge of the statutes related to administering an estate or trust.

To report on the stewardship function of the fiduciary, an estate or trust is accounted for as a separate entity. Unlike a separate business entity, however, the activities of the fiduciary are restricted by law and the provisions of the will or the trust instrument. The focus of the accounting system is therefore to facilitate reporting on the accountability of the fiduciary to the court or various interested parties. In general, the accounting does not adhere to the accrual basis of accounting and other generally accepted accounting practices associated with business organizations. Nor are the traditional balance sheet and income statement prepared. Specialized procedures for recording and reporting the activities of an estate or trust are covered in this chapter. Because statutes differ from state to state, the *Uniform Probate Code* will be used as a basis to illustrate statutory provisions.[1]

ESTATE PLANNING

Accountants are increasingly called on to participate in estate planning. The objective of estate planning is to maximize the amount of the estate assets distributed to the beneficiaries. An important consideration in reaching this objective is to minimize the amount of estate assets needed to satisfy federal and state estate and gift taxes. This requires careful planning and knowledge of the tax laws and specialized areas of law related to estate planning. Because of the complexity of the federal tax codes and the variety of state laws, an extensive discussion of estate planning is beyond the scope of this text. However, it should be pointed out that it is the estate of the decedent, not the recipient of the property, that is subject to estate and gift taxes. However, if the estate does not pay the taxes, the appropriate governmental agency may proceed against the recipient.

ADMINISTRATION OF AN ESTATE

On the death of a person, a personal representative is named or appointed to administer and dispose of the estate assets. The representative comes under the jurisdiction of a state court, frequently referred to as a *probate court*, which is directed by a set of statutes called the *probate code*. One of the first legal steps to be taken is to determine if the decedent has left a valid will.[2] The probate court will rule on the validity of the will. If a valid will has been left directing the disposal of the estate, the decedent is referred to as the *testator* if a male and a *testatrix* if a female, and is said to have died *testate*. In such cases, the provisions of the will normally govern the disposition of the decedent's property. The decedent may name a party in the will to carry out its provisions. The named party is referred to as an *executor*, if male; *executrix*, if female.

In the absence of a will, the decedent is said to have died *intestate*, and the probate statutes of the appropriate state will prescribe the disposition of the prop-

---

[1]The *Uniform Probate Code* has been approved by the American Bar Association, and has been adopted by approximately 15 states, including Alaska, Arizona, Colorado, Florida, Hawaii, Idaho, Maine, Michigan, Minnesota, Montana, Nebraska, New Mexico, North Dakota, and Utah.

[2]Proceedings are generally initiated by the personal administrator named in the will or by a party involved in action concerning the estate. In Sections 2–501 and 502, the *Uniform Probate Code* provides that in general a will is valid if

(*a*) The person is 18 years or more of age,

(*b*) The person is sound of mind,

(*c*) The will is in writing signed by the decedent, and

(*d*) The will was witnessed by at least two persons.

erty. If there is not a valid will, or if an executor is not named, or if the executor is not willing or qualified to administer the estate, the court will appoint an ***administrator*** (male) or an ***administratix*** (female). The *Uniform Probate Code* uses the term ***personal representative*** to refer to the person administering the estate. Hereafter, we will use that term whether a will exists or not.

If the decedent died intestate, the personal representative disposes of the property as prescribed by state laws. Real property of the decedent is distributed in accordance with the ***laws of descent*** of the jurisdiction where the property is located. The ***laws of distribution*** of the jurisdiction where the decedent resided at the time of death control the distribution of personal property. Persons receiving real property of the decedent are called ***heirs***; persons receiving personal property are referred to as ***next of kin***.

When a valid will does exist, the personal representative is responsible for distributing the estate assets as prescribed by the will. The disposition of real property in accordance with provisions of the will is called a ***devise***, and the recipient of real property is called a ***devisee***. The distribution of personal property is known as a ***legacy*** or ***bequest***, and the person named to receive the personal property is called the ***legatee***. The relationship of these legal terms is diagrammed below:

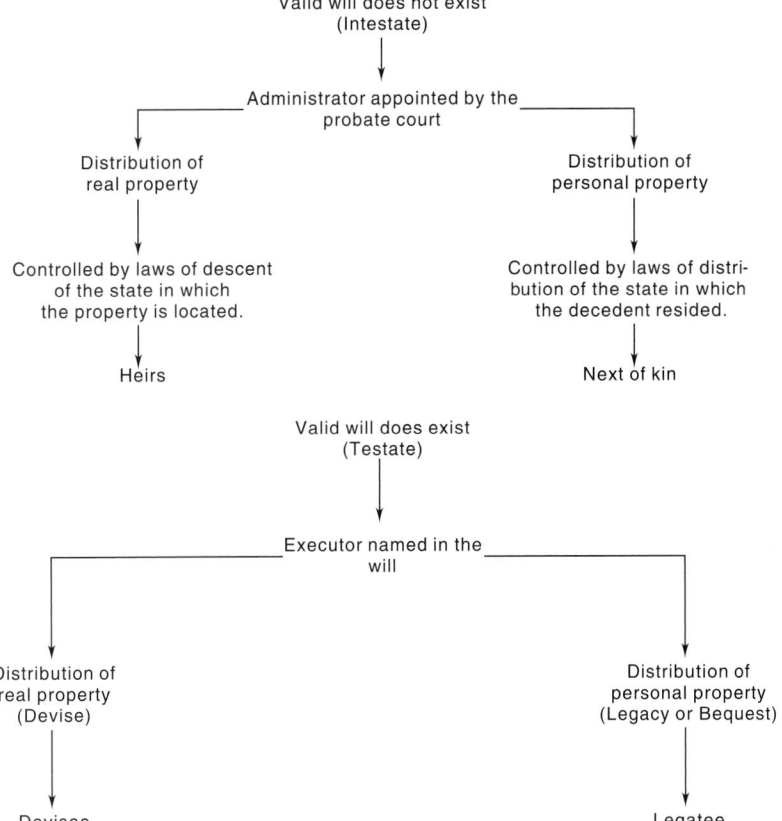

The decedent may provide for one or more of the following types of legacies in the will:

1. *Specific.* Disposition of a specifically identified asset, for example, a diamond ring to a daughter.

2. *Demonstrative.* Disposition of an amount from a specific source, for example, $2,000 from a savings account with the United Bank to the decedent's grandson Edward.

3. *General.* Disposition of an indicated amount of cash or personal property without specifying the particular source, for example, $5,000 to the Sierra Club.

4. *Residuary.* Disposition of all remaining personal property.

As can be seen, some legacies may provide for the distribution of assets other than cash. To the extent possible, the personal representative should distribute to the legatees cash and noncash assets as specified in the will. In other words, it is not necessary to convert all noncash assets into cash before a distribution is made. If a distribution of property is made, the personal representative must execute an instrument transferring title to the asset to the legatee as evidence of ownership.

DUTIES OF THE PERSONAL REPRESENTATIVE

The primary duties of the personal representative are to collect the assets of the decedent and file an inventory of the estate assets, pay the valid claims against the estate, and distribute any remaining property in the estate to the individuals entitled thereto, subject to approval of the probate court.

Preparing an Inventory of Estate Property

After appointment by the court, the personal representative normally takes title to all the decedent's assets except insurance policies that provide for payment to a beneficiary other than the estate. The personal representative takes title to real property and executes a deed to the recipient except when it is owned in joint tenancy or tenancy by the entirety and the other owner is still living. The personal representative prepares a complete inventory with a detailed description of the estate property, which will be submitted to the probate court and other interested parties.[3] Each item included in the inventory must be valued. For a complete record, items assigned a zero value should also be included in the inventory. The fair value at the time of death is assigned to each item contained in the list if such information is available at the time of filing. In this regard, it may be necessary to obtain the services of professional appraisers if the personal representative is unable to ascertain a satisfactory value.

The personal representative is responsible for seeking out any properties belonging to the estate that were not included in the initial inventory. If an asset is subsequently discovered, the court must be notified of the item and its assigned

---

[3]The estate assets make up the **principal** or **corpus** of the estate.

value. All properties controlled by the personal representative must be prudently managed and cared for until distributed.

Settlement of Claims Against the Estate

The personal representative is also responsible for satisfying all valid claims against the estate. Most state laws require that the personal representative publish notices requesting that all claims against the estate be filed. A limited period is established for filing claims. After this period all claims are forfeited. The *Uniform Probate Code* (Section 3–801, 803) requires that notices be published once a week for three successive weeks and that claims be filed within four months after the first notice is published. The personal representative is responsible for reviewing all claims and establishing the validity of each one before payment is made. Debts and expenses of the estate may include such items as funeral expenses, expenses related to the administration of the estate, income taxes of the decedent, estate taxes, and amounts due unpaid creditors of the decedent.

State laws normally provide that some estate assets are exempt from claims against the estate. One responsibility of the personal representative is to assure that these exemptions are recognized. Exemptions are defined in the *Uniform Probate Code* as

1. *Homestead Allowance*—A surviving spouse of a decedent is entitled to a homestead allowance of $5,000. If there is no surviving spouse, each minor child and each dependent child of the decedent is entitled to a homestead allowance amounting to $5,000 divided by the number of minor and dependent children of the decedent. The homestead allowance is exempt from and has priority over all claims against the estate. Homestead allowance is in addition to any share passing to the surviving spouse or minor or dependent child by the will of the decedent unless otherwise provided, by intestate succession or by way of elective share. (Section 2–401)

2. *Exempt Property*—In addition to the homestead allowance, the surviving spouse is entitled to receive from the estate an amount not exceeding $3,500 in excess of any security interest therein in household furniture, automobiles, furnishings, appliances and personal effects. If there is no surviving spouse, children of the decedent are entitled jointly to the same value. (Section 2–402)

3. *Family Allowance*—The surviving spouse and minor children whom the decedent was obligated to support and children who were in fact being supported by him are entitled to a reasonable allowance in money out of the estate for their maintenance during the period of administration (not to exceed $6,000 per year), which allowance may not continue for longer than one year if the estate is inadequate to discharge allowed claims (Section 2–403)

In some cases, the liquid assets of the estate may be sufficient to settle claims against the estate and legacies. In other cases, it may be necessary for the personal representative to convert some noncash assets not bequested into cash in order to satisfy claims and legacies prescribed in the will. (The reader is reminded that some assets, such as the assets used to satisfy the family and homestead allowance, are exempt from claims.) The remaining assets are then distributed according to the intent of the decedent. In still other cases, the settlement of creditors' claims filed against the estate may not leave sufficient estate assets to satisfy all legacies provided for in the will. In such cases, the personal representative must reduce proportionately certain classes of legacies. This process is referred to as ***abatement***. Depending on the size of the deficiency, the abatement may result in a complete revocation of a certain class of legacies. If the will is silent as to the order of abatement, state laws govern. The *Uniform Probate Code* (Section 3–805) provides the following abatement sequence:

1. Property not disposed of by will.
2. Residuary devises.
3. General devises.
4. Specific devises.

Properties that are not realized are held for distribution in accordance with provisions of the will.

If the applicable assets are insufficient to settle claims against the estate, state statutes will provide an order of settlement. The *Uniform Probate Code* (Section 3–805) directs the personal representative to pay claims in the following order:

1. Costs and expenses of administering the estate.

2. Reasonable funeral expenses and reasonable and necessary medical and hospital expenses of the last illness of the decedent, including compensation of persons attending him.

3. Debts and taxes with preference under federal law or the laws of the state.

4. All other claims (Section 3–805).

The probate court may also approve the disposal of devised real estate to satisfy the claims against the estate.

Distribution of Estate Assets After Settlement of Claims

After the claims against and expenses of the estate have been settled or provided for, the personal representative proceeds with the distribution of the assets to the appropriate beneficiaries. A distribution to a beneficiary should normally be deferred until the personal representative is assured that estate assets are sufficient to satisfy claims against the estate. A distribution to a beneficiary and a subsequent inadequacy in the estate assets to settle claims against the estate may result in personal liability of the personal representative.[4]

---

[4]The personal representative should always request a waiver for estate taxes on the federal level, state waiver of estate taxes, and a waiver for the last three years for income taxes. Otherwise, the personal representative may be personally liable for unpaid taxes.

Reporting on Estate Activities

The personal representative is normally required to file periodic reports with the probate court summarizing the transactions completed during the period. This report is commonly referred to as a ***Charge and Discharge Statement***. Although the form of the report depends on state requirements, the report frequently contains two sections, one to summarize the activities during the period related to the estate principal and the other to summarize activities related to estate income. (The distinction between estate principal and income is discussed later in this chapter.) Within each section, the personal representative reports the assets to which he or she was entrusted and the manner in which this accountability was discharged.

ACCOUNTING FOR AN ESTATE

A personal representative of an estate is entrusted with the safekeeping, management, and disposition of assets on behalf of others. In this capacity the personal representative is a steward or fiduciary and is accountable to various parties, such as the probate court, beneficiaries, and federal and state taxing agencies. The personal representative's accountability is increased by the receipt of assets and is decreased by the disposition of assets either as prescribed by law or in accordance with provisions of the will. Obligations of the decedent or claims resulting from the operation of the estate normally are not recorded until they are paid, since the accounting records are designed to account for the personal representative's accountability and this accountability is not reduced until payment is made. Thus, the fundamental accounting equation for an estate becomes

$$\text{Assets} = \text{Accountability}$$

From a reporting point of view, the personal representative is concerned primarily with reporting on the fulfillment of the fiduciary responsibility, not on reporting the complete financial position of the estate. The accounting system designed to account for the transactions of an estate should provide sufficient detail to facilitate the preparation of the required accountability reports. Thus the records are designed to provide a complete record of the estate assets controlled by the personal representative and the disposition of such assets.

Distinguishing Between Estate Principal and Income

The accounting records designed for an estate should also permit the personal representative to distinguish between estate principal and income transactions. ***Principal assets*** are cash and other assets originally received or subsequently discovered by the personal representative and designated to be held for eventual disposition to the principal beneficiaries. ***Estate income*** is an increase in estate assets resulting from the use of estate principal after the date of the decedent's death. This distinction is particularly important if the decedent provides that certain beneficiaries are to receive income earned, but the principal is to remain intact to be distributed to other parties, or is to be used to establish a trust. In addition, certain expenses of the estate may be paid only from principal assets, while other expenses may be paid only from income assets. Procedurally, the distinction is accomplished by maintaining separate accounts for principal and income.

Distinguishing between principal and income transactions is one of the most intricate and important aspects of accounting for an estate or trust. The decedent or creator of a trust may include in the will or trust instrument a method or a set of criteria to be used in making this distinction. If provisions are not made in the respective instruments, then the personal representative or trustee must rely on the appropriate statutes or obtain a ruling from the court to identify whether a receipt or a disbursement is an income or a principal transaction. Because of the wide variety of possible transactions, it is beyond the scope of this discussion to provide a detailed list of criteria here. The following are presented to illustrate the **general rules** for some of the most commonly encountered transactions:

1. Accrued interest earned before the date of death is principal; interest earned after the date of death is income. The same rules normally apply when determining whether accrued interest payable should be charged against income or principal. Interest accruing on savings accounts or certificates of deposit is classified as income (principal) if it becomes available to the depositor after (before) the date of death.

2. Cash dividends declared before the date of death are principal; cash dividends declared after the date of death are income. In other words, the declaration date, rather than the actual receipt, is normally the relevant date when classifying cash dividends. However, in some states the relevant date is the date of record.

3. Expenses incurred in connection with settlement of the estate are charged against principal, for example, debts of the decedent, funeral expenses, estate taxes, court costs, attorney fees, and family allowances.

4. Ordinary expenses identified with operation of income-producing properties are debited to an income-expense account, for example, normal recurring repairs, insurance premiums, and taxes.

In practice, a wide variety of classification problems may be encountered in addition to those discussed above. Items such as the amortization of bond discounts and premiums, depreciation of estate property, and the allocation of partnership earnings between principal and income require careful analysis. The personal representative must be familiar with the probate statutes when attempting to determine the proper treatment of certain transactions.

Account Titles

The opening entry on the estate books records the inventory of assets filed with the probate court. There should be a sufficient number of accounts to maintain a separate classification for each type of asset. Each account is debited for the respective amount assigned in the inventory list, which should approximate the fair value of each asset at the date of the decedent's death. The sum of these individual debits is offset by a credit to Estate Principal, which reflects the personal representative's accountability at this point.

Subsequent changes in principal assets increase or decrease the personal representative's accountability and are recorded in accounts separate from the estate principal account. Recording the changes in principal assets that result from alternative types of transactions makes it easier to prepare and reconcile reports filed by the personal representative. The two most common types of changes in estate principal are the discovery of assets after filing the initial inventory list and selling assets for an amount that is greater than (increase in accountability) or less than (decrease in accountability) the assets' carrying value. Accounts with titles such as Assets Subsequently Discovered and Gain (Loss) on Disposal of Principal Assets are created to record the changes in the personal representative's accountability as a result of such transactions. Income earned from assets constituting the estate principal should be recorded in accounts designated as income, such as

Cash—Income	XX	
Estate Income		XX

The number of income accounts created will depend on the variety of income sources.

As noted earlier, obligations of the decedent or claims resulting from the operation of the estate normally are not recorded until they are paid. The settlement of approved claims is recorded by a debit to an accountability account and a credit to an appropriate asset, usually cash. The debit is not made to Estate Principal; instead, new accounts are created to facilitate accumulating information on how the personal representative discharged his or her responsibility. Two common examples are (1) Debts of Decedent Paid and (2) Funeral and Administrative Expenses. The number of such accounts could, of course, be increased depending on the amount of detail desired and the variety of transactions. If there are numerous creditors and types of expenses, the two accounts could serve as controlling accounts with the detail recorded in subsidiary ledger accounts. Expenses to be paid out of income assets should be recorded by a debit to a separate expense account, such as Expenses—Income, and a credit to Cash—Income.

Distribution of estate assets to legatees also reduces the personal representative's accountability. The distribution of assets is recorded by a debit to Legacy Distributed and a credit to the asset account distributed. A legacy distributed account may be established for each individual legatee, or the account may serve as a controlling account. The distribution should be identified in the accounts as to principal or income assets.

ACCOUNTING FOR AN ESTATE ILLUSTRATED

To illustrate the accounting for an estate, assume that Jerry Reagan, a bachelor, died testate on May 15, 1995. In his will, Reagan named Frank Bush personal representative of the estate. The probate court determined the will to be valid and approved of Bush as personal representative. In the will, the following legacies were specified:

1. Joyce Jones, the housekeeper, and Chester Martin, the groundskeeper are to receive $10,000 each for their many years of service to Mr. Reagan.

2. Five hundred shares of AB Company common stock is granted to a niece, Ann Meyers.

3. All paintings are bequested to Reagan's only sister, Alison Smith.

4. Reagan's nephew, Tucker Smith, is to receive the automobile plus one-half of the income earned from the date of death on the 12% corporate bonds. The residual of the estate is to be placed in trust for Tucker Smith. First National Bank is to serve as trustee.

The required notices were published by the personal representative, and all claims against the estate assets filed within the statutory period were determined to be valid claims by Bush.

Entries to Record Transactions of the Estate

On June 10, Frank Bush filed an inventory of the estate assets with the probate court. This listing and the assigned fair values at the date of death are the basis for the following opening entry on the estate books:

June 10 Cash—Principal	12,000	
12% Northface Company Bonds—Market value		
is equal to par value of $20,000	20,000	
AB Company Common Stock—500 shares	13,000	
Grover Corp. Common Stock—100 shares	4,200	
Dividends Receivable (AB Common Stock)	800	
Interest Receivable (12% Bonds)	300	
Life Insurance Claim	60,000	
Automobile	7,000	
Personal Effects	1,000	
Residence	72,000	
Paintings	4,000	
Estate Principal		194,300
To record inventory of estate assets.		

Note that in this initial entry, interest earned and dividends declared before the decedent's death are accrued and constitute a part of the estate principal. Unless provided for in the will, this may be the only time the accrual basis of accounting is employed. Using the accrual basis at the date of death aids in distinguishing principal assets from income assets when recording subsequent transactions.

Bush filed with the probate court a schedule of his planned distribution of the estate assets. Entries to record the transactions completed by the personal representative follow:

June 12 Cash—Principal	800	
Dividends Receivable		800
Dividends that were declared on AB Company common stock before the date of death were received.		

13	Funeral and Administrative Expenses	4,300	
	Cash—Principal		4,300
	Paid funeral and medical expenses.		
28	Cash—Principal	4,000	
	Assets Subsequently Discovered		4,000
	Personal representative discovered cash in safety deposit box that was located after filing initial inventory.		

July	28	Cash—Principal	60,000	
		Life Insurance Claim		60,000
		Received life insurance benefit on policy in which estate was named beneficiary.		
Oct.	15	Debts of Decedent Paid	57,300	
		Cash—Principal		57,300
		Paid approved debts of decedent.		
	19	Legacy Distributed—Ann Meyers	13,000	
		AB Company Common Stock		13,000
		Delivered common stock to legatee.		
	21	Legacy Distributed—Alison Smith	4,000	
		Paintings		4,000
		Delivered paintings to legatee.		
Nov.	5	Cash—Principal	300	
		Cash—Income	900	
		Interest Receivable		300
		Estate Income		900
		Received interest on 12% Northface company bonds.		
	6	Legacy Distributed—Tucker Smith	7,000	
		Estate Income Distributed	450	
		Cash—Income		450
		Automobile		7,000
		Distributed principal asset (automobile) and one-half of interest earned to legatee.		
	28	Cash—Principal	3,600	
		Loss on Disposal of Principal Assets	600	
		Grover Corp. Common Stock		4,200
		Disposed of 100 shares of Grover Corp. common stock.		

Note that a gain or loss resulting from the disposal of an estate asset is identified as to principal or income.

Dec.	5	Funeral and Administrative Expenses	7,200	
		Expenses—Income	200	
		Cash—Principal		7,200
		Cash—Income		200
		Paid attorney's fees, court costs, estate taxes, and other administrative expenses, of which $200 were related to estate income.		
	23	Cash—Principal	84,000	
		Residence		72,000
		Personal Effects		1,000
		Gain on Disposal of Principal Assets		11,000
		Disposed of residence after an improvement in market conditions.		
	28	Legacy Distributed—Joyce Jones	10,000	
		Legacy Distributed—Chester Martin	10,000	
		Cash—Principal		20,000
		Paid cash to legatees.		

Jan.	7	Principal Assets Transferred to First National Bank	95,900	
		Cash—Principal		75,900
		12% Northface Company Bonds		20,000
		To record transfer of principal assets to trustee.		
	7	Income Assets Transferred to First National Bank	250	
		Cash—Income		250
		To record transfer of income assets to trustee.		

After these entries are posted, a trial balance of the principal and income accounts could be taken to assist in the preparation of the required reports.

Reports Filed by the Executor

A Charge and Discharge Statement for the estate of Jerry Reagan as of January 2 may be prepared in the form presented in Illustration 23-1. For a more complex estate, details of the individual items may be presented in supplementary schedules such as in Schedule 1 for the original inventory.

Closing Entries

Once all the estate assets have been distributed, the estate ceases to exist. The final act of the personal representative is the filing of a final report with the probate court. Once the final report is accepted, the estate accounts are closed. Closing entries for the Jerry Reagan estate are:

Jan. 25	Estate Principal	194,300	
	Assets Subsequently Discovered	4,000	
	Gain on Disposal of Principal Assets	11,000	
	Funeral and Administrative Expenses		11,500
	Debts of Decedent Paid		57,300
	Legacy Distributed—Ann Meyers		13,000
	Legacy Distributed—Joyce Jones		10,000
	Legacy Distributed—Chester Martin		10,000
	Legacy Distributed—Alison Smith		4,000
	Legacy Distributed—Tucker Smith		7,000
	Loss on Disposal of Principal Assets		600
	Principal Assets Transferred to First National Bank		95,900
	To close accounts related to estate principal.		
25	Estate Income	900	
	Estate Income Distributed		450
	Expenses—Income		200
	Income Assets Transferred to First National Bank		250
	To close accounts related to estate income.		

Note that Estate Principal and Estate Income serve as clearing accounts. After the closing entries are posted, every account should have a zero balance, since all the estate assets have been distributed. In this illustration, the life of the estate was approximately nine months. In some cases, the life of the estate may extend over a longer period, and the closing process may be performed on an interim basis. In such cases, the balances remaining in Estate Principal and Estate Income should equal the sum of the balances in the remaining asset accounts.

ILLUSTRATION 23-1
Estate of Jerry Reagan
Frank Bush, Personal Representative
Charge and Discharge Statement
For the Period May 15, 1995, to January 2, 1996

AS TO PRINCIPAL

I charge myself with		
Assets per original inventory (Schedule 1)	$194,300	
Assets discovered after initial inventory	4,000	
Gain on disposal of principal assets	11,000	
Total charges		$209,300
I credit myself with		
Funeral, estate taxes, and other administrative expenses	11,500	
Debts of decedent paid	57,300	
Loss on disposal of principal assets	600	
Legacies distributed		
Ann Meyers	13,000	
Joyce Jones	10,000	
Chester Martin	10,000	
Alison Smith	4,000	
Tucker Smith	7,000	
Total credits		113,400
Balance of estate principal		$ 95,900
Consisting of		
Cash—Principal		$ 75,900
12% Northface Company Bonds		20,000
Total		$ 95,900

AS TO INCOME

I charge myself with		
Estate income received		$ 900
I credit myself with		
Distribution to income beneficiary (Tucker Smith)		450
Expenses chargeable to income		200
Balance of estate income consisting of cash		$ 250

Schedule 1
Inventory of Original Assets

Cash	$ 12,000
Northface Company Bonds	20,000
AB Company Common Stock	13,000
Grover Corp. Common Stock	4,200
Dividends Receivable	800
Accrued Interest Receivable	300
Life Insurance Claim	60,000
Automobile	7,000
Personal Effects	1,000
Residence	72,000
Paintings	4,000
Total	$194,300

ACCOUNTING FOR A TRUST ARRANGEMENT

A trust is an entity created when a person (the **donor, creator, founder, trustor, grantor,** or **settler**) transfers a property interest to another person or persons (the **trustee**) to be used for the benefit of another person or persons (the **beneficiary**). A trust may be created by a will (a **testamentary trust**) or by a living person (a **living** or **inter vivos trust**). In a testamentary trust the assets, or portion thereof, left by the decedent are transferred to a trustee to be used for the benefit of the designated beneficiaries. A living trust is a trust arrangement made by a living person.

A trust agreement may provide that income earned from the trust assets is to be distributed to one class of beneficiaries (**income beneficiaries**), whereas the assets constituting the principal of the trust are to be distributed eventually to another class of beneficiaries (**principal** or **remainderman beneficiaries**). Of course, the agreement may provide that one class of beneficiaries is to receive both income and principal.

The trustee may be an individual or a corporation. The trustee is a fiduciary and, accordingly, has the powers and duties conveyed in the document creating the trust and is governed by the laws of a trust relationship. Thus, a trustee and other parties associated with administration of the trust assets must be familiar with the appropriate state laws. The primary powers and duties of the trustee are similar to those discussed earlier for a personal representative.

The procedures established to account for a trust are similar to those discussed and illustrated for an estate. This is because the primary objectives of accounting for both entities are to account for and report on the assets conveyed to the fiduciary and to report the manner in which the responsibility for the management and disposition of these assets is discharged. When trust transactions are recorded, separate accounts are used to distinguish between principal and income. For example, in the estate illustration presented earlier, the last distribution of the estate assets was to the First National Bank to create a testamentary trust for Tucker Smith. Assume further that Tucker was the income beneficiary and another party was the principal beneficiary. The receipt of the assets would be recorded by the trustee as follows:

Cash—Principal	75,900	
12% Northface Company Bonds	20,000	
Trust Principal		95,900
To record receipt of trust principal.		
Cash—Income	250	
Trust Income		250
To record receipt of income assets.		

In the case of a testamentary trust, the trust usually becomes effective at the date of the decedent's death, even though the trustee does not assume fiduciary responsibility for the assets until they are received. Thus, in the entry above, interest earned on the bonds after the decedent's death was accounted for as part of the trust income. Recall that income accrued at the date of death was reported as part of the estate principal.

Following the receipt of the resources above, the trustee will invest in appropriate income-producing assets, pay expenses of the trust, and distribute trust assets in accordance with the trust agreement. Journal entries to record these transactions are similar to those illustrated for an estate. A cash basis of accounting is frequently used to account for a trust, unless the trust instrument provides otherwise.

The trustee must exercise reasonably prudent care in the selection and disposal of investments. The selection of individual investments may be constrained by state law as to what constitutes an acceptable investment to be made by a trustee, as well as by provisions of the document creating the trust agreement.

The trustee is required to submit periodic reports to interested parties such as the income and principal beneficiaries. Generally, for a testamentary trust, a report must be filed with the original court probating the will. The form of the report(s) required by states varies, but may resemble a Charge and Discharge Statement prepared for an estate. Normally, the following information is included in the report, with the trust principal and income reported separately:

1. The period covered by the report.

2. The composition of the trust principal and income at the beginning of the period.

3. Changes in the trust principal and income that occurred during the period covered by the report.

4. The composition of the trust principal and income at the end of the period.

5. Estimated market values of the individual trust assets at the end of the period.

To facilitate the preparation of subsequent reports, the trustee may prefer to complete the closing process each time a report is filed. Procedures for doing so are similar to those for an estate, with the Trust Principal and Trust Income accounts serving as clearing accounts. The balance in the two accounts should equal the sum of the account balances of the remaining assets still on hand.

Questions

1. Where does a fiduciary derive his powers and duties pertaining to a certain estate or trust?

2. What is the objective of estate planning?

3. What determines whether or not the decedent is referred to as the testator?

4. If no party is named in the will to carry out its provisions, or if the party named is unable to administer the estate, what course of action will be taken?

5. How is the value that is to be assigned to the assets of the estate determined?

6. What responsibility does the executor have toward the claims against the estate?

7. Differentiate between principal assets and income assets.

8. What are the two ways in which a trust may be created?

9. What is the primary objective of accounting for estates and trusts?

10. Under whose jurisdiction does an appointed fiduciary come?

11. What is meant by the term *abatement* and when may it result?

12. Is the accrual basis of accounting employed when accounting for an estate? If so, when and for what items?

Exercises

Exercise 23-1

George Jones was named personal representative of the estate of Phil Top, who died February 28, 1995. On December 31, 1995, John prepared the following trial balance.

Cash—Principal	$ 4,900	
Cash—Income	2,000	
Stock	15,000	
Bonds	45,000	
Automobile	3,500	
Loss on Sale of Principal Assets	1,000	
Gain on Sale of Principal Assets		$ 2,000
Assets Subsequently Discovered		3,250
Funeral Expenses	2,500	
Debts of Decedent Paid	6,500	
Estate Principal		73,150
Estate Income		2,150
Expenses—Income	100	
Distribution to Income Beneficiary	50	
	$80,550	$80,550

Required:

Prepare a Charge and Discharge Statement for the estate of Phil Top.

Exercise 23-2

Sam Hill, CPA, is trustee of a testamentary trust established by John Davis' will. The trust principal consists of cash, securities, and a large office building. The will provides that trust income is to be paid to Davis' wife during her lifetime, that the trust will terminate on her death, and that the principal is then to be distributed to Davis' daughter, Linda.

Required:

Indicate whether each of the following statements is true or false:

1. Davis' widow would be considered the remainderman beneficiary.

2. A dividend declared on some of the securities would never be considered part of the principal.

3. The costs that Hill incurs in administering this trust should be deducted from the trust income before it is distributed to the widow.

4. If some of the securities were sold and a gain was realized, Hill would distribute the gain to the widow.

5. If it was discovered that Davis' debts exceeded the fair value of the trust assets, the widow and the daughter would have no claim to any of these assets.

Exercise 23-3

Refer to Exercise 23-2. Indicate whether the following items would be related to the principal or the income of the trust.

1. Estate and trust taxes.
2. Attorney fees in handling the trust.
3. Regular upkeep and maintenance of the office building.
4. Proceeds from fire insurance on the office building.
5. Fee payment to managers of the office building.

Exercise 23-4

You have been assigned by a CPA firm to work with the trustees of a large trust in preparing the first annual accounting to the court. The income beneficiaries and the remaindermen (those who are to receive the principal of the trust upon its termination) are in dispute as to the proper allocation of the following items on which the trust indenture is silent:

1. Costs incurred in expanding the garage facilities of an apartment house owned by the trust and held for rental income.
2. Real estate taxes on the apartment house.
3. Cost of casualty insurance premiums on the apartment house.
4. Costs incurred by the trust in the sale of a tract of land.
5. Interest earned on bonds held by the trust. (One-third of the interest had accrued before the date of death.)
6. Cost of legal counsel incurred by the trustee in administering the trust.

Required:

A. Explain briefly the nature of a trust, the concepts underlying the allocation between principal and income, and the importance of such allocations.

B. Indicate the allocations between principal and income to be made for each of the items above.

(AICPA adapted)

Exercise 23-5

Listed below are the transactions for the estate of Maria Lopez, who died April 15, 1995.

1. Inventory filed with the court on April 20:

Cash	$ 90,000
Condominium	120,000
Capital stock of Smith Corporation	130,000
9% bonds of Auto Company	
($100,000 principal amount)	100,000
Interest receivable on Auto Company bonds	1,500
Personal and household effects	57,000

2. On April 26 a certificate for 100 shares of Jennifer Corporation preferred stock valued at $22,000 was found in a closet where Maria lived.
3. On May 16 a dividend of $1,500 was received on the capital stock of Smith Corporation. The stock was willed as a specific legacy to John Kirklan.
4. Liabilities of Maria Lopez in the amount of $75,000 were paid on May 19.
5. On May 29 the 9% bonds of Auto Company were sold at 98, plus accrued interest of $2,825.
6. The capital stock of Smith Corporation and the cash dividend of $1,500 were transferred to Paul Lopez on May 31.

Required:

Prepare entries in general journal form for the transactions above.

Exercise 23-6

On February 1, 1995, Linda Cole was appointed to act as trustee for a trust fund consisting of the following.

1. Real estate valued at $60,000.
2. 1,000 shares of Water Company stock valued at $225,000. Dividends of $1.25 a share were declared January 25, 1995, but have not been received.
3. Ten bonds of June Corporation valued at $900 each, principal amount $10,000. Interest at an annual rate of 10% is paid on January 15 and July 15.
4. Cash of $25,000.

Required:

Prepare the initial entry that Linda Cole would make on the books of the trust.

Exercise 23-7

Select the best answer for each of the following:

1. Accrued interest earned before the date of death is recorded by
   (a) A debit to estate income.
   (b) A debit to estate principal.
   (c) A credit to estate income.
   (d) A credit to estate principal.
2. According to the Uniform Probate Code, the personal representative must pay this claim first:
   (a) Specific devises.
   (b) Costs of administering the estate.
   (c) Debts and taxes.
   (d) Funeral expenses.
3. Which of the following is not a primary duty of the personal representative?
   (a) Pay valid claims against the estate.
   (b) Collect the assets of the decedent.
   (c) Earn income on estate assets.
   (d) Distribute estate assets.

4. Valley Bank created a testamentary trust for Jane Tash on May 6, 1995, with the 100,000 shares of Jones Corporation left by her father, James. On May 10, 1995, Jones Corporation declared and paid a $1.00 per share dividend. The dividend is recorded with a
   (a) Credit to trust income.
   (b) Debit to trust income.
   (c) Credit to trust principal.
   (d) Debit to trust income.
5. Which of the following is not usually recorded as estate principal?
   (a) Interest accrued before the date of death.
   (b) Dividends declared before the date of death.
   (c) Expenses incurred in settlement of the estate.
   (d) Ordinary expenses identified with income-producing assets.

Exercise 23-8

Match the list of terms given below with the following list of definitions.

1. Testate	6. Trust
2. Administrator	7. Intestate
3. Executor	8. Legacy
4. Estate	9. Beneficiary
5. Devise	10. Trustee.

A. Party named by the decedent in the will to carry out its provisions.

B. The distribution of personal property.

C. An entity created when a person transfers property to another person to be used for the benefit of a third person.

D. The term used to denote that a valid will has been left by the decedent.

E. Party named by a court to carry out the provisions of a will.

F. The person who receives the benefits of a trust.

G. The disposition of real property in accordance with provisions of the will.

H. A legal entity that holds title to the property of a deceased person.

I. The person responsible for the management and distribution of trust property.

J. The absence of a will.

Problems

Problem 23-1

Brian Simms, a partner in a local law firm, died on February 28, 1995. Beth Young was named in the will as the personal representative of Simms' estate. Upon investigation, Young determined that the estate consisted of

Cash	$ 55,000
Certificates of deposit	30,000
9% Reynold Company debentures (interest paid September 30 and April 30)	150,000
Interest receivable on Reynold Company bonds	5,625
TSI common stock (1,000 shares)	35,000
One-third interest in Lea & Arthur Partnership (appraised value)	150,000

Legacies are to be distributed as follows:

1. Reynold Company debentures to widow Mary.
2. TSI common stock and estate earnings to son Ted.
3. A sum of $20,000 to the St. Jude Home for the Mentally Disturbed.
4. Estate residue to widow Mary.

Transactions of the personal representative were:

March	5	Filed the February 28 inventory of the deceased	
	10	Paid funeral and administrative expenses	$ 20,000
	28	Received cash from liquidation of partnership	147,500
April	6	Paid debts of decedent	10,000
	12	Paid federal estate and state inheritance taxes	15,000
	25	Received dividends declared March 15 on the TSI stock	500
May	1	Received interest on Reynold Co. bonds	6,750
	1	Distributed estate income, legacies, and residual estate properties as provided in the will	

Required:

A. Prepare entries on the books of the personal representative through May 15.

B. Show journal entries to close the estate's books.

Problem 23-2

On July 15, 1995, Tom Gray died, leaving a sizable estate. Bill Black was appointed personal representative of the estate. Transactions for the estate are as follows:

1. The following inventory of Gray's assets was filed with the court:

Balance in checking account	$ 22,200
Rental property	233,000
Rent receivable	5,000
Stamp collection	3,500
Life insurance policy, payable to the estate	100,000
Preferred stock, Green Corporation (1,800 shares, $20 each)	36,000
Dividends receivable on Green Corporation stock, $1.50 a share	2,700

One-quarter interest in Gray and Sons	
Partnership	225,000
6% bonds of MAC Corporation	
(50 bonds, $800 each, par $1,000 each)	40,000
Interest receivable on MAC Corporation	
bonds	125
Household furnishings	14,000

2. Funeral expenses of $14,200 were paid by Black.
3. A suitcase full of cash totaling $3,200 was found by Black.
4. The life insurance policy proceeds were collected.
5. The stamp collection was sold for $5,200.
6. Rent in the amount of $10,000 was collected.
7. The dividend on the Green Corporation stock was collected.
8. Accountant fees of $1,500 were paid by Black.
9. The interest in the Gray and Sons Partnership was sold for $221,700.
10. The September 30 interest collection was made on the MAC Corporation bonds. (Interest is paid quarterly.)
11. The household furnishings were given to the Cedarville Orphanage.
12. All estate income was distributed to Ron Gray; all other assets were distributed to the widow, Kerry.

Required:

A. Journalize the transactions on the books of Black.

B. Prepare closing entries on the books of the estate.

Problem 23-3

Paula Roads died on May 6, 1995. Her accountant, Christy Nash was appointed personal representative of her estate and filed with the probate court on June 1, the following inventory of assets:

Cash	$ 5,000
1,000 shares of common stock of Tandy	
Company, $20.80 each	20,800
Automobile	7,400
Condominium	95,000
Personal and household furnishings	9,000
Marketable securities	35,000

Other information:

1. Funeral expenses were $8,000.
2. Authorized claims against the estate were $6,900.
3. The condominium was sold for $86,500.
4. The marketable securities were sold for $32,500.
5. The Tandy Company common stock was sold for $23,100.
6. The will left by Roads provided for the following legacies.

Specific legacy to Mary, proceeds from the sale of
Tandy Company common stock.
Specific legacy to John, the automobile.
Specific legacy to charities as described in the will,
personal and household items.
General legacies to children:

Mary	$85,000
John	95,000

Required:

Prepare the journal entries on the books of the personal representative through the distribution of the legacies. Assume pro-rata abatement of general legacies in the event that the legacies cannot be met.

Problem 23-4

The will of Jim Elder, deceased, directed that his personal representative, Joe Young, liquidate the entire estate within two years of the date of Mr. Elder's death. Twenty thousand dollars of the proceeds and the estate income are to be paid to St. John's Home and the remainder of the estate principal to be paid to Rick Elder, the decedent's nephew. Mr. Elder, who was a bachelor, died on February 1, 1995, after a brief illness.

An inventory of the decedent's property was prepared, and the fair market value of all items was determined. The preliminary inventory, before the computation of any appropriate income accruals on inventory items, follows:

	FAIR VALUE
Valley National Bank checking account	$ 15,000
$80,000 par value City of Sunrise School Bonds, interest rate 9% payable January 1 and July 1, maturity date July 1, 1999	79,000
3,000 shares Brown Corporation capital stock	330,000
Term life insurance. Beneficiary—Estate of Jim Elder	75,000
Personal residence ($110,000) and furnishings ($2,000)	112,000

During 1995 the following transactions occurred:

1. The interest on the City of Sunrise School Bonds was collected. The bonds were sold on July 1 for $79,000, and the interest was paid to the home.
2. The Brown Corporation paid cash dividends of $1.50 per share on March 1 and December 1, as well as a 10% stock dividend on July 1. All dividends were declared 45 days before each payment date and were payable to holders of record as of 40 days before each payment date. On September 2, 1,000 shares were sold at $125 per share.
3. Because of a depressed real estate market, the personal residence was rented furnished at $350 per month commencing April 1. The rent is paid monthly in advance on the first day of each month. Real estate taxes of $900 for the calendar year of 1995 were paid. The house and furnishings have estimated lives of 45 years and 10 years, respectively. The part-time gardener-handyman was paid four months' wages totaling $1,200 on April 30 for services performed, and then released.

4. The Valley National Bank checking account was closed, and the balance of $15,000 was transferred to an estate bank account.
5. The term life insurance was received on March 1 and deposited in the estate bank account.
6. The following disbursements were made.
   (a) Funeral expenses, $6,500.
   (b) Final illness expenses, $2,250.
   (c) April 15 income tax remittance, $1,500.
   (d) Attorney's and accountant's fees, $20,000.
7. On December 31, the balance of the undistributed income was paid to the beneficiary. The legacies were distributed as specified.

Required:

As of December 31, 1995, the personal representative resigned and waived all commissions. Prepare a Charge and Discharge Statement separately stated as to principal and income, together with its supporting schedules, on behalf of the personal representative of the estate of Jim Elder for the period from February 1, 1995, through December 31, 1995.

(AICPA adapted)

Problem 23-5

Randy Wells died on March 29, 1995, after a long illness. His will provided for the following:

1. Personal residence is devised to Cal Wells.
2. The certificates of deposit are to be held in trust. All interest is to go to Cal Wells' 17-year-old daughter, Kim, until she reaches the age of 18, at which time the certificates will be distributed. Kim's birthday is October 1.
3. The personal representative and trustee is allowed 5% of income as a fee, payable December 31.
4. The remainder of the estate is to be divided equally between his 15-year-old sons, John and Brian, and placed in trust until their eighteenth birthdays.
5. Rex Martin, Randy Wells' attorney, was designated personal representative and trustee.

A preliminary inventory of the decedent's property, before computation of any accruals, was prepared as follows.

Checking account	$ 15,000
Personal residence	150,000
Prudent Life Insurance Company policy, payable to the estate	150,000
Certificates of deposit, 8% interest payable quarterly on March 31, June 30, September 30, and December 31.	10,000
Pyle Company bonds, 5% interest payable March 1 and September 1	100,000
500 shares 3M Corporation common stock	15,500

Other information:

1. Dividends of $.75 a share on the 3M Corporation stock were declared on March 13, 1995, payable to holders of record March 30, 1995.
2. Funeral expenses of $3,000 were paid by Martin on April 3, 1995.
3. Randy Wells' 1994 income taxes of $8,700 were paid on April 15, 1995.
4. Dividends on the 3M Corporation stock were received on June 18, 1995.
5. On July 1, 1995, the specific legacy was delivered and the remainder of the estate was transferred to a trust.

Required:

Prepare journal entries to record all events related to the estate and the trust of Randy Wells for 1995, including closing entries for the estate.

24

ACCOUNTING FOR INSTALLMENT SALES AND CONSIGNMENT TRANSACTIONS

Real or personal property is often sold on contract under which a down payment is made and the remainder of the sales price is collected in a series of installment payments. Because payments may be deferred for an extended period, there may be uncertainty as to the collectibility of the sales price. Uncertainty about collectibility may justify departure from the accrual basis of accounting. Circumstances in which such a departure is considered appropriate are discussed in the first section of this chapter, and alternative methods of reporting income are illustrated.

A consignment arrangement is a method of marketing a product in which the possession of goods is transferred to another party who is to act as an agent in selling the goods. The transfer of goods on consignment is not considered a sales transaction. However, both parties must establish adequate procedures to control and account for goods on consignment. Accounting for goods shipped on consignment is illustrated in the second section of this chapter.

ACCOUNTING FOR INSTALLMENT SALES

An installment sale is a sales contract that contains a financing arrangement whereby the sales price is received in a series of payments made over an extended period of time. Typically, the buyer makes a down payment and agrees to pay the remaining sales price in a series of specified payments at specified times. The payment period frequently ranges from 6 months to 5 years on the sale of personal property items such as furniture and automobiles, and up to 30 years or more on the sale of real property. Because the payments may extend over a period of months, an interest factor is normally included in computing the total cash payments.

Because of the length of the collection period and the deferral of much of the cash to be received, the risk of loss from installment sales is normally greater than that from ordinary sales in which credit terms of 30–60 days are granted. To provide some protection to the seller, a variety of legal devices are used that will enable the seller to recover the property in the event the buyer does not satisfy the terms of the installment sales contract. For example, title to the item sold may be retained by the seller, or a lien against the property may be held, until the final installment payment is received. This is in contrast to a cash sale or a short-term credit sale in which the title to the goods normally transfers at the point of sale.

Regardless of the legal steps taken to protect the seller, bad debt losses as a percentage of sales tend to be higher for installment sales than for normal short-term credit sales. Customers purchasing goods on installment generally represent higher credit risk. Furthermore, the customers' financial position and ability to pay may change during the extended payment period. The seller's right to repossess may constitute inadequate protection for the receivable balance, because the market value of the item sold, especially personal property, may decline faster than the receivable balance. Ideally, the amount of the down payment and subsequent installment payments would be large enough to ensure that this will not occur. However, a business may be limited in the action it can take by business practices established by competitors.

Despite this disadvantage to the seller, the practice of selling on an installment basis continues to grow in significance. Although credit losses resulting from installment sales are often significant, and processing and collection costs are increased, the profitability of the firm may still be improved through an increase in installment sales volume.

METHODS OF ACCOUNTING FOR INSTALLMENT SALES

Three methods have evolved to account for and report the effects of installment sales of inventory on a firm's financial statements. One method, the point-of-sale, is consistent with the conventional income measurement method related to the accrual basis of accounting. The other two methods (cost recovery and installment) are used to account for installment sales when the collection of the sales price is highly uncertain. In such cases, profit recognition is deferred and associated with the collection of cash.

Gross Profit Recognized at the Time of Sale

Revenue is geneally recognized from the sale of a tangible asset at a specific point in the earnings process of a business, typically when "(1) the earnings process is complete or virtually complete, and (2) an exchange has taken place."[1] In the case

---

[1] *Accounting Principles Board Statement No. 4*, "Basic Concepts and Accounting Principles Underlying Financial Statements of Business Enterprises" (New York: AICPA, 1970), par. 50.

of a cash sale or a short-term credit sale, revenue is generally recognized when title to the goods transfers or, from a practical point of view, when the goods are shipped to the customer. Related expenses are matched against the reported revenue to determine profit. To provide a complete measure of profitability, it may be necessary to establish allowances and accrue expenses in the current period for expenses expected to be incurred in future periods (for example, warranty expenses) or to recognize losses from the failure to collect the full sales price.

Theoretically, accounting for installment sales should parallel the accounting procedures considered acceptable for accounting for short-term credit sales, even though title to the asset may not transfer until some point in the future. In other words, total revenue and current and future expenses related to the sale should be reported in the accounting period in which the goods are delivered by the seller to the buyer and a claim is established against the buyer. The passing of title is not considered relevant when determining the point at which profit should be recognized from the sale. Both parties to the transaction intend and expect to fulfill the terms of the agreement, and the transfer of title from the seller to the buyer is expected at some future time.

Gross Profit Recognized as Cash Is Collected

In most circumstances, recognizing revenue and matching related expenses at the point of sale is considered the appropriate method of accounting for an installment sale. However, for some installment sales, bad debt losses on installment receivables may be significant and, more importantly from an income determination point of view, may be difficult to estimate because of the extended period of collection and lack of prior experience. Because of the uncertainty of these future losses and expenses, and in recognition of the diverse conditions under which installment sales are made, several alternatives to the point-of-sale method of recognizing revenue have evolved. These methods recognize profit in the period in which the sales price is collected, rather than in the period in which the sale is made.

Cost Recovery Method   When the cost recovery method is used, collections of the sales price are accounted for first as a recovery of cost. No gross profit is recognized from the sale until the amounts collected equal the cost of the asset sold. Once the product cost is recovered, subsequent receipts are reported as profit. Many accountants consider this method too conservative for most firms engaging in installment sales on a regular basis. However, the method is used when there is a great deal of uncertainty as to the collectibility of the receivable balance or the recovery of the receivable balance by repossessing the goods sold.

Installment Method   Under the installment method of accounting, each collection of the sales price is accounted for both as a partial recovery of cost and as a partial realization of the gross profit. The allocation of the cash payment is made using the same percentages in which these two elements were included in the original sales price. Thus, the gross profit on an installment sale is deferred and recognized in the periods in which cash is collected. The amount reported as profit in each period is dependent on the amount of cash collected in that period and the gross profit percentage applicable to the year of the original sale.

ACCEPTABILITY OF THE CASH BASIS METHODS

In many kinds of retail businesses, inventory is sold on installment contracts. Installment contracts are also used widely in the real estate field. Circumstances in which methods other than the full accrual method are considered appropriate in accounting for installment sales are discussed in this section.

Recurring Sales of Inventory

The installment method has been approved for use in computing taxable income by the Internal Revenue Service. For tax purposes, a firm is thus permitted to defer the recognition of a portion of gross profit until cash is collected and is available for payment of taxes. Because of this advantage, the installment method is used frequently to compute taxable income on installment sales of inventory, real property, and personal property. However, the Tax Reform Act of 1986 limits the use of the installment sales method on sales of personal and real property by dealers and on casual sales of real property (if the selling price exceeds $150,000) used in a trade or business when the seller has debt outstanding related to the installment obligation.

Although the installment method is acceptable for tax purposes, its general use for financial reporting purposes has been challenged primarily because the method is not in accordance with the accrual basis of accounting. Accountants oppose the general use of the installment method of accounting and consider it acceptable only when there is no reasonable basis for estimating the degree of collectibility. In paragraph 12 of *APB Opinion No. 10*, "Omnibus Opinion—1966," the Board stated.

> Chapter 1A of ARB No. 43, paragraph 1, states that "Profit is deemed to be realized when a sale in the ordinary course of business is effected, unless the circumstances are such that the collection of the sales price is not reasonably assured." The Board reaffirms this statement; it believes that revenue should ordinarily be accounted for at the time a transaction is completed, with appropriate provision for uncollectible accounts. Accordingly, it concludes that in the absence of the circumstances referred to above, the installment method of recognizing revenue is not acceptable.

In a footnote to paragraph 12, the Board added:

> The Board recognizes that there are exceptional cases where receivables are collectible over an extended period of time and, because of the terms of the transactions or other conditions, there is no reasonable basis for estimating the degree of collectibility. When such circumstances exist, and as long as they exist, either the installment method or the cost recovery method of accounting may be used.

Although the recognition of profit at the time of sale is clearly preferred, both the installment method and the cost recovery method are considered acceptable methods of reporting in "exceptional cases." These alternative methods of accounting should be viewed as exceptions to the accrual method of accounting. An accountant must evaluate the circumstances in a particular situation to determine if variation from the accrual method is warranted. For financial reporting purposes, it is difficult to justify departure from the accrual basis when inventory is sold on a recurring basis.

SALES OF REAL ESTATE

During the 1960s retail land sales activities increased significantly. The complexity of land development activities and the variety of financial agreements also increased, and in many cases, the legal form of the transaction obscured its economic substance. The absence of authoritative literature led to a diversity in accounting practices in recognizing sales and profits. Concerned with the variety of income recognition methods and other questionable practices that had evolved, the AICPA established two committees to evaluate the accounting practices used in the industry and recommend changes in existing practices. The efforts of the two committees resulted in the issuance of the following two *Industry Accounting Guides:*

1. "Accounting for Retail Land Sales," *Industry Accounting Guide* (New York: AICPA, 1973).

2. "Accounting for Profit Recognition on Sales of Real Estate," *Industry Accounting Guide* (New York: AICPA, 1973).

Interpretations of the two guides were issued in the form of two AICPA *Statements of Position (SOP).*

In *Statement of Financial Accounting Standards (SFAS) No. 32,* issued in 1979, the FASB agreed to exercise responsibility for all the specialized accounting and reporting principles and practices contained in the existing *Industry Accounting Guides* and *SOPs* by extracting those principles and practices from the *Guides* and *SOPs* and issuing them as *SFASs* after appropriate due process.[2] As part of the extraction project, the specialized profit recognition principles contained in the real estate guides and related *SOPs* were essentially adopted in *SFAS No. 66,* "Accounting for Sales of Real Estate."[3]

SFAS No. 66 establishes accounting and reporting standards for recognizing profit and loss on sales of real estate without regard to the nature of the seller's business. A separate set of standards addressing the problems of recording and reporting real estate transactions has evolved because real estate sales differ from most other business transactions. In paragraph 15 of the *Industry Accounting Guide,* "Accounting for Profit Recognition of Sales of Real Estate," the Committee noted:

[2]*Statement of Financial Accounting Standards No. 32,* "Specialized Accounting and Reporting Principles and Practices in AICPA Statements of Position and Guides on Accounting and Auditing Matters" (Stamford, Conn.: FASB, 1979), par. 10–11.

[3]*Statement of Financial Accounting Standards No. 66,* "Accounting for Sales of Real Estate" (Norwalk, Conn.: FASB, 1982).

A real estate sale differs from most business transactions because a significant portion of the consideration is often a note or other receivable collectible over a relatively long period, and the receivable is normally not supported by the full faith and credit of the buyer. Thus, often the only recourse of the seller on default by the buyer is to recover the property sold. For legal and business reasons, sellers usually limit themselves to foreclosure to remedy defaults, even if the terms of the agreements provide for full recourse against the buyer.

These characteristics result in considerable uncertainty as to the collectibility of the sales price. Furthermore, some real estate projects require the seller's continual involvement with the property for extended periods to satisfy obligations agreed to at the time of sale. The length of time required to satisfy the seller's obligations and the magnitude of the future costs and expenses to be incurred by the seller to fulfill the commitments are often either uncertain or difficult to estimate reliably. This creates problems in accounting for the transaction because the earnings process may not be complete at the time of sale. Given the nature and complexity of real estate transactions, a single method of accounting is not considered appropriate for all circumstances. What has evolved is a number of methods that are appropriate to a given set of circumstances.

For accounting purposes, *SFAS No. 66* distinguishes between retail land sales on a volume basis of lots that are subdivisions of large tracts of land, and all other sales of real estate. The two categories of real estate sales are distinguished because differences in terms of sales and selling procedures lead to different revenue recognition criteria and to the implementation of alternative accounting methods for recognizing profit. The *Statement* prescribes criteria for determining when the economic substance, as opposed to the legal form, of a real estate transaction indicates the consummation of a sale for accounting purposes and when collectibility of the sales price is reasonably assured. It requires the deferral of all or a portion of the profit in instances where the earnings process is not complete or virtually complete.

The specific rules and procedures set out in *SFAS NO. 66* are complex, and a detailed discussion is beyond the scope of this text. Our purpose in discussing the *Statement* is to point out the acceptability of alternative revenue recognition methods when accounting for the sales of real estate. The focus of the subsequent discussion is on the nonretail sales of real estate. The part of the *Statement* related to the retail sale of land is not discussed because it establishes standards for a specialized industry. The reader is cautioned that this is a highly technical area, and *SFAS No. 66* and related authoritative literature should be carefully reviewed before selecting the specific accounting procedures and revenue recognition methods to be used when accounting for and reporting on the sales of real estate.

Sales of Real Estate Other than Retail Land Sales   The provision of *SFAS No. 66* that apply to nonretail sales of real estate apply to all real estate transactions other than retail land sales, including sales of lots to builders, and sales of homes, buildings, and parcels of land to developers and others. The *Statement* provides that before profit can be recognized, a sale must be consummated, that is, an exchange transaction must occur. A sale is considered consummated when all the following conditions are met:

1. The parties are bound by the terms of a contract.

2. All consideration has been exchanged.

3. Any permanent financing for which the seller is responsible has been arranged.

4. All conditions precedent to closing have been performed.[4]

Generally, these conditions are met at the time of closing or later, not when an agreement to sell is signed.

To recognize all the profit when real estate is sold (the full accrual method) the *Statement* provides:

> Profit shall be recognized in full when real estate is sold, provided (a) the profit is determinable, that is, the collectibility of the sales price is reasonably assured or the amount that will not be collectible can be estimated, and (b) the earnings process is virtually complete, that is, the seller is not obligated to perform significant activities after the sale to earn the profit.[5]

Once a sale is consummated, *SFAS No. 66* establishes the following criteria for determining if both of the conditions exist for using the full accrual method:

1. The buyer's initial and continuing investments are adequate to demonstrate a commitment to pay for the property.

2. The seller's receivable is not subject to future subordination.

3. The seller has transferred to the buyer the usual risks and rewards of ownership in a transaction that is in substance a sale and the seller does not have a substantial continuing involvement with the property.[6]

The first criterion requires that additional assurance as to the collectibility of the sales price be obtained before profit on a real estate transaction is recognized in full. Added assurance that the sales price will be collected is evidenced by a significant initial and continuing investment in the property by the buyer. If a buyer has a significant investment in the property, it is considered unlikely that he or she will default on the loan and incur a loss on return of the property to the seller. The second criterion recognizes that a receivable that is subject to future subordination usually cannot be reasonably evaluated as to its collectibility. In such cases, it is considered appropriate to limit profit recognition to amounts calculated using the cost recovery method, as described later.

Under the third criterion, a real estate transaction should not be accounted for as a sale if it does not transfer to the buyer the risks and rewards of ownership. Furthermore, the earnings process is not complete if the sales agreement contains provisions that require the seller to complete significant parts of the contract in the future. There are many variations in real estate contracts and each contract must be analyzed carefully to determine the economic substance of the agreement.

---

[4]Ibid., par. 6.
[5]Ibid., par. 3.
[6]Ibid., par. 5.

For example, the rights of ownership to property legally sold may not be transferred to the buyer if the seller is obligated to repurchase the property at a price greater than the original sales price. Such an agreement may in substance be a financing arrangement rather than a sale.

If the conditions for use of the full accrual method are not satisfied, income recognition is postponed and either the deposit method, the installment method, the cost recovery method, or the reduced profit method is considered appropriate for use in a particular set of circumstances. A decision tree providing an overview of the major provisions of *SFAS No. 66* that relate to nonretail sales of real estate and the various questions that must be addressed in order to determine the appropriate accounting method to be used in certain circumstances are set forth in Illustration 24-1. The essence of the series of tests contained in the illustration is to require that the economic substance of the sales agreement shall govern the related accounting treatment.

Note that the first test is whether a sale has been consummated. If not, profit is deferred and any cash down payment received is accounted for as a deposit (liability) until the substance of the transaction indicates that a sale has occurred. If a sale is consummated, the full accrual method is considered appropriate if the criteria discussed earlier are met. Profit is recognized as cash is received when the substance of the real estate transaction indicates that a sale has been made for accounting purposes, but the buyer's initial investment is inadequate to provide evidence that the collectibility of the sales price is reasonably assured.[7] In general, the installment method is appropriate when recovery of the real estate is provided for in the sales agreement. The cost recovery method is used when there is uncertainty as to whether the cost of the property will be recovered on default by the buyer. An insignificant investment is recorded as a deposit until the substance of the transaction supports the use of one of the profit recognition methods. In other words, a small down payment is viewed in substance as an option arrangement and recognition of the sale and profit is postponed.

In addition to making an adequate initial investment, a buyer is required to increase the investment in the property each year before the seller is permitted to recognize the full profit on the sale. In assessing the adequacy of the continuing investment, paragraph 12 of *SFAS No. 66* provides:

> The buyer's continuing investment in real estate transactions shall not qualify unless the buyer is contractually required to pay each year on its total debt for the purchase price of the property an amount at least equal to the level annual payment that would be needed to pay that debt and interest on the unpaid balance over no more than (a) 20 years for debt for land and (b) the customary amortization term of a first mortgage loan by an independent established lending institution for other real estate.

The intent of the continuing investment requirement is to provide additional as-

---

[7]Guidance on minimum initial investments in various types of property is provided in paragraphs 53 and 54 of *SFAS No. 66*. Depending on the nature of the property, a minimum down payment ranging from 5% to 25% of the sales value is stipulated.

ILLUSTRATION 24-1
FASB Statement No. 66
Sales of Real Estate Other Than Retail Land Sales

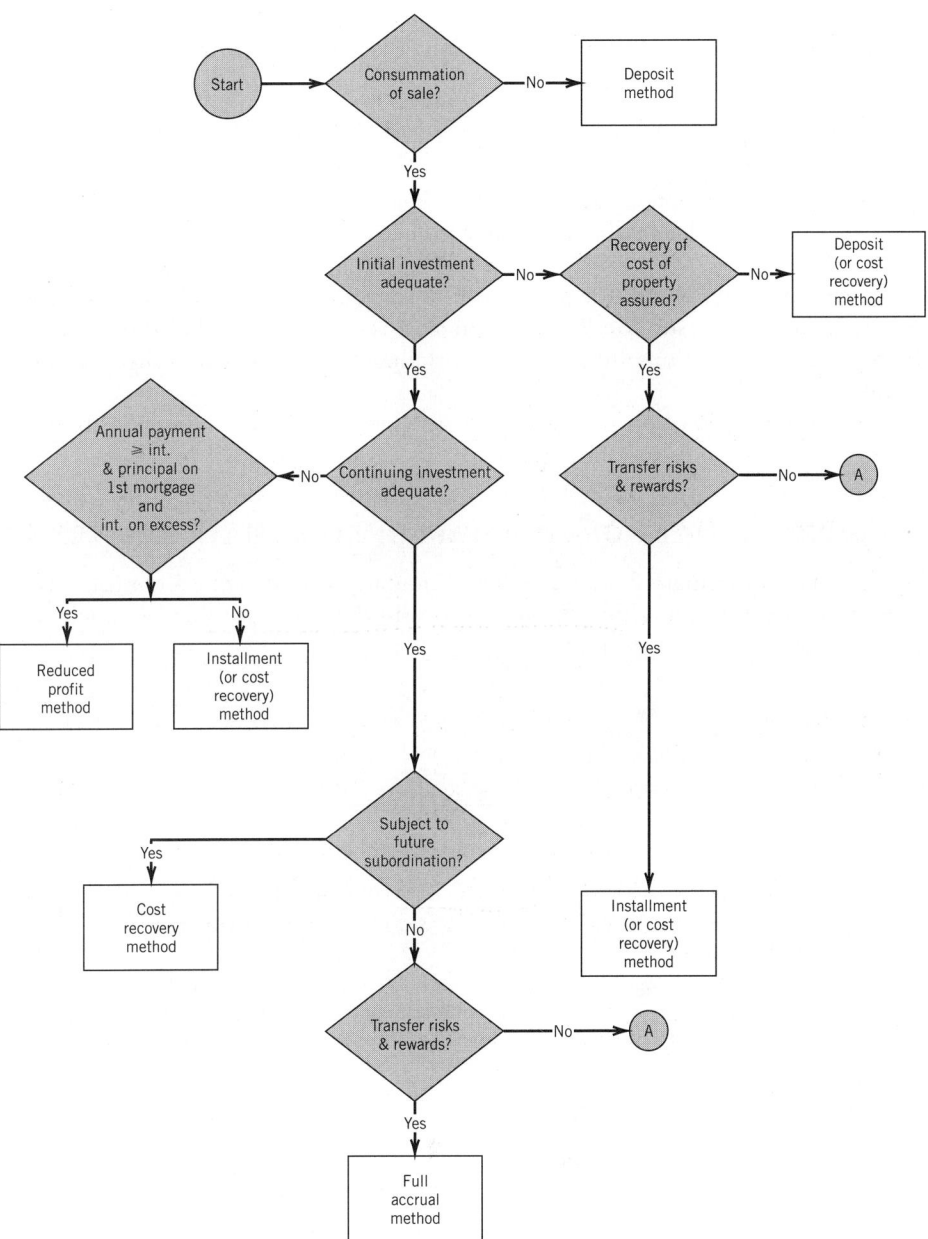

The decision tree should not be used without further reference to the statement. Ⓐ Transaction is in essence not a sale and should be accounted for according to the nature of the transaction (e.g., financing, leasing, or profit-sharing arrangement).

SOURCE: SFAS No. 66, par. 123.

surance that the sales price will be collected. Failure to reduce the debt on the property within the customary terms granted on a mortgage raises questions about the buyer's commitment to pay the full amount owed to the seller. If the continuing investment requirement is not met, the seller recognizes profit using the reduced profit method (discussed later in this chapter) if payments by the buyer each year are at least equal to the sum of

1. The interest and principal amortization on the maximum first mortgage loan that could be obtained on the property; plus,

2. Interest, at an appropriate rate, on' the excess of the aggregate actual debt on the property over such a maximum first mortgage loan.[8]

If these requirements are not met, profit is recognized by use of the installment method. Note in Illustration 24-1 that the cost recovery method also may be used in reporting transactions in which the installment method is considered appropriate.

A nonretail sale of property will now be used to illustrate the various methods used to account for an installment sale.

ACCOUNTING FOR A NONRETAIL SALE OF REAL ESTATE ILLUSTRATED

Assume that on January 2, 1995, Gilbert Company entered into a contract to sell land it had been holding for 15 years for possible plant expansion. Financial data related to the sale are as follows:

		%
1. Sales price	$200,000	100
Book value of the land sold	120,000	60
Gross profit on the sale	$ 80,000	40

2. Down payment received on January 2; $60,000.

3. The contract provides for 10 consecutive payments of $28,968 to be received on December 31. The interest rate of 16% is considered appropriate.[9]

---

[8]Ibid., par. 23. The provisions of *APB Opinion No. 21*, "Interest on Receivables and Payables," should be considered in selecting an appropriate interest rate for present value calculations.

[9]The required interest payments were computed as follows:

Reasonable rate of interest, 16%.

Annuity factor for 10 periods at 16%, 4.833.

Let X = Required annual payments

$$4.833(X) = \$140,000^*$$
$$X = \$28,968$$

*Sales price of $200,000 minus down payment of $60,000.

If the provision for interest is not explicitly stated, or if the stated rate is unreasonable, *APB Opinion No. 21*, "Interest on Receivables and Payables," requires that interest be imputed and accounted for over the life of the contract.

4. The substance of the transaction indicates that a sale has been consummated for accounting purposes.

5. The company's fiscal year-end is December 31.

In order to compare the three methods most commonly used to account for installment sales, journal entries for the accrual, installment, and cost recovery methods are presented in Illustration 24-2 on the basis of the sales agreement above. For each method it is assumed that the conditions for use of that method as required by *SFAS No. 66* are met.

ILLUSTRATION 24-2
Journal Entries to Record Nonretail Sale of Land

1995		ACCRUAL METHOD		INSTALLMENT METHOD		COST RECOVERY METHOD	
Jan. 2	Cash	60,000		60,000		60,000	
	Notes Receivable	140,000		140,000		140,000	
	Land		120,000		120,000		120,000
	Realized Profit on Sale of Land		80,000		—		—
	Deferred Profit on Sale of Land		—		80,000		80,000
	To record installment sale of land.						
Dec. 31	Cash	28,968		28,968		28,968	
	Notes Receivable		6,568		6,568		6,568
	Interest Revenue (140,000 × 16%)		22,400		22,400		—
	Deferred Profit on Sale of Land		—		—		22,400
	To record receipt of annual payment.						
	Deferred Profit on Sale of Land	—		26,627		—	
	Realized Profit on Sale of Land		—		26,627		—
	To record realized profit on sale of land [($60,000 + $6,568) × .40 = $26,627].						
1996							
Dec. 31	Cash	28,968		28,968		28,968	
	Notes Receivable		7,619		7,619		7,619
	Interest Revenue (140,000 − 6,568) × 16%		21,349		21,349		—
	Deferred Profit on Sale of Land		—		—		21,349
	To record receipt of annual payment.						
	Deferred Profit on Sale of Land	—		3,048		—	
	Realized Profit on Sale of Land		—		3,048		—
	To record realized profit on sale of land ($7,619 × .40 = $3,048).						
1997							
Dec. 31	Cash	28,968		28,968		28,968	
	Notes Receivable		8,838		8,838		8,838
	Interest Revenue		20,130		20,130		20,130
	To record receipt of annual payment.						
	Deferred Profit on Sale of Land	—		3,535		6,774*	
	Realized Profit on Sale of Land		—		3,535		6,774
	To record realized profit on sale of land ($8,838 × .40 = $3,535).						

*See Illustration 24-3.

8838
−6774
2064

Accrual Method

When the accrual method is used, the full gross profit of $80,000 is reported in the year of the sale. Subsequent cash receipts are allocated between principal and interest revenue as shown in the first three columns of Illustration 24-3. Over the life of the contract, income of $229,680, consisting of gross profit of $80,000 and interest of $149,680, is recorded.

Installment Method

When the installment method is used to account for the sale, the difference between the contracted sales price and book value of the item sold is deferred. The deferred gross profit ($80,000) is reported subsequently as realized in the periods that cash is received. The amount of gross profit realized each period is computed by multiplying the portion of the cash payments allocated to principal during the period by the gross profit percentage [(Sales price − book value) ÷ sales price]. Thus, each payment is considered to represent interest revenue, a partial recovery of cost, and a partial realization of gross profit. The amount reported as profit each year increases as the portion of the payment allocated to the reduction of principal increases. Interest revenue is recognized as earned and is accounted for separately

ILLUSTRATION 24-3
Cost Recovery Method

| | CASH RECEIVED | INTEREST PORTION | PRINCIPAL PAYMENT | UNRECOVERED COST | REVENUE | | NOTES RECEIVABLE | DEFERRED PROFIT | NET RECEIVABLE |
					INTEREST	DEFERRED PROFIT			
				$120,000			$200,000	$ 80,000	$120,000
1/2/95	$ 60,000		$ 60,000 (1)	60,000			140,000	80,000	60,000
12/31/95	28,968 (2)	$22,400	6,568 (1)	31,032			133,432 (3)	102,400	31,032
12/31/96	28,968	21,349	7,619	2,064	—	—	125,813	123,749	2,064
12/31/97	28,968	20,130	8,838	—	$ 20,130 (4)	$ 6,774	116,975	116,975	–0–
12/31/98	28,968	18,716	10,252	—	18,716 (5)	10,252	106,723	106,723	–0–
12/31/99	28,968	17,076	11,892	—	17,076	11,892	94,831	94,831	–0–
12/31/00	28,968	15,173	13,795	—	15,173	13,795	81,036	81,036	–0–
12/31/01	28,968	12,966	16,002	—	12,966	16,002	65,034	65,034	–0–
12/31/02	28,968	10,405	18,563	—	10,405	18,563	46,471	46,471	–0–
12/31/03	28,968	7,435	21,533	—	7,435	21,533	24,938	24,938	–0–
12/31/04	28,968	4,030	24,938	—	4,030	24,938	—	—	–0–
Totals	$349,680	$149,680	$200,000	$ —	$105,931	$123,749			

(1) $120,000 − $60,000 = $60,000; $60,000 − $28,968 = $31,032
(2) $140,000 × .16 = $22,400
(3) $80,000 + $22,400 = $102,400
(4) Principal payment—12/31/97 $8,838
     Unrecovered cost—1/1/97   2,064
     Deferred profit recognized $6,774
(5) That portion of each cash payment allocated to principal.

from the gross profit realized during the period. Again, total income of $229,680 is recorded over the life of the sales contract. However, in contrast to the accrual method in which the full $80,000 was reported as income in the year of sale, the $80,000 is reported as income under the installment method as cash is received during years 1–10.

If after adoption of the installment method, the transaction later satisfies the criteria for using the full accrual method, the seller may change to the full accrual method. The remaining deferred profit that has not been recognized as income is reported as income in the year of the change.[10]

Cost Recovery Method

Assume now that the sales agreement negotiated by Gilbert Company provides that the notes received in connection with the land sale may be subordinated to a construction loan. This provision enables the buyer to finance development of the land without first paying off the amount owed to Gilbert Company. In this case the cost recovery method should be used to determine the amount of income to be reported each period since it is doubtful that Gilbert could recover its cost in the event of default by the buyer. (The cost recovery method may also be used as an alternative to the installment method.) Under this method, cash received for both principal and interest is considered initially to be a recovery of the cost of the property. After the recovery of cost, all receipts are reported as revenue in the period received.

A schedule of cash receipts, unrecovered cost, revenue reported, and the net receivable balance each period for the term of the sale by Gilbert Company is presented in Illustration 24-3. Note that the principal portion of each cash receipt reduces the receivable balance, whereas the interest portion increases the deferred gross profit of $80,000 until the cost of the property is recovered. As a result of this procedure, the deferred profit account contains the deferred gross profit of $80,000 plus the accumulated deferred interest of $43,749 ($22,400 in 1995 + $21,349 in 1996) for a total of $123,749. In the balance sheet, the deferred profit account is reported as a reduction in the related receivable balance, which results in the net receivable balance being equal to the unrecovered cost of the property. Once the cost of the property is fully recovered, subsequent receipts for accrued interest may be recorded as interest revenue. Beginning in 1997 a portion of the accumulated deferred profit equal to the principal payment in excess of the unrecovered cost is recognized each year as revenue by making an entry debiting the deferred profit account and crediting realized profit. Thus, interest of $105,931 and deferred profit of $123,749 for a total of $229,680 is reported as revenue over the life of the contract.

If, after adoption of the cost recovery method, the transaction satisfies the criteria for using the full accrual method, the seller may change to the full accrual method. Any remaining deferred profit is reported in income in the year of the change.[11]

---

[10]*Statement of Financial Accounting Standards No. 66*, par. 61.
[11]Ibid., par. 64.

Reduced Profit Method

Recall that for a continuing investment to be adequate for full profit recognition at the time of sale, *SFAS No. 66* specifies that the buyer must reduce the debt annually over a maximum term of 20 years for the sale of land and the customary lending terms for a first mortgage for other real estate transactions. If these conditions are not satisfied, a reduced profit is recognized at the time of sale if the payments each year (excluding lump-sum payments) are at least equal to the sum of the interest and principal on the maximum available on a first mortgage plus the interest at an appropriate rate on the remaining debt. The reduced profit is determined by reducing the seller's receivable from the buyer to the present value of the lowest annual payments required by the sales contract over the maximum period specified in the continuing investment test. The discount rate to use is determined from the criteria established in paragraphs 13 and 14 of *APB Opinion No. 21*, but it should not be less than the rate stated in the sales contract.

To illustrate the reduced profit method, assume that Gilbert Company sold land that cost $120,000 for $200,000 with the following financing arrangement:

Down payment	$ 40,000
First mortgage note payable to an independent bank (Terms: interest rate, 16%; term, 20 years; annual payments of principal and interest, $16,867)	100,000
Second mortgage note payable to seller (Terms: interest rate, 12%; term, 25 years; annual payments of principal and interest, $7,650)	60,000
Sales price	$200,000

In this illustration, the financing arrangement does not meet the continuing investment test because the 25-year term for the second mortgage exceeds the 20-year amortization period permitted for the sale of land. Assuming that the payments by the buyer satisfy the criteria for using the reduced profit method and that the appropriate interest rate to use in discounting the receivable is the market rate of 16%, the profit to be recognized at the time of sale is computed as follows.

Down payment		$ 40,000
First mortgage note		100,000
Present value of seller's receivable		
Lowest level of annual payments	$7,650	
Present value of an annuity		
factor—20 periods @ 16%	5.92884	45,356
Adjusted sales price		185,356
Cost of the land sold		120,000
Profit recognized at the time of sale		$ 65,356

Note that the seller's receivable is discounted for the maximum amortization period permitted for land, not for the actual term agreed to in the contract. As a result, the profit recognized at the time of sale is reduced by $14,644 ($80,000 − $65,356), which is also the difference between the face amount ($60,000) and present value ($45,356) of the seller's receivable. This reduced profit is deferred and recognized in years 21–25 as the payments on the second mortgage are received.

Deposit Method

The deposit method is considered the appropriate method of accounting when analysis of the real estate transaction indicates that in substance a sale has not taken place for accounting purposes (for example, a sale is not consummated or the buyer's initial investment is inadequate). When the deposit method is used, recognition of the sale and profit is deferred until the transaction qualifies as a sale for accounting purposes. Until such time, all cash collections (including principal and interest) are accounted for as a deposit (a liability) on the contract, except that the portion of the payment designated as interest and nonrefundable may be used to offset carrying charges on the property, such as property taxes and interest on existing debt. The seller continues to report the property as an asset, discloses the status of the property, and reports existing debt on the property to be assumed by the buyer as a liability in the financial statements. Accordingly, a note receivable from the buyer is not recorded until the conditions are met for recording a sale. If a contract is canceled, nonrefundable deposits are recorded as income.

FINANCIAL STATEMENT PRESENTATION

In the period that a nonretail sale of real estate is consummated, the seller should disclose in the income statement, or related footnotes, the total sales value from which any deferred gross profit and related cost of sales is deducted. In each period, the deferred gross profit earned is presented as a separate item of revenue. Interest revenue would be reported in the appropriate section depending on whether the company uses a single-step or multiple-step format for the income statement. Other information that is required for a fair presentation of the financial statements, such as the terms of the sale, should be disclosed in a footnote. The criteria established in *APB Opinion No. 30* should be considered in determining whether a material gain or loss on the nonretail sale of real estate not used in the business should be reported as an extraordinary item, an unusual or infrequent item, or a customary business activity.[12]

On the balance sheet, receivables resulting from nonrecurring transactions should be reported as long-term if they are not expected to be realized within one year or the normal operating cycle, whichever is longer. There has been disagreement in the accounting literature and in practice as to the preferred manner of reporting the deferred gross profit balance. The account has been reported as a liability or a deferred credit on the basis that the balance consisted of unearned revenue. However, some have argued that the account does not represent an

---

[12]*Opinions of the Accounting Principles Board No. 30,* "Reporting the Results of Operations" (New York: AICPA, 1973).

amount owed by the firm to an outside party, but is more in the nature of an asset valuation account and should be deducted from the related installment receivable balance. This latter approach is supported in *SFAS No. 66*.[13] Thus, under the installment method, Gilbert Company would report the following balances in its balance sheet at the end of 1995 and 1996:

	DECEMBER 31	
	1995	1996
Notes receivable	$133,432	$125,813
Less: Deferred profit on sale of land	53,373	50,325
Net receivable	$ 80,059	$ 75,488

ACCOUNTING FOR THE INSTALLMENT SALE OF INVENTORY

If the installment sales method is used for tax purposes, the firm needs to maintain a record of gross profit percentages by year and the amount collected on receivables by year of sale. To illustrate, assume that Spencer Company sells merchandise on short-term credit and also provides financing for major purchases on an installment plan. The company adopted the installment sales method of accounting for tax purposes. The following information related to installment sales for the last three years was provided by the firm's accountant.

	1995	1996	1997
Installment sales	$300,000	$390,000	$360,000
Cost of goods sold on installment plan	180,000	237,900	226,800
Gross profit	$120,000	$152,100	$133,200
Gross profit percentage	40%	39%	37%
Cash receipts—1995 sales	$ 80,000	$120,000	$100,000
1996 sales		110,000	130,000
1997 sales			90,000

The gross profit reported as taxable income during each period is as follows:

	1995	1996	1997
Collection of 1995 sales	$32,000	$48,000	$ 40,000
Collection of 1996 sales		42,900	50,700
Collection of 1997 sales			33,300
	$32,000	$90,900	$124,000

The reported gross profit realized each period is computed by multiplying the cash collections for each respective year's sales by the gross profit percentage related to that year's sales.

---

[13]The deferred gross profit balance is offset against the receivable balance in an illustration of accounting for retail land sales contained in par. 96, which is required (see par. 63) when using the cost recovery method, and is implied in par. 58 in the discussion of the installment method.

A temporary difference will result if the company elects to use the installment sales method for tax purposes, but reports the total gross profit in the period of sale for financial reporting purposes. When a single installment sales contract is considered, book income will exceed taxable income in the year of the sale. In subsequent periods, the difference will reverse as taxable income computed using the installment sales method exceeds accounting income. Thus, the difference between accounting and taxable income satisfies the definition of a temporary difference. Accordingly, interperiod tax allocation procedures are necessary.

DEFAULTS AND REPOSSESSIONS

SFAS No. 66 does not address the issue of recording the repossession of real estate on default by the buyer on a nonretail sales contract. One approach to accounting for the repossession is to write off the balance in the receivable account, eliminate the remaining deferred profit related to the receivable, if any, and record the repossessed real estate at an amount equal to the net receivable balance. A loss is recorded if the fair value of the repossessed real estate is less than the net receivable balance. The result of this approach is to substitute the repossessed real estate for the net receivable balance. This is a conservative approach in which the firm's financial position is not improved by accepting a long-term nonmonetary asset in full satisfaction of a receivable.

To illustrate, assume that the buyer of the Gilbert Company land defaulted in January 1997 after making the second installment payment on December 31, 1996. The fair value of the land had declined to $70,000 after the land began to sink as a result of pumping too much ground water. Assuming that the installment method is used to account for the transaction, appropriate balances as of January 2, 1997, are:

Notes receivable ($140,000 − $6,568 − $7,619)	$125,813
Deferred profit ($80,000 − $26,627 − $3,048)	50,325

The journal entry to record the default and repossession is:

Land	70,000	
Deferred Profit on Sale of Land	50,325	
Loss on Repossession of Land	5,488	
Notes Receivable		125,813

In this illustration, a loss of $5,488 is recognized at the time of repossession. In certain situations, the loss may have been recognized in prior periods when it became evident that an asset had been impaired.

In the approach illustrated above, the repossessed land was recorded at the lower of its fair value or the net receivable balance. An alternative method is to record the repossessed asset at fair value even when fair value is greater than the net receivable. It could be argued that the original contract must have satisifed the conditions of a sale in order for the receivable and a portion or all of the profit to have been recorded. If not, the seller should have accounted for the cash receipts as deposits and not recognized the receivable and profit. The subsequent repossession, therefore, justifies the establishment of a new basis, assuming the series of transactions are arm's-length in nature.[14]

If the repossessed asset is recorded at fair value, the entry to record the repossession will appear as follows, assuming a fair value of $120,000:

Land	120,000	
Deferred Profit on Sale of Land	50,325	
Gain on Repossession of Land		44,512
Notes Receivable		125,813

Obviously, the difficult aspect of this approach to accounting for the repossession is ascertaining the fair value of the real estate. It is unlikely that the gain under this approach will exceed the deferred profit $50,325 by a material amount, because if the fair value of the land was in excess of the $125,813 due on the contract, the buyer would probably dispose of the property to settle the account, if permitted to do so by the contract.

ACCOUNTING FOR CONSIGNMENT TRANSACTIONS

Nature of the Consignment Agreement

A *consignment* constitutes the transfer of possession of merchandise without the transfer of title from the owner, called the *consignor*, to another person, called the *consignee*. The consignee acts as an agent on behalf of the consignor for the purpose of selling the goods for a commission. Legally, the consignment is a bailment and, accordingly, the laws of agency and bailment apply in the determination of the rights and responsibilities of both the consignor and the consignee.

The shipment of consigned goods to the consignee is not treated as a sale. Although a transfer of goods has taken place, it is not the intent of either the consignor or the consignee that a sale and purchase transaction take place. Title to the goods remains with the consignor, and recognition of the sale is deferred until the goods are transferred to a third party by the consignee. In other words,

---

[14]The use of market value also appears to be consistent with the provisions of *SFAS No. 15*, "Accounting by Debtors and Creditors for Troubled Debt Restructurings." Application of the *Statement* is justified by footnote 1:

> *Although troubled debt that is fully satisfied by foreclosure, repossession, or other transfer of assets or by grant of equity securities by the debtor is, in a technical sense, not restructured, that kind of event is included in the term troubled debt restructuring in this Statement.*

In paragraph 34 the Board states:

> *A troubled debt restructuring that is in substance a repossession or foreclosure by the creditor, or in which the creditor otherwise obtains one or more of the debtor's assets in place of all or part of the receivable, shall be accounted for according to the provisions of paragraphs 28 and 33, and, if appropriate, 39.*

Paragraph 28 provides that the assets received to settle the receivable should be accounted for at their fair value at the time of restructuring.

the intent of the parties is to transfer title directly from the consignor to the third party. At that time, the transaction is recorded as a sale on the books of the consignor. Accordingly, inventory on consignment must be reported as part of the consignor's inventory until it is sold by the consignee to a third party.

Advantages of a Consignment Arrangement

A consignment arrangement offers certain advantages to both the consignor and the consignee. A consignor may prefer shipping goods on consignment for the following reasons:

1. ***Wider Markets for a Product.***   Dealers may not be willing to assume the risk of purchasing certain goods, such as a new product or an item that may become obsolete, but may be willing to carry them on consignment.

2. ***Control over Selling Price.***   If goods are sold directly to the consignee, the consignor may find it difficult to establish and control the selling price of goods.

3. ***Recovery of an Asset.***   Since legal title does not transfer to the consignee, the consignor has the right to possession of all unsold goods or the right to payment for goods sold if the consignee declares bankruptcy. Creditors of the consignee do not have the claim against the consigned assets that they would have if the goods had been sold to the consignee.

The consignee may find a consignment arrangement attractive primarily for the following reasons:

1. ***Avoids Risk of Ownership.***   Goods that do not sell or that become obsolete, deteriorate, or decline in market value may be returned to the consignor.

2. ***Requires Less Capital.***   The consignee does not incur a liability and does not make a cash payment on the goods until they are sold. Thus, the consignee's capital investment will be lower if the goods are held on consignment.

Even with these advantages, consignment arrangements have been declining in use as a result of changing business practices, such as the tendency toward more liberal return policies on nonconsignment sales.

RIGHTS AND RESPONSIBILITIES OF THE CONSIGNEE

Before goods are transferred on consignment, a written agreement should specify clearly the intent of the parties. The agreement should address such issues as the amount and type of the consignee's expenses to be reimbursed by the consignor, how the consignee's commissions are to be computed, when commissions are to be paid, the credit terms and conditions, if any, to be considered by the consignee in granting credit, and the responsibility for collection of receivables and losses on receivables. The agreement should be complete and attempt to avoid potential points of conflict. For items not provided for in the agreement that result in litigation, the laws of bailment and agency apply.

Rights of the Consignee

Some of the more important rights and responsibilities of the consignee are:

1. *Compensation.* The consignee has a right to be compensated for services performed. Usually this compensation is stated as a percentage of the sales price, or the consignee is permitted to retain all the sales price above a specified amount.

2. *Reimbursement for Advances and Necessary Expenses.* Unless otherwise provided for in the agreement, the consignor, as owner of the goods, is responsible for all costs incurred that are directly related to the sale of the goods (for example, freight and insurance on the goods while in transit to the consignee's place of business). Before the goods are sold, several expenses that are directly related to the sale may be paid by the consignee for the convenience of the consignor. In addition, in some cases the consignee may make an advance to the consignor before the sale is made to a third party. The consignee has the right to be reimbursed for such advances and expenses. Normally, recovery is made by deducting the expenses and advances from the amounts collected from the sale of the consigned goods. If the collections are insufficient to cover these expenses and advances, the consignee has a direct claim against either unsold goods or receivable balances on items already sold.

3. *Granting of Credit.* Unless limited by an express agreement, the consignee has the right to sell goods on credit and extend normal credit terms. Of course, the consignee must exercise due care and act prudently in the granting of credit. A consignee may guarantee the collection of the receivable balance. The consignee is referred to in such cases as a *del credere* agent and generally receives additional compensation for assuming this risk.

4. *Warranty of Consigned Goods.* The consignee has the right to make warranties that are normal for the product being sold.

Responsibilities of the Consignee

1. *Care and Protection for Consigned Goods.* The consignee must provide care and protection reasonable for the type of goods being held and care for the goods in accordance with specific instructions of the consignor.

2. *Identification of Consigned Goods and Receivables.* Although physical separation is not required, the consignee must establish sufficient controls and provide adequate accounting records to identify consigned goods and consignment receivables.

3. *Due Care in Granting and Collecting Receivables.* The consignee must exercise reasonable effort to assure that the goods are sold at the specified price, that normal credit terms are granted, that a normal warranty is made, and that a reasonable effort is made to collect the sales price.

4. *Timely Periodic Reporting of Sales and Collections.* The consignee must report the sales and collections activities during the period and settle the account with the consignor as provided for in the consignment agreement The report rendered by

ILLUSTRATION 24-4
Example of an Account
Sales Made by Consignee

ACCOUNT SALES
Starbuck, Inc.
Phoenix, Arizona

No. ___22___

___June 30___, 1995

Sales for account of _____Mackie Sales Co._____

Account sales of _____Video recorders, Model VR 1100_____

DATE	EXPLANATION		AMOUNT
June 1	Consigned units on hand—0		$ –0–
June 10	Consigned units received—10		
June 1—30	Sales—9 units @ $1,200 each		10,800
	Expenses Incurred:		
	Freight	$ 500	
	Repairs needed on 2 units sold	60	
	Advertising in local newspaper	80	
	Commission (20% × $10,800)	2,160	2,800
	Net amount due		8,000
	Remittance enclosed		8,000
June 30	Ending Balance—1 unit		$ –0–

the consignee is referred to as an ***account sales***. Typically, it is similar in format to the one presented in Illustration 24-4. The report lists the goods received on consignment, the goods sold, the sales price, the expenses incurred by the consignee chargeable to the consignor, any advances made by the consignee, and the amount owed to or due from the consignor.

ACCOUNTING FOR CONSIGNED GOODS

Accounting by the Consignee

Accounting procedures established by the consignee must recognize that goods received on consignment are not owned. However, as noted earlier, the consignee must (1) maintain records and controls that permit the identification of (a) goods held on consignment and (b) related receivables and reimbursable expenses, and (2) prepare periodic reports. The consignee normally creates a special account, Consignment—In, which is debited for reimbursable expenses related to the consigned inventory, commissions earned by the consignee, and cash remittances to the consignor. The account is credited for the proceeds of consignment sales to third parties.

If the consignee transacts business with more than one consignor, a separate Consignment—In account should be established for each consignor. If the consignee deals with a number of consignors, a controlling account could be established in the general ledger and supporting information recorded in individual accounts in a subsidiary ledger. At the end of the period, a Consignment—In account may contain a debit balance, representing a net receivable due from the consignor, or the account may contain a credit balance, representing a net payable due to the consignor. The sum of receivable balances and payable balances should be reported separately and should not be offset against one another. Thus, the sum of the accounts with the debit balances should be reported on the balance sheet as a current asset; the sum of the accounts with credit balances should be reported on the balance sheet as a current liability.

Recording Consignment Transactions—An Illustration

To illustrate accounting by the consignee, the account sales report presented in Illustration 24-4 will be used as the basis for the journal entries.

(1)	June 10	Memorandum—Received 10 video recorders on consignment, Model Number VR1100, from Mackie Sales Co.		
(2)	10	Consignment—In—Mackie Sales Co.	500	
		Cash		500
		To record payment of freight charges for 10 video recorders received on consignment.		
(3)	12	Consignment—In—Mackie Sales Co.	60	
		Cash		60
		To record payment for repairs needed on two video recorders.		
(4)	12	Consignment—In—Mackie Sales Co.	80	
		Cash		80
		To record payment for advertising chargeable to consignor.		
(5)	10–30	Cash	10,800	
		Consignment—In—Mackie Sales Co.		10,800
		To record sale of 9 video recorders @ $1,200 each.		
(6)	30	Consignment—In—Mackie Sales Co.	2,160	
		Commissions Earned on Consignment Sales		2,160
		To record 20% commission earned on total consignment sales of $10,800.		
(7)	30	Consignment—In—Mackie Sales Co.	8,000	
		Cash		8,000
		To record cash remitted to consignor.		

Entry (6) must be made before the financial statements are prepared in order to reflect the revenue earned during this period by the consignee.

The entry to record the consignment sales [entry (5)] was based on the assumption that the sales were cash sales only. A memorandum entry could be made for those sales on account if the consignor were responsible for receivable collections. In such cases, the account sales report would reflect settlement in the form of cash for the balance in the Consignment—In account, and receivable balances transferred to the consignor would be listed. If receivables are transferred to the consignor, it is possible, of course, that the Consignment—In account will report a debit balance reflecting cash due from the consignor.

After the foregoing journal entries are posted to the general ledger, the Consignment—In account appears as follows:

CONSIGNMENT—IN—MACKIE SALES CO.

6/1	Units on hand	0	6/10–6/30	Sold 9 units	10,800
6/10	Units received	10			
6/10	Freight charges	500			
6/12	Repairs	60			
6/12	Advertising	80			
6/30	Commission earned	2,160			
6/30	Cash remitted to consignor	8,000			
		10,800			10,800
7/1	Units on hand	1			

Observe that the dollar value of the inventory held on consignment is not carried on the books of the consignee.

Accounting by the Consignor

The journal entries to be made on the books of the consignor vary, depending on (1) whether consignment transactions are recorded in separate ledger accounts for the purpose of determining profits on consignment sales or are simply combined with the regular account balances and (2) whether a perpetual or periodic inventory system is used.

If consignment transactions are recorded in separate accounts, a Consignment—Out account is established for each consignment shipment. If consignment shipments are too numerous, the account may serve as a controlling account for individual consignments that are recorded in a subsidiary ledger. Practice may vary as to the type of transactions charged to this account. One commonly used alternative is to debit Consignment—Out for the cost of goods shipped on consignment and all other expenses related to the consignment sales incurred by both the consignor and consignee; the account is credited for the amount of consignment sales. The Consignment—Out account is in the nature of an inventory account rather than a receivable account, since title to the goods is retained by the consignor.

The consignor may establish an accounting system in which the revenue and expenses related to the consignment transactions are recorded in the regular accounts, rather than in separate accounts as discussed before. If this is the case, then some modification is required in the accounting methods and control procedures adopted by the consignor. The modifications, identified in Illustration 24-5, are necessary to provide a record of the goods on consignment, to identify inventoriable cost related to goods on consignment, and to maintain a record of the relative position with each consignee.

Illustration—Perpetual Inventory System Maintained by the Consignor

The journal entries on the books of the consignor for the two alternatives discussed in the two preceding paragraphs are presented in Illustration 24-5. The transactions reported in the account sales report to Mackie Sales Co. presented in Illustration 24-4 constitute the primary support for these entries. It is assumed in this illustration that the consignor has adopted a perpetual inventory system. The modifications required when a periodic inventory system is used are discussed in a later section.

ILLUSTRATION 24-5
Journal Entries on Consignor's Books
Perpetual Inventory System

CONSIGNMENT TRANSACTIONS RECORDED IN SEPARATE ACCOUNTS			CONSIGNMENT TRANSACTIONS RECORDED IN REGULAR ACCOUNTS		
(1) JUNE 6					
Consignment—Out—			Consignment—Out—		
Starbuck, Inc.	7,500		Starbuck, Inc.	7,500	
Inventory		7,500	Inventory		7,500
To transfer cost of 10 video recorders shipped on consignment to separate asset account.					
(2) JUNE 6					
Consignment—Out—					
Starbuck, Inc.	400		Packing Expense (1)	400	
Cash		400	Cash		400
To record payment of packing expense incurred by consignor.					
(3) JUNE 30					
Cash	(2) 8,000		Cash	(2) 8,000	
Consignment—Out—			Freight Expense (1)	500	
Starbuck, Inc.	2,800		Repairs Expense	60	
Consignment—Out—			Advertising Expense	80	
Starbuck, Inc.		10,800	Commission Expense	2,160	
To record transactions as reported per Account Sales report.			Sales		10,800
(4) JUNE 30					
Consignment—Out—			Cost of Goods Sold	6,750	
Starbuck, Inc.	940		Consignment—Out—		
Profit on Consignment			Starbuck, Inc.		6,750
Sales		940	To adjust Consignment—Out for cost of consignment sales.		
To adjust Consignment—Out account for profit on consignment sales. (See illustration of allocation of cost in determination of profit on consignment sales on p. 978 for support of recorded amounts.)			Consignment—Out—		
			Starbuck, Inc. (3)	90	
			Packing Expense		40
			Freight Expense		50
			To adjust expense accounts for inventoriable cost of goods held on consignment at end of period. (One unit in consignment inventory at end of period.)		

(5) JUNE 30

Profit on Consignment		
Sales	940	
Income Summary		940
To close revenue and expense		
accounts.		

Sales	10,800	
Packing Expense		360
Freight Expense		450
Repairs Expense		60
Advertising Expense		80
Commission Expense		2,160
Cost of Goods Sold		6,750
Income Summary		940
(If regular sales had been recorded in this illustration, account balances would reflect both consignment and regular sales.)		

(1) Inventoriable costs are sometimes charged to a deferred cost account that is adjusted at the end of the period.

(2) This could include a debit to Accounts Receivable if there were sales on account and the consignor is responsible for collection.

(3) Costs may be expensed currently and not deferred if immaterial in amount.

After the journal entries listed in the first set of columns are posted, the Consignment—Out account will appear as follows:

CONSIGNMENT—OUT—STARBUCK,INC.

6/6	Shipped 10 video recorders to Starbuck, Inc.		7,500	6/30	Consignment Sales—9 units	10,800
6/6	Packing expense		400			
6/30	Transactions reported by Consignee					
	Freight	500				
	Repairs	60				
	Advertising	80				
	Commissions	2,160	2,800			
			10,700			
6/30	Profits on 9 units sold (10,800 − 9,860)		940	6/30	Balance—Cost allocated to one unsold unit	840
			11,640			11,640
7/1	Beginning balance—Inventoriable cost allocated to one unit		840			

The Consignment—Out account provides a summary of the consignment transactions that have occurred during the period. After the transactions reflected in the account sales report have been posted, the balance in the account must be adjusted to recognize the profit earned during the current period on the units sold by the consignee. The balance remaining in the account after this adjustment is posted represents the cost to be deferred as an asset on the unsold units.

In order to determine the profit from sales in this period and the cost to be deferred, it is necessary to allocate the total cost identified with the goods on consignment between the units sold in this period (to be matched against consignment sales in this period) and the units still on hand at the end of the period (to be reported as inventory on the consignor's balance sheet). The allocation of costs and the amount of the consignment profit were determined as follows.

	TOTAL COSTS	COSTS ASSOCIATED WITH CONSIGNMENT SALES—9 UNITS	COSTS ASSOCIATED WITH ENDING INVENTORY 1 UNIT
Cost of 10 video recorders	$ 7,500	$ 6,750	$750
Packing expense	400	360	40
Freight expense	500	450	50
Repairs expense—on units sold	60	60	—
Advertising expense	80	80	—
Commission expense	2,160	2,160	—
Total	$10,700	9,860	$840
Consignment sales		10,800	
Consignment profit		$ 940	

When this allocation is made, costs are classified as either inventoriable or non-inventoriable.

Inventoriable costs (product costs) are those considered necessary to acquire the product, get it to the location of sale, and prepare it for sale. Inventoriable costs are said to attach to the inventory and become a part of the total cost, or total valuation, of the inventory. In this illustration the cost of the goods, the packing, and the freight expenditures were considered costs necessary to get the goods to a location for sale and in a salable condition. Such costs are deducted from (matched against) consignment revenues in the accounting period in which the individual units are sold.

Other costs incurred by the consignee and consignor do not add to the utility of the goods and are considered noninventoriable or period costs. Period costs are expensed in the accounting period in which the expense is incurred. Costs such as commissions earned by the consignee and the cost of repairing two of the units sold did not add to the value of the unsold units and were expensed currently. Advertising is considered a period expense, even though there may be some future benefit. Freight on shipments to the consignee is considered an inventoriable cost to the extent that it does not exceed the normal costs of direct shipment for the consignor. Excessive freight on consignments should not be included in the value of the unsold units, but should be expensed currently as a period charge.

Other inventoriable costs may be incurred by the consignor when unsold units are returned by the consignee. The amount restored to the inventory account (that is, a credit is made to Consignment—Out) should not exceed the original cost of the inventory, and in some situations may be less if the goods have a lower value. After this entry, the balance remaining in Consignment—Out is expensed in the current period. Failure to do so would result in an overstated value for the retained goods. In addition, cost incurred to restore the inventory to a salable condition should be accounted for as a period expense.

The journal entries when the regular accounts are used to record the consignment transactions are self-explanatory and are based on the allocation of costs discussed before. It should be noted that the increase in net income of $940 and the deferred cost of $840 ($750 + $90) are the same for both alternatives.

Periodic Inventory System Maintained by the Consignor

Only minor changes are needed in the journal entries presented in Illustration 24-5 if the consignor uses a periodic inventory system. If consignment transactions are kept in separate accounts, the entry to record the shipment of goods [entry (1)] becomes:

Consignment—Out—Starbuck, Inc.	7,500	
Consignment Shipments		7,500

The Consignment Shipments account is viewed as a reduction in the cost of goods available for sale in order to determine the cost of goods available for regular sales. This account is, of course, closed at the end of the period. The remainder of the entries are the same as those in the first set of columns.

If consignment transactions are recorded in the regular accounts, a memorandum entry may be made in the journal to create a record of the goods shipped on consignment. This entry is in the form presented in the preceding paragraph, except that the two accounts are considered memorandum accounts.[15] This entry would be reversed for the cost of goods sold ($750 × 9 units) by the consignee. The ending balance of $750 in Consignment Shipments is offset against the ending balance of $750 in Consignment—Out. In other words, these accounts are simply memorandum accounts used to provide a record of goods still on consignment. The balances in the accounts will not be reported in the financial statements of the consignor. All other entries are once again the same, except that one additional entry is necessary to record a deferred inventory cost equal to the original purchase price of the one unsold unit of $750.

Reporting Consignment Transactions in the Financial Statements of the Consignor

A consignee may advance a portion of the anticipated sales price to the consignor or may remit more than the amount due based on the consignment transactions up to the end of the period. The amount of these advances or excess remittances should be credited to a liability account rather than the Consignment—Out account. Conversely, a receivable from the consignee should be established if the consignee remits less than the amount disclosed by the account sales report. The inclusion of these balances in Consignment—Out would be contrary to the purpose of this account, which is to report the inventoriable costs of goods held on con-

---

[15]Memorandum accounts are accounts with equal but opposite balances that offset each other and, accordingly, are not reported on the financial statements.

signment. The balance of Consignment—Out and other deferred costs related to consignment sales, if reported in a separate account, should be reported with the inventory of the consignor.

The income statement may take various forms, depending on the degree of detail that is desired in the disclosure of consignment sales. This, of course, should be influenced by the significance of consignment sales to the consignor. Two possible forms are presented in Illustration 24-6. The amounts reported for the non-consignment transactions are assumed; the amounts reported for the consignment sales are based on the preceding illustration.

ILLUSTRATION 24-6
Income Statement Presentation
of Consignment Sales

Mackie Sales Co.
Income Statement
For the Year Ended June 30, 1995

	CONSIGNMENT SALES	REGULAR SALES	TOTAL
Sales	$10,800	$60,000	$70,800
Cost of Goods Sold	7,560*	40,000	47,560
Gross Profit	3,240	20,000	23,240
Operating Expenses			
Selling Expenses	2,240	6,000	8,240
Other Expenses	60	7,000	7,060
Total	2,300	13,000	15,300
Net Income	$ 940	$ 7,000	$ 7,940

Mackie Sales Co.
Income Statement
For the Year Ended June 30, 1995

Sales	$60,000
Cost of Goods Sold	40,000
Gross Profit on Regular Sales	20,000
Gross Profit on Consignment Sales	3,240
Total Gross Profit	23,240
Operating Expenses	
Selling Expenses	8,240
Other Expenses	7,060
Total Expenses	15,300
Net Income	$ 7,940

*Inventoriable costs = $6,750 + $360 + $450

It should be pointed out that in the first alternative, the net income from the consignment sales is overstated, since none of the administrative costs have been allocated to consignment sales, but are charged totally against regular sales. Although it may be desirable to derive a more accurate measurement of net income on consignment sales, it is neither practical nor feasible to allocate administrative costs because of the arbitrary nature of such allocation and the additional cost that would be incurred in doing so.

Before closing this chapter, it should be emphasized that there is wide variation in practice in accounting for and reporting on consignment transactions. The procedures illustrated in this chapter can be modified to satisfy the particular needs of the consignee and consignor. Any variation adopted, of course, must report assets, liabilities, revenue, and expenses in a way that is supported by sound logic and accounting theory and that satisfies all legal requirements.

Questions

1. What is an installment sale? What are its risks?

2. What is the theoretical justification for departing from the accrual basis of accounting for installment sales?

3. Distinguish between the terms *installment sale* and *installment method.*

4. Why is it difficult to justify departing from the accrual basis of accounting when inventory is sold on a recurring basis?

5. Explain the relative effects on income from using each of the following methods: (a) accrual, (b) installment, and (c) cost recovery.

6. What two basic conditions should be met to ensure that the buyer will not default on an installment sale?

7. Under what conditions is the use of the cost recovery method appropriate?

8. In what circumstance could the net receivable balance on an installment sale exceed what the depreciated asset balance would have been had the asset not been sold?

9. What is a consignment transaction?

10. What are the advantages of a consignment arrangement to the consignor?

11. What are the advantages of a consignment arrangement to the consignee?

12. What are the specific rights and responsibilities of the consignee as a party to the consignment transaction?

13. What is an "account sales"?

14. When should gross profit on consignment sales be recognized by the consignor?

15. What is the nature of a remaining debit or credit balance in the Consignment—In account on the books of the consignee?

Exercises

Exercise 24-1

On March 30, 1995, Best Incorporated contracted to sell a parcel of investment property for $400,000. The land originally cost $240,000. The two-year contract called for a down payment of $130,000 and four semiannual payments of $77,920. Assume that the significant uncertainty about recovering all of the cost of the land warrants using the cost recovery method of profit recognition. The interest rate of 12% per annum is considered reasonable. Best Incorporated has a September 30 fiscal year-end.

Required:

A. Prepare journal entries related to the sale of the land through September 30, 1995.

B. Prepare the journal entry for March 30, 1996.

Exercise 24-2

On September 30, 1995, Jones Co., a calendar-year corporation, sold for $740,000 land with a book value of $518,000. The sales contract stipulated that Jones Co. was to receive a 25% down payment and the balance of the sales price in 16 quarterly payments of $47,630 each. Assume that Jones Co. uses the installment method to account for the sale.

Required:

A. Prepare journal entries related to the sale for the periods ending December 31, 1995, and December 31, 1996. (The first installment was paid on December 31, 1995.) Round all numbers to the nearest dollar.

B. What is the preferred method of presenting the deferred gross profit balance on the balance sheet?

Exercise 24-3

Systems, Inc. sells office automation systems on the installment basis. On July 1, 1995, Systems entered into an installment sales contract with INFO, Inc. for a five-year period. Under the contract, INFO must make 10 note payments of $10,000 plus interest of 12% per annum on the unpaid balance. The payments are due on January 1 and July 1, with the first installment payment due on January 1, 1996. INFO made a $40,000 down payment on July 1, 1995. Systems, Inc. is a calendar-year company. The gross profit on the sale is 40%.

Required:

A. Compute the effect of the sale on income before taxes for 1995, using each of the following methods:
   (1) The accrual method.
   (2) The installment sales method.
   (3) The cost recovery method.

B. Compute the net receivable balance on December 31, 1996, assuming the use of (1) the installment sales method and (2) the cost recovery method. Also assume that the deferred gross profit is reported in the preferred manner.

Exercise 24-4

On September 1, 1995, FutureVision Company sold a widescreen television costing $2,309 to Ray Jones. Jones made a down payment of $300 and signed an installment contract. The contract called for payments of $200 on the first of each of the next 18 months beginning on October 1. The list price of the television was $3,298 and the monthly interest percentage imputed in the installment contract was 2%.

Jones made payments from October 1, 1995, through March 1, 1996, but owing to financial difficulties, he had to default on the balance of the payments. On May 1, 1996, FutureVision repossessed the television, which then had a fair market value of $2,045.

Required:

A. Compute the amount of interest income and gross profit related to this transaction that would be reported for the year ended December 31, 1995, under each of the following accounting methods. Ignore income taxes and round all computations to the nearest dollar.
   (1) Accrual.
   (2) Installment sales.
   (3) Cost recovery.

B. Assuming that FutureVision records the repossessed television at fair value, prepare the journal entries on May 1 to reflect the effect of the default under the installment sales method. Ignore interest accruals after March 1, 1995.

Exercise 24-5

Select the best answer for each of the following items.

1. The method of accounting for installment sales which reports the full gross profit in the year of sale is
   (a) Installment method.
   (b) Cost recovery method.
   (c) Reduced profit method.
   (d) Accrual method.
2. The method to be used when it is doubtful the seller could recover her costs in the event of default is
   (a) Accrual method.
   (b) Deposit method.
   (c) Cost recovery method.
3. Darwin sold a piece of land to Jim for $500,000. The land originally cost Darwin $350,000. Jim made a down payment of $50,000 and signed an installment contract calling for annual payments of $25,000 and 10% interest on the outstanding balance. The gross profit percentage is
   (a) 40%.
   (b) 30%.
   (c) 60%.
   (d) 20%.
4. On January 1, 1995, Kim sold Rick a machine that cost her $50,000 for a down payment of $35,000 and three annual payments of $18,000. Payments begin December 31, 1995. If Kim uses the cost recovery method, how much profit will she report in 1995?
   (a) $–0–.

    (b) $3,000.

    (c) $35,000.

    (d) $18,000.

5. On January 1, 1995, John sold Tom a piece of land for $100,000. The land cost John $60,000. Tom is paying in five equal installments of $20,000 a year plus 10% interest on the unpaid balance. The first payment is due on December 31, 1995. How much gross profit from the sale of the land should John report in the first year if he uses the installment method?

    (a) $–0–.

    (b) $40,000.

    (c) $8,000.

    (d) $20,000.

Exercise 24-6

consignee = người nhận hàng gửi đến bán

Green, Inc. consigned out 100 lawn mowers to Lawn Care Co. on April 1, 1995. Green, whose cost per lawn mower is $200, received this information from Lawn Care concerning the year ended December 31, 1995.

Sales	$38,000 (95 lawn mowers) *400 each*
Commission	10% of sales
Freight	$30 per lawn mower × 10 = 300
Advertising	$1,500
Repairs on units sold	$800

Required:

Prepare the journal entries on the books of Green, Inc. for the year ended December 31, 1995, under the perpetual and periodic inventory systems assuming that the transactions are not recorded in the regular accounts.

Exercise 24-7

On February 1, 1995, All Carts, Inc. shipped 50 golf carts to Natural Greens on consignment. Each cart cost All Carts $2,000 to manufacture. Freight charges of $50 per unit were paid to the common carrier by the consignor. On July 1, 1995, an account sales report remitted by the consignee disclosed the following information:

Cash sales for the period: 45 units @ $3,250 each	
Sales commission: 15% of retail selling price	
Expenses paid by the consignee:	
2/12/95—Repairs/painting	$400
Various dates—Newspaper advertising	$800

Required:

(*Note:* Assume the use of the perpetual inventory method by the consignor.)

A. Compute the amount of cash remitted by the consignee with the account sales report.

B. Compute the inventory value of the remaining five unsold units. On whose books will this inventory value appear? In which account?

C. Compute the consignor's profit for the 45 units sold.

Exercise 24-8

Refer to the factual situation in Exercise 24-7.

Required:

A. Record all appropriate journal entries for the consignee during the period February 1, 1995, through July 1, 1995.

B. Post the journal entries above to a Consignment—In T account. Determine the account balance as of July 1, 1995.

Exercise 24-9

Refer to the factual situation in Exercise 24-7.

Required:

A. Record all appropriate journal entries for the consignor during the period February 1, 1995, through July 1, 1995.

B. Post the journal entries above to a Consignment—Out T account. Determine the account balance as of July 1, 1995. Assume that all consignment transactions are recorded in separate accounts and consignment profit is shown separately on the income statement.

Exercise 24-10

Becker Enterprises entered into the following consignment sales transactions during the year ended December 31, 1995:

1. Merchandise with a cost of $40,000 was shipped on consignment to a retail outlet. The controller's year-end inventory count excluded the shipped merchandise. Twenty percent of the shipment had been sold by the consignee and the profit was accounted for at December 31, 1995.
2. Freight expenses of $3,200 incurred to ship consigned merchandise were expensed when paid. As of December 31, 1995, none of the consigned merchandise relating to the shipment had been sold.
3. Receipt of $35,000 in merchandise inventory at December 31, 1995, was entirely included in the year-end inventory count. Of this shipment, $10,000 of the merchandise was received on a consignment basis. The terms of shipment were F.O.B. destination.
4. The account sales report for consignment sales made in December was not received from a consignee until January 18, 1996. The information contained in the report was omitted from Becker's financial statements as of December 31, 1995.

Required:

Discuss the effect of the errors listed above on the balance sheet and income statement of Becker Enterprises for the year ending December 31, 1995. Assume the use of the periodic inventory method by Becker and ignore income taxes.

Problems

Problem 24-1

On October 1, 1995, Hall Incorporated sold land near Green Lake that it had originally purchased for $280,000. The selling price of the land, $400,000, was to be collected on an installment basis subject to the following terms:

1. Principal payments of $37,500 plus interest of 14% per annum on the unpaid balance of the note are to be received in eight semiannual installments. The interest rate is considered reasonable.
2. A down payment of $100,000 was received on October 1, 1995.
3. Hall Incorporated is a calendar-year company, but the buyer's fiscal year-end is June 30.
4. The substance of the transaction indicates that for accounting purposes a sale has occurred.

Required:

A. Prepare the journal entries for Hall related to the sale for 1995 and 1996, assuming the use of (1) the accrual method, (2) the installment method, and (3) the cost recovery method.

B. The buyer defaults in December 1996 after making the second installment payment on October 1, 1996. Prepare the entry to record the default, assuming that the fair value of the repossessed land is (1) $150,000 and (2) $290,000. Also assume that the installment method has been used to account for the sale. Ignore accrued interest from October 1, 1996.

Problem 24-2

On January 1, 1995, Seller Company sold a piece of land to Buyer Company. The land was sold for $654,544 and had a book value of $458,181. The sales contract stipulated that Seller was to receive a 25% down payment and the balance of the sales price in 20 semiannual payments (June 30 and December 31) at 16% yearly interest.

Required:

Prepare the journal entries for the year ended December 31, 1995, under the accrual, installment, and cost recovery methods.

Problem 24-3

Prime Real Estate, Inc. recently sold a large piece of land to a development company for $886,009. This land had a book value $550,000. The company received a down payment of $150,000 on July 1, 1995, the date of sale, and will be receiving equal semiannual payments over the next five years at a 10% annual interest rate for the remainder of the receivable. Payments will be made on December 31 and June 30.

Required:

Prepare a schedule showing the gross profit realized for the years 1995 through 1997, and prepare the journal entries for the same years using the cost recovery method.

Problem 24-4

On April 1, 1995, Electronics, Inc. sold four used industrial robots to Computer Company for a total of $550,000. Computer signed a financing agreement on the sale that called for a 20% down payment and 12 equal quarterly payments on January 1, April 1, July 1, and October 1. The contract provides for 16% annual interest. Each robot originally cost Electronics $68,750 and was 20% depreciated at the time of the sale. The down payment was received on April 1, 1995, and the first installment was due on July 1, 1995.

Required:

A. Prepare the journal entries related to the sale for the years ending December 31, 1995, and December 31, 1996. Assume that Computer Company does not demonstrate reasonable ability to ensure recovery of the cost of the robots.

B. Assume that Electronics is reasonably assured of the collectibility of the installments due under the contract. Prepare the journal entries related to the sale for the periods ended December 31, 1995, and December 31, 1996.

C. Assuming that Electronics is reasonably assured that Computer can make enough payments to cover the cost of the robots, prepare the journal entries related to the sale for the years ended December 31, 1995, and December 31, 1996. Round the gross profit percentage and realized gross profit to the nearest whole number.

D. Compute the effects on income from using each of the methods to account for the sale in the situations above. Assuming one method is used for reporting taxable income and another method for financial reporting, are the differences permanent or are they timing differences?

Problem 24-5

On March 1, 1995, Discount Land Company sold undeveloped investment property on an installment basis. Pertinent financial data follow.

1. The land originally cost Discount $106,455.
2. The installment sale contract stipulated annual payments of $22,500 over a 10-year period. The first payment was made on the date of sale.
3. The stated interest rate included in the payments of 4% per annum is an unreasonable amount.
4. The estimated fair market value of the property on March 1, 1994, was $132,242. It appreciated in value 15% during the 12-month period following March 1, 1994.

Required:

A. Prepare the journal entries related to the sale for the period ending December 31, 1995, and on March 1, 1996, assuming that (1) the accrual method is used to account for the sale, and (2) the installment method is used to account for the sale. Round all numbers to the nearest dollar.

B. Assuming that the cost recovery method is used to account for the sale, prepare a schedule of collections indicating the portions of collections to be applied to notes receivable, unrecovered cost, deferred profit, and realized gross profit for the life of the note. Round all numbers to the nearest dollar.

Problem 24-6

The following consignment transactions of White, Inc., the consignor, occurred during June of the current year:

June 2   Shipped 1,000 units, each costing $125, to Joan Co. on consignment.
June 4   Paid $1,375 freight on the shipment above.
June 30   Received the following account sales from Joan Co.:

Units received	1,000	
Units on hand	450	
Units sold @ $175 each	550	$96,250
Less		
Local freight charges on 1,000 units	$ 200	
Advertising	500	
Repairs on units sold	650	
Commission—20% of sales	19,250	20,600
Net cash remitted		$75,650

Required:

A. Prepare appropriate journal entries for the information above on the books of White, Inc. Assume the use of the perpetual inventory method and that the consignment transactions are recorded in separate accounts.

B. Compute and journalize the amount of profit on consignment sales to be recognized during the month of June.

C. Construct a Consignment—Out account for the consignor, White, Inc., and post all appropriate information to it. Compute the dollar value of the ending inventory as of June 30.

D. Construct a Consignment—In account for the consignee, Joan Co., and post all appropriate information to it for the month of June.

Problem 24-7

Sara Lee, Inc., consignor, had the following consignment transactions during August 1995.

Aug. 5   Shipped 200 units, each costing $260, to Hummel Corporation on consignment.
Aug. 7   Shipped 150 units, each costing $435, to Bowers Company on consignment.
Aug. 10   Paid the following freight charges on the two shipments above:

Hummel Corporation	$ 500
Bowers Company	1,000

Aug. 30   Received the following account sales from Hummel Corporation:

Units received	200	
Units on hand	36	
Units sold @ $500 each	164	$82,000
Less		
Local freight on units received	$ 300	
Advertising	300	
Commission—17% of sales	13,940	14,540
Net cash remitted		$67,460

Aug. 31   Received the following account sales from Bowers Company:

Units received	150	
Units on hand	35	
Units sold @ $725 each	115	$83,375
Less		
Advertising	$ 400	
Repairs on units sold	700	
Commission—15% of sales	12,506	13,606
Net cash remitted		$69,769

Required:

Prepare all necessary journal entries to record the transactions above on the books of Sara Lee, Inc., including any gross profit to be recognized. Assume the use of the perpetual inventory method by the consignor and the right to extend normal credit terms by the consignee. Consignment transactions are recorded in regular accounts.

Problem 24-8

Spring, Inc., the consignor, and Market Company, the consignee, engaged in the following consignment transactions during 1995.

Feb. 3   Market received 250 units (unit cost, $117) from Spring.
Feb. 4   Market paid the shipping charges of $5.00 per unit to the common carrier.
Feb. 7   Market incurred $500 of repair cost on units subsequently sold during February.
Feb. 9   Market paid $1,000 in advertising to promote the sale of the consigned merchandise.
Feb. 28   Market sent and Spring received the following account sales for the month of February. Market is a *del credere* consignee.

Units received	250	
Units on hand	28	
Units sold @ $285 each	222	$63,270
Less		
Freight	$1,250	
Repairs	500	
Advertising	1,000	
Commission—15% of sales	9,490	12,240
Net cash remitted		$51,030

Feb. 28   Recognized gross profit on the foregoing account sales.
Mar. 31   Market sent and Spring received the following account sales for the remainder of the previously unsold consigned inventory.

Units on hand 3/1	28	
Units on hand 3/31	0	
Units sold @ $285 each	28	$7,980
Less		
Commission—15% of sales		1,197
Net cash remitted		$6,783

Mar. 31   Recognized gross profit on the March consignment sales.

Required:

Prepare appropriate journal entries related to the transactions above for the books of Spring, Inc. and Market Company, respectively. Assume the use of the perpetual inventory method by both companies. Consignment transactions are recorded in separate accounts.

Problem 24-9

Risky Corporation has requested a local CPA firm to audit its financial statements for the year ended December 31, 1995. The income statement presented to the auditors was as follows:

Risky Corporation
Income Statement
For the Year Ended December 31, 1995

Sales		$1,508,420
Cost of goods sold:		
Beginning inventory	$ 661,233	
Purchases (including freight)	571,243	
Goods available for sale	1,232,476	
Ending inventory	204,725	
Cost of goods sold		1,027,751
Gross profit on sales		480,669
Selling and administrative expenses		
(including freight-out)		101,150
Net income before income taxes		379,519
Provision for income taxes (46%)		174,579
Net income		$ 204,940

Subsequently, the auditors discovered the following information:

1. The year-end physical inventory count excluded 150 units out on consignment. The consigned goods were purchased by Risky during 1995 at a cost of $2,500 each. No entry was made to record the transfer between the consignor and consignee.
2. Freight charges of $5.00 per unit for consigned goods had been charged to the regular Freight-Out account during 1995.
3. Cash amounts remitted on consigned units sold during the year had been recorded as credits to the regular Sales account.
4. A summary of all account sales received from the consignee during the year appears here.

Account Sales Summary

Units received on consignment		150	
Units on hand		25	
Units sold @ $3,250 each		125	$406,250
Less			
Local freight	$	300	
Advertising		1,010	
Repairs on units sold		730	
Commission—10% of sales		40,625	42,665
Net cash remitted			$363,585

Required:

A. Prepare all necessary journal entries to correct the Consignment—Out and other accounts of Risky Corporation regarding the foregoing consignment transactions. Assume that inventories and related accounts have been closed to Cost of Goods Sold.

B. Prepare a corrected income statement for the year ended December 31, 1995, separating consignment gross profit from gross profit on regular sales.

APPENDIX:
TABLES OF AMOUNTS AND
PRESENT VALUES

TABLE A1 Amount of 1

$$a = (1 + i)^n$$

(n) PERIODS	2%	2½%	3%	4%	5%	6%
1	1.02000	1.02500	1.03000	1.04000	1.05000	1.06000
2	1.04040	1.05063	1.06090	1.08160	1.10250	1.12360
3	1.06121	1.07689	1.09273	1.12486	1.15763	1.19102
4	1.08243	1.10381	1.12551	1.16986	1.21551	1.26248
5	1.10408	1.13141	1.15927	1.21665	1.27628	1.33823
6	1.12616	1.15969	1.19405	1.26532	1.34010	1.41852
7	1.14869	1.18869	1.22987	1.31593	1.40710	1.50363
8	1.17166	1.21840	1.26677	1.36857	1.47746	1.59385
9	1.19509	1.24886	1.30477	1.42331	1.55133	1.68948
10	1.21899	1.28008	1.34392	1.48024	1.62889	1.79085
11	1.24337	1.31209	1.38423	1.53945	1.71034	1.89830
12	1.26824	1.34489	1.42576	1.60103	1.79586	2.01220
13	1.29361	1.37851	1.46853	1.66507	1.88565	2.13293
14	1.31948	1.41297	1.51259	1.73168	1.97993	2.26090
15	1.34587	1.44830	1.55797	1.80094	2.07893	2.39656
16	1.37279	1.48451	1.60471	1.87298	2.18287	2.54035
17	1.40024	1.52162	1.65285	1.94790	2.29202	2.69277
18	1.42825	1.55966	1.70243	2.02582	2.40662	2.85434
19	1.45681	1.59865	1.75351	2.10685	2.52695	3.02560
20	1.48595	1.63862	1.80611	2.19112	2.65330	3.20714
21	1.51567	1.67958	1.86029	2.27877	2.78596	3.39956
22	1.54598	1.72157	1.91610	2.36992	2.92526	3.60354
23	1.57690	1.76461	1.97359	2.46472	3.07152	3.81975
24	1.60844	1.80873	2.03279	2.56330	3.22510	4.04893
25	1.64061	1.85394	2.09378	2.66584	3.38635	4.29187
26	1.67342	1.90029	2.15659	2.77247	3.55567	4.54938
27	1.70689	1.94780	2.22129	2.88337	3.73346	4.82235
28	1.74102	1.99650	2.28793	2.99870	3.92013	5.11169
29	1.77584	2.04641	2.35657	3.11865	4.11614	5.41839
30	1.81136	2.09757	2.42726	3.24340	4.32194	5.74349
31	1.84759	2.15001	2.50008	3.37313	4.53804	6.08810
32	1.88454	2.20376	2.57508	3.50806	4.76494	6.45339
33	1.92223	2.25885	2.65234	3.64838	5.00319	6.84059
34	1.96068	2.31532	2.73191	3.79432	5.25335	7.25103
35	1.99989	2.37321	2.81386	3.94609	5.51602	7.68609
36	2.03989	2.43254	2.89828	4.10393	5.79182	8.14725
37	2.08069	2.49335	2.98523	4.26809	6.08141	8.63609
38	2.12230	2.55568	3.07478	4.43881	6.38548	9.15425
39	2.16474	2.61957	3.16703	4.61637	6.70475	9.70351
40	2.20804	2.68506	3.26204	4.80102	7.03999	10.28572

8%	9%	10%	12%	15%	(n) PERIODS
1.08000	1.09000	1.10000	1.12000	1.15000	1
1.16640	1.18810	1.21000	1.25440	1.32250	2
1.25971	1.29503	1.33100	1.40493	1.52088	3
1.36049	1.41158	1.46410	1.57352	1.74901	4
1.46933	1.53862	1.61051	1.76234	2.01136	5
1.58687	1.67710	1.77156	1.97382	2.31306	6
1.71382	1.82804	1.94872	2.21068	2.66002	7
1.85093	1.99256	2.14359	2.47596	3.05902	8
1.99900	2.17189	2.35795	2.77308	3.51788	9
2.15892	2.36736	2.59374	3.10585	4.04556	10
2.33164	2.58043	2.85312	3.47855	4.65239	11
2.51817	2.81267	3.13843	3.89598	5.35025	12
2.71962	3.06581	3.45227	4.36349	6.15279	13
2.93719	3.34173	3.79750	4.88711	7.07571	14
3.17217	3.64248	4.17725	5.47357	8.13706	15
3.42594	3.97031	4.59497	6.13039	9.35762	16
3.70002	4.32763	5.05447	6.86604	10.76126	17
3.99602	4.71712	5.55992	7.68997	12.37545	18
4.31570	5.14166	6.11591	8.61276	14.23177	19
4.66096	5.60441	6.72750	9.64629	16.36654	20
5.03383	6.10881	7.40025	10.80385	18.82152	21
5.43654	6.65860	8.14028	12.10031	21.64475	22
5.87146	7.25787	8.95430	13.55235	24.89146	23
6.34118	7.91108	9.84973	15.17863	28.62518	24
6.84847	8.62308	10.83471	17.00000	32.91895	25
7.39635	9.39916	11.91818	19.04007	37.85680	26
7.98806	10.24508	13.10999	21.32488	43.53532	27
8.62711	11.16714	14.42099	23.88387	50.06561	28
9.31727	12.17218	15.86309	26.74993	57.57545	29
10.06266	13.26768	17.44940	29.95992	66.21177	30
10.86767	14.46177	19.19434	33.55511	76.14354	31
11.73708	15.76333	21.11378	37.58173	87.56507	32
12.67605	17.18203	23.22515	42.09153	100.69983	33
13.69013	18.72841	25.54767	47.14252	115.80480	34
14.78534	20.41397	28.10244	52.79962	133.17552	35
15.96817	22.25123	30.91268	59.13557	153.15185	36
17.24563	24.25384	34.00395	66.23184	176.12463	37
18.62528	26.43668	37.40434	74.17966	202.54332	38
20.11530	28.81598	41.14479	83.08122	232.92482	39
21.72452	31.40942	45.25926	93.05097	267.86355	40

TABLE A2 Present Value of 1

$$p^n = \frac{1}{(1 + i)^n} = (1 + i)^{-n}$$

(n) PERIODS	2%	2½%	3%	4%	5%	6%
1	.98039	.97561	.97087	.96154	.95238	.94340
2	.96117	.95181	.94260	.92456	.90703	.89000
3	.94232	.92860	.91514	.88900	.86384	.83962
4	.92385	.90595	.88849	.85480	.82270	.79209
5	.90573	.88385	.86261	.82193	.78353	.74726
6	.88797	.86230	.83748	.79031	.74622	.70496
7	.87056	.84127	.81309	.75992	.71068	.66506
8	.85349	.82075	.78941	.73069	.67684	.62741
9	.83676	.80073	.76642	.70259	.64461	.59190
10	.82035	.78120	.74409	.67556	.61391	.55839
11	.80426	.76214	.72242	.64958	.58468	.52679
12	.78849	.74356	.70138	.62460	.55684	.49697
13	.77303	.72542	.68095	.60057	.53032	.46884
14	.75788	.70773	.66112	.57748	.50507	.44230
15	.74301	.69047	.64186	.55526	.48102	.41727
16	.72845	.67362	.62317	.53391	.45811	.39365
17	.71416	.65720	.60502	.51337	.43630	.37136
18	.70016	.64117	.58739	.49363	.41552	.35034
19	.68643	.62553	.57029	.47464	.39573	.33051
20	.67297	.61027	.55368	.45639	.37689	.31180
21	.65978	.59539	.53755	.43883	.35894	.29416
22	.64684	.58086	.52189	.42196	.34185	.27751
23	.63416	.56670	.50669	.40573	.32557	.26180
24	.62172	.55288	.49193	.39012	.31007	.24698
25	.60953	.53939	.47761	.37512	.29530	.23300
26	.59758	.52623	.46369	.36069	.28124	.21981
27	.58586	.51340	.45019	.34682	.26785	.20737
28	.57437	.50088	.43708	.33348	.25509	.19563
29	.56311	.48866	.42435	.32065	.24295	.18456
30	.55207	.47674	.41199	.30832	.23138	.17411
31	.54125	.46511	.39999	.29646	.22036	.16425
32	.53063	.45377	.38834	.28506	.20987	.15496
33	.52023	.44270	.37703	.27409	.19987	.14619
34	.51003	.43191	.36604	.26355	.19035	.13791
35	.50003	.42137	.35538	.25342	.18129	.13011
36	.49022	.41109	.34503	.24367	.17266	.12274
37	.48061	.40107	.33498	.23430	.16444	.11579
38	.47119	.39128	.32523	.22529	.15661	.10924
39	.46195	.38174	.31575	.21662	.14915	.10306
40	.45289	.37243	.30656	.20829	.14205	.09722

8%	9%	10%	12%	15%	(n) PERIODS
.92593	.91743	.90909	.89286	.86957	1
.85734	.84168	.82645	.79719	.75614	2
.79383	.77218	.75132	.71178	.65752	3
.73503	.70843	.68301	.63552	.57175	4
.68058	.64993	.62092	.56743	.49718	5
.63017	.59627	.56447	.50663	.43233	6
.58349	.54703	.51316	.45235	.37594	7
.54027	.50187	.46651	.40388	.32690	8
.50025	.46043	.42410	.36061	.28426	9
.46319	.42241	.38554	.32197	.24719	10
.42888	.38753	.35049	.28748	.21494	11
.39711	.35554	.31863	.25668	.18691	12
.36770	.32618	.28966	.22917	.16253	13
.34046	.29925	.26333	.20462	.14133	14
.31524	.27454	.23939	.18270	.12289	15
.29189	.25187	.21763	.16312	.10687	16
.27027	.23107	.19785	.14564	.09293	17
.25025	.21199	.17986	.13004	.08081	18
.23171	.19449	.16351	.11611	.07027	19
.21455	.17843	.14864	.10367	.06110	20
.19866	.16370	.13513	.09256	.05313	21
.18394	.15018	.12285	.08264	.04620	22
.17032	.13778	.11168	.07379	.04017	23
.15770	.12641	.10153	.06588	.03493	24
.14602	.11597	.09230	.05882	.03038	25
.13520	.10639	.08391	.05252	.02642	26
.12519	.09761	.07628	.04689	.02297	27
.11591	.08955	.06934	.04187	.01997	28
.10733	.08216	.06304	.03738	.01737	29
.09938	.07537	.05731	.03338	.01510	30
.09202	.06915	.05210	.02980	.01313	31
.08520	.06344	.04736	.02661	.01142	32
.07889	.05820	.04306	.02376	.00993	33
.07305	.05340	.03914	.02121	.00864	34
.06763	.04899	.03558	.01894	.00751	35
.06262	.04494	.03235	.01691	.00653	36
.05799	.04123	.02941	.01510	.00568	37
.05369	.03783	.02674	.01348	.00494	38
.04971	.03470	.02430	.01204	.00429	39
.04603	.03184	.02210	.01075	.00373	40

TABLE A3 Amount of an Ordinary Annuity of 1

$$A_{\overline{n}|i} = \frac{(1 + i)^n - 1}{i}$$

(n) PERIODS	2%	2½%	3%	4%	5%	6%
1	1.00000	1.00000	1.00000	1.00000	1.00000	1.00000
2	2.02000	2.02500	2.03000	2.04000	2.05000	2.06000
3	3.06040	3.07563	3.09090	3.12160	3.15250	3.18360
4	4.12161	4.15252	4.18363	4.24646	4.31013	4.37462
5	5.20404	5.25633	5.30914	5.41632	5.52563	5.63709
6	6.30812	6.38774	6.46841	6.63298	6.80191	6.97532
7	7.43428	7.54743	7.66246	7.89829	8.14201	8.39384
8	8.58297	8.73612	8.89234	9.21423	9.54911	9.89747
9	9.75463	9.95452	10.15911	10.58280	11.02656	11.49132
10	10.94972	11.20338	11.46338	12.00611	12.57789	13.18079
11	12.16872	12.48347	12.80780	13.48635	14.20679	14.97164
12	13.41209	13.79555	14.19203	15.02581	15.91713	16.86994
13	14.68033	15.14044	15.61779	16.62684	17.71298	18.88214
14	15.97394	16.51895	17.08632	18.29191	19.59863	21.01507
15	17.29342	17.93193	18.59891	20.02359	21.57856	23.27597
16	18.63929	19.38022	20.15688	21.82453	23.65749	25.67253
17	20.01207	20.86473	21.76159	23.69751	25.84037	28.21288
18	21.41231	22.38635	23.41444	25.64541	28.13238	30.90565
19	22.84056	23.94601	25.11687	27.67123	30.53900	33.75999
20	24.29737	25.54466	26.87037	29.77808	33.06595	36.78559
21	25.78332	27.18327	28.67649	31.96920	35.71925	39.99273
22	27.29898	28.86286	30.53678	34.24797	38.50521	43.39229
23	28.84496	30.58443	32.45288	36.61789	41.43048	46.99583
24	30.42186	32.34904	34.42647	39.08260	44.50200	50.81558
25	32.03030	34.15776	36.45926	41.64591	47.72710	54.86451
26	33.67091	36.01171	38.55304	44.31174	51.11345	59.15638
27	35.34432	37.91200	40.70963	47.08421	54.66913	63.70577
28	37.05121	39.85980	42.93092	49.96758	58.40258	68.52811
29	38.79223	41.85630	45.21885	52.96629	62.32271	73.63980
30	40.56808	43.90270	47.57542	56.08494	66.43885	79.05819
31	42.37944	46.00027	50.00268	59.32834	70.76079	84.80168
32	44.22703	48.15028	52.50276	62.70147	75.29883	90.88978
33	46.11157	50.35403	55.07784	66.20953	80.06377	97.34316
34	48.03380	52.61289	57.73018	69.85791	85.06696	104.18376
35	49.99448	54.92821	60.46208	73.65222	90.32031	111.43478
36	51.99437	57.30141	63.27594	77.59831	95.83632	119.12087
37	54.03425	59.73395	66.17422	81.70225	101.62814	127.26812
38	56.11494	62.22730	69.15945	85.97034	107.70955	135.90421
39	58.23724	64.78298	72.23423	90.40915	114.09502	145.05846
40	60.40198	67.40255	75.40126	95.02552	120.79977	154.76197

8%	9%	10%	12%	15%	(n) PERIODS
1.00000	1.00000	1.00000	1.00000	1.00000	1
2.08000	2.09000	2.10000	2.12000	2.15000	2
3.24640	3.27810	3.31000	3.37440	3.47250	3
4.50611	4.57313	4.64100	4.77933	4.99338	4
5.86660	5.98471	6.10510	6.35285	6.74238	5
7.33592	7.52334	7.71561	8.11519	8.75374	6
8.92280	9.20044	9.48717	10.08901	11.06680	7
10.63663	11.02847	11.43589	12.29969	13.72682	8
12.48756	13.02104	13.57948	14.77566	16.78584	9
14.48656	15.19293	15.93743	17.54874	20.30372	10
16.64549	17.56029	18.53117	20.65458	24.34928	11
18.97713	20.14072	21.38428	24.13313	29.00167	12
21.49530	22.95339	24.52271	28.02911	34.35192	13
24.21492	26.01919	27.97498	32.39260	40.50471	14
27.15211	29.36092	31.77248	37.27972	47.58041	15
30.32428	33.00340	35.94973	42.75328	55.71747	16
33.75023	36.97371	40.54470	48.88367	65.07509	17
37.45024	41.30134	45.59917	55.74972	75.83636	18
41.44626	46.01846	51.15909	63.43968	88.21181	19
45.76196	51.16012	57.27500	72.05244	102.44358	20
50.42292	56.76453	64.00250	81.69874	118.81012	21
55.45676	62.87334	71.40275	92.50258	137.63164	22
60.89330	69.53194	79.54302	104.60289	159.27638	23
66.76476	76.78981	88.49733	118.15524	184.16784	24
73.10594	84.70090	98.34706	133.33387	212.79302	25
79.95442	93.32398	109.18177	150.33393	245.71197	26
87.35077	102.72314	121.09994	169.37401	283.56877	27
95.33883	112.96822	134.20994	190.69889	327.10408	28
103.96594	124.13536	148.63093	214.58275	377.16969	29
113.28321	136.30754	164.49402	241.33268	434.74515	30
123.34587	149.57522	181.94343	271.29261	500.95692	31
134.21354	164.03699	201.13777	304.84772	577.10046	32
145.95062	179.80032	222.25154	342.42945	644.66553	33
158.62667	196.98234	245.47670	384.52098	765.36535	34
172.31680	215.71076	271.02437	431.66350	881.17016	35
187.10215	236.12472	299.12681	484.46312	1014.34568	36
203.07032	258.37595	330.03949	543.59869	1167.49753	37
220.31595	282.62978	364.04343	609.83053	1343.62216	38
238.94122	309.06646	401.44778	684.01020	1546.16549	39
259.05652	337.88245	442.59256	767.09142	1779.09031	40

TABLE A4 Present Value of an Ordinary Annuity of 1

$$P_{\overline{n}|i} = \frac{1 - \dfrac{1}{(1 + i)^n}}{i} = \frac{1 - v^n}{i}$$

(n) PERIODS	2%	2½%	3%	4%	5%	6%
1	.98039	.97561	.97087	.96154	.95238	.94340
2	1.94156	1.92742	1.91347	1.88609	1.85941	1.83339
3	2.88388	2.85602	2.82861	2.77509	2.72325	2.67301
4	3.80773	3.76197	3.71710	3.62990	3.54595	3.46511
5	4.71346	4.64583	4.57971	4.45182	4.32948	4.21236
6	5.60143	5.50813	5.41719	5.24214	5.07569	4.91732
7	6.47199	6.34939	6.23028	6.00205	5.78637	5.58238
8	7.32548	7.17014	7.01969	6.73274	6.46321	6.20979
9	8.16224	7.97087	7.78611	7.43533	7.10782	6.80169
10	8.98259	8.75206	8.53020	8.11090	7.72173	7.36009
11	9.78685	9.51421	9.25262	8.76048	8.30641	7.88687
12	10.57534	10.25776	9.95400	9.38507	8.86325	8.38384
13	11.34837	10.98319	10.63496	9.98565	9.39357	8.85268
14	12.10625	11.69091	11.29607	10.56312	9.89864	9.29498
15	12.84926	12.38138	11.93794	11.11839	10.37966	9.71225
16	13.57771	13.05500	12.56110	11.65230	10.83777	10.10590
17	14.29187	13.71220	13.16612	12.16567	11.27407	10.47726
18	14.99203	14.35336	13.75351	12.65930	11.68959	10.82760
19	15.67846	14.97889	14.32380	13.13394	12.08532	11.15812
20	16.35143	15.58916	14.87747	13.59033	12.46221	11.46992
21	17.01121	16.18455	15.41502	14.02916	12.82115	11.76408
22	17.65805	16.76541	15.93692	14.45112	13.16300	12.04158
23	18.29220	17.33211	16.44361	14.85684	13.48857	12.30338
24	18.91393	17.88499	16.93554	15.24696	13.79864	12.55036
25	19.52346	18.42438	17.41315	15.62208	14.09394	12.78336
26	20.12104	18.95061	17.87684	15.98277	14.37519	13.00317
27	20.70690	19.46401	18.32703	16.32959	14.64303	13.21053
28	21.28127	19.96489	18.76411	16.66306	14.89813	13.40616
29	21.84438	20.45355	19.18845	16.98371	15.14107	13.59072
30	22.39646	20.93029	19.60044	17.29203	15.37245	13.76483
31	22.93770	21.39541	20.00043	17.58849	15.59281	13.92909
32	23.46833	21.84918	20.38877	17.87355	15.80268	14.08404
33	23.98856	22.29188	20.76579	18.14765	16.00255	14.23023
34	24.49859	22.72379	21.13184	18.41120	16.19290	14.36814
35	24.99862	23.14516	21.48722	18.66461	16.37419	14.49825
36	25.48884	23.55625	21.83225	18.90828	16.54685	14.62099
37	25.96945	23.95732	22.16724	19.14258	16.71129	14.73678
38	26.44064	24.34860	22.49246	19.36786	16.86789	14.84602
39	26.90259	24.73034	22.80822	19.58448	17.01704	14.94907
40	27.35548	25.10278	23.11477	19.79277	17.15909	15.04630

8%	9%	10%	12%	15%	(n) PERIODS
.92593	.91743	.90909	.89286	.86957	1
1.78326	1.75911	1.73554	1.69005	1.62571	2
2.57710	2.53130	2.48685	2.40183	2.28323	3
3.31213	3.23972	3.16986	3.03735	2.85498	4
3.99271	3.88965	3.79079	3.60478	3.35216	5
4.62288	4.48592	4.35526	4.11141	3.78448	6
5.20637	5.03295	4.86842	4.56376	4.16042	7
5.74664	5.53482	5.33493	4.96764	4.48732	8
6.24689	5.99525	5.75902	5.32825	4.77158	9
6.71008	6.41766	6.14457	5.65022	5.01877	10
7.13896	6.80519	6.49506	5.93770	5.23371	11
7.53608	7.16073	6.81369	6.19437	5.42062	12
7.90378	7.48690	7.10336	6.42355	5.58315	13
8.24424	7.78615	7.36669	6.62817	5.72448	14
8.55948	8.06069	7.60608	6.81086	5.84737	15
8.85137	8.31256	7.82371	6.97399	5.95424	16
9.12164	8.54363	8.02155	7.11963	6.04716	17
9.37189	8.75563	8.20141	7.24967	6.12797	18
9.60360	8.95012	8.36492	7.36578	6.19823	19
9.81815	9.12855	8.51356	7.46944	6.25933	20
10.01680	9.29224	8.64869	7.56200	6.31246	21
10.20074	9.44243	8.77154	7.64465	6.35866	22
10.37106	9.58021	8.88322	7.71843	6.39884	23
10.52876	9.70661	8.98474	7.78432	6.43377	24
10.67478	9.82258	9.07704	7.84314	6.46415	25
10.80998	9.92897	9.16095	7.89566	6.49056	26
10.93516	10.02658	9.23722	7.94255	6.51353	27
11.05108	10.11613	9.30657	7.98442	6.53351	28
11.15841	10.19828	9.36961	8.02181	6.55088	29
11.25778	10.27365	9.42691	8.05518	6.56598	30
11.34980	10.34280	9.47901	8.08499	6.57911	31
11.43500	10.40624	9.52638	8.11159	6.59053	32
11.51389	10.46444	9.56943	8.13535	6.60046	33
11.58693	10.51784	9.60858	8.15656	6.60910	34
11.65457	10.56682	9.64416	8.17550	6.61661	35
11.71719	10.61176	9.67651	8.19241	6.62314	36
11.77518	10.65299	9.70592	8.20751	6.62882	37
11.82887	10.69082	9.73265	8.22099	6.63375	38
11.87858	10.72552	9.75697	8.23303	6.63805	39
11.92461	10.75736	9.77905	8.24378	6.64178	40

INDEX